Pro WPF 4.5 in VB

Matthew MacDonald

Pro WPF 4.5 in VB

ISBN-13 (pbk): 978-1-4302-4683-1

ISBN-13 (electronic): 978-1-4302-4684-8

President and Publisher: Paul Manning
Lead Editor: Ewan Buckingham
Technical Reviewer: Fabio Claudio Ferracchiati
Editorial Board: Steve Anglin, Ewan Buckingham, Gary Cornell, Louise Corrigan, Morgan Ertel,
    Jonathan Gennick, Jonathan Hassell, Robert Hutchinson, Michelle Lowman, James Markham,
    Matthew Moodie, Jeff Olson, Jeffrey Pepper, Douglas Pundick, Ben Renow-Clarke, Dominic Shakeshaft,
    Gwenan Spearing, Matt Wade, Tom Welsh
Coordinating Editor: Mark Powers
Copy Editors: Sharon Wilkey and Linda Seifert
Compositor: SPi Global
Indexer: SPi Global
Artist: SPi Global
Cover Designer: Anna Ishchenko

Distributed to the book trade worldwide by Springer Science+Business Media New York, 233 Spring Street, 6th Floor, New York, NY 10013. Phone 1-800-SPRINGER, fax (201) 348-4505, e-mail orders-ny@springer-sbm.com, or visit www.springeronline.com.

For information on translations, please e-mail rights@apress.com, or visit www.apress.com.

Apress and friends of ED books may be purchased in bulk for academic, corporate, or promotional use. eBook versions and licenses are also available for most titles. For more information, reference our Special Bulk Sales–eBook Licensing web page at www.apress.com/bulk-sales.

Any source code or other supplementary materials referenced by the author in this text is available to readers at www.apress.com/9781430246831. For detailed information about how to locate your book's source code, go to www.apress.com/source-code.

For my wonderful family,
Faria, Maya, and Brenna

Contents at a Glance

Contents

About the Author

Matthew MacDonald is an author, educator, and three-time Microsoft MVP. He's the author of more than a dozen books about .NET programming, including *Pro Silverlight 5 in C#* (Apress, 2012) and *Beginning ASP.NET 4.5 in C#* (Apress, 2012). He's also the author of *Your Brain: Th e Missing Manual* (O'Reilly Media, 2008), a popular look at getting the most from your squishy gray matter. Matthew lives in Toronto with his wife and two daughters.

About the Technical Reviewer

Fabio Claudio Ferracchiati, a prolific writer on cutting-edge technologies, has contributed to more than a dozen books on .NET, C#, Visual Basic, and ASP.NET. He is a .NET Microsoft Certified Solution Developer and lives in Milan, Italy. You can read his blog at Ferracchiati.com.

Acknowledgments

No author can complete a book without a small army of helpful individuals. I'm deeply indebted to the whole Apress team, including Mark Powers, who shepherded this edition through production; Sharon Wilkey and Linda Seifert, who speedily performed the copy edit; and many other individuals who worked behind the scenes indexing pages, drawing figures, and proofreading the final copy.

Fabio Claudio Ferracchiati deserves my sincere thanks for his insightful and timely tech review comments. I'm also thankful for the legions of die-hard bloggers on the various WPF teams, who never fail to shed light on the deepest recesses of WPF. I encourage anyone who wants to learn more about the future of WPF to track them down. Finally, I'd never write any book without the support of my wife and these special individuals: Nora, Razia, Paul, and Hamid. Thanks everyone!

—Matthew MacDonald

Introduction

When .NET first appeared, it introduced a small avalanche of new technologies. There was a whole new way to write web applications (ASP.NET), a whole new way to connect to databases (ADO.NET), new typesafe languages (C# and VB .NET), and a managed runtime (the CLR). Not least among these new technologies was Windows Forms, a library of classes for building Windows applications.

Although Windows Forms is a full-featured toolkit, it's hardwired to old, essential bits of Windows plumbing. Most significantly, Windows Forms relies on the Windows API to create the visual appearance of standard user interface elements such as buttons, text boxes, check boxes, and so on. As a result, these ingredients are essentially uncustomizable. For example, if you want to create a stylish glow button you need to create a custom control and paint every aspect of the button (in all its different states) using a lower-level drawing model. Even worse, ordinary windows are carved up into distinct regions, with each control getting its own piece of real estate. As a result, there's no good way for the painting in one control (for example, the glow effect behind a button) to spread into the area owned by another control. And don't even think about introducing animated effects such as spinning text, shimmering buttons, shrinking windows, or live previews because you'll have to paint every detail by hand.

The Windows Presentation Foundation (WPF) changed all this by introducing a model with entirely different plumbing. Although WPF includes the standard controls you're familiar with, it draws every text, border, and background fill *itself*. As a result, WPF can provide much more powerful features that let you alter the way any piece of screen content is rendered. Using these features, you can restyle common controls such as buttons, often without writing any code. Similarly, you can use transformation objects to rotate, stretch, scale, and skew anything in your user interface, and you can even use WPF's baked-in animation system to do it right before the user's eyes. And because the WPF engine renders the content for a window as part of a single operation, it can handle unlimited layers of overlapping controls, even if these controls are irregularly shaped and partially transparent.

Underlying WPF is a powerful infrastructure based on DirectX, the hardware-accelerated graphics API that's commonly used in cutting-edge computer games. This means that you can use rich graphical effects without incurring the performance overhead that you'd suffer with Windows Forms. In fact, you even get advanced features such as support for video files and 3-D content. Using these features (and a good design tool), it's possible to create eye-popping user interfaces and visual effects that would have been all but impossible with Windows Forms.

It's also important to note that you can use WPF to build an ordinary Windows application with standard controls and a straightforward visual appearance. In fact, it's just as easy to use common controls in WPF as it is in the older Windows Forms model. Even better, WPF enhances features that appeal directly to business developers, including a vastly improved data binding model, a set of classes for printing content and managing print queues, and a document feature for displaying large amounts of formatted text. You'll even get a model for building page-based applications that run seamlessly in Internet Explorer and can be launched from a website, all without the usual security warnings and irritating installation prompts. Overall, WPF combines the best of the old world of Windows development with new innovations for building modern, graphically rich user interfaces.

About This Book

This book is an in-depth exploration of WPF for professional developers who know the .NET platform, the VB language, and the Visual Studio development environment. Experience with previous versions of WPF is not required, although new features are highlighted with a "What's New" box at the beginning of each chapter for more seasoned WPF developers.

This book provides a complete description of every major WPF feature, from XAML (the markup language used to define WPF user interfaces) to 3-D drawing and animation. Along the way, you'll occasionally work with code that involves other features of the .NET Framework, such as the ADO.NET classes you use to query a database. These features aren't discussed here. Instead, if you want more information about .NET features that aren't specific to WPF, you can refer to one of the many dedicated .NET titles from Apress.

Chapter Overview

This book includes 33 chapters. If you're just starting out with WPF, you'll find it's easiest to read them in order, as later chapters often draw on the techniques demonstrated in earlier chapters.

The following list gives you a quick preview of each chapter:

Chapter 1: Introducing WPF describes the architecture of WPF, its DirectX plumbing, and the new device-independent measurement system that resizes user interfaces automatically.

Chapter 2: XAML describes the XAML standard that you use to define user interfaces. You'll learn why it was created and how it works, and you'll create a basic WPF window using different coding approaches.

Chapter 3: Layout delves into the layout panels that allow you to organize elements in a WPF window. You'll consider different layout strategies, and you'll build some common types of windows.

Chapter 4: Dependency Properties describes how WPF uses dependency properties to provide support for key features such as data binding and animation.

Chapter 5: Routed Events describes how WPF uses event routing to send events bubbling or tunneling through the elements in your user interface. It also describes the basic set of mouse, keyboard, and multitouch events that all WPF elements support.

Chapter 6: Controls considers the controls every Windows developer is familiar with, such as buttons, text boxes, and labels—and their WPF twists.

Chapter 7: The Application introduces the WPF application model. You'll see how to create single-instance and document-based WPF applications.

Chapter 8: Element Binding introduces WPF data binding. You'll see how to bind any type of object to your user interface.

Chapter 9: Commands introduces the WPF command model, which allows you to wire multiple controls to the same logical action.

Chapter 10: Resources describes how resources let you embed binary files in your assembly and reuse important objects throughout your user interface.

Chapter 11: Styles and Behaviors explains the WPF style system, which lets you apply a set of common property values to an entire group of controls.

Chapter 12: Shapes, Brushes, and Transforms introduces the 2-D drawing model in WPF. You'll learn to create shapes, alter elements with transforms, and paint exotic effects with gradients, tiles, and images.

Chapter 13: Geometries and Drawings delves deeper into 2-D drawing. You'll learn to create complex paths that incorporate arcs and curves and how to use complex graphics efficiently.

Chapter 14: Effects and Visuals describes lower-level graphics programming. You'll apply Photoshop-style effects with pixel shaders, build a bitmap by hand, and use WPF's visual layer for optimized drawing.

Chapter 15: Animation Basics explores WPF's animation framework, which lets you integrate dynamic effects into your application using straightforward, declarative markup.

Chapter 16: Advanced Animations explore more sophisticated animation techniques like key-frame animation, path-based animation, and frame-based animation. You'll also consider a detailed example that shows how to create and manage dynamic animations with code.

Chapter 17: Control Templates shows you how you can give any WPF control a dramatic new look (and new behavior) by plugging in a customized template. You'll also see how templates allow you to build a skinnable application.

Chapter 18: Custom Elements explores how you can extend the existing WPF controls and create your own. You'll see several examples, including a template-based color picker, a flippable panel, a custom layout container, and a decorator that performs custom drawing.

Chapter 19: Data Binding shows you how to fetch information from a database, insert it into a custom data objects, and bind these objects to WPF controls. You'll also learn how to improve the performance of huge data-bound lists with virtualization, and catch editing mistakes with validation.

Chapter 20: Formatting Bound Data shows some of the tricks for turning raw data into rich data displays that incorporate pictures, controls, and selection effects.

Chapter 21: Data Views explores how you use the view in a data-bound window to navigate through a list of data items, and to apply filtering, sorting, and grouping.

Chapter 22: Lists, Grids, and Trees gives you a tour of WPF's rich data controls, including the ListView, TreeView, and DataGrid.

Chapter 23: Windows examines how windows work in WPF. You'll also learn how to create irregularly shaped windows and use Vista glass effects. You'll also make the most of Windows 7 features by customizing taskbar jump lists, thumbnails, and icon overlays.

Chapter 24: Pages and Navigation describes how you can build pages in WPF and keep track of navigation history. You'll also see how to build a browser-hosted WPF application that can be launched from a website.

Chapter 25: Menus, Toolbars, and Ribbons considers command-oriented controls such as menus and toolbars. You'll also get a taste of more modern user interface with the freely downloadable Ribbon control.

Chapter 26: Sound and Video describes WPF's media support. You'll see how to control playback for sound and video, and how to throw in synchronized animations and live effects.

Chapter 27: 3-D Drawing explores the support for drawing 3-D shapes in WPF. You'll learn how to create, transform, and animate 3-D objects. You'll even see how to place interactive 2-D controls on 3-D surfaces.

Chapter 28: Documents introduces WPF's rich document support. You'll learn to use flow documents to present large amounts of text in the most readable way possible, and you'll use fixed documents to show print-ready pages. You'll even use the RichTextBox to provide document editing.

Chapter 29: Printing demonstrates WPF's printing model, which lets you draw text and shapes in a print document. You'll also learn how to manage page settings and print queues.

Chapter 30: Interacting with Windows Forms examines how you can combine WPF and Windows Forms content in the same application—and even in the same window.

Chapter 31: Multithreading describes how to create responsive WPF applications that perform time-consuming work in the background.

Chapter 32: The Add-In Model shows you how to create an extensible application that can dynamically discover and load separate components.

Chapter 33: ClickOnce Deployment shows how you can deploy WPF applications using the ClickOnce setup model.

What You Need to Use This Book

In order to *run* a WPF 4.5 application, your computer must have Windows 7, Windows 8, or Windows Vista with Service Pack 2. You also need the .NET Framework 4.5. In order to *create* a WPF 4.5 application (and open the sample projects included with this book), you need Visual Studio 2012, which includes the .NET Framework 4.5.

There's one other option. Instead of using any version of Visual Studio, you can use Expression Blend—a graphically oriented design tool—to build and test WPF applications. Overall, Expression Blend is intended for graphic designers who spend their time creating serious eye candy, while Visual Studio is ideal for code-heavy application programmers. This book assumes you're using Visual Studio. If you do plan to use Expression Blend, make sure you are using a version that explicitly supports WPF (the version that's bundled with some versions of Visual Studio is for Metro development only, and doesn't support WPF). At the time of this writing, the version of Expression Blend that supports WPF is available as a preview called Blend + Sketchflow Preview for Visual Studio 2012, and it's available at `http://tinyurl.com/cgar5lz`.

Code Samples and URLs

It's a good idea to check the Apress website or `http://www.prosetech.com` to download the most recent up-to-date code samples. You'll need to do this to test most of the more sophisticated code examples described in this book because the less significant details are usually left out. This book focuses on the most important sections so that you don't need to wade through needless extra pages to understand a concept.

To download the source code, surf to `http://www.prosetech.com` and look for the page for this book. You'll also find a list of links that are mentioned in this book, so you can find important tools and examples without needless typing.

Feedback

This book has the ambitious goal of being the best tutorial and reference for programming WPF. Toward that end, your comments and suggestions are extremely helpful. You can send complaints, adulation, and everything in between directly to apress@prosetech.com. I can't solve your .NET problems or critique your code, but I will benefit from information about what this book did right and wrong (or what it may have done in an utterly confusing way).

PART 1

Fundamentals

■ ■ ■

Introducing WPF

The Windows Presentation Foundation (WPF) is a modern graphical display system for Windows. It's a radical change from the technologies that came before it, with innovative features such as built-in hardware acceleration and resolution independence, both of which you'll explore in this chapter.

WPF is the best toolkit to use if you want to build a rich desktop application that runs on Windows Vista, Windows 7, and Windows 8 in desktop mode (as well as the corresponding versions of Windows Server). In fact, it's the *only* general-purpose toolkit that targets these versions of Windows. By comparison, Microsoft's new Metro toolkit—although exciting—is limited to Windows 8 systems only. (WPF applications can even be made to run on ancient Windows XP computers, which are still found in many businesses. The only limitation is that you must configure Visual Studio to target the slightly older .NET 4.0 Framework, rather than .NET 4.5.)

In this chapter, you'll take your first look at the architecture of WPF. You'll learn how it deals with varying screen resolutions, and you'll get a high-level survey of its core assemblies and classes. You'll also consider how WPF has evolved from its initial release to version 4.5.

The Evolution of Windows Graphics

Before WPF, Windows developers spent nearly 15 years using essentially the same display technology. That's because every traditional, pre-WPF Windows application relies on two well-worn parts of the Windows operating system to create its user interface:

- *User32*: This provides the traditional Windows look and feel for elements such as windows, buttons, text boxes, and so on.
- *GDI/GDI+*: This provides drawing support for rendering shapes, text, and images at the cost of additional complexity (and often lackluster performance).

Over the years, both technologies have been refined, and the APIs that developers use to interact with them have changed dramatically. But whether you're crafting an application with .NET and Windows Forms or even Visual Basic 6 or MFC-based C++ code, behind the scenes the same parts of the Windows operating system are at work. Different frameworks simply provide different wrappers for interacting with User32 and GDI/GDI+. They can provide improvements in efficiency, reduce complexity, and add prebaked features so you don't have to code them yourself; but they can't remove the fundamental limitations of a system component that was designed more than a decade ago.

■ **Note** The basic division of labor between User32 and GDI/GDI+ was introduced more than 15 years ago and was well established in Windows 3.0. Of course, User32 was simply User at that point, because software hadn't yet entered the 32-bit world.

DirectX: The New Graphics Engine

Microsoft created one way around the limitations of the User32 and GDI/GDI+ libraries: *DirectX*. DirectX began as a cobbled-together, error-prone toolkit for creating games on the Windows platform. Its design mandate was speed, and so Microsoft worked closely with video card vendors to give DirectX the hardware acceleration needed for complex textures, special effects such as partial transparency, and three-dimensional graphics.

Over the years since it was first introduced (shortly after Windows 95), DirectX has matured. It's now an integral part of Windows, with support for all modern video cards. However, the programming API for DirectX still reflects its roots as a game developer's toolkit. Because of its raw complexity, DirectX is almost never used in traditional types of Windows applications (such as business software).

WPF changes all this. In WPF, the underlying graphics technology isn't GDI/GDI+. Instead, it's DirectX. In fact, WPF applications use DirectX no matter what type of user interface you create. That means that whether you're designing complex three-dimensional graphics (DirectX's forte) or just drawing buttons and plain text, all the drawing work travels through the DirectX pipeline. As a result, even the most mundane business applications can use rich effects such as transparency and anti-aliasing. You also benefit from hardware acceleration, which simply means DirectX hands off as much work as possible to the graphics processing unit (GPU), which is the dedicated processor on the video card.

■ **Note**   DirectX is more efficient because it understands higher-level ingredients such as textures and gradients that can be rendered directly by the video card. GDI/GDI+ doesn't, so it needs to convert them to pixel-by-pixel instructions, which are rendered much more slowly by modern video cards.

One component that's still in the picture (to a limited extent) is User32. That's because WPF still relies on User32 for certain services, such as handling and routing input and sorting out which application owns which portion of screen real estate. However, all the drawing is funneled through DirectX.

Hardware Acceleration and WPF

Video cards differ in their support for specialized rendering features and optimizations. Fortunately, this isn't a problem, for two reasons. First, most modern computers have video hardware that's more than powerful enough for WPF features such as 3-D drawing and animation. This is true even of laptops and desktop computers with integrated graphics (graphics processors that are built in to the motherboard, rather than on a separate card). Second, WPF has a software fallback for everything it does. That means WPF is intelligent enough to use hardware optimizations where possible, but can perform the same work using software calculations if necessary. So if you run a WPF application on a computer with a legacy video card, the interface will still appear the way you designed it. Of course, the software alternative may be much slower, so you'll find that computers with older video cards won't run rich WPF applications very well, especially ones that incorporate complex animations or other intense graphical effects.

WPF: A Higher-Level API

If the only thing WPF offered was hardware acceleration through DirectX, it would be a compelling improvement but a limited one. But WPF includes a basket of high-level services designed for application programmers.

The following are some of the most dramatic changes that WPF ushers into the Windows programming world:

- *A web-like layout model*: Rather than fix controls in place with specific coordinates, WPF emphasizes flexible flow layout that arranges controls based on their content. The result is a user interface that can adapt to show highly dynamic content or different languages.

- *A rich drawing model*: Rather than painting pixels, in WPF you deal with *primitives*—basic shapes, blocks of text, and other graphical ingredients. You also have new features, such as true transparent controls, the ability to stack multiple layers with different opacities, and native 3-D support.

- *A rich text model*: WPF gives Windows applications the ability to display rich, styled text anywhere in a user interface. You can even combine text with lists, floating figures, and other user interface elements. And if you need to display large amounts of text, you can use advanced document display features such as wrapping, columns, and justification to improve readability.

- *Animation as a first-class programming concept*: In WPF, there's no need to use a timer to force a form to repaint itself. Instead, animation is an intrinsic part of the framework. You define animations with declarative tags, and WPF puts them into action automatically.

- *Support for audio and video media*: Previous user interface toolkits, such as Windows Forms, were surprisingly limited when dealing with multimedia. But WPF includes support for playing any audio or video file supported by Windows Media Player, and it allows you to play more than one media file at once. Even more impressively, it gives you the tools to integrate video content into the rest of your user interface, allowing you to pull off exotic tricks such as placing a video window on a spinning 3-D cube.

- *Styles and templates*: Styles allow you to standardize formatting and reuse it throughout your application. Templates allow you to change the way any element is rendered, even a core control such as the button. It has never been easier to build modern skinned interfaces.

- *Commands*: Most users realize that it doesn't matter whether they trigger the Open command through a menu or through a toolbar; the end result is the same. Now that abstraction is available to your code, you can define an application command in one place and link it to multiple controls.

- *Declarative user interface*: Although you can construct a WPF window with code, Visual Studio takes a different approach. It serializes each window's content to a set of XML tags in a XAML document. The advantage is that your user interface is completely separated from your code, and graphic designers can use professional tools to edit your XAML files and refine your application's front end. (*XAML* is short for Extensible Application Markup Language, and it's described in detail in Chapter 2.)

- *Page-based applications*: Using WPF, you can build a browser-like application that lets you move through a collection of pages, complete with forward and back navigation buttons. WPF handles the messy details such as the page history. You can even deploy your project as a browser-based application that runs right inside Internet Explorer.

Resolution Independence

Traditional Windows applications are bound by certain assumptions about resolution. Developers usually assume a standard monitor resolution (such as 1366 × 768 pixels), design their windows with that in mind, and try to ensure reasonable resizing behavior for smaller and larger dimensions.

The problem is that the user interface in traditional Windows applications isn't scalable. As a result, if you use a high monitor resolution that crams in pixels more densely, your application windows become smaller and more difficult to read. This is particularly a problem with newer monitors that have high pixel densities and run at correspondingly high resolutions. For example, it's common to find consumer monitors (particularly on laptops) that have pixel densities of 120 dpi or 144 dpi (dots per inch), rather than the more traditional 96 dpi. At their native resolution, these displays pack the pixels in much more tightly, creating eye-squintingly small controls and text.

Ideally, applications would use higher pixel densities to show more detail. For example, a high-resolution monitor could display similarly sized toolbar icons but use the extra pixels to render sharper graphics. That way, you could keep the same basic layout but offer increased clarity and detail. For a variety of reasons, this solution hasn't been possible in the past. Although you can resize graphical content that's drawn with GDI/GDI+, User32 (which generates the visuals for common controls) doesn't support true scaling.

WPF doesn't suffer from this problem because it renders all user interface elements itself, from simple shapes to common controls such as buttons. As a result, if you create a button that's 1 inch wide on your computer monitor, it can remain 1 inch wide on a high-resolution monitor—WPF will simply render it in greater detail and with more pixels.

This is the big picture, but it glosses over a few details. Most importantly, you need to realize that WPF bases its scaling on the *system* DPI setting, not the DPI of your physical display device. This makes perfect sense—after all, if you're displaying your application on a 100-inch projector, you're probably standing several feet back and expecting to see a jumbo-size version of your windows. You don't want WPF to suddenly scale down your application to "normal" size. Similarly, if you're using a laptop with a high-resolution display, you probably expect to have slightly smaller windows—it's the price you pay to fit all your information onto a smaller screen. Furthermore, different users have different preferences. Some want richer detail, while others prefer to cram in more content.

So, how does WPF determine how big an application window *should* be? The short answer is that WPF uses the system DPI setting when it calculates sizes. But to understand how this really works, it helps to take a closer look at the WPF measurement system.

WPF Units

A WPF window and all the elements inside it are measured using *device-independent units*. A single device-independent unit is defined as 1/96 of an inch. To understand what this means in practice, you'll need to consider an example.

Imagine that you create a small button in WPF that's 96 by 96 units in size. If you're using the standard Windows DPI setting (96 dpi), each device-independent unit corresponds to one real, physical pixel. That's because WPF uses this calculation:

```
[Physical Unit Size] = [Device-Independent Unit Size] × [System DPI]
                     = 1/96 inch × 96 dpi
                     = 1 pixel
```

Essentially, WPF assumes it takes 96 pixels to make an inch because Windows tells it that through the system DPI setting. However, the reality depends on your display device.

For example, consider a 19-inch LCD monitor with a maximum resolution of 1600 by 1200 pixels. Using a dash of Pythagoras, you can calculate the pixel density for this monitor, as shown here:

$$[\text{screenDPI}] = \frac{\sqrt{1600^2 + 1200^2}\ \text{pixels}}{19\ \text{inches}}$$
$$= 100\ \text{dpi}$$

In this case, the pixel density works out to 100 dpi, which is slightly higher than what Windows assumes. As a result, on this monitor a 96-by-96-pixel button will be slightly smaller than 1 inch.

On the other hand, consider a 15-inch LCD monitor with a resolution of 1024 by 768. Here, the pixel density drops to about 85 dpi, so the 96-by-96-pixel button appears slightly *larger* than 1 inch.

In both these cases, if you reduce the screen size (say, by switching to 800 by 600 resolution), the button (and every other screen element) will appear proportionally larger. That's because the system DPI setting remains at 96 dpi. In other words, Windows continues to assume it takes 96 pixels to make an inch, even though at a lower resolution it takes far fewer pixels.

■ **Tip** As you no doubt know, LCD monitors are designed to work best at a specific resolution, which is called the *native resolution*. If you lower the resolution, the monitor must use interpolation to fill in the extra pixels, which can cause blurriness. To get the best display, it's always best to use the native resolution. If you want larger windows, buttons, and text, consider modifying the system DPI setting instead (as described next).

System DPI

So far, the WPF button example works exactly the same as any other user interface element in any other type of Windows application. The difference is the result if you change the system DPI setting. In the previous generation of Windows, this feature was sometimes called *large fonts*. That's because the system DPI affects the system font size but often leaves other details unchanged.

■ **Note** Many Windows applications don't fully support higher DPI settings. At worst, increasing the system DPI can result in windows that have some content that's scaled up and other content that isn't, which can lead to obscured content and even unusable windows.

This is where WPF is different. WPF respects the system DPI setting natively and effortlessly. For example, if you change the system DPI setting to 120 dpi (a common choice for users of large high-resolution screens), WPF assumes that it needs 120 pixels to fill an inch of space. WPF uses the following calculation to figure out how it should translate its logical units to physical device pixels:

```
[Physical Unit Size] = [Device-Independent Unit Size] × [System DPI]
                     = 1/96 inch × 120 dpi
                     = 1.25 pixels
```

In other words, when you set the system DPI to 120 dpi, the WPF rendering engine assumes one device-independent unit equals 1.25 pixels. If you show a 96-by-96 button, the physical size will actually be 120 by 120 pixels (because 96 × 1.25 = 120). This is the result you expect—a button that's 1 inch on a standard monitor remains 1 inch in size on a monitor with a higher pixel density.

This automatic scaling wouldn't help much if it applied only to buttons. But WPF uses device-independent units for everything it displays, including shapes, controls, text, and any other ingredient you put in a window. As a result, you can change the system DPI to whatever you want, and WPF adjusts the size of your application seamlessly.

■ **Note** Depending on the system DPI, the calculated pixel size may be a fractional value. You might assume that WPF simply rounds off your measurements to the nearest pixel. However, by default, WPF does something different. If an edge of an element falls between pixels, it uses anti-aliasing to blend that edge into the adjacent pixels. This might seem like an odd choice, but it actually makes a fair bit of sense. Your controls won't necessarily have straight, clearly defined edges if you use custom-drawn graphics to skin them; so some level of anti-aliasing is already necessary.

The steps for adjusting the system DPI depend on the operating system. The following sections explain what to do, depending on your operating system.

Windows Vista

1. Right-click your desktop and choose Personalize.

2. In the list of links on the left, choose Adjust Font Size (DPI).

3. Choose between 96 or 120 dpi. Or click Custom DPI to use a custom DPI setting. You can then specify a percentage value, as shown in Figure 1-1. (For example, 175% scales the standard 96 dpi to 168 dpi.) In addition, when using a custom DPI setting, you have an option named Use Windows XP Style DPI Scaling, which is described in the sidebar "DPI Scaling."

Figure 1-1. *Changing the system DPI*

Windows 7 and Windows 8

1. Right-click your desktop and choose Personalize.

2. In the list of links at the bottom-left of the window, choose Display.

3. Choose between Smaller (the default option), Medium, or Larger. Although these options are described by scaling percentages (100%, 125%, or 150%), they actually correspond to the DPI values 96, 120, and 144. You'll notice that the first two are the same standards found in Windows Vista and Windows XP, while the third one is larger still. Alternatively, you can click Set Custom Text Size to use a custom DPI percentage, as shown in Figure 1-1. (For example, 175% scales the standard 96 dpi to 168 dpi.) When using a custom DPI setting, you have an option named Use Windows XP Style DPI Scaling, which is described in the following sidebar.

DPI SCALING

Because older applications are notoriously lacking in their support for high DPI settings, Windows Vista introduced a technique called *bitmap scaling*. Later versions of Windows also support this feature.

With bitmap scaling, when you run an application that doesn't appear to support high DPI settings, Windows resizes it as though it were an image. The advantage of this approach is that the application still believes it's running at the standard 96 dpi. Windows seamlessly translates input (such as mouse clicks) and routes them to the right place in the application's "real" coordinate system.

The scaling algorithm that Windows uses is a fairly good one—it respects pixel boundaries to avoid blurry edges and uses the video card hardware where possible to increase speed—but it inevitably leads to a fuzzier display. It also has a serious limitation in that Windows can't recognize older applications that *do* support high DPI settings. That's because applications need to include a manifest or call SetProcessDPIAware (in User32) to advertise their high DPI support. Although WPF applications handle this step correctly, applications created prior to Windows Vista won't use either approach and will be stuck with bitmap scaling even when they support higher DPIs.

There are two possible solutions. If you have a few specific applications that support high DPI settings but don't indicate it, you can configure that detail manually. To do so, right-click the shortcut that starts the application (in the Start menu) and choose Properties. On the Compatibility tab, enable the option named Disable Display Scaling on High DPI Settings. If you have a lot of applications to configure, this gets tiring fast.

The other possible solution is to disable bitmap scaling altogether. To do so, choose the Use Windows XP Style DPI Scaling option in the Custom DPI Setting dialog box shown in Figure 1-1. The only limitation of this approach is there may be some applications that won't display properly (and possibly won't be usable) at high DPI settings. By default, Use Windows XP Style DPI Scaling is checked for DPI sizes of 120 or less but unchecked for DPI sizes that are greater.

Bitmap and Vector Graphics

When you work with ordinary controls, you can take WPF's resolution independence for granted. WPF takes care of making sure that everything has the right size automatically. However, if you plan to incorporate images into your application, you can't be quite as casual. For example, in traditional Windows applications, developers use tiny bitmaps for toolbar commands. In a WPF application, this approach is not ideal because the bitmap may display artifacts (becoming blurry) as it's scaled up or down according to the system DPI. Instead, when designing a WPF user interface, even the smallest icon is generally implemented as a vector graphic. *Vector graphics* are defined as a set of shapes, and as such they can be easily scaled to any size.

■ **Note** Of course, drawing a vector graphic takes more time than painting a basic bitmap, but WPF includes optimizations that are designed to lessen the overhead to ensure that drawing performance is always reasonable.

It's difficult to overestimate the importance of resolution independence. At first glance, it seems like a straightforward, elegant solution to a time-honored problem (which it is). However, in order to design interfaces that are fully scalable, developers need to embrace a new way of thinking.

The Architecture of WPF

WPF uses a multilayered architecture. At the top, your application interacts with a high-level set of services that are completely written in managed C# code. The actual work of translating .NET objects into Direct3D textures and triangles happens behind the scenes, using a lower-level unmanaged component called milcore.dll. milcore. dll is implemented in unmanaged code because it needs tight integration with Direct3D and because it's extremely performance-sensitive.

Figure 1-2 shows the layers at work in a WPF application.

Figure 1-2. The architecture of WPF

Figure 1-2 includes these key components:

- *PresentationFramework.dll*: This holds the top-level WPF types, including those that represent windows, panels, and other types of controls. It also implements higher-level programming abstractions such as styles. Most of the classes you'll use directly come from this assembly.

- *PresentationCore.dll*: This holds base types, such as UIElement and Visual, from which all shapes and controls derive. If you don't need the full window and control abstraction layer, you can drop down to this level and still take advantage of WPF's rendering engine.

- *WindowsBase.dll*: This holds even more basic ingredients that have the potential to be reused outside of WPF, such as DispatcherObject and DependencyObject, which introduces the plumbing for dependency properties (a topic you'll explore in detail in Chapter 4).

- *milcore.dll*: This is the core of the WPF rendering system and the foundation of the Media Integration Layer (MIL). Its composition engine translates visual elements into the triangle and textures that Direct3D expects. Although milcore.dll is considered part of WPF, it's also an essential system component for Windows Vista and Windows 7. In fact, the Desktop Window Manager (DWM) uses milcore.dll to render the desktop.

■ **Note**   milcore.dll is sometimes referred to as the engine for "managed graphics." Much as the common language runtime (CLR) manages the lifetime of a .NET application, milcore.dll manages the display state. And just as the CLR saves you from worrying about releasing objects and reclaiming memory, milcore.dll saves you from thinking about invalidating and repainting a window. You simply create the objects with the content you want to show, and milcore.dll paints the appropriate portions of the window as it is dragged around, covered and uncovered, minimized and restored, and so on.

- *WindowsCodecs.dll*: This is a low-level API that provides imaging support (for example, processing, displaying, and scaling bitmaps and JPEGs).
- *Direct3D*: This is the low-level API through which all the graphics in a WPF application are rendered.
- *User32*: This is used to determine what program gets what real estate. As a result, it's still involved in WPF, but it plays no part in rendering common controls.

The most important fact that you should realize is Direct3D renders *all* the drawing in WPF. It doesn't matter whether you have a modest video card or a much more powerful one, whether you're using basic controls or drawing more complex content, or whether you're running your application on Windows XP, Windows Vista, or Windows 7. Even two-dimensional shapes and ordinary text are transformed into triangles and passed through the 3-D pipeline. There is no fallback to GDI+ or User32.

The Class Hierarchy

Throughout this book, you'll spend most of your time exploring the WPF namespaces and classes. But before you begin, it's helpful to take a first look at the hierarchy of classes that leads to the basic set of WPF controls.

Figure 1-3 shows a basic overview with some of the key branches of the class hierarchy. As you continue through this book, you'll dig into these classes (and their relatives) in more detail.

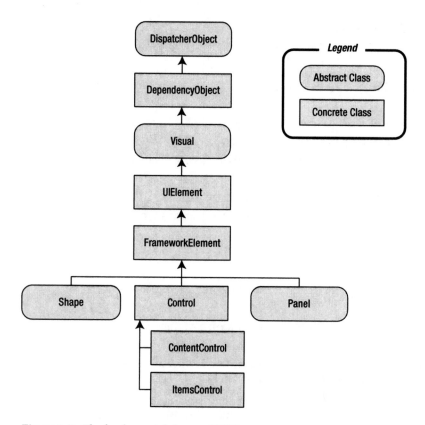

Figure 1-3. *The fundamental classes of WPF*

The following sections describe the core classes in this diagram. Many of these classes lead to whole branches of elements (such as shapes, panels, and controls).

■ **Note** The core WPF namespaces begin with System.Windows (for example, System.Windows, System.Windows. Controls, and System.Windows.Media). The sole exception is namespaces that begin with System.Windows.Forms, which are part of the Windows Forms toolkit.

System.Threading.DispatcherObject

WPF applications use the familiar single-thread affinity (STA) model, which means the entire user interface is owned by a single thread. It's not safe to interact with user interface elements from another thread. To facilitate this model, each WPF application is governed by a *dispatcher* that coordinates messages (which result from keyboard input, mouse movements, and framework processes such as layout). By deriving from DispatcherObject, every element in your user interface can verify whether code is running on the correct thread and access the dispatcher to marshal code to the user interface thread. You'll learn more about the WPF threading model in Chapter 31.

System.Windows.DependencyObject

In WPF, the central way of interacting with onscreen elements is through properties. Early on in the design cycle, the WPF architects decided to create a more powerful property model that baked in features such as change notification, inherited default values, and more economical property storage. The ultimate result is the *dependency property* feature, which you'll explore in Chapter 4. By deriving from DependencyObject, WPF classes get support for dependency properties.

System.Windows.Media.Visual

Every element that appears in a WPF window is, at heart, a Visual. You can think of the Visual class as a single drawing object that encapsulates drawing instructions, additional details about how the drawing should be performed (such as clipping, opacity, and transformation settings), and basic functionality (such as hit testing). The Visual class also provides the link between the managed WPF libraries and the milcore.dll that renders your display. Any class that derives from Visual has the ability to be displayed on a window. If you prefer to create your user interface using a lightweight API that doesn't have the higher-level framework features of WPF, you can program directly with Visual objects, as described in Chapter 14.

System.Windows.UIElement

UIElement adds support for WPF essentials such as layout, input, focus, and events (which the WPF team refers to by the acronym *LIFE*). For example, it's here that the two-step measure and arrange layout process is defined, which you'll learn about in Chapter 18. It's also here that raw mouse clicks and key presses are transformed to more useful events such as MouseEnter. As with properties, WPF implements an enhanced event-passing system called *routed events*. You'll learn how it works in Chapter 5. Finally, UIElement adds supports for commands (Chapter 9).

System.Windows.FrameworkElement

FrameworkElement is the final stop in the core WPF inheritance tree. It implements some of the members that are merely defined by UIElement. For example, UIElement sets the foundation for the WPF layout system, but FrameworkElement includes the key properties (such as HorizontalAlignment and Margin) that support it. UIElement also adds support for data binding, animation, and styles, all of which are core features.

System.Windows.Shapes.Shape

Basic shapes classes, such as Rectangle, Polygon, Ellipse, Line, and Path, derive from this class. These shapes can be used alongside more traditional Windows widgets such as buttons and text boxes. You'll start building shapes in Chapter 12.

System.Windows.Controls.Control

A *control* is an element that can interact with the user. It obviously includes classes such as TextBox, Button, and ListBox. The Control class adds additional properties for setting the font and the foreground and background colors. But the most interesting detail it provides is template support, which allows you to replace the standard appearance of a control with your own stylish drawing. You'll learn about control templates in Chapter 17.

▒ **Note**   In Windows Forms programming, every visual item in a form is referred to as a *control*. In WPF, this isn't the case. Visual items are called *elements*, and only some elements are actually controls (those that can receive focus and interact with the user). To make this system even more confusing, many elements are defined in the System.Windows. Controls namespace, even though they don't derive from System.Windows.Controls.Control and aren't considered controls. One example is the Panel class.

System.Windows.Controls.ContentControl

This is the base class for all controls that have a single piece of content. This includes everything from the humble Label to the Window. The most impressive part of this model (which is described in more detail in Chapter 6) is the fact that this single piece of content can be anything from an ordinary string to a layout panel with a combination of other shapes and controls.

System.Windows.Controls.ItemsControl

This is the base class for all controls that show a collection of items, such as the ListBox and TreeView. List controls are remarkably flexible—for example, using the features that are built into the ItemsControl class, you can transform the lowly ListBox into a list of radio buttons, a list of check boxes, a tiled display of images, or a combination of completely different elements that you've chosen. In fact, in WPF, menus, toolbars, and status bars are actually specialized lists, and the classes that implement them all derive from ItemsControl. You'll start using lists in Chapter 19 when you consider data binding. You'll learn to enhance them in Chapter 20, and you'll consider the most specialized list controls in Chapter 22.

System.Windows.Controls.Panel

This is the base class for all layout containers—elements that can contain one or more children and arrange them according to specific layout rules. These containers are the foundation of the WPF layout system, and using them is the key to arranging your content in the most attractive, flexible way possible. Chapter 3 explores the WPF layout system in more detail.

WPF 4.5

WPF is a mature technology. It's been part of several releases of .NET, with steady enhancements along the way:

- *WPF 3.0*: The first version of WPF was released with two other new technologies: Windows Communication Foundation (WCF) and Windows Workflow Foundation (WF). Together, these three technologies were called the .NET Framework 3.0.

- *WPF 3.5*: A year later, a new version of WPF was released as part of the .NET Framework 3.5. The new features in WPF are mostly minor refinements, including bug fixes and performance improvements.

- *WPF 3.5 SP1*: When the .NET Framework Service Pack 1 (SP1) was released, the designers of WPF had a chance to slip in a few new features, such as slick graphical effects (courtesy of pixel shaders) and the sophisticated DataGrid control.

- *WPF 4*: This release added a number of refinements, including better text rendering, more natural animation, and support for multitouch.

- *WPF 4.5*: The latest version of WPF has the fewest changes yet, which reflects its status as a mature technology. Along with the usual bug fixes and performance tweaks, WPF 4.5 adds a number of refinements to that data binding system, including improvements to data binding expressions, virtualization, support for the INotifyDataError interface, and data view synchronization. You'll see these new features in Chapter 8, Chapter 19, and Chapter 22.

The WPF Toolkit

Before a new control makes its way into the WPF libraries of the .NET platform, it often begins in a separate Microsoft download known as the WPF Toolkit. But the WPF Toolkit isn't just a place to preview the future direction of WPF—it's also a great source of practical components and controls that are made available outside the normal WPF release cycle. For example, WPF doesn't include any sort of charting tools, but the WPF Toolkit includes a set of controls for creating bar, pie, bubble, scatter, and line graphs.

This book occasionally references the WPF Toolkit to point out a useful piece of functionality that's not available in the core .NET runtime. To download the WPF Toolkit, review its code, or read its documentation, surf to `http://wpf.codeplex.com`. There, you'll also find links to other Microsoft-managed WPF projects, including WPF Futures (which provides more experimental WPF features) and WPF testing tools.

Visual Studio 2012

Although you can craft WPF user interfaces by hand or using the graphic-design-oriented tool Expression Blend, most developers will start in Visual Studio and spend most (or all) of their time there. This book assumes you're using Visual Studio and occasionally explains how to use the Visual Studio interface to perform an important task, such as adding a resource, configuring project properties, or creating a control library assembly. However, you won't spend much time exploring Visual Studio's design-time frills. Instead, you'll focus on the underlying markup and code you need to create professional applications.

■ **Note** You probably already know how to create a WPF project in Visual Studio, but here's a quick recap. First, select File ➤ New ➤ TRA Project. Then, pick the Visual Basic ➤ Windows group (in the tree on the left), and choose the WPF Application template (in the list on the right). You'll learn about the more specialized WPF Browser Application template in Chapter 24. After you pick a directory, enter a project name, and click OK, you'll end up with the basic skeleton of a WPF application.

Multitargeting

In the past, each version of Visual Studio was tightly coupled to a specific version of .NET. Visual Studio 2012 doesn't have this restriction—it allows you to design an application that targets any version of .NET from 2.0 to 4.5.

Although it's obviously not possible to create a WPF application with .NET 2.0, all later versions have WPF support. You may choose to target an older version, such as .NET 3.5 or .NET 4 to get the broadest possible compatibility. For example, a .NET 3.5 application can run on the .NET 3.5, 4, and 4.5 runtimes. Or, you may choose to target .NET 4.5 to get access to newer features in WPF or in the .NET platform. However, if you need to support legacy Windows XP computers, you can't target a version part of .NET 4, because this is the last .NET release that supports Windows XP.

When you create a new project in Visual Studio, you can choose the version of the .NET Framework that you're targeting from a drop-down list at the top of the New Project dialog box, just above the list of project templates (see Figure 1-4).

Figure 1-4. *Choosing the target version of the .NET Framework*

You can also change the version you're targeting at any point afterward. Just double-click the My Project node in the Solution Explorer, choose the Compile tab, click the Advanced Compile Options button, and change the selection in the Target Framework list.

To provide accurate multitargeting, Visual Studio includes *reference assemblies* for each version of .NET. These assemblies include the metadata of every type but none of the code that's required to implement it. That means Visual Studio can use the reference assembly to tailor its IntelliSense and error checking, ensuring that you aren't able to use controls, classes, or members that aren't available in the version of .NET that you're targeting. It also uses this metadata to determine what controls should appear in the Toolbox, what members should appear in the Properties window and Object Browser, and so on, ensuring that the entire IDE is limited to the version you've chosen.

The Visual Studio Designer

Visual Studio includes a rich designer for creating WPF user interfaces. But just because Visual Studio 2012 allows you to drag and drop WPF windows into existence doesn't mean you should start doing that right now—or at all. As you'll learn in Chapter 3, WPF uses a flexible and nuanced layout model that allows you to use different strategies for sizing and positioning the elements in your user interface. To get the result you need, you'll need to choose the right combination of layout containers, arrange them appropriately, and configure their properties. Visual Studio can help you out in this task, but it's far easier if you learn the basics of XAML markup and WPF layout *first*. Then, you'll be able to watch as Visual Studio's visual designer generates your markup, and you can modify it by hand as needed.

After you've mastered the syntax of XAML (Chapter 2) and you've learned about the family of WPF layout controls (Chapter 3), it's up to you to choose how you want to create your windows. There are professional developers who use Visual Studio, those who use Expression Blend, those who write XAML by hand, and those who use a combination of both methods (for example, creating the basic layout structure by hand and then configuring it with the Visual Studio designer).

The Last Word

In this chapter, you took your first look at WPF and the promise it holds. You considered the underlying architecture and briefly considered the core classes.

Clearly, WPF introduces many significant changes. However, there are five key principles that immediately stand out because they are so different from previous Windows user interface toolkits such as Windows Forms. These principles are the following:

- *Hardware acceleration*: All WPF drawing is performed through DirectX, which allows it to take advantage of the latest in modern video cards.

- *Resolution independence*: WPF is flexible enough to scale up or down to suit your monitor and display preferences, depending on the system DPI setting.

- *No fixed control appearance*: In traditional Windows development, there's a wide chasm between controls that can be tailored to suit your needs (which are known as *owner-drawn* controls) and those that are rendered by the operating system and essentially fixed in appearance. In WPF, everything from a basic Rectangle to a standard Button or more complex Toolbar is drawn using the same rendering engine and completely customizable. For this reason, WPF controls are often called *lookless controls*—they define the functionality of a control, but they don't have a hardwired "look."

- *Declarative user interfaces*: In the next chapter, you'll consider XAML, the markup standard you use to define WPF user interfaces. XAML allows you to build a window without using code. Impressively, XAML doesn't limit you to fixed, unchanging user interfaces. You can use tools such as data binding and triggers to automate basic user interface behavior (such as text boxes that update themselves when you page through a record source, or labels that glow when you hover overtop with the mouse), all without writing a single line of Visual Basic.

- *Object-based drawing*: Even if you plan to work at the lower-level visual layer (rather than the higher-level element layer), you won't work in terms of painting and pixels. Instead, you'll create shape objects and let WPF maintain the display in the most optimized manner possible.

You'll see these principles at work throughout this book. But before you go any further, it's time to learn about a complementary standard. The next chapter introduces XAML, the markup language used to define WPF user interfaces.

CHAPTER 2

XAML

XAML (short for *Extensible Application Markup Language* and pronounced *zammel*) is a markup language used to instantiate .NET objects. Although XAML is a technology that can be applied to many problem domains, its primary role in life is to construct WPF user interfaces. In other words, XAML documents define the arrangement of panels, buttons, and controls that make up the windows in a WPF application.

It's unlikely that you'll write XAML by hand. Instead, you'll use a tool that generates the XAML you need. If you're a graphic designer, that tool is likely to be a graphical design program such as Microsoft Expression Blend. If you're a developer, you'll probably start with Microsoft Visual Studio. Because both tools are equally at home with XAML, you can create a basic user interface with Visual Studio and then hand it off to a crack design team that can polish it up with custom graphics in Expression Blend. In fact, this ability to integrate the workflow between developers and designers is one of the key reasons that Microsoft created XAML.

This chapter presents a detailed introduction to XAML. You'll consider its purpose, its overall architecture, and its syntax. Once you understand the broad rules of XAML, you'll know what is and isn't possible in a WPF user interface—and how to make changes by hand when it's necessary. More important, by exploring the tags in a WPF XAML document, you can learn a bit about the object model that underpins WPF user interfaces and get ready for the deeper exploration to come.

What's New   WPF 4.5 adds nothing new to the XAML standard. In fact, even the minor refinements of XAML 2009 still aren't fully implemented. They're supported only in loose XAML files, not compiled XAML resources (which is what virtually every WPF application uses). In fact, XAML 2009 will probably never become a fully integrated part of WPF, because its improvements aren't terribly important, and any change to the XAML compiler raises security and performance concerns. For that reason, XAML 2009 isn't covered in this book.

Understanding XAML

Developers realized long ago that the most efficient way to tackle complex, graphically rich applications is to separate the graphical portion from the underlying code. That way, artists can own the graphics, and developers can own the code. Both pieces can be designed and refined separately, without any versioning headaches.

Graphical User Interfaces Before WPF

With traditional display technologies, there's no easy way to separate the graphical content from the code. The key problem with a Windows Forms application is that every form you create is defined entirely in VB code. As you drop controls onto the design surface and configure them, Visual Studio quietly adjusts the code in the corresponding form class. Sadly, graphic designers don't have any tools that can work with VB code.

Instead, artists are forced to take their content and export it to a bitmap format. These bitmaps can then be used to skin windows, buttons, and other controls. This approach works well for straightforward interfaces that don't change much over time, but it's extremely limiting in other scenarios. Some of its problems include the following:

- Each graphical element (background, button, and so on) needs to be exported as a separate bitmap. That limits the ability to combine bitmaps and use dynamic effects such as antialiasing, transparency, and shadows.

- A fair bit of user interface logic needs to be embedded in the code by the developer. This includes button sizes, positioning, mouse over effects, and animations. The graphic designer can't control any of these details.

- There's no intrinsic connection between the different graphical elements, so it's easy to end up with an unmatched set of images. Tracking all these items adds complexity.

- Bitmaps can't be resized without compromising their quality. For that reason, a bitmap-based user interface is resolution-dependent. That means it can't accommodate large monitors and high-resolution, which is a major violation of the WPF design philosophy.

If you've ever been through the process of designing a Windows Forms application with custom graphics in a team setting, you've put up with a lot of frustration. Even if the interface is designed from scratch by a graphic designer, you'll need to re-create it with VB code. Usually, the graphic designer will simply prepare a mock-up that you need to translate painstakingly into your application.

WPF solves this problem with XAML. When designing a WPF application in Visual Studio, the window you're designing isn't translated into code. Instead, it's serialized into a set of XAML tags. When you run the application, these tags are used to generate the objects that compose the user interface.

■ **Note** It's important to understand that WPF doesn't require XAML. There's no reason Visual Studio couldn't use the Windows Forms approach and create code statements that construct your WPF windows. But if it did, your window would be locked into the Visual Studio environment and available to programmers only.

In other words, WPF doesn't require XAML. However, XAML opens up worlds of possibilities for collaboration, because other design tools understand the XAML format. For example, a savvy designer can use a tool such as Microsoft Expression Design to fine-tune the graphics in your WPF application or a tool such as Expression Blend to build sophisticated animations for it. After you've finished this chapter, you may want to read a Microsoft white paper at http://windowsclient.net/wpf/white-papers/thenewiteration.aspx that reviews XAML and explores some of the ways developers and designers can collaborate on a WPF application.

■ **Tip** XAML plays the same role for Windows applications as control tags do for ASP.NET web applications. The difference is that the ASP.NET tagging syntax is designed to look like HTML, so designers can craft web pages by using ordinary web design applications such as Microsoft Expression and Adobe Dreamweaver. As with WPF, the actual code for an ASP.NET web page is usually placed in a separate file to facilitate this design.

The Variants of XAML

People use the term *XAML* in various ways. So far, I've used it to refer to the entire language of XAML which is an all-purpose XML-based syntax for representing a tree of .NET objects. (These objects could be buttons and text boxes in a window or custom classes you've defined. In fact, XAML could even be used on other platforms to represent non-.NET objects.)

There are also several subsets of XAML:

- *WPF XAML* encompasses the elements that describe WPF content, such as vector graphics, controls, and documents. Currently, it's the most significant application of XAML, and it's the subset you'll explore in this book.

- *XPS XAML* is the part of WPF XAML that defines an XML representation for formatted electronic documents. It's been published as the separate XML Paper Specification (XPS) standard. You'll explore XPS in Chapter 28.

- *Silverlight XAML* is a subset of WPF XAML that's intended for Microsoft Silverlight applications. Silverlight is a cross-platform browser plug-in that allows you to create rich web content with two-dimensional graphics, animation, and audio and video. Chapter 1 has more about Silverlight, or you can visit http://silverlight.net to learn about it in detail.

- *WF XAML* encompasses the elements that describe Windows Workflow Foundation (WF) content. You can learn more about WF at http://tinyurl.com/d9xr2nv.

XAML Compilation

The creators of WPF knew that XAML needed to not only solve the problem of design collaboration—it also needed to be fast. And though XML-based formats such as XAML are flexible and easily portable to other tools and platforms, they aren't always the most efficient option. XML was designed to be logical, readable, and straightforward, but not compact.

WPF addresses this shortcoming with Binary Application Markup Language (BAML. BAML is really nothing more than a binary representation of XAML. When you compile a WPF application in Visual Studio, all your XAML files are converted into BAML, and that BAML is then embedded as a resource into the final DLL or EXE assembly. BAML is *tokenized*, which means lengthier bits of XAML are replaced with shorter tokens. Not only is BAML significantly smaller, but it's also optimized in a way that makes it faster to parse at runtime.

Most developers won't worry about the conversion of XAML to BAML because the compiler performs it behind the scenes. However, it is possible to use XAML without compiling it first. This might make sense in scenarios that require some of the user interface to be supplied just in time (for example, pulled out of a database as a block of XAML tags). You'll see how this works in the upcoming section "Loading and Compiling XAML."

CREATING XAML WITH VISUAL STUDIO

In this chapter, you'll take a look at all the details of XAML markup. Of course, when you're designing an application, you won't write all your XAML by hand. Instead, you'll use a tool such as Visual Studio that can drag and drop your user interface into existence. Based on that, you might wonder whether it's worth spending so much time studying the syntax of XAML.

The answer is a resounding *yes*. Understanding XAML is critical to WPF application design. It will help you learn key WPF concepts, such as attached properties (in this chapter), layout (Chapter 3), routed events (Chapter 4), the content model (Chapter 6), and so on. More important, a whole host of tasks are possible—or are far easier to accomplish—with handwritten XAML. They include the following:

Wiring up event handlers: Attaching event handlers in the most common places—for example, to the Click event of a button—is easy to do in Visual Studio. However, once you understand how events are wired up in XAML, you'll be able create more-sophisticated connections. For example, you can set up an event handler that responds to the Click event of every button in a window. Chapter 5 has more about this technique.

Writing data-binding expressions: Data binding allows you to extract data from an object and display it in a linked element. To set up this relationship and configure how it works, you must add a data-binding expression to your XAML markup. Chapter 8 introduces data binding.

Defining resources: Resources are objects that you define once in a special section of your XAML and then reuse in various places in your markup. Resources allow you to centralize and standardize formatting and create nonvisual objects such as templates and animations. Chapter 10 shows how to create and use resources.

Defining animations: Animations are a common ingredient in XAML applications. Usually, they're defined as resources, constructed using XAML markup, and then linked to other controls (or triggered through code). Visual Studio has no design-time support for crafting animations. Chapter 15 delves into animation.

Defining control templates: WPF controls are designed to be *lookless*, which means you can substitute your custom visuals in place of the standard appearance. To do so, you must create your own control template, which is nothing more than a block of XAML markup. Chapter 17 tackles control templates.

Most WPF developers use a combination of techniques, laying out some of their user interface with a design tool (Visual Studio or Expression Blend) and then fine-tuning it by editing the XAML markup by hand. However, you'll probably find that it's easiest to write all your XAML by hand until you learn about layout containers in Chapter 3. That's because you need to use a layout container to properly arrange multiple controls in a window.

XAML Basics

The XAML standard is quite straightforward once you understand a few ground rules:

- Every element in a XAML document maps to an instance of a .NET class. The name of the element matches the name of the class *exactly*. For example, the element <Button instructs WPF to create a Button object.

- As with any XML document, you can nest one element inside another. As you'll see, XAML gives every class the flexibility to decide how it handles this situation. However, nesting is usually a way to express *containment*—in other words, if you find a Button element inside a Grid element, your user interface probably includes a grid that contains a button inside.

- You can set the properties of each class through attributes. However, in some situations, an attribute isn't powerful enough to handle the job. In these cases, you'll use nested tags with a special syntax.

■ **Tip**   If you're completely new to XML, you'll probably find it easier to review the basics before you tackle XAML. To get up to speed quickly, try the free web-based tutorial at www.w3schools.com/xml.

Before continuing, take a look at this bare-bones XAML document, which represents a new blank window (as created by Visual Studio). The lines have been numbered for easy reference:

```
1  <Window x:Class="Window1"
2      xmlns="http://schemas.microsoft.com/winfx/2006/xaml/presentation"
3      xmlns:x="http://schemas.microsoft.com/winfx/2006/xaml"
4      Title="Window1" Height="300" Width="300">
5
6      <Grid>
7      </Grid>
8  </Window>
```

This document includes only two elements—the top-level Window element, which represents the entire window, and the Grid, in which you can place all your controls. Although you could use any top-level element, WPF applications rely on just a few:

- Window
- Page (which is similar to Window but used for navigable applications)
- Application (which defines application resources and startup settings)

As in all XML documents, there can be only one top-level element. In the previous example, that means that as soon as you close the Window element with the </Window> tag, you end the document. No more content can follow.

Looking at the start tag for the Window element, you'll find several interesting attributes, including a class name and two XML namespaces (described in the following sections). You'll also find the three properties shown here:

```
4      Title="Window1" Height="300" Width="300">
```

Each attribute corresponds to a separate property of the Window class. All in all, this tells WPF to create a window with the caption Window1 and to make it 300 by 300 units large.

▨ **Note**   As you learned in Chapter 1, WPF uses a relative measurement system that isn't what most Windows developers expect. Rather than letting you set sizes using physical pixels, WPF uses *device-independent units* that can scale to fit different monitor resolutions and are defined as 1/96 of an inch. That means the 300-by-300-unit window in the previous example will be rendered as a 300-by-300-*pixel* window if your system DPI setting is the standard 96 dpi. However, on a system with a higher system DPI, more pixels will be used. Chapter 1 has the full story.

XAML Namespaces

Clearly, it's not enough to supply just a class name. The XAML parser also needs to know the .NET namespace where this class is located. For example, the Window class could exist in several places—it might refer to the System.Windows.Window class, or it could refer to a Window class in a third-party component or one you've defined in your application. To figure out which class you really want, the XAML parser examines the XML namespace that's applied to the element.

Here's how it works. In the sample document shown earlier, two namespaces are defined:

```
2      xmlns="http://schemas.microsoft.com/winfx/2006/xaml/presentation"
3      xmlns:x="http://schemas.microsoft.com/winfx/2006/xaml"
```

■ **Note**   XML namespaces are declared by using *attributes*. These attributes can be placed inside any element start tag. However, convention dictates that all the namespaces you need to use in a document should be declared in the very first tag, as they are in this example. After a namespace is declared, it can be used anywhere in the document.

The *xmlns attribute* is a specialized attribute in the world of XML that's reserved for declaring namespaces. This snippet of markup declares two namespaces that you'll find in every WPF XAML document you create:

- `http://schemas.microsoft.com/winfx/2006/xaml/presentation` is the core WPF namespace. It encompasses all the WPF classes, including the controls you use to build user interfaces. In this example, this namespace is declared without a namespace prefix, so it becomes the default namespace for the entire document. In other words, every element is automatically placed in this namespace unless you specify otherwise.

- `http://schemas.microsoft.com/winfx/2006/xaml` is the XAML namespace. It includes various XAML utility features that allow you to influence how your document is interpreted. This namespace is mapped to the prefix *x*. That means you can apply it by placing the namespace prefix before the element name (as in **<x:ElementName>**).

As you can see, the XML namespace name doesn't match any particular .NET namespace. There are a couple of reasons the creators of XAML chose this design. By convention, XML namespaces are often uniform resource identifiers (URIs) as they are here. These URIs look like they point to a location on the Web, but they don't. The URI format is used because it makes it unlikely that different organizations will inadvertently create different XML-based languages with the same namespace. Because the domain `schemas.microsoft.com` is owned by Microsoft, only Microsoft will use it in an XML namespace name.

The other reason that there isn't a one-to-one mapping between the XML namespaces used in XAML and .NET namespaces is because it would significantly complicate your XAML documents. The problem here is that WPF encompasses well over a dozen namespaces (all of which start with System.Windows). If each .NET namespace had a different XML namespace, you'd need to specify the right namespace for each and every control you use, which quickly gets messy. Instead, the creators of WPF chose to combine all of these .NET namespaces into a single XML namespace. This works because within the different .NET namespaces that are part of WPF, there aren't any classes that have the same name.

The namespace information allows the XAML parser to find the right class. For example, when it looks at the Window and Grid elements, it sees that they are placed in the default WPF namespace. It then searches the corresponding .NET namespaces until it finds System.Windows.Window and System.Windows.Controls.Grid.

The Code-Behind Class

XAML allows you to construct a user interface, but in order to make a functioning application, you need a way to connect the event handlers that contain your application code. XAML makes this easy by using the Class attribute that's shown here:

```
1  <Window x:Class="Window1"
```

The *x* namespace prefix places the Class attribute in the XAML namespace, which means this is a more general part of the XAML language. In fact, the Class attribute tells the XAML parser to generate a new class with the specified name. That class derives from the class that's named by the XML element. In other words, this example creates a new class named Window1, which derives from the base Window class.

The Window1 class is generated automatically at compile time. But here's where things get interesting. You can supply a piece of the Window1 class that will be merged into the automatically generated portion. The piece you specify is the perfect container for your event-handling code.

■ **Note** This magic happens through the VB feature known as *partial classes*. Partial classes allow you to split a class into two or more separate pieces for development and fuse them together in the compiled assembly. Partial classes can be used in a variety of code management scenarios, but they're most useful in situations like these, where your code needs to be merged with a designer-generated file.

When you compile your application, the XAML that defines your user interface (such as Window1.xaml) is translated into a CLR (common language runtime) type declaration that is merged with the logic in your code-behind class file (such as Window1.xaml.vb) to form one single unit. Initially, the code-behind class that Visual Studio creates is empty:

```
Class Window1

End Class
```

The InitializeComponent() Method

Currently, the Window1 class code doesn't include any code. However, one detail is completely hidden—the default constructor. If you could see the constructor that Visual Studio generates at compile time, it would look like this:

```
Public Sub New()
    InitializeComponent()
End Sub
```

The InitializeComponent() method is another piece of automatically generated code that doesn't appear in your class. It loads the BAML (the compiled XAML) from your assembly and uses it to build your user interface. As it parses the BAML, it creates each control object, sets its properties, and attaches any event handlers. (You'll see an example of the code that ends up in the InitializeComponent() method later in this chapter, in "Code and Compiled XAML.")

At this point, you're probably wondering why it's important to understand a detail that Visual Studio hides from you completely. The reason becomes apparent if you create a custom constructor for your window. In this case, you need to explicitly call the InitializeComponent() method. If you don't, the window won't be initialized, and none of your controls will appear.

Naming Elements

There's one more detail to consider. In your code-behind class, you'll often want to manipulate controls programmatically. For example, you might want to read or change properties or attach and detach event handlers on the fly. To make this possible, the control must include a XAML Name attribute. In the previous example, the Grid control does not include a Name attribute, so you won't be able to manipulate it in your code-behind file.

Here's how you can attach a name to the Grid:

```
6    <Grid x:Name="grid1">
7    </Grid>
```

You can make this change by hand in the XAML document, or you can select the grid in the Visual Studio designer and set the Name property by using the Properties window.

Either way, the Name attribute tells the XAML parser to add a field like this to the automatically generated portion of the Window1 class:

```
Friend WithEvents grid1 As System.Windows.Controls.Grid
```

Now you can interact with the grid in your Window1 class code by using the name grid1:

```
MessageBox.Show(String.Format("The grid is {0}x{1} units in size.", _
    grid1.ActualWidth, grid1.ActualHeight))
```

This technique doesn't add much for the simple grid example, but it becomes much more important when you need to read values in input controls such as text boxes and list boxes.

The Name property shown previously is part of the XAML language, and it's used to help integrate your code-behind class. Somewhat confusingly, many classes define their own Name property. (One example is the base FrameworkElement class from which all WPF elements derive.) XAML parsers have a clever way of handling this. You can set either the XAML Name property (using the x prefix) or the Name property that belongs to the actual element (by leaving out the prefix). Either way, the result is the same—the name you specify is used in the automatically generated code file *and* it's used to set the Name property.

That means the following markup is equivalent to what you've already seen:

```
<Grid Name="grid1">
</Grid>
```

This bit of magic works only if the class that includes the Name property decorates itself with the RuntimeNameProperty attribute. The RuntimeNameProperty indicates which property should be treated as the name for instances of that type. (Obviously, it's usually the property that's named Name.) The FrameworkElement class includes the RuntimeNameProperty attribute, so there's no problem.

▓ **Tip** In an old-fashioned Windows Forms application, every control has a name. In a WPF application, there's no such requirement. The examples in this book usually omit element names when they aren't needed, which makes the markup more concise.

By now, you should have a basic understanding of how to interpret a XAML document that defines a window and how that XAML document is converted into a final compiled class (with the addition of any code you've written). In the next section, you'll look at the property syntax in more detail and learn to wire up event handlers.

Properties and Events in XAML

So far, you've considered a relatively unexciting example—a blank window that hosts an empty Grid control. Before going any further, it's worth introducing a more realistic window that includes several controls. Figure 2-1 shows an example with an automatic question answerer.

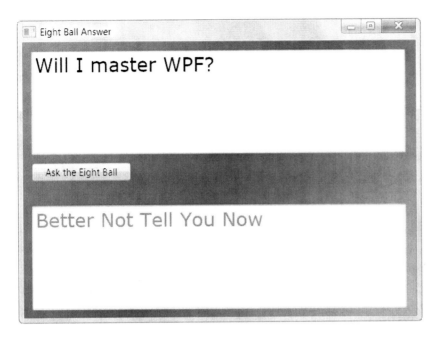

Figure 2-1. *Ask the eight ball, and all will be revealed*

The eight-ball window includes four controls: a Grid (the most common tool for arranging layout in WPF), two TextBox objects, and a Button. The markup that's required to arrange and configure these controls is significantly longer than the previous examples. Here's an abbreviated listing that replaces some of the details with an ellipsis (. . .) to expose the overall structure:

```
<Window x:Class=" Window1"
    xmlns="http://schemas.microsoft.com/winfx/2006/xaml/presentation"
    xmlns:x="http://schemas.microsoft.com/winfx/2006/xaml"
    Title="Eight Ball Answer" Height="328" Width="412">
  <Grid Name="grid1">
    <Grid.Background>
      ...
    </Grid.Background>
    <Grid.RowDefinitions>
      ...
    </Grid.RowDefinitions>

    <TextBox Name="txtQuestion" ... >
      ...
    </TextBox>

    <Button Name="cmdAnswer" ... >
      ...
    </Button>
```

```
    <TextBox Name="txtAnswer" ... >
        ...
    </TextBox>
  </Grid>
</Window>
```

In the following sections, you'll explore the parts of this document—and learn the syntax of XAML along the way.

■ **Note**   XAML isn't limited to the classes that are part of WPF. You can use XAML to create an instance of any class that meets a few ground rules. You'll learn how to use your own classes with XAML later in this chapter.

Simple Properties and Type Converters

As you've already seen, the attributes of an element set the properties of the corresponding object. For example, the text boxes in the eight-ball example configure the alignment, margin, and font:

```
<TextBox Name="txtQuestion"
  VerticalAlignment="Stretch" HorizontalAlignment="Stretch"
  FontFamily="Verdana" FontSize="24" Foreground="Green" ... >
```

For this to work, the System.Windows.Controls.TextBox class must provide the following properties: VerticalAlignment, HorizontalAlignment, FontFamily, FontSize, and Foreground. You'll learn the specific meaning for each of these properties in the following chapters.

To support this system, the XAML parser needs to perform a bit more work than you might initially realize. The value in an XML attribute is always a plain-text string. However, object properties can be any .NET type. In the previous example, there are two properties that use enumerations (VerticalAlignment and HorizontalAlignment), one string (FontFamily), one integer (FontSize), and one Brush object (Foreground).

To bridge the gap between string values and nonstring properties, the XAML parser needs to perform a conversion. The conversion is performed by *type converters*, a basic piece of .NET infrastructure that's existed since .NET 1.0.

Essentially, a type converter has one role in life—it provides utility methods that can convert a specific .NET data type to and from any other .NET type, such as a string representation in this case. The XAML parser follows two steps to find a type converter:

1. It examines the property declaration, looking for a TypeConverter attribute. (If present, the TypeConverter attribute indicates what class can perform the conversion.) For example, when you use a property such as Foreground, .NET checks the declaration of the Foreground property.

2. If there's no TypeConverter attribute on the property declaration, the XAML parser checks the class declaration of the corresponding data type. For example, the Foreground property uses a Brush object. The Brush class (and its derivatives) use the BrushConverter because the Brush class is decorated with the TypeConverter(GetType(BrushConverter)) attribute declaration.*converters.*

If there's no associated type converter on the property declaration or the class declaration, the XAML parser generates an error.

This system is simple but flexible. If you set a type converter at the class level, that converter applies to every property that uses that class. On the other hand, if you want to fine-tune the way type conversion works for a particular property, you can use the TypeConverter attribute on the property declaration instead.

It's technically possible to use type converters in code, but the syntax is a bit convoluted. It's almost always better to set a property directly—not only is it faster, but it also avoids potential errors from mistyping strings, which won't be caught until runtime. (This problem doesn't affect XAML, because the XAML is parsed and validated at compile time.) Of course, before you can set the properties on a WPF element, you need to know a bit more about the basic WPF properties and data types—a job you'll tackle in the next few chapters.

■ **Note**   XAML, like all XML-based languages, is *case-sensitive*. That means you can't substitute <button> for <Button>. However, type converters usually aren't case-sensitive, which means both Foreground="White" and Foreground="white" have the same result.

Complex Properties

As handy as type converters are, they aren't practical for all scenarios. For example, some properties are full-fledged objects with their own set of properties. Although it's possible to create a string representation that the type converter could use, that syntax might be difficult to use and prone to error.

Fortunately, XAML provides another option: *property-element syntax*. With property-element syntax, you add a child element with a name in the form Parent.PropertyName. For example, the Grid has a Background property that allows you to supply a brush that's used to paint the area behind the controls. If you want to use a complex brush— one more advanced than a solid-color fill—you'll need to add a child tag named Grid.Background, as shown here:

```
<Grid Name="grid1">
  <Grid.Background>
    ...
  </Grid.Background>
  ...
</Grid>
```

The key detail that makes this work is the period (.) in the element name. This distinguishes properties from other types of nested content.

This still leaves one detail—namely, after you've identified the complex property you want to configure, how do you set it? Here's the trick: inside the nested element, you can add another tag to instantiate a specific class. In the eight-ball example (shown in Figure 2-1), the background is filled with a gradient. To define the gradient you want, you need to create a LinearGradientBrush object.

Using the rules of XAML, you can create the LinearGradientBrush object by using an element with the name LinearGradientBrush:

```
<Grid Name="grid1">
  <Grid.Background>
    <LinearGradientBrush>
    </LinearGradientBrush>
  </Grid.Background>
  ...
</Grid>
```

The LinearGradientBrush class is part of the WPF set of namespaces, so you can keep using the default XML namespace for your tags.

However, it's not enough to simply create the LinearGradientBrush object—you also need to specify the colors in that gradient. You do this by filling the LinearGradientBrush.GradientStops property with a collection of GradientStop objects. Once again, the GradientStops property is too complex to be set with an attribute value alone. Instead, you need to rely on the property-element syntax:

```
<Grid Name="grid1">
  <Grid.Background>
    <LinearGradientBrush>
      <LinearGradientBrush.GradientStops>
      </LinearGradientBrush.GradientStops>
    </LinearGradientBrush>
  </Grid.Background>
  ...
</Grid>
```

Finally, you can fill the GradientStops collection with a series of GradientStop objects. Each GradientStop object has an Offset and Color property. You can supply these two values by using the ordinary property-attribute syntax:

```
<Grid Name="grid1">
  <Grid.Background>
    <LinearGradientBrush>
      <LinearGradientBrush.GradientStops>
        <GradientStop Offset="0.00" Color="Red" />
        <GradientStop Offset="0.50" Color="Indigo" />
        <GradientStop Offset="1.00" Color="Violet" />
      </LinearGradientBrush.GradientStops>
    </LinearGradientBrush>
  </Grid.Background>
  ...
</Grid>
```

■ **Note**   You can use property-element syntax for any property. But usually you'll use the simpler property-attribute approach if the property has a suitable type converter. Doing so results in more compact code.

Any set of XAML tags can be replaced with a set of code statements that performs the same task. The tags shown previously, which fill the background with a gradient of your choice, are equivalent to the following code:

```
Dim brush As New LinearGradientBrush()

Dim gradientStop1 As New GradientStop()
gradientStop1.Offset = 0
gradientStop1.Color = Colors.Red
brush.GradientStops.Add(gradientStop1)

Dim gradientStop2 As New GradientStop()
gradientStop2.Offset = 0.5
gradientStop2.Color = Colors.Indigo
brush.GradientStops.Add(gradientStop2)

Dim gradientStop3 As New GradientStop()
gradientStop3.Offset = 1
```

```
gradientStop3.Color = Colors.Violet
brush.GradientStops.Add(gradientStop3)

grid1.Background = brush
```

Markup Extensions

For most properties, the XAML property syntax works perfectly well. But in some cases, it just isn't possible to hard-code the property value. For example, you may want to set a property value to an object that already exists. Or you may want to set a property value *dynamically* by binding it to a property in another control. In both of these cases, you need to use a *markup extension*—specialized syntax that sets a property in a nonstandard way.

Markup extensions can be used in nested tags or in XML attributes, which is more common. When they're used in attributes, they are always bracketed by curly braces {}. For example, here's how you can use , which allows you to refer to a shared property in another class:

```
<Button ... Foreground="{x:Static SystemColors.ActiveCaptionBrush}" >
```

Markup extensions use the syntax {MarkupExtensionClass Argument}. In this case, the markup extension is the StaticExtension class. (By convention, you can drop the final word *Extension* when referring to an extension class.) The x prefix indicates that StaticExtension is found in one of the XAML namespaces. You'll also encounter markup extensions that are part of the WPF namespaces and don't have the x prefix.

All markup extensions are implemented by classes that derive from System.Windows.Markup.MarkupExtension. The base MarkupExtension class is extremely simple—it provides a single ProvideValue method that gets the value you want. In other words, when the XAML parser encounters the previous statement, it creates an instance of the StaticExtension class (passing in the string "SystemColors.ActiveCaptionBrush" as an argument to the constructor) and then calls ProvideValue() to get the object returned by the SystemColors.ActiveCaption.Brush shared property. The Foreground property of the cmdAnswer button is then set with the retrieved object.

The end result of this piece of XAML is the same as if you'd written this:

```
cmdAnswer.Foreground = SystemColors.ActiveCaptionBrush
```

Because markup extensions map to classes, they can also be used as nested properties, as you learned in the previous section. For example, you can use StaticExtension with the Button.Foreground property like this:

```
<Button ... >
  <Button.Foreground>
    <x:Static Member="SystemColors.ActiveCaptionBrush"></x:Static>
  </Button.Foreground>
</Button>
```

Depending on the complexity of the markup extension and the number of properties you want to set, this syntax is sometimes simpler.

Like most markup extensions, StaticExtension needs to be evaluated at runtime because only then can you determine the current system colors. Some markup extensions can be evaluated at compile time. These include NullExtension (which constructs an object that represents a .NET type). Throughout this book, you'll see many examples of markup extensions at work, particularly with resources and data binding.

Attached Properties

Along with ordinary properties, XAML also includes the concept of *attached properties*—properties that may apply to several controls but are defined in a different class. In WPF, attached properties are frequently used to control layout.

31

Here's how it works. Every control has its own set of intrinsic properties. (For example, a text box has a specific font, text color, and text content as dictated by properties such as FontFamily, Foreground, and Text.) When you place a control inside a container, it gains additional features, depending on the type of container. (For example, if you place a text box inside a grid, you need to be able to choose the grid cell where it's positioned.) These additional details are set by using attached properties.

Attached properties always use a two-part name in this form: DefiningType.PropertyName. This two-part naming syntax allows the XAML parser to distinguish between a normal property and an attached property.

In the eight-ball example, attached properties allow the individual controls to place themselves on separate rows in the (invisible) grid:

```
<TextBox ... Grid.Row="0">
  [Place question here.]
</TextBox>

<Button ... Grid.Row="1">
  Ask the Eight Ball
</Button>

<TextBox ... Grid.Row="2">
  [Answer will appear here.]
</TextBox>
```

Attached properties aren't really properties at all. They're translated into method calls. The XAML parser calls the shared method that has this form: *DefiningType.SetPropertyName*(). For example, in the previous XAML snippet, the defining type is the Grid class, and the property is Row, so the parser calls Grid.SetRow().

When calling SetPropertyName(), the parser passes two parameters: the object that's being modified and the property value that's specified. For example, when you set the Grid.Row property on the TextBox control, the XAML parser executes this code:

```
Grid.SetRow(txtQuestion, 0)
```

This pattern (calling a shared method of the defining type) is a convenience that conceals what's really taking place. To the casual eye, this code implies that the row number is stored in the Grid object. However, the row number is actually stored in the object that it *applies to*—in this case, the TextBox object.

This sleight of hand works because TextBox derives from the DependencyObject base class, as do all WPF controls. And as you'll learn in Chapter 4, the DependencyObject is designed to store a virtually unlimited collection of dependency properties. (The attached properties that were discussed earlier are a special type of dependency property.)

In fact, the Grid.SetRow() method is a shortcut that's equivalent to calling the DependencyObject.SetValue() method, as shown here:

```
txtQuestion.SetValue(Grid.RowProperty, 0)
```

Attached properties are a core ingredient of WPF. They act as an all-purpose extensibility system. For example, by defining the Row property as an attached property, you guarantee that it's usable with any control. The other option, making the property part of a base class such as FrameworkElement, complicates life. Not only would it clutter the public interface with properties that have meaning in only certain circumstances (in this case, when an element is being used inside a Grid), but it would also make it impossible to add new types of containers that require new properties.

Nesting Elements

As you've seen, XAML documents are arranged as a heavily nested tree of elements. In the current example, a Window element contains a Grid element, which contains TextBox and Button elements.

XAML allows each element to decide how it deals with nested elements. This interaction is mediated through one of three mechanisms that are evaluated in this order:

- If the parent implements IList, the parser calls IList.Add() and passes in the child.

- If the parent implements IDictionary, the parser calls IDictionary.Add() and passes in the child. When using a dictionary collection, you must also set the x:Key attribute to give a key name to each item.

- If the parent is decorated with the ContentProperty attribute, the parser uses the child to set that property.

For example, earlier in this chapter, you saw how LinearGradientBrush can hold a collection of GradientStop objects by using syntax like this:

```
<LinearGradientBrush>
  <LinearGradientBrush.GradientStops>
    <GradientStop Offset="0.00" Color="Red" />
    <GradientStop Offset="0.50" Color="Indigo" />
    <GradientStop Offset="1.00" Color="Violet" />
  </LinearGradientBrush.GradientStops>
</LinearGradientBrush>
```

The XAML parser recognizes that the LinearGradientBrush.GradientStops element is a complex property because it includes a period. However, the parser needs to process the tags inside (the three GradientStop elements) a little differently. In this case, it recognizes that the GradientStops property returns a GradientStopCollection object, and that GradientStopCollection implements the IList interface. Thus, it assumes (quite rightly) that each GradientStop should be added to the collection by using the IList.Add() method:

```
Dim gradientStop1 As New GradientStop()
gradientStop1.Offset = 0
gradientStop1.Color = Colors.Red
Dim list As IList = brush.GradientStops
list.Add(gradientStop1)
```

Some properties might support more than one type of collection. In this case, you need to add a tag that specifies the collection class, like this:

```
<LinearGradientBrush>
  <LinearGradientBrush.GradientStops>
    <GradientStopCollection>
      <GradientStop Offset="0.00" Color="Red" />
      <GradientStop Offset="0.50" Color="Indigo" />
      <GradientStop Offset="1.00" Color="Violet" />
    </GradientStopCollection>
  </LinearGradientBrush.GradientStops>
</LinearGradientBrush>
```

33

> ■ **Note**   If the collection defaults to a null reference (Nothing), you need to include the tag that specifies the collection class, thereby creating the collection object. If there's a default instance of the collection and you simply need to fill it, you can omit that part.

Nested content doesn't always indicate a collection. For example, consider the Grid element, which contains several other controls:

```
<Grid Name="grid1">
  ...
  <TextBox Name="txtQuestion" ... >
    ...
  </TextBox>
  <Button Name="cmdAnswer" ... >
    ...
  </Button>
  <TextBox Name="txtAnswer" ... >
    ...
  </TextBox>
</Grid>
```

These nested tags don't correspond to complex properties because they don't include the period. Furthermore, the Grid control isn't a collection and so it doesn't implement IList or IDictionary. What the Grid *does* support is the ContentProperty attribute, which indicates the property that should receive any nested content. Technically, the ContentProperty attribute is applied to the Panel class, from which the Grid derives, and looks like this:

```
<ContentProperty("Children")> _
Public MustInherit Class Panel
```

This indicates that any nested elements should be used to set the Children property. The XAML parser treats the content property differently depending on whether it's a collection property (in which case it implements the IList or IDictionary interface). Because the Panel.Children property returns a UIElementCollection and because UIElementCollection implements IList, the parser uses the IList.Add() method to add nested content to the grid.

In other words, when the XAML parser meets the previous markup, it creates an instance of each nested element and passes it to the Grid by using the Grid.Children.Add() method:

```
txtQuestion = New TextBox()
...
grid1.Children.Add(txtQuestion)

cmdAnswer = New Button()
...
grid1.Children.Add(cmdAnswer)

txtAnswer = New TextBox()
...
grid1.Children.Add(txtAnswer)
```

What happens next depends entirely on how the control implements the content property. The Grid displays all the controls it holds in an invisible layout of rows and columns, as you'll see in Chapter 3.

The ContentProperty attribute is frequently used in WPF. Not only is it used for container controls (such as Grid) and controls that contain a collection of visual items (such as ListBox and TreeView), it's also used for controls that contain singular content. For example, the TextBox and Button controls are able to hold only a single element or piece of text, but they both use a content property to deal with nested content like this:

```
<TextBox Name="txtQuestion" ... >
  [Place question here.]
</TextBox>
<Button Name="cmdAnswer" ... >
  Ask the Eight Ball
</Button>
<TextBox Name="txtAnswer" ... >
  [Answer will appear here.]
</TextBox>
```

The TextBox class uses the ContentProperty attribute to flag the TextBox.Text property. The Button class uses the ContentProperty attribute to flag the Button.Content property. The XAML parser uses the supplied text to set these properties.

The TextBox.Text property allows only strings. However, Button.Content is much more interesting. As you'll learn in Chapter 6, the Content property accepts any element. For example, here's a button that contains a shape object:

```
<Button Name="cmdAnswer" ... >
  <Rectangle Fill="Blue" Height="10" Width="100" />
</Button>
```

Because the Text and Content properties don't use collections, you can't include more than one piece of content. For example, if you attempt to nest multiple elements inside a Button, the XAML parser will throw an exception. The parser also throws an exception if you supply nontext content (such as a Rectangle).

■ **Note** As a general rule of thumb, all controls that derive from ContentControl allow a single nested element. All controls that derive from ItemsControl allow a collection of items that map to some part of the control (such as a list of items or a tree of nodes). All controls that derive from Panel are containers that are used to organize groups of controls. The ContentControl, ItemsControl, and Panel base classes all use the ContentProperty attribute.

Special Characters and Whitespace

XAML is bound by the rules of XML. For example, XML pays special attention to a few specific characters, such as & and <and>. If you try to use these values to set the content of an element, you'll run into trouble because the XAML parser assumes you're trying to do something else—such as create a nested element.

For example, imagine you want to create a button that contains the text <Click Me>. The following markup won't work:

```
<Button ... >
  <Click Me>
</Button>
```

The problem here is that it looks like you're trying to create an element named Click with an attribute named Me. The solution is to replace the offending characters with entity references—specific codes that the XAML parser will interpret correctly. Table 2-1 lists the character entities you might choose to use. Note that the quotation mark character entity is required only when setting values by using an attribute, because the quotation mark indicates the beginning and ending of an attribute value.

Table 2-1. XML Character Entities

Special Character	Character Entity
Less than (<)	&lt;
Greater than (>)	&gt;
Ampersand (&)	&amp;
Quotation mark (")	&quot;

Here's the corrected markup that uses the appropriate character entities:

```
<Button ... >
  &lt;Click Me&gt;
</Button>
```

When the XAML parser reads this, it correctly understands that you want to add the text <Click Me>, and it passes a string with this content, complete with angle brackets, to the Button.Content property.

■ **Note**   This limitation is a XAML detail, and it won't affect you if you want to set the Button.Content property in code.

Special characters aren't the only stumbling block you'll run into with XAML. Another issue is whitespace handling By default, XML collapses all whitespace, which means a long string of spaces, tabs, and hard returns is reduced to a single space. Furthermore, if you add whitespace before or after your element content, this space is ignored completely. You can see this in the eight-ball example. The text in the button and the two text boxes is separated from the XAML tags by using a hard return and tab to make the markup more readable. However, this extra space doesn't appear in the user interface.

Sometimes this isn't what you want. For example, you may want to include a series of several spaces in your button text. In this case, you need to use the xml:space="preserve" attribute on your element.

The xml:space attribute is part of the XML standard, and it's an all-or-nothing setting. After you switch it on, all the whitespace inside that element is retained. For example, consider this markup:

```
<TextBox Name="txtQuestion" xml:space="preserve" ...>
    [There is a lot of space inside these quotation marks "        ".]
</TextBox>
```

In this example, the text in the text box will include the hard return and tab that appear before the actual text. It will also include the series of spaces inside the text and the hard return that follows the text.

If you just want to keep the spaces inside, you'll need to use this less-readable markup:

```
<TextBox Name="txtQuestion" xml:space="preserve" ...
 >[There is a lot of space inside these quotation marks "        ".]</TextBox>
```

The trick here is to make sure no whitespace appears between the opening > and your content, or between your content and the closing <.

Once again, this issue applies only to XAML markup. If you set the text in a text box programmatically, all the spaces you include are used.

Events

So far, all the attributes you've seen map to properties. However, attributes can also be used to attach event handlers. The syntax for this is EventName = "EventHandlerMethodName".

For example, the Button control provides a Click event. You can attach an event handler like this:

```
<Button ... Click="cmdAnswer_Click">
```

This assumes that there is a method with the name cmdAnswer_Click in the code-behind class. The event handler must have the correct signature (that is, it must match the delegate for the Click event). Here's the method that does the trick:

```
Private Sub cmdAnswer_Click(ByVal sender As Object, ByVal e As RoutedEventArgs)
    Me.Cursor = Cursors.Wait

    ' Dramatic delay...
    System.Threading.Thread.Sleep(TimeSpan.FromSeconds(3))

    Dim generator As New AnswerGenerator()
    txtAnswer.Text = generator.GetRandomAnswer(txtQuestion.Text)
    Me.Cursor = Nothing
End Sub
```

The event model in WPF is different than in other types of .NET applications, because it relies on *event* . You'll learn more in Chapter 5.

In many situations, you'll use attributes to set properties and attach event handlers on the same element. WPF always follows the same sequence: first it sets the Name property (if set); then it attaches any event handlers; and finally it sets the properties. This means that any event handlers that respond to property changes will fire when the property is set for the first time.

■ **Note**   It's possible to embed code (such as event handlers) directly in a XAML document by using the Code element. However, this technique is thoroughly discouraged, and it doesn't have any practical application in WPF. This approach isn't supported by Visual Studio and isn't discussed in this book.

Visual Studio helps you out with IntelliSense when you add an event handler attribute. After you enter the equal sign (for example, after you've typed **Click=** in the <Button> element), IntelliSense shows a drop-down list with all the suitable event handlers in your code-behind class, as shown in Figure 2-2. If you need to create a new event handler to handle this event, you simply choose <New Event Handler> from the top of the list. Alternatively, you can attach and create event handlers by using the Events tab of the Properties window.

```
            </Grid.Background>
            <TextBox VerticalAlignment="Stretch" HorizontalAlignment="Stretch" Margin="10
                     TextWrapping="Wrap" FontFamily="Verdana" FontSize="24"
                     Grid.Row="0" >
              [Place question here.]
            </TextBox>
            <Button VerticalAlignment="Top" HorizontalAlignment="Left" Margin="10,0,0,20"
                     Click=""
                     Grid.Ro ⊞ <New Event Handler>
             Ask the Eight ⊞ cmdAnswer_Click
            </Button>
            <TextBox VerticalAlignment="Stretch" HorizontalAlignment="Stretch" Margin="10
                     TextWrapping="Wrap" IsReadOnly="True" FontFamily="Verdana" FontSize="
                     Grid.Row="2">
              [Answer will appear here.]
            </TextBox>
          </Grid>
        </Window>
```
100 %

Figure 2-2. *Attaching an event with Visual Studio IntelliSense*

There's one wrinkle in the way that WPF event handlers work with VB. As you no doubt know, Visual Basic defines a Handles statement that allows you to hook up events declaratively in code. WPF supports this convention.

To use the Handles statement, your element must have a name. Provided this requirement is met, you can use the Handles statement in the familiar form, supplying *ElementName.EventName*, as shown here:

```
Private Sub cmdAnswer_Click(ByVal sender As Object, _
   ByVal e As RoutedEventArgs e) Handles cmdAnswer.Click
   ...
End Sub
```

In this case, no event attribute is required in the XAML. (In fact, you must be careful not to supply an event attribute, or you'll end up connecting the same event handler twice.) If you double-click an element on the Visual Studio design surface, Visual Studio creates this type of event handler automatically. It even assigns an automatically generated name to the element if it doesn't already have a name to ensure that this system works.

At first glance, this seems like a perfect solution, because it preserves the convenient VB event-handling approach with minimum fuss. However, the Handles statement is somewhat limited. As you'll discover in Chapter 5, WPF uses a routed event model that allows you to handle events at different places in your markup. For example, instead of handling a Click event on the Button control where it occurs, you can handle it after it bubbles up through your layout to a containing element. Similarly, you can preview events (such as key presses) in a containing element before they're received by the control that actually has focus. Both of these techniques are useful in a variety of situations. However, in many scenarios they don't work with the Handles statement.

It's up to you whether you want to use a mix of approaches, with the Handles statement for straightforward event hookup and the event attributes for more-complicated examples that won't work with Handles. In this book, all the code examples use event attributes for consistency.

The Full Eight-Ball Example

Now that you've considered the fundamentals of XAML, you know enough to walk through the definition for the window in Figure 2-1. Here's the complete XAML markup:

```
<Window x:Class=" Window1"
 xmlns="http://schemas.microsoft.com/winfx/2006/xaml/presentation"
 xmlns:x="http://schemas.microsoft.com/winfx/2006/xaml"
 Title="Eight Ball Answer" Height="328" Width="412" >
  <Grid Name="grid1">
    <Grid.RowDefinitions>
      <RowDefinition Height="*" />
      <RowDefinition Height="Auto" />
      <RowDefinition Height="*" />
    </Grid.RowDefinitions>
    <TextBox VerticalAlignment="Stretch" HorizontalAlignment="Stretch"
     Margin="10,10,13,10" Name="txtQuestion"
     TextWrapping="Wrap" FontFamily="Verdana" FontSize="24"
     Grid.Row="0">
      [Place question here.]
    </TextBox>
    <Button VerticalAlignment="Top" HorizontalAlignment="Left"
     Margin="10,0,0,20" Width="127" Height="23" Name="cmdAnswer"
     Click="cmdAnswer_Click" Grid.Row="1">
      Ask the Eight Ball
    </Button>
    <TextBox VerticalAlignment="Stretch" HorizontalAlignment="Stretch"
     Margin="10,10,13,10" Name="txtAnswer" TextWrapping="Wrap"
     IsReadOnly="True" FontFamily="Verdana" FontSize="24" Foreground="Green"
     Grid.Row="2">
      [Answer will appear here.]
    </TextBox>

    <Grid.Background>
      <LinearGradientBrush>
        <LinearGradientBrush.GradientStops>
          <GradientStop Offset="0.00" Color="Red" />
          <GradientStop Offset="0.50" Color="Indigo" />
          <GradientStop Offset="1.00" Color="Violet" />
        </LinearGradientBrush.GradientStops>
      </LinearGradientBrush>
    </Grid.Background>
  </Grid>
</Window>
```

Remember, you probably won't write the XAML for an entire user interface by hand—doing so would be unbearably tedious. However, you might have good reason to edit the XAML code to make a change that would be awkward to accomplish in the designer. You might also find yourself reviewing XAML to get a better idea of how a window works.

Using Types from Other Namespaces

So far, you've seen how to create a basic user interface in XAML by using the classes that are part of WPF. However, XAML is designed as an all-purpose way to instantiate .NET objects, including ones that are in other non-WPF namespaces and those you create yourself.

It might seem odd to consider creating objects that aren't designed for onscreen display in a XAML window, but it makes sense in a number of scenarios. One example is when you use data binding and you want to draw information from another object to display in a control. Another example is if you want to set the property of a WPF object by using a non-WPF object.

For example, you can fill a WPF ListBox with data objects. The ListBox will call the ToString() method to get the text to display for each item in the list. (Or for an even better list, you can create a *data template* that extracts multiple pieces of information and formats them appropriately. This technique is described in Chapter 20.)

To use a class that isn't defined in one of the WPF namespaces, you need to map the .NET namespace to an XML namespace. XAML has a special syntax for doing this, which looks like this:

```
xmlns:Prefix="clr-namespace:Namespace;assembly=AssemblyName"
```

Typically, you'll place this namespace mapping in the root element of your XAML document, right after the attributes that declare the WPF and XAML namespaces. You'll also fill in the three italicized bits with the appropriate information, as explained here:

> *Prefix*: This is the XML prefix you want to use to indicate that namespace in your XAML markup. For example, the XAML language uses the x prefix.

> *Namespace*: This is the fully qualified .NET namespace name.

> *AssemblyName*: This is the assembly where the type is declared, without the .dll extension. This assembly must be referenced in your project. If you want to use your project assembly, leave this out.

For example, here's how you would gain access to the basic types in the System namespace and map them to the prefix *sys*:

```
xmlns:sys="clr-namespace:System;assembly=mscorlib"
```

Here's how you would gain access to the types you've declared in the My Project namespace of the current project and map them to the prefix *local*:

```
xmlns:local="clr-namespace:MyNamespace"
```

Now, to create an instance of a class in one of these namespaces, you use the namespace prefix:

```
<local:MyObject ...></local:MyObject>
```

■ **Tip**　Remember, you can use any namespace prefix you want, as long as you are consistent throughout your XAML document. However, the sys and local prefixes are commonly used when importing the System namespace and the namespace for the current project. You'll see them used throughout this book.

Ideally, every class you want to use in XAML will have a no-argument constructor. If it does, the XAML parser can create the corresponding object, set its properties, and attach any event handlers you supply. XAML doesn't support parameterized constructors, and all the elements in WPF elements include a no-argument constructor. Additionally, you need to be able to set all the details you want by using public properties. XAML doesn't allow you to set public fields or call methods.

If the class you want to use doesn't have a no-argument constructor, you're in a bit of a bind. If you're trying to create a simple primitive (such as a string, date, or numeric type), you can supply the string representation of your data as content inside your tag. The XAML parser will then use the type converter to convert that string into the appropriate object. Here's an example with the DateTime structure:

```
<sys:DateTime>10/30/2013 4:30 PM</sys:DateTime>
```

This works because the DateTime class uses the TypeConverter attribute to link itself to the DateTimeConverter. The DateTimeConverter recognizes this string as a valid DateTime object and converts it. When you're using this technique, you can't use attributes to set any properties for your object.

If you want to create a class that doesn't have a no-argument constructor and there isn't a suitable type converter to use, you're out of luck.

■ **Note** Some developers get around these limitations by creating custom wrapper classes. For example, the FileStream class doesn't include a no-argument constructor. However, you could create a wrapper class that does. Your wrapper class would create the required FileStream object in its constructor, retrieve the information it needs, and then close the FileStream. This type of solution is seldom ideal because it invites hard-coding information in your class constructor and complicates exception handling. In most cases, it's a better idea to manipulate the object with a little event-handling code and leave it out of your XAML entirely.

The following example puts these concepts together. It maps the sys prefix to the System namespace and uses the System namespace to create three DateTime objects, which are used to fill a list:

```
<Window x:Class=" Window1"
    xmlns="http://schemas.microsoft.com/winfx/2006/xaml/presentation"
    xmlns:x="http://schemas.microsoft.com/winfx/2006/xaml"
    xmlns:sys="clr-namespace:System;assembly=mscorlib"
    Width="300" Height="300"
    >
  <ListBox>
    <ListBoxItem>
      <sys:DateTime>10/13/2013 4:30 PM</sys:DateTime>
    </ListBoxItem>
    <ListBoxItem>
      <sys:DateTime>10/29/2013 12:30 PM</sys:DateTime>
    </ListBoxItem>
    <ListBoxItem>
      <sys:DateTime>10/30/2013 2:30 PM</sys:DateTime>
    </ListBoxItem>
  </ListBox>
</Window>
```

Loading and Compiling XAML

As you've already learned, XAML and WPF are separate, albeit complementary, technologies. As a result, it's quite possible to create a WPF application that doesn't use the faintest bit of XAML.

Altogether, there are three distinct coding styles that you can use to create a WPF application:

> *Code-only*: This is the traditional approach used in Visual Studio for Windows Forms applications. It generates a user interface through code statements.

> *Code and uncompiled markup (XAML)*: This is a specialized approach that makes sense when you need highly dynamic user interfaces. You load part of the user interface from a XAML file at runtime by using the XamlReader class from the System.Windows.Markup namespace.

> *Code and compiled markup (BAML)*: This is the preferred approach for WPF and the one that Visual Studio supports. You create a XAML template for each window, and this XAML is compiled into BAML and embedded in the final assembly. At runtime the compiled BAML is extracted and used to regenerate the user interface.

In the following sections, you'll dig deeper into these three models and how they work. You'll also see how you can open loose XAML files in a browser, provided they don't use any code.

Code-Only

Code-only development is a less common (but still fully supported) avenue for writing a WPF application without any XAML. The obvious disadvantage to code-only development is that it has the potential to be extremely tedious. WPF controls don't include parameterized constructors, so even adding a simple button to a window requires several lines of code.

One potential advantage is that code-only development offers unlimited avenues for customization. For example, you could generate a form full of input controls based on the information in a database record, or you could conditionally decide to add or substitute controls depending on the current user. All you need is a sprinkling of conditional logic. By contrast, when you use XAML documents, they're embedded in your assembly as fixed, unchanging resources.

■ **Note**   Even though you probably won't create a code-only WPF application, you probably will use the code-only approach to creating a WPF control at some point when you need an adaptable chunk of user interface.

The following code is for a modest window with a single button and an event handler (see Figure 2-3). When the window is created, the constructor calls an InitializeComponent method that instantiates and configures the button and the form and hooks up the event handler.

■ **Note**   To create this example, you must code the Window1 class from scratch (right-click the Solution Explorer and choose Add ➤ Class to get started). You can't choose Add ➤ Window, because that will add a code file *and* a XAML template for your window, complete with an automatically generated InitializeComponent() method.

```vb
Imports System.Windows.Markup

Public Class Window1
    Inherits Window

    Private button1 As Button

    Public Sub New()
        InitializeComponent()
    End Sub

    Private Sub InitializeComponent()
        ' Configure the form.
        Me.Width = Me.Height = 285
        Me.Left = Me.Top = 100
        Me.Title = "Code-Only Window"

        ' Create a container to hold a button.
        Dim panel As New DockPanel()

        ' Create the button.
        button1 = New Button()
        button1.Content = "Please click me."
        button1.Margin = New Thickness(30)

        ' Attach the event handler.
        AddHandler button1.Click, AddressOf button1_Click

        ' Place the button in the panel.
        Dim container As IAddChild = panel
        container.AddChild(button1)

        ' Place the panel in the form.
        container = Me
        container.AddChild(panel)
    End Sub

    Private Sub button1_Click(ByVal sender As Object, _
      ByVal e As RoutedEventArgs)
        button1.Content = "Thank you."
    End Sub

End Class
```

Conceptually, the Window1 class in this example is a lot like a form in a traditional Windows Forms application. It derives from the base Window class and adds a private member variable for every control. For clarity, this class performs its initialization work in a dedicated InitializeComponent() method.

To get this application started, you can use a Main() method with code like this:

```
Public Class Program
    Inherits Application

    Public Shared Sub Main()
        Dim app As New Program()
        app.MainWindow = New Window1()
        app.MainWindow.ShowDialog()
    End Sub

End Sub
```

Code and Uncompiled XAML

One of the most interesting ways to use XAML is to parse it on the fly with the XamlReader. For example, imagine you start with this XAML content in a file named Window1.xaml:

```
<DockPanel xmlns="http://schemas.microsoft.com/winfx/2006/xaml/presentation">
  <Button Name="button1" Margin="30">Please click me.</Button>
</DockPanel>
```

At runtime, you can load this content into a live window to create the same window shown in Figure 2-3. Here's the code that does it:

Figure 2-3. *A single-button window*

```
Imports System.IO
Imports System.Windows.Markup

Public Class Window1
    Inherits Window
```

```
    Private WithEvents button1 As Button

    Public Sub New(ByVal xamlFile As String)
        InitializeComponent(xamlFile)
    End Sub

    Private Sub InitializeComponent(ByVal xamlFile As String)
        ' Configure the form.
        Me.Height = 285
        Me.Width = Me.Height
        Me.Top = 100
        Me.Left = Me.Top
        Me.Title = "Dynamically Loaded XAML"

        ' Get the XAML content from an external file.
        Dim rootElement As DependencyObject
        Using fs As New FileStream(xamlFile, FileMode.Open)
            rootElement = CType(XamlReader.Load(fs), DependencyObject)
        End Using

        Me.Content = rootElement

        ' Find the control with the appropriate name.
        button1 = (Button)LogicalTreeHelper.FindLogicalNode(rootElement, "button1");
    End Sub

    Private Sub button1_Click(ByVal sender As Object, ByVal e As RoutedEventArgs) _
      Handles button1.Click
        button1.Content = "Thank you."
    End Sub
End Class
```

Here, the constructor receives the name of the XAML file as an argument (in this case, Window1.xaml). It then opens a FileStream and uses the XamlReader.Load() method to convert the content in this file into a DependencyObject, which is the base from which all WPF controls derive. The DependencyObject can be placed inside any type of container (for example, a Panel), but in this example it's used as the entire content inside the window.

■ **Note**   In this example, you're loading an element—the DockPanel object—from the XAML file. Alternatively, you could load an entire XAML window. In this case, you would cast the object returned by XamlReader.Load() to the Window type and then call its Show() or ShowDialog() method to show it.

To manipulate an element—for example, the button in the Window1.xaml file—you need to find the corresponding control object in the dynamically loaded content. LogicalTreeHelper serves this purpose because it has the ability to search an entire tree of control objects, digging down as many layers as necessary until it finds the object with the name you've specified. Although you could use explicit event wire-up (as in the previous example), this example attaches the event handler to the Button.Click event by using the Handles clause. As a result, the event handler will be connected as soon as the button1 reference is set.

Another alternative is to use the FrameworkElement.FindName() method. In this example, the root element is a DockPanel object. Like all the controls in a WPF window, DockPanel derives from FrameworkElement. That means you can replace this code:

```
button1 = CType( _
  LogicalTreeHelper.FindLogicalNode(rootElement, "button1"), _
  Button)
```

with this equivalent approach:

```
Dim frameworkElement As FrameworkElement = CType(rootElement, FrameworkElement)
button1 = CType(frameworkElement.FindName("button1"), Button)
```

In this example, the Window1.xaml file is distributed alongside the application executable, in the same folder. However, even though it isn't compiled as part of the application, you can still add it to your Visual Studio project. Doing so allows you to manage the file more easily and design the user interface with Visual Studio (assuming you use the file extension .xaml so Visual Studio recognizes that it's a XAML document).

If you use this approach, just make sure that the loose XAML file isn't compiled or embedded in your project like a traditional XAML file. After you add it to your project, select it in the Solution Explorer, and use the Properties window to set the Build Action option to None and the Copy to Output Directory option to Copy Always.

Obviously, loading XAML dynamically won't be as efficient as compiling the XAML to BAML and then loading the BAML at runtime, particularly if your user interface is complex. However, it opens up a number of possibilities for building dynamic user interfaces. For example, you could create an all-purpose survey application that reads a form file from a web service and then displays the corresponding survey controls (labels, text boxes, check boxes, and so on). The form file would be an ordinary XML document with WPF tags, which you load into an existing form by using the XamlReader. To collect the results after the survey is filled out, you simply need to enumerate over all the input controls and grab their content.

Code and Compiled XAML

You've already seen the most common way to use XAML with the eight-ball example shown in Figure 2-1 and dissected throughout this chapter. This is the method used by Visual Studio, and it has several advantages that this chapter has touched on already:

- Some of the plumbing is automatic. There's no need to perform ID lookup with LogicalTreeHelper or wire up event handlers in code.

- Reading BAML at runtime is faster than reading XAML.

- Deployment is easier. Because BAML is embedded in your assembly as one or more resources, there's no way to lose it.

- XAML files can be edited in other programs, such as design tools. This opens up the possibility for better collaboration between programmers and designers. (You also get this benefit when using uncompiled XAML, as described in the previous section.)

Visual Studio uses a two-stage compilation process when you're compiling a WPF application. The first step is to compile the XAML files into BAML. For example, if your project includes a file name Window1.xaml, the compiler will create a temporary file named Window1.baml and place it in the obj\Debug subfolder (in your project folder). At the same time, a partial class is created for your window, using the language of your choice. For example, if you're using VB, the compiler will create a file named Window1.g.vb in the obj\Debug folder. The *g* stands for *generated*.

The partial class includes three things:

- Fields for all the controls in your window.

- Code that loads the BAML from the assembly, thereby creating the tree of objects. This happens when the constructor calls InitializeComponent().

- Code that assigns the appropriate control object to each field and connects all the event handlers. This happens in a method named Connect, which the BAML parser calls every time it finds a named object.

The partial class does *not* include code to instantiate and initialize your controls, because that task is performed by the WPF engine when the BAML is processed by the Application.LoadComponent() method.

Note As part of the XAML compilation process, the XAML compiler needs to create a partial class. This is possible only if the language you're using supports the .NET CodeDOM model. C# and VB support CodeDOM, but if you're using a third-party language, you'll need to make sure this support exists before you can create compiled XAML applications.

Here's the (slightly abbreviated) Window1.g.vb file from the eight-ball example shown in Figure 2-1:

```vb
Partial Public Class Window1
    Inherits System.Windows.Window
    Implements System.Windows.Markup.IComponentConnector

    ' The control fields.
    Friend WithEvents txtQuestion As System.Windows.Controls.TextBox
    Friend WithEvents cmdAnswer As System.Windows.Controls.Button
    Friend WithEvents txtAnswer As System.Windows.Controls.TextBox

    Private _contentLoaded As Boolean

    ' Load the BAML.
    Public Sub InitializeComponent() _
      Implements IComponentConnector.InitializeComponent
        If _contentLoaded Then
            Return
        End If
        _contentLoaded = True

        Dim resourceLocater As New System.Uri( _
          "/EightBall;component/window1.xaml", System.UriKind.Relative)
        System.Windows.Application.LoadComponent(Me, resourceLocater)
    End Sub

    ' Hook up each control.
    Sub System_Windows_Markup_IComponentConnector_Connect( _
      ByVal connectionId As Integer, ByVal target As Object) _
      Implements System.Windows.Markup.IComponentConnector.Connect
```

```
        If (connectionId = 1) Then
            Me.txtQuestion = CType(target, System.Windows.Controls.TextBox)
            Return
        End If
        If (connectionId = 2) Then
            Me.cmdAnswer = CType(target, System.Windows.Controls.Button)
            AddHandler Me.cmdAnswer.Click, AddressOf Me.cmdAnswer_Click
            Return
        End If
        If (connectionId = 3) Then
            Me.txtAnswer = CType(target,System.Windows.Controls.TextBox)
            Return
        End If
        Me._contentLoaded = true
    End Sub

End Class
```

When the XAML-to-BAML compilation stage is finished, Visual Studio uses the appropriate language compiler to compile your code and the generated partial class files. In the case of a VB application, it's the vbc.exe compiler that handles this task. The compiled code becomes a single assembly (EightBall.exe), and the BAML for each window is embedded as a separate resource.

XAML Only

The previous sections show you how to use XAML from a code-based application. As a .NET developer, this is what you'll spend most of your time doing. However, it's also possible to use a XAML file without creating any code. This is called a *loose* XAML file. Loose XAML files can be opened directly in Internet Explorer.

■ **Note** If your XAML file uses code, it can't be opened in Internet Explorer. However, you can build a browser-based application called an *XBAP* that breaks through this boundary. Chapter 24 describes how.

At this point, it probably seems relatively useless to create a loose XAML file—after all, what's the point of a user interface with no code to drive it? However, as you explore XAML, you'll discover several features that are entirely declarative. These include features such as animation, triggers, data binding, and links (which can point to other loose XAML files). Using these features, you can build a few very simple no-code XAML files. They won't seem like complete applications, but they can accomplish quite a bit more than static HTML pages.

To try a loose XAML page, take a XAML file and make these changes:

- Remove the Class attribute on the root element.

- Remove any attributes that attach event handlers (such as the Button.Click attribute).

- Change the name of the opening and closing tag from Window to Page. Internet Explorer can show only hosted pages, not stand-alone windows.

You can then double-click your XAML file to load it in Internet Explorer. Figure 2-4 shows a converted EightBall.xaml page, which is included with the downloadable code for this chapter. You can type in the top text box, but because the application lacks the code-behind file, nothing happens when you click the button. If you want to create a more capable browser-based application that can include code, you'll need to use the XBAP model described in Chapter 24.

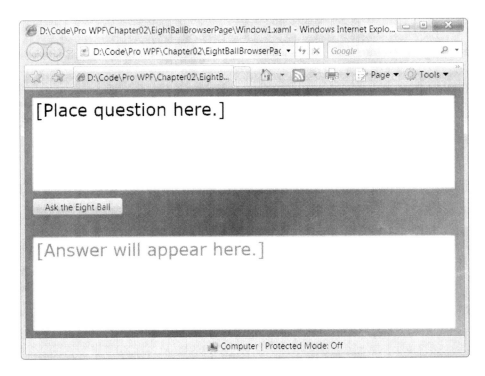

Figure 2-4. *A XAML page in a browser*

The Last Word

In this chapter, you took a tour through a simple XAML file and learned its syntax at the same time. Here's what you saw:

- You considered key XAML ingredients, such as type converters, markup extensions, and attached properties.

- You learned how to wire up a code-behind class that can handle the events raised by your controls.

- You considered the compilation process that takes a standard WPF application into a compiled executable file. At the same time, you took a look at three variants: creating a WPF application through code alone, creating a WPF page with nothing but XAML, and loading XAML manually at runtime.

Although you haven't had an exhaustive look at every detail of XAML markup, you've learned enough to reap all its benefits. Now your attention can shift to the WPF technology itself, which holds some of the most interesting surprises. In the next chapter, you'll consider how controls are organized into realistic windows by using the WPF layout panels.

Layout

Half the battle in any user interface design is organizing the content in a way that's attractive, practical, and flexible. But the real challenge is making sure that your layout can adapt itself gracefully to different window sizes.

In WPF, you shape layout by using different *containers*. Each container has its own layout logic—some stack elements, others arrange them in a grid of invisible cells, and so on. But coordinate-based layout is strongly discouraged in WPF. Instead, the emphasis is on creating more-flexible layouts that can adapt to changing content, different languages, and a variety of window sizes. For many developers moving to WPF, the layout system is a great surprise—and the first real challenge.

In this chapter, you'll see how the WPF layout model works, and you'll begin using the basic layout containers. You'll also consider several common layout examples—everything from a basic dialog box to a resizable split window—in order to learn the fundamentals of WPF layout.

Understanding Layout in WPF

The WPF layout model represents a dramatic shift in the way Windows developers approach user interfaces. In the past, Windows developers used strict coordinate-based layouts to anchor controls into place. Although this approach is possible in WPF, it's far less common. Most applications will use weblike *flow* layouts, which let controls grow and bump other controls out of the way. This model allows developers to create resolution-independent, size-independent interfaces that scale well on different monitors, adjust themselves when content changes, and handle the transition to other languages effortlessly. However, before you can take advantage of this system, you need to understand a bit more about its underlying concepts and assumptions.

The WPF Layout Philosophy

A WPF window can hold only a single element. To fit in more than one element and create a more practical user interface, you need to place a container in your window and then add other elements to that container.

Note   This limitation stems from the fact that the Window class is derived from ContentControl, which you'll study more closely in Chapter 6.

In WPF, layout is determined by the container that you use. Although there are several containers to choose from, the "ideal" WPF window follows a few key principles:

- *Elements (such as controls) should not be explicitly sized.* Instead, they grow to fit their content. For example, a button expands as you add more text. You can limit controls to acceptable sizes by setting a maximum and minimum size.

- *Elements do not indicate their position with screen coordinates.* Instead, they are arranged by their container based on their size, order, and (optionally) other information that's specific to the layout container. If you need to add whitespace between elements, you use the Margin property.

■ **Tip**   Hard-coded sizes and positions are evil because they limit your ability to localize your interface, and they make it much more difficult to deal with dynamic content.

- *Layout containers "share" the available space among their children.* They attempt to give each element its preferred size (based on its content) if the space is available. They can also distribute extra space to one or more children.

- *Layout containers can be nested.* A typical user interface begins with the Grid, WPF's most capable container, and contains other layout containers that arrange smaller groups of elements, such as captioned text boxes, items in a list, icons on a toolbar, a column of buttons, and so on.

Although there are exceptions to these rules, they reflect the overall design goals of WPF. In other words, if you follow these guidelines when you build a WPF application, you'll create a better, more flexible user interface. If you break these rules, you'll end up with a user interface that isn't well suited to WPF and is much more difficult to maintain.

The Layout Process

WPF layout takes place in two stages: a measure stage and an arrange stage. In the *measure stage*, the container loops through its child elements and asks them to provide their preferred size. In the *arrange stage*, the container places the child elements in the appropriate position.

Of course, an element can't always get its preferred size—sometimes the container isn't large enough to accommodate it. In this case, the container must truncate the offending element to fit the visible area. As you'll see, you can often avoid this situation by setting a minimum window size.

■ **Note**   Layout containers don't provide any scrolling support. Instead, scrolling is provided by a specialized content control—the ScrollViewer—that can be used just about anywhere. You'll learn about the ScrollViewer in Chapter 6.

The Layout Containers

All the WPF layout containers are panels that derive from the abstract System.Windows.Controls.Panel class (see Figure 3-1). The Panel class adds a small set of members, including the three public properties that are detailed in Table 3-1.

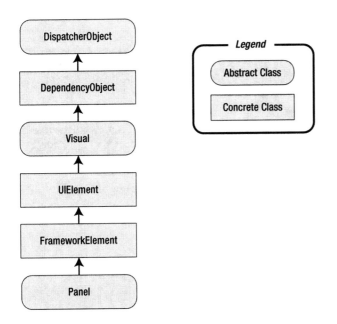

Figure 3-1. *The hierarchy of the Panel class*

Table 3-1. *Public Properties of the Panel Class*

Name	Description
Background	The brush that's used to paint the panel background. You must set this property to a non-null value if you want to receive mouse events. (If you want to receive mouse events but you don't want to display a solid background, just set the background color to Transparent.) You'll learn more about basic brushes in Chapter 6 (and about advanced brushes in Chapter 12).
Children	The collection of items that's stored in the panel. This is the first level of items—in other words, these items may themselves contain more items.
IsItemsHost	A Boolean value that's True if the panel is being used to show the items that are associated with an ItemsControl (such as the nodes in a TreeViewor the list entries in a ListBox). Most of the time you won't even be aware that a list control is using a behind-the-scenes panel to manage the layout of its items. However, this detail becomes more important if you want to create a customized list that lays out children in a different way (for example, a ListBox that tiles images). You'll use this technique in Chapter 20.

░ **Note** The Panel class also has a bit of internal plumbing you can use if you want to create your own layout container. Most notably, you can override the MeasureOverride() and ArrangeOverride methods inherited from FrameworkElement to change the way the panel handles the measure stage and the arrange stage when organizing its child elements. You'll learn how to create a custom panel in Chapter 18.

On its own, the base Panel class is nothing but a starting point for other, more-specialized classes. WPF provides a number of Panel-derived classes that you can use to arrange layout. The most fundamental of these are listed in Table 3-2. As with all WPF controls and most visual elements, these classes are found in the System.Windows.Controls namespace.

Table 3-2. *Core Layout Panels*

Name	Description
StackPanel	Places elements in a horizontal or vertical stack. This layout container is typically used for small sections of a larger, more complex window.
WrapPanel	Places elements in a series of wrapped lines. In horizontal orientation, the WrapPanel lays items out in a row from left to right and then onto subsequent lines. In vertical orientation, the WrapPanel lays out items in a top-to-bottom column and then uses additional columns to fit the remaining items.
DockPanel	Aligns elements against an entire edge of the container.
Grid	Arranges elements in rows and columns according to an invisible table. This is one of the most flexible and commonly used layout containers.
UniformGrid	Places elements in an invisible table but forces all cells to have the same size. This layout container is used infrequently.
Canvas	Allows elements to be positioned absolutely by using fixed coordinates. This layout container is the most similar to old-fashioned Windows Forms applications, without the anchoring and docking features. As a result, it's an unsuitable choice for a resizable window unless you're willing to do a fair bit of work.

Along with these core containers, you'll encounter several more specialized panels in various controls. These include panels that are dedicated to holding the child items of a particular control, such as TabPanel (the tabs in a TabControl), ToolbarPanel (the buttons in a Toolbar), and ToolbarOverflowPanel (the commands in a Toolbar's overflow menu). There's also a VirtualizingStackPanel, which data-bound list controls use to dramatically reduce their overhead, and an InkCanvas, which is similar to the Canvas but has support for handling stylus input on the TabletPC. (For example, depending on the mode you choose, the InkCanvas supports drawing with the pointer to select onscreen elements. And although it's a little counterintuitive, you can use the InkCanvas with an ordinary computer and a mouse.) You'll learn about the InkCanvas in this chapter, and you'll take a closer look at the VirtualizingStackPanel in Chapter 19. You'll learn about the other specialized panels when you consider the related control, elsewhere in this book.

Simple Layout with the StackPanel

The StackPanel is one of the simplest layout containers. It simply stacks its children in a single row or column.

For example, consider this window, which contains a stack of four buttons:

```
<Window x:Class=" SimpleStack"
    xmlns="http://schemas.microsoft.com/winfx/2006/xaml/presentation"
    xmlns:x="http://schemas.microsoft.com/winfx/2006/xaml"
    Title="Layout" Height="223" Width="354"
    >
  <StackPanel>
    <Label>A Button Stack</Label>
    <Button>Button 1</Button>
    <Button>Button 2</Button>
    <Button>Button 3</Button>
    <Button>Button 4</Button>
  </StackPanel>
</Window>
```

Figure 3-2 shows the window that results.

Figure 3-2. *The StackPanel in action*

ADDING A LAYOUT CONTAINER IN VISUAL STUDIO

It's relatively easy to create this example by using the designer in Visual Studio. Begin by deleting the root Grid element (if it's there). Then, drag a StackPanel into the window. Next, drag the other elements (the label and four buttons) into the window, in the top-to-bottom order you want. If you want to rearrange the order of elements in the StackPanel, you can simply drag any one to a new position.

Although we won't spend much time discussing Visual Studio's design-time support in this book, it's improved greatly since the first versions of WPF. For example, Visual Studio no longer assigns names to every new control you add in the designer, and it no longer adds hard-coded Width and Height values, unless you manually resize the control.

By default, a StackPanel arranges elements from top to bottom, making each one as tall as is necessary to display its content. In this example, that means the labels and buttons are sized just large enough to comfortably accommodate the text inside. All elements are stretched to the full width of the StackPanel, which is the width of the window. If you widen the window, the StackPanel widens as well, and the buttons stretch themselves to fit.

The StackPanel can also be used to arrange elements horizontally by setting the Orientation property:

```
<StackPanel Orientation="Horizontal">
```

Now elements are given their minimum width (wide enough to fit their text) and are stretched to the full height of the containing panel. Depending on the current size of the window, this may result in some elements that don't fit, as shown in Figure 3-3.

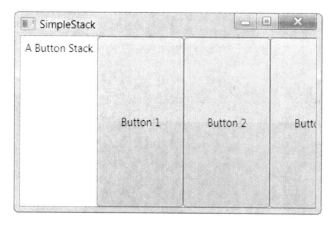

Figure 3-3. *The StackPanel with horizontal orientation*

Clearly, this doesn't provide the flexibility real applications need. Fortunately, you can fine-tune the way the StackPanel and other layout containers work by using layout properties, as described next.

Layout Properties

Although layout is determined by the container, the child elements can still get their say. In fact, layout panels work in concert with their children by respecting a small set of layout properties, listed in Table 3-3.

Table 3-3. *Layout Properties*

Name	Description
HorizontalAlignment	Determines how a child is positioned inside a layout container when there's extra horizontal space available. You can choose Center, Left, Right, or Stretch.
VerticalAlignment	Determines how a child is positioned inside a layout container when there's extra vertical space available. You can choose Center, Top, Bottom, or Stretch.
Margin	Adds a bit of breathing room around an element. The Margin property is an instance of the System.Windows.Thickness structure, with separate components for the top, bottom, left, and right edges.
MinWidth and MinHeight	Sets the minimum dimensions of an element. If an element is too large for its layout container, it will be cropped to fit.
MaxWidth and MaxHeight	Sets the maximum dimensions of an element. If the container has more room available, the element won't be enlarged beyond these bounds, even if the HorizontalAlignment and VerticalAlignment properties are set to Stretch.
Width and Height	Explicitly sets the size of an element. This setting overrides a Stretch value for the HorizontalAlignment or VerticalAlignment properties. However, this size won't be honored if it's outside of the bounds set by the MinWidth, MinHeight, MaxWidth, and MaxHeight.

All of these properties are inherited from the base FrameworkElement class and are therefore supported by all the graphical widgets you can use in a WPF window.

> ▓ **Note** As you learned in Chapter 2, different layout containers can provide *attached properties* to their children. For example, all the children of a Grid object gain Row and Column properties that allow them to choose the cell where they're placed. Attached properties allow you to set information that's specific to a particular layout container. However, the layout properties in Table 3-3 are generic enough that they apply to many layout panels. Thus, these properties are defined as part of the base FrameworkElement class.

This list of properties is just as notable for what it *doesn't* contain. If you're looking for familiar position properties, such as Top, Right, and Location, you won't find them. That's because most layout containers (all except the Canvas) use automatic layout and don't give you the ability to explicitly position elements.

Alignment

To understand how these properties work, take another look at the simple StackPanel shown in Figure 3-2. In this example—a StackPanel with vertical orientation—the VerticalAlignment property has no effect because each element is given as much height as it needs and no more. However, the HorizontalAlignment *is* important. It determines where each element is placed in its row.

Ordinarily, the default HorizontalAlignment is Left for a label and Stretch for a Button. That's why every button takes the full column width. However, you can change these details:

```
<StackPanel>
  <Label HorizontalAlignment="Center">A Button Stack</Label>
  <Button HorizontalAlignment="Left">Button 1</Button>
  <Button HorizontalAlignment="Right">Button 2</Button>
  <Button>Button 3</Button>
  <Button>Button 4</Button>
</StackPanel>
```

Figure 3-4 shows the result. The first two buttons are given their minimum sizes and aligned accordingly, while the bottom two buttons are stretched over the entire StackPanel. If you resize the window, you'll see that the label remains in the middle and the first two buttons stay stuck to either side.

Figure 3-4. *A StackPanel with aligned buttons*

▨ **Note**   The StackPanel also has its own HorizontalAlignment and VerticalAlignment properties. By default, both of these are set to Stretch, and so the StackPanel fills its container completely. In this example, that means the StackPanel fills the window. If you use different settings, the StackPanel will be made just large enough to fit the widest control.

Margin

There's an obvious problem with the StackPanel example in its current form. A well-designed window doesn't just contain elements—it also includes a bit of extra space between the elements. To introduce this extra space and make the StackPanel example less cramped, you can set control margins.

When setting margins, you can set a single width for all sides, like this:

```
<Button Margin="5">Button 3</Button>
```

Alternatively, you can set different margins for each side of a control in the order *left, top, right, bottom*:

```
<Button Margin="5,10,5,10">Button 3</Button>
```

In code, margins are set by using the Thickness structure:

```
cmd.Margin = New Thickness(5)
```

Getting the right control margins is a bit of an art because you need to consider how the margin settings of adjacent controls influence one another. For example, if you have two buttons stacked on top of each other, and the topmost button has a bottom margin of 5, and the bottommost button has a top margin of 5, you have a total of 10 units of space between the two buttons.

Ideally, you'll be able to keep different margin settings as consistent as possible and avoid setting distinct values for the different margin sides. For instance, in the StackPanel example, it makes sense to use the same margins on the buttons and on the panel itself, as shown here:

```
<StackPanel Margin="3">
  <Label Margin="3" HorizontalAlignment="Center">
   A Button Stack</Label>
  <Button Margin="3" HorizontalAlignment="Left">Button 1</Button>
  <Button Margin="3" HorizontalAlignment="Right">Button 2</Button>
  <Button Margin="3">Button 3</Button>
  <Button Margin="3">Button 4</Button>
</StackPanel>
```

This way, the total space between two buttons (the sum of the two button margins) is the same as the total space between the button at the edge of the window (the sum of the button margin and the StackPanel margin). Figure 3-5 shows this more respectable window, and Figure 3-6 shows how the margin settings break down.

Figure 3-5. *Adding margins between elements*

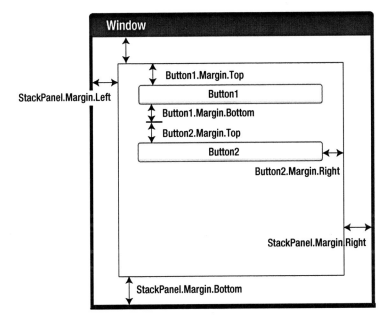

Figure 3-6. *How margins are combined*

Minimum, Maximum, and Explicit Sizes

Finally, every element includes Height and Width properties that allow you to give it an explicit size. However, it's rarely a good idea to take this step. Instead, use the maximum and minimum size properties to lock your control into the right range, if necessary.

■ **Tip** Think twice before setting an explicit size in WPF. In a well-designed layout, it shouldn't be necessary. If you do add size information, you risk creating a more brittle layout that can't adapt to changes (such as different languages and window sizes) and truncates your content.

For example, you might decide that the buttons in your StackPanel should stretch to fit the StackPanel but be made no larger than 200 units wide and no smaller than 100 units wide. (By default, buttons start with a minimum width of 75 units.) Here's the markup you need:

```
<StackPanel Margin="3">
  <Label Margin="3" HorizontalAlignment="Center">
   A Button Stack</Label>
  <Button Margin="3" MaxWidth="200" MinWidth="100">Button 1</Button>
  <Button Margin="3" MaxWidth="200" MinWidth="100">Button 2</Button>
  <Button Margin="3" MaxWidth="200" MinWidth="100">Button 3</Button>
  <Button Margin="3" MaxWidth="200" MinWidth="100">Button 4</Button>
</StackPanel>
```

▓ **Tip**   At this point, you might be wondering if there's an easier way to set properties that are standardized across several elements, such as the button margins in this example. The answer is *styles*—a feature that allows you to reuse property settings and even apply them automatically. You'll learn about styles in Chapter 11.

When the StackPanel sizes a button, it considers several pieces of information:

The minimum size: Each button will always be at least as large as the minimum size.

The maximum size: Each button will always be smaller than the maximum size (unless you've incorrectly set the maximum size to be smaller than the minimum size).

The content: If the content inside the button requires a greater width, the StackPanel will attempt to enlarge the button. (You can find out the size that the button wants by examining the DesiredSize property, which returns the minimum width or the content width, whichever is greater.)

The size of the container: If the minimum width is larger than the width of the StackPanel, a portion of the button will be cut off. Otherwise, the button will not be allowed to grow wider than the StackPanel, even if it can't fit all its text on the button surface.

The horizontal alignment: Because the button uses a HorizontalAlignment of Stretch (the default), the StackPanel will attempt to enlarge the button to fill the full width of the StackPanel.

The trick to understanding this process is to realize that the minimum and maximum size set the absolute bounds. Within those bounds, the StackPanel tries to respect the button's desired size (to fit its content) and its alignment settings.

Figure 3-7 sheds some light on how this works with the StackPanel. On the left is the window at its minimum size. The buttons are 100 units each, and the window cannot be resized to be narrower. If you shrink the window from this point, the right side of each button will be clipped off. (You can prevent this possibility by applying the MinWidth property to the window itself, so the window can't go below a minimum width.)

Figure 3-7. *Constrained button sizing*

As you enlarge the window, the buttons grow with it until they reach their maximum of 200 units. From this point on, if you make the window any larger, the extra space is added to either side of the button (as shown on the right).

■ **Note**   In some situations, you might want to use code that checks how large an element is in a window. The Height and Width properties are no help because they indicate your desired size settings, which might not correspond to the actual rendered size. In an ideal scenario, you'll let your elements size to fit their content, and the Height and Width properties won't be set at all. However, you can find out the actual size used to render an element by reading the ActualHeight and ActualWidth properties. But remember, these values may change when the window is resized or the content inside it changes.

AUTOMATICALLY SIZED WINDOWS

In this example, there's still one element that has hard-coded sizes: the top-level window that contains the StackPanel (and everything else inside). For a number of reasons it still makes sense to hard-code window sizes:

- In many cases, you want to make a window *smaller* than the desired size of its child elements. For example, if your window includes a container of scrollable text, you'll want to constrain the size of that container so that scrolling is possible. You *don't* want to make the window ridiculously large so that no scrolling is necessary, which is what the container will request. (You'll learn more about scrolling in Chapter 6.)

- The minimum window size may be usable, but it might not give you the most attractive proportions. Some window dimensions just look better.

- Automatic window sizing isn't constrained by the display size of your monitor. So, an automatically sized window might be too large to view.

However, automatically sized windows are possible, and they do make sense if you are constructing a simple window with dynamic content. To enable automatic window sizing, remove the Height and Width properties and set the Window.SizeToContent property to WidthAndHeight. The window will make itself just large enough to accommodate all its content. You can also allow a window to resize itself in just one dimension by using a SizeToContent value of Width or Height.

The Border

The Border isn't one of the layout panels, but it's a handy element that you'll often use alongside them. For that reason, it makes sense to introduce it now, before you go any further.

The Border class is pure simplicity. It takes a single piece of nested content (which is often a layout panel) and adds a background or border around it. To master the Border, you need nothing more than the properties listed in Table 3-4.

Table 3-4. *Properties of the Border Class*

Name	Description
Background	Sets a background that appears behind all the content in the border by using a Brush object. You can use a solid color or something more exotic.
BorderBrush and BorderThickness	Sets the color of the border that appears at the edge of the Border object, using a Brush object, and sets the width of the border, respectively. To show a border, you must set both properties.
CornerRadius	Allows you to gracefully round the corners of your border. The greater the CornerRadius, the more dramatic the rounding effect is.
Padding	Adds spacing between the border and the content inside. (By contrast, Margin adds spacing outside the border.)

Here's a straightforward slightly rounded border around a group of buttons in a StackPanel:

```
<Border Margin="5" Padding="5" Background="LightYellow"
 BorderBrush="SteelBlue" BorderThickness="3,5,3,5" CornerRadius="3"
 VerticalAlignment="Top">
  <StackPanel>
    <Button Margin="3">One</Button>
    <Button Margin="3">Two</Button>
    <Button Margin="3">Three</Button>
  </StackPanel>
</Border>
```

Figure 3-8 shows the result.

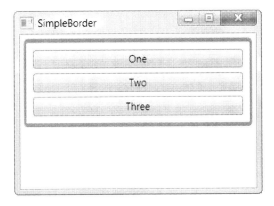

Figure 3-8. *A basic border*

Chapter 6 has more details about brushes and the colors you can use to set BorderBrush and Background.

▓ **Note** Technically, the Border is a *decorator*, which is a type of element that's typically used to add some sort of graphical embellishment around an object. All decorators derive from the System.Windows.Controls.Decorator class. Most decorators are designed for use with specific controls. For example, the Button uses a ButtonChrome decorator to get its trademark rounded corner and shaded background, while the ListBox uses the ListBoxChrome decorator. There are also two more general decorators that are useful when composing user interfaces: the Border discussed here and the Viewbox you'll explore in Chapter 12.

The WrapPanel and DockPanel

Obviously, the StackPanel alone can't help you create a realistic user interface. To complete the picture, the StackPanel needs to work with other, more-capable layout containers. Only then can you assemble a complete window.

The most sophisticated layout container is the Grid, which you'll consider later in this chapter. But first, it's worth looking at the WrapPanel and DockPanel, which are two more of the simple layout containers provided by WPF. They complement the StackPanel by offering different layout behavior.

The WrapPanel

The WrapPanel lays out controls in the available space, one line or column at a time. By default, the WrapPanel.Orientation property is set to Horizontal; controls are arranged from left to right and then on subsequent rows. However, you can use Vertical to place elements in multiple columns.

▓ **Tip** Like the StackPanel, the WrapPanel is really intended for control over small-scale details in a user interface, not complete window layouts. For example, you might use a WrapPanel to keep together the buttons in a toolbar-like control.

Here's an example that defines a series of buttons with different alignments and places them into the WrapPanel:

```
<WrapPanel Margin="3">
  <Button VerticalAlignment="Top">Top Button</Button>
  <Button MinHeight="60">Tall Button 2</Button>
  <Button VerticalAlignment="Bottom">Bottom Button</Button>
  <Button>Stretch Button</Button>
  <Button VerticalAlignment="Center">Centered Button</Button>
</WrapPanel>
```

Figure 3-9 shows how the buttons are wrapped to fit the current size of the WrapPanel (which is determined by the size of the window that contains it). As this example demonstrates, a WrapPanel in horizontal mode creates a series of imaginary rows, each of which is given the height of the tallest contained element. Other controls may be stretched to fit or aligned according to the VerticalAlignment property. In the example on the left in Figure 3-9, all the buttons fit into one tall row and are stretched or aligned to fit. In the example on the right, several buttons have been bumped to the second row. Because the second row does not include an unusually tall button, the row height is kept at the minimum button height. As a result, it doesn't matter what VerticalAlignment setting the various buttons in this row use.

Figure 3-9. *Wrapped buttons*

■ **Note**   The WrapPanel is the only panel that can't be duplicated with a crafty use of the Grid.

The DockPanel

The DockPanel is a more interesting layout option. It stretches controls against one of its outside edges. The easiest way to visualize this is to think of the toolbars that sit at the top of many Windows applications. These toolbars are docked to the top of the window. As with the StackPanel, docked elements get to choose one aspect of their layout. For example, if you dock a button to the top of a DockPanel, it's stretched across the entire width of the DockPanel but given whatever height it requires (based on the content and the MinHeight property). On the other hand, if you dock a button to the left side of a container, its height is stretched to fit the container, but its width is free to grow as needed.

The obvious question is, How do child elements choose the side where they want to dock? The answer is through an attached property named Dock, which can be set to Left, Right, Top, or Bottom. Every element that's placed inside a DockPanel automatically acquires this property.

Here's an example that puts one button on every side of a DockPanel:

```
<DockPanel LastChildFill="True">
  <Button DockPanel.Dock="Top">Top Button</Button>
```

```
    <Button DockPanel.Dock="Bottom">Bottom Button</Button>
    <Button DockPanel.Dock="Left">Left Button</Button>
    <Button DockPanel.Dock="Right">Right Button</Button>
    <Button>Remaining Space</Button>
</DockPanel>
```

This example also sets the LastChildFill to True, which tells the DockPanel to give the remaining space to the last element. Figure 3-10 shows the result.

Figure 3-10. *Docking to every side*

Clearly, when docking controls, the order is important. In this example, the top and bottom buttons get the full edge of the DockPanel because they're docked first. When the left and right buttons are docked next, they fit between these two buttons. If you reversed this order, the left and right buttons would get the full sides, and the top and bottom buttons would become narrower because they'd be docked between the two side buttons.

You can dock several elements against the same side. In this case, the elements simply stack up against the side in the order they're declared in your markup. And if you don't like the spacing or the stretch behavior, you can tweak the Margin, HorizontalAlignment, and VerticalAlignment properties, just as you did with the StackPanel. Here's a modified version of the previous example that adjusts the alignment:

```
<DockPanel LastChildFill="True">
    <Button DockPanel.Dock="Top">A Stretched Top Button</Button>
    <Button DockPanel.Dock="Top" HorizontalAlignment="Center">
     A Centered Top Button</Button>
    <Button DockPanel.Dock="Top" HorizontalAlignment="Left">
     A Left-Aligned Top Button</Button>
    <Button DockPanel.Dock="Bottom">Bottom Button</Button>
    <Button DockPanel.Dock="Left">Left Button</Button>
    <Button DockPanel.Dock="Right">Right Button</Button>
    <Button>Remaining Space</Button>
</DockPanel>
```

The docking behavior is still the same. First the top buttons are docked, and then the bottom button is docked, and finally the remaining space is divided between the side buttons and a final button in the middle. Figure 3-11 shows the resulting window.

Figure 3-11. *Docking multiple elements to the top*

Nesting Layout Containers

The StackPanel, WrapPanel, and DockPanel are rarely used on their own. Instead, they're used to shape portions of your interface. For example, you could use a DockPanel to place different StackPanel and WrapPanel containers in the appropriate regions of a window.

For example, imagine you want to create a standard dialog box with an OK and Cancel button in the bottom-right corner and a large content region in the rest of the window. You can model this interface with WPF in several ways, but the easiest option that uses the panels you've seen so far is as follows:

1. Create a horizontal StackPanel to wrap the OK and Cancel buttons together.

2. Place the StackPanel in a DockPanel and use that to dock it to the bottom of the window.

3. Set DockPanel.LastChildFill to True so you can use the rest of the window to fill in other content. You can add another layout control here or just an ordinary TextBox control (as in this example).

4. Set the margin properties to give the right amount of whitespace.

Here's the final markup:

```
<DockPanel LastChildFill="True">
  <StackPanel DockPanel.Dock="Bottom" HorizontalAlignment="Right"
   Orientation="Horizontal">
    <Button Margin="10,10,2,10" Padding="3">OK</Button>
    <Button Margin="2,10,10,10" Padding="3">Cancel</Button>
  </StackPanel>
  <TextBox DockPanel.Dock="Top" Margin="10">This is a test.</TextBox>
</DockPanel>
```

In this example, the Padding property adds some minimum space between the button border and the content inside (the word *OK* or *Cancel*). Figure 3-12 shows the rather pedestrian dialog box this creates.

Figure 3-12. *A basic dialog box*

At first glance, this seems like a fair bit more work than placing controls in precise positions by using coordinates. And in many cases, it is. However, the longer setup time is compensated by the ease with which you can change the user interface in the future. For example, if you decide you want the OK and Cancel buttons to be centered at the bottom of the window, you simply need to change the alignment of the StackPanel that contains them:

```
<StackPanel DockPanel.Dock="Bottom" HorizontalAlignment="Center" ... >
```

Compared to older user interface frameworks such as Windows Forms, the markup used here is cleaner, simpler, and more compact. If you add a dash of styles to this window (Chapter 11), you can improve it even further and remove other extraneous details (such as the margin settings) to create a truly adaptable user interface.

■ **Tip** If you have a densely nested tree of elements, it's easy to lose sight of the overall structure. Visual Studio provides a handy feature that shows you a tree representation of your elements and allows you to click your way down to the element you want to look at (or modify). This feature is the Document Outline window, and you can show it by choosing View ➤ Other Windows ➤ Document Outline from the menu.

The Grid

The Grid is the most powerful layout container in WPF. Much of what you can accomplish with the other layout controls is also possible with the Grid. The Grid is also an ideal tool for carving your window into smaller regions that you can manage with other panels. In fact, the Grid is so useful that when you add a new XAML document for a window in Visual Studio, it automatically adds the Grid tags as the first-level container, nested inside the root Window element.

The Grid separates elements into an invisible grid of rows and columns Although more than one element can be placed in a single cell (in which case they overlap), it generally makes sense to place just a single element per cell. Of course, that element may itself be another layout container that organizes its own group of contained controls.

■ **Tip** Although the Grid is designed to be invisible, you can set the Grid.ShowGridLines property to True to take a closer look. This feature isn't really intended for prettying up a window. Instead, it's a debugging convenience that's designed to help you understand how the Grid has subdivided itself into smaller regions. This feature is important because you have the ability to control exactly how the Grid chooses column widths and row heights.

Creating a Grid-based layout is a two-step process. First, you choose the number of columns and rows that you want. Next, you assign the appropriate row and column to each contained element, thereby placing it in just the right spot.

You create grids and rows by filling the Grid.ColumnDefinitions and Grid.RowDefinitions collections with objects. For example, if you decide you need two rows and three columns, you'd add the following tags:

```
<Grid ShowGridLines="True">
  <Grid.RowDefinitions>
    <RowDefinition></RowDefinition>
    <RowDefinition></RowDefinition>
  </Grid.RowDefinitions>
  <Grid.ColumnDefinitions>
    <ColumnDefinition></ColumnDefinition>
    <ColumnDefinition></ColumnDefinition>
    <ColumnDefinition></ColumnDefinition>
  </Grid.ColumnDefinitions>

  ...
</Grid>
```

As this example shows, it's not necessary to supply any information in a RowDefinition or ColumnDefinition element. If you leave them empty (as shown here), the Grid will share the space evenly between all rows and columns. In this example, each cell will be exactly the same size, depending on the size of the containing window.

To place individual elements into a cell, you use the attached Row and Column properties. Both these properties take 0-based index numbers. For example, here's how you could create a partially filled grid of buttons:

```
<Grid ShowGridLines="True">
  ...

  <Button Grid.Row="0" Grid.Column="0">Top Left</Button>
  <Button Grid.Row="0" Grid.Column="1">Middle Left</Button>
  <Button Grid.Row="1" Grid.Column="2">Bottom Right</Button>
  <Button Grid.Row="1" Grid.Column="1">Bottom Middle</Button>
</Grid>
```

Each element must be placed into its cell explicitly. This allows you to place more than one element into a cell (which rarely makes sense) or leave certain cells blank (which is often useful). It also means you can declare your elements out of order, as with the final two buttons in this example. However, it makes for clearer markup if you define your controls row by row, and from right to left in each row.

There is one exception. If you don't specify the Grid.Row property, the Grid assumes that it's 0. The same behavior applies to the Grid.Column property. Thus, you leave both attributes off of an element to place it in the first cell of the Grid.

■ **Note** The Grid fits elements into predefined rows and columns. This is different from layout containers such as the WrapPanel and StackPanel that create implicit rows or columns as they lay out their children. If you want to create a grid that has more than one row and one column, you must define your rows and columns explicitly by using RowDefinition and ColumnDefinition objects.

Figure 3-13 shows how this simple grid appears at two sizes. Notice that the ShowGridLines property is set to True so that you can see the separation between each column and row.

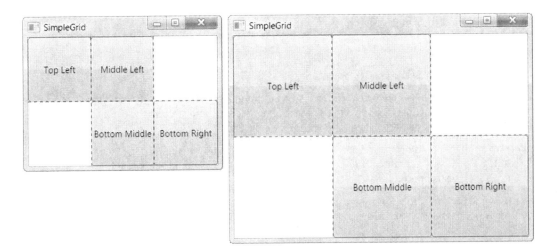

Figure 3-13. *A simple grid*

As you would expect, the Grid honors the basic set of layout properties listed in Table 3-3. That means you can add margins around the content in a cell, you can change the sizing mode so an element doesn't grow to fill the entire cell, and you can align an item along one of the edges of a cell. If you force an element to have a size that's larger than the cell can accommodate, part of the content will be chopped off.

USING THE GRID IN VISUAL STUDIO

When you use a Grid on the Visual Studio design surface, you'll find that it works a bit differently than other layout containers. As you drag an element into a Grid, Visual Studio allows you to place it in a precise position. Visual Studio works this magic by setting the Margin property of your element.

When setting margins, Visual Studio uses the closest corner. For example, if your element is nearest to the top-left corner of the Grid, Visual Studio pads the top and left margins to position the element (and leaves the right and bottom margins at 0). If you drag your element down closer to the bottom-left corner, Visual Studio sets the bottom and left margins instead and sets the VerticalAlignment property to Bottom. This obviously affects how the element will move when the Grid is resized.

Visual Studio's margin-setting process seems straightforward enough, but most of the time it won't create the results you want. Usually, you'll want a more flexible flow layout that allows some elements to expand dynamically and push others out of the way. In this scenario, you'll find that hard-coding a position with the Margin property is extremely inflexible. The problems get worse when you add multiple elements, because Visual Studio won't automatically add new cells. As a result, all the elements will be placed in the same cell. Different elements may be aligned to different corners of the Grid, which will cause them to move with respect to one another (and even overlap each other) as the window is resized.

Once you understand how the Grid works, you can correct these problems. The first trick is to configure your Grid before you begin adding elements by defining its rows and columns. (You can edit the RowDefinitions and ColumnDefinitions collections by using the Properties window.) After you've set up the Grid, you can drag and drop the elements you want into the Grid and configure their margin and alignment settings in the Properties window or by editing the XAML by hand.

Fine-Tuning Rows and Columns

If the Grid were simply a proportionately sized collection of rows and columns, it wouldn't be much help. Fortunately, it's not. To unlock the full potential of the Grid, you can change the way each row and column is sized.

The Grid supports three sizing strategies:

Absolute sizes: You choose the exact size by using device-independent units. This is the least useful strategy because it's not flexible enough to deal with changing content size, changing container size, or localization.

Automatic sizes: Each row or column is given exactly the amount of space it needs, and no more. This is one of the most useful sizing modes.

Proportional sizes: Space is divided between a group of rows or columns. This is the standard setting for all rows and columns. For example, in Figure 3-13 you'll see that all cells increase in size proportionately as the Grid expands.

For maximum flexibility, you can mix and match these sizing modes. For example, it's often useful to create several automatically sized rows and then let one or two remaining rows get the leftover space through proportional sizing.

You set the sizing mode by using the Width property of the ColumnDefinition object or the Height property of the RowDefinition object to a number. For example, here's how you set an absolute width of 100 device-independent units:

```
<ColumnDefinition Width="100"></ColumnDefinition>
```

To use automatic sizing, you use a value of Auto:

```
<ColumnDefinition Width="Auto"></ColumnDefinition>
```

Finally, to use proportional sizing, you use an asterisk (*):

```
<ColumnDefinition Width="*"></ColumnDefinition>
```

If you use a mix of proportional sizing and other sizing modes, the proportionally sized rows or columns get whatever space is left over.

If you want to divide the remaining space unequally, you can assign a *weight* which you must place before the asterisk. For example, if you have two proportionately sized rows and you want the first to be half as high as the second, you could share the remaining space like this:

```
<RowDefinition Height="*"></RowDefinition>
<RowDefinition Height="2*"></RowDefinition>
```

This tells the Grid that the height of the second row should be twice the height of the first row. You can use whatever numbers you like to portion out the extra space.

■ **Note** It's easy to interact with ColumnDefinition and RowDefinition objects programmatically. You simply need to know that the Width and Height properties are GridLength objects. To create a GridLength that represents a specific size, just pass the appropriate value to the GridLength constructor. To create a GridLength that represents a proportional (*) size, pass the number to the GridLength constructor, and pass GridUnitType.Star as the second constructor argument. To indicate automatic sizing, use the shared property GridLength.Auto.

Using these size modes, you can duplicate the simple dialog box example shown in Figure 3-12 by using a top-level Grid container to split the window into two rows, rather than a DockPanel. Here's the markup you'd need:

```
<Grid ShowGridLines="True">
  <Grid.RowDefinitions>
    <RowDefinition Height="*"></RowDefinition>
    <RowDefinition Height="Auto"></RowDefinition>
  </Grid.RowDefinitions>
  <TextBox Margin="10" Grid.Row="0">This is a test.</TextBox>
  <StackPanel Grid.Row="1" HorizontalAlignment="Right" Orientation="Horizontal">
    <Button Margin="10,10,2,10" Padding="3">OK</Button>
    <Button Margin="2,10,10,10" Padding="3">Cancel</Button>
  </StackPanel>
</Grid>
```

■ **Tip** This Grid doesn't declare any columns. This is a shortcut you can take if your Grid uses just one column and that column is proportionately sized (so it fills the entire width of the Grid).

This markup is slightly longer, but it has the advantage of declaring the controls in the order they appear, which makes it easier to understand. In this case, the approach you take is simply a matter of preference. And if you want, you could replace the nested StackPanel with a one-row, two-column Grid.

■ **Note** You can create almost any interface by using nested Grid containers. (One exception is wrapped rows or columns that use the WrapPanel.) However, when you're dealing with small sections of user interface or laying out a small number of elements, it's often simpler to use the more specialized StackPanel and DockPanel containers.

Layout Rounding

As you learned in Chapter 1, WPF uses a resolution-independent system of measurement. Although this gives it the flexibility to work on a variety of hardware, it also sometimes introduces a few quirks. One of these is that elements can be aligned on subpixel boundaries—in other words, positioned with fractional coordinates that don't exactly line up with physical pixels. You can force this to happen by giving adjacent layout containers nonintegral sizes. But this quirk also crops up in some situations when you might not expect it, such as when creating a proportionately sized Grid.

For example, imagine that a two-column Grid has 200 pixels to work with. If you've split it evenly into two proportional columns, that means each gets 100 pixels. But if you have 175 pixels, the division isn't as clean, and each column gets 87.5 pixels. That means the second column is slightly displaced from the ordinary pixel boundaries. Ordinarily, this isn't a problem, but if that column contains one of the shape elements, a border, or an image, that content may appear blurry because WPF uses anti-aliasing to "blend" what would otherwise be sharp edges over pixel boundaries. Figure 3-14 shows the problem in action. It magnifies a portion of a window that contains two Grid containers. The topmost Grid does not use layout rounding, and as a result, the sharp edge of the rectangle inside becomes blurry at certain window sizes.

No layout
rounding:

With layout
rounding:

Figure 3-14. *Blur from proportionate sizing*

If this problem affects your layout, there's an easy fix. Just set the UseLayoutRounding property to True on your layout container:

```
<Grid UseLayoutRounding="True">
```

Now WPF will ensure that all the content in that layout container is snapped to the nearest pixel boundary, removing any blurriness.

Spanning Rows and Columns

You've already seen how to place elements in cells by using the Row and Column attached properties. You can also use two more attached properties to make an element stretch over several cells: RowSpan and ColumnSpan. These properties take the number of rows or columns that the element should occupy.

For example, this button will take all the space that's available in the first and second cell of the first row:

```
<Button Grid.Row="0" Grid.Column="0" Grid.RowSpan="2">Span Button</Button>
```

And this button will stretch over four cells in total by spanning two columns and two rows:

```
<Button Grid.Row="0" Grid.Column="0" Grid.RowSpan="2" Grid.ColumnSpan="2">
  Span Button</Button>
```

Row and column spanning can achieve some interesting effects and is particularly handy when you need to fit elements in a tabular structure that's broken up by dividers or longer sections of content.

Using column spanning, you could rewrite the simple dialog box example from Figure 3-12 by using just a single Grid. This Grid divides the window into three columns, spreads the text box over all three, and uses the last two columns to align the OK and Cancel buttons.

```
<Grid ShowGridLines="True">
  <Grid.RowDefinitions>
    <RowDefinition Height="*"></RowDefinition>
    <RowDefinition Height="Auto"></RowDefinition>
  </Grid.RowDefinitions>
  <Grid.ColumnDefinitions>
    <ColumnDefinition Width="*"></ColumnDefinition>
    <ColumnDefinition Width="Auto"></ColumnDefinition>
    <ColumnDefinition Width="Auto"></ColumnDefinition>
  </Grid.ColumnDefinitions>
  <TextBox Margin="10" Grid.Row="0" Grid.Column="0" Grid.ColumnSpan="3">
    This is a test.</TextBox>
  <Button Margin="10,10,2,10" Padding="3"
    Grid.Row="1" Grid.Column="1">OK</Button>
  <Button Margin="2,10,10,10" Padding="3"
    Grid.Row="1" Grid.Column="2">Cancel</Button>
</Grid>
```

Most developers will agree that this layout isn't clear or sensible. The column widths are determined by the size of the two buttons at the bottom of the window, which makes it difficult to add new content into the existing Grid structure. If you make even a minor addition to this window, you'll probably be forced to create a new set of columns.

As this shows, when you choose the layout containers for a window, you aren't simply interested in getting the correct layout behavior—you also want to build a layout structure that's easy to maintain and enhance in the future. A good rule of thumb is to use smaller layout containers such as the StackPanel for one-off layout tasks, such as arranging a group of buttons. On the other hand, if you need to apply a consistent structure to more than one area of your window (as with the text box column shown later in Figure 3-22), the Grid is an indispensable tool for standardizing your layout.

Splitting Windows

Every Windows user has seen *splitter bars*—draggable dividers that separate one section of a window from another. For example, when you use Windows Explorer, you're presented with a list of folders (on the left) and a list of files (on the right). You can drag the splitter bar in between to determine what proportion of the window is given to each pane.

In WPF, splitter bars are represented by the GridSplitter class and are a feature of the Grid. By adding a GridSplitter to a Grid, you give the user the ability to resize rows or columns. Figure 3-15 shows a window that has a GridSplitter between two columns. By dragging the splitter bar, the user can change the relative widths of both columns.

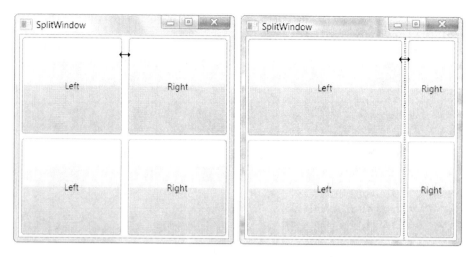

Figure 3-15. *Moving a splitter bar*

Most programmers find that the GridSplitter isn't the most intuitive part of WPF. Understanding how to use it to get the effect you want takes a little experimentation. Here are a few guidelines:

- The GridSplitter must be placed in a Grid cell. You can place the GridSplitter in a cell with existing content, in which case you need to adjust the margin settings so it doesn't overlap. A better approach is to reserve a dedicated column or row for the GridSplitter, with a Height or Width value of Auto.

- The GridSplitter always resizes entire rows or columns (not single cells). To make the appearance of the GridSplitter consistent with this behavior, you should stretch the GridSplitter across an entire row or column, rather than limit it to a single cell. To accomplish this, you use the RowSpan or ColumnSpan properties you considered earlier. For example, the GridSplitter in Figure 3-15 has a RowSpan of 2. As a result, it stretches over the entire column. If you didn't add this setting, it would appear only in the top row (where it's placed), *even though* dragging the splitter bar would resize the entire column.

- Initially, the GridSplitter is invisibly small. To make it usable, you need to give it a minimum size. In the case of a vertical splitter bar (like the one in Figure 3-15), you need to set VerticalAlignment to Stretch (so it fills the whole height of the available area) and Width to a fixed size (such as 10 device-independent units). In the case of a horizontal splitter bar, you need to set HorizontalAlignment to Stretch and set Height to a fixed size.

- The GridSplitter alignment also determines whether the splitter bar is horizontal (used to resize rows) or vertical (used to resize columns). In the case of a horizontal splitter bar, you should set VerticalAlignment to Center (which is the default value) to indicate that dragging the splitter resizes the rows that are above and below. In the case of a vertical splitter bar (like the one in Figure 3-15), you should set HorizontalAlignment to Center to resize the columns on either side.

▮ **Note**   You can change the resizing behavior by using the ResizeDirection and ResizeBehavior properties of the GridSplitter. However, it's simpler to let this behavior depend entirely on the alignment settings, which is the default.

Dizzy yet? To reinforce these rules, it helps to take a look at the markup for the example shown in Figure 3-15. In the following listing the GridSplitter details are highlighted:

```
<Grid>
  <Grid.RowDefinitions>
    <RowDefinition></RowDefinition>
    <RowDefinition></RowDefinition>
  </Grid.RowDefinitions>
  <Grid.ColumnDefinitions>
    <ColumnDefinition MinWidth="100"></ColumnDefinition>
    <ColumnDefinition Width="Auto"></ColumnDefinition>
    <ColumnDefinition MinWidth="50"></ColumnDefinition>
  </Grid.ColumnDefinitions>

  <Button Grid.Row="0" Grid.Column="0" Margin="3">Left</Button>
  <Button Grid.Row="0" Grid.Column="2" Margin="3">Right</Button>
  <Button Grid.Row="1" Grid.Column="0" Margin="3">Left</Button>
  <Button Grid.Row="1" Grid.Column="2" Margin="3">Right</Button>

  <GridSplitter Grid.Row="0" Grid.Column="1" Grid.RowSpan="2"
    Width="3" VerticalAlignment="Stretch" HorizontalAlignment="Center"
    ShowsPreview="False"></GridSplitter>

</Grid>
```

■ **Tip** To create a successful GridSplitter, make sure you supply values for the VerticalAlignment, HorizontalAlignment, and Width (or Height) properties.

This markup includes one additional detail. When the GridSplitter is declared, the ShowsPreview property is set to False. As a result, when the splitter bar is dragged from one side to another, the columns are resized immediately. But if you set ShowsPreview to True, when you drag, you'll see a gray shadow follow your mouse pointer to show you where the split will be. The columns won't be resized until you release the mouse button. It's also possible to use the arrow keys to resize a GridSplitter once it receives focus.

ShowsPreview isn't the only GridSplitter property that you can set. You can also adjust the DragIncrement property if you want to force the splitter to move in coarser "chunks" (such as 10 units at a time). If you want to control the maximum and minimum allowed sizes of the columns, you simply make sure the appropriate properties are set in the ColumnDefinitions section, as shown in the previous example.

■ **Tip** You can change the fill that's used for the GridSplitter so that it isn't just a shaded gray rectangle. The trick is to apply a fill by using the Background property, which accepts simple colors and more-complex brushes.

A Grid usually contains no more than a single GridSplitter. However, you can nest one Grid inside another, and if you do, each Grid may have its own GridSplitter. This allows you to create a window that's split into two regions (for example, a left and right pane) and then further subdivide one of these regions (say, the pane on the right) into more sections (such as a resizable top and bottom portion). Figure 3-16 shows an example.

Figure 3-16. Resizing a window with two splits

Creating this window is fairly straightforward, although it's a chore to keep track of the three Grid containers that are involved: the overall Grid, the nested Grid on the left, and the nested Grid on the right. The only trick is to make sure the GridSplitter is placed in the correct cell and given the correct alignment. Here's the complete markup:

```
<!-- This is the Grid for the entire window. -->
<Grid>
  <Grid.ColumnDefinitions>
    <ColumnDefinition></ColumnDefinition>
    <ColumnDefinition Width="Auto"></ColumnDefinition>
    <ColumnDefinition></ColumnDefinition>
  </Grid.ColumnDefinitions>

  <!-- This is the nested Grid on the left.
       It isn't subdivided further with a splitter. -->
  <Grid Grid.Column="0" VerticalAlignment="Stretch">
    <Grid.RowDefinitions>
      <RowDefinition></RowDefinition>
      <RowDefinition></RowDefinition>
    </Grid.RowDefinitions>
    <Button Margin="3" Grid.Row="0">Top Left</Button>
    <Button Margin="3" Grid.Row="1">Bottom Left</Button>
  </Grid>

  <!-- This is the vertical splitter that sits between the two nested
       (left and right) grids. -->
  <GridSplitter Grid.Column="1"
   Width="3" HorizontalAlignment="Center" VerticalAlignment="Stretch"
   ShowsPreview="False"></GridSplitter>

  <!-- This is the nested Grid on the right. -->
  <Grid Grid.Column="2">
    <Grid.RowDefinitions>
      <RowDefinition></RowDefinition>
```

```
    <RowDefinition Height="Auto"></RowDefinition>
    <RowDefinition></RowDefinition>
  </Grid.RowDefinitions>

  <Button Grid.Row="0" Margin="3">Top Right</Button>
  <Button Grid.Row="2" Margin="3">Bottom Right</Button>

  <!-- This is the horizontal splitter that subdivides it into
       a top and bottom region.. -->
  <GridSplitter Grid.Row="1"
    Height="3" VerticalAlignment="Center" HorizontalAlignment="Stretch"
    ShowsPreview="False"></GridSplitter>
  </Grid>
</Grid>
```

■ **Tip**   Remember, if a Grid has just a single row or column, you can leave out the RowDefinitions section. Also, elements that don't have their row position explicitly set are assumed to have a Grid.Row value of 0 and are placed in the first row. The same holds true for elements that don't supply a Grid.Column value.

Shared Size Groups

As you've seen, a Grid contains a collection of rows and columns, which are sized explicitly, proportionately, or based on the size of their children. There's one other way to size a row or a column—to match the size of another row or column. This works through a feature called *shared-size groups.*

The goal of shared-size groups is to keep separate portions of your user interface consistent. For example, you might want to size one column to fit its content and size another column to match that size exactly. However, the real benefit of shared-size groups is to give the same proportions to separate Grid controls.

To understand how this works, consider the example shown in Figure 3-17. This window features two Grid objects—one at the top of the window (with three columns) and one at the bottom (with two columns). The leftmost column of the first Grid is sized proportionately to fit its content (a long text string). The leftmost column of the second Grid has exactly the same width, even though it contains less content. That's because it shares the same size group. No matter how much content you stuff in the first column of the first Grid, the first column of the second Grid stays synchronized.

Figure 3-17. *Two grids that share a column definition*

As this example demonstrates, a shared column can be used in otherwise different grids. In this example, the top Grid has an extra column, and so the remaining space is divided differently. Similarly, the shared columns can occupy different positions, so you could create a relationship between the first column in one Grid and the second column in another. And obviously, the columns can host completely different content.

When you use a shared-size group, it's as if you've created one column (or row) definition, which is reused in more than one place. It's not a simple one-way copy of one column to another. You can test this with the previous example by changing the content in the shared column of the second Grid. Now, the column in the first Grid will be lengthened to match (Figure 3-18).

Figure 3-18. *Shared-size columns remain synchronized*

You can even add a GridSplitter to one of the Grid objects. As the user resizes the column in one Grid, the shared column in the other Grid will follow along, resizing itself at the same time.

Creating a shared group is easy. You simply need to set the SharedSizeGroup propertyon both columns, using a matching string. In the current example both columns use a group named TextLabel:

```
<Grid Margin="3" Background="LightYellow" ShowGridLines="True">
  <Grid.ColumnDefinitions>
    <ColumnDefinition Width="Auto" SharedSizeGroup="TextLabel"></ColumnDefinition>
    <ColumnDefinition Width="Auto"></ColumnDefinition>
    <ColumnDefinition></ColumnDefinition>
  </Grid.ColumnDefinitions>

  <Label Margin="5">A very long bit of text</Label>
  <Label Grid.Column="1" Margin="5">More text</Label>
  <TextBox Grid.Column="2" Margin="5">A text box</TextBox>
</Grid>
...
<Grid Margin="3" Background="LightYellow"  ShowGridLines="True">
  <Grid.ColumnDefinitions>
    <ColumnDefinition Width="Auto" SharedSizeGroup="TextLabel"></ColumnDefinition>
    <ColumnDefinition></ColumnDefinition>
  </Grid.ColumnDefinitions>

  <Label Margin="5">Short</Label>
  <TextBox Grid.Column="1" Margin="5">A text box</TextBox>
</Grid>
```

There's one other detail. Shared-size groups aren't global to your entire application because more than one window might inadvertently use the same name. You might assume that shared-size groups are limited to the current window, but WPF is even more stringent than that. To share a group, you need to explicitly set the attached Grid.IsSharedSizeScope property to True on a container somewhere upstream that holds the Grid objects with the shared column. In the current example, the top and bottom Grid are wrapped in another Grid that accomplishes this purpose, although you could just as easily use a different container such as a DockPanel or StackPanel.

Here's the markup for the top-level Grid:

```
<Grid Grid.IsSharedSizeScope="True" Margin="3">
  <Grid.RowDefinitions>
    <RowDefinition></RowDefinition>
    <RowDefinition Height="Auto"></RowDefinition>
    <RowDefinition></RowDefinition>
  </Grid.RowDefinitions>

  <Grid Grid.Row="0" Margin="3" Background="LightYellow" ShowGridLines="True">
    ...
  </Grid>
  <Label Grid.Row="1" >Some text in between the two grids...</Label>
  <Grid Grid.Row="2" Margin="3" Background="LightYellow" ShowGridLines="True">
    ...
  </Grid>
</Grid>
```

■ **Tip**   You could use a shared-size group to synchronize a separate Grid with column headers. The width of each column can then be determined by the content in the column, which the header will share. You could even place a GridSplitter in the header, which the user could drag to resize the header and the entire column underneath.

The UniformGrid

There is a grid that breaks all the rules you've learned about so far: the UniformGrid. Unlike the Grid, the UniformGrid doesn't require (or even support) predefined columns and rows. Instead, you simply set the Rows and Columns properties to set its size. Each cell is always the same size because the available space is divided equally. Finally, elements are placed into the appropriate cell based on the order in which you define them. There are no attached Row and Column properties, and no blank cells.

Here's an example that fills a UniformGrid with four buttons:

```
<UniformGrid Rows="2" Columns="2">
  <Button>Top Left</Button>
  <Button>Top Right</Button>
  <Button>Bottom Left</Button>
  <Button>Bottom Right</Button>
</UniformGrid>
```

The UniformGrid is used far less frequently than the Grid. The Grid is an all-purpose tool for creating window layouts from the simple to the complex. The UniformGrid is a much more specialized layout container that's primarily useful when quickly laying out elements in a rigid grid (for example, when building a playing board for certain games). Many WPF programmers will never use the UniformGrid.

Coordinate-Based Layout with the Canvas

The only layout container you haven't considered yet is the Canvas. It allows you to place elements by using exact coordinates, which is a poor choice for designing rich data-driven forms and standard dialog boxes, but a valuable tool if you need to build something a little different (such as a drawing surface for a diagramming tool). The Canvas is also the most lightweight of the layout containers. That's because it doesn't include any complex layout logic to negotiate the sizing preferences of its children. Instead, it simply lays them all out at the position they specify, with the exact size they want.

To position an element on the Canvas, you set the attached Canvas.Left and Canvas.Top properties. Canvas.Left sets the number of units between the left edge of your element and the left edge of the Canvas. Canvas.Top sets the number of units between the top of your element and the top of the Canvas. As always, these values are set in device-independent units, which line up with ordinary pixels exactly when the system DPI is set to 96 dpi.

■ **Note**   Alternatively, you can use Canvas.Right instead of Canvas.Left to space an element from the right edge of the Canvas, and Canvas.Bottom instead of Canvas.Top to space it from the bottom. You just can't use both Canvas.Right and Canvas.Left at once, or both Canvas.Top and Canvas.Bottom.

Optionally, you can size your element explicitly by using its Width and Height properties. This is more common when using the Canvas than it is in other panels because the Canvas has no layout logic of its own. (And often you'll use the Canvas when you need precise control over how a combination of elements is arranged.) If you don't set the

Width and Height properties, your element will get its desired size—in other words, it will grow just large enough to fit its content.

Here's a simple Canvas that includes four buttons:

```
<Canvas>
  <Button Canvas.Left="10" Canvas.Top="10">(10,10)</Button>
  <Button Canvas.Left="120" Canvas.Top="30">(120,30)</Button>
  <Button Canvas.Left="60" Canvas.Top="80" Width="50" Height="50">
    (60,80)</Button>
  <Button Canvas.Left="70" Canvas.Top="120" Width="100" Height="50">
    (70,120)</Button>
</Canvas>
```

Figure 3-19 shows the result.

Figure 3-19. *Explicitly positioned buttons in a Canvas*

If you resize the window, the Canvas stretches to fill the available space, but none of the controls in the Canvas moves or changes size. The Canvas doesn't include any of the anchoring or docking features that were provided with coordinate layout in Windows Forms. Part of the reason for this gap is to keep the Canvas lightweight. Another reason is to prevent people from using the Canvas for purposes for which it's not intended (such as laying out a standard user interface).

Like any other layout container, the Canvas can be nested inside a user interface. That means you can use the Canvas to draw some detailed content in a portion of your window, while using more standard WPF panels for the rest of your elements.

░ **Tip** If you use the Canvas alongside other elements, you may want to consider setting its ClipToBounds to True. That way, elements inside the Canvas that stretch beyond its bounds are clipped off at the edge of the Canvas. (This prevents them from overlapping other elements elsewhere in your window.) All the other layout containers always clip their children to fit, regardless of the ClipToBounds setting.

Z-Order

If you have more than one overlapping element, you can set the attached Canvas.ZIndex property to control how they are layered.

Ordinarily, all the elements you add have the same ZIndex—0. When elements have the same ZIndex, they're displayed in the same order that they exist in the Canvas.Children collection, which is based on the order that they're defined in the XAML markup. Elements declared later in the markup—such as button (70,120)—are displayed on top of elements that are declared earlier—such as button (120,30).

However, you can promote any element to a higher level by increasing its ZIndex. That's because higher ZIndex elements *always* appear over lower ZIndex elements. Using this technique, you could reverse the layering in the previous example:

```
<Button Canvas.Left="60" Canvas.Top="80" Canvas.ZIndex="1" Width="50" Height="50">
 (60,80)</Button>
<Button Canvas.Left="70" Canvas.Top="120" Width="100" Height="50">
 (70,120)</Button>
```

▓ **Note** The values you use for the Canvas.ZIndex property have no meaning. The important detail is how the ZIndex value of one element compares to the ZIndex value of another. You can set the ZIndex by using any positive or negative integer.

The ZIndex property is particularly useful if you need to change the position of an element programmatically. Just call Canvas.SetZIndex and pass in the element you want to modify and the new ZIndex you want to apply. Unfortunately, there is no BringToFront() or SendToBack() method—it's up to you to keep track of the highest and lowest ZIndex values if you want to implement this behavior.

The InkCanvas

WPF also includes an InkCanvas element that's similar to the Canvas in some respects (and wholly different in others). Like the Canvas the InkCanvas defines four attached properties that you can apply to child elements for coordinate-based positioning (Top, Left, Bottom, and Right). However, the underlying plumbing is quite a bit different—in fact, the InkCanvas doesn't derive from Canvas or even from the base Panel class. Instead, it derives directly from FrameworkElement.

The primary purpose of the InkCanvas is to allow stylus input. A *stylus* is a pen-like input device that's used in tablet PCs. However, the InkCanvas works with the mouse in the same way as it works with the stylus. Thus, a user can draw lines or select and manipulate elements in the InkCanvas by using the mouse.

The InkCanvas holds two collections of child content. The familiar Children collection holds arbitrary elements, just as with the Canvas. Each element can be positioned based on the Top, Left, Bottom, and Right properties. The Strokes collection holds System.Windows.Ink.Stroke objects, which represent graphical input that the user has drawn in the InkCanvas. Each line or curve that the user draws becomes a separate Stroke object. Thanks to these dual collections, you can use the InkCanvas to let the user annotate content (stored in the Children collection) with strokes (stored in the Strokes collection).

For example, Figure 3-20 shows an InkCanvas that contains a picture that has been annotated with extra strokes. Here's the markup for the InkCanvas in this example, which defines the image:

```
<InkCanvas Name="inkCanvas" Background="LightYellow"
 EditingMode="Ink">
  <Image Source="office.jpg" InkCanvas.Top="10" InkCanvas.Left="10"
```

```
  Width="287" Height="319"></Image>
</InkCanvas>
```

The strokes are drawn at runtime by the user.

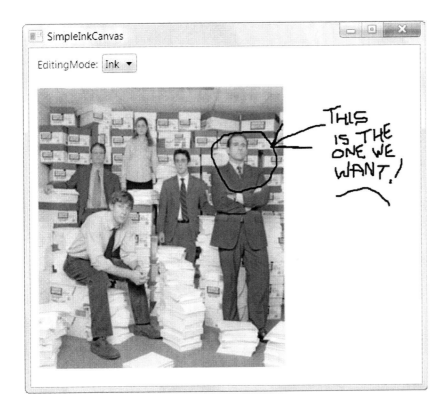

Figure 3-20. *Adding strokes in an InkCanvas*

The InkCanvas can be used in some significantly different ways, depending on the value you set for the InkCanvas.EditingMode property. Table 3-5 lists all your options.

Table 3-5. *Values of the InkCanvasEditingMode Enumeration*

Name	Description
Ink	The InkCanvas allows the user to draw annotations. This is the default mode. When the user draws with the mouse or stylus, a stroke is drawn.
GestureOnly	The InkCanvas doesn't allow the user to draw stroke annotations but pays attention to specific predefined *gestures* (such as dragging the stylus in one direction or scratching out content). The full list of recognized gestures is listed by the System.Windows.Ink.ApplicationGesture enumeration.
InkAndGesture	The InkCanvas allows the user to draw stroke annotations and also recognizes predefined gestures.

(continued)

Table 3-5. (*continued*)

Name	Description
EraseByStroke	The InkCanvas erases a stroke when it's clicked. A user can switch to this mode by using the back end of a stylus. (You can determine the current mode by using the read-only ActiveEditingMode property, and you can change the mode used for the back end of the stylus by changing the EditingModeInverted property.)
EraseByPoint	The InkCanvas erases a portion of a stroke (a point in a stroke) when that portion is clicked.
Select	The InkCanvas allows the user to select elements that are stored in the Children collection. To select an element, the user must click it or drag a selection "lasso" around it. After an element is selected, it can be moved, resized, or deleted.
None	The InkCanvas ignores mouse and stylus input.

The InkCanvas raises events when the editing mode changes (ActiveEditingModeChanged), a gesture is detected in GestureOnly or InkAndGesture mode (Gesture), a stroke is drawn (StrokeCollected), a stroke is erased (StrokeErasing and StrokeErased), and an element is selected or changed in Select mode (SelectionChanging, SelectionChanged, SelectionMoving, SelectionMoved, SelectionResizing, and SelectionResized). The events that end in *ing* represent an action that is about to take place but can be canceled by setting the Cancel property of the EventArgs object.

In Select mode, the InkCanvas provides a fairly capable design surface for dragging content around and manipulating it. Figure 3-21 shows a Button control in an InkCanvas as it's being selected (on the left) and then repositioned and resized (on the right).

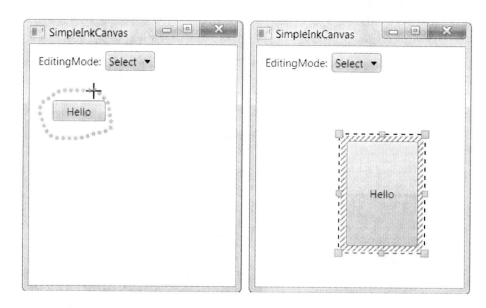

Figure 3-21. *Moving and resizing an element in the InkCanvas*

As interesting as Select mode is, it isn't a perfect fit if you're building a drawing or diagramming tool. You'll see a better example of how to create a custom drawing surface in Chapter 14.

Layout Examples

You've now spent a considerable amount of time poring over the intricacies of the WPF layout containers. With this low-level knowledge in mind, it's worth looking at a few complete layout examples. Doing so will give you a better sense of how the various WPF layout concepts (such as size-to-content, stretch, and nesting) work in real-world windows.

A Column of Settings

Layout containers such as the Grid make it dramatically easier to create an overall structure to a window. For example, consider the window with settings shown in Figure 3-22. This window arranges its individual components—labels, text boxes, and buttons—into a tabular structure.

Figure 3-22. *Folder settings in a column*

To create this table, you begin by defining the rows and columns of the grid. The rows are easy enough—each one is simply sized to the height of the containing content. That means the entire row will get the height of the largest element, which in this case is the Browse button in the third column.

```
<Grid Margin="3,3,10,3">
  <Grid.RowDefinitions>
    <RowDefinition Height="Auto"></RowDefinition>
    <RowDefinition Height="Auto"></RowDefinition>
    <RowDefinition Height="Auto"></RowDefinition>
    <RowDefinition Height="Auto"></RowDefinition>
  </Grid.RowDefinitions>
  ...
```

Next, you need to create the columns. The first and last columns are sized to fit their content (the label text and the Browse button, respectively). The middle column gets all the remaining room, which means it grows as the window is resized larger, giving you more room to see the selected folder. (If you want this stretching to top out at some extremely wide maximum value, you can use the MaxWidth property when defining the column, just as you do with individual elements.)

```
...
<Grid.ColumnDefinitions>
  <ColumnDefinition Width="Auto"></ColumnDefinition>
  <ColumnDefinition Width="*"></ColumnDefinition>
  <ColumnDefinition Width="Auto"></ColumnDefinition>
</Grid.ColumnDefinitions>
...
```

■ **Tip**   The Grid needs some minimum space—enough to fit the full label text, the browse button, and a few pixels in the middle column to show the text box. If you shrink the containing window to be smaller than this, some content will be cut off. As always, it makes sense to use the MinWidth and MinHeight properties on the window to prevent this from occurring.

Now that you have your basic structure, you simply need to slot the elements into the right cells. However, you also need to think carefully about margins and alignment. Each element needs a basic margin (a good value is 3 units) to give some breathing room. In addition, the label and text box need to be centered vertically because they aren't as tall as the Browse button. Finally, the text box needs to use automatic sizing mode, so it stretches to fit the entire column.

Here's the markup you need to define the first row in the grid:

```
...
<Label Grid.Row="0" Grid.Column="0" Margin="3"
  VerticalAlignment="Center">Home:</Label>
<TextBox Grid.Row="0" Grid.Column="1" Margin="3"
  Height="Auto" VerticalAlignment="Center"></TextBox>
<Button Grid.Row="0" Grid.Column="2" Margin="3" Padding="2">Browse</Button>
  ...
</Grid>
```

You can repeat this markup to add all your rows by simply incrementing the value of the Grid.Row attribute.

One fact that's not immediately obvious is how flexible this window is because of the use of the Grid control. None of the individual elements—the labels, text boxes, and buttons—have hard-coded positions or sizes. As a result, you can quickly make changes to the entire grid simply by tweaking the ColumnDefinition elements. Furthermore, if you add a row that has longer label text (necessitating a wider first column), the entire grid is adjusted to be consistent, including the rows that you've already added. And if you want to add elements between the rows—such as separator lines to divide sections of the window—you can keep the same columns but use the ColumnSpan property to stretch a single element over a larger area.

Dynamic Content

As the column of settings demonstrates, windows that use the WPF layout containers are easy to change and adapt as you revise your application. This flexibility doesn't just benefit you at design time. It's also a great asset if you need to display content that changes dramatically.

One example is *localized text*—text that appears in your user interface and needs to be translated into different languages for different geographic regions. In old-style coordinate-based applications, changing the text can wreak havoc in a window, particularly because a short amount of English text becomes significantly larger in many languages. Even if elements are allowed to resize themselves to fit larger text, doing so often throws off the whole balance of a window.

Figure 3-23 demonstrates how this isn't the case when you use the WPF layout containers intelligently. In this example, the user interface has a short text and a long text option. When the long text is used, the buttons that contain the text are resized automatically and other content is bumped out of the way. And because the resized buttons share the same layout container (in this case, a table column), that entire section of the user interface is resized. The end result is that all buttons keep a consistent size—the size of the largest button.

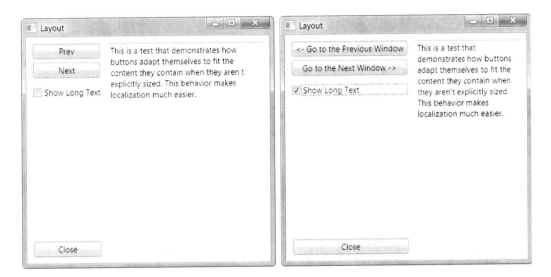

Figure 3-23. *A self-adjusting window*

To make this work, the window is carved into a table with two columns and two rows. The column on the left takes the resizable buttons, while the column on the right takes the text box. The bottom row is used for the Close button. It's kept in the same table so that it resizes along with the top row.

Here's the complete markup:

```
<Grid>
  <Grid.RowDefinitions>
    <RowDefinition Height="*"></RowDefinition>
    <RowDefinition Height="Auto"></RowDefinition>
  </Grid.RowDefinitions>
  <Grid.ColumnDefinitions>
    <ColumnDefinition Width="Auto"></ColumnDefinition>
    <ColumnDefinition Width="*"></ColumnDefinition>
  </Grid.ColumnDefinitions>

  <StackPanel Grid.Row="0" Grid.Column="0">
    <Button Name="cmdPrev" Margin="10,10,10,3">Prev</Button>
    <Button Name="cmdNext" Margin="10,3,10,3">Next</Button>
    <CheckBox Name="chkLongText" Margin="10,10,10,10"
```

```
        Checked="chkLongText_Checked" Unchecked="chkLongText_Unchecked">
        Show Long Text</CheckBox>
    </StackPanel>
    <TextBox Grid.Row="0" Grid.Column="1" Margin="0,10,10,10"
      TextWrapping="WrapWithOverflow" Grid.RowSpan="2">This is a test that demonstrates
      how buttons adapt themselves to fit the content they contain when they aren't
      explicitly sized. This behavior makes localization much easier.</TextBox>
    <Button Grid.Row="1" Grid.Column="0" Name="cmdClose"
      Margin="10,3,10,10">Close</Button>
</Grid>
```

The event handlers for the CheckBox aren't shown here. They simply change the text in the two buttons.

A Modular User Interface

Many of the layout containers gracefully "flow" content into the available space, such as the StackPanel, DockPanel, and WrapPanel. One advantage of this approach is that it allows you to create truly modular interfaces. In other words, you can plug in different panels with the appropriate user interface sections you want to show and leave out those that don't apply. The entire application can shape itself accordingly, somewhat like a portal site on the Web.

Figure 3-24 demonstrates this. It places several separate panels into a WrapPanel. The user can choose which of these panels are visible by using the check boxes at the top of the window.

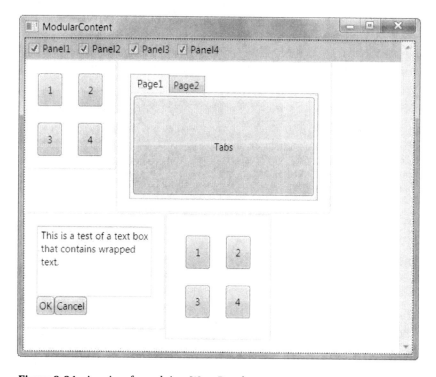

Figure 3-24. *A series of panels in a WrapPanel*

■ **Note** Although you can set the background of a layout panel, you can't set a border around it. This example overcomes that limitation by wrapping each panel in a Border element that outlines the exact dimensions.

As different panels are hidden, the remaining panels reflow themselves to fit the available space (and the order in which they're declared). Figure 3-25 shows a different permutation of panels.

Figure 3-25. *Hiding some panels*

To hide and show the individual panels, a small bit of code handles check box clicks. Although you haven't considered the WPF event-handling model in any detail (Chapter 5 has the full story), the trick is to set the Visibility property:

```
panel.Visibility = Visibility.Collapsed
```

The Visibility property is a part of the base UIElement class and is therefore supported by just about everything you'll put in a WPF window. It takes one of three values, from the System.Windows.Visibility enumeration, as listed in Table 3-6.

Table 3-6. *Values of the Visibility Enumeration*

Value	Description
Visible	The element appears as normal in the window.
Collapsed	The element is not displayed and doesn't take up any space.
Hidden	The element is not displayed, but the space it would otherwise use is still reserved. (In other words, there's a blank space where it would have appeared.) This setting is handy if you need to hide and show elements without changing the layout and the relative positioning of the elements in the rest of your window.

■ **Tip** You can use the Visibility property to dynamically tailor a variety of interfaces. For example, you could make a collapsible pane that can appear at the side of your window. All you need to do is wrap all the contents of that pane in some sort of layout container and set its Visibility property to suit. The remaining content will be rearranged to fit the available space.

The Last Word

In this chapter, you took a detailed tour of the WPF layout model and learned how to place elements in stacks, grids, and other arrangements. You built more-complex layouts by using nested combinations of the layout containers, and you threw the GridSplitter into the mix to make resizable split windows. And all along, you kept close focus on the reasons for this dramatic change—namely, the benefits you'll get when maintaining, enhancing, and localizing your user interface.

The layout story is still far from over. In the following chapters, you'll see many more examples that use the layout containers to organize groups of elements. You'll also learn about a few additional features that let you arrange content in a window:

Specialized containers: The ScrollViewer, TabItem, and Expander controls give you the ability to scroll content, place it in separate tabs, and collapse it out of sight. Unlike the layout panels, these containers can hold only a single piece of content. However, you can easily use them in concert with a layout panel to get exactly the effect you need. You'll try these containers in Chapter 6.

The Viewbox: Need a way to resize graphical content (such as images and vector drawings)? The Viewbox is yet another specialized container that can help you out, and it has built-in scaling. You'll take your first look at the Viewbox in Chapter 12.

Text layout: WPF adds tools for laying out large blocks of styled text. You can use floating figures and lists and use paging, columns, and sophisticated wrapping intelligence to get remarkably polished results. You'll see how in Chapter 28.

CHAPTER 4

■ ■ ■

Dependency Properties

Every .NET programmer is familiar with *properties* and *events*, which are core parts of .NET's object abstraction. Few would expect WPF, a user interface technology, to change either of these fundamentals. But surprisingly enough, that's exactly what WPF does.

In this chapter, you'll learn how WPF replaces ordinary .NET properties with a higher-level *dependency property* feature. Dependency properties use more-efficient storage and support additional features such as change notification and property value inheritance (the ability to propagate default values down the element tree). Dependency properties are also the basis for a number of key WPF features, including animation, data binding, and styles. Fortunately, even though the plumbing has changed, you can read and set dependency properties in code in exactly the same way as traditional .NET properties.

In the following pages, you'll take a close look at dependency properties. You'll see how they're defined, registered, and consumed. You'll also learn what features they support and what problems they solve.

■ **Note** Understanding dependency properties requires a heavy dose of theory, which you might not want to slog through just yet. If you can't wait to get started building an application, feel free to skip ahead to the following chapters and then return to this one when you need a deeper understanding of how WPF ticks and you want to build dependency properties of your own.

Understanding Dependency Properties

Dependency properties are a new implementation of standard .NET properties—one that has a significant amount of added value. You need dependency properties to plug into core WPF features such as animation, data binding, and styles.Most of the properties that are exposed by WPF elements are dependency properties. In all the examples you've seen up to this point, you've been using dependency properties without realizing it. That's because dependency properties are designed to be consumed in the same way as normal properties.

However, dependency properties are *not* normal properties. It's comforting to think of a dependency property as a normal property (defined in the typical .NET fashion) with a set of WPF features added on. Conceptually, dependency features behave this way, but that's not how they're implemented behind the scenes. The simple reason is performance. If the designers of WPF simply added extra features on top of the .NET property system, they'd need to create a complex, bulky layer for your code to travel through. Ordinary properties could not support all the features of dependency properties without this extra overhead.

Dependency properties are a WPF-specific creation. However, the dependency properties in the WPF libraries are always wrapped by ordinary .NET property procedures. This makes them usable in the normal way, even with code that has no understanding of the WPF dependency property system. It seems odd to think of an older technology wrapping a newer one, but that's how WPF is able to change a fundamental ingredient such as properties without disrupting the rest of the .NET world.

Defining a Dependency Property

You'll spend much more time using dependency properties than creating them. However, there are still many reasons that you'll need to create your own dependency properties. Obviously, they're a key ingredient if you're designing a custom WPF element. However, they're also required in some cases if you want to add data binding, animation, or another WPF feature to a portion of code that wouldn't otherwise support it. Creating a dependency property isn't difficult, but the syntax takes a little getting used to. It's thoroughly different from creating an ordinary .NET property.

■ **Note**   You can add dependency properties only to dependency objects—classes that derive from DependencyObject. Fortunately, most of the key pieces of WPF infrastructure derive indirectly from DependencyObject, with the most obvious example being elements.

The first step is to define an object that *represents* your property. This is an instance of the DependencyProperty class. The information about your property needs to be available all the time, and possibly even shared among classes (as is common with WPF elements). For that reason, your DependencyProperty object must be defined as a shared field in the associated class.

For example, the FrameworkElement class defines a Margin property that all elements share. Unsurprisingly, Margin is a dependency property. That means it's defined in the FrameworkElement class like this:

```
Public Class FrameworkElement
    Inherits UIElement
    Implements ...

    Public Shared ReadOnly MarginProperty As DependencyProperty
    ...
End Class
```

By convention, the field that defines a dependency property has the name of the ordinary property, plus the word *Property* at the end. That way, you can separate the dependency property definition from the name of the actual property. The field is defined with the ReadOnly keyword, which means it can be set only in the shared constructor for the FrameworkElement, which is the task you'll undertake next.

Registering a Dependency Property

Defining the DependencyProperty object is just the first step. For it to become usable, you need to register your dependency property with WPF. This step needs to be completed before any code uses the property, so it must be performed in a shared constructor for the associated class.

WPF ensures that DependencyProperty objects can't be instantiated directly, because the DependencyProperty class has no public constructor. Instead, a DependencyObject instance can be created only by using the shared DependencyProperty.Register() method. WPF also ensures that DependencyProperty objects can't be changed after they're created, because all DependencyProperty members are read-only. Instead, their values must be supplied as arguments to the Register() method.

The following code shows an example of how a DependencyProperty must be created. Here, the FrameworkElement class uses a shared constructor to initialize the MarginProperty:

```
Shared Sub New()
    Dim metadata As new FrameworkPropertyMetadata( _
      New Thickness(), FrameworkPropertyMetadataOptions.AffectsMeasure)
```

```
MarginProperty = DependencyProperty.Register("Margin", _
    GetType(Thickness), GetType(FrameworkElement), metadata, _
    AddressOf FrameworkElement.IsMarginValid)
  ...
End Sub
```

There are two steps involved in registering a dependency property. First, you create a FrameworkPropertyMetadata object that indicates what services you want to use with your dependency property (such as support for data binding, animation, and journaling). Next, you register the property by calling the shared DependencyProperty.Register() method. At this point, you are responsible for supplying a few key ingredients:

- The property name (Margin in this example)
- The data type used by the property (the Thickness structure in this example)
- The type that owns this property (the FrameworkElement class in this example)
- Optionally, a FrameworkPropertyMetadata object with additional property settings
- Optionally, a callback that performs validation for the property

The first three details are all straightforward. The FrameworkPropertyMetadata object and the validation callback are more interesting.

You use FrameworkPropertyMetadata to configure additional features for your dependency property. Most of the properties of the FrameworkPropertyMetadata class are simple Boolean flags that you set to flip on a feature. (The default value for each Boolean flag is False.) A few are callbacks that point to custom methods that you create to perform a specific task. One—FrameworkPropertyMetadata.DefaultValue—sets the default value that WPF will apply when the property is first initialized. Table 4-1 lists all the FrameworkPropertyMetadata properties.

Table 4-1. *Properties of the FrameworkPropertyMetadata Class*

Name	Description
AffectsArrange, AffectsMeasure, AffectsParentArrange, and AffectsParentMeasure	If True, the dependency property may affect how adjacent elements (or the parent element) are placed during the measure pass and the arrange pass of a layout operation. For example, the Margin dependency property sets AffectsMeasure to True, signaling that if the margin of an element changes, the layout container needs to repeat the measure step to determine the new placement of elements.
AffectsRender	If True, the dependency property may affect something about the way an element is drawn, requiring that the element be repainted.
BindsTwoWayByDefault	If True, this dependency property will use two-way data binding instead of one-way data binding by default. However, you can specify the binding behavior you want explicitly when you create the binding.
Inherits	If True, the dependency property value propagates through the element tree and can be inherited by nested elements. For example, Font is an inheritable dependency property—if you set it on a higher-level element, it's inherited by nested elements, unless they explicitly override it with their own font settings.
IsAnimationProhibited	If True, the dependency property can't be used in an animation.
IsNotDataBindable	If True, the dependency property can't be set with a binding expression.

(continued)

93

Table 4-1. (*continued*)

Name	Description
Journal	If True, this dependency property will be persisted to the journal (the history of visited pages) in a page-based application.
SubPropertiesDoNotAffectRender	If True, WPF will not rerender an object if one of its subproperties (the property of a property) changes.
DefaultUpdateSourceTrigger	This sets the default value for the Binding.UpdateSourceTrigger property when this property is used in a binding expression. The UpdateSourceTrigger determines when a data-bound value applies its changes. You can set the UpdateSourceTrigger property manually when you create the binding.
DefaultValue	This sets the default value for the dependency property.
CoerceValueCallback	This provides a callback that attempts to "correct" a property value before it's validated.
PropertyChangedCallback	This provides a callback that is called when a property value is changed.

In the following sections, you'll take a closer look at the validation callback and some of the metadata options. You'll also see a few more of them at work in examples throughout this book. But first, you need to understand how you can make sure every dependency property can be accessed in the same way as a traditional .NET property.

Adding a Property Wrapper

The final step to creating a dependency property is to wrap it in a traditional .NET property. However, whereas typical property procedures retrieve or set the value of a private field, the property procedures for a WPF property use the GetValue() and SetValue() methods that are defined in the base DependencyObject class. Here's an example:

```
Public Property Margin As Thickness
    Get
        Return CType(GetValue(MarginProperty),Thickness)
    End Get
    Set
        SetValue(MarginProperty, value)
    End Set
End Property
```

When you create the property wrapper, you should include nothing more than a call to SetValue() and a call to GetValue(), as in the previous example. You should *not* add any extra code to validate values, raise events, and so on. That's because other features in WPF may bypass the property wrapper and call SetValue() and GetValue() directly. (One example is when a compiled XAML file is parsed at runtime.) Both SetValue() and GetValue() are public.

■ **Note**   The property wrapper isn't the right place to validate data or raise an event. However, WPF does provide a place for this code; the trick is to use dependency property callbacks. Validation should be performed through the DependencyProperty.ValidateValueCallback shown previously, while events can be raised from the FrameworkPropertyMetadata.PropertyChangedCallback shown in the next section.

You now have a fully functioning dependency property, which you can set just like any other .NET property, using the property wrapper:

```
myElement.Margin = New Thickness(5)
```

There's one extra detail. Dependency properties follow strict rules of precedence to determine their current value. Even if you don't set a dependency property directly, it may already have a value—perhaps one that's applied by a binding, style, or animation, or one that's inherited through the element tree. (You'll learn more about these rules of precedence in the next section, "How WPF Uses Dependency Properties.") However, as soon as you set the value directly, it overrides all these other influences.

At some point later, you may want to remove your local value setting and let the property value be determined as though you never set it. Obviously, you can't accomplish this by setting a new value. Instead, you need to use another method that's inherited from DependencyObject: the ClearValue() method. Here's how it works:

```
myElement.ClearValue(FrameworkElement.MarginProperty)
```

How WPF Uses Dependency Properties

As you'll discover throughout this book, dependency properties are required for a range of WPF features. However, all of these features work through two key behaviors that every dependency property supports—change notification and dynamic value resolution.

Contrary to what you might expect, dependency properties do *not* automatically fire events to let you know when a property value changes. Instead, they trigger a protected method named OnPropertyChangedCallback(). This method passes the information along to two WPF services (data binding and triggers). It also calls the PropertyChangedCallback, if one is defined.

In other words, if you want to react when a property changes, you have two choices—you can create a binding that uses the property value (Chapter 8), or you can write a trigger that automatically changes another property or starts an animation (Chapter 11). However, dependency properties don't give you a general-purpose way to fire off some code to respond to a property change.

■ **Note** If you're dealing with a control that you've created, you can use the property callback mechanism to react to property changes and even raise an event. Many common controls use this technique for properties that correspond to user-supplied information. For example, the TextBox provides a TextChanged event, and the ScrollBar provides a ValueChanged event. A control can implement functionality like this by using the PropertyChangedCallback, but this functionality isn't exposed from dependency properties in a general way for performance reasons.

The second feature that's key to the way dependency properties work is dynamic value resolution. This means when you retrieve the value from a dependency property, WPF takes several factors into consideration.

This behavior gives dependency properties their name—in essence, a dependency property *depends* on multiple property providers, each with its own level of precedence. When you retrieve a value from a property value, the WPF property system goes through a series of steps to arrive at the final value. First, it determines the base value for the property by considering the following factors, arranged from lowest to highest precedence:

1. The default value (as set by the FrameworkPropertyMetadata object)

2. The inherited value (if the FrameworkPropertyMetadata.Inherits flag is set and a value has been applied to an element somewhere up the containment hierarchy)

3. The value from a theme style (as discussed in Chapter 18)

4. The value from a project style (as discussed in Chapter 11)

5. The local value (in other words, a value you've set directly on this object by using code or XAML)

As this list shows, you override the entire hierarchy by applying a value directly. If you don't, the value is determined by the next applicable item up on the list.

■ **Note**   One of the advantages of this system is that it's very economical. If the value of a property has not been set locally, WPF will retrieve its value from a style, another element, or the default. In this case, no memory is required to store the value. You can quickly see the savings if you add a few buttons to a form. Each button has dozens of properties, which, if they are set through one of these mechanisms, use no memory at all.

WPF follows the previous list to determine the *base value* of a dependency property. However, the base value is not necessarily the final value that you'll retrieve from a property. That's because WPF considers several other providers that can change a property's value.

Here's the four-step process WPF follows to determine a property value:

1. Determine the base value (as described previously).

2. If the property is set by using an expression, evaluate that expression. Currently, WPF supports two types of expressions: data binding (Chapter 8) and resources (Chapter 10).

3. If this property is the target of animation, apply that animation.

4. Run CoerceValueCallback to "correct" the value. (You'll learn how to use this technique later, in the "Property Validation" section.)

Essentially, dependency properties are hardwired into a small set of WPF services. If it weren't for this infrastructure, these features would add unnecessary complexity and significant overhead.

■ **Tip**   In future versions of WPF, the dependency property pipeline could be extended to include additional services. When you design custom elements (a topic covered in Chapter 18), you'll probably use dependency properties for most (if not all) of their public properties.

Shared Dependency Properties

Some classes share the same dependency property, even though they have separate class hierarchies. For example, both TextBlock.FontFamily and Control.FontFamily point to the same shared dependency property, which is actually defined in the TextElement class and TextElement.FontFamilyProperty. The shared constructor of TextElement registers the property, but the shared constructors of TextBlock and Control simply reuse it by calling the DependencyProperty.AddOwner() method:

```
TextBlock.FontFamilyProperty = _
    TextElement.FontFamilyProperty.AddOwner(GetType(TextBlock))
```

You can use the same technique when you create your own custom classes (assuming the property is not already provided in the class you're inheriting from, in which case you get it for free). You can also use an overload of the AddOwner() method that allows you to supply a validation callback and a new FrameworkPropertyMetadata that will apply only to this new use of the dependency property.

Reusing dependency properties can lead to some strange side effects in WPF, most notably with styles. For example, if you use a style to set the TextBlock.FontFamily property automatically, your style will also affect the Control.FontFamily property, because behind the scenes both classes use the same dependency property. You'll see this phenomenon in action in Chapter 11.

Attached Dependency Properties

Chapter 2 introduced a special type of dependency property called an *attached property*. An attached property is a dependency property, and it's managed by the WPF property system. The difference is that an attached property applies to a class other than the one where it's defined.

The most common example of attached properties is found in the layout containers described in Chapter 3. For example, the Grid class defines the attached properties Row and Column, which you set on the contained elements to indicate where they should be positioned. Similarly, the DockPanel defines the attached property Dock, and the Canvas defines the attached properties Left, Right, Top, and Bottom.

To define an attached property, you use the RegisterAttached() method instead of Register(). Here's an example that registers the Grid.Row property:

```
Dim metadata As New FrameworkPropertyMetadata(0, _
    AddressOf Grid.OnCellAttachedPropertyChanged)
Grid.RowProperty = DependencyProperty.RegisterAttached("Row", _
    GetType(System.Int32), GetType(Grid), metadata, _
    AddressOf Grid.IsIntValueNotNegative)
```

As with an ordinary dependency property, you can supply a FrameworkPropertyMetadata object and a ValidateValueCallback.

When creating an attached property, you don't define the .NET property wrapper. That's because attached properties can be set on *any* dependency object. For example, the Grid.Row property may be set on a Grid object (if you have one Grid nested inside another) or on some other element. In fact, the Grid.Row property can be set on an element even if that element isn't in a Grid—and even if there isn't a single Grid object in your element tree.

Instead of using a .NET property wrapper, attached properties require a pair of shared methods that can be called to set and get the property value. These methods use the familiar SetValue() and GetValue() methods (inherited from the DependencyObject class). The shared methods should be named Set*PropertyName*() and Get*PropertyName*().

Here are the shared methods that implement the Grid.Row attached property:

```
Public Shared Function GetRow(ByVal element As UIElement) As Integer
    If element Is Nothing Then
        Throw New ArgumentNullException(...)
    End If
    Return CType(element.GetValue(Grid.RowProperty),Integer)
End Function

Public Shared Sub SetRow(ByVal element As UIElement, ByVal value As Integer)
    If element Is Nothing Then
        Throw New ArgumentNullException(...)
    End If
    element.SetValue(Grid.RowProperty, value)
End Sub
```

Here's an example that uses code to position an element in the first row of a Grid:

```
Grid.SetRow(txtElement, 0)
```

Alternatively, you can call the SetValue() or GetValue() method directly and bypass the shared methods:

```
txtElement.SetValue(Grid.RowProperty, 0)
```

The SetValue() method also provides one brain-twisting oddity. Although XAML doesn't allow it, you can use an overloaded version of the SetValue() method in code to attach a value for any dependency property, *even if that property isn't defined as an attached property*. For example, the following code is perfectly legitimate:

```
Dim comboBox As New ComboBox()
...
comboBox.SetValue(PasswordBox.PasswordCharProperty, "*")
```

Here, a value for the PasswordBox.PasswordChar property is set for a ComboBox object, even though PasswordBox.PasswordCharProperty is registered as an ordinary dependency property, not an attached property. This action won't change the way the ComboBox works—after all, the code inside the ComboBox won't look for the value of a property that it doesn't know exists—but you could act upon the PasswordChar value in your own code.

Although rarely used, this quirk provides some more insight into the way the WPF property system works, and it demonstrates its remarkable extensibility. It also shows that even though attached properties are registered with a different method than normal dependency properties, in the eyes of WPF there's no real distinction. The only difference is what the XAML parser allows. Unless you register your property as an attached property, you won't be able to set it on other elements in your markup.

Property Validation

When defining any sort of property, you need to face the possibility that it may be set incorrectly. With traditional .NET properties, you might try to catch this sort of problem in the property setter. With dependency properties, this isn't appropriate, because the property may be set directly through the WPF property system by using the SetValue() method.

Instead, WPF provides two ways to prevent invalid values:

> *ValidateValueCallback*: This callback can accept or reject new values. Usually, this callback is used to catch obvious errors that violate the constraints of the property. You can supply it as an argument to the DependencyProperty.Register() method.

> *CoerceValueCallback*: This callback can change new values into something more acceptable. Usually, this callback is used to deal with conflicting dependency property values that are set on the same object. These values might be independently valid but aren't consistent when applied together. To use this callback, supply it as a constructor argument when creating the FrameworkPropertyMetadata object, which you then pass to the DependencyProperty.Register() method.

Here's how all the pieces come into play when an application attempts to set a dependency property:

1. First, the CoerceValueCallback method has the opportunity to modify the supplied value (usually, to make it consistent with other properties) or return DependencyProperty.UnsetValue, which rejects the change altogether.

2. Next, the ValidateValueCallback is fired. This method returns True to accept a value as valid or returns False to reject it. Unlike the CoerceValueCallback, the ValidateValueCallback does not have access to the actual object on which the property is being set, which means you can't examine other property values.

3. Finally, if both these previous stages succeed, the PropertyChangedCallback is triggered. At this point, you can raise a change event if you want to provide notification to other classes.

The Validation Callback

As you saw earlier, the DependencyProperty.Register() method accepts an optional validation callback:

```
MarginProperty = DependencyProperty.Register("Margin", _
  GetType(Thickness), GetType(FrameworkElement), metadata, _
  AddressOf FrameworkElement.IsMarginValid)
```

You can use this callback to enforce the validation that you'd normally add in the set portion of a property procedure. The callback you supply must point to a method that accepts an object parameter and returns a Boolean value. You return True to accept the object as valid and False to reject it.

The validation of the FrameworkElement.Margin property isn't terribly interesting because it relies on a Thickness.IsValid() method that has Friend accessibility (and so isn't available to classes outside of the assembly where it's compiled). This method makes sure the Thickness object is valid for its current use (representing a margin). For example, it may be possible to construct a perfectly acceptable Thickness object that isn't acceptable for setting the margin. One example is a Thickness object with negative dimensions. If the supplied Thickness object isn't valid for a margin, the IsMarginValid property returns False:

```
Private Shared Function IsMarginValid(ByVal value As Object) As Boolean
    Dim thickness1 As Thickness = CType(value, Thickness)
    Return thickness1.IsValid(True, False, True, False)
End Function
```

There's one limitation with validation callbacks: they are shared methods that don't have access to the object that's being validated. All you get is the newly applied value. Although that makes them easier to reuse, it also makes it impossible to create a validation routine that takes other properties into account. The classic example is an element with Maximum and Minimum properties. Clearly, it should not be possible to set the Maximum to a value that's less than the Minimum. However, you can't enforce this logic with a validation callback because you'll have access to only one property at a time.

Note The preferred approach to solve this problem is to use value coercion. *Coercion* is a step that occurs just before validation, and it allows you to modify a value to make it more acceptable (for example, raising the Maximum so it's at least equal to the Minimum) or disallow the change altogether. The coercion step is handled through another callback, but this one is attached to the FrameworkPropertyMetadata object, which is described in the next section.

The Coercion Callback

You use the CoerceValueCallback through the FrameworkPropertyMetadata object. Here's an example:

```
Dim metadata As New FrameworkPropertyMetadata()
metadata.CoerceValueCallback = AddressOf CoerceMaximum

DependencyProperty.Register("Maximum", GetType(Double), _
  GetType(RangeBase), metadata)
```

The CoerceValueCallback allows you to deal with interrelated properties. For example, the ScrollBar provides Maximum, Minimum, and Value properties, all of which are inherited from the RangeBase class. One way to keep these properties aligned is to use property coercion.

CHAPTER 4 ▓ DEPENDENCY PROPERTIES

For example, when the Maximum is set, it must be coerced so that it can't be less than the Minimum:

```
Private Shared Function CoerceMaximum(ByVal d As DependencyObject, _
   ByVal value As Object) As Object
    Dim base1 As RangeBase = CType(d, RangeBase)
    If CType(value, Double) < base1.Minimum Then
        Return base1.Minimum
    End If
    Return value
End Function
```

In other words, if the value that's applied to the Maximum property is less than the Minimum, the Minimum value is used instead to cap the Maximum. Notice that the CoerceValueCallback passes two parameters—the value that's being applied *and* the object to which it's being applied.

When the Value is set, a similar coercion takes place. The Value property is coerced so that it can't fall outside the range defined by the Minimum and Maximum, using this code:

```
Friend Shared Function ConstrainToRange(ByVal d As DependencyObject, _
   ByVal value As Object) As Object
    Dim newValue As Double = CType(value, Double)
    Dim base1 As RangeBase = CType(d, RangeBase)

    Dim minimum As Double = base1.Minimum
    If newValue < minimum Then
        Return minimum
    End If
    Dim maximum As Double = base1.Maximum
    If newValue > maximum Then
        Return maximum
    End If
    Return newValue
End Function
```

The Minimum property doesn't use value coercion at all. Instead, after it has been changed, it triggers a PropertyChangedCallback which forces the Maximum and Value properties to follow along by manually triggering *their* coercion:

```
Private Shared Sub OnMinimumChanged(ByVal d As DependencyObject, _
   ByVal e As DependencyPropertyChangedEventArgs)
    Dim base1 As RangeBase = CType(d, RangeBase)
    ...
    base1.CoerceMaximum(RangeBase.MaximumProperty)
    base1.CoerceValue(RangeBase.ValueProperty)
End Sub
```

Similarly, after the Maximum has been set and coerced, it manually coerces the Value property to fit:

```
Private Shared Sub OnMaximumChanged(ByVal d As DependencyObject, _
   ByVal e As DependencyPropertyChangedEventArgs)
    Dim base1 As RangeBase = CType(d, RangeBase)
    ...
    base1.CoerceValue(RangeBase.ValueProperty)
```

```
    base1.OnMaximumChanged(CType(e.OldValue, Double), _
        CType(e.NewValue, Double))
End Sub
```

The end result is that if you set conflicting values, the Minimum takes precedence, the Maximum gets its say next (and may possibly be coerced by the Minimum), and then the Value is applied (and may be coerced by both the Maximum and the Minimum).

The goal of this somewhat confusing sequence of steps is to ensure that the ScrollBar properties can be set in various orders without causing an error. This is an important consideration for initialization, such as when a window is being created for a XAML document. All WPF controls guarantee that their properties can be set in any order, without causing any change in behavior.

A careful review of the previous code calls this goal into question. For example, consider this code:

```
Dim bar As New ScrollBar()
bar.Value = 100
bar.Minimum = 1
bar.Maximum = 200
```

When the ScrollBar is first created, Value is 0, Minimum is 0, and Maximum is 1.

After the second line of code, the Value property is coerced to 1 (because initially the Maximum property is set to the default value 1). But something remarkable happens when you reach the fourth line of code. When the Maximum property is changed, it triggers coercion on both the Minimum and Value properties. This coercion acts on the values you specified *originally*. In other words, the local value of 100 is still stored by the WPF dependency property system, and now that it's an acceptable value, it can be applied to the Value property. Thus, after this single line of code executes, two properties have changed. Here's a closer look at what's happening:

```
Dim bar As New ScrollBar()
bar.Value = 100
' (Right now bar.Value returns 1.)
bar.Minimum = 1
' (bar.Value still returns 1.)
bar.Maximum = 200
' (Now now bar.Value returns 100.)
```

This behavior persists no matter when you set the Maximum property. For example, if you set a Value of 100 when the window loads and set the Maximum property later when the user clicks a button, the Value property is still restored to its rightful value of 100 at that point. (The only way to prevent this from taking place is to set a different value or remove the local value that you've applied by using the ClearValue() method that all elements inherit from DependencyObject.)

This behavior is due to WPF's property resolution system, which you learned about earlier. Although WPF stores the exact local value you've set internally, it *evaluates* what the property should be (using coercion and a few other considerations) when you read the property.

The Last Word

In this chapter, you took a deep look at WPF dependency properties. First, you saw how dependency properties are defined and registered. Next, you learned how they plug into other WPF services and support validation and coercion. In the next chapter, you'll explore another WPF feature that extends a core part of the traditional .NET infrastructure: routed events.

▓ **Tip**   One of the best ways to learn more about the internals of WPF is to browse the code for basic WPF elements, such as Button, UIElement, and FrameworkElement. One of the best tools to perform this browsing is Reflector, which is available at www.reflector.net. Using Reflector, you can see the definitions for dependency properties, browse through the shared constructor code that initializes them, and even explore how they're used in the class code. You can also get similar low-level information about routed events, which are described in the next chapter.

CHAPTER 5

■ ■ ■

Routed Events

In the previous chapter, you saw how WPF created a new dependency property system, reworking traditional .NET properties to improve performance and integrate new capabilities such as data binding and animation. In this chapter, you'll learn about the second shift: replacing ordinary .NET events with a higher-level routed event feature.

Routed events are events with more traveling power—they can tunnel down or bubble up the element tree and be processed by event handlers along the way. A routed event can be handled on one element (such as a label) even though it originates on another (such as an image inside that label). As with dependency properties, routed events can be consumed in the traditional way—by connecting an event handler with the right signature—but you need to understand how they work to unlock all their features.

In this chapter, you'll explore the WPF event system and learn how to fire and handle routed events. Once you've learned the basics, you'll consider the family of events that WPF elements provide. These include events for dealing with initialization, mouse and keyboard input, and multitouch devices.

Understanding Routed Events

Every .NET developer is familiar with the idea of *events*—messages that are sent by an object (such as a WPF element) to notify your code when something significant occurs. WPF enhances the .NET event model with the concept of *event routing*. Event routing allows an event to originate in one element but be raised by another one. For example, event routing allows a click that begins in a toolbar button to rise up to the toolbar and then to the containing window before it's handled by your code.

Event routing gives you the flexibility to write tight, well-organized code that handles events in the most convenient place. It's also a necessity for working with the WPF content model, which allows you to build simple elements (such as a button) out of dozens of distinct ingredients, each of which has its own independent set of events.

Defining, Registering, and Wrapping a Routed Event

The WPF event model is quite similar to the WPF property model. As with dependency properties, routed events are represented by read-only shared fields, registered in a shared constructor, and wrapped by a standard .NET event definition.

For example, the WPF Button class provides the familiar Click event, which is inherited from the abstract ButtonBase class. Here's how the event is defined and registered:

```
Public MustInherit Class ButtonBase
    Inherits ContentControl
    Implements ...

    ' The event definition.
    Public Shared ClickEvent As RoutedEvent
```

103

```
' The event registration.
Shared Sub New()
    ButtonBase.ClickEvent = EventManager.RegisterRoutedEvent( _
      "Click", RoutingStrategy.Bubble, GetType(RoutedEventHandler), _
      GetType(ButtonBase))
    ...
End Sub

' The traditional event wrapper.
Public Event Click As RoutedEventHandler
    AddHandler(ByVal value As RoutedEventHandler)
        MyBase.AddHandler(ButtonBase.ClickEvent, value)
    End AddHandler
    RemoveHandler(ByVal value As RoutedEventHandler)
        MyBase.RemoveHandler(ButtonBase.ClickEvent, value)
    End RemoveHandler
End Event

End Class
```

Whereas dependency properties are registered with the DependencyProperty.Register() method, routed events are registered with the EventManager.RegisterRoutedEvent() method. When registering an event, you need to specify the name of the event, the type of routine (more on that later), the delegate that defines the syntax of the event handler (in this example, RoutedEventHandler), and the class that owns the event (in this example, ButtonBase).

Usually, routed events are wrapped by ordinary .NET events to make them accessible to all .NET languages. The event wrapper includes custom AddHandler and RemoveHandler logic, which is not commonly seen in ordinary VB code. Rather than simply attaching the event subscriber to the event through the ordinary .NET event system, this code adds and removes registered callers by using the AddHandler() and RemoveHandler() methods, both of which are defined in the base FrameworkElement class and inherited by every WPF element. This way, they will receive event notification through the richer WPF routed event system.

■ **Note** It's easy to confuse the AddHandler() and RemoveHandler() methods of the FrameworkElement class with the AddHandler and RemoveHandler statements in the Visual Basic language. Although they have similar names, they work a bit differently. The FrameworkElement methods offer the most direct approach—they plug directly into the routed event model. The VB statements use the event wrapper, which then calls the FrameworkElement methods. Both approaches have the same end result.

Sharing Routed Events

As with dependency properties, the definition of a routed event can be shared between classes. For example, two base classes use the MouseUp event: UIElement (which is the starting point for ordinary WPF elements) and ContentElement (which is the starting point for content elements, which are individual bits of content that can be placed in a flow document). The MouseUp event is defined by the System.Windows.Input.Mouse class. The UIElement and ContentElement classes simply reuse the event with the RoutedEvent.AddOwner() method:

```
UIElement.MouseUpEvent = Mouse.MouseUpEvent.AddOwner(GetType(UIElement))
```

Raising a Routed Event

Of course, as with any event, the defining class needs to raise the routed event at some point. Exactly where this takes place is an implementation detail. However, the important factor is that your event is *not* raised through the traditional .NET event wrapper. Instead, you use the RaiseEvent() method that every element inherits from the UIElement class. Here's the appropriate code from deep inside the ButtonBase class:

```
Dim e As New RoutedEventArgs(ButtonBase.ClickEvent, Me)
MyBase.RaiseEvent(e)
```

The RaiseEvent() method takes care of firing the event to every caller that's been registered with the AddHandler() method. Because AddHandler() is public, callers have a choice—they can register themselves directly by calling AddHandler(), or they can use the event wrapper. (The following section demonstrates both approaches.) Either way, they'll be notified when the RaiseEvent() method is invoked.

All WPF events use the familiar .NET convention for event signatures. That first parameter of every event handler provides a reference to the object that fired the event (the sender). The second parameter is an EventArgs object that bundles together any additional details that might be important. For example, the MouseUp event provides a MouseEventArgs object that indicates what mouse buttons were pressed when the event occurred:

```
Private Sub img_MouseUp(ByVal sender As Object, ByVal e As MouseButtonEventArgs)
End Sub
```

In WPF, if an event doesn't need to send any additional details, it uses the RoutedEventArgs class, which includes some details about how the event was routed. If the event *does* need to transmit extra information, it uses a more specialized RoutedEventArgs-derived object (such as MouseButtonEventArgs in the previous example). Because every WPF event argument class derives from RoutedEventArgs, every WPF event handler has access to information about event routing.

Handling a Routed Event

As you learned in Chapter 2, there are several ways to attach an event handler. The most common approach is to add an event attribute to your XAML markup. The event attribute is named after the event you want to handle, and its value is the name of the event handler method. Here's an example that uses this syntax to connect the MouseUp event of the Image to an event handler named img_MouseUp:

```
<Image Source="happyface.jpg" Stretch="None"
  Name="img" MouseUp="img_MouseUp" />
```

Although it's not required, it's a common convention to name event handler methods in the form *ElementName_EventName*. If the element doesn't have a defined name (presumably because you don't need to interact with it in any other place in your code), consider using the name it *would* have:

```
<Button Click="cmdOK_Click">OK</Button>
```

> **Tip** It may be tempting to attach an event to a high-level method that performs a task, but you'll have more flexibility if you keep an extra layer of event-handling code. For example, clicking a button named cmdUpdate shouldn't trigger a method named UpdateDatabase() directly. Instead, it should call an event handler such as cmdUpdate_Click(), which can then call the UpdateDatabase() method that does the real work. This pattern gives you the flexibility to change where your database code is located, replace the update button with a different control, and wire several controls to the same process, all without limiting your ability to change the user interface later. If you want a simpler way to deal with actions that can be triggered from various places in a user interface (toolbar buttons, menu commands, and so on), you'll want to add the WPF command feature that's described in Chapter 9.

You can also connect an event with . Here's the code equivalent of the XAML markup shown previously:

```
AddHandler img.MouseUp, AddressOf img_MouseUp
```

The code approach is useful if you need to dynamically create a control and attach an event handler at some point during the lifetime of your window. By comparison, the events you hook up in XAML are always attached when the window object is first instantiated. The code approach also allows you to keep your XAML simpler and more streamlined, which is perfect if you plan to share it with nonprogrammers, such as a design artist. The drawback is a significant amount of boilerplate code that will clutter up your code files.

The previous code approach relies on the event wrapper, which calls the UIElement.AddHandler() method, as shown in the previous section. You can also connect an event directly by calling the UIElement.AddHandler() method yourself. Here's an example:

```
img.AddHandler(Image.MouseUpEvent, _
  New MouseButtonEventHandler(AddressOf img_MouseUp))
```

When you use this approach, you always need to create the appropriate delegate type (such as MouseButtonEventHandler). You can't create the delegate object implicitly, as you can when hooking up an event through the property wrapper. That's because the UIElement.AddHandler() method supports all WPF events and doesn't know the delegate type that you want to use.

Some developers prefer to use the name of the class where the event is defined, rather than the name of the class that is firing the event. Here's the equivalent syntax that makes it clear that the MouseUp event is defined in UIElement:

```
img.AddHandler(UIElement.MouseUpEvent, _
  New MouseButtonEventHandler(AddressOf img_MouseUp))
```

> **Note** Which approach you use is largely a matter of taste. However, the drawback to this second approach is that it doesn't make it obvious that the Image class *provides* a MouseUp event. It's possible to confuse this code and assume it's attaching an event handler that's meant to deal with the MouseUp event in a nested element. You'll learn more about this technique in the section "Attached Events" later in this chapter.

If you want to detach an event handler, code is your only option. You can use the RemoveHandler statement, as shown here:

```
RemoveHandler img.MouseUp, AddressOf img_MouseUp
```

Or you can use the UIElement.RemoveHandler() method:

```
img.RemoveHandler(Image.MouseUpEvent, _
  New MouseButtonEventHandler(AddressOf img_MouseUp))
```

It is technically possible to connect an event handler to the same event more than once. This is usually the result of a coding mistake. (In this case, the event handler will be triggered multiple times.) If you attempt to remove an event handler that's been connected twice, the event will still trigger the event handler, but just once.

Event Routing

As you learned in the previous chapter, many controls in WPF are content controls, and content controls can hold any type and amount of nested content. For example, you can build a graphical button out of shapes, create a label that mixes text and pictures, or put content in a specialized container to get a scrollable or collapsible display. You can even repeat this nesting process to go as many layers deep as you want.

This ability for arbitrary nesting raises an interesting question. For example, imagine you have a label like this one, which contains a StackPanel that brings together two blocks of text and an image:

```
<Label BorderBrush="Black" BorderThickness="1">
  <StackPanel>
    <TextBlock Margin="3">
     Image and text label</TextBlock>
    <Image Source="happyface.jpg" Stretch="None" />
    <TextBlock Margin="3">
     Courtesy of the StackPanel</TextBlock>
  </StackPanel>
</Label>
```

As you already know, every ingredient you place in a WPF window derives from UIElement at some point, including Label, StackPanel, TextBlock, and Image. UIElement defines some core events. For example, every class that derives from UIElement provides a MouseDown and MouseUp event.

But consider what happens when you click the image part of the fancy label shown here. Clearly, it makes sense for the Image.MouseDown and Image.MouseUp events to fire. But what if you want to treat all label clicks in the same way? In this case, it shouldn't matter whether the user clicks the image, some of the text, or part of the blank space inside the label border. In every case, you'd like to respond with the same code.

Clearly, you could wire up the same event handler to the MouseDown or MouseUp event of each element, but that would result in a significant amount of clutter and make your markup more difficult to maintain. WPF provides a better solution with its routed event model.

Routed events come in the following three flavors:

> *Direct events*: These are like ordinary .NET events. They originate in one element and don't pass to any other. For example, MouseEnter (which fires when the mouse pointer moves over an element) is a direct event.

> *Bubbling events*: These events travel *up* the containment hierarchy. For example, MouseDown is a bubbling event. It's raised first by the element that is clicked. Next, it's raised by that element's parent, then by *that* element's parent, and so on, until WPF reaches the top of the element tree.

Tunneling events: These events travel *down* the containment hierarchy. They give you the chance to preview (and possibly stop) an event before it reaches the appropriate control. For example, PreviewKeyDown allows you to intercept a key press, first at the window level and then in increasingly more-specific containers until you reach the element that had focus when the key was pressed.

When you register a routed event by using the EventManager.RegisterEvent() method, you pass a value from the RoutingStrategy enumeration that indicates the event behavior you want to use for your event.

Because MouseUp and MouseDown are bubbling events, you can now determine what happens in the fancy label example. When the happy face is clicked, the MouseDown event fires in this order:

1. Image.MouseDown

2. StackPanel.MouseDown

3. Label.MouseDown

After the MouseDown event is raised for the label, it's passed on to the next control (which in this case is the Grid that lays out the containing window) and then to its parent (the window). The window is the top level of the containment hierarchy and the final stop in the event-bubbling sequence. It's your last chance to handle a bubbling event such as MouseDown. If the user releases the mouse button, the MouseUp event fires in the same sequence.

■ **Note**   In Chapter 24, you'll learn how to create a page-based WPF application. In this situation, the top-level container isn't a window but an instance of the Page class.

You aren't limited to handling a bubbling event in one place. In fact, there's no reason you can't handle the MouseDown or MouseUp event at every level. But usually you'll choose the most appropriate level of event routing for the task at hand.

The RoutedEventArgs Class

When you handle a bubbling event, the sender parameter provides a reference to the last link in the chain. For example, if an event bubbles up from an image to a label before you handle it, the sender parameter references the label object.

In some cases, you'll want to determine where the event originally took place. You can get that information and other details from the properties of the RoutedEventArgs class (which are listed in Table 5-1). Because all WPF event argument classes inherit from RoutedEventArgs, these properties are available in any event handler.

Table 5-1. *Properties of the RoutedEventArgs Class*

Name	Description
Source	Indicates what object raised the event. In the case of a keyboard event, this is the control that had focus when the event occurred (for example, when the key was pressed). In the case of a mouse event, this is the topmost element under the mouse pointer when the event occurred (for example, when a mouse button was clicked).
OriginalSource	Indicates what object originally raised the event. Usually, the OriginalSource is the same as the source. However, in some cases the OriginalSource goes deeper in the object tree to get a behind-the-scenes element that's part of a higher-level element. For example, if you click close to the border of a window, you'll get a Window object for the event source but a Border object for the original source. That's because a Window is composed of individual, smaller components. To take a closer look at this composition model (and learn how to change it), head to Chapter 17, which discusses control templates.
RoutedEvent	Provides the RoutedEvent object for the event triggered by your event handler (such as the shared UIElement.MouseUpEvent object). This information is useful if you're handling different events with the same event handler.
Handled	Allows you to halt the event bubbling or tunneling process. When a control sets the Handled property to True, the event doesn't travel any further and isn't raised for any other elements. (As you'll see in the section "Handling a Suppressed Event," there is one way around this limitation.)

Bubbling Events

Figure 5-1 shows a simple window that demonstrates event bubbling. When you click a part of the label, the event sequence is shown in a list box. Figure 5-1 shows the appearance of this window immediately after you click the image in the label. The MouseUp event travels through five levels, ending up at the custom BubbledLabelClick form.

Figure 5-1. *A bubbled image click*

To create this test form, the image and every element above it in the element hierarchy are wired up to the same event handler—a method named SomethingClicked(). Here's the XAML that does it:

```
<Window x:Class=" BubbledLabelClick"
 xmlns="http://schemas.microsoft.com/winfx/2006/xaml/presentation"
 xmlns:x="http://schemas.microsoft.com/winfx/2006/xaml"
 Title="BubbledLabelClick" Height="359" Width="329"
 MouseUp="SomethingClicked">
  <Grid Margin="3" MouseUp="SomethingClicked">
    <Grid.RowDefinitions>
      <RowDefinition Height="Auto"></RowDefinition>
      <RowDefinition Height="*"></RowDefinition>
      <RowDefinition Height="Auto"></RowDefinition>
```

```
            <RowDefinition Height="Auto"></RowDefinition>
        </Grid.RowDefinitions>

        <Label Margin="5" Grid.Row="0" HorizontalAlignment="Left"
          Background="AliceBlue" BorderBrush="Black" BorderThickness="1"
          MouseUp="SomethingClicked">
          <StackPanel MouseUp="SomethingClicked">
            <TextBlock Margin="3"
              MouseUp="SomethingClicked">
              Image and text label</TextBlock>
            <Image Source="happyface.jpg" Stretch="None"
              MouseUp="SomethingClicked" />
            <TextBlock Margin="3"
              MouseUp="SomethingClicked">
              Courtesy of the StackPanel</TextBlock>
          </StackPanel>
        </Label>

        <ListBox Grid.Row="1" Margin="5" Name="lstMessages"></ListBox>
        <CheckBox Grid.Row="2"  Margin="5" Name="chkHandle">
          Handle first event</CheckBox>
        <Button Grid.Row="3" Margin="5" Padding="3" HorizontalAlignment="Right"
          Name="cmdClear" Click="cmdClear_Click">Clear List</Button>
    </Grid>
</Window>
```

The SomethingClicked() method simply examines the properties of the RoutedEventArgs object and adds a message to the list box:

```
Protected eventCounter As Integer = 0

Private Sub SomethingClicked(ByVal sender As Object, _
  ByVal e As RoutedEventArgs)
    eventCounter += 1
    Dim message As String = "#" & eventCounter.ToString() & ":" & _
      Constants.vbCrLf & " Sender: " & sender.ToString() & _
      Constants.vbCrLf & " Source: " & e.Source.ToString() & _
      Constants.vbCrLf & " Original Source: " & _
      e.OriginalSource.ToString()
    lstMessages.Items.Add(message)
    e.Handled = CBool(chkHandle.IsChecked)
End Sub
```

▓ **Note** Technically, the MouseUp event provides a MouseButtonEventArgs object with additional information about the mouse state at the time of the event. However, the MouseButtonEventArgs object derives from MouseEventArgs, which in turn derives from RoutedEventArgs. As a result, it's possible to use RoutedEventArgs when declaring the event handler (as shown here) if you don't need additional information about the mouse.

There's one other detail in this example. If you've selected the chkHandle check box, the SomethingClicked() method sets the RoutedEventArgs.Handled property to True, which stops the event-bubbling sequence the first time an event occurs. As a result, you'll see only the first event appear in the list, as shown in Figure 5-2.

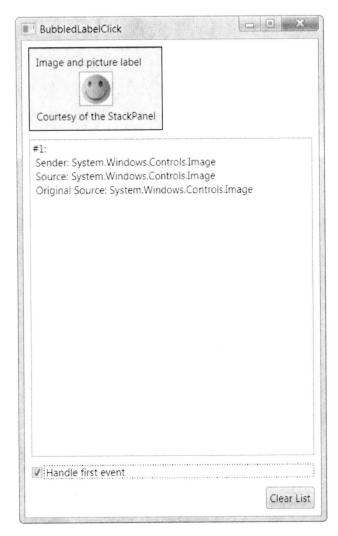

Figure 5-2. *Marking an event as handled*

■ **Note** There's an extra cast required here because the CheckBox.IsChecked property is a nullable Boolean value (a Nullable(Of Boolean) rather than a Boolean). The null value (Nothing) represents an indeterminate state for the check box, which means it's neither checked or unchecked. This feature isn't used in this example, so a simple cast solves the problem.

Because the SomethingClicked() method handles the MouseUp event that's fired by the Window, you'll be able to intercept clicks on the list box and the blank window surface. However, the MouseUp event doesn't fire when you click the Clear button (which removes all the list box entries). That's because the button includes an interesting bit of code that suppresses the MouseUp event and raises a higher-level Click event. At the same time, the Handled flag is set to True, which prevents the MouseUp event from going any further.

■ **Tip**   Most WPF elements don't expose a Click event. Instead, they include the more straightforward MouseDown and MouseUp events. Click is reserved for button-based controls.

Handling a Suppressed Event

Interestingly, there *is* a way to receive events that are marked as handled. Instead of attaching the event handler through XAML, you must use the AddHandler() method described earlier. The AddHandler() method provides an overload that accepts a Boolean value for its third parameter. Set this to True, and you'll receive the event even if the Handled flag has been set:

```
cmdClear.AddHander(UIElement.MouseUpEvent, _
  New MouseButtonEventHandler(cmdClear_MouseUp), True)
```

This is rarely a good design decision. The button is designed to suppress the MouseUp event for a reason: to prevent possible confusion. After all, it's a common Windows convention that buttons can be "clicked" with the keyboard in several ways. If you make the mistake of handling the MouseUp event in a Button instead of the Click event, your code will respond only to mouse clicks, not the equivalent keyboard actions.

Attached Events

The fancy label example is a fairly straightforward example of event bubbling because all the elements support the MouseUp event. However, many controls have their own more specialized events. The button is one example—it adds a Click event that isn't defined by any base class.

This introduces an interesting dilemma. Imagine that you wrap a stack of buttons in a StackPanel. You want to handle all the button clicks in one event handler. The crude approach is to attach the Click event of each button to the same event handler. But the Click event supports event bubbling, which gives you a better option. You can handle all the button clicks by handling the Click event at a higher level (such as the containing StackPanel).

Unfortunately, this apparently obvious code doesn't work:

```
<StackPanel Click="DoSomething" Margin="5">
  <Button Name="cmd1">Command 1</Button>
  <Button Name="cmd2">Command 2</Button>
  <Button Name="cmd3">Command 3</Button>
  ...
</StackPanel>
```

The problem is that the StackPanel doesn't include a Click event, so this is interpreted by the XAML parser as an error. The solution is to use a different attached-event syntax in the form *ClassName.EventName*. Here's the corrected example:

```
<StackPanel Button.Click="DoSomething" Margin="5">
  <Button Name="cmd1">Command 1</Button>
  <Button Name="cmd2">Command 2</Button>
```

```
    <Button Name="cmd3">Command 3</Button>
    ...
</StackPanel>
```

Now your event handler receives the click for all contained buttons.

▓ **Note**   The Click event is actually defined in the ButtonBase class and inherited by the Button class. If you attach an event handler to ButtonBase.Click, that event handler will be used when any ButtonBase-derived control is clicked (including the Button, RadioButton, and CheckBox classes). If you attach an event handler to Button.Click, it's used only for Button objects.

You can wire up an attached event in code, but you need to use the UIElement.AddHandler() method rather than the AddHandler() statement that's part of the Visual Basic language. Here's an example (which assumes that the StackPanel has been given the name pnlButtons):

```
pnlButtons.AddHandler(Button.Click, New RoutedEventHandler(DoSomething))
```

In the DoSomething() event handler, you have several options for determining which button fired the event. You can compare its text (which will cause problems for localization) or its name (which is fragile because you won't catch mistyped names when you build the application). The best approach is to make sure each button has a Name property set in XAML so that you can access the corresponding object through a field in your window class and compare that reference with the event sender. Here's an example:

```
Private Sub DoSomething(ByVal sender As Object, ByVal e As RoutedEventArgs)
    If e.Source Is cmd1 Then
        ...
    ElseIf e.Source Is cmd2 Then
        ...
    ElseIf e.Source Is cmd3 Then
        ...
    End If
End Sub
```

Another option is to simply send a piece of information along with the button that you can use in your code. For example, you could set the Tag property of each button, as shown here:

```
<StackPanel Button.Click="DoSomething" Margin="5">
  <Button Name="cmd1" Tag="The first button.">Command 1</Button>
  <Button Name="cmd2" Tag="The second button.">Command 2</Button>
  <Button Name="cmd3" Tag="The third button.">Command 3</Button>
  ...
</StackPanel>
```

You can then access the Tag property in your code:

```
Private Sub DoSomething(ByVal sender As Object, ByVal e As RoutedEventArgs)
    Dim tag As Object = CType(sender,FrameworkElement).Tag
    MessageBox.Show(CType(tag,String))
End Sub
```

Tunneling Events

Tunneling events work the same as bubbling events but in the opposite direction. For example, if MouseUp was a tunneled event (which it isn't), clicking the image in the fancy label example would cause MouseUp to fire first in the window, then in the Grid, then in the StackPanel, and so on, until it reaches the actual source, which is the image in the label.

Tunneling events are easy to recognize because they begin with the word *Preview*. Furthermore, WPF usually defines bubbling and tunneling events in pairs. That means if you find a bubbling MouseUp event, you can probably also find a tunneling PreviewMouseUp event. The tunneling event always fires before the bubbling event, as shown in Figure 5-3.

Figure 5-3. *Tunneling and bubbling events*

To make life more interesting, if you mark the tunneling event as handled, the bubbling event won't occur. That's because the two events share the same instance of the RoutedEventArgs class.

Tunneling events are useful if you need to perform some preprocessing that acts on certain keystrokes or filters out certain mouse actions. Figure 5-4 shows an example that tests tunneling with the PreviewKeyDown event When you press a key in the text box, the event is fired first in the window and then down through the hierarchy. And if you mark the PreviewKeyDown event as handled at any point, the bubbling KeyDown event won't occur.

Figure 5-4. *A tunneled key press*

■ **Tip** Be careful about marking a tunneling event as handled. Depending on the way the control is written, this may prevent the control from handling its own event (the related bubbling event) to perform some task or update its state.

IDENTIFYING THE ROUTING STRATEGY OF AN EVENT

Clearly the different routing strategies affect how you'll use an event. But how do you determine what type of routing a given event uses?

Tunneling events are straightforward. By .NET convention, a tunneling event always begins with the word *Preview* (as in PreviewKeyDown). However, there's no similar mechanism to distinguish bubbling events from direct events. For developers exploring WPF, the easiest approach is to find the event in the Visual Studio documentation. You'll see Routed Event Information that indicates the shared field for the event, the type of routing, and the event signature.

You can get the same information programmatically by examining the shared field for the event. For example, the ButtonBase.ClickEvent.RoutingStrategy property provides an enumerated value that tells you what type of routing the Click event uses.

WPF Events

Now that you've learned how WPF events work, it's time to consider the rich variety of events that you can respond to in your code. Although every element exposes a dizzying array of events, the most important events usually fall into one of five categories:

> *Lifetime events*: These events occur when the element is initialized, loaded, or unloaded.
>
> *Mouse events*: These events are the result of mouse actions.
>
> *Keyboard events*: These events are the result of keyboard actions (such as key presses).
>
> *Stylus events*: These events are the result of using the pen-like stylus, which takes the place of a mouse on a Tablet PC.
>
> *Multitouch events*: These events are the result of touching down with one or more fingers on a multitouch screen. They're supported only in Windows 7 and Windows 8.

Taken together, mouse, keyboard, stylus, and multitouch events are known as *input events*.

Lifetime Events

All elements raise events when they are first created and when they are released. You can use these events to initialize a window. Table 5-2 lists these events which are defined in the FrameworkElement class.

Table 5-2. *Lifetime Events for All Elements*

Name	Description
Initialized	Occurs after the element is instantiated and its properties have been set according to the XAML markup. At this point, the element is initialized, but other parts of the window may not be. Also, styles and data binding haven't been applied yet. At this point, the IsInitialized property is True. Initialized is an ordinary .NET event, not a routed event.
Loaded	Occurs after the entire window has been initialized and styles and data binding have been applied. This is the last stop before the element is rendered. At this point, the IsLoaded property is True.
Unloaded	Occurs when the element has been released, either because the containing window has been closed or the specific element has been removed from the window.

To understand how the Initialized and Loaded events relate, it helps to consider the rendering process. The FrameworkElement implements the ISupportInitialize interface, which provides two methods for controlling the initialization process. The first, BeginInit(), is called immediately after the element is instantiated. After BeginInit() is called, the XAML parser sets all the element properties (and adds any content). The second method, EndInit(), is called when initialization is complete, at which point the Initialized event fires.

■ **Note** This is a slight simplification. The XAML parser takes care of calling the BeginInit() and EndInit() methods, as it should. However, if you create an element by hand and add it to a window, it's unlikely that you'll use this interface. In this case, the element raises the Initialized event after you add it to the window, just before the Loaded event.

When you create a window, each branch of elements is initialized in a bottom-up fashion. That means deeply nested elements are initialized before their containers. When the Initialized event fires, you are guaranteed that the tree of elements from the current element down is completely initialized. However, the element that *contains* your element probably isn't initialized, and you can't assume that any other part of the window is initialized.

After each element is initialized, it's also laid out in its container, styled, and bound to a data source, if required. After the Initialized event fires for the window, it's time to go on to the next stage.

After the initialization process is complete, the Loaded event is fired. The Loaded event follows the reverse path of the Initialized event—in other words, the containing window fires the Loaded event first, followed by more deeply nested elements. When the Loaded event has fired for all elements, the window becomes visible and the elements are rendered.

The lifetime events listed in Table 5-2 don't tell the whole story. The containing window also has its own more specialized lifetime events. These events are listed in Table 5-3.

Table 5-3. *Lifetime Events for the Window Class*

Name	Description
SourceInitialized	Occurs when the HwndSource property of the window is acquired (but before the window is made visible). The HwndSource is a window handle that you may need to use if you're calling legacy functions in the Win32 API.
ContentRendered	Occurs immediately after the window has been rendered for the first time. This isn't a good place to perform any changes that might affect the visual appearance of the window, or you'll force a second render operation. (Use the Loaded event instead.) However, the ContentRendered event does indicate that your window is fully visible and ready for input.
Activated	Occurs when the user switches to this window (for example, from another window in your application or from another application). Activated also fires when the window is loaded for the first time. Conceptually, the Activated event is the window equivalent of a control's GotFocus event.
Deactivated	Occurs when the user switches away from this window (for example, by moving to another window in your application or another application). Deactivated also fires when the window is closed by a user, after the Closing event but before Closed. Conceptually, the Deactivated event is the window equivalent of a control's LostFocus event.
Closing	Occurs when the window is closed, either by a user action or programmatically by using the Window.Close() method or the Application.Shutdown() method. The Closing event gives you the opportunity to cancel the operation and keep the window open by setting the CancelEventArgs.Cancel property to True. However, you won't receive the Closing event if your application is ending because the user is shutting down the computer or logging off. To deal with these possibilities, you need to handle the Application.SessionEnding event described in Chapter 7.
Closed	Occurs after the window has been closed. However, the element objects are still accessible, and the Unloaded event hasn't fired yet. At this point, you can perform cleanup, write settings to a persistent storage place (such as a configuration file or the Windows Registry), and so on.

If you're simply interested in performing first-time initializing for your controls, the best time to take care of this task is when the Loaded event fires. Usually, you can perform all your initialization in one place, which is typically an event handler for the Window.Loaded event.

■ **Tip**   You can also use the window constructor to perform your initialization (just add your code immediately after the InitializeComponent() call). However, it's always better to use the Loaded event. That's because if an exception occurs in the constructor of the Window, it's thrown while the XAML parser is parsing the page. As a result, your exception is wrapped in an unhelpful XamlParseException object (with the original exception in the InnerException property).

Input Events

Input events are events that occur when the user interacts with some sort of peripheral hardware, such as a mouse, keyboard, stylus, or multitouch screen. Input events can pass along extra information by using a custom event argument class that derives from InputEventArgs. Figure 5-5 shows the inheritance hierarchy.

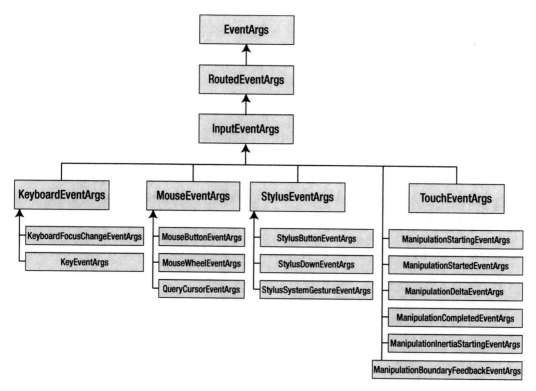

Figure 5-5. *The EventArgs classes for input events*

The InputEventArgs class adds just two properties: Timestamp and Device. Timestamp provides an integer that indicates when the event occurred as a number of milliseconds. (The actual time that this represents isn't terribly important, but you can compare different timestamp values to determine what event took place first. Larger timestamps signify more-recent events.) The Device returns an object that provides more information about the device that triggered the event, which could be the mouse, the keyboard, or the stylus. Each of these three possibilities is represented by a different class, all of which derive from the abstract System.Windows.Input.InputDevice class.

In the following sections, you'll take a closer look at how you handle mouse, keyboard, and multitouch actions in a WPF application.

Keyboard Input

When the user presses a key, a sequence of events unfolds. Table 5-4 lists these events in the order that they occur.

Table 5-4. *Keyboard Events for All Elements (in the Order They Occur)*

Name	Routing Type	Description
PreviewKeyDown	Tunneling	Occurs when a key is pressed.
KeyDown	Bubbling	Occurs when a key is pressed.
PreviewTextInput	Tunneling	Occurs when a keystroke is complete and the element is receiving the text input. This event isn't fired for keystrokes that don't result in text being "typed" (for example, it doesn't fire when you press Ctrl, Shift, Backspace, the arrow keys, the function keys, and so on).
TextInput	Bubbling	Occurs when a keystroke is complete and the element is receiving the text input. This event isn't fired for keystrokes that don't result in text.
PreviewKeyUp	Tunneling	Occurs when a key is released.
KeyUp	Bubbling	Occurs when a key is released.

Keyboard handling is never quite as straightforward as it seems. Some controls may suppress some of these events so they can perform their own more specialized keyboard handling. The most notorious example is the TextBox control, which suppresses the TextInput event. The TextBox also suppresses the KeyDown event for some keystrokes, such as the arrow keys. In cases like these, you can usually still use the tunneling events (PreviewTextInput and PreviewKeyDown).

The TextBox control also adds one new event, named TextChanged. This event fires immediately after a keystroke causes the text in the text box to change. At this point, the new text is already visible in the text box, so it's too late to prevent a keystroke you don't want.

Handling a Key Press

The best way to understand the key events is to use a sample program such as the one shown in Figure 5-6. It monitors a text box for all the possible key events and reports when they occur. Figure 5-6 shows the result of typing a capital *S* in a text box.

Figure 5-6. *Watching the keyboard*

This example illustrates an important point. The PreviewKeyDown and KeyDown events fire every time a key is pressed. However, the TextInput event fires only when a character is "typed" into an element. This action may actually involve multiple key presses. In the example in Figure 5-5, two key presses are needed to create the capital letter *S*. First, the Shift key is pressed, followed by the S key. As a result, you'll see two KeyDown and KeyUp events but only one TextInput event.

The PreviewKeyDown, KeyDown, PreviewKeyUp, and KeyUp events all provide the same information through the KeyEventArgs object. The most important detail is the Key property, which returns a value from the System. Windows.Input.Key enumeration that identifies the key that was pressed or released. Here's the event handler that handles key events for the example in Figure 5-6:

```
Private Sub KeyEvent(ByVal sender As Object, ByVal e As KeyEventArgs)
    Dim message As String = "Event: " & e.RoutedEvent.ToString() & _
        " " & " Key: " & e.Key
    lstMessages.Items.Add(message)
End Sub
```

The Key value doesn't take into account the state of any other keys. For example, it doesn't matter whether the Shift key is currently pressed when you press the S key; either way you'll get the same Key value (Key.S).

There's one more wrinkle. Depending on your Windows keyboard settings, pressing a key causes the keystroke to be repeated after a short delay. For example, holding down the S key obviously puts a stream of *S* characters in the text box. Similarly, pressing the Shift key causes multiple keystrokes and a series of KeyDown events. In a real-world test in which you press Shift+S, your text box will actually fire a series of KeyDown events for the Shift key, followed by a KeyDown event for the S key, a TextInput event (or TextChanged event in the case of a text box), and then a KeyUp event for the Shift and S keys. If you want to ignore these repeated Shift keys, you can check if a keystroke is the result of a key that's being held down by examining the KeyEventArgs.IsRepeat property, as shown here:

```
If CBool(chkIgnoreRepeat.IsChecked) AndAlso e.IsRepeat Then
    Return
End If
```

■ **Tip** The PreviewKeyDown, KeyDown, PreviewKeyUp, and KeyUp events are best for writing low-level keyboard handling (which you'll rarely need outside a custom control) and handling special keystrokes, such as the function keys.

After the KeyDown event occurs, the PreviewTextInput event follows. (The TextInput event doesn't occur, because the TextBox suppresses this event.) At this point, the text has not yet appeared in the control.

The TextInput event provides your code with a TextCompositionEventArgs object. This object includes a Text property that gives you the processed text that's about to be received by the control. Here's the code that adds this text to the list shown in Figure 5-6:

```
Private Sub TextInputPreview(ByVal sender As Object, _
  ByVal e As TextCompositionEventArgs)
    Dim message As String = "Event: " & e.RoutedEvent.ToString() & _
      " " & " Text: " & e.Text
    lstMessages.Items.Add(message)
End Sub
```

Ideally, you'd use PreviewTextInput to perform validation in a control such as the TextBox. For example, if you're building a numeric-only text box, you could make sure that the current keystroke isn't a letter and set the Handled flag if it is. Unfortunately, the PreviewTextInput event doesn't fire for some keys that you may need to handle. For example, if you press the spacebar in a text box, you'll bypass PreviewTextInput altogether. That means you also need to handle the PreviewKeyDown event.

Unfortunately, it's difficult to write robust validation logic in a PreviewKeyDown event handler because all you have is the Key value, which is a fairly low-level piece of information. For example, the Key enumeration distinguishes between the numeric key pad and the number keys that appear just above the letters on a typical keyboard. That means depending on how you press the number 9, you might get a value of Key.D9 or Key.NumPad9. Checking for all the allowed key values is tedious, to say the least.

One option is to use the KeyConverter to convert the Key value into a more useful string. For example, using KeyConverter.ConvertToString() on both Key.D9 and Key.NumPad9 returns "9" as a string. If you just use the Key.ToString() conversion, you'll get the much less useful enumeration name (either "D9" or "NumPad9"):

```
Dim converter As New KeyConverter()
Dim key As String = converter.ConvertToString(e.Key)
```

However, even using the KeyConverter is a bit awkward because you'll end up with longer bits of text (such as "Backspace") for keystrokes that don't result in text input.

The best compromise is to handle both PreviewTextInput (which takes care of most of the validation) and use PreviewKeyDown for keystrokes that don't raise PreviewTextInput in the text box (such as the spacebar). Here's a simple solution that does it:

```
Private Sub pnl_PreviewTextInput(ByVal sender As Object, _
  ByVal e As TextCompositionEventArgs)
    Dim val As Short
```

123

```
    If Not Int16.TryParse(e.Text, val) Then
        e.Handled = True
    End If
End Sub

Private Sub pnl_PreviewKeyDown(ByVal sender As Object, _
  ByVal e As KeyEventArgs)
    If e.Key = Key.Space Then
        e.Handled = True
    End If
End Sub
```

You can attach these event handlers to a single text box, or you can wire them up to a container (such as a StackPanel that contains several numeric-only text boxes) for greater efficiency.

■ **Note** This key-handling behavior may seem unnecessarily awkward (and it is). One of the reasons that the TextBox doesn't provide better key handling is that WPF focuses on data binding, a feature that lets you wire up controls such as the TextBox to custom objects. When you use this approach, validation is usually provided by the bound object, errors are signaled by an exception, and bad data triggers an error message that appears somewhere in the user interface. Unfortunately, there's no easy way (at present) to combine the useful, high-level data-binding feature with the lower-level keyboard handling that would be necessary to prevent the user from typing invalid characters altogether.

Focus

In the Windows world, a user works with one control at a time. The control that is currently receiving the user's key presses is the control that has *focus*. Sometimes this control is drawn slightly differently. For example, the WPF button uses blue shading to show that it has the focus.

For a control to be able to accept the focus, its Focusable property must be set to True. This is the default for all controls.

Interestingly enough, the Focusable property is defined as part of the UIElement class, which means that other noncontrol elements can also be focusable. Usually, in noncontrol classes, Focusable will be False by default. However, you can set it to True. Try this with a layout container such as the StackPanel—when it receives the focus, a dotted border will appear around the panel's edge.

To move the focus from one element to another, the user can click the mouse or use the Tab and arrow keys. In previous development frameworks, programmers have been forced to take great care to make sure that the Tab key moves focus in a logical manner (generally from left to right and then down the window) and that the correct control has focus when the window first appears. In WPF, this extra work is seldom necessary because WPF uses the hierarchical layout of your elements to implement a tabbing sequence. Essentially, when you press the Tab key, you'll move to the first child in the current element or, if the current element has no children, to the next child at the same level. For example, if you tab through a window with two StackPanel containers, you'll move through all the controls in the first StackPanel and then through all the controls in the second container.

If you want to take control of tab sequence, you can set the TabIndex property for each control to place it in numerical order. The control with a TabIndex of 0 gets the focus first, followed by the next highest TabIndex value (for example, 1, then 2, then 3, and so on). If more than one element has the same TabIndex value, WPF uses the automatic tab sequence, which means it jumps to the nearest subsequent element.

■ **Tip** By default, the TabIndex property for all controls is set to Int32.MaxValue. That means you can designate a specific control as the starting point for a window by setting its TabIndex to 0 but rely on automatic navigation to guide the user through the rest of the window from that starting point, according to the order that your elements are defined.

The TabIndex property is defined in the Control class, along with an IsTabStop property. You can set IsTabStop to False to prevent a control from being included in the tab sequence. The difference between IsTabStop and Focusable is that a control with an IsTabStop value of False can still get the focus in another way—either programmatically (when your code calls its Focus() method) or by a mouse click.

Controls that are invisible or disabled ("grayed out") are generally skipped in the tab order and are not activated regardless of the TabIndex, IsTabStop, and Focusable settings. To hide or disable a control, you set the Visibility and IsEnabled properties, respectively.

Getting Key State

When a key press occurs, you often need to know more than just what key was pressed. It's also important to find out what other keys were held down at the same time. That means you might want to investigate the state of other keys, particularly modifiers such as Shift, Ctrl, and Alt.

The key events (PreviewKeyDown, KeyDown, PreviewKeyUp, and KeyUp) make this information easy to get. First, the KeyEventArgs object includes a KeyStates property that reflects the property of the key that triggered the event. More usefully, the KeyboardDevice property provides the same information for any key on the keyboard.

Not surprisingly, the KeyboardDevice property provides an instance of the KeyboardDevice class. Its properties include information about which element currently has the focus (FocusedElement) and what modifier keys were pressed when the event occurred (Modifiers). The modifier keys include Shift, Ctrl, and Alt, and you can check their status by using bitwise logic like this:

```
If (e.KeyboardDevice.Modifiers And ModifierKeys.Control) = _
   ModifierKeys.Control Then
      lblInfo.Text = "You held the Control key."
End If
```

The KeyboardDevice property also provides a few handy methods, listed in Table 5-5. For each of these methods, you pass in a value from the Key enumeration.

Table 5-5. *KeyboardDevice Methods*

Name	Description
IsKeyDown()	Tells you whether this key was pressed down when the event occurred.
IsKeyUp()	Tells you whether this key was up (not pressed) when the event occurred.
IsKeyToggled()	Tells you whether this key was in a "switched on" state when the event occurred. This has a meaning only for keys that can be toggled on or off, such as Caps Lock, Scroll Lock, and Num Lock.
GetKeyStates()	Returns one or more values from the KeyStates enumeration that tell you whether this key is currently up, pressed, or in a toggled state. This method is essentially the same as calling both IsKeyDown() and IsKeyToggled() on the same key.

When you use the KeyEventArgs.KeyboardDevice property, your code gets the *virtual key state*. This means it gets the state of the keyboard at the time the event occurred. This is not necessarily the same as the current keyboard state. For example, consider what happens if the user types faster than your code executes. Each time your KeyPress event fires, you'll have access to the keystroke that fired the event, not the typed-ahead characters. This is almost always the behavior you want.

However, you aren't limited to getting key information in the key events. You can also get the state of the keyboard at any time. The trick is to use the Keyboard class, which is very similar to KeyboardDevice except it's made up of shared members. Here's an example that uses the Keyboard class to check the current state of the left Shift key:

```
If Keyboard.IsKeyDown(Key.LeftShift) Then
    lblInfo.Text = "The left Shift is held down."
End If
```

■ **Note**   The Keyboard class also has methods that allow you to attach application-wide keyboard event handlers, such as AddKeyDownHandler() and AddKeyUpHandler(). However, these methods aren't recommended. A better approach to implementing application-wide functionality is to use the WPF command system, as described in Chapter 9.

Mouse Input

Mouse events perform several related tasks. The most fundamental mouse events allow you to react when the mouse is moved over an element. These events are MouseEnter (which fires when the mouse pointer moves over the element) and MouseLeave (which fires when the mouse pointer moves away). Both are *direct events*, which means they don't use tunneling or bubbling. Instead, they originate in one element and are raised by just that element. This makes sense because of the way controls are nested in a WPF window.

For example, if you have a StackPanel that contains a button and you move the mouse pointer over the button, the MouseEnter event will fire first for the StackPanel (as you enter its borders) and then for the button (as you move directly over it). As you move the mouse away, the MouseLeave event will fire first for the button and then for the StackPanel.

You can also react to two events that fire whenever the mouse moves: PreviewMouseMove (a tunneling event) and MouseMove (a bubbling event). All of these events provide your code with the same information: a MouseEventArgs object. The MouseEventArgs object includes properties that tell you the state that the mouse buttons were in when the event fired, and it includes a GetPosition() method that tells you the coordinates of the mouse in relation to an element of your choosing. Here's an example that displays the position of the mouse pointer in device-independent pixels relative to the form:

```
Private Sub MouseMoved(ByVal sender As Object, ByVal e As MouseEventArgs)
    Dim pt As Point = e.GetPosition(Me)
    lblInfo.Text = _
      String.Format("You are at ({0},{1}) in window coordinates", pt.X, pt.Y)
End Sub
```

In this case, the coordinates are measured from the top-left corner of the client area (just below the title bar). Figure 5-7 shows this code in action.

Figure 5-7. Watching the mouse

You'll notice that the mouse coordinates in this example are not whole numbers. That's because this screen capture was taken on a system running at 120 dpi, not the standard 96 dpi. As explained in Chapter 1, WPF automatically scales up its units to compensate, using more physical pixels. Because the size of a screen pixel no longer matches the size of the WPF unit system, the physical mouse position may be translated to a fractional number of WPF units, as shown here.

■ **Tip** The UIElement class also includes two useful properties that can help with mouse hit-testing. Use IsMouseOver to determine whether a mouse is currently over an element or one of its children, and use IsMouseDirectlyOver to find out whether the mouse is over an element but not one of its children. Usually, you won't read and act on these values in code. Instead, you'll use them to build style triggers that automatically change elements as the mouse moves over them. Chapter 11 demonstrates this technique.

Mouse Clicks

Mouse clicks unfold in a similar way to key presses. The difference is that there are distinct events for the left mouse button and the right mouse button. Table 5-6 lists these events in the order they occur. Along with these are two events that react to the mouse wheel: PreviewMouseWheel and MouseWheel.

Table 5-6. *Mouse Click Events for All Elements (in Order)*

Name	Routing Type	Description
PreviewMouseLeftButtonDown and PreviewMouseRightButtonDown	Tunneling	Occurs when a mouse button is pressed
MouseLeftButtonDown and MouseRightButtonDown	Bubbling	Occurs when a mouse button is pressed
PreviewMouseLeftButtonUp and PreviewMouseRightButtonUp	Tunneling	Occurs when a mouse button is released
MouseLeftButtonUp and MouseRightButtonUp	Bubbling	Occurs when a mouse button is released

All mouse button events provide a MouseButtonEventArgs object. The MouseButtonEventArgs class derives from MouseEventArgs (which means it includes the same coordinate and button state information), and it adds a few members. The less important of these are MouseButton (which tells you which button triggered the event) and ButtonState (which tells you whether the button was pressed or unpressed when the event occurred). The more interesting property is ClickCount, which tells you how many times the button was clicked, allowing you to distinguish single clicks (where ClickCount is 1) from double-clicks (where ClickCount is 2).

■ **Tip**   Usually, Windows applications react when the mouse key is raised after being clicked (the "up" event rather than the "down" event).

Some elements add higher-level mouse events. For example, the Control class adds PreviewMouseDoubleClick and MouseDoubleClick events that take the place of the MouseLeftButtonUp event. Similarly, the Button class raises a Click event that can be triggered by the mouse or keyboard.

■ **Note**   As with key press events, the mouse events provide information about where the mouse was and what buttons were pressed when the mouse event occurred. To get the current mouse position and mouse button state, you can use the shared members of the Mouse class, which are similar to those of the MouseButtonEventArgs.

Capturing the Mouse

Ordinarily, every time an element receives a mouse button "down" event, it will receive a corresponding mouse button "up" event shortly thereafter. However, this isn't always the case. For example, if you click an element, hold down the mouse, and then move the mouse pointer off the element, the element won't receive the mouse up event.

In some situations, you may want to have a notification of mouse up events, even if they occur after the mouse has moved off your element. To do so, you need to *capture* the mouse by calling the Mouse.Capture() method and passing in the appropriate element. From that point on, you'll receive mouse down and mouse up events until you call Mouse.Capture() again and pass in a null reference (Nothing). Other elements won't receive mouse events while the mouse is captured. That means the user won't be able to click buttons elsewhere in the window, click inside text boxes, and so on. Mouse capturing is sometimes used to implement draggable and resizable elements. You'll see an example with the custom-drawn resizable window in Chapter 23.

■ **Tip**   When you call Mouse.Capture(), you can pass in an optional CaptureMode value as the second parameter. Ordinarily, when you call Mouse.Capture(), you use CaptureMode.Element, which means your element always receives the mouse events. However, you can use CaptureMode.SubTree to allow mouse events to pass through to the clicked element if that clicked element is a child of the element that's performing the capture. This makes sense if you're already using event bubbling or tunneling to watch mouse events in child elements.

In some cases, you may lose a mouse capture through no fault of your own. For example, Windows may free the mouse if it needs to display a system dialog box. You'll also lose the mouse capture if you don't free the mouse after a mouse up event occurs and the user carries on to click a window in another application. Either way, you can react to losing the mouse capture by handling the LostMouseCapture event for your element.

Although the mouse has been captured by an element, you won't be able to interact with other elements. (For example, you won't be able to click another element on your window.) Mouse capturing is generally used for short-term operations such as drag-and-drop.

■ **Note**   Instead of using Mouse.Capture(), you can use two methods that are built into the UIElement class: CaptureMouse() and ReleaseMouseCapture(). Just call these methods on the appropriate element. The only limitation of this approach is that it doesn't allow you to use the CaptureMode.SubTree option.

Drag-and-Drop

Drag-and-drop operations (a technique for pulling information out of one place in a window and depositing it in another) aren't quite as common today as they were a few years ago. Programmers have gradually settled on other methods of copying information that don't require holding down the mouse button (a technique that many users find difficult to master). Programs that do support drag-and-drop often use it as a shortcut for advanced users, rather than a standard way of working.

Essentially, a drag-and-drop operation unfolds in three steps:

1. The user clicks an element (or selects a specific region inside it) and holds the mouse button down. At this point, some information is set aside, and a drag-and-drop operation begins.

2. The user moves the mouse over another element. If this element can accept the type of content that's being dragged (for example, a bitmap or a piece of text), the mouse cursor changes to a drag-and-drop icon. Otherwise, the mouse cursor becomes a circle with a line drawn through it.

3. When the user releases the mouse button, the element receives the information and decides what to do with it. The operation can be canceled by pressing the Esc key (without releasing the mouse button).

You can try the way drag-and-drop is supposed to work by adding two text boxes to a window, because the TextBox control has built-in logic to support drag-and-drop. If you select some text inside a text box, you can drag it to another text box. When you release the mouse button, the text will be moved. The same technique works between applications—for example, you can drag some text from a Word document and drop it into a WPF TextBox object, or vice versa.

Sometimes, you might want to allow drag and drop between elements that don't have the built-in functionality. For example, you might want to allow the user to drag content from a text box and drop it in a label. Or you might want to create the example shown in Figure 5-8, which allows a user to drag text from a Label or TextBox object and drop it into a different label. In this situation, you need to handle the drag-and-drop events.

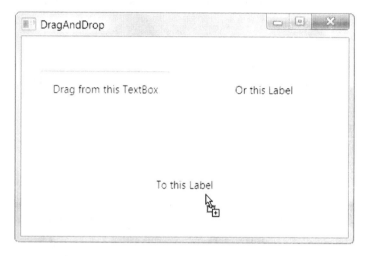

Figure 5-8. *Dragging content from one element to another*

■ **Note**   The methods and events that are used for drag-and-drop operations are centralized in the System.Windows. DragDrop class. That way, any element can participate in a drag-and-drop operation by using this class.

There are two sides to a drag-and-drop operation: the source and target. To create a drag-and-drop source, you need to call the DragDrop.DoDragDrop() method at some point to initiate the drag-and-drop operation. At this point you identify the source of the drag-and-drop operation, set aside the content you want to transfer, and indicate what drag-and-drop effects are allowed (copying, moving, and so on).

Usually, the DoDragDrop() method is called in response to the MouseDown or PreviewMouseDown event. Here's an example that initiates a drag-and-drop operation when a label is clicked. The text content from the label is used for the drag-and-drop operation:

```
Private Sub lblSource_MouseDown(ByVal sender As Object, _
  ByVal e As MouseButtonEventArgs)
    Dim lbl As Label = CType(sender, Label)
    DragDrop.DoDragDrop(lbl, lbl.Content, DragDropEffects.Copy)
End Sub
```

The element that receives the data needs to set its AllowDrop property to True. Additionally, it needs to handle the Drop event to deal with the data:

```
<Label Grid.Row="1" AllowDrop="True" Drop="lblTarget_Drop">To Here</Label>
```

When you set AllowDrop to True, you configure an element to allow any type of information. If you want to be pickier, you can handle the DragEnter event. At this point, you can check the type of data that's being dragged and then determine what type of operation to allow. The following example allows only text content—if you drag something that cannot be converted to text, the drag-and-drop operation won't be allowed, and the mouse pointer will change to the forbidding circle-with-a-line cursor:

```
Private Sub lblTarget_DragEnter(ByVal sender As Object, _
   ByVal e As DragEventArgs)
     If e.Data.GetDataPresent(DataFormats.Text) Then
         e.Effects = DragDropEffects.Copy
     Else
         e.Effects = DragDropEffects.None
     End If
End Sub
```

Finally, when the operation completes, you can retrieve the data and act on it. The following code takes the dropped text and inserts it into the label:

```
Private Sub lblTarget_Drop(ByVal sender As Object, ByVal e As DragEventArgs)
    CType(sender, Label).Content = e.Data.GetData(DataFormats.Text)
End Sub
```

You can exchange any type of object through a drag-and-drop operation. However, although this free-spirited approach is perfect for your applications, it isn't wise if you need to communicate with other applications. If you want to drag and drop into other applications, you should use a basic data type (such as string, int, and so on) or an object that implements ISerializable or IDataObject (which allows .NET to transfer your object into a stream of bytes and reconstruct the object in another application domain). One interesting trick is to convert a WPF element into XAML and reconstitute it somewhere else. All you need is the XamlWriter and XamlReader objects described in Chapter 2.

Note   If you want to transfer data between applications, be sure to check out the System.Windows.Clipboard class, which provides shared methods for placing data on the Windows clipboard and retrieving it in a variety of formats.

Multitouch Input

Multitouch is a way of interacting with an application by touching a screen. What distinguishes multitouch input from old-fashioned pen input is that multitouch recognizes *gestures*—specific ways the user can move more than one finger to perform a common operation. For example, placing two fingers on the touch screen and moving them together is generally accepted to mean *zoom in*, while pivoting one finger around another means *rotate*. And because the user makes these gestures directly on the application window, each gesture is naturally connected to a specific object. For example, a simple multitouch-enabled application might show multiple pictures on a virtual desktop and allow the user to drag, resize, and rotate each image to create a new arrangement.

Tip   For a list of standard multitouch gestures that Windows can recognize, see `http://tinyurl.com/yawwhw2`.

Multitouch screens are nearly ubiquitous on smartphones and tablets. However, they're far less common on ordinary computers. Although hardware manufacturers have created touch-screen laptops and touch-screen LCD monitors, conventional laptops and monitors are still far more popular.

This presents a challenge for developers who want to experiment with multitouch applications. Currently, the best approach is to invest in a basic multitouch laptop. However, with a bit of work, you can use an *emulator* to simulate multitouch input. The basic approach is to connect more than one mouse to your computer and install the drivers from the Multi-Touch Vista open source project (which also works with Windows 7). To get started, surf to `http://multitouchvista.codeplex.com`. But be warned—you'll probably need to follow the tutorial videos to make sure you get the rather convoluted setup procedure done right, and it doesn't work on all systems.

■ **Note** Although some applications may support multitouch on Windows Vista, the support that's built into WPF requires Windows 7 or Windows 8, regardless of whether you have supported hardware or use an emulator.

The Levels of Multitouch Support

As you've seen, WPF allows you to work with keyboard and mouse input at a high level (for example, clicks and text changes) or a low level (mouse movements and key presses). This is important, because some applications need a much finer degree of control. The same applies to multitouch input, and WPF provides three layers of multitouch support:

> *Raw touch*: This is the lowest level of support, and it gives you access to every touch the user makes. The disadvantage is that it's up to your application to combine separate touch messages and interpret them. Raw touch makes sense if you don't plan to recognize the standard touch gestures but instead want to create an application that reacts to multitouch input in a unique way. One example is a painting program such as Windows 7 Paint, which lets users "finger paint" on a touch screen with several fingers at once.

> *Manipulation*: This is a convenient abstraction that translates raw multitouch input into meaningful gestures, much like WPF controls interpret a sequence of MouseDown and MouseUp events as a higher-level MouseDoubleClick. The common gestures that WPF elements support include pan, zoom, rotate, and tap.

> *Built-in element support*: Some elements already react to multitouch events, with no code required. For example, scrollable controls such as the ListBox, ListView, DataGrid, TextBox, and ScrollViewer support touch panning.

The following sections show examples of both raw-touch and manipulation with gestures.

Raw Touch

As with the basic mouse and keyboard events, touch events are built into the low-level UIElement and ContentElement classes. Table 5-7 lists them all.

Table 5-7. *Raw Touch Events for All Elements*

Name	Routing Type	Description
PreviewTouchDown	Tunneling	Occurs when the user touches down on this element
TouchDown	Bubbling	Occurs when the user touches down on this element
PreviewTouchMove	Tunneling	Occurs when the user moves the touched-down finger
TouchMove	Bubbling	Occurs when the user moves the touched-down finger
PreviewTouchUp	Tunneling	Occurs when the user lifts the finger, ending the touch
TouchUp	Bubbling	Occurs when the user lifts the finger, ending the touch
TouchEnter	None	Occurs when a contact point moves from outside this element into this element
TouchLeave	None	Occurs when a contact point moves out of this element

All of these events provide a TouchEventArgs object, which includes two important members. First, the GetTouchPoint() method gives you the screen coordinates where the touch event occurred (along with less commonly used data, such as the size of the contact point). Second, the TouchDevice property returns a TouchDevice object. The trick here is that every contact point is treated as a separate device. So if a user presses two fingers down at different positions (either simultaneously or one after the other), WPF treats it as two touch devices and assigns a unique ID to each. As the user moves these fingers and the touch events occur, your code can distinguish between the two contact points by paying attention to the TouchDevice.Id property.

The following example shows how this works with a simple demonstration of raw-touch programming (see Figure 5-9). When the user touches down on the Canvas, the application adds a small ellipse element to show the contact point. Then, as the user moves the finger, the code moves the ellipse so it follows along.

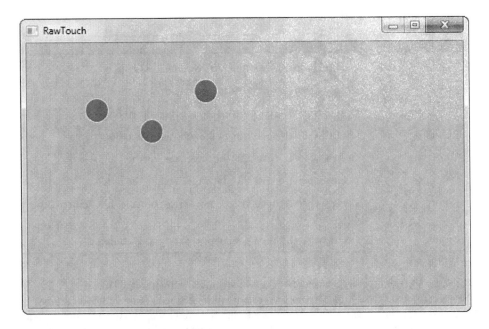

Figure 5-9. *Dragging circles with multitouch*

What distinguishes this example from a similar mouse event test is that the user can touch down with several fingers at once, causing multiple ellipses to appear, each of which can be dragged about independently.

To create this example, you need to handle the TouchDown, TouchUp, and TouchMove events:

```
<Canvas x:Name="canvas" Background="LightSkyBlue"
  TouchDown="canvas_TouchDown" TouchUp="canvas_TouchUp"
  TouchMove="canvas_TouchMove">
</Canvas>
```

To keep track of all the contact points, you need to store a collection as a window member variable. The cleanest approach is to store a collection of UIElement objects (one for each active ellipse), indexed by the touch device ID (which is an integer):

```
Private movingEllipses As New Dictionary(Of Integer, UIElement)()
```

When the user touches a finger down, the code creates and configures a new Ellipse element (which looks like a small circle). It places the ellipse at the appropriate coordinates by using the touch point, adds it to the collection (indexed by the touch device ID), and then shows it in the Canvas:

```
Private Sub canvas_TouchDown(ByVal sender As Object, ByVal e As TouchEventArgs)
    ' Create an ellipse to draw at the new contact point.
    Dim ellipse As New Ellipse()
    ellipse.Width = 30
    ellipse.Height = 30
    ellipse.Stroke = Brushes.White
    ellipse.Fill = Brushes.Green
```

```
    ' Position the ellipse at the contact point.
    Dim touchPoint As TouchPoint = e.GetTouchPoint(canvas)
    Canvas.SetTop(ellipse, touchPoint.Bounds.Top)
    Canvas.SetLeft(ellipse, touchPoint.Bounds.Left)

    ' Store the ellipse in the active collection.
    movingEllipses(e.TouchDevice.Id) = ellipse

    ' Add the ellipse to the Canvas.
    canvas.Children.Add(ellipse)
End Sub
```

When the user moves a touched-down finger, the TouchMove event fires. At this point, you can determine which point is moving by using the touch device ID. All the code needs to do is find the corresponding ellipse and update its coordinates:

```
Private Sub canvas_TouchMove(ByVal sender As Object, ByVal e As TouchEventArgs)
    ' Get the ellipse that corresponds to the current contact point.
    Dim element As UIElement = movingEllipses(e.TouchDevice.Id)

    ' Move it to the new contact point.
    Dim touchPoint As TouchPoint = e.GetTouchPoint(canvas)
    Canvas.SetTop(ellipse, touchPoint.Bounds.Top)
    Canvas.SetLeft(ellipse, touchPoint.Bounds.Left)
End Sub
```

Finally, when the user lifts the finger, the ellipse is removed from the tracking collection. Optionally, you may want to remove it from the Canvas now as well.

```
Private Sub canvas_TouchUp(ByVal sender As Object, ByVal e As TouchEventArgs)
    ' Remove the ellipse from the Canvas.
    Dim element As UIElement = movingEllipses(e.TouchDevice.Id)
    canvas.Children.Remove(element)

    ' Remove the ellipse from the tracking collection.
    movingEllipses.Remove(e.TouchDevice.Id)
End Sub
```

■ **Note** The UIElement also adds the CaptureTouch() and ReleaseTouchCapture() methods, which are analogous to the CaptureMouse() and ReleaseMouseCapture() methods. When touch input is captured by an element, that element receives all the touch events from that touch device, even if the touch events happen in another part of the window. But because there can be multiple touch devices, several elements can capture touch input at once, as long as each captures the input from a different device.

Manipulation

Raw touch is great for applications that use touch events in a direct, straightforward way, like the dragging circles example or a painting program. But if you want to support the standard touch gestures, raw touch doesn't make it easy. For example, to support a rotation, you'd need to detect two contact points on the same element, keep track of how they move, and use some sort of calculation to determine that one is rotating around the other. Even then, you still need to add the code that actually applies the corresponding rotation effect.

Fortunately, WPF doesn't leave you completely on your own. It includes higher-level support for gestures, called touch *manipulation*. You configure an element to opt in to manipulation by setting its IsManipulationEnabled property to True. You can then react to four manipulation events: ManipulationStarting, ManipulationStarted, ManipulationDelta, and ManipulationCompleted.

Figure 5-10 shows a manipulation example. Here, three images are shown in a Canvas in a basic arrangement. The user can then use panning, rotating, and zooming gestures to move, turn, shrink, or expand them.

Figure 5-10. *Before and after: three images manipulated with multitouch*

The first step to create this example is to define the Canvas and place the three Image elements. To make life easy, the ManipulationStarting and ManipulationDelta events are handled in the Canvas, after they bubble up from the appropriate Image element inside.

```
<Canvas x:Name="canvas" ManipulationStarting="image_ManipulationStarting"
 ManipulationDelta="image_ManipulationDelta">
  <Image Canvas.Top="10" Canvas.Left="10" Width="200"
   IsManipulationEnabled="True" Source="koala.jpg">
    <Image.RenderTransform>
      <MatrixTransform></MatrixTransform>
    </Image.RenderTransform>
  </Image>
  <Image Canvas.Top="30" Canvas.Left="350" Width="200"
   IsManipulationEnabled="True" Source="penguins.jpg">
    <Image.RenderTransform>
      <MatrixTransform></MatrixTransform>
    </Image.RenderTransform>
  </Image>
  <Image Canvas.Top="100" Canvas.Left="200" Width="200"
   IsManipulationEnabled="True" Source="tulips.jpg">
    <Image.RenderTransform>
      <MatrixTransform></MatrixTransform>
    </Image.RenderTransform>
  </Image>
</Canvas>
```

There's one new detail in this markup. Each image includes a MatrixTransform, which gives the code an easy way to apply a combination of movement, rotation, and zoom manipulations. Currently, the MatrixTransform objects don't do anything, but the code will alter them when the manipulation events occur. (You'll get the full details about how transforms work in Chapter 12.)

When the user touches down on one of the images, the ManipulationStarting event fires. At this point, you need to set the manipulation container, which is the reference point for all manipulation coordinates you'll get later. In this case, the Canvas that contains the images is the natural choice. Optionally, you can choose what types of manipulations should be allowed. If you don't, WPF will watch for any gesture it recognizes: pan, zoom, and rotate.

```
Private Sub image_ManipulationStarting(ByVal sender As Object, _
  ByVal e As ManipulationStartingEventArgs)
    ' Set the container (used for coordinates.)
    e.ManipulationContainer = canvas

    ' Choose what manipulations to allow.
    e.Mode = ManipulationModes.All
End Sub
```

The ManipulationDelta event fires when a manipulation is taking place (but not necessarily finished). For example, if the user begins to rotate an image, the ManipulationDelta event will fire continuously, until the user rotation is finished and the user raises up the touched-down fingers.

The current state of the gesture is recorded by a ManipulationDelta object, which is exposed through the ManipulationDeltaEventArgs.DeltaManipulation property. Essentially, the ManipulationDelta object records the amount of zooming, rotating, and panning that should be applied to an object and exposes that information through three straightforward properties: Scale, Rotation, and Translation. The trick is to use this information to adjust the element in your user interface.

In theory, you could deal with the scale and rotation details by changing the element's size and position. But this still doesn't apply a rotation (and the code is somewhat messy). A far better approach is to use *transforms*—objects that allow you to mathematically warp the appearance of any WPF element. The idea is to take the information supplied by the ManipulationDelta object and use it to configure a MatrixTransform. Although this sounds complicated, the code you need to use is essentially the same in every application that uses this feature. It looks like this:

```
Private Sub image_ManipulationDelta(ByVal sender As Object, _
  ByVal e As ManipulationDeltaEventArgs)
    ' Get the image that's being manipulated.
    Dim element As UIElement = CType(e.Source, UIElement)

    ' Use the matrix of the transform to manipulate the element's appearance.
    Dim matrix As Matrix = (CType(element.RenderTransform, MatrixTransform)).Matrix

    ' Get the ManipulationDelta object.
    Dim deltaManipulation As ManipulationDelta = e.DeltaManipulation

    ' Find the old center, and apply any previous manipulations.
    Dim center As New Point(element.ActualWidth / 2, element.ActualHeight / 2)
    center = matrix.Transform(center)

    ' Apply new zoom manipulation (if it exists).
    matrix.ScaleAt(deltaManipulation.Scale.X, deltaManipulation.Scale.Y, _
        center.X, center.Y)

    ' Apply new rotation manipulation (if it exists).
    matrix.RotateAt(e.DeltaManipulation.Rotation, center.X, center.Y)

    ' Apply new panning manipulation (if it exists).
    matrix.Translate(e.DeltaManipulation.Translation.X, _
        e.DeltaManipulation.Translation.Y)

    ' Set the final matrix.
    CType(element.RenderTransform, MatrixTransform).Matrix = matrix
End Sub
```

This code allows you to manipulate all the images, as shown in Figure 5-10.

Inertia

WPF has another layer of features that build on its basic manipulation support, called *inertia*. Essentially, inertia allows a more realistic, fluid manipulation of elements.

Right now, if a user drags one of the images in Figure 5-10 by using a panning gesture, the image stops moving the moment the fingers are raised from the touch screen. But if inertia is enabled, the movement would continue for a very short period, decelerating gracefully. This gives manipulation a presence and sense of momentum. And inertia also causes elements to bounce back when they are dragged into a boundary they can't cross, allowing them to act like real, physical objects.

To add inertia to the previous example, you simply need to handle the ManipulationInertiaStarting event. Like the other manipulation event, it will begin in one of the images and bubble up to the Canvas. The ManipulationInertiaStarting event fires when the user ends the gesture and releases the element by raising the fingers.

At this point, you can use the ManipulationInertiaStartingEventArgs object to determine the current velocity—the speed at which the element was moving when the manipulation ended—and set the deceleration speed you want. Here's an example that adds inertia to translation, zooming, and rotation gestures:

```
Private Sub image_ManipulationInertiaStarting(ByVal sender As Object, _
   ByVal e As ManipulationInertiaStartingEventArgs)
     ' If the object is moving, decrease its speed by
     ' 10 inches per second every second.
     ' deceleration = 10 inches * 96 units per inch / (1000 milliseconds)^2
     e.TranslationBehavior = New InertiaTranslationBehavior()
     e.TranslationBehavior.InitialVelocity = e.InitialVelocities.LinearVelocity
     e.TranslationBehavior.DesiredDeceleration = 10.0 * 96.0 / (1000.0 * 1000.0)

     ' Decrease the speed of zooming by 0.1 inches per second every second.
     ' deceleration = 0.1 inches * 96 units per inch / (1000 milliseconds)^2
     e.ExpansionBehavior = New InertiaExpansionBehavior()
     e.ExpansionBehavior.InitialVelocity = e.InitialVelocities.ExpansionVelocity
     Dim DesiredDeceleration As e.ExpansionBehavior. = 0.1 * 96 / 1000.0 * 1000.0

     ' Decrease the rotation rate by 2 rotations per second every second.
     ' deceleration = 2 * 360 degrees / (1000 milliseconds)^2
     e.RotationBehavior = New InertiaRotationBehavior()
     e.RotationBehavior.InitialVelocity = e.InitialVelocities.AngularVelocity
     Dim DesiredDeceleration As e.RotationBehavior. = 720 / (1000.0 * 1000.0)
End Sub
```

To make elements bounce back naturally from barriers, you need to check whether they've drifted into the wrong place in the ManipulationDelta event. If a boundary is crossed, it's up to you to report it by calling ManipulationDeltaEventArgs.ReportBoundaryFeedback().

At this point, you might be wondering why you need to write so much of the manipulation code if it's standard boilerplate that all multitouch developers need. One obvious advantage is that it allows you to easily tweak some of the details (such as the amount of deceleration in the inertia settings). However, in many situations, you may be able to get exactly what you need with prebuilt manipulation support, in which case you should check out the WPF Multitouch project at http://multitouch.codeplex.com. It includes two convenient ways that you can add manipulation support to a container without writing it yourself—either by using a behavior that applies it automatically (see Chapter 11) or by using a custom control that has the logic hardwired (see Chapter 18). Best of all, it's free to download, and the source code is ready for tweaking.

The Last Word

In this chapter, you took a deep look at routed events. First, you explored routed events and saw how they allow you to deal with events at different levels—either directly at the source or in a containing element. Next, you saw how these routing strategies are implemented in the WPF elements to allow you to deal with keyboard, mouse, and multitouch input.

It may be tempting to begin writing event handlers that respond to common events such as mouse movements to apply simple graphical effects or otherwise update the user interface. But don't start writing this logic just yet. As you'll see later in Chapter 11, you can automate many simple program operations with declarative markup by using WPF styles and triggers. But before you branch out to this topic, the next chapter takes a short detour to show you how many of the most fundamental controls (things such as buttons, labels, and text boxes) work in the WPF world.

Deeper into WPF

CHAPTER 6

Controls

Now that you've learned the fundamentals of layout, content, and event handling, you're ready to take a closer look at WPF's family of elements. In this chapter, you'll consider *controls*—elements that derive from the System.Windows. Control class. You'll begin by examining the base Control class, and learning how it supports brushes and fonts. Then you'll explore the full catalog of WPF controls, including the following:

> *Content controls*: These controls can contain nested elements, giving them nearly unlimited display capabilities. They include the Label, Button, ToolTip, and ScrollViewer classes.

> *Headered content controls*: These are content controls that allow you to add a main section of content and a separate title portion. They are usually intended to wrap larger blocks of user interface. They include the TabItem, GroupBox, and Expander classes.

> *Text controls*: This is the small set of controls that allow users to enter input. The text controls support ordinary text (the TextBox), passwords (the PasswordBox), and formatted text (the RichTextBox, which is discussed in Chapter 28).

> *List controls*: These controls show collections of items in a list. They include the ListBox and ComboBox classes.

> *Range-based controls*: These controls have just one thing in common: a Value property that can be set to any number in a prescribed range. Examples include the Slider and ProgressBar classes.

> *Date controls*: This category includes two controls that allow users to select dates: the Calendar and DatePicker.

There are several types of controls that you won't see in this chapter, including those that create menus, toolbars, and ribbons; those that show grids and trees of bound data; and those that allow rich document viewing and editing. You'll consider these more advanced controls throughout this book, as you explore the related WPF features.

The Control Class

WPF windows are filled with elements, but only some of these elements are *controls*. In the world of WPF, a control is generally described as a *user-interactive* element—that is, an element that can receive focus and accept input from the keyboard or mouse. Obvious examples include text boxes and buttons. However, the distinction is sometimes a bit blurry. A tooltip is considered to be a control because it appears and disappears depending on the user's mouse movements. A label is considered to be a control because of its support for *mnemonics* (shortcut keys that transfer the focus to related controls).

All controls derive from the System.Windows.Control class, which adds a bit of basic infrastructure:

- The ability to set the alignment of content inside the control

- The ability to set the tab order

- Support for painting a background, foreground, and border

- Support for formatting the size and font of text content

Background and Foreground Brushes

All controls include the concept of a background and foreground. Usually, the background is the surface of the control (think of the white or gray area inside the borders of a button), and the foreground is the text. In WPF, you set the color of these two areas (but not the content) by using the Background and Foreground properties.

It's natural to expect that the Background and Foreground properties would use color objects. However, these properties actually use something much more versatile: a Brush object. That gives you the flexibility to fill your background and foreground content with a solid color (by using the SolidColorBrush) or something more exotic (for example, by using a LinearGradientBrush or TileBrush). In this chapter, you'll consider only the simple SolidColorBrush, but you'll try fancier brushwork in Chapter 12.

Setting Colors in Code

Imagine you want to set a blue surface area inside a button named cmd. Here's the code that does the trick:

```
cmd.Background = New SolidColorBrush(Colors.AliceBlue)
```

This code creates a new SolidColorBrush by using a ready-made color via a shared property of the handy Colors class. (The names are based on the color names supported by most web browsers.) It then sets the brush as the background brush for the button, which causes its background to be painted a light shade of blue.

■ **Note** This method of styling a button isn't completely satisfactory. If you try it, you'll find that it configures the background color for a button in its normal (unpressed) state, but it doesn't change the color that appears when you press the button (which is a darker gray). To really customize every aspect of a button's appearance, you need to delve into templates, as discussed in Chapter 17.

You can also grab system colors (which may be based on user preferences) from the System.Windows. SystemColors enumeration. Here's an example:

```
cmd.Background = New SolidColorBrush(SystemColors.ControlColor)
```

Because system brushes are used frequently, the SystemColors class also provides ready-made properties that return SolidColorBrush objects. Here's how to use them:

```
cmd.Background = SystemColors.ControlBrush
```

As written, both of these examples suffer from a minor problem. If the system color is changed *after* you run this code, your button won't be updated to use the new color. In essence, this code grabs a snapshot of the current color or brush. To make sure your program can update itself in response to configuration changes, you need to use dynamic resources, as described in Chapter 10.

The Colors and SystemColors classes offer handy shortcuts, but they're not the only way to set a color. You can also create a Color object by supplying the R, G, B values (red, green, and blue). Each one of these values is a number from 0 to 255:

```
Dim red As Integer = 0
Dim green As Integer = 255
Dim blue As Integer = 0
cmd.Foreground = New SolidColorBrush(Color.FromRgb(red, green, blue))
```

You can also make a color partly transparent by supplying an alpha value and calling the Color.FromArgb() method. An alpha value of 255 is completely opaque, while 0 is completely transparent.

RGB AND SCRGB

The RGB standard is useful because it's used in many other programs. For example, you can get the RGB value of a color in a graphic in a paint program and use the same color in your WPF application. However, other devices (such as printers) might support a richer range of colors. Therefore, an alternative scRGB standard has been created. This standard uses 64-bit values to represent each color component (alpha, red, green, and blue).

The WPF Color structure supports either approach. It includes a set of standard RGB properties (A, R, G, and B) and a set of properties for scRGB (ScA, ScR, ScG, and ScB). These properties are linked, so that if you set the R property, the ScR property is changed accordingly.

The relationship between the RGB values and the scRGB values is not linear. A 0 value in the RGB system is 0 in scRGB, 255 in RGB becomes 1 in scRGB, and all values between 0 and 255 in RGB are represented as decimal values between 0 and 1 in scRGB.

Setting Colors in XAML

When you set the background or foreground in XAML, you can use a helpful shortcut. Rather than define a Brush object, you can supply a color name or color value. The WPF parser will automatically create a SolidColorBrush object using the color you specify, and it will use that brush object for the foreground or background. Here's an example that uses a color name:

```
<Button Background="Red">A Button</Button>
```

It's equivalent to this more verbose syntax:

```
<Button>A Button
  <Button.Background>
    <SolidColorBrush Color="Red" />
  </Button.Background>
</Button>
```

You need to use the longer form if you want to create a different type of brush, such as a LinearGradientBrush, and use that to paint the background.

If you want to use a color code, you need to use a slightly less convenient syntax that puts the R, G, and B values in hexadecimal notation. You can use one of two formats—either #rrggbb or #aarrggbb (the difference being that the latter includes the alpha value). You need only two digits to supply the A, R, G, and B values because they're all in hexadecimal notation. Here's an example that uses the #aarrggbb notation to create the same color as in the previous code snippets:

```
<Button Background="#FFFF0000">A Button</Button>
```

Here, the alpha value is FF (255), the red value is FF (255), and the green and blue values are 0.

■ **Note** Brushes support automatic change notification. In other words, if you attach a brush to a control and change the brush, the control updates itself accordingly. This works because brushes derive from the System.Windows. Freezable class. The name stems from the fact that all freezable objects have two states—a readable state and a read-only (or "frozen") state.

The Background and Foreground properties are not the only details you can set with a brush. You can also paint a border around controls (and some other elements, such as the Border element) by using the BorderBrush and BorderThickness properties. BorderBrush takes a brush of your choosing, and BorderThickness takes the width of the border in device-independent units. You need to set both properties before you'll see the border.

■ **Note** Some controls don't respect the BorderBrush and BorderThickness properties. The Button object ignores them completely because it defines its background and border by using the ButtonChrome decorator. However, you can give a button a new face (with a border of your choosing) by using templates, as described in Chapter 17.

Fonts

The Control class defines a small set of font-related properties that determine how text appears in a control. These properties are outlined in Table 6-1.

Table 6-1. *Font-Related Properties of the Control Class*

Name	Description
FontFamily	The name of the font you want to use.
FontSize	The size of the font in device-independent units (each of which is 1/96 inch). This is a bit of a change from tradition that's designed to support WPF's new resolution-independent rendering model. Ordinary Windows applications measure fonts by using *points*, which are assumed to be 1/72 inch on a standard PC monitor. If you want to turn a WPF font size into a more familiar point size, you can use a handy trick—just multiply by 3/4. For example, a traditional 38-point font is equivalent to 48 units in WPF.
FontStyle	The angling of the text, as represented as a FontStyle object. You get the FontSyle preset you need from the shared properties of the FontStyles class, which includes Normal, Italic, or Oblique lettering. (*Oblique* is an artificial way to create italic text on a computer that doesn't have the required italic font. Letters are taken from the normal font and slanted by using a transform. This usually creates a poor result.)
FontWeight	The heaviness of text, as represented as a FontWeight object. You get the FontWeight preset you need from the shared properties of the FontWeights class. Bold is the most obvious of these, but some typefaces provide other variations, such as Heavy, Light, ExtraBold, and so on.
FontStretch	The amount that text is stretched or compressed, as represented by a FontStretch object. You get the FontStretch preset you need from the shared properties of the FontStretches class. For example, UltraCondensed reduces fonts to 50% of their normal width, while UltraExpanded expands them to 200%. Font stretching is an OpenType feature that is not supported by many typefaces. (To experiment with this property, try using the Rockwell font, which does support it.)

■ **Note** The Control class doesn't define any properties that *use* its font. While many controls include a property such as Text, that isn't defined as part of the base Control class. Obviously, the font properties don't mean anything unless they're used by the derived class.

Font Family

A *font family* is a collection of related typefaces. For example, Arial Regular, Arial Bold, Arial Italic, and Arial Bold Italic are all part of the Arial font family. Although the typographic rules and characters for each variation are defined separately, the operating system realizes they are related. As a result, you can configure an element to use Arial Regular, set the FontWeight property to Bold, and be confident that WPF will switch over to the Arial Bold typeface.

When choosing a font, you must supply the full family name, as shown here:

```
<Button Name="cmd" FontFamily="Times New Roman" FontSize="18">A Button</Button>
```

It's much the same in code:

```
cmd.FontFamily = "Times New Roman"
cmd.FontSize = "18"
```

When identifying a FontFamily, a shortened string is not enough. That means you can't substitute Times or Times New instead of the full name Times New Roman.

Optionally, you can use the full name of a typeface to get italic or bold, as shown here:

```
<Button FontFamily="Times New Roman Bold">A Button</Button>
```

However, it's clearer and more flexible to use just the family name and set other properties (such as FontStyle and FontWeight) to get the variant you want. For example, the following markup sets the FontFamily to Times New Roman and sets the FontWeight to FontWeights.Bold:

```
<Button FontFamily="Times New Roman" FontWeight="Bold">A Button</Button>
```

Text Decorations and Typography

Some elements also support more-advanced text manipulation through the TextDecorations and Typography properties. These allow you to add embellishments to text. For example, you can set the TextDecorations property by using a shared property from the TextDecorations class. It provides just four decorations, each of which allows you to add some sort of line to your text. They include Baseline, OverLine, Strikethrough, and Underline. The Typography property is more advanced—it lets you access specialized typeface variants that only some fonts will provide. Examples include different number alignments, ligatures (connections between adjacent letters), and small caps.

For the most part, the TextDecorations and Typography features are found only in flow document content—which you use to create rich, readable documents. (Chapter 28 describes documents in detail.) However, the frills also turn up on the TextBox class. Additionally, they're supported by the TextBlock, which is a lighter-weight version of the Label that's perfect for showing small amounts of wrappable text content. Although you're unlikely to use text decorations with the TextBox or change its typography, you may want to use underlining in the TextBlock, as shown here:

```
<TextBlock TextDecorations="Underline">Underlined text</TextBlock>
```

If you're planning to place a large amount of text content in a window and you want to format individual portions (for example, underline important words), you should refer to Chapter 28, where you'll learn about many more flow elements. Although flow elements are designed for use with documents, you can nest them directly inside a TextBlock.

Font Inheritance

When you set any of the font properties, the values flow through to nested objects. For example, if you set the FontFamily property for the top-level window, every control in that window gets the same FontFamily value (unless the control explicitly sets a different font). This works because the font properties are dependency properties, and one of the features that dependency properties can provide is property value inheritance—the magic that passes your font settings down to nested controls.

It's worth noting that property value inheritance can flow through elements that don't even support that property. For example, imagine you create a window that holds a StackPanel, inside of which are three Label controls. You can set the FontSize property of the window because the Window class derives from the Control class. You can't set the FontSize property for the StackPanel because it isn't a control. However, if you set the FontSize property of the window, your property value is still able to flow through the StackPanel to get to your labels inside and change their font sizes.

Along with the font settings, several other base properties use property value inheritance. In the Control class, the Foreground property uses inheritance. The Background property does not. (However, the default background is a null reference that's rendered by most controls as a transparent background. That means the parent's background will still show through.) In the UIElement class, AllowDrop, IsEnabled, and IsVisible use property inheritance. In the FrameworkElement, the CultureInfo and FlowDirection properties do.

■ **Note** A dependency property supports inheritance only if the FrameworkPropertyMetadata.Inherits flag is set to True, which is not the default. Chapter 4 discusses the FrameworkPropertyMetadata class and property registration in detail.

Font Substitution

When you're setting fonts, you need to be careful to choose a font that you know will be present on the user's computer. However, WPF does give you a little flexibility with a font fallback system. You can set FontFamily to a comma-separated list of font options. WPF will then move through the list in order, trying to find one of the fonts you've indicated.

Here's an example that attempts to use Technical Italic font but falls back to Comic Sans MS or Arial if that isn't available:

```
<Button FontFamily="Technical Italic, Comic Sans MS, Arial">A Button</Button>
```

If a font family really does contain a comma in its name, you'll need to escape the comma by including it twice in a row.

Incidentally, you can get a list of all the fonts that are installed on the current computer by using the shared SystemFontFamilies collection of the System.Windows.Media.Fonts class. Here's an example that uses the collection to add fonts to a list box:

```
For Each fontFamily As FontFamily In Fonts.SystemFontFamilies
    lstFonts.Items.Add(fontFamily.Source)
Next
```

The FontFamily object also allows you to examine other details, such as the line spacing and associated typefaces.

■ **Note** One of the ingredients that WPF doesn't include is a dialog box for choosing a font. The WPF Text team has posted two much more attractive WPF font pickers, including a no-code version that uses data binding (http://blogs.msdn.com/text/archive/2006/06/20/592777.aspx) and a more sophisticated version that supports the optional typographic features that are found in some OpenType fonts (http://blogs.msdn.com/text/archive/2006/11/01/sample-font-chooser.aspx).

Font Embedding

Another option for dealing with unusual fonts is to embed them in your application. That way, your application never has a problem finding the font you want to use.

The embedding process is simple. First, you add the font file (typically, a file with the extension .ttf) to your application and set the Build Action option to Resource. (You can do this in Visual Studio by selecting the font file in the Solution Explorer and changing its Build Action in the Properties window.)

Next, when you use the font, you need to add the character sequence ./# before the font family name, as shown here:

```
<Label FontFamily="./#Bayern" FontSize="20">This is an embedded font</Label>
```

The `./` characters are interpreted by WPF to mean *the current folder*. To understand what this means, you need to know a little more about XAML's packaging system.

As you learned in Chapter 2, you can run stand-alone (known as *loose*) XAML files directly in your browser without compiling them. The only limitation is that your XAML file can't use a code-behind file. In this scenario, the current folder is exactly that, and WPF looks at the font files that are in the same directory as the XAML file and makes them available to your application.

More commonly, you'll compile your WPF application to a .NET assembly before you run it. In this case, the current folder is still the location of the XAML document, only now that document has been compiled and embedded in your assembly. WPF refers to compiled resources by using a specialized URI syntax that's discussed in Chapter 7. All application URIs start with `pack://application`. If you create a project named ClassicControls and add a window named EmbeddedFont.xaml, the URI for that window is this:

```
pack://application:,,,/ClassicControls/embeddedfont.xaml
```

This URI is made available in several places, including through the FontFamily.BaseUri property. WPF uses this URI to base its font search. Thus, when you use the `./` syntax in a compiled WPF application, WPF looks for fonts that are embedded as resources alongside your compiled XAML.

After the `./` character sequence, you can supply the file name, but you'll usually just add the number sign (#) and the font's real family name. In the previous example, the embedded font is named Bayern.

■ **Note** Setting up an embedded font can be a bit tricky. You need to make sure you get the font family name exactly right, and you need to make sure you choose the correct build action for the font file. To see an example of the correct setup, refer to the sample code for this chapter.

Embedding fonts raises obvious licensing concerns. Unfortunately, most font vendors allow their fonts to be embedded in documents (such as PDF files) but not applications (such as WPF assemblies), even though an embedded WPF font isn't directly accessible to the end user. WPF doesn't make any attempt to enforce font licensing, but you should make sure you're on solid legal ground before you redistribute a font.

You can check a font's embedding permissions by using Microsoft's free font properties extension utility, which is available at www.microsoft.com/typography/TrueTypeProperty21.mspx. After you install this utility, right-click any font file and choose Properties to see more-detailed information about it. In particular, check the Embedding tab for information about the allowed embedding for this font. Fonts marked with Installed Embedding Allowed are suitable for WPF applications; fonts with Editable Embedding Allowed may not be. Consult with the font vendor for licensing information about a specific font.

Text Formatting Mode

The text rendering in WPF is significantly different from the rendering in older GDI-based applications. A large part of the difference is due to WPF's device-independent display system, but there are also significant enhancements that allow text to appear clearer and crisper, particularly on LCD monitors.

However, WPF text rendering has one well-known shortcoming. At small text sizes, text can become blurry and show undesirable artifacts (such as color fringing around the edges). These problems don't occur with GDI text display, because GDI uses tricks to optimize the clarity of small text. For example, GDI can change the shapes of small letters, adjust their positions, and line up everything on pixel boundaries. These steps cause the typeface to lose its distinctive character, but they make for a better onscreen reading experience when dealing with very small text.

So how can you fix WPF's small-text display problem? The best solution is to scale up your text (on a 96 dpi monitor, the effect should disappear at a text size of about 15 device-independent units) or use a high-dpi monitor that has enough resolution to show sharp text at any size. But because these options often aren't practical, WPF also has the ability to selectively use GDI-like text rendering.

To use GDI-style text rendering, you add the TextOptions.TextFormattingMode attached property to a text-displaying element such as the TextBlock or Label, and set it to Display (rather than the standard value, Ideal). Here's an example:

```
<TextBlock FontSize="12" Margin="5">
This is a Test. Ideal text is blurry at small sizes.
</TextBlock>

<TextBlock FontSize="12" Margin="5" TextOptions.TextFormattingMode="Display">
This is a Test. Display text is crisp at small sizes.
</TextBlock>
```

It's important to remember that the TextFormattingMode property is a solution for small text only. If you use it on larger text (text above 15 points), the text will not be as clear, the spacing will not be as even, and the typeface will not be rendered as accurately. And if you use text in conjunction with a transform (discussed in Chapter 12) that rotates, resizes, or otherwise changes its appearance, you should always use WPF's standard text display mode. That's because the GDI-style optimization for display text is applied before any transforms. After a transform is applied, the result will no longer be aligned on pixel boundaries, and the text will appear blurry.

Mouse Cursors

A common task in any application is to adjust the mouse cursor to show when the application is busy or to indicate how different controls work. You can set the mouse pointer for any element by using the Cursor property, which is inherited from the FrameworkElement class.

Every cursor is represented by a System.Windows.Input.Cursor object. The easiest way to get a Cursor object is to use the shared properties of the Cursors class (from the System.Windows.Input namespace). The cursors include all the standard Windows cursors, such as the hourglass, the hand, the resizing arrows, and so on. Here's an example that sets the hourglass for the current window:

```
Me.Cursor = Cursors.Wait
```

Now when you move the mouse over the current window, the mouse pointer changes to the familiar swirl.

▓ **Note** The properties of the Cursors class draw on the cursors that are defined on the computer. If the user has customized the set of standard cursors, the application you create will use those customized cursors.

If you set the cursor in XAML, you don't need to use the Cursors class directly. That's because the TypeConverter for the Cursor property is able to recognize the property names and retrieve the corresponding Cursor object from the Cursors class. That means you can write markup like this to show the help cursor (a combination of an arrow and a question mark) when the mouse is positioned over a button:

```
<Button Cursor="Help">Help</Button>
```

It's possible to have overlapping cursor settings. In this case, the most specific cursor wins. For example, you could set a different cursor on a button and on the window that contains the button. The button's cursor will be shown when you move the mouse over the button, and the window's cursor will be used for every other region in the window.

However, there's one exception. A parent can override the cursor settings of its children by using the ForceCursor property. When this property is set to True, the child's Cursor property is ignored, and the parent's Cursor property applies everywhere inside.

If you want to apply a cursor setting to every element in every window of an application, the FrameworkElement. Cursor property won't help you. Instead, you need to use the shared Mouse.OverrideCursor property, which overrides the Cursor property of every element:

```
Mouse.OverrideCursor = Cursors.Wait
```

To remove this application-wide cursor override, set the Mouse.OverrideCursor property to Nothing.

Lastly, WPF supports custom cursors without any fuss. You can use both ordinary .cur cursor files (which are essentially small bitmaps) and .ani animated cursor files. To use a custom cursor, you pass the file name of your cursor file or a stream with the cursor data to the constructor of the Cursor object:

```
Dim customCursor As New Cursor(Path.Combine(applicationDir, "stopwatch.ani"))
Me.Cursor = customCursor
```

The Cursor object doesn't directly support the URI resource syntax that allows other WPF elements (such as the Image) to use files that are stored in your compiled assembly. However, it's still quite easy to add a cursor file to your application as a resource and then retrieve it as a stream that you can use to construct a Cursor object. The trick is using the Application.GetResourceStream() method:

```
Dim sri As StreamResourceInfo = Application.GetResourceStream( _
  New Uri("stopwatch.ani", UriKind.Relative))
Dim customCursor As New Cursor(sri.Stream)
Me.Cursor = customCursor
```

This code assumes that you've added a file named stopwatch.ani to your project and set its Build Action to Resource. You'll learn more about the GetResourceStream() method in Chapter 7.

Content Controls

A content control is a still more specialized type of control that is able to hold (and display) a piece of content. Technically, a content control is a control that can contain a single nested element. The one-child limit is what differentiates content controls from layout containers, which can hold as many nested elements as you want.

■ **Tip**   Of course, you can still pack a lot of content in a single content control. The trick is to wrap everything in a single container, such as a StackPanel or a Grid. For example, the Window class is itself a content control. Obviously, windows often hold a great deal of content, but it's all wrapped in one top-level container (typically a Grid).

As you learned in Chapter 3, all WPF layout containers derive from the abstract Panel class, which gives the support for holding multiple elements. Similarly, all content controls derive from the abstract ContentControl class. Figure 6-1 shows the class hierarchy.

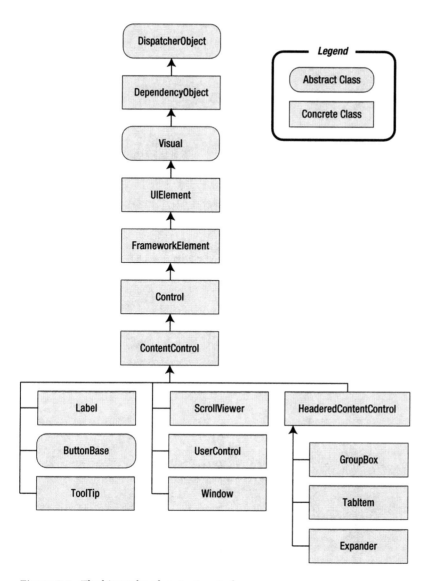

Figure 6-1. *The hierarchy of content controls*

As Figure 6-1 shows, several common controls are content controls, including the Label and the ToolTip. Additionally, all types of buttons are content controls, including the familiar Button, the RadioButton, and the CheckBox. There are also a few more specialized content controls, such as ScrollViewer (which allows you to create a scrollable panel) and UserControl class (which allows you to reuse a custom grouping of controls). The Window class, which is used to represent each window in your application, is itself a content control.

Finally, there is a subset of content controls that goes through one more level of inheritance by deriving from the HeaderedContentControl class. These controls have both a content region and a header region, which can be used to display some sort of title. They include the GroupBox, TabItem (a page in a TabControl), and Expander controls.

■ **Note** Figure 6-1 leaves out just a few elements. It doesn't show the Frame element, which is used for navigation (discussed in Chapter 24), and it omits a few elements that are used inside other controls (such as list box and status bar items).

The Content Property

Whereas the Panel class adds the Children collection to hold nested elements, the ContentControl class adds a Content property, which accepts a single object. The Content property supports any type of object, but it separates objects into two groups and gives each group different treatment:

Objects that don't derive from UIElement: The content control calls ToString() to get the text for these controls and then displays that text.

Objects that derive from UIElement: These objects (which include all the visual elements that are a part of WPF) are displayed inside the content control by using the UIElement. OnRender() method.

■ **Note** Technically, the OnRender() method doesn't draw the object immediately. It simply generates a graphical representation, which WPF paints on the screen as needed.

To understand how this works, consider the humble button. So far, the examples that you've seen that include buttons have simply supplied a string:

```
<Button Margin="3">Text content</Button>
```

This string is set as the button content and displayed on the button surface. However, you can get more ambitious by placing other elements inside the button. For example, you can place an image inside a button by using the Image class:

```
<Button Margin="3">
  <Image Source="happyface.jpg" Stretch="None" />
</Button>
```

Or you could combine text and images by wrapping them all in a layout container such as the StackPanel:

```
<Button Margin="3">
  <StackPanel>
    <TextBlock Margin="3">Image and text button</TextBlock>
    <Image Source="happyface.jpg" Stretch="None" />
    <TextBlock Margin="3">Courtesy of the StackPanel</TextBlock>
  </StackPanel>
</Button>
```

> **Note** It's acceptable to place text content inside a content control because the XAML parser converts that to a string object and uses that to set the Content property. However, you can't place string content directly in a layout container. Instead, you need to wrap it in a class that derives from UIElement, such as TextBlock or Label.

If you wanted to create a truly exotic button, you could even place other content controls such as text boxes and buttons inside the button (and still nest elements inside these). It's doubtful that such an interface would make much sense, but it's possible. Figure 6-2 shows some sample buttons.

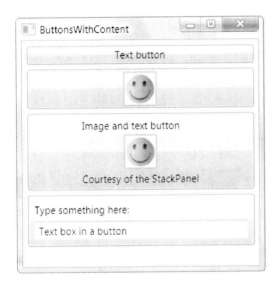

Figure 6-2. *Buttons with different types of nested content*

This is the same content model you saw with windows. Just like the Button class, the Window class allows a single nested element, which can be a piece of text, an arbitrary object, or an element.

> **Note** One of the few elements that is *not* allowed inside a content control is the Window. When you create a Window, it checks to see whether it's the top-level container. If it's placed inside another element, the Window throws an exception.

Aside from the Content property, the ContentControl class adds very little. It includes a HasContent property that returns True if there is content in the control, and a ContentTemplate that allows you to build a template telling the control how to display an otherwise unrecognized object. Using a ContentTemplate, you can display non-UIElement-derived objects more intelligently. Instead of just calling ToString() to get a string, you can take various property values and arrange them into more-complex markup. You'll learn more about data templates in Chapter 20.

Aligning Content

In Chapter 3, you learned how to align different controls in a container by using the HorizontalAlignment and VerticalAlignment properties, which are defined in the base FrameworkElement class. However, once a control contains content, you need to consider another level of organization. You need to decide how the content inside your content control is aligned with its borders. This is accomplished by using the HorizontalContentAlignment and VerticalContentAlignment properties.

HorizontalContentAlignment and VerticalContentAlignment support the same values as HorizontalAlignment and VerticalAlignment. That means you can line up content on the inside of any edge (Top, Bottom, Left, or Right), you can center it (Center), or you can stretch it to fill the available space (Stretch). These settings are applied directly to the nested content element, but you can use multiple levels of nesting to create a sophisticated layout. For example, if you nest a StackPanel in a Label element, the Label.HorizontalContentAlignment property determines where the StackPanel is placed, but the alignment and sizing options of the StackPanel and its children will determine the rest of the layout.

In Chapter 3, you also learned about the Margin property, which allows you to add whitespace between adjacent elements. Content controls use a complementary property named Padding, which inserts space between the edges of the control and the edges of the content. To see the difference, compare the following two buttons:

```
<Button>Absolutely No Padding</Button>
<Button Padding="3">Well Padded</Button>
```

The button that has no padding (the default) has its text crowded against the button edge. The button that has a padding of 3 units on each side gets a more respectable amount of breathing space. Figure 6-3 highlights the difference.

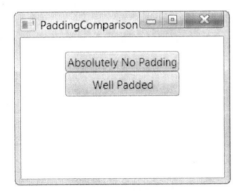

Figure 6-3. *Padding the content of the button*

■ **Note** The HorizontalContentAlignment, VerticalContentAlignment, and Padding properties are defined as part of the Control class, not the more specific ContentControl class. That's because some controls that aren't content controls could still have some sort of content. One example is the TextBox—its contained text (stored in the Text property) is adjusted by using the alignment and padding settings you've applied.

The WPF Content Philosophy

At this point, you might be wondering if the WPF content model is really worth all the trouble. After all, you might choose to place an image inside a button, but you're unlikely to embed other controls and entire layout panels. However, there are a few important reasons driving the shift in perspective.

Consider the example shown in Figure 6-2, which includes a simple image button that places an Image element inside the Button control. This approach is less than ideal, because bitmaps are not resolution-independent. On a high-dpi display, the bitmap may appear blurry because WPF must add more pixels by interpolation to make sure the image stays the correct size. More-sophisticated WPF interfaces avoid bitmaps and use a combination of vector shapes to create custom-drawn buttons and other graphical frills (as you'll see in Chapter 12).

This approach integrates nicely with the content control model. Because the Button class is a content control, you are not limited to filling it with a fixed bitmap; instead, you can include other content. For example, you can use the classes in the System.Windows.Shapes namespace to draw a vector image inside a button. Here's an example that creates a button with two diamond shapes (as shown in Figure 6-4):

```
<Button Margin="3">
  <Grid>
    <Polygon Points="100,25 125,0 200,25 125,50"
     Fill="LightSteelBlue" />
    <Polygon Points="100,25 75,0 0,25 75,50"
     Fill="White"/>
  </Grid>
</Button>
```

Figure 6-4. *A button with shape content*

Clearly, in this case, the nested content model is simpler than adding extra properties to the Button class to support the different types of content. Not only is the nested content model more flexible, but it also allows the Button class to expose a simpler interface. And because all content controls support content nesting in the same way, there's no need to add different content properties to multiple classes.

In essence, the nested content model is a trade-off. It simplifies the class model for elements because there's no need to use additional layers of inheritance to add properties for different types of content. However, you need to use a slightly more complex *object* model—elements that can be built from other nested elements.

■ **Note**   You can't always get the effect you want by changing the content of a control. For example, even though you can place any content in a button, a few details never change, such as the button's shaded background, its rounded border, and the mouse-over effect that makes it glow when you move the mouse pointer over it. However, another way to change these built-in details is to apply a new control template. Chapter 17 shows how you can change all aspects of a control's look and feel by using a control template.

Labels

The simplest of all content controls is the Label control. Like any other content control, it accepts any single piece of content you want to place inside. But what distinguishes the Label control is its support for *mnemonics*, which are essentially shortcut keys that set the focus to a linked control.

To support this functionality, the Label control adds a single property, named Target. To set the Target property, you need to use a binding expression that points to another control. Here's the syntax you must use:

```
<Label Target="{Binding ElementName=txtA}">Choose _A</Label>
<TextBox Name="txtA"></TextBox>
<Label Target="{Binding ElementName=txtB}">Choose _B</Label>
<TextBox Name="txtB"></TextBox>
```

The underscore in the label text indicates the shortcut key. (If you really *do* want an underscore to appear in your label, you must add two underscores instead.) All mnemonics work with Alt and the shortcut key you've identified. For example, if the user presses Alt+A in this example, the first label transfers focus to the linked control, which is txtA. Similarly, Alt+B takes the user to txtB.

Usually, the shortcut letters are hidden until the user presses Alt, at which point they appear as underlined letters (Figure 6-5). However, this behavior depends on system settings.

■ **Tip** If all you need to do is display content without support for mnemonics, you may prefer to use the more lightweight TextBlock element. Unlike the Label, the TextBlock also supports wrapping through its TextWrapping property.

Figure 6-5. Shortcuts in a label

Buttons

WPF recognizes three types of button controls: the familiar Button, the CheckBox, and the RadioButton. All of these controls are content controls that derive from ButtonBase.

The ButtonBase class includes only a few members. It defines the Click event and adds support for commands, which allow you to wire buttons to higher-level application tasks (a feat you'll consider in Chapter 9). Finally, the ButtonBase class adds a ClickMode property, which determines when a button fires its Click event in response to mouse actions. The default value is ClickMode.Release, which means the Click event fires when the mouse is clicked and released. However, you can also choose to fire the Click event when the mouse button is first pressed (ClickMode. Press) or, oddly enough, whenever the mouse moves over the button and pauses there (ClickMode.Hover).

▓ **Note** All button controls support access keys, which work similarly to mnemonics in the Label control. You add the underscore character to identify the access key. If the user presses Alt and the access key, a button click is triggered.

The Button

The Button class represents the ever-present Windows push button. It adds just two writeable properties, IsCancel and IsDefault:

- *When IsCancel is True*, this button is designated as the cancel button for a window. If you press the Esc key while positioned anywhere on the current window, this button is triggered.

- *When IsDefault is True*, this button is designated as the default button (also known as the *accept button*). Its behavior depends on your current location in the window. If you're positioned on a non-Button control (such as a TextBox, RadioButton, CheckBox, and so on), the default button is given a blue shading, almost as though it has focus. If you press Enter, this button is triggered. However, if you're positioned on another Button control, the current button gets the blue shading, and pressing Enter triggers that button, not the default button.

Many users rely on these shortcuts (particularly the Esc key to close an unwanted dialog box), so it makes sense to take the time to define these details in every window you create. It's still up to you to write the event-handling code for the cancel and default buttons, because WPF won't supply this behavior.

In some cases, it may make sense for the same button to be the cancel button *and* the default button for a window. One example is the OK button in an About box. However, there should be only a single cancel button and a single default button in a window. If you designate more than one cancel button, pressing Esc will simply move the focus to the next default button, but it won't trigger that button. If you have more than one default button, pressing Enter has a somewhat more confusing behavior. If you're on a non-Button control, pressing Enter moves you to the next default button. If you're on a Button control, pressing Enter triggers it.

ISDEFAULT AND ISDEFAULTED

The Button class also includes the horribly confusing IsDefaulted property, which is read-only. IsDefaulted returns True for a default button if another control has focus and that control doesn't accept the Enter key. In this situation, pressing the Enter key will trigger the button.

For example, a TextBox does not accept the Enter key, unless you've set TextBox.AcceptsReturn to True. When a TextBox with an AcceptsReturn value of True has focus, IsDefaulted is False for the default button. When a TextBox with an AcceptsReturns value of False has focus, the default button has IsDefaulted set to True. If this isn't confusing enough, the IsDefaulted property returns False when the button itself has focus, even though hitting Enter at this point will trigger the button.

Although it's unlikely that you'll want to use the IsDefaulted property, this property does allow you to write certain types of style triggers, as you'll see in Chapter 11. If that doesn't interest you, just add it to your list of obscure WPF trivia, which you can use to puzzle your colleagues.

The ToggleButton and RepeatButton

Along with Button, three more classes derive from ButtonBase. These include the following:

- *GridViewColumnHeader* represents the clickable header of a column when you use a grid-based ListView. The ListView is described in Chapter 22.

- *RepeatButton* fires Click events continuously, as long as the button is held down. Ordinary buttons fire one Click event per user click.

- *ToggleButton* represents a button that has two states (pushed or unpushed). When you click a ToggleButton, it stays in its pushed state until you click it again to release it. This is sometimes described as *sticky click* behavior.

Both RepeatButton and ToggleButton are defined in the System.Windows.Controls.Primitives namespace, which indicates they aren't often used on their own. Instead, they're used to build more-complex controls by composition, or extended with features through inheritance. For example, the RepeatButton is used to build the higher-level ScrollBar control (which, ultimately, is a part of the even higher-level ScrollViewer). The RepeatButton gives the arrow buttons at the ends of the scrollbar their trademark behavior—scrolling continues as long as you hold it down. Similarly, ToggleButton is used to derive the more useful CheckBox and RadioButton classes described next.

However, neither RepeatButton nor ToggleButton is an abstract class, so you can use both of them directly in your user interfaces. The ToggleButton is genuinely useful inside a ToolBar, which you'll use in Chapter 25.

The CheckBox

Both the CheckBox and the RadioButton are buttons of a different sort. They derive from ToggleButton, which means they can be switched on or off by the user, hence their "toggle" behavior. In the case of the CheckBox, switching the control on means placing a check mark in it.

The CheckBox class doesn't add any members, so the basic CheckBox interface is defined in the ToggleButton class. Most important, ToggleButton adds an IsChecked property. IsChecked is a nullable Boolean, which means it can be set to True, False, or a null reference (Nothing). Obviously, True represents a checked box, while False represents an empty one. The Nothing value is a little trickier—it represents an indeterminate state, which is displayed as a shaded box. The indeterminate state is commonly used to represent values that haven't been set or areas where some discrepancy exists. For example, if you have a check box that allows you to apply bold formatting in a text application, and the current selection includes both bold and regular text, you might set the check box to Nothing to show an indeterminate state.

To assign a null value in WPF markup, you need to use the null markup extension, as shown here:

```
<CheckBox IsChecked="{x:Null}">A check box in indeterminate state</CheckBox>
```

Along with the IsChecked property, the ToggleButton class adds a property named IsThreeState, which determines whether the user is able to place the check box into an indeterminate state. If IsThreeState is False (the default), clicking the check box alternates its state between checked and unchecked, and the only way to place it in an indeterminate state is through code. If IsThreeState is True, clicking the check box cycles through all three possible states.

The ToggleButton class also defines three events that fire when the check box enters specific states: Checked, Unchecked, and Indeterminate. In most cases, it's easier to consolidate this logic into one event handler by handling the Click event that's inherited from ButtonBase. The Click event fires whenever the button changes state.

The RadioButton

The RadioButton also derives from ToggleButton and uses the same IsChecked property and the same Checked, Unchecked, and Indeterminate events. Along with these, the RadioButton adds a single property named GroupName, which allows you to control how radio buttons are placed into groups.

Ordinarily, radio buttons are grouped by their container. That means if you place three RadioButton controls in a single StackPanel, they form a group from which you can select just one of the three. On the other hand, if you place a combination of radio buttons in two separate StackPanel controls, you have two independent groups on your hands.

The GroupName property allows you to override this behavior. You can use it to create more than one group in the same container or to create a single group that spans multiple containers. Either way, the trick is simple—just give all the radio buttons that belong together the same group name.

Consider this example:

```
<StackPanel>
  <GroupBox Margin="5">
    <StackPanel>
      <RadioButton>Group 1</RadioButton>
      <RadioButton>Group 1</RadioButton>
      <RadioButton>Group 1</RadioButton>
      <RadioButton Margin="0,10,0,0" GroupName="Group2">Group 2</RadioButton>
    </StackPanel>
  </GroupBox>
  <GroupBox Margin="5">
    <StackPanel>
      <RadioButton>Group 3</RadioButton>
      <RadioButton>Group 3</RadioButton>
      <RadioButton>Group 3</RadioButton>
      <RadioButton Margin="0,10,0,0" GroupName="Group2">Group 2</RadioButton>
    </StackPanel>
  </GroupBox>
</StackPanel>
```

Here, there are two containers holding radio buttons, but three groups. The final radio button at the bottom of each group box is part of a third group. In this example, it makes for a confusing design, but at times you might want to separate a specific radio button from the pack in a subtle way without causing it to lose its group membership.

■ **Tip** You don't need to use the GroupBox container to wrap your radio buttons, but it's a common convention. The GroupBox shows a border and gives you a caption that you can apply to your group of buttons.

Tooltips

WPF has a flexible model for *tooltips* (those infamous yellow boxes that pop up when you hover over something interesting). Because tooltips in WPF are content controls, you can place virtually anything inside a tooltip. You can also tweak various timing settings to control how quickly tooltips appear and disappear.

The easiest way to show a tooltip doesn't involve using the ToolTip class directly. Instead, you simply set the ToolTip propertyof your element. The ToolTip property is defined in the FrameworkElement class, so it's available on anything you'll place in a WPF window.

For example, here's a button that has a basic tooltip:

```
<Button ToolTip="This is my tooltip">I have a tooltip</Button>
```

When you hover over this button, the text *This is my tooltip* appears in the familiar yellow box.

If you want to supply more-ambitious tooltip content, such as a combination of nested elements, you need to break the ToolTip property out into a separate element. Here's an example that sets the ToolTip property of a button by using more-complex nested content:

```
<Button>
  <Button.ToolTip>
    <StackPanel>
      <TextBlock Margin="3" >Image and text</TextBlock>
      <Image Source="happyface.jpg" Stretch="None" />
      <TextBlock Margin="3" >Image and text</TextBlock>
    </StackPanel>
  </Button.ToolTip>
  <Button.Content>I have a fancy tooltip</Button.Content>
</Button>
```

As in the previous example, WPF implicitly creates a ToolTip object. The difference is that, in this case, the ToolTip object contains a StackPanel rather than a simple string. Figure 6-6 shows the result.

Figure 6-6. *A fancy tooltip*

If more than one tooltip overlaps, the most specific tooltip wins. For example, if you add a tooltip to the StackPanel container in the previous example, this tooltip appears when you hover over an empty part of the panel or a control that doesn't have its own tooltip.

■ **Note**   Don't put user-interactive controls in a tooltip because the ToolTip window can't accept focus. For example, if you place a button in a ToolTip control, the button will appear, but it isn't clickable. (If you attempt to click it, your mouse click will just pass through to the window underneath.) If you want a tooltip-like window that can hold other controls, consider using the Popup control instead, which is discussed shortly, in the section named "The Popup."

Setting ToolTip Properties

The previous example shows how you can customize the content of a tooltip, but what if you want to configure other ToolTip-related settings? You have two options. The first technique you can use is to explicitly define the ToolTip object. That gives you the chance to directly set a variety of ToolTip properties.

The ToolTip is a content control, so you can adjust standard properties such as the Background (so it isn't a yellow box), Padding, and Font. You can also modify the members that are defined in the ToolTip class (listed in Table 6-2). Most of these properties are designed to help you place the tooltip exactly where you want it.

Table 6-2. *ToolTip Properties*

Name	Description
HasDropShadow	Determines whether the tooltip has a diffuse black drop shadow that makes it stand out from the window underneath.
Placement	Determines how the tooltip is positioned, using one of the values from the PlacementMode enumeration. The default value is Mouse, which means that the top-left corner of the tooltip is placed relative to the current mouse position. (The actual position of the tooltip may be offset from this starting point based on the HorizontalOffset and VerticalOffset properties.) Other possibilities allow you to place the tooltip by using absolute screen coordinates or place it relative to some element (which you indicate using the PlacementTarget property).
HorizontalOffset and VerticalOffset	Allow you to nudge the tooltip into the exact position you want. You can use positive or negative values.
PlacementTarget	Allows you to place a tooltip relative to another element. In order to use this property, the Placement property must be set to Left, Right, Top, Bottom, or Center. (This is the edge of the element to which the tooltip is aligned.)
PlacementRectangle	Allows you to offset the position of the tooltip. This works in much the same way as the HorizontalOffset and VerticalOffest properties. This property doesn't have an effect if Placement property is set to Mouse.
CustomPopupPlacementCallback	Allows you to position a tooltip dynamically using code. If the Placement property is set to Custom, this property identifies the method that will be called by the ToolTip to get the position where the ToolTip should be placed. Your callback method receives three pieces of information: popupSize (the size of the ToolTip), targetSize (the size of the PlacementTarget, if it's used), and offset (a point that's created based on HorizontalOffset and VerticalOffset properties). The method returns a CustomPopupPlacement object that tells WPF where to place the tooltip.
StaysOpen	Has no effect in practice. The intended purpose of this property is to allow you to create a tooltip that remains open until the user clicks somewhere else. However, the ToolTipService.ShowDuration property overrides the StaysOpen property. As a result, tooltips always disappear after a configurable amount of time (usually about 5 seconds) or when the user moves the mouse away. If you want to create a tooltip-like window that stays open indefinitely, the easiest approach is to use the Popup control.
IsEnabled and IsOpen	Allow you to control the tooltip in code. IsEnabled allows you to temporarily disable a ToolTip. IsOpen allows you to programmatically show or hide a tooltip (or just check whether the tooltip is open).

Using the ToolTip properties, the following markup creates a tooltip that has no drop shadow but uses a transparent red background, which lets the underlying window (and controls) show through:

```
<Button>
  <Button.ToolTip>
    <ToolTip Background="#60AA4030" Foreground="White"
    HasDropShadow="False" >
```

```
    <StackPanel>
      <TextBlock Margin="3" >Image and text</TextBlock>
      <Image Source="happyface.jpg" Stretch="None" />
      <TextBlock Margin="3" >Image and text</TextBlock>
    </StackPanel>
  </ToolTip>
 </Button.ToolTip>
 <Button.Content>I have a fancy tooltip</Button.Content>
</Button>
```

In most cases, you'll be happy enough to use the standard tooltip placement, which puts it at the current mouse position. However, the various ToolTip properties give you many more options. Here are some strategies you can use to place a tooltip:

Based on the current position of the mouse: This is the standard behavior, which relies on Placement being set to Mouse. The top-left corner of the tooltip box is lined up with the bottom-left corner of the invisible bounding box around the mouse pointer.

Based on the position of the moused-over element: Set the Placement property to Left, Right, Top, Bottom, or Center, depending on the edge of the element you want to use. The top-left corner of the tooltip box will be lined up with that edge.

Based on the position of another element (or the window): Set the Placement property as if you were lining up the tooltip with the current element. (Use the value Left, Right, Top, Bottom, or Center.) Then choose the element by setting the PlacementTarget property. Remember to use the {Binding ElementName=*Name*} syntax to identify the element you want to use.

With an offset: Use any of the strategies described previously, but set the HorizontalOffset and VerticalOffset properties to add a little extra space.

Using absolute coordinates: Set Placement to Absolute and use the HorizontalOffset and VerticalOffset properties (or the PlacementRectangle) to set some space between the tooltip and the top-left corner of the window.

Using a calculation at runtime: Set Placement to Custom. Set the CustomPopupPlacementCallback property to point to a method that you've created.

Figure 6-7 shows how different placement properties stack up. Note that when lining up a tooltip against an element along the tooltip's bottom or right edge, you'll end up with a bit of extra space. That's because of the way that the ToolTip measures its content.

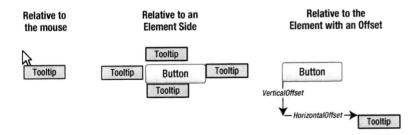

Figure 6-7. *Placing a tooltip explicitly*

Setting ToolTipService Properties

There are some tooltip properties that can't be configured using the properties of the ToolTip class. In this case, you need to use a different class, which is named ToolTipService. ToolTipService allows you to configure the time delays associated with the display of a tooltip. All the properties of the ToolTipService class are attached properties, so you can set them directly in your control tag, as shown here:

```
<Button ToolTipService.InitialShowDelay="1">
  ...
</Button>
```

The ToolTipService class defines many of the same properties as ToolTip. This allows you to use a simpler syntax when you're dealing with text-only tooltips. Rather than adding a nested ToolTip element, you can set everything you need using attributes:

```
<Button ToolTip="This tooltip is aligned with the bottom edge"
  ToolTipService.Placement="Bottom">I have a tooltip</Button>
```

Table 6-3 lists the properties of the ToolTipService class. The ToolTipService class also provides two routed events: ToolTipOpening and ToolTipClosing. You can react to these events to fill a tooltip with just-in-time content or to override the way tooltips work. For example, if you set the handled flag in both events, tooltips will no longer be shown or hidden automatically. Instead, you'll need to show and hide them manually by setting the IsOpen property.

Table 6-3. *ToolTipService Properties*

Name	Description
InitialShowDelay	Sets the delay (in milliseconds) before this tooltip is shown when the mouse hovers over the element.
ShowDuration	Sets the amount of time (in milliseconds) that this tooltip is shown before it disappears, if the user does not move the mouse.
BetweenShowDelay	Sets a time window (in milliseconds) during which the user can move between tooltips without experiencing the InitialShowDelay. For example, if BetweenShowDelay is 5000, the user has 5 seconds to move to another control that has a tooltip. If the user moves to another control within that time period, the new tooltip is shown immediately. If the user takes longer, the BetweenShowDelay window expires, and the InitialShowDelay kicks into action. In this case, the second tooltip isn't shown until after the InitialShowDelay period.
ToolTip	Sets the content for the tooltip. Setting ToolTipService.ToolTip is equivalent to setting the FrameworkElement.ToolTip property of an element.
HasDropShadow	Determines whether the tooltip has a diffuse black drop shadow that makes it stand out from the window underneath.
ShowOnDisabled	Determines the tooltip behavior when the associated element is disabled. If True, the tooltip will appear for disabled elements (elements that have their IsEnabled property set to False). The default is False, in which case the tooltip appears only if the associated element is enabled.
Placement, PlacementTarget, PlacementRectangle, and VerticalOffset	Allow you to control the placement of the tooltip. These properties work in the same way as the matching properties of the ToolTipHorizontalOffset class.

⬛ **Tip**   It makes little sense to duplicate the same tooltip settings for several controls. If you plan to adjust the way tooltips are handled in your entire application, use styles so that your settings are applied automatically, as described in Chapter 11. Unfortunately, the ToolTipService property values are not inherited, which means if you set them at the window or container level, they don't flow through to the nested elements.

The Popup

The Popup control has a great deal in common with the ToolTip, although neither one derives from the other. Like the ToolTip, the Popup can hold a single piece of content, which can include any WPF element. (This content is stored in the Popup.Child property, unlike the ToolTip content, which is stored in the ToolTip.Content property.) Also, like the ToolTip, the content in the Popup can extend beyond the bounds of the window. Lastly, the Popup can be placed using the same placement properties and shown or hidden using the same IsOpen property.

The differences between the Popup and ToolTip are more important. They include the following:

- The Popup is never shown automatically. You must set the IsOpen property for it to appear.

- By default, the Popup.StaysOpen property is set to True, and the Popup does not disappear until you explicitly set its IsOpen property to False. If you set StaysOpen to False, the Popup disappears when the user clicks somewhere else.

⬛ **Note**   A pop-up that stays open can be a bit jarring because it behaves like a separate stand-alone window. If you move the window underneath, the pop-up remains fixed in its original position. You won't witness this behavior with the ToolTip or with a Popup that sets StaysOpen to False, because as soon as you click to move the window, the tooltip or pop-up window disappears.

- The Popup provides a PopupAnimation property that lets you control how it comes into view when you set IsOpen to True. Your options include None (the default), Fade (the opacity of the pop-up gradually increases), Scroll (the pop-up slides in from the upper-left corner of the window, space permitting), and Slide (the pop-up slides down into place, space permitting). In order for any of these animations to work, you must also set the AllowsTransparency property to True.

- The Popup can accept focus. Thus, you can place user-interactive controls in it, such as a Button. This functionality is one of the key reasons to use the Popup instead of the ToolTip.

- The Popup control is defined in the System.Windows.Controls.Primitives namespace because it is most commonly used as a building block for more-complex controls. You'll find that the Popup is not quite as polished as other controls. Notably, you must set the Background property if you want to see your content, because it won't be inherited from your window and you need to add the border yourself (the Border element works perfectly well for this purpose).

Because the Popup must be shown manually, you may choose to create it entirely in code. However, you can define it just as easily in XAML markup—just make sure to include the Name property so you can manipulate it in code.

Figure 6-8 shows an example. Here, when the user moves the mouse over an underlined word, a pop-up appears with more information and a link that opens an external web browser window.

Figure 6-8. *A pop-up with a hyperlink*

To create this window, you need to include a TextBlock with the initial text and a Popup with the additional content that you'll show when the user moves the mouse into the correct place. Technically, it doesn't matter where you define the Popup tag, because it's not associated with any particular control. Instead, it's up to you to set the placement properties to position the Popup in the correct spot. In this example, the Popup appears at the current mouse position, which is the simplest option.

```
<TextBlock TextWrapping="Wrap">You can use a Popup to provide a link for a
  specific <Run TextDecorations="Underline" MouseEnter="run_MouseEnter">term</Run>
  of interest.</TextBlock>

<Popup Name="popLink" StaysOpen="False" Placement="Mouse" MaxWidth="200"
  PopupAnimation="Slide" AllowsTransparency="True">
  <Border BorderBrush="Beige" BorderThickness="2" Background="White">
    <TextBlock Margin="10" TextWrapping="Wrap">
      For more information, see
      <Hyperlink NavigateUri="http://en.wikipedia.org/wiki/Term"
       Click="lnk_Click">Wikipedia</Hyperlink>
    </TextBlock>
  </Border>
</Popup>
```

This example presents two elements that you might not have seen before. The Run element allows you to apply formatting to a specific part of a TextBlock—it's a piece of flow content that you'll learn about in Chapter 28 when you consider documents. The Hyperlink allows you to provide a clickable piece of text. You'll take a closer look at it in Chapter 24, when you consider page-based applications.

The only remaining details are the relatively trivial code that shows the Popup when the mouse moves over the correct word and the code that launches the web browser when the link is clicked:

```
Private Sub run_MouseEnter(ByVal sender As Object, ByVal e As MouseEventArgs)
    popLink.IsOpen = true
End Sub
```

```
Private Sub lnk_Click(ByVal sender As Object, ByVal e As RoutedEventArgs)
    Hyperlink lnk = CType(sender, Hyperlink)
    Process.Start(lnk.NavigateUri.ToString())
End Sub
```

■ **Note**   You can show and hide a Popup by using a *trigger*—an action that takes place automatically when a specific property hits a specific value. You simply need to create a trigger that reacts when Popup.IsMouseOver is True and sets the Popup.IsOpen property to True. Chapter 11 has the details.

Specialized Containers

Content controls aren't just for basics such as labels, buttons, and tooltips. They also include specialized containers that allow you to shape large portions of your user interface.

In the following sections, you'll meet these more ambitious content controls. You'll start with the ScrollViewer control, which derives directly from ContentControl and provides a virtual surface that lets users scroll around a much larger element. And although the ScrollViewer can only hold a single element (like all content controls), you can place a layout container inside to hold any assortment of elements you need.

Next you'll look at three more controls that go through an extra layer of inheritance: the GroupBox, TabItem, and Expander. All of these controls derive from HeaderedContentControl (which, in turn, derives from ContentControl). The role of HeaderedContentControl is simple—it represents a container that has both single-element content (as stored in the Content property) and a single-element header (as stored in the Header property). The addition of the header is what distinguishes HeaderedContentControl from the content controls you've seen so far. Once again, you can pack the content into a HeaderedContentControl using a layout container for its content, its header, or both.

The ScrollViewer

Scrolling is a key feature if you want to fit large amounts of content in a limited amount of space. In order to get scrolling support in WPF, you need to wrap the content you want to scroll inside a ScrollViewer.

Although the ScrollViewer can hold anything, you'll typically use it to wrap a layout container. For example, in Chapter 3, you saw an example that used a Grid element to create a three-column display of text, text boxes, and buttons. To make this Grid scrollable, you simply need to wrap the Grid in a ScrollViewer, as shown in this slightly shortened markup:

```
<ScrollViewer>
  <Grid Margin="3,3,10,3">
    <Grid.RowDefinitions>
      ...
    </Grid.RowDefinitions>
    <Grid.ColumnDefinitions>
      ...
    </Grid.ColumnDefinitions>

    <Label Grid.Row="0" Grid.Column="0" Margin="3"
      VerticalAlignment="Center">Home:</Label>
    <TextBox Grid.Row="0" Grid.Column="1" Margin="3"
```

```
        Height="Auto" VerticalAlignment="Center"></TextBox>
      <Button Grid.Row="0" Grid.Column="2" Margin="3" Padding="2">
        Browse</Button>
      ...

    </Grid>
</ScrollViewer>
```

The result is shown in Figure 6-9.

Figure 6-9. *A scrollable window*

If you resize the window in this example so that it's large enough to fit all its content, the scrollbar becomes disabled. However, the scrollbar will still be visible. You can control this behavior by setting the VerticalScrollBarVisibility property, which takes a value from the ScrollBarVisibility enumeration. The default value of Visible makes sure the vertical scrollbar is always present. Use Auto if you want the scrollbar to appear when it's needed and disappear when it's not. Or use Disabled if you don't want the scrollbar to appear at all.

■ **Note** You can also use Hidden, which is similar to Disabled but subtly different. First, content with a hidden scrollbar is still scrollable. (For example, you can scroll through the content by using the arrow keys.) Second, the content in a ScrollViewer is laid out differently. When you use Disabled, you tell the content in the ScrollViewer that it has only as much space as the ScrollViewer itself. On the other hand, if you use Hidden, you tell the content that it has an infinite amount of space. That means it can overflow and stretch off into the scrollable region. Ordinarily, you'll use Hidden only if you plan to allow scrolling by another mechanism (such as the custom scrolling buttons described next). You'll use Disabled only if you want to temporarily prevent the ScrollViewer from doing anything at all.

The ScrollViewer also supports horizontal scrolling. However, the HorizontalScrollBarVisibility property is Hidden by default. To use horizontal scrolling, you need to change this value to Visible or Auto.

Programmatic Scrolling

To scroll through the window shown in Figure 6-9, you can click the scrollbar with the mouse, you can move over the grid and use a mouse scroll wheel, you can tab through the controls, or you can click somewhere on the blank surface of the grid and use the up and down arrow keys. If this still doesn't give you the flexibility you crave, you can use the methods of the ScrollViewer class to scroll your content programmatically:

- The most obvious are LineUp() and LineDown(), which are equivalent to clicking the arrow buttons on the vertical scrollbar to move up or down once.

- You can also use PageUp() and PageDown(), which scroll an entire screenful up or down and are equivalent to clicking the surface of the scrollbar, above or below the scrollbar thumb.

- Similar methods allow horizontal scrolling, including LineLeft(), LineRight(), PageLeft(), and PageRight().

- Finally, you can use the ScrollTo*Xxx*() methods to go somewhere specific. For vertical scrolling, they include ScrollToEnd() and ScrollToHome(), which take you to the top or bottom of the scrollable content, and ScrollToVerticalOffset(), which takes you to a specific position. There are horizontal versions of the same methods, including ScrollToLeftEnd(), ScrollToRightEnd(), and ScrollToHorizontalOffset().

In the example in Figure 6-10, several custom buttons allow you to move through the ScrollViewer. Each button triggers a simple event handler that uses one of the methods in the previous list.

Figure 6-10. *Programmatic scrolling*

Custom Scrolling

The built-in scrolling in the ScrollViewer is quite useful. It allows you to scroll slowly through any content, from a complex vector drawing to a grid of elements. However, one of the most intriguing features of the ScrollViewer is its ability to let its content participate in the scrolling process. Here's how it works:

1. You place a scrollable element inside the ScrollViewer. This is any element that implements IScrollInfo.

2. You tell the ScrollViewer that the content knows how to scroll itself by setting the ScrollViewer.CanContentScroll property to True.

3. When you interact with the ScrollViewer (by using the scrollbar, the mouse wheel, the scrolling methods, and so on), the ScrollViewer calls the appropriate methods on your element by using the IScrollInfo interface. The element then performs its own custom scrolling.

■ **Note** The IScrollInfo interface defines a set of methods that react to different scrolling actions. For example, it includes many of the scrolling methods exposed by the ScrollViewer, such as LineUp(), LineDown(), PageUp(), and PageDown(). It also defines methods that handle the mouse wheel.

Very few elements implement IScrollInfo. One element that does is the StackPanel container. Its IScrollInfo implementation uses *logical scrolling*, which is scrolling that moves from element to element, rather than from line to line.

If you place a StackPanel in a ScrollViewer and you don't set the CanContentScroll property, you get the ordinary behavior. Scrolling up and down moves you a few pixels at a time. However, if you set CanContentScroll to True, each time you click down, you scroll to the beginning of the next element:

```
<ScrollViewer CanContentScroll="True">
  <StackPanel>
    <Button Height="100">1</Button>
    <Button Height="100">2</Button>
    <Button Height="100">3</Button>
    <Button Height="100">4</Button>
  </StackPanel>
</ScrollViewer>
```

You may or may not find that the StackPanel's logical scrolling system is useful in your application. However, it's indispensable if you want to create a custom panel with specialized scrolling behavior.

The GroupBox

The GroupBox is the simplest of the three controls that derives from HeaderedContentControl. It's displayed as a box with rounded corners and a title. Here's an example (shown in Figure 6-11):

```
<GroupBox Header="A GroupBox Test" Padding="5"
  Margin="5" VerticalAlignment="Top">
  <StackPanel>
    <RadioButton Margin="3">One</RadioButton>
    <RadioButton Margin="3">Two</RadioButton>
    <RadioButton Margin="3">Three</RadioButton>
    <Button Margin="3">Save</Button>
  </StackPanel>
</GroupBox>
```

Figure 6-11. *A basic group box*

Notice that the GroupBox still requires a layout container (such as a StackPanel) to arrange its contents. The GroupBox is often used to group small sets of related controls, such as radio buttons. However, the GroupBox has no built-in functionality, so you can use it however you want. (RadioButton objects are grouped by placing them into any panel. A GroupBox is not required, unless you want the rounded, titled border.)

The TabItem

The TabItem represents a page in a TabControl. The only significant member that the TabItem class adds is the IsSelected property, which indicates whether the tab is currently being shown in the TabControl. Here's the markup that's required to create the simple example shown in Figure 6-12:

```
<TabControl Margin="5">
  <TabItem Header="Tab One">
    <StackPanel Margin="3">
      <CheckBox Margin="3">Setting One</CheckBox>
      <CheckBox Margin="3">Setting Two</CheckBox>
      <CheckBox Margin="3">Setting Three</CheckBox>
    </StackPanel>
  </TabItem>
  <TabItem Header="Tab Two">
    ...
  </TabItem>
</TabControl>
```

Figure 6-12. *A set of tabs*

■ **Tip**   You can use the TabStripPlacement property to make the tabs appear on the side of the tab control, rather than in their normal location at the top.

As with the Content property, the Header property can accept any type of object. It displays UIElement-derived classes by rendering them and uses the ToString() method for inline text and all other objects. That means you can create a group box or a tab with graphical content or arbitrary elements in its title. Here's an example:

```
<TabControl Margin="5">
  <TabItem>
    <TabItem.Header>
      <StackPanel>
        <TextBlock Margin="3" >Image and Text Tab Title</TextBlock>
        <Image Source="happyface.jpg" Stretch="None" />
      </StackPanel>
    </TabItem.Header>

    <StackPanel Margin="3">
      <CheckBox Margin="3">Setting One</CheckBox>
      <CheckBox Margin="3">Setting Two</CheckBox>
      <CheckBox Margin="3">Setting Three</CheckBox>
    </StackPanel>
  </TabItem>

  <TabItem Header="Tab Two"></TabItem>
</TabControl>
```

Figure 6-13 shows the somewhat garish result.

Figure 6-13. *An exotic tab title*

The Expander

The most exotic headered content control is the Expander. It wraps a region of content that the user can show or hide by clicking a small arrow button. This technique is used frequently in online help and on web pages, to allow them to include large amounts of content without overwhelming users with information they don't want to see.

Figure 6-14 shows two views of a window with three expanders. In the version on the left, all three expanders are collapsed. In the version on the right, all the regions are expanded. (Of course, users are free to expand or collapse any combination of expanders individually.)

Figure 6-14. *Hiding content with expandable regions*

Using an Expander is extremely simple—you just need to wrap the content you want to make collapsible inside. Ordinarily, each Expander begins collapsed, but you can change this in your markup (or in your code) by setting the IsExpanded property. Here's the markup that creates the example shown in Figure 6-14:

```
<StackPanel>
  <Expander Margin="5" Padding="5" Header="Region One">
    <Button Padding="3">Hidden Button One</Button>
  </Expander>
  <Expander Margin="5" Padding="5" Header="Region Two" >
    <TextBlock TextWrapping="Wrap">
      Lorem ipsum dolor sit amet, consectetuer adipiscing elit ...
    </TextBlock>
  </Expander>
  <Expander Margin="5" Padding="5" Header="Region Three">
    <Button Padding="3">Hidden Button Two</Button>
  </Expander>
</StackPanel>
```

You can also choose in which direction the expander expands. In Figure 6-14, the standard value (Down) is used, but you can also set the ExpandDirection property to Up, Left, or Right. When the Expander is collapsed, the arrow always points in the direction where it will expand.

Life gets a little interesting when using different ExpandDirection values, because the effect on the rest of your user interface depends on the type of container. Some containers, such as the WrapPanel, simply bump other elements out of the way. Others, such as Grid, have the option of using proportional or automatic sizing. Figure 6-15 shows an example with a four-cell grid in various degrees of expansion. In each cell is an Expander with a different ExpandDirection. The columns are sized proportionately, which forces the text in the Expander to wrap. (An autosized column would simply stretch to fit the text, making it larger than the window.) The rows are set to automatic sizing, so they expand to fit the extra content.

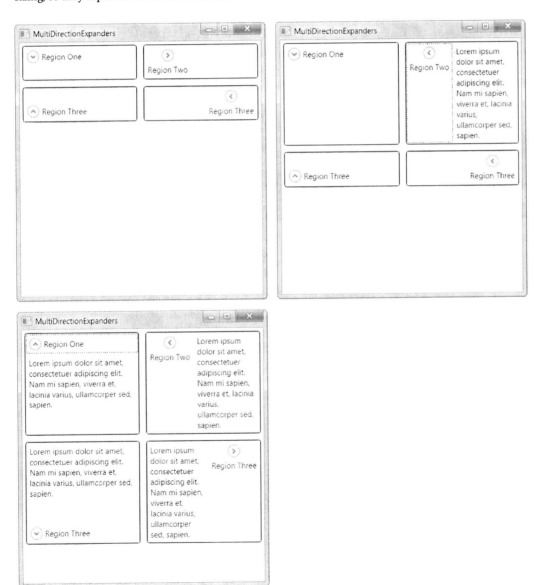

Figure 6-15. *Expanding in different directions*

The Expander is a particularly nice fit in WPF because WPF encourages you to use a flowing layout model that can easily handle content areas that grow or shrink dynamically.

If you need to synchronize other controls with an Expander, you can handle the Expanded and Collapsed events. Contrary to what the naming of these events implies, they fire just *before* the content appears or disappears. This gives you a useful way to implement a lazy load. For example, if the content in an Expander is expensive to create, you might wait until it's shown to retrieve it. Or perhaps you want to update the content just before it's shown. Either way, you can react to the Expanded event to perform your work.

■ **Note** If you like the functionality of the Expander but aren't impressed with the built-in appearance, don't worry. Using the template system in WPF, you can completely customize the expand and collapse arrows so they match the style of the rest of your application. You'll learn how in Chapter 17.

Ordinarily, when you expand an Expander, it grows to fit its content. This may create a problem if your window isn't large enough to fit all the content when everything is expanded. You can use several strategies to handle this problem:

- Set a minimum size for the window (using MinWidth and MinHeight) to make sure it will fit everything even at its smallest.

- Set the SizeToContent property of the window so that it expands automatically to fit the exact dimensions you need when you open or close an Expander. Ordinarily, SizeToContent is set to Manual, but you can use Width or Height to make it expand or contract in either dimension to accommodate its content.

- Limit the size of the Expander by hard-coding its Height and Width. Unfortunately, this is likely to truncate the content that's inside if it's too large.

- Create a scrollable expandable region by using the ScrollViewer.

For the most part, these techniques are quite straightforward. The only one that requires any further exploration is the combination of an Expander and a ScrollViewer. In order for this approach to work, you need to hard-code the size for the ScrollViewer. Otherwise, it will simply expand to fit its content. Here's an example:

```
<Expander Margin="5" Padding="5" Header="Region Two">
  <ScrollViewer Height="50">
    <TextBlock TextWrapping="Wrap">
      ...
    </TextBlock>
  </ScrollViewer>
</Expander>
```

It would be nice to have a system in which an Expander could set the size of its content region based on the available space in a window. However, this would present obvious complexities. (For example, how would space be shared between multiple regions when an Expander expands?) The Grid layout container might seem like a potential solution, but unfortunately, it doesn't integrate well with the Expander. If you try it out, you'll end up with oddly spaced rows that don't update their heights properly when an Expander is collapsed.

Text Controls

WPF includes three text-entry controls: TextBox, RichTextBox, and PasswordBox. The PasswordBox derives directly from Control. The TextBox and RichTextBox controls go through another level and derive from TextBoxBase.

Unlike the content controls you've seen, the text boxes are limited in the type of content they can contain. The TextBox always stores a string (provided by the Text property). The PasswordBox also deals with string content (provided by the Password property), although it uses a SecureString internally to mitigate against certain types of attacks. Only the RichTextBox has the ability to store more-sophisticated content: a FlowDocument that can contain a complex combination of elements.

In the following sections, you'll consider the core features of the TextBox. You'll end by taking a quick look at the security features of the PasswordBox.

■ **Note** The RichTextBox is an advanced control design for displaying FlowDocument objects. You'll learn how to use it when you tackle documents in Chapter 28.

Multiple Lines of Text

Ordinarily, the TextBox control stores a single line of text. (You can limit the allowed number of characters by setting the MaxLength property.) However, in many cases you'll want to create a multiline text box for dealing with large amounts of content. In this case, set the TextWrapping property to Wrap or WrapWithOverflow. Wrap always breaks at the edge of the control, even if it means severing an extremely long word in two. WrapWithOverflow allows some lines to stretch beyond the right edge if the line-break algorithm can't find a suitable place (such as a space or a hyphen) to break the line.

For multiple lines to be visible in a text box, it needs to be sized large enough. Rather than setting a hard-coded height (which won't adapt to different font sizes and may cause layout problems), you can use the handy MinLines and MaxLines properties. MinLines is the minimum number of lines that must be visible in the text box. For example, if MinLines is 2, the text box will grow to be at least two lines tall. If its container doesn't have enough room, part of the text box may be clipped. MaxLines sets the maximum number of lines that will be displayed. Even if a text box expands to fit its container (for example, a proportionally sized Grid row or the last element in a DockPanel), it won't grow beyond this limit.

■ **Note** The MinLines and MaxLines properties have no effect on the amount of content you can place in a text box. They simply help you size the text box. In your code, you can examine the LineCount property to find out exactly how many lines are in a text box.

If your text box supports wrapping, the odds are good that the user can enter more text than can be displayed at once in the visible lines. For this reason, it usually makes sense to add an always-visible or on-demand scrollbar by setting the VerticalScrollBarVisibility property to Visible or Auto. (You can also set the HorizontalScrollBarVisibility property to show a less common horizontal scrollbar.)

You may want to allow the user to enter hard returns in a multiline text box by pressing the Enter key. (Ordinarily, pressing the Enter key in a text box triggers the default button.) To make sure a text box supports the Enter key, set AcceptsReturn to True. You can also set AcceptsTab to allow the user to insert tabs. Otherwise, the Tab key moves to the next focusable control in the tab sequence.

■ **Tip** The TextBox class also includes a host of methods that let you move through the text content programmatically in small or large steps. They include LineUp(), LineDown(), PageUp(), PageDown(), ScrollToHome(), ScrollToEnd(), and ScrollToLine().

Sometimes, you'll create a text box purely for the purpose of displaying text. In this case, set the IsReadOnly property to True to prevent editing. This is preferable to disabling the text box by setting IsEnabled to False, because a disabled text box shows grayed-out text (which is more difficult to read), does not support selection (or copying to the clipboard), and does not support scrolling.

Text Selection

As you already know, you can select text in any text box by clicking and dragging with the mouse or holding down Shift while you move through the text with the arrow keys. The TextBox class also gives you the ability to determine or change the currently selected text programmatically, using the SelectionStart, SelectionLength, and SelectedText properties.

SelectionStart identifies the zero-based position where the selection begins. For example, if you set this property to 10, the first selected character is the 11th character in the text box. SelectionLength indicates the total number of selected characters. (A value of 0 indicates no selected characters.) Finally, the SelectedText property allows you to quickly examine or change the selected text in the text box. You can react to the selection being changed by handling the SelectionChanged event. Figure 6-16 shows an example that reacts to this event and displays the current selection information.

Figure 6-16. *Selecting text*

The TextBox class also includes one property that lets you control its selection behavior: AutoWordSelection. If this is True, the text box selects entire words at a time as you drag through the text.

Another useful feature of the TextBox control is Undo, which allows the user to reverse recent changes. The Undo feature is available programmatically (using the Undo() method), and it's available using the Ctrl+Z keyboard shortcut, as long as the CanUndo property has not been set to False.

■ **Tip**   When manipulating text in the text box programmatically, you can use the BeginChange() and EndChange() methods to bracket a series of actions that the TextBox will treat as a single block of changes. These actions can then be undone in a single step.

Spell Checking

The TextBox includes an unusual frill: an integrated spell-check feature, which underlines unrecognized words with a red squiggly line. The user can right-click an unrecognized word and choose from a list of possibilities, as shown in Figure 6-17.

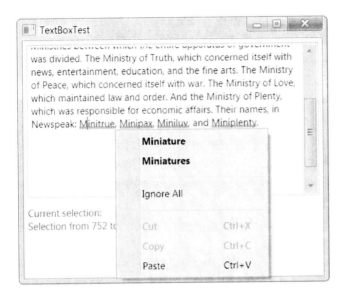

Figure 6-17. *Spell-checking a text box*

To turn on the spell-check functionality for the TextBox control, you simply need to set the SpellCheck.IsEnabled dependency property, as shown here:

```
<TextBox SpellCheck.IsEnabled="True">...</TextBox>
```

The spelling checker is WPF-specific and doesn't depend on any other software (such as Office). The spelling checker determines which dictionary to use based on the input language that's configured for the keyboard. You can override this default by setting the Language property of the TextBox, which is inherited from the FrameworkElement class, or you can set the xml:lang attribute on the <TextBox> element. However, the WPF spelling checker is currently limited to just four languages: English, Spanish, French, and German. You can use the SpellingReform property to set whether post-1990 spelling rule changes are applied to French and German languages.

WPF allows you to customize the dictionary by adding a list of words that will not be treated as errors (and will be used as right-click suggestions, when appropriate). To do so, you must first create a lexicon file, which is nothing more than a text file with the extension .lex. In the lexicon file, you add the list of words. Place each word on a separate line, in any order, as shown here:

```
acantholysis
atypia
bulla
chromonychia
dermatoscopy
desquamation
...
```

In this example, the words are used regardless of the current language setting. However, you can specify that a lexicon should be used only for a specific language by adding a locale ID. Here's how you would specify that the custom words should be used only when the current language is English:

```
#LID 1033
acantholysis
atypia
bulla
chromonychia
dermatoscopy
desquamation
...
```

The other supported locale IDs are 3082 (Spanish), 1036 (French), and 1031 (German).

■ **Note**   The custom dictionary feature is not designed to allow you to use additional languages. Instead, it simply augments an already supported language (such as English) with the words you supply. For example, you can use a custom dictionary to recognize proper names or to allow medical terms in a medical application.

Once you've created the lexicon file, make sure the SpellCheck.IsEnabled property is set to True for your TextBox. The final step is to attach a Uri object that points to your custom dictionary, using the SpellCheck.CustomDictionaries property. If you choose to specify it in XAML, as in the following example, you must first import the System namespace so that you can declare a Uri object in markup:

```
<Window xmlns:sys="clr-namespace:System;assembly=system" ... >
```

You can use multiple custom dictionaries at once, as long as you add a Uri object for each one. Each Uri can use a hard-coded path to the file on a local drive or network share. But the safest approach is to use an application resource. For example, if you've added the file CustomWords.lex to a project named SpellTest, and you've set the Build Action of that file to Resource (using the Solution Explorer), you will use markup like this:

```
<TextBox TextWrapping="Wrap" SpellCheck.IsEnabled="True"
 Text="Now the spell checker recognizes acantholysis and offers the right correction
for acantholysi">
  <SpellCheck.CustomDictionaries>
    <sys:Uri>pack://application:,,,/SpellTest;component/CustomWords.lex</sys:Uri>
  </SpellCheck.CustomDictionaries>
</TextBox>
```

The odd pack://application:,,,/ portion at the beginning of the URI is the pack URI syntax that WPF uses to refer to an assembly resource. You'll take a closer look at it when you consider resources in detail in Chapter 7.

If you need to load the lexicon file from the application directory, the easiest option is to create the URI you need by using code, and add it to the SpellCheck.CustomDictionaries collection when the window is initialized.

The PasswordBox

The PasswordBox looks like a TextBox, but it displays a string of circle symbols to mask the characters it shows. (You can choose a different mask character by setting the PasswordChar property.) Additionally, the PasswordBox does not support the clipboard, so you can't copy the text inside.

Compared to the TextBox class, the PasswordBox has a much simpler, stripped-down interface. Much like the TextBox class, it provides a MaxLength property; Clear(), Paste() and SelectAll() methods; and an event that fires when the text is changed (named PasswordChanged). But that's it. Still, the most important difference between the TextBox and the PasswordBox is on the inside. Although you can set text and read it as an ordinary string by using the Password property, internally the PasswordBox uses a System.Security.SecureString object exclusively.

A SecureString is a text-only object much like the ordinary string. The difference is how it's stored in memory. A SecureString is stored in memory in an encrypted form. The key that's used to encrypt the string is generated randomly and stored in a portion of memory that's never written to disk. The end result is that even if your computer crashes, malicious users won't be able to examine the paging file to retrieve the password data. At best, they will find the encrypted form.

The SecureString class also includes on-demand disposal. When you call SecureString.Dispose(), the in-memory password data is overwritten. This guarantees that all password information has been wiped out of memory and is no longer subject to any kind of exploit. As you would expect, the PasswordBox is conscientious enough to call Dispose() on the SecureString that it stores internally when the control is destroyed.

List Controls

WPF includes many controls that wrap a collection of items, ranging from the simple ListBox and ComboBox that you'll examine here to more specialized controls such as the ListView, the TreeView, and the ToolBar, which are covered in future chapters. All of these controls derive from the ItemsControl class (which itself derives from Control).

The ItemsControl class fills in the basic plumbing that's used by all list-based controls. Notably, it gives you two ways to fill the list of items. The most straightforward approach is to add them directly to the Items collection, using code or XAML. However, in WPF, it's more common to use data binding. In this case, you set the ItemsSource property to the object that has the collection of data items you want to display. (You'll learn more about data binding with a list in Chapter 19.)

The class hierarchy that leads from ItemsControls is a bit tangled. One major branch is the *selectors*, which includes the ListBox, the ComboBox, and the TabControl. These controls derive from Selector and have properties that let you track down the currently selected item (SelectedItem) or its position (SelectedIndex). Separate from these are controls that wrap lists of items but don't support selection in the same way. These include the classes for menus, toolbars, and trees—all of which are ItemsControls but aren't selectors.

In order to unlock most of the features of any ItemsControl, you'll need to use data binding. This is true even if you aren't fetching your data from a database or an external data source. WPF data binding is general enough to work with data in a variety of forms, including custom data objects and collections. But you won't consider the details of data binding just yet. For now, you'll take only a quick look at the ListBox and ComboBox.

The ListBox

The ListBox class represents a common staple of Windows design—the variable-length list that allows the user to select an item.

■ **Note** The ListBox class also allows multiple selection if you set the SelectionMode property to Multiple or Extended. In Multiple mode, you can select or deselect any item by clicking it. In Extended mode, you need to hold down the Ctrl key to select additional items or the Shift key to select a range of items. In either type of multiple-selection list, you use the SelectedItems collection instead of the SelectedItem property to get all the selected items.

To add items to the ListBox, you can nest ListBoxItem elements inside the ListBox element. For example, here's a ListBox that contains a list of colors:

```
<ListBox>
  <ListBoxItem>Green</ListBoxItem>
  <ListBoxItem>Blue</ListBoxItem>
  <ListBoxItem>Yellow</ListBoxItem>
  <ListBoxItem>Red</ListBoxItem>
</ListBox>
```

As you'll remember from Chapter 2, different controls treat their nested content in different ways. The ListBox stores each nested object in its Items collection.

The ListBox is a remarkably flexible control. Not only can it hold ListBoxItem objects, but it can also host any arbitrary element. This works because the ListBoxItem class derives from ContentControl, which gives it the ability to hold a single piece of nested content. If that piece of content is a UIElement-derived class, it will be rendered in the ListBox. If it's some other type of object, the ListBoxItem will call ToString() and display the resulting text.

For example, if you decided you want to create a list with images, you could create markup like this:

```
<ListBox>
  <ListBoxItem>
    <Image Source="happyface.jpg"></Image>
  </ListBoxItem>
  <ListBoxItem>
    <Image Source="happyface.jpg"></Image>
  </ListBoxItem>
</ListBox>
```

The ListBox is intelligent enough to create the ListBoxItem objects it needs implicitly. That means you can place your objects directly inside the ListBox element. Here's a more ambitious example that uses nested StackPanel objects to combine text and image content:

```
<ListBox>
  <StackPanel Orientation="Horizontal">
    <Image Source="happyface.jpg"  Width="30" Height="30"></Image>
    <Label VerticalContentAlignment="Center">A happy face</Label>
  </StackPanel>
  <StackPanel Orientation="Horizontal">
    <Image Source="redx.jpg" Width="30" Height="30"></Image>
    <Label VerticalContentAlignment="Center">A warning sign</Label>
  </StackPanel>
  <StackPanel Orientation="Horizontal">
    <Image Source="happyface.jpg"  Width="30" Height="30"></Image>
    <Label VerticalContentAlignment="Center">A happy face</Label>
  </StackPanel>
</ListBox>
```

In this example, the StackPanel becomes the item that's wrapped by the ListBoxItem. This markup creates the rich list shown in Figure 6-18.

Figure 6-18. *A list of images*

■ **Note**   One flaw in the current design is that the text color doesn't change when the item is selected. This isn't ideal, because it's difficult to read the black text with a blue background. To solve this problem, you need to use a data template, as described in Chapter 20.

This ability to nest arbitrary elements inside list box items allows you to create a variety of list-based controls without needing to use other classes. For example, the Windows Forms toolkit includes a CheckedListBox class that's displayed as a list with a check box next to every item. No such specialized class is required in WPF because you can quickly build one by using the standard ListBox:

```
<ListBox Name="lst" SelectionChanged="lst_SelectionChanged"
  CheckBox.Click="lst_SelectionChanged">
  <CheckBox Margin="3">Option 1</CheckBox>
  <CheckBox Margin="3">Option 2</CheckBox>
</ListBox>
```

There's one caveat to be aware of when you use a list with different elements inside. When you read the SelectedItem value (and the SelectedItems and Items collections), you won't see ListBoxItem objects; instead, you'll see whatever objects you placed in the list. In the CheckedListBox example, that means SelectedItem provides a CheckBox object.

For example, here's some code that reacts when the SelectionChanged event fires. It then gets the currently selected CheckBox and displays whether that item has been selected:

```
Private Sub lst_SelectionChanged(ByVal sender As Object, _
  ByVal e As SelectionChangedEventArgs)
    If lst.SelectedItem Is Nothing Then Return
```

```
    txtSelection.Text = String.Format( _
        "You chose item at position {0}." & vbCrLf & "Checked state is {1}.", _
        lst.SelectedIndex, CType(lst.SelectedItem, CheckBox).IsChecked)
End Sub
```

■ **Tip**   If you want to find the current selection, you can read it directly from the SelectedItem or SelectedItems property, as shown here. If you want to determine which item (if any) was *unselected*, you can use the RemovedItems property of the SelectionChangedEventArgs object. Similarly, the AddedItems property tells you which items were added to the selection. In single-selection mode, one item is always added and one item is always removed whenever the selection changes. In multiple or extended mode, this isn't necessarily the case.

In the following code snippet, similar code loops through the collection of items to determine which ones are selected. (You could write similar code that loops through the collection of selected items in a multiple-selection list with check boxes.)

```
Private Sub cmd_CheckAllItems(ByVal sender As Object, _
  ByVal e As RoutedEventArgs)
    Dim sb As New StringBuilder()
    For Each item As CheckBox In lst.Items
        If item.IsChecked = True Then
            sb.Append(item.Content.ToString() & " is checked.")
            sb.Append(Constants.vbCrLf)
        End If
    Next
    txtSelection.Text = sb.ToString()
End Sub
```

Figure 6-19 shows the list box that uses this code.

Figure 6-19. *A check box list*

When manually placing items in a list, it's up to you whether you want to insert the items directly or explicitly wrap each one in a ListBoxItem object. The second approach is often cleaner, albeit more tedious. The most important consideration is to be consistent. For example, if you place StackPanel objects in your list, the ListBox.SelectedItem object will be a StackPanel. If you place StackPanel objects wrapped by ListBoxItem objects, the ListBox.SelectedItem object will be a ListBoxItem, so code accordingly.

The ListBoxItem offers a little extra functionality from what you get with directly nested objects. Namely, it defines an IsSelected property that you can read (or set) and a Selected and Unselected event that tells you when that item is highlighted. However, you can get similar functionality by using the members of the ListBox class, such as the SelectedItem (or SelectedItems) property, and the SelectionChanged event.

Interestingly, there's a technique to retrieve a ListBoxItem wrapper for a specific object when you use the nested object approach. The trick is the often overlooked ContainerFromElement() method. Here's the code that uses this technique to check whether the first item is selected in a list:

```
Dim selectedObject As DependencyObject
selectedObject = CType(lst.SelectedItems(0), DependencyObject))

Dim selectedItem As ListBoxItem
selectedItem = CType(lst.ContainerFromElement(selectedItem, ListBoxItem)
MessageBox.Show(("IsSelected: " + selectedItem.IsSelected.ToString))
```

The ComboBox

The ComboBox is similar to the ListBox control. It holds a collection of ComboBoxItem objects, which are created either implicitly or explicitly. As with the ListBoxItem, the ComboBoxItem is a content control that can contain any nested element.

The key difference between the ComboBox and ListBox classes is the way they render themselves in a window. The ComboBox control uses a drop-down list, which means only one item can be selected at a time.

If you want to allow the user to type text in the combo box to select an item, you must set the IsEditable property to True, and you must make sure you are storing ordinary text-only ComboBoxItem objects or an object that provides a meaningful ToString() representation. For example, if you fill an editable combo box with Image objects, the text that appears in the upper portion is simply the fully qualified Image class name, which isn't much use.

One limitation of the ComboBox is the way it sizes itself when you use automatic sizing. The ComboBox widens itself to fit its content, which means that it changes size as you move from one item to the next. Unfortunately, there's no easy way to tell the ComboBox to take the size of its largest contained item. Instead, you may need to supply a hard-coded value for the Width property, which isn't ideal.

Range-Based Controls

WPF includes three controls that use the concept of a *range*. These controls take a numeric value that falls between a specific minimum and maximum value. These controls—ScrollBar, ProgressBar, and Slider—all derive from the RangeBase class (which itself derives from the Control class). But although they share an abstraction (the range), they work quite differently.

The RangeBase class defines the properties shown in Table 6-4.

Table 6-4. *Properties of the RangeBase Class*

Name	Description
Value	The current value of the control (which must fall between the minimum and maximum). By default, it starts at 0. Contrary to what you might expect, Value isn't an Integer—it's a Double, so it accepts fractional values. You can react to the ValueChanged event if you want to be notified when the value is changed.
Maximum	The upper limit (the largest allowed value).
Minimum	The lower limit (the smallest allowed value).
SmallChange	The amount the Value property is adjusted up or down for a small change. The meaning of a "small change" depends on the control (and may not be used at all). For the ScrollBar and Slider, this is the amount the value changes when you use the arrow keys. For the ScrollBar, you can also use the arrow buttons at either end of the bar.
LargeChange	The amount the Value property is adjusted up or down for a large change. The meaning of a "large change" depends on the control (and may not be used at all). For the ScrollBar and Slider, this is the amount the value changes when you use the Page Up and Page Down keys or when you click the bar on either side of the thumb (which indicates the current position).

Ordinarily, there's no need to use the ScrollBar control directly. The higher-level ScrollViewer control, which wraps two ScrollBar controls, is typically much more useful. The Slider and ProgressBar are more practical, and are often useful on their own.

The Slider

The Slider is a specialized control that's occasionally useful—for example, you might use it to set numeric values when the number itself isn't particularly significant. For example, it makes sense to set the volume in a media player by dragging the thumb in a slider bar from side to side. The general position of the thumb indicates the relative loudness (normal, quiet, or loud), but the underlying number has no meaning to the user.

The key Slider properties are defined in the RangeBase class. Along with these, you can use all the properties listed in Table 6-5.

Table 6-5. *Additional Properties in the Slider Class*

Name	Description
Orientation	Switches between a vertical and a horizontal slider.
Delay and Interval	Control how fast the thumb moves along the track when you click and hold down either side of the slider. Both are millisecond values. The Delay is the time before the thumb moves one (small change) unit after you click, and the Interval is the time before it moves again if you continue holding down the mouse button.
TickPlacement	Determines where the tick marks appear. (*Tick marks* are notches that appear near the bar to help you visualize the scale.) By default, TickPlacement is set to None, and no tick marks appear. If you have a horizontal slider, you can place the tick marks above (TopLeft) or below (BottomRight) the track. With a vertical slider, you can place them on the left (TopLeft) and right (BottomRight). (The TickPlacement names are a bit confusing because two values cover four possibilities, depending on the orientation of the slider.)

(continued)

Table 6-5. (*continued*)

Name	Description
TickFrequency	Sets the interval between ticks, which determines how many ticks appear. For example, you could place them every 5 numeric units, every 10, and so on.
Ticks	If you want to place ticks in specific, irregular positions, you can use the Ticks collection. Simply add one number (as a Double) to this collection for each tick mark. For example, you could place ticks at the positions 1, 1.5, 2, and 10 on the scale by adding these numbers.
IsSnapToTickEnabled	If True, when you move the slider, it automatically snaps into place, jumping to the nearest tick mark. The default is False.
IsSelectionRangeEnabled	If True, you can use a selection range to shade in a portion of the slider bar. You set the position selection range by using the SelectionStart and SelectionEnd properties. The selection range has no intrinsic meaning, but you can use it for whatever purpose makes sense. For example, media players sometimes use a shaded background bar to indicate the download progress for a media file.

Figure 6-20 compares Slider controls with different tick settings.

Figure 6-20. *Adding ticks to a slider*

The ProgressBar

The ProgressBar indicates the progress of a long-running task. Unlike the slider, the ProgressBar isn't user-interactive. Instead, it's up to your code to periodically increment the Value property. (Technically speaking, WPF rules suggest that the ProgressBar shouldn't be a control because it doesn't respond to mouse actions or keyboard input.) The ProgressBar has a minimum height of four device-independent units. It's up to you to set the Height property (or put it in the appropriate fixed-size container) if you want to see a larger, more traditional bar.

One neat trick that you can perform with the ProgressBar is using it to show a long-running status indicator, even if you don't know how long the task will take. Interestingly (and oddly), you do this by setting the IsIndeterminate property to True:

```
<ProgressBar Height="18" Width="200" IsIndeterminate="True"></ProgressBar>
```

When setting IsIndeterminate, you no longer use the Minimum, Maximum, and Value properties. Instead, this ProgressBar shows a periodic green pulse that travels from left to right, which is the universal Windows convention indicating that there's work in progress. This sort of indicator makes sense in an application's status bar. For example, you could use it to indicate that you're contacting a remote server for information.

Date Controls

WPF includes two date controls: the Calendar and the DatePicker. Both are designed to allow the user to choose a single date.

The Calendar control displays a calendar that's similar to what you see in the Windows operating system (for example, when you configure the system date). It shows a single month at a time and allows you to step through from month to month (by clicking the arrow buttons) or jump to a specific month (by clicking the month header to view an entire year, and then clicking the month).

The DatePicker requires less space. It's modeled after a simple text box, which holds a date string in long or short date format. The DatePicker provides a drop-down arrow that, when clicked, pops open a full calendar view that's identical to that shown by the Calendar control. This pop-up is displayed on top of any other content, just like a drop-down combo box.

Figure 6-21 shows the two display modes that the Calendar supports, as well as the two date formats that the DatePicker allows.

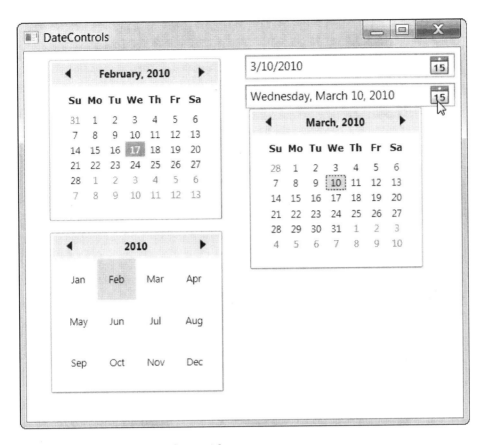

Figure 6-21. The Calendar and DatePicker

The Calendar and DatePicker include properties that allow you to determine which dates are shown and which dates are selectable (provided they fall in a contiguous range). Table 6-6 lists the properties you can use.

Table 6-6. Properties of the Calendar and DatePicker Classes

Property	Description
DisplayDateStart and DisplayDateEnd	Set the range of dates that are displayed in the calendar view, from the first, earliest date (DisplayDateStart) to the last, most recent date (DisplayDateEnd). The user won't be able to navigate to months that don't have any displayable dates. To show all dates, set DisplayDateStart to DateTime.MinValue and DisplayDateEnd to DateTime.MaxValue.
BlackoutDates	Holds a collection of dates that will be disabled in the calendar and won't be selectable. If these dates are not in the range of displayed dates, or if one of these dates is already selected, you'll receive an exception. To prevent selection of any date in the past, call the BlackoutDates.AddDatesInPast() method.

(continued)

Table 6-6. (*continued*)

Property	Description
SelectedDate	Provides the selected date as a DateTime object (or Nothing if no date is selected). It can be set programmatically, by the user clicking the date in the calendar, or by the user typing in a date string (in the DatePicker). In the calendar view, the selected date is marked by a shaded square, which is visible only when the date control has focus.
SelectedDates	Provides the selected dates as a collection of DateTime objects. This property is supported by the Calendar, and it's useful only if you've changed the SelectionMode property to allow multiple date selection.
DisplayDate	Determines the date that's displayed initially in the calendar view (using a DateTime object). If it's a null value (Nothing), the SelectedDate is shown. If DisplayDate and SelectedDate are both null, the current date is used. The display date determines the initial month page of the calendar view. When the date control has focus, a square outline is displayed around the appropriate day in that month (which is different from the shaded square used for the currently selected date).
FirstDayOfWeek	Determines the day of the week that will be displayed at the start of each calendar row, in the leftmost position.
IsTodayHighlighted	Determines whether the calendar view uses highlighting to point out the current date.
DisplayMode (Calendar only)	Determines the initial display month of the calendar. If set to Month, the Calendar shows the standard single-month view. If set to Year, the Calendar shows the months in the current year (similar to when the user clicks the month header). After the user clicks a month, the Calendar shows the full calendar view for that month.
SelectionMode (Calendar only)	Determines the type of date selections that are allowed. The default is SingleDate, which allows a single date to be selected. Other options include None (selection is disabled entirely), SingleRange (a contiguous group of dates can be selected), and MultipleRange (any combination of dates can be selected). In SingleRange or MultipleRange modes, the user can drag to select multiple dates, or click while holding down the Ctrl key. You can use the SelectedDates property to get a collection with all the selected dates.
IsDropDownOpen (DatePicker only)	Determines whether the calendar view drop-down is open in the DatePicker. You can set this property programmatically to show or hide the calendar.
SelectedDateFormat (DatePicker only)	Determines how the selected date will be displayed in the text part of the DatePicker. You can choose Short or Long. The actual display format is based on the client computer's regional settings. For example, if you use Short, the date might be rendered in the yyyy/mm/dd format or dd/mm/yyyy. The long format generally includes the month and day names.

The date controls also provide a few events. Most useful is SelectedDateChanged (in the DatePicker) or the similar SelectedDatesChanged (in the Calendar), which adds support for multiple date selection. You can react to these events to reject specific date selections, such as dates that fall on a weekend:

```
Private Sub Calendar_SelectedDatesChanged(ByVal sender As Object, _
  ByVal e As CalendarDateChangedEventArgs)
    ' Check all the newly added items.
    For Each selectedDate As DateTime In e.AddedItems
        If (selectedDate.DayOfWeek = DayOfWeek.Saturday) OrElse _
           (selectedDate.DayOfWeek = DayOfWeek.Sunday) Then
            lblError.Text = "Weekends are not allowed"

            ' Remove the selected date.
            CType(sender, Calendar).SelectedDates.Remove(selectedDate)
        End If
    Next
End Sub
```

You can try this out with a Calendar that supports single or multiple selection. If it supports multiple selection, try dragging the mouse over an entire week of dates. All the dates will remain highlighted except for the disallowed weekend dates, which will be unselected automatically.

The Calendar also adds a DisplayDateChanged event (when the user browses to a new month). The DatePicker adds CalendarOpened and CalendarClosed events (which fire when the calendar drop-down is displayed and closed) and a DateValidationError event (which fires when the user types a value in the text-entry portion that can't be interpreted as a valid date). Ordinarily, invalid values are discarded when the user opens the calendar view, but here's an option that fills in some text to inform the user of the problem:

```
Private Sub DatePicker_DateValidationError(ByVal sender As Object, _
  ByVal e As DatePickerDateValidationErrorEventArgs)
    lblError.Text = "'" & e.Text & "' is not a valid value because " & _
        e.Exception.Message
End Sub
```

The Last Word

In this chapter, you took a tour of the fundamental WPF controls, including basic ingredients such as labels, buttons, text boxes, and lists. Along the way, you learned about some important WPF concepts that underlie the control model, such as brushes, fonts, and the content model. Although most WPF controls are quite easy to use, developers who have this additional understanding—and know how all the different branches of WPF elements relate together—will have an easier time creating well-designed windows.

The Application

While it's running, every WPF application is represented by an instance of the System.Windows.Application class. This class tracks all the open windows in your application, decides when your application shuts down, and fires application events that you can handle to perform initialization and cleanup.

In this chapter, you'll explore the Application class in detail. You'll learn how you can use it to perform tasks such as catching unhandled errors, showing a splash screen, and retrieving command-line parameters. You'll even consider an ambitious example that uses instance handling and registered file types, allowing the application to manage an unlimited number of documents under one roof.

Once you understand the infrastructure that underpins the Application class, you'll consider how to create and use *assembly resources*. Every resource is a chunk of binary data that you embed in your compiled application. As you'll see, this makes resources the perfect repository for pictures, sounds, and even localized data in multiple languages.

The Application Life Cycle

In WPF, applications go through a straightforward life cycle. Shortly after your application begins, the application object is created. As your application runs, various application events fire, which you may choose to monitor. Finally, when the application object is released, your application ends.

Note WPF allows you to create full-fledged applications that give the illusion of running inside a web browser. These applications are called XAML Browser Applications (XBAPs), and you'll learn how to create them (and how to take advantage of the browser's page-based navigation system) in Chapter 24. However, it's worth noting that XBAPs use the same Application class, fire the same lifetime events, and use assembly resources in the same way as standard window-based WPF applications.

Creating an Application Object

If you want to do all the heavy lifting yourself, you can create an instance of the WPF Application class by hand. To do so, you must configure your application to start by running a shared Main() method. (This is the same technique you used in Chapter 2 when loading XAML dynamically.) The following Program class shows an example. It includes a Main() method that creates a window named Window1 and fires up a new application.

```
Public Class Startup
    Inherits Application
```

```
Shared Sub Main()
    ' Create the application.
    Dim app As New Application()

    ' Create the main window.
    Dim win As New Window1()

    ' Launch the application and show the main window.
    app.Run(win)
End Sub

End Class
```

When you pass a window to the Application.Run() method, that window is set as the main window and exposed to your entire application through the Application.MainWindow property. The Run() method then fires the Application.Startup event and shows the main window.

When started in this way, your application continues running until the main window *and every other window* are closed. At that point, the Run() method returns, and any additional code in your Main() method is executed before the application winds down.

■ **Note**   If you want to start your application by using a Main() method, you need to designate the class that contains the Main() method as the startup object in Visual Studio. To do so, double-click the My Project node in the Solution Explorer. In the Application tab, remove the check mark next to the Enable Application Framework setting. You can then choose Sub Main in the Startup Object list. Ordinarily, you don't need to take this step, because Visual Studio creates the Main() method for you based on the XAML application template. You'll learn about the application template in the next section.

Deriving a Custom Application Class

Although the approach shown in the previous section—instantiating the base Application class and calling the Run() method—works perfectly well, it's not the pattern that Visual Studio uses when you create a new WPF application.

Instead, Visual Studio derives a custom class from the Application class. In a simple application, this approach has no meaningful effect. However, if you're planning to handle application events, it provides a neater model, because you can place all your event-handling code in the Application-derived class.

The model Visual Studio uses for the Application class is essentially the same as the model it uses for the windows. The starting point is a XAML template, which is named Application.xaml by default. Here's what it looks like (without the resources section, which you'll learn about in Chapter 10):

```
<Application x:Class="Application"
    xmlns="http://schemas.microsoft.com/winfx/2006/xaml/presentation"
    xmlns:x="http://schemas.microsoft.com/winfx/2006/xaml"
    StartupUri="Window1.xaml"
    >
</Application>
```

As you might remember from Chapter 2, the Class attribute is used in XAML to create a class derived from the element. Thus, this markup creates a class that derives from System.Windows.Application, with (confusingly enough) the name Application. If you want, you can change the class name to something else.

The Application tag not only creates a custom application class, but also sets the StartupUri property to identify the XAML document that represents the main window. As a result, you don't need to explicitly instantiate this window by using code—the XAML parser will do it for you.

As with windows, the application class is defined in two separate portions that are fused together at compile time. The automatically generated portion isn't visible in your project, but it contains the Main() entry point and the code for starting the application. It looks something like this:

```
Partial Public Class Application
    Inherits System.Windows.Application

    Public Shared Sub Main()
        Dim app As New Application
        app.InitializeComponent()
        app.Run()
    End Sub

    Public Sub InitializeComponent()
        Me.StartupUri = New System.Uri("Window1.xaml", System.UriKind.Relative)
    End Sub

End Class
```

If you're really interested in seeing the custom application class that the XAML template creates, look for the Application.g.vb file in the obj\Debug folder inside your project directory.

The only difference between the automatically generated code shown here and a custom application class that you might create on your own is that the automatically generated class uses the StartupUri property instead of setting the MainWindow property or passing the main window as a parameter to the Run() method. You're free to create a custom application class that uses this approach, as long as you use the same URI format. You need to create a relative Uri object that names a XAML document that's in your project. (This XAML document is compiled and embedded in your application assembly as a BAML resource. The resource name is the name of the original XAML file. In the previous example, the application contains a resource named Window1.xaml with the compiled XAML.)

■ **Note** The URI system you see here is an all-purpose way to refer to resources in your application. You'll learn more about how it works in the "Pack URIs" section later in this chapter.

The second portion of the custom application class is stored in your project in a file such as Application.xaml.vb. It contains the event-handling code you add. Initially, it's empty aside from a comment:

```
Class Application

    ' Application-level events, such as Startup, Exit, and
    ' DispatcherUnhandledException can be handled in this file.

End Class
```

This file is merged with the automatically generated application code through the magic of partial classes.

Application Shutdown

Ordinarily, the Application class keeps your application alive as long as at least one window is still open. If this isn't the behavior you want, you can adjust the Application.ShutdownMode. If you're instantiating your Application object by hand, you need to set the ShutdownMode property before you call Run(). If you're using the Application.xaml file, you can simply set the ShutdownMode property in the XAML markup.

You have three choices for the shutdown mode, as listed in Table 7-1.

Table 7-1. *Values from the ShutdownMode Enumeration*

Value	Description
OnLastWindowClose	This is the default behavior—your application keeps running as long as there is at least one window in existence. If you close the main window, the Application.MainWindow property still refers to the object that represents the closed window. (Optionally, you can use code to reassign the MainWindow property to point to a different window.)
OnMainWindowClose	This is the traditional approach—your application stays alive only as long as the main window is open.
OnExplicitShutdown	The application never ends (even if all the windows are closed) unless you call Application.Shutdown(). This approach might make sense if your application is a front end for a long-running background task or if you just want to use more-complex logic to decide when your application should close (at which point you'll call the Application.Shutdown() method).

For example, if you want to use the OnMainWindowClose approach and you're using the Application.xaml file, you need to make this addition:

```
<Application x:Class="Application"
    xmlns="http://schemas.microsoft.com/winfx/2006/xaml/presentation"
    xmlns:x="http://schemas.microsoft.com/winfx/2006/xaml"
    StartupUri="Window1.xaml" ShutdownMode="OnMainWindowClose"
    >
</Application>
```

Alternatively, you can apply the same setting through your project properties. To do so, double-click the My Project node in the Solution Explorer, choose the Application tab, and choose an option for the Shutdown Mode setting. You have three choices, which correspond to the values in the ShutdownMode enumeration.

No matter which shutdown method you choose, you can always use the Application.Shutdown() method to end your application immediately. (Of course, when you call the Shutdown() method, your application doesn't necessarily stop running right away. Calling Application.Shutdown() causes the Application.Run() method to return immediately, but there may be additional code that runs in the Main() method or responds to the Application.Exit event.)

■ **Note** When ShutdownMode is OnMainWindowClose and you close the main window, the Application object will automatically close all the other windows before the Run() method returns. The same is true if you call Application. Shutdown(). This is significant, because these windows may have event-handling code that fires when they are being closed.

Application Events

Initially, the Application.xaml.vb file doesn't contain any code. Although no code is required, you can add code that handles application events. The Application class provides a small set of useful events. Table 7-2 lists the most important ones. It leaves out the events that are used solely for navigation applications (which are discussed in Chapter 24).

Table 7-2. *Application Events*

Name	Description
Startup	Occurs after the Application.Run() method is called and just before the main window is shown (if you passed the main window to the Run() method). You can use this event to check for any command-line arguments, which are provided as an array through the StartupEventArgs.Args property. You can also use this event to create and show the main window (instead of using the StartupUri property in the Application.xaml file).
Exit	Occurs when the application is being shut down for any reason, just before the Run() method returns. You can't cancel the shutdown at this point, although the code in your Main() method could relaunch the application. You can use the Exit event to set the integer exit code that's returned from the Run() method.
SessionEnding	Occurs when the Windows session is ending—for example, when the user is logging off or shutting down the computer. (You can find out which one it is by examining the SessionEndingCancelEventArgs. ReasonSessionEnding property.) You can also cancel the shutdown by setting SessionEndingCancelEventArgs.Cancel to True. If you don't, WPF will call the Application.Shutdown() method when your event handler ends.
Activated	Occurs when one of the windows in the application is activated. This occurs when you switch from another Windows program to this application. It also occurs the first time you show a window.
Deactivated	Occurs when a window in the application is deactivated. This occurs when you switch to another Windows program.
DispatcherUnhandledException	Occurs when an unhandled exception is generated anywhere in your application (on the main application thread). The application dispatcher catches these exceptions. By responding to this event, you can log critical errors, and you can even choose to neutralize the exception and continue running your application by setting the DispatcherUnhandledExceptionEventArgs. Handled property to True. You should take this step only if you can be guaranteed that the application is still in a valid state and can continue.

WPF gives you several equivalent options for handling application events:

- You can use the AddHandler statement in your code.
- You can add the Handles clause to a method definition.
- You can set the corresponding event attribute in the Application.xaml file.

All of these options are equivalent. Unlike the events that take place in a WPF window (where the Handles clause sacrifices some capabilities), there's no difference when dealing with application events.

For example, if you create this event handler to respond to unhandled exceptions:

```
Private Sub Application_DispatcherUnhandledException(ByVal sender As Object, _
  ByVal e As DispatcherUnhandledExceptionEventArgs)

    MessageBox.Show("An unhandled " & e.Exception.GetType().ToString() & _
      " exception was caught and ignored.")
    e.Handled = True
End Sub
```

you can connect to the Application.DispatcherUnhandled event by adding the Handles keyword:

```
Private Sub Application_DispatcherUnhandledException(ByVal sender As Object, _
  ByVal e As DispatcherUnhandledExceptionEventArgs) _
  Handles Me.DispatcherUnhandledException
```

Or you can connect it by adding the DispatcherUnhandledException attribute to the Application tag in the Application.xaml file:

```
<Application x:Class="Application"
    xmlns="http://schemas.microsoft.com/winfx/2006/xaml/presentation"
    xmlns:x="http://schemas.microsoft.com/winfx/2006/xaml"
    StartupUri="Window1.xaml"
    DispatcherUnhandledException="Application_DispatcherUnhandledException"
    >
</Application>
```

Application Tasks

Now that you understand how the Application object fits into a WPF application, you're ready to take a look at how you can apply it to a few common scenarios. In the following sections, you'll consider how you can show a splash screen, process command-line arguments, support interaction between windows, add document tracking, and create a single-instance application.

■ **Note** The following sections work perfectly well for ordinary window-based WPF applications, but don't apply to browser-based WPF applications (XBAPs), which are discussed in Chapter 24. XBAPs have a built-in browser splash screen, can't receive command-line arguments, don't use multiple windows, and don't make sense as single-instance applications.

Showing a Splash Screen

As fast as they are, WPF applications don't start instantaneously. When you first fire up an application, there's a delay while the common language runtime (CLR) initializes the .NET environment and then starts your application.

This delay isn't necessarily a problem. Ordinarily, this small span of time passes, and then your first window appears. But if you have more time-consuming initialization steps to take care of, or if you just want the professional polish of showing an opening graphic, you can use WPF's simple splash-screen feature.

Here's how to add a splash screen:

1. Add an image file to your project. (Typically, this is a .bmp, .png, or .jpg.)

2. Select the file in the Solution Explorer.

3. Change the Build Action to SplashScreen.

The next time you run your application, this graphic will be shown immediately, in the center of the screen. Once the runtime environment is ready, and after the Application_Startup method has finished, your application's first window appears, and the splash-screen graphic fades away quickly (in about 300 milliseconds).

This feature sounds straightforward, and it is. Just remember that the splash screen is shown without any adornments. No window border is drawn around it, so it's up to you to make sure that's a part of your splash-screen graphic. There's also no way to get fancy with a splash-screen graphic by showing a sequence of multiple images or an animation. If you want that, you need to take the traditional approach: create a startup window that runs your initialization code while showing the graphical display you want.

Incidentally, when you add a splash screen, the WPF compiler adds code like this to the automatically generated Application.g.vb file:

```
Dim splashScreen As New SplashScreen("splashScreenImage.png")

' Show the splash screen.
' The true parameter sets the splashScreen to fade away automatically
' after the first window appears.
splashScreen.Show(True)

' Start the application.
Dim app As New MyApplication.App()
app.InitializeComponent()
app.Run()
' The splash screen begins its automatic fade-out now.
```

You could write this sort of logic yourself instead of using the SplashScreen build action. But there's little point, as the only detail you can change is the speed with which the splash screen fades. To do that, you pass False to the SpashScreen.Show() method (so WPF won't fade it automatically). It's then up to you to hide the splash screen at the appropriate time by calling SplashScreen.Close() and supplying a TimeSpan that indicates how long the fadeout should take.

Handling Command-Line Arguments

To process command-line arguments, you react to the Application.Startup event. The arguments are provided as an array of strings through the StartupEventArgs.Args property.

For example, imagine you want to load a document when its name is passed as a command-line argument. In this case, it makes sense to read the command-line arguments and perform the extra initialization you need. The following example implements this pattern by responding to the Application.Startup event. It doesn't set the Application.StartupUri property at any point; instead, the main window is instantiated by using code.

```
Public Class Application

    Private Sub Application_Startup(ByVal sender As Object, _
      ByVal e As System.Windows.StartupEventArgs) Handles Me.Startup
```

```
        ' Create, but don't show the main window.
        Dim win As New FileViewer()

        If e.Args.Length > 0 Then
            Dim file As String = e.Args(0)
            If System.IO.File.Exists(file) Then
                ' Configure the main window.
                win.LoadFile(file)
            End If
        Else
            ' (Perform alternate initialization here when
            '  no command-line arguments are supplied.)
        End If

        ' This window will automatically be set as the Application.MainWindow.
        win.Show()
    End Sub

End Class
```

This method initializes the main window, which is then shown when the Application_Startup()method ends. This code assumes that the FileViewer class has a public method (that you've added) named LoadFile(). Here's one possible example, which simply reads (and displays) the text in the file you've identified:

```
Public Class FileViewer

    ...

    Public Sub LoadFile(ByVal path As String)
        Me.Content = File.ReadAllText(path)
        Me.Title = path
    End Sub
End Class
```

You can try an example of this technique with the sample code for this chapter.

■ **Note**   At first glance, the code in the LoadFile() method looks a little strange. It sets the Content property of the current Window, which determines what the window displays in its client area. Interestingly enough, WPF windows are actually a type of content control (meaning they derive from the ContentControl class). As a result, they can contain (and display) a single object. It's up to you whether that object is a string, a control, or (more usefully) a panel that can host multiple controls.

Accessing the Current Application

You can get the current application instance from anywhere in your application by using the shared Application. Current property. This allows rudimentary interaction between windows, because any window can get access to the current Application object, and through that, obtain a reference to the main window.

```
Dim main As Window = Application.Current.MainWindow
MessageBox.Show("The main window is " & main.Title)
```

Of course, if you want to access any methods, properties, or events that you've added to your custom main window class, you need to cast the window object to the right type. If the main window is an instance of a custom MainWindow class, you can use code like this:

```
Dim main As MainWindow = CType(Application.Current.MainWindow, MainWindow)
main.DoSomething()
```

A window can also examine the contents of the Application.Windows collection, which provides references to *all* the currently open windows:

```
For Each window As Window In Application.Current.Windows
    MessageBox.Show(window.Title & " is open.")
Next
```

In practice, most applications prefer to use a more structured form of interaction between windows. If you have several long-running windows that are open at the same time and they need to communicate in some way, it makes more sense to hold references to these windows in a custom application class. That way, you can always find the exact window you need. Similarly, if you have a document-based application, you might choose to create a collection that tracks document windows but nothing else. The next section considers this technique.

▪ **Note** Windows (including the main window) are added to the Windows collection as they're shown, and they're removed when they're closed. For this reason, the position of windows in the collection may change, and you can't assume you'll find a specific window object at a specific position.

Interacting Between Windows

As you've seen, the custom application class is a great place to put code that reacts to different application events. There's one other purpose that an Application class can fill quite nicely: storing references to important windows so one window can access another.

▪ **Tip** This technique makes sense when you have a modeless window that lives for a long period of time and might be accessed in various classes (not just the class that created it). If you're simply showing a modal dialog box as part of your application, this technique is overkill. In this situation, the window won't exist for very long, and the code that creates the window is the only code that needs to access it. (To brush up on the difference between modal windows, which interrupt application flow until they're closed, and modeless windows, which don't, refer to Chapter 23.)

For example, imagine you want to keep track of all the document windows that your application uses. To that end, you might create a dedicated collection in your custom application class. Here's an example that uses a generic

List collection to hold a group of custom window objects. In this example, each document window is represented by an instance of a class named Document:

```
Public Class ApplicationCore

    Private _documents As New List(Of Document)()

    Public Property Documents() As List(Of Document)
        Get
            Return _documents
        End Get
        Set(ByVal value As List(Of Document))
            _documents = value
        End Set
    End Property
End Class
```

Notice that the application class has been named ApplicationCore instead of the standard Application, which avoids confusion with the System.Windows.Application base class.

Now, when you create a new document, you simply need to remember to add it to the Documents collection. Here's an event handler that responds to a button click and does the deed:

```
Private Sub cmdCreate_Click(ByVal sender As Object, ByVal e As RoutedEventArgs)
    Dim doc As New Document()
    doc.Owner = Me
    doc.Show()
    CType(Application.Current, ApplicationCore).Documents.Add(doc)
End Sub
```

Alternatively, you could respond to an event such as Window.Loaded in the Document class to make sure the document object always registers itself in the Documents collection when it's created.

■ **Note** This code also sets the Window.Owner property so that all the document windows are displayed on top of the main window that creates them. You'll learn more about the Owner property when you consider windows in detail in Chapter 23.

Now you can use that collection elsewhere in your code to loop over all the documents and use public members. In this case, the Document class includes a custom SetContent() method that updates its display:

```
Private Sub cmdUpdate_Click(ByVal sender As Object, ByVal e As RoutedEventArgs)
    Dim app As ApplicationCore = CType(Application.Current, ApplicationCore)
    For Each doc As Document In app.Documents
        doc.SetContent("Refreshed at " & DateTime.Now.ToLongTimeString() & ".")
    Next
End Sub
```

Figure 7-1 demonstrates this application. The actual end result isn't terribly impressive, but the interaction is worth noting. This is a safe, disciplined way for your windows to interact through a custom application class. It's superior to using the Windows property, because it's strongly typed, and it holds only Document windows (not a collection of all the windows in your application). It also gives you the ability to categorize the windows in another, more useful way—for example, in a Dictionary collection with a key name for easy lookup. In a document-based application, you might choose to index windows in a collection by file name.

Figure 7-1. *Allowing windows to interact*

■ **Note** When interacting between windows, don't forget your object-oriented smarts. Always use a layer of custom methods, properties, and events that you've added to the window classes. Never expose the fields or controls of a form to other parts of your code. If you do, you'll quickly wind up with a tightly coupled interface where one window reaches deep into the inner workings of another, and you won't be able to enhance either class without breaking the murky interdependencies between them.

Single-Instance Applications

Ordinarily, you can launch as many copies of a WPF application as you want. In some scenarios, this design makes perfect sense. However, in other cases it's a problem, particularly when building document-based applications.

For example, consider Microsoft Word. No matter how many documents you open (or how you open them), only a single instance of winword.exe is loaded at a time. As you open new documents, they appear in the new windows, but a single application remains in control of all the document windows. This design is the best approach if you want to reduce the overhead of your application, centralize certain features (for example, create a single print queue manager), or integrate disparate windows (for example, offer a feature that tiles all the currently open document windows next to each other).

WPF doesn't provide a native solution for single-instance applications, but you can use several workarounds. The basic technique is to check whether another instance of your application is already running when the Application. Startup event fires. The simplest way to do this is to use a systemwide *mutex* (a synchronization object provided by the operating system that allows for interprocess communication). This approach is simple but limited. Most significantly, there's no way for the new instance of an application to communicate with the existing instance. This is a problem in a document-based application, because the new instance may need to tell the existing instance to open a specific document if it's passed on the command line. (For example, when you double-click a .doc file in Windows Explorer and Word is already running, you expect Word to load the requested file.) This communication is more complex, and it's usually performed through remoting or Windows Communication Foundation (WCF). A proper implementation needs to include a way to discover the remoting server and use it to transfer command-line arguments.

But the simplest approach, and the one that's currently recommended by the WPF team, is to use the built-in support that's provided in Windows Forms and tailored to Visual Basic applications. This approach handles the messy plumbing behind the scenes.

So, how can you use a feature that's designed for Windows Forms to manage a WPF application? Essentially, the old-style application class acts as a wrapper for your WPF application class. When your application is launched, you'll create the old-style application class, which will then create the WPF application class. The old-style application class handles the instance management, while the WPF application class handles the real application. Figure 7-2 shows how these parts interact.

Figure 7-2. *Wrapping the WPF application with a WindowsFormsApplicationBase*

Creating the Single-Instance Application Wrapper

The first step to use this approach is to derive a custom class from the Microsoft.VisualBasic.ApplicationServices. WindowsFormsApplicationBase class. This class provides three important members that you use for instance management:

- The IsSingleInstance property enables a single-instance application. You set this property to True in the constructor.

- The OnStartup() method is triggered when the application starts. You override this method and create the WPF application object at this point.

■ **Note** Ordinarily, all applications that derive from WindowsFormsApplicationBase designate a main form. However, your application uses the WPF model, so it won't include any forms. To prevent an error, you must replace the default startup logic by overriding OnStartup(). It's not enough to simply handle the Startup event.

- The StartupNextInstance event is fired when another instance of the application starts up. This event provides access to the command-line arguments. At this point, you'll probably call a method in your WPF application class to show a new window but not create another application object.

Here's the code for the custom class that's derived from WindowsFormsApplicationBase:

```
Public Class SingleInstanceApplicationWrapper
    Inherits
    Microsoft.VisualBasic.ApplicationServices.WindowsFormsApplicationBase

    Public Sub New()
        ' Enable single-instance mode.
        Me.IsSingleInstance = True
    End Sub

    ' Create the WPF application class.
    Private app As WpfApp

    Protected Overrides Function OnStartup(ByVal eventArgs As
        Microsoft.VisualBasic.ApplicationServices.StartupEventArgs) As Boolean
        app = New WpfApp()
        app.Run()

        Return False
    End Function

    ' Direct multiple instances
    Private Sub StartupNextInstance(ByVal sender As Object, ByVal e As
        Microsoft.VisualBasic.ApplicationServices.StartupNextInstanceEventArgs)
        Handles Me.StartupNextInstance
        If e.CommandLine.Count > 0 Then
            app.ShowDocument(e.CommandLine(0))
        End If
    End Sub

End Class
```

When the application starts, this class creates an instance of WpfApp, which is a custom WPF application class (a class that derives from System.Windows.Application). The WpfApp class includes some startup logic that shows a main window, along with a custom ShowDocument() window that loads a document window for a given file. Every time a file name is passed to SingleInstanceApplicationWrapper through the command line, SingleInstanceApplicationWrapper calls WpfApp.ShowDocument().

Here's the code for the WpfApp class:

```
Public Class WpfApp
    Inherits System.Windows.Application

    Private Sub Application_Startup(ByVal sender As Object,
        ByVal e As System.Windows.StartupEventArgs)
        Handles Me.Startup
```

```
    ' Load the main window.
    Dim list As New DocumentList()
    Me.MainWindow = list
    list.Show()

    ' Load the document that was specified as an argument.
    If e.Args.Length > 0 Then
        ShowDocument(e.Args(0))
    End If
End Sub

Public Sub ShowDocument(ByVal filename As String)
    Try
        Dim doc As New Document()
        Dim docRef As New DocumentReference(doc, filename)
        doc.LoadFile(docRef)
        doc.Owner = Me.MainWindow
        doc.Show()
        doc.Activate()
    Catch
        MessageBox.Show("Could not load document.")
    End Try
End Sub

End Class
```

The only missing detail now (aside from the DocumentList and Document windows) is the entry point for the application. Because the application needs to create the SingleInstanceApplicationWrapper class before the App class, the application must start with a traditional Main() method, rather than an Application.xaml file. Here's the code you need:

```
Public Class Startup
    Public Shared Sub Main(ByVal args As String())
        Dim wrapper As New SingleInstanceApplicationWrapper()
        wrapper.Run(args)
    End Sub
End Class
```

These three classes—SingleInstanceApplicationWrapper, WpfApp, and Startup—form the basis for a single-instance WPF application. Using this bare-bones model, it's possible to create a more sophisticated example. For example, the downloadable code for this chapter modifies the WpfApp class so it maintains a list of open documents (as demonstrated earlier). Using WPF data binding with a list (a feature described in Chapter 19), the DocumentList window displays the currently open documents. Figure 7-3 shows an example with three open documents.

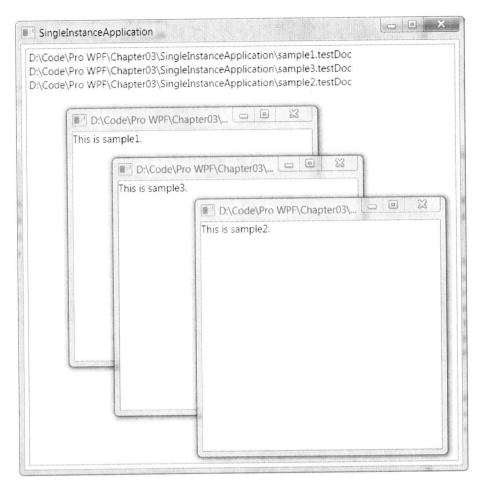

Figure 7-3. *A single-instance application with a central window*

■ **Note**   Single-instance application support will eventually make its way to WPF in a future version. For now, this workaround provides the same functionality with only a little more work required.

Registering the File Type

To test the single-instance application, you need to register its file extension (.testDoc) with Windows and associate it with your application. That way, when you click a .testDoc file, your application will start up immediately.

One way to create this file-type registration is by hand, using Windows Explorer:

1. Right-click a .testDoc file and choose Open With ➤ Choose Default Program.

2. In the Open With dialog box, click Browse, find your application's .exe file, and double-click it.

3. If you don't want to make your application the default handler for this file type, make sure the option "Always use the selected program to open this type of file" isn't selected in the Open With dialog box. In this case, you won't be able to launch your application by double-clicking the file. However, you will be able to open it by right-clicking the file, choosing Open With, and selecting your application from the list.

4. Click OK.

The other way to create the file-type registration is to run some code that edits the registry. The SingleInstanceApplication example includes a FileRegistrationHelper class that does exactly that:

```
Dim extension As String = ".testDoc"
Dim title As String = "SingleInstanceApplication"
Dim extensionDescription As String = "A Test Document"
FileRegistrationHelper.SetFileAssociation( _
  extension, title & "." & extensionDescription)
```

The FileRegistrationHelper registers the .testDoc file extension by using the classes in the Microsoft.Win32 namespace. To see the full code, refer to the downloadable examples for this chapter.

The registration process needs to be executed just once. After the registration is in place, every time you double-click a file with the extension .testDoc, the SingleInstanceApplication is started, and the file is passed as a command-line argument. If the SingleInstanceApplication is already running, the SingleInstanceApplicationWrapper. StartupNextInstance event is triggered, and the new document is loaded by the existing application.

▓ **Tip** When creating a document-based application with a registered file type, you may be interested in using the jump list feature (which is available in Windows 7 or Windows 8). To learn more about this feature, see Chapter 23.

WINDOWS AND UAC

File registration is a task that's usually performed by a setup program. One problem with including it in your application code is that it requires elevated permissions that the user running the application might not have. In fact, even if the user *does* has these privileges, the Windows User Account Control (UAC) feature will still prevent your code from accessing them.

To understand why, you need to realize that in the eyes of UAC, all applications have one of three *run levels*:

asInvoker. The application inherits the process token of the parent process (the process that launched it). The application won't get administrator privileges unless the user specifically requests them, even if the user is logged on as an administrator. This is the default.

requireAdministrator. If the current user is a member of the Administrators group, a UAC confirmation dialog box appears. After the user accepts this confirmation, the application gets administrator privileges. If the user is not a member of the Administrators group, a dialog box appears, enabling the user to enter the username and password of an account that does have administrator privileges.

highestAvailable: The application gets the highest privileges according to its group membership. For example, if the current user is a member of the Administrators group, the application gets administrator privileges (after the user accepts the UAC confirmation). The advantage of this run level is that the application will still run if administrator privileges aren't available, unlike requireAdministrator.

Ordinarily, your application runs with the asInvoker run level. To request administrator privileges, you must right-click the application EXE file and choose Run As Administrator when you start it. To get administrator privileges when testing your application in Visual Studio, you must right-click the Visual Studio shortcut and choose Run As Administrator.

If your application needs administrator privileges, you can choose to require them with the requireAdministrator run level or request them with the highestAvailable run level. Either way, you need to create a *manifest*, which is a file with a block of XML that will be embedded in your compiled assembly. To edit the manifest for your application, double-click the My Project node. On the Application tab, click the View UAC Settings button.

The content of the manifest file is a relatively simple block of XML:

```xml
<?xml version="1.0" encoding="utf-8"?>
<asmv1:assembly manifestVersion="1.0"
 xmlns="urn:schemas-microsoft-com:asm.v1"
 xmlns:asmv1="urn:schemas-microsoft-com:asm.v1"
 xmlns:asmv2="urn:schemas-microsoft-com:asm.v2">
  <assemblyIdentity version="1.0.0.0" name="MyApplication.app"/>
  <trustInfo>
    <security>
      <requestedPrivileges>
        <requestedExecutionLevel level="asInvoker" />
      </requestedPrivileges>
    </security>
  </trustInfo>
</asmv1:assembly>
```

To change the run level, simply modify the level attribute of the <requestedExecutionLevel> element. Valid values are asInvoker, requireAdministrator, and highestAvailable.

In some cases, you might want to request administrator privileges in specific scenarios. In the file registration example, you might choose to request administrator privileges only when the application is run for the first time and needs to create the registration. This allows you to avoid unnecessary UAC warnings. The easiest way to implement this pattern is to put the code that requires higher privileges in a separate executable, which you can then call when necessary.

Assembly Resources

Assembly resources in a WPF application work in essentially the same way as assembly resources in other .NET applications. The basic concept is that you add a file to your project, so that Visual Studio can embed it into your compiled application's EXE or DLL file. The key difference between WPF assembly resources and those in other applications is the addressing system that you use to refer to them.

▓ **Note**   Assembly resources are also known as *binary resources* because they're embedded in compiled assembly as an opaque blob of binary data.

You've already seen assembly resources at work in Chapter 2. That's because every time you compile your application, each XAML file in your project is converted to a BAML file that's more efficient to parse. These BAML files are embedded in your assembly as individual resources. It's just as easy to add your own resources.

Adding Resources

You can add your own resources by adding a file to your project and setting its Build Action property (in the Properties window) to Resource. Here's the good news: that's all you need to do.

For better organization, you can create subfolders in your project (right-click the Solution Explorer and choose Add New ➤ Folder) and use these to organize different types of resources. In the example in Figure 7-4, several image resources are grouped in a folder named Images, and two audio fields appear in a folder named Sounds.

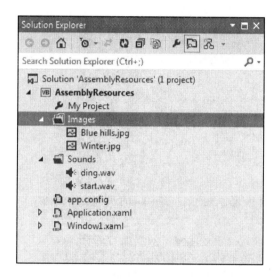

Figure 7-4. *An application with assembly resources*

Resources that you add in this way are easy to update. All you need to do is replace the file and recompile your application. For example, if you create the project shown in Figure 7-4, you could copy all new files to the Images folder by using Windows Explorer. As long as you're replacing the contents of files that are included in your project, you don't need to take any special step in Visual Studio (aside from actually compiling your application).

There are a couple of things that you must *not* do in order to use assembly resources successfully:

- Don't make the mistake of setting the Build Action property to Embedded Resource. Even though all assembly resources are embedded resources by definition, the Embedded Resource build action places the binary data in another area where it's more difficult to access. In WPF applications, it's assumed that you always use a build type of Resource.

- Don't use the Resources tab in the Project Properties window. WPF does not support this type of resource URI.

Curious programmers naturally want to know what happens to the resources they embed in their assemblies. WPF merges them all into a single stream (along with BAML resources). This single resource stream is named in this format: *AssemblyName*.g.resources. In Figure 7-5, the application is named AssemblyResources and the resource stream is named AssemblyResources.g.resources.

Figure 7-5. *Assembly resources in .NET Reflector*

If you want to actually *see* the embedded resources in a compiled assembly, you can use a disassembler. Unfortunately, the .NET staple—ildasm—doesn't have this feature. However, you can use a more elegant tool such as Reflector (http://reflector.net) to dig into your resources. Figure 7-5 shows the resources for the project shown in Figure 7-4, using Reflector.

You'll see the BAML resource for the only window in the application, along with all the images and audio files. The spaces in the file names don't cause a problem in WPF, because Visual Studio is intelligent enough to escape them properly. You'll also notice that the file names are changed to lowercase when your application is compiled.

Retrieving Resources

Adding resources is clearly easy enough, but how do you actually *use* them? There's more than one approach that you can use.

The low-level choice is to retrieve a StreamResourceInfo object that wraps your data, and then decide what to do with it. You can do this through code, using the shared Application.GetResourceStream() method.

For example, here's the code that gets the StreamResourceInfo object for the winter.jpg image:

```
Dim sri As StreamResourceInfo = Application.GetResourceStream( _
  New Uri("images/winter.jpg", UriKind.Relative))
```

Once you have a StreamResourceInfo object, you can get two pieces of information. The ContentType property returns a string describing the type of data—in this example, it's image/jpg. The Stream property returns an UnmanagedMemoryStream object, which you can use to read the data, one byte at a time.

The GetResourceStream() method is really just a helper method that wraps a ResourceManager and ResourceSet classes. These classes are a core part of the .NET Framework resource system, and they've existed since version 1.0. Without the GetResourceStream() method, you would need to specifically access the AssemblyName.g.resources resource stream (which is where all WPF resources are stored) and search for the object you want. Here's the far uglier code that does the trick:

```
Dim asm As System.Reflection.Assembly
asm = System.Reflection.Assembly.GetAssembly(Me.GetType())

Dim resourceName As string = asm.GetName().Name & ".g"
Dim rm As New ResourceManager(resourceName, asm)

Using resSet As ResourceSet = _
  rm.GetResourceSet(CultureInfo.CurrentCulture, True, True)

    ' The second parameter of the GetObject() method is set to True,
    ' which performs a case-insensitive resource lookup.
    Dim obj As Object = resSet.GetObject("images/winter.jpg", True)
    Dim s As UnmanagedMemoryStream = CType(obj, UnmanagedMemoryStream)
    ...
End Using
```

The ResourceManager and ResourceSet classes also allow you to do a few things you can't do with the Application class alone. For example, the following snippet of code shows you the name of all the embedded resources in the AssemblyName.g.resources stream:

```
Dim asm As System.Reflection.Assembly
asm = System.Reflection.Assembly.GetAssembly(Me.GetType())

Dim resourceName As string = asm.GetName().Name & ".g"
Dim rm As New ResourceManager(resourceName, asm)

Using resSet As ResourceSet = _
  rm.GetResourceSet(CultureInfo.CurrentCulture, True, True)
    For Each res As DictionaryEntry In resSet
        MessageBox.Show(res.Key.ToString())
    Next
End Using
```

Resource-Aware Classes

Even with the help of the GetResourceStream() method, you're unlikely to bother retrieving a resource directly. The problem is that this approach gets you a relatively low-level UnmanagedMemoryStream object, which isn't much use on its own. Instead, you'll want to translate the data into something more meaningful, such as a higher-level object with properties and methods.

WPF provides a few classes that work with resources natively. Rather than forcing you to do the work of resource extraction (which is messy and not typesafe), they take the name of the resource you want to use. For example, if you want to show the Blue hills.jpg image in the WPF Image element, you could use this markup:

```
<Image Source="Images/Blue hills.jpg"></Image>
```

Notice that the backslash becomes a forward slash because that's the convention WPF uses with its URIs. (It works *both* ways, but the forward slash is recommended for consistency.)

You can perform the same trick in code. In the case of an Image element, you simply need to set the Source property with a BitmapImage object that identifies the location of the image you want to display as a URI. You could specify a fully qualified file path like this:

```
img.Source = New BitmapImage(New Uri("d:\Photo\Backgrounds\arch.jpg"))
```

But if you use a relative URI, you can pull a different resource out of the assembly and pass it to the image, with no UnmanagedMemoryStream object required:

```
img.Source = New BitmapImage(New Uri("images/winter.jpg", UriKind.Relative))
```

This technique constructs a URI that consists of the base application URI with images/winter.jpg added on the end. Most of the time, you don't need to think about this URI syntax—as long as you stick to relative URIs, it all works seamlessly. However, in some cases it's important to understand the URI system in a bit more detail, particularly if you want to access a resource that's embedded in another assembly. The following section digs into WPF's URI syntax.

Pack URIs

WPF lets you address compiled resources (such as the BAML for a page) by using the *pack URI* syntax. The Image and tag in the previous section referenced a resource by using a relative URI, like this:

```
images/winter.jpg
```

This is equivalent to the more cumbersome absolute URI shown here:

```
pack://application:,,,/images/winter.jpg
```

You can use this absolute URI when setting the source of an image, although it doesn't provide any advantage:

```
img.Source = New BitmapImage( _
  New Uri("pack://application:,,,/images/winter.jpg"))
```

■ **Tip** When using an absolute URI, you can use a file path, a UNC path to a network share, a website URL, or a pack URI that points to an assembly resource. Just be aware that if your application can't retrieve the resource from the expected location, an exception will occur. If you've set the URI in XAML, the exception will happen when the page is being created.

The pack URI syntax is borrowed from the XML Paper Specification (XPS) standard. The reason it looks so strange is that it embeds one URI inside another. The three commas are actually three escaped slashes. In other words, the pack URI shown previously contains an application URI that starts with application:///.

Resources in Other Assemblies

Pack URIs also allow you to retrieve resources that are embedded in another library (in other words, in a DLL assembly that your application uses). In this case, you need to use the following syntax:

```
pack://application:,,,/AssemblyName;component/ResourceName
```

For example, if your image is embedded in a referenced assembly named ImageLibrary, you would use a URI like this:

```
img.Source = New BitmapImage( _
  New Uri("pack://application:,,,/ImageLibrary;component/images/winter.jpg"))
```

Or, more practically, you would use the equivalent relative URI:

```
img.Source = New BitmapImage( _
  New Uri("ImageLibrary;component/images/winter.jpg", UriKind.Relative))
```

If you're using a strong-named assembly, you can replace the assembly name with a qualified assembly reference that includes the version, the public key token, or both. You separate each piece of information by using a semicolon and precede the version number with the letter v. Here's an example with just a version number:

```
img.Source = New BitmapImage( _
  New Uri("ImageLibrary;v1.25;component/images/winter.jpg", _
  UriKind.Relative))
```

And here's an example with both the version number and the public-key token:

```
img.Source = New BitmapImage( _
  New Uri("ImageLibrary;v1.25;dc642a7f5bd64912;component/images/winter.jpg", _
  UriKind.Relative))
```

Content Files

When you embed a file as a resource, you place it into the compiled assembly and ensure it's always available. This is an ideal choice for deployment, and it side-steps possible problems. However, there are some situations where it isn't practical:

- You want to change the resource file without recompiling the application.
- The resource file is very large.
- The resource file is optional and may not be deployed with the assembly.
- The resource is a sound file.

> ■ **Note** As you'll discover in Chapter 26, the WPF sound classes don't support assembly resources. As a result, there's no way to pull an audio file out of a resource stream and play it—at least not without saving it first. This is a limitation of the underlying bits of technology on which these classes are based (namely, the Win32 API and Media Player).

Obviously, you can deal with this issue by deploying the files with your application and adding code to your application to read these files from the hard drive. However, WPF has a convenient option that can make this process easier to manage. You can specifically mark these noncompiled files as *content* files.

Content files won't be embedded in your assembly. However, WPF adds an AssemblyAssociatedContentFile attribute to your assembly that advertises the existence of each content file. This attribute also records the location of each content file relative to your executable file (indicating whether the content file is in the same folder as the executable file or in a subfolder). Best of all, you can use the same URI system to use content files with resource-aware elements such as the Image class.

To try this out, add a sound file to your project, select it in the Solution Explorer, and change the Build Action in the Properties window to Content. Make sure that the Copy to Output Directory setting is set to Copy Always, so that the sound file is copied to the output directory when you build your project.

Now you can use a relative URI to point a MediaElement to your content file:

```
<MediaElement Name="Sound" Source="Sounds/start.wav"
  LoadedBehavior="Manual"></MediaElement>
```

To see an application that uses both application resources and content files, check out the downloadable code for this chapter.

Localization

Assembly resources also come in handy when you need to localize a window. Using resources, you allow controls to change according to the current culture settings of the Windows operating system. This is particularly useful with text labels and images that need to be translated into different languages.

In some frameworks, localization is performed by providing multiple copies of user-interface details such as string tables and images. In WPF, localization isn't this fine-grained. Instead, the unit of localization is the XAML file (technically, the compiled BAML resource that's embedded in your application). If you want to support three languages, you need to include three BAML resources. WPF chooses the correct one based on the current culture on the computer that's executing the application. (Technically, WPF bases its decision on the CurrentUICulture property of the thread that's hosting the user interface.)

Of course, this process wouldn't make much sense if you need to create (and deploy) an all-in-one assembly with *all* the localized resources. This wouldn't be much better than creating separate versions of your application for every language, because you would need to rebuild your entire application every time you wanted to add support for a new culture (or if you needed to tweak the text in one of the existing resources). Fortunately, .NET solves this problem by using *satellite assemblies*, which are assemblies that work with your application but are stored in separate subfolders. When you create a localized WPF application, you place each localized BAML resource in a separate satellite assembly. To allow your application to use this assembly, you place it in a subfolder under the main application folder, such as fr-FR for French (France). Your application can then bind to this satellite assembly automatically using a technique called *probing*, which has been a part of the .NET Framework since version 1.0.

The challenge in localizing an application is in the workflow—in other words, how do you pull your XAML files out of your project, get them localized, compile them into satellite assemblies, and then bring them back to your application? This is the shakiest part of the localization story in WPF, because tools such as Visual Studio don't have built-in design support for localization. That means you'll need to do a bit more work, and you may want to create your own localization tools.

Building Localizable User Interfaces

Before you begin to translate anything, you need to consider how your application will respond to changing content. For example, if you double the length of all the text in your user interface, how will the overall layout of your window be adjusted? If you've built a truly adaptable layout (as described in Chapter 3), you shouldn't have a problem. Your interface should be able to adjust itself to fit dynamic content. Some good practices that suggest you're on the right track include the following:

- Not using hard-coded widths or heights (or at least not using them with elements that contain nonscrollable text content)

- Setting the Window.SizeToContent property to Width, Height, or WidthAndHeight so it can grow as needed (not always required, depending on the structure of your window, but sometimes useful)

- Using the ScrollViewer to wrap large amounts of text

OTHER CONSIDERATIONS FOR LOCALIZATION

Depending on the languages in which you want to localize your application, there are other considerations that you might need to take into account. Although a discussion of user interface layout in different languages is beyond the scope of this book, here are a couple issues to consider:

- If you want to localize your application into a language that has a dramatically different character set, you'll need to use a different font. You can do this by localizing the FontFamily property in your user interface, or you can use a composite font such as Global User Interface, Global Sans Serif, or Global Serif, which support all languages.

- You may also need to think about how your layout works in a right-to-left layout (rather than the standard English left-to-right layout). For example, Arabic and Hebrew use a right-to-left layout. You can control this behavior by setting the FlowDirection property on each page or window in your application. For more information about right-to-left layouts, see the Bidirectional Features topic in the MSDN help (http://tinyurl.com/cx5ynbl).

Localization is a complex topic. WPF has a solution that's workable, but it's not fully mature. After you've learned the basics, you may want to take a look at Microsoft's slightly dated, but still useful, 66-page WPF localization white paper, which is available at http://wpflocalization.codeplex.com along with sample code.

Preparing an Application for Localization

The next step is to switch on localization support for your project. This takes just one change—add the following element to the .vbproj file for your project anywhere in the first <PropertyGroup> element:

```
<UICulture>en-US</UICulture>
```

This tells the compiler that the default culture for your application is US English (obviously, you could choose something else if that's appropriate). Once you make this change, the build process changes. The next time you compile your application, you'll end up with a subfolder named en-US. Inside that folder is a satellite assembly with the same name as your application and the extension .resources.dll (for example, LocalizableApplication.resources.dll). This assembly contains all the compiled BAML resources for your application, which were previously stored in your main application assembly.

UNDERSTANDING CULTURES

Technically, you don't localize an application for a specific language but for a *culture*, which takes into account regional variation. Cultures are identified by two identifiers separated by a hyphen. The first portion identifies the language. The second portion identifies the country. Thus, fr-CA is French as spoken in Canada, while fr-FR represents French in France. For a full list of culture names and their two-part identifiers, refer to the System. Globalization.CultureInfo class in the MSDN help (http://tinyurl.com/cuyhe6p).

This presumes a fine-grained localization that might be more than you need. Fortunately, you can localize an application based just on a language. For example, if you want to define settings that will be used for any French-language region, you could use fr for your culture. This works as long as there isn't a more specific culture available that matches the current computer exactly.

Now, when you run this application, the CLR automatically looks for satellite assemblies in the correct directory, based on the computer's regional settings, and loads the correct localized resource. For example, if you're running in the fr-FR culture, the CLR will look for an fr-FR subdirectory and use the satellite assemblies it finds there. So, if you want to add support for more cultures to a localized application, you simply need to add more subfolders and satellite assemblies without disturbing the original application executable.

When the CLR begins probing for a satellite assembly, it follows a few simple rules of precedence:

1. It checks for the most specific directory that's available. That means it looks for a satellite assembly that's targeted for the current language and region (such as fr-FR).

2. If it can't find this directory, it looks for a satellite assembly that's targeted for the current language (such as fr).

3. If it can't find this directory, an IOException exception is thrown.

This list is slightly simplified. If you decide to use the Global Assembly Cache (GAC) to share some components over the entire computer, you'll need to realize that .NET actually checks the GAC at the beginning of step 1 and step 2. In other words, in step 1, the CLR checks whether the language- and region-specific version of the assembly is in the GAC and uses it if it is. The same is true for step 2.

Managing the Translation Process

Now you have all the infrastructure you need for localization. All you need to do is create the appropriate satellite assemblies with the alternate versions of your windows (in BAML form) and put these assemblies in the correct folders. Doing this by hand would obviously be a lot of work. Furthermore, localization usually involves a third-party translation service that needs to work with your original text. Obviously, it's too much to expect that your translators will be skilled programmers who can find their way around a Visual Studio project (and you're unlikely to trust them with the code anyway). For all these reasons, you need a way to manage the localization process.

Currently, WPF has a partial solution. It works, but it requires a few trips to the command line, and one piece isn't finalized. The basic process works like this:

1. You flag the elements in your application that need to be localized. Optionally, you may add comments to help the translator.

2. You extract the localizable details to a .csv file (a comma-separated text file) and send it off to your translation service.

3. After you receive the translated version of this file, you run LocBaml again to generate the satellite assembly you need.

You'll follow these steps in the following sections.

Preparing Markup Elements for Localization

The first step is to add a specialized Uid attribute to all the elements you want to localize. Here's an example:

```
<Button x:Uid="Button_1" Margin="10" Padding="3">A button</Button>
```

The Uid attribute plays a role similar to that of the Name attribute—it uniquely identifies a button in the context of a single XAML document. That way, you can specify localized text for just this button. However, there are a few reasons why WPF uses a Uid instead of just reusing the Name value: the name might not be assigned, it might be set according to different conventions and used in code, and so on. In fact, the Name property is itself a localizable piece of information.

■ **Note** Obviously, text isn't the only detail you need to localize. You also need to think about fonts, font sizes, margins, padding, other alignment-related details, and so on. In WPF, every property that may need to be localized is decorated with the System.Windows.LocalizabilityAttribute.

Although you don't need to, you should add the Uid to *every* element in every window of a localizable application. This could add up to a lot of extra work, but the MSBuild tool can do it automatically. Use it like this:

```
msbuild /t:updateuid LocalizableApplication.vbproj
```

This assumes you wish to add Uids to an application named LocalizableApplication.

And if you want to check whether your elements all have Uids (and make sure you haven't accidentally duplicated one), you can use MSBuild like this:

```
msbuild /t:checkuid LocalizableApplication.vbproj
```

■ **Tip** The easiest way to run MSBuild is to launch the Visual Studio Command Prompt (Start ➤ All ➤ Programs ➤ Microsoft Visual Studio 2012 ➤ Visual Studio Tools ➤ Developer Command Prompt for VS2012) so that the path is set to give you easy access. Then you can quickly move to your project folder to run MSBuild.

When you generate Uids by using MSBuild, your Uids are set to match the name of the corresponding control. Here's an example:

```
<Button x:Uid="cmdDoSomething" Name="cmdDoSomething"  Margin="10" Padding="3">
```

If your element doesn't have a name, MSBuild creates a less helpful Uid based on the class name, with a numeric suffix:

```
<TextBlock x:Uid="TextBlock_1" Margin="10">
```

■ **Note** Technically, this step is how you globalize an application—in other words, prepare it for localization into different languages. Even if you don't plan to localize your application right away, there's an argument to be made that you should prepare it for localization anyway. If you do, you may be able to update your application to a different language simply by deploying a satellite assembly. Of course, globalization is not worth the effort if you haven't taken the time to assess your user interface and make sure it uses an adaptable layout that can accommodate changing content (such as buttons with longer captions, and so on).

Extracting Localizable Content

To extract the localizable content of all your elements, you need to use the LocBaml command-line tool. Currently, LocBaml isn't included as a compiled tool. Instead, the source code is available as a sample at http://tinyurl.com/df3bqg (look for the "LocBaml Tool Sample" link). The LocBaml sample must be compiled by hand.

When using LocBaml, you *must* be in the folder that contains your compiled assembly (for example, LocalizableApplication\bin\Debug). To extract a list of localizable details, you point LocBaml to your satellite assembly and use the /parse parameter, as shown here:

```
locbaml /parse en-US\LocalizableApplication.resources.dll
```

The LocBaml tool searches your satellite assembly for all its compiled BAML resources and generates a .csv file that has the details. In this example, the .csv file will be named LocalizationApplication.resources.csv.

Each line in the extracted file represents a single localizable property that you've used on an element in your XAML document. Each line consists of the following seven values:

- The name of the BAML resource (for example, LocalizableApplication.g.en-US. resources:window1.baml).

- The Uid of the element and the name of the property to localize. Here's an example: StackPanel_1:System.Windows.FrameworkElement.Margin.

- The localization category. This is a value from the LocalizationCategory enumeration that helps to identify the type of content that this property represents (long text, a title, a font, a button caption, a tooltip, and so on).

- Whether the property is readable (essentially, visible as text in the user interface). All readable values always need to be localized; nonreadable values may or may not require localization.

- Whether the property value can be modified by the translator. This value is always True unless you specifically indicate otherwise.

- Additional comments that you've provided for the translator. If you haven't provided comments, this value is blank.

- The value of the property. This is the detail that needs to be localized.

For example, imagine you have the window shown in Figure 7-6. Here's the XAML markup:

```
<Window x:Uid="Window_1" x:Class=" Window1"
    xmlns="http://schemas.microsoft.com/winfx/2006/xaml/presentation"
    xmlns:x="http://schemas.microsoft.com/winfx/2006/xaml"
    Title="LocalizableApplication" Height="300" Width="300"
    SizeToContent="WidthAndHeight"
    >
```

```
<StackPanel x:Uid="StackPanel_1" Margin="10">
  <TextBlock x:Uid="TextBlock_1" Margin="10">One line of text.</TextBlock>
  <Button x:Uid="cmdDoSomething" Name="cmdDoSomething"  Margin="10" Padding="3">
   A button</Button>
  <TextBlock x:Uid="TextBlock_2" Margin="10">
   This is another line of text.</TextBlock>
</StackPanel>
</Window>
```

Figure 7-6. *A window that can be localized*

When you run this through LocBaml, you'll get the information shown in Table 7-3. (For the sake of brevity, the BAML name has been left out, because it's always the same window; the resource key has been shortened so it doesn't use fully qualified names; and the comments, which are blank, have been left out.)

Table 7-3. *A Sample List of Localizable Properties*

Resource Key	Localization Category	Readable	Modifiable	Value
Window_1:LocalizableApplication. Window1.$Content	None	True	True	#StackPanel_1;
Window_1:Window.Title	Title	True	True	LocalizableApplication
Window_1:FrameworkElement.Height	None	False	True	300
Window_1:FrameworkElement.Width	None	False	True	300
Window_1:Window.SizeToContent	None	False	True	WidthAndHeight
StackPanel_1:FrameworkElement.Margin	None	False	True	10
TextBlock_1:TextBlock.$Content	Text	True	True	One line of text
TextBlock_1:FrameworkElement.Margin	None	False	True	10
cmdDoSomething:Button.$Content	Button	True	True	A button
cmdDoSomething:FrameworkElement.Margin	None	False	True	10
cmdDoSomething:Padding	None	False	True	3
TextBlock_2:TextBlock.$Content	Text	True	True	Another line of text
TextBlock_2:FrameworkElement.Margin	None	False	True	10

Here's where the current tool support is a bit limited. It's unlikely that a translation service will want to work directly with the .csv file, because it presents information in a rather awkward way. Instead, another tool is needed that parses this file and allows the translator to review it more efficiently. You could easily build a tool that pulls out all this information, displays the values where Readable and Modifiable are True, and allows the user to edit the corresponding value. However, at the time of this writing, WPF doesn't include such a tool.

To perform a simple test, you can open this file directly (use Notepad or Excel) and modify the last piece of information—the value—to supply translated text instead. Here's an example:

```
LocalizableApplication.g.en-US.resources:window1.baml,
TextBlock_1:System.Windows.Controls.TextBlock.$Content,
Text,True,True,,
Une ligne de texte.
```

■ **Note**   Although this is really a single line of code, it's broken here to fit on the page.

You don't specify which culture you're using at this point. You do that when you compile the new satellite assembly in the next step.

Building a Satellite Assembly

Now you're ready to build the satellite assemblies for other cultures. Once again, the LocBaml tool takes care of this task, but this time, you use the /generate parameter.

Remember that the satellite assembly will contain an alternate copy of each *complete* window as an embedded BAML resource. In order to create these resources, the LocBaml tool needs to take a look at the original satellite assembly, substitute all the new values from the translated .csv file, and then generate a new satellite assembly. That means you need to point LocBaml to the original satellite assembly and (using the /trans: parameter) the translated list of values. You also need to tell LocBaml which culture this assembly represents (using the /cul: parameter). Remember that cultures are defined using two-part identifiers that are listed in the description of the System.Globalization.CultureInfo class.

Here's an example that pulls it all together:

```
locbaml /generate en-US\LocalizableApplication.resources.dll
        /trans:LocalizableApplication.resources.French.csv
        /cul:fr-FR /out:fr-FR
```

This command does the following:

- Uses the original satellite assembly en-US\LocalizedApplication.resources.dll.

- Uses the translates .csv file French.csv.

- Uses the France French culture.

- Outputs to the fr-FR subfolder (which must already exist). Though this seems implicit based on the culture you're using, you need to supply this detail.

When you run this command line, LocBaml creates a new version of the LocalizableApplication.resources.dll assembly with the translated values and places it in the fr-FR subfolder of the application.

Now when you run the application on a computer that has its culture set to France French, the alternate version of the window will be shown automatically. You can change the culture by using the Regional and Language Options section of the Control Panel. Or for an easier approach to testing, you can use code to change the culture of the current thread. You need to do this before you create or show any windows, so it makes sense to use an application event, or just use your application class constructor, as shown here:

```
Public Class Application

    Public Sub New()
        'Thread.CurrentThread.CurrentUICulture = New CultureInfo("fr-FR")
    End Sub

End Class
```

Figure 7-7 shows the result.

Figure 7-7. *A window that's localized in French*

Not all localizable content is defined as a localizable property in your user interface. For example, you might need to show an error message when something occurs. The best way to handle this situation is to use XAML resources (as described in Chapter 10). For example, you could store your error message strings as resources in a specific window, in the resources for an entire application, or in a resource dictionary that's shared across multiple applications. Here's an example:

```
<Window.Resources>
  <s:String x:Uid="s:String_1" x:Key="Error">Something bad happened.</s:String>
</Window.Resources>
```

When you run LocBaml, the strings in this file are also added to the content that needs to be localized. When compiled, this information is added to the satellite assembly, ensuring that error messages are in the correct language (as shown in Figure 7-8).

Figure 7-8. *Using a localized string*

Note An obvious weakness in the current system is that it's difficult to keep up with an evolving user interface. The LocBaml tool always creates a new file, so if you end up moving controls to different windows or replacing one control with another, you'll probably be forced to create a new list of translations from scratch.

The Last Word

In this chapter, you took a detailed look at the WPF application model.

To manage a simple WPF application, you need to do nothing more than create an instance of the Application class and call the Run() method. However, most applications go further and derive a custom class from the Application class. And as you saw, this custom class is an ideal tool for handling application events and an ideal place to track the windows in your application or implement a single-instance pattern.

In the second half of this chapter, you considered assembly resources that allow you to package binary data and embed it in your application. You also took a look at localization and learned how a few command-line tools (msbuild.exe and locbaml.exe) allow you to provide culture-specific versions of your user interface, albeit with a fair bit of manual labor.

CHAPTER 8

■ ■ ■

Element Binding

At its simplest, data binding is a relationship that tells WPF to extract some information from a *source* object and use it to set a property in a *target* object. The target property is always a dependency property, and it's usually in a WPF element—after all, the ultimate goal of WPF data binding is to display some information in your user interface. However, the source object can be just about anything, ranging from another WPF element to an ADO.NET data object (such as DataTable and DataRow) or a data-only object of your own creation.

In this chapter, you'll begin your exploration of data binding by considering the simplest approach: element-to-element binding. In Chapter 19, you'll revisit the data-binding story, and learn the most efficient way to shuttle data from a database to your data forms.

■ **What's New**   WPF 4.5 has made several improvements to the data-binding system, most of which you'll consider in Chapter 19. In this chapter, you'll see two of the more minor changes. First, you'll consider the Delay property that allows you to add a pause before a data-binding expression is evaluated (see the "Binding Delays" section). Second, you'll look at WPF's enhanced ability to get binding information programmatically (see the "Retrieving Bindings in Code" section).

Binding Elements Together

The simplest data-binding scenario occurs when your source object is a WPF element and your source property is a dependency property. That's because dependency properties have built-in support for change notification, as explained in Chapter 4. As a result, when you change the value of the dependency property in the source object, the bound property in the target object is updated immediately. This is exactly what you want, and it happens without requiring you to build any additional infrastructure.

■ **Note**   Although it's nice to know that element-to-element binding is the simplest approach, most developers are more interested in finding out which approach is most common in the real world. Overall, the bulk of your data-binding work will be spent binding elements to data objects. This allows you to display the information that you've extracted from an external source (such as a database or file). However, element-to-element binding is often useful. For example, you can use element-to-element binding to automate the way elements interact so that when a user modifies a control, another element is updated automatically. This is a valuable shortcut that can save you from writing boilerplate code.

To understand how you can bind an element to another element, consider the simple window shown in Figure 8-1. It contains two controls: a Slider and a TextBlock with a single line of text. If you pull the thumb in the slider to the right, the font size of the text is increased immediately. If you pull it to the left, the font size is reduced.

Figure 8-1. *Linked controls through data binding*

Clearly, it wouldn't be difficult to create this behavior by using code. You would simply react to the Slider. ValueChanged event and copy the current value from the slider to the TextBlock. However, data binding makes it even easier.

■ **Tip** Data binding also has another benefit: it allows you to create simple XAML pages that you can run in the browser without compiling them into applications. (As you learned in Chapter 2, if your XAML file has a linked code-behind file, it can't be opened in a browser.)

The Binding Expression

When using data binding, you don't need to make any changes to your source object (which is the Slider in this example). Just configure it to take the correct range of values, as you would usually:

```
<Slider Name="sliderFontSize" Margin="3"
 Minimum="1" Maximum="40" Value="10"
 TickFrequency="1" TickPlacement="TopLeft">
</Slider>
```

The binding is defined in the TextBlock element. Instead of using a literal value to set the FontSize , you use a binding expression, as shown here:

```
<TextBlock Margin="10" Text="Simple Text" Name="lblSampleText"
 FontSize="{Binding ElementName=sliderFontSize, Path=Value}" >
</TextBlock>
```

Data-binding expressions use a XAML markup extension (and hence have curly braces). You begin with the word *Binding*, because you're creating an instance of the System.Windows.Data.Binding class. Although you can configure a Binding object in several ways, in this situation, you need to set just two properties: the ElementName that indicates the source element and a Path that indicates the property in the source element.

The name Path is used instead of Property because the Path might point to a property of a property (for example, FontFamily.Source) or an indexer used by a property (for example, Content.Children[0]). You can build up a path with multiple periods to dig into a property of a property of a property, and so on.

If you want to refer to an attached property (a property that's defined in another class but applied to the bound element), you need to wrap the property name in parentheses. For example, if you're binding to an element that's placed in a Grid, the path (Grid.Row) retrieves the row number where you've placed it.

Binding Errors

WPF doesn't raise exceptions to notify you about data-binding problems. If you specify an element or a property that doesn't exist, you won't receive any indication; instead, the data will simply fail to appear in the target property.

At first glance, this seems like a debugging nightmare. Fortunately, WPF *does* output trace information that details binding failures. This information appears in Visual Studio's Output window when you're debugging the application. For example, if you try to bind to a nonexistent property, you'll see a message like this in the Output window:

```
System.Windows.Data Error: 35 : BindingExpression path error:
 'Tex' property not found on 'object' ''TextBox' (Name='txtFontSize')'.
 BindingExpression:Path=Text; DataItem='TextBox' (Name='txtFontSize');
 target element is 'TextBox' (Name='');
 target property is 'Text' (type 'String')
```

WPF also ignores any exception that's thrown when you attempt to read the source property and quietly swallows the exception that occurs if the source data can't be cast to the data type of the target property. However, there is another option when dealing with these problems—you can tell WPF to change the appearance of the source element to indicate that an error has occurred. For example, this allows you to flag invalid input with an exclamation icon or a red outline. You'll learn more about validation in Chapter 19.

Binding Modes

One of the neat features of data binding is that your target is updated automatically, no matter how the source is modified. In this example, the source can be modified in only one way—by the user's interaction with the slider thumb. However, consider a slightly revamped version of this example that adds a few buttons, each of which applies a preset value to the slider. Figure 8-2 shows the new window.

Figure 8-2. *Modifying the data-binding source programmatically*

When you click the Set to Large button, this code runs:

```
Private Sub cmd_SetLarge(ByVal sender As Object, ByVal e As RoutedEventArgs)
    sliderFontSize.Value = 30
End Sub
```

This code sets the value of the slider, which in turn forces a change to the font size of the text through data binding. It's the same as if you had moved the slider thumb yourself.

However, this code doesn't work as well:

```
Private Sub cmd_SetLarge(ByVal sender As Object, ByVal e As RoutedEventArgs)
    lblSampleText.FontSize = 30
End Sub
```

It sets the font of the text box directly. As a result, the slider position isn't updated to match. Even worse, this has the effect of wiping out your font size binding and replacing it with a literal value. If you move the slider thumb now, the text block won't change at all.

Interestingly, there's a way to force values to flow in both directions: from the source to the target *and* from the target to the source. The trick is to set the Mode property of the Binding. Here's a revised bidirectional binding that allows you to apply changes to either the source or the target and have the other piece of the equation update itself automatically:

```
<TextBlock Margin="10" Text="Simple Text" Name="lblSampleText"
 FontSize="{Binding ElementName=sliderFontSize, Path=Value, Mode=TwoWay}" >
</TextBlock>
```

In this example, you have no reason to use a two-way binding (which requires more overhead) because you can solve the problem by using the correct code. However, consider a variation of this example that includes a text box where the user can set the font size precisely. This text box needs to use a two-way binding, so it can both apply the user's changes and display the most recent size value in the text box when it's changed through another avenue. You'll see this example in the next section.

WPF allows you to use one of five values from the System.Windows.Data.BindingMode enumeration when setting the Binding.Mode property. Table 8-1 has the full list.

Table 8-1. *Values from the BindingMode Enumeration*

Name	Description
OneWay	The target property is updated when the source property changes.
TwoWay	The target property is updated when the source property changes, and the source property is updated when the target property changes.
OneTime	The target property is set initially based on the source property value. However, changes are ignored from that point onward (unless the binding is set to a completely different object or you call BindingExpression.UpdateTarget(), as described later in this chapter). Usually, you'll use this mode to reduce overhead if you know the source property won't change.
OneWayToSource	Similar to OneWay but in reverse. The source property is updated when the target property changes (which might seem a little backward), but the target property is never updated.
Default	The type of binding depends on the target property. It's either TwoWay (for user-settable properties, such as the TextBox.Text) or OneWay (for everything else). All bindings use this approach unless you specify otherwise.

Figure 8-3 illustrates the difference. You've already seen OneWay and TwoWay. OneTime is fairly straightforward. The other two choices warrant some additional investigation.

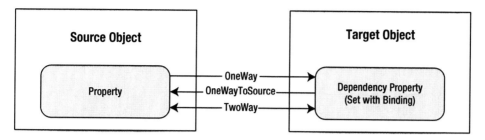

Figure 8-3. *Different ways to bind two properties*

OneWayToSource

You might wonder why there's both a OneWay and a OneWayToSource option—after all, both values create a one-way binding that works in the same way. The only difference is where the binding expression is placed. Essentially, OneWayToSource allows you to flip the source and target by placing the expression in what would ordinarily be considered the binding source.

The most common reason to use this trick is to set a property that isn't a dependency property. As you learned at the beginning of this chapter, binding expressions can be used only to set dependency properties. But by using OneWayToSource, you can overcome this limitation, provided the property that's supplying the value is itself a dependency property.

Default

Initially, it seems logical to assume that all bindings are one-way unless you explicitly specify otherwise. (After all, that's the way the simple slider example works.) However, this isn't the case. To demonstrate this fact to yourself, return to the example with the bound text box that allows you to edit the current font size. If you remove the Mode=TwoWay setting, this example still works just as well. That's because WPF uses a different Mode default depending on the property you're binding. (Technically, there's a bit of metadata on every dependency property—the FrameworkPropertyMetadata.BindsTwoWayByDefault flag—that indicates whether that property should use one-way or two-way binding.)

Often, the default is exactly what you want. However, you can imagine an example with a read-only text box that the user can't change. In this case, you can reduce the overhead slightly by setting the mode to use one-way binding.

As a general rule of thumb, it's never a bad idea to explicitly set the mode. Even in the case of a text box, it's worth emphasizing that you want a two-way binding by including the Mode property.

Creating Bindings with Code

When you're building a window, it's usually most efficient to declare your binding expression in the XAML markup by using the Binding markup extension. However, you can also create a binding by using code.

Here's how you could create the binding for the TextBlock shown in the previous example:

```
Dim binding As New Binding()
binding.Source = sliderFontSize
binding.Path = New PropertyPath("Value")
binding.Mode = BindingMode.TwoWay
lblSampleText.SetBinding(TextBlock.FontSizeProperty, binding)
```

You can also remove a binding with code by using two static methods of the BindingOperations class. The ClearBinding() method takes a reference to the dependency property that has the binding you want to remove, while ClearAllBindings() removes all the data binding for an element:

```
BindingOperations.ClearAllBindings(lblSampleText)
```

Both ClearBinding() and ClearAllBindings() use the ClearValue() method that every element inherits from the based DependencyObject class. ClearValue() simply removes a property's local value (which, in this case, is a data-binding expression).

Markup-based binding is far more common than programmatic binding, because it's cleaner and requires less work. In this chapter, all the examples use markup to create their bindings. However, you will want to use code to create a binding in some specialized scenarios:

Creating a dynamic binding: If you want to tailor a binding based on other runtime information or create a different binding depending on the circumstances, it often makes sense to create your binding in code. (Alternatively, you could define every binding you might want to use in the Resources collection of your window and just add the code that calls SetBinding() with the appropriate binding object.)

Removing a binding: If you want to remove a binding so that you can set a property in the usual way, you need the help of the ClearBinding() or ClearAllBindings() method. It isn't enough to simply apply a new value to the property. If you're using a two-way binding, the value you set is propagated to the linked object, and both properties remain synchronized.

■ **Note**   You can remove any binding by using the ClearBinding() and ClearAllBindings() methods. It doesn't matter whether the binding was applied programmatically or in XAML markup.

Creating custom controls: To make it easier for other people to modify the visual appearance of a custom control you build, you'll need to move certain details (such as event handlers and data-binding expressions) into your code and out of your markup. Chapter 18 includes a custom color-picking control that uses code to create its bindings.

Retrieving Bindings in Code

You can also use code to retrieve a binding and examine its properties, regardless of whether that binding was originally created with code or markup.

There are two ways to get information about a binding. The first option is to use the static BindingOperations. GetBinding() method to retrieve the corresponding Binding object. You need to supply two arguments: the bound element, and the property that has the binding expression.

For example, if you have a binding like this:

```
<TextBlock Margin="10" Text="Simple Text" Name="lblSampleText"
 FontSize="{Binding ElementName=sliderFontSize, Path=Value}" >
</TextBlock>
```

You can use code like this to get the binding:

```
Dim binding As Binding = BindingOperations.GetBinding(lblSampleText, TextBlock.FontSize)
```

Once you have the Binding object, you can examine its properties. For example, Binding.ElementName provides the name of the bound element that supplies the value for your binding expression (in this case, it's "sliderFontSize"). Binding.Path provides the PropertyPath object that extracts the bound value from the bound object, and Binding.Path. Path gets the name of the bound property (in this case, "Value"). There's also a Binding.Mode property that tells you when the binding updates the target element.

The Binding object may be of some interest if you have to add diagnostic code while testing. But WPF also lets you get a more practical BindingExpression object by calling the BindingOperations.GetBindingExpression() method with the same arguments you used for the GetBinding() method:

```
Dim expression As BindingExpression = BindingOperations.GetBindingExpression( _
  lblSampleText, TextBlock.FontSize)
```

The BindingExpression object includes a few properties that duplicate the information provided by the Binding object. But by far its most interesting feature is the ResolvedSource property, which allows you to evaluate the binding expression and get its result—the bound data that it's passing along. Here's an example:

```
' Get the source element.
Dim boundObject As Slider = CType(expression.ResolvedSource, Slider)

' Get any data you need from the source element, including its bound property.
Dim boundData As String = boundObject.FontSize
```

This technique becomes more useful when you start binding data objects, as you'll do later in this chapter. Then, you can use the ResolvedSource property to get a reference to the bound data object whenever you need it.

Multiple Bindings

Although the previous example includes just a single binding, you don't need to stop there. If you wanted, you could set up the TextBlock to draw its text from a text box, its current foreground and background color from separate lists of colors, and so on. Here's an example:

```
<TextBlock Margin="3" Name="lblSampleText"
  FontSize="{Binding ElementName=sliderFontSize, Path=Value}"
  Text="{Binding ElementName=txtContent, Path=Text}"
  Foreground="{Binding ElementName=lstColors, Path=SelectedItem.Tag}" >
</TextBlock>
```

Figure 8-4 shows the triple-bound TextBlock.

Figure 8-4. *A TextBlock that's bound to three elements*

You can also chain data bindings. For example, you could create a binding expression for the TextBox.Text property that links to the TextBlock.FontSize property, which contains a binding expression that links to the Slider. Value property. In this case, when the user drags the slider thumb to a new position, the value flows from the Slider to the TextBlock and then from the TextBlock to the TextBox. Although this works seamlessly, a cleaner approach is to bind your elements as closely as possible to the data they use. In the example described here, you should consider binding both the TextBlock and the TextBox directly to the Slider.Value property.

Life becomes a bit more interesting if you want a target property to be influenced by more than one source—for example, if you want there to be two equally legitimate bindings that set its property. At first glance, this doesn't seem possible. After all, when you create a binding, you can point to only a single target property. However, you can get around this limitation in several ways.

The easiest approach is to change the data-binding mode. As you've already learned, the Mode property allows you to change the way a binding works so that values aren't just pushed from the source to the target but also from target to the source. Using this technique, you can create multiple binding expressions that set the same property. The last-set property is the one that comes into effect.

To understand how this works, consider a variation of the slider bar example that introduces a text box where you can set the exact font size. In this example (shown in Figure 8-5), you can set the TextBlock.FontSize property in two ways: by dragging the slider thumb or by typing a font size into the text box. All the controls are synchronized so that if you type a new number in the text box, the font size of the sample text is adjusted *and* the slider thumb is moved to the corresponding position.

Figure 8-5. *Linking two properties to the font size*

As you know, you can apply only a single data binding to the TextBlock.FontSize property. It makes sense to leave the TextBlock.FontSize property as is, so that it binds directly to the slider:

```
<TextBlock Margin="10" Text="Simple Text" Name="lblSampleText"
 FontSize="{Binding ElementName=sliderFontSize, Path=Value, Mode=TwoWay}" >
</TextBlock>
```

Although you can't add another binding to the FontSize property, you *can* bind the new control—the TextBox—to the TextBlock.FontSize property. Here's the markup you need:

```
<TextBox Text="{Binding ElementName=lblSampleText, Path=FontSize, Mode=TwoWay}">
</TextBox>
```

Now, whenever the TextBlock.FontSize property changes, the current value is inserted into the text box. Even better, you can edit the value in the text box to apply a specific size. Notice that in order for this example to work, the TextBox.Text property must use a two-way binding so that values travel both ways. Otherwise, the text box will be able to display the TextBlock.FontSize value but won't be able to change it.

This example has a few quirks:

- Because the Slider.Value property is a Double, you'll end up with a fractional font size when you drag the slider thumb. You can constrain the slider to whole numbers by setting the TickFrequency property to 1 (or some other whole number interval) and setting the IsSnapToTickEnabled property to True.

- The text box allows letters and other non-numeric characters. If you enter any, the text box value can no longer be interpreted as a number. As a result, the data binding silently fails, and the font size is set to 0. Another approach would be to handle key presses in the text box to prevent invalid input altogether or to use validation, as discussed in Chapter 19.

- The changes you make in the text box aren't applied until the text box loses focus (for example, when you tab to another control). If this isn't the behavior you want, you can get an instantaneous refresh by using the UpdateSourceTrigger property of the Binding object, as you'll learn shortly in the "Binding Updates" section.

Interestingly, the solution shown here isn't the only way to connect the text box. It's just as reasonable to configure the text box so that it changes the Slider.Value property instead of the TextBlock.FontSize property:

```
<TextBox Text="{Binding ElementName=sliderFontSize, Path=Value, Mode=TwoWay}">
</TextBox>
```

Now changing the text box triggers a change in the slider, which then applies the new font to the text. Once again, this approach works only if you use two-way data binding.

And lastly, you can swap the roles of the slider and text box so that the slider binds to the text box. To do this, you need to create an unbound TextBox and give it a name:

```
<TextBox Name="txtFontSize" Text="10">
</TextBox>
```

Then you can bind the Slider.Value property, as shown here:

```
<Slider Name="sliderFontSize" Margin="3"
 Minimum="1" Maximum="40"
 Value="{Binding ElementName=txtFontSize, Path=Text, Mode=TwoWay}"
 TickFrequency="1" TickPlacement="TopLeft">
</Slider>
```

Now the slider is in control. When the window is first shown, it retrieves the TextBox.Text property and uses that to set its Value property. When the user drags the slider thumb to a new position, it uses the binding to update the text box. Alternatively, the user can update the slider value (and the font size of the sample text) by typing in the text box.

■ **Note** If you bind the Slider.Value property, the text box behaves slightly differently than the previous two examples. Any edits you make in the text box are applied immediately, rather than waiting until the text box loses focus. You'll learn more about controlling when an update takes place in the next section.

As this example demonstrates, two-way bindings give you remarkable flexibility. You can use them to apply changes from the source to the target and from the target to the source. You can also apply them in combination to create a surprisingly complex code-free window.

Usually, the decision of where to place a binding expression is driven by the logic of your coding model. In the previous example, it probably makes more sense to place the binding in the TextBox.Text property rather than the Slider.Value property, because the text box is an optional add-on to an otherwise complete example, not a core ingredient that the slider relies on. It also makes more sense to bind the text box directly to the TextBlock.FontSize property rather than the Slider.Value property. (Conceptually, you're interested in reporting the current font size, and the slider is just one of the ways this font size can be set. Even though the slider position is the same as the font size, it's an unnecessary extra detail if you're trying to write the cleanest possible markup.) Of course, these decisions are subjective and a matter of coding style. The most important lesson is that all three approaches can give you the same behavior.

In the following sections, you'll explore two details that apply to this example. First, you'll consider your choices for setting the direction of a binding. Then you'll see how you can tell WPF exactly when it should update the source property in a two-way binding.

Binding Updates

In the example shown in Figure 8-5 (which binds TextBox.Text to TextBlock.FontSize), there's another quirk. As you change the displayed font size by typing in the text box, nothing happens. The change is not applied until you tab to another control. This behavior is different from the behavior you see with the slider control. With that control, the new font size is applied as you drag the slider thumb—there's no need to tab away.

To understand this difference, you need to take a closer look at the binding expressions used by these two controls. When you use OneWay or TwoWay binding, the changed value is propagated from the source to the target immediately. In the case of the slider, there's a one-way binding expression in the TextBlock. Thus, changes in the Slider.Value property are immediately applied to the TextBlock.FontSize property. The same behavior takes place in the text box example—changes to the source (which is TextBlock.FontSize) affect the target (TextBox.Text) immediately.

However, changes that flow in the reverse direction—from the target to the source—don't necessarily happen immediately. Instead, their behavior is governed by the Binding.UpdateSourceTrigger property, which takes one of the values listed in Table 8-2. When the text is taken from the text box and used to update the TextBlock.FontSize property, you're witnessing an example of a target-to-source update that uses the UpdateSourceTrigger.LostFocus behavior.

Table 8-2. *Values from the UpdateSourceTrigger Enumeration*

Name	Description
PropertyChanged	The source is updated immediately when the target property changes.
LostFocus	The source is updated when the target property changes and the target loses focus.
Explicit	The source is not updated unless you call the BindingExpression.UpdateSource() method.
Default	The updating behavior is determined by the metadata of the target property (technically, its FrameworkPropertyMetadata.DefaultUpdateSourceTrigger property). For most properties, the default behavior is PropertyChanged, although the TextBox.Text property has a default behavior of LostFocus.

Remember that the values in Table 8-2 have no effect over how the target is updated. They simply control how the *source* is updated in a TwoWay or OneWayToSource binding.

With this knowledge, you can improve the text box example so that changes are applied to the font size as the user types in the text box. Here's how:

```
<TextBox Text="{Binding ElementName=txtSampleText, Path=FontSize, Mode=TwoWay,
 UpdateSourceTrigger=PropertyChanged}" Name="txtFontSize"></TextBox>
```

▓ **Tip** The default behavior of the TextBox.Text property is LostFocus, simply because the text in a text box will change repeatedly as the user types, causing multiple refreshes. Depending on how the source control updates itself, the PropertyChanged update mode can make the application feel more sluggish. Additionally, it might cause the source object to refresh itself before an edit is complete, which can cause problems for validation.

For complete control over when the source object is updated, you can choose the UpdateSourceTrigger.Explicit mode. If you use this approach in the text box example, nothing happens when the text box loses focus. Instead, it's up to your code to manually trigger the update. For example, you could add an Apply button that calls the BindingExpression.UpdateSource() method, triggering an immediate refresh and updating the font size.

Of course, before you can call BindingExpression.UpdateSource(), you need a way to get a BindingExpression object. A BindingExpression object is a slim package that wraps together two things: the Binding object you've already learned about (provided through the BindingExpression.ParentBinding property) and the object that's being bound from the source (BindingExpression.DataItem). In addition, the BindingExpression object provides two methods for triggering an immediate update for one part of the binding: UpdateSource() and UpdateTarget().

To get a BindingExpression object, you use the GetBindingExpression() method, which every element inherits from the base FrameworkElement class, and pass in the target property that has the binding. Here's an example that changes the font size in the TextBlock based on the current text in the text box:

```
' Get the binding that's applied to the text box.
Dim binding As BindingExpression
binding = txtFontSize.GetBindingExpression(TextBox.TextProperty)

' Update the linked source (the TextBlock).
binding.UpdateSource()
```

Binding Delays

In some rare cases, you might want to prevent data binding from springing into action and modifying the source object—at least, for a certain interval of time. For example, you might want to pause briefly before copying information from a text box, rather than grabbing it after every keystroke. Or perhaps your source object performs a processor-intensive operation when its data-bound property is changed. In this case, you might want to introduce a small delay so the operation isn't triggered quite as often.

In these specialized scenarios, you can make use of the Delay property of the Binding. It takes a number of milliseconds to wait, after which it commits the change. Here's a revised version of the text box example that waits for the user to stop typing for 500 milliseconds (half a second) before updating the source object:

```
<TextBox Text="{Binding ElementName=txtSampleText, Path=FontSize, Mode=TwoWay,
  UpdateSourceTrigger=PropertyChanged, Delay=500}" Name="txtFontSize"></TextBox>
```

Binding to Objects That Aren't Elements

So far, you've focused on adding bindings that link two elements. But in data-driven applications, it's more common to create binding expressions that draw their data from a nonvisual object. The only requirement is that the information you want to display must be stored in *public properties*. The WPF data-binding infrastructure won't pick up private information or public fields.

When binding to an object that isn't an element, you need to give up the Binding.ElementName property and use one of the following properties instead:

Source: This is a reference that points directly to the source object—in other words, the object that's supplying the data.

RelativeSource: This is a reference that points to the source object by using a RelativeSource object. This extra layer allows you to base the reference on the current element (the element that holds the binding expression). Although this sounds needlessly complicated, the RelativeSource property is a specialized tool that's handy when writing control templates and data templates.

DataContext: If you don't specify a source by using the Source or RelativeSource property, WPF searches up the element tree, starting at the current element. It examines the DataContext property of each element and uses the first one that isn't a null reference (Nothing). The DataContext property is extremely useful if you need to bind several properties of the same object to different elements, because you can set the DataContext property of a higher-level container object, rather than setting it directly on the target element.

The following sections fill in a few more details about these three options.

Source

The Source property is quite straightforward. The only catch is that you need to have your data object handy in order to bind it. As you'll see, you can use several approaches for getting the data object: pull it out of a resource, generate it programmatically, or get it with the help of a data provider.

The simplest option is to point the Source to some static object that's readily available. For example, you could create a static object in your code and use that. Or, you could use an ingredient from the .NET class library, as shown here:

```
<TextBlock Text="{Binding Source={x:Static SystemFonts.IconFontFamily},
 Path=Source}"></TextBlock>
```

This binding expression gets the FontFamily object that's provided by the static SystemFonts.IconFontFamily property. (Notice that you need the help of the static markup extension to set the Binding.Source property.) It then sets the Binding.Path property to the FontFamily.Source property, which gives the name of the font family. The result is a single line of text—typically, the font name Segoe UI appears.

Another option is to bind to an object that you've previously created as a resource. For example, this markup creates a FontFamily object that points to the Calibri font:

```
<Window.Resources>
  <FontFamily x:Key="CustomFont">Calibri</FontFamily>
</Window.Resources>
```

And here's a TextBlock that binds to this resource:

```
<TextBlock Text="{Binding Source={StaticResource CustomFont},
 Path=Source}"></TextBlock>
```

Now the text you'll see is *Calibri*.

RelativeSource

The RelativeSource property allows you to point to a source object based on its relation to the target object. For example, you can use the RelativeSource property to bind an element to itself or to bind to a parent element that's found an unknown number of steps up the element tree.

To set the Binding.RelativeSource property, you use a RelativeSource object. This makes the syntax a little more convoluted, because you need to create a Binding object and create a nested RelativeSource object inside. One option is to use the property-setting syntax instead of the Binding markup extension. For example, the following code creates a Binding object for the TextBlock.Text property. The Binding object uses a RelativeSource that searches out the parent window and displays the window title.

```
<TextBlock>
  <TextBlock.Text>
    <Binding Path="Title">
      <Binding.RelativeSource>
        <RelativeSource Mode="FindAncestor" AncestorType="{x:Type Window}" />
      </Binding.RelativeSource>
    </Binding>
  </TextBlock.Text>
</TextBlock>
```

The RelativeSource object uses the FindAncestor mode, which tells it to search up the element tree until it finds the type of element defined by the AncestorType property.

The more common way to write this binding is to combine it into one string by using the Binding and RelativeSource markup extensions, as shown here:

```
<TextBlock Text="{Binding Path=Title,
    RelativeSource={RelativeSource FindAncestor, AncestorType={x:Type Window}} }">
</TextBlock>
```

The FindAncestor mode is only one of four options when you create a RelativeSource object. Table 8-3 lists all four modes.

Table 8-3. *Values from the RelativeSourceMode Enumeration*

Name	Description
Self	The expression binds to another property in the same element.
FindAncestor	The expression binds to a parent element. WPF will search up the element tree until it finds the parent you want. To specify the parent, you must also set the AncestorType property to indicate the type of parent element you want to find. Optionally, you can use the AncestorLevel property to skip a certain number of occurrences of the specified element. For example, if you want to bind to the third element of type ListBoxItem when going up the tree, you would set AncestorType={x:Type ListBoxItem} and AncestorLevel=3, thereby skipping the first two ListBoxItems. By default, AncestorLevel is 1, and the search stops at the first matching element.
PreviousData	The expression binds to the previous data item in a data-bound list. You would use this in a list item.
TemplatedParent	The expression binds to the element on which the template is applied. This mode works only if your binding is located inside a control template or data template.

At first glance, the RelativeSource property seems like a way to unnecessarily complicate your markup. After all, why not bind directly to the source you want by using the Source or ElementName property? However, this isn't always possible, usually because the source and target objects are in distinct sections of markup. This happens when you're creating control templates and data templates. For example, if you're building a data template that changes the way items are presented in a list, you might need to access the top-level ListBox object to read a property.

DataContext

In some cases, you'll have a number of elements that bind to the same object. For example, consider the following group of TextBlock elements, each of which uses a similar binding expression to pull out different details about the default icon font, including its line spacing and the style and weight of the first typeface it provides (both of which are simply Regular). You can use the Source property for each one, but this results in fairly lengthy markup:

```
<StackPanel>
  <TextBlock Text="{Binding Source={x:Static SystemFonts.IconFontFamily},
    Path=Source}"></TextBlock>
  <TextBlock Text="{Binding Source={x:Static SystemFonts.IconFontFamily},
    Path=LineSpacing}"></TextBlock>
  <TextBlock Text="{Binding Source={x:Static SystemFonts.IconFontFamily},
    Path=FamilyTypefaces[0].Style}"></TextBlock>
  <TextBlock Text="{Binding Source={x:Static SystemFonts.IconFontFamily},
    Path=FamilyTypefaces[0].Weight}"></TextBlock>
</StackPanel>
```

In this situation, it's cleaner and more flexible to define the binding source once by using the FrameworkElement. DataContext property. In this example, it makes sense to set the DataContext property of the StackPanel that contains all the TextBlock elements. (You could also set the DataContext property at an even higher level—for example, the entire window—but it's better to define it as narrowly as possible to make your intentions clear.)

You can set the DataContext property of an element in the same way that you set the Binding.Source property. In other words, you can supply your object inline, pull it out of a static property, or pull it out of a resource, as shown here:

```
<StackPanel DataContext="{x:Static SystemFonts.IconFontFamily}">
```

Now you can streamline your binding expressions by leaving out the source information:

```
<TextBlock Margin="5" Text="{Binding Path=Source}"></TextBlock>
```

When the source information is missing from a binding expression, WPF checks the DataContext property of that element. If it's a null reference (Nothing), WPF searches up the element tree, looking for the first data context that isn't null. (Initially, the DataContext property of all elements is null.) If WPF finds a data context, it uses that for the binding. If it doesn't, the binding expression doesn't apply any value to the target property.

▓ **Note** If you create a binding that explicitly specifies a source by using the Source property, your element uses that source instead of any data context that might be available.

This example shows how you can create a basic binding to an object that isn't an element. However, to use this technique in a realistic application, you need to pick up a few more skills. In Chapter 19, you'll learn how to display information drawn from a database by building on these data-binding techniques.

The Last Word

In this chapter, you took a quick look at data-binding fundamentals. You learned how to pull information out of one element and display it in another without a single line of code. And although this technique seems fairly modest right now, it's an essential skill that will allow you to perform much more impressive feats, such as restyling controls with custom control templates (discussed in Chapter 17).

In Chapters 19 and 20, you'll greatly extend your data-binding skills. You'll learn how to show entire collections of data objects in a list, handle edits with validation, and turn ordinary text into a richly formatted data display. But for now, you have all the data-binding experience you need to tackle the chapters ahead.

CHAPTER 9

■ ■ ■

Commands

In Chapter 5, you learned about routed events, which you can use to respond to a wide range of mouse and keyboard actions. However, events are a fairly low-level ingredient. In a realistic application, functionality is divided into higher-level *tasks*. These tasks may be triggered by a variety of actions and through a variety of user-interface elements, including main menus, context menus, keyboard shortcuts, and toolbars.

WPF allows you to define these tasks—known as *commands*—and connect controls to them so you don't need to write repetitive event-handling code. Even more important, the command feature manages the state of your user interface by automatically disabling controls when the linked commands aren't available. It also gives you a central place to store (and localize) the text captions for your commands.

In this chapter, you'll learn how to use the prebuilt command classes in WPF, wire them up to controls, and define your own commands. You'll also consider the limitations of the command model—namely, the lack of a command history and the lack of support for an application-wide Undo feature—and you'll see how you can build your own system for tracking and reversing commands.

Understanding Commands

In a well-designed Windows application, the application logic doesn't sit in the event handlers but is coded in higher-level methods. Each one of these methods represents a single application *task*. Each task may rely on other libraries (such as separately compiled components that encapsulate business logic or database access). Figure 9-1 shows this relationship.

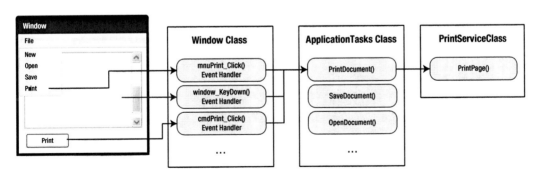

Figure 9-1. Mapping event handlers to a task

The most obvious way to use this design is to add event handlers wherever they're needed, and use each event handler to call the appropriate application method. In essence, your window code becomes a stripped-down switchboard that responds to input and forwards requests to the heart of the application.

Although this design is perfectly reasonable, it doesn't save you any work. Many application tasks can be triggered through a variety of routes, so you'll often need to code several event handlers that call the same application method. This in itself isn't much of a problem (because the switchboard code is so simple), but life becomes much more complicated when you need to deal with user interface *state*.

A simple example shows the problem. Imagine you have a program that includes an application method named PrintDocument(). This method can be triggered in four ways: through a main menu (by choosing File ➤ Print), through a context menu (by right-clicking somewhere and choosing Print), through a keyboard shortcut (Ctrl+P), and through a toolbar button. At certain points in your application's lifetime, you need to temporarily disable the PrintDocument() task. That means you need to disable the two menu commands and the toolbar button so they can't be clicked, and you need to ignore the Ctrl+P shortcut. Writing the code that does this (and adding the code that enables these controls later) is messy. Even worse, if it's not done properly, you might wind up with different blocks of state code overlapping incorrectly, causing a control to be switched on even when it shouldn't be available. Writing and debugging this sort of code is one of the least glamorous aspects of Windows development.

WPF includes a command model that can help you deal with these issues. It adds two key features:

- It delegates events to the appropriate commands.

- It keeps the enabled state of a control synchronized with the state of the corresponding command.

The WPF command model isn't quite as straightforward as you might expect. Plugging into the routed event model requires several separate ingredients, which you'll learn about in this chapter. However, the command model is *conceptually* simple. Figure 9-2 shows how a command-based application changes the design shown in Figure 9-1. Now each action that initiates printing (clicking the button, clicking the menu item, or pressing Ctrl+P) is mapped to the same command. A command binding links that command to a single event handler in your code.

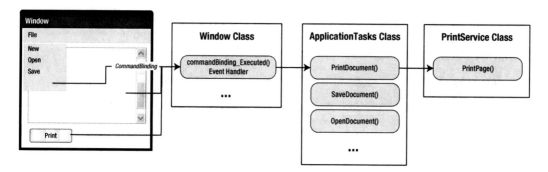

Figure 9-2. *Mapping events to a command*

The WPF command system is a great tool for simplifying application design. However, it still has some fairly significant gaps. Notably, WPF doesn't have any support for the following:

- Command tracking (for example, keeping a history of recent commands)

- Undoable commands

- Commands that have state and can be in different modes (for example, a command that can be toggled on or off)

The WPF Command Model

The WPF command model consists of a surprising number of moving parts. All together, it has four key ingredients:

Commands: A command *represents* an application task and keeps track of whether it can be executed. However, commands don't actually contain the code that *performs* the application task.

Command bindings: Each command binding links a command to the related application logic, for a particular area of your user interface. This factored design is important, because a single command might be used in several places in your application and have a different significance in each place. To handle this, you use the same command with different command bindings.

Command sources: A command source triggers a command. For example, a MenuItem and a Button can both be command sources. Clicking them executes the bound command.

Command targets: A command target is the element on which the command is being performed. For example, a Paste command might insert text into a TextBox, and an OpenFile command might pop a document into a DocumentViewer. The target may or may not be important, depending on the nature of the command.

In the following sections, you'll dig into the first ingredient: the WPF command.

The ICommand Interface

The heart of the WPF command model is the System.Windows.Input.ICommand interface, which defines how commands work. This interface includes two methods and an event:

```
Public Interface ICommand
    Private Event CanExecuteChanged As EventHandler
    Sub Execute(ByVal parameter As Object)

    Function CanExecute(ByVal parameter As Object) As Boolean
End Interface
```

In a simple implementation, the Execute() method would contain the application task logic (for example, printing the document). However, as you'll see in the next section, WPF is a bit more elaborate. It uses the Execute() method to fire off a more complicated process that eventually raises an event that's handled elsewhere in your application. This gives you the ability to use ready-made command classes and plug in your own logic. It also gives you the flexibility to use one command (such as Print) in several places.

The CanExecute() method returns the state of the command: True if it's enabled and False if it's disabled. Both Execute() and CanExecute() accept an additional parameter object that you can use to pass along any extra information you need.

Finally, the CanExecuteChanged event is raised when the state changes. This is a signal to any controls using the command that they should call the CanExecute() method to check the command's state. This is part of the glue that allows command sources (such as a Button or MenuItem) to automatically enable themselves when the command is available and to disable themselves when it's not available.

The RoutedCommand Class

When creating your own commands, you won't implement ICommand directly. Instead, you'll use the System. Windows.Input.RoutedCommand class, which implements this interface for you. The RoutedCommand class is the only class in WPF that implements ICommand. In other words, all WPF commands are instances of RoutedCommand (or a derived class).

One of the key concepts behind the command model in WPF is that the RoutedUICommand class doesn't contain any application logic. It simply *represents* a command. This means one RoutedCommand object has the same capabilities as another.

The RoutedCommand class adds a fair bit of extra infrastructure for event tunneling and bubbling. Whereas the ICommand interface encapsulates the idea of a command—an action that can be triggered and may or may not be enabled—the RoutedCommand modifies the command so that it can bubble through the WPF element hierarchy to get to the correct event handler.

WHY WPF COMMANDS NEED EVENT BUBBLING

When looking at the WPF command model for the first time, it's tricky to grasp exactly why WPF commands require routed events. After all, shouldn't the command object take care of performing the command, regardless of how it's invoked?

If you were using the ICommand interface directly to create your own command classes, this would be true. The code would be hardwired into the command, so it would work the same way no matter what triggered the command. You wouldn't need event bubbling.

However, WPF uses a number of *prebuilt* commands. These command classes don't contain any real code. They're just conveniently defined objects that represent a common application task (such as printing a document). To act on these commands, you need to use a command binding, which raises an event to your code (as shown in Figure 9-2). To make sure you can handle this event in one place, even if it's fired by different command sources in the same window, you need the power of event bubbling.

This raises an interesting question: why use prebuilt commands at all? Wouldn't it be clearer to have custom command classes do all the work, instead of relying on an event handler? In many ways, this design would be simpler. However, the advantage of prebuilt commands is that they provide much better possibilities for integration. For example, a third-party developer could create a document viewer control that uses the prebuilt Print command. As long as your application uses the same prebuilt command, you won't need to do any extra work to wire up printing in your application. Seen this way, commands are a major piece of WPF's pluggable architecture.

To support routed events, the RoutedCommand class implements the ICommand interface privately and then adds slightly different versions of its methods. The most obvious change you'll notice is that the Execute() and CanExecute() methods take an extra parameter. Here are their new signatures:

```
Public Sub Execute(ByVal parameter As Object, ByVal target As IInputElement)
  ...
End Sub

Public Function CanExecute(ByVal parameter As Object, _
  ByVal target As IInputElement) As Boolean
  ...
End Function
```

The *target* is the element where the event handling begins. This event begins at the target element and bubbles up to higher-level containers until your application handles it to perform the appropriate task. (To handle the Executed event, your element needs the help of yet another class—CommandBinding.)

Along with this shift, the RoutedElement also introduces three properties: the command name (Name), the class that this command is a member of (OwnerType), and any keystrokes or mouse actions that can also be used to trigger the command (in the InputGestures collection).

The RoutedUICommand Class

Most of the commands you'll deal with won't be RoutedCommand objects; rather, they will be instances of the RoutedUICommand class, which derives from RoutedCommand. (In fact, all the ready-made commands that WPF provides are RoutedUICommand objects.)

RoutedUICommand is intended for commands with text that is displayed somewhere in the user interface (for example, the text of a menu item or the tooltip for a toolbar button). The RoutedUICommand class adds a single property—Text—which is the display text for that command.

The advantage of defining the command text with the command (rather than directly on the control) is that you can perform your localization in one place. However, if your command text never appears anywhere in the user interface, the RoutedCommand class is equivalent.

▓ **Note** You don't need to use the RoutedUICommand text in your user interface. In fact, there may be good reasons to use something else. For example, you might prefer *Print Document* to just *Print*, and in some cases you might replace the text altogether with a tiny graphic.

The Command Library

The designers of WPF realized that every application is likely to have a large number of commands and that many commands are common to many different applications. For example, all document-based applications will have their own versions of the New, Open, and Save commands. To save you the work of creating those commands, WPF includes a basic command library that's stocked with more than 100 commands. These commands are exposed through the shared properties of five dedicated shared classes:

> *ApplicationCommands*: This class provides the common commands, including clipboard commands (such as Copy, Cut, and Paste) and document commands (such as New, Open, Save, SaveAs, Print, and so on).

> *NavigationCommands*: This class provides commands used for navigation, including some that are designed for page-based applications (such as BrowseBack, BrowseForward, and NextPage) and others that are suitable for document-based applications (such as IncreaseZoom and Refresh).

> *EditingCommands*: This class provides a long list of mostly document-editing commands, including commands for moving around (MoveToLineEnd, MoveLeftByWord, MoveUpByPage, and so on), selecting content (SelectToLineEnd, SelectLeftByWord), and changing formatting (ToggleBold and ToggleUnderline).

> *ComponentCommands*: This includes commands that are used by user-interface components, including commands for moving around and selecting content that are similar to (and even duplicate) some of the commands in the EditingCommands class.

> *MediaCommands*: This class includes a set of commands for dealing with multimedia (such as Play, Pause, NextTrack, and IncreaseVolume).

The ApplicationCommands class exposes a set of basic commands that are commonly used in all types of applications, so it's worth a quick look. Here's the full list:

New	Copy	Replace
Open	Cut	SelectAll
Save	Paste	Stop
SaveAs	Delete	ContextMenu
Close	Undo	CorrectionList
Print	Redo	Properties
PrintPreview	Find	Help
CancelPrint		

For example, ApplicationCommands.Open is a shared property that exposes a RoutedUICommand object. This object represents the Open command in an application. Because ApplicationCommands.Open is a shared property, there is only one instance of the Open command for your entire application. However, you may treat it differently depending on its source—in other words, where it occurs in the user interface.

The RoutedUICommand.Text property for every command matches its name, with the addition of spaces between words. For example, the text for the ApplicationCommands.SelectAll command is *Select All*. (The Name property gives you the same text without the spaces.) The RoutedUICommand.OwnerType property returns a type object for the ApplicationCommands class, because the Open command is a shared property of that class.

■ **Tip** You can modify the Text property of a command before you bind it in a window (for example, using code in the constructor of your window or application class). Because commands are shared objects that are global to your entire application, changing the text affects the command everywhere it appears in your user interface. Unlike the Text property, the Name property cannot be modified.

As you've already learned, these individual command objects are just markers with no real functionality. However, many of the command objects have one extra feature: default input bindings. For example, the ApplicationCommands.Open command is mapped to the keystroke Ctrl+O. As soon as you bind that command to a command source and add that command source to a window, the key combination becomes active, even if the command doesn't appear anywhere in the user interface.

Executing Commands

So far, you've taken a close look at commands, considering both the base classes and interfaces and the command library that WPF provides for you to use. However, you haven't yet seen any examples of how to use these commands.

As explained earlier, the RoutedUICommand doesn't have any hardwired functionality. It simply represents a command. To trigger this command, you need a command *source* (or you can use code). To respond to this command, you need a command *binding* that forwards execution to an ordinary event handler. You'll see both ingredients in the following sections.

Command Sources

The commands in the command library are always available. The easiest way to trigger them is to hook them up to a control that implements the ICommandSource interface, which includes controls that derive from ButtonBase (Button, CheckBox, and so on), individual ListBoxItem objects, the Hyperlink, and the MenuItem.

The ICommandSource interface defines three properties, as listed in Table 9-1.

Table 9-1. *Properties of the ICommandSource Interface*

Name	Description
Command	Points to the linked command. This is the only required detail.
CommandParameter	Supplies any other data you want to send with the command.
CommandTarget	Identifies the element on which the command is being performed.

For example, here's a button that links to the ApplicationCommands.New command by using the Command property:

```
<Button Command="ApplicationCommands.New">New</Button>
```

WPF is intelligent enough to search all five command container classes described earlier, which means you can use the following shortcut:

```
<Button Command="New">New</Button>
```

However, you may find that this syntax is less explicit and therefore less clear because it doesn't indicate which class contains the command.

Command Bindings

When you attach a command to a command source, you'll see something interesting. The command source will be automatically disabled.

For example, if you create the New button shown in the previous section, the button will appear dimmed and won't be clickable, just as if you had set IsEnabled to False (see Figure 9-3). That's because the button has queried the state of the command. Because the command has no attached binding, it's considered to be disabled.

Figure 9-3. *A command without a binding*

To change this state of affairs, you need to create a binding for your command that indicates three things:

- What to do when the command is triggered.

- How to determine whether the command can be performed. (This is optional. If you leave out this detail, the command is always enabled as long as there is an attached event handler.)

- Where the command is in effect. For example, the command might be limited to a single button, or it might be enabled over the entire window (which is more common).

Here's a snippet of code that creates a binding for the New command. You can add this code to the constructor of your window:

```
' Create the binding.
' When referring to the ApplicationCommands.New property in code, you must
' use square brackets around the word New, because New is a reserved
' Visual Basic keyword.
Dim binding As New CommandBinding(ApplicationCommands.[New])

' Attach the event handler.
AddHandler binding.Executed, AddressOf NewCommand_Executed

' Register the binding.
Me.CommandBindings.Add(binding)
```

Notice that the completed CommandBinding object is added to the CommandBindings collection of the containing window. This works through event bubbling. Essentially, when the button is clicked, the CommandBinding.Executed event bubbles up from the button to the containing elements.

Although it's customary to add all the bindings to the window, the CommandBindings property is actually defined in the base UIElement class. That means it's supported by any element. For example, this example would work just as well if you added the command binding directly to the button that uses it (although then you wouldn't be able to reuse it with another higher-level element). For greatest flexibility, command bindings are usually added to the top-level window. If you want to use the same command from more than one window, you'll need to create a binding in both windows.

■ **Note** You can also handle the CommandBinding.PreviewExecuted event, which is fired first in the highest-level container (the window) and then tunnels down to the button. As you learned in Chapter 4, you use event tunneling to intercept and stop an event before it's completed. If you set the RoutedEventArgs.Handled property to True, the Executed event will never take place.

The previous code assumes that you have an event handler named NewCommand_Executed in the same class, which is ready to receive the command. Here's an example of some simple code that displays the source of the command:

```
Private Sub NewCommand_Executed(ByVal sender As Object, _
  ByVal e As ExecutedRoutedEventArgs)
    MessageBox.Show(("New command triggered by " & e.Source.ToString()))
End Sub
```

Now, when you run the application, the button is enabled (see Figure 9-4). If you click it, the Executed event fires, bubbles up to the window, and is handled by the NewCommand() handler shown earlier. At this point, WPF tells you the source of the event (the button). The ExecutedRoutedEventArgs object also allows you to get a reference to the command that was invoked (ExecutedRoutedEventArgs.Command) and any extra information that was passed along (ExecutedRoutedEventArgs.Parameter). In this example, the parameter is a null reference (Nothing) because you haven't passed any extra information. (If you wanted to pass additional information, you would set the CommandParameter property of the command source. And if you wanted to pass a piece of information drawn from another control, you would need to set CommandParameter by using a data-binding expression, as shown later in this chapter.)

Figure 9-4. *A command with a binding*

■ **Note**   In this example, the event handler that responds to the command is still code inside the window where the command originates. The same rules of good code organization still apply to this example; in other words, your window should delegate its work to other components where appropriate. For example, if your command involves opening a file, you may use a custom file helper class that you've created to serialize and deserialize information. Similarly, if you create a command that refreshes a data display, you'll use it to call a method in a database component that fetches the data you need. See Figure 9-2 for a refresher.

In the previous example, the command binding was generated using code. However, it's just as easy to wire up commands declaratively using XAML if you want to streamline your code-behind file. Here's the markup you need:

```
<Window x:Class="TestNewCommand"
    xmlns="http://schemas.microsoft.com/winfx/2006/xaml/presentation"
    xmlns:x="http://schemas.microsoft.com/winfx/2006/xaml"
    Title="TestNewCommand">

  <Window.CommandBindings>
    <CommandBinding Command="ApplicationCommands.New"
      Executed="NewCommand_Executed"></CommandBinding>
  </Window.CommandBindings>

  <StackPanel Margin="5">
    <Button Padding="5" Command="ApplicationCommands.New">New</Button>
  </StackPanel>
</Window>
```

Unfortunately, Visual Studio does not have any design-time support for defining command bindings. It also provides relatively feeble support for connecting controls and commands. You can set the Command property of a control by using the Properties window, but it's up to you to type the exact name of the command—there's no handy drop-down list of commands from which to choose.

Using Multiple Command Sources

The button example seems like a somewhat roundabout way to trigger an ordinary event. However, the extra command layer starts to make more sense when you add more controls that use the same command. For example, you might add a menu item that also uses the New command:

```
<Menu>
  <MenuItem Header="File">
    <MenuItem Command="New"></MenuItem>
  </MenuItem>
</Menu>
```

Note that this MenuItem object for the New command doesn't set the Header property. That's because the MenuItem is intelligent enough to pull the text out of the command if the Header property isn't set. (The Button control lacks this feature.) This might seem like a minor convenience, but it's an important consideration if you plan to localize your application in different languages. In this case, being able to modify the text in one place (by setting the Text property of your commands) is easier than tracking it down in your windows.

The MenuItem class has another frill. It automatically picks up the first shortcut key that's in the Command. InputBindings collection (if there is one). In the case of the ApplicationsCommands.New command object, that means the Ctrl+O shortcut appears in the menu alongside the menu text (see Figure 9-5).

Figure 9-5. *A menu item that uses a command*

■ **Note** One frill you *don't* get is an underlined access key. WPF has no way of knowing what commands you might place together in a menu, so it can't determine the best access keys to use. This means if you want to use the N key as a quick access key (so that it appears underlined when the menu is opened with the keyboard, and the user can trigger the New command by pressing N), you need to set the menu text manually, preceding the access key with an underscore. The same is true if you want to use a quick access key for a button.

Note that you don't need to create another command binding for the menu item. The single command binding you created in the previous section is now being used by two different controls, both of which hand their work off to the same command event handler.

Fine-Tuning Command Text

Based on the ability of the menu to pull out the text of the command item automatically, you might wonder whether you can do the same with other ICommandSource classes, such as the Button control. You can, but it requires a bit of extra work.

You can use two techniques to reuse the command text. One option is to pull the text directly from the shared command object. XAML allows you to do this with the Static markup extension. Here's an example that gets the command name New and uses that as the text for a button:

```
<Button Command="New" Content="{x:Static ApplicationCommands.New}"></Button>
```

The problem with this approach is that it simply calls ToString() on the command object. As a result, you get the command name but not the command text. (For commands that have multiple words, the command text is nicer because it includes spaces.) You could correct this problem, but it's significantly more work. There's also another issue in the way that one button uses the same command twice, introducing the possibility that you'll inadvertently grab the text from the wrong command.

The preferred solution is to use a data-binding expression. This data binding is a bit unusual, because it binds to the current element, grabs the Command object you're using, and pulls out the Text property. Here's the terribly long-winded syntax:

```
<Button Margin="5" Padding="5" Command="ApplicationCommands.New" Content=
  "{Binding RelativeSource={RelativeSource Self}, Path=Command.Text}"
</Button>
```

You can use this technique in other, more imaginative ways. For example, you can set the content of a button with a tiny image but use the binding expression to show the command name in a tooltip:

```
<Button Margin="5" Padding="5" Command="ApplicationCommands.New"
  ToolTip="{Binding RelativeSource={RelativeSource Self}, Path=Command.Text}">
<Image ... />
</Button>
```

The content of the button (which isn't shown here) will be a shape or bitmap that appears as a thumbnail icon.

Clearly, this approach is wordier than just putting the command text directly in your markup. However, it's worth considering if you are planning to localize your application in different languages. You simply need to set the command text for all your commands when your application starts. (If you change the command text after you've created a command binding, it won't have any effect. That's because the Text property isn't a dependency property, so there's no automatic change notification to update the user interface.)

Invoking a Command Directly

You aren't limited to the classes that implement ICommandSource if you want to trigger a command. You can also call a method directly from any event handler by using the Execute() method. At that point, you need to pass in the parameter value (or Nothing) and a reference to the target element:

```
ApplicationCommands.[New].Execute(Nothing, targetElement)
```

The target element is simply the element where WPF begins looking for the command binding. You can use the containing window (which has the command binding) or a nested element (such as the actual element that fired the event).

You can also go through the Execute() method in the associated CommandBinding object. In this case, you don't need to supply the target element, because it's automatically set to the element that exposes the CommandBindings collection that you're using.

```
Me.CommandBindings(0).Command.Execute(Nothing)
```

This approach uses only half the command model. It allows you to trigger the command, but it doesn't give you a way to respond to the command's state change. If you want this feature, you may also want to handle the RoutedCommand.CanExecuteChanged to react when the command becomes disabled or enabled. When the CanExecuteChanged event fires, you need to call the RoutedCommand.CanExecute() method to check whether the commands are in a usable state. If not, you can disable or change the content in a portion of your user interface.

COMMAND SUPPORT IN CUSTOM CONTROLS

WPF includes controls that implement ICommandSupport and have the ability to raise commands. (It also includes some controls that have the ability to *handle* commands, as you'll see shortly in the section "Using Controls with Built-in Commands.") Despite this support, you may come across a control that you would like to use with the command model, even though it doesn't implement ICommandSource. In this situation, the easiest option is to handle one of the control's events and execute the appropriate command by using code. However, another option is to build a new control of your own—one that has the command-executing logic built in.

The downloadable code for this chapter includes an example that uses this technique to create a slider that triggers a command when its value changes. This control derives from the Slider class you learned about in Chapter 6; implements ICommand; defines the Command, CommandTarget, and CommandParameter dependency properties; and monitors the RoutedCommand.CanExecuteChanged event internally. Although the code is straightforward, this solution is a bit over the top for most scenarios. Creating a custom control is a fairly significant step in WPF, and most developers prefer to restyle existing controls with templates (discussed in Chapter 17) rather than add an entirely new class. However, if you're designing a custom control from scratch and you want it to provide command support, this example is worth exploring.

Disabling Commands

You'll see the real benefits of the command model when you create a command that varies between an enabled and disabled state. For example, consider the one-window application shown in Figure 9-6, which is a basic text editor that consists of a menu, a toolbar, and a large text box. It allows you to open files, create new (blank) documents, and save your work.

Figure 9-6. *A simple text editor*

In this case, it's perfectly reasonable to make the New, Open, Save, SaveAs, and Close commands perpetually available. But a different design might enable the Save command only if the text has been changed in some way from the original file. By convention, you can track this detail in your code by using a simple Boolean value:

```
Private isDirty As Boolean = False
```

You would then set this flag whenever the text is changed:

```
Private Sub txt_TextChanged(ByVal sender As Object, ByVal e As RoutedEventArgs)
    isDirty = true
End Sub
```

Now you need a way for the information to make its way from your window to the command binding so that the linked controls can be updated as necessary. The trick is to handle the CanExecute event of the command binding. You can attach an event handler to this event through code:

```
Dim binding As CommandBinding = New CommandBinding(ApplicationCommands.Save)
AddHandler binding.Executed, AddressOf SaveCommand_Executed
AddHandler binding.CanExecute, AddressOf SaveCommand_CanExecute
Me.CommandBindings.Add(binding)
```

or declaratively:

```
<Window.CommandBindings>
  <CommandBinding Command="ApplicationCommands.Save"
    Executed="SaveCommand_Executed" CanExecute="SaveCommand_CanExecute">
  </CommandBinding>
</Window.CommandBindings>
```

In your event handler, you simply need to check the isDirty variable and set the CanExecuteRoutedEventArg. CanExecute property accordingly:

```
Private Sub SaveCommand_CanExecute(ByVal sender As Object, _
  ByVal e As CanExecuteRoutedEventArgs)
    e.CanExecute = isDirty
End Sub
```

If isDirty is False, the command is disabled. If it's True, the command is enabled. (If you don't set the CanExecute flag, it keeps its most recent value.)

There's one issue to be aware of when using CanExecute. It's up to WPF to call the RoutedCommand.CanExecute() method to trigger your event handler and determine the status of your command. The WPF command manager does this when it detects a change it believes is significant—for example, when the focus moves from one control to another, or after you execute a command. Controls can also raise the CanExecuteChanged event to tell WPF to reevaluate a command—for example, this occurs when you press a key in the text box. All in all, the CanExecute event will fire quite frequently, and you shouldn't use time-consuming code inside it.

However, other factors might affect the command state. In the current example, the isDirty flag could be modified in response to another action. If you notice that the command state is not being updated at the correct time, you can force WPF to call CanExecute() on all the commands you're using. You do this by calling the shared CommandManager.InvalidateRequerySuggested() method. The command manager then fires the RequerySuggested event to notify the command sources in your window (buttons, menu items, and so on). The command sources will then requery their linked commands and update themselves accordingly.

THE LIMITS OF WPF COMMANDS

WPF commands are able to change only one aspect of the linked element's state: the value of its IsEnabled property. It's not hard to imagine situations where you need something a bit more sophisticated. For example, you might want to create a PageLayoutView command that can be switched on or off. When switched on, the corresponding controls should be adjusted accordingly. (For example, a linked menu item should be checked (displayed with a checkmark next to it), and a linked toolbar button should be highlighted, as a CheckBox is when you add it to a ToolBar.) Unfortunately, there's no way to keep track of the "checked" state of a command. That means you're forced to handle an event for that control and update its state and that of any other linked controls by hand.

There's no easy way to solve this problem. Even if you created a custom class that derives from RoutedUICommand and gave it the functionality for tracking its checked/unchecked state (and raising an event when this detail changes), you would also need to replace some of the related infrastructure. For example, you would need to create a custom CommandBinding class that could listen to notifications from your custom command, react when the checked/unchecked state changes, and then update the linked controls.

Checked buttons are an obvious example of user-interface state that falls outside the WPF command model. However, other details might suit a similar design. For example, you might create some sort of a split button that can be switched to different modes. Once again, there's no way to propagate this change to other linked controls through the command model.

Controls with Built-in Commands

Some input controls handle command events on their own. For example, the TextBox class handles the Cut, Copy, and Paste commands (as well as Undo and Redo commands and some of the commands from the EditingCommands class that select text and move the cursor to different positions).

When a control has its own hardwired command logic, you don't need to do anything to make your command work. For example, if you took the simple text editor shown in Figure 9-6 and added the following toolbar buttons, you would get automatic support for cutting, copying, and pasting text.

```
<ToolBar>
  <Button Command="Cut">Cut</Button>
  <Button Command="Copy">Copy</Button>
  <Button Command="Paste">Paste</Button>
</ToolBar>
```

You can click any of these buttons (while the text box has focus) to copy, cut, or paste text from the clipboard. Interestingly, the text box also handles the CanExecute event. If nothing is currently selected in the text box, the Cut and Copy commands will be disabled. All three commands will be automatically disabled when the focus changes to another control that doesn't support these commands (unless you've attached your own CanExecute event handler that enables them).

This example has an interesting detail. The Cut, Copy, and Paste commands are handled by the text box that has focus. However, the command is triggered by the button in the toolbar, which is a completely separate element. In this example, this process works seamlessly because the button is placed in a toolbar, and the ToolBar class includes some built-in magic that dynamically sets the CommandTarget property of its children to the control that currently has focus. (Technically, the ToolBar looks at the parent, which is the window, and finds the most recently focused control in that context, which is the text box. The ToolBar has a separate *focus scope*, and in that context, the button is focused.)

If you place your buttons in a different container (other than a ToolBar or Menu), you won't have this benefit. That means your buttons won't work unless you set the CommandTarget property manually. To do so, you must use a binding expression that names the target element. For example, if the text box is named txtDocument, you would define the buttons like this:

```
<Button Command="Cut"
 CommandTarget="{Binding ElementName=txtDocument}">Cut</Button>
<Button Command="Copy"
 CommandTarget="{Binding ElementName=txtDocument}">Copy</Button>
<Button Command="Paste"
 CommandTarget="{Binding ElementName=txtDocument}">Paste</Button>
```

Another, simpler option is to create a new focus scope by using the attached FocusManager.IsFocusScope property. This tells WPF to look for the element in the parent's focus scope when the command is triggered:

```
<StackPanel FocusManager.IsFocusScope="True">
  <Button Command="Cut">Cut</Button>
  <Button Command="Copy">Copy</Button>
  <Button Command="Paste">Paste</Button>
</StackPanel>
```

This approach has the added advantage that the same commands will apply to multiple controls, unlike the previous example where the CommandTarget was hard-coded. Incidentally, the Menu and ToolBar set the FocusManager.IsFocusScope property to True by default, but you can set it to False if you want the simpler command-routing behavior that doesn't hunt down the focused element in the parent's context.

In some rare cases, you might find that a control has built-in command support you don't want to enable. In this situation, you have three options for disabling the command.

Ideally, the control will provide a property that allows you to gracefully switch off the command support. This ensures that the control will remove the feature and adjust itself consistently. For example, the TextBox control provides an IsUndoEnabled property that you can set to False to prevent the Undo feature. (If IsUndoEnabled is True, the Ctrl+Z keystroke triggers it.)

If that fails, you can add a new binding for the command you want to disable. This binding can then supply a new CanExecute event handler that always responds False. Here's an example that uses this technique to remove support for the Cut feature of the text box:

```
Dim commandBinding As New CommandBinding( _
   ApplicationCommands.Cut, Nothing, AddressOf SuppressCommand)
txt.CommandBindings.Add(commandBinding)
```

and here's the event handler that sets the CanExecute state:

```
Private Sub SuppressCommand(ByVal sender As Object, _
   ByVal e As CanExecuteRoutedEventArgs)
      e.CanExecute = false
      e.Handled = true
End Sub
```

Notice that this code sets the Handled flag to prevent the text box from performing its own evaluation, which might set CanExecute to True.

This approach isn't perfect. It successfully disables both the Cut keystroke (Ctrl+X) and the Cut command in the context menu for the text box. However, the option will still appear in the context menu in a disabled state.

The final option is to remove the input that triggers the command by using the InputBindings collections. For example, you could disable the Ctrl+C keystroke that triggers the Copy command in a TextBox by using code like this:

```
Dim keyBinding As New KeyBinding( _
   ApplicationCommands.NotACommand, Key.C, ModifierKeys.Control)
txt.InputBindings.Add(keyBinding)
```

The trick is to use the special ApplicationCommands.NotACommand value, which is a command that does nothing. It's specifically intended for disabling input bindings.

When you use this approach, the Copy command is still enabled. You can trigger it through buttons of your own creation (or the context menu for the text box, unless you remove that as well by setting the ContextMenu property to Nothing).

■ **Note** You always need to add new command bindings or input bindings to disable features. You can't remove existing bindings. That's because existing bindings don't show up in the public CommandBinding and InputBinding collection. Instead, they're defined through a separate mechanism, called *class bindings*. In Chapter 18, you'll learn how to wire up commands in this way to the custom controls you build.

Advanced Commands

Now that you've seen the basics of commands, it's worth considering a few more sophisticated implementations. In the following sections, you'll learn how to use your own commands, treat the same command differently depending on the target, and use command parameters. You'll also consider how you can support a basic undo feature.

Custom Commands

As well stocked as the five command classes (ApplicationCommands, NavigationCommands, EditingCommands, ComponentCommands, and MediaCommands) are, they obviously can't provide everything your application might need. Fortunately, it's easy to define your own custom commands. All you need to do is instantiate a new RoutedUICommand object.

The RoutedUICommand class provides several constructors. You can create a RoutedUICommand with no additional information, but you'll almost always want to supply the command name, the command text, and the owning type. In addition, you may want to supply a keyboard shortcut for the InputGestures collection.

The best design is to follow the example of the WPF libraries and expose your custom commands through shared properties. Here's an example with a command named Requery:

```
Public Class DataCommands

    Private Shared requery As RoutedUICommand

    Shared Sub New()
        ' Initialize the command.
        Dim inputs As New InputGestureCollection()
        inputs.Add(New KeyGesture(Key.R, ModifierKeys.Control, "Ctrl+R"))
        requery = New RoutedUICommand("Requery", "Requery", _
          GetType(DataCommands), inputs)
    End Sub

    Public Shared ReadOnly Property Requery As RoutedUICommand
        Get
            Return requery
        End Get
    End Property

End Class
```

■ **Tip** You can also modify the RoutedCommand.InputGestures collection of an existing command—for example, by removing existing key bindings or adding new ones. You can even add mouse bindings, so a command is triggered when a combination of a mouse button and modifier key is pressed (although, in this case, you'll want to place the command binding on just the element where the mouse handling should come into effect).

Once you've defined a command, you can use it in your command bindings in the same way as any of the ready-made commands that are provided by WPF. However, there's one twist. If you want to use your command in XAML, you need to first map your .NET namespace to an XML namespace. For example, if your class is in a namespace named Commands (the default for a project named Commands), you would add this namespace mapping:

```
xmlns:local="clr-namespace:Commands"
```

In this example, *local* is chosen as the namespace alias. You can use any alias you want, as long as you are consistent in your XAML file.

Now you can access your command through the local namespace:

```
<CommandBinding Command="local:DataCommands.Requery"
  Executed="RequeryCommand_Executed"></CommandBinding>
```

Here's a complete example of a simple window that includes a button that triggers the Requery command:

```
<Window x:Class="CustomCommand"
    xmlns="http://schemas.microsoft.com/winfx/2006/xaml/presentation"
    xmlns:x="http://schemas.microsoft.com/winfx/2006/xaml"
    Title="CustomCommand" Height="300" Width="300">

  <Window.CommandBindings>
    <CommandBinding Command="local:DataCommands.Requery"
      Executed="RequeryCommand_Executed"></CommandBinding>
  </Window.CommandBindings>

  <Button Margin="5" Command="local:DataCommands.Requery">Requery</Button>
</Window>
```

To complete this example, you simply need to implement the RequeryCommand_Executed() event handler in your code. Optionally, you can also use the CanExecute event to selectively enable or disable this command.

■ **Tip** When using custom commands, you may need to call the shared CommandManager.InvalidateRequerySuggested() method to tell WPF to reevaluate the state of your command. WPF will then trigger the CanExecute event and update any command sources that use that command.

Using the Same Command in Different Places

One of the key ideas in the WPF command model is *scope*. Although there is exactly one copy of every command, the effect of using the command varies depending on where it's triggered. For example, if you have two text boxes, they both support the Cut, Copy, and Paste commands, but the operation happens only in the text box that currently has focus.

You haven't yet learned how to do this with the commands that you wire up yourself. For example, imagine you create a window with space for two documents, as shown in Figure 9-7.

Figure 9-7. *A two-files-at-once text editor*

If you use the Cut, Copy, and Paste commands, you'll find they automatically work on the correct text box. However, the commands you've implemented yourself—New, Open, and Save—do not. The problem is that when the Executed event fires for one of these commands, you have no idea whether it pertains to the first or second text box. Although the ExecutedRoutedEventArgs object provides a Source property, this property reflects the element that has the command binding (just like the sender reference). So far, all your command bindings have been attached to the containing window.

The solution to this problem is to bind the command differently in each text box by using the CommandBindings collection for the text box. Here's an example:

```
<TextBox.CommandBindings>
  <CommandBinding Command="ApplicationCommands.Save"
    Executed="SaveCommand_Executed"
    CanExecute="SaveCommand_CanExecute"></CommandBinding>
</TextBox.CommandBindings>
```

Now the text box handles the Executed event. In your event handler, you can use this information to make sure the correct information is saved:

```
Private Sub SaveCommand_Executed(ByVal sender As Object, _
  ByVal e As ExecutedRoutedEventArgs)
    Dim text As String = (CType(sender, TextBox)).Text
    MessageBox.Show("About to save: " & text)
    . . .
    isDirty = False
End Sub
```

This implementation has two minor issues. First, the simple isDirty flag no longer works, because you must keep track of two text boxes. This problem has several solutions. You could use the TextBox.Tag property to store the isDirty flag. That way, whenever the CanExecuteSave() method is called, you simply look at the Tag property of the sender. Or, you could create a private dictionary collection that stores the isDirty value, indexed by the control reference. When the CanExecuteSave() method is triggered, you simply look for the isDirty value that belongs to the sender. Here's the full code you would use:

```
Private isDirty As New Dictionary(Of Object, Boolean) ()

Private Sub txt_TextChanged(ByVal sender As Object, ByVal e As RoutedEventArgs)
    isDirty(sender) = True
End Sub

Private Sub SaveCommand_CanExecute(ByVal sender As Object, _
  ByVal e As CanExecuteRoutedEventArgs)
    If isDirty.ContainsKey(sender) AndAlso isDirty(sender) = True Then
        e.CanExecute = True
    Else
        e.CanExecute = False
    End If
End Sub
```

The other issue with the current implementation is that it creates two command bindings where you really need only one. This adds clutter to your XAML file and makes it more difficult to maintain. This problem is especially bad if you have a large number of commands that are shared between both text boxes.

The solution is to create a single command binding and add that same binding to the CommandBindings collection of both text boxes. This is easy to accomplish in code. If you want to polish it off in XAML, you need to use WPF resources. You simply add a section to the top of your window that creates the CommandBinding object you need to use and gives it a key name:

```
<Window.Resources>
  <CommandBinding x:Key="binding" Command="ApplicationCommands.Save"
    Executed="SaveCommand" CanExecute="CanExecuteSave">
  </CommandBinding>
</Window.Resources>
```

To insert the object into another place in your markup, you use the StaticResource extension and supply the key name:

```
<TextBox.CommandBindings>
  <StaticResource ResourceKey="binding"></StaticResource>
</TextBox.CommandBindings>
```

Using a Command Parameter

So far, the examples you've seen haven't used the command parameter to pass extra information. However, some commands always require some extra information. For example, the NavigationCommands.Zoom command needs a percentage value to use for its zoom. Similarly, you can imagine that some of the commands you're already using might require extra information in certain scenarios. For example, if you use the Save command with the two-file text editor in Figure 9-7, you need to know which file to use when saving the document.

The solution is to set the CommandParameter property. You can set this directly on an ICommandSource control (and you can even use a binding expression that gets a value from another control). For example, here's how you might set the zoom percentage for a button that's linked to the Zoom command by reading the value from another text box:

```
<Button Command="NavigationCommands.Zoom"
  CommandParameter="{Binding ElementName=txtZoom, Path=Text}">
  Zoom To Value
</Button>
```

Unfortunately, that approach doesn't always work. For example, in the two-file text editor, the Save button is reused for each text box, but each text box needs to use a different file name. In situations like these, you're forced to store the information somewhere else (for example, in the TextBox.Tag property or in a separate collection that indexes file names to line up with your text boxes), or you need to trigger the command programmatically like this:

```
ApplicationCommands.[New].Execute(theFileName, CType(sender, Button))
```

Either way, the parameter is made available in the Executed event handler through the ExecutedRoutedEventArgs.Parameter property.

Tracking and Reversing Commands

One feature that the command model lacks is the ability to make a command reversible. Although there is an ApplicationCommands.Undo command, this command is generally used by edit controls (such as the TextBox) that maintain their own Undo histories. If you want to support an application-wide Undo feature, you need to track the previous state internally and restore it when the Undo command is triggered.

Unfortunately, it's not easy to extend the WPF command system. Relatively few entry points are available for you to connect custom logic, and those that exist are not documented. To create a general-purpose, reusable Undo feature, you would need to create a whole new set of "undoable" command classes and a specialized type of command binding. In essence, you would be forced to replace the WPF command system with a new one of your own creation.

A better solution is to design your own system for tracking and reversing commands, but use the CommandManager class to keep a command history. Figure 9-8 shows an example that does exactly that. The window consists of two text boxes, where you can type freely, and a list box that keeps track of every command that has taken place in both text boxes. You can reverse the last command by clicking the Reverse Last Action button.

Figure 9-8. *An application-wide Undo feature*

To build this solution, you need to use a few new techniques. The first detail is a class for tracking the command history. It might occur to you to build an undo system that stores a list of recent commands. (Perhaps you would even like to create a derived ReversibleCommand class that exposes a method such as Unexecute() for reversing the task it did previously.) Unfortunately, this system won't work, because all WPF commands are treated like singletons. That means there is only one instance of each command in your application.

To understand the problem, imagine you support the EditingCommands.Backspace command, and the user performs several backspaces in a row. You can register that fact by adding the Backspace command to a stack of recent commands, but you're actually adding the same command object several times. As a result, there's no easy way to store other information along with that command, such as the character that has just been deleted. If you want to store this state, you'll need to build your own data structure to do it. This example uses a class named CommandHistoryItem.

Every CommandHistoryItem object tracks several pieces of information:

- The command name.

- The element on which the command was performed. In this example, there are two text boxes, so it could be either one.

- The property that was changed in the target element. In this example, it will be the Text property of the TextBox class.

- An object that you can use to store the previous state of the affected element (for example, the text the text box had before the command was executed).

263

■ **Note** This design is fairly crafty in that it stores the state for one element. If you stored a snapshot of the state in the entire window, you would use significantly more memory. However, if you have large amounts of data (such as text boxes with dozens of lines), the Undo overhead could be more than trivial. The solution is to limit the number of items you keep in the history, or to use a more intelligent (and more complex) routine that stores information about only the changed data, rather than *all* the data.

The CommandHistoryItem also includes one method: an all-purpose Undo() method. This method uses reflection to apply the previous value to the modified property. This works for restoring the text in a TextBox, but in a more complex application, you would need a hierarchy of CommandHistoryItem classes, each of which is able to revert a different type of action in a different way.

Here's the complete code for the CommandHistoryItem class:

```
Public Class CommandHistoryItem

    Private _commandName As String
    Public Property CommandName() As String
        Get
            Return _commandName
        End Get
        Set(ByVal value As String)
            _commandName = value
        End Set
    End Property

    Private _elementActedOn As UIElement
    Public Property ElementActedOn() As UIElement
        Get
            Return _elementActedOn
        End Get
        Set(ByVal value As UIElement)
            _elementActedOn = value
        End Set
    End Property

    Private _propertyActedOn As String
    Public Property PropertyActedOn() As String
        Get
            Return _propertyActedOn
        End Get
        Set(ByVal value As String)
            _propertyActedOn = value
        End Set
    End Property

    Private _previousState As Object
    Public Property PreviousState() As Object
        Get
            Return _previousState
        End Get
```

```
        Set(ByVal value As Object)
            _previousState = value
        End Set
    End Property


    Public Sub New(ByVal commandName As String)
        Me.New(commandName, Nothing, "", Nothing)
    End Sub


    Public Sub New(ByVal commandName As String, _
      ByVal elementActedOn As UIElement, ByVal propertyActedOn As String, _
      ByVal previousState As Object)
        Me.CommandName = commandName
        Me.ElementActedOn = elementActedOn
        Me.PropertyActedOn = propertyActedOn
        Me.PreviousState = previousState
    End Sub


    Public ReadOnly Property CanUndo() As Boolean
        Get
            Return (Not ElementActedOn Is Nothing AndAlso PropertyActedOn <> "")
        End Get
    End Property


    Public Sub Undo()
        Dim elementType As Type = ElementActedOn.GetType()
        Dim propInfo As PropertyInfo = elementType.GetProperty(PropertyActedOn)
        propInfo.SetValue(ElementActedOn, PreviousState, Nothing)
    End Sub

End Class
```

The next ingredient you need is a command that performs the application-wide Undo action. The ApplicationCommands.Undo command isn't suitable, because it's already used for individual controls for a different purpose (reverting the last editing change). Instead, you need to create a new command, as shown here:

```
Private Shared _applicationUndo As RoutedUICommand

Public Shared ReadOnly Property ApplicationUndo() As RoutedUICommand
    Get
        Return _applicationUndo
    End Get
End Property

Shared Sub New()
    _applicationUndo = New RoutedUICommand("ApplicationUndo", _
      "Application Undo", GetType(MonitorCommands))
End Sub
```

In this example, the command is defined in a window class named MonitorCommands.

So far, this code is relatively unremarkable (aside from the nifty bit of reflection code that performs the undo operation). The more difficult part is integrating this command history into the WPF command model. An ideal solution would do this in such a way that you can track any command, regardless of how it's triggered and how it's bound. In a poorly designed solution, you would be forced to rely on a whole new set of custom command objects that have this logic built in or to manually handle the Executed event of every command.

It's easy enough to react to a specific command, but how can you react when *any* command executes? The trick is to use the CommandManager, which exposes a few shared events. These events include CanExecute, PreviewCanExecute, Executed, and PreviewCanExecuted. In this example, the last two are the most interesting, because they fire whenever any command is executed.

The Executed event is suppressed by the CommandManager, but you can still attach an event handler by using the UIElement.AddHandler() method and passing in a value of True for the optional third parameter. This allows you to receive the event even though it's handled, as described in Chapter 4. However, the Executed event fires *after* the event is executed, at which point it's too late to save the state of the affected control in your command history. Instead, you need to respond to the PreviewExecuted event, which fires just before.

Here's the code that attaches the PreviewExecuted event handler in the window constructor and removes it when the window is closed:

```
Public Sub New()
    InitializeComponent()

    Me.AddHandler(CommandManager.PreviewExecutedEvent, _
        New ExecutedRoutedEventHandler(AddressOf CommandExecuted))
End Sub

Private Sub window_Unloaded(ByVal sender As Object, ByVal e As RoutedEventArgs)
    Me.RemoveHandler(CommandManager.PreviewExecutedEvent, _
        New ExecutedRoutedEventHandler(AddressOf CommandExecuted))
End Sub
```

When the PreviewExecuted event fires, you need to determine whether it's a command that deserves your attention. If so, you can create the CommandHistoryItem and add it to the Undo stack. You also need to watch out for two potential problems. First, when you click a toolbar button to perform a command on the text box, the CommandExecuted event is raised twice: once for the toolbar button and once for the text box. This code avoids duplicate entries in the Undo history by ignoring the command if the sender is ICommandSource. Second, you need to explicitly ignore the commands you don't want to add to the Undo history. One example is the ApplicationUndo command, which allows you to reverse the previous action.

```
Private Sub CommandExecuted(ByVal sender As Object, _
  ByVal e As ExecutedRoutedEventArgs)
    ' Ignore menu button source.
    If TypeOf e.Source Is ICommandSource Then
        Return
    End If

    ' Ignore the ApplicationUndo command.
    If e.Command Is MonitorCommands.ApplicationUndo Then
        Return
    End If

    Dim txt As TextBox = TryCast(e.Source, TextBox)
    If Not txt Is Nothing Then
```

```
        Dim cmd As RoutedCommand = CType(e.Command, RoutedCommand)
        Dim historyItem As New CommandHistoryItem( _
          cmd.Name, txt, "Text", txt.Text)

        Dim item As New ListBoxItem()
        item.Content = historyItem
        lstHistory.Items.Add(historyItem)
    End If
End Sub
```

This example stores all CommandHistoryItem objects in a ListBox. The ListBox has DisplayMember set to Name so that it shows the CommandHistoryItem.Name property of each item. This code supports the Undo feature only if the command is being fired for a text box. However, it's generic enough to work with any text box in the window. You could extend this code to support other controls and properties.

The last detail is the code that performs the application-wide Undo. Using a CanExecute handler, you can make sure that this code is executed only when there is at least one item in the Undo history:

```
Private Sub ApplicationUndoCommand_CanExecute(ByVal sender As Object, _
  ByVal e As CanExecuteRoutedEventArgs)
    If lstHistory Is Nothing OrElse lstHistory.Items.Count = 0 Then
        e.CanExecute = False
    Else
        e.CanExecute = True
    End If
End Sub
```

To revert the last change, you simply call the Undo() method of the CommandHistoryItem and then remove it from the list:

```
Private Sub ApplicationUndoCommand_Executed(ByVal sender As Object, _
  ByVal e As RoutedEventArgs)
    Dim historyItem As CommandHistoryItem = _
      CType(lstHistory.Items(lstHistory.Items.Count - 1), CommandHistoryItem)

    If historyItem.CanUndo Then
        historyItem.Undo()
    End If
    lstHistory.Items.Remove(historyItem)
End Sub
```

Although this example demonstrates the concept and presents a simple application with multiple controls that fully support the Undo feature, you would need to make many refinements before you would use an approach like this in a real-world application. For example, you would need to spend considerable time refining the event handler for the CommandManager.PreviewExecuted event to ignore commands that clearly shouldn't be tracked. (Currently, events such as selecting text with the keyboard and hitting the spacebar raise commands.) Similarly, you probably would want to add CommandHistoryItem objects for actions that should be reversible but aren't represented by commands, such as typing a bunch of text and then navigating to another control. Finally, you probably would want to limit the Undo history to just the most recent commands.

The Last Word

In this chapter, you explored the WPF command model. You learned how to hook controls to commands, respond when the commands are triggered, and handle commands differently based on where they occur. You also designed your own custom commands and learned how to extend the WPF command system with a basic command history and Undo feature.

As you've seen in this chapter, the WPF command model isn't quite as streamlined as other bits of WPF architecture. The way that it plugs into the routed event model requires a fairly complex assortment of classes, and its inner workings aren't easy to customize. In fact, to get the most out of WPF commands, you probably need to use a separate toolkit that *extends* WPF by using the Model View ViewModel (MVVM) pattern. The most popular example is Prism (see `http://compositewpf.codeplex.com`).

■ **Tip** Even if you're building huge WPF applications with a team of developers, and Prism interests you, don't delve into it just yet. It's best to learn the fundamentals of WPF first (by reading this book), before you add a whole new layer of complexity.

CHAPTER 10

Resources

WPF's resource system is simply a way of keeping around a set of useful objects, such as commonly used brushes, styles, or templates, so you can reuse them more easily.

Although you can create and manipulate resources in code, you'll usually define them in your XAML markup. After a resource is defined, you can use it throughout the rest of the markup in your window (or, in the case of an application resource, throughout the rest of your application). This technique simplifies your markup, saves repetitive coding, and allows you to store user interface details (such as your application's color scheme) in a central place so they can be modified easily. Object resources are also the basis for reusing WPF styles, as you'll see in the next chapter.

Note Don't confuse WPF's *object* resources with the *assembly* resources you learned about in Chapter 7. An assembly resource is a chunk of binary data that's embedded in your compiled assembly. You can use an assembly resource to make sure your application has an image or sound file it needs. An object resource, on the other hand, is a .NET object that you want to define in one place and use in several others.

Resource Basics

WPF allows you to define resources in code or in a variety of places in your markup (along with specific controls, in specific windows, or across the entire application).

Resources have these important benefits:

> *Efficiency*: Resources let you define an object once and use it in several places in your markup. This streamlines your code and makes it marginally more efficient.

> *Maintainability*: Resources let you take low-level formatting details (such as font sizes) and move them to a central place where they're easy to change. It's the XAML equivalent of creating constants in your code.

> *Adaptability*: Once certain information is separated from the rest of your application and placed in a resource section, it becomes possible to modify it dynamically. For example, you may want to change resource details based on user preferences or the current language.

The Resources Collection

Every element includes a Resources property, which stores a dictionary collection of resources. (It's an instance of the ResourceDictionary class.) The resources collection can hold any type of object, indexed by string.

Although every element includes the Resources property (which is defined as part of the FrameworkElement class), the most common way to define resources is at the window level. That's because every element has access to the resources in its own resource collection and the resources in all of its parents' resource collections.

For example, consider the window with three buttons shown in Figure 10-1. Two of the three buttons use the same brush—an image brush that paints a tile pattern of happy faces.

Figure 10-1. *A window that reuses a brush*

In this case, it's clear that you want both the top and bottom buttons to have the same styling. However, you might want to change the characteristics of the image brush later. For that reason, it makes sense to define the image brush in the resources for the window and reuse it as necessary.

Here's how you define the brush:

```
<Window.Resources>
  <ImageBrush x:Key="TileBrush" TileMode="Tile"
    ViewportUnits="Absolute" Viewport="0 0 32 32"
    ImageSource="happyface.jpg" Opacity="0.3">
  </ImageBrush>
</Window.Resources>
```

The details of the image brush aren't terribly important (although Chapter 12 has the specifics). What *is* important is the first attribute, named Key (and preceded by the *x* namespace prefix, which puts it in the XAML namespace rather than the WPF namespace). This assigns the name under which the brush will be indexed in the Window.Resources collection. You can use whatever you want, so long as you use the same name when you need to retrieve the resource.

■ **Note**   You can instantiate any .NET class in the resources section (including your own custom classes), as long as it's XAML-friendly. That means it needs to have a few basic characteristics, such as a public zero-argument constructor and writeable properties.

To use a resource in your XAML markup, you need a way to refer to it. This is accomplished using a markup extension. In fact, there are two markup extensions that you can use: one for dynamic resources and one for static resources. Static resources are set once, when the window is first created. Dynamic resources are reapplied if the resource is changed. (You'll study the difference more closely a little bit later in this chapter.) In this example, the image brush never changes, so the static resource is fine.

Here's one of the buttons that uses the resource:

```
<Button Background="{StaticResource TileBrush}"
  Margin="5" Padding="5" FontWeight="Bold" FontSize="14">
  A Tiled Button
</Button>
```

In this case, the resource is retrieved and used to assign the Button.Background property. You could perform the same feat (with slightly more overhead) by using a dynamic resource:

```
<Button Background="{DynamicResource TileBrush}"
```

Using a simple .NET object for a resource really is this easy. However, there are a few finer points you need to consider. The following sections will fill you in.

The Hierarchy of Resources

Every element has its own resource collection, and WPF performs a recursive search up your element tree to find the resource you want. In the current example, you could move the image brush from the Resources collection of the window to the Resources collection of the StackPanel that holds all three buttons without changing the way the application works. You could also put the image brush in the Button.Resources collection, but then you'd need to define it twice—once for each button.

There's another issue to consider. When using a static resource, you must always define a resource in your markup *before* you refer to it. That means that even though it's perfectly valid (from a markup perspective) to put the Windows.Resources section after the main content of the window (the StackPanel that contains all the buttons), this change will break the current example. When the XAML parser encounters a static reference to a resource it doesn't know, it throws an exception. (You can get around this problem by using a dynamic resource, but there's no good reason to incur the extra overhead.)

As a result, if you want to place your resource in the button element, you need to rearrange your markup a little so that the resource is defined before the background is set. Here's one way to do it:

```
<Button Margin="5" Padding="5" FontWeight="Bold" FontSize="14">
  <Button.Resources>
    <ImageBrush x:Key="TileBrush" TileMode="Tile"
      ViewportUnits="Absolute" Viewport="0 0 10 10"
      ImageSource="happyface.jpg" Opacity="0.3"></ImageBrush>
  </Button.Resources>

  <Button.Background>
    <StaticResource ResourceKey="TileBrush"/>
  </Button.Background>

  <Button.Content>Another Tiled Button</Button.Content>
</Button>
```

The syntax for the static resource markup extension looks a bit different in this example because it's set in a nested element (not an attribute). The resource key is specified using the ResourceKey property to point to the right resource.

Interestingly, you can reuse resource names as long as you don't use the same resource name more than once in the same collection. That means you could create a window like this, which defines the image brush in two places:

```
<Window x:Class="TwoResources"
    xmlns="http://schemas.microsoft.com/winfx/2006/xaml/presentation"
    xmlns:x="http://schemas.microsoft.com/winfx/2006/xaml"
    Title="Resources" Height="300" Width="300" >

    <Window.Resources>
        <ImageBrush x:Key="TileBrush" TileMode="Tile"
                ViewportUnits="Absolute" Viewport="0 0 32 32"
                ImageSource="happyface.jpg" Opacity="0.3"></ImageBrush>
    </Window.Resources>

    <StackPanel Margin="5">
        <Button Background="{StaticResource TileBrush}" Padding="5"
          FontWeight="Bold" FontSize="14" Margin="5" >A Tiled Button</Button>

        <Button Padding="5" Margin="5"
          FontWeight="Bold" FontSize="14">A Normal Button</Button>
        <Button Background="{DynamicResource TileBrush}" Padding="5" Margin="5"
          FontWeight="Bold" FontSize="14">

            <Button.Resources>
              <ImageBrush x:Key="TileBrush" TileMode="Tile"
                ViewportUnits="Absolute" Viewport="0 0 32 32"
                ImageSource="sadface.jpg" Opacity="0.3"></ImageBrush>
            </Button.Resources>

            <Button.Content>Another Tiled Button</Button.Content>
        </Button>

    </StackPanel>
</Window>
```

In this case, the button uses the resource it finds first. Because it begins by searching its own Resources collection, the second button uses the sadface.jpg graphic, while the first button gets the brush from the containing window and uses the happyface.jpg image.

Static and Dynamic Resources

You might assume that because the previous example used a static resource, it's immune to any changes you make to your resource (in this case, the image brush). However, that's not the case.

For example, imagine you execute this code at some point after the resource has been applied and the window has been displayed:

```
Dim brush As ImageBrush
brush = CType(Me.Resources("TileBrush"), ImageBrush)
brush.Viewport = New Rect(0, 0, 5, 5)
```

This code retrieves the brush from the Window.Resources collection and manipulates it. (Technically, the code changes the size of each tile, shrinking the happy face and packing the image pattern more tightly.) When you run this code, you probably don't expect any reaction in your user interface—after all, it's a static resource. However, this change does propagate to the two buttons. In fact, the buttons are updated with the new Viewport property setting, *regardless* of whether they use the brush through a static resource or a dynamic resource.

The reason this works is because the Brush class derives from a class named Freezable. The Freezable class has basic-change tracking features (and it can be "frozen" to a read-only state if it doesn't need to change). What that means is that whenever you change a brush in WPF, any controls that use that brush refresh themselves automatically. It doesn't matter whether they get their brushes through a resource.

At this point, you're probably wondering what the difference is between a static and dynamic resource. The difference is that a static resource grabs the object from the resources collection once. Depending on the type of object (and the way it's used), any changes you make to that object may be noticed right away. However, the dynamic resource looks the object up in the resources collection every time it's needed. That means you could place an entirely new object under the same key, and the dynamic resource would pick up your change.

To see an example that illustrates the difference, consider the following code, which replaces the current image brush with a completely new (and boring) solid blue brush:

```
Me.Resources("TileBrush") = New SolidColorBrush(Colors.LightBlue)
```

A dynamic resource picks up this change, while a static resource has no idea that its brush has been replaced in the Resources collection by something else. It continues using the original ImageBrush instead.

Figure 10-2 shows this example in a window that includes a dynamic resource (the top button) and a static resource (the bottom button).

Figure 10-2. *Dynamic and static resources*

Usually, you don't need the overhead of a dynamic resource, and your application will work perfectly well with a static resource. One notable exception is if you're creating resources that depend on Windows settings (such as system colors). In this situation, you need to use dynamic resources if you want to be able to react to any change in the current color scheme. (Or if you use static resources, you'll keep using the old color scheme until the user restarts the application.) You'll learn more about how this works when you tackle system resources a bit later in this chapter.

As a general guideline, use dynamic properties only when you have these conditions:

- Your resource has properties that depend on system settings (such as the current Windows colors or fonts).

- You plan to replace your resource objects programmatically (for example, to implement some sort of dynamic skinning feature, as demonstrated in Chapter 17).

However, you shouldn't get overly ambitious with dynamic resources. The primary issue is that changing a resource doesn't necessarily trigger a refresh in your user interface. (It does in the brush example because of the way brush objects are constructed—namely, they have this notification support built in.) When you need dynamic updates (in other words, the ability to change your content and have a control adjust itself automatically), data binding is usually a much better choice.

■ **Note** On rare occasions, dynamic resources are also used to improve the first-time load performance of a window. That's because static resources are always loaded when the window is created, while dynamic resources are loaded when they're first used. However, you won't see any benefit unless your resource is extremely large and complex (in which case parsing its markup takes a nontrivial amount of time).

Nonshared Resources

Ordinarily, when you use a resource in multiple places, you're using the same object instance. This behavior—called *sharing*—is usually what you want. However, it's also possible to tell the parser to create a separate instance of your object each time it's used.

To turn off sharing, you use the Shared attribute, as shown here:

```
<ImageBrush x:Key="TileBrush" x:Shared="False" ...></ImageBrush>
```

There are few good reasons for using nonshared resources. You might consider nonshared resources if you want to modify your resource instances separately later. For example, you could create a window that has several buttons that use the same brush but turn off sharing so that you can change each brush individually. This approach isn't very common because it's inefficient. In this example, it would be better to let all the buttons use the same brush initially and then create and apply new brush objects as needed. That way, you're incurring the overhead of extra brush objects only when you really need to do so.

Another reason you might use nonshared resources is if you want to reuse an object in a way that otherwise wouldn't be allowed. For example, using this technique, you could define an element (such as an Image or a Button) as a resource and then display that element in several places in a window.

Once again, this usually isn't the best approach. For example, if you want to reuse an Image element, it makes more sense to store the relevant piece of information (such as the BitmapImage object that identifies the image source) and share that between multiple Image elements. And if you simply want to standardize controls so they share the same properties, you're far better off using styles, which are described in the next chapter. Styles give you the ability to create identical or nearly identical copies of any element, but they also allow you to override property values when they don't apply and attach distinct event handlers, two features you'd lose if you simply cloned an element by using a nonshared resource.

Accessing Resources in Code

Usually, you'll define and use resources in your markup. However, if the need arises, you can work with the resources collection in code.

As you've already seen, you can pull items out of the resources collection by name. However, to use this approach, you need to use the resource collection of the right element. This limitation doesn't apply to your markup. A control such as a button can retrieve a resource without specifically knowing where it's defined. When it attempts to assign the brush to its Background property, WPF checks the resources collection of the button for a resource named TileBrush, and then it checks the resources collection of the containing StackPanel and then the containing window. (This process actually continues to look at application and system resources, as you'll see in the next section.)

You can hunt for a resource in the same way using the FrameworkElement.FindResource() method. Here's an example that looks for the resource of a button (or one of its higher-level containers) when a Click event fires:

```
Private Sub cmdChange_Click(ByVal sender As object, ByVal e As RoutedEventArgs)
    Dim cmd As Button = CType(sender, Button)
    Dim brush As ImageBrush = CType(sender.FindResource("TileBrush"), _
      ImageBrush)
    ...
End Sub
```

Instead of FindResource(), you can use the TryFindResource() method that returns a null reference (Nothing) if a resource can't be found, rather than throwing an exception.

Incidentally, you can also add resources programmatically. Pick the element where you want to place the resource, and use the Add() method of the resources collection. However, it's much more common to define resources in markup.

Application Resources

The Window isn't the last stop in the resource search. If you indicate a resource that can't be found in a control or any of its containers (up to the containing window or page), WPF continues to check the set of resources you've defined for your application. In Visual Studio, these are the resources you've defined in the markup for your App.xaml file, as shown here:

```
<Application x:Class="Application"
    xmlns="http://schemas.microsoft.com/winfx/2006/xaml/presentation"
    xmlns:x="http://schemas.microsoft.com/winfx/2006/xaml"
    StartupUri="Menu.xaml"
    >
    <Application.Resources>
      <ImageBrush x:Key="TileBrush" TileMode="Tile"
        ViewportUnits="Absolute" Viewport="0 0 32 32"
        ImageSource="happyface.jpg" Opacity="0.3">
      </ImageBrush>
    </Application.Resources>
</Application>
```

As you've probably already guessed, application resources give you a great way to reuse an object across your entire application. In this example, it's a good choice if you plan to use the image brush in more than one window.

■ **Note** Before creating an application resource, consider the trade-off between complexity and reuse. Adding an application resource gives you better reuse, but it adds complexity because it's not immediately clear which windows use a given resource. (It's conceptually the same as an old-style C++ program with too many global variables.) A good guideline is to use application resources if your object is reused widely (for example, in many windows). If it's used in just two or three, consider defining the resource in each window.

It turns out that application resources *still* aren't the final stop when an element searches for a resource. If the resource can't be found in the application resources, the element continues to look at the system resources.

System Resources

As you learned earlier, dynamic resources are primarily intended to help your application respond to changes in system environment settings. However, this raises a question—how do you retrieve the system environment settings and use them in your code in the first place?

The secret is a set of three classes named SystemColors, SystemFonts, and SystemParameters, all of which are in the System.Windows namespace. SystemColors gives you access to color settings; SystemFonts gives you access to font settings; and SystemParameters wraps a huge list of settings that describe the standard size of various screen elements, keyboard and mouse settings, and screen size, and whether various graphical effects (such as hot tracking, drop shadows, and showing window contents while dragging) are switched on.

■ **Note**   There are two versions of the SystemColors and SystemFonts classes. They're found in the System.Windows namespace and the System.Drawing namespace. Those in the System.Windows namespace are part of WPF. They use the right data types and support the resource system. The ones in the System.Drawing namespace are part of Windows Forms. They aren't useful in a WPF application.

The SystemColors, SystemFonts, and SystemParameters classes expose all their details through shared properties. For example, SystemColors.WindowTextColor gets you a Color structure that you can use as you please. Here's an example that uses it to create a brush and fill the foreground of an element:

```
label.Foreground = New SolidBrush(SystemColors.WindowTextColor)
```

Or to be a bit more efficient, you can just use the ready-made brush property:

```
label.Foreground = SystemColors.WindowTextBrush
```

In WPF, you can access shared properties by using the static markup extension. For example, here's how you could set the foreground of the same label by using XAML:

```
<Label Foreground="{x:Static SystemColors.WindowTextBrush}">
  Ordinary text
</Label>
```

This example doesn't use a resource. It also suffers from a minor failing—when the window is parsed and the label is created, a brush is created based on the current "snapshot" of the window text color. If you change the Windows colors while this application is running (after the window containing the label has been shown), the label won't update itself. Applications that behave this way are considered to be a bit rude.

To solve this problem, you can't set the Foreground property directly to a brush object. Instead, you need to set it to a DynamicResource object that wraps this system resource. Fortunately, all the System*Xxx* classes provide a complementary set of properties that return ResourceKey objects—references that let you pull the resource out of the collection of system resources. These properties have the same name as the ordinary property that returns the object directly, with the word *Key* added to the end. For example, the resource key for the SystemColors.WindowTextBrush is SystemColors.WindowTextBrushKey.

■ Note Resource keys aren't simple names—they're references that tell WPF where to look to find a specific resource. The ResourceKey class is opaque, so it doesn't show you the low-level details about how system resources are identified. However, there's no need to worry about your resources conflicting with the system resources because they are in separate assemblies and are treated differently.

Here's how you can use a resource from one of the System*Xxx* classes:

```
<Label Foreground="{DynamicResource {x:Static SystemColors.WindowTextBrushKey}}">
  Ordinary text
</Label>
```

This markup is a bit more complex than the previous example. It begins by defining a dynamic resource. However, the dynamic resource isn't pulled out of the resource collection in your application. Instead, it uses a key that's defined by the SystemColors.WindowTextBrushKey property. Because this property is shared, you also need to throw in the static markup extension so that the parser understands what you're trying to do.

Now that you've made this change, you have a label that can update itself seamlessly when system settings change.

Resource Dictionaries

If you want to share resources between multiple projects, you can create a *resource dictionary*. A resource dictionary is simply a XAML document that does nothing but store the resources you want to use.

Creating a Resource Dictionary

Here's an example of a resource dictionary that has one resource:

```
<ResourceDictionary
 xmlns="http://schemas.microsoft.com/winfx/2006/xaml/presentation"
 xmlns:x="http://schemas.microsoft.com/winfx/2006/xaml">

  <ImageBrush x:Key="TileBrush" TileMode="Tile"
    ViewportUnits="Absolute" Viewport="0 0 32 32"
    ImageSource="happyface.jpg" Opacity="0.3">
  </ImageBrush>
</ResourceDictionary>
```

When you add a resource dictionary to an application, make sure the Build Action is set to Page (as it is for any other XAML file). This ensures that your resource dictionary is compiled to BAML for best performance. However, it's perfectly allowed to have a resource dictionary with a Build Action of Resource, in which case it's embedded in the assembly but not compiled. Parsing it at runtime is then imperceptibly slower.

Using a Resource Dictionary

To use a resource dictionary, you need to merge it into a resource collection somewhere in your application. You could do this in a specific window, but it's more common to merge it into the resources collection for the application, as shown here:

```
<Application x:Class="Application"
    xmlns="http://schemas.microsoft.com/winfx/2006/xaml/presentation"
    xmlns:x="http://schemas.microsoft.com/winfx/2006/xaml"
    StartupUri="Menu.xaml" >
  <Application.Resources>
    <ResourceDictionary>
      <ResourceDictionary.MergedDictionaries>
        <ResourceDictionary Source="AppBrushes.xaml"/>
        <ResourceDictionary Source="WizardBrushes.xaml"/>
      </ResourceDictionary.MergedDictionaries>
    </ResourceDictionary>
  </Application.Resources>
</Application>
```

This markup works by explicitly creating a ResourceDictionary object. The resources collection is always a ResourceDictionary object, but this is one case where you need to specify that detail explicitly so that you can also set the ResourceDictionary.MergedDictionaries property. If you don't take this step, the MergedDictionaries property will be a null reference (Nothing).

The MergedDictionaries collection is a collection of ResourceDictionary objects that you want to use to supplement your resource collection. In this example, there are two: one that's defined in the AppBrushes.xaml resource dictionary and another that's defined in the WizardBrushes.xaml.

If you want to add your own resources *and* merge in resource dictionaries, you simply need to place your resources before or after the MergedProperties section, as shown here:

```
<Application.Resources>
  <ResourceDictionary>
    <ResourceDictionary.MergedDictionaries>
      <ResourceDictionary Source="AppBrushes.xaml"/>
      <ResourceDictionary Source="WizardBrushes.xaml"/>
    </ResourceDictionary.MergedDictionaries>
    <ImageBrush x:Key="GraphicalBrush1" ... ></ImageBrush>
    <ImageBrush x:Key="GraphicalBrush2" ... ></ImageBrush>
  </ResourceDictionary>
</Application.Resources>
```

■ **Note** As you learned earlier, it's perfectly reasonable to have resources with the same name stored in different but overlapping resource collections. However, it's not acceptable to merge resource dictionaries that use the same resource names. If there's a duplicate, you'll receive a XamlParseException when you compile your application.

One reason to use resource dictionaries is to define one or more reusable application "skins" that you can apply to your controls. (You'll learn how to develop this technique in Chapter 17.) Another reason is to store content that needs to be localized (such as error message strings).

Sharing Resources Between Assemblies

If you want to share a resource dictionary between multiple applications, you could copy and distribute the XAML file that contains the resource dictionary. This is the simplest approach, but it doesn't give you any version control. A more structured approach is to compile your resource dictionary in a separate class library assembly and distribute that component instead.

When sharing a compiled assembly with one or more resource dictionaries, there's another challenge to face—namely, you need a way to extract the resource you want and use it in your application. There are two approaches you can take. The most straightforward solution is to use code that creates the appropriate ResourceDictionary object. For example, if you have a resource dictionary in a class library assembly named ReusableDictionary.xaml, you could use the following code to create it manually:

```
Dim resourceDictionary As New ResourceDictionary()
resourceDictionary.Source = New Uri( _
  "ResourceLibrary;component/ReusableDictionary.xaml", UriKind.Relative)
```

This code snippet uses the pack URI syntax you learned about earlier in this chapter. It constructs a relative URI that points to the compiled XAML resource named ReusableDictionary.xaml in the other assembly. Once you've created the ResourceDictionary object, you can manually retrieve the resource you want from the collection:

```
cmd.Background = CType(resourceDictionary("TileBrush"), Brush)
```

However, you don't need to assign resources manually. Any DynamicResource references you have in your window will be automatically reevaluated when you load a new resource dictionary. You'll see an example of this technique in Chapter 17, when you build a dynamic skinning feature.

If you don't want to write any code, you have another choice. You can use the ComponentResourceKey markup extension, which is designed for just this purpose. You use the ComponentResourceKey to create the key name for your resource. By taking this step, you indicate to WPF that you plan to share your resource between assemblies.

▧ **Note** Up until this point, you've seen only resources that use strings (such as "TileBrush") for key names. Using a string is the most common way to name a resource. However, WPF has some clever resource extensibility that kicks in automatically when you use certain types of key names that aren't strings. For example, in the next chapter you'll see that you can use a Type object as a key name for a style. This tells WPF to apply the style to the appropriate type of element automatically. Similarly, you can use an instance of ComponentResourceKey as a key name for any resource you want to share between assemblies.

Before you go any further, you need to make sure you've given your resource dictionary the right name. For this trick to work, your resource dictionary must be in a file named generic.xaml, and that file must be placed in a Themes subfolder in your application. The resources in the generic.xaml files are considered part of the default theme, and they're always made available. You'll use this trick many more times, particularly when you build custom controls in Chapter 18.

Figure 10-3 shows the proper organization of files. The top project, named ResourceLibrary, includes the generic.xaml file in the correct folder. The bottom project, named Resources, has a reference to ResourceLibrary, so it can use the resources it contains.

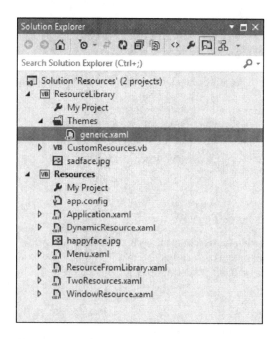

Figure 10-3. *Sharing resources with a class library*

■ **Tip** If you have a lot of resources and you want to organize them in the best way possible, you can create individual resource dictionaries, just as you did before. However, make sure you merge these dictionaries into the generic.xaml file so that they're readily available.

The next step is to create the key name for the resource you want to share, which is stored in the ResourceLibrary assembly. When using a ComponentResourceKey, you need to supply two pieces of information: a reference to a class in your class library assembly and a descriptive resource ID. The class reference is part of the magic that allows WPF to share your resource with other assemblies. When they use the resource, they'll supply the same class reference and the same resource ID.

It doesn't matter what this class actually looks like, and it doesn't need to contain code. The assembly where this type is defined is the same assembly where ComponentResourceKey will find the resource. The example shown in Figure 10-3 uses a class named CustomResources, which has no code:

```
Public Class CustomResources
End Class
```

Now you can create a key name using this class and a resource ID:

```
x:Key="{ComponentResourceKey TypeInTargetAssembly={x:Type local:CustomResources},
  ResourceId=SadTileBrush}"
```

Here's the complete markup for the generic.xaml file, which includes a single resource—an ImageBrush that uses a different graphic:

```
<ResourceDictionary
 xmlns="http://schemas.microsoft.com/winfx/2006/xaml/presentation"
 xmlns:x="http://schemas.microsoft.com/winfx/2006/xaml"
 xmlns:local="clr-namespace:ResourceLibrary">

  <ImageBrush
    x:Key="{ComponentResourceKey TypeInTargetAssembly={x:Type local:CustomResources},
ResourceId=SadTileBrush}"
    TileMode="Tile" ViewportUnits="Absolute" Viewport="0 0 32 32"
    ImageSource="ResourceLibrary;component/sadface.jpg" Opacity="0.3">
  </ImageBrush>
</ResourceDictionary>
```

Keen eyes will notice one unexpected detail in this example. The ImageSource property is no longer set with the image name (sadface.jpg). Instead, a more complex relative URI is used that clearly indicates the image is a part of the ResourceLibrary component. This is a required step because this resource will be used in the context of another application. If you simply use the image name, that application will search its own resources to find the image. What you really need is a relative URI that indicates the component where the image is stored.

Now that you've created the resource dictionary, you can use it in another application. First, make sure you've defined a prefix for the class library assembly, as shown here:

```
<Window x:Class="ResourceFromLibrary"
 xmlns="http://schemas.microsoft.com/winfx/2006/xaml/presentation"
 xmlns:x="http://schemas.microsoft.com/winfx/2006/xaml"
 xmlns:res="clr-namespace:ResourceLibrary;assembly=ResourceLibrary"
 ... >
```

You can then use a DynamicResource that contains a ComponentResourceKey. (This makes sense because the ComponentResourceKey *is* the resource name.) The ComponentResourceKey you use in the consumer is the same as the ComponentResourceKey you use in the class library. You supply a reference to the same class and the same resource ID. The only difference is that you may not use the same XML namespace prefix. This example uses res instead of local, so as to emphasize the fact that the CustomResources class is defined in a different assembly:

```
<Button Background="{DynamicResource {ComponentResourceKey
 TypeInTargetAssembly={x:Type res:CustomResources}, ResourceId=SadTileBrush}}"
 Padding="5" Margin="5" FontWeight="Bold" FontSize="14">
  A Resource From ResourceLibrary
</Button>
```

■ **Note** You must use a dynamic resource, not a static resource, when using a ComponentResourceKey.

This completes the example. However, you can take one additional step to make it easier to use your resource. You can define a shared property that returns the correct ComponentResourceKey that you need to use. Typically, you'll define this property in a class in your component, as shown here:

```
Public Class CustomResources
    Public Shared ReadOnly Property SadTileBrush() As ComponentResourceKey
        Get
            Return New ComponentResourceKey( _
                GetType(CustomResources), "SadTileBrush")
        End Get
    End Property
End Class
```

Now you use the Static markup extension to access this property and apply the resource without using the long-winded ComponentResourceKey in your markup:

```
<Button
 Background="{DynamicResource {x:Static res:CustomResources.SadTileBrushKey}}"
 Padding="5" Margin="5" FontWeight="Bold" FontSize="14">
  A Resource From ResourceLibrary
</Button>
```

This handy shortcut is essentially the same technique that's used by the System*Xxx* classes that you saw earlier. For example, when you retrieve SystemColors.WindowTextBrushKey, you are receiving the correct resource key object. The only difference is that it's an instance of the private SystemResourceKey rather than ComponentResourceKey. Both classes derive from the same ancestor: an abstract class named ResourceKey.

The Last Word

In this chapter, you explored how the WPF resource system lets you reuse the same objects in different parts of your application. You saw how to declare resources in code and markup, how to draw on system resources, and how to share resources between applications with class library assemblies.

You're not done looking at resources just yet. One of the most practical uses of object resources is to store *styles*—collections of property settings that you can apply to multiple elements. In the next chapter, you'll learn how to define styles, store them as resources, and reuse them effortlessly.

CHAPTER 11

■ ■ ■

Styles and Behaviors

WPF applications would be a drab bunch if you were limited to the plain, gray look of ordinary buttons and other common controls. Fortunately, WPF has several features that allow you to inject some flair into basic elements and standardize the visual appearance of your application. In this chapter, you'll learn about two of the most important: styles and behaviors.

Styles are an essential tool for organizing and reusing for formatting choices. Rather than filling your XAML with repetitive markup to set details such as margins, padding, colors, and fonts, you can create a set of styles that encompass all these details. You can then apply the styles where you need them by setting a single property.

Behaviors are a more ambitious tool for reusing user interface code. The basic idea is that a behavior encapsulates a common bit of UI functionality (for example, the code that makes an element draggable). If you have the right behavior, you can attach it to any element with a line or two of XAML markup, saving you the effort of writing and debugging the code yourself.

Style Basics

In the previous chapter, you learned about the WPF resource system, which lets you define objects in one place and reuse them throughout your markup. Although you can use resources to store a wide variety of objects, one of the most common reasons you'll use them is to hold *styles*.

A style is a collection of property values that can be applied to an element. The WPF style system plays a similar role to the Cascading Style Sheets (CSS) standard in HTML markup. Like CSS, WPF styles allow you to define a common set of formatting characteristics and apply them throughout your application to ensure consistency. And as with CSS, WPF styles can work automatically, target specific element types, and cascade through the element tree. However, WPF styles are more powerful because they can set *any* dependency property. That means you can use them to standardize characteristics that have nothing to do with formatting, such as properties that control the behavior of a control. WPF styles also support *triggers*, which allow you to change the style of a control when another property is changed (as you'll see in this chapter), and they can use *templates* to redefine the built-in appearance of a control (as you'll see in Chapter 17). Once you've learned how to use styles, you'll be sure to include them in all your WPF applications.

To understand how styles fit in, it helps to consider a simple example. Imagine you need to standardize the font that's used in a window. The simplest approach is to set the font properties of the containing window. These properties, which are defined in the Control class, include FontFamily, FontSize, FontWeight (for bold), FontStyle (for italics), and FontStretch (for compressed and expanded variants). Thanks to the property value inheritance feature, when you set these properties at the window level, all the elements inside the window will acquire the same values, unless they explicitly override them.

■ **Note** Property value inheritance is one of the many optional features that dependency properties can provide. Dependency properties are described in Chapter 4.

Now consider a different situation, one in which you want to lock down the font that's used for just a portion of your user interface. If you can isolate these elements in a specific container (for example, if they're all inside one Grid or StackPanel), you can use essentially the same approach and set the font properties of the container. However, life is not usually that easy. For example, you may want to give all buttons a consistent typeface and text size independent from the font settings that are used in other elements. In this case, you need a way to define these details in one place and reuse them wherever they apply.

Resources give you a solution, but it's somewhat awkward. Because there's no Font object in WPF (just a collection of font-related properties), you're stuck defining several related resources, as shown here:

```
<Window.Resources>
  <FontFamily x:Key="ButtonFontFamily">Times New Roman</FontFamily>
  <sys:Double x:Key="ButtonFontSize">18</s:Double>
  <FontWeight x:Key="ButtonFontWeight">Bold</FontWeight>
</Window.Resources>
```

This snippet or markup adds three resources to a window: a FontFamily object with the name of the font you want to use, a Double that stores the number 18, and the enumerated value FontWeight.Bold. It assumes you've mapped the .NET namespace System to the XML namespace prefix sys, as shown here:

```
<Window xmlns:sys="clr-namespace:System;assembly=mscorlib" ... >
```

■ **Tip** When setting properties using a resource, it's important that the data types match exactly. WPF won't use a type converter in the same way it does when you set an attribute value directly. For example, if you're setting the FontFamily attribute in an element, you can use the string "Times New Roman" because the FontFamilyConverter will create the FontFamily object you need. However, the same magic won't happen if you try to set the FontFamily property using a string resource—in this situation, the XAML parser throws an exception.

Once you've defined the resources you need, the next step is to actually use these resources in an element. Because the resources are never changed over the lifetime of the application, it makes sense to use static resources, as shown here:

```
<Button Padding="5" Margin="5" Name="cmd"
  FontFamily="{StaticResource ButtonFontFamily}"
  FontWeight="{StaticResource ButtonFontWeight}"
  FontSize="{StaticResource ButtonFontSize}">
  A Customized Button
</Button>
```

This example works, and it moves the font details (the so-called magic numbers) out of your markup. However, it also presents two new problems:

- There's no clear indication that the three resources are related (other than the similar resource names). This complicates the maintainability of the application. It's especially a problem if you need to set more font properties or if you decide to maintain different font settings for different types of elements.

- The markup you need to use your resources is quite verbose. In fact, it's less concise than the approach it replaces (defining the font properties directly in the element).

You could improve on the first issue by defining a custom class (such as FontSettings) that bundles all the font details together. You could then create one FontSettings object as a resource and use its various properties in your markup. However, this still leaves you with verbose markup—and it makes for a fair bit of extra work.

Styles provide the perfect solution. You can define a single style that wraps all the properties you want to set. Here's how:

```
<Window.Resources>
  <Style x:Key="BigFontButtonStyle">
    <Setter Property="Control.FontFamily" Value="Times New Roman" />
    <Setter Property="Control.FontSize" Value="18" />
    <Setter Property="Control.FontWeight" Value="Bold" />
  </Style>
</Window.Resources>
```

This markup creates a single resource: a System.Windows.Style object. This style object holds a Setters collection with three Setter objects, one for each property you want to set. Each Setter object names the property that it acts on and the value that it applies to that property. Like all resources, the style object has a key name so you can pull it out of the collection when needed. In this case, the key name is BigFontButtonStyle. (By convention, the key names for styles usually end with *Style*.)

Every WPF element can use a single style (or no style). The style plugs into an element through the element's Style property (which is defined in the base FrameworkElement class). For example, to configure a button to use the style you created previously, you'd point the button to the style resource like this:

```
<Button Padding="5" Margin="5" Name="cmd"
 Style="{StaticResource BigFontButtonStyle}">
  A Customized Button
</Button>
```

Of course, you could also set a style programmatically. All you need to do is pull the style out of the closest Resources collection using the familiar FindResource() method. Here's the code you'd use for a Button object named cmd:

```
cmd.Style = CType(cmd.FindResource("BigFontButtonStyle"), Style)
```

Figure 11-1 shows a window with two buttons that use the BigFontButtonStyle.

Figure 11-1. *Reusing button settings with a style*

The style system adds many benefits. Not only does it allow you to create groups of settings that are clearly related, it also streamlines your markup by making it easier to apply these settings. Best of all, you can apply a style without worrying about what properties it sets. In the previous example, the font settings were organized into a style named BigFontButtonStyle. If you decide later that your big-font buttons also need more padding and margin space, you can add setters for the Padding and Margin properties as well. All the buttons that use the style automatically acquire the new style settings.

The Setters collection is the most important property of the Style class. But there are five key properties altogether, which you'll consider in this chapter. Table 11-1 shows a snapshot.

Table 11-1. *Properties of the Style Class*

Property	Description
Setters	A collection of Setter or EventSetter objects that set property values and attach event handlers automatically.
Triggers	A collection of objects that derive from TriggerBase and allow you to change style settings automatically. For example, you can modify a style when another property changes or when an event occurs.
Resources	A collection of resources that you want to use with your styles. For example, you might need to use a single object to set more than one property. In that case, it's more efficient to create the object as a resource and then use that resource in your Setter object (rather than create the object as part of each Setter, using nested tags).
BasedOn	A property that allows you to create a more specialized style that inherits (and optionally overrides) the settings of another style.
TargetType	A property that identifies the element type that this style acts upon. This property allows you to create setters that only affect certain elements, and it allows you to create setters that spring into action automatically for the right element type.

Now that you've seen a basic example of a style at work, you're ready to look into the style model more deeply.

Creating a Style Object

In the previous example, the style object is defined at the window level and then reused in two buttons inside that window. Although that's a common design, it's certainly not your only choice.

If you want to create more finely targeted styles, you could define them using the Resources collection of their container, such as a StackPanel or a Grid. If you want to reuse styles across an application, you can define them using the Resources collection of your application. These are also common approaches.

Strictly speaking, you don't need to use styles and resources together. For example, you could define the style of a particular button by filling its Style collection directly, as shown here:

```
<Button Padding="5" Margin="5">
  <Button.Style>
    <Style>
      <Setter Property="Control.FontFamily" Value="Times New Roman" />
      <Setter Property="Control.FontSize" Value="18" />
      <Setter Property="Control.FontWeight" Value="Bold" />
    </Style>
  </Button.Style>
  <Button.Content>A Customized Button</Button.Content>
</Button>
```

This works, but it's obviously a lot less useful. Now there's no way to share this style with other elements.

This approach isn't worth the trouble if you're simply using a style to set some properties (as in this example) because it's easier to set the properties directly. However, this approach is occasionally useful if you're using another feature of styles and you want to apply it to a single element only. For example, you can use this approach to attach triggers to an element. This approach also allows you to modify a part of an element's control template. (In this case, you use the Setter.TargetName property to apply a setter to a specific component inside the element, such as the scroll bar buttons in a list box. You'll learn more about this technique in Chapter 17.)

Setting Properties

As you've seen, every Style object wraps a collection of Setter objects. Each Setter object sets a single property in an element. The only limitation is that a setter can only change a dependency property—other properties can't be modified.

In some cases, you won't be able to set the property value using a simple attribute string. For example, an ImageBrush object can't be created with a simple string. In this situation, you can use the familiar XAML trick of replacing the attribute with a nested element. Here's an example:

```
<Style x:Key="HappyTiledElementStyle">
  <Setter Property="Control.Background">
    <Setter.Value>
      <ImageBrush TileMode="Tile"
        ViewportUnits="Absolute" Viewport="0 0 32 32"
        ImageSource="happyface.jpg" Opacity="0.3">
      </ImageBrush>
    </Setter.Value>
  </Setter>
</Style>
```

■ **Tip** If you want to reuse the same image brush in more than one style (or in more than one setter in the same style), you can define it as a resource and then use that resource in your style.

To identify the property you want to set, you need to supply both a class and a property name. However, the class name you use doesn't need to be the class where the property is defined. It can also be a derived class that inherits the property. For example, consider the following version of the BigFontButton style, which replaces the references to the Control class with references to the Button class:

```
<Style x:Key="BigFontButtonStyle">
  <Setter Property="Button.FontFamily" Value="Times New Roman" />
  <Setter Property="Button.FontSize" Value="18" />
  <Setter Property="Button.FontWeight" Value="Bold" />
</Style>
```

If you substitute this style in the same example (Figure 11-1), you'll get the same result. So, why the difference? In this case, the distinction is how WPF handles other classes that may include the same FontFamily, FontSize, and FontWeight properties but that don't derive from Button. For example, if you apply this version of the BigFontButton style to a Label control, it has no effect. WPF simply ignores the three properties because they don't apply. But if you use the original style, the font properties will affect the label because the Label class derives from Control.

■ **Tip** The fact that WPF ignores properties that don't apply means you can also set properties that won't necessarily be available in the element to which you apply the style. For example, if you set the ButtonBase.IsCancel property, it will have an effect only when you set the style on a button.

There are some cases in WPF where the same properties are defined in more than one place in the element hierarchy. For example, the full set of font properties (such as FontFamily) is defined in both the Control class and the

TextBlock class. If you're creating a style that applies to TextBlock objects and elements that derive from Control, it might occur to you to create markup like this:

```
<Style x:Key="BigFontStyle">
  <Setter Property="Button.FontFamily" Value="Times New Roman" />
  <Setter Property="Button.FontSize" Value="18" />

  <Setter Property="TextBlock.FontFamily" Value="Arial" />
  <Setter Property="TextBlock.FontSize" Value="10" />
</Style>
```

However, this won't have the desired effect. The problem is that although Button.FontFamily and TextBlock.FontFamily are declared separately in their respective base classes, they are both references to the same dependency property. (In other words, TextBlock.FontSizeProperty and Control.FontSizeProperty are references that point to the same DependencyProperty object. You first learned about this possible issue in Chapter 4.) As a result, when you use this style, WPF sets the FontFamily and FontSize property twice. The last-applied settings (in this case, 10-unit Arial) take precedence and are applied to both Button and TextBlock objects. Although this problem is fairly specific and doesn't occur with many properties, it's important to be on the lookout for it if you often create styles that apply different formatting to different element types.

There's one more trick that you can use to simplify style declarations. If all your properties are intended for the same element type, you can set the TargetType property of the Style object to indicate the class to which your properties apply. For example, if you're creating a button-only style, you could create the style like this:

```
<Style x:Key="BigFontButtonStyle" TargetType="Button">
  <Setter Property="FontFamily" Value="Times New Roman" />
  <Setter Property="FontSize" Value="18" />
  <Setter Property="FontWeight" Value="Bold" />
</Style>
```

This is a relatively minor convenience. As you'll discover later, the TargetType property also doubles as a shortcut that allows you to apply styles automatically if you leave out the style key name.

Attaching Event Handlers

Property setters are the most common ingredient in any style, but you can also create a collection of EventSetter objects that wire up events to specific event handlers. Here's an example that attaches the event handlers for the MouseEnter and MouseLeave events:

```
<Style x:Key="MouseOverHighlightStyle">
  <EventSetter Event="TextBlock.MouseEnter" Handler="element_MouseEnter" />
  <EventSetter Event="TextBlock.MouseLeave" Handler="element_MouseLeave" />
  <Setter Property="TextBlock.Padding" Value="5"/>
</Style>
```

Here's the event handling code:

```
Private Sub element_MouseEnter(ByVal sender As Object, _
  ByVal e As MouseEventArgs)
    CType(sender, TextBlock).Background = _
      New SolidColorBrush(Colors.LightGoldenrodYellow)
End Sub
```

```
Private Sub element_MouseLeave(ByVal sender As Object, _
  ByVal e As MouseEventArgs)
    CType(sender, TextBlock).Background = Nothing
End Sub
```

MouseEnter and MouseLeave use direct event routing, which means they don't bubble up or tunnel down the element tree. If you want to apply a mouseover effect to a large number of elements (for example, you want to change the background color of an element when the mouse moves overtop of it), you need to add the MouseEnter and MouseLeave event handlers to each element. The style-based event handlers simplify this task. Now you simply need to apply a single style, which can include property setters and event setters:

```
<TextBlock Style="{StaticResource MouseOverHighlightStyle}">
  Hover over me.
</TextBlock>
```

Figure 11-2 shows a simple demonstration of this technique with three elements, two of which use the MouseOverHighlightStyle.

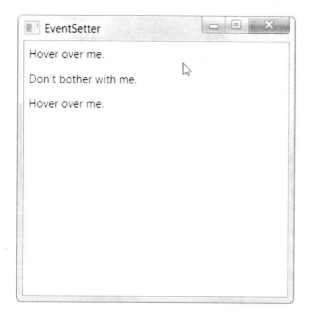

Figure 11-2. *Handling the MouseEnter and MouseLeave events with a style*

Event setters are a rare technique in WPF. If you need the functionality shown here, you're more likely to use event triggers, which define the action you want declaratively (and so require no code). Event triggers are designed to implement animations, which makes them more useful when creating mouseover effects.

Event setters aren't a good choice when handling an event that uses bubbling. In this situation, it's usually easier to handle the event you want on a higher-level element. For example, if you want to link all the buttons in a toolbar to the same event handler for the Click event, the best approach is to attach a single event handler to the Toolbar element that holds all the buttons. In this situation, an event setter is an unnecessary complication.

▪ **Tip** In many cases it's clearer to explicitly define all your events and avoid event setters altogether. If you need to link several events to the same event handler, do it by hand. You can also use tricks such as attaching an event handler at the container level and centralizing logic with commands (Chapter 9).

The Many Layers of Styles

Although you can define an unlimited number of styles at many different levels, each WPF element can use only a single style object at once. Although this might appear to be a limitation at first, it usually isn't because of property value inheritance and style inheritance.

For example, imagine you want to give a group of controls the same font without applying the same style to each one. In this case, you may be able to place them in a single panel (or another type of container) and set the style of the container. As long as you're setting properties that use the property value inheritance feature, these values will flow down to the children. Properties that use this model include IsEnabled, IsVisible, Foreground, and all the font properties.

In other cases, you might want to create a style that builds upon another style. You can use this sort of style inheritance by setting the BasedOn attribute of a style. For example, consider these two styles:

```
<Window.Resources>
  <Style x:Key="BigFontButtonStyle">
    <Setter Property="Control.FontFamily" Value="Times New Roman" />
    <Setter Property="Control.FontSize" Value="18" />
    <Setter Property="Control.FontWeight" Value="Bold" />
  </Style>

  <Style x:Key="EmphasizedBigFontButtonStyle"
    BasedOn="{StaticResource BigFontButtonStyle}">
    <Setter Property="Control.Foreground" Value="White" />
    <Setter Property="Control.Background" Value="DarkBlue" />
  </Style>
</Window.Resources>
```

The first style (BigFontButtonStyle) defines three font properties. The second style (EmphasizedBigFontButtonStyle) acquires these aspects from BigFontButtonStyle and then supplements them with two more properties that change the foreground and the background brushes. This two-part design gives you the ability to apply just the font settings or the font-and-color combination. This design also allows you to create more styles that incorporate the font or color details you've defined (but not necessarily both).

▪ **Note** You can use the BasedOn property to create an entire chain of inherited styles. The only rule is that if you set the same property twice, the last property setter (the one in the derived class furthest down the inheritance chain) overrides any earlier definitions.

Figure 11-3 shows style inheritance at work in a simple window that uses both styles.

Figure 11-3. *Creating a style based on another style*

STYLE INHERITANCE ADDS COMPLEXITY

Although style inheritance seems like a great convenience at first glance, it's usually not worth the trouble. That's because style inheritance is subject to the same problems as code inheritance: dependencies that make your application more fragile. For example, if you use the markup shown previously, you're forced to keep the same font characteristics for two styles. If you decide to change BigFontButtonStyle, EmphasizedBigFontButtonStyle changes as well—unless you explicitly add more setters that override the inherited values.

This problem is trivial enough in the two-style example, but it becomes a significant issue if you use style inheritance in a more realistic application. Usually, styles are categorized based on different types of content and the role that the content plays. For example, a sales application might include styles such as ProductTitleStyle, ProductTextStyle, HighlightQuoteStyle, NavigationButtonStyle, and so on. If you base ProductTitleStyle on ProductTextStyle (perhaps because they both share the same font), you'll run into trouble if you apply settings to ProductTextStyle later that you don't want to apply to ProductTitleStyle (such as different margins). In this case, you'll be forced to define your settings in ProductTextStyle and explicitly override them in ProductTitleStyle. At the end, you'll be left with a more complicated model and very few style settings that are actually reused.

Unless you have a specific reason to base one style on another (for example, the second style is a special case of the first and changes just a few characteristics out of a large number of inherited settings), don't use style inheritance.

Automatically Applying Styles by Type

So far, you've seen how to create named styles and refer to them in your markup. However, there's another approach. You can apply a style automatically to elements of a certain type.

Doing this is quite easy. You simply need to set the TargetType property to indicate the appropriate type (as described earlier) and leave out the key name altogether. When you do this, WPF actually sets the key name implicitly using the type markup extension, as shown here:

```
x:Key="{x:Type Button}"
```

Now the style is automatically applied to any buttons all the way down the element tree. For example, if you define a style in this way on the window, it applies to every button in that window (unless there's a style further downstream that replaces it).

Here's an example with a window that sets the button styles automatically to get the same effect you saw in Figure 11-1:

```
<Window.Resources>
  <Style TargetType="Button">
    <Setter Property="FontFamily" Value="Times New Roman" />
    <Setter Property="FontSize" Value="18" />
    <Setter Property="FontWeight" Value="Bold" />
  </Style>
</Window.Resources>

<StackPanel Margin="5">
  <Button Padding="5" Margin="5">Customized Button</Button>
  <TextBlock Margin="5">Normal Content.</TextBlock>
  <Button Padding="5" Margin="5" Style="{x:Null}">A Normal Button</Button>
  <TextBlock Margin="5">More normal Content.</TextBlock>
  <Button Padding="5" Margin="5">Another Customized Button</Button>
</StackPanel>
```

In this example, the middle button explicitly replaces the style. But rather than supply a new style of its own, this button sets the Style property to a null reference (Nothing), which effectively removes the style.

Although automatic styles are convenient, they can complicate your design. Here are a few reasons why:

- In a complex window with many styles and multiple layers of styles, it becomes difficult to track down whether a given property is set through property value inheritance or a style (and if it's a style, which one). As a result, if you want to change a simple detail, you may need to wade through the markup of your entire window.

- The formatting in a window often starts out more general and becomes increasingly fine-tuned. If you apply automatic styles to the window early on, you'll probably need to override the styles in many places with explicit styles. This complicates the overall design. It's much more straightforward to create named styles for every combination of formatting characteristics you want and apply them by name.

- For example, if you create an automatic style for the TextBlock element, you'll wind up modifying other controls that use the TextBlock (such as a template-driven ListBox control).

To avoid problems, it's best to apply automatic styles judiciously. If you do decide to give your entire user interface a single, consistent look using automatic styles, try to limit your use of explicit styles to special cases.

Triggers

One of the themes in WPF is extending what you can do *declaratively*. Whether you're using styles, resources, or data binding, you'll find that you can do quite a bit without resorting to code.

Triggers are another example of this trend. Using triggers, you can automate simple style changes that would ordinarily require boilerplate event handling logic. For example, you can react when a property is changed and adjust a style automatically.

Triggers are linked to styles through the Style.Triggers collection. Every style can have an unlimited number of triggers, and each trigger is an instance of a class that derives from System.Windows.TriggerBase. WPF gives you the choices listed in Table 11-2.

Table 11-2. *Classes That Derive from TriggerBase*

Name	Description
Trigger	This is the simplest form of trigger. It watches for a change in a dependency property and then uses a setter to change the style.
MultiTrigger	This is similar to Trigger but combines multiple conditions. All the conditions must be met before the trigger springs into action.
DataTrigger	This trigger works with data binding. It's similar to Trigger, except it watches for a change in any bound data.
MultiDataTrigger	This combines multiple data triggers.
EventTrigger	This is the most sophisticated trigger. It applies an animation when an event occurs.

You can apply triggers directly to elements, without needing to create a style, by using the FrameworkElement. Triggers collection. However, there's a sizable catch. This Triggers collection supports event triggers only. (There's no technical reason for this limitation; it's simply a feature the WPF team didn't have time to implement and may include in future versions.)

A Simple Trigger

You can attach a simple trigger to any dependency property. For example, you can create mouseover and focus effects by responding to changes in the IsFocused, IsMouseOver, and IsPressed properties of the Control class.

Every simple trigger identifies the property you're watching and the value that you're waiting for. When this value occurs, the setters you've stored in the Trigger.Setters collection are applied. (Unfortunately, it isn't possible to use more sophisticated trigger logic that compares a value to see how it falls in a range, performs a calculation, and so on. In these situations, you're better off using an event handler.)

Here's a trigger that waits for a button to get the keyboard focus, at which point it's given a dark red background:

```
<Style x:Key="BigFontButton">
  <Style.Setters>
    <Setter Property="Control.FontFamily" Value="Times New Roman" />
    <Setter Property="Control.FontSize" Value="18" />
  </Style.Setters>
```

```
      <Style.Triggers>
        <Trigger Property="Control.IsFocused" Value="True">
          <Setter Property="Control.Foreground" Value="DarkRed" />
        </Trigger>
      </Style.Triggers>
  </Style>
```

The nice thing about triggers is that there's no need to write any logic to reverse them. As soon as the trigger stops applying, your element reverts to its normal appearance. In this example, that means the button gets its ordinary gray background as soon as the user tabs away.

■ **Note** To understand how this works, you need to remember the dependency property system that you learned about in Chapter 4. Essentially, a trigger is one of the many property providers that can override the value that's returned by a dependency property. However, the original value (whether it is set locally or by a style) still remains. As soon as the trigger becomes deactivated, the pre-trigger value is available again.

It's possible to create multiple triggers that may apply to the same element at once. If these triggers set different properties, there's no ambiguity in this situation. However, if you have more than one trigger that modifies the same property, the last trigger in the list wins.

For example, consider the following triggers, which adjust a control depending on whether it is focused, whether the mouse is hovering over it, and whether it's been clicked:

```
<Style x:Key="BigFontButton">
  <Style.Setters>
    ...
  </Style.Setters>
  <Style.Triggers>
    <Trigger Property="Control.IsFocused" Value="True">
      <Setter Property="Control.Foreground" Value="DarkRed" />
    </Trigger>
    <Trigger Property="Control.IsMouseOver" Value="True">
      <Setter Property="Control.Foreground" Value="LightYellow" />
      <Setter Property="Control.FontWeight" Value="Bold" />
    </Trigger>
    <Trigger Property="Button.IsPressed" Value="True">
      <Setter Property="Control.Foreground" Value="Red" />
    </Trigger>
  </Style.Triggers>
</Style>
```

Obviously, it's possible to hover over a button that currently has the focus. This doesn't pose a problem because these triggers modify different properties. But if you click the button, there are two different triggers attempting to set the foreground. Now the trigger for the Button.IsPressed property wins because it's last in the list. It doesn't matter which trigger *occurs* first—for example, WPF doesn't care that a button gets focus before you click it. The order in which the triggers are listed in your markup is all that matters.

■ **Note** In this example, triggers aren't all you need to get a nice-looking button. You're also limited by the button's control template, which locks down certain aspects of its appearance. For best results when customizing elements to this degree, you need to use a control template. However, control templates don't replace triggers—in fact, control templates often use triggers to get the best of both worlds: controls that can be completely customized *and* react to mouseovers, clicks, and other events to change some aspect of their visual appearance.

If you want to create a trigger that switches on only if several criteria are true, you can use a MultiTrigger. It provides a Conditions collection that lets you define a series of property and value combinations. Here's an example that applies formatting only if a button has focus and the mouse is over it:

```
<Style x:Key="BigFontButton">
  <Style.Setters>
    ...
  </Style.Setters>
  <Style.Triggers>
    <MultiTrigger>
      <MultiTrigger.Conditions>
        <Condition Property="Control.IsFocused" Value="True">
        <Condition Property="Control.IsMouseOver" Value="True">
      </MultiTrigger.Conditions>
      <MultiTrigger.Setters>
        <Setter Property="Control.Foreground" Value="DarkRed" />
      </MultiTrigger.Setters>
    </MultiTrigger>
  </Style.Triggers>
</Style>
```

In this case, it doesn't matter what order you declare the conditions in because they must all hold true before the background is changed.

An Event Trigger

While an ordinary trigger waits for a property change to occur, an event trigger waits for a specific event to be fired. You might assume that at this point you use setters to change the element, but that's not the case. Instead, an event trigger requires that you supply a series of actions that modify the control. These actions are used to apply an animation.

Although you won't consider animations in detail until Chapter 15, you can get the idea with a basic example. The following event trigger waits for the MouseEnter event and then animates the FontSize property of the button, enlarging it to 22 units for 0.2 seconds:

```
<Style x:Key="BigFontButtonStyle">
  <Style.Setters>
    ...
  </Style.Setters>

  <Style.Triggers>
    <EventTrigger RoutedEvent="Mouse.MouseEnter">
      <EventTrigger.Actions>
        <BeginStoryboard>
```

```
      <Storyboard>
        <DoubleAnimation
          Duration="0:0:0.2"
          Storyboard.TargetProperty="FontSize"
          To="22"  />
      </Storyboard>
    </BeginStoryboard>
  </EventTrigger.Actions>
</EventTrigger>
...
```

In XAML, every animation must be defined in a storyboard, which provides the timeline for the animation. Inside the storyboard, you define the animation object (or objects) that you want to use. Every animation object performs essentially the same task: it modifies a dependency property over some time period.

In this example, a prebuilt animation class named DoubleAnimation is being used (which is found in the System. Windows.Media.Animation namespace, like all animation classes). DoubleAnimation can gradually change any Double value (such as FontSize) to a set target over a given period of time. Because the Double value is changed in small fractional units, you'll see the font grow gradually. The actual size of the change depends on the total amount of time and the total change you need to make. In this example, the font changes from its current set value to 22 units, over a time period of 0.2 seconds. (You can fine-tune details such as these and create an animation that accelerates or decelerates by tweaking the properties of the DoubleAnimation class.)

Unlike property triggers, you need to reverse event triggers if you want the element to return to its original state. (That's because the default animation behavior is to remain active once the animation is complete, holding the property at the final value. You'll learn more about how this system works in Chapter 15.)

To reverse the font size in this example, the style uses an event trigger that reacts to the MouseLeave event and shrinks the font back to its original size over a full two seconds. You don't need to indicate the target font size in this case—if you don't, WPF assumes you want the original font size that the button had before the first animation kicked in:

```
...
<EventTrigger RoutedEvent="Mouse.MouseLeave">
  <EventTrigger.Actions>
    <BeginStoryboard>
      <Storyboard>
        <DoubleAnimation
          Duration="0:0:1"
          Storyboard.TargetProperty="FontSize"  />
      </Storyboard>
    </BeginStoryboard>
  </EventTrigger.Actions>
</EventTrigger>
</Style.Triggers>
</Style>
```

Interestingly, you can also perform an animation when a dependency property hits a specific value. This is useful if you want to perform an animation and there isn't a suitable event to use.

To use this technique you need a property trigger, as described in the previous section. The trick is to not supply any Setter objects for your property trigger. Instead, you set the Trigger.EnterActions and Trigger.ExitActions properties. Both properties take a collection of actions, such as the BeginStoryboard action that starts an animation. The EnterActions are performed when the property reaches the designated value, and ExitActions are performed when the property changes away from the designated value.

You'll learn much more about using event triggers and property triggers to launch animations in Chapter 15.

Behaviors

Styles give you a practical way to reuse groups of property settings. They're a great first step that can help you build consistent, well-organized interfaces—but they're also broadly limited.

The problem is that property settings are only a small part of the user-interface infrastructure in a typical application. Even the most basic program usually needs reams of user-interface code that has nothing to do with the application's functionality. In many programs, the code that's used for UI tasks (such as driving animations, powering slick effects, maintaining user-interface state, and supporting user-interface features such as dragging, zooming, and docking) far outweighs the business code in both size and complexity. Much of this code is generic, meaning you end up writing the same thing in every WPF project you create. Almost all of it is tedious.

In response to this challenge, the creators of Expression Blend have developed a feature called *behaviors*. The idea is simple: you (or another developer) create a behavior that encapsulates a common bit of user-interface functionality. This functionality can be basic (such as starting a storyboard or navigating to a hyperlink). Or, it can be complex (such as handling multitouch interactions or modeling a collision with a real-time physics engine). Once built, you can add this functionality to another control in any application by hooking that control to the right behavior and setting the behavior's properties. In Expression Blend, using a behavior takes little more than a drag-and-drop operation.

■ **Note** Custom controls are another technique for reusing user-interface functionality in an application (or among multiple applications). However, a custom control must be developed as a tightly linked package of visuals and code. Although custom controls are extremely powerful, they don't address situations where you need to equip many different controls with similar functionality (for example, adding a mouseover rendering effect to a group of different elements). For that reason, styles, behaviors, and custom controls are all complementary.

Getting Support for Behaviors

There's one catch. The infrastructure for reusing common blocks of user-interface code isn't part of WPF. Instead, it's bundled with Expression Blend. This is because behaviors began as a design-time feature for Expression Blend. In fact, Expression Blend is still the only tool that lets you add behaviors by dragging them onto the controls that need them. But that doesn't mean behaviors are useful only in Expression Blend. You can create and use them in a Visual Studio application with only slightly more effort. You simply need to write the markup by hand rather than using the Toolbox.

To get the assemblies that support for behaviors, you have two options:

- You can install Expression Blend 3, Expression Blend 4, or Expression Blend for Visual Studio 2012 (which is currently available only as a preview, at http://tinyurl.com/c5u84uc). All these versions include the assemblies you need for the behavior feature in Visual Studio, but Expression Blend for Visual Studio 2012 is the only version that allows you to create and edit WPF 4.5 applications in the Blend environment.

- You can install the Expression Blend 3 SDK (which is available at http://tinyurl.com/kkp4g8).

░ **Note** Microsoft's naming system for Expression Blend is hugely confusing. Many versions of Visual Studio 2012 include a limited version of Expression Blend, which is called Expression Blend for Visual Studio 2012. This limited version only allows the creation of Metro-style applications, and it only works on Windows 8. However, the full version of Blend has the same name (Expression Blend for Visual Studio 2012), even though it supports Silverlight and WPF. At the time of this writing, the full version is available as a free preview only (`http://tinyurl.com/c5u84uc`).

Whether you use an old version of Expression Blend, the new preview, or the SDK, you'll find the same two important assemblies that you need, in a folder like c:\Program Files (x86)\Microsoft SDKs\Expression\Blend 3\Interactivity\Libraries\WPF. They are

- *System.Windows.Interactivity.dll*: This assembly defines the base classes that support behaviors. It's the cornerstone of the behavior feature.

- *Microsoft.Expression.Interactions.dll*: This assembly adds some useful extensions, with optional action and trigger classes that are based on the core behavior classes.

Understanding the Behavior Model

The behavior feature comes in two versions (both of which are included with Expression Blend or the Expression Blend SDK). One version is designed to add behavior support to Silverlight, Microsoft's rich client plug-in for the browser, while the other is designed for WPF. Although both offer identical features, the behavior feature meshes more neatly into the Silverlight world, because it fills a bigger gap. Unlike WPF, Silverlight has no support for triggers, so it makes sense that the assemblies that implement behaviors also implement triggers. However, WPF *does* support triggers, which makes it more than a little confusing to find that the behavior feature includes its own trigger system, which doesn't match the WPF model.

The problem is that these two similarly named features overlap partly but not completely. In WPF, the most important role for triggers is building flexible styles and control templates (as you'll see in Chapter 17). With the help of triggers, your styles and template become more intelligent; for example, you can apply a visual effect when some property changes. However, the trigger system in Expression Blend has a different purpose. It allows you to add simple functionality to an application using a visual design tool. In other words, WPF triggers support more powerful styles and control templates. Expression Blend triggers support quick code-free application design.

So, what does all this mean for the average WPF developer? Here are a few guidelines:

- The behavior model is not a core part of WPF, so it's not as established as styles and templates. In other words, you can program WPF applications without using behaviors, but you won't be able to create much more than a Hello World demonstration without styles and templates.

- The trigger feature in Expression Blend may interest you if you spend a lot of time in Expression Blend or you want to develop components for other Expression Blend users. Even though it shares a name with the trigger system in WPF, there's no overlap, and you can use both.

- If you don't work with Expression Blend, you can skip the trigger feature altogether—but you should still look at Expression Blend's full-fledged behavior classes. That's because behaviors are both more powerful and more common than Expression Blend triggers. Eventually, you're bound to find a third-party component that includes a nice, neat behavior for you to use in your own applications. (For example, in Chapter 5 you explored multitouch and learned about a free behavior that you can use to give your elements automatic behavior support.)

In this chapter, you won't look at the Expression Blend trigger system, but you will consider the full-fledged behavior classes. To learn more about Expression Blend triggers and see additional behavior examples (some of which are intended for Silverlight rather than WPF), you can read through the posts at `http://tinyurl.com/yfvakl3`. The downloadable code for this chapter also includes two custom trigger examples.

Creating a Behavior

Behaviors aim to encapsulate bits of UI functionality so you can apply them to elements without writing the code yourself. Another way of looking at is that every behavior provides a service to an element. This service usually involves listening to several different events and performing several related operations. For example, an example at `http://tinyurl.com/9kwdnsc` provides a watermark behavior for text boxes. If the text box is empty and doesn't currently have focus, a prompt message (like "[Enter text here]") is shown in light lettering. When the text box gets focus, the behavior springs into action and removes the watermark text.

The best way to gain a better understanding of behaviors is to create one of your own. Imagine that you want to give any element the ability to be dragged around a Canvas with the mouse. The basic steps for a single element are easy enough—your code listens for mouse events and changes the attached properties that set the Canvas coordinates appropriately. But with a bit more effort, you can turn that code into a reusable behavior that can give dragging support to any element on any Canvas.

Before you go any further, create a WPF class library assembly. (In this example, it's called CustomBehaviorsLibrary.) In it, add a reference to the System.Windows.Interactivity.dll assembly. Then, create a class that derives from the base Behavior class. Behavior is a generic class that takes a type argument. You can use this type argument to restrict your behavior to specific elements, or you can use UIElement or FrameworkElement to include them all, as shown here:

```
Public Class DragInCanvasBehavior
    Inherits Behavior(Of UIElement)
    ...
End Class
```

■ **Note** Ideally, you won't need to create a behavior yourself. Instead, you'll use a ready-made behavior that someone else has created.

The first step in any behavior is to override the OnAttached() and OnDetaching() methods. When OnAttached() is called, you can access the element where the behavior is placed (through the AssociatedObject property) and attach event handlers. When OnDetaching() is called, you remove your event handlers.

Here's the code that the DragInCanvasBehavior uses to monitor the MouseLeftButtonDown, MouseMove, and MouseLeftButtonUp events:

```
Protected Overrides Sub OnAttached()
    MyBase.OnAttached()

    ' Hook up event handlers.
    AddHandler AssociatedObject.MouseLeftButtonDown, _
      AddressOf AssociatedObject_MouseLeftButtonDown
    AddHandler AssociatedObject.MouseMove, AddressOf AssociatedObject_MouseMove
    AddHandler AssociatedObject.MouseLeftButtonUp, _
      AddressOf AssociatedObject_MouseLeftButtonUp
End Sub
```

```vb
Protected Overrides Sub OnDetaching()
    MyBase.OnDetaching()

    ' Detach event handlers.
    RemoveHandler AssociatedObject.MouseLeftButtonDown, _
      AddressOf AssociatedObject_MouseLeftButtonDown
    RemoveHandler AssociatedObject.MouseMove, AddressOf AssociatedObject_MouseMove
    RemoveHandler AssociatedObject.MouseLeftButtonUp, _
      AddressOf AssociatedObject_MouseLeftButtonUp
End Sub
```

The final step is to run the appropriate code in the event handlers. For example, when the user clicks the left mouse button, DragInCanvasBehavior starts a dragging operation, records the offset between the upper-left corner of the element and the mouse pointer, and captures the mouse:

```vb
' Keep track of the Canvas where this element is placed.
Private canvas As Canvas

' Keep track of when the element is being dragged.
Private isDragging As Boolean = False

' When the element is clicked, record the exact position
' where the click is made.
Private mouseOffset As Point

Private Sub AssociatedObject_MouseLeftButtonDown(ByVal sender As Object, _
  ByVal e As MouseButtonEventArgs)
    ' Find the Canvas.
    If canvas Is Nothing Then
      canvas = CType(VisualTreeHelper.GetParent(Me.AssociatedObject), Canvas)
    End If

    ' Dragging mode begins.
    isDragging = True

    ' Get the position of the click relative to the element
    ' (so the top-left corner of the element is (0,0).
    mouseOffset = e.GetPosition(AssociatedObject)

    ' Capture the mouse. This way you'll keep receiving
    ' the MouseMove event even if the user jerks the mouse
    ' off the element.
    AssociatedObject.CaptureMouse()
End Sub
```

When the element is in dragging mode and the mouse moves, the element is repositioned:

```vb
Private Sub AssociatedObject_MouseMove(ByVal sender As Object, _
  ByVal e As MouseEventArgs)
    If isDragging Then
        ' Get the position of the element relative to the Canvas.
        Dim point As Point = e.GetPosition(canvas)
```

```
       ' Move the element.
       AssociatedObject.SetValue(Canvas.TopProperty, point.Y - mouseOffset.Y)
       AssociatedObject.SetValue(Canvas.LeftProperty, point.X - mouseOffset.X)
   End If
End Sub
```

And when the mouse button is released, dragging ends:

```
Private Sub AssociatedObject_MouseLeftButtonUp(ByVal sender As Object, _
  ByVal e As MouseButtonEventArgs)
    If isDragging Then
        AssociatedObject.ReleaseMouseCapture()
        isDragging = False
    End If
End Sub
```

Using a Behavior

To test your behavior, being by creating a new WPF Application project. Then, add a reference to the class library that defines the DragInCanvasBehavior class (which you created in the previous section) and the System.Windows.Interactivity.dll assembly. Next, map both namespaces in your XML. Assuming the DragInCanvasBehavior class is stored in a class library named CustomBehaviorsLibrary, you'll need markup like this:

```
<Window xmlns:i=
"clr-namespace:System.Windows.Interactivity;assembly=System.Windows.Interactivity"
 xmlns:custom=
"clr-namespace:CustomBehaviorsLibrary;assembly=CustomBehaviorsLibrary" ... >
```

To use this behavior, you simply need to add to any element inside a Canvas using the Interaction.Behaviors attached property. The following markup creates a Canvas with three shapes. The two Ellipse elements use the DragInCanvasBehavior and can be dragged around the Canvas. The Rectangle element does not and so cannot be moved.

```
<Canvas>
  <Rectangle Canvas.Left="10" Canvas.Top="10" Fill="Yellow" Width="40" Height="60">
  </Rectangle>

  <Ellipse Canvas.Left="10" Canvas.Top="70" Fill="Blue" Width="80" Height="60">
    <i:Interaction.Behaviors>
       <custom:DragInCanvasBehavior></custom:DragInCanvasBehavior>
    </i:Interaction.Behaviors>
  </Ellipse>
```

```
  <Ellipse Canvas.Left="80" Canvas.Top="70" Fill="OrangeRed" Width="40" Height="70">
    <i:Interaction.Behaviors>
      <custom:DragInCanvasBehavior></custom:DragInCanvasBehavior>
    </i:Interaction.Behaviors>
  </Ellipse>
</Canvas>
```

Figure 11-4 shows this example in action.

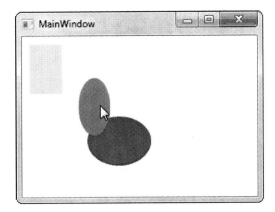

Figure 11-4. *Making elements draggable with a behavior*

But this isn't the whole story. If you're developing in Expression Blend, behaviors give you an even better design experience—one that can save you from writing any markup at all.

Design-Time Behavior Support in Blend

In Expression Blend, working with behaviors is a drag-and-drop-and-configure operation. First, you need to make sure your application has a reference to the assembly that has the behaviors you want to use. (In this case, that's the class library assembly where DragInCanvasBehavior is defined.) Next, you need to ensure that it also has a reference to the System.Windows.Interactivity.dll assembly.

Expression Blend automatically searches all referenced assemblies for behaviors and displays them in the Asset Library (the same panel you use for choosing elements when designing a Silverlight page). It also adds the behaviors from the Microsoft.Expression.Interactions.dll assembly, even if they aren't yet referenced by your project.

To see the behaviors you have to choose from, start by drawing a button on the design surface of your page, click the Asset Library button, and click the Behaviors tab (see Figure 11-5).

Figure 11-5. *Actions in the Asset Library*

To add an action to a control, drag it from the Asset Library, and drop it onto your control (in this case, one of the shapes in the Canvas). When you take this step, Expression Blend automatically creates the behavior, which you can then configure (if it has any properties).

The Last Word

In this chapter, you saw how to use styles to reuse formatting settings with elements. You also considered how to use behaviors to develop tidy packages of user interface functionality, which can then be wired up to any element. Both tools give you a way to make more intelligent, maintainable user interfaces—ones that centralize formatting details and complex logic rather than forcing you to distribute it throughout your application and repeat it many times over.

Drawing

CHAPTER 12

■ ■ ■

Shapes, Brushes, and Transforms

In many user interface technologies, there's a clear distinction between ordinary controls and custom drawing. Often the drawing features are used only in specialized applications—for example, games, data visualization, physics simulations, and so on.

WPF has a dramatically different philosophy. It handles prebuilt controls and custom-drawn graphics in the same way. Not only will you use WPF's drawing support to create graphically rich visuals for your user interface, but you'll also use it to get the most out of other features such as animation (Chapter 15) and control templates (Chapter 17). In fact, WPF's drawing support is equally important whether you're creating a dazzling new game or just adding polish to an ordinary business application.

In this chapter, you'll explore WPF's 2-D drawing features, starting with the basic elements for shape drawing. Next, you'll consider how to paint their borders and interiors with brushes. Then you'll learn how to rotate, skew, and otherwise manipulate shapes and elements by using transforms. Finally, you'll see how to make shapes and other elements partially transparent.

Understanding Shapes

The simplest way to draw 2-D graphical content in a WPF user interface is to use *shapes*—dedicated classes that represent simple lines, ellipses, rectangles, and polygons. Technically, shapes are known as drawing *primitives*. You can combine these basic ingredients to create more-complex graphics.

The most important detail about shapes in WPF is that they all derive from FrameworkElement. As a result, shapes *are* elements. This has the following important consequences:

- *Shapes draw themselves.* You don't need to manage the invalidation and painting process. For example, you don't need to manually repaint a shape when content moves, the window is resized, or the shape's properties change.

- *Shapes are organized in the same way as other elements.* In other words, you can place a shape in any of the layout containers you learned about in Chapter 3. (Although the Canvas is obviously the most useful container, because it allows you to place shapes at specific coordinates, which is important when you're building a complex drawing out of multiple pieces.)

- *Shapes support the same events as other elements.* That means you don't need to go to any extra work to deal with focus, key presses, mouse movements, and mouse clicks. You can use the same set of events you would use with any element, and you have the same support for tooltips, context menus, and drag-and-drop operations.

■ **Tip** As you'll see in Chapter 14, it's possible to program at a lower level in WPF by using the *visual layer*. This lightweight model improves performance if you need to create huge numbers of elements (say, thousands of shapes), and you don't need all the features of the UIElement and FrameworkElement classes (such as data binding and event handling).

The Shape Classes

Every shape derives from the abstract System.Windows.Shapes.Shape class. Figure 12-1 shows the inheritance hierarchy for shapes.

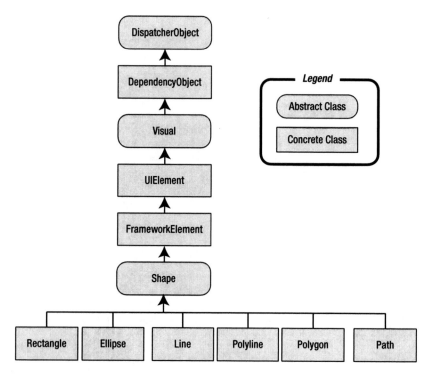

Figure 12-1. *The WPF shape classes*

As you can see, a relatively small set of classes derive from the Shape class. Line, Ellipse, and Rectangle are straightforward. Polyline is a connected series of straight lines. Polygon is a closed shape made up of a connected series of straight lines. Finally, the Path class is an all-in-one superpower that can combine basic shapes in a single element.

Although the Shape class can't do anything on its own, it defines a small set of important properties, which are listed in Table 12-1.

Table 12-1. *Shape Properties*

Name	Description
Fill	Sets the brush object that paints the surface of the shape (everything inside its borders).
Stroke	Sets the brush object that paints the edge of the shape (its border).
StrokeThickness	Sets the thickness of the border, in device-independent units. When drawing a line, WPF splits the width on each side. So a line that's 10 units wide gets 5 units of space on each side of where a single-unit line would be drawn. If you give a line an odd-number thickness, the line will have a fractional width on each side. For example, an 11-unit line has 5.5 units of space on each side. This pretty much guarantees that the line won't line up evenly with the display pixels of your monitor, even if it's running at 96 dpi resolution, so you'll end up with a slightly fuzzy anti-aliased edge. You can use the SnapsToDevicePixels property to clean this up if it bothers you (as described in the section "Pixel Snapping" later in this chapter).
StrokeStartLineCap and StrokeEndLineCap	Determine the contour of the edge of the beginning and end of the line. These properties have an effect only for the Line, the Polyline, and (sometimes) the Path shapes. All other shapes are closed, and so have no starting and ending point.
StrokeDashArray, StrokeDashOffset, and StrokeDashCap	Allow you to create a dashed border around a shape. You can control the size and frequency of the dashes, and the contour of the edge where each dash line begins and ends.
StrokeLineJoin and StrokeMiterLimit	Determine the contour of the shape's corners. Technically, these properties affect the *vertices* where different lines meet, such as the corners of a Rectangle. These properties have no effect for shapes without corners, such as Line and Ellipse.
Stretch	Determines how a shape fills its available space. You can use this property to create a shape that expands to fit its container. You can also force a shape to expand in one direction by using a Stretch value for the HorizontalAlignment or VerticalAlignment properties (which are inherited from the FrameworkElement class).
DefiningGeometry	Provides a Geometry object for the shape. A Geometry object describes the coordinates and size of a shape without including the UIElement plumbing, such as the support for keyboard and mouse events. You'll use geometries in Chapter 13.
GeometryTransform	Allows you to apply a Transform object that changes the coordinate system that's used to draw a shape. This allows you to skew, rotate, or displace a shape. Transforms are particularly useful when animating graphics. You'll learn about transforms later in this chapter.
RenderedGeometry	Provides a Geometry object that describes the final, rendered shape. Geometries are described in Chapter 13.

In the following sections, you'll consider the Rectangle, Ellipse, Line, and Polyline. Along the way, you'll learn the following fundamentals:

- How to size shapes and organize them in a layout container

- How to control which regions of a complex shape are filled in

- How to use dashed lines and different line ends (or *caps*)

- How to neatly align shape edges along pixel boundaries

You'll take a look at the more sophisticated Path class in Chapter 13.

Rectangle and Ellipse

The Rectangle and Ellipse are the two simplest shapes. To create either one, set the familiar Height and Width properties (inherited from FrameworkElement) to define the size of your shape, and then set the Fill or Stroke property (or both) to make the shape visible. You're also free to use properties such as MinHeight, MinWidth, HorizontalAlignment, VerticalAlignment, and Margin.

■ **Note** If you fail to set the Stroke or Fill property, your shape won't appear at all.

Here's a simple example that stacks an ellipse on a rectangle (see Figure 12-2) by using a StackPanel:

```
<StackPanel>
  <Ellipse Fill="Yellow" Stroke="Blue"
   Height="50" Width="100" Margin="5" HorizontalAlignment="Left"></Ellipse>
  <Rectangle Fill="Yellow" Stroke="Blue"
   Height="50" Width="100" Margin="5" HorizontalAlignment="Left"></Rectangle>
</StackPanel>
```

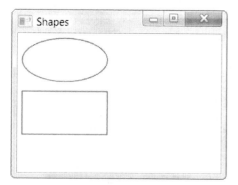

Figure 12-2. *Two simple shapes*

The Ellipse class doesn't add any properties. The Rectangle class adds just two: RadiusX and RadiusY. When set to nonzero values, these properties allow you to create nicely rounded corners.

You can think of RadiusX and RadiusY as describing an ellipse that's used just to fill in the corners of the rectangle. For example, if you set both properties to 10, WPF draws your corners by using the edge of a circle that's 10 units wide. As you make your radius larger, more of your rectangle will be rounded off. If you increase RadiusY more than RadiusX, your corners will round off more gradually along the left and right sides and more sharply along the top and bottom edge. If you increase the RadiusX property to match your rectangle's width, and increase RadiusY to match its height, you'll end up converting your rectangle into an ordinary ellipse.

Figure 12-3 shows a few rectangles with rounded corners.

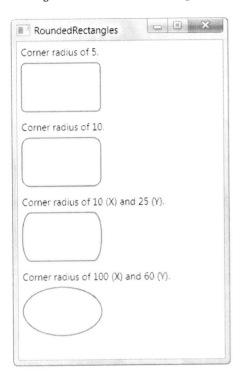

Figure 12-3. *Rounded corners*

Sizing and Placing Shapes

As you already know, hard-coded sizes are usually not the ideal approach to creating user interfaces. They limit your ability to handle dynamic content, and they make it more difficult to localize your application into other languages.

When drawing shapes, these concerns don't always apply. Often you'll need tighter control over shape placement. However, in many cases you can make your design a little more flexible. Both the Ellipse and the Rectangle have the ability to size themselves to fill the available space.

If you don't supply the Height and Width properties, the shape is sized based on its container. In the previous example, removing the Height and Width values (and leaving out the MinHeight and MinWidth values) will cause the shapes to shrink to a vanishingly small size, because the StackPanel is sized to fit its content. However, if you force the StackPanel to take the full width of the window (by setting its HorizontalAlignment property to Stretch), and then also set the HorizontalAlignment property of the ellipse to Stretch and remove the ellipse's Width property, the ellipse will take the full width of the window.

A better example can be made with the Grid container. If you use the proportional row-sizing behavior (which is the default), you can create an ellipse that fills a window with this stripped-down markup:

```
<Grid>

  <Ellipse Fill="Yellow" Stroke="Blue"></Ellipse>

</Grid>
```

Here, the Grid fills the entire window. The Grid contains a single proportionately sized row, which fills the entire Grid. Finally, the ellipse fills the entire row.

This sizing behavior depends on the value of the Stretch property (which is defined in the Shape class). By default, it's set to Fill, which stretches a shape to fill its container if an explicit size isn't indicated. Table 12-2 lists all your possibilities.

Table 12-2. *Values for the Stretch Enumeration*

Name	Description
Fill	Your shape is stretched in width and height to fit its container exactly. (If you set an explicit height and width, this setting has no effect.)
None	The shape is not stretched. Unless you set a nonzero width and height (using the Height and Width or MinHeight and MinWidth properties), your shape won't appear.
Uniform	The width and height are sized up proportionately until the shape reaches the edge of the container. If you use this with an ellipse, you'll end up with the biggest circle that fits in the window. If you use it with a rectangle, you'll get the biggest possible square. (If you set an explicit height and width, your shape is sized within those bounds. For example, if you set a Width of 10 and a Height of 100 for a rectangle, you'll get only a 10 × 10 square.)
UniformToFill	The width and height are sized proportionately until the shape fills all the available height and width. For example, if you place a rectangle with this size setting into a window that's 100 × 200 units, you'll get a 200 × 200 rectangle, and part of it will be clipped off. (If you set an explicit height and width, your shape is sized within those bounds. For example, if you set a Width of 10 and a Height of 100 for a rectangle, you'll get a 100 × 100 rectangle that's clipped to fit an invisible 10 × 100 box.)

Figure 12-4 shows the difference between Fill, Uniform, and UniformToFill.

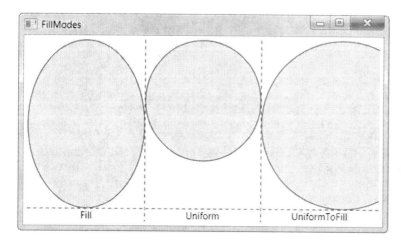

Figure 12-4. *Filling three cells in a Grid*

Usually, a Stretch value of Fill is the same as setting both HorizontalAlignment and VerticalAlignment to Stretch. The difference occurs if you choose to set a fixed Width or Height on your shape. In this case, the HorizontalAlignment and VerticalAlignment values are simply ignored. However, the Stretch setting still has an effect—it determines how your shape content is sized within the bounds you've given it.

■ **Tip**   In most cases, you'll size a shape explicitly or allow it to stretch to fit. You won't combine both approaches.

So far, you've seen how to size a Rectangle and an Ellipse, but what about placing them exactly where you want them? WPF shapes use the same layout system as any other element. However, some layout containers aren't as appropriate. For example, the StackPanel, DockPanel, and WrapPanel often aren't what you want because they're designed to separate elements. The Grid is a bit more flexible because it allows you to place as many elements as you want in the same cell (although it doesn't let you position squares and ellipses in different parts of that cell). The ideal container is the Canvas, which forces you to specify the coordinates of each shape by using the attached Left, Top, Right, or Bottom properties. This gives you complete control over how shapes overlap:

```
<Canvas>
  <Ellipse Fill="Yellow" Stroke="Blue" Canvas.Left="100" Canvas.Top="50"
    Width="100" Height="50"></Ellipse>
    <Rectangle Fill="Yellow" Stroke="Blue" Canvas.Left="30" Canvas.Top="40"
      Width="100" Height="50"></Rectangle>
</Canvas>
```

With a Canvas, the order of your tags is important. In the previous example, the rectangle is superimposed on the ellipse because the ellipse appears first in the list, and so is drawn first (see Figure 12-5).

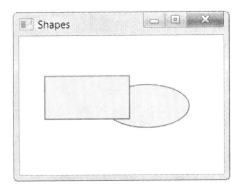

Figure 12-5. *Overlapping shapes in a Canvas*

Remember that a Canvas doesn't need to occupy an entire window. For example, there's no reason that you can't create a Grid that uses a Canvas in one of its cells. This gives you the perfect way to lock down fixed bits of drawing logic in a dynamic, free-flowing user interface.

Scaling Shapes with a Viewbox

The only limitation to using the Canvas is that your graphics won't be able to resize themselves to fit larger or smaller windows. This makes perfect sense for buttons (which don't change size in these situations), but not necessarily for other types of graphical content. For example, you might create a complex graphic that you want to be resizable so it can take advantage of the available space.

In situations like these, WPF has an easy solution. If you want to combine the precise control of the Canvas with easy resizability, you can use the Viewbox element.

The Viewbox is a simple class that derives from Decorator (much like the Border class you first encountered in Chapter 3). It accepts a single child, which it stretches or shrinks to fit the available space. Of course, that single child can be a layout container, which can hold a number of shapes (or other elements) that will be resized in sync. However, it's more common to use the Viewbox for vector graphics than for ordinary controls.

Although you could place a single shape in a Viewbox, that doesn't provide any real advantage. Instead, the Viewbox shines when you need to wrap a group of shapes that make up a drawing. Typically, you'll place a Canvas inside a Viewbox, and place your shapes inside the Canvas.

The following example puts a Canvas-containing Viewbox in the second row of a Grid. The Viewbox takes the full height and width of the row. The row takes whatever space is left over after the first autosized row is rendered. Here's the markup:

```
<Grid Margin="5">
  <Grid.RowDefinitions>
    <RowDefinition Height="Auto"></RowDefinition>
    <RowDefinition Height="*"></RowDefinition>
  </Grid.RowDefinitions>

  <TextBlock>The first row of a Grid.</TextBlock>

  <Viewbox Grid.Row="1" HorizontalAlignment="Left" >
    <Canvas Width="200" Height="150">
      <Ellipse Fill="Yellow" Stroke="Blue" Canvas.Left="10"  Canvas.Top="50"
        Width="100" Height="50" HorizontalAlignment="Left"></Ellipse>
      <Rectangle Fill="Yellow" Stroke="Blue" Canvas.Left="30"  Canvas.Top="40"
        Width="100" Height="50" HorizontalAlignment="Left"></Rectangle>
    </Canvas>
  </Viewbox>
</Grid>
```

Figure 12-6 shows how the Viewbox adjusts itself as the window is resized. The first row is unchanged. However, the second row expands to fill the extra space. As you can see, the shape in the Viewbox changes proportionately as the window grows.

Figure 12-6. *Resizing with a Viewbox*

> **Note**   The scaling that the Viewbox does is similar to the scaling you see in WPF if you increase the system DPI setting. It changes every onscreen element proportionally, including images, text, lines, and shapes. For example, if you place an ordinary button in a Viewbox, the sizing will affect its overall size, the text inside, and the thickness of the border around it. If you place a shape element inside, the Viewbox resizes its inside area and its border proportionately, so the larger your shape grows, the thicker its border will be.

By default, the Viewbox performs proportional scaling that preserves the aspect ratio of its contents. In the current example, that means that even if the shape of the containing row changes (growing wider or taller), the shapes inside won't be distorted. Instead, the Viewbox uses the largest scaling factor that fits inside the available space. However, you can change this behavior by using the Viewbox.Stretch property. By default, it's set to Uniform, but you can use any of the values from Table 12-2. Change it to Fill, and the content inside the Viewbox is stretched in both directions to fit the available space exactly, even if it mangles your original drawing. You can also get slightly more control by using the StretchDirection property. By default, this property takes the value Both, but you can use UpOnly to create content that can grow but won't shrink beyond its original size, and use DownOnly to create content that can shrink but not grow.

In order for the Viewbox to perform its scaling magic, it needs to be able to determine two pieces of information: the ordinary size that your content would have (if it weren't in a Viewbox) and the new size that you want it to have.

The second detail—the new size—is simple enough. The Viewbox gives the inner content all the space that's available, based on its Stretch property. That means the bigger the Viewbox, the bigger your content.

The first detail—the ordinary, non-Viewbox size, is implicit in the way you define the nested content. In the previous example, the Canvas is given an explicit size of 200×150 units. Thus, the Viewbox scales the image from that starting point. For example, the ellipse is initially 100 units wide, which means it takes up half the allotted Canvas drawing space. As the Canvas grows larger, the Viewbox respects these proportions, and the ellipse continues to take half the available space.

However, consider what happens if you remove the Width and Height properties from the Canvas. Now the Canvas is given a size of 0×0 units, so the Viewbox cannot resize it, and your nested content won't appear. (This is different from the behavior you get if you have the Canvas on its own. That's because even though the Canvas is still given a size of 0×0, your shapes are allowed to draw outside the Canvas area as long as the Canvas.ClipToBounds property hasn't been set to True. The Viewbox isn't as tolerant of this error.)

Now consider what happens if you wrap the Canvas inside a proportionately sized Grid cell and you don't specify the size of the Canvas. If you aren't using the Viewbox, this approach works perfectly well—the Canvas is stretched to fill the cell, and the content inside is visible. But if you place all this content in a Viewbox, this strategy fails. The Viewbox can't determine the initial size, so it can't resize the Grid appropriately.

You can get around this problem by placing certain shapes (such as the Rectangle and Ellipse) directly in an autosized container (such as the Grid). The Viewbox can then evaluate the minimum size the Grid needs to fit its content and scale it up to fit what's available. However, the easiest way to get the size you really want in a Viewbox is to wrap your content in an element that has a fixed size, whether it's a Canvas, a button, or something else. This fixed size then becomes the initial size that the Viewbox uses for its calculations. Hard-coding a size in this way won't limit the flexibility of your layout, because the Viewbox is sized proportionally based on the available space and its layout container.

Line

The Line shape represents a straight line that connects one point to another. The starting and ending points are set by four properties: X1 and Y1 (for the first point) and X2 and Y2 (for the second point). For example, here's a line that stretches from (0, 0) to (10, 100):

```
<Line Stroke="Blue" X1="0" Y1="0" X2="10" Y2="100"></Line>
```

The Fill property has no effect for a line. You must set the Stroke property.

The coordinates you use in a line are relative to the top-left corner where the line is placed. For example, if you place the previous line in a StackPanel, the coordinate (0, 0) points to wherever that item in the StackPanel is placed. It might be the top-left corner of the window, but it probably isn't. If the StackPanel uses a nonzero Margin, or if the line is preceded by other elements, the line will begin at a point (0, 0) some distance down from the top of the window.

However, it's perfectly reasonable to use negative coordinates for a line. In fact, you can use coordinates that take your line out of its allocated space and draw on top of any other part of the window. This isn't possible with the Rectangle and Ellipse shapes you've seen so far. However, there's also a drawback to this model, which is that lines can't use the flow content model. That means there's no point setting properties such as Margin, HorizontalAlignment, and VerticalAlignment on a line, because they won't have any effect. The same limitation applies to the Polyline and Polygon shapes.

▓ **Note** You can use the Height, Width, and Stretch properties with a line, although it's not terribly common. The basic technique is to use the Height and Width to determine the space that's allocated to the line, and then use the Stretch property to resize the line to fill this area.

If you place a Line in a Canvas, the attached position properties (such as Top and Left) still apply. They determine the starting position of the line. In other words, the two line coordinates are offset by that amount. Consider this line:

```
<Line Stroke="Blue" X1="0" Y1="0" X2="10" Y2="100"
 Canvas.Left="5" Canvas.Top="100"></Line>
```

It stretches from (0, 0) to (10, 100), using a coordinate system that treats the point (5, 100) on the Canvas as (0, 0). That makes it equivalent to this line, which doesn't use the Top and Left properties:

```
<Line Stroke="Blue" X1="5" Y1="100" X2="15" Y2="200"></Line>
```

It's up to you whether you use the position properties when you place a Line on a Canvas. Often you can simplify your line drawing by picking a good starting point. You also make it easier to move parts of your drawing. For example, if you draw several lines and other shapes at a specific position in a Canvas, it's a good idea to draw them relative to a nearby point (by using the same Top and Left coordinates). That way, you can shift that entire part of your drawing to a new position as needed.

▓ **Note** There's no way to create a curved line with Line or Polyline shapes. Instead, you need the more advanced Path class described in Chapter 13.

Polyline

The Polyline class allows you to draw a sequence of connected straight lines. You simply supply a list of X and Y coordinates by using the Points property. Technically, the Points property requires a PointCollection object, but you fill this collection in XAML by using a lean string-based syntax. You simply need to supply a list of points and add a space or a comma between each coordinate.

A Polyline can have as few as two points. For example, here's a Polyline that duplicates the first line you saw in this section, which stretches from (5, 100) to (15, 200):

```
<Polyline Stroke="Blue" Points="5 100 15 200"></Polyline>
```

For better readability, use commas between each X and Y coordinate:

```
<Polyline Stroke="Blue" Points="5,100 15,200"></Polyline>
```

And here's a more complex Polyline that begins at (10, 150). The points move steadily to the right, oscillating between higher Y values such as (50, 160) and lower ones such as (70, 130):

```
<Canvas>
  <Polyline Stroke="Blue" StrokeThickness="5" Points="10,150 30,140 50,160 70,130
90,170 110,120 130,180 150,110 170,190 190,100 210,240" >
  </Polyline>
</Canvas>
```

Figure 12-7 shows the final line.

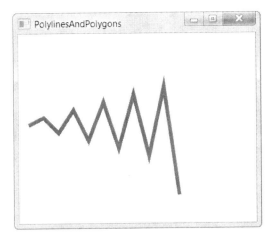

Figure 12-7. *A line with several segments*

At this point, it might occur to you that it would be easier to fill the Points collection programmatically, using some sort of loop that automatically increments X and Y values accordingly. This is true if you need to create highly dynamic graphics—for example, a chart that varies its appearance based on a set of data you extract from a database. But if you simply want to build a fixed piece of graphical content, you won't want to worry about the specific coordinates of your shapes at all. Instead, you (or a designer) will use another tool, such as Expression Design, to draw the appropriate graphics, and then export to XAML.

Polygon

The Polygon is virtually the same as the Polyline. Like the Polyline class, the Polygon class has a Points collection that takes a list of coordinates. The only difference is that the Polygon adds a final line segment that connects the final point to the starting point. (If your final point is already the same as the first point, the Polygon class has no difference from the Polyline class.) You can fill the interior of this shape by using the Fill brush. Figure 12-8 shows the previous Polyline as a Polygon with a yellow fill.

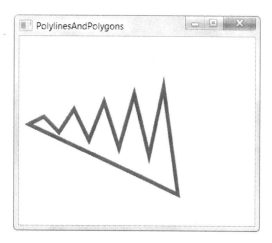

Figure 12-8. A filled polygon

■ **Note** Technically, you can set the Fill property of a Polyline as well. In this situation, the Polyline fills itself as though it were a Polygon—in other words, as though it had an invisible line segment connecting the last point to the first point. This effect is of limited use.

In a simple shape with lines that never cross, it's easy to fill the interior. However, sometimes you'll have a more complex Polygon where it's not necessarily obvious which portions are "inside" the shape (and should be filled) and which portions are outside.

For example, consider Figure 12-9, which features a line that crosses more than one other line, leaving an irregular region at the center that you may or may not want to fill. Obviously, you can control exactly what gets filled by breaking this drawing down into smaller shapes, but you may not need to do that.

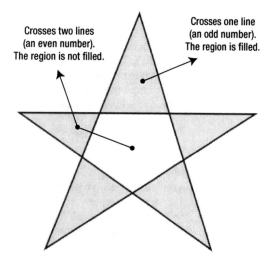

Figure 12-9. Determining fill areas when FillRule is EvenOdd

Every Polygon and Polyline includes a FillRule property, which lets you choose between two approaches for filling in regions. By default, FillRule is set to EvenOdd. In order to decide whether to fill a region, WPF counts the number of lines that must be crossed to reach the outside of the shape. If this number is odd, the region is filled in; if it's even, the region isn't filled. In the center area of Figure 12-9, you must cross two lines to get out of the shape, so it's not filled.

WPF also supports the Nonzero fill rule, which is a little trickier. Essentially, with Nonzero, WPF follows the same line-counting process as EvenOdd, but it takes into account the direction that each crossed line flows. If the number of lines going in one direction (say, left to right) is equal to the number going in the opposite direction (right to left), the region is not filled. If the difference between these two counts is not zero, the region is filled. In the shape from the previous example, the interior region is filled if you set the FillRule property to Nonzero. Figure 12-10 shows why. (In this example, the points are numbered in the order they are drawn, and arrows show the direction in which each line is drawn.)

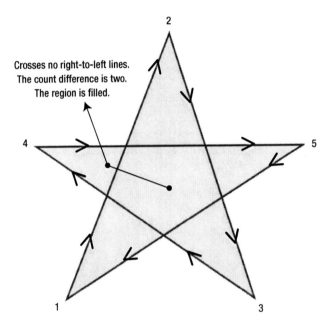

Figure 12-10. *Determining fill areas when FillRule is Nonzero*

■ **Note**   If an odd number of lines are crossed to reach the outside of the shape, the difference between the two counts can't be zero. Thus, the Nonzero fill rule always fills at least as much as the EvenOdd rule, plus possibly a bit more.

The tricky part about Nonzero is that its fill settings depend on *how* you draw the shape, not what the shape itself looks like. For example, you could draw the same shape in such a way that the center isn't filled (although it's much more awkward—you would begin by drawing the inner region, and then you would draw the outside spikes in the reverse direction).

Here's the markup that draws the star shown in Figure 12-10:

```
<Polygon Stroke="Blue" StrokeThickness="1" Fill="Yellow"
  Canvas.Left="10" Canvas.Top="175" FillRule="Nonzero"
  Points="15,200 68,70 110,200 0,125 135,125">
</Polygon>
```

Line Caps and Line Joins

When drawing with the Line and Polyline shapes, you can choose how the starting and ending edge of the line is drawn by using the StartLineCap and EndLineCap properties. (These properties have no effect on other shapes because they're closed.)

Ordinarily, both StartLineCap and EndLineCap are set to Flat, which means the line ends immediately at its final coordinate. Your other choices are Round (which rounds the corner off gently), Triangle (which draws the two sides of the line together in a point), and Square (which ends the line with a sharp edge). All of these values add length to the line—in other words, they take it beyond the position where it would otherwise end. The extra distance is half the thickness of the line.

■ **Note**   The only difference between Flat and Square is that the square-edged line extends this extra distance. In all other respects, the edge looks the same.

Figure 12-11 shows different line caps at the end of a line.

Figure 12-11. *Line caps*

All shapes except Line allow you to use the StrokeLineJoin property to tweak how their corners are shaped. You have four choices: Miter (the default) uses sharp edges, Bevel cuts off the point edge, Round rounds it out gently, and Triangle brings it to a sharp point. Figure 12-12 shows a comparison.

Figure 12-12. *Line joins*

When using mitered edges with thick lines and very small angles, the sharp corner can extend an impractically long distance. In this case, you can use Bevel or Round to pare down the corner. Or you could use the StrokeMiterLimit, which automatically bevels the edge when it reaches a certain maximum length. The StrokeMiterLimit is a ratio that compares the length used to miter the corner to half the thickness of the line. If you set this to 1 (which is the default value), you're allowing the corner to extend half the thickness of the line. If you set it to 3, you're allowing the corner to extend to 1.5 times the thickness of the line. The last line in Figure 12-12 uses a higher miter limit with a narrow corner.

Dashes

Instead of drawing boring solid lines for the borders of your shape, you can draw *dashed lines*—lines that are broken with spaces according to a pattern you specify. When creating a dashed line in WPF, you aren't limited to specific presets. Instead, you choose the length of the solid segment of the line and the length of the broken (blank) segment by setting the StrokeDashArray property. For example, consider this line:

```
<Polyline Stroke="Blue" StrokeThickness="14" StrokeDashArray="1 2"
  Points="10,30 60,0 90,40 120,10 350,10">
</Polyline>
```

It has a line value of 1 and a gap value of 2. These values are interpreted relative to the thickness of the line. So if the line is 14 units thick (as in this example), the solid portion is 14 units, followed by a blank portion of 28 units. The line repeats this pattern for its entire length.

On the other hand, if you swap these values around like so:

```
StrokeDashArray="2 1"
```

you get a line that has 28-unit solid portions broken by 12-unit spaces. Figure 12-13 shows both lines. As you'll notice, when a very thick line segment falls on a corner, it may be broken unevenly.

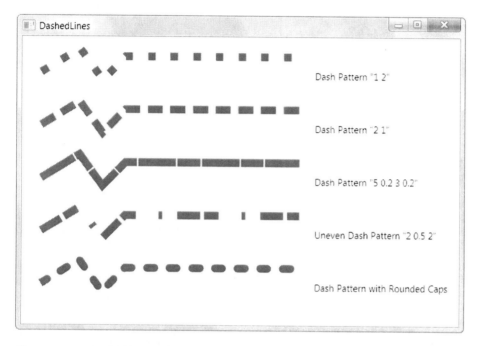

Figure 12-13. *Dashed lines*

There's no reason that you need to stick with whole-number values. For example, this StrokeDashArray is perfectly reasonable:

```
StrokeDashArray="5 0.2 3 0.2"
```

It supplies a more complex sequence—a dashed line that's 5×14 length, then a 0.2×15 break, followed by a 3×14 length and another 0.2×14 length. At the end of this sequence, the line repeats the pattern from the beginning.

An interesting thing happens if you supply an odd number of values for the StrokeDashArray. Take this one, for example:

```
StrokeDashArray="3 0.5 2"
```

When drawing this line, WPF begins with a 3-times-thickness line, followed by a 0.5-times-thickness space, followed by a 2-times-thickness line. But when it repeats the pattern, it starts with a gap, meaning you get a 3-times-thickness *space*, followed by a 0.5-times-thickness line, and so on. Essentially, the dashed line alternates its pattern between line segments and spaces.

If you want to start midway into your pattern, you can use the StrokeDashOffset property, which is a 0-based index number that points to one of the values in your StrokeDashArray. For example, if you set StrokeDashOffset to 1 in the previous example, the line will begin with the 0.5-thickness space. Set it to 2, and the line begins with the 2-thickness segment.

Finally, you can control how the broken edges of your line are capped. Ordinarily, it's a straight edge, but you can set the StrokeDashCap to the Bevel, Square, and Triangle values you considered in the previous section. Remember that all of these settings add one-half the line thickness to the end of your dash. If you don't take this into account, you might end up with dashes that overlap one another. The solution is to add extra space to compensate.

■ **Tip** When using the StrokeDashCap property with a line (not a shape), it's often a good idea to set the StartLineCap and EndLineCap to the same values. This makes the line look consistent.

Pixel Snapping

As you know, WPF uses a device-independent drawing system. You specify sizes for things like fonts and shapes by using "virtual" pixels, which are the same size as normal pixels on ordinary 96 dpi displays but are scaled up on higher-DPI displays. In other words, a rectangle you draw that's 50 pixels wide might be rendered using more or fewer pixels, depending on the device. This conversion between device-independent units and physical pixels happens automatically, and you usually don't need to think about it.

The ratio of pixels between different DPI settings is rarely a whole number. For example, 50 pixels at 96 dpi become 62.4996 pixels on a 120 dpi monitor. (This isn't an error condition; in fact, WPF always allows you to use fractional Double values when supplying a value in device-independent units.) Obviously, there's no way to place an edge on a point that's between pixels. WPF compensates by using anti-aliasing. For example, when drawing a red line that's 62.4992 pixels long, WPF might fill the first 62 pixels normally and then shade the 63rd pixel with a value that's between the line color (red) and the background. However, there's a catch. If you're drawing straight lines, rectangles, or polygons with square corners, this automatic anti-aliasing can introduce a tinge of blurriness at the edges of your shape.

You might assume that this problem appears only when you're running an application on a display that has display resolution that's *not* 96 dpi. However, that's not necessarily the case, because all shapes can be sized using fractional lengths and coordinates, which causes the same issue. And although you probably won't use fractional values in your shape drawing, *resizable* shapes—shapes that are stretched because they size along with their container or they're placed in a Viewbox—will almost always end up with fractional sizes. Similarly, odd-numbered line thicknesses create a line that has a fractional number of pixels on either side.

The fuzzy edge issue isn't necessarily a problem. In fact, depending on the type of graphic you're drawing, it might look quite normal. However, if you don't want this behavior, you can tell WPF not to use anti-aliasing for a specific shape. Instead, WPF will round the measurement to the nearest device pixel. You turn on this feature, which is called *pixel snapping*, by setting the SnapsToDevicePixels property of a UIElement to True.

To see the difference, look at the magnified window in Figure 12-14, which compares two rectangles. The bottom one uses pixel snapping, and the top one doesn't. If you look carefully, you'll see a thin edge of lighter color along the top and left edges of the unsnapped rectangle.

Figure 12-14. The effect of pixel snapping

Using Brushes

Brushes fill an area—whether it's the background, foreground, or border of an element, or the fill or stroke of a shape. The simplest type of brush is SolidColorBrush, which paints a solid, continuous color. When you set the Stroke or Fill property of a shape in XAML, there's a SolidColorBrush at work, doing the painting behind the scenes.

Here are a few more fundamental facts about brushes:

- Brushes support change notification because they derive from Freezable. As a result, if you change a brush, any elements that use that brush repaint themselves automatically.

- Brushes support partial transparency. All you need to do is modify the Opacity property to let the background show through. You'll try out this approach at the end of this chapter.

- The SystemBrushes class provides access to brushes that use the colors defined in the Windows system preferences for the current computer.

Although SolidColorBrush is indisputably useful, several other classes inherit from System.Windows.Media. Brush and give you more-exotic effects. Table 12-3 lists them all.

Table 12-3. *Brush Classes*

Name	Description
SolidColorBrush	Paints an area using a single continuous color.
LinearGradientBrush	Paints an area using a gradient fill, a gradually shaded fill that changes from one color to another (and, optionally, to another and then another, and so on).
RadialGradientBrush	Paints an area using a radial gradient fill, which is similar to a linear gradient, except that it radiates out in a circular pattern starting from a center point.
ImageBrush	Paints an area using an image that can be stretched, scaled, or tiled.
DrawingBrush	Paints an area using a Drawing object. This object can include shapes you've defined and bitmaps.
VisualBrush	Paints an area using a Visual object. Because all WPF elements derive from the Visual class, you can use this brush to copy part of your user interface (such as the face of a button) to another area. This is useful when creating fancy effects, such as partial reflections.
BitmapCacheBrush	Paints an area using the cached content from a Visual object. This makes it similar to VisualBrush, but more efficient if the graphical content needs to be reused in multiple places or repainted frequently.

The DrawingBrush is covered in Chapter 13, when you consider more optimized ways to deal with large numbers of graphics. In this section, you'll learn how to use the brushes that fill areas with gradients, images, and visual content copied from other elements.

■ **Note** All Brush classes are found in the System.Windows.Media namespace.

The SolidColorBrush

You've already seen how SolidColorBrush objects work with controls in Chapter 6. In most controls, setting the Foreground property paints the text color, and setting the Background property paints the space behind it. Shapes use similar but different properties: Stroke for painting the shape border and Fill for painting the shape interior.

As you've seen throughout this chapter, you can set both Stroke and Fill in XAML using color names, in which case the WPF parser automatically creates the matching SolidColorBrush object for you. You can also set Stroke and Fill in code, but you'll need to create the SolidColorBrush explicitly:

```
' Create a brush from a named color:
cmd.Background = New SolidColorBrush(Colors.AliceBlue)

' Create a brush from a system color:
cmd.Background = SystemColors.ControlBrush

' Create a brush from color values:
Dim red As Integer = 0
Dim green As Integer = 255
Dim blue As Integer = 0
cmd.Foreground = New SolidColorBrush(Color.FromRgb(red, green, blue))
```

The LinearGradientBrush

The LinearGradientBrush allows you to create a blended fill that changes from one color to another.

Here's the simplest possible gradient. It shades a rectangle diagonally from blue (in the top-left corner) to white (in the bottom-right corner):

```
<Rectangle Width="150" Height="100">
  <Rectangle.Fill>
    <LinearGradientBrush >
      <GradientStop Color="Blue" Offset="0"/>
      <GradientStop Color="White" Offset="1" />
    </LinearGradientBrush>
  </Rectangle.Fill>
</Rectangle>
```

The top gradient in Figure 12-15 shows the result.

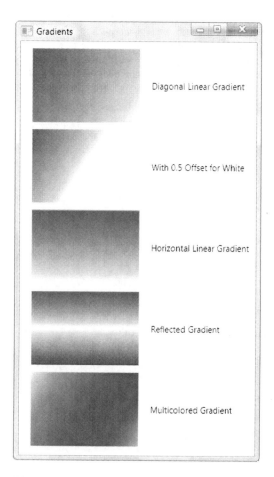

Figure 12-15. *A rectangle with different linear gradients*

To create this gradient, you need to add one GradientStop for each color. You also need to place each color in your gradient by using an Offset value from 0 to 1. In this example, the GradientStop for the blue color has an offset of 0, which means it's placed at the very beginning of the gradient. The GradientStop for the white color has an offset of 1, which places it at the end. By changing these values, you can adjust how quickly the gradient switches from one color to the other. For example, if you set the GradientStop for the white color to 0.5, the gradient would blend from blue (in the top-left corner) to white in the middle (the point between the two corners). The right side of the rectangle would be completely white. (The second gradient in Figure 12-15 shows this example.)

The previous markup creates a gradient with a diagonal fill that stretches from one corner to another. However, you might want to create a gradient that blends from top to bottom or side to side, or uses a different diagonal angle. You control these details by using the StartPoint and EndPoint properties of the LinearGradientBrush. These properties allow you to choose the point where the first color begins to change and the point where the color change ends with the final color. (The area in between is blended gradually.) However, there's one quirk: the coordinates you use for the starting and ending point aren't real coordinates. Instead, the LinearGradientBrush assigns the point (0, 0) to the top-left corner and (1, 1) to the bottom-right corner of the area you want to fill, no matter how high and wide it actually is.

To create a top-to-bottom horizontal fill, you can use a start point of (0, 0) for the top-left corner, and an end point of (0, 1), which represents the bottom-left corner. To create a side-to-side vertical fill (with no slant), you can use a start point of (0, 0) and an end point of (1, 0) for the bottom-left corner. Figure 12-15 shows a horizontal gradient (it's the third one).

You can get a little craftier by supplying start points and end points that aren't quite aligned with the corners of your gradient. For example, you could have a gradient stretch from (0, 0) to (0, 0.5), which is a point on the left edge, halfway down. This creates a compressed linear gradient—one color starts at the top, blending to the second color in the middle. The bottom half of the shape is filled with the second color. But wait—you can change this behavior by using the LinearGradientBrush.SpreadMethod property. It's Pad by default (which means areas outside the gradient are given a solid fill with the appropriate color), but you can also use Reflect (to reverse the gradient, going from the second color back to the first) or Repeat (to duplicate the same color progression). Figure 12-15 shows the Reflect effect (it's the fourth gradient).

The LinearGradientBrush also allows you to create gradients with more than two colors by adding more than two GradientStop objects. For example, here's a gradient that moves through a rainbow of colors:

```
<Rectangle Width="150" Height="100">
  <Rectangle.Fill>
    <LinearGradientBrush StartPoint="0,0" EndPoint="1,1">
      <GradientStop Color="Yellow" Offset="0.0" />
      <GradientStop Color="Red" Offset="0.25" />
      <GradientStop Color="Blue" Offset="0.75" />
      <GradientStop Color="LimeGreen" Offset="1.0" />
    </LinearGradientBrush>
  </Rectangle.Fill>
</Rectangle>
```

The only trick is to set the appropriate offset for each GradientStop. For example, if you want to transition through five colors, you might give your first color an offset of 0, the second 0.25, the third 0.5, the fourth 0.75, and the fifth 1. Or if you want the colors to blend more quickly at the beginning and then end more gradually, you could set the offsets to 0, 0.1, 0.2, 0.4, 0.6, and 1.

Remember that Brushes aren't limited to shape drawing. You can substitute the LinearGradientBrush anytime you would use the SolidColorBrush—for example, when filling the background surface of an element (using the Background property), the foreground color of its text (using the Foreground property), or the fill of a border (using the BorderBrush property). Figure 12-16 shows an example of a gradient-filled TextBlock.

Figure 12-16. *Using the LinearGradientBrush to set the TextBlock.Foreground property*

The RadialGradientBrush

The RadialGradientBrush works similarly to the LinearGradientBrush. It also takes a sequence of colors with different offsets. As with the LinearGradientBrush, you can use as many colors as you want. The difference is how you place the gradient.

To identify the point where the first color in the gradient starts, you use the GradientOrigin property. By default, it's (0.5, 0.5), which represents the middle of the fill region.

■ **Note**   As with the LinearGradientBrush, the RadialGradientBrush uses a proportional coordinate system that acts as though the top-left corner of your rectangular fill area is (0, 0) and the bottom-right corner is (1, 1). That means you can pick any coordinate from (0, 0) to (1, 1) to place the starting point of the gradient. In fact, you can even go beyond these limits if you want to locate the starting point outside the fill region.

The gradient radiates out from the starting point in a circular fashion. Eventually, your gradient reaches the edge of an inner gradient circle, where it ends. This center of this circle may or may not line up with the gradient origin, depending on the effect you want. The area beyond the edge of the inner gradient circle and the outermost edge of the fill region is given a solid fill using the last color that's defined in the RadialGradientBrush.GradientStops collection. Figure 12-17 illustrates how a radial gradient is filled.

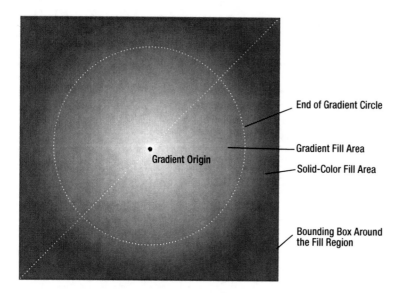

Figure 12-17. *How a radial gradient is filled*

You set the edge of the inner gradient circle by using three properties: Center, RadiusX, and RadiusY. By default, the Center property is (0.5, 0.5), which places the center of the limiting circle in the middle of your fill region and in the same position as the gradient origin.

RadiusX and RadiusY determine the size of the limiting circle, and by default, they're both set to 0.5. These values can be a bit unintuitive, because they're measured in relation to the *diagonal* span of your fill area (the length of an imaginary line stretching from the top-left corner to the bottom-right corner of your fill area). That means a radius of 0.5

defines a circle that has a radius that's half the length of this diagonal. If you have a square fill region, you can use a dash of Pythagoras to calculate that this is about 0.7 times the width (or height) of your region. Thus, if you're filling a square region with the default settings, the gradient begins in the center and stretches to its outermost edge at about 0.7 times the width of the square.

> **Note** If you trace the largest possible ellipse that fits in your fill area, that's the place where the gradient ends with your second color.

The radial gradient is a particularly good choice for filling rounded shapes and creating lighting effects. (Master artists use a combination of gradients to create buttons with a glow effect.) A common trick is to offset the GradientOrigin point slightly to create an illusion of depth in your shape. Here's an example:

```
<Ellipse Margin="5" Stroke="Black" StrokeThickness="1" Width="200" Height="200">
  <Ellipse.Fill>
    <RadialGradientBrush RadiusX="1" RadiusY="1" GradientOrigin="0.7,0.3">
      <GradientStop Color="White" Offset="0" />
      <GradientStop Color="Blue" Offset="1" />
    </RadialGradientBrush>
  </Ellipse.Fill>
</Ellipse>
```

Figure 12-18 shows this gradient, along with an ordinary radial gradient that has the standard GradientOrigin (0.5, 0.5).

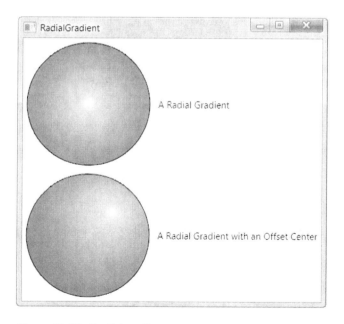

Figure 12-18. *Radial gradients*

The ImageBrush

The ImageBrush allows you to fill an area with a bitmap image. You can use most common file types, including BMP, PNG, GIF, and JPEG files. You identify the image you want to use by setting the ImageSource property. For example, this brush paints the background of a Grid by using an image named logo.jpg that's included in the assembly as a resource:

```
<Grid>
  <Grid.Background>
    <ImageBrush ImageSource="logo.jpg"></ImageBrush>
  </Grid.Background>
</Grid>
```

The ImageBrush.ImageSource property works in the same way as the Source property of the Image element, which means you can also set it by using a URI that points to a resource, an external file, or a web location. You can also create an ImageBrush that uses XAML-defined vector content by supplying a DrawingImage object for the ImageSource property. You might take this approach to reduce overhead (by avoiding the more costly Shape-derived classes), or if you want to use a vector image to create a tiled pattern. You'll learn more about the DrawingImage class in Chapter 13.

■ **Note**   WPF respects any transparency information that it finds in an image. For example, WPF supports transparent areas in a GIF file and transparent or partially transparent areas in a PNG file.

In this example, the ImageBrush is used to paint the background of a cell. As a result, the image is stretched to fit the fill area. If the Grid is larger than the original size of the image, you may see resizing artifacts in your image (such as a general fuzziness). If the shape of the Grid doesn't match the aspect ratio of the picture, the picture will be distorted to fit.

You can control this behavior by modifying the ImageBrush.Stretch property, and assigning one of the values listed in Table 12-2, shown earlier in the chapter. For example, use Uniform to scale the image to fit the container, but keep the aspect ratio or None to paint the image at its natural size (in which case, part of it may be clipped to fit).

■ **Note**   Even with a Stretch of None setting, your image may still be scaled. For example, if you've set your Windows system DPI setting to 120 dpi (also known as *large fonts*), WPF will scale up your bitmap proportionately. This may introduce some fuzziness, but it's a better solution than having your image sizes (and the alignment of your overall user interface) change on monitors with different DPI settings.

If the image is painted smaller than the fill region, the image is aligned according to the AlignmentX and AlignmentY properties. The unfilled area is left transparent. This occurs if you're using Uniform scaling and the region you're filling has a different shape (in which case, you'll get blank bars on the top or the sides). It also occurs if you're using None and the fill region is larger than the image.

You can also use the Viewbox property to clip out a smaller portion of the picture that you're interested in using. To do so, you specify four numbers that describe the rectangle you want to clip out of the source picture. The first two identify the top-left corner where your rectangle begins, and the following two numbers specify the width and height of the rectangle. The only catch is that the Viewbox uses a relative coordinate system, just like the gradient brushes. This coordinate system designates the top-left corner of your picture as (0, 0) and the bottom-right corner as (1, 1).

To understand how Viewbox works, take a look at this markup:

```
<ImageBrush ImageSource="logo.jpg" Stretch="Uniform"
  Viewbox="0.4,0.5 0.2,0.2"></ImageBrush>
```

Here, the Viewbox starts at (0.4, 0.5), which is almost halfway into the picture. (Technically, the X coordinate is 0.4× width and the Y coordinate is 0.5× width.) The rectangle then extends to fill a small box that's 20 percent as wide and tall as the total image (technically, the rectangle is 0.2× width long and 0.2× height tall). The cropped-out portion is then stretched or centered, based on the Stretch, AlignmentX, and AlignmentY properties. Figure 12-19 shows two rectangles that use different ImageBrush objects to fill themselves. The topmost rectangle shows the full image, while the rectangle underneath uses the Viewbox to magnify a small section. Both are given a solid black border.

■ **Note** The Viewbox property is occasionally useful when reusing parts of the same picture in different ways to create certain effects. However, if you know in advance that you need to use only a portion of an image, it obviously makes more sense to crop it down in your favorite graphics software.

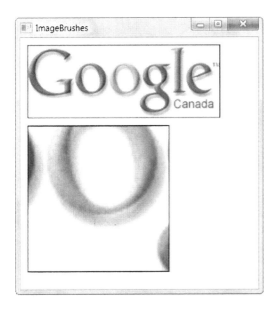

Figure 12-19. *Different ways to use an ImageBrush*

A Tiled ImageBrush

An ordinary ImageBrush isn't all that exciting. However, you can get some interesting effects by tiling your image across the surface of the brush.

When tiling an image, you have two options:

Proportionally sized tiles: Your fill area always has the same number of tiles. The tiles expand and shrink to fit the fill region.

Fixed-sized tiles: Your tiles are always the same size. The size of your fill area determines the number of tiles that appear.

Figure 12-20 compares the difference when a tile-filled rectangle is resized.

Figure 12-20. *Different ways to tile a rectangle*

To tile an image, you need to set the ImageSource property (to identify the image you want to tile) and the Viewport, ViewportUnits, and TileMode properties. These latter three properties determine the size of your tile and the way it's arranged.

You use the Viewport property to set the size of each tile. To use proportionately sized tiles, ViewportUnits must be set to RelativeToBoundingBox (which is the default). Then you define the tile size by using a proportional coordinate system that stretches from 0 to 1 in both dimensions. In other words, a tile that has a top-left corner at (0, 0) and a bottom-right corner at (1, 1) occupies the entire fill area. To get a tiled pattern, you need to define a Viewport that's smaller than the total size of the fill area, as shown here:

```
<ImageBrush ImageSource="tile.jpg" TileMode="Tile"
  Viewport="0,0 0.5,0.5"></ImageBrush>
```

This creates a Viewport box that begins at the top-left corner of the fill area (0, 0) and stretches down to the midpoint (0.5, 0.5). As a result, the fill region will always hold four tiles, no matter how big or small it is. This behavior is nice because it ensures that there's no danger of having part of a tile chopped off at the edge of a shape. (Of course, this isn't the case if you're using the ImageBrush to fill a nonrectangular area.)

Because the tile in this example is relative to the size of the fill area, a larger fill area will use a larger tile, and you may wind up with some blurriness from image resizing. Furthermore, if your fill area isn't perfectly square, the relative coordinate system is squashed accordingly, so each tiled square becomes a rectangle. This behavior is shown in the second tiled pattern in Figure 12-20.

You can alter this behavior by changing the Stretch property (which is Fill by default). Use None to ensure that tiles are never distorted and keep their proper shape. However, if the fill area isn't square, whitespace will appear between your tiles. This detail is shown in the third tiled pattern in Figure 12-20.

A third option is to use a Stretch value of UniformToFill, which crops your tile image as needed. That way, your tiled image keeps the correct aspect ratio and you don't have any whitespace between your tiles. However, if your fill area isn't a square, you won't see the complete tile image.

The automatic tile resizing is a nifty feature, but there's a price to pay. Some bitmaps may not resize properly. To some extent, you can prepare for this situation by supplying a bitmap that's bigger than what you need, but this technique can result in a blurrier bitmap when it's scaled down.

An alternate solution is to define the size of your tile in absolute coordinates, based on the size of your original image. To take this step, you set ViewportUnits to Absolute (instead of RelativeToBoundBox). Here's an example that defines a 32 × 32 unit size for each tile and starts them at the top-left corner:

```
<ImageBrush ImageSource="tile.jpg" TileMode="Tile"
  ViewportUnits="Absolute" Viewport="0,0 32,32"></ImageBrush>
```

This type of tiled pattern is shown in the first rectangle in Figure 12-20. The drawback here is that the height and width of your fill area must be divisible by 32. Otherwise, you'll get a partial tile at the edge. If you're using the ImageBrush to fill a resizable element, there's no way around this problem, so you'll need to accept that the tiles won't always line up with the edges of the fill region.

So far, all the tiled patterns you've seen have used a TileMode value of Tile. You can change the TileMode to set how alternate tiles are flipped. Table 12-4 lists your choices.

Table 12-4. *Values from the TileMode Enumeration*

Name	Description
Tile	Copies the image across the available area
FlipX	Copies the image, but flips each second column vertically
FlipY	Copies the image, but flips each second row horizontally
FlipXY	Copies the image, but flips each second column vertically and each second row horizontally

This flipping behavior is often useful if you need to make tiles blend more seamlessly. For example, if you use FlipX, tiles that are side by side will always line up seamlessly. Figure 12-21 compares the tiling options.

Figure 12-21. *Flipping tiles*

The VisualBrush

The VisualBrush is an unusual brush that allows you to take the visual content of an element and use it to fill any surface. For example, using a VisualBrush, you could copy the appearance of a button in a window to a region somewhere else in that same window. However, the button copy won't be clickable or interactive in any way. It's simply a copy of how your element looks.

For example, here's a snippet of markup that defines a button and a VisualBrush that duplicates the button:

```
<Button Name="cmd" Margin="3" Padding="5">Is this a real button?</Button>
<Rectangle Margin="3" Height="100">
  <Rectangle.Fill>
    <VisualBrush Visual="{Binding ElementName=cmd}"></VisualBrush>
  </Rectangle.Fill>
</Rectangle>
```

Although you could define the element you want to use in the VisualBrush itself, it's much more common to use a binding expression to refer to an element in the current window, as in this example. Figure 12-22 shows the original button (at the top of the window) and several differently shaped regions that are painted with a VisualBrush based on that button.

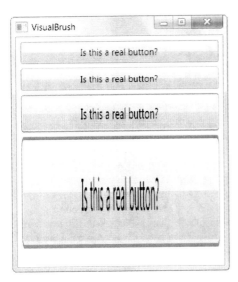

Figure 12-22. *Copying the visual for a button*

A VisualBrush watches for changes in the appearance of your element. For example, if you copy the visual for a button, and that button then receives focus, the VisualBrush repaints its fill area with the new visual—a focused button. The VisualBrush derives from TileBrush, so it also supports all the cropping, stretching, and flipping features you learned about in the previous section. If you combine these details with the transforms that you will learn about later in this chapter, you can easily use a VisualBrush to take element content and manipulate it beyond all recognition.

Because the content of a VisualBrush isn't interactive, you might wonder what purpose it has. In fact, the VisualBrush is useful in a number of situations where you need to create static content that duplicates the "real" content that's featured elsewhere. For example, you can take an element that contains a significant amount of nested content (even an entire window), shrink it down to a smaller size, and use it for a live preview. Some document programs do this to show formatting, Internet Explorer uses it to show previews of the documents in different tabs on the Quick Tabs view (hit Ctrl+Q), and Windows uses it to show previews of different applications in the taskbar.

You can use a VisualBrush in combination with animation to create certain effects (such as a document shrinking down to the bottom of your main application window). The VisualBrush is also the foundation for one of WPF's most notoriously overused effects—the live reflection, which you'll see in the following section (and the even worse live reflection of video content, which you'll see in Chapter 26).

The BitmapCacheBrush

The BitmapCacheBrush resembles the VisualBrush in many ways. While the VisualBrush provides a Visual property that refers to another element, the BitmapCacheBrush includes a Target property that serves the same purpose.

The key difference is that the BitmapCacheBrush takes the visual content (after it has been altered by any transforms, clipping, effects, and opacity settings) and asks the video card to store it in video memory. This way, the content can be redrawn quickly when needed, without requiring any extra work from WPF.

To configure bitmap caching, you set the BitmapCacheBrush.BitmapCache property (using, predictably, a BitmapCache object). Here's the simplest possible usage:

```
<Button Name="cmd" Margin="3" Padding="5">Is this a real button?</Button>
<Rectangle Margin="3" Height="100">
  <Rectangle.Fill>
```

```
  <BitmapCacheBrush Target="{Binding ElementName=cmd}"
   BitmapCache="BitmapCache"></BitmapCacheBrush>
 </Rectangle.Fill>
</Rectangle>
```

The BitmapCacheBrush has a significant drawback: the initial step of rendering the bitmap and copying it to video memory takes a short but noticeable amount of extra time. If you use the BitmapCacheBrush in a window, you'll probably notice that there's a lag before the window draws itself for the first time, while the BitmapCacheBrush is rendering and copying its bitmap. For this reason, the BitmapCacheBrush isn't much help in a traditional window.

However, bitmap caching is worth considering if you're making heavy use of animation in your user interface. That's because an animation can force your window to be repainted many times each second. If you have complex vector content, it may be faster to paint it from a cached bitmap than to redraw it from scratch. But even in this situation, you shouldn't jump to the BitmapCacheBrush just yet. You're much more likely to apply caching by setting the higher-level UIElement.CacheMode property on each element you want to cache (a technique described in Chapter 15). In this case, WPF uses the BitmapCacheBrush behind the scenes to get the same effect, but with less work.

Based on these details, it may seem that the BitmapCacheBrush isn't particularly useful on its own. However, it may make sense if you have a single piece of complex visual content that you need to paint in several places. In this case, you can save memory by caching it once with the BitmapCacheBrush, rather than separately for each element. Once again, the savings are not likely to be worth it, unless your user interface is also using animation. To learn more about bitmap caching and when to use it, refer to Chapter 15.

Using Transforms

Many drawing tasks can be made simpler with the use of a *transform*—an object that alters the way a shape or element is drawn by quietly shifting the coordinate system it uses. In WPF, transforms are represented by classes that derive from the abstract System.Windows.Media.Transform class, as listed in Table 12-5.

Table 12-5. *Transform Classes*

Name	Description	Important Properties
TranslateTransform	Displaces your coordinate system by some amount. This transform is useful if you want to draw the same shape in different places.	X, Y
RotateTransform	Rotates your coordinate system. The shapes you draw normally are turned around a center point you choose.	Angle, CenterX, CenterY
ScaleTransform	Scales your coordinate system up or down, so that your shapes are drawn smaller or larger. You can apply different degrees of scaling in the X and Y dimensions, thereby stretching or compressing your shape.	ScaleX, ScaleY, CenterX, CenterY
SkewTransform	Warps your coordinate system by slanting it a number of degrees. For example, if you draw a square, it becomes a parallelogram.	AngleX, AngleY, CenterX, CenterX
MatrixTransform	Modifies your coordinate system by using matrix multiplication with the matrix you supply. This is the most complex option; it requires some mathematical skill.	Matrix

(continued)

Table 12-5. (*continued*)

Name	Description	Important Properties
TransformGroup	Combines multiple transforms so they can all be applied at once. The order in which you apply transformations is important because it affects the final result. For example, rotating a shape (with RotateTransform) and then moving it (with TranslateTransform) sends the shape off in a different direction than if you move it and *then* rotate it.	N/A

Technically, all transforms use matrix math to alter the coordinates of your shape. However, using the prebuilt transforms such as TranslateTransform, RotateTransform, ScaleTransform, and SkewTransform is far simpler than using the MatrixTransform and trying to work out the correct matrix for the operation you want to perform. When you perform a series of transforms with the TransformGroup, WPF fuses your transforms together into a single MatrixTransform, ensuring optimal performance.

▨ **Note** All transforms derive from Freezable (through the Transform class). That means they have automatic change notification support. If you change a transform that's being used in a shape, the shape will redraw itself immediately.

Transforms are one of those quirky concepts that turn out to be extremely useful in a variety of contexts. Some examples include the following:

Angling a shape: So far, you've been stuck with horizontally aligned rectangles, ellipses, lines, and polygons. Using the RotateTransform, you can turn your coordinate system to create certain shapes more easily.

Repeating a shape: Many drawings are built using a similar shape in several places. Using a transform, you can take a shape and then move it, rotate it, resize it, and so on.

▨ **Tip** To use the same shape in multiple places, you'll need to duplicate the shape in your markup (which isn't ideal), use code (to create the shape programmatically), or use the Path shape described in Chapter 13. The Path shape accepts Geometry objects, and you can store a Geometry object as a resource so it can be reused throughout your markup.

Animation: You can create sophisticated effects with the help of a transform, such as by rotating a shape, moving it from one place to another, and warping it dynamically.

You'll use transforms throughout this book, particularly when you create animations (Chapter 16) and manipulate 3-D content (Chapter 27). For now, you can learn all you need to know by considering how to apply a basic transform to an ordinary shape.

Transforming Shapes

To transform a shape, you assign the RenderTransform property to the transform object you want to use. Depending on the transform object you're using, you'll need to fill in different properties to configure it, as detailed in Table 12-5.

For example, if you're rotating a shape, you need to use the RotateTransform, and supply the angle in degrees. Here's an example that rotates a square by 25 degrees:

```
<Rectangle Width="80" Height="10" Stroke="Blue" Fill="Yellow"
  Canvas.Left="100" Canvas.Top="100">
  <Rectangle.RenderTransform>
    <RotateTransform Angle="25" />
  </Rectangle.RenderTransform>
</Rectangle>
```

When you transform a shape in this way, you rotate it about the shape's origin (the top-left corner). Figure 12-23 illustrates this by rotating the same square 25, 50, 75, and then 100 degrees.

Figure 12-23. *Rotating a rectangle four times*

Sometimes you'll want to rotate a shape around a different point. The RotateTransform, like many other transform classes, provides a CenterX property and a CenterY property. You can use these properties to indicate the center point around which the rotation should be performed. Here's a rectangle that uses this approach to rotate itself 25 degrees around its center point:

```
<Rectangle Width="80" Height="10" Stroke="Blue" Fill="Yellow"
  Canvas.Left="100" Canvas.Top="100">
  <Rectangle.RenderTransform>
    <RotateTransform Angle="25" CenterX="45" CenterY="5" />
  </Rectangle.RenderTransform>
</Rectangle>
```

Figure 12-24 shows the result of performing the same sequence of rotations featured in Figure 12-23, but around the designated center point.

Figure 12-24. Rotating a rectangle around its middle

There's a clear limitation to using the CenterX and CenterY properties of the RotateTransform. These properties are defined using absolute coordinates, which means you need to know the exact center point of your content. If you're displaying dynamic content (for example, pictures of varying dimensions or elements that can be resized), this introduces a problem. Fortunately, WPF has a solution with the handy RenderTransformOrigin property, which is supported by all shapes. This property sets the center point by using a proportional coordinate system that stretches from 0 to 1 in both dimensions. In other words, the point (0, 0) is designated as the top-left corner and (1, 1) is the bottom-right corner. (If the shape region isn't square, the coordinate system is stretched accordingly.)

With the help of the RenderTransformOrigin property, you can rotate any shape around its center point by using markup like this:

```
<Rectangle Width="80" Height="10" Stroke="Blue" Fill="Yellow"
  Canvas.Left="100" Canvas.Top="100" RenderTransformOrigin="0.5,0.5">
  <Rectangle.RenderTransform>
    <RotateTransform Angle="25" />
  </Rectangle.RenderTransform>
</Rectangle>
```

This works because the point (0.5, 0.5) designates the center of the shape, regardless of its size. In practice, RenderTransformOrigin is generally more useful than the CenterX and CenterY properties, although you can use either one (or both) depending on your needs.

■ **Tip** You can use values greater than 1 or less than 0 when setting the RenderTransformOrigin property to designate a point that appears outside the bounding box of your shape. For example, you can use this technique with a Rotate Transform to rotate a shape in a large arc around a very distant point, such as (5, 5).

Transforming Elements

The RenderTransform and RenderTransformOrigin properties aren't limited to shapes. In fact, the Shape class inherits them from the UIElement class, which means they're supported by all WPF elements, including buttons, text boxes, the TextBlock, entire layout containers full of content, and so on. Amazingly, you can rotate, skew, and scale any piece of WPF user interface (although in most cases you shouldn't).

RenderTransform isn't the only transform-related property that's defined in the base WPF classes. The FrameworkElement also defines a LayoutTransform property. LayoutTransform alters the element in the same way, but it performs its work before the layout pass. This results in slightly more overhead, but it's critical if you're using a layout container to provide automatic layout with a group of controls. (The shape classes also include the LayoutTransform property, but you'll rarely need to use it. You'll usually place your shapes specifically using a container such as the Canvas, rather than using automatic layout.)

To understand the difference, consider Figure 12-25, which includes two StackPanel containers (represented by the shaded areas), both of which contain a rotated button and a normal button. The rotated button in the first StackPanel uses the RenderTransform approach. The StackPanel lays out the two buttons as though the first button were positioned normally, and the rotation happens just before the button is rendered. As a result, the rotated button overlaps the one underneath. In the second StackPanel, the rotated button uses the LayoutTransform approach. The StackPanel gets the bounds that are required for the rotated button and lays out the second button accordingly.

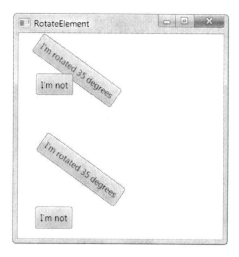

Figure 12-25. *Rotating buttons*

A few rare elements can't be transformed because their rendering work isn't native to WPF. Two examples are the WindowsFormsHost, which lets you place a Windows Forms control in a WPF window (a feat demonstrated in Chapter 30) and the WebBrowser element, which allows you to show HTML content.

To a certain degree, WPF elements aren't aware that they're being modified when you set the LayoutTransform or RenderTransform properties. Notably, transforms don't affect the ActualHeight and ActualWidth properties of the element, which continue to report their untransformed dimensions. This is part of how WPF ensures that features such as flow layout and margins continue to work with the same behavior, even when you apply one or more transforms.

Transparency

WPF supports true transparency. That means if you layer several shapes (or other elements) on top of one another and give them all varying levels of transparency, you'll see exactly what you expect. At its simplest, this feature gives you the ability to create graphical backgrounds that "show through" the elements you place on top. At its most complex, this feature allows you to create multilayered animations and other effects that would be extremely difficult in other frameworks.

Making an Element Partially Transparent

There are several ways to make an element semitransparent:

Set the Opacity property of your element: Every element, including shapes, inherits the Opacity property from the base UIElement class. *Opacity* is a fractional value from 0 to 1, where 1 is completely solid (the default) and 0 is completely transparent. For example, an opacity of 0.9 creates a 90 percent visible (10 percent transparency) effect. When you set the opacity this way, it applies to the visual content of the entire element.

Set the Opacity property of your brush: Every brush also inherits an Opacity property from the base Brush class. You can set this property from 0 to 1 to control the opacity of the content the brush paints—whether it's a solid color, gradient, or some sort of texture or image. Because you use a different brush for the Stroke and Fill properties of a shape, you can give different amounts of transparency to the border and surface area.

Use a color that has a nonopaque alpha value: Any color that has an alpha value less than 255 is semitransparent. For example, you could use a partially transparent color in a SolidColorBrush, and use that to paint the foreground content or background surface of an element. In some situations, using partially transparent colors will perform better than setting the Opacity property.

Figure 12-26 shows an example that has several semitransparent layers:

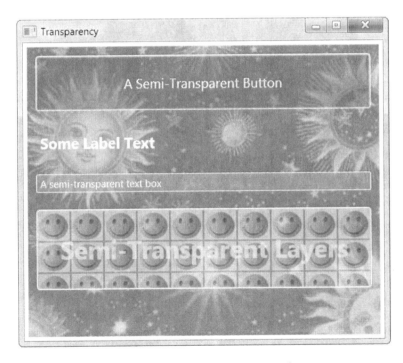

Figure 12-26. *A window with several semitransparent layers*

- The window has an opaque white background.

- The top-level StackPanel that contains all the elements has an ImageBrush that applies a picture. The Opacity of this brush is reduced to lighten it, allowing the white window background to show through.

- The first button uses a semitransparent red background color. (Behind the scenes, WPF creates a SolidColorBrush to paint this color.) The image shows through in the button background, but the text is opaque.

- The label (under the first button) is used as is. By default, all labels have a completely transparent background color.

- The text box uses opaque text and an opaque border but a semitransparent background color.

- Another StackPanel under the text box uses a TileBrush to create a pattern of happy faces. The TileBrush has a reduced Opacity, so the other background shows through. For example, you can see the sun at the bottom-right corner of the form.

- In the second StackPanel is a TextBlock with a completely transparent background (the default) and semitransparent white text. If you look carefully, you can see both backgrounds show through under some letters.

Here are the contents of the window in XAML:

```
<StackPanel Margin="5">
  <StackPanel.Background>
    <ImageBrush ImageSource="celestial.jpg" Opacity="0.7" />
  </StackPanel.Background>

  <Button Foreground="White" FontSize="16" Margin="10"
    BorderBrush="White" Background="#60AA4030"
    Padding="20">A Semi-Transparent Button</Button>
  <Label Margin="10" FontSize="18" FontWeight="Bold" Foreground="White">
    Some Label Text</Label>
  <TextBox Margin="10" Background="#AAAAAAAA" Foreground="White"
    BorderBrush="White">A semi-transparent text box</TextBox>

  <Button Margin="10" Padding="25" BorderBrush="White">
    <Button.Background>
      <ImageBrush ImageSource="happyface.jpg" Opacity="0.6"
        TileMode="Tile" Viewport="0,0,0.1,0.3"/>
    </Button.Background>

    <StackPanel>
      <TextBlock Foreground="#75FFFFFF" TextAlignment="Center"
        FontSize="30" FontWeight="Bold" TextWrapping="Wrap">
        Semi-Transparent Layers</TextBlock>
    </StackPanel>
  </Button>
</StackPanel>
```

Transparency is a popular WPF feature. In fact, it's so easy and works so well that it's a bit of a WPF user-interface cliché. For that reason, be careful not to overuse it.

Using Opacity Masks

The Opacity property makes *all* the content of an element partially transparent. The OpacityMask property gives you more flexibility. It makes specific regions of an element transparent or partially transparent, allowing you to achieve a variety of common and exotic effects. For example, you can use it to fade a shape gradually into transparency.

The OpacityMask property accepts any brush. The alpha channel of the brush determines where the transparency occurs. For example, if you use a SolidColorBrush that's set to a transparent color for your OpacityMask, your entire element will disappear. If you use a SolidColorBrush that's set to use a nontransparent color, your element will remain completely visible. The other details of the color (the red, green, and blue components) aren't important and are ignored when you set the OpacityMask property.

Using OpacityMask with a SolidColorBrush doesn't make much sense, because you can accomplish the same effect more easily with the Opacity property. However, OpacityMask becomes more useful when you use more exotic types of brushes, such as the LinearGradient or RadialGradientBrush. Using a gradient that moves from a solid to a transparent color, you can create a transparency effect that fades in over the surface of your element, like the one used by this button:

```
<Button FontSize="14" FontWeight="Bold">
  <Button.OpacityMask>
    <LinearGradientBrush StartPoint="0,0" EndPoint="1,0">
      <GradientStop Offset="0" Color="Black"></GradientStop>
      <GradientStop Offset="1" Color="Transparent"></GradientStop>
    </LinearGradientBrush>
  </Button.OpacityMask>
  <Button.Content>A Partially Transparent Button</Button.Content>
</Button>
```

Figure 12-27 shows this button over a window that displays a picture of a grand piano.

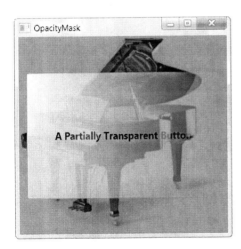

Figure 12-27. *A button that fades from solid to transparent*

You can also use the OpacityMask property in conjunction with the VisualBrush to create a reflection effect. For example, the following markup creates one of WPF's most common effects—a text box with mirrored text.

As you type, the VisualBrush paints a reflection of the text underneath. The VisualBrush paints a rectangle that uses the OpacityMask property to fade the reflection out, which distinguishes it from the real element above:

```
<TextBox Name="txt" FontSize="30">Here is some reflected text</TextBox>
<Rectangle Grid.Row="1" RenderTransformOrigin="1,0.5">
  <Rectangle.Fill>
    <VisualBrush Visual="{Binding ElementName=txt}"></VisualBrush>
  </Rectangle.Fill>
  <Rectangle.OpacityMask>
    <LinearGradientBrush StartPoint="0,0" EndPoint="0,1">
      <GradientStop Offset="0.3" Color="Transparent"></GradientStop>
      <GradientStop Offset="1" Color="#44000000"></GradientStop>
    </LinearGradientBrush>
  </Rectangle.OpacityMask>
  <Rectangle.RenderTransform>
    <ScaleTransform ScaleY="-1"></ScaleTransform>
  </Rectangle.RenderTransform>
</Rectangle>
```

This example uses a LinearGradientBrush that fades from a completely transparent color to a partially transparent color, to make the reflected content more faded. It also adds a RenderTransform that flips the rectangle so the reflection is upside down. As a result of this transformation, the gradient stops must be defined in the reverse order. Figure 12-28 shows the result.

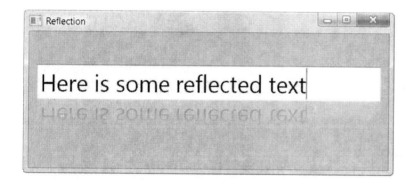

Figure 12-28. *VisualBrush + OpacityMask + RenderTransform = reflection effect*

Along with the gradient brushes and the VisualBrush, the OpacityMask property is often used with the DrawingBrush you'll learn about in the next chapter. This allows you to apply a shaped transparent region to an element.

The Last Word

In this chapter, you took a detailed look at WPF's support for basic 2-D drawing. You began by considering the simple shape classes. Next, you learned how to outline and fill shapes with brushes both simple and complex, and how to move, resize, rotate, and warp shapes with transforms. Finally, you took a quick look at transparency.

Your journey isn't finished yet. In the next chapter, you'll take a look at the Path, the most sophisticated of the shape classes, which lets you combine the shapes you've seen so far and add arcs and curves. You'll also consider how you can make more-efficient graphics with the help of WPF's Geometry and Drawing objects, and how you can export clip art from other programs.

CHAPTER 13

■ ■ ■

Geometries and Drawings

In the preceding chapter, you started your exploration of WPF's 2-D drawing features. You considered how you can use simple Shape-derived classes in combination with brushes and transforms to create a variety of graphical effects. However, the concepts you learned still fall far short of what you need to create (and manipulate) detailed 2-D scenes made up of vector art. That's because there's a wide gap between rectangles, ellipses, and polygons and the sort of clip art you see in graphically rich applications.

In this chapter, you'll extend your skills with a few more concepts. You'll learn how more-complex drawings are defined in WPF, how to model arcs and curves, and how you can convert existing vector art to the XAML format you need. You'll also consider the most efficient ways to work with complex images—in other words, how you can reduce the overhead involved in managing hundreds or thousands of shapes. This begins with replacing the simple shapes you learned about in the previous chapter with the more powerful Path class, which can wrap complex geometries.

Paths and Geometries

In the previous chapter, you took a look at a number of classes that derive from Shape, including Rectangle, Ellipse, Polygon, and Polyline. However, there's one Shape-derived class that you haven't considered yet, and it's the most powerful by far. The Path class has the ability to encompass any simple shape, groups of shapes, and more-complex ingredients such as curves.

The Path class includes a single property, named Data, that accepts a Geometry object that defines the shape (or shapes) the path includes. You can't create a Geometry object directly, because it's an abstract class. Instead, you need to use one of the seven derived classes listed in Table 13-1.

Table 13-1. *Geometry Classes*

Name	Description
LineGeometry	Represents a straight line. The geometry equivalent of the Line shape.
RectangleGeometry	Represents a rectangle (optionally with rounded corners). The geometry equivalent of the Rectangle shape.
EllipseGeometry	Represents an ellipse. The geometry equivalent of the Ellipse shape.
GeometryGroup	Adds any number of Geometry objects to a single path, using the EvenOdd or Nonzero fill rule to determine what regions to fill.
CombinedGeometry	Merges two geometries into one shape. The CombineMode property allows you to choose how the two are combined.

(*continued*)

Table 13-1. (*continued*)

Name	Description
PathGeometry	Represents a more complex figure that's composed of arcs, curves, and lines, and can be open or closed.
StreamGeometry	A read-only lightweight equivalent to PathGeometry. StreamGeometry saves memory because it doesn't hold the individual segments of your path in memory all at once. However, it can't be modified after it has been created.

At this point, you might be wondering what the difference is between a path and a geometry. The geometry *defines* a shape. A path allows you to *draw* the shape. Thus, the Geometry object defines details such as the coordinates and size of your shape, and the Path object supplies the Stroke and Fill brushes you'll use to paint it. The Path class also includes the features it inherits from the UIElement infrastructure, such as mouse and keyboard handling.

However, the geometry classes aren't quite as simple as they seem. For one thing, they all inherit from Freezable (through the base Geometry class), which gives them support for change notification. As a result, if you use a geometry to create a path, and then modify the geometry after the fact, your path will be redrawn automatically. The geometry classes can also be used to define drawings that you can apply through a brush, which gives you an easy way to paint complex content that doesn't need the user-interactivity features of the Path class. You'll consider this ability in the "Drawings" section later in this chapter.

In the following sections, you'll explore all the classes that derive from Geometry.

Line, Rectangle, and Ellipse Geometries

The LineGeometry, RectangleGeometry, and EllipseGeometry classes map directly to the Line, Rectangle, and Ellipse shapes that you learned about in Chapter 12. For example, you can convert this markup that uses the Rectangle element:

```
<Rectangle Fill="Yellow" Stroke="Blue"
  Width="100" Height="50" ></Rectangle>
```

to this markup that uses the Path element:

```
<Path Fill="Yellow" Stroke="Blue">
  <Path.Data>
    <RectangleGeometry Rect="0,0 100,50"></RectangleGeometry>
  </Path.Data>
</Path>
```

The only real difference is that the Rectangle shape takes Height and Width values, while the RectangleGeometry takes four numbers that describe the size *and* location of the rectangle. The first two numbers describe the X and Y coordinates point where the top-left corner will be placed, and the last two numbers set the width and height of the rectangle. You can start the rectangle out at (0, 0) to get the same effect as an ordinary Rectangle element, or you can offset the rectangle by using different values. The RectangleGeometry class also includes the RadiusX and RadiusY properties, which let you round the corners (as described in the preceding chapter).

Similarly, you can convert the following Line:

```
<Line Stroke="Blue" X1="0" Y1="0" X2="10" Y2="100"></Line>
```

to this LineGeometry:

```
<Path Fill="Yellow" Stroke="Blue">
  <Path.Data>
    <LineGeometry StartPoint="0,0" EndPoint="10,100"></LineGeometry>
  </Path.Data>
</Path>
```

and you can convert an Ellipse like this:

```
<Ellipse Fill="Yellow" Stroke="Blue"
  Width="100" Height="50" HorizontalAlignment="Left"></Ellipse>
```

to this EllipseGeometry:

```
<Path Fill="Yellow" Stroke="Blue">
  <Path.Data>
    <EllipseGeometry RadiusX="50" RadiusY="25" Center="50,25"></EllipseGeometry>
  </Path.Data>
</Path>
```

Notice that the two radius values are simply half of the width and height values. You can also use the Center property to offset the location of the ellipse. In this example, the center is placed in the exact middle of the ellipse bounding box, so that it's drawn in exactly the same way as the Ellipse shape.

Overall, these simple geometries work in the same way as the corresponding shapes. You get the added ability to offset rectangles and ellipses, but that's not necessary if you're placing your shapes on a Canvas, which already gives you the ability to position your shapes at a specific point In fact, if this were all you could do with geometries, you probably wouldn't bother to use the Path element. The difference appears when you decide to combine more than one geometry in the same path, as described in the next section.

Combining Shapes with GeometryGroup

The simplest way to combine geometries is to use the GeometryGroup, and nest the other Geometry-derived objects inside. Here's an example that places an ellipse next to a square:

```
<Path Fill="Yellow" Stroke="Blue" Margin="5" Canvas.Top="10" Canvas.Left="10" >
  <Path.Data>
    <GeometryGroup>
      <RectangleGeometry Rect="0,0 100,100"></RectangleGeometry>
      <EllipseGeometry Center="150,50" RadiusX="35" RadiusY="25"></EllipseGeometry>
    </GeometryGroup>
  </Path.Data>
</Path>
```

The effect of this markup is the same as if you had supplied two Path elements, one with the RectangleGeometry and one with the EllipseGeometry (and that's the same as if you had used a Rectangle and Ellipse shape instead). However, there's one advantage to this approach. You've replaced two elements with one, which means you've reduced the overhead of your user interface. In general, a window that uses a smaller number of elements with more-complex geometries will perform faster than a window that has a large number of elements with simpler geometries. This effect won't be apparent in a window that has just a few dozen shapes, but it may become significant in one that requires hundreds or thousands.

Of course, there's also a drawback to combining geometries in a single Path element: you won't be able to perform event handling of the different shapes separately. Instead, the Path element will fire all mouse events. However, you can still manipulate the nested RectangleGeometry and EllipseGeometry objects independently to change the overall path. For example, each geometry provides a Transform property, which you can set to stretch, skew, or rotate that part of the path.

Another advantage of geometries is that you can reuse the same geometry in several separate Path elements. No code is necessary—you simply need to define the geometry in a Resources collection and refer to it in your path with the StaticExtension or DynamicExtension markup extensions. Here's an example that rewrites the markup shown previously to show instances of the CombinedGeometry, at two locations on a Canvas and with two fill colors:

```
<Window.Resources>
  <GeometryGroup x:Key="Geometry">
    <RectangleGeometry Rect="0 ,0 100 ,100"></RectangleGeometry>
    <EllipseGeometry Center="150, 50" RadiusX="35" RadiusY="25"></EllipseGeometry>
  </GeometryGroup>
</Window.Resources>

<Canvas>
  <Path Fill="Yellow" Stroke="Blue" Margin="5" Canvas.Top="10" Canvas.Left="10"
  Data="{StaticResource Geometry}">
  </Path>
  <Path Fill="Green" Stroke="Blue" Margin="5" Canvas.Top="150" Canvas.Left="10"
  Data="{StaticResource Geometry}">
  </Path>
</Canvas>
```

The GeometryGroup becomes more interesting when your shapes intersect. Rather than simply treating your drawing as a combination of solid shapes, the GeometryGroup uses its FillRule property (which can be EvenOdd or Nonzero, as described in Chapter 12) to decide which shapes to fill. Consider what happens if you alter the markup shown earlier like this, placing the ellipse over the square:

```
<Path Fill="Yellow" Stroke="Blue" Margin="5" Canvas.Top="10" Canvas.Left="10" >
  <Path.Data>
    <GeometryGroup>
      <RectangleGeometry Rect="0,0 100,100"></RectangleGeometry>
      <EllipseGeometry Center="50,50" RadiusX="35" RadiusY="25"></EllipseGeometry>
    </GeometryGroup>
  </Path.Data>
</Path>
```

This markup creates a square with an ellipse-shaped hole in it. If you change FillRule to Nonzero, you'll get a solid ellipse over a solid rectangle, both with the same yellow fill.

You could create the square-with-a-hole effect by simply superimposing a white-filled ellipse over your square. However, the GeometryGroup class becomes more useful if you have content underneath, which is typical in a complex drawing. Because the ellipse is treated as a hole in your shape (not another shape with a different fill), any content underneath shows through. For example, if you add this line of text:

```
<TextBlock Canvas.Top="50" Canvas.Left="20" FontSize="25" FontWeight="Bold">
  Hello There</TextBlock>
```

you'll get the result shown in Figure 13-1.

Figure 13-1. *A path that uses two shapes*

■ Note   Remember that objects are drawn in the order they are processed. In other words, if you want the text to appear underneath your shape, make sure you add the TextBlock to your markup before the Path element. Or if you're using a Canvas or Grid to hold your content, you can set the attached Panel.ZIndex property on your elements to place them explicitly, as described in Chapter 3.

Fusing Geometries with CombinedGeometry

The GeometryGroup class is an invaluable tool for building complex shapes out of the basic primitives (rectangle, ellipse, and line). However, it has obvious limitations. It works great for creating a shape by drawing one shape and "subtracting" other shapes from inside. However, it's difficult to get the result you want if the shape borders intersect one another, and it's no help if you want to remove part of a shape.

The CombinedGeometry class is tailor-made for combining shapes that overlap, and where neither shape contains the other completely. Unlike GeometryGroup, CombinedGeometry takes just two geometries, which you supply by using the Geometry1 and Geometry2 properties. CombinedGeometry doesn't include the FillRule property. Instead, it has the much more powerful GeometryCombineMode property, which takes one of four values, as described in Table 13-2.

Table 13-2. *Values from the GeometryCombineMode Enumeration*

Name	Description
Union	Creates a shape that includes all the areas of the two geometries.
Intersect	Creates a shape that contains the area that's shared between the two geometries.
Xor	Creates a shape that contains the area that isn't shared between the two geometries. In other words, it's as if the shapes were combined (using a Union) and then the shared part (the Intersect) were removed.
Exclude	Creates a shape that includes all the area from the first geometry, not including the area that's in the second geometry.

For example, here's how you can merge two shapes to create one shape with the total area by using GeometryCombineMode.Union:

```
<Path Fill="Yellow" Stroke="Blue" Margin="5">
  <Path.Data>
    <CombinedGeometry GeometryCombineMode="Union">
      <CombinedGeometry.Geometry1>
        <RectangleGeometry Rect="0,0 100,100"></RectangleGeometry>
      </CombinedGeometry.Geometry1>
      <CombinedGeometry.Geometry2>
        <EllipseGeometry Center="85,50" RadiusX="65" RadiusY="35"></EllipseGeometry>
      </CombinedGeometry.Geometry2>
    </CombinedGeometry>
  </Path.Data>
</Path>
```

Figure 13-2 shows this shape, as well as the result of combining the same shapes in every other way possible.

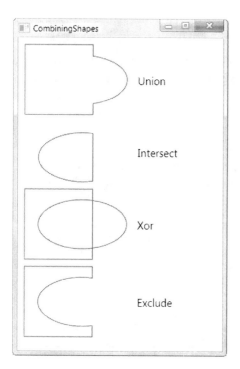

Figure 13-2. *Combining shapes*

The fact that a CombinedGeometry can combine only two shapes may seem like a significant limitation, but it's not. You can build a shape that involves dozens of distinct geometries or more—you simply need to use nested CombinedGeometry objects. For example, one CombinedGeometry object might combine two other CombinedGeometry objects, which themselves can combine more geometries. Using this technique, you can build up detailed shapes.

To understand how this works, consider the simple "no" sign (a circle with a slash through it) shown in Figure 13-3. Although there isn't any WPF primitive that resembles this shape, you can assemble it quite quickly using CombinedGeometry objects.

Figure 13-3. *Several combined shapes*

It makes sense to start by drawing the ellipse that represents the outer edge of the shape. Then, using a CombinedGeometry with the GeometryCombineMode.Exclude, you can remove a smaller ellipse from the inside. Here's the markup that you need:

```
<Path Fill="Yellow" Stroke="Blue">
  <Path.Data>
    <CombinedGeometry GeometryCombineMode="Exclude">
      <CombinedGeometry.Geometry1>
        <EllipseGeometry Center="50,50" RadiusX="50" RadiusY="50"></EllipseGeometry>
      </CombinedGeometry.Geometry1>
      <CombinedGeometry.Geometry2>
        <EllipseGeometry Center="50,50" RadiusX="40" RadiusY="40"></EllipseGeometry>
      </CombinedGeometry.Geometry2>
    </CombinedGeometry>
  </Path.Data>
</Path>
```

This gets you part of the way, but you still need the slash through the middle. The easiest way to add this element is to use a rectangle that's tilted to the side. You can accomplish this using the RectangleGeometry with a RotateTransform of 45 degrees:

```
<RectangleGeometry Rect="44,5 10,90">
  <RectangleGeometry.Transform>
    <RotateTransform Angle="45" CenterX="50" CenterY="50"></RotateTransform>
  </RectangleGeometry.Transform>
</RectangleGeometry>
```

■ **Note** When applying a transform to a geometry, you use the Transform property (not RenderTransform or LayoutTransform). That's because the geometry defines the shape, and any transforms are always applied before the path is used in your layout.

The final step is to combine this geometry with the combined geometry that created the hollow circle. In this case, you need to use GeometryCombineMode.Union to add the rectangle to your shape.

Here's the complete markup for the symbol:

```
<Path Fill="Yellow" Stroke="Blue">
  <Path.Data>
    <CombinedGeometry GeometryCombineMode="Union">
      <CombinedGeometry.Geometry1>
        <CombinedGeometry GeometryCombineMode="Exclude">
          <CombinedGeometry.Geometry1>
            <EllipseGeometry Center="50,50"
              RadiusX="50" RadiusY="50"></EllipseGeometry>
          </CombinedGeometry.Geometry1>
          <CombinedGeometry.Geometry2>
            <EllipseGeometry Center="50,50"
              RadiusX="40" RadiusY="40"></EllipseGeometry>
          </CombinedGeometry.Geometry2>
        </CombinedGeometry>
      </CombinedGeometry.Geometry1>

      <CombinedGeometry.Geometry2>
        <RectangleGeometry Rect="44,5 10,90">
          <RectangleGeometry.Transform>
            <RotateTransform Angle="45" CenterX="50" CenterY="50"></RotateTransform>
          </RectangleGeometry.Transform>
        </RectangleGeometry>
      </CombinedGeometry.Geometry2>
    </CombinedGeometry>
  </Path.Data>
</Path>
```

■ **Note** A GeometryGroup object can't influence the fill or stroke brushes used to color your shape. These details are set by the path. Therefore, you need to create separate Path objects if you want to color parts of your path differently.

Drawing Curves and Lines with PathGeometry

PathGeometry is the superpower of geometries. It can draw anything that the other geometries can, and much more. The only drawback is a lengthier (and somewhat more complex) syntax.

Every PathGeometry object is built out of one or more PathFigure objects (which are stored in the PathGeometry. Figures collection). Each PathFigure is a continuous set of connected lines and curves that can be closed or open. The figure is closed if the end of the last line in the figure connects to the beginning of the first line.

The PathFigure class has four key properties, as described in Table 13-3.

Table 13-3. *PathFigure Properties*

Name	Description
StartPoint	This is a point that indicates where the line for the figure begins.
Segments	This is a collection of PathSegment objects that are used to draw the figure.
IsClosed	If True, WPF adds a straight line to connect the starting and ending points (if they aren't the same).
IsFilled	If True, the area inside the figure is filled in using the Path.Fill brush.

So far, this all sounds fairly straightforward. The PathFigure is a shape that's drawn using an unbroken line that consists of a number of segments. However, the trick is that there are several type of segments, all of which derive from the PathSegment class. Some are simple, like the LineSegment that draws a straight line. Others, like the BezierSegment, draw curves and are correspondingly more complex.

You can mix and match different segments freely to build your figure. Table 13-4 lists the segment classes you can use.

Table 13-4. *PathSegment Classes*

Name	Description
LineSegment	Creates a straight line between two points.
ArcSegment	Creates an elliptical arc between two points.
BezierSegment	Creates a Bézier curve between two points.
QuadraticBezierSegment	Creates a simpler form of Bézier curve that has one control point instead of two, and is faster to calculate.
PolyLineSegment	Creates a series of straight lines. You can get the same effect by using multiple LineSegment objects, but a single PolyLineSegment is more concise.
PolyBezierSegment	Creates a series of Bézier curves.
PolyQuadraticBezierSegment	Creates a series of simpler quadratic Bézier curves.

Straight Lines

It's easy enough to create simple lines by using the LineSegment and PathGeometry classes. You simply set the StartPoint and add one LineSegment for each section of the line. The LineSegment.Point property identifies the end point of each segment.

For example, the following markup begins at (10, 100), draws a straight line to (100, 100), and then draws a line from that point to (100, 50). Because the PathFigure.IsClosed property is set to True, a final line segment is added, connecting (100, 50) to (0, 0). The final result is a right-angled triangle.

```
<Path Stroke="Blue">
  <Path.Data>
    <PathGeometry>
      <PathFigure IsClosed="True" StartPoint="10,100">
        <LineSegment Point="100,100" />
        <LineSegment Point="100,50" />
      </PathFigure>
    </PathGeometry>
  </Path.Data>
</Path>
```

■ **Note** Remember that each PathGeometry can contain an unlimited number of PathFigure objects. That means you can create several separate open or closed figures that are all considered part of the same path.

Arcs

Arcs are a little more interesting than straight lines. You identify the end point of the line by using the ArcSegment.Point property, just as you would with a LineSegment. However, the PathFigure draws a curved line from the starting point (or the end point of the previous segment) to the end point of your arc. This curved connecting line is actually a portion of the edge of an ellipse.

Obviously, the end point doesn't provide enough information to draw the arc, because many curves (some gentle, some more extreme) could connect two points. You also need to indicate the size of the imaginary ellipse that's being used to draw the arc. You do this by using the ArcSegment.Size property, which supplies the X radius and the Y radius of the ellipse. The larger the ellipse size of the imaginary ellipse, the more gradually its edge curves.

■ **Note** For any two points, there is a practical maximum and minimum size for the ellipse. The maximum occurs when you create an ellipse so large that the line segment you're drawing appears straight. Increasing the size beyond this point has no effect. The minimum occurs when the ellipse is small enough that a full semicircle connects the two points. Shrinking the size beyond this point also has no effect.

Here's an example that creates the gentle arc shown in Figure 13-4:

```
<Path Stroke="Blue" StrokeThickness="3">
  <Path.Data>
    <PathGeometry>
      <PathFigure IsClosed="False" StartPoint="10,100" >
        <ArcSegment Point="250,150" Size="200,300" />
      </PathFigure>
    </PathGeometry>
  </Path.Data>
</Path>
```

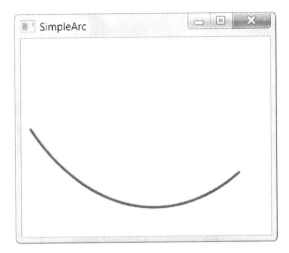

Figure 13-4. *A simple arc*

So far, arcs sound fairly straightforward. However, it turns out that even with the start and end points and the size of the ellipse, you still don't have all the information you need to draw your arc unambiguously. In the previous example, you're relying on two default values that may not be set to your liking.

To understand the problem, you need to consider the other ways that an arc can connect the same two points. If you picture two points on an ellipse, it's clear that you can connect them in two ways: by going around the short side, or by going around the long side. Figure 13-5 illustrates these choices.

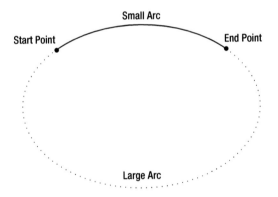

Figure 13-5. *Two ways to trace a curve along an ellipse*

You set the direction by using the ArcSegment.IsLargeArc property, which can be True or False. The default value is False, which means you get the shorter of the two arcs.

Even after you've set the direction, there is still one point of ambiguity: where the ellipse is placed. For example, imagine you draw an arc that connects a point on the left with a point on the right, using the shortest possible arc. The curve that connects these two points could be stretched down and then up (as it does in Figure 13-4), or it could be flipped so that it curves up and then down. The arc you get depends on the order in which you define the two points in the arc and the ArcSegment.SweepDirection property, which can be Counterclockwise (the default) or Clockwise. Figure 13-6 shows the difference.

Figure 13-6. *Two ways to flip a curve*

Bézier Curves

Bézier curves connect two line segments by using a complex mathematical formula that incorporates two *control points* that determine how the curve is shaped. Bézier curves are an ingredient in virtually every vector drawing application ever created because they're remarkably flexible. Using nothing more than a start point, an end point, and two control points, you can create a surprisingly wide variety of smooth curves (including loops). Figure 13-7 shows a classic Bézier curve. Two small circles indicate the control points, and a dashed line connects each control point to the end of the line it affects the most.

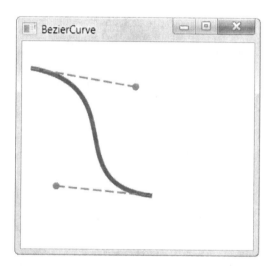

Figure 13-7. *A Bézier curve*

Even without understanding the math underpinnings, it's fairly easy to get the "feel" of how Bézier curves work. Essentially, the two control points do all the magic. They influence the curve in two ways:

- At the starting point, a Bézier curve runs parallel with the line that connects it to the first control point. At the ending point, the curve runs parallel with the line that connects it to the end point. (In between, it curves.)

- The degree of curvature is determined by the distance to the two control points. If one control point is farther away, it exerts a stronger "pull."

To define a Bézier curve in markup, you supply three points. The first two points (BezierSegment.Point1 and BezierSegment.Point2) are the control points. The third point (BezierSegment.Point3) is the end point of the curve. As always, the starting point is that starting point of the path or wherever the previous segment leaves off.

The example shown in Figure 13-7 includes three separate components, each of which uses a different stroke and thus requires a separate Path element. The first path creates the curve, the second adds the dashed lines, and the third applies the circles that indicate the control points. Here's the complete markup:

```
<Canvas>
  <Path Stroke="Blue" StrokeThickness="5" Canvas.Top="20">
    <Path.Data>
      <PathGeometry>
        <PathFigure StartPoint="10,10">
          <BezierSegment Point1="130,30" Point2="40,140"
            Point3="150,150"></BezierSegment>
        </PathFigure>
      </PathGeometry>
    </Path.Data>
  </Path>
  <Path Stroke="Green" StrokeThickness="2" StrokeDashArray="5 2" Canvas.Top="20">
    <Path.Data>
      <GeometryGroup>
        <LineGeometry StartPoint="10,10" EndPoint="130,30"></LineGeometry>
        <LineGeometry StartPoint="40,140" EndPoint="150,150"></LineGeometry>
      </GeometryGroup>
    </Path.Data>
  </Path>
  <Path Fill="Red" Stroke="Red" StrokeThickness="8"  Canvas.Top="20">
    <Path.Data>
      <GeometryGroup>
        <EllipseGeometry Center="130,30"></EllipseGeometry>
        <EllipseGeometry Center="40,140"></EllipseGeometry>
      </GeometryGroup>
    </Path.Data>
  </Path>
</Canvas>
```

Trying to code Bézier paths is a recipe for many thankless hours of trial-and-error computer coding. You're much more likely to draw your curves (and many other graphical elements) in a dedicated drawing program that has an export-to-XAML feature or in Expression Design.

▨ **Tip** To learn more about the algorithm that underlies the Bézier curve, you can read an informative Wikipedia article on the subject at http://en.wikipedia.org/wiki/Bezier_curve.

Using the Geometry Mini-Language

The geometries you've seen so far have been relatively concise, with only a few points. More-complex geometries are conceptually the same but can easily require hundreds of segments. Defining each line, arc, and curve in a complex path is extremely verbose and unnecessary. After all, it's likely that complex paths will be generated by a design tool, rather than written by hand, so the clarity of the markup isn't all that important. With this in mind, the creators of WPF added a more concise alternate syntax for defining geometries that allows you to represent detailed figures with much smaller amounts of markup. This syntax is often described as the *geometry mini-language* (and sometimes the *path mini-language* because of its application with the Path element).

To understand the mini-language, you need to realize that it is essentially a long string holding a series of commands. These commands are read by a type converter, which then creates the corresponding geometry. Each command is a single letter and is optionally followed by a few bits of numeric information (such as X and Y coordinates) separated by spaces. Each command is also separated from the previous command with a space.

For example, a bit earlier, you created a basic triangle by using a closed path with two line segments. Here's the markup that did the trick:

```
<Path Stroke="Blue">
  <Path.Data>
    <PathGeometry>
      <PathFigure IsClosed="True" StartPoint="10,100">
        <LineSegment Point="100,100" />
        <LineSegment Point="100,50" />
      </PathFigure>
    </PathGeometry>
  </Path.Data>
</Path>
```

Here's how you could duplicate this figure by using the mini-language:

```
<Path Stroke="Blue" Data="M 10,100 L 100,100 L 100,50 Z"/>
```

This path uses a sequence of four commands. The first command (M) creates the PathFigure and sets the starting point to (10, 100). The following two commands (L) create line segments. The final command (Z) ends the PathFigure and sets the IsClosed property to True. The commas in this string are optional, as are the spaces between the command and its parameters, but you must leave at least one space between adjacent parameters and commands. That means you can reduce the syntax even further to this less-readable form:

```
<Path Stroke="Blue" Data="M10 100 L100 100 L100 50 Z"/>
```

When creating a geometry with the mini-language, you are actually creating a StreamGeometry object, not a PathGeometry. As a result, you won't be able to modify the geometry later in your code. If this isn't acceptable, you can create a PathGeometry explicitly but use the same syntax to define its collection of PathFigure objects. Here's how:

```
<Path Stroke="Blue">
  <Path.Data>
    <PathGeometry Figures="M 10,100 L 100,100 L 100,50 Z" />
  </Path.Data>
</Path>
```

The geometry mini-language is easy to grasp. It uses a fairly small set of commands, which are detailed in Table 13-5. Parameters are shown in italics.

Table 13-5. *Commands for the Geometry Mini-Language*

Command	Description
F *value*	Sets the Geometry.FillRule property. Use 0 for EvenOdd or 1 for Nonzero. This command must appear at the beginning of the string (if you decide to use it).
M *x,y*	Creates a new PathFigure for the geometry and sets its start point. This command must be used before any other commands except F. However, you can also use it during your drawing sequence to move the origin of your coordinate system. (The M stands for *move*.)

(*continued*)

Table 13-5. (*continued*)

Command	Description
L *x,y*	Creates a LineSegment to the specified point.
H *x*	Creates a horizontal LineSegment by using the specified X value and keeping the Y value constant.
V *y*	Creates a vertical LineSegment by using the specified Y value and keeping the X value constant.
A *radiusX, radiusY degrees isLargeArc, isClockwise x,y*	Creates an ArcSegment to the indicated point. You specify the radii of the ellipse that describes the arc, the number of degrees the arc is rotated, and Boolean flags that set the IsLargeArc and SweepDirection properties described earlier.
C *x1,y1 x2,y2 x,y*	Creates a BezierSegment to the indicated point, using control points at (x1, y1) and (x2, y2).
Q *x1, y1 x,y*	Creates a QuadraticBezierSegment to the indicated point, with one control point at (x1, y1).
S *x2,y2 x,y*	Creates a smooth BezierSegment by using the second control point from the previous BezierSegment as the first control point in the new BezierSegment.
Z	Ends the current PathFigure and sets IsClosed to True. You don't need to use this command if you don't want to set IsClosed to True. Instead, simply use M if you want to start a new PathFigure or end the string.

■ **Tip** There's one more trick in the geometry mini-language. You can use a command in lowercase if you want its parameters to be evaluated relative to the previous point rather than using absolute coordinates.

Clipping with Geometry

As you've seen, geometries are the most powerful way to create a shape. However, geometries aren't limited to the Path element. They're also used anywhere you need to supply the abstract definition of a shape (rather than draw a real, concrete shape in a window).

Another place geometries are used is to set the Clip property, which is provided by all elements. The Clip property allows you to constrain the outer bounds of an element to fit a specific geometry. You can use the Clip property to create exotic effects. Although it's commonly used to trim image content in an Image element, you can use the Clip property with any element. The only limitation is that you'll need a closed geometry if you actually want to see anything—individual curves and line segments aren't of much use.

The following example defines a single geometry that's used to clip two elements: an Image element that contains a bitmap, and a standard Button element. The results are shown in Figure 13-8.

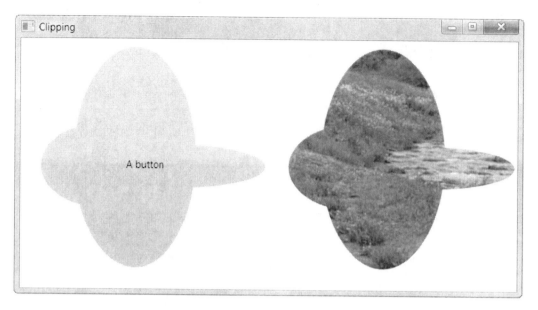

Figure 13-8. *Clipping two elements*

Here's the markup for this example:

```
<Window.Resources>
  <GeometryGroup x:Key="clipGeometry" FillRule="Nonzero">
    <EllipseGeometry RadiusX="75" RadiusY="50" Center="100,150"></EllipseGeometry>
    <EllipseGeometry RadiusX="100" RadiusY="25" Center="200,150"></EllipseGeometry>
    <EllipseGeometry RadiusX="75" RadiusY="130" Center="140,140"></EllipseGeometry>
  </GeometryGroup>
</Window.Resources>
<Grid>
  <Grid.ColumnDefinitions>
    <ColumnDefinition></ColumnDefinition>
    <ColumnDefinition></ColumnDefinition>
  </Grid.ColumnDefinitions>

  <Button Clip="{StaticResource clipGeometry}">A button</Button>
  <Image Grid.Column="1" Clip="{StaticResource clipGeometry}"
   Stretch="None" Source="creek.jpg"></Image>
</Grid>
```

There's one limitation with clipping. The clipping you set doesn't take the size of the element into account. In other words, if the button in Figure 13-8 becomes larger or smaller when the window is resized, the clipped region will remain the same and show a different portion of the button. One possible solution is to wrap the element in a Viewbox to provide automatic rescaling. However, this causes *everything* to resize proportionately, including the details you do want to resize (the clip region and button surface) and those you might not (the button text and the line that draws the button border).

In the next section, you'll go a bit further with Geometry objects and use them to define a lightweight drawing that can be used in a variety of ways.

Drawings

As you've learned, the abstract Geometry class represents a shape or a path. The abstract Drawing class plays a complementary role. It represents a 2-D drawing; in other words, it contains all the information you need to display a piece of vector or bitmap art.

Although there are several types of drawing classes, the GeometryDrawing is the one that works with the geometries you've learned about so far. It adds the stroke and fill details that determine how the geometry should be painted. You can think of a GeometryDrawing as a single shape in a piece of vector clip art. For example, it's possible to convert a standard Windows Metafile Format (.wmf) into a collection of GeometryDrawing objects that are ready to insert into your user interface. (In fact, you'll learn how to do exactly this in the "Exporting Clip Art" section a little later in this chapter.)

It helps to consider a simple example. Earlier, you saw how to define a simple PathGeometry that represents a triangle:

```
<PathGeometry>
  <PathFigure IsClosed="True" StartPoint="10,100">
    <LineSegment Point="100,100" />
    <LineSegment Point="100,50" />
  </PathFigure>
</PathGeometry>
```

You can use this PathGeometry to build a GeometryDrawing like so:

```
<GeometryDrawing Brush="Yellow">
  <GeometryDrawing.Pen>
    <Pen Brush="Blue" Thickness="3"></Pen>
  </GeometryDrawing.Pen>
<GeometryDrawing.Geometry>
  <PathGeometry>
    <PathFigure IsClosed="True" StartPoint="10,100">
      <LineSegment Point="100,100" />
      <LineSegment Point="100,50" />
    </PathFigure>
  </PathGeometry>
  </GeometryDrawing.Geometry>
</GeometryDrawing>
```

Here, the PathGeometry defines the shape (a triangle). The GeometryDrawing defines the shape's appearance (a yellow triangle with a blue outline). Neither the PathGeometry nor the GeometryDrawing is an element, so you can't use either one directly to add your custom-drawn content to a window. Instead, you'll need to use another class that supports drawings, as described in the next section.

▨ **Note**   The GeometryDrawing class introduces a new detail: the System.Windows.Media.Pen class. The Pen class provides the Brush and Thickness properties used in the previous example, along with all the stroke-related properties you learned about with shapes (StartLine, EndLineCap, DashStyle, DashCap, LineJoin, and MiterLimit). In fact, most Shape-derived classes use Pen objects internally in their drawing code but expose pen-related properties directly for ease of use.

GeometryDrawing isn't the only drawing class in WPF (although it is the most relevant one when considering 2-D vector graphics). In fact, the Drawing class is meant to represent *all* types of 2-D graphics, and there's a small group of classes that derive from it. Table 13-6 lists them all.

Table 13-6. *The Drawing Classes*

Class	Description	Properties
GeometryDrawing	Wraps a geometry with the brush that fills it and the pen that outlines it.	Geometry, Brush, Pen
ImageDrawing	Wraps an image (typically, a file-based bitmap image) with a rectangle that defines its bounds.	ImageSource, Rect
VideoDrawing	Combines a MediaPlayer that's used to play a video file with a rectangle that defines its bounds. Chapter 26 has the details about WPF's multimedia support.	Player, Rect
GlyphRunDrawing	Wraps a low-level text object known as a GlyphRun with a brush that paints it.	GlyphRun, ForegroundBrush
DrawingGroup	Combines a collection of Drawing objects of any type. The DrawingGroup allows you to create composite drawings, and apply effects to the entire collection at once using one of its properties.	BitmapEffect, BitmapEffectInput, Children, ClipGeometry, GuidelineSet, Opacity, OpacityMask, Transform

Displaying a Drawing

Because Drawing-derived classes are not elements, they can't be placed in your user interface. Instead, to display a drawing, you need to use one of three classes listed in Table 13-7.

Table 13-7. *Classes for Displaying a Drawing*

Class	Derives From	Description
DrawingImage	ImageSource	Allows you to host a drawing inside an Image element.
DrawingBrush	Brush	Allows you to wrap a drawing with a brush, which you can then use to paint any surface.
DrawingVisual	Visual	Allows you to place a drawing in a lower-level visual object. Visuals don't have the overhead of true elements, but can still be displayed if you implement the required infrastructure. You'll learn more about using visuals in Chapter 14.

There's a common theme in all of these classes. Quite simply, they give you a way to display your 2-D content with less overhead.

For example, imagine you want to use a piece of vector art to create the icon for a button. The most convenient (and resource-intensive) way to do this is to place a Canvas inside the button, and place a series of Shape-derived elements inside the Canvas:

```
<Button ... >
  <Canvas ... >
    <Polyline ... >
    <Polyline ... >
```

```
    <Rectangle ... >
    <Ellipse ... >
    <Polygon ... >
    ...
  </Canvas>
</Button>
```

As you already know, if you take this approach, each element is completely independent, with its own memory footprint, event handling, and so on. A better approach is to reduce the number of elements by using the Path element. Because each path has a single stroke and fill, you'll still need a large number of Path objects, but you'll probably be able to reduce the number of elements somewhat:

```
<Button ... >
  <Canvas ... >
    <Path ... >
    <Path ... >
    ...
  </Canvas>
</Button>
```

Once you start using the Path element, you've made the switch from separate shapes to distinct geometries. You can carry the abstraction one level further by extracting the geometry, stroke, and fill information from the path, and turning it into a drawing. You can then fuse your drawings together in a DrawingGroup and place that DrawingGroup in a DrawingImage, which can in turn be placed in an Image element. Here's the new markup this process creates:

```
<Button ... >
  <Image ... >
    <Image.Source>
      <DrawingImage>
        <DrawingImage.Drawing>
          <DrawingGroup>
            <GeometryDrawing ... >
            <GeometryDrawing ... >
            <GeometryDrawing ... >
            ...
          </DrawingGroup>
        </DrawingImage.Drawing>
      </DrawingImage>
    <Image.Source>
  </Image>
</Button>
```

This is a significant change. It hasn't simplified your markup, as you've simply substituted one GeometryDrawing object for each Path object. However, it *has* reduced the number of elements and hence the overhead that's required. The previous example created a Canvas inside the button and added a separate element for each path. This example requires just one nested element: the Image inside the button. The trade-off is that you no longer have the ability to handle events for each distinct path (for example, you can't detect mouse clicks on separate regions of the drawing). But in a static image that's used for a button, it's unlikely that you want this ability anyway.

■ **Note** It's easy to confuse DrawingImage and ImageDrawing, two WPF classes with awkwardly similar names. DrawingImage is used to place a drawing inside an Image element. Typically, you'll use it to put vector content in an Image. ImageDrawing is completely different—it's a Drawing-derived class that accepts bitmap content. This allows you to combine GeometryDrawing and ImageDrawing objects in one DrawingGroup, thereby creating a drawing with vector and bitmap content that you can use however you want.

Although the DrawingImage gives you the majority of the savings, you can still get a bit more efficient and remove one more element with the help of the DrawingBrush.

The basic idea is to wrap your DrawingImage in a DrawingBrush, like so:

```
<Button ... >
  <Button.Background>
    <DrawingBrush>
      <DrawingBrush.Drawing>
        <DrawingGroup>
          <GeometryDrawing ... >
          <GeometryDrawing ... >
          <GeometryDrawing ... >
          ...
        </DrawingGroup>
      </DrawingBrush.Drawing>
    </DrawingBrush>
  </Button.Background>
</Button>
```

The DrawingBrush approach isn't exactly the same as the DrawingImage approach shown earlier, because the default way that an Image sizes its content is different. The default Image.Stretch property is Uniform, which scales the image up or down to fit the available space. The default DrawingBrush.Stretch property is Fill, which may distort your image.

When changing the Stretch property of a DrawingBrush, you may also want to adjust the Viewport setting to explicitly tweak the location and size of the drawing in the fill region. For example, this markup scales the drawing used by the drawing brush to take 90 percent of the fill area:

```
<DrawingBrush Stretch="Fill" Viewport="0,0 0.9,0.9">
```

This is useful with the button example because it gives some space for the border around the button. Because the DrawingBrush isn't an element, it won't be placed using the WPF layout process. That means that unlike the Image, the placement of the content in the DrawingBrush won't take the Button.Padding value into account.

■ **Tip** Using DrawingBrush objects also allows you to create some effects that wouldn't otherwise be possible, such as tiling. Because DrawingBrush derives from TileBrush, you can use the TileMode property to repeat a drawing in a pattern across your fill region. Chapter 12 has the full details about tiling with the TileBrush.

One quirk with the DrawingBrush approach is that the content disappears when you move the mouse over the button and a new brush is used to paint its surface. But when you use the Image approach, the picture remains unaffected. To deal with this issue, you need to create a custom control template for the button that doesn't paint its background in the same way. This technique is demonstrated in Chapter 17.

Either way, whether you use a DrawingImage on its own or wrapped in a DrawingBrush, you should also consider refactoring your markup by using *resources*. The basic idea is to define each DrawingImage or DrawingBrush as a distinct resource, which you can then refer to when needed. This is a particularly good idea if you want to show the same content in more than one element or in more than one window, because you simply need to reuse the resource, rather than copy a whole block of markup.

Exporting Clip Art

Although all of these examples have declared their drawings inline, a more common approach is to place some portion of this content in a resource dictionary so it can be reused throughout your application (and modified in one place). It's up to you how you break down this markup into resources, but two common choices are to store a dictionary full of DrawingImage objects or a dictionary stocked with DrawingBrush objects. Optionally, you can factor out the Geometry objects and store them as separate resources. (This is handy if you use the same geometry in more than one drawing, with different colors.)

Of course, very few developers will code much (if any) art by hand. Instead, they'll use dedicated design tools that export the XAML content they need. Most design tools don't support XAML export yet, although there are a wide variety of plug-ins and converters that fill the gaps. Here are some examples:

- www.mikeswanson.com/XAMLExport has a free XAML plug-in for Adobe Illustrator.

- www.mikeswanson.com/swf2xaml has a free XAML converter for Adobe Flash files.

- Expression Design, Microsoft's illustration and graphic design program, has a built-in XAML export feature. In can read a variety of vector art file formats, including the Windows Metafile Format (.wmf), which allows you to import existing clip art and export it as XAML.

However, even if you use one of these tools, the knowledge you've learned about geometries and drawings is still important for several reasons.

First, many programs allow you to choose whether you want to export a drawing as a combination of separate elements in a Canvas or as a collection of DrawingBrush or DrawingImage resources. Usually, the Canvas choice is the default, because it preserves more features. However, if you're using a large number of drawings, your drawings are complex, or you simply want to use the least amount of memory for static graphics such as button icons, it's a much better idea to use DrawingBrush or DrawingImage resources. Better still, these formats are separated from the rest of your user interface, so it's easier to update them later. (In fact, you could even place your DrawingBrush or DrawingImage resources in a separately compiled DLL assembly, as described in Chapter 10.)

▒ **Tip**   To save resources in Expression Design, you must explicitly choose Resource Dictionary instead of Canvas in the Document Format list box.

Another reason that it's important to understand the plumbing behind 2-D graphics is that it makes it far easier for you to manipulate them. For example, you can alter a standard 2-D graphic by modifying the brushes used to paint various shapes, applying transforms to individual geometries, or altering the opacity or transform of an entire layer of shapes (through a DrawingGroup object). More dramatically, you can add, remove, or alter individual geometries. These techniques can be easily combined with the animation skills you'll pick up in Chapter 15 and Chapter 16. For example, it's easy to rotate a Geometry object by modifying the Angle property of a RotateTransform, fade a layer of shapes into existence by using DrawingGroup.Opacity, or create a swirling gradient effect by animating a LinearGradientBrush that paints the fill for a GeometryDrawing.

■ **Tip** If you're really curious, you can hunt down the resources used by other WPF applications. The basic technique is to use a tool such as Reflector (`www.reflector.net`) and open the assembly with the resources. You can extract one of the BAML resources and decompile it back to XAML. Of course, most companies won't take kindly to developers who steal their handcrafted graphics to use in their own applications!

The Last Word

In this chapter, you delved deeper into WPF's 2-D drawing model. You began with a thorough look at the Path class, the most powerful of WPF's shape classes, and the geometry model that it uses. Then you considered how you could use a geometry to build a drawing, and to use that drawing to display lightweight, noninteractive graphics. In the next chapter, you'll consider an even leaner approach—forgoing elements and using the lower-level Visual class to perform your rendering by hand.

CHAPTER 14

∎ ∎ ∎

Effects and Visuals

In the previous two chapters, you explored the core concepts of 2-D drawing in WPF. Now that you have a solid understanding of the fundamentals—such as shapes, brushes, transforms, and drawings—it's worth digging down to WPF's lower-level graphics features.

Usually, you'll turn to these features when raw performance becomes an issue, or when you need access to individual pixels (or both). In this chapter, you'll consider three WPF techniques that can help you out:

> *Visuals*: If you want to build a program for drawing vector art, or you plan to create a canvas with thousands of shapes that can be manipulated individually, WPF's element system and shape classes will only slow you down. Instead, you need a leaner approach, which is to use the lower-level Visual class to perform your rendering by hand.

> *Effects*: If you want to apply complex visual effects (such as blurs and color tuning) to an element, the easiest approach is to alter individual pixels with a specialized tool called a *pixel shader*. Pixel shaders are hardware-accelerated for blistering performance, and there are plenty of ready-made effects that you can drop into your applications with minimal effort.

> *The WriteableBitmap*: It's far more work, but the WriteableBitmap class lets you own a bitmap in its entirety—meaning you can set and inspect any of its pixels. You can use this feature in complex data-visualization scenarios (for example, when graphing scientific data), or just to generate an eye-popping effect from scratch.

Visuals

In the previous chapter, you learned the best ways to deal with modest amounts of graphical content. By using geometries, drawings, and paths, you reduce the overhead of your 2-D art. Even if you're using complex compound shapes with layered effects and gradient brushes, this is an approach that performs well.

However, this design isn't suitable for drawing-intensive applications that need to render a huge number of graphical elements. For example, consider a mapping program, a physics modeling program that demonstrates particle collisions, or a side-scrolling game. The problem posed by these applications isn't the complexity of the art, but the sheer number of individual graphical elements. Even if you replace your Path elements with lighter-weight Geometry objects, the overhead will still hamper the application's performance.

The WPF solution for this sort of situation is to use the lower-level *visual layer* model. The basic idea is that you define each graphical element as a Visual object, which is an extremely lightweight ingredient that has less overhead than a Geometry object or a Path object. You can then use a single element to render all your visuals in a window.

In the following sections, you'll learn how to create visuals, manipulate them, and perform hit testing. Along the way, you'll build a basic vector-based drawing application that lets you add squares to a drawing surface, select them, and drag them around.

Drawing Visuals

Visual is an abstract class, so you can't create an instance of it. Instead, you need to use one of the classes that derive from Visual. These include UIElement (which is the root of WPF's element model), Viewport3DVisual (which allows you to display 3-D content, as described in Chapter 27), and ContainerVisual (which is a basic container that holds other visuals). But the most useful derived class is DrawingVisual, which derives from ContainerVisual and adds the support you need to "draw" the graphical content you want to place in your visual.

To draw content in a DrawingVisual, you call the DrawingVisual.RenderOpen() method. This method returns a DrawingContext that you can use to define the content of your visual. When you're finished, you call DrawingContext. Close(). Here's how it all unfolds:

```
Dim visual As New DrawingVisual()
Dim dc As DrawingContext = visual.RenderOpen()
' (Perform drawing here.)
dc.Close()
```

Essentially, the DrawingContext class is made up of methods that add some graphical detail to your visual. You call these methods to draw various shapes, apply transforms, change the opacity, and so on. Table 14-1 lists the methods of the DrawingContext class.

Table 14-1. *DrawingContext Methods*

Name	Description
DrawLine(), DrawRectangle(), DrawRoundedRectangle(), and DrawEllipse()	Draw the specified shape at the point you specify, with the fill and outline you specify. These methods mirror the shapes you saw in Chapter 12.
DrawGeometry () and DrawDrawing()	Draw more-complex Geometry objects and Drawing objects.
DrawText()	Draws text at the specified location. You specify the text, font, fill, and other details by passing a FormattedText object to this method. You can use DrawText() to draw wrapped text if you set the FormattedText.MaxTextWidth property.
DrawImage()	Draws a bitmap image in a specific region (as defined by a Rect).
DrawVideo()	Draws video content (wrapped in a MediaPlayer object) in a specific region. Chapter 26 has the full details about video rendering in WPF.
Pop()	Reverses the last Push*Xxx*() method that was called. You use the Push*Xxx*() method to temporarily apply one or more effects, and the Pop() method to reverse them.
PushClip()	Limits drawing to a specific clip region. Content that falls outside this region isn't drawn.
PushEffect()	Applies a BitmapEffect to subsequent drawing operations.
PushOpacity() and PushOpacityMask()	Apply a new opacity setting or opacity mask (see Chapter 12) to make subsequent drawing operations partially transparent.
PushTransform()	Sets a Transform object that will be applied to subsequent drawing operations. You can use a transformation to scale, displace, rotate, or skew content.

Here's an example that creates a visual containing a basic black triangle with no fill:

```
Dim visual As New DrawingVisual()
Using dc As DrawingContext = visual.RenderOpen()
    Dim drawingPen As New Pen(Brushes.Black, 3)
    dc.DrawLine(drawingPen, New Point(0, 50), New Point(50, 0))
    dc.DrawLine(drawingPen, New Point(50, 0), New Point(100, 50))
    dc.DrawLine(drawingPen, New Point(0, 50), New Point(100, 50))
End Using
```

As you call the DrawingContext methods, you aren't actually painting your visual; rather, you're defining its visual appearance. When you finish by calling Close(), the completed drawing is stored in the visual and exposed through the read-only DrawingVisual.Drawing property. WPF retains the Drawing object so that it can repaint the window when needed.

The order of your drawing code is important. Later drawing actions can write content on top of what already exists. The Push*Xxx*() methods apply settings that will apply to future drawing operations. For example, you can use PushOpacity() to change the opacity level, which will then affect all subsequent drawing operations. You can use Pop() to reverse the most recent Push*Xxx*() method. If you call more than one Push*Xxx*() method, you can switch them off one at a time with subsequent Pop() calls.

After you've closed the DrawingContext, you can't modify your visual any further. However, you can apply a transform or change a visual's overall opacity (using the Transform and Opacity properties of the DrawingVisual class). If you want to supply completely new content, you can call RenderOpen() again and repeat the drawing process.

▓ **Tip** Many drawing methods use Pen and Brush objects. If you plan to draw many visuals with the same stroke and fill, or if you expect to render the same visual multiple times (in order to change its content), it's worth creating the Pen and Brush objects you need up front and holding on to them over the lifetime of your window.

Visuals are used in several ways. In the remainder of this chapter, you'll learn how to place a DrawingVisual in a window and perform hit testing for it. You can also use a DrawingVisual to define content you want to print, as you'll see in Chapter 29. Finally, you can use visuals to render a custom-drawn element by overriding the OnRender() method, as you'll see in Chapter 18. In fact, that's exactly how the shape classes that you learned about in Chapter 12 do their work. For example, here's the rendering code that the Rectangle element uses to paint itself:

```
Protected Overrides Sub OnRender(ByVal drawingContext As DrawingContext)
    Dim pen As Pen = MyBase.GetPen()
    drawingContext.DrawRoundedRectangle(MyBase.Fill, pen, _
      Me._rect, Me.RadiusX, Me.RadiusY)
End Sub
```

Wrapping Visuals in an Element

Defining a visual is the most important step in visual-layer programming, but it's not enough to actually show your visual content onscreen. To display a visual, you need the help of a full-fledged WPF element that can add it to the visual tree. At first glance, this seems to reduce the benefit of visual-layer programming—after all, isn't the whole point to avoid elements and their high overhead? However, a single element has the ability to display an unlimited number of visuals. Thus, you can easily create a window that holds only one or two elements but hosts thousands of visuals.

To host a visual in an element, you need to perform the following tasks:

- Call the AddVisualChild() and AddLogicalChild() methods of your element to register your visual. Technically speaking, these tasks aren't required to make the visual appear, but they are required to ensure it is tracked correctly, appears in the visual and logical tree, and works with other WPF features such as hit testing.

- Override the VisualChildrenCount property and return the number of visuals you've added.

- Override the GetVisualChild() method and add the code needed to return your visual when it's requested by index number.

When you override VisualChildrenCount and GetVisualChild(), you are essentially hijacking that element. If you're using a content control, decorator, or panel that can hold nested elements, these elements will no longer be rendered. For example, if you override these two methods in a custom window, you won't see the rest of the window content. Instead, you'll see only the visuals that you've added.

For this reason, it's common to create a dedicated custom class that wraps the visuals you want to display. For example, consider the window shown in Figure 14-1. It allows the user to add squares (each of which is a visual) to a custom Canvas.

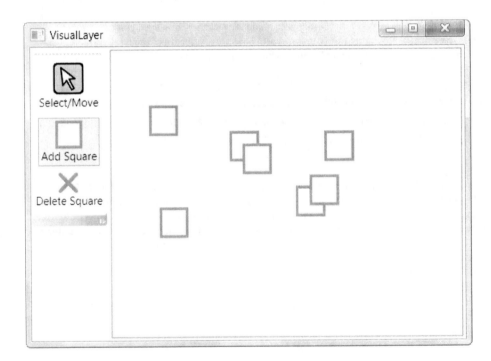

Figure 14-1. *Drawing visuals*

On the left side of the window in Figure 14-1 is a toolbar with three RadioButton objects. As you'll discover in Chapter 25, the ToolBar changes the way some basic controls are rendered, such as buttons. By using a group of RadioButton objects, you can create a set of linked buttons. When you click one of the buttons in this set, it is selected and remains "pushed," while the previously selected button reverts to its normal appearance.

On the right side of the window in Figure 14-1 is a custom Canvas named DrawingCanvas, which stores a collection of visuals internally. DrawingCanvas returns the total number of squares in the VisualChildrenCount property, and uses the GetVisualChild() method to provide access to each visual in the collection. Here's how these details are implemented:

```
Public Class DrawingCanvas
    Inherits Canvas

    Private visuals As New List(Of Visual)()

    Protected Overrides ReadOnly Property VisualChildrenCount() As Integer
        Get
            Return visuals.Count
        End Get
    End Property

    Protected Overrides Function GetVisualChild(ByVal index As Integer) _
      As Visual
        Return visuals(index)
    End Function
    ...
```

Additionally, the DrawingCanvas includes an AddVisual() method and a DeleteVisual() method to make it easy for the consuming code to insert visuals into the collection, with the appropriate tracking:

```
    ...
    Public Sub AddVisual(ByVal visual As Visual)
        visuals.Add(visual)

        MyBase.AddVisualChild(visual)
        MyBase.AddLogicalChild(visual)
    End Sub

    Public Sub DeleteVisual(ByVal visual As Visual)
        visuals.Remove(visual)

        MyBase.RemoveVisualChild(visual)
        MyBase.RemoveLogicalChild(visual)
    End Sub
End Class
```

The DrawingCanvas doesn't include the logic for drawing squares, selecting them, and moving them. That's because this functionality is controlled at the application layer. This makes sense because there might be several drawing tools, all of which work with the same DrawingCanvas. Depending on which button the user clicks, the user might be able to draw different types of shapes or use different stroke and fill colors. All of these details are specific to the window. The DrawingCanvas simply provides the functionality for hosting, rendering, and tracking your visuals.

Here's how the DrawingCanvas is declared in the XAML markup for the window:

```
<local:DrawingCanvas x:Name="drawingSurface" Background="White" ClipToBounds="True"
  MouseLeftButtonDown="drawingSurface_MouseLeftButtonDown"
  MouseLeftButtonUp="drawingSurface_MouseLeftButtonUp"
  MouseMove="drawingSurface_MouseMove" />
```

371

■ **Tip** By setting the background to white (rather than transparent), it's possible to intercept all mouse clicks on the canvas surface.

Now that you've considered the DrawingCanvas container, it's worth considering the event-handling code that creates the squares. The starting point is the event handler for the MouseLeftButton. It's at this point that the code determines what operation is being performed—square creation, square deletion, or square selection. At the moment, we're interested in just the first task:

```
Private Sub drawingSurface_MouseLeftButtonDown(ByVal sender As Object, _
  ByVal e As MouseButtonEventArgs)
    Dim pointClicked As Point = e.GetPosition(drawingSurface)

    If cmdAdd.IsChecked = True Then
        Dim visual As New DrawingVisual()
        DrawSquare(visual, pointClicked, False)
        drawingSurface.AddVisual(visual)
        ...
    End If
End Sub
```

The actual work is performed by a custom method named DrawSquare(). This approach is useful because the square drawing needs to be triggered at several points in the code. Obviously, DrawSquare() is required when the square is first created. It's also used when the appearance of the square changes for any reason (such as when it's selected).

The DrawSquare() method accepts three parameters: the DrawingVisual to draw, the point for the top-left corner of the square, and a Boolean flag that indicates whether the square is currently selected, in which case it is given a different fill color.

Here's the modest rendering code:

```
' Drawing constants.
Private drawingBrush As Brush = Brushes.AliceBlue
Private selectedDrawingBrush As Brush = Brushes.LightGoldenrodYellow
Private drawingPen As New Pen(Brushes.SteelBlue, 3)
Private squareSize As New Size(30, 30)

Private Sub DrawSquare(ByVal visual As DrawingVisual, _
  ByVal topLeftCorner As Point, ByVal isSelected As Boolean)

    Using dc As DrawingContext = visual.RenderOpen()
        Dim brush As Brush = drawingBrush
        If isSelected Then
            brush = selectedDrawingBrush
        End If
        dc.DrawRectangle(brush, drawingPen, New Rect(topLeftCorner, squareSize))
    End Using
End Sub
```

This is all you need to display a visual in a window: some code that renders the visual, and a container that handles the necessary tracking details. However, there's a bit more work to do if you want to add interactivity to your visuals, as you'll see in the following section.

Hit Testing

The square-drawing application not only allows users to draw squares, but it also allows them to move and delete existing squares. To perform either of these tasks, your code needs to be able to intercept a mouse click and find the visual at the clicked location. This task is called *hit testing*.

To support hit testing, it makes sense to add a GetVisual() method to the DrawingCanvas class. This method takes a point and returns the matching DrawingVisual. To do its work, it uses the shared VisualTreeHelper.HitTest() method. Here's the complete code for the GetVisual() method:

```
Public Function GetVisual(ByVal point As Point) As DrawingVisual
    Dim hitResult As HitTestResult = VisualTreeHelper.HitTest(Me, point)
    Return TryCast(hitResult.VisualHit, DrawingVisual)
End Function
```

In this case, the code ignores any hit object that isn't a DrawingVisual, including the DrawingCanvas itself. If no squares are clicked, the GetVisual() method returns a null reference (Nothing).

The delete feature makes use of the GetVisual() method. When the delete command is selected and a square is clicked, the MouseLeftButtonDown event handler uses this code to remove it:

```
ElseIf cmdDelete.IsChecked = True Then
    Dim visual As DrawingVisual = drawingSurface.GetVisual(pointClicked)
    If Not visual Is Nothing Then
        drawingSurface.DeleteVisual(visual)
    End If
End If
```

Similar code supports the dragging feature, but it needs a way to keep track of the fact that dragging is underway. Three fields in the window class serve this purpose—isDragging, clickOffset, and selectedVisual:

```
Private isDragging As Boolean = False
Private clickOffset As Vector
Private selectedVisual As DrawingVisual
```

When the user clicks a shape, the isDragging field is set to True, the selectedVisual is set to the visual that was clicked, and the clickOffset records the space between the top-left corner of the square and the point where the user clicked. Here's the code from the MouseLeftButtonDown event handler:

```
ElseIf cmdSelectMove.IsChecked = True Then
    Dim visual As DrawingVisual = drawingSurface.GetVisual(pointClicked)
    If visual IsNot Nothing Then
        ' Calculate the top-left corner of the square.
        ' This is done by looking at the current bounds and
        ' removing half the border (pen thickness).
        ' An alternate solution would be to store the top-left
        ' point of every visual in a collection in the
        ' DrawingCanvas, and provide this point when hit testing.
        Dim topLeftCorner As New Point( _
            visual.ContentBounds.TopLeft.X + drawingPen.Thickness / 2, _
            visual.ContentBounds.TopLeft.Y + drawingPen.Thickness / 2)
        DrawSquare(visual, topLeftCorner, True)
```

```
                clickOffset = topLeftCorner - pointClicked
                isDragging = True

                If (selectedVisual IsNot Nothing) AndAlso _
                  (selectedVisual IsNot visual) Then
                    ' The selection has changed. Clear the previous selection.
                    ClearSelection()
                End If
                selectedVisual = visual
            End If
        End If
    End If
End If
```

Along with basic bookkeeping, this code calls DrawSquare() to rerender the DrawingVisual, giving it the new color. The code also uses another custom method, named ClearSelection(), to repaint the previously selected square so it returns to its normal appearance:

```
Private Sub ClearSelection()
    Dim topLeftCorner As New Point( _
        selectedVisual.ContentBounds.TopLeft.X + drawingPen.Thickness / 2, _
        selectedVisual.ContentBounds.TopLeft.Y + drawingPen.Thickness / 2)

    DrawSquare(selectedVisual, topLeftCorner, False)
    selectedVisual = Nothing
End Sub
```

■ **Note** Remember that the DrawSquare() method defines the content for the square—it doesn't actually paint it in the window. For that reason, you don't need to worry about inadvertently painting on top of another square that should be underneath. WPF manages the painting process, ensuring that visuals are painted in the order they are returned by the GetVisualChild() method (which is the order in which they are defined in the visuals collection).

Next, you need to actually move the square as the user drags, and end the dragging operation when the user releases the left mouse button. Both of these tasks are accomplished with some straightforward event-handling code:

```
Private Sub drawingSurface_MouseMove(ByVal sender As Object, _
   ByVal e As MouseEventArgs)
    If isDragging Then
        Dim pointDragged As Point = e.GetPosition(drawingSurface) + clickOffset
        DrawSquare(selectedVisual, pointDragged, True)
    End If
End Sub

Private Sub drawingSurface_MouseLeftButtonUp(ByVal sender As Object, _
   ByVal e As MouseButtonEventArgs)
    isDragging = False
End Sub
```

Complex Hit Testing

In the previous example, the hit-testing code always returns the topmost visual (or a null reference if the space is empty). However, the VisualTreeHelper class includes two overloads to the HitTest() method that allow you to perform more-sophisticated hit testing. Using these methods, you can retrieve all the visuals that are at a specified point, even if they're obscured underneath other visuals. You can also find all the visuals that fall in a given geometry.

To use this more advanced hit-testing behavior, you need to create a callback. The VisualTreeHelper will then walk through your visuals from top to bottom (in the reverse order that you created them). Each time it finds a match, it calls your callback with the details. You can then choose to stop the search (if you've dug down enough levels) or continue until no more visuals remain.

The following code implements this technique by adding a GetVisuals() method to the DrawingCanvas. GetVisuals() accepts a Geometry object, which it uses for hit testing. It creates the callback delegate, clears the collection of hit-test results, and then starts the hit-testing process by calling the VisualTreeHelper.HitTest() method. When the process is finished, it returns a collection with all the visuals that were found:

```
Private hits As New List(Of DrawingVisual)()

Public Function GetVisuals(ByVal region As Geometry) As List(Of DrawingVisual)
    ' Remove matches from the previous search.
    hits.Clear()

    ' Prepare the parameters for the hit test operation
    ' (the geometry and callback).
    Dim parameters As New GeometryHitTestParameters(region)
    Dim callback As New HitTestResultCallback(AddressOf Me.HitTestCallback)

    ' Search for hits.
    VisualTreeHelper.HitTest(Me, Nothing, callback, parameters)
    Return hits
End Function
```

Tip   In this example, the callback is implemented by a separately defined method named HitTestResultCallback(). Both HitTestResultCallback() and GetVisuals() use the hits collection, so it must be defined as a member field. However, you could remove this requirement by using an anonymous method for the callback, which you would declare inside the GetVisuals() method.

The callback method implements your hit-testing behavior. Ordinarily, the HitTestResult object provides just a single property (VisualHit), but you can cast it to one of two derived types depending on the type of hit test you're performing.

If you're hit testing a point, you can cast HitTestResult to PointHitTestResult, which provides a relatively uninteresting PointHit property that returns the original point you used to perform the hit test. But if you're hit testing a Geometry object, as in this example, you can cast HitTestResult to GeometryHitTestResult and get access to the IntersectionDetail property. This property tells you whether your geometry completely wraps the visual (FullyInside), the geometry and visual simply overlap (Intersects), or your hit-tested geometry falls within the visual (FullyContains). In this example, hits are counted only if the visual is completely inside the hit-tested region. Finally, at the end of the callback, you can return one of two values from the HitTestResultBehavior enumeration: Continue to keep looking for hits, or Stop to end the process.

```
Private Function HitTestCallback(ByVal result As HitTestResult) _
  As HitTestResultBehavior
    Dim geometryResult As GeometryHitTestResult
    geometryResult = CType(result, GeometryHitTestResult)
    Dim visual As DrawingVisual = TryCast(result.VisualHit, DrawingVisual)

    ' Only include matches that are DrawingVisual objects and
    ' that are completely inside the geometry.
    If (visual IsNot Nothing) AndAlso _
      (geometryResult.IntersectionDetail = IntersectionDetail.FullyInside) Then
        hits.Add(visual)
    End If

    Return HitTestResultBehavior.Continue
End Function
```

Using the GetVisuals() method, you can create the sophisticated selection box effect shown in Figure 14-2. Here, the user draws a box around a group of squares. The application then reports the number of squares in the region.

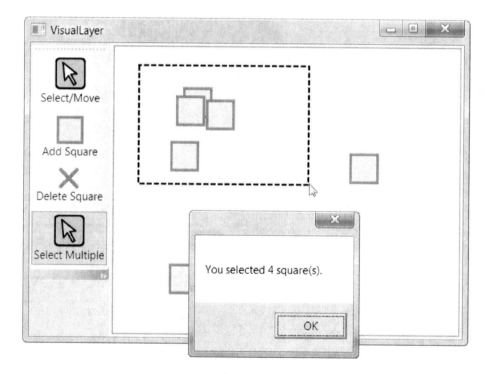

Figure 14-2. *Advanced hit testing*

To create the selection square, the window simply adds another DrawingVisual to the DrawingCanvas. The window also stores a reference to the selection square as a member field, along with a flag named isMultiSelecting that keeps track of when the selection box is being drawn, and a field named selectionSquareTopLeft that tracks the top-left corner of the current selection box:

```
Private selectionSquare As DrawingVisual
Private isMultiSelecting As Boolean = False
Private selectionSquareTopLeft As Point
```

To implement the selection box feature, you need to add some code to the event handlers you've already seen. When the mouse is clicked, you need to create the selection box, switch isMultiSelecting to True, and capture the mouse. Here's the code that does this work in the MouseLeftButtonDown event handler:

```
ElseIf cmdSelectMultiple.IsChecked = True Then
    selectionSquare = New DrawingVisual()
    drawingSurface.AddVisual(selectionSquare)

    selectionSquareTopLeft = pointClicked
    isMultiSelecting = True

    ' Make sure we get the MouseLeftButtonUp event even if the user
    ' moves off the Canvas. Otherwise, two selection squares could
    ' be drawn at once.
    drawingSurface.CaptureMouse()
End If
```

Now, when the mouse moves, you can check whether the selection box is currently active, and draw it if it is. To do so, you need this code in the MouseMove event handler:

```
ElseIf isMultiSelecting Then
    Dim pointDragged As Point = e.GetPosition(drawingSurface)
    DrawSelectionSquare(selectionSquareTopLeft, pointDragged)
End If
```

The actual drawing takes place in a dedicated method named DrawSelectionSquare(), which looks a fair bit like the DrawSquare() method you considered earlier:

```
Private selectionSquareBrush As Brush = Brushes.Transparent
Private selectionSquarePen As New Pen(Brushes.Black, 2)

Private Sub DrawSelectionSquare(ByVal point1 As Point, ByVal point2 As Point)
    selectionSquarePen.DashStyle = DashStyles.Dash

    Using dc As DrawingContext = selectionSquare.RenderOpen()
        dc.DrawRectangle(selectionSquareBrush, selectionSquarePen, _
          New Rect(point1, point2))
    End Using
End Sub
```

Finally, when the mouse is released, you can perform the hit testing, show the message box, and then remove the selection square. To do so, you need this code in the MouseLeftButtonUp event handler:

```
If isMultiSelecting Then
    ' Display all the squares in this region.
    Dim geometry As New RectangleGeometry( _
        New Rect(selectionSquareTopLeft, e.GetPosition(drawingSurface)))
    Dim visualsInRegion As List(Of DrawingVisual) = _
        drawingSurface.GetVisuals(geometry)

    MessageBox.Show(String.Format("You selected {0} square(s).", _
        visualsInRegion.Count))

    isMultiSelecting = False
    drawingSurface.DeleteVisual(selectionSquare)
    drawingSurface.ReleaseMouseCapture()
End If
```

Effects

WPF provides visual effects that you can apply to any element. The goal of effects is to give you an easy, declarative way to enhance the appearance of text, images, buttons, and other controls. Rather than write your own drawing code, you simply use one of the classes that derives from Effect (in the System.Windows.Media.Effects namespace) to get instant effects such as blurs, glows, and drop shadows.

Table 14-2 lists the effect classes that you can use.

Table 14-2. *Effects*

Name	Description	Properties
BlurEffect	Blurs the content in your element	Radius, KernelType, RenderingBias
DropShadowEffect	Adds a rectangular drop shadow behind your element	BlurRadius, Color, Direction, Opacity, ShadowDepth, RenderingBias
ShaderEffect	Applies a pixel shader, which is a ready-made effect that's defined in High Level Shading Language (HLSL) and already compiled	PixelShader

The Effect-derived classes listed in Table 14-2 shouldn't be confused with bitmap effects, which derive from the BitmapEffect class in the same namespace. Although bitmap effects have a similar programming model, they have several significant limitations:

- Bitmap effects don't support pixel shaders, which are the most powerful and flexible way to create reusable effects.

- Bitmap effects are implemented in unmanaged code, and so require a fully trusted application. Therefore, you can't use bitmap effects in a browser-based XBAP application (Chapter 24).

- Bitmap effects are always rendered in software and don't use the resources of the video card. This makes them slow, especially when dealing with large numbers of elements or elements that have a large visual surface.

The BitmapEffect class dates back to the first version of WPF, which didn't include the Effect class. Bitmap effects remain only for backward compatibility.

The following sections dig deeper into the effect model and demonstrate the three Effect-derived classes: BlurEffect, DropShadowEffect, and ShaderEffect.

BlurEffect

WPF's simplest effect is the BlurEffect class. It blurs the content of an element, as though you're looking at it through an out-of-focus lens. You increase the level of blur by increasing the value of the Radius property (the default value is 5).

To use any effect, you create the appropriate effect object and set the Effect property of the corresponding element:

```
<Button Content="Blurred (Radius=2)" Padding="5" Margin="3">
  <Button.Effect>
    <BlurEffect Radius="2"></BlurEffect>
  </Button.Effect>
</Button>
```

Figure 14-3 shows three blurs (where Radius is 2, 5, and 20) applied to a stack of buttons.

Figure 14-3. *Blurred buttons*

DropShadowEffect

DropShadowEffect adds a slightly offset shadow behind an element. You have several properties to play with, as listed in Table 14-3.

Table 14-3. *DropShadowEffect Properties*

Name	Description
Color	Sets the color of the drop shadow (the default is Black).
ShadowDepth	Determines how far the shadow is from the content, in pixels (the default is 5). Use a ShadowDepth of 0 to create an outer-glow effect, which adds a halo of color around your content.
BlurRadius	Blurs the drop shadow, much like the Radius property of BlurEffect (the default is 5).
Opacity	Makes the drop shadow partially transparent, using a fractional value between 1 (fully opaque, the default) and 0 (fully transparent).
Direction	Specifies where the drop shadow should be positioned relative to the content, as an angle from 0 to 360. Use 0 to place the shadow on the right side, and increase the value to move the shadow counterclockwise. The default is 315, which places it to the lower right of the element.

Figure 14-4 shows several drop-shadow effects on a TextBlock. Here's the markup for all of them:

```
<TextBlock FontSize="20" Margin="5">
  <TextBlock.Effect>
    <DropShadowEffect></DropShadowEffect>
  </TextBlock.Effect>
  <TextBlock.Text>Basic dropshadow</TextBlock.Text>
</TextBlock>

<TextBlock FontSize="20" Margin="5">
  <TextBlock.Effect>
    <DropShadowEffect Color="SlateBlue"></DropShadowEffect>
  </TextBlock.Effect>
  <TextBlock.Text>Light blue dropshadow</TextBlock.Text>
</TextBlock>

<TextBlock FontSize="20" Foreground="White" Margin="5">
  <TextBlock.Effect>
    <DropShadowEffect BlurRadius="15"></DropShadowEffect>
  </TextBlock.Effect>
  <TextBlock.Text>Blurred dropshadow with white text</TextBlock.Text>
</TextBlock>

<TextBlock FontSize="20" Foreground="Magenta" Margin="5">
  <TextBlock.Effect>
    <DropShadowEffect ShadowDepth="0"></DropShadowEffect>
  </TextBlock.Effect>
  <TextBlock.Text>Close dropshadow</TextBlock.Text>
</TextBlock>

<TextBlock FontSize="20" Foreground="LimeGreen" Margin="5">
  <TextBlock.Effect>
    <DropShadowEffect ShadowDepth="25"></DropShadowEffect>
  </TextBlock.Effect>
  <TextBlock.Text>Distant dropshadow</TextBlock.Text>
</TextBlock>
```

Figure 14-4. *Drop shadows*

There is no class for grouping effects, which means you can apply only a single effect to an element at a time. However, you can sometimes simulate multiple effects by adding them to higher-level containers (for example, using the drop-shadow effect for a TextBlock and then placing it in a Stack Panel that uses the blur effect). In most cases, you should avoid this workaround, because it multiplies the rendering work and reduces performance. Instead, look for a single effect that can do everything you need.

ShaderEffect

The ShaderEffect class doesn't represent a ready-to-use effect. Instead, it's a MustInherit class from which you derive your own custom pixel shaders. By using ShaderEffect (or a custom effect that derives from it), you gain the ability to go far beyond mere blurs and drop shadows.

Contrary to what you may expect, the logic that implements a pixel shader isn't written in VB code directly in the effect class. Instead, pixel shaders are written using High Level Shader Language (HLSL), which was created as part of Microsoft DirectX. (The benefit is obvious—because DirectX and HLSL have been around for many years, graphics developers have already created scores of pixel-shader routines that you can use in your own code.)

To create a pixel shader, you need to be able to write and compile HLSL code. To perform the compilation, you can use Microsoft's fxc.exe command-line tool, which is included with the Windows SDK for Windows 8 at http://tinyurl.com/8ea7r43. (Despite the name, the Windows SDK for Windows 8 supports Windows 7 as well.) A more convenient option is to use the free Shazzam tool (http://shazzam-tool.com). Shazzam provides an editor for HLSL files, which includes the ability to try them on sample images. It also includes several sample pixel shaders that you can use as the basis for custom effects.

Although authoring your own HLSL files is beyond the scope of this book, using an existing HLSL file isn't. After you've compiled your HLSL file to a .ps file, you can use it in a project. Simply add the file to an existing WPF project, select it in the Solution Explorer, and set its Build Action to Resource. Finally, you must create a custom class that derives from ShaderEffect and uses this resource.

For example, if you're using a custom pixel shader that's compiled in a file named Effect.ps, you can use the following code:

```
Public Class CustomEffect
    Inherits ShaderEffect

    Public Sub New()
        ' Use the URI syntax described in Chapter 7 to refer to your resource.
        ' AssemblyName;component/ResourceFileName
        Dim pixelShaderUri As New Uri("Effect.ps", UriKind.Relative)

        ' Load the information from the .ps file.
        PixelShader = New PixelShader()
        PixelShader.UriSource = pixelShaderUri
    End Sub
End Class
```

You can now use the custom pixel shader in any window. First, make the namespace available by adding a mapping like this:

```
<Window xmlns:local="clr-namespace:CustomEffectTest" ...>
```

Now, create an instance of the custom effect class, and use it to set the Effect property of an element:

```
<Image>
  <Image.Effect>
    <local:CustomEffect></local:CustomEffect>
  </Image.Effect>
</Image>
```

You can get a bit more complicated than this if you use a pixel shader that takes certain input arguments. In this case, you need to create the corresponding dependency properties by calling the shared RegisterPixelShaderSamplerProperty() method.

A crafty pixel shader is as powerful as the plug-ins used in graphics software such as Adobe Photoshop. It can do anything from adding a basic drop shadow to imposing more-ambitious effects such as blurs, glows, watery ripples, embossing, sharpening, and so on. Pixel shaders can also create eye-popping effects when they're combined with animation that alters their parameters in real time, as you'll see in Chapter 16.

▦ **Tip** Unless you're a hard-core graphics programmer, the best way to get more-advanced pixel shaders isn't to write the HLSL yourself. Instead, look for existing HLSL examples or, even better, third-party WPF components that provide custom-effect classes. The gold standard is the free Windows Presentation Foundation Pixel Shader Effects Library at http://codeplex.com/wpffx. It includes a long list of dazzling effects such as swirls, color inversion, and pixelation. Even more useful, it includes transition effects that combine pixel shaders with the animation capabilities described in Chapter 15.

The WriteableBitmap Class

WPF allows you to show bitmaps with the Image element. However, displaying a picture this way is a strictly one-way affair. Your application takes a ready-made bitmap, reads it, and displays it in the window. On its own, the Image element doesn't give you a way to create or edit bitmap information.

This is where WriteableBitmap fits in. It derives from BitmapSource, which is the class you use when setting the Image.Source property (either directly, when you set the image in code, or implicitly, when you set it in XAML). But whereas BitmapSource is a read-only reflection of bitmap data, WriteableBitmap is a modifiable array of pixels that opens up many interesting possibilities.

■ **Note**   It's important to realize that the WriteableBitmap isn't the best way for most applications to draw graphical content. If you need a lower-level alternative to WPF's element system, you should begin by checking out the Visual class demonstrated earlier in this chapter. For example, the Visual class is the perfect tool for creating a charting tool or a simple animated game. The WriteableBitmap is better suited to applications that need to manipulate individual pixels— for example, a fractal generator, a sound analyzer, a visualization tool for scientific data, or an application that processes raw image data from an external hardware device (for example, a webcam). Although the WriteableBitmap gives you fine-grained control, it's complex and requires much more code than the other approaches.

Generating a Bitmap

To generate a bitmap with WriteableBitmap, you must supply a few key pieces of information: its width and height in pixels, its DPI resolution in both dimensions, and the image format.

Here's an example that creates an image as big as the current window:

```
Dim wb As New WriteableBitmap(CInt(Me.ActualWidth), CInt(Me.ActualHeight), _
  96, 96, PixelFormats.Bgra32, Nothing)
```

The PixelFormats enumeration has a long list of pixel formats, but only about half are considered writeable formats and are supported by the WriteableBitmap class. Here are the ones you can use:

Bgra32: This format (the one used in the current example) uses 32-bit sRGB color. That means that each pixel is represented by 32 bits, or 4 bytes. The first byte represents the contribution of the blue channel (as a number from 0 to 255). The second byte is for the green channel, the third is for the red channel, and the fourth is for the alpha value (where 0 is completely transparent and 255 is completely opaque). As you can see, the order of the colors (blue, green, red, alpha) matches the letters in the name *Bgra32*.

Bgr32: This format uses 4 bytes per pixel, just like Bgra32. The difference is that the alpha channel is ignored. You can use this format when transparency is not required.

Pbgra32: This format uses 4 bytes per pixel, just like Bgra32. The difference is the way it handles semitransparent pixels. In order to optimize the performance of opacity calculations, each color byte is *premultiplied* (hence the *P* in Pbgra32). This means each color byte is multiplied by the alpha value and divided by 255. So a partially transparent pixel that has the B, G, R, A values (255, 100, 0, 200) in Bgra32 would become (200, 78, 0, 200) in Pbgra32.

BlackWhite, Gray2, Gray4, Gray8: These are the black-and-white and grayscale formats. The number following the word *Gray* corresponds to the number of bits per pixel. Thus, these formats are compact, but they don't support color.

Indexed1, Indexed2, Indexed4, Indexed8: These are indexed formats, which means that each pixel points to a value in a color palette. When using one of these formats, you must pass the corresponding ColorPalette object as the last WriteableBitmap constructor argument. The number following the word *Indexed* corresponds to the number of bits per pixel. The indexed formats are compact, slightly more complex to use, and support far fewer colors—2, 14, 16, or 256 colors, respectively.

The top three formats—Bgra32, Bgr32, and Pbgra32—are by far the most common choices.

Writing to a WriteableBitmap

A WriteableBitmap begins with 0 values for all its bytes. Essentially, it's a big, black rectangle.

To fill a WriteableBitmap with content, you use the WritePixels() method. WritePixels() copies an array of bytes into the bitmap at the position you specify. You can call WritePixels() to set a single pixel, the entire bitmap, or a rectangular region that you choose. To get pixels out of the WriteableBitmap, you use the CopyPixels() method, which transfers the bytes you want into a byte array. Taken together, the WritePixels() and CopyPixels() methods don't give you the most convenient programming model to work with, but that's the cost of low-level pixel access.

To use WritePixels() successfully, you need to understand your image format and how it encodes pixels into bytes. For example, in the 32-bit bitmap type Bgra32, each pixel requires 4 bytes, one each for the blue, green, red, and alpha components. Here's how you can set them by hand, and then transfer them into an array:

```
Dim blue As Byte = 100
Dim green As Byte = 50
Dim red As Byte = 50
Dim alpha As Byte = 255

Dim colorData As Byte() = {blue, green, red, alpha}
```

Note that the order is critical here. The byte array must follow the blue, green, red, alpha sequence set out in the Bgra32 standard.

When you call WritePixels(), you supply an Int32Rect that indicates the rectangular region of the bitmap that you want to update. The Int32Rect wraps four pieces of information: the X and Y coordinate of the top-left corner of the update region, and the width and height of the update region.

The following code takes the colorData array shown in the preceding code and uses it to set the first pixel in the WriteableBitmap:

```
' Update a single pixel. It's a region starting at (0,0)
' that's 1 pixel wide and 1 pixel high.
Dim rect As New Int32Rect(0, 0, 1, 1)

' Write the 4 bytes from the array into the bitmap.
wb.WritePixels(rect, colorData, 4, 0)
```

Using this approach, you could create a code routine that generates a WriteableBitmap. It simply needs to loop over all the columns and rows in the image, updating a single pixel in each iteration.

```
For x As Integer = 0 To wb.PixelWidth - 1
    For y As Integer = 0 To wb.PixelHeight - 1
        ' Pick a pixel color using a formula of your choosing.
        Dim blue As Byte = ...
        Dim green As Byte = ...
        Dim red As Byte = ...
        Dim alpha As Byte = ...

        ' Create the byte array.
        Dim colorData As Byte() = {blue, green, red, alpha}

        ' Pick the position where the pixel will be drawn.
        Dim rect As New Int32Rect(x, y, 1, 1)

        ' Calculate the stride.
        Dim stride As Integer = CInt(wb.PixelWidth * wb.Format.BitsPerPixel / 8)

        ' Write the pixel.
        wb.WritePixels(rect, colorData, stride, 0)
    Next
Next
```

This code includes one additional detail: a calculation for the *stride*, which the WritePixels() method requires. Technically, the stride is the number of bytes required for each row of pixel data. You can calculate this by multiplying the number of pixels in a row by the number of bits in a pixel for your format (usually 4, as with the Bgra32 format used in this example), and then dividing the result by 8 to convert it from bits to bytes.

After the pixel-generating process is finished, you need to display the final bitmap. Typically, you'll use an Image element to do the job:

```
img.Source = wb
```

Even after writing and displaying a bitmap, you're still free to read and modify pixels in the WriteableBitmap. This gives you the ability to build more-specialized routines for bitmap editing and bitmap hit testing.

Using More-Efficient Pixel Writing

Although the code shown in the previous section works, it's not the best approach. If you need to write a large amount of pixel data at once—or even the entire image—you're better off using bigger chunks That's because there's a certain amount of overhead for calling WritePixels(), and the more often you call it, the longer you'll delay your application.

Figure 14-5 shows a test application that's included with the samples for this chapter. It creates a dynamic bitmap by filling pixels with a mostly random pattern interspersed with regular gridlines. The downloadable code performs this task in two ways: using the pixel-by-pixel approach explained in the previous section and using the single-write strategy you'll see next. If you test this application, you'll find that the single-write technique is far faster.

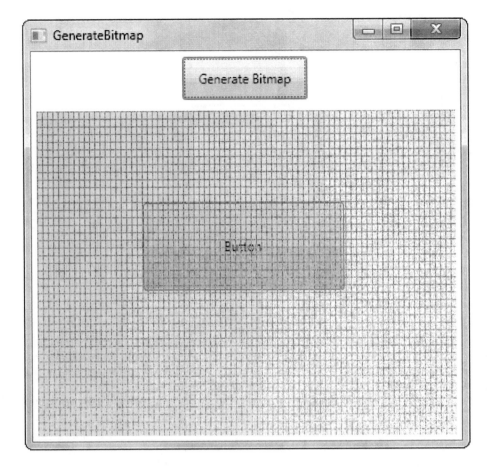

Figure 14-5. *A dynamically generated bitmap*

To update more than one pixel at once, you need to understand how the pixels are packaged together in your byte array. Regardless of the format you're using, your update buffer will hold a one-dimensional array of bytes. This array supplies values for the pixels in a rectangular section of the image, stretching from left to right to fill each row, and then from top to bottom.

To find a specific pixel, you need to use the following formula, which steps down the number of rows and then moves to the appropriate position in that row:

```
(y * wb.PixelWidth + x) * BytesPerPixel
```

For example, to set the pixel (40, 100) in a Bgra32 bitmap (which has 4 bytes per pixel), you use this code:

```
Dim pixelOffset As Integer = CInt((40 + 100 * wb.PixelWidth) * _
  wb.Format.BitsPerPixel/8)
pixels(pixelOffset) = blue
pixels(pixelOffset + 1) = green
pixels(pixelOffset + 2) = red
pixels(pixelOffset + 3) = alpha
```

With that in mind, here's the complete code that creates the bitmap shown in Figure 14-5, by first filling all the data in a single array, and then copying it to the WriteableBitmap with just one call to WritePixels():

```
' Create the bitmap, with the dimensions of the image placeholder.
Dim wb As New WriteableBitmap(CInt(img.Width), CInt(img.Height), _
  96, 96, PixelFormats.Bgra32, Nothing)

Dim rand As New Random()
For x As Integer = 0 To wb.PixelWidth - 1
    For y As Integer = 0 To wb.PixelHeight - 1
        Dim alpha As Integer = 0
        Dim red As Integer = 0
        Dim green As Integer = 0
        Dim blue As Integer = 0

        ' Determine the pixel's color.
        If (x Mod 5 = 0) OrElse (y Mod 7 = 0) Then
            red = CInt(y / wb.PixelHeight * 255)
            green = rand.Next(100, 255)
            blue = CInt(x / wb.PixelWidth * 255)
            alpha = 255
        Else
            red = CInt(x / wb.PixelWidth * 255)
            green = rand.Next(100, 255)
            blue = CInt(y / wb.PixelHeight * 255)
            alpha = 50
        End If

        ' Set the pixel value.
        Dim colorData As Byte() = {CByte(blue), CByte(green), _
          CByte(red), CByte(alpha)}

        Dim rect As New Int32Rect(x, y, 1, 1)
        Dim stride As Integer = CInt((wb.PixelWidth * wb.Format.BitsPerPixel) / 8)
        wb.WritePixels(rect, colorData, stride, 0)
    Next
Next

' Show the bitmap in an Image element.
img.Source = wb
```

In a realistic application, you're likely to choose an approach that falls somewhere in between. You won't write one pixel a time if you need to update large sections of a bitmap, because that approach would probably be prohibitively slow. But you won't hold all of the image data in memory at once, because it could be very large. (After all, a 1000×1000 pixel image that requires 4 bytes per pixel needs nearly 4 MB of memory, which is not yet excessive but not trivial either.) Instead, you should aim to write large chunks of image data rather than individual pixels, especially if you're generating an entire bitmap at once.

The Last Word

In this chapter, you looked at three topics that go beyond WPF's standard 2-D drawing support. First, you tackled the lower-level visual layer, which is the most efficient way to display graphics in WPF. Using the visual layer, you saw how you could build a basic drawing application that uses sophisticated hit testing. Next, you learned about pixel shaders, a way to fuse graphical effects originally designed for next-generation games into any WPF application. Not only are pixel shaders nearly effortless to use, but there's already a huge library of free pixel shaders that you can drop into your applications right now. Finally, you considered the WriteableBitmap, a powerful but more limited tool that lets you create a bitmap image, and directly manipulate the individual pixels that compose it.

CHAPTER 15

Animation Basics

Animation allows you to create truly *dynamic* user interfaces. It's often used to apply effects—for example, icons that grow when you move over them, logos that spin, text that scrolls into view, and so on. Sometimes these effects seem like excessive glitz. But used properly, animations can enhance an application in several ways. They can make an application seem more responsive, natural, and intuitive. (For example, a button that slides in when you click it feels like a real, physical button—not just another gray rectangle.) Animations can also draw attention to important elements and guide the user through transitions to new content. (For example, an application could advertise newly downloaded content with a twinkling icon in a status bar.)

Animations are a core part of the WPF model. That means you don't need to use timers and event-handling code to put them into action. Instead, you can create them declaratively, configure them by using one of a handful of classes, and put them into action without writing a single line of VB code. Animations also integrate themselves seamlessly into ordinary WPF windows and pages. For example, if you animate a button so it drifts around the window, the button still behaves like a button. It can be styled, it can receive focus, and it can be clicked to fire off the typical event-handling code. This is what separates animation from traditional media files, such as video. (In Chapter 26, you'll learn how to put a video window in your application. A video window is a completely separate region of your application—it's able to play video content, but it's not user interactive.)

In this chapter, you'll consider the rich set of animation classes that WPF provides. You'll see how to use them in code and (more commonly) how to construct and control them with XAML. Along the way, you'll see a wide range of animation examples, including fading pictures, rotating buttons, and expanding elements.

Understanding WPF Animation

In many user frameworks (particularly ones that predate WPF, such as Windows Forms and MFC), developers need to build their own animation systems from scratch. The most common technique is to use a timer in conjunction with some custom painting logic. WPF is different—it includes a built-in *property-based* animation system. The following two sections describe the difference.

Timer-Based Animation

Imagine you need to make a piece of text spin in the About box of a Windows Forms application. Here's the traditional way you would structure your solution:

1. Create a timer that fires periodically (say, every 50 milliseconds).

2. When the timer fires, use an event handler to calculate some animation-related details, such as the new degree of rotation. Then invalidate part or all of the window.

3. Shortly thereafter, Windows will ask the window to repaint itself, triggering your custom painting code.

4. In your painting code, render the rotated text.

Although this timer-based solution isn't difficult to implement, integrating it into an ordinary application window is more trouble than it's worth. Here are some of the problems:

- *It paints pixels, not controls.* To rotate text in Windows Forms, you need the lower-level GDI+ drawing support. It's easy enough to use, but it doesn't mix well with ordinary window elements, such as buttons, text boxes, labels, and so on. As a result, you need to segregate your animated content from your controls, and you can't incorporate any user-interactive elements into an animation. If you want a rotating button, you're out of luck.

- *It assumes a single animation.* If you decide you want to have two animations running at the same time, you need to rewrite all your animation code—and it could become much more complex. WPF is much more powerful in this regard, allowing you to build more-complex animations out of individual, simpler animations.

- *The animation frame rate is fixed.* It's whatever the timer is set at. And if you change the timer interval, you might need to change your animation code (depending on how your calculations are performed). Furthermore, the fixed frame rate you choose is not necessarily the ideal one for the computer's video hardware.

- *Complex animations require exponentially more complex code.* The spinning text example is easy enough, but moving a small vector drawing along a path is quite a bit more difficult. In WPF, even intricate animations can be defined in XAML (and generated with a third-party design tool).

Timer-based animation still suffers from several flaws: it results in code that isn't very flexible, it becomes messy for complex effects, and it doesn't get the best possible performance.

Property-Based Animation

WPF uses a higher-level model that allows you to focus on *defining* your animations, without worrying about the way they're rendered. This model is based on the dependency property infrastructure. Essentially, a WPF animation is simply a way to modify the value of a dependency property over an interval of time.

For example, to make a button that grows and shrinks, you can modify its Width property in an animation. To make it shimmer, you could change the properties of the LinearGradientBrush that it uses for its background. The secret to creating the right animation is determining what properties you need to modify.

If you want to make other changes that can't be made by modifying a property, you're out of luck. For example, you can't add or remove elements as part of animation. Similarly, you can't ask WPF to perform a transition between a starting scene and an ending scene (although some crafty workarounds can simulate this effect). And finally, you can use animation only with a dependency property, because only dependency properties use the dynamic property-resolution system (described in Chapter 4) that takes animations into account.

At first glance, the property-focused nature of WPF animations seems terribly limiting. However, as you work with WPF, you'll find that it's surprisingly capable. In fact, you can create a wide range of animated effects by using common properties that every element supports.

That said, in many cases the property-based animation system won't work. As a rule of thumb, property-based animation is a great way to add dynamic effects to otherwise ordinary Windows applications. For example, if you want a slick front end for your interactive shopping tool, property-based animations will work perfectly well. However, if you need to use animations as part of the core purpose of your application and you want them to continue running over the lifetime of your application, you probably need something more flexible and more powerful. For example, if you're creating a basic arcade game or using complex physics calculations to model collisions, you'll need greater control over the animation. In these situations, you'll be forced to do most of the work yourself by using WPF's lower-level frame-based rendering support, which is described in Chapter 16.

Basic Animation

You've already learned the first rule of WPF animation—every animation acts on a single dependency property. However, there's another restriction. To animate a property (in other words, change its value in a time-dependent way), you need to have an animation class that supports its data type. For example, the Button.Width property uses the Double data type. To animate it, you use the DoubleAnimation class. However, Button.Padding uses the Thickness structure, so it requires the ThicknessAnimation class.

This requirement isn't as absolute as the first rule of WPF animation, which limits animations to dependency properties. That's because you can animate a dependency property that doesn't have a corresponding animation class by creating your *own* animation class for that data type. However, you'll find that the System.Windows.Media. Animation namespace includes animation classes for most of the data types that you'll want to use.

Many data types don't have a corresponding animation class because it wouldn't be practical. A prime example is enumerations. For example, you can control how an element is placed in a layout panel by using the HorizontalAlignment property, which takes a value from the HorizontalAlignment enumeration. However, the HorizontalAlignment enumeration allows you to choose between only four values (Left, Right, Center, and Stretch), which greatly limits its use in an animation. Although you can swap between one orientation and another, you can't smoothly transition an element from one alignment to another. For that reason, there's no animation class for the HorizontalAlignment data type. You can build one yourself, but you're still constrained by the four values of the enumeration.

Reference types are not usually animated. However, their subproperties are. For example, all content controls sport a Background property that allows you to set a Brush object that's used to paint the background. It's rarely efficient to use animation to switch from one brush to another, but you can use animation to vary the properties of a brush. For example, you could vary the Color property of a SolidColorBrush (using the ColorAnimation class) or the Offset property of a GradientStop in a LinearGradientBrush (using the DoubleAnimation class). This extends the reach of WPF animation, allowing you to animate specific aspects of an element's appearance.

The Animation Classes

Based on the animation types mentioned so far—DoubleAnimation and ColorAnimation—you might assume that all animation classes are named in the form *TypeName*Animation. This is close but not exactly true.

There are actually two types of animations—those that vary a property incrementally between the starting and finishing values (a process called *linear interpolation*) and those that abruptly change a property from one value to another. DoubleAnimation and ColorAnimation are examples of the first category; they use interpolation to smoothly change the value. However, interpolation doesn't make sense when changing certain data types, such as strings and reference type objects. Rather than use interpolation, these data types are changed abruptly at specific times by using a technique called *key-frame animation*. All key-frame animation classes are named in the form *TypeName*AnimationUsingKeyFrames, as in StringAnimationUsingKeyFrames and ObjectAnimationUsingKeyFrames.

Some data types have a key-frame animation class but no interpolation animation class. For example, you can animate a string by using key frames, but you can't animate a string by using interpolation. However, *every* data type supports key-frame animations, unless they have no animation support at all. In other words, every data type that has a normal animation class that uses interpolation (such as DoubleAnimation and ColorAnimation) also has a corresponding animation type for key-frame animation (such as DoubleAnimationUsingKeyFrames and ColorAnimationUsingKeyFrames).

Truthfully, there's still one more type of animation. The third type is called *path-based animation,* and it's much more specialized than animation that uses interpolation or key frames. A path-based animation modifies a value to correspond with the shape that's described by a PathGeometry object, and it's primarily useful for moving an element along a path. The classes for path-based animations have names in the form *TypeName*AnimationUsingPath, such as DoubleAnimationUsingPath and PointAnimationUsingPath.

■ **Note** Although WPF currently uses three approaches to animation (linear interpolation, key frames, and paths), there's no reason you can't create more animation classes that modify values using a completely different approach. The only requirement is that your animation class must modify values in a time-dependent way.

All in all, you'll find the following in the System.Windows.Media.Animation namespace:

- Seventeen *TypeName*Animation classes, which use interpolation
- Twenty-two *TypeName*AnimationUsingKeyFrames classes, which use key-frame animation
- Three *TypeName*AnimationUsingPath classes, which use path-based animation

Every one of these animation classes derives from an abstract *TypeName*AnimationBase class that implements a few fundamentals. This gives you a shortcut to creating your own animation classes. If a data type supports more than one type of animation, both animation classes derive from the abstract animation base class. For example, DoubleAnimation and DoubleAnimationUsingKeyFrames both derive from DoubleAnimationBase.

■ **Note** These 42 classes aren't the only things you'll find in the System.Windows.Media.Animation namespace. Every key-frame animation also works with its own key-frame class and key-frame collection classes, which adds to the clutter. In total, there are more than 100 classes in System.Windows.Media.Animation.

You can quickly determine what data types have native support for animation by reviewing these 42 classes. The following is the complete list:

BooleanAnimationUsingKeyFrames	DoubleAnimationUsingPath
ByteAnimation	Int16Animation
ByteAnimationUsingKeyFrames	Int16AnimationUsingKeyFrames
CharAnimationUsingKeyFrames	Int32Animation
ColorAnimation	Int32AnimationUsingKeyFrames
ColorAnimationUsingKeyFrames	Int64Animation
DecimalAnimation	Int64AnimationUsingKeyFrames
DecimalAnimationUsingKeyFrames	MatrixAnimationUsingKeyFrames
DoubleAnimation	MatrixAnimationUsingPath
DoubleAnimationUsingKeyFrames	ObjectAnimationUsingKeyFrames

PointAnimation

PointAnimationUsingKeyFrames

PointAnimationUsingPath

Point3DAnimation

Point3DAnimationUsingKeyFrames

QuarternionAnimation

QuarternionAnimationUsingKeyFrames

RectAnimation

RectAnimationUsingKeyFrames

Rotation3DAnimation

Rotation3DAnimationUsingKeyFrames

SingleAnimation

SingleAnimationUsingKeyFrames

SizeAnimation

SizeAnimationUsingKeyFrames

StringAnimationUsingKeyFrames

ThicknessAnimation

ThicknessAnimationUsingKeyFrames

VectorAnimation

VectorAnimationUsingKeyFrames

Vector3DAnimation

Vector3DAnimationUsingKeyFrames

Many of these types are self-explanatory. For example, after you master the DoubleAnimation class, you won't think twice about SingleAnimation, Int16Animation, Int32Animation, and all the other animation classes for simple numeric types, which work in the same way. Along with the animation classes for numeric types, you'll find a few that work with other basic data types (byte, bool, string, and char) and many more that deal with two-dimensional and three-dimensional Drawing primitives (Point, Size, Rect, Vector, and so on). You'll also find an animation class for the Margin and Padding properties of any element (ThicknessAnimation), one for color (ColorAnimation), and one for any reference type object (ObjectAnimationUsingKeyFrames). You'll consider many of these animation types as you work through the examples in this chapter.

THE CLUTTERED ANIMATION NAMESPACE

If you look in the System.Windows.Media.Animation namespace, you may be a bit shocked. It's packed full, with different animation classes for different data types. The effect is a bit overwhelming. It would be nice if there were a way to combine all the animation features into a few core classes. And what developer wouldn't appreciate a generic Animate(Of T) that could work with any data type? However, this model isn't currently possible, for a variety of reasons. First, different animation classes may perform their work in slightly different ways, which means the code required will differ. For example, the way a color value is blended from one shade to another by the ColorAnimation class differs from the way a single numeric value is modified by the DoubleAnimation class. In other words, although the animation classes expose the same public interface for you to use, their internal workings may differ. Their interface is standardized through inheritance, because all animation classes derive from the same base classes (beginning with Animatable).

However, this isn't the full story. Certainly, many animation classes *do* share a significant amount of code, and a few areas absolutely cry out for a dash of generics, such as the 100 or so classes used to represent key frames and key-frame collections. In an ideal world, animation classes would be distinguished by the type of animation they perform, so you could use classes such as NumericAnimation(Of T), KeyFrameAnimation(Of T), or LinearInterpolationAnimation(Of T). One can only assume that the deeper reason that prevents solutions like these is that XAML lacks direct support for generics.

Animations in Code

As you've already learned, the most common animation technique is linear interpolation, which modifies a property smoothly from its starting point to its end point. For example, if you set a starting value of 1 and an ending value of 10, your property might be rapidly changed from 1 to 1.1, 1.2, 1.3, and so on, until the value reaches 10.

At this point, you're probably wondering how WPF determines the increments it will use when performing interpolation. Happily, this detail is taken care of automatically. WPF uses whatever increment it needs to ensure a smooth animation at the currently configured frame rate. The standard frame rate WPF uses is 60 frames per second. (You'll learn how to tweak this detail later in this chapter.) In other words, every 1/60th of a second, WPF calculates all animated values and updates the corresponding properties.

The simplest way to use an animation is to instantiate one of the animation classes listed earlier, configure it, and then use the BeginAnimation() method of the element you want to modify. All WPF elements inherit BeginAnimation(), which is part of the IAnimatable interface, from the base UIElement class. Other classes that implement IAnimatable include ContentElement (the base class for bits of document flow content) and Visual3D (the base class for 3D visuals).

■ **Note** Using the BeginAnimation() method isn't the most common approach—it most situations, you'll create animations declaratively by using XAML, as described later in the "Working with Storyboards and Event Triggers" section. However, using XAML is slightly more involved because you need another object—called a *storyboard*—to connect the animation to the appropriate property. Code-based animations are also useful in certain scenarios in which you need to use complex logic to determine the starting and ending values for your animation.

Figure 15-1 shows an extremely simple animation that widens a button. When you click the button, WPF smoothly extends both sides until the button fills the window.

Figure 15-1. *An animated button*

To create this effect, you use an animation that modifies the Width property of the button. Here's the code that creates and launches this animation when the button is clicked:

```
Dim widthAnimation As New DoubleAnimation()
widthAnimation.From = 160
widthAnimation.To = Me.Width - 30
widthAnimation.Duration = TimeSpan.FromSeconds(5)
cmdGrow.BeginAnimation(Button.WidthProperty, widthAnimation)
```

Three details are the bare minimum of any animation that uses linear interpolation: the starting value (From), the ending value (To), and the time that the entire animation should take (Duration). In this example, the ending value is based on the current width of the containing window. These three properties are found in all the animation classes that use interpolation.

The From, To, and Duration properties seem fairly straightforward, but you should note a few important details. The following sections explore these properties more closely.

From

The From value is the starting value for the Width property. If you click the button multiple times, each time you click it the Width is reset to 160, and the animation runs again. This is true even if you click the button while an animation is already underway.

▪ **Note** This example exposes another detail about WPF animations; namely, every dependency property can be acted on by only one animation at a time. If you start a second animation, the first one is automatically discarded.

In many situations, you don't want an animation to begin at the original From value. There are two common reasons:

- *You have an animation that can be triggered multiple times in a row for a cumulative effect.* For example, you might want to create a button that grows a bit more each time it's clicked.

- *You have animations that may overlap.* For example, you might use the MouseEnter event to trigger an animation that expands a button, and the MouseLeave event to trigger a complementary animation that shrinks it back. (This is often known as a *fish-eye effect.*) If you move the mouse over and off this sort of button several times in quick succession, each new animation will interrupt the previous one, causing the button to "jump" back to the size that's set by the From property.

The current example falls into the second category. If you click the button while it's already growing, the width is reset to 160 pixels—which can be a bit jarring. To correct the problem, just leave out the code statement that sets the From property:

```
Dim widthAnimation As New DoubleAnimation()
widthAnimation.To = Me.Width - 30
widthAnimation.Duration = TimeSpan.FromSeconds(5)
cmdGrow.BeginAnimation(Button.WidthProperty, widthAnimation)
```

There's one catch. For this technique to work, the property you're animating must have a previously set value. In this example, that means the button must have a hard-coded width (whether it's defined directly in the button tag or applied through a style setter). The problem is that in many layout containers, it's common not to specify a width and to allow the container to control it based on the element's alignment properties. In this case, the default width applies, which is the special value Double.NaN (where NaN stands for *not a number*). You can't animate a property that has this value by using linear interpolation.

So, what's the solution? In many cases, the answer is to hard-code the button's width. As you'll see, animations often require a more fine-grained control of element sizing and positioning than you'd otherwise use. In fact, the most common layout container for "animatable" content is the Canvas, because it makes it easy to move content around (with possible overlap) and resize it. The Canvas is also the most lightweight layout container, because no extra layout work is needed when a property such as Width is changed.

In the current example, there's another option. You could retrieve the current value of the button by using its ActualWidth property, which indicates the current rendered width. You can't animate ActualWidth (it's read-only), but you can use it to set the From property of your animation:

```
widthAnimation.From = cmdGrow.ActualWidth
```

This technique works for both code-based animations (such as the current example) and the declarative animations you'll see later (which require the use of a binding expression to get the ActualWidth value).

■ **Note**   It's important to use the ActualWidth property in this example rather than the Width property. That's because Width reflects the desired width that you choose, while ActualWidth indicates the rendered width that was used. If you're using automatic layout, you probably won't set a hard-coded Width at all, so the Width property will simply return Double. NaN, and an exception will be raised when you attempt to start the animation.

You need to be aware of another issue when you use the current value as a starting point for an animation—it may change the speed of your animation. That's because the duration isn't adjusted to take into account that there's a smaller spread between the initial value and the final value. For example, imagine that you create a button that doesn't use the From value and instead animates from its current position. If you click the button when it has almost reached its maximum width, a new animation begins. This animation is configured to take 5 seconds (through the Duration property), even though there are only a few more pixels to go. As a result, the growth of the button will appear to slow down.

This effect appears only when you restart an animation that's almost complete. Although it's a bit odd, most developers don't bother trying to code around it. Instead, it's considered to be an acceptable quirk.

■ **Note**   You could compensate for this problem by writing some custom logic that modifies the animation duration, but it's seldom worth the effort. To do so, you'd need to make assumptions about the standard size of the button (which limits the reusability of your code), and you'd need to create your animations programmatically so that you could run this code (rather than declaratively, which is the more common approach you'll see a bit later).

To

Just as you can omit the From property, you can omit the To property. In fact, you could leave out both the From and To properties to create an animation like this:

```
Dim widthAnimation As New DoubleAnimation()
widthAnimation.Duration = TimeSpan.FromSeconds(5)
cmdGrow.BeginAnimation(Button.WidthProperty, widthAnimation)
```

At first glance, this animation seems like a long-winded way to do nothing at all. It's logical to assume that because both the To and From properties are left out, they'll both use the same value. But there's a subtle and important difference.

When you leave out From, the animation uses the current value and takes animation into account. For example, if the button is midway through a grow operation, the From value uses the expanded width. However, when you leave out To, the animation uses the current value *without taking animation into account.* Essentially, that means the To value becomes the *original* value—whatever you last set in code, on the element tag, or through a style. (This works thanks to WPF's property-resolution system, which is able to calculate a value for a property based on several overlapping property providers, without discarding any information. Chapter 4 describes this system in more detail.)

In the button example, that means if you start a grow animation and then interrupt it with the animation shown previously (perhaps by clicking another button), the button will shrink from its half-grown size until it reaches the original width that's set in the XAML markup. On the other hand, if you run this code while no other animation is underway, nothing will happen. That's because the From value (the animated width) and the To value (the original width) are the same.

By

Instead of using To, you can use the By property. The By property is used to create an animation that changes a value *by* a set amount, rather than *to* a specific target. For example, you could create an animation that enlarges a button by 10 units more than its current size, as shown here:

```
Dim widthAnimation As New DoubleAnimation()
widthAnimation.By = 10
widthAnimation.Duration = TimeSpan.FromSeconds(0.5)
cmdGrowIncrementally.BeginAnimation(Button.WidthProperty, widthAnimation)
```

This approach isn't necessary in the button example, because you could achieve the same result by using a simple calculation to set the To property, like this:

```
widthAnimation.To = cmdGrowIncrementally.Width + 10
```

However, the By value makes more sense when you're defining your animation in XAML, because XAML doesn't provide a way to perform simple calculations.

■ **Note**   You can use By and From in combination, but it doesn't save you any work. The By value is simply added to the From value to arrive at the To value.

The By property is offered by most, but not all, animation classes that use interpolation. For example, it doesn't make sense with non-numeric data types, such as a Color structure (as used by ColorAnimation).

There's one other way to get similar behavior without using the By property—you can create an *additive* animation by setting the IsAdditive property. When you do, the current value is added to both the From and To values automatically. For example, consider this animation:

```
Dim widthAnimation As New DoubleAnimation()
widthAnimation.From = 0
widthAnimation.To = -10
widthAnimation.Duration = TimeSpan.FromSeconds(0.5)
widthAnimation.IsAdditive = True
```

It starts from the current value and finishes at a value that's reduced by 10 units. On the other hand, if you use this animation:

```
Dim widthAnimation As New DoubleAnimation()
widthAnimation.From = 10
widthAnimation.To = 50
widthAnimation.Duration = TimeSpan.FromSeconds(0.5)
widthAnimation.IsAdditive = True
```

the property jumps to the new value (which is 10 units greater than the current value) and then increases until it reaches a final value that is 50 units more than the current value before the animation began.

Duration

The Duration property is straightforward enough—it takes the time interval (in milliseconds, minutes, hours, or whatever else you'd like to use) between the time the animation starts and the time it ends. Although the duration of the animations in the previous examples is set by using a TimeSpan, the Duration property actually requires a Duration object. Fortunately, Duration and TimeSpan are quite similar, and the Duration structure defines an implicit cast that can convert System.TimeSpan to System.Windows.Duration as needed. That's why this line of code is perfectly reasonable:

```
widthAnimation.Duration = TimeSpan.FromSeconds(5)
```

So, why bother introducing a whole new type? The Duration also includes two special values that can't be represented by a TimeSpan object—Duration.Automatic and Duration.Forever. Neither of these values is useful in the current example. (Automatic simply sets the animation to a 1-second duration, and Forever makes the animation infinite in length, which prevents it from having any effect.) However, these values become useful when creating more-complex animations.

Simultaneous Animations

You can use BeginAnimation() to launch more than one animation at a time. The BeginAnimation() method returns almost immediately, allowing you to use code like this to animate two properties simultaneously:

```
Dim widthAnimation As New DoubleAnimation()
widthAnimation.From = 160
widthAnimation.To = Me.Width - 30
widthAnimation.Duration = TimeSpan.FromSeconds(5)

Dim heightAnimation As New DoubleAnimation()
heightAnimation.From = 40
heightAnimation.To = Me.Height - 50
heightAnimation.Duration = TimeSpan.FromSeconds(5)

cmdGrow.BeginAnimation(Button.WidthProperty, widthAnimation)
cmdGrow.BeginAnimation(Button.HeightProperty, heightAnimation)
```

In this example, the two animations are not synchronized. That means the width and height won't grow at exactly the same intervals. (Typically, you'll see the button grow wider and then grow taller just after.) You can overcome this limitation by creating animations that are bound to the same timeline. You'll learn this technique later in this chapter, when you consider storyboards.

Animation Lifetime

Technically, WPF animations are *temporary*, which means they don't change the value of the underlying property. While an animation is active, it simply overrides the property value. This is because of the way that dependency properties work (as described in Chapter 4), and it's an often overlooked detail that can cause significant confusion.

A one-way animation (such as the button-growing animation) remains active after it finishes running. That's because the animation needs to hold the button's width at the new size. This can lead to an unusual problem—namely, if you try to modify the value of the property by using code after the animation has completed, your code will appear to have no effect. That's because your code simply assigns a new local value to the property, but the animated value still takes precedence.

You can solve this problem in several ways, depending on what you're trying to accomplish:

- Create an animation that resets your element to its original state. You do this by not setting the To property. For example, the button-shrinking animation reduces the width of the button to its last set size, after which you can change it in your code.

- Create a reversible animation. You do this by setting the AutoReverse property to True. For example, when the button-growing animation finishes widening the button, it will play out the animation in reverse, returning it to its original width. The total duration of your animation will be doubled.

- Change the FillBehavior property. Ordinarily, FillBehavior is set to HoldEnd, which means that when an animation ends, it continues to apply its final value to the target property. If you change FillBehavior to Stop, as soon as the animation ends, the property reverts to its original value.

- Remove the animation object when the animation is complete by handling the Completed event of the animation object.

The first three options change the behavior of your animation. One way or another, they return the animated property to its original value. If this isn't what you want, you need to use the last option.

First, before you launch the animation, attach an event handler that reacts when the animation finishes:

```
AddHandler widthAnimation.Completed, AddressOf animation_Completed
```

■ **Note** The Completed event is a normal .NET event that takes an ordinary EventArgs object with no additional information. It's not a routed event.

When the Completed event fires, you can render the animation inactive by calling the BeginAnimation() method. You simply need to specify the property and pass in a null reference (Nothing) for the animation object:

```
cmdGrow.BeginAnimation(Button.WidthProperty, Nothing)
```

When you call BeginAnimation(), the property returns to the value it had before the animation started. If this isn't what you want, you can take note of the current value that's being applied by the animation, remove the animation, and then manually set the new property, like so:

```
Dim currentWidth As Double = cmdGrow.Width
cmdGrow.BeginAnimation(Button.WidthProperty, Nothing)
cmdGrow.Width = currentWidth
```

Keep in mind that this changes the local value of the property. That may affect how other animations work. For example, if you animate this button with an animation that doesn't specify the From property, it uses this newly applied value as a starting point. In most cases, this is the behavior you want.

The Timeline Class

As you've seen, every animation revolves around a few key properties. You've seen several of these properties: From and To (which are provided in animation classes that use interpolation) and Duration and FillBehavior (which are provided in all animation classes). Before going any further, it's worth taking a closer look at the properties you have to work with.

Figure 15-2 shows the inheritance hierarchy of the WPF animation types. It includes all the base classes, but it leaves out the full 42 animation types (and the corresponding *TypeName*AnimationBase classes).

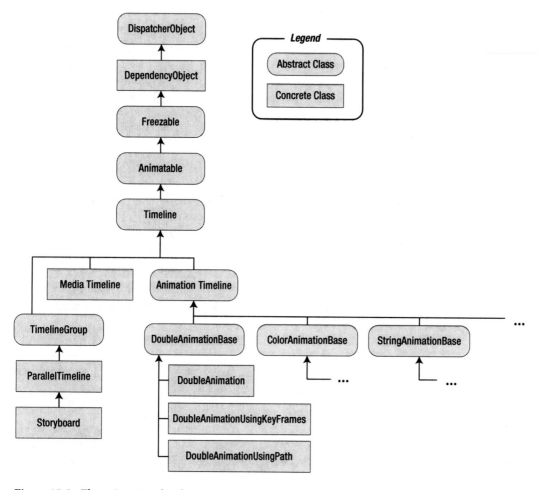

Figure 15-2. *The animation class hierarchy*

The class hierarchy includes three main branches that derive from the abstract Timeline class. MediaTimeline is used when playing audio or video files—it's described in Chapter 26. AnimationTimeline is used for the property-based animation system you've considered so far. And TimelineGroup allows you to synchronize timelines and control their playback. It's described later in this chapter in the "Synchronized Animations" section, when you tackle storyboards.

The first useful members appear in the Timeline class, which defines the Duration property you've already considered and a few more. Table 15-1 lists its properties.

Table 15-1. *Timeline Properties*

Name	Description
BeginTime	Sets a delay that will be added before the animation starts (as a TimeSpan). This delay is added to the total time, so a 5-second animation with a 5-second delay takes 10 seconds. BeginTime is useful when synchronizing different animations that start at the same time but should apply their effects in sequence.
Duration	Sets the length of time the animation runs, from start to finish, as a Duration object.
SpeedRatio	Increases or decreases the speed of the animation. Ordinarily, SpeedRatio is 1. If you increase it, the animation completes more quickly (for example, a SpeedRatio of 5 completes five times faster). If you decrease it, the animation is slowed down (for example, a SpeedRatio of 0.5 takes twice as long). You can change the Duration of your animation for an equivalent result. The SpeedRatio is not taken into account when applying the BeginTime delay.
AccelerationRatio and DecelerationRatio	Makes an animation nonlinear, so it starts off slow and then speeds up (by increasing the AccelerationRatio) or slows down at the end (by increasing the DecelerationRatio). Both values are set from 0 to 1 and begin at 0. Furthermore, the total of both values cannot exceed 1.
AutoReverse	If True, the animation will play out in reverse after it's complete, reverting to the original value. This also doubles the time the animation takes. If you've increased the SpeedRatio, it applies to both the initial playback of the animation and the reversal. The BeginTime applies only to the very beginning of the animation—it doesn't delay the reversal.
FillBehavior	Determines what happens when the animation ends. Usually, it keeps the property fixed at the ending value (FillBehavior.HoldEnd), but you can also choose to return it to its original value (FillBehavior.Stop).
RepeatBehavior	Allows you to repeat an animation a specific number of times or for a specific time interval. The RepeatBehavior object that you use to set this property determines the exact behavior.

Although BeginTime, Duration, SpeedRatio, and AutoReverse are all fairly straightforward, some of the other properties warrant closer examination. The following sections delve into AccelerationRatio, DecelerationRatio, and RepeatBehavior.

AccelerationRatio and DecelerationRatio

AccelerationRatio and DecelerationRatio allow you to compress part of the timeline so it passes by more quickly. The rest of the timeline is stretched to compensate so that the total time is unchanged.

Both of these properties represent a percentage value. For example, an AccelerationRatio of 0.3 indicates that you want to spend the first 30 percent of the duration of the animation accelerating. For example, in a 10-second animation, the first 3 seconds would be taken up with acceleration, and the remaining 7 seconds would pass at a consistent speed. (Obviously, the speed in the last 7 seconds is faster than the speed of a nonaccelerated animation, because the animation needs to make up for the slow start.) If you set AccelerationRatio to 0.3 and DecelerationRatio to 0.3, acceleration takes place for the first 3 seconds, the middle 4 seconds are at a fixed maximum speed, and deceleration takes place for the last 3 seconds. Viewed this way, it's obvious that the total of AccelerationRatio and DecelerationRatio can't top 1, because that would require more than 100 percent of the available time to perform the

401

requested acceleration and deceleration. Of course, you could set AccelerationRatio to 1 (in which case the animation speeds up from start to finish) or DecelerationRatio to 1 (in which case the animation slows down from start to finish).

Animations that accelerate and decelerate are often used to give a more natural appearance. However, AccelerationRatio and DecelerationRatio give you only relatively crude control. For example, they don't let you vary the acceleration or set it specifically. If you want to have an animation that uses varying degrees of acceleration, you'll need to define a series of animations, one after the other, and set the AccelerationRatio and DecelerationRatio property of each one, or you'll need to use a key-frame animation with key spline frames (as described in Chapter 16). Although this technique gives you plenty of flexibility, keeping track of all the details is a headache, and it's a perfect case for using a design tool to construct your animations.

RepeatBehavior

The RepeatBehavior property allows you to control how an animation is repeated. If you want to repeat it a fixed number of times, pass the appropriate number of times to the RepeatBehavior constructor. For example, this animation repeats twice:

```
Dim widthAnimation As New DoubleAnimation()
widthAnimation.To = Me.Width - 30
widthAnimation.Duration = TimeSpan.FromSeconds(5)
widthAnimation.RepeatBehavior = New RepeatBehavior(2)
cmdGrow.BeginAnimation(Button.WidthProperty, widthAnimation)
```

When you run this animation, the button will increase in size (over 5 seconds), jump back to its original value, and then increase in size again (over 5 seconds), ending at the full width of the window. If you've set AutoReverse to True, the behavior is slightly different—the entire animation is completed forward and backward (meaning the button expands and then shrinks), and *then* it's repeated again.

■ **Note**   Animations that use interpolation provide an IsCumulative property, which tells WPF how to deal with each repetition. If IsCumulative is True, the animation isn't repeated from start to finish. Instead, each subsequent animation adds to the previous one. For example, if you use IsCumulative with the animation shown earlier, the button will expand twice as wide over twice as much time. To put it another way, the first iteration is treated normally, but every repetition after that is treated as though you set IsAdditive to True.

Rather than using RepeatBehavior to set a repeat count, you can use it to set a repeat *interval*. To do so, simply pass a TimeSpan to the RepeatBehavior constructor. For example, the following animation repeats itself for 13 seconds:

```
Dim widthAnimation As New DoubleAnimation()
widthAnimation.To = Me.Width - 30
widthAnimation.Duration = TimeSpan.FromSeconds(5)
widthAnimation.RepeatBehavior = New RepeatBehavior(TimeSpan.FromSeconds(13))
cmdGrow.BeginAnimation(Button.WidthProperty, widthAnimation)
```

In this example, the Duration property specifies that the entire animation takes 5 seconds. As a result, the RepeatBehavior of 13 seconds will trigger two repeats and then leave the button halfway through a third repeat (at the 3-second mark).

■ **Tip** You can use RepeatBehavior to perform just part of an animation. To do so, use a fractional number of repetitions, or use a TimeSpan that's less than the duration.

Finally, you can cause an animation to repeat itself endlessly with the RepeatBehavior.Forever value:

```
widthAnimation.RepeatBehavior = RepeatBehavior.Forever
```

Storyboards

As you've seen, WPF animations are represented by a group of animation classes. You set the relevant information, such as the starting value, ending value, and duration, using a handful of properties. This obviously makes them a great fit for XAML. What's less clear is how you wire an animation up to a particular element and property and how you trigger it at the right time.

It turns out that two ingredients are at work in any declarative animation:

A storyboard: It's the XAML equivalent of the BeginAnimation() method. It allows you to direct an animation to the right element and property.

An event trigger: It responds to a property change or event (such as the Click event of a button) and controls the storyboard. For example, to start an animation, the event trigger must *begin* the storyboard.

You'll learn how both pieces work in the following sections.

The Storyboard

A storyboard is an enhanced timeline. You can use it to group multiple animations as well as to control the playback of animation—pausing it, stopping it, and changing its position. However, the most basic feature provided by the Storyboard class is its ability to point to a specific property and specific element by using the TargetProperty and TargetName properties. In other words, the storyboard bridges the gap between your animation and the property you want to animate.

Here's how you might define a storyboard that manages a DoubleAnimation:

```
<Storyboard TargetName="cmdGrow" TargetProperty="Width">
  <DoubleAnimation From="160" To="300" Duration="0:0:5"></DoubleAnimation>
</Storyboard>
```

Both TargetName and TargetProperty are attached properties. That means you can apply them directly to the animation, as shown here:

```
<Storyboard>
  <DoubleAnimation
    Storyboard.TargetName="cmdGrow" Storyboard.TargetProperty="Width"
    From="160" To="300" Duration="0:0:5"></DoubleAnimation>
</Storyboard>
```

This syntax is more common, because it allows you to put several animations in the same storyboard but allow each animation to act on a different element and property.

Defining a storyboard is the first step to creating an animation. To actually put this storyboard into action, you need an event trigger.

Event Triggers

You first learned about event triggers in Chapter 11, when you considered styles. Styles give you one way to attach an event trigger to an element. However, you can define an event trigger in four places:

- In a style (the Styles.Triggers collection)

- In a data template (the DataTemplate.Triggers collection)

- In a control template (the ControlTemplate.Triggers collection)

- In an element directly (the FrameworkElement.Triggers collection)

When creating an event trigger, you need to indicate the routed event that starts the trigger and the action (or actions) that are performed by the trigger. With animations, the most common action is BeginStoryboard, which is equivalent to calling BeginAnimation().

The following example uses the Triggers collection of a button to attach an animation to the Click event. When the button is clicked, it grows.

```
<Button Padding="10" Name="cmdGrow" Height="40" Width="160"
 HorizontalAlignment="Center" VerticalAlignment="Center">
  <Button.Triggers>
    <EventTrigger RoutedEvent="Button.Click">
      <EventTrigger.Actions>
        <BeginStoryboard>
          <Storyboard>
            <DoubleAnimation Storyboard.TargetProperty="Width"
              To="300" Duration="0:0:5"></DoubleAnimation>
          </Storyboard>
        </BeginStoryboard>
      </EventTrigger.Actions>
    </EventTrigger>
  </Button.Triggers>

  <Button.Content>
    Click and Make Me Grow
  </Button.Content>
</Button>
```

■ **Tip**   To create an animation that fires when the window first loads, add an event trigger in the Window.Triggers collection that responds to the Window.Loaded event.

The Storyboard.TargetProperty property identifies the property you want to change (in this case, Width). If you don't supply a class name, the storyboard uses the parent element, which is the button you want to expand. If you want to set an attached property (for example, Canvas.Left or Canvas.Top), you need to wrap the entire property in brackets, like this:

```
<DoubleAnimation Storyboard.TargetProperty="(Canvas.Left)" ... />
```

The Storyboard.TargetName property isn't required in this example. When you leave it out, the storyboard uses the parent element, which is the button.

■ **Note** All an event trigger is able to do is launch *actions*. All actions are represented by classes that derive from System.Windows.TriggerAction. Currently, WPF includes a very small set of actions that are designed for interacting with a storyboard and controlling media playback.

There's one difference between the declarative approach shown here and the code-only approach demonstrated earlier. Namely, the To value is hard-coded at 300 units, rather than set relative to the size of the containing window. If you wanted to use the window width, you'd need to use a data-binding expression, like so:

```
<DoubleAnimation Storyboard.TargetProperty="Width"
 To="{Binding ElementName=window,Path=Width}" Duration="0:0:5">
</DoubleAnimation>
```

This still doesn't produce exactly the result you need. Here, the button grows from its current size to the full width of the window. The code-only approach enlarges the button to 30 units less than the full size, using a trivial calculation. Unfortunately, XAML doesn't support inline calculations. One solution is to build an IValueConverter that does the work for you. Fortunately, this odd trick is easy to implement (and many developers have). You can find one example in the downloadable examples for this chapter.

■ **Note** Another option is to create a custom dependency property in your window class that performs the calculation. You can then bind your animation to the custom dependency property. For more information about creating dependency properties, see Chapter 4.

You can now duplicate all the examples you've seen so far by creating triggers and storyboards and setting the appropriate properties of the DoubleAnimation object.

Attaching Triggers with a Style

The FrameworkElement.Triggers collection is a bit of an oddity. It supports only event triggers. The other trigger collections (Styles.Triggers, DataTemplate.Triggers, and ControlTemplate.Triggers) are more capable. They support the three basic types of WPF triggers: property triggers, data triggers, and event triggers.

■ **Note** There's no technical reason why the FrameworkElement.Triggers collection shouldn't support additional trigger types, but this functionality wasn't implemented in time for the first version of WPF.

Using an event trigger is the most common way to attach an animation. However, it's not your only option. If you're using the Triggers collection in a style, data template, or control template, you can also create a property trigger that reacts when a property value changes. For example, here's a style that duplicates the example shown earlier. It triggers a storyboard when IsPressed is True:

```
<Window.Resources>
  <Style x:Key="GrowButtonStyle">
    <Style.Triggers>
      <Trigger Property="Button.IsPressed" Value="True">
```

```
      <Trigger.EnterActions>
        <BeginStoryboard>
          <Storyboard>
            <DoubleAnimation Storyboard.TargetProperty="Width"
              To="250" Duration="0:0:5"></DoubleAnimation>
          </Storyboard>
        </BeginStoryboard>
      </Trigger.EnterActions>
    </Trigger>
  </Style.Triggers>
</Style>
</Window.Resources>
```

You can attach actions to a property trigger in two ways. You can use Trigger.EnterActions to set actions that will be performed when the property changes to the value you specify (in the previous example, when IsPressed becomes True) and use Trigger.ExitActions to set actions that will be performed when the property changes back (when the value of IsPressed returns False false). This is a handy way to wrap together a pair of complementary animations.

Here's the button that uses the style shown earlier:

```
<Button Padding="10" Name="cmdGrow" Height="40" Width="160"
 Style="{StaticResource GrowButtonStyle}"
 HorizontalAlignment="Center" VerticalAlignment="Center">
 Click and Make Me Grow
</Button>
```

Remember, you don't need to use property triggers in a style. You can also use event triggers, as you saw in the previous section. Finally, you don't need to define a style separately from the button that uses it (you can set the Button.Style property with an inline style), but this two-part separation is more common, and it gives you the flexibility to apply the same animation to multiple elements.

■ **Note**   Triggers are also handy when you fuse them into a control template, which allows you to add visual pizzazz to a standard WPF control. Chapter 17 shows numerous examples of control templates that use animations, including a ListBox that animates its child items with triggers.

Overlapping Animations

The storyboard gives you the ability to change the way you deal with animations that overlap—in other words, when a second animation is applied to a property that is already being animated. You do this using the BeginStoryboard. HandoffBehavior property.

Ordinarily, when two animations overlap, the second animation overrides the first one immediately. This behavior is known as *snapshot-and-replace* (and represented by the SnapshotAndReplace value in the HandoffBehavior enumeration). When the second animation starts, it takes a snapshot of the property as it currently is (based on the first animation), stops the animation, and replaces it with the new animation.

The only other HandoffBehavior option is Compose, which fused the second animation into the first animation's timeline. For example, consider a revised version of the ListBox example that uses HandoffBehavior.Compose when shrinking the button:

```
<EventTrigger RoutedEvent="ListBoxItem.MouseLeave">
  <EventTrigger.Actions>
    <BeginStoryboard HandoffBehavior="Compose">
      <Storyboard>
        <DoubleAnimation Storyboard.TargetProperty="FontSize"
         BeginTime="0:0:0.5" Duration="0:0:0.2"></DoubleAnimation>
      </Storyboard>
    </BeginStoryboard>
  </EventTrigger.Actions>
</EventTrigger>
```

Now, if you move the mouse onto a ListBoxItem and off it, you'll see a different behavior. When you move the mouse off the item, it will continue expanding, which will be clearly visible until the second animation reaches its begin time delay of 0.5 seconds. Then, the second animation will shrink the button. Without the Compose behavior, the button would simply wait, fixed at its current size, for the 0.5-second time interval before the second animation kicks in.

Using a HandoffBehavior of compose requires more overhead. That's because the clock that's used to run the original animation won't be released when the second animation starts. Instead, it will stay alive until the ListBoxItem is garbage collected or a new animation is used on the same property.

■ **Tip**   If performance becomes an issue, the WPF team recommends that you manually release the animation clock for your animations as soon as they are complete (rather than waiting for the garbage collector to find them). To do this, you need to handle an event such as Storyboard.Completed. Then, call BeginAnimation() on the element that has just finished its animation, supplying the appropriate property and a null reference (Nothing) in place of an animation.

Synchronized Animations

The Storyboard class derives indirectly from TimelineGroup, which gives it the ability to hold more than one animation. Best of all, these animations are managed as one group—meaning they're started at the same time.

To see an example, consider the following storyboard. It starts two animations, one that acts on the Width property of a button and the other that acts on the Height property. Because the animations are grouped into one storyboard, they increment the button's dimensions in unison, which gives a more synchronized effect than simply calling BeginAnimation() multiple times in your code.

```
<EventTrigger RoutedEvent="Button.Click">
  <EventTrigger.Actions>
    <BeginStoryboard>
      <Storyboard>
        <DoubleAnimation Storyboard.TargetProperty="Width"
         To="300" Duration="0:0:5"></DoubleAnimation>
        <DoubleAnimation Storyboard.TargetProperty="Height"
         To="300" Duration="0:0:5"></DoubleAnimation>
      </Storyboard>
    </BeginStoryboard>
  </EventTrigger.Actions>
</EventTrigger>
```

In this example, both animations have the same duration, but this isn't a requirement. The only consideration with animations that end at different times is their FillBehavior. If an animation's FillBehavior property is set to HoldEnd, it holds the value until all the animations in the storyboard are completed. If the storyboard's FillBehavior property is HoldEnd, the final animated values are held indefinitely (until a new animation replaces this one or until you manually remove the animation).

It's at this point that the Timeline properties you learned about in Table 15-1 start to become particularly useful. For example, you can use SpeedRatio to make one animation in a storyboard run faster than the other. Or you can use BeginTime to offset one animation relative to another so that it starts at a specific point.

■ **Note**   Because Storyboard derives from Timeline, you can use all the properties that were described in Table 15-1 to configure its speed, use acceleration or deceleration, introduce a delay time, and so on. These properties will affect all the contained animations, and they're cumulative. For example, if you set the Storyboard.SpeedRatio to 2 and the DoubleAnimation.SpeedRatio to 2, that animation will run four times faster than usual.

Controlling Playback

So far, you've been using one action in your event triggers—the BeginStoryboard action that launches an animation. However, you can use several other actions to control a storyboard after it's created. These actions, which derive from the ControllableStoryboardAction class, are listed in Table 15-2.

Table 15-2. *Action Classes for Controlling a Storyboard*

Name	Description
PauseStoryboard	Stops playback of an animation and keeps it at the current position.
ResumeStoryboard	Resumes playback of a paused animation.
StopStoryboard	Stops playback of an animation and resets the animation clock to the beginning.
SeekStoryboard	Jumps to a specific position in an animation's timeline. If animation is currently playing, it continues playback from the new position. If the animation is currently paused, it remains paused.
SetStoryboardSpeedRatio	Changes the SpeedRatio of the entire storyboard (rather than just one animation inside).
SkipStoryboardToFill	Moves the storyboard to the end of its timeline. Technically, this period is known as the *fill region*. For a standard animation, with FillBehavior set to HoldEnd, the animation continues to hold the final value.
RemoveStoryboard	Removes a storyboard, halting any in-progress animation and returning the property to its original, last-set value. This has the same effect as calling BeginAnimation() on the appropriate element with a null animation object.

■ **Note** Stopping an animation is not equivalent to completing an animation (unless FillBehavior is set to Stop). That's because even when an animation reaches the end of its timeline, it continues to apply its final value. Similarly, when an animation is paused, it continues to apply the most recent intermediary value. However, when an animation is stopped, it no longer applies any value, and the property reverts to its preanimation value.

There's an undocumented stumbling block to using these actions. For them to work successfully, you must define all the triggers in one Triggers collection. If you place the BeginStoryboard action in a different trigger collection than the PauseStoryboard action, the PauseStoryboard action won't work. To see the design you need to use, it helps to consider an example.

Consider the window shown in Figure 15-3. It superimposes two Image elements in exactly the same position, using a grid. Initially, only the topmost image—a day scene of a Toronto city landmark—is visible. But as the animation runs, the opacity is reduced from 1 to 0, eventually allowing the night scene to show through completely. The effect is as if the image is changing from day to night, like a sequence of time-lapse photography.

Figure 15-3. *A controllable animation*

Here's the markup that defines the Grid with its two images:

```
<Grid>
  <Image Source="night.jpg"></Image>
  <Image Source="day.jpg" Name="imgDay"></Image>
</Grid>
```

and here's the animation that fades from one to the other:

```
<DoubleAnimation
  Storyboard.TargetName="imgDay" Storyboard.TargetProperty="Opacity"
  From="1" To="0" Duration="0:0:10">
</DoubleAnimation>
```

To make this example more interesting, it includes several buttons at the bottom that allow you to control the playback of this animation. Using these buttons, you can perform the typical media player actions, such as pausing, resuming, and stopping. (You could add other buttons to change the speed ratio and seek out specific times.)

Here's the markup that defines these buttons:

```
<StackPanel Orientation="Horizontal" HorizontalAlignment="Center" Margin="5">
  <Button Name="cmdStart">Start</Button>
  <Button Name="cmdPause">Pause</Button>
  <Button Name="cmdResume">Resume</Button>
  <Button Name="cmdStop">Stop</Button>
  <Button Name="cmdMiddle">Move To Middle</Button>
</StackPanel>
```

Ordinarily, you might choose to place the event trigger in the Triggers collection of each individual button. However, as explained earlier, that doesn't work for animations. The easiest solution is to define all the event triggers in one place, such as the Triggers collection of a containing element, and wire them up using the EventTrigger. SourceName property. As long as the SourceName matches the Name property you've given the button, the trigger will be applied to the appropriate button.

In this example, you could use the Triggers collection of the StackPanel that holds the buttons. However, it's often easier to use the Triggers collection of the top-level element, which is the window in this case. That way, you can move your buttons to different places in your user interface without disabling their functionality.

```
<Window.Triggers>
  <EventTrigger SourceName="cmdStart" RoutedEvent="Button.Click">
    <BeginStoryboard Name="fadeStoryboardBegin">
      <Storyboard>
        <DoubleAnimation
          Storyboard.TargetName="imgDay" Storyboard.TargetProperty="Opacity"
          From="1" To="0" Duration="0:0:10">
        </DoubleAnimation>
      </Storyboard>
    </BeginStoryboard>
  </EventTrigger>

  <EventTrigger SourceName="cmdPause" RoutedEvent="Button.Click">
    <PauseStoryboard BeginStoryboardName="fadeStoryboardBegin"></PauseStoryboard>
  </EventTrigger>
  <EventTrigger SourceName="cmdResume" RoutedEvent="Button.Click">
    <ResumeStoryboard BeginStoryboardName="fadeStoryboardBegin"></ResumeStoryboard>
  </EventTrigger>
  <EventTrigger SourceName="cmdStop" RoutedEvent="Button.Click">
    <StopStoryboard BeginStoryboardName="fadeStoryboardBegin"></StopStoryboard>
```

```
    </EventTrigger>
    <EventTrigger SourceName="cmdMiddle" RoutedEvent="Button.Click">
      <SeekStoryboard BeginStoryboardName="fadeStoryboardBegin"
      Offset="0:0:5"></SeekStoryboard>
    </EventTrigger>
</Window.Triggers>
```

Notice that you must give a name to the BeginStoryboard action. (In this example, it's fadeStoryboardBegin). The other triggers specify this name in the BeginStoryboardName property to link up to the same storyboard.

You'll encounter one limitation when using storyboard actions. The properties they provide (such as SeekStoryboard.Offset and SetStoryboardSpeedRatio.SpeedRatio) are not dependency properties. That limits your ability to use data-binding expressions. For example, you can't automatically read the Slider.Value property and apply it to the SetStoryboardSpeedRatio.SpeedRatio action, because the SpeedRatio property doesn't accept a data-binding expression. You might think you could code around this problem by using the SpeedRatio property of the Storyboard object, but this won't work. When the animation starts, the SpeedRatio value is read and used to create an animation clock. If you change it after that point, the animation continues at its normal pace.

If you want to adjust the speed or position dynamically, the only solution is to use code. The Storyboard class exposes methods that provide the same functionality as the triggers described in Table 15-2, including Begin(), Pause(), Resume(), Seek(), Stop(), SkipToFill(), SetSpeedRatio(), and Remove().

To access the Storyboard object, you need to make sure you set its Name property in the markup:

```
<Storyboard Name="fadeStoryboard">
```

■ **Note** Don't confuse the name of the Storyboard object (which is required to use the storyboard in your code) with the name of the BeginStoryboard action (which is required to wire up other trigger actions that manipulate the storyboard). To prevent confusion, you may want to adopt a convention such as adding the word *Begin* to the end of the BeginStoryboard name.

Now you simply need to write the appropriate event handler and use the methods of the Storyboard object. (Remember, simply changing storyboard properties such as SpeedRatio won't have any effect. They simply configure the settings that will be used when the animation starts.)

Here's an event handler that reacts when you drag the thumb on a Slider. The code then takes the value of the slider (which ranges from 0 to 3) and uses it to apply a new speed ratio:

```
Private Sub sldSpeed_ValueChanged(ByVal sender As Object, _
  ByVal e As RoutedEventArgs)
    fadeStoryboard.SetSpeedRatio(Me, sldSpeed.Value)
End Sub
```

Notice that the SetSpeedRatio() requires two arguments. The first argument is the top-level animation container (in this case, the current window). All the storyboard methods require this reference. The second argument is the new speed ratio.

THE WIPE EFFECT

The previous example provides a gradual transition between the two images you're using by varying the Opacity of the topmost image. Another common way to transition between images is to perform a "wipe" that unveils the new image on top of the existing one.

The trick to using this technique is to create an opacity mask for the topmost image. Here's an example:

```
<Image Source="day.jpg" Name="imgDay">
  <Image.OpacityMask>
    <LinearGradientBrush StartPoint="0,0" EndPoint="1,0">
      <GradientStop Offset="0" Color="Transparent" x:Name="transparentStop" />
      <GradientStop Offset="0" Color="Black" x:Name="visibleStop" />
    </LinearGradientBrush>
  </Image.OpacityMask>
</Image>
```

This opacity mask uses a gradient that defines two gradient stops, Black (where the image will be completely visible) and Transparent (where the image will be completely transparent). Initially, both stops are positioned at the left edge of the image. Because the visible stop is declared last, it takes precedence, and the image will be completely opaque. Notice that both stops are named so they can be easily accessed by your animation.

Next, you need to perform your animation on the offsets of the LinearGradientBrush. In this example, both offsets are moved from the left side to the right side, allowing the image underneath to appear. To make this example a bit fancier, the offsets don't occupy the same position while they move. Instead, the visible offset leads the way, followed by the transparent offset after a short delay of 0.2 seconds. This creates a blended fringe at the edge of the wipe while the animation is underway.

```
<Storyboard>
  <DoubleAnimation
    Storyboard.TargetName="visibleStop"
    Storyboard.TargetProperty="Offset"
    From="0" To="1.2" Duration="0:0:1.2" ></DoubleAnimation>
  <DoubleAnimation
    Storyboard.TargetName="transparentStop"
    Storyboard.TargetProperty="Offset" BeginTime="0:0:0.2"
    From="0" To="1" Duration="0:0:1" ></DoubleAnimation>
</Storyboard>
```

There's one odd detail here. The visible stop moves to 1.2 rather than simply 1, which denotes the right edge of the image. This ensures that both offsets move at the same speed, because the total distance each one must cover is proportional to the duration of its animation.

Wipes commonly work from left to right or top to bottom, but more-creative effects are possible by using different opacity masks. For example, you could use a DrawingBrush for your opacity mask and modify its geometry to let the content underneath show through in a tiled pattern. You'll see more examples that animate brushes in Chapter 16.

Monitoring Progress

The animation player shown in Figure 15-3 still lacks one feature that's common in most media players—the ability to determine your current position. To make it a bit fancier, you can add some text that shows the time offset and a progress bar that provides a visual indication of how far you are in the animation. Figure 15-4 shows a revised animation player with both details (along with the Slider for controlling speed that was explained in the previous section).

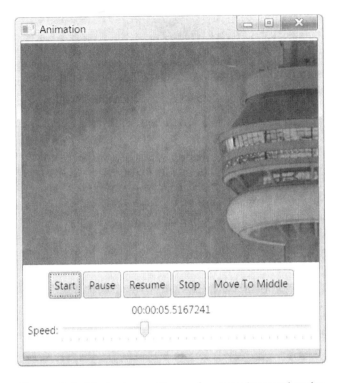

Figure 15-4. *Displaying position and progress in an animation*

Adding these details is fairly straightforward. First you need a TextBlock element to show the time and a ProgressBar control to show the graphical bar. You might assume you could set the TextBlock value and the ProgressBar content by using a data-binding expression, but this isn't possible. That's because the only way to retrieve the information about the current animation clock from the Storyboard is to use methods such as GetCurrentTime() and GetCurrentProgress(). There isn't any way to get the same information from properties.

The easiest solution is to react to one of the storyboard events listed in Table 15-3.

Table 15-3. *Storyboard Events*

Name	Description
Completed	The animation has reached its ending point.
CurrentGlobalSpeedInvalidated	The speed has changed, or the animation has been paused, resumed, stopped, or moved to a new position. This event also occurs when the animation clock reverses (at the end of a reversible animation) and when it accelerates or decelerates.
CurrentStateInvalidated	The animation has started or ended.
CurrentTimeInvalidated	The animation clock has moved forward an increment, changing the animation. This event also occurs when the animation starts, stops, or ends.
RemoveRequested	The animation is being removed. The animated property will subsequently return to its original value.

In this case, the event you need is CurrentTimeInvalidated, which fires every time the animation clock moves forward. (Typically, this will be 60 times per second, but if your code takes more time to execute, you may miss clock ticks.)

When the CurrentTimeInvalidated event fires, the sender is a Clock object (from the System.Windows.Media. Animation namespace). The Clock object allows you to retrieve the current time as a TimeSpan and the current progress as a value from 0 to 1.

Here's the code that updates the label and the progress bar:

```
Private Sub storyboard_CurrentTimeInvalidated(ByVal sender As Object, _
  ByVal e As EventArgs)
    ' Sender is the clock that was created for this storyboard.
    Dim storyboardClock As Clock = CType(sender, Clock)

    If storyboardClock.CurrentProgress Is Nothing Then
        lblTime.Text = "[[ stopped ]]"
        progressBar.Value = 0
    Else
        lblTime.Text = storyboardClock.CurrentTime.ToString()
        progressBar.Value = CDbl(storyboardClock.CurrentProgress)
    End If
End Sub
```

■ **Tip** If you use the Clock.CurrentProgress property, you don't need to perform any calculation to determine the value for your progress bar. Instead, simply configure your progress bar with a minimum of 0 and a maximum of 1. That way, you can simply use the Clock.CurrentProgress to set the ProgressBar.Value, as in this example.

Animation Easing

One of the shortcomings of linear animation is that it often feels mechanical and unnatural. By comparison, sophisticated user interfaces have animated effects that model real-world systems. For example, they may use tactile push-buttons that jump back quickly when clicked but slow down as they come to rest, creating the illusion of true movement. Or they may use maximize and minimize effects as in the Windows operating system, where the speed at which the window grows or shrinks accelerates as the window nears its final size. These details are subtle, and you're not likely to notice them when they're implemented well. However, you'll almost certainly notice the clumsy feeling of less-refined animations that lack these finer points.

The secret to improving your animations and creating more-natural animations is to vary the rate of change. Instead of creating animations that change properties at a fixed, unchanging rate, you need to design animations that speed up or slow down along the way. WPF gives you several options. In the next chapter, you'll learn about frame-based animation and key-frame animation, two techniques that give you more-nuanced control over your animations (and require significantly more work). But the simplest way to make a more natural animation is to use a prebuilt *easing function*.

When using an easing function, you still define your animation normally by specifying the starting and ending property values. But in addition to these details, you add a ready-made mathematical function that alters the progression of your animation, causing it to accelerate or decelerate at different points. This is the technique you'll study in the following sections.

Using an Easing Function

The best part about animation easing is that it requires much less work than other approaches such as frame-based animation and key frames. To use animation easing, you set the EasingFunction property of an animation object with an instance of an easing function class (a class that derives from EasingFunctionBase). You'll usually need to set a few properties on the easing function, and you may be forced to play around with different settings to get the effect you want, but you'll need no code and very little additional XAML.

For example, consider the two animations shown here, which act on a button. When the user moves the mouse over the button, a small snippet of code calls the growStoryboard animation into action, stretching the button to 400 units. When the user moves the mouse off the button, the buttons shrinks back to its normal size.

```
<Storyboard x:Name="growStoryboard">
  <DoubleAnimation
    Storyboard.TargetName="cmdGrow" Storyboard.TargetProperty="Width"
    To="400" Duration="0:0:1.5"></DoubleAnimation>
</Storyboard>

<Storyboard x:Name="revertStoryboard">
  <DoubleAnimation
    Storyboard.TargetName="cmdGrow" Storyboard.TargetProperty="Width"
    Duration="0:0:3"></DoubleAnimation>
</Storyboard>
```

Right now, the animations use linear interpolation, which means the growing and shrinking happen in a steady, mechanical way. For a more natural effect, you can add an easing function. The following example adds an easing function named ElasticEase. The end result is that the button springs beyond its full size, snaps back to a value that's somewhat less, swings back over its full size again (but a little less than before), snaps back a bit less, and so on, repeating its bouncing pattern as the movement diminishes. It gradually comes to rest ten oscillations later. The Oscillations property controls the number of bounces at the end. The ElasticEase class provides one other property that's not used in this example: Springiness. This higher this value, the more each subsequent oscillation dies down (the default value is 3).

```
<Storyboard x:Name="growStoryboard">
  <DoubleAnimation
    Storyboard.TargetName="cmdGrow" Storyboard.TargetProperty="Width"
    To="400" Duration="0:0:1.5">
    <DoubleAnimation.EasingFunction>
```

```
      <ElasticEase EasingMode="EaseOut" Oscillations="10"></ElasticEase>
    </DoubleAnimation.EasingFunction>
  </DoubleAnimation>
</Storyboard>
```

To really appreciate the difference between this markup and the earlier example that didn't use an easing function, you need to try this animation (or run the companion examples for this chapter). It's a remarkable change. With one line of XAML, a simple animation changes from amateurish to a slick effect that would feel at home in a professional application.

■ **Note** Because the EasingFunction property accepts a single easing function object, you can't combine different easing functions for the same animation.

Easing In and Easing Out

Before you consider the different easing functions, it's important to understand *when* an easing function is applied. Every easing function class derives from EasingFunctionBase and inherits a single property named EasingMode. This property has three possible values: EaseIn (which means the effect is applied to the beginning of the animation), EaseOut (which means it's applied to the end), and EaseInOut (which means it's applied at both the beginning and the end—the easing in takes place in the first half of the animation, and the easing out takes place in the second half).

In the previous example, the animation in the growStoryboard animation uses EaseOut mode. Thus, the sequence of gradually diminishing bounces takes place at the end of the animation. If you were to graph the changing button width as the animation progresses, you'd see something like the graph shown in Figure 15-5.

Figure 15-5. Oscillating to a stop by using EaseOut with ElasticEase

---

■ **Note** The duration of an animation doesn't change when you apply an easing function. In the case of the growStoryboard animation, the ElasticEase function doesn't just change the way the animation ends—it also makes the initial portion of the animation (when the button expands normally) run more quickly so that there's more time left for the oscillations at the end.

If you switch the ElasticEase function to use EaseIn mode, the bounces happen at the beginning of the animation. The button shrinks below its starting value a bit, expands a bit over, shrinks back a little more, and continues this pattern of gradually increasing oscillations until it finally breaks free and expands the rest of the way. (You use the ElasticEase.Oscillations property to control the number of bounces.) Figure 15-6 shows this very different pattern of movement.

Figure 15-6. *Oscillating to a start by using EaseIn with ElasticEase*

Finally, EaseInOut creates a stranger effect, with oscillations that start the animation in its first half followed by oscillations that stop it in the second half. Figure 15-7 illustrates.

Figure 15-7. *Oscillating to a start and to a stop by using EaseInOut with ElasticEase*

Easing Function Classes

WPF has 11 easing functions, all of which are found in the familiar System.Windows.Media.Animation namespace. Table 15-4 describes them all and lists their important properties. Remember, every animation also provides the EasingMode property, which allows you to control whether it affects that animation as it starts (EaseIn), ends (EaseOut), or both (EaseInOut).

Table 15-4. *Easing Functions*

Name	Description	Properties
BackEase	When applied with EaseIn, pulls the animation back before starting it. When applied with EaseOut, this function allows the animation to overshoot slightly and then pulls it back.	Amplitude determines the amount of pullback or overshoot. The default value is 1, and you can decrease it (to any value greater than 0) to reduce the effect or increase it to amplify the effect.
ElasticEase	When applied with EaseOut, makes the animation overshoot its maximum and swing back and forth, gradually slowing. When applied with EaseIn, the animation swings back and forth around its starting value, gradually increasing.	Oscillations controls the number of times the animation swings back and forth (the default is 3), and Springiness controls how quickly the oscillations increase or diminish (the default is 3).
BounceEase	Performs an effect similar to ElasticEase, except the bounces never overshoot the initial or final values.	Bounces controls the number of times the animation bounces back (the default is 2), and Bounciness determines how quickly the bounces increase or diminish (the default is 2).

(continued)

Table 15-4. (*continued*)

Name	Description	Properties
CircleEase	Accelerates (with EaseIn) or decelerates (with EaseOut) the animation by using a circular function.	None
CubicEase	Accelerates (with EaseIn) or decelerates (with EaseOut) the animation by using a function based on the cube of time. The effect is similar to CircleEase, but the acceleration is more gradual.	None
QuadraticEase	Accelerates (with EaseIn) or decelerates (with EaseOut) the animation by using a function based on the square of time. The effect is similar to CubicEase but even more gradual.	None
QuarticEase	Accelerates (with EaseIn) or decelerates (with EaseOut) the animation by using a function based on time to the power of 4. The effect is similar to CubicEase and QuadraticEase, but the acceleration is more pronounced.	None
QuinticEase	Accelerates (with EaseIn) or decelerates (with EaseOut) the animation by using a function based on time to the power of 5. The effect is similar to CubicEase, QuadraticEase, and QuinticEase, but the acceleration is more pronounced.	None
SineEase	Accelerates (with EaseIn) or decelerates (with EaseOut) the animation by using a function that includes a sine calculation. The acceleration is very gradual and closer to linear interpolation than any of the other easing functions.	None
PowerEase	Accelerates (with EaseIn) or decelerates (with EaseOut) the animation by using the power function $f(t) = t^p$. Depending on the value you use for the exponent p, you can duplicate the effect of the Cubic, QuadraticEase, QuarticEase, and QuinticEase functions.	Power sets the value of the exponent in the formula. Use 2 to duplicate QuadraticEase ($f(t) = t^2$), 3 for CubicEase ($f(t) = t^3$), 4 for QuarticEase ($f(t) = t^4$), and 5 for QuinticEase ($f(t) = t^5$), or choose something different. The default is 2.
ExponentialEase	Accelerates (with EaseIn) or decelerates (with EaseOut) the animation by using the exponential function $f(t)=(e(at) - 1)/(e(a) - 1)$.	Exponent allows you to set the value of the exponent (2 is the default).

Many of the easing functions provide similar but subtly different results. To use animation easing successfully, you need to decide which easing function to use and how to configure it. Often this process requires a bit of trial-and-error experimentation. Two good resources can help you.

First, the WPF documentation charts example behavior for each easing function, showing how the animated value changes as time progresses. Reviewing these charts is a good way to develop a sense of what the easing function does. Figure 15-8 shows the charts for the most popular easing functions.

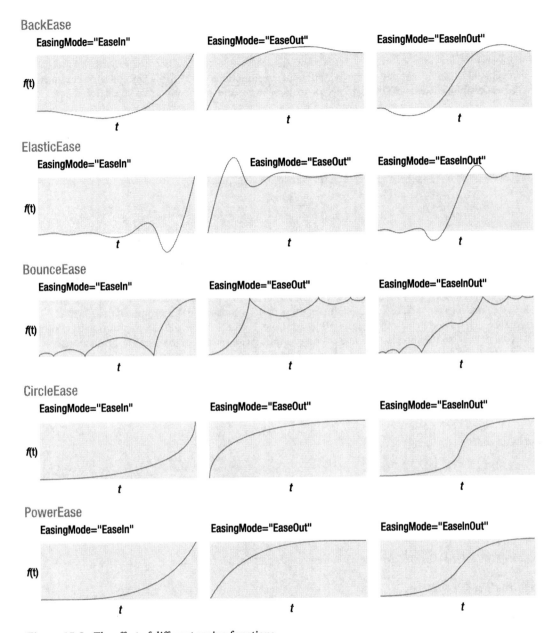

Figure 15-8. *The effect of different easing functions*

Second, Microsoft provides several sample applications that you can use to play with the easing functions and try different property values. One of the handiest is a Silverlight application that you can run in the browser by surfing to http://tinyurl.com/animationeasing. It allows you to observe the effect of any easing function on a falling square, and it shows the automatically generated XAML markup needed to duplicate the effect.

Creating a Custom Easing Function

You can create a custom easing effect by deriving your own class from EasingFunctionBase and overriding the EaseInCore() and CreateInstanceCore() methods. This is a fairly specialized technique, because most developers will be able to get the results they want by configuring the standard easing functions (or by using key spline animations, as described in the next chapter). However, if you do decide to create a custom easing function, you'll find that it's surprisingly easy.

Virtually all the logic you need to write runs in the EaseInCore() method. It accepts a normalized time value—essentially, a value from 0 to 1 that represents the progress of the animation. When the animation first begins, the normalized time is 0. It increases from that point on, until it reaches 1 at the end of the animation.

```
Protected Overrides Function EaseInCore(ByVal normalizedTime As Double) _
  As Double
    ...
End Function
```

During an animation, WPF calls the EaseInCore() method each time it updates the animated value. The exact frequency depends on the animation's frame rate, but you can expect it to call EaseInCore() close to 60 times each second.

To perform easing, the EaseInCore() method takes the normalized time and adjusts it in some way. The adjusted value that EaseInCore() returns is then used to adjust the progress of the animation. For example, if EaseInCore() returns 0, the animation is returned to its starting point. If EaseInCore() returns 1, the animation jumps to its ending point. However, EaseInCore() isn't limited to this range—for example, it can return 1.5 to cause the animation to overrun itself by an additional 50 percent. (You've already seen this effect with easing functions such as ElasticEase.)

Here's a version of EaseInCore() that does nothing at all. It returns the normalized time, meaning the animation will unfold evenly, just as if there were no easing:

```
Protected Overrides Function EaseInCore(ByVal normalizedTime As Double) _
  As Double
    Return normalizedTime
End Function
```

And here's a version of EaseInCore() that duplicates the CubicEase function, by cubing the normalized time. Because the normalized time is a fractional value, cubing it produces a smaller fraction. Thus, this method has the effect of initially slowing down the animation and causing it to accelerate as the normalized time (and its cubed value) approaches 1.

```
Protected Overrides Function EaseInCore(ByVal normalizedTime As Double) _
  As Double
    Return Math.Pow(normalizedTime, 3)
End Function
```

▓ **Note** The easing you perform in the EaseInCore() method is what you'll get when you use an EasingMode of EaseIn. Interestingly, that's all the work you need to do, because WPF is intelligent enough to calculate complementary behavior for the EaseOut and EaseInOut settings.

Finally, here's a custom easing function that does something more interesting—it offsets the normalized value a random amount, causing a sporadic jittering effect. You can adjust the magnitude of the jitter (within a narrow range) by using the provide Jitter dependency property, which accepts a value from 0 to 2000.

```vb
Public Class RandomJitterEase
    Inherits EasingFunctionBase
    ' Store a random number generator.
    Private rand As New Random()

    ' Allow the amount of jitter to be configured.
    Public Shared ReadOnly JitterProperty As DependencyProperty = _
      DependencyProperty.Register("Jitter", GetType(Integer), _
      GetType(RandomJitterEase), New UIPropertyMetadata(1000), _
      New ValidateValueCallback(AddressOf ValidateJitter))

    Public Property Jitter() As Integer
        Get
            Return CInt(GetValue(JitterProperty))
        End Get
        Set(ByVal value As Integer)
            SetValue(JitterProperty, value)
        End Set
    End Property

    Private Shared Function ValidateJitter(ByVal value As Object) As Boolean
        Dim jitterValue As Integer = CInt(value)
        Return ((jitterValue <= 2000) AndAlso (jitterValue >= 0))
    End Function

    ' Perform the easing.
    Protected Overrides Function EaseInCore(ByVal normalizedTime As Double) _
      As Double
        ' Make sure there's no jitter in the final value.
        If normalizedTime = 1 Then
            Return 1
        End If

        ' Offset the value by a random amount.
        Return Math.Abs(normalizedTime - CDbl(rand.Next(0, 10)) / (2010 - Jitter))
    End Function

    ' This required override simply provides a live instance of your
    ' easing function.
    Protected Overrides Function CreateInstanceCore() As Freezable
        Return New RandomJitterEase()
    End Function
End Class
```

■ **Tip** If you want to see the eased values that you're calculating as your animation runs, use the WriteLine() method of the System.Diagnostics.Debug class in the EaseInCore() method. This writes the value you supply to the Output window while you're debugging your application in Visual Studio.

Using this easing function is easy. First, map the appropriate namespace in your XAML:

```
<Window x:Class="CustomEasingFunction"
 xmlns="http://schemas.microsoft.com/winfx/2006/xaml/presentation"
 xmlns:x="http://schemas.microsoft.com/winfx/2006/xaml"
 Title="CustomEasingFunction" Height="300" Width="600"
 xmlns:local="clr-namespace:Animation">
```

Then you can create a RandomJitterEase object in your markup, like this:

```
<DoubleAnimation
 Storyboard.TargetName="ellipse2" Storyboard.TargetProperty="(Canvas.Left)"
 To="500" Duration="0:0:10">

  <DoubleAnimation.EasingFunction>
    <local:RandomJitterEase EasingMode="EaseIn" Jitter="1000">
    </local:RandomJitterEase>
  </DoubleAnimation.EasingFunction>

</DoubleAnimation>
```

The online samples for this chapter feature an example that compares an animation with no easing (the movement of a small ellipse across a Canvas) to one that uses the RandomJitterEase.

Animation Performance

Often an animated user interface requires little more than creating and configuring the right animation and storyboard objects. But in other scenarios, particularly ones in which you have multiple animations taking place at the same time, you may need to pay more attention to performance. Certain effects are more likely to cause these issues—for example, those that involve video, large bitmaps, and multiple levels of transparency typically demand more from the computer's CPU. If they're not implemented carefully, they may run with notable jerkiness, or they may steal CPU time away from other applications that are running at the same time.

Fortunately, WPF has a few tricks that can help you. In the following sections, you'll learn to slow down the maximum frame rate and cache bitmaps on the computer's video card, two techniques that can lessen the load on the CPU.

Desired Frame Rate

As you learned earlier in this chapter, WPF attempts to keep animations running at 60 frames per second. This ensures smooth, fluid animations from start to finish. Of course, WPF might not be able to deliver on its intentions. If you have multiple complex animations running at once and the CPU or video card can't keep up, the overall frame rate may drop (in the best-case scenario), or it may jump to catch up (in the worst-case scenario).

Although it's rare to increase the frame rate, you may choose to *decrease* the frame rate. You might take this step for one of two reasons:

- Your animation looks good at a lower frame rate, so you don't want to waste the extra CPU cycles.

- Your application is running on a less powerful CPU or video card, and you know your complete animation won't be rendered as well at a high frame rate as it would at a lower rate.

■ **Note** Developers sometimes assume that WPF includes code that scales the frame rate down based on the video card hardware. It does not. Instead, WPF always attempts 60 frames per second, unless you tell it otherwise. To evaluate how your animations are performing and whether WPF is able to achieve 60 frames per second on a specific computer, you can use the Perforator tool, which is included as part of the Microsoft Windows SDK v7.0. For a download link, installation instructions, and documentation, see `http://tinyurl.com/9kzmv9s`.

Adjusting the frame rate is easy. You simply use the Timeline.DesiredFrameRate attached property on the storyboard that contains your animations. Here's an example that halves the frame rate:

```
<Storyboard Timeline.DesiredFrameRate="30">
```

Figure 15-9 shows a simple test application that animates a circle so that it arcs across a Canvas.

Figure 15-9. *Testing frame rates with a simple animation*

The application begins with an Ellipse object in a Canvas. The Canvas.ClipToBounds property is set to True so the edges of the circle won't leak over the edge of the Canvas into the rest of the window.

```
<Canvas ClipToBounds="True">
  <Ellipse Name="ellipse" Fill="Red" Width="10" Height="10"></Ellipse>
</Canvas>
```

To move the circle across the Canvas, two animations take place at once—one that updates the Canvas.Left property (moving it from left to right) and one that changes the Canvas.Top property (causing it to rise up and then fall back down). The Canvas.Top animation is reversible—after the circle reaches its highest point, it falls back down. The Canvas.Left animation is not, but it takes twice as long, so both animations move the circle simultaneously. The final trick is using the DecelerationRatio property on the Canvas.Top animation. That way, the circle rises more slowly as it reaches the summit, which creates a more realistic effect.

Here's the complete markup for the animation:

```
<Window.Resources>
  <BeginStoryboard x:Key="beginStoryboard">
    <Storyboard Timeline.DesiredFrameRate=
      "{Binding ElementName=txtFrameRate,Path=Text}">
      <DoubleAnimation Storyboard.TargetName="ellipse"
       Storyboard.TargetProperty="(Canvas.Left)"
       From="0" To="300" Duration="0:0:5">
      </DoubleAnimation>
      <DoubleAnimation Storyboard.TargetName="ellipse"
       Storyboard.TargetProperty="(Canvas.Top)"
       From="300" To="0" AutoReverse="True" Duration="0:0:2.5"
       DecelerationRatio="1">
      </DoubleAnimation>
    </Storyboard>
  </BeginStoryboard>
</Window.Resources>
```

Notice that the Canvas.Left and Canvas.Top properties are wrapped in brackets—this indicates that they aren't found on the target element (the ellipse) but are attached properties. You'll also see that the animation is defined in the Resources collection for the window. This allows the animation to be started in more than one way. In this example, the animation is started when the Repeat button is clicked and when the window is first loaded, using code like this:

```
<Window.Triggers>
  <EventTrigger RoutedEvent="Window.Loaded">
    <EventTrigger.Actions>
      <StaticResource ResourceKey="beginStoryboard"></StaticResource>
    </EventTrigger.Actions>
  </EventTrigger>
</Window.Triggers>
```

The real purpose of this example is to try different frame rates. To see the effect of a particular frame rate, you simply need to type the appropriate number in the text box and click Repeat. The animation is then triggered with the new frame rate (which it picks up through a data-binding expression), and you can watch the results. At lower frame rates, the ellipse won't appear to move evenly—instead, it will hop across the Canvas.

You can also adjust the Timeline.DesiredFrame property in code. For example, you may want to read the shared RenderCapability.Tier to determine the level of video card support.

Bitmap Caching

Bitmap caching tells WPF to take a bitmap image of your content as it currently is and copy that to the memory on your video card. From this point on, the video card can take charge of manipulating the bitmap and refreshing the display. This process is far faster than getting WPF to do all the work and communicate continuously with the video card.

In the right situation, bitmap caching improves the drawing performance of your application. But in the wrong situation, it wastes video card memory and actually *slows* performance. Thus, before you use bitmap caching, you need to make sure that it's truly suitable. Here are some guidelines:

- If the content you're painting needs to be redrawn frequently, bitmap caching may make sense. That's because each subsequent redraw will happen much faster. One example is using a BitmapCacheBrush to paint the surface of a shape, while some other animated objects float on top. Even though your shape isn't changing, different parts of it are being obscured or revealed, necessitating a redraw.

- If the content in your element changes often, bitmap caching probably doesn't make sense. That's because each time the visual changes, WPF needs to rerender the bitmap and send it to the video card cache, which takes time. This rule is a bit tricky, because certain changes won't invalidate the cache. Examples of safe operations include rotating and rescaling your element with a transform, clipping it, changing its opacity, or applying an effect. On the other hand, changing its content, layout, and formatting will force the bitmap to be rerendered.

- Cache the smallest amount of content possible. The larger the bitmap, the longer WPF takes to store the cached copy, and the more video card memory it requires. After the video card memory is exhausted, WPF will be forced to fall back on slower software rendering.

■ **Tip** A poor caching strategy can cause more performance problems that an application that isn't fully optimized. So don't apply caching unless you're sure you meet these guidelines. Also, use a profiling tool such as Perforator (`http://tinyurl.com/9kzmv9s`) to verify that your strategy is improving performance.

To get a better understanding, it helps to play with a simple example. Figure 15-10 shows a project that's included with the downloadable samples for this chapter. Here, an animation pushes a simple shape—a square—over a Canvas that contains a Path with a complex geometry. As the square moves over its surface, WPF is forced to recalculate the path and fill in the missing sections. This imposes a surprisingly heavy CPU load, and the animation may even begin to become choppy.

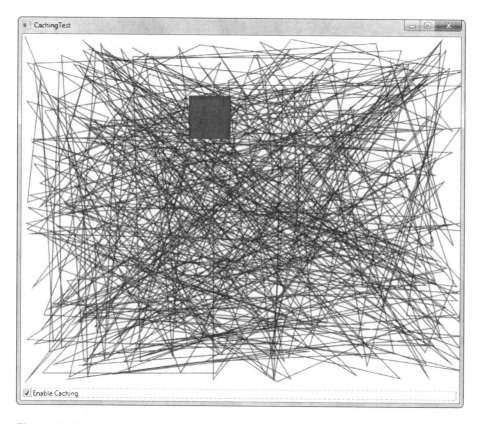

Figure 15-10. *Animating over a complex piece of vector art*

There are several ways to solve this problem. One option is to replace the background with a bitmap, which WPF can manage more efficiently. A more flexible option is to use bitmap caching, which preserves the background as a live, interactive element.

To switch on bitmap caching, you set the CacheMode property of the corresponding element to BitmapCache. Every element provides this property, which means you have a fine-grained ability to choose exactly which elements use this feature:

```
<Path CacheMode="BitmapCache" ...></Path>
```

■ **Note**   If you cache an element that contains other elements, such as a layout container, all the elements will be cached in a single bitmap. Thus, you need to be extremely careful about adding caching to something like a Canvas—do it only if the Canvas is small and its content will not change.

With this single, simple change, you'll see an immediate difference. First, the window will take slightly longer to appear. But the animation will run more smoothly, and the CPU load will decrease dramatically. Check it out in Windows Task Manager—it's not unusual to see it drop from close to 100 percent to less than 20 percent.

Ordinarily, when you enable bitmap caching, WPF takes a snapshot of the element at its current size and copies that bitmap to the video card. This can become a problem if you then use a ScaleTransform to make the element bigger. In this situation, you'll be enlarging the cached bitmap, not the actual element, which will cause it to grow fuzzy and pixelated as it grows.

For example, imagine a revised example in which a second simultaneous animation expands the Path to ten times its original size and then shrinks it back. To ensure good quality, you can cache a bitmap of the Path at five times its current size:

```
<Path ...>
  <Path.CacheMode>
    <BitmapCache RenderAtScale="5"></BitmapCache>
  </Path.CacheMode>
</Path>
```

This resolves the pixelation problem. The cached bitmap is still smaller than the maximum animated size of the Path (which reaches ten times its original size), but the video card is able to double the size of the bitmap from five to ten times its original size without any obvious scaling artifacts. More important, this still keeps your application from using an excessive amount of video memory.

The Last Word

In this chapter, you explored WPF's animation support in detail. You learned about the basic animation classes and the concept of linear interpolation. You also saw how to control the playback of one or more animations with a storyboard and how to create more-natural effects with animation easing.

Now that you've mastered the basics, you can spend more time with the art of animation—deciding what properties to animate and how to modify them to get the effect you want. In the next chapter, you'll learn how to create a variety of effects by applying animations to transforms, brushes, and pixel shaders. You'll also learn to create key-frame animations that contain multiple segments and frame-based animations that break free from the standard property-based animation model. Finally, you'll see how to create and manage storyboards with code rather than XAML.

CHAPTER 16

■ ■ ■

Advanced Animation

You now know the fundamentals of WPF's property animation system—how animations are defined, how they're connected to elements, and how you can control playback with a storyboard. Now is a good time to take a closer look at the practical animation techniques you can use in an application.

In this chapter, you'll begin by considering what you should animate to get the results you want. You'll see examples that animate transforms, brushes, and pixel shaders. Next, you'll learn how key-frame and path-based animations allow you to shape the acceleration and deceleration of your animations, in a way that's similar to animation easing but far more flexible. Then you'll learn how frame-based animation lets you break free of the animation model altogether to create complex effects such as realistic collisions. Finally, you'll examine another example—a bomb-dropping game—that shows how you can integrate animations into the overall flow of an application, by creating and managing them with code.

Animation Types Revisited

The first challenge in creating any animation is choosing the right property to animate. Making the leap between the result you want (for example, an element moving across the window) and the property you need to use (in this case, Canvas.Left and Canvas.Top) isn't always intuitive. Here are a few guidelines:

- If you want to use an animation to make an element appear or disappear, don't use the Visibility property (which allows you to switch only between completely visible or completely invisible). Instead, use the Opacity property to fade the element in or out.

- If you want to animate the position of an element, consider using a Canvas. It provides the most direct properties (Canvas.Left and Canvas.Top) and requires the least overhead. Alternatively, you can get similar effects in other layout containers by using the ThicknessAnimation class to animate properties such as Margin and Padding. You can also animate the MinWidth or MinHeight or a column or row in a Grid.

■ **Tip**   Many animation effects are designed to progressively "reveal" an element. Common options include making an element fade into visibility, slide into view, or expand from a tiny point. However, there are many alternatives. For example, you could blur out an element by using the BlurEffect described in Chapter 14 and animate the Radius property to reduce the blur and allow the element to come gradually into focus.

- The most common properties to animate are render transforms. You can use them to move or flip an element (TranslateTransform), rotate it (RotateTransform), resize or stretch it (ScaleTransform), and more. Used carefully, they can sometimes allow you to avoid hard-coding sizes and positions in your animation. They also bypass the WPF layout system, making them faster than other approaches that act directly on element size or position.

- One good way to change the surface of an element through an animation is to modify the properties of the brush. You can use a ColorAnimation to change the color or another animation object to transform a property of a more complex brush, like the offset in a gradient.

The following examples demonstrate how to animate transforms and brushes and how to use a few more animation types. You'll also learn how to create multisegmented animations with key frames, path-based animations, and frame-based animations.

Animating Transforms

Transforms offer one of the most powerful ways to customize an element. When you use transforms, you don't simply change the bounds of an element. Instead, the entire visual appearance of the element is moved, flipped, skewed, stretched, enlarged, shrunk, or rotated. For example, if you animate the size of a button by using a ScaleTransform, the entire button is resized, including its border and its inner content. The effect is much more impressive than if you animate its Width and Height or the FontSize property that affects its text.

As you learned in Chapter 12, every element has the ability to use transforms in two ways: the RenderTransform property and the LayoutTransform property. RenderTransform is more efficient, because it's applied after the layout pass and used to transform the final rendered output. LayoutTransform is applied before the layout pass, and as a result, other controls are rearranged to fit. Changing the LayoutTransform property triggers a new layout operation (unless you're using your element in a Canvas, in which case RenderTransform and LayoutTransform are equivalent).

To use a transform in animation, the first step is to define the transform. (An animation can change an existing transform but not create a new one.) For example, imagine you want to allow a button to rotate. This requires the RotateTransform:

```
<Button Content="A Button">
  <RenderTransform>
    <RotateTransform></RotateTransform>
  </RenderTransform>
</Button>
```

Now here's an event trigger that makes the button rotate when the mouse moves over it. It uses the target property RenderTransform.Angle—in other words, it reads the button's RenderTransform property and modifies the Angle property of the RotateTransform object that's defined there. The fact that the RenderTransform property can hold a variety of transform objects, each with different properties, doesn't cause a problem. As long as you're using a transform that has an angle property, this trigger will work.

```
<EventTrigger RoutedEvent="Button.MouseEnter">
  <EventTrigger.Actions>
    <BeginStoryboard>
      <Storyboard>
        <DoubleAnimation Storyboard.TargetProperty="RenderTransform.Angle"
        To="360" Duration="0:0:0.8" RepeatBehavior="Forever"></DoubleAnimation>
      </Storyboard>
    </BeginStoryboard>
  </EventTrigger.Actions>
</EventTrigger>
```

The button rotates one revolution every 0.8 seconds and continues rotating perpetually. While the mouse is rotating, it's still completely usable—for example, you can click it and handle the Click event.

To make sure the button rotates around its center point (not the top-left corner), you need to set the RenderTransformOrigin property as shown here:

```
<Button RenderTransformOrigin="0.5,0.5">
```

Remember, the RenderTransformOrigin property uses relative units from 0 to 1, so 0.5 represents a midpoint.

To stop the rotation, you can use a second trigger that responds to the MouseLeave event. At this point, you could remove the storyboard that performs the rotation, but this causes the button to jump back to its original orientation in one step. A better approach is to start a second animation that replaces the first. This animation leaves out the To and From properties, which means it seamlessly rotates the button back to its original orientation in a snappy 0.2 seconds:

```
<EventTrigger RoutedEvent="Button.MouseLeave">
  <EventTrigger.Actions>
    <BeginStoryboard>
      <Storyboard>
        <DoubleAnimation Storyboard.TargetProperty="LayoutTransform.Angle"
        Duration="0:0:0.2"></DoubleAnimation>
      </Storyboard>
    </BeginStoryboard>
  </EventTrigger.Actions>
</EventTrigger>
```

To create your rotating button, you'll need to add both these triggers to the Button.Triggers collection. Or you could pull them (and the transform) into a style and apply that style to as many buttons as you want. For example, here's the markup for the window full of "rotatable" buttons shown in Figure 16-1:

```
<Window x:Class="RotateButton" ... >
  <Window.Resources>
    <Style TargetType="{x:Type Button}">
      <Setter Property="HorizontalAlignment" Value="Center"></Setter>
      <Setter Property="RenderTransformOrigin" Value="0.5,0.5"></Setter>
      <Setter Property="Padding" Value="20,15"></Setter>
      <Setter Property="Margin" Value="2"></Setter>
      <Setter Property="LayoutTransform">
        <Setter.Value>
          <RotateTransform></RotateTransform>
        </Setter.Value>
      </Setter>
      <Style.Triggers>
        <EventTrigger RoutedEvent="Button.MouseEnter">
          ...
        </EventTrigger>
        <EventTrigger RoutedEvent="Button.MouseLeave">
          ...
        </EventTrigger>
      </Style.Triggers>
    </Style>
```

```
    </Window.Resources>
    <StackPanel Margin="5" Button.Click="cmd_Clicked">
      <Button>One</Button>
      <Button>Two</Button>
      <Button>Three</Button>
      <Button>Four</Button>
      <TextBlock Name="lbl" Margin="5"></TextBlock>
    </StackPanel>
</Window>
```

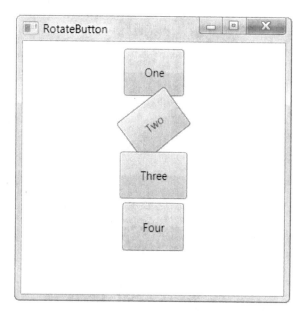

Figure 16-1. *Using a render transform*

When any button is clicked, a message is displayed in the TextBlock.

This example also gives you a great chance to consider the difference between the RenderTransform and the LayoutTransform. If you modify the code to use a LayoutTransform, you'll see that the other buttons are pushed out of the way as a button spins (see Figure 16-2). For example, if the topmost button turns, the buttons underneath bounce up and down to avoid it.

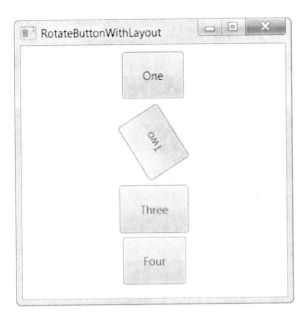

Figure 16-2. *Using a layout transform*

Of course, to get a sense of how the buttons "feel," it's worth trying this example with the downloadable code.

Animating Multiple Transforms

You can easily use transforms in combination. In fact, it's easy—you simply need to use the TransformGroup to set the LayoutTransform or RenderTransform property. You can nest as many transforms as you need inside the TransformGroup.

Figure 16-3 shows an interesting effect that was created using two transforms. A document window begins as a small thumbnail in the top-left corner of the main window. When the document window appears, this content rotates, expands, and fades into view rapidly. This is conceptually similar to the effect that Windows uses when you maximize a window. In WPF, you can use this trick with any element using transforms.

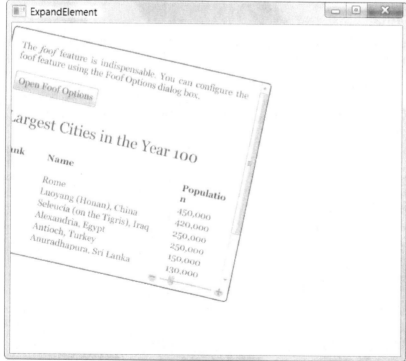

Figure 16-3. Content that "jumps" into view

To create this effect, two transforms are defined in a TransformGroup and used to set the RenderTransform property of a Border object that contains all the content:

```
<Border.RenderTransform>
  <TransformGroup>
    <ScaleTransform></ScaleTransform>
      <RotateTransform></RotateTransform>
    </TransformGroup>
</Border.RenderTransform>
```

Your animation can interact with both of these transform objects by specifying a numeric offset (0 for the ScaleTransform that appears first and 1 for the RotateTransform that's next). For example, here's the animation that enlarges the content:

```
<DoubleAnimation Storyboard.TargetName="element"
  Storyboard.TargetProperty="RenderTransform.Children[0].ScaleX"
  From="0" To="1" Duration="0:0:2" AccelerationRatio="1">
</DoubleAnimation>
<DoubleAnimation Storyboard.TargetName="element"
  Storyboard.TargetProperty="RenderTransform.Children[0].ScaleY"
  From="0" To="1" Duration="0:0:2" AccelerationRatio="1">
</DoubleAnimation>
```

and here's the animation in the same storyboard that rotates it:

```
<DoubleAnimation Storyboard.TargetName="element"
  Storyboard.TargetProperty="RenderTransform.Children[1].Angle"
  From="70" To="0" Duration="0:0:2" >
</DoubleAnimation>
```

The animation is slightly more involved than shown here. For example, there's an animation that increases the Opacity property at the same time, and when the Border reaches full size, it briefly "bounces" back, creating a more natural feel. Creating the timeline for this animation and tweaking the various animation object properties takes time—ideally, you'll perform tasks like this using a design tool such as Expression Blend rather than code them by hand. An even better scenario would be having a third-party developer group this logic into a single custom animation that you could then reuse and apply to your objects as needed. (As it currently stands, you could reuse this animation by storing the Storyboard as an application-level resource.)

This effect is surprisingly practical. For example, you could use it to draw attention to new content—such as a file that the user has just opened. The possible variations are endless. For example, a retail company could create a product catalog that slides a panel with product details or rolls a product image into view when you hover over the corresponding product name.

Animating Brushes

Animating brushes is another common technique in WPF animations, and it's just as easy as animating transforms. Once again, the technique is to dig into the particular subproperty you want to change, using the appropriate animation type.

Figure 16-4 shows an example that tweaks a RadialGradientBrush. As the animation runs, the center point of the radial gradient drifts along the ellipse, giving it a three-dimensional effect. At the same time, the outer color of the gradient changes from blue to black.

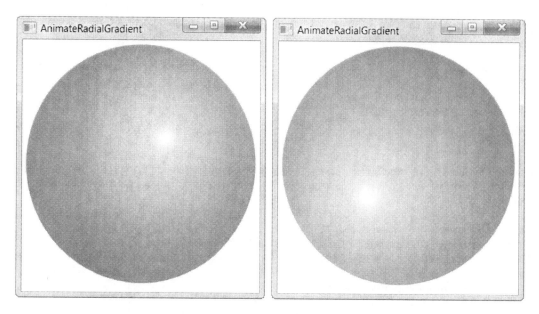

Figure 16-4. *Altering a radial gradient*

To perform this animation, you need to use two animation types that you haven't considered yet. ColorAnimation blends gradually between two colors, creating a subtle color-shift effect. PointAnimation allows you to move a point from one location to another. (It's essentially the same as if you modified both the X coordinate and the Y coordinate by using a separate DoubleAnimation, with linear interpolation.) You can use a PointAnimation to deform a figure that you've constructed out of points or to change the location of the radial gradient's center point, as in this example.

Here's the markup that defines the ellipse and its brush:

```
<Ellipse Name="ellipse" Margin="5" Grid.Row="1" Stretch="Uniform">
  <Ellipse.Fill>
    <RadialGradientBrush
     RadiusX="1" RadiusY="1" GradientOrigin="0.7,0.3">
      <GradientStop Color="White" Offset="0"></GradientStop>
      <GradientStop Color="Blue" Offset="1"></GradientStop>
    </RadialGradientBrush>
  </Ellipse.Fill>
</Ellipse>
```

and here are the two animations that move the center point and change the second color:

```
<PointAnimation Storyboard.TargetName="ellipse"
 Storyboard.TargetProperty="Fill.GradientOrigin"
 From="0.7,0.3" To="0.3,0.7" Duration="0:0:10" AutoReverse="True"
 RepeatBehavior="Forever">
</PointAnimation>
<ColorAnimation Storyboard.TargetName="ellipse"
 Storyboard.TargetProperty="Fill.GradientStops[1].Color"
 To="Black" Duration="0:0:10" AutoReverse="True"
 RepeatBehavior="Forever">
</ColorAnimation>
```

You can create a huge range of hypnotic effects by varying the colors and offsets in LinearGradientBrush and RadialGradientBrush. And if that's not enough, gradient brushes also have their own RelativeTransform property that you can use to rotate, scale, stretch, and skew them. The WPF team has a fun tool called Gradient Obsession for building gradient-based animations. You can find it (and the C# source code) at `http://tinyurl.com/yc5fjpm`. For some additional ideas, check out the animation examples Charles Petzold provides at `http://tinyurl.com/y92mf8a`, which change the geometry of different DrawingBrush objects, creating tiled patterns that morph into different shapes.

VisualBrush

As you learned in Chapter 12, a VisualBrush allows you to take the appearance of any element and use it to fill another surface. That other surface can be anything from an ordinary rectangle to letters of text.

Figure 16-5 shows a basic example. On top sits a real, live button. Underneath, a VisualBrush is used to fill a rectangle with a picture of the button that stretches and rotates under the effect of various transforms.

Figure 16-5. *Animating an element that's filled with a VisualBrush*

The VisualBrush also opens up some interesting possibilities for animation. For example, instead of animating the live, real element, you can animate a simple rectangle that has the same fill.

To understand how this works, consider the example shown earlier in Figure 16-3, which pops an element into view. While this animation is underway, the animated element is treated the same as any other WPF element, which means it's possible to click the button inside or scroll through the content with the keyboard (if you're fast enough). In some situations, this could cause confusion. In other situations, it might result in worse performance because of the extra overhead required to transform input (for example, mouse clicks) and pass it along to the original element.

Replacing this effect with a VisualBrush is easy. First you need to create another element that fills itself by using a VisualBrush. That VisualBrush must draw its visual from the element you want to animate (which, in this example, is the border named element).

```
<Rectangle Name="rectangle">
  <Rectangle.Fill>
    <VisualBrush Visual="{Binding ElementName=element}">
    </VisualBrush>
  </Rectangle.Fill>
  <Rectangle.RenderTransform>
    <TransformGroup>
      <ScaleTransform></ScaleTransform>
      <RotateTransform></RotateTransform>
    </TransformGroup>
  </Rectangle.RenderTransform>
</Rectangle>
```

To place the rectangle into the same position as the original element, you can place them both into the same cell of a Grid. The cell is sized to fit the original element (the border), and the rectangle is stretched to match. Another option is to overlay a Canvas on top of your real application layout container. (You could then bind your animation properties to the ActualWidth and ActualHeight properties of the real element underneath to make sure it lines up.)

After you've added the rectangle, you simply need to adjust your animations to animate its transforms. The final step is to hide the rectangle when the animations are complete:

```
Private Sub storyboardCompleted(ByVal sender As Object, ByVal e As EventArgs)
    rectangle.Visibility = Visibility.Collapsed
End Sub
```

Animating Pixel Shaders

In Chapter 14, you learned about pixel shaders—low-level routines that can apply bitmap-style effects such as blurs, glows, and warps to any element. On their own, pixel shaders are an interesting but only occasionally useful tool. But combined with animation, they become much more versatile. You can use them to design eye-catching transitions (for example, by blurring out one control, hiding it, and then removing the blur in another one). Or you can use them to create impressive user-interactivity effects (for example, by increasing the glow on a button when the user moves the mouse over it). Best of all, you can animate the properties of a pixel shader just as easily as you animate anything else.

Figure 16-6 shows a page that's based on the rotating button example shown earlier. It contains a sequence of buttons, and when the user moves the mouse over one of the buttons, an animation is attached and started. The difference is that the animation in this example doesn't rotate the button—instead, it reduces the blur radius to 0. The result is that as you move the mouse, the nearest control slides sharply and briskly into focus.

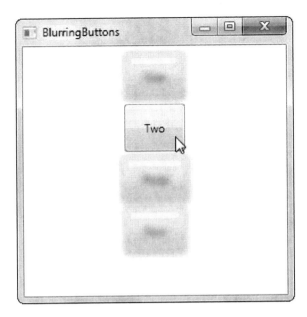

Figure 16-6. *Animating a pixel shader*

The code is the same as in the rotating button example. You need to give each button a BlurEffect instead of a RotateTransform:

```
<Button Content="A Button">
  <Button.Effect>
    <BlurEffect Radius="10"></BlurEffect>
  </Button.Effect>
</Button>
```

You also need to change the animation accordingly:

```
<EventTrigger RoutedEvent="Button.MouseEnter">
  <EventTrigger.Actions>
    <BeginStoryboard>
      <Storyboard>
        <DoubleAnimation Storyboard.TargetProperty="Effect.Radius"
          To="0" Duration="0:0:0.4"></DoubleAnimation>
      </Storyboard>
    </BeginStoryboard>
  </EventTrigger.Actions>
</EventTrigger>

<EventTrigger RoutedEvent="Button.MouseLeave">
  <EventTrigger.Actions>
    <BeginStoryboard>
      <Storyboard>
        <DoubleAnimation Storyboard.TargetProperty="Effect.Radius" To="10"
          Duration="0:0:0.2"></DoubleAnimation>
      </Storyboard>
```

```
    </BeginStoryboard>
  </EventTrigger.Actions>
</EventTrigger>
```

You could use the same approach in reverse to highlight a button. For example, you could use a pixel shader that applies a glow effect to highlight the moused-over button. And if you're interested in using pixel shaders to animate page transitions, check out the WPF Shader Effects Library at http://codeplex.com/wpffx. It includes a range of eye-popping pixel shaders and a set of helper classes for performing transitions with them.

Key-Frame Animation

All the animations you've seen so far have used linear interpolation to move from a starting point to an ending point. But what if you need to create an animation that has multiple segments and moves less regularly? For example, you might want to create an animation that slides an element into view quickly and then slowly moves it the rest of the way into place. You could achieve this effect by creating a sequence of two animations and using the BeginTime property to start the second animation after the first one. However, there's an easier approach—you can use a key-frame animation.

A *key-frame animation* is an animation that's made up of many short segments. Each segment represents an initial, final, or intermediary value in the animation. When you run the animation, it moves smoothly from one value to another.

For example, consider the Point animation that allowed you to move the center point of a RadialGradientBrush from one spot to another:

```
<PointAnimation Storyboard.TargetName="ellipse"
 Storyboard.TargetProperty="Fill.GradientOrigin"
 From="0.7,0.3" To="0.3,0.7" Duration="0:0:10" AutoReverse="True"
 RepeatBehavior="Forever">
</PointAnimation>
```

You can replace this PointAnimation object with an equivalent PointAnimationUsingKeyFrames object, as shown here:

```
<PointAnimationUsingKeyFrames Storyboard.TargetName="ellipse"
 Storyboard.TargetProperty="Fill.GradientOrigin"
 AutoReverse="True" RepeatBehavior="Forever" >
  <LinearPointKeyFrame Value="0.7,0.3" KeyTime="0:0:0"></LinearPointKeyFrame>
  <LinearPointKeyFrame Value="0.3,0.7" KeyTime="0:0:10"></LinearPointKeyFrame>
</PointAnimationUsingKeyFrames>
```

This animation includes two key frames. The first sets the Point value when the animation first starts. (If you want to use the current value that's set in the RadialGradientBrush, you can leave out this key frame.) The second key frame defines the end value, which is reached after 10 seconds. The PointAnimationUsingKeyFrames object performs linear interpolation to move smoothly from the first key-frame value to the second, just as the PointAnimation does with the From and To values.

■ **Note** Every key-frame animation uses its own key-frame animation object (for example, LinearPointKeyFrame). For the most point, these classes are the same—they include a Value property that stores the target value and a KeyTime property that indicates when the frame reaches the target value. The only difference is the data type of the Value property. In a LinearPointKeyFrame it's a Point, in a DoubleKeyFrame it's a Double, and so on.

You can create a more interesting example by using a series of key frames. The following animation walks the center point through a series of positions that are reached at different times. The speed that the center point moves will change depending on the length of time between key frames and the amount of distance that needs to be covered.

```
<PointAnimationUsingKeyFrames Storyboard.TargetName="ellipse"
 Storyboard.TargetProperty="Fill.GradientOrigin"
 RepeatBehavior="Forever" >
  <LinearPointKeyFrame Value="0.7,0.3" KeyTime="0:0:0"></LinearPointKeyFrame>
  <LinearPointKeyFrame Value="0.3,0.7" KeyTime="0:0:5"></LinearPointKeyFrame>
  <LinearPointKeyFrame Value="0.5,0.9" KeyTime="0:0:8"></LinearPointKeyFrame>
  <LinearPointKeyFrame Value="0.9,0.6" KeyTime="0:0:10"></LinearPointKeyFrame>
  <LinearPointKeyFrame Value="0.8,0.2" KeyTime="0:0:12"></LinearPointKeyFrame>
  <LinearPointKeyFrame Value="0.7,0.3" KeyTime="0:0:14"></LinearPointKeyFrame>
</PointAnimationUsingKeyFrames>
```

This animation isn't reversible, but it does repeat. To make sure there's no jump between the final value of one iteration and the starting value of the next iteration, the animation ends at the same center point that it began.

Chapter 27 shows another key-frame example. It uses a Point3DAnimationUsingKeyFrames animation to move the camera through a 3-D scene and a Vector3DAnimationUsingKeyFrames to rotate the camera at the same time.

■ **Note**   Using key-frame animation isn't quite as powerful as using a sequence of multiple animations. The most important difference is that you can't apply different AccelerationRatio and DecelerationRatio values to each key frame. Instead, you can apply only a single value to the entire animation.

Discrete Key-Frame Animations

The key-frame animation you saw in the previous example uses *linear* key frames. As a result, it transitions smoothly between the key-frame values. Another option is to use *discrete* key frames. In this case, no interpolation is performed. When the key time is reached, the property changes abruptly to the new value.

Linear key-frame classes are named in the form Linear*DataType*KeyFrame. Discrete key-frame classes are named in the form Discrete*DataType*KeyFrame. Here's a revised version of the RadialGradientBrush example that uses discrete key frames:

```
<PointAnimationUsingKeyFrames Storyboard.TargetName="ellipse"
 Storyboard.TargetProperty="Fill.GradientOrigin"
 RepeatBehavior="Forever" >
  <DiscretePointKeyFrame Value="0.7,0.3" KeyTime="0:0:0"></DiscretePointKeyFrame>
  <DiscretePointKeyFrame Value="0.3,0.7" KeyTime="0:0:5"></DiscretePointKeyFrame>
  <DiscretePointKeyFrame Value="0.5,0.9" KeyTime="0:0:8"></DiscretePointKeyFrame>
  <DiscretePointKeyFrame Value="0.9,0.6" KeyTime="0:0:10"></DiscretePointKeyFrame>
  <DiscretePointKeyFrame Value="0.8,0.2" KeyTime="0:0:12"></DiscretePointKeyFrame>
  <DiscretePointKeyFrame Value="0.7,0.3" KeyTime="0:0:14"></DiscretePointKeyFrame>
</PointAnimationUsingKeyFrames>
```

When you run this animation, the center point will jump from one position to the next at the appropriate time. It's a dramatic (but jerky) effect.

All key-frame animation classes support discrete key frames, but only some support linear key frames. It all depends on the data type. The data types that support linear key frames are the same ones that support linear interpolation and provide a *DataType*Animation class. Examples include Point, Color, and Double. Data types that don't support linear interpolation include string and object. You'll see an example in Chapter 26 that uses the StringAnimationUsingKeyFrames class to display different pieces of text as an animation progresses.

■ **Tip** You can combine both types of key frame—linear and discrete—in the same key-frame animation.

Easing Key Frames

In the previous chapter, you saw how easing functions can improve ordinary animations. Even though key-frame animations are split into multiple segments, each of these segments uses ordinary, boring linear interpolation.

If this isn't what you want, you can use animation easing to add acceleration or deceleration to individual key frames. However, the ordinary linear key frame and discrete key-frame classes don't support this feature. Instead, you need to use an *easing* key frame, such as EasingDoubleKeyFrame, EasingColorKeyFrame, or EasingPointKeyFrame. Each one works the same way as its linear counterpart but exposes an additional EasingFunction property.

Here's an example that uses animation easing to apply an accelerating effect to the first 5 seconds of the key-frame animation:

```
<PointAnimationUsingKeyFrames Storyboard.TargetName="ellipseBrush"
 Storyboard.TargetProperty="GradientOrigin"
 RepeatBehavior="Forever" >
  <LinearPointKeyFrame Value="0.7,0.3" KeyTime="0:0:0"></LinearPointKeyFrame>
  <EasingPointKeyFrame Value="0.3,0.7" KeyTime="0:0:5">
    <EasingPointKeyFrame.EasingFunction>
      <CircleEase></CircleEase>
    </EasingPointKeyFrame.EasingFunction>
  </EasingPointKeyFrame>
  <LinearPointKeyFrame Value="0.5,0.9" KeyTime="0:0:8"></LinearPointKeyFrame>
  <LinearPointKeyFrame Value="0.9,0.6" KeyTime="0:0:10"></LinearPointKeyFrame>
  <LinearPointKeyFrame Value="0.8,0.2" KeyTime="0:0:12"></LinearPointKeyFrame>
  <LinearPointKeyFrame Value="0.7,0.3" KeyTime="0:0:14"></LinearPointKeyFrame>
</PointAnimationUsingKeyFrames>
```

The combination of key frames and animation easing is a convenient way to model complex animations, but it still may not give you the control you need. Instead of using animation easing, you can create a mathematical formula that dictates the progression of your animation. This is the technique you'll learn in the next section.

Spline Key-Frame Animations

There's one more type of key frame: a *spline* key frame. Every class that supports linear key frames also supports spline key frames, and they're named in the form Spline*DataType*KeyFrame.

Like linear key frames, spline key frames use interpolation to move smoothly from one key value to another. The difference is that every spline key frame sports a KeySpline property. Using the KeySpline property, you define a cubic Bézier curve that influences the way interpolation is performed. Although it's tricky to get the effect you want (at least without an advanced design tool to help you), this technique enables you to create more-seamless acceleration and deceleration and more-lifelike motion.

As you may remember from Chapter 13, a Bézier curve is defined by a start point, an end point, and two control points. In the case of a key spline, the start point is always (0,0), and the end point is always (1,1). You simply supply the two control points. The curve that you create describes the relationship between time (in the X axis) and the animated value (in the Y axis).

Here's an example that demonstrates a key spline animation by comparing the motion of two ellipses across a Canvas. The first ellipse uses a DoubleAnimation to move slowly and evenly across the window. The second ellipse uses a DoubleAnimationUsingKeyFrames with two SplineDoubleKeyFrame objects. It reaches the destination at the same time as the first ellipse (after 10 seconds), but it accelerates and decelerates during its travel, pulling ahead and dropping behind the other ellipse.

```
<DoubleAnimation Storyboard.TargetName="ellipse1"
 Storyboard.TargetProperty="(Canvas.Left)"
 To="500" Duration="0:0:10">
</DoubleAnimation>

<DoubleAnimationUsingKeyFrames Storyboard.TargetName="ellipse2"
 Storyboard.TargetProperty="(Canvas.Left)" >
  <SplineDoubleKeyFrame KeyTime="0:0:5" Value="250"
    KeySpline="0.25,0 0.5,0.7"></SplineDoubleKeyFrame>
  <SplineDoubleKeyFrame KeyTime="0:0:10" Value="500"
    KeySpline="0.25,0.8 0.2,0.4"></SplineDoubleKeyFrame>
</DoubleAnimationUsingKeyFrames>
```

The fastest acceleration occurs shortly after the 5-second mark, when the second SplineDoubleKeyFrame kicks in. Its first control point matches a relatively large Y axis value, which represents the animation progress (0.8) against a correspondingly smaller X axis value, which represents the time. As a result, the ellipse increases its speed over a small distance, before slowing down again.

Figure 16-7 shows a graphical depiction of the two curves that control the movement of the ellipse. To interpret these curves, remember that they chart the progress of the animation from top to bottom. Looking at the first curve, you can see that it follows a fairly even progress downward, with a short pause at the beginning and a gradual leveling off at the end. However, the second curve plummets downward quite quickly, achieving the bulk of its progress, and then levels off for the remainder of the animation.

Figure 16-7. *Charting the progress of a key spline animation*

Path-Based Animation

A path-based animation uses a PathGeometry object to set a property. Although a path-based animation can, in principle, be used to modify any property that has the right data type, it's most useful when animating position-related properties. In fact, the path-based animation classes are primarily intended to help you move a visual object along a path.

As you learned in Chapter 13, a PathGeometry object describes a figure that can include lines, arcs, and curves. Figure 16-8 shows an example with a PathGeometry object that consists of two arcs and a straight line segment that joins the last-defined point to the starting point. This creates a closed route over which a small vector image travels at a constant rate.

Figure 16-8. *Moving an image along a path*

Creating this example is easy. The first step is to build the path you want to use. In this example, the path is defined as a resource:

```
<Window.Resources>
  <PathGeometry x:Key="path">
    <PathFigure IsClosed="True">
      <ArcSegment Point="100,200" Size="15,10"
        SweepDirection="Clockwise"></ArcSegment>
      <ArcSegment Point="400,50" Size="5,5" ></ArcSegment>
    </PathFigure>
  </PathGeometry>
</Window.Resources>
```

Although it's not necessary, this example displays the path. That way, you can clearly see that the image follows the route you've defined. To show the path, you simply need to add a Path element that uses the geometry you've defined:

```
<Path Stroke="Red" StrokeThickness="1" Data="{StaticResource path}"
 Canvas.Top="10" Canvas.Left="10">
</Path>
```

The Path element is placed in a Canvas, along with the Image element that you want to move around the path:

```
<Image Name="image">
  <Image.Source>
    <DrawingImage>
      <DrawingImage.Drawing>
        <GeometryDrawing Brush="LightSteelBlue">
          <GeometryDrawing.Geometry>
            <GeometryGroup>
              <EllipseGeometry Center="10,10" RadiusX="9" RadiusY="4" />
              <EllipseGeometry Center="10,10" RadiusX="4" RadiusY="9" />
            </GeometryGroup>
          </GeometryDrawing.Geometry>
          <GeometryDrawing.Pen>
            <Pen Thickness="1" Brush="Black" />
          </GeometryDrawing.Pen>
        </GeometryDrawing>
      </DrawingImage.Drawing>
    </DrawingImage>
  </Image.Source>
</Image>
```

The final step is to create the animations that move the image. To move the image, you need to adjust the Canvas. Left and Canvas.Top properties. The DoubleAnimationUsingPath does the trick, but you'll need two—one to work on the Canvas.Left property and one to deal with the Canvas.Top property. Here's the complete storyboard:

```
<Storyboard>
  <DoubleAnimationUsingPath Storyboard.TargetName="image"
    Storyboard.TargetProperty="(Canvas.Left)"
    PathGeometry="{StaticResource path}"
    Duration="0:0:5" RepeatBehavior="Forever" Source="X" />
  <DoubleAnimationUsingPath Storyboard.TargetName="image"
    Storyboard.TargetProperty="(Canvas.Top)"
    PathGeometry="{StaticResource path}"
    Duration="0:0:5" RepeatBehavior="Forever" Source="Y" />
</Storyboard>
```

As you can see, when creating a path-based animation, you don't supply starting and ending values. Instead, you indicate the PathGeometry that you want to use with the PathGeometry property. Some path-based animation classes, such as PointAnimationUsingPath, apply both the X and Y components to the destination property. The DoubleAnimationUsingPath class doesn't have this ability, because it sets just one Double value. As a result, you also need to set the Source property to X or Y to indicate whether you're using the X coordinate or the Y coordinate from the path.

Although a path-based animation can use a path that includes a Bézier curve, it's quite a bit different from the key spline animations you learned about in the previous section. In a key spline animation, the Bézier curve describes the relationship between animation progress and time, allowing you to create an animation that changes speed. But in a path-based animation, the collection of lines and curves that constitutes the path determines the *values* that will be used for the animated property.

■ **Note** A path-based animation always runs at a continuous speed. WPF considers the total length of the path and the duration you've specified to determine that speed.

Frame-Based Animation

Along with the property-based animation system, WPF provides a way to create frame-based animation using nothing but code. All you need to do is respond to the shared CompositionTarget.Rendering event, which is fired to get the content for each frame. This is a far lower-level approach, which you won't want to tackle unless you're sure the standard property-based animation model won't work for your scenario (for example, if you're building a simple side-scrolling game, creating physics-based animations, or modeling particle effects such as fire, snow, and bubbles).

The basic technique for building a frame-based animation is easy. You simply need to attach an event handler to the shared CompositionTarget.Rendering event. After you do, WPF will begin calling this event handler continuously. (As long as your rendering code executes quickly enough, WPF will call it 60 times each second.) In the rendering event handler, it's up to you to create or adjust the elements in the window accordingly. In other words, you need to manage all the work yourself. When the animation has ended, detach the event handler.

Figure 16-9 shows a straightforward example. Here, a random number of circles fall from the top of a Canvas to the bottom. They fall at different speeds (based on a random starting velocity), but they accelerate downward at the same rate. The animation ends when all the circles reach the bottom.

Figure 16-9. *A frame-based animation of falling circles*

In this example, each falling circle is represented by an Ellipse element. A custom class named EllipseInfo keeps a reference to the ellipse and tracks the details that are important for the physics model. In this case, there's only one piece of information—the velocity at which the ellipse is moving along the X axis. (You could easily extend this class to include a velocity along the Y axis, additional acceleration information, and so on.)

```
Public Class EllipseInfo
    Private _ellipse As Ellipse
    Public Property Ellipse() As Ellipse
        Get
            Return _ellipse
        End Get
        Set(ByVal value As Ellipse)
            _ellipse = value
        End Set
    End Property

    Private _velocityY As Double
    Public Property VelocityY() As Double
        Get
            Return _velocityY
        End Get
        Set(ByVal value As Double)
            _velocityY = value
        End Set
    End Property

    Public Sub New(ByVal ellipse As Ellipse, ByVal velocityY As Double)
        Me.VelocityY = velocityY
        Me.Ellipse = ellipse
    End Sub
End Class
```

The application keeps track of the EllipseInfo object for each ellipse by using a collection. There are several more window-level fields, which record various details that are used when calculating the fall of the ellipse. You could easily make these details configurable.

```
Private ellipses As List(Of EllipseInfo) = New List(Of EllipseInfo)()

Private accelerationY As Double = 0.1
Private minStartingSpeed As Integer = 1
Private maxStartingSpeed As Integer = 50
Private speedRatio As Double = 0.1
Private minEllipses As Integer = 20
Private maxEllipses As Integer = 100
Private ellipseRadius As Integer = 10
```

When a button is clicked, the collection is cleared, and the event handler is attached to the CompositionTarget.
Rendering event:

```
Private rendering As Boolean = False

Private Sub cmdStart_Clicked(ByVal sender As Object, ByVal e As RoutedEventArgs)
    If Not rendering Then
        ellipses.Clear()
        canvas.Children.Clear()

        AddHandler CompositionTarget.Rendering, AddressOf RenderFrame
        rendering = True
    End If
End Sub
```

If the ellipses don't exist, the rendering code creates them automatically. It creates a random number of ellipses
(currently, between 20 and 100) and gives each of them the same size and color. The ellipses are placed at the top of
the Canvas, but they're offset randomly along the X axis.

```
Private Sub RenderFrame(ByVal sender As Object, ByVal e As EventArgs)
    If ellipses.Count = 0 Then
        ' Animation just started. Create the ellipses.
        Dim halfCanvasWidth As Integer = CInt(Fix(canvas.ActualWidth)) / 2

        Dim rand As New Random()
        Dim ellipseCount As Integer = rand.Next(minEllipses, maxEllipses + 1)
        For i As Integer = 0 To ellipseCount - 1
            ' Create the ellipse.
            Dim ellipse As New Ellipse()
            ellipse.Fill = Brushes.LimeGreen
            ellipse.Width = ellipseRadius
            ellipse.Height = ellipseRadius

            ' Place the ellipse.
            canvas.SetLeft(ellipse, _
              halfCanvasWidth + rand.Next(-halfCanvasWidth, halfCanvasWidth))
            canvas.SetTop(ellipse, 0)
            canvas.Children.Add(ellipse)

            ' Track the ellipse.
            Dim info As New EllipseInfo(ellipse, _
              speedRatio * rand.Next(minStartingSpeed, maxStartingSpeed))
            ellipses.Add(info)
        Next
    ...
```

If the ellipses already exist, the code tackles the more interesting job of animating them. Each ellipse is moved slightly by using the Canvas.SetTop() method. The amount of movement depends on the assigned velocity.

```
...
Else
    For i As Integer = ellipses.Count - 1 To 0 Step -1
        Dim info As EllipseInfo = ellipses(i)
        Dim top As Double = canvas.GetTop(info.Ellipse)
        canvas.SetTop(info.Ellipse, top + 1 * info.VelocityY)
        ...
```

To improve performance, the ellipses are removed from the tracking collection as soon as they've reached the bottom of the Canvas. That way, you don't need to process them again. To allow this to work without causing you to lose your place while stepping through the collection, you need to iterate backward, from the end of the collection to the beginning.

If the ellipse hasn't yet reached the bottom of the Canvas, the code increases the velocity. (Alternatively, you could set the velocity based on how close the ellipse is to the bottom of the Canvas for a magnet-like effect.)

```
        ...
        If top >= (canvas.ActualHeight - ellipseRadius * 2 - 10) Then
            ' This circle has reached the bottom.
            ' Stop animating it.
            ellipses.Remove(info)
        Else
            ' Increase the velocity.
            info.VelocityY += accelerationY
        End If
        ...
```

Finally, if all the ellipses have been removed from the collection, the event handler is removed, allowing the animation to end:

```
        ...
        If ellipses.Count = 0 Then
            ' End the animation.
            ' There's no reason to keep calling this method
            ' if it has no work to do.
            StopRendering()
        End If
    Next
    End If
End Sub
```

Obviously, you could extend this animation to make the circles bounce, scatter, and so on. The technique is the same—you simply need to use more-complex formulas to arrive at the velocity.

There's one caveat to consider when building frame-based animations: they aren't time-dependent. In other words, your animation may run faster on fast computers, because the frame rate will increase and your CompositionTarget.Rendering event will be called more frequently. To compensate for this effect, you need to write code that takes the current time into account.

Storyboards in Code

In the previous chapter, you saw how to create simple one-off animations in code and how to build more-sophisticated storyboards—complete with multiple animations and playback controls—with XAML markup. But sometimes, it makes sense to take the more sophisticated storyboard route but do all the hard work in code. In fact, this scenario is fairly common. It occurs anytime you have multiple animations to deal with and you don't know in advance how many animations there will be or how they should be configured. (This is the case with the simple bomb-dropping game you'll see in this section.) It also occurs if you want to use the same animation in different windows or you simply want the flexibility to separate all the animation-related details from your markup for easier reuse.

It isn't difficult to create, configure, and launch a storyboard programmatically. You just need to create the animation and storyboard objects, add the animations to the storyboard, and start the storyboard. You can perform any cleanup work after your animation ends by reacting to the Storyboard.Completed event.

In the following example, you'll see how to create the game shown in Figure 16-10. Here, a series of bombs are dropped at ever-increasing speeds. The player must click each bomb to defuse it. When a set limit is reached—by default, five dropped bombs—the game ends.

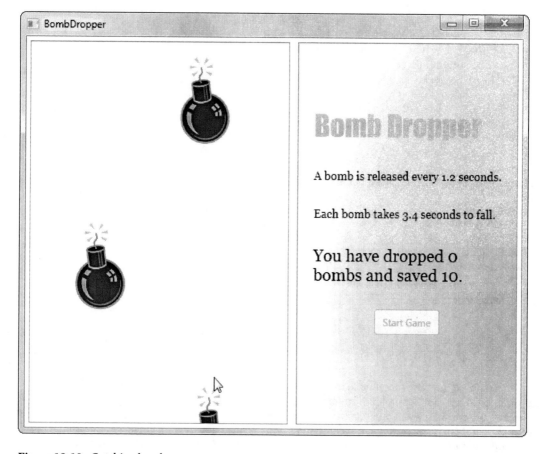

Figure 16-10. *Catching bombs*

In this example, every dropped bomb has its own storyboard with two animations. The first animation drops the bomb (by animating the Canvas.Top property), and the second animation rotates the bomb slightly back and forth, giving it a realistic wiggle effect. If the user clicks a dropping bomb, these animations are halted and two more take place that send the bomb careening harmlessly off the side of the Canvas. Finally, every time an animation ends, the application checks to see whether it represents a bomb that fell down or one that was saved, and it updates the count accordingly.

In the following sections, you'll see how to create each part of this example.

Creating the Main Window

The main window in the BombDropper example is straightforward. It contains a two-column Grid. On the left side is a Border element, which contains the Canvas that represents the game surface:

```
<Border Grid.Column="0" BorderBrush="SteelBlue" BorderThickness="1" Margin="5">
  <Grid>
    <Canvas x:Name="canvasBackground" SizeChanged="canvasBackground_SizeChanged"
      MinWidth="50">
      <Canvas.Background>
        <RadialGradientBrush>
          <GradientStop Color="AliceBlue" Offset="0"></GradientStop>
          <GradientStop Color="White" Offset="0.7"></GradientStop>
        </RadialGradientBrush>
      </Canvas.Background>
    </Canvas>
  </Grid>
</Border>
```

When the Canvas is sized for the first time or resized (when the user changes the size of the window), the following code runs and sets the clipping region:

```
Private Sub canvasBackground_SizeChanged(ByVal sender As Object, _
  ByVal e As SizeChangedEventArgs)
    ' Set the clipping region to match the current display region of the Canvas.
    Dim rect As New RectangleGeometry()
    rect.Rect = New Rect(0, 0, _
      canvasBackground.ActualWidth, canvasBackground.ActualHeight)
    canvasBackground.Clip = rect
End Sub
```

This is required because otherwise the Canvas draws its children even if they lie outside its display area. In the bomb-dropping game, this would cause the bombs to fly out of the box that delineates the Canvas.

■ **Note** Because the user control is defined without explicit sizes, it's free to resize itself to match the window. The game logic uses the current window dimensions without attempting to compensate for them in any way. Thus, if you have a very wide window, bombs are spread across a wide area, making the game more difficult. Similarly, if you have a very tall window, bombs fall faster so they can complete their trajectory in the same interval of time. You could get around this issue by using a fixed-size region, which you could then center in the middle of your user control. However, a resizable window makes the example more adaptable and more interesting.

On the right side of the main window is a panel that shows the game statistics, the current bomb-dropped and bomb-saved count, and a button for starting the game:

```
<Border Grid.Column="1" BorderBrush="SteelBlue" BorderThickness="1" Margin="5">
  <Border.Background>
    <RadialGradientBrush GradientOrigin="1,0.7" Center="1,0.7"
      RadiusX="1" RadiusY="1">
      <GradientStop Color="Orange"  Offset="0"></GradientStop>
      <GradientStop Color="White" Offset="1"></GradientStop>
    </RadialGradientBrush>
  </Border.Background>

  <StackPanel Margin="15" VerticalAlignment="Center" HorizontalAlignment="Center">
    <TextBlock FontFamily="Impact" FontSize="35" Foreground="LightSteelBlue">
    Bomb Dropper</TextBlock>
    <TextBlock x:Name="lblRate" Margin="0,30,0,0" TextWrapping="Wrap"
    FontFamily="Georgia" FontSize="14"></TextBlock>
    <TextBlock x:Name="lblSpeed" Margin="0,30" TextWrapping="Wrap"
    FontFamily="Georgia" FontSize="14"></TextBlock>
    <TextBlock x:Name="lblStatus" TextWrapping="Wrap"
    FontFamily="Georgia" FontSize="20">No bombs have dropped.</TextBlock>
    <Button x:Name="cmdStart" Padding="5" Margin="0,30" Width="80"
    Content="Start Game" Click="cmdStart_Click"></Button>
  </StackPanel>
</Border>
```

Creating the Bomb User Control

The next step is to create the graphical image of the bomb. Although you can use a static image (as long as it has a transparent background), it's always better to deal with more-flexible WPF shapes. By using shapes, you gain the ability to resize the bomb without introducing distortion, and you can animate or alter individual parts of the drawing. The bomb shown in this example is drawn straight from Microsoft Word's online clip-art collection. The bomb was converted to XAML by inserting it into a Word document and then saving that document as an XPS file, a process described in Chapter 12. The full XAML, which uses a combination of Path elements, isn't shown here. But you can see it by downloading the BombDropper game along with the samples for this chapter.

The XAML for the Bomb class was then simplified slightly (by removing the unnecessary extra Canvas elements around it and the transforms for scaling it). The XAML was then inserted into a new user control named Bomb. This way, the main page can show a bomb by creating the Bomb user control and adding it to a layout container (such as a Canvas).

Placing the graphic in a separate user control makes it easy to instantiate multiple copies of that graphic in your user interface. It also lets you encapsulate related functionality by adding to the user control's code. In the bomb-dropping example, only one detail is added to the code—a Boolean property that tracks whether the bomb is currently falling:

```
Public Partial Class Bomb
    Inherits UserControl

    Public Sub New()
        InitializeComponent()
    End Sub
```

```
        Private _isFalling As Boolean
        Public Property IsFalling() As Boolean
            Get
                Return _isFalling
            End Get
            Set(ByVal value As Boolean)
                _isFalling = value
            End Set
        End Property
End Class
```

The markup for the bomb includes a RotateTransform, which the animation code can use to give the bomb a wiggling effect as it falls. Although you could create and add this RotateTransform programmatically, it makes more sense to define it in the XAML file for the bomb:

```
<UserControl x:Class="BombDropper.Bomb"
    xmlns="http://schemas.microsoft.com/winfx/2006/xaml/presentation"
    xmlns:x="http://schemas.microsoft.com/winfx/2006/xaml"
    >
  <UserControl.RenderTransform>
    <TransformGroup>
      <RotateTransform Angle="20" CenterX="50" CenterY="50"></RotateTransform>
      <ScaleTransform ScaleX="0.5" ScaleY="0.5"></ScaleTransform>
    </TransformGroup>
  </UserControl.RenderTransform>

  <Canvas>
    <!-- The Path elements that draw the bomb graphic are defined here. -->
  </Canvas>
</UserControl>
```

With this code in place, you could insert a bomb into your window by using a <bomb:Bomb> element, much as the main window inserts the Title user control (as described in the previous section). However, in this case it makes far more sense to create the bombs programmatically.

Dropping the Bombs

To drop the bombs, the application uses DispatcherTimer, a timer that plays nicely with the WPF user interface because it triggers events on the user-interface thread (saving you the multithreaded programming challenges that are described in Chapter 31). You choose a time interval, and then the DispatcherTimer fires a periodic Tick event at that interval.

```
Private bombTimer As New DispatcherTimer()

Public Sub New()
    InitializeComponent()
    AddHandler bombTimer.Tick, AddressOf bombTimer_Tick
End Sub
```

In the BombDropper game, the timer initially fires every 1.3 seconds. When the user clicks the button to start the game, the timer is started:

```
' Keep track of how many bombs are dropped and stopped.
Private droppedCount As Integer = 0
Private savedCount As Integer = 0

' Initially, bombs fall every 1.3 seconds, and hit the ground after 3.5 seconds.
Private initialSecondsBetweenBombs As Double = 1.3
Private initialSecondsToFall As Double = 3.5
Private secondsBetweenBombs As Double
Private secondsToFall As Double

Private Sub cmdStart_Click(ByVal sender As Object, ByVal e As RoutedEventArgs)
    cmdStart.IsEnabled = False

    ' Reset the game.
    droppedCount = 0
    savedCount = 0
    secondsBetweenBombs = initialSecondsBetweenBombs
    secondsToFall = initialSecondsToFall

    ' Start the bomb-dropping timer.
    bombTimer.Interval = TimeSpan.FromSeconds(secondsBetweenBombs)
    bombTimer.Start()
End Sub
```

Every time the timer fires, the code creates a new Bomb object and sets its position on the Canvas. The bomb is placed just above the top edge of the Canvas so it can fall seamlessly into view. It's given a random horizontal position that falls somewhere between the left and right sides:

```
Private Sub bombTimer_Tick(ByVal sender As Object, ByVal e As EventArgs)
    ' Create the bomb.
    Dim bomb As New Bomb()
    bomb.IsFalling = True

    ' Position the bomb.
    Dim random As New Random()
    bomb.SetValue(Canvas.LeftProperty, _
      CDbl(random.Next(0, canvasBackground.ActualWidth - 50)))
    bomb.SetValue(Canvas.TopProperty, -100.0)

    ' Add the bomb to the Canvas.
    canvasBackground.Children.Add(bomb)
    ...
```

The code then dynamically creates a storyboard to animate the bomb. Two animations are used: one that drops the bomb by changing the attached Canvas.Top property and one that wiggles the bomb by changing the angle of its rotate transform. Because Storyboard.TargetElement and Storyboard.TargetProperty are attached properties, you must set them using the Storyboard.SetTargetElement() and Storyboard.SetTargetProperty() methods:

```
...
' Attach mouse click event (for defusing the bomb).
AddHandler bomb.MouseLeftButtonDown, AddressOf bomb_MouseLeftButtonDown

' Create the animation for the falling bomb.
Dim storyboard As New Storyboard()
Dim fallAnimation As New DoubleAnimation()
fallAnimation.To = canvasBackground.ActualHeight
fallAnimation.Duration = TimeSpan.FromSeconds(secondsToFall)

Storyboard.SetTarget(fallAnimation, bomb)
Storyboard.SetTargetProperty(fallAnimation, New PropertyPath("(Canvas.Top)"))
storyboard.Children.Add(fallAnimation)

' Create the animation for the bomb "wiggle."
Dim wiggleAnimation As New DoubleAnimation()
wiggleAnimation.To = 30
wiggleAnimation.Duration = TimeSpan.FromSeconds(0.2)
wiggleAnimation.RepeatBehavior = RepeatBehavior.Forever
wiggleAnimation.AutoReverse = True

Storyboard.SetTarget(wiggleAnimation, _
    (CType(bomb.RenderTransform, TransformGroup)).Children(0))
Storyboard.SetTargetProperty(wiggleAnimation, New PropertyPath("Angle"))
storyboard.Children.Add(wiggleAnimation)
...
```

Both of these animations could use animation easing for more-realistic behavior, but this example keeps the code simple by using basic linear animations.

The newly created storyboard is stored in a dictionary collection so it can be retrieved easily in other event handlers. The collection is stored as a field in the main window class:

```
' Make it possible to look up a storyboard based on a bomb.
Private storyboards As New Dictionary(Of Bomb, Storyboard) ()
```

Here's the code that adds the storyboard to the tracking collection:

```
...
storyboards.Add(bomb, storyboard)
...
```

Next, you attach an event handler that reacts when the storyboard finishes the fallAnimation, which occurs when the bomb hits the ground. Finally, the storyboard is started, and the animations are put in motion:

```
...
storyboard.Duration = fallAnimation.Duration
AddHandler storyboard.Completed, AddressOf storyboard_Completed
storyboard.Begin()
...
```

The bomb-dropping code needs one last detail. As the game progresses, it becomes more difficult. The timer begins to fire more frequently, the bombs begin to appear more closely together, and the fall time is reduced. To implement these changes, the timer code makes adjustments whenever a set interval of time has passed. By default, BombDropper makes an adjustment every 15 seconds. Here are the fields that control the adjustments:

```
' Perform an adjustment every 15 seconds.
Private secondsBetweenAdjustments As Double = 15
Private lastAdjustmentTime As DateTime = DateTime.MinValue

' After every adjustment, shave 0.1 seconds off both.
Private secondsBetweenBombsReduction As Double = 0.1
Private secondsToFallReduction As Double = 0.1
```

And here's the code at the end of the DispatcherTimer.Tick event handler, which checks whether an adjustment is needed and makes the appropriate changes:

```
...
' Perform an "adjustment" when needed.
If (DateTime.Now.Subtract(lastAdjustmentTime).TotalSeconds > _
    secondsBetweenAdjustments) Then
        lastAdjustmentTime = DateTime.Now

        secondsBetweenBombs -= secondsBetweenBombsReduction
        secondsToFall -= secondsToFallReduction

        ' (Technically, you should check for 0 or negative values.
        ' However, in practice these won't occur because the game will
        ' always end first.)

        ' Set the timer to drop the next bomb at the appropriate time.
        bombTimer.Interval = TimeSpan.FromSeconds(secondsBetweenBombs)

        ' Update the status message.
        lblRate.Text = String.Format("A bomb is released every {0} seconds.", _
            secondsBetweenBombs)
        lblSpeed.Text = String.Format("Each bomb takes {0} seconds to fall.", _
            secondsToFall)
    End If
End Sub
```

With this code in place, there's enough functionality to drop bombs at an ever-increasing rate. However, the game still lacks the code that responds to dropped and saved bombs.

Intercepting a Bomb

The user saves a bomb by clicking it before it reaches the bottom of the Canvas. Because each bomb is a separate instance of the Bomb user control, intercepting mouse clicks is easy—all you need to do is handle the MouseLeftButtonDown event, which fires when any part of the bomb is clicked (but doesn't fire if you click somewhere in the background, such as around the edges of the bomb circle).

When a bomb is clicked, the first step is to get the appropriate bomb object and set its IsFalling property to indicate that it's no longer falling. (The IsFalling property is used by the event handler that deals with completed animations.)

```
Private Sub bomb_MouseLeftButtonDown(ByVal sender As Object, _
  ByVal e As MouseButtonEventArgs)
    ' Get the bomb.
    Dim bomb As Bomb = CType(sender, Bomb)
    bomb.IsFalling = False

    ' Record the bomb's current (animated) position.
    Dim currentTop As Double = Canvas.GetTop(bomb)
    ...
```

The next step is to find the storyboard that controls the animation for this bomb so it can be stopped. To find the storyboard, you need to look it up in the collection that this game uses for tracking. Currently, WPF doesn't include any standardized way to find the animations that are acting on a given element.

```
    ...
    ' Stop the bomb from falling.
    Dim storyboard As Storyboard = storyboards(bomb)
    storyboard.Stop()
    ...
```

After a button is clicked, another set of animations moves the bomb off the screen, throwing it up and left or right (depending on which side is closest). Although you could create an entirely new storyboard to implement this effect, the BombDropper game clears the current storyboard that's being used for the bomb and adds new animations to it. When this process is completed, the new storyboard is started:

```
    ...
    ' Reuse the existing storyboard, but with new animations.
    ' Send the bomb on a new trajectory by animating Canvas.Top
    ' and Canvas.Left.
    storyboard.Children.Clear()

    Dim riseAnimation As New DoubleAnimation()
    riseAnimation.From = currentTop
    riseAnimation.To = 0
    riseAnimation.Duration = TimeSpan.FromSeconds(2)

    Storyboard.SetTarget(riseAnimation, bomb)
    Storyboard.SetTargetProperty(riseAnimation, New PropertyPath("(Canvas.Top)"))
    storyboard.Children.Add(riseAnimation)
```

```
    Dim slideAnimation As New DoubleAnimation()
    Dim currentLeft As Double = Canvas.GetLeft(bomb)

    ' Throw the bomb off the closest side.
    If currentLeft < canvasBackground.ActualWidth / 2 Then
        slideAnimation.To = -100
    Else
        slideAnimation.To = canvasBackground.ActualWidth + 100
    End If
    slideAnimation.Duration = TimeSpan.FromSeconds(1)
    Storyboard.SetTarget(slideAnimation, bomb)
    Storyboard.SetTargetProperty(slideAnimation, New PropertyPath("(Canvas.Left)"))
    storyboard.Children.Add(slideAnimation)

    ' Start the new animation.
    storyboard.Duration = slideAnimation.Duration
    storyboard.Begin()
End Sub
```

Now the game has enough code to drop bombs and bounce them off the screen when the user saves them. However, to keep track of which bombs are saved and which ones are dropped, you need to react to the Storyboard. Completed event that fires at the end of an animation.

Counting Bombs and Cleaning Up

As you've seen, the BombDropper uses storyboards in two ways: to animate a falling bomb and to animate a defused bomb. You could handle the completion of these storyboards with different event handlers, but to keep things simple, the BombDropper uses just one. It tells the difference between an exploded bomb and a rescued bomb by examining the Bomb.IsFalling property.

```
' End the game when 5 bombs have fallen.
Private maxDropped As Integer = 5

Private Sub storyboard_Completed(ByVal sender As Object, ByVal e As EventArgs)
    Dim clockGroup As ClockGroup = CType(sender, ClockGroup)

    ' Get the first animation in the storyboard, and use it to find the
    ' bomb that's being animated.
    Dim completedAnimation As DoubleAnimation
    completedAnimation = CType(clockGroup.Children(0).Timeline, DoubleAnimation)
    Dim completedBomb As Bomb
    completedBomb = CType(Storyboard.GetTarget(completedAnimation), Bomb)

    ' Determine if a bomb fell or flew off the Canvas after being clicked.
    If completedBomb.IsFalling Then
        droppedCount += 1
    Else
        savedCount += 1
    End If
    ...
```

Either way, the code then updates the display test to indicate the number of bombs that have been dropped and saved:

```
...
' Update the display.
lblStatus.Text = String.Format("You have dropped {0} bombs and saved {1}.", _
    droppedCount, savedCount)
...
```

At this point, the code checks to see whether the maximum number of dropped bombs has been reached. If it has, the game ends, the timer is stopped, and all the bombs and storyboards are removed:

```
...
' Check if it's game over.
If droppedCount >= maxDropped Then
    bombTimer.Stop()
    lblStatus.Text &= Environment.NewLine & Environment.NewLine & "Game over."

    ' Find all the storyboards that are underway.
    For Each item As KeyValuePair(Of Bomb, Storyboard) In storyboards
        Dim storyboard As Storyboard = item.Value
        Dim bomb As Bomb = item.Key

        storyboard.Stop()
        canvasBackground.Children.Remove(bomb)
    Next

    ' Empty the tracking collection.
    storyboards.Clear()

    ' Allow the user to start a new game.
    cmdStart.IsEnabled = True
Else
    ' Clean up just this bomb, and let the game continue.
    Dim storyboard As Storyboard = CType(clockGroup.Timeline, Storyboard)
    storyboard.Stop()

    storyboards.Remove(completedBomb)
    canvasBackground.Children.Remove(completedBomb)
End If
End Sub
```

This completes the code for BombDropper game. However, you can make plenty of refinements. Some examples include the following:

> *Animate a bomb explosion effect*: This effect can make the flames around the bomb twinkle or send small pieces of shrapnel flying across the Canvas.

> *Animate the background*: This change is easy, and it adds pizzazz. For example, you can create a linear gradient that shifts up, creating an impression of movement, or one that transitions between two colors.

Add depth: It's easier than you think. The basic technique is to give the bombs different sizes. Bombs that are bigger should have a higher ZIndex, ensuring that they overlap smaller bombs, and should be given a shorter animation time, ensuring that they fall faster. You can also make the bombs partially transparent, so as one falls, the others behind it are visible.

Add sound effects: In Chapter 26, you'll learn to use sound and other media in WPF. You can use well-timed sound effects to punctuate bomb explosions or rescued bombs.

Use animation easing: If you want bombs to accelerate as they fall, bounce off the screen, or wiggle more naturally, you can add easing functions to the animations used here. And, as you'd expect, easing functions can be constructed in code just as easily as in XAML.

Fine-tune the parameters: You can provide more dials to tweak behavior (for example, variables that set how the bomb times, trajectories, and frequencies that are altered as the game processes). You can also inject more randomness (for example, allowing saved bombs to bounce off the Canvas in slightly different ways).

The Last Word

In this chapter, you learned the techniques needed to make practical animations and integrate them into your applications. The only missing ingredient is the eye candy—in other words, making sure the animated effects are as polished as your code.

As you've seen over the past two chapters, the animation model in WPF is surprisingly full-featured. However, getting the result you want isn't always easy. If you want to animate separate portions of your interface as part of a single animated "scene," you're often forced to write a fair bit of markup with interdependent details that aren't always clear. In more-complex animations, you may be forced to hard-code details and fall back to code to perform calculations for the ending value of animation. And if you need fine-grained control over an animation, such as when modeling a physical particle system, you'll need to control every step of the way by using frame-based animation.

The future of WPF animation promises higher-level classes that are built on the basic plumbing you've learned about in this chapter. Ideally, you'll be able to plug animations into your application simply by using prebuilt animation classes, wrapping your elements in specialized containers, and setting a few attached properties. The actual implementation that generates the effect you want—whether it's a smooth dissolve between two images or a series of animated fly-ins that builds a window—will be provided for you.

Templates and Custom Elements

CHAPTER 17

■ ■ ■

Control Templates

In the past, Windows developers were forced to choose between convenience and flexibility. For maximum convenience, they could use prebuilt controls. These controls worked well enough, but they offered limited customization and almost always had a fixed visual appearance. Occasionally, some controls provided a less-than-intuitive "owner drawing" mode that allowed developers to paint a portion of the control by responding to a callback. But the basic controls—buttons, text boxes, check boxes, list boxes, and so on—were completely locked down.

As a result, developers who wanted a bit more pizzazz were forced to build custom controls from scratch. This was a problem—not only was it slow and difficult to write the required drawing logic by hand, but custom control developers also needed to implement basic functionality from scratch (such as selection in a text box or key handling in a button). And even after the custom controls were perfected, inserting them into an existing application involved a fairly significant round of editing, which would usually necessitate changes in the code (and more rounds of testing). In short, custom controls were a necessary evil—they were the only way to get a modern, distinctive interface, but they were also a headache to integrate into an application and support.

WPF solves the control customization problem with styles (which you considered in Chapter 11) and templates (which you'll begin exploring in this chapter). These features work so well because of the dramatically different way that controls are implemented in WPF. In previous user interface technologies, such as Windows Forms, commonly used controls aren't actually implemented in .NET code. Instead, the Windows Forms control classes wrap core ingredients from the Win32 API, which are untouchable. But as you've already learned, in WPF every control is composed in pure .NET code, with no Win32 API glue in the background. As a result, it's possible for WPF to expose mechanisms (styles and templates) that allow you to reach into these elements and tweak them. In fact, *tweak* is the wrong word because, as you'll see in this chapter, WPF controls allow the most radical redesigns you can imagine.

Understanding Logical Trees and Visual Trees

Earlier in this book, you spent a great deal of time considering the content model of a window—in other words, how you can nest elements inside other elements to build a complete window.

For example, consider the extremely simple two-button window shown in Figure 17-1. To create this window, you nest a StackPanel control inside a Window. In the StackPanel, you place two Button controls, and inside of each you can add some content of your choice (in this case, two strings). Here's the markup:

```
<Window x:Class="Window1"
    xmlns="http://schemas.microsoft.com/winfx/2006/xaml/presentation"
    xmlns:x="http://schemas.microsoft.com/winfx/2006/xaml"
    Title="SimpleWindow" Height="338" Width="356"
    >
```

```
    <StackPanel Margin="5">
      <Button Padding="5" Margin="5">First Button</Button>
      <Button Padding="5" Margin="5">Second Button</Button>
    </StackPanel>
</Window>
```

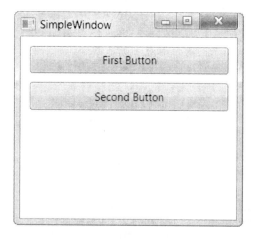

Figure 17-1. *A window with three elements*

The assortment of elements that you've added is called the *logical tree*, and it's shown in Figure 17-2. As a WPF programmer, you'll spend most of your time building the logical tree and then backing it up with event-handling code. In fact, all of the features you've considered so far (such as property value inheritance, event routing, and styling) work through the logical tree.

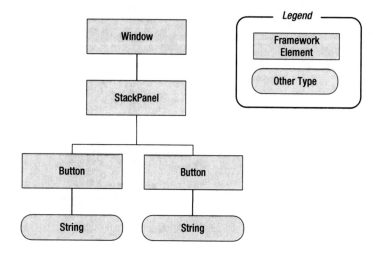

Figure 17-2. *The logical tree for SimpleWindow*

However, if you want to customize your elements, the logical tree isn't much help. Obviously, you could replace an entire element with another element (for example, you could substitute a custom FancyButton class in place of the current Button), but this requires more work, and it could disrupt your application's interface or its code. For that reason, WPF goes deeper with the visual tree.

A *visual tree* is an expanded version of the logical tree. It breaks elements down into smaller pieces. In other words, instead of seeing a carefully encapsulated black box such as the Button control, you see the visual components of that button—the border that gives buttons their signature shaded background (represented by the ButtonChrome class), the container inside (a ContentPresenter), and the block that holds the button text (represented by the familiar TextBlock). Figure 17-3 shows the visual tree for Figure 17-1.

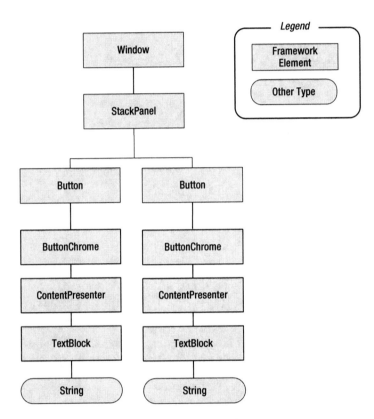

Figure 17-3. *The visual tree for SimpleWindow*

All of these details are themselves elements—in other words, every individual detail in a control such as Button is represented by a class that derives from FrameworkElement.

■ **Note** It's important to realize that there is more than one possible way to expand a logical tree into a visual tree. Details such as the styles you've used and the properties you've set can affect the way a visual tree is composed. For instance, in the previous example, the button holds text content, and as a result, it automatically creates a nested TextBlock element. But as you know, the Button control is a content control, so it can hold any other element you want to use, as long as you nest it inside the button.

So far, this doesn't seem that remarkable. You've just seen that all WPF elements can be decomposed into smaller parts. But what's the advantage for a WPF developer? The visual tree allows you to do two useful things:

- You can alter one of the elements in the visual tree by using styles. You can select the specific element you want to modify by using the Style.TargetType property. You can even use triggers to make changes automatically when control properties change. However, certain details are difficult or impossible to modify.

- You can create a new template for your control. In this case, your control template will be used to build the visual tree exactly the way you want it.

Interestingly enough, WPF provides two classes that let you browse through the logical and visual trees. These classes are System.Windows.LogicalTreeHelper and System.Windows.Media.VisualTreeHelper.

You've already seen the LogicalTreeHelper in Chapter 2, where it allowed you to hook up event handlers in a WPF application with a dynamically loaded XAML document. The LogicalTreeHelper provides the relatively sparse set of methods listed in Table 17-1. Although these methods are occasionally useful, in most cases you'll use the methods of a specific FrameworkElement instead.

Table 17-1. *LogicalTreeHelper Methods*

Name	Description
FindLogicalNode()	Finds a specific element by name, starting at the element you specify and searching down the logical tree.
BringIntoView()	Scrolls an element into view (if it's in a scrollable container and isn't currently visible). The FrameworkElement.BringIntoView() method performs the same trick.
GetParent()	Gets the parent element of a specific element.
GetChildren()	Gets the child element of a specific element. As you learned in Chapter 2, different elements support different content models. For example, panels support multiple children, while content controls support only a single child. However, the GetChildren() method abstracts away this difference and works with any type of element.

The VisualTreeHelper provides a few similar methods—GetChildrenCount(), GetChild(), and GetParent()—along with a small set of methods that are designed for performing lower-level drawing. (For example, you'll find methods for hit testing and bounds checking, which you considered in Chapter 14.)

The VisualTreeHelper also doubles as an interesting way to study the visual tree in your application. Using the GetChild() method, you can drill down through the visual tree of any window and display it for your consideration. This is a great learning tool, and it requires nothing more than a dash of recursive code.

Figure 17-4 shows one possible implementation. Here, a separate window displays an entire visual tree, starting at any supplied object. In this example, another window (named SimpleWindow) uses the VisualTreeDisplay window to show its visual tree.

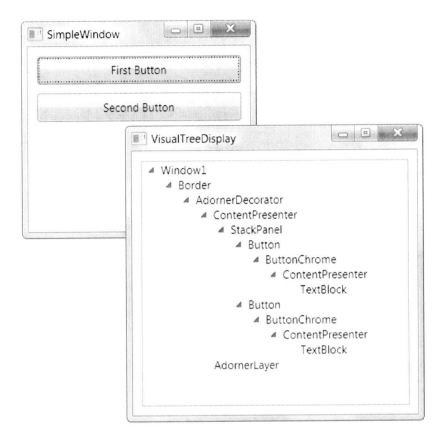

Figure 17-4. *Programmatically examining the visual tree*

Here, a window named Window1 contains a Border, which in turn holds an AdornerDecorator. (The AdornerDecorator class adds support for drawing content in the adorner layer, which is a special invisible region that overlays your element content. WPF uses the adorner layer to draw details such as focus cues and drag-and-drop indicators.) Inside the AdornerDecorator is a ContentPresenter, which hosts the content of the window. That content includes StackPanel with two Button controls, each of which comprises a ButtonChrome (which draws the standard visual appearance of the button) and a ContentPresenter (which holds the button content). Finally, inside the ContentPresenter of each button is a TextBlock that wraps the text you see in the window.

■ **Note** In this example, the code builds a visual tree in another window. If you place the TreeView in the same window as the one you're examining, you'd inadvertently change the visual tree as you fill the TreeView with items.

Here's the complete code for the VisualTreeDisplay window:

```
Public Class VisualTreeDisplay

    Public Sub ShowVisualTree(ByVal element As DependencyObject)
        ' Clear the tree.
        treeElements.Items.Clear()
```

```
      ' Start processing elements, begin at the root.
      ProcessElement(element, Nothing)
   End Sub

   Private Sub ProcessElement(ByVal element As DependencyObject, _
     ByVal previousItem As TreeViewItem)
      ' Create a TreeViewItem for the current element.
      Dim item As New TreeViewItem()
      item.Header = element.GetType().Name
      item.IsExpanded = True

      ' Check whether this item should be added to the root of the tree
      '(if it's the first item), or nested under another item.
      If previousItem Is Nothing Then
          treeElements.Items.Add(item)
      Else
          previousItem.Items.Add(item)
      End If

      ' Check if this element contains other elements.
      For i As Integer = 0 To VisualTreeHelper.GetChildrenCount(element) - 1
          ' Process each contained element recursively.
          ProcessElement(VisualTreeHelper.GetChild(element, i), item)
      Next
   End Sub

End Class
```

Once you've added this tree to a project, you can use this code from any other window to display its visual tree:

```
Dim treeDisplay As New VisualTreeDisplay()
treeDisplay.ShowVisualTree(Me)
treeDisplay.Show()
```

■ **Tip**   You can delve into the visual tree of other applications by using the remarkable Snoop utility, which is available at http://snoopwpf.codeplex.com. Using Snoop, you can examine the visual tree of any currently running WPF application. You can also zoom in on any element, survey routed events as they're being executed, and explore and even modify element properties.

Understanding Templates

This look at the visual tree raises a few interesting questions. For example, how is a control translated from the logical tree into the expanded representation of the visual tree?

It turns out that every control has a built-in recipe that determines how it should be rendered (as a group of more fundamental elements). That recipe is called a *control template*, and it's defined by using a block of XAML markup.

▓ **Note** Every WPF control is designed to be *lookless*, which means that its visuals (the "look") can be completely redefined. What doesn't change is the control's behavior, which is hardwired into the control class (although it can often be fine-tuned using various properties). When you choose to use a control such as the Button, you choose it because you want button-like behavior (in other words, an element that presents content can be clicked to trigger an action and can be used as the default or cancel button on a window). However, you're free to change the way a button looks and how it reacts when you mouse over it or press it, as well as any other aspect of its appearance and visual behavior.

Here's a simplified version of the template for the common Button class. It omits the XML namespace declarations, the attributes that set the properties of the nested elements, and the triggers that determine how the button behaves when it's disabled, focused, or clicked:

```
<ControlTemplate ... >
  <mwt:ButtonChrome Name="Chrome" ... >
    <ContentPresenter Content="{TemplateBinding ContentControl.Content}" ... />
  </mwt:ButtonChrome>
  <ControlTemplate.Triggers>
    ...
  </ControlTemplate.Triggers>
</ControlTemplate>
```

Although we haven't yet explored the ButtonChrome and ContentPresenter classes, you can easily recognize that the control template provides the expansion you saw in the visual tree. The ButtonChrome class defines the standard button visuals, while the ContentPresenter holds whatever content you've supplied. If you wanted to build a completely new button (as you'll see later in this chapter), you simply need to create a new control template. In place of ButtonChrome, you'd use something else—perhaps your own custom element or a shape-drawing element like the ones described in Chapter 12.

▓ **Note** ButtonChrome derives from Decorator (much like the Border class). That means it's designed to add a graphical embellishment around another element—in this case, around the content of a button.

The triggers control how the button changes when it is focused, clicked, and disabled. There's actually nothing particularly interesting in these triggers. Rather than perform the heavy lifting themselves, the focus and click triggers simply modify a property of the ButtonChrome class that provides the visuals for the button:

```
<Trigger Property="UIElement.IsKeyboardFocused">
  <Setter Property="mwt:ButtonChrome.RenderDefaulted" TargetName="Chrome">
    <Setter.Value>
      <s:Boolean>True</s:Boolean>
    </Setter.Value>
  </Setter>
  <Trigger.Value>
    <s:Boolean>True</s:Boolean>
  </Trigger.Value>
```

```
</Trigger>
<Trigger Property="ToggleButton.IsChecked">
  <Setter Property="mwt:ButtonChrome.RenderPressed" TargetName="Chrome">
    <Setter.Value>
      <s:Boolean>True</s:Boolean>
    </Setter.Value>
  </Setter>
  <Trigger.Value>
    <s:Boolean>True</s:Boolean>
  </Trigger.Value>
</Trigger>
```

The first trigger ensures that when the button receives focus, the RenderDefaulted property is set to True. The Second trigger ensures that when the button is clicked, the RenderPressed property is set to True. Either way, it's up to the ButtonChrome class to adjust itself accordingly. The graphical changes that take place are too complex to be represented by a few property setter statements.

Both of the Setter objects in this example use the TargetName property to act upon a specific piece of a control template. This technique is possible only when working with a control template. In other words, you can't write a style trigger that uses the TargetName property to access the ButtonChrome object, because the name *Chrome* isn't in scope in your style. This is just one of the ways that templates give you more power than styles alone.

Triggers don't always need to use the TargetName property. For example, the trigger for the IsEnabled property simply adjusts the foreground color of any text content in the button. This trigger does its work by setting the attached TextElement.Foreground property without the help of the ButtonChrome class:

```
<Trigger Property="UIElement.IsEnabled">
  <Setter Property="TextElement.Foreground">
    <Setter.Value>
      <SolidColorBrush>#FFADADAD</SolidColorBrush>
    </Setter.Value>
  </Setter>
  <Trigger.Value>
    <s:Boolean>False</s:Boolean>
  </Trigger.Value>
</Trigger>
```

You'll see the same division of responsibilities when you build your own control templates. If you're lucky enough to be able to do all your work directly with triggers, you may not need to create custom classes and add code. On the other hand, if you need to provide more-complex visual tailoring, you may need to derive a custom chrome class of your own. The ButtonChrome class itself provides no customization—it's dedicated to rendering the standard theme-specific appearance of a button.

▓ **Note** All the XAML that you see in this section is extracted from the standard Button control template. A bit later, in the "Dissecting Controls" section, you'll learn how to view a control's default control template.

TYPES OF TEMPLATES

This chapter focuses on control templates, which allow you to define the elements that make up a control. However, there are actually three types of templates in the WPF world, all of which derive from the base FrameworkTemplate class. Along with control templates (represented by the ControlTemplate class), there are data templates (represented by DataTemplate and HierarchicalDataTemplate) and the more specialized panel template for an ItemsControl (ItemsPanelTemplate).

Data templates are used to extract data from an object and display it in a content control or in the individual items of a list control. Data templates are ridiculously useful in data-binding scenarios, and they're described in detail in Chapter 20. To a certain extent, data templates and control templates overlap. For example, both types of templates allow you to insert additional elements, apply formatting, and so on. However, data templates are used to add elements *inside* an existing control. The prebuilt aspects of that control aren't changed. On the other hand, control templates are a much more drastic approach that allows you to completely rewrite the content model of a control.

Finally, panel templates are used to control the layout of items in a list control (a control that derives from the ItemsControl class). For example, you can use them to create a list box that tiles its items from right to left and then down (rather than the standard top-to-bottom single-line display). Panel templates are described in Chapter 20.

You can certainly combine template types in the same control. For example, if you want to create a slick list control that is bound to a specific type of data, lays its items out in a nonstandard way, and replaces the stock border with something more exciting, you'll want to create your own data templates, panel template, and control template.

The Chrome Classes

The ButtonChrome class is defined in the Microsoft.Windows.Themes namespace, which holds a relatively small set of similar classes that render basic Windows details. Along with ButtonChrome, these classes include BulletChrome (for check boxes and radio buttons), ScrollChrome (for scrollbars), ListBoxChrome, and SystemDropShadowChrome. This is the lowest level of the public control API. At a slightly higher level, you'll find that the System.Windows. Controls.Primitives namespace includes a number of basic elements that you can use independently but are more commonly wrapped into more-useful controls. These include ScrollBar, ResizeGrip (for sizing a window), Thumb (the draggable button on a scrollbar), TickBar (the optional set of ticks on a slider), and so on. Essentially, System. Windows.Controls.Primitives provides bare-bones ingredients that can be used in a variety of controls and aren't very useful on their own, while Microsoft.Windows.Themes contains the down-and-dirty drawing logic for rendering these details.

There's one more difference. The types in System.Windows.Controls.Primitives are, like most WPF types, defined in the PresentationFramework.dll assembly. However, those in the Microsoft.Windows.Themes are defined separately in *three* assemblies: PresentationFramework.Aero.dll, PresentationFramework.Luna.dll, and PresentationFramework. Royale.dll. Each assembly includes its own version of the ButtonChrome class (and other chrome classes), with slightly different rendering logic. The one that WPF uses depends on your operating system and theme settings.

■ **Note** You'll learn more about the internal workings of a chrome class in Chapter 18, and you'll learn to build your own chrome class with custom rendering logic.

Although control templates often draw on the chrome classes, they don't always need to do so. For example, the ResizeGrip element (which is to create the grid of dots in the bottom-right corner of a resizable window) is simple enough that its template can use the drawing classes you learned about in Chapter 12 and Chapter 13, such as Path, DrawingBrush, and LinearGradientBrush. Here's the (somewhat convoluted) markup that it uses:

```
<ControlTemplate TargetType="{x:Type ResizeGrip}" ... >
  <Grid Background="{TemplateBinding Panel.Background}" SnapsToDevicePixels="True">
    <Path Margin="0,0,2,2" Data="M9,0L11,0 11,11 0,11 0,9 3,9 3,6 6,6 6,3 9,3z"
      HorizontalAlignment="Right" VerticalAlignment="Bottom">
      <Path.Fill>
        <DrawingBrush ViewboxUnits="Absolute" TileMode="Tile" Viewbox="0,0,3,3"
          Viewport="0,0,3,3" ViewportUnits="Absolute">
          <DrawingBrush.Drawing>
            <DrawingGroup>
              <DrawingGroup.Children>
                <GeometryDrawing Geometry="M0,0L2,0 2,2 0,2z">
                  <GeometryDrawing.Brush>
                    <LinearGradientBrush EndPoint="1,0.75" StartPoint="0,0.25">
                      <LinearGradientBrush.GradientStops>
                        <GradientStop Offset="0.3" Color="#FFFFFFFF" />
                        <GradientStop Offset="0.75" Color="#FFBBC5D7" />
                        <GradientStop Offset="1" Color="#FF6D83A9" />
                      </LinearGradientBrush.GradientStops>
                    </LinearGradientBrush>
                  </GeometryDrawing.Brush>
                </GeometryDrawing>
              </DrawingGroup.Children>
            </DrawingGroup>
          </DrawingBrush.Drawing>
        </DrawingBrush>
      </Path.Fill>
    </Path>
  </Grid>
</ControlTemplate>
```

■ **Note**   It's common to see the SnapsToDevicePixels setting in a prebuilt control template (and it's useful in the one you create as well). As you learned in Chapter 12, SnapsToDevicePixels ensures that single-pixel lines aren't placed "between" pixels because of WPF's resolution independence, which creates a fuzzy 2-pixel line.

Dissecting Controls

When you create a control template (as you'll see in the next section), your template replaces the existing template completely. This gives you a high level of flexibility, but it also makes life a little more complex. In most cases, you'll need to see the standard template that a control uses before you can create your own adapted version. In some cases, your control template might mirror the standard template with only a minor change.

The WPF documentation doesn't list the XAML for standard control templates. However, you can get the information you need programmatically. The basic idea is to grab a control's template from its Template property (which is defined as part of the Control class) and then serialize it to XAML by using the XamlWriter class. Figure 17-5 shows an example with a program that lists all the WPF controls and lets you view each one's control template.

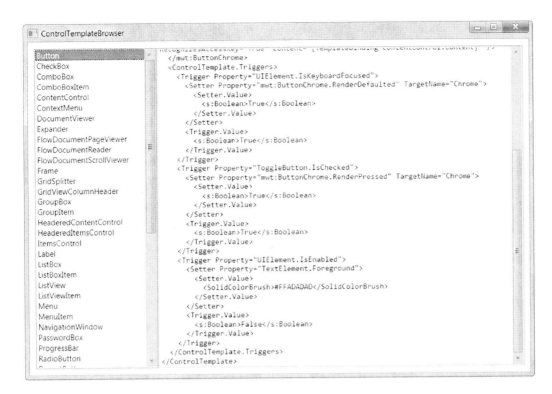

Figure 17-5. *Browsing WPF control templates*

The secret to building this application is a healthy dose of *reflection*, the .NET API for examining types. When the main window in this application is first loaded, it scans all the types in the core PresentationFramework.dll assembly (which is where the Control class is defined). It then adds these types to a collection, which it sorts by type name, and then binds that collection to a list.

```
Private Sub Window_Loaded(ByVal sender As Object, ByVal e As EventArgs)
    Dim controlType As Type = GetType(Control)
    Dim derivedTypes As List(Of Type) = New List(Of Type)()

    ' Search all the types in the assembly where the Control class is defined.
    Dim controlAssembly As System.Reflection.Assembly
    controlAssembly = System.Reflection.Assembly.GetAssembly(GetType(Control))

    For Each type As Type In controlAssembly.GetTypes()
        ' Only add a type of the list if it's a Control, a concrete class,
        ' and public.
        If type.IsSubclassOf(controlType) And (Not type.IsAbstract) _
          And type.IsPublic Then
            derivedTypes.Add(type)
        End If
    Next
```

```
      ' Sort the types. The custom TypeComparer class orders types
      ' alphabetically by type name.
      derivedTypes.Sort(New TypeComparer())

      ' Show the list of types.
      lstTypes.ItemsSource = derivedTypes
End Sub
```

Whenever a control is selected from the list, the corresponding control template is shown in the text box on the right. This step takes a bit more work. The first challenge is that a control template is null (Nothing) until the control is displayed in a window. Using reflection, the code attempts to create an instance of the control and add it to the current window (albeit with a Visibility of Collapse so it can't be seen). The second challenge is that you need to convert the live ControlTemplate object to the familiar XAML markup. The shared XamlWriter.Save() method takes care of this task, although the code uses the XmlWriter and XmlWriterSettings objects to make sure the XAML is indented so that it's easier to read. All of this code is wrapped in an exception-handling block, which catches the problems that result from controls that can't be created or can't be added to a Grid (such as another Window or a Page):

```
Private Sub lstTypes_SelectionChanged(ByVal sender As Object, _
  ByVal e As SelectionChangedEventArgs)
    Try
        ' Get the selected type.
        Dim type As Type = CType(lstTypes.SelectedItem, Type)

        ' Instantiate the type.
        Dim info As ConstructorInfo
        info = type.GetConstructor(System.Type.EmptyTypes)
        Dim control As Control = CType(info.Invoke(Nothing), Control)

        ' Add it to the grid (but keep it hidden).
        control.Visibility = Visibility.Collapsed
        grid.Children.Add(control)

        ' Get the template.
        Dim template As ControlTemplate = control.Template

        ' Get the XAML for the template.
        Dim settings As New XmlWriterSettings()
        settings.Indent = True
        Dim sb As New StringBuilder()
        Dim writer As XmlWriter = XmlWriter.Create(sb, settings)
        XamlWriter.Save(template, writer)

        ' Display the template.
        txtTemplate.Text = sb.ToString()

        ' Remove the control from the grid.
        grid.Children.Remove(control)

    Catch err As Exception
        txtTemplate.Text = "<< Error generating template: " & err.Message & ">>"
    End Try
End Sub
```

It wouldn't be much more difficult to extend this application so you can edit the template in the text box, convert it back to a ControlTemplate object (using the XamlReader), and then assign that to a control to see its effect. However, you'll have an easier time testing and refining templates by putting them into action in a real window, as described in the next section.

■ **Tip**   If you're using Expression Blend, you can also use a handy feature that lets you edit the template for any control that you're working with. (Technically, this step grabs the default template, creates a copy of it for your control, and then lets you edit the copy.) To try this, right-click a control on the design surface and choose Edit Control Parts (Template) ➤ Edit a Copy. Your control template copy will be stored as a resource (see Chapter 10), so you'll be prompted to choose a descriptive resource key, and you'll need to choose between storing your resource in the current window or in the global application resources so you can use your control template throughout your application.

Creating Control Templates

So far, you've learned a fair bit about the way templates work, but you haven't built a template of your own. In the following sections, you'll build a simple custom button and learn a few of the finer details about control templates in the process.

As you've already seen, the basic Button control uses the ButtonChrome class to draw its distinctive background and border. One of the reasons that the Button class uses ButtonChrome instead of the WPF drawing primitives is that a standard button's appearance depends on a few obvious characteristics (whether it's disabled, focused, or in the process of being clicked) and other subtler factors (such as the current Windows theme). Implementing this sort of logic with triggers alone would be awkward.

However, when you build your own custom controls, you're probably not as worried about standardization and theme integration. (In fact, WPF doesn't emphasize user interface standardization nearly as strongly as previous user interface technologies.) Instead, you're more concerned with creating attractive, distinctive controls that blend in with the rest of your user interface. For that reason, you might not need to create classes such as ButtonChrome. Instead, you can use the elements you already know (along with the drawing elements you learned about in Chapter 12 and Chapter 13, and the animation skills you picked in Chapter 15 and Chapter 16) to design a self-sufficient control template with no code.

■ **Note**   For an alternate approach, check out Chapter 18, which explains how to build your own chrome with custom rendering logic and integrate it into a control template.

A Simple Button

To apply a custom control template, you simply set the Template property of your control. Although you can define an inline template (by nesting the control template tag inside the control tag), this approach rarely makes sense. That's because you'll almost always want to reuse your template to skin multiple instances of the same control. To accommodate this design, you need to define your control template as a resource and refer to it by using a StaticResource reference, as shown here:

```
<Button Margin="10" Padding="5" Template="{StaticResource ButtonTemplate}">
 A Simple Button with a Custom Template</Button>
```

Not only does this approach make it easier to create a whole host of customized buttons, it also gives you the flexibility to modify your control template later without disrupting the rest of your application's user interface.

In this particular example, the ButtonTemplate resource is placed in the Resources collection of the containing window. However, in a real application, you're much more likely to use application resources. The reasons (and a few design tips) are discussed a bit later in the "Organizing Template Resources" section.

Here's the basic outline for the control template:

```
<Window.Resources>
  <ControlTemplate x:Key="ButtonTemplate" TargetType="{x:Type Button}">
    ...
  </ControlTemplate>
</Window.Resources>
```

You'll notice that this control template sets the TargetType property to explicitly indicate it's designed for buttons. As a matter of style, this is always a good convention to follow. In content controls, such as the button, it's also a requirement, or the ContentPresenter won't work.

To create a template for a basic button, you need to draw your own border and background and then place the content inside the button. Two possible candidates for drawing the border are the Rectangle class and the Border class. The following example uses the Border class to combine a rounded orange outline with an eye-catching red background and white text:

```
<ControlTemplate x:Key="ButtonTemplate" TargetType="{x:Type Button}">
  <Border BorderBrush="Orange" BorderThickness="3" CornerRadius="2"
    Background="Red" TextBlock.Foreground="White">
    ...
  </Border>
</ControlTemplate>
```

This takes care of the background, but you still need a way to display the button content. You may remember from your earlier exploration that the Button class includes a ContentPresenter in its control template. The ContentPresenter is required for all content controls—it's the "insert content here" marker that tells WPF where to stuff the content:

```
<ControlTemplate x:Key="ButtonTemplate" TargetType="{x:Type Button}">
  <Border BorderBrush="Orange" BorderThickness="3" CornerRadius="2"
    Background="Red" TextBlock.Foreground="White">
    <ContentPresenter RecognizesAccessKey="True"></ContentPresenter>
  </Border>
</ControlTemplate>
```

This ContentPresenter sets the RecognizesAccessKey property to True. Although this isn't required, it ensures that the button supports *access keys*—underlined letters that you can use to quickly trigger the button. In this case, if your button has text such as *Click _Me*, the user can trigger the button by pressing Alt+M. (Under standard Windows settings, the underscore is hidden, and the access key—in this case, *M*—appears underlined as soon as you press the Alt key.) If you don't set RecognizesAccessKey to True, this detail will be ignored, and any underscores will be treated as ordinary underscores and displayed as part of the button content.

> **Note** If a control derives from ContentControl, its template will include a ContentPresenter that specifies where the content will be placed. If the control derives from ItemsControl, its template will include an ItemsPresenter that indicates where the panel that contains the list of items will be placed. In rare cases, the control may use a derived version of one of these classes—for example, the ScrollViewer's control template uses a ScrollContentPresenter, which derives from ContentPresenter.

Template Bindings

There's still one minor issue with this example. Right now the tag you've added for your button specifies a Margin value of 10 and a Padding of 5. The StackPanel pays attention to the Margin property of the button, but the Padding property is ignored, leaving the contents of your button scrunched up against the sides. The problem here is that the Padding property doesn't have any effect unless you specifically heed it in your template. In other words, it's up to your template to retrieve the padding value and use it to insert some extra space around your content.

Fortunately, WPF has a tool that's designed exactly for this purpose: *template bindings*. By using a template binding, your template can pull out a value from the control to which you're applying the template. In this example, you can use a template binding to retrieve the value of the Padding property and use it to create a margin around the ContentPresenter:

```
<ControlTemplate x:Key="ButtonTemplate" TargetType="{x:Type Button}">
  <Border BorderBrush="Orange" BorderThickness="3" CornerRadius="2"
    Background="Red" TextBlock.Foreground="White">
    <ContentPresenterRecognizesAccessKey="True"
      Margin="{TemplateBinding Padding}"></ContentPresenter>
  </Border>
</ControlTemplate>
```

This achieves the desired effect of adding some space between the border and the content. Figure 17-6 shows your modest new button.

Figure 17-6. A button with a customized control template

Template bindings are similar to ordinary data bindings, but they're lighter weight because they're specifically designed for use in a control template. They support only one-way data binding (in other words, they can pass information from the control to the template but not the other way around), and they can't be used to draw information from a property of a class that derives from Freezable. If you run into a situation where template bindings won't work, you can use a full-fledged data binding instead. Chapter 18 includes a sample color picker that runs into this problem and uses a combination of template bindings and regular bindings.

■ **Note** Template bindings support the WPF change-monitoring infrastructure that's built into all dependency properties. That means that if you modify a property in a control, the template takes it into account automatically. This detail is particularly useful when you're using animations that change a property value repeatedly in a short space of time.

The only way you can anticipate what template bindings are needed is to check the default control template. If you look at the control template for the Button class, you'll find that it uses a template binding in exactly the same way as this custom template—it takes the padding specified on the button and converts it to a margin around the ContentPresenter. You'll also find that the standard button template includes a few more template bindings that aren't used in the simple customized template, such as HorizontalAlignment, VerticalAlignment, and Background. That means if you set these properties on the button, they'll have no effect on the simple custom template.

■ **Note** Technically, the ContentPresenter works because it has a template binding that sets the ContentPresenter. Content property to the Button.Content property. However, this binding is implicit, so you don't need to add it yourself.

In many cases, leaving out template bindings isn't a problem. In fact, you don't need to bind a property if you don't plan to use it or don't want it to change your template. For example, it makes sense that the current simple button sets the Foreground property for text to white and ignores any value you've set for the Background property because the foreground and background are intrinsic parts of this button's visual appearance.

There's another reason you might choose to avoid template bindings—your control may not be able to support them adequately. For example, if you've ever set the Background property of a button, you've probably noticed that this background isn't handled consistently when the button is pressed (in fact, it disappears at this point and is replaced with the default visual for pressed buttons). The custom template shown in this example is similar. Although it doesn't yet have any mouseover and mouse-pressed behavior, after you add these details you'll want to take complete control over the colors and how they change in different states.

Triggers That Change Properties

If you try the button that you created in the previous section, you'll find it's a major disappointment. Essentially, it's nothing more than a rounded red rectangle—as you move the mouse over it or click it, there's no visual feedback. The button simply lies there inert.

This problem is easily fixed by adding triggers to your control template. You first considered triggers with styles in Chapter 11. As you know, you can use triggers to change one or more properties when another property changes. The bare minimums that you'll want to respond to in your button are IsMouseOver and IsPressed. Here's a revised version of the control template that changes the colors when these properties change:

```
<ControlTemplate x:Key="ButtonTemplate" TargetType="{x:Type Button}">
  <Border Name="Border" BorderBrush="Orange" BorderThickness="3" CornerRadius="2"
    Background="Red" TextBlock.Foreground="White">
```

```
        <ContentPresenter RecognizesAccessKey="True"
          Margin="{TemplateBinding Padding}"></ContentPresenter>
      </Border>
      <ControlTemplate.Triggers>
        <Trigger Property="IsMouseOver" Value="True">
          <Setter TargetName="Border" Property="Background" Value="DarkRed" />
        </Trigger>
        <Trigger Property="IsPressed" Value="True">
          <Setter TargetName="Border" Property="Background" Value="IndianRed" />
          <Setter TargetName="Border" Property="BorderBrush" Value="DarkKhaki" />
        </Trigger>
      </ControlTemplate.Triggers>
    </ControlTemplate>
```

There's one other change that makes this template work. The Border element has been given a name, and that name is used to set the TargetName property of each Setter. This way, the Setter can update the Background and BorderBrush properties of the Border that's specified in the template. Using names is the easiest way to make sure a single specific part of a template is updated. You could create an element-typed rule that affects all Border elements (because you know there is only a single border in the button template), but this approach is both clearer and more flexible if you change the template later.

There's one more required element in any button (and most other controls)—a focus indicator. There's no way to change the existing border to add a focus effect, but you can easily add another element that shows it and simply show or hide this element based on the Button.IsKeyboardFocused property by using a trigger. Although you could create a focus effect in many ways, the following example simply adds a transparent Rectangle element with a dashed border. The Rectangle doesn't have the ability to hold child content, so you need to make sure the Rectangle overlaps the rest of the content. The easiest way to do this is to wrap the Rectangle and the ContentPresenter in a one-cell Grid, with both elements in the same cell.

Here's the revised template with focus support:

```
<ControlTemplate x:Key="ButtonTemplate" TargetType="{x:Type Button}">
  <Border Name="Border" BorderBrush="Orange" BorderThickness="3" CornerRadius="2"
    Background="Red" TextBlock.Foreground="White">
    <Grid>
      <Rectangle Name="FocusCue" Visibility="Hidden" Stroke="Black"
        StrokeThickness="1" StrokeDashArray="1 2"
        SnapsToDevicePixels="True"></Rectangle>
      <ContentPresenter RecognizesAccessKey="True"
        Margin="{TemplateBinding Padding}"></ContentPresenter>
    </Grid>
  </Border>
  <ControlTemplate.Triggers>
    <Trigger Property="IsMouseOver" Value="True">
      <Setter TargetName="Border" Property="Background" Value="DarkRed" />
    </Trigger>
    <Trigger Property="IsPressed" Value="True">
      <Setter TargetName="Border" Property="Background" Value="IndianRed" />
      <Setter TargetName="Border" Property="BorderBrush" Value="DarkKhaki" />
    </Trigger>
```

```
    <Trigger Property="IsKeyboardFocused" Value="True">
      <Setter TargetName="FocusCue" Property="Visibility" Value="Visible" />
    </Trigger>
  </ControlTemplate.Triggers>
</ControlTemplate>
```

Once again, the Setter finds the element it needs to change by using the TargetName property (which points to the FocusCue rectangle in this example).

■ **Note**   This technique of hiding or showing elements in response to a trigger is a useful building block in many templates. You can use it to replace the visuals of a control with something completely different when its state changes. (For example, a clicked button could change from a rectangle to an ellipse by hiding the former and showing the latter.)

Figure 17-7 shows three buttons that use the revised template. The second button currently has focus (as represented by the dashed rectangle), while the mouse is hovering over the third button.

Figure 17-7. *Buttons with focus and mouseover support*

To really round out this button, you'll add an additional trigger that changes the button background (and possibly the text foreground) when the IsEnabled property of the button becomes False:

```
<Trigger Property="IsEnabled" Value="False">
  <Setter TargetName="Border" Property="TextBlock.Foreground" Value="Gray" />
  <Setter TargetName="Border" Property="Background" Value="MistyRose" />
</Trigger>
```

To make sure that this rule takes precedence over any conflicting trigger settings, you should define it at the end of the list of triggers. That way, it doesn't matter if the IsMouseOver property is also True; the IsEnabled property trigger takes precedence, and the button remains inactive.

<hr>

TEMPLATES VS. STYLES

It might have occurred to you that there's a similarity between templates and styles. Both allow you to change the appearance of an element, usually throughout your application. However, styles are far more limited in scope. They're able to adjust properties of the control but not replace it with an entirely new visual tree that's made up of different elements.

Already, the simple button you've seen includes features that couldn't be duplicated with styles alone. Although you could use styles to set the background of a button, you'd have more trouble adjusting the background when the button was pressed because the built-in template for the button already includes a trigger for that purpose. You also wouldn't have an easy way to add the focus rectangle.

Control templates also open the door to many more exotic types of buttons that are unthinkable with styles. For example, rather than using a rectangular border, you can create a button that's shaped like an ellipse or uses a path to draw a more complex shape. All you need are the drawing classes from Chapter 12. The rest of your markup—even the triggers that switch the background from one state to another—require relatively few changes.

<hr>

Triggers That Use Animation

As you learned in Chapter 11, triggers aren't limited to setting properties. You can also use event triggers to run animations when specific properties change.

At first glance, this may seem like a frill, but it's actually a key ingredient in all but the simplest WPF controls. For example, consider the button you've studied so far. Currently, it switches instantaneously from one color to another when the mouse moves over the top. However, a more modern button might use a very brief animation to *blend* from one color to the other, which creates a subtle but refined effect. Similarly, the button might use an animation to change the opacity of the focus cue rectangle, fading it quickly into view when the button gains focus rather than showing it in one step. In other words, event triggers allow controls to change from one state to another more gradually and more gracefully, which gives them that extra bit of polish.

Here's a revamped button template that uses triggers to make the button color pulse (shift continuously between red and blue) when the mouse is over it. When the mouse moves away, the button background returns to its normal color by using a separate 1-second animation:

```
<ControlTemplate x:Key="ButtonTemplate" TargetType="{x:Type Button}">
  <Border BorderBrush="Orange" BorderThickness="3" CornerRadius="2"
  Background="Red" TextBlock.Foreground="White" Name="Border">
    <Grid>
      <Rectangle Name="FocusCue" Visibility="Hidden" Stroke="Black"
       StrokeThickness="1" StrokeDashArray="1 2"
       SnapsToDevicePixels="True" ></Rectangle>
      <ContentPresenter RecognizesAccessKey="True"
        Margin="{TemplateBinding Padding}"></ContentPresenter>
    </Grid>
  </Border>

  <ControlTemplate.Triggers>
   <EventTrigger RoutedEvent="MouseEnter">
    <BeginStoryboard>
     <Storyboard>
```

```
          <ColorAnimation Storyboard.TargetName="Border"
            Storyboard.TargetProperty="Background.Color"
            To="Blue" Duration="0:0:1" AutoReverse="True"
            RepeatBehavior="Forever"></ColorAnimation>
        </Storyboard>
      </BeginStoryboard>
    </EventTrigger>
    <EventTrigger RoutedEvent="MouseLeave">
      <BeginStoryboard>
        <Storyboard>
          <ColorAnimation Storyboard.TargetName="Border"
            Storyboard.TargetProperty="Background.Color"
            Duration="0:0:0.5"></ColorAnimation>
        </Storyboard>
      </BeginStoryboard>
    </EventTrigger>
  </ControlTemplate.Triggers>
</ControlTemplate>
```

You can add the mouseover animation in two equivalent ways—by creating an event trigger that responds to the MouseEnter and MouseLeave events (as demonstrated here) or by creating a property trigger that adds enter and exit actions when the IsMouseOver property changes.

This example uses two ColorAnimation objects to change the button. Here are some other tasks you might want to perform with an EventTrigger-driven animation:

- *Show or hide an element*: To do this, you need to change the Opacity property of an element in the control template.

- *Change the shape or position*: You can use a TranslateTransform to tweak the positioning of an element (for example, offsetting it slightly to give the impression that the button has been pressed). You can use a ScaleTransform or a RotateTransform to twiddle the element's appearance slightly as the user moves the mouse over it.

- *Change the lighting or coloration*: To do this, you need an animation that acts on the brush that you use to paint the background. You can use a ColorAnimation to change colors in a SolidBrush, but more-advanced effects are possible by animating more-complex brushes. For example, you can change one of the colors in a LinearGradientBrush (which is what the default button control template does), or you can shift the center point of a RadialGradientBrush.

■ **Tip** Some advanced lighting effects use multiple layers of transparent elements. In this case, your animation modifies the opacity of one layer to let other layers show through.

Organizing Template Resources

When using control templates, you need to decide how broadly you want to share your templates and whether you want to apply them automatically or explicitly.

The first question asks you to think about where you want to use your templates. For example, are they limited to a specific window? In most situations, control templates apply to multiple windows and possibly even the entire application. To avoid defining them more than once, you can define them in the Resources collection of the Application class.

However, this raises another consideration. Often control templates are shared between applications. It's quite possible that a single application might use templates that have been developed separately. However, an application can have only a single Application.xaml file and a single Application.Resources collection. For that reason, it's a better idea to define your resources in separate resource dictionaries. That gives you the flexibility to bring them into action in specific windows or in the entire application. It also allows you to combine styles because any application can hold multiple resource dictionaries. To add a resource dictionary in Visual Studio, right-click your project in the Solution Explorer window, choose Add ➤ New Item, and then select Resource Dictionary (WPF).

You've already learned about resource dictionaries in Chapter 10. Using them is easy. You simply need to add a new XAML file to your application with content like this:

```
<ResourceDictionary
  xmlns="http://schemas.microsoft.com/winfx/2006/xaml/presentation"
  xmlns:x="http://schemas.microsoft.com/winfx/2006/xaml" >
  <ControlTemplate x:Key="ButtonTemplate" TargetType="{x:Type Button}">
    ...
  </ControlTemplate>
</ResourceDictionary>
```

Although you could combine all your templates into a single resource dictionary file, experienced developers prefer to create a separate resource dictionary for each control template. That's because a control template can quickly become quite complex and can draw on a host of other related resources. Keeping these together in one place, but separate from other controls, is good organization.

To use your resource dictionary, you simply add it to the Resources collection of a specific window or, more commonly, your application. You do this by using the MergedDictionaries collection. For example, if your button template is in a file named Button.xaml in a project subfolder named Resources, you could use this markup in your Application.xaml file:

```
<Application x:Class="Application"
 xmlns="http://schemas.microsoft.com/winfx/2006/xaml/presentation"
 xmlns:x="http://schemas.microsoft.com/winfx/2006/xaml"
 StartupUri="Window1.xaml">
  <Application.Resources>
    <ResourceDictionary>
      <ResourceDictionary.MergedDictionaries>
        <ResourceDictionary Source="Resources\Button.xaml" />
      </ResourceDictionary.MergedDictionaries>
    </ResourceDictionary>
  </Application.Resources>
</Application>
```

Refactoring the Button Control Template

As you enhance and extend a control template, you may find that it wraps various details, including specialized shapes, geometries, and brushes. It's a good idea to pull these details out of your control template and define them as separate resources. One reason you'll take this step is to make it easier to reuse these brushes among a set of related controls. For example, you might decide that you want to create a customized Button, CheckBox, and RadioButton that use a similar set of colors. To make this easier, you could create a separate resource dictionary for your brushes (named Brushes.xaml) and merge that into the resource dictionary for each of your controls (such as Button.xaml, CheckBox.xaml, and RadioButton.xaml).

To see this technique in action, consider the following markup. It presents the complete resource dictionary for a button, including the resources that the control template uses, the control template, and the style rule that applies the control template to every button in the application. This is the order that you always need to follow because a resource needs to be defined before it can be used. (If you defined one of the brushes after the template, you'd receive an error because the template wouldn't be able to find the brush it requires.)

```
<ResourceDictionary
    xmlns="http://schemas.microsoft.com/winfx/2006/xaml/presentation"
    xmlns:x="http://schemas.microsoft.com/winfx/2006/xaml">

  <!-- Resources used by the template. -->
  <RadialGradientBrush RadiusX="1" RadiusY="5" GradientOrigin="0.5,0.3"
   x:Key="HighlightBackground">
    <GradientStop Color="White" Offset="0" />
    <GradientStop Color="Blue" Offset=".4" />
  </RadialGradientBrush>

  <RadialGradientBrush RadiusX="1" RadiusY="5" GradientOrigin="0.5,0.3"
   x:Key="PressedBackground">
    <GradientStop Color="White" Offset="0" />
    <GradientStop Color="Blue" Offset="1" />
  </RadialGradientBrush>

  <SolidColorBrush Color="Blue" x:Key="DefaultBackground"></SolidColorBrush>
  <SolidColorBrush Color="Gray" x:Key="DisabledBackground"></SolidColorBrush>

  <RadialGradientBrush RadiusX="1" RadiusY="5" GradientOrigin="0.5,0.3"
   x:Key="Border">
    <GradientStop Color="White" Offset="0" />
    <GradientStop Color="Blue" Offset="1" />
  </RadialGradientBrush>

  <!-- The button control template. -->
  <ControlTemplate x:Key="GradientButtonTemplate" TargetType="{x:Type Button}">
    <Border Name="Border" BorderBrush="{StaticResource Border}" BorderThickness="2"
     CornerRadius="2" Background="{StaticResource DefaultBackground}"
     TextBlock.Foreground="White">
      <Grid>
        <Rectangle Name="FocusCue" Visibility="Hidden" Stroke="Black"
         StrokeThickness="1" StrokeDashArray="1 2" SnapsToDevicePixels="True">
        </Rectangle>
        <ContentPresenter Margin="{TemplateBinding Padding}"
         RecognizesAccessKey="True"></ContentPresenter>
      </Grid>
    </Border>
    <ControlTemplate.Triggers>
      <Trigger Property="IsMouseOver" Value="True">
        <Setter TargetName="Border" Property="Background"
         Value="{StaticResource HighlightBackground}" />
      </Trigger>
```

```
      <Trigger Property="IsPressed" Value="True">
        <Setter TargetName="Border" Property="Background"
        Value="{StaticResource PressedBackground}" />
      </Trigger>
      <Trigger Property="IsKeyboardFocused" Value="True">
        <Setter TargetName="FocusCue" Property="Visibility"
          Value="Visible"></Setter>
      </Trigger>
      <Trigger Property="IsEnabled" Value="False">
        <Setter TargetName="Border" Property="Background"
        Value="{StaticResource DisabledBackground}"></Setter>
      </Trigger>
    </ControlTemplate.Triggers>
  </ControlTemplate>
</ResourceDictionary>
```

Figure 17-8 shows the button that this template defines. In this example, a gradient fill is used when the user moves the mouse over the button. However, the gradient is always centered in the middle of the button. If you want to create a more exotic effect, such as a gradient that follows the position of the mouse, you'll need to use an animation or write code. Chapter 18 shows an example with a custom chrome class that implements this effect.

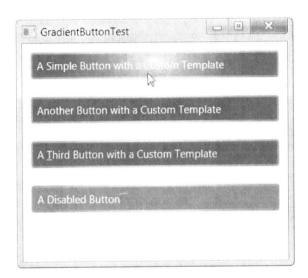

Figure 17-8. *A gradient button*

Applying Templates with Styles

There's one limitation in this design. The control template essentially hard-codes quite a few details, such as the color scheme. That means that if you want to use the same combination of elements in your button (Border, Grid, Rectangle, and ContentPresenter) and arrange them in the same way but you want to supply a different color scheme, you'll be forced to create a new copy of the template that references different brush resources.

This isn't necessarily a problem (after all, the layout and formatting details may be so closely related that you don't want to separate them anyway). However, it does limit your ability to reuse your control template. If your template uses a complex arrangement of elements that you know you'll want to reuse with a variety of formatting details (usually colors and fonts), you can pull these details out of your template and put them into a style.

To make this work, you'll need to rework your template. Instead of using hard-coded colors, you need to pull the information out of control properties by using template bindings. The following example defines a streamlined template for the fancy button you saw earlier. The control template treats some details as fundamental, unchanging ingredients—namely, the focus box and the rounded 2-unit-thick border. The background and border brushes are configurable. The only trigger that remains is the one that shows the focus box:

```
<ControlTemplate x:Key="CustomButtonTemplate" TargetType="{x:Type Button}">
  <Border Name="Border" BorderThickness="2" CornerRadius="2"
    Background="{TemplateBinding Background}"
    BorderBrush="{TemplateBinding BorderBrush}">
    <Grid>
      <Rectangle Name="FocusCue" Visibility="Hidden" Stroke="Black"
        StrokeThickness="1" StrokeDashArray="1 2" SnapsToDevicePixels="True">
      </Rectangle>
      <ContentPresenter Margin="{TemplateBinding Padding}"
        RecognizesAccessKey="True"></ContentPresenter>
    </Grid>
  </Border>
  <ControlTemplate.Triggers>
    <Trigger Property="IsKeyboardFocused" Value="True">
      <Setter TargetName="FocusCue" Property="Visibility"
        Value="Visible"></Setter>
    </Trigger>
  </ControlTemplate.Triggers>
</ControlTemplate>
```

The associated style applies this control template, sets the border and background colors, and adds triggers that change the background depending on the state of the button:

```
<Style x:Key="CustomButtonStyle" TargetType="{x:Type Button}">
  <Setter Property="Control.Template"
    Value="{StaticResource CustomButtonTemplate}"></Setter>
  <Setter Property="BorderBrush"
    Value="{StaticResource Border}"></Setter>
  <Setter Property="Background"
      Value="{StaticResource DefaultBackground}"></Setter>
        <Setter Property="TextBlock.Foreground"
        Value="White"></Setter>
  <Style.Triggers>
    <Trigger Property="IsMouseOver" Value="True">
      <Setter Property="Background"
        Value="{StaticResource HighlightBackground}" />
    </Trigger>
    <Trigger Property="IsPressed" Value="True">
      <Setter Property="Background"
        Value="{StaticResource PressedBackground}" />
```

```
    </Trigger>
    <Trigger Property="IsEnabled" Value="False">
      <Setter Property="Background"
        Value="{StaticResource DisabledBackground}"></Setter>
    </Trigger>
  </Style.Triggers>
</Style>
```

Ideally, you'd be able to keep all the triggers in the control template because they represent control behavior and use the style simply to set basic properties. Unfortunately, that's not possible here if you want to give the style the ability to set the color scheme.

■ **Note** If you set triggers in both the control template and style, the style triggers win out.

To use this new template, you need to set the Style property of a button rather than the Template property:

```
<Button Margin="10" Padding="5" Style="{StaticResource CustomButtonStyle}">
 A Simple Button with a Custom Template</Button>
```

You can now create new styles that use the same template but bind to different brushes to apply a new color scheme.

There's one significant limitation in this approach. You can't use the Setter.TargetName property in this style because the style doesn't contain the control template (it simply references it). As a result, your style and its triggers are somewhat limited. They can't reach deep into the visual tree to change the aspect of a nested element. Instead, your style needs to set a property of the control, and the element in the control needs to bind the property by using a template binding.

CONTROL TEMPLATES VS. CUSTOM CONTROLS

You can get around both of the problems discussed here—being forced to define control behavior in the style with triggers and not being able to target specific elements—by creating a custom control. For example, you could build a class that derives from Button and adds properties such as HighlightBackground, DisabledBackground, and PressedBackground. You could then bind to these properties in the control template and simply set them in the style with no triggers required. However, this approach has its own drawback. It forces you to use a different control in your user interface (such as CustomButton instead of just Button). This is more trouble when designing the application.

Usually, you'll switch from custom control templates to custom controls in one of two situations:

- Your control represents a significant change in functionality. For example, you have a custom button, and that button adds new functionality that requires new properties or methods.

- You plan to distribute your control in a separate class library assembly so it can be used in (and customized for) a wide range of applications. In this situation, you need a higher level of standardization than is possible with control templates alone.

If you decide to create a custom control, Chapter 18 has all the information you need.

Applying Templates Automatically

In the current example, each button is responsible for hooking itself up to the appropriate template by using the Template or Style property. This makes sense if you're using your control template to create a specific effect in a specific place in your application. It's less convenient if you want to re-skin every button in your entire application with a custom look. In this situation, it's more likely that you want all the buttons in your application to acquire your new template automatically. To make this a reality, you need to apply your control template with a style.

The trick is to use a typed style that affects the appropriate element type automatically and sets the Template property. Here's an example of the style you'd place in the resources collection of your resource dictionary to give your buttons a new look:

```
<Style TargetType="{x:Type Button}">
  <Setter Property="Control.Template" Value="{StaticResource ButtonTemplate}"
</Style>
```

This works because the style doesn't specify a key name, which means the element type (Button) is used instead. Remember, you can still opt out of this style by creating a button that explicitly sets its Style to a null value:

```
<Button Style="{x:Null}" ... ></Button>
```

■ **Tip** This technique works even better if you've followed good design practices and defined your button in a separate resource dictionary. In this situation, the style doesn't sprint into action until you add a ResourceDictionary tag that imports your resources into the entire application or a specific window, as described earlier.

A resource dictionary that contains a combination of type-based styles is often called (informally) a *theme*. The possibilities of themes are remarkable. They allow you to take an existing WPF application and completely re-skin all its controls without changing the user interface markup at all. All you need to do is add the resource dictionaries to your project and merge them into the Application.Resources collection in the Application.xaml file.

If you hunt around the Web, you'll find more than a few themes that you can use to revamp a WPF application. For example, you can download several sample themes as part of the WPF Futures release at `http://tinyurl.com/ylojdry`.

To use a theme, add the .xaml file that contains the resource dictionary to your project. For example, WPF Futures includes a theme file named ExpressionDark.xaml. Then you need to make the styles active in your application. You could do this on a window-by-window basis, but it's quicker to import them at the application level by adding markup like this:

```
<Application ... >
  <Application.Resources>
    <ResourceDictionary Source="ExpressionDark.xaml"/>
  </Application.Resources>
</Application>
```

Now the type-based styles in the resource dictionary will be in full force and will automatically change the appearance of every common control in every window of your application. If you're an application developer in search of a hot new user interface but you don't have the design skills to build it yourself, this trick makes it easy to plug in third-party pizzazz with almost no effort.

Working with User-Selected Skins

In some applications, you might want to alter templates dynamically, usually in response to user preferences. This is easy enough to accomplish, but it's not well-documented. The basic technique is to load a new resource dictionary at runtime and use it to replace the current resource dictionary. (It's not necessary to replace all your resources, just those that are used for your skin.)

The trick is retrieving the ResourceDictionary object, which is compiled and embedded as a resource in your application. The easiest approach is to use the ResourceManager class described in Chapter 10 to load up the resources you want.

For example, imagine you've created two resources that define alternate versions of the same button control template. One is stored in a file named GradientButton.xaml, while the other is in a file named GradientButtonVariant. xaml. Both files are placed in the Resources subfolder in the current project for better organization.

Now you can create a simple window that uses one of these resources, using a Resources collection like this:

```
<Window.Resources>
  <ResourceDictionary>
    <ResourceDictionary.MergedDictionaries>
      <ResourceDictionary
        Source="Resources/GradientButton.xaml"></ResourceDictionary>
    </ResourceDictionary.MergedDictionaries>
  </ResourceDictionary>
</Window.Resources>
```

Now you can swap in a different resource dictionary by using code like this:

```
Dim newDictionary As New ResourceDictionary()
newDictionary.Source = New Uri( _
  "Resources/GradientButtonVariant.xaml", UriKind.Relative)
Me.Resources.MergedDictionaries(0) = newDictionary
```

This code loads the resource dictionary named GradientButtonVariant and places it into the first slot in the MergedDictionaries collection. It doesn't clear the MergedDictionaries collection (or any other window resources) because it's possible that you might be linking to other resource dictionaries that you want to continue using. It doesn't add a new entry to the MergedDictionaries collection because there could then be conflict between resources with the same name but in different collections.

If you were changing the skin for an entire application, you'd use the same approach, but you'd use the resource dictionary of the application. You could update this resource dictionary by using code like this:

```
Application.Current.Resources.MergedDictionaries(0) = newDictionary
```

You can also load a resource dictionary that's defined in another assembly by using the pack URI syntax described in Chapter 7:

```
Dim newDictionary As New ResourceDictionary()
newDictionary.Source = new Uri( _
  "ControlTemplateLibrary;component/GradientButtonVariant.xaml", _
  UriKind.Relative)
Me.Resources.MergedDictionaries(0) = newDictionary
```

When you load a new resource dictionary, all the buttons are automatically updated to use the new template. You can also include basic styles as part of your skin if you don't need to be quite as ambitious when modifying a control.

This example assumes that the GradientButton.xaml and GradientButtonVariant.xaml resources use an element-typed style to change your buttons automatically. As you know, there's another approach—you can opt in to a new template by manually setting the Template or Style property of your Button objects. If you take this approach, make sure you use a DynamicResource reference instead of a StaticResource. If you use a StaticResource, the button template won't be updated when you switch skins.

Note When using a DynamicResource reference, you're making an assumption that the resource you need will appear somewhere in the resource hierarchy. If it doesn't, the resource is simply ignored, and the buttons revert to their standard appearance without generating an error.

There's another way to load resource dictionaries programmatically. You can create a code-behind class for your resource dictionary in much the same way you create code-behind classes for windows. You can then instantiate that class directly rather than using the ResourceDictionary.Source property. This approach has the benefit of being strongly typed (there's no chance of entering an invalid URI for the Source property), and it allows you to add properties, methods, and other functionality to your resource class. For example, you'll use this ability to create a resource that has event-handling code for a custom window template in Chapter 23.

To use this approach, you must first add the Class attribute to the root element of your resource dictionary:

```
<ResourceDictionary x:Class="GradientButtonVariant" ... >
```

You don't actually need to create the resource dictionary class (which is named GradientButtonVariant in this example). If you don't, the Visual Basic compiler will automatically generate a code-behind class with a public constructor that calls InitializeComponent(). However, if you want to add public members that provide additional features, you can create the code-behind class like this:

```
Public Class GradientButtonVariant
End Class
```

After you've set the Class attribute, you can use code like this to create your resource dictionary and apply it to a window:

```
Dim newDictionary As New GradientButtonVariant()
Me.Resources.MergedDictionaries(0) = newDictionary
```

If you want your GradientButtonVariant.xaml.vb file to appear nested under the GradientButtonVariant.xaml file in the Solution Explorer, you need to modify the .vbproj project file in a text editor. Find the code-behind file in the <ItemGroup> section and change this:

```
<Compile Include="Resources\GradientButtonVariant.xaml.vb" />
```

to this:

```
<Compile Include="Resources\GradientButtonVariant.xaml.vb">
  <DependentUpon> Resources\GradientButtonVariant.xaml</DependentUpon>
</Compile>
```

Building More Complex Templates

There is an implicit contract between a control's template and the code that underpins it. If you're replacing a control's standard template with one of your own, you need to make sure your new template meets all the requirements of the control's implementation code.

In simple controls, this process is easy, because there are few (if any) real requirements on the template. In a complex control, the issue is subtler, because it's impossible for the visuals and the implementation to be completely separated. In this situation, the control needs to make some assumptions about its visual display, no matter how well it has been designed.

You've already seen two examples of the requirements a control can place on its control template, with placeholder elements (such as ContentPresenter and ItemsPresenter) and template bindings. In the following sections, you'll see two more: elements with specific names (starting with *PART_*) and elements that are specially designed for use in a particular control's template (such as Track in the ScrollBar control). To create a successful control template, you need to look carefully at the standard template for the control in question, make note of how these four techniques are used, and then duplicate them in your own templates.

■ **Note** There's another way to get comfortable with the interaction between controls and control templates. You can create your own custom control. In this case, you'll have the reverse challenge—you'll need to create code that uses a template in a standardized way and that can work equally well with templates supplied by other developers. You'll tackle this challenge in Chapter 18 (which makes a great complement to the perspective you'll get in this chapter).

Nested Templates

The template for the button control can be decomposed into a few relatively simple pieces. However, many templates aren't so simple. In some cases, a control template will contain a number of elements that every custom template will require as well. And in some cases, changing the appearance of a control involves creating more than one template.

For example, imagine you're planning to revamp the familiar ListBox control. The first step to create this example is to design a template for the ListBox and (optionally) add a style that applies the template automatically. Here are both ingredients rolled into one:

```
<Style TargetType="{x:Type ListBox}">
  <Setter Property="Template">
    <Setter.Value>
      <ControlTemplate TargetType="{x:Type ListBox}">
        <Border
          Name="Border"
          Background="{StaticResource ListBoxBackgroundBrush}"
          BorderBrush="{StaticResource StandardBorderBrush}"
          BorderThickness="1" CornerRadius="3">
          <ScrollViewer Focusable="False">
            <ItemsPresenter Margin="2"></ItemsPresenter>
          </ScrollViewer>
        </Border>
      </ControlTemplate>
    </Setter.Value>
  </Setter>
</Style>
```

This style draws on two brushes for painting the border and the background. The actual template is a simplified version of the standard ListBox template, but it avoids the ListBoxChrome class in favor of a simpler Border. Inside the Border is the ScrollViewer that provides the list scrolling, and an ItemsPresenter that holds all the items of the list.

This template is most notable for what it doesn't let you do—namely, configure the appearance of individual items in the list. Without this ability, the selected item is always highlighted with the familiar blue background. To change this behavior, you need to add a control template for the ListBoxItem, which is a content control that wraps the content of each individual item in the list.

As with the ListBox template, you can apply the ListBoxItem template by using an element-typed style. The following basic template wraps each item in an invisible border. Because the ListBoxItem is a content control, you use the ContentPresenter to place the item content inside. Along with these basics are triggers that react when an item is moused over or clicked:

```
<Style TargetType="{x:Type ListBoxItem}">
  <Setter Property="Template">
    <Setter.Value>
      <ControlTemplate TargetType="{x:Type ListBoxItem}">
        <Border ... >
          <ContentPresenter />
        </Border>
        <ControlTemplate.Triggers>
          <EventTrigger RoutedEvent="ListBoxItem.MouseEnter">
            <EventTrigger.Actions>
              <BeginStoryboard>
                <Storyboard>
                  <DoubleAnimation Storyboard.TargetProperty="FontSize"
                    To="20" Duration="0:0:1"></DoubleAnimation>
                </Storyboard>
              </BeginStoryboard>
            </EventTrigger.Actions>
          </EventTrigger>
          <EventTrigger RoutedEvent="ListBoxItem.MouseLeave">
            <EventTrigger.Actions>
              <BeginStoryboard>
                <Storyboard>
                  <DoubleAnimation Storyboard.TargetProperty="FontSize"
                    BeginTime="0:0:0.5" Duration="0:0:0.2"></DoubleAnimation>
                </Storyboard>
              </BeginStoryboard>
            </EventTrigger.Actions>
          </EventTrigger>

          <Trigger Property="IsMouseOver" Value="True">
            <Setter TargetName="Border" Property="BorderBrush" ... />
          </Trigger>
          <Trigger Property="IsSelected" Value="True">
            <Setter TargetName="Border" Property="Background" ... />
            <Setter TargetName="Border" Property="TextBlock.Foreground" ... />
          </Trigger>
        </ControlTemplate.Triggers>
```

```
      </ControlTemplate>
    </Setter.Value>
  </Setter>
</Style>
```

Together, these two templates allow you to create a list box that uses animation to enlarge the item over which the mouse is currently positioned. Because each ListBoxItem can have its own animation, when you run your mouse up and down the list, you'll see several items start to grow and then shrink back again, creating an intriguing "fish-eye" effect. (A more extravagant fish-eye effect would enlarge and warp the item over which you're hovering, using animated transforms.)

Although it's not possible to capture this effect in a single image, Figure 17-9 shows a snapshot of this list after the mouse has moved rapidly over several items.

Figure 17-9. *Using a custom template for the ListBoxItem*

You won't reconsider the entire template ListBoxItem example here, because it's built from many pieces that style the ListBox, the ListBoxItem, and the various constituents of the ListBox (such as the scrollbar). The important piece is the style that changes the ListBoxItem template.

In this example, the ListBoxItem enlarges relatively slowly (over 1 second) and then decreases much more quickly (in 0.2 seconds). However, there is a 0.5-second delay before the shrinking animation begins.

Note that the shrinking animation leaves out the From and To properties. That way, it always shrinks the text from its current size to its original size. If you move the mouse on and off a ListBoxItem, you'll get the result you expect—it appears as though the item simply continues expanding while the mouse is on top and continues shrinking when the mouse is moved away.

■ **Tip** As always, the best way to get used to these conventions is to play with the template browser shown earlier to look at the control templates for basic controls. You can then copy and edit the template to use it as a basis for your custom work.

Modifying the Scrollbar

There's one aspect of the list box that's remained out of touch: the scrollbar on the right. It's part of the ScrollViewer, which is part of the ListBox template. Even though this example redefines the ListBox template, it doesn't alter the ScrollViewer of the ScrollBar.

To customize this detail, you could create a new ScrollViewer template for use with the ListBox. You could then point the ScrollViewer template to your custom ScrollBar template. However, there's an easier option. You can create an element-typed style that changes the template of all the ScrollBar controls it comes across. This avoids the extra work of creating the ScrollViewer template.

Of course, you also need to think about how this design affects the rest of your application. If you create an element-typed style ScrollBar and add it to the Resources collection of a window, all the controls in that window will have the newly styled scrollbars whenever they use the ScrollBar control, which may be exactly what you want. On the other hand, if you want to change only the scrollbar in the ListBox, you must add the element-typed ScrollBar style to the resources collection of the ListBox itself. And finally, it you want to change the way scrollbars look in your entire application, you can add it to the resources collection in the Application.xaml file.

The ScrollBar control is surprisingly sophisticated. It's actually built out of a collection of smaller pieces, as shown in Figure 17-10.

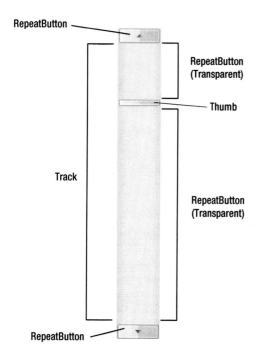

Figure 17-10. *Dissecting the scrollbar*

The background of the scrollbar is represented by the Track class—it's usually a shaded rectangle that's stretched out over the length of the scrollbar. At the far ends of the scrollbar are buttons that allow you to move one increment up or down (or to the left or right). These are instances of the RepeatButton class, which derives from ButtonBase. The key difference between a RepeatButton and the ordinary Button class is that if you hold the mouse down on a RepeatButton, the Click event fires over and over again (which is handy for scrolling).

In the middle of the scrollbar is a Thumb that represents the current position in the scrollable content. And, most interesting of all, the blank space on either side of the thumb is made up of two more RepeatButton objects, which are transparent. When you click either one of these, the scrollbar scrolls an entire *page* (a page is defined as the amount that fits in the visible window of the scrollable content). This gives you the familiar ability to jump quickly through scrollable content by clicking the bar on either side of the thumb.

Here's the template for a vertical scrollbar:

```
<ControlTemplate x:Key="VerticalScrollBar" TargetType="{x:Type ScrollBar}">
  <Grid>
    <Grid.RowDefinitions>
      <RowDefinition MaxHeight="18"/>
      <RowDefinition Height="*"/>
      <RowDefinition MaxHeight="18"/>
    </Grid.RowDefinitions>

    <RepeatButton Grid.Row="0" Height="18"
      Style="{StaticResource ScrollBarLineButtonStyle}"
      Command="ScrollBar.LineUpCommand" >
      <Path Fill="{StaticResource GlyphBrush}"
      Data="M 0 4 L 8 4 L 4 0 Z"></Path>
    </RepeatButton>

    <Track Name="PART_Track" Grid.Row="1"
      IsDirectionReversed="True" ViewportSize="0">
      <Track.DecreaseRepeatButton>
        <RepeatButton Command="ScrollBar.PageUpCommand"
         Style="{StaticResource ScrollBarPageButtonStyle}">
        </RepeatButton>
      </Track.DecreaseRepeatButton>
      <Track.Thumb>
        <Thumb Style="{StaticResource ScrollBarThumbStyle}">
        </Thumb>
      </Track.Thumb>
      <Track.IncreaseRepeatButton>
        <RepeatButton Command="ScrollBar.PageDownCommand"
         Style="{StaticResource ScrollBarPageButtonStyle}">
        </RepeatButton>
      </Track.IncreaseRepeatButton>
    </Track>

    <RepeatButton
      Grid.Row="3" Height="18"
      Style="{StaticResource ScrollBarLineButtonStyle}"
      Command="ScrollBar.LineDownCommand"
      Content="M 0 0 L 4 4 L 8 0 Z">
    </RepeatButton>

    <RepeatButton
      Grid.Row="3" Height="18"
      Style="{StaticResource ScrollBarLineButtonStyle}"
      Command="ScrollBar.LineDownCommand">
```

```
    <Path Fill="{StaticResource GlyphBrush}"
      Data="M 0 0 L 4 4 L 8 0 Z"></Path>
  </RepeatButton>
 </Grid>
</ControlTemplate>
```

This template is fairly straightforward, once you understand the multipart structure of the scrollbar (as shown in Figure 17-10). There are a few key points to note:

- The vertical scrollbar consists of a three-row grid. The top and bottom rows hold the buttons at either end (and appear as arrows). They're fixed at 18 units. The middle section, which holds the track, takes the rest of the space.

- The RepeatButton elements at both ends use the same style. The only difference is the Content property that contains a Path that draws the arrow—because the top button has an up arrow, while the bottom button has a down arrow. For conciseness, these arrows are represented by using the path mini-language described in Chapter 13. The other details, such as the background fill and the circle that appears around the arrow, are defined in the control template, which is set out in the ScrollButtonLineStyle.

- Both buttons are linked to a command in the ScrollBar class (LineUpCommand and LineDownCommand). This is how they do their work. As long as you provide a button that's linked to this command, it doesn't matter what its name is, what it looks like, or what specific class it uses. (Commands are covered in detail in Chapter 9.)

- The Track has the name PART_Track. You must use this name in order for the ScrollBar class to hook up its code successfully. If you look at the default template for the ScrollBar class (which is similar, but lengthier), you'll see it appears there as well.

■ **Note** If you're examining a control with reflection (or using a tool such as Reflector), you can look for the TemplatePart attributes attached to the class declaration. There should be one TemplatePart attribute for each named part. The TemplatePart attribute indicates the name of the expected element (through the Name property) and its class (through the Type property). In Chapter 18, you'll see how to apply the TemplatePart attribute to your own custom control classes.

- The Track.ViewportSize property is set to 0. This is a specific implementation detail in this template. It ensures that the Thumb always has the same size. (Ordinarily, the thumb is sized proportionally based on the content so that if you're scrolling through content that mostly fits in the window, the thumb becomes much larger.)

- The Track wraps two RepeatButton objects (whose style is defined separately) and the Thumb. Once again, these buttons are wired up to the appropriate functionality by using commands.

You'll also notice that the template uses a key name that specifically identifies it as a vertical scrollbar. As you learned in Chapter 11, when you set a key name on a style, you ensure that it isn't applied automatically, even if you've also set the TargetType property. The reason this example uses this approach is that the template is suitable only for scrollbars in the vertical orientation. Another, element-typed style uses a trigger to automatically apply the control template if the ScrollBar.Orientation property is set to Vertical:

```
<Style TargetType="{x:Type ScrollBar}">
  <Setter Property="SnapsToDevicePixels" Value="True"/>
  <Setter Property="OverridesDefaultStyle" Value="true"/>
```

```
      <Style.Triggers>
        <Trigger Property="Orientation" Value="Vertical">
          <Setter Property="Width" Value="18"/>
          <Setter Property="Height" Value="Auto" />
          <Setter Property="Template" Value="{StaticResource VerticalScrollBar}" />
        </Trigger>
      </Style.Triggers>
    </Style>
```

Although you could easily build a horizontal scrollbar out of the same basic pieces, this example doesn't take that step (and so retains the normally styled horizontal scrollbar).

The final task is to fill in the styles that format the various RepeatButton objects and the Thumb. These styles are relatively modest, but they do change the standard look of the scrollbar. First, the Thumb is shaped like an ellipse:

```
<Style x:Key="ScrollBarThumbStyle" TargetType="{x:Type Thumb}">
  <Setter Property="IsTabStop" Value="False"/>
  <Setter Property="Focusable" Value="False"/>
  <Setter Property="Margin" Value="1,0,1,0" />
  <Setter Property="Background" Value="{StaticResource StandardBrush}" />
  <Setter Property="BorderBrush" Value="{StaticResource StandardBorderBrush}" />
  <Setter Property="Template">
    <Setter.Value>
      <ControlTemplate TargetType="{x:Type Thumb}">
        <Ellipse Stroke="{StaticResource StandardBorderBrush}"
         Fill="{StaticResource StandardBrush}"></Ellipse>
      </ControlTemplate>
    </Setter.Value>
  </Setter>
</Style>
```

Next, the arrows at either end are drawn inside nicely rounded circles. The circles are defined in the control template, while the arrows are provided from the content of the RepeatButton and inserted into the control template by using the ContentPresenter:

```
<Style x:Key="ScrollBarLineButtonStyle" TargetType="{x:Type RepeatButton}">
  <Setter Property="Focusable" Value="False"/>
  <Setter Property="Template">
    <Setter.Value>
      <ControlTemplate TargetType="{x:Type RepeatButton}">
        <Grid Margin="1">
          <Ellipse Name="Border" StrokeThickness="1"
           Stroke="{StaticResource StandardBorderBrush}"
           Fill="{StaticResource StandardBrush}"></Ellipse>
          <ContentPresenter HorizontalAlignment="Center"
           VerticalAlignment="Center"></ContentPresenter>
        </Grid>
        <ControlTemplate.Triggers>
          <Trigger Property="IsPressed" Value="true">
            <Setter TargetName="Border" Property="Fill"
             Value="{StaticResource PressedBrush}" />
```

```
        </Trigger>
      </ControlTemplate.Triggers>
    </ControlTemplate>
  </Setter.Value>
</Setter>
</Style>
```

The RepeatButton objects that are displayed over the track aren't changed. They simply use a transparent background so the track shows through:

```
<Style x:Key="ScrollBarPageButtonStyle" TargetType="{x:Type RepeatButton}">
  <Setter Property="IsTabStop" Value="False"/>
  <Setter Property="Focusable" Value="False"/>
  <Setter Property="Template">
    <Setter.Value>
      <ControlTemplate TargetType="{x:Type RepeatButton}">
        <Border Background="Transparent" />
      </ControlTemplate>
    </Setter.Value>
  </Setter>
</Style>
```

Unlike the normal scrollbar, in this template no background is assigned to the Track, which leaves it transparent. That way, the gently shaded gradient of the list box shows through. Figure 17-11 shows the final list box.

Figure 17-11. *A list box with a customized scrollbar*

Exploring the Control Template Examples

As you've seen, giving a new template to a common control can be a detailed task. That's because all the requirements of a control template aren't always obvious. For example, a typical ScrollBar requires a combination of two RepeatButton objects and a Track. Other control templates need elements with specific PART_ names. In the case of a custom window, you need to make sure the adorner layer is defined because some controls will require it.

Although you can discover these details by exploring the default template for a control, these default templates are often complicated and include details that aren't important and bindings that you probably won't support anyway. Fortunately, there's a better place to get started: the ControlTemplateExamples sample project (formerly known as *SimpleStyles*).

The control template examples provide a collection of simple, streamlined templates for all WPF's standard controls, which makes them a useful jumping-off point for any custom control designer. Unlike the default control templates, these use standard colors, perform all their work declaratively (with no chrome classes), and leave out optional parts such as template bindings for less commonly used properties. The goal of control template examples is to give developers a practical starting point that they can use to design their own graphically enhanced control templates. Figure 17-12 shows about half of the control template examples.

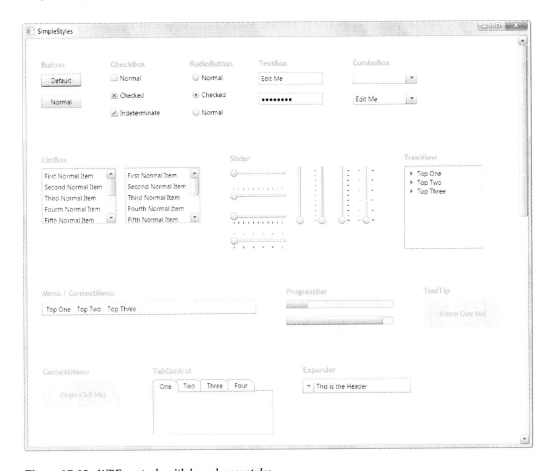

Figure 17-12. *WPF controls with bare-bones styles*

The SimpleStyles examples are included with the .NET Framework SDK. The easiest way to get them is to download them directly from http://tinyurl.com/9jtk93x.

■ **Tip** The SimpleStyles are one of the hidden gems of WPF. They provide templates that are easier to understand and enhance than the default control templates. If you need to enhance a common control with a custom look, this project should be your first stop.

Visual States

So far, you've learned the most direct (and most popular) way to craft a control template: using a mix of elements, binding expressions, and triggers. The elements create the overall visual structure of the control. The bindings pull information from the properties of the control class and apply it to the elements inside. And the triggers create the interactivity, allowing the control to change its appearance when its state changes.

The advantage of this model is that it's extremely powerful and extremely flexible. You can do just about anything you want. This isn't immediately apparent in the button example, because the control template relies on built-in properties such as IsMouseOver and IsPressed. But even if these properties weren't available, you could still craft a control template that changes itself in response to mouse movements and button clicks. The trick would be to use event triggers that apply animations. For example, you could add an event trigger that reacts to the Border.MouseOver by starting an animation that changes the border background color. This animation doesn't even need to look like an animation—if you give it a duration of 0 seconds, it will apply itself immediately, just like the property triggers you're using now. In fact, this exact technique is used in a number of professional template examples.

Despite their capabilities, trigger-based templates have a downside: they require that the template designer has a detailed understanding of the way the control works. In the button example, the template designer needs to know about the existence of the IsMouseOver and IsPressed properties, for example, and how to use them. And these aren't the only details—for example, most controls need to react visually to mouse movements, being disabled, getting focus, and many other state changes. When these states are applied in combination, it can be difficult to determine exactly how the control should look. The trigger-based model is also notoriously awkward with *transitions*. For example, imagine you want to create a button that pulses while the mouse is over it. To get a professional result, you may need two animations—one that changes the state of the button from normal to mouseover and one that applies the continuous pulsing effect immediately after that. Managing all these details with a trigger-based template can be a challenge.

In WPF 4, Microsoft added a feature called *visual states*, which addresses this challenge. Using named parts (which you've already seen) and visual states, a control can provide a standardized visual contract. Rather than understanding the entire control, a template designer simply needs to understand the rules of the visual contract. As a result, it's much easier to design a simple control template—especially when it's for a control you've never worked with before.

Much as controls can use the TemplatePart attribute to indicate specific named elements (or parts) that the control template should include, they can use the TemplateVisualState attribute to indicate the visual states they support. For example, an ordinary button would provide a set of visual states like this:

```
<TemplateVisualState(Name:="Normal", GroupName:="CommonStates"), _
 TemplateVisualState(Name:="MouseOver", GroupName:="CommonStates"), _
 TemplateVisualState(Name:="Pressed", GroupName:="CommonStates"), _
 TemplateVisualState(Name:="Disabled", GroupName:="CommonStates"), _
 TemplateVisualState(Name:="Unfocused", GroupName:="FocusStates"), _
 TemplateVisualState(Name:="Focused", GroupName:="FocusStates")> _
Public Class Button
    Inherits ButtonBase
    ...
End Class
```

States are placed together in *groups*. Groups are mutually exclusive, which means a control has one state in each group. For example, the button shown here has two state groups: CommonStates and FocusStates. At any given time, the button has one of the states from the CommonStates group *and* one of the states from the FocusStates group.

For example, if you tab to the button, its states will be Normal (from CommonStates) and Focused (from FocusStates). If you then move the mouse over the button, its states will be MouseOver (from CommonStates) and Focused (from FocusStates). Without state groups, you'd have trouble dealing with this situation. You'd either be forced to make some states dominate others (so a button in the MouseOver state would lose its focus indicator) or need to create many more states (such as FocusedNormal, UnfocusedNormal, FocusedMouseOver, UnfocusedMouseOver, and so on).

At this point, you can already see the appeal of the visual states model. From the template, it's immediately clear that a control template needs to address six state possibilities. You also know the name of each state, which is the only essential detail. You don't need to know what properties the Button class provides or understand the inner workings of the control. Best of all, if you use Expression Blend, you'll get enhanced design-time support when creating control templates for a control that supports visual states. Blend will show you the named parts and visual states the control supports (as defined with the TemplatePart and TemplateVisualState attributes), and you can then add the corresponding elements and storyboards.

In the next chapter, you'll see a custom control named the FlipPanel that puts the visual state model into practice.

The Last Word

In this chapter, you learned how to use basic template-building techniques to re-skin core WPF controls like the button, without being forced to reimplement any core button functionality. These custom buttons support all the normal button behavior—you can tab from one to the next, you can click them to fire an event, you can use access keys, and so on. Best of all, you can reuse your button template throughout your application and still replace it with a whole new design at a moment's notice.

So, what more do you need to know before you can skin all the basic WPF controls? To get the snazzy look you probably want, you might need to spend more time studying the details of WPF drawing (Chapter 12 and Chapter 13) and animation (Chapter 15 and Chapter 16). It might surprise you to know that you can use the shapes and brushes you've already learned about to build sophisticated controls with glass-style blurs and soft glow effects. The secret is in combining multiple layers of shapes, each with a different gradient brush. The best way to get this sort of effect is to learn from the control template examples others have created. Here are two good examples to check out:

- There are plenty of handcrafted, shaded buttons with glass and soft glow effects on the Web. You can find an old (but still useful) tutorial that walks you through the process of creating a snazzy glass button in Expression Blend at `http://tinyurl.com/3bk26g`.

- An MSDN Magazine article about control templates provides examples of templates that incorporate simple drawings in innovative ways. For example, a CheckBox is replaced by an up-down lever, a slider is rendered with a three-dimensional tab, a ProgressBar is changed into a thermometer, and so on. Check it out at `http://msdn.microsoft.com/magazine/cc163497.aspx`.

CHAPTER 18

■ ■ ■

Custom Elements

In previous Windows development frameworks, custom controls played a central role. But in WPF, the emphasis has shifted. Custom controls are still a useful way to build custom widgets that you can share between applications, but they're no longer a requirement when you want to enhance and customize core controls. (To understand how remarkable this change is, it helps to point out that this book's predecessor, *Pro .NET 2.0 Windows Forms and Custom Controls* in *VB 2005*, had nine complete chapters about custom controls and additional examples in other chapters. But in this book, you've made it to Chapter 18 without a single custom control sighting!)

WPF de-emphasizes custom controls because of its support for styles, content controls, and templates. These features give every developer several ways to refine and extend standard controls without deriving a new control class. Here are your possibilities:

> *Styles:* You can use a style to painlessly reuse a combination of control properties. You can even apply effects by using triggers.

> *Content controls:* Any control that derives from ContentControl supports nested content. Using content controls, you can quickly create compound controls that aggregate other elements. (For example, you can transform a button into an image button or a list box into an image list.)

> *Control templates:* All WPF controls are *lookless*, which means they have hardwired functionality but their appearance is defined separately through the control template. Replace the default template with something new, and you can revamp basic controls such as buttons, check boxes, radio buttons, and even windows.

> *Data templates:* All ItemsControl-derived classes support data templates, which allow you to create a rich list representation of some type of data object. Using the right data template, you can display each item by using a combination of text, images, and even editable controls, all in a layout container of your choosing.

If possible, you should pursue these avenues before you decide to create a custom control or another type of custom element. That's because these solutions are simpler, easier to implement, and often easier to reuse.

So, when *should* you create a custom element? Custom elements aren't the best choice when you want to fine-tune the appearance of an element, but they do make sense when you want to change its underlying functionality. For example, there's a reason that WPF has separate classes for the TextBox and PasswordBox classes. They handle key presses differently, store their data internally in a different way, interact with other components such as the clipboard differently, and so on. Similarly, if you want to design a control that has its own distinct set of properties, methods, and events, you'll need to build it yourself.

In this chapter, you'll learn how to create custom elements and how to make them into first-class WPF citizens. That means you'll outfit them with dependency properties and routed events to get support for essential WPF services such as data binding, styles, and animation. You'll also learn how to create a *lookless* control—a template-driven control that allows the control consumer to supply different visuals for greater flexibility.

Understanding Custom Elements in WPF

Although you can code a custom element in any WPF project, you'll usually want to place custom elements in a dedicated class library (DLL) assembly. That way, you can share your work with multiple WPF applications.

To make sure you have the right assembly references and namespace imports, you should choose the Custom Control Library (WPF) project type when you create your application in Visual Studio. Inside your class library, you can create as many or as few controls as you like.

■ **Tip** As with all class library development, it's often a good practice to place both your class library and the application that uses your class library in the same Visual Studio solution. That way, you can easily modify and debug both pieces at once.

The first step in creating a custom control is choosing the right base class to inherit from. Table 18-1 lists some commonly used classes for creating custom controls, and Figure 18-1 shows where they fit into the element hierarchy.

Table 18-1. *Base Classes for Creating a Custom Element*

Name	Description
FrameworkElement	This is the lowest level you'll typically use when creating a custom element. Usually, you'll take this approach only if you want to draw your content from scratch by overriding OnRender()and using the System.Windows.Media.DrawingContext. It's similar to the approach you saw in Chapter 14, where a user interface was constructed by using Visual objects. The FrameworkElement class provides the basic set of properties and events for elements that aren't intended to interact with the user.
Control	This is the most common starting point when building a control from scratch. It's the base class for all user-interactive widgets. The Control class adds properties for setting the background and foreground, as well as the font and alignment of content. The control class also places itself into the tab order (through the IsTabStop property) and introduces the notion of double-clicking (through the MouseDoubleClick and PreviewMouseDoubleClick events). But most important, the Control class defines the Template property that allows its appearance to be swapped out with a customized element tree for endless flexibility.
ContentControl	This is the base class for controls that can display a single piece of arbitrary content. That content can be an element or a custom object that's used in conjunction with a template. (The content is set through the Content property, and an optional template can be provided in the ContentTemplate property.) Many controls wrap a specific, limited type of content (such as a string of text in a text box). Because these controls don't support all elements, they shouldn't be defined as content controls.
UserControl	This is a content control that can be configured using a design-time surface. Although a user control isn't that different from an ordinary content control, it's typically used when you want to quickly reuse an unchanging block of user interface in more than one window (rather than create a true stand-alone control that can be transported from one application to another).

(continued)

Table 18-1. (*continued*)

Name	Description
ItemsControl or Selector	ItemsControl is the base class for controls that wrap a list of items but don't support selection, while Selector is the more specialized base class for controls that do support selection. These classes aren't often used to create custom controls, because the data-templating features of the ListBox, ListView, and TreeView provide a great deal of flexibility.
Panel	This is the base class for controls with layout logic. A layout control can hold multiple children and arranges them according to specific layout semantics. Often panels include attached properties that can be set on the children to configure how the children are arranged.
Decorator	This is the base class for elements that wrap another element and provide a graphical effect or specific feature. Two prominent examples are the Border, which draws a line around an element, and the Viewbox, which scales its content dynamically using a transform. Other decorators include the chrome classes used to give the familiar border and background to common controls such as the button.
A specific control class	If you want to introduce a refinement to an existing control, you can derive directly from that control. For example, you can create a TextBox with built-in validation logic. However, before you take this step, consider whether you could accomplish the same thing by using event-handling code or a separate component. Both approaches allow you to decouple your logic from the control and reuse it with other controls.

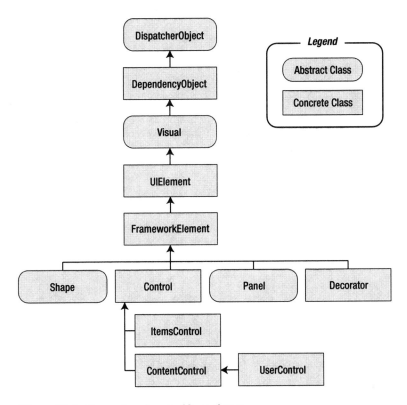

Figure 18-1. *Element and control base classes*

■ **Note**   Although you can create a custom element that isn't a control, most custom elements you create in WPF will be controls—that is to say they'll be able to receive focus, and they'll interact with the user's key presses and mouse actions. For that reason, the terms *custom elements* and *custom controls* are sometimes used interchangeably in WPF development.

In this chapter, you'll see a user control, a lookless color picker that derives directly from the Control class, a lookless FlipPanel that uses visual states, a custom layout panel, and a custom-drawn element that derives from FrameworkElement and overrides OnRender(). Many of the examples are quite lengthy. Although you'll walk through almost all of the code in this chapter, you'll probably want to follow up by downloading the samples and playing with the custom controls yourself.

Building a Basic User Control

A good way to get started with custom controls is to take a crack at creating a straightforward user control. In this section, we'll begin by creating a basic color picker. Later, you'll see how to refactor this control into a more capable template-based control.

Creating a basic color picker is easy. However, creating a custom color picker is still a worthy exercise. Not only does it demonstrate a variety of important control-building concepts, but it also gives you a practical piece of functionality.

You could create a custom dialog box for your color picker. But if you want to create a color picker that you can integrate into different windows, a custom control is a far better choice. The most straightforward type of custom control is a *user control*, which allows you to assemble a combination of elements in the same way as when you design a window or page. Because the color picker appears to be little more than a fairly straightforward grouping of existing controls with added functionality, a user control seems like a perfect choice.

A typical color picker allows a user to select a color by clicking somewhere in a color gradient or specifying individual red, green, and blue components. Figure 18-2 shows the basic color picker you'll create in this section (at the top of the window). It consists of three Slider controls for adjusting color components, along with a Rectangle that shows a preview of the selected color.

Figure 18-2. *A color picker user control*

> ■ **Note** The user control approach has one significant flaw—it limits your ability to customize the appearance of your color picker to suit different windows, applications, and uses. Fortunately, it's not much harder to step up to a more template-based control, as you'll see a bit later.

Defining Dependency Properties

The first step in creating the color picker is to add a user control to your custom control library project. When you do, Visual Studio creates a XAML markup file and a corresponding custom class to hold your initialization and event-handling code. This is the same experience as when you create a new window or page—the only difference is that the top-level container is the UserControl class.

The easiest starting point is to design the public interface that the user control exposes to the outside world. In other words, it's time to create the properties, methods, and events that the control consumer (the application that uses the control) will rely on to interact with the color picker.

The most fundamental detail is the Color property—after all, the color picker is nothing more than a specialized tool for displaying and choosing a color value. To support WPF features such as data binding, styles, and animation, writeable control properties are almost always dependency properties.

As you learned in Chapter 4, the first step to creating a dependency property is to define a shared field for it, with the word *Property* added to the end of your property name:

```
Public Shared ColorProperty As DependencyProperty
```

The Color property will allow the control consumer to set or retrieve the color value programmatically. However, the sliders in the color picker also allow the user to modify one aspect of the current color. To implement this design, you could use event handlers that respond when a slider value is changed and update the Color property accordingly. But it's cleaner to wire the sliders up by using data binding. To make this possible, you need to define each of the color components as a separate dependency property:

```
Public Shared RedProperty As DependencyProperty
Public Shared GreenProperty As DependencyProperty
Public Shared BlueProperty As DependencyProperty
```

Although the Color property will store a System.Windows.Media.Color object, the Red, Green, and Blue properties will store individual byte values that represent each color component. (You could also add a slider and a property for managing the alpha value, which allows you to create a partially transparent color, but this example doesn't add this detail.)

Defining the shared fields for your properties is just the first step. You also need a shared constructor in your user control that registers them, specifying the property name, the data type, and the control class that owns the property. As you learned in Chapter 4, this is the point where you can opt in to specific property features (such as value inheritance) by passing a FrameworkPropertyMetadata object with the right flags set. It's also the point where you can attach callbacks for validation, value coercion, and property change notifications.

In the color picker, you have just one consideration—you need to attach callbacks that respond when the various properties are changed. That's because the Red, Green, and Blue properties are really a different representation of the Color property, and if one property changes, you need to make sure the others stay synchronized.

Here's the shared constructor code that registers the four dependency properties of the color picker:

```
Shared Sub New()
    ColorProperty = DependencyProperty.Register( _
      "Color", GetType(Color), GetType(ColorPickerUserControl), _
      New FrameworkPropertyMetadata(Colors.Black, _
        New PropertyChangedCallback(AddressOf OnColorChanged)))
```

507

```vbnet
    RedProperty = DependencyProperty.Register( _
      "Red", GetType(Byte), GetType(ColorPickerUserControl), _
      New FrameworkPropertyMetadata( _
        New PropertyChangedCallback(AddressOf OnColorRGBChanged)))

    GreenProperty = DependencyProperty.Register( _
      "Green", GetType(Byte), GetType(ColorPickerUserControl), _
      New FrameworkPropertyMetadata( _
      New PropertyChangedCallback(AddressOf OnColorRGBChanged)))

    BlueProperty = DependencyProperty.Register( _
      "Blue", GetType(Byte), GetType(ColorPickerUserControl), _
      New FrameworkPropertyMetadata( _
        New PropertyChangedCallback(AddressOf OnColorRGBChanged)))
End Sub
```

Now that you have your dependency properties defined, you can add standard property wrappers that make them easier to access and usable in XAML:

```vbnet
Public Property Color() As Color
    Get
        Return CType(GetValue(ColorProperty), Color)
    End Get
    Set(ByVal value As Color)
        SetValue(ColorProperty, value)
    End Set
End Property

Public Property Red() As Byte
    Get
        Return CByte(GetValue(RedProperty))
    End Get
    Set(ByVal value As Byte)
        SetValue(RedProperty, value)
    End Set
End Property

Public Property Green() As Byte
    Get
        Return CByte(GetValue(GreenProperty))
    End Get
    Set(ByVal value As Byte)
        SetValue(GreenProperty, value)
    End Set
End Property

Public Property Blue() As Byte
    Get
        Return CByte(GetValue(BlueProperty))
    End Get
```

```
      Set(ByVal value As Byte)
          SetValue(BlueProperty, value)
      End Set
End Property
```

Remember, the property wrappers shouldn't contain any logic, because properties may be set and retrieved directly by using the SetValue() and GetValue() methods of the base DependencyObject class. For example, the property synchronization logic in this example is implemented by using callbacks that fire when the property changes through the property wrapper or a direct SetValue() call.

The property change callbacks are responsible for keeping the Color property consistent with the Red, Green, and Blue properties. Whenever the Red, Green, or Blue property is changed, the Color property is adjusted accordingly:

```
Private Shared Sub OnColorRGBChanged(ByVal sender As DependencyObject, _
  ByVal e As DependencyPropertyChangedEventArgs)
    Dim colorPicker As ColorPickerUserControl
    colorPicker = CType(sender, ColorPickerUserControl)

    Dim color As Color = colorPicker.Color
    If e.Property Is RedProperty Then
        color.R = CByte(e.NewValue)
    ElseIf e.Property Is GreenProperty Then
        color.G = CByte(e.NewValue)
    ElseIf e.Property Is BlueProperty Then
        color.B = CByte(e.NewValue)
    End If

    colorPicker.Color = color
End Sub
```

and when the Color property is set, the Red, Green, and Blue values are also updated:

```
Private Shared Sub OnColorChanged(ByVal sender As DependencyObject, _
  ByVal e As DependencyPropertyChangedEventArgs)
    Dim newColor As Color = CType(e.NewValue, Color)
    Dim oldColors As Color = CType(e.OldValue, Color)

    Dim colorPicker As ColorPickerUserControl
    colorPicker = CType(sender, ColorPickerUserControl)
    colorPicker.Red = newColor.R
    colorPicker.Green = newColor.G
    colorPicker.Blue = newColor.B
End Sub
```

Despite its appearances, this code won't cause an infinite series of calls as each property tries to change the other. That's because WPF doesn't allow reentrancy in the property change callbacks. For example, if you change the Color property, the OnColorChanged() method will be triggered. The OnColorChanged() method will modify the Red, Green, and Blue properties, triggering the OnColorRGBChanged() callback three times (once for each property). However, the OnColorRBGChanged() will not trigger the OnColorChanged() method again.

■ **Tip** It might occur to you to use the coercion callbacks discussed in Chapter 4 to deal with the color properties. However, this approach isn't appropriate. Property coercion callbacks are designed for properties that are interrelated and may override or influence one another. They don't make sense for properties that expose the same data in different ways. If you used property coercion in this example, it would be possible to set different values in the Red, Green, and Blue properties and have that color information *override* the Color property. The behavior you really want is to set the Red, Green, and Blue properties and use that color information to permanently *change* the value of the Color property.

Defining Routed Events

You might also want to add routed events that can be used to notify the control consumer when something happens. In the color picker example, it's useful to have an event that fires when the color is changed. Although you could define this event as an ordinary .NET event, using a routed event allows you to provide event bubbling and tunneling, so the event can be handled in a higher-level parent, such as the containing window.

As with the dependency properties, the first step to defining a routed event is to create a shared property for it, with the word *Event* added to the end of the event name:

```
Public Shared ReadOnly ColorChangedEvent As RoutedEvent
```

You can then register the event in the shared constructor. At this point, you specify the event name, the routing strategy, the signature, and the owning class:

```
ColorChangedEvent = EventManager.RegisterRoutedEvent( _
  "ColorChanged", RoutingStrategy.Bubble, _
  GetType(RoutedPropertyChangedEventHandler(Of Color)), _
  GetType(ColorPickerUserControl))
```

Rather than going to the work of creating a new delegate for your event signature, you can sometimes reuse existing delegates. The two useful delegates are RoutedEventHandler (for a routed event that doesn't pass along any extra information) and RoutedPropertyChangedEventHandler (for a routed event that provides the old and new values after a property has been changed). The RoutedPropertyChangedEventHandler, which is used in the previous example, is a generic delegate that's parameterized by type. As a result, you can use it with any property data type without sacrificing type safety.

After you've defined and registered the event, you need to create a standard .NET event wrapper that exposes your event. This event wrapper can be used to attach (and remove) event listeners:

```
Public Custom Event ColorChanged As RoutedPropertyChangedEventHandler(Of Color)
    AddHandler(ByVal value As RoutedPropertyChangedEventHandler(Of Color))
        MyBase.AddHandler(ColorChangedEvent, value)
    End AddHandler
    RemoveHandler(ByVal value As RoutedPropertyChangedEventHandler(Of Color))
        MyBase.RemoveHandler(ColorChangedEvent, value)
    End RemoveHandler
    RaiseEvent(ByVal sender As System.Object, _
      ByVal e As RoutedPropertyChangedEventArgs(Of Color))
    End RaiseEvent
End Event
```

The final detail is the code that raises the event at the appropriate time. This code must call the RaiseEvent() method that's inherited from the base DependencyObject class.

In the color picker example, you simply need to add this line of code to the end of the OnColorChanged() method:

```
Dim oldColor As Color = CType(e.OldValue, Color)
Dim args As New RoutedPropertyChangedEventArgs(Of Color)(oldValue, newValue)
args.RoutedEvent = ColorPickerUserControl.ColorChangedEvent
colorPicker.RaiseEvent(args)
```

Remember, the OnColorChanged() callback is triggered whenever the Color property is modified, either directly or by modifying the Red, Green, and Blue color components.

Adding Markup

Now that your user control's public interface is in place, all you need is the markup that creates the control's appearance. In this case, a basic Grid is all that's needed to bring together the three Slider controls and the Rectangle with the color preview. The trick is the data-binding expressions that tie these controls to the appropriate properties, with no event-handling code required.

All in all, four data-binding expressions are at work in the color picker. The three sliders are bound to the Red, Green, and Blue properties and are allowed to range from 0 to 255 (the acceptable values for a byte). The Rectangle.Fill property is set using a SolidColorBrush, and the Color property of that brush is bound to the Color property of the user control.

Here's the complete markup:

```xml
<UserControl x:Class="ColorPicker"
    xmlns="http://schemas.microsoft.com/winfx/2006/xaml/presentation"
    xmlns:x="http://schemas.microsoft.com/winfx/2006/xaml" Name="colorPicker">
  <Grid>
    <Grid.RowDefinitions>
      <RowDefinition Height="Auto"></RowDefinition>
      <RowDefinition Height="Auto"></RowDefinition>
      <RowDefinition Height="Auto"></RowDefinition>
    </Grid.RowDefinitions>
    <Grid.ColumnDefinitions>
      <ColumnDefinition></ColumnDefinition>
      <ColumnDefinition Width="Auto"></ColumnDefinition>
    </Grid.ColumnDefinitions>

    <Slider Name="sliderRed" Minimum="0" Maximum="255"
     Value="{Binding ElementName=colorPicker,Path=Red}"></Slider>
    <Slider Grid.Row="1" Name="sliderGreen" Minimum="0" Maximum="255"
     Value="{Binding ElementName=colorPicker,Path=Green}"></Slider>
    <Slider Grid.Row="2" Name="sliderBlue" Minimum="0" Maximum="255"
     Value="{Binding ElementName=colorPicker,Path=Blue}"></Slider>

    <Rectangle Grid.Column="1" Grid.RowSpan="3"
     Width="50" Stroke="Black" StrokeThickness="1">
      <Rectangle.Fill>
        <SolidColorBrush Color="{Binding ElementName=colorPicker,Path=Color}">
        </SolidColorBrush>
      </Rectangle.Fill>
    </Rectangle>

  </Grid>
</UserControl>
```

The markup for a user control plays the same role as the control template for a lookless control. If you want to make some of the details in your markup configurable, you can use binding expressions that link them to control properties. For example, currently the Rectangle's width is hard-coded at 50 units. However, you could replace this detail with a data-binding expression that pulls the value from a dependency property in your user control. That way, the control consumer could modify that property to choose a different width. Similarly, you could make the stroke color and thickness variable. However, if you want to make a control with real flexibility, you're much better off to create a lookless control and define the markup in a template, as described later in this chapter.

Occasionally, you might choose to use binding expressions to repurpose one of the core properties that's already defined in your control. For example, the UserControl class uses its Padding property to add space between the outer edge and the inner content that you define. (This detail is implemented through the control template for the UserControl.) However, you could also use the Padding property to set the spacing around each slider, as shown here:

```
<Slider Name="sliderRed" Minimum="0" Maximum="255"
  Margin="{Binding ElementName=colorPicker,Path=Padding}"
  Value="{Binding ElementName=colorPicker,Path=Red}"></Slider>
```

Similarly, you could grab the border settings for the Rectangle from the BorderThickness and BorderBrush properties of the UserControl. Once again, this is a shortcut that may make perfect sense for creating simple controls but can be improved by introducing additional properties (for example, SliderMargin, PreviewBorderBrush, and PreviewBorderThickness) or creating a full-fledged template-based control.

NAMING A USER CONTROL

In the example shown here, the top-level UserControl is assigned a name (colorPicker). This allows you to write straightforward data-binding expressions that bind to properties in the custom user control class. However, this technique raises an obvious question. Namely, what happens when you create an instance of the user control in a window (or page) and assign a new name to it?

Fortunately, this situation works without a hitch, because the user control performs its initialization before that of the containing window. First, the user control is initialized, and its data bindings are connected. Next, the window is initialized, and the name that's set in the window markup is applied to the user control. The data-binding expressions and event handlers in the window can now use the window-defined name to access the user control, and everything works the way you'd expect.

Although this sounds straightforward, you might notice a couple of quirks if you use code that examines the UserControl.Name property directly. For example, if you examine the Name property in an event handler in the user control, you'll see the new name that was applied by the window. Similarly, if you don't set a name in the window markup, the user control will retain the original name from the user control markup. You'll then see this name if you examine the Name property in the window code.

Neither of these quirks represents a problem, but a better approach would be to avoid naming the user control in the user control markup and use the Binding.RelativeSource property to search up the element tree until you find the UserControl parent. Here's the lengthier syntax that does this:

```
<Slider Name="sliderRed" Minimum="0" Maximum="255"
      Value="{Binding Path=Red,
            RelativeSource={RelativeSource FindAncestor,
                          AncestorType={x:Type UserControl}}
            }">
</Slider>
```

You'll see this approach later, when you build a template-based control in the section "Refactoring the Color Picker Markup."

Using the Control

Now that you've completed the control, using it is easy. To use the color picker in another window, you need to begin by mapping the assembly and .NET namespace to an XML namespace, as shown here:

```
<Window x:Class=" ColorPickerUserControlTest"
  xmlns:lib="clr-namespace:CustomControls;assembly=CustomControls" ... >
```

Using the XML namespace you've defined and the user control class name, you can create your user control exactly as you create any other type of object in XAML markup. You can also set its properties and attach event handlers directly in the control tag, as shown here:

```
<lib:ColorPickerUserControl Name="colorPicker" Color="Beige"
 ColorChanged="colorPicker_ColorChanged"></lib:ColorPickerUserControl>
```

Because the Color property uses the Color data type and the Color data type is decorated with a TypeConverter attribute, WPF knows to use the ColorConverter to change the string color name into the corresponding Color object before setting the Color property.

The code that handles the ColorChanged event is straightforward:

```
Private Sub colorPicker_ColorChanged(ByVal sender As Object, _
  ByVal e As RoutedPropertyChangedEventArgs(Of Color))
    lblColor.Text = "The new color is " & e.NewValue.ToString()
End Sub
```

This completes your custom control. However, there's still one frill worth adding. In the next section, you'll enhance the color picker with support for WPF's command feature.

Supporting Commands

Many controls have baked-in command support. You can add this to your controls in two ways:

- Add command bindings that link your control to specific commands. That way, your control can respond to a command without the help of any external code.

- Create a new RoutedUICommand object for your command as a shared field in your control. Then add a command binding for that command. This allows your control to automatically support commands that aren't already defined in the basic set of command classes that you learned about in Chapter 9.

In the following example, you'll use the first approach to add support for the ApplicationCommands.Undo command.

■ **Tip**   For more information about commands and how to create custom RoutedUICommand objects, refer to Chapter 9.

To support an Undo feature in the color picker, you need to track the previous color in a member field:

```
Private previousColor As Nullable(Of Color)
```

It makes sense to make this field nullable, because when the control is first created, there shouldn't be a previous color set. (You can also clear the previous color programmatically after an action that you want to make irreversible.)

When the color is changed, you simply need to record the old value. You can take care of this task by adding this line to the end of the OnColorChanged() method:

```
colorPicker.previousColor = CType(e.OldValue, Color)
```

Now you have the infrastructure in place that you need to support the Undo command. All that's left is to create the command binding that connects your control to the command and handle the CanExecute and Executed events.

The best place to create command bindings is when the control is first created. For example, the following code uses the color picker's constructor to add a command binding to the ApplicationCommands.Undo command:

```
Public Sub New()
    InitializeComponent()
    SetUpCommands()
End Sub

Private Sub SetUpCommands()
    ' Set up command bindings.
    Dim binding As New CommandBinding(ApplicationCommands.Undo, _
        AddressOf UndoCommand_Executed, AddressOf UndoCommand_CanExecute)
    Me.CommandBindings.Add(Binding)
End Sub
```

To make your command functional, you need to handle the CanExecute event and allow the command as long as there is a previous value:

```
Private Sub UndoCommand_CanExecute(ByVal sender As Object, _
  ByVal e As CanExecuteRoutedEventArgs)
        e.CanExecute =previousColor.HasValue
End Sub
```

Finally, when the command is executed, you can swap in the new color.

```
Private Sub UndoCommand_Executed(ByVal sender As Object, _
  ByVal e As ExecutedRoutedEventArgs)
    Me.Color = CType(previousColor, Color)
End Sub
```

You can trigger the Undo command in two ways. You can use the default Ctrl+Z key binding when an element in the user control has focus, or you can add a button to the client that triggers the command, like this one:

```
<Button Command="Undo" CommandTarget="{Binding ElementName=colorPicker}">
  Undo
</Button>
```

Either way, the current color is abandoned and the previous color is applied.

■ **Tip** The current example stores just one level of undo information. However, it's easy to create an undo stack that stores a series of values. You just need to store Color values in the appropriate type of collection. The Stack collection in the System.Collections.Generic namespaces is a good choice, because it implements a last-in first-out approach that makes it easy to grab the most recent Color object when performing an undo operation.

More Robust Commands

The technique described earlier is a perfectly legitimate way to connect commands to controls, but it's not the technique that's used in WPF elements and professional controls. These elements use a more robust approach and attach shared command handlers by using the CommandManager.RegisterClassCommandBinding() method.

The problem with the implementation shown in the previous example is that it uses the public CommandBindings collection. This makes it a bit fragile, because the client can modify the CommandBindings collection freely. This isn't possible if you use the RegisterClassCommandBinding() method. This is the approach that WPF controls use. For example, if you look at the CommandBindings collection of a TextBox, you won't find any of the bindings for hardwired commands such as Undo, Redo, Cut, Copy, and Paste, because these are registered as class bindings.

The technique is fairly straightforward. Instead of creating the command binding in the instance constructor, you must create the command binding in the shared constructor, using code like this:

```
CommandManager.RegisterClassCommandBinding(GetType(ColorPickerUserControl), _
  New CommandBinding(ApplicationCommands.Undo, _
  AddressOf UndoCommand_Executed, AddressOf UndoCommand_CanExecute))
```

Although this code hasn't changed much, there's an important shift. Because the UndoCommand_Executed() and UndoCommand_CanExecute() methods are referred to in the constructor, they must both be shared methods. To retrieve instance data (such as the current color and the previous color information), you need to cast the event sender to a ColorPicker object and use it.

Here's the revised command-handling code:

```
Private Shared Sub UndoCommand_CanExecute(ByVal sender As Object, _
  ByVal e As CanExecuteRoutedEventArgs)
    Dim colorPicker As ColorPickerUserControl = _
      CType(sender, ColorPickerUserControl)
    e.CanExecute = colorPicker.previousColor.HasValue
End Sub
```

```
Private Shared Sub UndoCommand_Executed(ByVal sender As Object, _
  ByVal e As ExecutedRoutedEventArgs)
    Dim colorPicker As ColorPickerUserControl = _
      CType(sender, ColorPickerUserControl)
    colorPicker.Color = CType(colorPicker.previousColor, Color)
End Sub
```

Incidentally, this technique isn't limited to commands. If you want to hardwire event-handling logic into your control, you can use a class event handler with the EventManager.RegisterClassHandler() method. Class event handlers are always invoked before instance event handlers, allowing you to easily suppress events.

Taking a Closer Look at User Controls

User controls provide a fairly painless but somewhat limited way to create a custom control. To understand why, it helps to take a closer look at how user controls work.

Behind the scenes, the UserControl class works a lot like the ContentControl class from which it derives. In fact, it has just a few key differences:

- The UserControl class changes some default values. Namely, it sets IsTabStop and Focusable to False (so it doesn't occupy a separate place in the tab order), and it sets HorizontalAlignment and VerticalAlignment to Stretch (rather than Left and Top) so it fills the available space.

- The UserControl class applies a new control template that consists of a Border element that wraps a ContentPresenter. The ContentPresenter holds the content you add by using markup.

- The UserControl class changes the source of routed events. When events bubble or tunnel from controls inside the user control to elements outside the user control, the source changes to point to the user control rather than the original element. This gives you a bit more encapsulation. (For example, if you handle the UIElement.MouseLeftButtonDown event in the layout container that holds the color picker, you'll receive an event when you click the Rectangle inside. However, the source of this event won't be the Rectangle element but the ColorPicker object that contains the Rectangle. If you create the same color picker as an ordinary content control, this isn't the case—it's up to you to intercept the event in your control, handle it, and reraise it.)

The most significant difference between user controls and other types of custom controls is the way that a user control is designed. Like all controls, user controls have a control template. However, you'll rarely change this template—instead, you'll supply the markup as part of your custom user control class, and this markup is processed using the InitializeComponent() method when the control is created. On the other hand, a lookless control has no markup—everything it needs is in the template.

An ordinary ContentControl has the following stripped-down template:

```
<ControlTemplate TargetType="ContentControl">
  <ContentPresenter
   ContentTemplate="{TemplateBinding ContentControl.ContentTemplate}"
   Content="{TemplateBinding ContentControl.Content}" />
</ControlTemplate>
```

This template does little more than fill in the supplied content and apply the optional content template. Properties such as Padding, Background, HorizontalAlignment, and VerticalAlignment won't have any effect unless you explicitly bind to it.

The UserControl has a similar template with a few more niceties. Most obviously, it adds a Border element and binds its properties to the BorderBrush, BorderThickness, Background, and Padding properties of the user control to make sure they have some meaning. Additionally, the ContentPresenter inside binds to the alignment properties.

```
<ControlTemplate TargetType="UserControl">
  <Border BorderBrush="{TemplateBinding Border.BorderBrush}"
    BorderThickness="{TemplateBinding Border.BorderThickness}"
    Background="{TemplateBinding Panel.Background}" SnapsToDevicePixels="True"
    Padding="{TemplateBinding Control.Padding}">

    <ContentPresenter
      HorizontalAlignment="{TemplateBinding Control.HorizontalContentAlignment}"
      VerticalAlignment="{TemplateBinding Control.VerticalContentAlignment}"
      SnapsToDevicePixels="{TemplateBinding UIElement.SnapsToDevicePixels}"
      ContentTemplate="{TemplateBinding ContentControl.ContentTemplate}"
      Content="{TemplateBinding ContentControl.Content}" />

  </Border>
</ControlTemplate>
```

Technically, you could change the template of a user control. In fact, you could move all your markup into the template, with only slight readjusting. But there's really no reason to take this step—if you want a more flexible control that separates the visual look from the interface that's defined by your control class, you'd be much better off creating a custom lookless control, as described in the next section.

Creating a Lookless Control

The goal of user controls is to provide a design surface that supplements the control template, giving you a quicker way to define the control at the price of future flexibility. This causes a problem if you're happy with the functionality of a user control, but you need to tailor its visual appearance. For example, imagine you want to use the same color picker but give it a different "skin" that blends better into an existing application window. You may be able to change some aspects of the user control through styles, but parts of it are locked away inside, hard-coded into the markup. For example, there's no way to move the preview rectangle to the left side of the sliders.

The solution is to create a lookless control—a control that derives from one of the control base classes but doesn't have a design surface. Instead, this control places its markup into a default template that can be replaced at will without disturbing the control logic.

Refactoring the Color Picker Code

Changing the color picker into a lookless control isn't too difficult. The first step is easy—you simply need to change the class declaration, as shown here:

```
Public Class ColorPicker
  Inherits System.Windows.Controls.Control
    ...
End Class
```

In this example, the ColorPicker class derives from Control. FrameworkElement isn't suitable, because the color picker does allow user interaction and the other higher-level classes don't accurately describe the color picker's behavior. For example, the color picker doesn't allow you to nest other content inside, so the ContentControl class isn't appropriate.

The code inside the ColorPicker class is the same as the code for the user control (aside from the fact that you must remove the call to InitializeComponent() in the constructor). You follow the same approach to define dependency properties and routed events. The only difference is that you need to tell WPF that you will be providing a new style for your control class. This style will provide the new control template. (If you don't take this step, you'll continue whatever template is defined in the base class.)

To tell WPF that you're providing a new style, you need to call the OverrideMetadata() method in the shared constructor of your class. You call this method on the DefaultStyleKeyProperty, which is a dependency property that defines the default style for your control. The code you need is as follows:

```
DefaultStyleKeyProperty.OverrideMetadata(GetType(ColorPicker), _
    New FrameworkPropertyMetadata(GetType(ColorPicker)))
```

You could supply a different type if you want to use the template of another control class, but you'll almost always create a specific style for each one of your custom controls.

Refactoring the Color Picker Markup

After you've added the call to OverrideMetadata, you simply need to plug in the right style. This style needs to be placed in a resource dictionary named generic.xaml, which must be placed in a Themes subfolder in your project. That way, your style will be recognized as the default style for your control. Here's how to add the generic.xaml file:

1. Right-click the class library project in the Solution Explorer, and choose Add ➤ New Folder.

2. Name the new folder Themes.

3. Right-click the Themes folder, and choose Add ➤ New Item.

4. In the Add New Item dialog box, pick the XML file template, enter the name generic.xaml, and click Add.

Figure 18-3 shows the generic.xaml file in the Themes folder.

Figure 18-3. *A WPF application and class library*

THEME-SPECIFIC STYLES AND GENERIC.XAML

As you've seen, the ColorPicker gets its default control template from a file named generic.xaml, which is placed in a project folder named Themes. This slightly strange convention is actually part of a legacy WPF feature: *Windows theme support.*

The original goal of Windows theme support was to let developers create customized versions of their controls to match different Windows themes. This goal made the most sense on old Windows XP computers, which used themes to control the overall color scheme of Windows applications. When Windows Vista was released, it introduced the Aero theme, which effectively replaced the old theme choices. The versions of Windows that followed haven't changed that state of affairs, and so the Windows theming feature in WPF (which was never much used) is now universally ignored.

The bottom line this: WPF developers creating applications today always use a generic.xaml file to set their default control styles. The name of the generic.xaml file (and the Themes folder in which it's placed) is a holdover from the past.

Often, a custom control library has several controls. To keep their styles separate for easier editing, the generic.xaml file often uses resource dictionary merging. The following markup shows a generic.xaml file that pulls in the resources from the ColorPicker.xaml resource dictionary in the same Themes subfolder of a control library named CustomControls:

```
<ResourceDictionary
 xmlns="http://schemas.microsoft.com/winfx/2006/xaml/presentation"
 xmlns:x="http://schemas.microsoft.com/winfx/2006/xaml" >
```

```
  <ResourceDictionary.MergedDictionaries>
    <ResourceDictionary Source="/CustomControls;component/themes/ColorPicker.xaml">
    </ResourceDictionary>
  </ResourceDictionary.MergedDictionaries>

</ResourceDictionary>
```

Your custom control style must use the TargetType attribute to attach itself to the color picker automatically. Here's the basic structure of the markup that appears in the ColorPicker.xaml file:

```
<ResourceDictionary
 xmlns="http://schemas.microsoft.com/winfx/2006/xaml/presentation"
 xmlns:x="http://schemas.microsoft.com/winfx/2006/xaml"
 xmlns:local="clr-namespace:CustomControls">
  <Style TargetType="{x:Type local:ColorPicker}">
    ...
  </Style>
</ResourceDictionary>
```

You can use your style to set any properties in the control class (whether they're inherited from the base class or new properties you've added). However, the most useful task that your style performs is to apply a new template that defines the default visual appearance of your control.

It's fairly easy to convert ordinary markup (such as that used by the color picker) into a control template. Keep these considerations in mind:

- When creating binding expressions that link to properties in the parent control class, you can't use the ElementName property. Instead, you need to use the RelativeSource property to indicate that you want to bind to the parent control. If one-way data binding is all that you need, you can usually use the lightweight TemplateBinding markup extension instead of the full-fledged Binding.

- You can't attach event handlers in the control template. Instead, you'll need to give your elements recognizable names and attach event handlers to them programmatically in the control constructor.

- Don't name an element in a control template unless you want to attach an event handler or interact with it programmatically. When naming an element you want to use, give it a name in the form PART_*ElementName*.

With these considerations in mind, you can create the following template for the color picker. The most important changed details are highlighted in bold.

```
<Style TargetType="{x:Type local:ColorPicker}">
  <Setter Property="Template">
    <Setter.Value>
      <ControlTemplate TargetType="{x:Type local:ColorPicker}">
        <Grid>
          <Grid.RowDefinitions>
            <RowDefinition Height="Auto"></RowDefinition>
            <RowDefinition Height="Auto"></RowDefinition>
            <RowDefinition Height="Auto"></RowDefinition>
          </Grid.RowDefinitions>
```

```xml
        <Grid.ColumnDefinitions>
          <ColumnDefinition></ColumnDefinition>
          <ColumnDefinition Width="Auto"></ColumnDefinition>
        </Grid.ColumnDefinitions>

        <Slider Minimum="0" Maximum="255"
         Margin="{TemplateBinding Padding}"
         Value="{Binding Path=Red,
                RelativeSource={RelativeSource TemplatedParent}}">
        </Slider>
        <Slider Grid.Row="1" Minimum="0" Maximum="255"
         Margin="{TemplateBinding Padding}"
         Value="{Binding Path=Red,
                RelativeSource={RelativeSource TemplatedParent}}">
        </Slider>
        <Slider Grid.Row="2" Minimum="0" Maximum="255"
         Margin="{TemplateBinding Padding}"
         Value="{Binding Path=Red,
                RelativeSource={RelativeSource TemplatedParent}}">
        </Slider>

        <Rectangle Grid.Column="1" Grid.RowSpan="3"
         Margin="{TemplateBinding Padding}"
         Width="50" Stroke="Black" StrokeThickness="1">
          <Rectangle.Fill>
            <SolidColorBrush
             Color="{Binding Path=Color,
                RelativeSource={RelativeSource TemplatedParent}}">
            </SolidColorBrush>
          </Rectangle.Fill>
        </Rectangle>
      </Grid>
    </ControlTemplate>
  </Setter.Value>
 </Setter>
</Style>
```

As you'll notice, some binding expressions have been replaced with the TemplateBinding extension. Others still use the Binding extension but have the RelativeSource set to point to the template parent (the custom control). Although both TemplateBinding and Binding with a RelativeSource of TemplatedParent are for the same purpose—extracting data from the properties of your custom control—the lighter-weight TemplateBinding is always appropriate. It won't work if you need two-way binding (as with the sliders) or when binding to the property of a class that derives from Freezable (such as the SolidColorBrush).

Streamlining the Control Template

As it stands, the color picker control template fills in everything you need, and you can use it in the same way that you use the color picker user control. However, it's still possible to simplify the template by removing some of the details.

Currently, any control consumer that wants to supply a custom template will be forced to add a slew of data-binding expressions to ensure that the control continues to work. This isn't difficult, but it is tedious. Another option is to configure all the binding expressions in the initialization code of the control itself. This way, the template doesn't need to specify these details.

■ **Note**   This is the same technique you use when attaching event handlers to the elements that make up a custom control. You attach each event handler programmatically, rather than use event attributes in the template.

Adding Part Names

For this system to work, your code needs to be able to find the elements it needs. WPF controls locate the elements they need by name. As a result, your element names become part of the public interface of your control and need suitably descriptive names. By convention, these names begin with the text *PART_* followed by the element name. The element name uses initial caps, just like a property name. PART_RedSlider is a good choice for a required element name, while PART_sldRed, PART_redSlider, and RedSlider are all poor choices.

For example, here's how you would prepare the three sliders for programmatic binding, by removing the binding expression from the Value property and adding a PART_ name:

```
<Slider Name="PART_RedSlider" Minimum="0" Maximum="255"
 Margin="{TemplateBinding Padding}"></Slider>
<Slider Grid.Row="1" Name="PART_GreenSlider" Minimum="0" Maximum="255"
 Margin="{TemplateBinding Padding}"></Slider>
<Slider Grid.Row="2" Name="PART_BlueSlider" Minimum="0" Maximum="255"
 Margin="{TemplateBinding Padding}"></Slider>
```

Notice that the Margin property still uses a binding expression to add padding, but this is an optional detail that can easily be left out of a custom template (which may choose to hard-code the padding or use a different layout).

To ensure maximum flexibility, the Rectangle isn't given a name. Instead, the SolidColorBrush inside is given a name. That way, the color preview feature can be used with any shape or an arbitrary element, depending on the template.

```
<Rectangle Grid.Column="1" Grid.RowSpan="3"
 Margin="{TemplateBinding Padding}"
 Width="50" Stroke="Black" StrokeThickness="1">
  <Rectangle.Fill>
    <SolidColorBrush x:Name="PART_PreviewBrush"></SolidColorBrush>
  </Rectangle.Fill>
</Rectangle>
```

Manipulating Template Parts

You could connect your binding expressions when the control is initialized, but there's a better approach. WPF has a dedicated OnApplyTemplate() method that you should override if you need to search for elements in the template and attach event handlers or add data-binding expressions. In that method, you can use the GetTemplateChild() method (which is inherited from FrameworkElement) to find the elements you need.

If you don't find an element that you want to work with, the recommended pattern is to do nothing. Optionally, you can add code that checks that the element, if present, is the correct type and raises an exception if it isn't. (The thinking here is that a missing element represents a conscious opting out of a specific feature, whereas an incorrect element type represents a mistake.)

Here's how you can connect the data-binding expression for a single slider in the OnApplyTemplate() method:

```
Public Overrides Sub OnApplyTemplate()
    MyBase.OnApplyTemplate()

    Dim slider As RangeBase
    slider = TryCast(GetTemplateChild("PART_RedSlider"), RangeBase)
    If slider IsNot Nothing Then
        ' Bind to the Red property in the control, using a two-way binding.
        Dim binding As New Binding("Red")
        binding.Source = Me
        binding.Mode = BindingMode.TwoWay
        slider.SetBinding(RangeBase.ValueProperty, binding)
    End If
    ...
End Sub
```

Notice that the code uses the System.Windows.Controls.Primitives.RangeBase class (from which Slider derives) instead of the Slider class. That's because the RangeBase class provides the minimum required functionality—in this case, the Value property. By making the code as generic as possible, the control consumer gains more freedom. For example, it's now possible to supply a custom template that uses a different RangeBase-derived control in place of the color sliders.

The code for binding the other two sliders is virtually identical. The code for binding the SolidColorBrush is slightly different, because the SolidColorBrush does not include the SetBinding() method (which is defined in the FrameworkElement class). One easy workaround is to create a binding expression for the ColorPicker.Color property, which uses the one-way-to-source direction. That way, when the color picker's color is changed, the brush is updated automatically.

```
Dim brush As SolidColorBrush
brush = TryCast(GetTemplateChild("PART_PreviewBrush"), SolidColorBrush)

If brush IsNot Nothing Then
    Dim binding As New Binding("Color")
    binding.Source = brush
    binding.Mode = BindingMode.OneWayToSource
    Me.SetBinding(ColorPicker.ColorProperty, binding)
End If
```

To see the benefit of this change in design, you need to create a control that uses the color picker but supplies a new control template. Figure 18-4 shows one possibility.

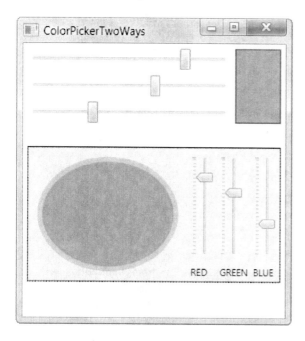

Figure 18-4. *A color picker custom control with two different templates*

Documenting Template Parts

There's one last refinement that you should make to the previous example. Good design guidelines suggest that you add the TemplatePart attribute to your control declaration to document what part names you use in your template and what type of control you use for each part. Technically, this step isn't required, but it's a piece of documentation that can help others who are using your class (and it can also be inspected by design tools that let you build customized control templates, such as Expression Blend).

Here are the TemplatePart attributes you should add to the ColorPicker control class:

```
<TemplatePart(Name:="PART_RedSlider", Type:=GetType(RangeBase)), _
TemplatePart(Name:="PART_BlueSlider", Type:=GetType(RangeBase)), _
TemplatePart(Name:="PART_GreenSlider", Type:=GetType(RangeBase)), _
TemplatePart(Name:="PART_PreviewBrush", Type:=GetType(SolidColorBrush))> _
Public Class ColorPicker
    Inherits System.Windows.Controls.Control
    ...
End Class
```

FINDING A CONTROL'S DEFAULT STYLE

Every control has a default style. You call DefaultStyleKeyProperty.OverrideMetadata() in the shared constructor of your control class to indicate what default style your custom control should use. If you don't, your control will simply use the default style that's defined for the control that your class derives from.

Contrary to what you might expect, the default theme style is not exposed through the Style property. All the controls in the WPF library return a null reference (Nothing) for their Style property.

Instead, the Style property is reserved for an *application style* (the type you learned to build in Chapter 11). If you set an application style, it's merged into the default theme style. If you set an application style that conflicts with the default style, the application style wins and overrides the property setter or trigger in the default style. However, the details you don't override remain. This is the behavior you want. It allows you to create an application style that changes just a few properties (for example, the text font in a button), without removing the other essential details that are supplied in the default theme style (such as the control template).

Incidentally, you can retrieve the default style programmatically. To do so, you can use the FindResource() method to search up the resource hierarchy for a style that has the right element-type key. For example, if you want to find the default style that's applied to the Button class, you can use this code statement:

```
Dim buttonStyle As Style
buttonStyle = Application.Current.FindResource(GetType(Button))
```

Supporting Visual States

The ColorPicker control is a good example of control design. Because its behavior and its visual appearance are carefully separated, other designers can develop new templates that change its appearance dramatically.

One of the reasons the ColorPicker is so simple is that it doesn't have a concept of states. In other words, it doesn't distinguish its visual appearance based on whether it has focus, whether the mouse is on top, whether it's disabled, and so on. The FlipPanel control in the following example is a bit different.

The basic idea behind the FlipPanel is that it provides two surfaces to host content, but only one is visible at a time. To see the other content, you "flip" between the sides. You can customize the flipping effect through the control template, but the default effect uses a simple fade that transitions between the front and back (see Figure 18-5). Depending on your application, you could use the FlipPanel to combine a data-entry form with some helpful documentation, to provide a simple or a more complex view on the same data, or to fuse together a question and an answer in a trivia game.

Figure 18-5. *Flipping the FlipPanel*

You can perform the flipping programmatically (by setting a property named IsFlipped), or the user can flip the panel by using a convenient button (unless the control consumer removes it from the template).

Clearly, the control template needs to specify two separate sections: the front and back content regions of the FlipPanel. However, there's an additional detail—namely, the FlipPanel needs a way to switch between its two states: flipped and not flipped. You could do the job by adding triggers to your template. One trigger would hide the front panel and show the second panel when a button is clicked, while the other would reverse these changes. Both could use any animations you like. But by using visual states, you clearly indicate to the control consumer that these two states are a required part of the template. Rather than writing triggers for the right property or event, the control consumer simply needs to fill in the appropriate state animations—a task that gets even easier with Expression Blend.

Starting the FlipPanel Class

Stripped down to its bare bones, the FlipPanel is surprisingly simple. It consists of two content regions that the user can fill with a single element (most likely, a layout container that contains an assortment of elements). Technically, that means the FlipPanel isn't a true panel, because it doesn't use layout logic to organize a group of child elements. However, this isn't likely to pose a problem, because the structure of the FlipPanel is clear and intuitive. The FlipPanel also includes a flip button that lets the user switch between the two content regions.

Although you can create a custom control by deriving from a control class such as ContentControl or Panel, the FlipPanel derives directly from the base Control class. If you don't need the functionality of a specialized control class, this is the best starting point. You shouldn't derive from the simpler FrameworkElement class unless you want to create an element without the standard control and template infrastructure:

```
Public Class FlipPanel
    Inherits Control
    ...
End Class
```

The first order of business is to create the properties for the FlipPanel. As with almost all the properties in a WPF element, you should use dependency properties. Here's how FlipPanel defines the FrontContent property that holds the element that's displayed on the front surface:

```
Public Shared ReadOnly FrontContentProperty As DependencyProperty = _
   DependencyProperty.Register("FrontContent", GetType(Object), _
   GetType(FlipPanel), Nothing)
```

Next, you need to add a traditional .NET property procedure that calls the base GetValue() and SetValue() methods to change the dependency property. Here's the property procedure implementation for the FrontContent property:

```
Public Property FrontContent() As Object
    Get
        Return MyBase.GetValue(FrontContentProperty)
    End Get
    Set(ByVal value As Object)
        MyBase.SetValue(FrontContentProperty, value)
    End Set
End Property
```

The BackContent property is virtually identical:

```
Public Shared ReadOnly BackContentProperty As DependencyProperty = _
  DependencyProperty.Register("BackContent", GetType(Object), _
  GetType(FlipPanel), Nothing)

Public Property BackContent() As Object
    Get
        Return MyBase.GetValue(BackContentProperty)
    End Get
    Set(ByVal value As Object)
        MyBase.SetValue(BackContentProperty, value)
    End Set
End Property
```

You need to add just one more essential property: IsFlipped. This Boolean property keeps track of the current state of the FlipPanel (forward-facing or backward-facing) and lets the control consumer flip it programmatically:

```
Public Shared ReadOnly IsFlippedProperty As DependencyProperty = _
  DependencyProperty.Register("IsFlipped", GetType(Boolean), _
  GetType(FlipPanel), Nothing)

Public Property IsFlipped() As Boolean
    Get
        Return CBool(MyBase.GetValue(IsFlippedProperty))
    End Get
    Set(ByVal value As Boolean)
        MyBase.SetValue(IsFlippedProperty, value)
        ChangeVisualState(True)
    End Set
End Property
```

The IsFlipped property setter calls a custom method called ChangeVisualState(). This method makes sure the display is updated to match the current flip state (forward-facing or backward-facing). You'll consider the code that takes care of this task a bit later.

The FlipPanel doesn't need many more properties, because it inherits virtually everything it needs from the Control class. One exception is the CornerRadius property. Although the Control class includes BorderBrush and BorderThickness properties, which you can use to draw a border around the FlipPanel, it lacks the CornerRadius property for rounding square edges into a gentler curve, as the Border element does. Implementing the same effect in the FlipPanel is easy, provided you add the CornerRadius dependency property and use it to configure a Border element in the FlipPanel's default control template:

```
Public Shared ReadOnly CornerRadiusProperty As DependencyProperty = _
  DependencyProperty.Register("CornerRadius", GetType(CornerRadius), _
  GetType(FlipPanel), Nothing)

Public Property CornerRadius() As CornerRadius
    Get
        Return CType(GetValue(CornerRadiusProperty), CornerRadius)
    End Get
```

```
        Set(ByVal value As CornerRadius)
            SetValue(CornerRadiusProperty, value)
        End Set
End Property
```

You also need to add a style that applies the default template for the FlipPanel. You place this style in the generic.xaml resource dictionary, as you did when developing the ColorPicker. Here's the basic skeleton you need:

```
<Style TargetType="{x:Type local:FlipPanel}">
  <Setter Property="Template">
    <Setter.Value>
      <ControlTemplate TargetType="local:FlipPanel">
        ...
      </ControlTemplate>
    </Setter.Value>
  </Setter>
</Style>
```

There's one last detail. To tell your control to pick up the default style from the generic.xaml file, you need to call the DefaultStyleKeyProperty.OverrideMetadata() method in the FlipPanel's shared constructor:

```
DefaultStyleKeyProperty.OverrideMetadata(GetType(FlipPanel), _
  New FrameworkPropertyMetadata(GetType(FlipPanel)))
```

Choosing Parts and States

Now that you have the basic structure in place, you're ready to identify the parts and states that you'll use in the control template.

Clearly, the FlipPanel requires two states:

Normal: This storyboard ensures that only the front content is visible. The back content is flipped, faded, or otherwise shuffled out of view.

Flipped: This storyboard ensures that only the back content is visible. The front content is animated out of the way.

In addition, you need two parts:

FlipButton: This is the button that, when clicked, changes the view from the front to the back (or vice versa). The FlipPanel provides this service by handling this button's events.

FlipButtonAlternate: This is an optional element that works in the same way as the FlipButton. Its inclusion allows the control consumer to use two approaches in a custom control template. One option is to use a single flip button outside the flippable content region. The other option is to place a separate flip button on both sides of the panel, in the flippable region.

▧ **Note** Keen eyes will notice a confusing design choice here. Unlike the custom ColorPicker, the named parts in the FlipPanel don't use the PART_ naming syntax (as in PART_FlipButton). That's because the PART_ naming system was introduced before the visual state model. With the visual state model, the conventions have changed to favor simpler names, although this is still an emerging standard, and it could change in the future. In the meantime, your custom controls should be fine as long as they use the TemplatePart attribute to point out all the named parts.

You could also add parts for the front content and back content regions. However, the FlipPanel control doesn't need to manipulate these regions directly, as long as the template includes an animation that hides or shows them at the appropriate time. (Another option is to define these parts so you can explicitly change their visibility in code. That way, the panel can still change between the front and back content region even if no animations are defined, by hiding one section and showing the other. For simplicity's sake, the FlipPanel doesn't go to these lengths.)

To advertise the fact that the FlipPanel uses these parts and states, you should apply the TemplatePart attribute to your control class, as shown here:

```
<TemplateVisualState(Name := "Normal", GroupName := "ViewStates"), _
 TemplateVisualState(Name := "Flipped", GroupName := "ViewStates"), _
 TemplatePart(Name := "FlipButton", Type := GetType(ToggleButton)), _
 TemplatePart(Name := "FlipButtonAlternate", Type := GetType(ToggleButton))> _
Public Class FlipPanel
    Inherits Control
    ...
End Class
```

The FlipButton and FlipButtonAlternate parts are restricted—each one can be only a ToggleButton or an instance of a ToggleButton-derived class. (As you may remember from Chapter 6, the ToggleButton is a clickable button that can be in one of two states. In the case of the FlipPanel control, the ToggleButton states correspond to normal front-forward view or a flipped back-forward view.)

▧ **Tip** To ensure the best, most flexible template support, use the least-specialized element type that you can. For example, it's better to use FrameworkElement than ContentControl, unless you need some property or behavior that ContentControl provides.

The Default Control Template

Now, you can slot these pieces into the default control template. The root element is a two-row Grid that holds the content area (in the top row) and the flip button (in the bottom row). The content area is filled with two overlapping Border elements, representing the front and back content, but only one of the two is ever shown at a time.

To fill in the front and back content regions, the FlipPanel uses the ContentPresenter. This technique is virtually the same as in the custom button example, except you need two ContentPresenter elements, one for each side of the FlipPanel. The FlipPanel also includes a separate Border element wrapping each ContentPresenter. This lets the control consumer outline the flippable content region by setting a few straightforward properties on the FlipPanel (BorderBrush, BorderThickness, Background, and CornerRadius), rather than being forced to add a border by hand.

Here's the basic skeleton for the default control template:

```
<ControlTemplate TargetType="{x:Type local:FlipPanel}">
  <Grid>
    <Grid.RowDefinitions>
      <RowDefinition Height="Auto"></RowDefinition>
      <RowDefinition Height="Auto"></RowDefinition>
    </Grid.RowDefinitions>

    <!-- This is the front content. -->
    <Border BorderBrush="{TemplateBinding BorderBrush}"
     BorderThickness="{TemplateBinding BorderThickness}"
     CornerRadius="{TemplateBinding CornerRadius}"
     Background="{TemplateBinding Background}">
      <ContentPresenter Content="{TemplateBinding FrontContent}">
      </ContentPresenter>
    </Border>

    <!-- This is the back content. -->
    <Border BorderBrush="{TemplateBinding BorderBrush}"
     BorderThickness="{TemplateBinding BorderThickness}"
     CornerRadius="{TemplateBinding CornerRadius}"
     Background="{TemplateBinding Background}">
      <ContentPresenter Content="{TemplateBinding BackContent}">
      </ContentPresenter>
    </Border>

    <!-- This the flip button. -->
    <ToggleButton Grid.Row="1" x:Name="FlipButton" Margin="0,10,0,0">
    </ToggleButton>

  </Grid>
</ControlTemplate>
```

When you create a default control template, it's best to avoid hard-coding details that the control consumer may want to customize. Instead, you need to use template-binding expressions. In this example, you set several properties by using template-binding expressions: BorderBrush, BorderThickness, CornerRadius, Background, FrontContent, and BackContent. To set the default value for these properties (and thereby ensure that you get the right visual even if the control consumer doesn't set them), you must add additional setters to your control's default style.

The Flip Button

The control template shown in the previous example includes a ToggleButton. However, it uses the ToggleButton's default appearance, which makes the ToggleButton look like an ordinary button, complete with the traditional shaded background. This isn't suitable for the FlipPanel.

Although you can place any content you want inside the ToggleButton, the FlipPanel requires a bit more. It needs to do away with the standard background and change the appearance of the elements inside depending on the state of the ToggleButton. As you saw earlier in Figure 18-5, the ToggleButton points the way the content will be flipped (right initially, when the front faces forward, and left when the back faces forward). This makes the purpose of the button clearer.

To create this effect, you need to design a custom control template for the ToggleButton. This control template can include the shape elements that draw the arrow you need. In this example, the ToggleButton is drawn using an Ellipse element for the circle and a Path element for the arrow, both of which are placed in a single-cell Grid:

```
<ToggleButton Grid.Row="1" x:Name="FlipButton" RenderTransformOrigin="0.5,0.5"
 Margin="0,10,0,0" Width="19" Height="19">
  <ToggleButton.Template>
    <ControlTemplate>
      <Grid>
        <Ellipse Stroke="#FFA9A9A9" Fill="AliceBlue"></Ellipse>
        <Path Data="M1,1.5L4.5,5 8,1.5" Stroke="#FF666666" StrokeThickness="2"
         HorizontalAlignment="Center" VerticalAlignment="Center"></Path>
      </Grid>
    </ControlTemplate>
  </ToggleButton.Template>
</ToggleButton>
```

The ToggleButton needs one more detail—a RotateTransform that turns the arrow away from one side to point at the other. This RotateTransform will be used when you create the state animations:

```
<ToggleButton.RenderTransform>
  <RotateTransform x:Name="FlipButtonTransform" Angle="-90"></RotateTransform>
</ToggleButton.RenderTransform>
```

Defining the State Animations

The state animations are the most interesting part of the control template. They're the ingredients that provide the flipping behavior. They're also the details that are most likely to be changed if a developer creates a custom template for the FlipPanel.

To define state groups, you must add the VisualStateManager.VisualStateGroups element in the root element of your control template, as shown here:

```
<ControlTemplate TargetType="{x:Type local:FlipPanel}">
  <Grid>
    <VisualStateManager.VisualStateGroups>

      ...

    </VisualStateManager.VisualStateGroups>


    ...

  </Grid>
</ControlTemplate>
```

■ **Note**   To add the VisualStateManager element to a template, your template must use a layout panel. This layout panel holds both the visuals for your control and the VisualStateManager, which is invisible. The VisualStateManager defines storyboards with the animations that the control can use at the appropriate time to alter its appearance.

Inside the VisualStateGroups element, you can create the state groups by using appropriately named VisualStateGroup elements. Inside each VisualStateGroup, you add a VisualState element for each visual state. In the case of the FlipPanel, there is one group that contains two visual states:

```
<VisualStateManager.VisualStateGroups>
  <VisualStateGroup x:Name="ViewStates">
    <VisualState x:Name="Normal">
      ...
    </VisualState>
  </VisualStateGroup>

  <VisualStateGroup x:Name="FocusStates">
    <VisualState x:Name="Flipped">
      ...
    </VisualState>
  </VisualStateGroup>
</VisualStateManager.VisualStateGroups>
```

Each state corresponds to a storyboard with one or more animations. If these storyboards exist, they're triggered at the appropriate times. (If they don't, the control should degrade gracefully, without raising an error.)

In the default control template, the animations use a simple fade to change from one content region to the other and use a rotation to flip the ToggleButton arrow around to point in the other direction. Here's the markup that takes care of both tasks:

```
<VisualState x:Name="Normal">
  <Storyboard>
    <DoubleAnimation Storyboard.TargetName="BackContent"
     Storyboard.TargetProperty="Opacity" To="0" Duration="0" ></DoubleAnimation>
  </Storyboard>
</VisualState>

<VisualState x:Name="Flipped">
  <Storyboard>
    <DoubleAnimation Storyboard.TargetName="FlipButtonTransform"
     Storyboard.TargetProperty="Angle" To="90" Duration="0"></DoubleAnimation>
    <DoubleAnimation Storyboard.TargetName="FrontContent"
     Storyboard.TargetProperty="Opacity" To="0" Duration="0"></DoubleAnimation>
  </Storyboard>
</VisualState>
```

You'll notice that the visual states set the animation duration to 0, which means the animation applies its effect instantaneously. This might seem a little odd—after all, don't you need a more gradual change to notice the animated effect?

In fact, this design is perfectly correct, because visual states are meant to indicate how the control looks while it's in the appropriate state. For example, a flipped panel simply shows its background content while in the flipped state. The flipping process is a *transition* that happens just before the FlipControl enters the flipped state, not part of the state itself. (This distinction between states and transitions is important, because some controls *do* have animations that run during a state. For example, think of the button example from Chapter 17 that featured the pulsing background color while the mouse hovers over it.)

Defining the State Transitions

A transition is an animation that starts from the current state and ends at the new state. One of the advantages of the transition model is that you don't need to create the storyboard for this animation. For example, if you add the markup shown here, WPF creates a 0.7-second animation to change the opacity of the FlipPanel, creating the pleasant fade effect you want:

```
<VisualStateGroup x:Name="ViewStates">
  <VisualStateGroup.Transitions>
    <VisualTransition GeneratedDuration="0:0:0.7"></VisualTransition>
  </VisualStateGroup.Transitions>

  <VisualState x:Name="Normal">
    ...
  </VisualState>

  <VisualState x:Name="Flipped">
    ...
  </VisualState>
</VisualStateGroup>
```

Transitions apply to state groups. When you define a transition, you must add it to the VisualStateGroup. Transitions collection. This example uses the simplest sort of transition: a *default transition*, which applies to all the state changes for that group.

A default transition is convenient, but it's a one-size-fits-all solution that's not always suitable. For example, you may want the FlipPanel to transition at different speeds depending on which state it's entering. To set this up, you need to define multiple transitions, and you need to set the To property to specify when the transition will come into effect.

For example, if you have these transitions

```
<VisualStateGroup.Transitions>
  <VisualTransition To="Flipped" GeneratedDuration="0:0:0.5" />
  <VisualTransition To="Normal" GeneratedDuration="0:0:0.1" />
</VisualStateGroup.Transitions>
```

the FlipPanel will switch to the Flipped state in 0.5 seconds, and it will enter the Normal state in 0.1 seconds.

This example shows transitions that apply when entering specific states, but you can also use the From property to create a transition that applies when leaving a state, and you can use the To and From properties in conjunction to create even more specific transitions that apply only when moving between two specific states. When applying transitions, WPF looks through the collection of transitions to find the most specific one that applies, and it uses only that one.

For even more control, you can create custom transition animations that take the place of the automatically generated transitions WPF would normally use. You may create a custom transition for several reasons. Here are some examples: to control the pace of the animation with a more sophisticated animation, to use an animation easing, to run several animations in succession, or to play a sound at the same time as an animation.

To define a custom transition, you place a storyboard with one or more animations inside the VisualTransition element. In the FlipPanel example, you can use custom transitions to make sure the ToggleButton arrow rotates itself quickly, while the fade takes place more gradually.

```
<VisualStateGroup.Transitions>
  <VisualTransition GeneratedDuration="0:0:0.7" To="Flipped">
    <Storyboard>
```

```
      <DoubleAnimation Storyboard.TargetName="FlipButtonTransform"
        Storyboard.TargetProperty="Angle" To="90"
        Duration="0:0:0.2"></DoubleAnimation>
    </Storyboard>
  </VisualTransition>
  <VisualTransition GeneratedDuration="0:0:0.7" To="Normal">
    <Storyboard>
      <DoubleAnimation Storyboard.TargetName="FlipButtonTransform"
        Storyboard.TargetProperty="Angle" To="-90"
        Duration="0:0:0.2"></DoubleAnimation>
    </Storyboard>
  </VisualTransition>
</VisualStateGroup.Transitions>
```

■ **Note**   When you use a custom transition, you must still set the VisualTransition.GeneratedDuration property to match the duration of your animation. Without this detail, the VisualStateManager can't use your transition, and it will apply the new state immediately. (The actual time value you use still has no effect on your custom transition, because it applies only to automatically generated animations.)

Unfortunately, many controls will require custom transitions, and writing them is tedious. You still need to keep the zero-length state animations, which also creates some unavoidable duplication of details between your visual states and your transitions.

Wiring Up the Elements

Now that you've polished off a respectable control template, you need to fill in the plumbing in the FlipPanel control to make it work.

The trick is the OnApplyTemplate(), which you also used to set bindings in the ColorPicker. The OnApplyTemplate() method for the FlipPanel retrieves the ToggleButton for the FlipButton and FlipButtonAlternate parts and attaches event handlers to each so it can react when the user clicks to flip the control. Finally, the OnApplyTemplate() method ends by calling a custom method named ChangeVisualState(), which ensures that the control's visuals match its current state:

```
Public Overrides Sub OnApplyTemplate()
    MyBase.OnApplyTemplate()

    ' Wire up the ToggleButton.Click event.
    Dim flipButton As ToggleButton = TryCast( _
      MyBase.GetTemplateChild("FlipButton"), ToggleButton)
    If flipButton IsNot Nothing Then
        AddHandler flipButton.Click, AddressOf flipButton_Click
    End If

    ' Allow for two flip buttons if needed (one for each side of the panel).
    Dim flipButtonAlternate As ToggleButton = TryCast( _
      MyBase.GetTemplateChild("FlipButtonAlternate"), ToggleButton)
    If flipButtonAlternate IsNot Nothing Then
        AddHandler flipButtonAlternate.Click, AddressOf flipButton_Click
    End If
```

```
' Make sure the visuals match the current state.
ChangeVisualState(False)
End Sub
```

■ Tip When calling GetTemplateChild(), you need to indicate the string name of the element you want. To avoid possible errors, you can declare this string as a constant in your control. You can then use that constant in the TemplatePart attribute and when calling GetTemplateChild().

Here's the very simple event handler that allows the user to click the ToggleButton and flip the panel:

```
Private Sub flipButton_Click(ByVal sender As Object, ByVal e As RoutedEventArgs)
    IsFlipped = Not IsFlipped
    ChangeVisualState(True)
End Sub
```

Fortunately, you don't need to manually trigger the state animations. Nor do you need to create or trigger the transition animations. Instead, to change from one state to another, you call the shared VisualStateManager. GoToState() method. When you do, you pass in a reference to the control object that's changing state, the name of the new state, and a Boolean value that determines whether a transition is shown. This value should be True when it's a user-initiated change (for example, when the user clicks the ToggleButton) but False when it's a property setting (for example, if the markup for your page sets the initial value of the IsFlipped property).

Dealing with all the different states a control supports can become messy. To avoid scattering GoToState() calls throughout your control code, most controls add a custom method such as the ChangeVisualState() method in the FlipPanel. This method has the responsibility of applying the correct state in each state group. The code inside uses one if block (or switch statement) to apply the current state in each state group. This approach works because it's completely acceptable to call GoToState() with the name of the current state. In this situation, when the current state and the requested state are the same, nothing happens.

Here's the code for the FlipPanel's version of the ChangeVisualState() method:

```
Private Sub ChangeVisualState(ByVal useTransitions As Boolean)
    If Not IsFlipped Then
        VisualStateManager.GoToState(Me, "Normal", useTransitions)
    Else
        VisualStateManager.GoToState(Me, "Flipped", useTransitions)
    End If
End Sub
```

Usually, you call the ChangeVisualState() method (or your equivalent) in the following places:

- After initializing the control at the end of the OnApplyTemplate() method.
- When reacting to an event that represents a state change, such as a mouse movement or a click of the ToggleButton.
- When reacting to a property change or a method that's triggered through code. (For example, the IsFlipped property setter calls ChangeVisualState() and always supplies true, thereby showing the transition animations. If you want to give the control consumer the choice of not showing the transition, you can add a Flip() method that takes the same Boolean parameter you pass to ChangeVisualState().

As written, the FlipPanel control is remarkably flexible. For example, you can use it without a ToggleButton and flip it programmatically (perhaps when the user clicks a different control). Or, you can include one or two flip buttons in the control template and allow the user to take control.

Using the FlipPanel

Now that you've completed the control template and code for the FlipPanel, you're ready to use it in an application. Assuming you've added the necessary assembly reference, you can then map an XML prefix to the namespace that holds your custom control:

```
<Window x:Class="FlipPanelTest.Page"
  xmlns:lib="clr-namespace:FlipPanelControl;assembly=FlipPanelControl" ... >
```

Next, you can add instances of the FlipPanel to your page. Here's an example that creates the FlipPanel shown earlier in Figure 18-5, using a StackPanel full of elements for the front content region and a Grid for the back:

```
<lib:FlipPanel x:Name="panel" BorderBrush="DarkOrange"
 BorderThickness="3" CornerRadius="4" Margin="10">
  <lib:FlipPanel.FrontContent>
    <StackPanel Margin="6">
      <TextBlock TextWrapping="Wrap" Margin="3" FontSize="16"
       Foreground="DarkOrange">This is the front side of the FlipPanel.</TextBlock>
      <Button Margin="3" Padding="3" Content="Button One"></Button>
      <Button Margin="3" Padding="3" Content="Button Two"></Button>
      <Button Margin="3" Padding="3" Content="Button Three"></Button>
      <Button Margin="3" Padding="3" Content="Button Four"></Button>
    </StackPanel>
  </lib:FlipPanel.FrontContent>

  <lib:FlipPanel.BackContent>
    <Grid Margin="6">
      <Grid.RowDefinitions>
        <RowDefinition Height="Auto"></RowDefinition>
        <RowDefinition></RowDefinition>
      </Grid.RowDefinitions>
      <TextBlock TextWrapping="Wrap" Margin="3" FontSize="16"
       Foreground="DarkMagenta">This is the back side of the FlipPanel.</TextBlock>
      <Button Grid.Row="2" Margin="3" Padding="10" Content="Flip Back to Front"
       HorizontalAlignment="Center" VerticalAlignment="Center"
       Click="cmdFlip_Click"></Button>
    </Grid>
  </lib:FlipPanel.BackContent>
</lib:FlipPanel>
```

When clicked, the button on the back side of the FlipPanel programmatically flips the panel:

```
Private Sub cmdFlip_Click(ByVal sender As Object, ByVal e As RoutedEventArgs)
    panel.IsFlipped = Not panel.IsFlipped
End Sub
```

This has the same result as clicking the ToggleButton with the arrow, which is defined as part of the default control template.

Using a Different Control Template

Custom controls that have been designed properly are extremely flexible. In the case of the FlipPanel, you can supply a new template to change the appearance and placement of the ToggleButton and the animated effects that are used when flipping between the front and back content regions.

Figure 18-6 shows one such example. Here, the flip button is placed in a special bar that's at the bottom of the front side and the top of the back side. And when the panel flips, it doesn't turn its content like a sheet of paper. Instead, it squares the front content into nothingness at the top of the panel while simultaneously expanding the back content underneath. When the panel flips the other way, the back content squishes back down, and the front content expands from the top. For even more visual pizzazz, the content that's being squashed is also blurred with the help of the BlurEffect class.

Figure 18-6. *The FlipPanel with a different control template*

Here's the portion of the template that defines the front content region:

```
<Border BorderBrush="{TemplateBinding BorderBrush}"
 BorderThickness="{TemplateBinding BorderThickness}"
 CornerRadius="{TemplateBinding CornerRadius}"
 Background="{TemplateBinding Background}">

  <Border.RenderTransform>
    <ScaleTransform x:Name="FrontContentTransform"></ScaleTransform>
  </Border.RenderTransform>
  <Border.Effect>
    <BlurEffect x:Name="FrontContentEffect" Radius="0"></BlurEffect>
  </Border.Effect>

  <Grid>
    <Grid.RowDefinitions>
      <RowDefinition></RowDefinition>
      <RowDefinition Height="Auto"></RowDefinition>
    </Grid.RowDefinitions>

    <ContentPresenter Content="{TemplateBinding FrontContent}"></ContentPresenter>
    <Rectangle Grid.Row="1" Stretch="Fill" Fill="LightSteelBlue"></Rectangle>
    <ToggleButton Grid.Row="1" x:Name="FlipButton" Margin="5" Padding="15,0"
     Content="^" FontWeight="Bold" FontSize="12" HorizontalAlignment="Right">
```

```
    </ToggleButton>
  </Grid>
</Border>
```

The back content region is almost the same. It consists of a Border that contains a ContentPresenter element, and it includes its own ToggleButton placed at the right edge of the shaded rectangle. It also defines the all-important ScaleTransform and BlurEffect on the Border, which is what the animations use to flip the panel.

Here are the animations that flip the panel. To see all the markup, refer to the downloadable code for this chapter.

```
<VisualState x:Name="Flipped">
  <Storyboard>
    <DoubleAnimation Storyboard.TargetName="FrontContentTransform"
      Storyboard.TargetProperty="ScaleY" To="0" ></DoubleAnimation>

    <DoubleAnimation Storyboard.TargetName="FrontContentEffect"
      Storyboard.TargetProperty="Radius" To="30" ></DoubleAnimation>

    <DoubleAnimation Storyboard.TargetName="BackContentTransform"
      Storyboard.TargetProperty="ScaleY" To="1" ></DoubleAnimation>

    <DoubleAnimation Storyboard.TargetName="BackContentEffect"
      Storyboard.TargetProperty="Radius" To="0" ></DoubleAnimation>
  </Storyboard>
</VisualState>
```

Because the animation that changes the front content region runs at the same time as the animation that changes the back content region, you don't need a custom transition to manage them.

Creating Custom Panels

So far, you've seen how to develop two custom controls from scratch, with a custom ColorPicker and FlipPanel. In the following sections, you'll consider two more specialized options: deriving a custom Panel and building a custom-drawn control.

Creating a custom panel is a specific but relatively common subset of custom control development. As you learned in Chapter 3, panels host one or more children and implement specific layout logic to arrange them appropriately. Custom panels are an essential ingredient if you want to build your own system for tear-off toolbars or dockable windows. Custom panels are often useful when creating composite controls that need a specific nonstandard layout, like fancy docking toolbars.

You're already familiar with the basic types of panels that WPF includes for organizing content (such as the StackPanel, DockPanel, WrapPanel, Canvas, and Grid). You've also seen that some WPF elements use their own custom panels (such as the TabPanel, ToolBarOverflowPanel, and VirtualizingPanel). If you don't mind C# code, you can find many more examples of custom panels online. Here are some worth exploring:

- A custom Canvas that allows its children to be dragged with no extra event-handling code (http://tinyurl.com/9s324ud)

- Two panels that implement fish-eye and fanning effects on a list of items (http://tinyurl.com/965bqt3)

- A panel that uses a frame-based animation to transition from one layout to another (http://tinyurl.com/95sdzgx)

In the next sections, you'll learn how to create a custom panel, and you'll consider two straightforward examples—a basic Canvas clone and an enhanced version of the WrapPanel.

The Two-Step Layout Process

Every panel uses the same plumbing: a two-step process that's responsible for sizing and arranging children. The first stage is the *measure* pass, and it's at this point that the panel determines how large its children want to be. The second stage is the *layout* pass, and it's at this point that each control is assigned its bounds. Two steps are required because the panel might need to take into account the desires of all its children before it decides how to partition the available space.

You add the logic for these two steps by overriding the oddly named MeasureOverride() and ArrangeOverride() methods, which are defined in the FrameworkElement class as part of the WPF layout system. The odd names represent that the MeasureOverride() and ArrangeOverride() methods replace the logic that's defined in the MeasureCore() and ArrangeCore() methods that are defined in the UIElement class. These methods are *not* overridable.

MeasureOverride()

The first step is to determine how much space each child wants by using the MeasureOverride() method. However, even in the MeasureOverride() method, children aren't given unlimited room. At a bare minimum, children are confined to fit in the space that's available to the panel. Optionally, you might want to limit them more stringently. For example, a Grid with two proportionally sized rows will give children half the available height. A StackPanel will offer the first element all the space that's available, then offer the second element whatever's left, and so on.

Every MeasureOverride() implementation is responsible for looping through the collection of children and calling the Measure() method of each one. When you call the Measure() method, you supply the bounding box—a Size object that determines the maximum available space for the child control. At the end of the MeasureOverride() method, the panel returns the space it needs to display all its children and their desired sizes.

Here's the basic structure of the MeasureOverride() method, without the specific sizing details:

```
Protected Overrides Function MeasureOverride(ByVal constraint As Size) As Size
    ' Examine all the children.
    For Each element As UIElement In MyBase.InternalChildren
        ' Ask each child how much space it would like, given the
        ' availableSize constraint.
        Dim availableSize As New Size(...)
        element.Measure(availableSize)
        ' (You can now read element.DesiredSize to get the requested size.)
    Next

    ' Indicate how much space this panel requires.
    ' This will be used to set the DesiredSize property of the panel.
    Return New Size(...)
End Function
```

The Measure() method doesn't return a value. After you call Measure() on a child, that child's DesiredSize property provides the requested size. You can use this information in your calculations for future children (and to determine the total space required for the panel).

You *must* call Measure() on each child, even if you don't want to constrain the child's size or use the DesiredSize property. Many elements will not render themselves until you've called Measure(). If you want to give a child free reign to take all the space it wants, pass a Size object with a value of Double.PositiveInfinity for both dimensions.

(The ScrollViewer is one element that uses this strategy, because it can handle any amount of content.) The child will then return the space it needs for all its content. Otherwise, the child will normally return the space it needs for its content or the space that's available—whichever is smaller.

At the end of the measuring process, the layout container must return its desired size. In a simple panel, you might calculate the panel's desired size by combining the desired size of every child.

■ **Note**   You can't simply return the constraint that's passed to the MeasureOverride() method for the desired size of your panel. Although this seems like a good way to take all the available size, it runs into trouble if the container passes in a Size object with Double.PositiveInfinity for one or both dimensions (which means "take all the space you want"). Although an infinite size is allowed as a sizing constraint, it's not allowed as a sizing result, because WPF won't be able to figure out how large your element should be. Furthermore, you really shouldn't take more space than you need. Doing so can cause extra whitespace and force elements that occur after your layout panel to be bumped further down the window.

Attentive readers may have noticed that there's a close similarity between the Measure() method that's called on each child and the MeasureOverride() method that defines the first step of the panel's layout logic. In fact, the Measure() method triggers the MeasureOverride() method. Thus, if you place one layout container inside another, when you call Measure(), you'll get the total size required for the layout container and all its children.

■ **Tip**   One reason the measuring process goes through two steps—a Measure() method that triggers the MeasureOverride() method—is to deal with margins. When you call Measure(), you pass in the total available space. When WPF calls the MeasureOverride() method, it automatically reduces the available space to take margin space into account (unless you've passed in an infinite size).

ArrangeOverride()

After every element has been measured, it's time to lay them out in the space that's available. The layout system calls the ArrangeOverride() method of your panel, and the panel calls the Arrange()method of each child to tell it how much space it's been allotted. (As you can probably guess, the Arrange() method triggers the ArrangeOverride() method, much as the Measure() method triggers the MeasureOverride() method.)

When measuring items with the Measure() method, you pass in a Size object that defines the bounds of the available space. When placing an item with the Arrange() method, you pass in a System.Windows.Rect object that defines the size *and* position of the item. At this point, it's as though every element is placed with Canvas-style X and Y coordinates that determine the distance between the top-left corner of your layout container and the element.

■ **Note**   Elements (and layout panels) are free to break the rules and attempt to draw outside of their allocated bounds. For example, in Chapter 12 you saw how the Line can overlap adjacent items. However, ordinary elements should respect the bounds they're given. Additionally, most containers will clip children that extend outside their bounds.

Here's the basic structure of the ArrangeOverride() method, without the specific sizing details:

```
Protected Overrides Function ArrangeOverride(ByVal arrangeSize As Size) As Size
    ' Examine all the children.
    For Each element As UIElement In MyBase.InternalChildren
        ' Assign the child its bounds.
        Dim bounds As New Rect(...)
        element.Arrange(bounds)
        ' (You can now read element.ActualHeight and element.ActualWidth
        '  to find out the size it used.)
    Next

    ' Indicate how much space this panel occupies.
    ' This will be used to set the ActualHeight and ActualWidth properties
    ' of the panel.
    Return arrangeSize
End Function
```

When arranging elements, you can't pass infinite sizes. However, you can give an element its desired size by passing in the value from its DesiredSize property. You can also give an element *more* space than it requires. In fact, this happens frequently. For example, a vertical StackPanel gives a child as much height as it requests but gives it the full width of the panel itself. Similarly, a Grid might use fixed or proportionally sized rows that are larger than the desired size of the element inside. And even if you've placed an element in a size-to-content container, that element can still be enlarged if an explicit size has been set using the Height and Width properties.

When an element is made larger than its desired size, the HorizontalAlignment and VerticalAlignment properties come into play. The element content is placed somewhere inside the bounds that it has been given.

Because the ArrangeOverride() method always receives a defined size (not an infinite size), you can return the Size object that's passed in to set the final size of your panel. In fact, many layout containers take this step to occupy all the space that's been given. (You aren't in danger of taking up space that could be needed for another control, because the measure step of the layout system ensures that you won't be given more space than you need unless that space is available.)

The Canvas Clone

The quickest way to get a grasp of these two methods is to explore the inner workings of the Canvas class, which is the simplest layout container. To create your own Canvas-style panel, you simply need to derive from Panel and add the MeasureOverride() and ArrangeOverride() methods shown next:

```
Public Class CanvasClone
    Inherits System.Windows.Controls.Panel
    ...
End Class
```

The Canvas places children where they want to be placed and gives them the size they want. As a result, it doesn't need to calculate how the available space should be divided. That makes its MeasureOverride() method extremely simple. Each child is given infinite space to work with:

```
Protected Overrides Function MeasureOverride(ByVal constraint As Size) As Size
    Dim maxSize As New Size(double.PositiveInfinity, double.PositiveInfinity)
    For Each element As UIElement In MyBase.InternalChildren
        element.Measure(maxSize)
```

```
      Next
      Return New Size()
End Function
```

Notice that the MeasureOverride() returns an empty Size object, which means the Canvas doesn't request any space at all. It's up to you to specify an explicit size for the Canvas or place it in a layout container that will stretch it to fill the available space.

The ArrangeOverride() method is only slightly more involved. To determine the proper placement of each element, the Canvas uses attached properties (Left, Right, Top, and Bottom). As you learned in Chapter 4 (and as you'll see in the WrapBreakPanel next), attached properties are implemented with two helper methods in the defining class: a Get*Property*() and a Set*Property*() method.

The Canvas clone that you're considering is a bit simpler—it respects only the Left and Top attached properties (not the redundant Right and Bottom properties). Here's the code it uses to arrange elements:

```
Protected Overrides Function ArrangeOverride(ByVal arrangeSize As Size) As Size
    For Each element As UIElement In MyBase.InternalChildren
        Dim x As Double = 0
        Dim y As Double = 0

        Dim left As Double = Canvas.GetLeft(element)
        If Not DoubleUtil.IsNaN(left) Then
            x = left
        End If

        Dim top As Double = Canvas.GetTop(element)
        If Not DoubleUtil.IsNaN(top) Then
            y = top
        End If

        element.Arrange(New Rect(New Point(x, y), element.DesiredSize))
    Next

    Return arrangeSize
End Function
```

A Better Wrapping Panel

Now that you've examined the panel system in a fair bit of detail, it's worth creating your own layout container that adds something you can't get with the basic set of WPF panels. In this section, you'll see an example that extends the capabilities of the WrapPanel.

The WrapPanel performs a simple function that's occasionally quite useful. It lays out its children one after the other, moving to the next line after the width in the current line is used up. However, occasionally you need a way to force an immediate line break, so you can start a specific control on a new line. Although the stock WrapPanel doesn't provide this capability, it's fairly easy to add one if you create a custom control. All you need to do is add an attached property that requests a line break. Then the child elements in the panel can use this property to start a new line at the right spot.

The following listing shows a WrapBreakPanel that adds an attached LineBreakBeforeProperty. When set to True, this property causes an immediate line break before the element.

```vbnet
Public Class WrapBreakPanel
    Inherits Panel

    Public Shared LineBreakBeforeProperty As DependencyProperty

    Shared Sub New()
        Dim metadata As New FrameworkPropertyMetadata()
        metadata.AffectsArrange = True
        metadata.AffectsMeasure = True
        LineBreakBeforeProperty = DependencyProperty.RegisterAttached( _
          "LineBreakBefore", GetType(Boolean), GetType(WrapBreakPanel), _
          metadata)
    End Sub
    ...
End Class
```

As with any dependency property, the LineBreakBefore property is defined as a shared field and then registered in the shared constructor for your class. The only difference is that you use the RegisterAttached() method rather than Register().

The FrameworkPropertyMetadata object for the LineBreakBefore property specifically indicates that it affects the layout process. As a result, a new layout pass will be triggered whenever this property is set.

Attached properties aren't wrapped by normal property wrappers, because they aren't set in the same class that defines them. Instead, you need to provide two shared methods that can use the DependencyObject.SetValue() method to set this property on any arbitrary element. Here's the code that you need for the LineBreakBefore property:

```vbnet
Public Shared Sub SetLineBreakBefore(ByVal element As UIElement, _
  ByVal value As Boolean)
    element.SetValue(LineBreakBeforeProperty, value)
End Sub

Public Shared Function GetLineBreakBefore(ByVal element As UIElement) As Boolean
    Return CBool(element.GetValue(LineBreakBeforeProperty))
End Function
```

The only remaining detail is to take this property into account when performing the layout logic. The layout logic of the WrapBreakPanel is based on the WrapPanel. During the measure stage, elements are arranged into lines so that the panel can calculate the total space it needs. Each element is added into the current line unless it's too large or the LineBreakBefore property is set to True. Here's the full code:

```vbnet
Protected Overrides Function MeasureOverride(ByVal constraint As Size) As Size
    Dim currentLineSize As New Size()
    Dim panelSize As New Size()

    For Each element As UIElement In MyBase.InternalChildren
        element.Measure(constraint)
        Dim desiredSize As Size = element.DesiredSize

        If GetLineBreakBefore(element) OrElse _
          (currentLineSize.Width + desiredSize.Width > constraint.Width) Then
            ' Switch to a new line (either because the element has requested it
            ' or space has run out).
```

```
        panelSize.Width = Math.Max(currentLineSize.Width, panelSize.Width)
        panelSize.Height += currentLineSize.Height
        currentLineSize = desiredSize

        ' If the element is too wide to fit using the maximum width of the
        ' line, just give it a separate line.
        If desiredSize.Width > constraint.Width Then
            panelSize.Width = Math.Max(desiredSize.Width, panelSize.Width)
            panelSize.Height += desiredSize.Height
            currentLineSize = New Size()
        End If
    Else
        ' Keep adding to the current line.
        currentLineSize.Width += desiredSize.Width

        ' Make sure the line is as tall as its tallest element.
        currentLineSize.Height = Math.Max(desiredSize.Height, _
            currentLineSize.Height)
    End If
Next

' Return the size required to fit all elements.
' Ordinarily, this is the width of the constraint, and the height
' is based on the size of the elements.
' However, if an element is wider than the width given to the panel,
' the desired width will be the width of that line.
panelSize.Width = Math.Max(currentLineSize.Width, panelSize.Width)
panelSize.Height += currentLineSize.Height
Return panelSize
End Function
```

The key detail in this code is the test that checks the LineBreakBefore property. This implements the additional logic that's not provided in the ordinary WrapPanel.

The code for ArrangeOverride() is almost the same but slightly more tedious. The difference is that the panel needs to determine the maximum height of the line (which is determined by the tallest element) before it begins laying out that line. That way, each element can be given the full amount of available space, which takes into account the full height of the line. This is the same process that's used to lay out an ordinary WrapPanel. To see the full details, refer to the downloadable code examples for this chapter.

Using the WrapBreakPanel is easy. Here's some markup that demonstrates that the WrapBreakPanel correctly separates lines and calculates the right desired size based on the size of its children:

```
<StackPanel>
  <StackPanel.Resources>
    <Style TargetType="{x:Type Button}">
      <Setter Property="Margin" Value="3"></Setter>
      <Setter Property="Padding" Value="3"></Setter>
    </Style>
  </StackPanel.Resources>

  <TextBlock Padding="5" Background="LightGray">
    Content above the WrapBreakPanel.
  </TextBlock>
```

```
<lib:WrapBreakPanel>
    <Button>No Break Here</Button>
    <Button>No Break Here</Button>
    <Button>No Break Here</Button>
    <Button>No Break Here</Button>
    <Button lib:WrapBreakPanel.LineBreakBefore="True" FontWeight="Bold">
     Button with Break
    </Button>
    <Button>No Break Here</Button>
    <Button>No Break Here</Button>
    <Button>No Break Here</Button>
    <Button>No Break Here</Button>
</lib:WrapBreakPanel>
<TextBlock Padding="5" Background="LightGray">
    Content below the WrapBreakPanel.
</TextBlock>
</StackPanel>
```

Figure 18-7 shows how this markup is interpreted.

Figure 18-7. *The WrapBreakPanel*

Custom-Drawn Elements

In the previous section, you began to explore the inner workings of WPF elements—namely, the MeasureOverride()
and ArrangeOverride() methods that allow every element to plug into WPF's layout system. In this section, you'll delve
a bit deeper and consider how elements render themselves.

Most WPF elements use *composition* to create their visual appearance. In other words, a typical element builds
itself out of other, more fundamental elements. You've seen this pattern at work throughout this chapter. For example,
you define the composite elements of a user control by using markup that's processed in the same way as the XAML
in a custom window. You define the visual tree for a custom control by using a control template. And when creating a

custom panel, you don't need to define any visual details at all. The composite elements are provided by the control consumer and added to the Children collection.

Of course, composition can take you only so far. Eventually, some class needs to take responsibility for drawing content. In WPF, this point is a long way down the element tree. In a typical window, the rendering is performed by individual bits of text, shapes, and bitmaps, rather than high-level elements.

The OnRender() Method

To perform custom rendering, an element must override the OnRender() method, which is inherited from the base UIElement class. The OnRender() method doesn't necessarily replace composition—some controls use OnRender() to paint a visual detail and use composition to layer other elements over it. Two examples are the Border class, which draws its border in the OnRender() method, and the Panel class, which draws its background in the OnRender() method. Both the Border and Panel support child content, and this content is rendered on top of the custom-drawn details.

The OnRender() method receives a DrawingContext object, which provides a set of useful methods for drawing content. You first learned about the DrawingContext class in Chapter 14, when you used it to draw the content for a Visual object. The key difference when performing drawing in the OnRender() method is that you don't explicitly create and close the DrawingContext. That's because several different OnRender() methods could conceivably use the same DrawingContext. For example, a derived element might perform some custom drawing and call the OnRender() implementation in the base class to draw additional content. This works because WPF automatically creates the DrawingContext object at the beginning of this process and closes it when it's no longer needed.

■ **Note** Technically, the OnRender() method doesn't actually *draw* your content to the screen. Instead, it draws your content to the DrawingContext object, and WPF then caches that information. WPF determines when your element needs to be repainted and paints the content that you created with the DrawingContext. This is the essence of WPF's retained graphics system—you define the content, and it manages the painting and refreshing process seamlessly.

The most surprising detail about WPF rendering is that so few classes actually do it. Most classes are built out of other simpler classes, and you need to dig quite a way down the element tree of a typical control before you discover a class that actually overrides OnRender(). Here are some that do:

> *The TextBlock class*: Wherever you place text, there's a TextBlock object using OnRender() to draw it.
>
> *The Image class*: The Image class overrides OnRender() to paint its image content by using the DrawingContext.DrawImage() method.
>
> *The MediaElement class:* The MediaElement overrides OnRender() to draw a frame of video, if it's being used to play a video file.
>
> *The shape classes*: The base Shape class overrides OnRender() to draw its internally stored Geometry object, with the help of the DrawingContext.DrawGeometry() method. This Geometry object could represent an ellipse, a rectangle, or a more complex path composed of lines and curves, depending on the specific Shape-derived class. Many elements use shapes to draw small visual details.
>
> *The chrome classes*: Classes such as ButtonChrome and ListBoxChrome draw the outer appearance of a common control and place the content you specify inside. Many other Decorator-derived classes, such as Border, also override OnRender().
>
> *The panel classes*: Although the content of a panel is supplied by its children, the OnRender() method takes care of drawing a rectangle with the background color if the Background property is set.

Often, the OnRender() implementation is deceptively simple. For example, here's the rendering code for any Shape-derived class:

```
Protected Overrides Sub OnRender(ByVal drawingContext As DrawingContext)
    Me.EnsureRenderedGeometry
    If (Me._renderedGeometry <> Geometry.Empty) Then
        drawingContext.DrawGeometry(Me.Fill, Me.GetPen, Me._renderedGeometry)
    End If
End Sub
```

Remember, overriding OnRender() isn't the only way to render content and add it to your user interface. You can also create a DrawingVisual object and add that visual to a UIElement by using the AddVisualChild() method (and implementing a few other details, as described in Chapter 14). You can then call DrawingVisual.RenderOpen() to retrieve a DrawingContext for your DrawingVisual and use it to render its content.

Some elements use this strategy in WPF to display some graphical detail on top of other element content. For example, you'll see it with drag-and-drop indicators, error indicators, and focus boxes. In all these cases, the DrawingVisual approach allows the element to draw content *over* other content, rather than *under* it. But for the most part, rendering takes place in the dedicated OnRender() method.

Evaluating Custom Drawing

When you create your own custom elements, you may choose to override OnRender() to draw custom content. You might override OnRender() in an element that contains content (most commonly, a Decorator-derived class) so you can add a graphical embellishment around that content. Or you might override OnRender() in an element that doesn't have any nested content so that you can draw its full visual appearance. For example, you might create a custom element that draws a small graphical detail, which you can then use in another control through composition. One example in WPF is the TickBar element, which draws the tick marks for a Slider. The TickBar is embedded in the visual tree of a Slider through the Slider's default control template (along with a Border and a Track that includes two RepeatButton controls and a Thumb).

The obvious question is when to use the comparatively low-level OnRender() approach and when to use composition with other classes (such as the Shape-derived elements) to draw what you need. To decide, you need to evaluate the complexity of the graphics you need and the interactivity you want to provide.

For example, consider the ButtonChrome class. In WPF's implementation of the ButtonChrome class, the custom rendering code takes various properties into account, including RenderDefaulted, RenderMouseOver, and RenderPressed. The default control template for the Button uses triggers to set these properties at the appropriate time, as you saw in Chapter 17. For example, when the mouse moves over the button, the Button class uses a trigger to set the ButtonChrome.RenderMouseOver property to True.

Whenever the RenderDefaulted, RenderMouseOver, or RenderPressed property is changed, the ButtonChrome calls the base InvalidateVisual() method to indicate that its current appearance is no longer valid. WPF then calls the ButtonChrome.OnRender() method to get its new graphical representation.

If the ButtonChrome class used composition, this behavior would be more difficult to implement. It's easy enough to create the standard appearance for the ButtonChrome class by using the right elements, but it's more work to modify it when the button's state changes. You'd need to dynamically change the nested elements that compose the ButtonChrome class or—if the appearance changes more dramatically—you'd be forced to hide one element and show another one in its place.

Most custom elements won't need custom rendering. But if you need to render complex visuals that change significantly when properties are changed or certain actions take place, the custom rendering approach just might be easier to use and more lightweight.

Creating a Custom-Drawn Element

Now that you know how the OnRender() method works and when to use it, the last step is to consider a custom control that demonstrates it in action.

The following code defines an element named CustomDrawnElement that demonstrates a simple effect. It paints a shaded background by using the RadialGradientBrush. The trick is that the highlight point where the gradient starts is set dynamically, so it follows the mouse. Thus, as the user moves the mouse over the control, the white glowing center point follows, as shown in Figure 18-8.

Figure 18-8. *A custom-drawn element*

The CustomDrawnElement doesn't need to contain any child content, so it derives directly from FrameworkElement. It allows only a single property to be set—the background color of the gradient. (The foreground color is hard-coded to be white, although you could easily change this detail.)

```vb
Public Class CustomDrawnElement
    Inherits FrameworkElement

    Public Shared BackgroundColorProperty As DependencyProperty

    Shared Sub New()
        Dim metadata As New FrameworkPropertyMetadata(Colors.Yellow)
        metadata.AffectsRender = True
        BackgroundColorProperty = DependencyProperty.Register( _
          "BackgroundColor", GetType(Color), _
          GetType(CustomDrawnElement), metadata)
    End Sub
```

```
Public Property BackgroundColor() As Color
    Get
        Return CType(GetValue(BackgroundColorProperty), Color)
    End Get
    Set(ByVal value As Color)
        SetValue(BackgroundColorProperty, value)
    End Set
End Property
...
```

The BackgroundColor dependency property is specifically marked with the FrameworkPropertyMetadata. AffectRender flag. As a result, WPF will automatically call OnRender() whenever the color is changed. However, you also need to make sure OnRender() is called when the mouse moves to a new position. This is handled by calling the InvalidateVisual() method at the right times:

```
...
Protected Overrides Sub OnMouseMove(ByVal e As MouseEventArgs)
    MyBase.OnMouseMove(e)
    Me.InvalidateVisual()
End Sub

Protected Overrides Sub OnMouseLeave(ByVal e As MouseEventArgs)
    MyBase.OnMouseLeave(e)
    Me.InvalidateVisual()
End Sub
...
```

The only remaining detail is the rendering code. It uses the DrawingContext.DrawRectangle() method to paint the element's background. The ActualWidth and ActualHeight properties indicate the final rendered dimensions of the control.

```
...
Protected Overrides Sub OnRender(ByVal dc As DrawingContext)
    MyBase.OnRender(dc)

    Dim bounds As New Rect(0, 0, MyBase.ActualWidth, MyBase.ActualHeight)
    dc.DrawRectangle(GetForegroundBrush(), Nothing, bounds)
End Sub
...
```

Finally, a private helper method named GetForegroundBrush() constructs the correct RadialGradientBrush based on the current position of the mouse. To calculate the center point, you need to convert the current position of the mouse over the element to a relative position from 0 to 1, which is what the RadialGradientBrush expects.

```
...
Private Function GetForegroundBrush() As Brush
    If Not IsMouseOver Then
        Return New SolidColorBrush(BackgroundColor)
    Else
        Dim brush As New RadialGradientBrush(Colors.White, BackgroundColor)
```

```
            ' Get the position of the mouse in device-independent units,
            ' relative to the control itself.
            Dim absoluteGradientOrigin As Point = Mouse.GetPosition(Me)

            ' Convert the point coordinates to proportional (0 to 1) values.
            Dim relativeGradientOrigin As New Point( _
                absoluteGradientOrigin.X / MyBase.ActualWidth, _
                absoluteGradientOrigin.Y / MyBase.ActualHeight)

            brush.GradientOrigin = relativeGradientOrigin
            brush.Center = relativeGradientOrigin
            brush.Freeze()
            Return brush
        End If
    End Function

End Class
```

This completes the example.

Creating a Custom Decorator

As a general rule, you should never use custom drawing in a control. If you do, you violate the premise of WPF's lookless controls. The problem is that after you hardwire in some drawing logic, you've ensured that a portion of your control's visual appearance cannot be customized through the control template.

A much better approach is to design a separate element that draws your custom content (such as the CustomDrawnElement class in the previous example) and then use that element inside the default control template for your control. That's the approach used in many WPF controls, and you saw it at work in the Button control in Chapter 17.

It's worth quickly considering how you can adapt the previous example so that it can function as part of a control template. Custom-drawn elements usually play two roles in a control template:

- They draw some small graphical detail (such as the arrow on a scroll button).

- They provide a more detailed background or frame around another element.

The second approach requires a custom decorator. You can change the CustomDrawnElement into a custom-drawn element by making two small changes. First, derive it from Decorator:

```
Public Class CustomDrawnDecorator
    Inherits Decorator
    ...
End Class
```

Next, override the OnMeasure() method to specify the required size. It's the responsibility of all decorators to consider their children, add the extra space required for their embellishments, and then return the combined size. The CustomDrawnDecorator doesn't need any extra space to draw a border. Instead, it simply makes itself as large as the content warrants by using this code:

```
Protected Overrides Function MeasureOverride(ByVal constraint As Size) As Size
    Dim child As UIElement = Me.Child
    If Not child Is Nothing Then
```

```
            child.Measure(constraint)
            Return child.DesiredSize
        Else
            Return New Size()
        End If
End Function
```

After you've created your custom decorator, you can use it in a custom control template. For example, here's a button template that places the mouse-tracking gradient background behind the button content. It uses template bindings to make sure the properties for alignment and padding are respected.

```
<ControlTemplate x:Key="ButtonWithCustomChrome">
  <lib:CustomDrawnDecorator BackgroundColor="LightGreen">
    <ContentPresenter Margin="{TemplateBinding Padding}"
      HorizontalAlignment="{TemplateBinding HorizontalContentAlignment}"
      VerticalAlignment="{TemplateBinding VerticalContentAlignment}"
      ContentTemplate="{TemplateBinding ContentControl.ContentTemplate}"
      Content="{TemplateBinding ContentControl.Content}"
      RecognizesAccessKey="True" />
  </lib:CustomDrawnDecorator>
</ControlTemplate>
```

You can now use this template to restyle your buttons with a new look. Of course, to make your decorator more practical, you'd probably want to vary its appearance when the mouse button is clicked. You can do this by using triggers that modify properties in your chrome class. Chapter 17 has a complete discussion of this design.

The Last Word

In this chapter, you took a detailed look at custom control development in WPF. You saw how to build basic user controls and extend existing WPF controls and how to create the WPF gold standard—a template-based lookless control. Finally, you considered custom drawing and how you can use custom-drawn content with a template-based control.

If you're planning to dive deeper into the world of custom control development, you'll find some excellent samples online. One good starting point is Microsoft's set of control customization samples that are available at http://tinyurl.com/9jtk93x. Another worthwhile download is the actively maintained Bag-o-Tricks sample project provided by Kevin Moore (a former program manager on the WPF team) at http://tinyurl.com/95sdzgx, which includes everything from basic date controls to a panel with built-in animation.

PART 5

Data

CHAPTER 19

Data Binding

Data binding is the time-honored tradition of pulling information out of an object and displaying it in your application's user interface, without writing the tedious code that does all the work. Often, rich clients use *two-way* data binding, which adds the ability to push information from the user interface back into some object—again, with little or no code. Because many Windows applications are all about data (and all of them need to deal with data some of the time), data binding is a top concern in a user interface technology like WPF.

Developers who are approaching WPF from a Windows Forms background will find that WPF data binding has many similarities. As in Windows Forms, WPF data binding allows you to create bindings that take information from just about any property of any object and stuff it into just about any property of any element. WPF also includes a set of list controls that can handle entire collections of information and allow you to navigate through them. However, there are significant changes in the way that data binding is implemented behind the scenes, some impressive new functionality, and a fair bit of tweaking and fine-tuning. Many of the same concepts apply, but the same code won't.

In this chapter, you'll learn how to use WPF data binding. You'll create declarative bindings that extract the information you need and display it in various types of elements. You'll also learn how to plug this system into a back-end database.

What's New   Although the data binding basics remain the same, WPF 4.5 adds a number of small refinements. In this chapter, you'll learn about the improved VirtualizationPanel, which allows more fine-tuning (see the section "Improving Performance in Long Lists"). You'll also consider the INotifyDataErrorInfo interface for validation (see the section "Validation"), which was brought over from Silverlight and replaces the IDataErrorInfo interface.

Binding to a Database with Custom Objects

When developers hear the term *data binding*, they often think of one specific application—pulling information out of a database and showing it onscreen with little or no code.

As you saw in Chapter 8, data binding in WPF is a much more general tool. Even if your application never comes into contact with a database, it's still likely to use data binding to automate the way elements interact or translate an object model into a suitable display.

However, you can learn a lot about the details of object binding by considering a traditional example that queries and updates a table in a database. In this chapter, you'll use an example that retrieves a catalog of products. The first step in building this example is to create a custom data access component.

■ **Note** The downloadable code for this chapter includes the custom data access component and a database script that installs the sample data, so you can test all the examples. But if you don't have a test database server or you don't want to go to the trouble of creating a new database, you can use an alternate version of the data access component that's also included with the code. This version simply loads the data from a file, while still exposing the same set of classes and methods. It's perfect for testing but obviously impractical for a real application.

Building a Data Access Component

In professional applications, database code is not embedded in the code-behind class for a window but encapsulated in a dedicated class. For even better componentization, these data access classes can be pulled out of your application altogether and compiled in a separate DLL component. This is particularly true when writing code that accesses a database (because this code tends to be extremely performance-sensitive), but it's a good design no matter where your data lives.

DESIGNING DATA ACCESS COMPONENTS

No matter how you plan to use data binding (or even if you don't), your data access code should always be coded in a separate class. This approach is the only way you have the slightest chance to make sure you can efficiently maintain, optimize, troubleshoot, and (optionally) reuse your data access code.

When creating a data class, you should follow a few basic guidelines in this section:

- *Open and close connections quickly*: Open the database connection in every method call, and close it before the method ends. This way, a connection can't be inadvertently left open. One way to ensure the connection is closed at the appropriate time is with a using block.

- *Implement error handling*: Use error handling to make sure that connections are closed even if an exception occurs.

- *Follow stateless design practices*: Accept all the information needed for a method in its parameters, and return all the retrieved data through the return value. This avoids complications in a number of scenarios (for example, if you need to create a multithreaded application or host your database component on a server).

- *Store the connection string in one place*: Ideally, this is the configuration file for your application.

The database component that's shown in the following example retrieves a table of product information from the Store database, which is a sample database for the fictional IBuySpy store included with some Microsoft case studies. Figure 19-1 shows two tables in the Store database and their schemas.

Figure 19-1. *A portion of the Store database*

The data access class is exceedingly simple—it provides just a single method that allows the caller to retrieve one product record. Here's the basic outline:

```
Public Class StoreDB
    ' Get the connection string from the current configuration file.
    Private connectionString As String = My.Settings.Default.StoreDatabase

    Public Function GetProduct(ByVal ID As Integer) As Product
        ...
    End Function
End Class
```

The query is performed through a stored procedure in the database named GetProduct. The connection string isn't hard-coded—instead, it's retrieved through an application setting in the .config file for this application. (To view or set application settings, double-click the My Project node in the Solution Explorer, and then click the Settings tab.)

When other windows need data, they call the StoreDB.GetProduct() method to retrieve a Product object. The Product object is a custom object that has a sole purpose in life—to represent the information for a single row in the Products table. You'll consider it in the next section.

You have several options for making the StoreDB class available to the windows in your application:

- The window could create an instance of StoreDB whenever it needs to access the database.

- You could change the methods in the StoreDB class to be static.

- You could create a single instance of StoreDB and make it available through a static property in another class (following the "factory" pattern).

The first two options are reasonable, but both of them limit your flexibility. The first choice prevents you from caching data objects for use in multiple windows. Even if you don't want to use that caching right away, it's worth designing your application in such a way that it's easy to implement later. Similarly, the second approach assumes you won't have any instance-specific state that you need to retain in the StoreDB class. Although this is a good design principle, you might want to retain some details (such as the connection string) in memory. If you convert the StoreDB class to use static methods, it becomes much more difficult to access different instances of the Store database in different back-end data stores.

Ultimately, the third option is the most flexible. It preserves the switchboard design by forcing all the windows to work through a single property. Here's an example that makes an instance of StoreDB available through the Application class:

```
Public Class Application
    Private Shared _storeDB As New StoreDB()
    Public Shared ReadOnly Property StoreDB() As StoreDB
```

```
        Get
            Return _storeDB
        End Get
    End Property
End Class
```

In this book, we're primarily interested with how data objects can be bound to WPF elements. The actual process that deals with creating and filling these data objects (as well as other implementation details, such as whether StoreDB caches the data over several method calls, whether it uses stored procedures instead of inline queries, whether it fetches the data from a local XML file when offline, and so on) isn't our focus. However, just to get an understanding of what's taking place, here's the complete code:

```
Public Class StoreDB
    Private connectionString As String = My.Settings.Default.StoreDatabase

    Public Function GetProduct(ByVal ID As Integer) As Product
        Dim con As New SqlConnection(connectionString)
        Dim cmd As New SqlCommand("GetProductByID", con)
        cmd.CommandType = CommandType.StoredProcedure
        cmd.Parameters.AddWithValue("@ProductID", ID)

        Try
            con.Open()

            Dim reader As SqlDataReader
            reader = cmd.ExecuteReader(CommandBehavior.SingleRow)
            If reader.Read() Then
                ' Create a Product object that wraps the
                ' current record.
                Dim product As New Product( _
                  CStr(reader("ModelNumber")), CStr(reader("ModelName")), _
                  CDec(reader("UnitCost")), CStr(reader("Description")), _
                  CStr(reader("ProductImage")))
                Return product
            Else
                Return Nothing
            End If

        Finally
            con.Close()
        End Try
    End Function

End Class
```

▨ **Note** Currently, the GetProduct() method doesn't include any exception handling code, so all exceptions will bubble up the calling code. This is a reasonable design choice, but you might want to catch the exception in GetProduct(), perform cleanup or logging as required, and then rethrow the exception to notify the calling code of the problem. This design pattern is called *caller inform*.

Building a Data Object

The data object is the information package that you plan to display in your user interface. Any class works, provided it consists of public properties (fields and private properties aren't supported). In addition, if you want to use this object to make changes (via two-way binding), the properties cannot be read-only.

Here's the Product object that's used by StoreDB:

```
Public Class Product

    Private _modelNumber As String
    Public Property ModelNumber() As String
        Get
            Return _modelNumber
        End Get
        Set(ByVal value As String)
            _modelNumber = value
        End Set
    End Property

    Private _modelName As String
    Public Property ModelName() As String
        Get
            Return _modelName
        End Get
        Set(ByVal value As String)
            _modelName = value
        End Set
    End Property

    Private _unitCost As Decimal
    Public Property UnitCost() As Decimal
        Get
            Return _unitCost
        End Get
        Set(ByVal value As Decimal)
            _unitCost = value
        End Set
    End Property

    Private _description As String
    Public Property Description() As String
        Get
            Return _description
        End Get
        Set(ByVal value As String)
            _description = value
        End Set
    End Property

    Public Sub New(ByVal modelNumber As String, ByVal modelName As String, _
        ByVal unitCost As Decimal, ByVal description As String)
        Me.ModelNumber = modelNumber
```

```
        Me.ModelName = modelName
        Me.UnitCost = unitCost
        Me.Description = description
    End Sub

End Class
```

Displaying the Bound Object

The final step is to create an instance of the Product object and then bind it to your controls. Although you could create a Product object and store it as a resource or a static property, neither approach makes much sense. Instead, you need to use StoreDB to create the appropriate object at runtime and then bind that to your window.

▨ **Note**   Although the declarative no-code approach sounds more elegant, there are plenty of good reasons to mix a little code into your data-bound windows. For example, if you're querying a database, you probably want to handle the connection in your code so that you can decide how to handle exceptions and inform the user of problems.

Consider the simple window shown in Figure 19-2. It allows the user to supply a product code, and it then shows the corresponding product in the Grid in the lower portion of the window.

Figure 19-2. *Querying a product*

When you design this window, you don't have access to the Product object that will supply the data at runtime. However, you can still create your bindings without indicating the data source. You simply need to indicate the property that each element uses from the Product class.

Here's the full markup for displaying a Product object:

```
<Grid Name="gridProductDetails">
  <Grid.ColumnDefinitions>
    <ColumnDefinition Width="Auto"></ColumnDefinition>
    <ColumnDefinition></ColumnDefinition>
  </Grid.ColumnDefinitions>
  <Grid.RowDefinitions>
    <RowDefinition Height="Auto"></RowDefinition>
    <RowDefinition Height="Auto"></RowDefinition>
    <RowDefinition Height="Auto"></RowDefinition>
    <RowDefinition Height="Auto"></RowDefinition>
    <RowDefinition Height="*"></RowDefinition>
  </Grid.RowDefinitions>

  <TextBlock Margin="7">Model Number:</TextBlock>
  <TextBox Margin="5" Grid.Column="1"
   Text="{Binding Path=ModelNumber}"></TextBox>
  <TextBlock Margin="7" Grid.Row="1">Model Name:</TextBlock>
  <TextBox Margin="5" Grid.Row="1" Grid.Column="1"
   Text="{Binding Path=ModelName}"></TextBox>
  <TextBlock Margin="7" Grid.Row="2">Unit Cost:</TextBlock>
  <TextBox Margin="5" Grid.Row="2" Grid.Column="1"
   Text="{Binding Path=UnitCost}"></TextBox>
  <TextBlock Margin="7,7,7,0" Grid.Row="3">Description:</TextBlock>
  <TextBox Margin="7" Grid.Row="4" Grid.Column="0" Grid.ColumnSpan="2"
   TextWrapping="Wrap" Text="{Binding Path=Description}"></TextBox>
</Grid>
```

Notice that the Grid wrapping all these details is given a name so that you can manipulate it in code and complete your data bindings.

When you first run this application, no information will appear. Even though you've defined your bindings, no source object is available.

When the user clicks the button at runtime, you use the StoreDB class to get the appropriate product data. Although you could create each binding programmatically, this wouldn't make much sense (and it wouldn't save much code over just populating the controls by hand). However, the DataContext property provides a perfect shortcut. If you set it for the Grid that contains all your data binding expressions, all your binding expressions will use it to fill themselves with data.

Here's the event handling code that reacts when the user clicks the button:

```
Private Sub cmdGetProduct_Click(ByVal sender As Object, _
  ByVal e As RoutedEventArgs)
    Dim ID As Integer
    If Int32.TryParse(txtID.Text, ID) Then
        Try
            gridProductDetails.DataContext = Application.StoreDB.GetProduct(ID)
        Catch
            MessageBox.Show("Error contacting database.")
        End Try
    Else
        MessageBox.Show("Invalid ID.")
    End If
End Sub
```

561

BINDING WITH NULL VALUES

The current Product class assumes that it will get a full complement of product data. However, database tables frequently include nullable fields, where a null value (Nothing) represents missing or inapplicable information. You can reflect this reality in your data classes by using nullable data types for simple value types such as numbers and dates. For example, in the Product class, you can use Nullable(Of Decimal) instead of Decimal. Of course, reference types, such as strings and full-fledged objects, always support null values.

The results of binding a null value are predictable: the target element shows nothing at all. For numeric fields, this behavior is useful because it distinguishes between a missing value (in which case the element shows nothing) and a zero value (in which case it shows the text "0"). However, it's worth noting that you can change how WPF handles null values by setting the TargetNullValue property in your binding expression. If you do, the value you supply will be displayed whenever the data source has a null value. Here's an example that shows the text "[No Description Provided]" when the Product.Description property is null:

```
Text="{Binding Path=Description, TargetNullValue=[No Description Provided]}"
```

The square brackets around the TargetNullValue text are optional. In this example, they're intended to help the user recognize that the displayed text isn't drawn from the database.

Updating the Database

You don't need to do anything extra to enable data object updates with this example. The TextBox.Text property uses two-way binding by default, which means that the bound Product object is modified as you edit the text in the text boxes. (Technically, each property is updated when you tab to a new field, because the default source update mode for the TextBox.Text property is LostFocus. To review the different update modes that binding expressions support, refer to Chapter 8.)

You can commit changes to the database at any time. All you need is to add an UpdateProduct() method to the StoreDB class and an Update button to the window. When clicked, your code can grab the current Product object from the data context and use it to commit the update:

```
Private Sub cmdUpdateProduct_Click(ByVal sender As Object, _
  ByVal e As RoutedEventArgs)
    Dim product As Product = CType(gridProductDetails.DataContext,Product)
    Try
        Application.StoreDB.UpdateProduct(product)
    Catch As System.Exception
        MessageBox.Show("Error contacting database.")
    End Try
End Sub
```

This example has one potential stumbling block. When you click the Update button, the focus changes to that button, and any uncommitted edit is applied to the Product object. However, if you set the Update button to be a default button (by setting IsDefault to True), there's another possibility. A user could make a change in one of the fields and hit Enter to trigger the update process without committing the last change. To avoid this possibility, you can explicitly force the focus to change before you execute any database code, like this:

```
FocusManager.SetFocusedElement(Me, CType(sender, Button))
```

Change Notification

The Product binding example works so well because each Product object is essentially fixed—it never changes (except if the user edits the text in one of the linked text boxes).

For simple scenarios, where you're primarily interested in displaying content and letting the user edit it, this behavior is perfectly acceptable. However, it's not difficult to imagine a different situation, where the bound Product object might be modified elsewhere in your code. For example, imagine an Increase Price button that executes this line of code:

```
product.UnitCost *= 1.1
```

■ **Note** Although you could retrieve the Product object from the data context, this example assumes you're also storing it as a member variable in your window class, which simplifies your code and requires less type casting.

When you run this code, you'll find that even though the Product object has been changed, the old value remains in the text box. That's because the text box has no way of knowing that you've changed a value.

You can use three approaches to solve this problem:

- You can make each property in the Product class a dependency property using the syntax you learned about in Chapter 4. (In this case, your class must derive from DependencyObject.) Although this approach gets WPF to do the work for you (which is nice), it makes the most sense in elements—classes that have a visual appearance in a window. It's not the most natural approach for data classes like Product.

- You can raise an event for each property. In this case, the event must have the name *PropertyName*Changed (for example, UnitCostChanged). It's up to you to fire the event when the property is changed.

- You can implement the System.ComponentModel.INotifyPropertyChanged interface, which requires a single event named PropertyChanged. You must then raise the PropertyChanged event whenever a property changes and indicate which property has changed by supplying the property name as a string. It's still up to you to raise this event when a property changes, but you don't need to define a separate event for each property.

The first approach relies on the WPF dependency property infrastructure, while both the second and the third rely on events. Usually, when creating a data object, you'll use the third approach. It's the simplest choice for non-element classes.

■ **Note** You can actually use one other approach. If you suspect a change has been made to a bound object and that bound object doesn't support change notifications in any of the proper ways, you can retrieve the BindingExpression object (using the FrameworkElement.GetBindingExpression() method) and call BindingExpression.UpdateTarget() to trigger a refresh. Obviously, this is the most awkward solution—you can almost see the duct tape that's holding it together.

Here's the definition for a revamped Product class that uses the INotifyPropertyChanged interface, with the code for the implementation of the PropertyChanged event:

```
Public Class Product
    Implements INotifyPropertyChanged

    Public Event PropertyChanged As PropertyChangedEventHandler _
      Implements INotifyPropertyChanged.PropertyChanged

    Public Sub OnPropertyChanged(ByVal e As PropertyChangedEventArgs)
        If Not PropertyChangedEvent Is Nothing Then
            RaiseEvent PropertyChanged(Me, e)
        End If
    End Sub
End Class
```

Now you simply need to fire the PropertyChanged event in all your property setters:

```
Private _unitCost As Decimal
Public Property UnitCost() As Decimal
    Get
        Return _unitCost
    End Get
    Set(ByVal value As Decimal)
      _unitCost = value
      OnPropertyChanged(New PropertyChangedEventArgs("UnitCost"))
    End Set
End Property
```

If you use this version of the Product class in the previous example, you'll get the behavior you expect. When you change the current Product object, the new information will appear in the text box immediately.

■ **Tip**   If several values have changed, you can call OnPropertyChanged() and pass in an empty string. This tells WPF to reevaluate the binding expressions that are bound to any property in your class.

Binding to a Collection of Objects

Binding to a single object is quite straightforward. But life gets more interesting when you need to bind to some collection of objects—for example, all the products in a table.

Although every dependency property supports the single-value binding you've seen so far, collection binding requires an element with a bit more intelligence. In WPF, all the classes that derive from ItemsControl have the ability to show an entire list of items. Data binding possibilities include the ListBox, ComboBox, ListView, and DataGrid (and the Menu and TreeView for hierarchical data).

■ **Tip**   Although it seems like WPF offers a relatively small set of list controls, these controls allow you to show your data in a virtually unlimited number of ways. That's because the list controls support data templates, which allow you to control exactly how items are displayed. You'll learn more about data templates in Chapter 20.

To support collection binding, the ItemsControl class defines the three key properties listed in Table 19-1.

Table 19-1. *Properties in the ItemsControl Class for Data Binding*

Name	Description
ItemsSource	Points to the collection that has all the objects that will be shown in the list.
DisplayMemberPath	Identifies the property that will be used to create the display text for each item.
ItemTemplate	Accepts a data template that will be used to create the visual appearance of each item. This property is far more powerful than DisplayMemberPath, and you'll learn how to use it in Chapter 20.

At this point, you're probably wondering exactly what type of collections you can stuff in the ItemSource property. Happily, you can use just about anything. All you need is support for the IEnumerable interface, which is provided by arrays, all types of collections, and many more specialized objects that wrap groups of items. However, the support you get from a basic IEnumerable interface is limited to read-only binding. If you want to edit the collection (for example, you want to allow inserts and deletions), you need a bit more infrastructure, as you'll see shortly.

Displaying and Editing Collection Items

Consider the window shown in Figure 19-3, which shows a list of products. When you choose a product, the information for that product appears in the bottom section of the window, where you can edit it. (In this example, a GridSplitter lets you adjust the space given to the top and bottom portions of the window.)

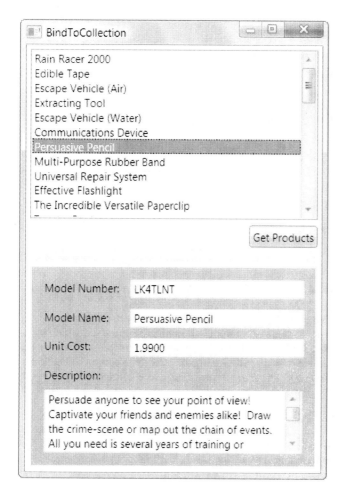

Figure 19-3. *A list of products*

To create this example, you need to begin by building your data access logic. In this case, the StoreDB. GetProducts() method retrieves the list of all the products in the database using the GetProducts stored procedure. A Product object is created for each record and added to a generic List collection. (You could use any collection here—for example, an array or a weakly typed ArrayList would work equivalently.)

Here's the GetProducts() code:

```
Public Function GetProducts() As List(Of Product)
    Dim con As New SqlConnection(connectionString)
    Dim cmd As New SqlCommand("GetProducts", con)
    cmd.CommandType = CommandType.StoredProcedure

    Dim products As New List(Of Product)()
    Try
        con.Open()
        Dim reader As SqlDataReader = cmd.ExecuteReader()
        Do While reader.Read()
```

```
            ' Create a Product object that wraps the
            ' current record.
            Dim product As New Product(CStr(reader("ModelNumber")), _
              CStr(reader("ModelName")), CDec(reader("UnitCost")), _
              CStr(reader("Description")))

            ' Add to collection
            products.Add(product)
        Loop
    Finally
        con.Close()
    End Try

    Return products
End Function
```

When the Get Products button is clicked, the event handling code calls the GetProducts() method and supplies it as the ItemsSource for list. The collection is also stored as a member variable in the window class for easier access elsewhere in your code.

```
Private products As List(Of Product)

Private Sub cmdGetProducts_Click(ByVal sender As Object, _
  ByVal e As RoutedEventArgs)
    products = Application.StoreDB.GetProducts()
    lstProducts.ItemsSource = products
End Sub
```

This successfully fills the list with Product objects. However, the list doesn't know how to display a product object, so it will simply call the ToString() method. Because this method hasn't been overridden in the Product class, this has the unimpressive result of showing the fully qualified class name for every item (see Figure 19-4).

Figure 19-4. *An unhelpful bound list*

You have three options to solve this problem:

- *Set the DisplayMemberPath property of the list*: For example, set this to ModelName to get the result shown in Figure 19-4.

- *Override the ToString() method to return more useful information*: For example, you could return a string with the model number and model name of each item. This approach gives you a way to show more than one property in the list (for example, it's great for combining the FirstName and LastName properties in a Customer class). However, you still don't have much control over how the data is presented.

- *Supply a data template*: This way, you can show any arrangement of property values (along with fixed text). You'll learn how to use this trick in Chapter 20.

After you've decided how to display information in the list, you're ready to move on to the second challenge: displaying the details for the currently selected item in the grid that appears below the list. You could handle this challenge by responding to the SelectionChanged event and manually changing the data context of the grid, but there's a quicker approach that doesn't require any code. You simply need to set a binding expression for the Grid. DataContent property that pulls the selected Product object out of the list, as shown here:

```
<Grid DataContext="{Binding ElementName=lstProducts, Path=SelectedItem}">
  ...
</Grid>
```

When the window first appears, nothing is selected in the list. The ListBox.SelectedItem property is a null reference (Nothing), and therefore the Grid.DataContext is too, and no information appears. As soon as you select an item, the data context is set to the corresponding object, and all the information appears.

If you try this example, you'll be surprised to see that it's already fully functional. You can edit product items, navigate away (using the list), and then return to see that your edits were successfully committed. In fact, you can even change a value that affects the display text in the list. If you modify the model name and tab to another control, the corresponding entry in the list is refreshed automatically. (Experienced developers will recognize this as a frill that Windows Forms applications lacked.)

■ **Tip** To prevent a field from being edited, set the IsLocked property of the text box to True, or, better yet, use a read-only control like a TextBlock.

MASTER-DETAILS DISPLAY

As you've seen, you can bind other elements to the SelectedItem property of your list to show more details about the currently selected item. Interestingly, you can use a similar technique to build a master-details display of your data. For example, you can create a window that shows a list of categories and a list of products. When the user chooses a category in the first list, you can show just the products that belong to that category in the second list.

To pull this off, you need to have a *parent* data object that provides a collection of related *child* data objects through a property. For example, you could build a Category product that provides a property named Category. Products with the products that belong to that category. (In fact, you can find an example of a Category class that's designed like this in Chapter 21.) You can then build a master-details display with two lists. Fill your first list with Category objects. To show the related products, bind your second list—the list that displays products—to the SelectedItem.Products property of the first list. This tells the second list to grab the current Category object, extract its collection of linked Product objects, and display them.

You can find an example that uses related data in Chapter 21, with a TreeView that shows a categorized list of products.

Of course, to complete this example, from an application perspective you'll need to supply some code. For example, you might need an UpdateProducts() method that accepts your collection or products and executes the appropriate statements. Because an ordinary .NET object doesn't provide any change tracking, this is a situation where you might want to consider using the ADO.NET DataSet (as described a little later in this chapter). Alternatively, you might want to force users to update records one at a time. (One option is to disable the list when text is modified in a text box and force the user to then cancel the change by clicking Cancel or apply it immediately by clicking Update.)

Inserting and Removing Collection Items

One limitation of the previous example is that it won't pick up changes you make to the collection. It notices changed Product objects, but it won't update the list if you add a new item or remove one through code.

For example, imagine you add a Delete button that executes this code:

```
Private Sub cmdDeleteProduct_Click(ByVal sender As Object, _
  ByVal e As RoutedEventArgs)
    products.Remove(CType(lstProducts.SelectedItem, Product))
End Sub
```

The deleted item is removed from the collection, but it remains stubbornly visible in the bound list.

To enable collection change tracking, you need to use a collection that implements the INotifyCollectionChanged interface. Most generic collections don't, including the List collection used in the current example. In fact, WPF includes a single collection that uses INotifyCollectionChanged: the ObservableCollection class.

■ **Note**   If you have an object model that you're porting over from the Windows Forms world, you can use the Windows Forms equivalent of ObservableCollection, which is BindingList. The BindingList collection implements IBindingList instead of INotifyCollectionChanged, which includes a ListChanged event that plays the same role as the INotifyCollectionChanged. CollectionChanged event.

You can derive a custom collection from ObservableCollection to customize the way it works, but that's not necessary. In the current example, it's enough to replace the List(Of Product) object with an ObservableCollection(Of Product), as shown here:

```
Public Function GetProducts() As List(Of Product)
    Dim con As New SqlConnection(connectionString)
    Dim cmd As New SqlCommand("GetProducts", con)
    cmd.CommandType = CommandType.StoredProcedure

    Dim products As New ObservableCollection(Of Product)()
    ...
```

The return type can be left as List(Of Product), because the ObservableCollection class derives from the List class. To make this example just a bit more generic, you could use ICollection(Of Product) for the return type, because the ICollection interface has all the members you need to use.

Now, if you remove or add an item programmatically, the list is refreshed accordingly. Of course, it's still up to you to create the data access code that takes place before the collection is modified—for example, the code that removes the product record from the back-end database.

Binding to the ADO.NET Objects

All the features you've learned about with custom objects also work with the ADO.NET disconnected data objects.

For example, you could create the same user interface you see in Figure 19-4 but use the DataSet, DataTable, and DataRow on the back end, rather than the custom Product class and the ObservableCollection.

To try it, start by considering a version of the GetProducts() method that extracts the same data but packages it into a DataTable:

```
Public Function GetProducts() As DataTable
    Dim con As New SqlConnection(connectionString)
    Dim cmd As New SqlCommand("GetProducts", con)
```

```
cmd.CommandType = CommandType.StoredProcedure
Dim adapter As New SqlDataAdapter(cmd)

Dim ds As New DataSet()
adapter.Fill(ds, "Products")
Return ds.Tables(0)
End Function
```

You can retrieve this DataTable and bind it to the list in almost the same way you did with the ObservableCollection. The only difference is that you can't bind directly to the DataTable itself. Instead, you need to go through an intermediary known as the DataView. Although you can create a DataView by hand, every DataTable has a ready-made DataView object available through the DataTable.DefaultView property.

Note   This limitation is nothing new. Even in a Windows Forms application, all DataTable data binding goes through a DataView. The difference is that the Windows Forms universe can conceal this fact. It allows you to write code that appears to bind directly to a DataTable, when in reality it uses the DataView that's provided by the DataTable.DefaultView property.

Here's the code you need:

```
private products As DataTable

Private Sub cmdGetProducts_Click(ByVal sender As Object, _
  ByVal e As RoutedEventArgs)
    products = Application.StoreDB.GetProducts()
    lstProducts.ItemsSource = products.DefaultView
End Sub
```

Now the list will create a separate entry for each DataRow object in the DataTable.Rows collection. To determine what content is shown in the list, you need to set DisplayMemberPath property with the name of the field you want to show or use a data template (as described in Chapter 20).

The nice aspect of this example is that once you've changed the code that fetches your data, you don't need to make any more modifications. When an item is selected in the list, the Grid underneath grabs the selected item for its data context. The markup you used with the ProductList collection still works, because the property names of the Product class match the field names of the DataRow.

Another nice feature in this example is that you don't need to take any extra steps to implement change notifications. That's because the DataView class implements the IBindingList interface, which allows it to notify the WPF infrastructure if a new DataRow is added or an existing one is removed.

However, you do need to be a little careful when removing a DataRow object. It might occur to you to use code like this to delete the currently selected record:

```
products.Rows.Remove(CType(lstProducts.SelectedItem, DataRow))
```

This code is wrong on two counts. First, the selected item in the list isn't a DataRow object—it's a thin DataRowView wrapper that's provided by the DataView. Second, you probably don't want to remove your DataRow from the collection of rows in the table. Instead, you probably want to mark it as deleted so that when you commit the changes to the database, the corresponding record is removed.

Here's the correct code, which gets the selected DataRowView, uses its Row property to find the corresponding DataRow object, and calls its Delete() method to mark the row for upcoming deletion:

```
CType(lstProducts.SelectedItem, DataRowView).Row.Delete()
```

At this point, the scheduled-to-be-deleted DataRow disappears from the list, even though it's technically still in the DataTable.Rows collection. That's because the default filtering settings in the DataView hide all deleted records. You'll learn more about filtering in Chapter 21.

Binding to a LINQ Expression

WPF supports Language Integrated Query (LINQ), which is an all-purpose query syntax that works across a variety of data sources and is closely integrated with the VB language. LINQ works with any data source that has a LINQ provider. Using the support that's included with .NET, you can use similarly structured LINQ queries to retrieve data from an in-memory collection, an XML file, or a SQL Server database. And as with other query languages, LINQ allows you to apply filtering, sorting, grouping, and transformations to the data you retrieve.

Although LINQ is somewhat outside the scope of this chapter, you can learn a lot from a simple example. For example, imagine you have a collection of Product objects, named *products*, and you want to create a second collection that contains only those products that exceed $100 in cost. Using procedural code, you can write something like this:

```
' Get the full list of products.
Dim products As List(Of Product) = Application.StoreDB.GetProducts()

' Create a second collection with matching products.
Dim matches As New List(Of Product)
For Each product As Product In products
    If product.UnitCost >= 100 Then
        matches.Add(product)
    End If
Next
```

Using LINQ, you can use the following *expression,* which is far more concise:

```
' Get the full list of products.
Dim products As List(Of Product)= Application.StoreDB.GetProducts()

' Create a second collection with matching products.
Dim matches As IEnumerable(Of Product)
matches = From product In products _
          Where product.UnitCost >= 100 _
          Select product
```

This example uses LINQ to Collections, which means it uses a LINQ expression to query the data in an in-memory collection. LINQ expressions use a set of new language keywords, including From, In, Where, and Select. These LINQ keywords are a genuine part of the VB language.

▓ **Note** A full discussion of LINQ is beyond the scope of this book. For a detailed treatment, refer to the huge catalog of LINQ examples at http://tinyurl.com/9la8jzg.

LINQ revolves around the IEnumerable(Of T) interface. No matter what data source you use, every LINQ expression returns some object that implements IEnumerable(Of T). Because IEnumerable(Of T) extends IEnumerable, you can bind it in a WPF window just as you bind an ordinary collection:

```
lstProducts.ItemsSource = matches
```

Unlike ObservableCollection and the DataTable classes, the IEnumerable(Of T) interface does not provide a way to add or remove items. If you need this capability, you need to first convert your IEnumerable(Of T) object into an array or List collection using the ToArray() or ToList() method.

Here's an example that uses ToList() to convert the result of a LINQ query (shown previously) into a strongly typed List collection of Product objects:

```
Dim productMatches As List(Of Product) = matches.ToList()
```

▓ **Note**   ToList() is an extension method, which means it's defined in a different class from the one in which is used. Technically, ToList() is defined in the System.Linq.Enumerable helper class, and it's available to all IEnumerable(Of T) objects. However, it won't be available if the Enumerable class isn't in scope, which means the code shown here will not work if you haven't imported the System.Linq namespace.

The ToList() method causes the LINQ expression to be evaluated immediately. The end result is an ordinary collection, which you can deal with in all the usual ways. For example, you can wrap it in an ObservableCollection to get notification events, so any changes you make are reflected in bound controls immediately:

```
Dim productMatchesTracked As _
  New ObservableCollection(Of Product)(productMatches)
```

You can then bind the productMatchesTracked collection to a control in your window.

DESIGNING DATA FORMS IN VISUAL STUDIO

Writing data access code and filling in dozens of binding expressions can take a bit of time. And if you create several WPF applications that work with databases, you're likely to find that you're writing similar code and markup in all of them. That's why Visual Studio includes the ability to generate data access code and insert data-bound controls *automatically*.

To use these features, you need to first create a Visual Studio *data source*. (A data source is a definition that allows Visual Studio to recognize your back-end data provider and provide code generation services that use it.) You can create a data source that wraps a database, a web service, an existing data access class, or a SharePoint server. The most common choice is to create an *entity data model*, which is a set of generated classes that models the tables in a database and allows you to query them, somewhat like the data access component used in this chapter. The benefit is obvious—the entity data model allows you to avoid writing the often tedious data code. The disadvantages are just as clear—if you want the data logic to work exactly the way you want, you'll need to spend some time tweaking options, finding the appropriate extensibility points, and wading through the lengthy code. Examples where you might want fine-grained control over data access logic include if you need to call specific stored procedures, cache the results of a query, use a specific concurrency strategy, or log your data access operations. These feats are usually possible with an entity data model, but they take more work and may mitigate the benefit of automatically generated code.

To create a data source, choose Data ➤ Add New Data Source to start the Data Source Configuration Wizard, which will ask you to choose your data source (in this case, a database) and then prompt you for additional information (such as the tables and fields you want to query). Once you've added your data source, you can use the Data Sources window to create bound controls. The basic approach is pure simplicity. First choose Data ➤ Show Data Sources to see the Data Source window, which outlines the tables and fields you've chosen to work with. Then you can drag an individual field from the Data Sources window onto the design surface of a window (to create a bound TextBlock, TextBox, ListBox, or other control) or drag entire tables (to create a bound DataGrid or ListView).

WPF's data form features give you a quick and nifty way to build data-driven applications, but they don't beat knowing what's actually going on. They may be a good choice if you need straightforward data viewing or data editing and you don't want to spend a lot of time fiddling with features and fine-tuning your user interface. They're often a good fit for conventional line-of-business applications. If you'd like to learn more, you can find the official documentation at `http://tinyurl.com/d2taskv`.

Improving Performance in Long Lists

If you deal with huge amounts of data—for example, tens of thousands of records rather than just a few hundred—you know that a good data binding system needs more than sheer features. It also needs to be able to handle a huge amount of data without slowing to a crawl or swallowing an inordinate amount of memory. Fortunately, WPF's list controls are optimized to help you.

In the following sections, you'll learn about several performance enhancements for large lists that are supported by all WPF's list controls (that is, all controls that derive from ItemsControl), including the lowly ListBox and ComboBox and the more specialized ListView, TreeView, and DataGrid that you'll meet in Chapter 22.

Virtualization

The most important feature that WPF's list controls provide is *UI virtualization*, a technique where the list creates container objects for the currently displayed items only. For example, if you have a ListBox control with 50,000 records but the visible area holds only 30 records, the ListBox will create just 30 ListBoxItem objects (plus a few more to ensure good scrolling performance). If the ListBox didn't support UI virtualization, it would need to generate a full set of 50,000 ListBoxItem objects, which would clearly take more memory. More significantly, allocating these objects would take a noticeable amount of time, briefly locking up the application when your code sets the ListBox.ItemsSource property.

The support for UI virtualization isn't actually built into the ListBox or the ItemsControl class. Instead, it's hardwired into the VirtualizingStackPanel container, which functions like a StackPanel except for the added benefit of virtualization support. The ListBox, ListView, and DataGrid automatically use a VirtualizingStackPanel to lay out their children. As a result, you don't need to take any additional steps to get virtualization support. However, the ComboBox class uses the standard nonvirtualized StackPanel. If you need virtualization support, you must explicitly add it by supplying a new ItemsPanelTemplate, as shown here:

```
<ComboBox>
  <ComboBox.ItemsPanel>
    <ItemsPanelTemplate>
      <VirtualizingStackPanel></VirtualizingStackPanel>
    </ItemsPanelTemplate>
  </ComboBox.ItemsPanel>
</ComboBox>
```

The TreeView (see Chapter 22) is another control that supports virtualization but, by default, has it switched off. The issue is that the VirtualizingStackPanel didn't support hierarchical data in early releases of WPF. Now it does, but the TreeView disables the feature to guarantee ironclad backward compatibility. Fortunately, you can turn it on with just a single property setting, which is always recommended in trees that contain large amounts of data:

```
<TreeView VirtualizingStackPanel.IsVirtualizing="True" ... >
```

■ **Note** Technically VirtualizingStackPanel inherits from the MustInherit class VirtualizingPanel. If you want to use a different type of virtualization panel (for example, a Grid that supports virtualization), you'll need to purchase one from a third-party component vendor.

A number of factors can break UI virtualization, sometimes when you don't expect it:

- *Putting your list control in a ScrollViewer*: The ScrollViewer provides a window onto its child content. The problem is that the child content is given unlimited "virtual" space. In this virtual space, the ListBox renders itself at full size, with all of its child items on display. As a side effect, each item gets its own memory-hogging ListBoxItem object. This problem occurs any time you place a ListBox in a container that doesn't attempt to constrain its size; for example, the same problem crops up if you pop it into a StackPanel instead of a Grid.

- *Changing the list's control template and failing to use the ItemsPresenter*: The ItemsPresenter uses the ItemsPanelTemplate, which specifies the VirtualizingStackPanel. If you break this relationship or if you change the ItemsPanelTemplate yourself so it doesn't use a VirtualizingStackPanel, you'll lose the virtualization feature.

- *Not using data binding*: It should be obvious, but if you fill a list programmatically—for example, by dynamically creating the ListBoxItem objects you need—no virtualization will occur. Of course, you can consider using your own optimization strategy, such as creating just those objects that you need and only creating them at the time they're needed. You'll see this technique in action with a TreeView that uses just-in-time node creation to fill a directory tree in Chapter 22.

If you have a large list, you need to avoid these practices to ensure good performance.

Even when you're using UI virtualization, you still have to pay the price of instantiating your in-memory data objects. For example, in the 50,000-item ListBox example, you'll have 50,000 data objects floating around, each with distinct data about one product, customer, order record, or something else. If you want to optimize this portion of your application, you can consider using *data virtualization*—a technique where you fetch only a batch of records at a time. Data virtualization is a more complex technique, because it assumes the cost of retrieving the data is lower than the cost of maintaining it. This might not be true, depending on the sheer size of the data and the time required to retrieve it. For example, if your application is continually connecting to a network database to fetch more product information as the user scrolls through a list, the end result may be slow scrolling performance and an increased load on the database server.

WPF does not have any controls or classes that support data virtualization. However, that hasn't stopped enterprising developers from creating the missing piece: a "fake" collection that pretends to have all the items but doesn't query the back-end data source until the control requires that data. You can find solid examples of this work at http://bea.stollnitz.com/blog/?p=344 and http://bea.stollnitz.com/blog/?p=378.

Item Container Recycling

Ordinarily, as you scroll through a virtualized list, the control continually creates new item container objects to hold the newly visible items. For example, as you scroll through the 50,000-item ListBox, the ListBox will generate new ListBoxItem objects. But if you enable item container recycling, the ListBox will keep a small set of ListBoxItem objects alive and simply reuse them for different rows by loading them with new data as you scroll.

```
<ListBox VirtualizingStackPanel.VirtualizationMode="Recycling" ... >
```

Item container recycling improves scrolling performance and reduces memory consumption, because there's no need for the garbage collector to find old item objects and release them. Once again, this feature is disabled by default for all controls except the DataGrid to ensure backward compatibility. If you have a large list, you should always turn it on.

Cache Length

As you've already learned, the VirtualizingStackPanel creates a few extra items beyond the ones it shows. That way, it's ready to show these items immediately, when you start scrolling.

In previous versions of WPF, the number of extra items was hard-coded into the VirtualizingStackPanel. But in WPF 4.5, you can fine tune the exact number using two VirtualizingStackPanel properties: CacheLength and CacheLengthUnit. CacheLengthUnit lets you choose how you want to specify the number of extra items—as a number of items, as a number of pages (where a single page includes all the items that fit into the visible "window" of the control), or as a number of pixels (which might make sense if your items show pictures and are different sizes).

The default CacheLength and CacheLengthUnit properties store an extra page of items before and after the currently visible items, like this:

```
<ListBox VirtualizingStackPanel.CacheLength="1"
 VirtualizingStackPanel.CacheLengthUnit="Page" ... />
```

Here's how you might store exactly 100 items before and 100 items after:

```
<ListBox VirtualizingStackPanel.CacheLength="100"
 VirtualizingStackPanel.CacheLengthUnit="Item" ... />
```

And here's how you might store 100 items before and 500 items after (perhaps because you expect users to spend most of their time scrolling down the list rather than up it):

```
<ListBox VirtualizingStackPanel.CacheLength="100,500"
 VirtualizingStackPanel.CacheLengthUnit="Item" ... />
```

It's worth noting that the cache of extra items is filled in the background. That means that the VirtualizingStackPanel will show the visible set of items immediately, as soon as it's created. After that, the VirtualizingStackPanel will begin filling the cache on a lower priority background thread, so it can't lock up your application.

Deferred Scrolling

To further improve scrolling performance, you can switch on *deferred scrolling*. With deferred scrolling, the list display isn't updated when the user drags the thumb along the scroll bar. It's refreshed only once the user releases the thumb. By comparison, when you use ordinary scrolling, the list is refreshed as you drag so that it shows your changing position.

As with item container recycling, you need to explicitly enable deferred scrolling:

```
<ListBox ScrollViewer.IsDeferredScrollingEnabled="True" ... />
```

Clearly, there's a trade-off here between responsiveness and ease of use. If you have complex templates and lots of data, deferred scrolling may be preferred for its blistering speed. But otherwise, your users may prefer the ability to see where they're going as they scroll.

Ordinarily, the VirtualizingStackPanel uses *item-based* scrolling. That means that when you scroll down a small amount, the next item pops into view. You can't scroll down to see just *part* of an item. The smallest amount the panel scrolls is one complete item, whether you click the scroll bar, click a scroll arrow, or call a method like ListBox. ScrollIntoView().

However, you can override this behavior and use *pixel-based* scrolling by setting the VirtualizingStackPanel. ScrollUnit property to Pixel:

```
<ListBox VirtualizingStackPanel.ScrollUnit="Pixel" ... />
```

Now clipping is allowed, which means that as you scroll down you may see just part of an item.

The choice between item-based and pixel-based scrolling depends on the type of content you're showing in the list and your personal preference. In general, pixel-based scrolling is smoother because it allows smaller scrolling intervals, while item-based scrolling is cleaner because the full content of an item is always visible.

Validation

Another key ingredient in any data binding scenario is *validation*—in other words, logic that catches incorrect values and refuses them. You can build validation directly into your controls (for example, by responding to input in the text box and refusing invalid characters), but this low-level approach limits your flexibility.

Fortunately, WPF provides a validation feature that works closely with the data binding system you've explored. Validation gives you two more options to catch invalid values:

- *You can raise errors in your data object*: To notify WPF of an error, simply throw an exception from a property set procedure. Ordinarily, WPF ignores any exceptions that are thrown when setting a property, but you can configure it to show a more helpful visual indication. Other options to implement include the INotifyDataErrorInfo or IDataErrorInfo interface in your data class, which gives you the ability to indicate errors without throwing exceptions.

- *You can define validation at the binding level*: This gives you the flexibility to use the same validation regardless of the input control. Even better, because you define your validation in a distinct class, you can easily reuse it with multiple bindings that store similar types of data.

In general, you'll use the first approach if your data objects already have hardwired validation logic in their property set procedures and you want to take advantage of that logic. You'll use the second approach when you're defining validation logic for the first time and you want to reuse it in different contexts and with different controls. However, some developers choose to use both techniques. They use validation in the data object to defend against a small set of fundamental errors and use validation in the binding to catch a wider set of user-entry errors.

■ **Note**   Validation applies only when a value from the target is being used to update the source—in other words, when you're using a TwoWay or OneWayToSource binding.

Validation in the Data Object

Some developers build error checking directly into their data objects. For example, here's a modified version of the Product.UnitPrice property that disallows negative numbers:

```
Public Property UnitCost As Decimal
    Get
        Return unitCost
    End Get
```

```
Set
    If value < 0 Then
        Throw New ArgumentException("UnitCost cannot be negative.")
    Else
        unitCost = value
        OnPropertyChanged(New PropertyChangedEventArgs("UnitCost"))
    End If
End Set
End Property
```

The validation logic shown in this example prevents negative price values, but it doesn't give the user any feedback about the problem. As you learned earlier, WPF quietly ignores data binding errors that occur when setting or getting properties. In this case, the user won't have any way of knowing that the update has been rejected. In fact, the incorrect value will remain in the text box—it just won't be applied to the bound data object. To improve this situation, you need the help of the ExceptionValidationRule, which is described next.

DATA OBJECTS AND VALIDATION

Whether it's a good approach to place validation logic in a data object is a matter of never-ending debate.

This approach has some advantages; for example, it catches all errors all the time, whether they occur because of an invalid user edit, a programming mistake, or a calculation that's based on other invalid data. However, this has the disadvantage of making the data objects more complex and moving validation code that's intended for an application's front end deeper into the back-end data model.

If applied carelessly, property validation can inadvertently rule out perfectly reasonable uses of the data object. They can also lead to inconsistencies and actually *compound* data errors. (For example, it might not make sense for the UnitsInStock to hold a value of −10, but if the underlying database stores this value, you might still want to create the corresponding Product object so you can edit it in your user interface.) Sometimes, problems like these are solved by creating yet another layer of objects—for example, in a complex system, developers might build a rich business object model overtop the bare-bones data object layer.

In the current example, the StoreDB and Product classes are designed to be part of a back-end data access component. In this context, the Product class is simply a glorified package that lets you pass information from one layer of code to another. For that reason, validation code really doesn't belong in the Product class.

The ExceptionValidationRule

The ExceptionValidationRule is a prebuilt validation rule that tells WPF to report all exceptions. To use the ExceptionValidationRule, you must add it to the Binding.ValidationRules collection, as shown here:

```
<TextBox Margin="5" Grid.Row="2" Grid.Column="1">
  <TextBox.Text>
    <Binding Path="UnitCost">
      <Binding.ValidationRules>
        <ExceptionValidationRule></ExceptionValidationRule>
      </Binding.ValidationRules>
    </Binding>
  </TextBox.Text>
</TextBox>
```

This example uses both a value converter and a validation rule. Usually, validation is performed before the value is converted, but the ExceptionValidationRule is a special case. It catches exceptions that occur at any point, including exceptions that occur if the edited value can't be cast to the correct data type, exceptions that are thrown by the property setter, and exceptions that are thrown by the value converter.

So, what happens when validation fails? Validation errors are recorded using the attached properties of the System.Windows.Controls.Validation class. For each failed validation rule, WPF takes three steps:

- It sets the attached Validation.HasError property to True on the bound element (in this case, the TextBox control).

- It creates a ValidationError object with the error details (as returned from the ValidationRule. Validate() method) and adds that to the attached Validation.Errors collection.

- If the Binding.NotifyOnValidationError property is set to True, WPF raises the Validation.Error attached event on the element.

The visual appearance of your bound control also changes when an error occurs. WPF automatically switches the template that a control uses when its Validation.HasError property is True to the template that's defined by the attached Validation.ErrorTemplate property. In a text box, the new template changes the outline of the box to a thin red border.

In most cases, you'll want to augment the error indication in some way and give specific information about the error that caused the problem. You can use code that handles the Error event, or you can supply a custom control template that provides a different visual indication. But before you tackle either of these tasks, it's worth considering two other ways WPF allows you to catch errors—by using the INotifyDataErrorInfo or IDataErrorInfo in your data objects and by writing custom validation rules.

The INotifyDataErrorInfo Interface

Many object-orientation purists prefer not to raise exceptions to indicate user input errors. There are several possible reasons, including the following: a user input error isn't an exceptional condition, error conditions may depend on the interaction between multiple property values, and it's sometimes worthwhile to hold on to incorrect values for further processing rather than reject them outright. WPF provides two interfaces that allow you to build objects that report errors without throwing exceptions. These interfaces are IDataErrorInfo and INotifyDataErrorInfo.

___

■ **Note** The IDataErrorInfo and INotifyDataErrorInfo interfaces have the same goal—they replace aggressive unhandled exceptions with a more polite system of error notification. The IDataErrorInfo interface is the original error-tracking interface, which dates back to the first version of .NET. WPF includes it for backward compatibility. The INotifyDataErrorInfo interface is a similar but richer interface that was created for Silverlight and ported to WPF for version 4.5. It has support for additional features, such as multiple errors per property and asynchronous validation. It's the one you'll use in this section.

___

The following example shows how to use the INotifyDataErrorInfo interface to detect problems with the Product object. The first step is to implement the interface:

```
Public Class Product
    Implements INotifyPropertyChanged, INotifyDataErrorInfo
    ...
End Class
```

The INotifyDataErrorInfo interface requires just three members. The ErrorsChanged event fires when an error is added or removed. The HasErrors property returns True or False to indicate whether the data object has errors. Finally, the GetErrors() method provides the full error information.

Before you can implement these methods, you need a way to track the errors in your code. The best bet is a private collection, like this:

```
Private errors As New Dictionary(Of String, List(Of String))()
```

At first glance, this collection looks a little odd. To understand why, you need to know two facts. First, the INotifyDataErrorInfo interface expects you to link your errors to a specific property. Second, each property can have one or more errors. The easiest way to track this error information is with a Dictionary(Of T, Of K) collection that's indexed by property name:

```
Private errors As New Dictionary(Of String, List(Of String))()
```

Each entry in the dictionary is itself a collection of errors. This example uses a simple List<Of T> List<T> of strings:

```
Private errors As New Dictionary(Of String, List(Of String))()
```

However, you could use a full-fledged error object to bundle together multiple pieces of information about the error, including details such as a text message, error code, severity level, and so on.

Once you have this collection in place, you simply need to add to it when an error occurs (and remove the error information if the error is corrected). To make this process easier, the Product class in this example adds a pair of private methods named SetErrors() and ClearErrors():

```
Public Event ErrorsChanged As EventHandler(Of DataErrorsChangedEventArgs) _
    Implements INotifyDataErrorInfo.ErrorsChanged

Private Sub SetErrors(ByVal propertyName As String, _
  ByVal propertyErrors As List(Of String))
    ' Clear any errors that already exist for this property.
    errors.Remove(propertyName)

    ' Add the list collection for the specified property.
    errors.Add(propertyName, propertyErrors)

    ' Raise the error-notification event.
    RaiseEvent ErrorsChanged(Me, New DataErrorsChangedEventArgs(propertyName))
End Sub

Private Sub ClearErrors(ByVal propertyName As String)
    ' Remove the error list for this property.
    errors.Remove(propertyName)

    ' Raise the error-notification event.
    RaiseEvent ErrorsChanged(Me, New DataErrorsChangedEventArgs(propertyName))
End Sub
```

And here's the error-handling logic that ensures that the Product.ModelNumber property is restricted to a string of alphanumeric characters. (Punctuation, spaces, and other special characters are not allowed.)

```
Private _modelNumber As String
Public Property ModelNumber() As String
    Get
        Return _modelNumber
    End Get
    Set(ByVal value As String)
        _modelNumber = value

        Dim valid As Boolean = True
        For Each c As Char In _modelNumber
            If (Not Char.IsLetterOrDigit(c)) Then
                valid = False
                Exit For
            End If
        Next
        If (Not valid) Then
            Dim errors As List(Of String) = New List(Of String)()
            errors.Add("The ModelNumber can only contain letters and numbers.")
            SetErrors("ModelNumber", errors)
        Else
            ClearErrors("ModelNumber")
        End If

        OnPropertyChanged(New PropertyChangedEventArgs("ModelNumber"))
    End Set
End Property
```

The final step is to implement the GetErrors() and HasErrors() methods. The GetErrors() method returns the list of errors for a specific property (or all the errors for all the properties). The HasErrors() property returns True if the Product class has one or more errors.

```
Public Function GetErrors(ByVal propertyName As String) As IEnumerable _
  Implements System.ComponentModel.INotifyDataErrorInfo.GetErrors

    If propertyName = "" Then
        ' Provide all the error collections.
        Return (errors.Values)
    Else
        ' Provice the error collection for the requested property
        ' (if it has errors).
        If errors.ContainsKey(propertyName) Then
            Return (errors(propertyName))
        Else
            Return Nothing
        End If
    End If
End Function
```

```
Public ReadOnly Property HasErrors As Boolean _
  Implements INotifyDataErrorInfo.HasErrors

    Get
        ' Indicate whether this entire object is error-free.
        Return (errors.Count > 0)
    End Get
End Property
```

To tell WPF to use the INotifyDataErrorInfo interface and use it to check for errors when a property is modified, the ValidatesOnNotifyDataErrors property of the binding must be True:

```
<TextBox Margin="5" Grid.Row="2" Grid.Column="1" x:Name="txtModelNumber"
  Text="{Binding Path=ModelNumber, Mode=TwoWay, ValidatesOnNotifyDataErrors=True,
NotifyOnValidationError=True}"></TextBox>
```

Technically, you don't need to explicitly set ValidatesOnNotifyDataErrors, because it's True by default (unlike the similar ValidatesOnDataErrors property that's used with the IDataErrorInfo interface). However, it's still a good idea to set it explicitly to make your intention to use it clear in the markup.

Incidentally, you can combine both approaches by creating a data object that throws exceptions for some types of errors and uses IDataErrorInfo or INotifyDataErrorInfo to report others. However, keep in mind that these two approaches have a broad difference. When an exception is triggered, the property is not updated in the data object. But when you use the IDataErrorInfo or INotifyDataErrorInfo interface, invalid values are allowed but flagged. The data object is updated, but you can use notifications and the BindingValidationFailed event to inform the user.

Custom Validation Rules

The approach for applying a custom validation rule is similar to applying a custom converter. You define a class that derives from ValidationRule (in the System.Windows.Controls namespace), and you override the Validate() method to perform your validation. If desired, you can add properties that accept other details that you can use to influence your validation (for example, a validation rule that examines text might include a Boolean CaseSensitive property).

Here's a complete validation rule that restricts decimal values to fall between some set minimum and maximum. By default, the minimum is set at 0, and the maximum is the largest number that will fit in the decimal data type, because this validation rule is intended for use with currency values. However, both these details are configurable through properties for maximum flexibility.

```
Public Class PositivePriceRule
    Inherits ValidationRule

    Private _min As Decimal = 0
    Private _max As Decimal = Decimal.MaxValue

    Public Property Min() As Decimal
        Get
            Return _min
        End Get
        Set(ByVal value As Decimal)
            _min = value
        End Set
    End Property
```

```
    Public Property Max() As Decimal
        Get
            Return _max
        End Get
        Set(ByVal value As Decimal)
            _max = value
        End Set
    End Property

    Public Overrides Function Validate(ByVal value As Object, _
      ByVal cultureInfo As CultureInfo) As ValidationResult
        Dim price As Decimal = 0

        Try
            If (CStr(value)).Length > 0 Then
                ' Allow number styles with currency symbols like $.
                price = Decimal.Parse(CStr(value), NumberStyles.Any, culture)
            End If
        Catch
            Return New ValidationResult(False, "Illegal characters.")
        End Try

        If (price < Min) OrElse (price > Max) Then
            Return New ValidationResult(False, _
               "Not in the range " & Min & " to " & Max & ".")
        Else
            Return New ValidationResult(True, Nothing)
        End If
    End Function

End Class
```

Notice that the validation logic uses the overloaded version of the Decimal.Parse() method that accepts a value from the NumberStyles enumeration. That's because validation is always performed *before* conversion. If you've applied both the validator and the converter to the same field, you need to be sure that your validation will succeed if there's a currency symbol present. The success or failure of the validation logic is indicated by returning a ValidationResult object. The IsValid property indicates whether the validation succeeded, and if it didn't, the ErrorContent property provides an object that describes the problem. In this example, the error content is set to a string that will be displayed in the user interface, which is the most common approach.

Once you've perfected your validation rule, you're ready to attach it to an element by adding it to the Binding.ValidationRules collection. Here's an example that uses the PositivePriceRule and sets the Maximum at 999.99:

```
<TextBlock Margin="7" Grid.Row="2">Unit Cost:</TextBlock>
  <TextBox Margin="5" Grid.Row="2" Grid.Column="1">
    <TextBox.Text>
      <Binding Path="UnitCost">
        <Binding.ValidationRules>
          <local:PositivePriceRule Max="999.99" />
        </Binding.ValidationRules>
      </Binding>
    </TextBox.Text>
  </TextBox>
</TextBox>
```

Often, you'll define a separate validation rule object for each element that uses the same type of rule. That's because you might want to adjust the validation properties (such as the minimum and maximum in the PositivePriceRule) separately. If you know that you want to use *exactly* the same validation rule for more than one binding, you can define the validation rule as a resource and simply point to it in each binding using the StaticResource markup extension.

As you've probably gathered, the Binding.ValidationRules collection can take an unlimited number of rules. When the value is committed to the source, WPF checks each validation rule, in order. (Remember, a value in a text box is committed to the source when the text box loses focus, unless you specify otherwise with the UpdateSourceTrigger property.) If all the validation succeeds, WPF then calls the converter (if one exists) and applies the value to the source.

▓ **Note** If you add the PositivePriceRule followed by the ExceptionValidationRule, the PositivePriceRule will be evaluated first. It will capture errors that result from an out-of-range value. However, the ExceptionValidationRule will catch type-casting errors that result if you type an entry that can't be cast to a decimal value (such as a sequence of letters).

When you perform validation with the PositivePriceRule, the behavior is the same as when you use the ExceptionValidationRule—the text box is outlined in red, the HasError and Errors properties are set, and the Error event fires. To provide the user with some helpful feedback, you need to add a bit of code or customize the ErrorTemplate. You'll learn how to take care of both approaches in the following sections.

▓ **Tip** Custom validation rules can be extremely specific so that they target a specific constraint for a specific property or much more general so that they can be reused in a variety of scenarios. For example, you could easily create a custom validation rule that validates a string using a regular expression you specify, with the help of .NET's System. Text.RegularExpressions.Regex class. Depending on the regular expression you use, you could use this validation rule with a variety of pattern-based text data, such as e-mail addresses, phone numbers, IP addresses, and ZIP codes.

Reacting to Validation Errors

In the previous example, the only indication the user receives about an error is a red outline around the offending text box. To provide more information, you can handle the Error event, which fires whenever an error is stored or cleared. However, you must first be sure you've set the Binding.NotifyOnValidationError property to True:

```
<Binding Path="UnitCost" NotifyOnValidationError="True">
```

The Error event is a routed event that uses bubbling, so you can handle the Error event for multiple controls by attaching an event handler in the parent container, as shown here:

```
<Grid Name="gridProductDetails" Validation.Error="validationError">
```

Here's the code that reacts to this event and displays a message box with the error information. (A less disruptive option would be to show a tooltip or display the error information somewhere else in the window.)

```
Private Sub validationError(ByVal sender As Object, _
  ByVal e As ValidationErrorEventArgs)
    If e.Action = ValidationErrorEventAction.Added Then
```

```
        MessageBox.Show(e.Error.ErrorContent.ToString())
    End If
End Sub
```

The ValidationErrorEventArgs.Error property provides a ValidationError object that bundles together several useful details, including the exception that caused the problem (Exception), the validation rule that was violated (ValidationRule), the associated Binding object (BindingInError), and any custom information that the ValidationRule object has returned (ErrorContent).

If you're using custom validation rules, you'll almost certainly choose to place the error information in the ValidationError.ErrorContent property. If you're using the ExceptionValidationRule, the ErrorContent property will return the Message property of the corresponding exception. However, there's a catch. If an exception occurs because the data type cannot be cast to the appropriate value, the ErrorContent works as expected and reports the problem. However, if the property setter in the data object throws an exception, this exception is wrapped in a TargetInvocationException, and the ErrorContent provides the text from the TargetInvocationException.Message property, which is the much less helpful warning "Exception has been thrown by the target of an invocation."

Thus, if you're using your property setters to raise exceptions, you'll need to add code that checks the InnerException property of the TargetInvocationException. If it's not a null reference (Nothing), you can retrieve the original exception object and use its Message property instead of the ValidationError.ErrorContent property.

Getting a List of Errors

At certain times, you might want to get a list of all the outstanding errors in your current window (or a given container in that window). This task is relatively straightforward—all you need to do is walk through the element tree testing the Validation.HasError property of each element.

The following code routine demonstrates an example that specifically searches out invalid data in TextBox objects. It uses recursive code to dig down through the entire element hierarchy. Along the way, the error information is aggregated into a single message that's then displayed to the user.

```
Private Sub cmdOK_Click(ByVal sender As Object, ByVal e As RoutedEventArgs)
    Dim message As String
    If FormHasErrors(message) Then
        ' Errors still exist.
        MessageBox.Show(message)
    Else
        ' There are no errors. You can continue on to complete the task
        ' (for example, apply the edit to the data source.).
    End If
End Sub

Private Function FormHasErrors(ByRef message As String) As Boolean
    Dim sb As New StringBuilder()
    GetErrors(sb, gridProductDetails)
    message = sb.ToString()
    Return (message <> "")
End Function

Private Sub GetErrors(ByVal sb As StringBuilder, ByVal obj As DependencyObject)
    For Each child As Object In LogicalTreeHelper.GetChildren(obj)
        Dim element As TextBox = CType(child,TextBox)
```

```
        If element Is Nothing Then
            Continue For
        End If

        If Validation.GetHasError(element) Then
            sb.Append((element.Text & " has errors:" & vbCrLf))
            For Each error As ValidationError In Validation.GetErrors(element)
                sb.Append("  " & error.ErrorContent.ToString())
                sb.Append("" & vbCrLf)
            Next
        End If

        ' Check the children of this object for errors.
        GetErrors(sb, element)
    Next
End Sub
```

In a more complete implementation, the FormHasErrors() method would probably create a collection of objects with error information. The cmdOK_Click() event handler would then be responsible for constructing an appropriate message.

Showing a Different Error Indicator

To get the most out of WPF validation, you'll want to create your own error template that flags errors in an appropriate way. At first glance, this seems like a fairly low-level way to go about reporting an error—after all, a standard control template gives you the ability to customize the composition of a control in minute detail. However, an error template isn't like an ordinary control template.

Error templates use the *adorner layer*, which is a drawing layer that exists just above ordinary window content. Using the adorner layer, you can add a visual embellishment to indicate an error without replacing the control template of the control underneath or changing the layout in your window. The standard error template for a text box works by adding a red Border element that floats just above the corresponding text box (which remains unchanged underneath). You can use an error template to add other details such as images, text, or some other sort of graphical detail that draws attention to the problem.

The following markup shows an example. It defines an error template that uses a green border and adds an asterisk next to the control with the invalid input. The template is wrapped in a style rule so that it's automatically applied to all the text boxes in the current window:

```
<Style TargetType="{x:Type TextBox}">
  <Setter Property="Validation.ErrorTemplate">
    <Setter.Value>
      <ControlTemplate>
        <DockPanel LastChildFill="True">
          <TextBlock DockPanel.Dock="Right" Foreground="Red"
          FontSize="14" FontWeight="Bold">*</TextBlock>
          <Border BorderBrush="Green" BorderThickness="1">
            <AdornedElementPlaceholder></AdornedElementPlaceholder>
          </Border>
        </DockPanel>
      </ControlTemplate>
    </Setter.Value>
  </Setter>
</Style>
```

The AdornedElementPlaceholder is the glue that makes this technique work. It represents the control itself, which exists in the element layer. By using the AdornedElementPlaceholder, you can arrange your content in relation to the text box underneath.

As a result, the border in this example is placed directly overtop of the text box, no matter what its dimensions are. The asterisk in this example is placed just to the right (as shown in Figure 19-5). Best of all, the new error template content is superimposed on top of the existing content without triggering any change in the layout of the original window. (In fact, if you're careless and include too much content in the adorner layer, you'll end up overwriting other portions of the window.)

Figure 19-5. *Flagging an error with an error template*

■ **Tip** If you want your error template to appear superimposed over the element (rather than positioned around it), you can place both your content and the AdornerElementPlaceholder in the same cell of a Grid. Alternatively, you can leave out the AdornerElementPlaceholder altogether, but then you lose the ability to position your content precisely in relation to the element underneath.

This error template still suffers from one problem—it doesn't provide any additional information about the error. To show these details, you need to extract them using data binding. One good approach is to take the error content of the first error and use it for tooltip text of your error indicator. Here's a template that does exactly that:

```
<ControlTemplate>
  <DockPanel LastChildFill="True">
    <TextBlock DockPanel.Dock="Right"
      Foreground="Red" FontSize="14" FontWeight="Bold"
      ToolTip="{Binding ElementName=adornerPlaceholder,
              Path=AdornedElement.(Validation.Errors)[0].ErrorContent}"
    >*</TextBlock>
```

```
    <Border BorderBrush="Green" BorderThickness="1">
      <AdornedElementPlaceholder Name="adornerPlaceholder">
      </AdornedElementPlaceholder>
    </Border>
  </DockPanel>
</ControlTemplate>
```

The Path of the binding expression is a little convoluted and bears closer examination. The source of this binding expression is the AdornedElementPlaceholder, which is defined in the control template:

```
ToolTip="{Binding ElementName=adornerPlaceholder, ...
```

The AdornedElementPlaceholder class provides a reference to the element underneath (in this case, the TextBox object with the error) through a property named AdornedElement:

```
ToolTip="{Binding ElementName=adornerPlaceholder,
         Path=AdornedElement ...
```

To retrieve the actual error, you need to check the Validation.Errors property of this element. However, you need to wrap the Validation.Errors property in parentheses to indicate that it's an attached property, rather than a property of the TextBox class:

```
ToolTip="{Binding ElementName=adornerPlaceholder,
         Path=AdornedElement.(Validation.Errors) ...
```

Finally, you need to use an indexer to retrieve the first ValidationError object from the collection and then extract its Error content property:

```
ToolTip="{Binding ElementName=adornerPlaceholder,
         Path=AdornedElement.(Validation.Errors)[0].ErrorContent}"
```

Now you can see the error message when you move the mouse over the asterisk.

Alternatively, you might want to show the error message in a tooltip for the Border or TextBox itself so that the error message appears when the user moves the mouse over any portion of the control. You can perform this trick without the help of a custom error template—all you need is a trigger on the TextBox control that reacts when Validation.HasError becomes True and applies the tooltip with the error message. Here's an example:

```
<Style TargetType="{x:Type TextBox}">
  ...
  <Style.Triggers>
    <Trigger Property="Validation.HasError" Value="True">
      <Setter Property="ToolTip"
        Value="{Binding RelativeSource={RelativeSource Self},
        Path=(Validation.Errors)[0].ErrorContent}" />
    </Trigger>
  </Style.Triggers>
</Style>
```

Figure 19-6 shows the result.

Figure 19-6. *Turning a validation error message into a tooltip*

Validating Multiple Values

The approaches you've seen so far allow you to validate individual values. However, there are many situations where you need to perform validation that incorporates two or more bound values. For example, a Project object isn't valid if its StartDate falls after its EndDate. An Order object shouldn't have a Status of Shipped and a blank ShipDate. A Product shouldn't have a ManufacturingCost greater than the RetailPrice. And so on.

There are various ways to design your application to deal with these limitations. In some cases, it makes sense to build a smarter user interface. (For example, if some fields aren't appropriate based on the information on other fields, you may choose to disable them.) In other situations, you'll build this logic into the data class itself. (However, this won't work if the data is valid in some situations but just not acceptable in a particular editing task.) And lastly, you can use *binding groups* to create custom validation rules that apply this sort of rule through WPF's data binding system.

The basic idea behind binding groups is simple. You create a custom validation rule that derives from the ValidationRule class, as you saw earlier. But instead of applying that validation rule to a single binding expression, you attach it to the container that holds all your bound controls. (Typically, this is the same container that has the DataContext set with the data object.) WPF then uses that to validate the entire data object when an edit is committed, which is known as *item-level validation*.

For example, the following markup creates a binding group for a Grid by setting the BindingGroup property (which all elements include). It then adds a single validation rule, named NoBlankProductRule. The rule automatically applies to the bound Product object that's stored in the Grid.DataContext property.

```
<Grid Name="gridProductDetails"
 DataContext="{Binding ElementName=lstProducts, Path=SelectedItem}">

  <Grid.BindingGroup>
    <BindingGroup x:Name="productBindingGroup">
      <BindingGroup.ValidationRules>
        <local:NoBlankProductRule></local:NoBlankProductRule>
      </BindingGroup.ValidationRules>
```

```
        </BindingGroup>
    </Grid.BindingGroup>

    <TextBlock Margin="7">Model Number:</TextBlock>
    <TextBox Margin="5" Grid.Column="1" Text="{Binding Path=ModelNumber}">
    </TextBox>

    ...
</Grid>
```

In the validation rules you've seen so far, the Validate() method receives a single value to inspect. But when using binding groups, the Validate() method receives a BindingGroup object instead. This BindingGroup wraps your bound data object (in this case, a Product).

Here's how the Validate() method begins in the NoBlankProductRule class:

```
Public Overloads Overrides Function Validate(ByVal value As Object, _
   ByVal cultureInfo As System.Globalization.CultureInfo) As ValidationResult
        Dim bindingGroup As BindingGroup = CType(value, BindingGroup)
        Dim product As Product = CType(bindingGroup.Items(0), Product)
    ...
End Function
```

You'll notice that the code retrieves the first object from the BindingGroup.Items collection. In this example, there is just a single data object. But it is possible (albeit less common) to create binding groups that apply to different data objects. In this case, you receive a collection with all the data objects.

▨ **Note** To create a binding group that applies to more than one data object, you must set the BindingGroup.Name property to give your binding group a descriptive name. You then set the BindingGroupName property in your binding expressions to match:

```
Text="{Binding Path=ModelNumber, BindingGroupName=MyBindingGroup}"
```

This way, each binding expression explicitly opts in to the binding group, and you can use the same binding group with expressions that work on different data objects.

There's another unexpected difference in the way the Validate() method works with a binding group. By default, the data object you receive is for the original object, with none of the new changes applied. To get the new values you want to validate, you need to call the BindingGroup.GetValue() method and pass in your data object and the property name:

```
Dim newModelName As String = CStr(bindingGroup.GetValue(product, "ModelName"))
```

This design makes a fair bit of sense. By holding off on actually applying the new value to the data object, WPF ensures that the change won't trigger other updates or synchronization tasks in your application before they make sense.

Here's the complete code for the NoBlankProductRule:

```
Public Class NoBlankProductRule
    Inherits ValidationRule

    Public Overloads Overrides Function Validate(ByVal value As Object, _
      ByVal cultureInfo As System.Globalization.CultureInfo) As ValidationResult
        Dim bindingGroup As BindingGroup = CType(value, BindingGroup)

        ' This product has the original values.
        Dim product As Product = CType(bindingGroup.Items(0), Product)

        ' Check the new values.
        Dim newModelName As String = CStr( _
          bindingGroup.GetValue(product, "ModelName"))
        Dim newModelNumber As String = CStr( _
          bindingGroup.GetValue(product, "ModelNumber"))

        If newModelName = "" And newModelNumber = "" Then
            Return New ValidationResult(False, _
              "A product requires a ModelName or ModelNumber.")
        Else
            Return New ValidationResult(True, Nothing)
        End If
    End Function
End Class
```

When using item-level validation, you'll usually need to create a tightly coupled validation rule like this one. That's because the logic doesn't usually generalize that easily (in other words, it's unlikely to apply to a similar but slightly different case with another data object). You also need to use the specific property name when calling GetValue(). As a result, the validation rules you create for item-level validation probably won't be as neat, streamlined, and reusable as those you create for validating individual values.

As it stands, the current example isn't quite finished. Binding groups use a transactional editing system, which means that it's up to you to officially commit the edit before your validation logic runs. The easiest way to do this is to call the BindingGroup.CommitEdit() method. You can use an event handler that runs when a button is clicked or when an editing control loses focus, as shown here:

```
<Grid Name="gridProductDetails" TextBox.LostFocus="txt_LostFocus"
 DataContext="{Binding ElementName=lstProducts, Path=SelectedItem}">
```

And here's the event handling code:

```
Private Sub txt_LostFocus(ByVal sender As Object, ByVal e As RoutedEventArgs)
    productBindingGroup.CommitEdit()
End Sub
```

If validation fails, the entire Grid is considered invalid and is outlined with a thin red border. As with edit controls like the TextBox, you can change the Grid's appearance by modifying its Validation.ErrorTemplate.

■ **Note** Item-level validation works more seamlessly with the DataGrid control you'll explore in Chapter 22. It handles the transactional aspects of editing, triggering field navigation when the user moves from one cell to another, and calling BindingGroup.CommitEdit() when the user moves from one row to another.

Data Providers

In most of the examples you've seen, the top-level data source has been supplied by programmatically setting the DataContext of an element or the ItemsSource property of a list control. In general, this is the most flexible approach, particularly if your data object is constructed by another class (such as StoreDB). However, you have other options.

One technique is to define your data object as a resource in your window (or some other container). This works well if you can construct your object declaratively, but it makes less sense if you need to connect to an outside data store (such as a database) at runtime. However, some developers still use this approach (often in a bid to avoid writing event handling code). The basic idea is to create a wrapper object that fetches the data you need in its constructor. For example, you could create a resource section like this:

```
<Window.Resources>
  <ProductListSource x:Key="products"></ProductListSource>
</Window.Resources>
```

Here, ProductListSource is a class that derives from ObservableCollection<Products>. Thus, it has the ability to store a list of products. It also has some basic logic in the constructor that calls StoreDB.GetProducts() to fill itself.

Now, other elements can use this in their binding:

```
<ListBox ItemsSource="{StaticResource products}" ... >
```

This approach seems tempting at first, but it's a bit risky. When you add error handling, you'll need to place it in the ProductListSource class. You may even need to show a message explaining the problem to the user. As you can see, this approach mingles the data model, the data access code, and the user interface code in a single muddle, so it doesn't make much sense when you need to access outside resources (files, databases, and so on).

Data providers are, in some ways, an extension of this model. A data provider gives you the ability to bind directly to an object that you define in the resources section of your markup. However, instead of binding directly to the data object itself, you bind to a data provider that's able to retrieve or construct that object. This approach makes sense if the data provider is full-featured—for example, if it can raise events when exceptions occur and provides properties that allow you to configure other details about its operation. Unfortunately, the data providers that are included in WPF aren't yet up to this standard. They're too limited to be worth the trouble in a situation with external data (for example, when fetching the information from a database or a file). They may make sense in simpler scenarios—for example, you could use a data provider to glue together some controls that supply input to a class that calculates a result. However, they add relatively little in this situation except the ability to reduce event handling code in favor of markup.

All data providers derive from the System.Windows.Data.DataSourceProvider class. Currently, WPF provides just two data providers:

- *ObjectDataProvider*, which gets information by calling a method in another class

- *XmlDataProvider*, which gets information directly from an XML file

The goal of both of these objects is to allow you to instantiate your data object in XAML, without resorting to event handling code.

▓ **Note** There's still one more option: you can explicitly create a view object as a resource in your XAML, bind your controls to the view, and fill your view with data in code. This option is primarily useful if you want to customize the view by applying sorting and filtering, although it's also preferred by some developers as a matter of taste. In Chapter 21, you'll learn how to use views.

The ObjectDataProvider

The ObjectDataProvider allows you to get information from another class in your application. It adds the following features:

- It can create the object you need and pass parameters to the constructor.
- It can call a method in that object and pass method parameters to it.
- It can create the data object asynchronously. (In other words, it can wait until after the window is loaded and then perform the work in the background.)

For example, here's a basic ObjectDataProvider that creates an instance of the StoreDB class, calls its GetProducts() method, and makes the data available to the rest of your window:

```
<Window.Resources>
  <ObjectDataProvider x:Key="productsProvider" ObjectType="{x:Type local:StoreDB}"
    MethodName="GetProducts"></ObjectDataProvider>
</Window.Resources>
```

You can now create a binding that gets the source from the ObjectDataProvider:

```
<ListBox Name="lstProducts" DisplayMemberPath="ModelName"
 ItemsSource="{Binding Source={StaticResource productsProvider}}"></ListBox>
```

This tag looks like it binds to the ObjectDataProvider, but the ObjectDataProvider is intelligent enough to know you really want to bind to the product list that it returns from the GetProducts() method.

▓ **Note** The ObjectDataProvider, like all data providers, is designed to retrieve data but not update it. In other words, there's no way to force the ObjectDataProvider to call a different method in the StoreDB class to trigger an update. This is just one example of how the data provider classes in WPF are less mature than other implementations in other frameworks, such as the data source controls in ASP.NET.

Error Handling

As written, this example has a giant limitation. When you create this window, the XAML parser creates the window and calls the GetProducts() method so it can set up the binding. Everything runs smoothly if the GetProducts() method returns the data you want, but the result isn't as nice if an unhandled exception is thrown (for example, if the database is too busy or isn't reachable). At this point, the exception bubbles up from the InitializeComponent() call in the window constructor. The code that's showing this window needs to catch this error, which is conceptually confusing. And there's no way to continue and show the window—even if you catch the exception in the constructor, the rest of the window won't be initialized properly.

Unfortunately, there's no easy way to solve this problem. The ObjectDataProvider class includes an IsInitialLoadEnabled property that you can set to False to prevent it from calling GetProducts() when the window is first created. If you set this, you can call Refresh() later to trigger the call. Unfortunately, if you use this technique, your binding expression will fail, because the list won't be able to retrieve its data source. (This is unlike most data binding errors, which fail silently without raising an exception.)

So, what's the solution? You can construct the ObjectDataProvider programmatically, although you'll lose the benefit of declarative binding, which is the reason you probably used the ObjectDataProvider in the first place. Another solution is to configure the ObjectDataProvider to perform its work asynchronously, as described in the next section. In this situation, exceptions cause a silent failure (although a trace message will still be displayed in the Debug window detailing the error).

Asynchronous Support

Most developers will find that there aren't many reasons for using the ObjectDataProvider. Usually, it's easier to simply bind directly to your data object and add the tiny bit of code that calls the class that queries the data (such as StoreDB). However, there is one reason that you might use the ObjectDataProvider—to take advantage of its support for asynchronous data querying.

```
<ObjectDataProvider IsAsynchronous="True" ... >
```

It's deceptively simple. As long as you set the ObjectDataProvider.IsAsynchronous property to True, the ObjectDataProvider performs its work on a background thread. As a result, your interface isn't tied up while the work is underway. Once the data object has been constructed and returned from the method, the ObjectDataProvider makes it available to all bound elements.

■ **Tip** If you don't want to use the ObjectDataProvider, you can still launch your data access code asynchronously. The trick is to use WPF's support for multithreaded applications. One useful tool is the BackgroundWorker component that's described in Chapter 31. When you use the BackgroundWorker, you gain the benefit of optional cancellation support and progress reporting. However, incorporating the BackgroundWorker into your user interface is more work than simply setting the ObjectDataProvider.IsAsynchronous property.

ASYNCHRONOUS DATA BINDINGS

WPF also provides asynchronous support through the IsAsync property of each Binding object. However, this feature is far less useful than the asynchronous support in the ObjectDataProvider. When you set Binding.IsAsync to True, WPF retrieves the bound property from the data object asynchronously. However, the data object itself is still created synchronously.

For example, imagine you create an asynchronous binding for the StoreDB example that looks like this:

```
<TextBox Text="{Binding Path=ModelNumber, IsAsync=True}" />
```

Even though you're using an asynchronous binding, you'll still be forced to wait while your code queries the database. Once the product collection is created, the binding will query the Product.ModelNumber property of the current product object asynchronously. This behavior has little benefit, because the property procedures in the Product class take a trivial amount of time to execute. In fact, all well-designed data objects are built out of lightweight properties such as this, which is one reason that the WPF team had serious reservations about providing the Binding.IsAsync property at all!

The only way to take advantage of Binding.IsAsync is to build a specialized class that includes time-consuming logic in a property get procedure. For example, consider an analysis application that binds to a data model. This data object might include a piece of information that's calculated using a time-consuming algorithm. You could bind to this property using an asynchronous binding but bind to all the other properties with synchronous bindings. That way, some information will appear immediately in your application, and the additional information will appear once it's ready.

WPF also includes a priority binding feature that builds on asynchronous bindings. Priority binding allows you to supply several asynchronous bindings in a prioritized list. The highest-priority binding is preferred, but if it's still being evaluated, a lower-priority binding is used instead. Here's an example:

```
<TextBox>
  <TextBox.Text>
    <PriorityBinding>
      <Binding Path="SlowSpeedProperty" IsAsync="True" />
      <Binding Path="MediumSpeedProperty" IsAsync="True" />
      <Binding Path="FastSpeedProperty" />
    </PriorityBinding>
  </TextBox.Text>
</TextBox>
```

This assumes that the current data context contains an object with three properties named SlowSpeedProperty, MediumSpeedProperty, and FastSpeedProperty. The bindings are placed in their order of importance. As a result, SlowSpeedProperty is always used to set the text, if it's available. But if the first binding is still in the midst of reading SlowSpeedProperty (in other words, there is time-consuming logic in the property get procedure), MediumSpeedProperty is used instead. If that's not available, FastSpeedProperty is used. For this approach to work, you must make all the binding asynchronous, except the fastest, lowest-priority binding at the end of the list. This binding can be asynchronous (in which case the text box will appear empty until the value is retrieved) or synchronous (in which case the window won't be frozen until the synchronous binding has finished its work).

The XmlDataProvider

The XmlDataProvider provides a quick and straightforward way to extract XML data from a separate file, web location, or application resource and make it available to the elements in your application. The XmlDataProvider is designed to be read-only (in other words, it doesn't provide the ability to commit changes), and it isn't able to deal with XML data that may come from other sources (such as a database record, a web service message, and so on). As a result, it's a fairly specific tool.

If you've used .NET to work with XML in the past, you already know that .NET provides a rich set of libraries for reading, writing, and manipulating XML. You can use streamlined reader and writer classes that allow you to step through XML files and handle each element with custom code, you can use XPath or the DOM to hunt for specific bits of content, and you can use serializer classes to convert entire objects to and from an XML representation. Each of these approaches has advantages and disadvantages, but all of them are more powerful than the XmlDataProvider.

If you foresee needing the ability to modify XML or to convert XML data into an object representation that you can work with in your code, you're better off using the extensive XML support that already exists in .NET. The fact that your data is stored in an XML representation then becomes a low-level detail that's irrelevant to the way you construct your user interface. (Your user interface can simply bind to data objects, as in the database-backed examples you've seen in this chapter.) However, if you absolutely must have a quick way to extract XML content and your requirements are relatively light, the XmlDataProvider is a reasonable choice.

To use the XmlDataProvider, you begin by defining it and pointing it to the appropriate file by setting the Source property.

```
<XmlDataProvider x:Key="productsProvider" Source="store.xml"></XmlDataProvider>
```

You can also set the Source programmatically (which is important if you aren't sure what the file name is that you need to use). By default, the XmlDataProvider loads the XML content asynchronously, unless you explicitly set XmlDataProvider.IsAsynchronous to False.

Here's a portion of the simple XML file used in this example. It wraps the entire document in a top-level Products element and places each product in a separate Product element. The individual properties for each product are provided as nested elements.

```
<Products>
  <Product>
    <ProductID>355</ProductID>
    <CategoryID>16</CategoryID>
    <ModelNumber>RU007</ModelNumber>
    <ModelName>Rain Racer 2000</ModelName>
    <ProductImage>image.gif</ProductImage>
    <UnitCost>1499.99</UnitCost>
    <Description>Looks like an ordinary bumbershoot ... </Description>
  </Product>
  <Product>
    <ProductID>356</ProductID>
    <CategoryID>20</CategoryID>
    <ModelNumber>STKY1</ModelNumber>
    <ModelName>Edible Tape</ModelName>
    <ProductImage>image.gif</ProductImage>
    <UnitCost>3.99</UnitCost>
    <Description>The latest in personal survival gear ... </Description>
  </Product>
  ...
</Products>
```

To pull information from your XML, you use XPath expressions. XPath is a powerful standard that allows you to retrieve the portions of a document that interest you. Although a full discussion of XPath is beyond the scope of this book, it's easy to sketch out the essentials.

XPath uses a pathlike notation. For example, the path / identifies the root of an XML document, and /Products identifies a root element named <Products>. The path /Products/Product selects every <Product> element inside the <Products> element.

When using XPath with the XmlDataProvider, your first task is to identify the root node. In this case, that means selecting the <Products> element that contains all the data. (If you wanted to focus on a specific section of the XML document, you would use a different top-level element.)

```
<XmlDataProvider x:Key="productsProvider" Source="/store.xml"
  XPath="/Products"></XmlDataProvider>
```

The next step is to bind your list. When working the XmlDataProvider, you use the Binding.XPath property instead of the Binding.Path property. This gives you the flexibility to dig into your XML as deeply as you need.

Here's the markup that pulls out all the <Product> elements:

```
<ListBox Name="lstProducts" Margin="5" DisplayMemberPath="ModelName"
 ItemsSource="{Binding Source={StaticResource products}, XPath=Product}" ></ListBox>
```

When setting the XPath property in a binding, you need to remember that your expression is relative to the current position in the XML document. For that reason, you don't need to supply the full path /Products/Product in the list binding. Instead, you can simply use the relative path Product, which starts from the <Products> node that was selected by the XmlDataProvider.

Finally, you need to wire up each of the elements that displays the product details. Once again, the XPath expression you write is evaluated relative to the current node (which will be the <Product> element for the current product). Here's an example that binds to the <ModelNumber> element:

```
<TextBox Text="{Binding XPath=ModelNumber}"></TextBox>
```

Once you make these changes, you'll be left with an XML-based example that's nearly identical to the object-based bindings you've seen so far. The only difference is that all the data is treated as ordinary text. To convert it to a different data type or a different representation, you'll need to use a value converter.

The Last Word

This chapter took a thorough look at data binding. You learned how to create data binding expressions that draw information from custom objects and how to push changes back to the source. You also learned how to use change notification, bind entire collections, and bind to the ADO.NET DataSet.

In many ways, WPF data binding is designed to be an all-purpose solution for automating the way that elements interact and for mapping the object model of an application to its user interface. Although WPF applications are still new, those that exist today use data binding much more frequently and thoroughly than their Windows Forms counterparts. In WPF, data binding is much more than an optional frill, and every professional WPF developer needs to master it.

You haven't reached the end of your data exploration yet. You still have several topics to tackle. In the following chapters, you'll build on the data binding basics you've learned here and tackle these new topics:

- *Data formatting*: You've learned how to get your data but not necessarily how to make it look good. In Chapter 20, you'll learn to format numbers and dates, and you'll go far further with styles and data templates that allow you to customize the way records are shown in a list.

- *Data views*: In every application that uses data binding, there's a data view at work. Often, you can ignore this piece of background plumbing. But if you take a closer look, you can use it to write navigation logic and apply filtering and sorting. Chapter 21 shows the way.

- *Advanced data controls*: For richer data display options, WPF gives you the ListView, TreeView, and DataGrid. All three support data binding with remarkable flexibility. Chapter 22 describes them all.

CHAPTER 20

Formatting Bound Data

In Chapter 19, you learned the essentials of WPF data binding—how to pull information out of an object and display it in a window, with little code required. Along the way, you considered how to make that information editable, how to deal with collections of data objects, and how to perform validation to catch bad edits. However, there's still a lot more to learn.

In this chapter, you'll continue your exploration by tackling several subjects that will allow you to build better bound windows. First you'll look at data conversion, the powerful and extensible system WPF uses to examine values and convert them. As you'll discover, this process of conversion goes far beyond simple conversion, giving you the ability to apply conditional formatting and deal with images, files, and other types of specialized content.

Next you'll look at how you can format entire lists of data. You'll review the infrastructure that supports bound lists, starting with the base ItemsControl class. Then you'll learn how to refine the appearance of lists with styles, along with triggers that apply alternating formatting and selection highlighting. Finally, you'll use the most powerful formatting tool of all, *data templates*, which let you customize the way each item is shown in an ItemsControl. Data templates are the secret to converting a basic list into a rich data presentation tool complete with custom formatting, picture content, and additional WPF controls.

Data Binding Redux

In most data-binding scenarios, you aren't binding to a single object but to an entire collection. Figure 20-1 shows a familiar example—a form with a list of products. When the user selects a product, its details appear on the right.

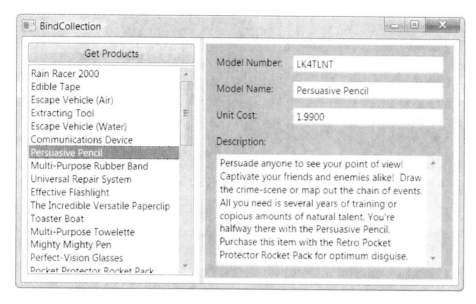

Figure 20-1. *Browsing a collection of products*

In Chapter 19, you learned to build exactly this sort of form. Here's a quick review of the basic steps:

1. First you need to create the list of items, which you can show in an ItemsControl. Set the DisplayMemberPath to indicate the property (or field) you want to show for each item in the list. This list shows the model name of each item:

```
<ListBox Name="lstProducts" DisplayMemberPath="ModelName"></ListBox>
```

2. To fill the list with data, set the ItemsSource property to your collection (or DataTable). Typically, you'll perform this step in code when your window loads or the user clicks a button. In this example, the ItemsControl is bound to an ObservableCollection of Product objects.

```
Dim products As ObservableCollection(Of Product)
products = Application.StoreDB.GetProducts()
lstProducts.ItemsSource = products
```

3. To show item-specific information, add as many elements as you need, each with a binding expression that identifies the property or field you want to display. In this example, each item in the collection is a Product object. Here's an example that shows the model number of an item by binding to the Product.ModelNumber property:

```
<TextBox Text="{Binding Path=ModelNumber}"></TextBox>
```

4. The easiest way to connect the item-specific elements to the currently selected item is to wrap them in a single container. Set the DataContext property of the container to refer to the selected item in the list:

```
<Grid DataContext="{Binding ElementName=lstProducts, Path=SelectedItem}">
```

So far, this is all review. However, what you haven't yet considered is how to tailor the appearance of the data list and the data fields. For example, you don't yet know how to format numeric values, how to create a list that shows multiple pieces of information at once (and arranges these pieces in a pleasing way), and how to deal with nontext content, such as picture data. In this chapter, you'll cover all these tasks as you begin to build more-respectable data forms.

Data Conversion

In a basic binding, the information travels from the source to the target without any change. This seems logical, but it's not always the behavior you want. Often your data source might use a low-level representation that you don't want to display directly in your user interface. For example, you might have numeric codes you want to replace with human-readable strings, numbers that need to be cut down to size, dates that need to be displayed in a long format, and so on. If so, you need a way to convert these values into the right display form. And if you're using a two-way binding, you also need to do the converse—take user-supplied data and convert it to a representation suitable for storage in the appropriate data object.

Fortunately, WPF has two tools that can help you:

String formatting: This feature allows you to convert data that's represented as text—for example, strings that contain dates and numbers—by setting the Binding.StringFormat property. It's a convenient technique that works for at least half of all formatting tasks.

Value converters: This is a far more powerful (and somewhat more complicated) feature that lets you convert any type of source data into any type of object representation, which you can then pass on to the linked control.

In the following sections, you'll consider both approaches.

Using the StringFormat Property

String formatting is the perfect tool for formatting numbers that need to be displayed as text. For example, consider the UnitCost property from the Product class introduced in the previous chapter. UnitCost is stored as a decimal, and, as a result, when it's displayed in a text box, you'll see values such as 3.9900. Not only does this display format show more decimal places than you'd probably like, it also leaves out the currency symbol. A more intuitive representation would be the currency-formatted value $3.99.

The easiest solution is to set the Binding.StringFormat property. WPF will use the format string to convert the raw text to its display value, just before it appears in the control. Just as important, WPF will (in most cases) use this string to perform the reverse conversion, taking any edited data and using it to update the bound property.

When setting the Binding.StringFormat property, you use standard .NET format strings, in the form {0:C}. Here, the *0* represents the first value, and the *C* refers to the format string you want to apply—which is, in this case, the standard local-specific currency format, which translates 3.99 to $3.99 on a US computer. The entire expression is wrapped in curly braces.

Here's an example that applies the format string to the UnitCost field so that it's displayed as a currency value:

```
<TextBox Margin="5" Grid.Row="2" Grid.Column="1"
 Text="{Binding Path=UnitCost, StringFormat={}{0:C}}">
</TextBox>
```

You'll notice that the StringFormat value is preceded with the curly braces {}. In full, it's {}{0:C} rather than just {0:C}. The slightly unwieldy pair of braces at the beginning is required to escape the string. Otherwise, the XAML parser can be confused by the curly brace at the beginning of {0:C}.

Incidentally, the {} escape sequence is required only when the StringFormat value begins with a brace. Consider this example, which adds a literal sequence of text before each formatted value:

```
<TextBox Margin="5" Grid.Row="2" Grid.Column="1"
 Text="{Binding Path=UnitCost, StringFormat=The value is {0:C}.}">
</TextBox>
```

This expression converts a value such as 3.99 to "The value is $3.99." Because the first character in the StringFormat value is an ordinary letter, not a brace, the initial escape sequence isn't required. However, this format string works in one direction only. If the user tries to supply an edited value that includes this literal text (such as "The value is $4.25"), the update will fail. On the other hand, if the user performs an edit with the numeric characters only (4.25) or with the numeric characters and the currency symbol ($4.25), the edit will succeed, and the binding expression will convert it to the display text "The value is $4.25" and show that in the text box.

To get the results you want with the StringFormat property, you need the right format string. You can learn about all the format strings that are available in the Visual Studio help. However, Table 20-1 and Table 20-2 show some of the most common options you'll use for numeric and date values, respectively. And here's a binding expression that uses a custom date format string to format the OrderDate property:

```
<TextBlock Text="{Binding Date, StringFormat={}{0:MM/dd/yyyy}}"></TextBlock>
```

Table 20-1. *Format Strings for Numeric Data*

Type	Format String	Example
Currency	C	$1,234.50. Parentheses indicate negative values: ($1,234.50). The currency sign is locale-specific.
Scientific (Exponential)	E	1.234.50E+004.
Percentage	P	45.6%.
Fixed Decimal	F?	Depends on the number of decimal places you set. F3 formats values such as 123.400. F0 formats values such as 123.

Table 20-2. *Format Strings for Times and Dates*

Type	Format String	Format
Short Date	d	M/d/yyyy For example: 10/30/2008
Long Date	D	dddd, MMMM dd, yyyy For example: Wednesday, January 30, 2008
Long Date and Short Time	f	dddd, MMMM dd, yyyy HH:mm aa For example: Wednesday, January 30, 2008 10:00 AM
Long Date and Long Time	F	dddd, MMMM dd, yyyy HH:mm:ss aa For example: Wednesday, January 30, 2008 10:00:23 AM
ISO Sortable Standard	s	yyyy-MM-dd HH:mm:ss For example: 2008-01-30 10:00:23
Month and Day	M	MMMM dd For example: January 30
General	G	M/d/yyyy HH:mm:ss aa (depends on locale-specific settings) For example: 10/30/2008 10:00:23 AM

The WPF list controls also support string formatting for list items. To use it, you simply set the ItemStringFormat property of the list (which is inherited from the base ItemsControl class). Here's an example with a list of product prices:

```
<ListBox Name="lstProducts" DisplayMemberPath="UnitCost" ItemStringFormat="{0:C}">
</ListBox>
```

The formatting string is automatically passed down to the binding that grabs the text for each item.

Introducing Value Converters

The Binding.StringFormat property is created for simple, standard formatting with numbers and dates. But many data-binding scenarios need a more powerful tool, called a *value converter* class.

A value converter plays a straightforward role. It's responsible for converting the source data just before it's displayed in the target and (in the case of a two-way binding) converting the new target value just before it's applied back to the source.

▓ **Note** This approach to conversion is similar to the way data binding worked in the world of Windows Forms with the Format and Parse binding events. The difference is that in a Windows Forms application, you could code this logic anywhere—you simply needed to attach both events to the binding. In WPF, this logic must be encapsulated in a value converter class, which makes for easier reuse.

Value converters are an extremely useful piece of the WPF data-binding puzzle. They can be used in several useful ways:

> *To format data to a string representation*: For example, you can convert a number to a currency string. This is the most obvious use of value converters, but it's certainly not the only one.

> *To create a specific type of WPF object*: For example, you could read a block of binary data and create a BitmapImage object that can be bound to an Image element.

> *To conditionally alter a property in an element based on the bound data*: For example, you might create a value converter that changes the background color of an element to highlight values in a specific range.

Formatting Strings with a Value Converter

To get a basic idea of how a value converter works, it's worth revisiting the currency-formatting example you looked at in the previous section. Although that example used the Binding.StringFormat property, you can accomplish the same thing—and more—with a value converter. For example, you could round or truncate values (changing 3.99 to 4), use number names (changing 1,000,000 into 1 million), or even add a dealer markup (multiplying 3.99 by 15%). You can also tailor the way that the reverse conversion works to change user-supplied values into the right data values in the bound object.

To create a value converter, you need to take four steps:

1. Create a class that implements IValueConverter.

2. Add the ValueConversion attribute to the class declaration, and specify the destination and target data types.

3. Implement a Convert() method that changes data from its original format to its display format.

4. Implement a ConvertBack() method that does the reverse and changes a value from display format to its native format.

Figure 20-2 shows how it works.

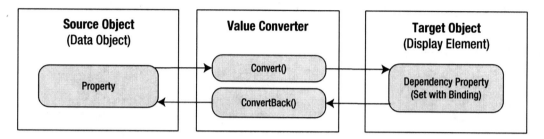

Figure 20-2. *Converting bound data*

In the case of the decimal-to-currency conversion, you can use the Decimal.ToString() method to get the formatted string representation you want. You simply need to specify the currency format string "C", as shown here:

```
Dim currencyText As String = decimalPrice.ToString("C")
```

This code uses the culture settings that apply to the current thread. A computer that's configured for the English (United States) region runs with a locale of en-US and displays currencies with the dollar sign ($). A computer that's configured for another locale might display a different currency symbol. (This is the same way that the {0:C} format string works when applied with the Binding.StringFormat property.) If this isn't the result you want (for example, you always want the dollar sign to appear), you can specify a culture by using the overload of the ToString() method shown here:

```
Dim culture As New CultureInfo("en-US")
string currencyText = decimalPrice.ToString("C", culture)
```

Converting from the display format back to the number you want is a little trickier. The Parse() and TryParse() methods of the Decimal type are logical choices to do the work, but ordinarily they can't handle strings that include currency symbols. The solution is to use an overloaded version of the Parse() or TryParse() method that accepts a System.Globalization.NumberStyles value. If you supply NumberStyles.Any, you'll be able to successfully strip out the currency symbol, if it exists.

Here's the complete code for the value converter that deals with price values such as the Product.UnitCost property:

```
<ValueConversion(GetType(Decimal), GetType(String))> _
Public Class PriceConverter
    Implements IValueConverter

    Public Function Convert(ByVal value As Object, ByVal targetType As Type, _
      ByVal parameter As Object, ByVal culture As CultureInfo) As Object _
      Implements IValueConverter.Convert
        Dim price As Decimal = CDec(value)
        Return price.ToString("c", culture)
    End Function
```

```
   Public Function ConvertBack(ByVal value As Object, _
     ByVal targetType As Type, ByVal parameter As Object, _
     ByVal culture As CultureInfo) As Object _
     Implements IValueConverter.ConvertBack
       Dim price As String = value.ToString(culture)

       Dim result As Decimal
       If Decimal.TryParse(price, NumberStyles.Any, culture, result) Then
           Return result
       End If
       Return value
   End Function

End Class
```

To put this converter into action, you need to begin by mapping your project namespace to an XML namespace prefix you can use in your markup. Here's an example that uses the namespace prefix *local* and assumes that your value converter is in the namespace DataBinding:

```
xmlns:local="clr-namespace:DataBinding"
```

Typically, you'll add this attribute to the <Window> tag that holds all your markup.

Now you simply need to create an instance of the PriceConverter class and assign it to the Converter property of your binding. To do this, you need the more long-winded syntax shown here:

```
<TextBlock Margin="7" Grid.Row="2">Unit Cost:</TextBlock>
<TextBox Margin="5" Grid.Row="2" Grid.Column="1">
  <TextBox.Text>
    <Binding Path="UnitCost">
      <Binding.Converter>
        <local:PriceConverter></local:PriceConverter>
      </Binding.Converter>
    </Binding>
  </TextBox.Text>
</TextBox>
```

In many cases, the same converter is used for multiple bindings. In this case, it doesn't make sense to create an instance of the converter for each binding. Instead, create one converter object in the Resources collection, as shown here:

```
<Window.Resources>
  <local:PriceConverter x:Key="PriceConverter"></local:PriceConverter>
</Window.Resources>
```

Then you can point to it in your binding by using a StaticResource reference, as described in Chapter 10:

```
<TextBox Margin="5" Grid.Row="2" Grid.Column="1"
 Text="{Binding Path=UnitCost, Converter={StaticResource PriceConverter}}">
</TextBox>
```

Creating Objects with a Value Converter

Value converters are indispensable when you need to bridge the gap between the way data is stored in your classes and the way it's displayed in a window. For example, imagine you have picture data stored as a byte array in a field in a database. You could convert the binary data into a System.Windows.Media.Imaging.BitmapImage object and store that as part of your data object. However, this design might not be appropriate.

For example, you might need the flexibility to create more than one object representation of your image, possibly because your data library is used in both WPF applications and Windows Forms applications (which use the System.Drawing.Bitmap class instead). In this case, it makes sense to store the raw binary data in your data object and convert it to a WPF BitmapImage object by using a value converter. (To bind it to a form in a Windows Forms application, you'd use the Format and Parse events of the System.Windows.Forms.Binding class.)

■ **Tip** To convert a block of binary data into an image, you must first create a BitmapImage object and read the image data into a MemoryStream. Then you can call the BitmapImage.BeginInit() method, set its StreamSource property to point to your MemoryStream, and call EndInit() to finish loading the image.

The Products table from the Store database doesn't include binary picture data, but it does include a ProductImage field that stores the file name of an associated product image. In this case, there's even more reason to delay creating the image object. First, the image might not be available, depending on where the application's running. Second, there's no point in incurring the extra memory overhead for storing the image unless it's going to be displayed.

The ProductImage field includes the file name but not the full path of an image file, which gives you the flexibility to put the image files in any suitable location. The value converter has the task of creating a URI that points to the image file based on the ProductImage field and the directory you want to use. The directory is stored by using a custom property named ImageDirectory, which defaults to the current directory.

Here's the complete code for the ImagePathConverter that performs the conversion:

```
Public Class ImagePathConverter
    Implements IValueConverter

    Private _imageDirectory As String = Directory.GetCurrentDirectory()
    Public Property ImageDirectory() As String
        Get
            Return _imageDirectory
        End Get
        Set(ByVal value As String)
            _imageDirectory = value
        End Set
    End Property

    Public Function Convert(ByVal value As Object, ByVal targetType As Type, _
      ByVal parameter As Object, ByVal culture As CultureInfo) As Object _
      Implements IValueConverter.Convert
        Dim imagePath As String
        imagePath = System.IO.Path.Combine(ImageDirectory, CStr(value))
        Return New BitmapImage(New Uri(imagePath))
    End Function
```

```
    Public Function ConvertBack(ByVal value As Object, _
      ByVal targetType As Type, ByVal parameter As Object, _
      ByVal culture As CultureInfo) As Object _
      Implements IValueConverter.ConvertBack
        Throw New NotSupportedException()
    End Function

End Class
```

To use this converter, begin by adding it to the Resources. In this example, the ImageDirectory property is not set, which means the ImagePathConverter defaults to the current application directory:

```
<Window.Resources>
  <local:ImagePathConverter x:Key="ImagePathConverter"></local:ImagePathConverter>
</Window.Resources>
```

Now it's easy to create a binding expression that uses this value converter:

```
<Image Margin="5" Grid.Row="2" Grid.Column="1" Stretch="None"
 HorizontalAlignment="Left" Source=
 "{Binding Path=ProductImagePath, Converter={StaticResource ImagePathConverter}}">
</Image>
```

This works because the Image.Source property expects an ImageSource object, and the BitmapImage class derives from ImageSource.

Figure 20-3 shows the result.

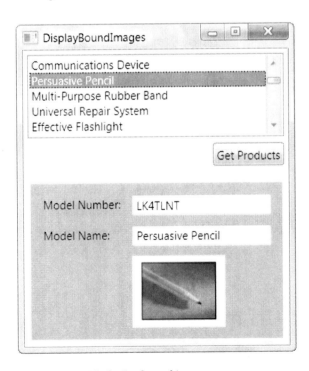

Figure 20-3. *Displaying bound images*

You might improve this example in a couple of ways. First, attempting to create a BitmapImage that points to a nonexistent file causes an exception, which you'll receive when setting the DataContext, ItemsSource, or Source property. Alternatively, you can add properties to the ImagePathConverter class that allow you to configure this behavior. For example, you might introduce a Boolean SuppressExceptions property. If set to True, you could catch exceptions in the Convert() method and then return the Binding.DoNothing value (which tells WPF to temporarily act as though no data binding is set). Or you could add a DefaultImage property that takes a placeholder BitmapImage. The ImagePathConverter could then return the default image if an exception occurs.

You'll also notice that this converter supports only one-way conversion. That's because it's not possible to change the BitmapImage object and use that to update the image path. However, you could take an alternate approach. Rather than return a BitmapImage from the ImagePathConverter, you could simply return the fully qualified URI from the Convert() method, as shown here:

```
Return New Uri(imagePath)
```

This works just as successfully, because the Image element uses a type converter to translate the Uri to the ImageSource object it really wants. If you take this approach, you could then allow the user to choose a new file path (perhaps using a TextBox that's set with the help of the OpenFileDialog class). You could then extract the file name in the ConvertBack() method and use that to update the image path that's stored in your data object.

Applying Conditional Formatting

Some of the most interesting value converters aren't designed to format data for presentation. Instead, they're intended to format some other appearance-related aspect of an element based on a data rule.

For example, imagine you want to flag high-priced items by giving them a different background color. You can easily encapsulate this logic with the following value converter:

```
Public Class PriceToBackgroundConverter
    Implements IValueConverter

    Private _minimumPriceToHighlight As Decimal
    Public Property MinimumPriceToHighlight() As Decimal
        Get
            Return _minimumPriceToHighlight
        End Get
        Set(ByVal value As Decimal)
            _minimumPriceToHighlight = value
        End Set
    End Property

    Private _highlightBrush As Brush
    Public Property HighlightBrush() As Brush
        Get
            Return _highlightBrush
        End Get
        Set(ByVal value As Brush)
            _highlightBrush = value
        End Set
    End Property
```

```
    Private _defaultBrush As Brush
    Public Property DefaultBrush() As Brush
        Get
            Return _defaultBrush
        End Get
        Set(ByVal value As Brush)
            _defaultBrush = value
        End Set
    End Property

    Public Function Convert(ByVal value As Object, ByVal targetType As Type, _
      ByVal parameter As Object, ByVal culture As CultureInfo) As Object _
      Implements IValueConverter.Convert
        Dim price As Decimal = CDec(value)
        If price >= MinimumPriceToHighlight Then
            Return HighlightBrush
        Else
            Return DefaultBrush
        End If
    End Function

    Public Function ConvertBack(ByVal value As Object, _
      ByVal targetType As Type, ByVal parameter As Object, _
      ByVal culture As CultureInfo) As Object _
      Implements IValueConverter.ConvertBack
        Throw New NotSupportedException()
    End Function

End Class
```

Once again, the value converter is carefully designed with reusability in mind. Rather than hard-coding the color highlights in the converter, they're specified in the XAML by the code that *uses* the converter:

```
<local:PriceToBackgroundConverter x:Key="PriceToBackgroundConverter"
  DefaultBrush="{x:Null}" HighlightBrush="Orange" MinimumPriceToHighlight="50">
</local:PriceToBackgroundConverter>
```

Brushes are used instead of colors so that you can create more-advanced highlight effects by using gradients and background images. And if you want to keep the standard, transparent background (so the background of the parent elements is used), just set the DefaultBrush or HighlightBrush property to a null reference (Nothing).

Now all that's left is to use this converter to set the background of some element, such as the Border that contains all the other elements:

```
<Border Background=
  "{Binding Path=UnitCost, Converter={StaticResource PriceToBackgroundConverter}}"
  ... >
```

OTHER WAYS TO APPLY CONDITIONAL FORMATTING

Using a custom value converter is only one of the ways to apply conditional formatting based on your data object. You can also use data triggers in a style, style selector, and template selector, all of which are described in this chapter. Each one of these approaches has its own advantages and disadvantages.

The value converter approach works best when you need to set a single property in an element based on the bound data object. It's easy, and it's automatically synchronized. If you make changes to the bound data object, the linked property is changed immediately.

Data triggers are similarly straightforward, but they support only extremely simple logic that tests for equality. For example, a data trigger can apply formatting that applies to products in a specific category, but it can't apply formatting that kicks in when the price is greater than a specific minimum value. The key advantage of data triggers is that you can use them to apply certain types of formatting and selection effects without writing any code.

Style selectors and template selectors are the most powerful options. They allow you to change multiple properties in the target element at once and change the way items are presented in the list. However, they introduce additional complexity. Also, you need to add code that reapplies your styles and templates if the bound data changes.

Evaluating Multiple Properties

So far, you've used binding expressions to convert one piece of source data into a single, formatted result. And although you can't change the second part of this equation (the result), you *can* create a binding that evaluates or combines the information in more than one source property, with a little craftiness.

The first trick is to replace your Binding object with a MultiBinding. Then you define the arrangement of bound properties by using the MultiBinding.StringFormat property. Here's an example that turns Joe and Smith into "Smith, Joe" and displays the result in a TextBlock:

```
<TextBlock>
  <TextBlock.Text>
    <MultiBinding StringFormat="{1}, {0}">
      <Binding Path="FirstName"></Binding>
      <Binding Path="LastName"></Binding>
    </MultiBinding>
  </TextBlock.Text>
</TextBlock>
```

You'll notice in this example that the two fields are used as is in the StringFormat property. Alternatively, you can use format strings to change it. For example, if you were combining a text value and a currency value with a MultiBinding, you might set StringFormat to "{0} costs {1:C}."

If you want to do anything more ambitious with the two source fields than simply stitching them together, you need the help of a value converter. You can use this technique to perform calculations (such as multiplying UnitPrice by UnitsInStock) or apply formatting that takes several details into consideration (such as highlighting all high-priced products in a specific category). However, your value converter must implement IMultiValueConverter rather than IValueConverter.

Here's an example in which a MultiBinding uses the UnitCost and UnitsInStock properties from the source object and combines them by using a value converter:

```
<TextBlock>Total Stock Value: </TextBlock>
<TextBox>
  <TextBox.Text>
    <MultiBinding Converter="{StaticResource ValueInStockConverter}">
      <Binding Path="UnitCost"></Binding>
      <Binding Path="UnitsInStock"></Binding>
    </MultiBinding>
  </TextBox.Text>
</TextBox>
```

The IMultiValueConverter interface defines similar Convert() and ConvertBack() methods as the IValueConverter interface. The main difference is that you're provided with an array of values rather than a single value. These values are placed in the same order that they're defined in your markup. Thus, in the previous example, you can expect UnitCost to appear first, followed by UnitsInStock.

Here's the code for the ValueInStockConverter:

```
Public Class ValueInStockConverter
    Implements IMultiValueConverter

    Public Function Convert(ByVal values As Object(), _
      ByVal targetType As Type, ByVal parameter As Object, _
      ByVal culture As CultureInfo) As Object _
      Implements IMultiValueConverter.Convert
        ' Return the total value of all the items in stock.
        Dim unitCost As Decimal = CDec(values(0))
        Dim unitsInStock As Integer = CInt(Fix(values(1)))
        Return unitCost * unitsInStock
    End Function

    Public Function ConvertBack(ByVal value As Object, _
      ByVal targetTypes As Type(), ByVal parameter As Object, _
      ByVal culture As CultureInfo) As Object() _
      Implements IMultiValueConverter.ConvertBack
        Throw New NotSupportedException()
    End Function

End Class
```

List Controls

String formatting and value converters are all you need to apply flexible formatting to individual bound values. But bound lists need a bit more. Fortunately, WPF provides no shortage of formatting choices. Most of these are built into the base ItemsControl class from which all list controls derive, so this is where your list-formatting exploration should start.

As you know, the ItemsControl class defines the basic functionality for controls that wrap a list of items. Those items can be entries in a list, nodes in a tree, commands in a menu, buttons in a toolbar, and so on. Figure 20-4 provides an at-a-glance overview of all the ItemsControl classes in WPF.

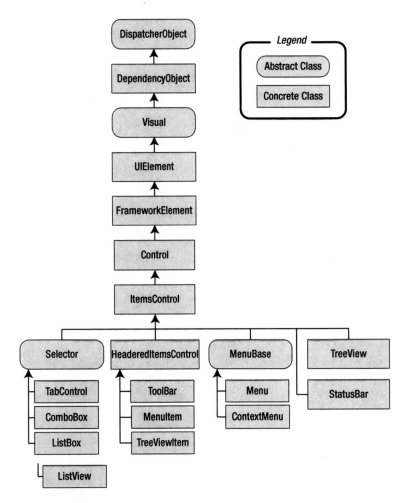

Figure 20-4. *Classes that derive from ItemsControl*

■ **Note**   You'll notice that some item wrappers appear in the hierarchy of classes that derive from ItemsControl. For example, not only will you see the expected Menu and TreeView classes, but you'll also see MenuItem and TreeViewItem. That's because these classes have the ability to contain their own collection of items—that's what gives trees and menus their nested, hierarchical structure. On the other hand, you won't find ComboBoxItem or ListBoxItem in this list, because they don't need to hold a child collection of items and so don't derive from ItemsControl.

The ItemsControl defines the properties that support data binding and two key formatting features: styles and data templates. You'll explore both features in the following sections, and Table 20-3 gives you a quick overview of the properties that support them. The table is loosely organized from more-basic features to more-advanced ones, and it also mirrors the order you'll explore them in this chapter.

Table 20-3. *Formatting-Related Properties of the ItemsControl Class*

Name	Description
ItemsSource	The bound data source (the collection or DataView that you want to display in the list).
DisplayMemberPath	The property that you want to display for each data item. For a more sophisticated representation or to use a combination of properties, use the ItemTemplate instead.
ItemStringFormat	A .NET format string that, if set, will be used to format the text for each item. Usually, this technique is used to convert numeric or date values into a suitable display representation, exactly as the Binding.StringFormat property does.
ItemContainerStyle	A style that allows you to set the properties of the container that wraps each item. The container depends on the type of list (for example, it's ListBoxItem for the ListBox class and ComboBoxItem for the ComboBox class). These wrapper objects are created automatically as the list is filled.
ItemContainerStyleSelector	A StyleSelector that uses code to choose a style for the wrapper of each item in the list. This allows you to give different styles to different items in the list. You must create a custom StyleSelector yourself.
AlternationCount	The number of alternating sets in your data. For example, an AlternationCount of 2 alternates between two row styles, an AlternationCount of 3 alternates between three row styles, and so on.
ItemTemplate	A template that extracts the appropriate data out of your bound object and arranges it into the appropriate combination of controls.
ItemTemplateSelector	A DataTemplateSelector that uses code to choose a template for each item in the list. This allows you to give different templates to different items. You must create a custom DataTemplateSelector class yourself.
ItemsPanel	Defines the panel that's created to hold the items of the list. All the item wrappers are added to this container. Usually, a VirtualizingStackPanel is used with a vertical (top-to-bottom) orientation.
GroupStyle	If you're using grouping, this is a style that defines how each group should be formatted. When using grouping, the item wrappers (ListBoxItem, ComboBoxItem, and so on) are added in GroupItem wrappers that represent each group, and these groups are then added to the list. Grouping is demonstrated in Chapter 21.
GroupStyleSelector	A StyleSelector that uses code to choose a style for each group. This allows you to give different styles to different groups. You must create a custom StyleSelector yourself.

The next rung in the ItemsControl inheritance hierarchy is the Selector class, which adds a straightforward set of properties for determining (and setting) a selected item. Not all ItemsControl classes support selection. For example, selection doesn't have any meaning for the ToolBar or Menu, so these classes derive from ItemsControl but not Selector.

The properties that the Selector class adds include SelectedItem (the selected data object), SelectedIndex (the position of the selected item), and SelectedValue (the "value" property of the selected data object, which you designate by setting SelectedValuePath). Notice that the Selector class doesn't provide support for multiple selection—that's added to the ListBox through its SelectionMode and SelectedItems properties (which is essentially all the ListBox class adds to this model).

List Styles

For the rest of this chapter, you'll be concentrating on two features that are provided by all the WPF list controls: styles and data templates.

Out of these two tools, styles are simpler (and less powerful). In many cases, they allow you to add a bit of formatting polish. In the following sections, you'll see how styles let you format list items, apply alternating-row formatting, and apply conditional formatting according to the criteria you specify.

The ItemContainerStyle

In Chapter 11, you learned how styles allow you to reuse formatting with similar elements in different places. Styles play much the same role with lists—they allow you to apply a set of formatting characteristics to each of the individual items.

This is important, because WPF's data-binding system generates list item objects automatically. As a result, it's not so easy to apply the formatting you want to individual items. The solution is the ItemContainerStyle property. If the ItemContainerStyle is set, the list control will pass it down to each of its items, as the item is created. In the case of a ListBox control, each item is represented by a ListBoxItem object. (In a ComboBox, it's ComboBoxItem, and so on.) Thus, any style you apply with the ListBox.ItemContainerStyle property is used to set the properties of each ListBoxItem object.

Here's one of the simplest possible effects that you can achieve with the ListBoxItem. It applies a blue-gray background to each item. To make sure the individual items stand apart from each other (rather than having their backgrounds merge together), the style also adds some margin space:

```
<ListBox Name="lstProducts" Margin="5" DisplayMemberPath="ModelName">
  <ListBox.ItemContainerStyle>
    <Style>
      <Setter Property="ListBoxItem.Background" Value="LightSteelBlue" />
      <Setter Property="ListBoxItem.Margin" Value="5" />
      <Setter Property="ListBoxItem.Padding" Value="5" />
    </Style>
  </ListBox.ItemContainerStyle>
</ListBox>
```

On its own, this isn't terribly interesting. However, the style becomes a bit more polished with the addition of triggers. In the following example, property triggers change the background color and add a solid border when the ListBoxItem.IsSelected property becomes True. Figure 20-5 shows the result.

```
<ListBox Name="lstProducts" Margin="5" DisplayMemberPath="ModelName">
  <ListBox.ItemContainerStyle>
    <Style TargetType="{x:Type ListBoxItem}">
      <Setter Property="Background" Value="LightSteelBlue" />
      <Setter Property="Margin" Value="5" />
      <Setter Property="Padding" Value="5" />

      <Style.Triggers>
        <Trigger Property="IsSelected" Value="True">
          <Setter Property="Background" Value="DarkRed" />
          <Setter Property="Foreground" Value="White" />
          <Setter Property="BorderBrush" Value="Black" />
          <Setter Property="BorderThickness" Value="1" />
        </Trigger>
```

```
          </Style.Triggers>
      </Style>
   </ListBox.ItemContainerStyle>
</ListBox>
```

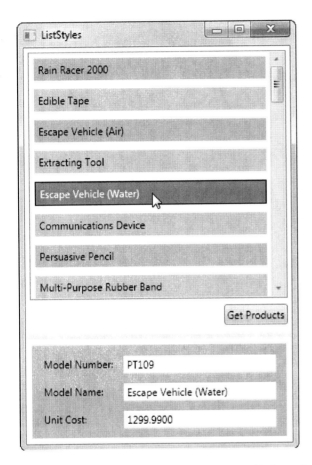

Figure 20-5. *Use style triggers to change the highlighting for the selected item*

For cleaner markup, this style uses the Style.TargetType property so that it can set properties without including the class name in each setter.

This use of triggers is particularly handy, because the ListBox doesn't provide any other way to apply targeted formatting to the selected item. In other words, if you don't use a style, you're stuck with the standard blue highlighting.

Later in this chapter, when you use data templates to completely revamp data lists, you'll once again rely on the ItemContainerStyle to change the selected item effect.

A ListBox with Check Boxes or Radio Buttons

The ItemContainerStyle is also important if you want to reach deep into a list control and change the control template that its items use. For example, you can use this technique to make every ListBoxItem display a radio button or a check box next to its item text.

Figure 20-6 and Figure 20-7 show two examples—one with a list filled with RadioButton elements (only one of which can be chosen at a time) and one with a list of CheckBox elements. The two solutions are similar, but the list with radio buttons is slightly easier to create.

Figure 20-6. *A radio button list using a template*

Figure 20-7. *A check box list using a template*

▓ **Note**   At first glance, using templates to change the ListBoxItem might seem like more work than it's worth. After all, it's easy enough to solve the problem by composition. All you need to do is fill a ScrollViewer with a series of CheckBox objects. However, this implementation doesn't provide the same programming model. There's no easy way to iterate through all the check boxes, and, more important, there's no way to use this implementation with data binding.

The basic technique in this example is to change the control template used as the container for each list item. You don't want to modify the ListBox.Template property, because this provides the template for the ListBox. Instead, you need to modify the ListBoxItem.Template property. Here's the template you need to wrap each item in a RadioButton element:

```
<ControlTemplate TargetType="{x:Type ListBoxItem}">
  <RadioButton Focusable="False" IsChecked="{Binding Path=IsSelected,
RelativeSource={RelativeSource TemplatedParent},Mode=TwoWay}">
    <ContentPresenter></ContentPresenter>
  </RadioButton>
</ControlTemplate>
```

This works because a RadioButton is a content control and can contain any content. Although you could use a binding expression to get the content, it's far more flexible to use the ContentPresenter element, as shown here. The ContentPresenter grabs whatever would ordinarily appear in the item, which might be property text (if you're using the ListBox.DisplayMemberPath property) or a more complex representation of the data (if you're using the ListBox.ItemTemplate property).

The real trick is the binding expression for the RadioButton.IsChecked property. This expression retrieves the value of the ListBoxItem.IsSelected property by using the Binding.RelativeSource property. That way, when you click a RadioButton to select it, the corresponding ListBoxItem is marked as selected. At the same time, all other items are deselected. This binding expression also works in the other direction, which means you can set the selection in code and the right RadioButton will be filled in.

To complete this template, you need to set the RadioButton.Focusable property to False. Otherwise, you'll be able to tab to the currently selected ListBoxItem (which is focusable) and then into the RadioButton itself, which doesn't make much sense.

To set the ListBoxItem.Template property, you need a style rule that can dig down to the right level. Thanks to the ItemContainerStyle property, this part is easy:

```
<Window.Resources>
  <Style x:Key="RadioButtonListStyle" TargetType="{x:Type ListBox}">
    <Setter Property="ItemContainerStyle">
      <Setter.Value>
        <Style TargetType="{x:Type ListBoxItem}" >
          <Setter Property="Margin" Value="2" />
          <Setter Property="Template">
            <Setter.Value>
              <ControlTemplate TargetType="{x:Type ListBoxItem}">
                <RadioButton Focusable="False"
                 IsChecked="{Binding Path=IsSelected, Mode=TwoWay,
                            RelativeSource={RelativeSource TemplatedParent} }">
                  <ContentPresenter></ContentPresenter>
                </RadioButton>
              </ControlTemplate>
            </Setter.Value>
```

```
          </Setter>
        </Style>
      </Setter.Value>
    </Setter>
  </Style>
</Window.Resources>
```

Although you could set the ListBox.ItemContainerStyle property directly, this example factors it out one more level. The style that sets the ListBoxItem.Control template is wrapped in another style that applies this style to the ListBox.ItemContainerStyle property. This makes the template reusable, allowing you to connect it to as many ListBox objects as you want.

```
<ListBox Style="{StaticResource RadioButtonListStyle}" Name="lstProducts"
 DisplayMemberPath="ModelName">
```

You could also use the same style to adjust other properties of the ListBox.

Creating a ListBox that shows check boxes is just as easy. In fact, you have to make only two changes. First, replace the RadioButton element with an identical CheckBox element. Then change the ListBox.SelectionMode property to allow simple multiple selection. Now the user can check as many or as few items as desired.

Here's the style rule that transforms an ordinary ListBox into a list of check boxes:

```
<Style x:Key="CheckBoxListStyle" TargetType="{x:Type ListBox}">
  <Setter Property="SelectionMode" Value="Multiple"></Setter>
  <Setter Property="ItemContainerStyle">
    <Setter.Value>
      <Style TargetType="{x:Type ListBoxItem}" >
        <Setter Property="Margin" Value="2" />
        <Setter Property="Template">
          <Setter.Value>
            <ControlTemplate TargetType="{x:Type ListBoxItem}">
              <CheckBox Focusable="False"
               IsChecked="{Binding Path=IsSelected, Mode=TwoWay,
                          RelativeSource={RelativeSource TemplatedParent} }">
                <ContentPresenter></ContentPresenter>
              </CheckBox>
            </ControlTemplate>
          </Setter.Value>
        </Setter>
      </Style>
    </Setter.Value>
  </Setter>
</Style>
```

Alternating Item Style

One common way to format a list is to use alternating row formatting—in other words, a set of formatting characteristics that distinguishes every second item in a list. Often, alternating rows are given subtly different background colors so that the rows are clearly separated, as shown in Figure 20-8.

Figure 20-8. *Alternating-row highlighting*

WPF has built-in support for alternating items through two properties: AlternationCount and AlternationIndex.

AlternationCount is the number of items that form a sequence, after which the style alternates. By default, AlternationCount is set to 0, and alternating formatting isn't used. If you set AlternationCount to 1, the list will alternate after every item, which allows you to apply the even-odd formatting pattern shown in Figure 20-8.

Every ListBoxItem is given an AlternationIndex, which allows you to determine how it's numbered in the sequence of alternating items. Assuming you've set AlternationCount to 2, the first ListBoxItem gets an AlternationIndex of 0, the second gets an AlternationIndex of 1, the third gets an AlternationIndex of 0, the fourth gets an AlternationIndex of 1, and so on. The trick is to use a trigger in your ItemContainerStyle that checks the AlternationIndex value and varies the formatting accordingly.

For example, the ListBox control shown here gives alternate items a slightly different background color (unless the item is selected, in which case the higher-priority trigger for ListBoxItem.IsSelected wins out):

```
<ListBox Name="lstProducts" Margin="5" DisplayMemberPath="ModelName"
 AlternationCount="2">
  <ListBox.ItemContainerStyle>
    <Style TargetType="{x:Type ListBoxItem}">
      <Setter Property="Background" Value="LightSteelBlue" />
      <Setter Property="Margin" Value="5" />
      <Setter Property="Padding" Value="5" />
        <Style.Triggers>
          <Trigger Property="ItemsControl.AlternationIndex" Value="1">
            <Setter Property="Background" Value="LightBlue" />
          </Trigger>
          <Trigger Property="IsSelected" Value="True">
            <Setter Property="Background" Value="DarkRed" />
            <Setter Property="Foreground" Value="White" />
            <Setter Property="BorderBrush" Value="Black" />
            <Setter Property="BorderThickness" Value="1" />
          </Trigger>
```

```
          </Style.Triggers>
        </Style>
    </ListBox.ItemContainerStyle>
</ListBox>
```

You'll notice that AlternationIndex is an attached property that's defined by the ListBox class (or, technically, the ItemsControl class that it derives from). It's not defined in the ListBoxItem class, so when you use it in a style trigger, you need to specify the class name.

Interestingly, alternating items don't need to be every second item. Instead, you can create more-complex alternating formatting that alternates in a sequence of three or more. For example, to use three groups, set AlternationCount to 3, and write triggers for any of the three possible AlternationIndex values (0, 1, or 2). In the list, items 1, 4, 7, 10, and so on, will have an AlternationIndex of 0. Items 2, 5, 8, 11, and so on, get an AlternationIndex of 1. And finally, items 3, 6, 9, 12, and so on, get an AltenationIndex of 2.

Style Selectors

You've now seen how to vary the style based on the selection state of the item or its position in the list. However, you might want to use a number of other conditions—criteria that depend on your data rather than the ListBoxItem container that holds it.

To deal with this situation, you need a way to give different items completely different styles. Unfortunately, there's no way to do this declaratively. Instead, you need to build a specialized class that derives from StyleSelector. This class has the responsibility of examining each data item and choosing the appropriate style. This work is performed in the SelectStyle() method, which you must override.

Here's a rudimentary selector that chooses between two styles:

```
Public Class ProductByCategoryStyleSelector
    Inherits StyleSelector

    Public Overrides Function SelectStyle(ByVal item As Object, _
      ByVal container As DependencyObject) As Style
        Dim product As Product = CType(item, Product)
        Dim window As Window = Application.Current.MainWindow

        If product.CategoryName = "Travel" Then
            Return CType(window.FindResource("TravelProductStyle"), _
              Style)
        Else
            Return CType(window.FindResource("DefaultProductStyle"), _
              Style)
        End If
    End Function
End Class
```

In this example, products that are in the Travel category get one style, while all other products get another. In this example, both styles you want to use must be defined in the Resources collection of the window, with the key names TravelProductStyle and DefaultProductStyle.

This style selector works, but it's not perfect. One problem is that your code depends on details that are in the markup, which means there's a dependency that isn't enforced at compile time and could easily be disrupted (for example, if you give your styles the wrong resource keys). The other problem is that this style selector hard-codes the value it's looking for (in this case, the category name), which limits reuse.

A better idea is to create a style selector that uses one or more properties to allow you to specify some of these details, such as the criteria you're using to evaluate your data items and the styles you want to use. The following style selector is still quite simple but extremely flexible. It's able to examine any data object, look for a given property, and compare that property against another value to choose between two styles. The property, property value, and styles are all specified as properties. The SelectStyle() method uses reflection to find the right property in a manner similar to the way data bindings work when digging out bound values.

Here's the complete code:

```vb
Public Class SingleCriteriaHighlightStyleSelector
    Inherits StyleSelector

    Private _defaultStyle As Style
    Public Property DefaultStyle() As Style
        Get
            Return _defaultStyle
        End Get
        Set(ByVal value As Style)
            _defaultStyle = value
        End Set
    End Property

    Private _highlightStyle As Style
    Public Property HighlightStyle() As Style
        Get
            Return _highlightStyle
        End Get
        Set(ByVal value As Style)
            _highlightStyle = value
        End Set
    End Property

    Private _propertyToEvaluate As String
    Public Property PropertyToEvaluate() As String
        Get
            Return _propertyToEvaluate
        End Get
        Set(ByVal value As String)
            _propertyToEvaluate = value
        End Set
    End Property

    Private _propertyValueToHighlight As String
    Public Property PropertyValueToHighlight() As String
        Get
            Return _propertyValueToHighlight
        End Get
        Set(ByVal value As String)
            _propertyValueToHighlight = value
        End Set
    End Property
```

```
      Public Overrides Function SelectStyle(ByVal item As Object, _
        ByVal container As DependencyObject) As Style
          Dim product As Product = CType(item, Product)

          ' Use reflection to get the property to check.
          Dim type As Type = product.GetType()
          Dim propertyInfo As PropertyInfo = type.GetProperty(PropertyToEvaluate)

          ' Decide if this product should be highlighted
          ' based on the property value.
          If propertyInfo.GetValue(product, Nothing).ToString() = _
            PropertyValueToHighlight Then
              Return HighlightStyle
          Else
              Return DefaultStyle
          End If
      End Function

End Class
```

To make this work, you'll need to create the two styles you want to use, and you'll need to create and initialize an instance of the SingleCriteriaHighlightStyleSelector.

Here are two similar styles, which are distinguished only by the background color and the use of bold formatting:

```
<Window.Resources>
  <Style x:Key="DefaultStyle" TargetType="{x:Type ListBoxItem}">
    <Setter Property="Background" Value="LightYellow" />
    <Setter Property="Padding" Value="2" />
  </Style>

  <Style x:Key="HighlightStyle" TargetType="{x:Type ListBoxItem}">
    <Setter Property="Background" Value="LightSteelBlue" />
    <Setter Property="FontWeight" Value="Bold" />
    <Setter Property="Padding" Value="2" />
  </Style>
</Window.Resources>
```

When you create the SingleCriteriaHighlightStyleSelector, you point it to these two styles. You can also create the SingleCriteriaHighlightStyleSelector as a resource (which is useful if you want to reuse it in more than one place), or you can define it inline in your list control, as in this example:

```
<ListBox Name="lstProducts" HorizontalContentAlignment="Stretch">
  <ListBox.ItemContainerStyleSelector>
    <local:SingleCriteriaHighlightStyleSelector
      DefaultStyle="{StaticResource DefaultStyle}"
      HighlightStyle="{StaticResource HighlightStyle}"
      PropertyToEvaluate="CategoryName"
      PropertyValueToHighlight="Travel"
    >
    </local:SingleCriteriaHighlightStyleSelector>
  </ListBox.ItemContainerStyleSelector>
</ListBox>
```

Here, the SingleCriteriaHighlightStyleSelector looks for a Category property in the bound data item and uses the HighlightStyle if it contains the text *Travel*. Figure 20-9 shows the result.

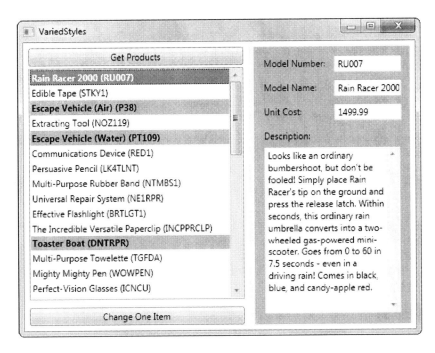

Figure 20-9. *A list with two item styles*

The style selection process is performed once, when you first bind the list. This is a problem if you're displaying editable data and it's possible for an edit to move the data item from one style category to another. In this situation, you need to force WPF to reapply the styles, and there's no graceful way to do it. The brute-force approach is to remove the style selector by setting the ItemContainerStyleSelector property to Nothing and then to reassign it:

```
Dim selector As StyleSelector = lstProducts.ItemContainerStyleSelector
lstProducts.ItemContainerStyleSelector = Nothing
lstProducts.ItemContainerStyleSelector = selector
```

You may choose to run this code automatically in response to certain changes by handling events such as PropertyChanged (which is raised by all classes that implement INotifyPropertyChanged, including Product), DataTable.RowChanged (if you're using the ADO.NET data objects), and, more generically, Binding.SourceUpdated (which fires only when Binding.NotifyOnSourceUpdated is True). When you reassign the style selector, WPF examines and updates every item in the list—a process that's quick for small or medium-size lists.

Data Templates

Styles give you some basic formatting abilities, but they don't address the most significant limitation of the lists you've seen so far: no matter how you tweak the ListBoxItem, it's only a ListBoxItem, not a more capable combination of elements. And because each ListBoxItem supports just a single bound field (as set through the DisplayMemberPath property), there's no room to make a rich list that incorporates multiple fields or images.

However, WPF does have another tool that can break out of this rather limiting box, allowing you to use a combination of properties from the bound object and lay them out in a specific way or to display a visual representation that's more sophisticated than a simple string. That tool is the data template.

A *data template* is a chunk of XAML markup that defines how a bound data object should be displayed. Two types of controls support data templates:

- Content controls support data templates through the ContentTemplate property. The content template is used to display whatever you've placed in the Content property.

- List controls (controls that derive from ItemsControl) support data templates through the ItemTemplate property. This template is used to display each item from the collection (or each row from a DataTable) that you've supplied as the ItemsSource.

The list-based template feature is actually based on content control templates. That's because each item in a list is wrapped by a content control, such as ListBoxItem for the ListBox, ComboBoxItem for the ComboBox, and so on. Whatever template you specify for the ItemTemplate property of the list is used as the ContentTemplate of each item in the list.

So, what can you put inside a data template? It's actually quite simple. A data template is an ordinary block of XAML markup. Like any other block of XAML markup, the template can include any combination of elements. It should also include one or more data-binding expressions that pull out the information that you want to display. (After all, if you don't include any data-binding expressions, each item in the list will appear the same, which isn't very helpful.)

The best way to see how a data template works is to start with a basic list that doesn't use them. For example, consider this list box, which was shown previously:

```
<ListBox Name="lstProducts" DisplayMemberPath="ModelName"></ListBox>
```

You can get the same effect with this list box that uses a data template:

```
<ListBox Name="lstProducts">
  <ListBox.ItemTemplate>
    <DataTemplate>
      <TextBlock Text="{Binding Path=ModelName}"></TextBlock>
    </DataTemplate>
  </ListBox.ItemTemplate>
</ListBox>
```

When the list is bound to the collection of products (by setting the ItemsSource property), a single ListBoxItem is created for each Product. The ListBoxItem.Content property is set to the appropriate Product object, and the ListBoxItem.ContentTemplate is set to the data template shown earlier, which extracts the value from the Product. ModelName property and displays it in a TextBlock.

So far, the results are underwhelming. But now that you've switched to a data template, there's no limit to how you can creatively present your data. Here's an example that wraps each item in a rounded border, shows two pieces of information, and uses bold formatting to highlight the model number:

```
<ListBox Name="lstProducts" HorizontalContentAlignment="Stretch">
  <ListBox.ItemTemplate>
    <DataTemplate>
      <Border Margin="5" BorderThickness="1" BorderBrush="SteelBlue"
      CornerRadius="4">
        <Grid Margin="3">
          <Grid.RowDefinitions>
            <RowDefinition></RowDefinition>
```

```
            <RowDefinition></RowDefinition>
          </Grid.RowDefinitions>
          <TextBlock FontWeight="Bold"
            Text="{Binding Path=ModelNumber}"></TextBlock>
          <TextBlock Grid.Row="1"
            Text="{Binding Path=ModelName}"></TextBlock>
        </Grid>
      </Border>
    </DataTemplate>
  </ListBox.ItemTemplate>
</ListBox>
```

When this list is bound, a separate Border object is created for each product. Inside the Border element is a Grid with two pieces of information, as shown in Figure 20-10.

Figure 20-10. *A list that uses a data template*

▨ **Tip**   When using Grid objects to lay out individual items in a list, you may want to use the SharedSizeGroup property described in Chapter 3. You can apply the SharedSizeGroup property (with a descriptive group name) to individual rows or columns to ensure that those rows and columns are made the same size for every item. Chapter 22 includes an example that uses this approach to build a rich view for the ListView that combines text and image content.

Separating and Reusing Templates

Like styles, templates are often declared as a window or application resource rather than defined in the list where you use them. This separation is often clearer, especially if you use long, complex templates or multiple templates in the same control (as described in the next section). It also gives you the ability to reuse your templates in more than one list or content control if you want to present your data the same way in different places in your user interface.

To make this work, all you need to do is to define your data template in a resources collection and give it a key name. Here's an example that extracts the template shown in the previous example:

```
<Window.Resources>
  <DataTemplate x:Key="ProductDataTemplate">
    <Border Margin="5" BorderThickness="1" BorderBrush="SteelBlue"
     CornerRadius="4">
      <Grid Margin="3">
        <Grid.RowDefinitions>
          <RowDefinition></RowDefinition>
          <RowDefinition></RowDefinition>
        </Grid.RowDefinitions>
        <TextBlock FontWeight="Bold"
         Text="{Binding Path=ModelNumber}"></TextBlock>
        <TextBlock Grid.Row="1"
         Text="{Binding Path=ModelName}"></TextBlock>
      </Grid>
    </Border>
  </DataTemplate>
</Window.Resources>
```

Now you can add your data template to the list using a StaticResource reference:

```
<ListBox Name="lstProducts" HorizontalContentAlignment="Stretch"
 ItemTemplate="{StaticResource ProductDataTemplate}"></ListBox>
```

You can use another interesting trick if you want to reuse the same data template in different types of controls automatically. You can set the DataTemplate.DataType property to identify the type of bound data for which your template should be used. For example, you could alter the previous example by removing the key and specifying that this template is intended for bound Product objects, no matter where they appear:

```
<Window.Resources>
  <DataTemplate DataType="{x:Type local:Product}">
  </DataTemplate>
</Window.Resources>
```

This assumes that you've defined an XML namespace prefix named *local* and mapped it to your project namespace.

Now this template will be used with any list or content control in this window that's bound to Product objects. You don't need to specify the ItemTemplate setting.

■ **Note** Data templates don't require data binding. In other words, you don't need to use the ItemsSource property to fill a template list. In the previous examples, you're free to add Product objects declaratively (in your XAML markup) or programmatically (by calling the ListBox.Items.Add() method). In both cases, the data template works in the same way.

Using More Advanced Templates

Data templates can be remarkably self-sufficient. Along with basic elements such as the TextBlock and data-binding expressions, they can also use more-sophisticated controls, attach event handlers, convert data to different representations, use animations, and so on.

It's worth considering a couple of quick examples that show how powerful data templates are. First, you can use value converter objects in your data binding to convert your data to a more useful representation. The following example uses the ImagePathConverter demonstrated earlier to show the image for each product in the list:

```
<Window.Resources>
  <local:ImagePathConverter x:Key="ImagePathConverter"></local:ImagePathConverter>
  <DataTemplate x:Key="ProductTemplate">
    <Border Margin="5" BorderThickness="1" BorderBrush="SteelBlue"
     CornerRadius="4">
      <Grid Margin="3">
        <Grid.RowDefinitions>
          <RowDefinition></RowDefinition>
          <RowDefinition></RowDefinition>
          <RowDefinition></RowDefinition>
        </Grid.RowDefinitions>
        <TextBlock FontWeight="Bold" Text="{Binding Path=ModelNumber}"></TextBlock>
        <TextBlock Grid.Row="1" Text="{Binding Path=ModelName}"></TextBlock>
        <Image Grid.Row="2" Grid.RowSpan="2" Source=
"{Binding Path=ProductImagePath, Converter={StaticResource ImagePathConverter}}">
        </Image>
      </Grid>
    </Border>
  </DataTemplate>
</Window.Resources>
```

Although this markup doesn't involve anything exotic, the result is a much more interesting list (see Figure 20-11).

Figure 20-11. *A list with image content*

Another useful technique is to place controls directly inside a template. For example, Figure 20-12 shows a list of categories. Next to each category is a View button that you can use to launch another window with just the matching products in that category.

Figure 20-12. *A list with button controls*

The trick in this example is handling the button clicks. Obviously, all of the buttons will be linked to the same event handler, which you define inside the template. However, you need to determine which item was clicked from the list. One solution is to store some extra identifying information in the Tag property of the button, as shown here:

```
<DataTemplate>
  <Grid Margin="3">
    <Grid.ColumnDefinitions>
      <ColumnDefinition></ColumnDefinition>
      <ColumnDefinition Width="Auto"></ColumnDefinition>
    </Grid.ColumnDefinitions>

    <TextBlock Text="{Binding Path=CategoryName}"></TextBlock>
    <Button Grid.Column="2" HorizontalAlignment="Right" Padding="2"
      Click="cmdView_Clicked" Tag="{Binding Path=CategoryID}">View ...</Button>
  </Grid>
</DataTemplate>
```

You can then retrieve the Tag property in the cmdView_Clicked event handler:

```
Private Sub cmdView_Clicked(ByVal sender As Object, ByVal e As RoutedEventArgs)
    Dim cmd As Button = CType(sender, Button)
    Dim categoryID As Integer = CType(cmd.Tag, Integer)
    ...
End Sub
```

You can use this information to take another action. For example, you might launch another window that shows products and pass the CategoryID value to that window, which can then use filtering to show only the products in that category. (One easy way to implement filtering is with data views, as described in Chapter 21.)

If you want all the information about the selected data item, you can grab the entire data object by leaving out the Path property when you define the binding:

```
<Button HorizontalAlignment="Right" Padding="1"
  Click="cmdView_Clicked" Tag="{Binding}">View ...</Button>
```

Now your event handler will receive the Product object (if you're binding a collection of Products). If you're binding to a DataTable, you'll receive a DataRowView object instead, which you can use to retrieve all the field values exactly as you would with a DataRow object.

Passing the entire object has another advantage: it makes it easier to update the list selection. In the current example, it's possible to click a button in any item, regardless of whether that item is selected. This is potentially confusing, because the user could select one item and click the View button of another item. When the user returns to the list window, the first item remains selected even though the second item was the one that was used by the previous operation. To remove the possibility for confusion, it's a good idea to move the selection to the new list item when the View button is clicked, as shown here:

```
Dim cmd As Button = CType(sender, Button)
Dim product As Product = CType(cmd.Tag, Product)
lstCategories.SelectedItem = product
```

Another option is to show the View button only in a selected item. This technique involves modifying or replacing the template you're using in this list, which is described in the "Templates and Selection" section a bit later in this chapter.

Varying Templates

One limitation with the templates you've seen so far is that you're limited to one template for the entire list. But in many situations, you'll want the flexibility to present different data items in different ways.

You can achieve this goal in several ways. Here are some common techniques:

Use a data trigger: You can use a trigger to change a property in the template based on the value of a property in the bound data object. Data triggers work like the property triggers you learned about with styles in Chapter 11, except they don't require dependency properties.

Use a value converter: A class that implements IValueConverter can convert a value from your bound object to a value you can use to set a formatting-related property in your template.

Use a template selector: A template selector examines the bound data object and chooses between several distinct templates.

Data triggers offer the simplest approach. The basic technique is to set a property of one of the elements in your template based on a property in your data item. For example, you could change the background of the custom border that wraps each list item based on the CategoryName property of the corresponding Product object. Here's an example that highlights products in the Tools category with red lettering:

```
<DataTemplate x:Key="DefaultTemplate">
  <DataTemplate.Triggers>
    <DataTrigger Binding="{Binding Path=CategoryName}" Value="Tools">
    <Setter Property="ListBoxItem.Foreground" Value="Red"></Setter>
    </DataTrigger>
  </DataTemplate.Triggers>
  <Border Margin="5" BorderThickness="1" BorderBrush="SteelBlue"
   CornerRadius="4">
    <Grid Margin="3">
      <Grid.RowDefinitions>
        <RowDefinition></RowDefinition>
        <RowDefinition></RowDefinition>
      </Grid.RowDefinitions>
      <TextBlock FontWeight="Bold"
       Text="{Binding Path=ModelNumber}"></TextBlock>
      <TextBlock Grid.Row="1"
       Text="{Binding Path=ModelName}"></TextBlock>
    </Grid>
  </Border>
</DataTemplate>
```

Because the Product object implements the INotifyPropertyChanged interface (as described in Chapter 19), any changes are picked up immediately. For example, if you modify the CategoryName property to move a product out of the Tools category, its text in the list changes at the same time.

This approach is useful but inherently limited. It doesn't allow you to change complex details about your template, only tweak individual properties of the elements in the template (or the container element). Also, as you learned in Chapter 11, triggers can test only for equality—they don't support more-complex comparison conditions. That means you can't use this approach to highlight prices that exceed a certain value, for example. And if you need to choose between a range of possibilities (for example, giving each product category a different background color), you'll need to write one trigger for each possible value, which is messy.

Another option is to create one template that's intelligent enough to adjust itself based on the bound object. To pull this trick off, you usually need to use a value converter that examines a property in your bound object and returns a more suitable value. For example, you could create a CategoryToColorConverter that examines a product's category and returns a corresponding Color object. That way, you can bind directly to the CategoryName property in your template, as shown here:

```
<Border Margin="5" BorderThickness="1" BorderBrush="SteelBlue" CornerRadius="4"
 Background=
 "{Binding Path=CategoryName, Converter={StaticResource CategoryToColorConverter}}">
```

Like the trigger approach, the value converter approach also prevents you from making dramatic changes, such as replacing a portion of your template with something completely different. However, it allows you to implement more-sophisticated formatting logic. Also, it allows you to base a single formatting property on several properties from the bound data object, if you use the IMultiValueConverter interface instead of the ordinary IValueConverter.

■ **Tip** Value converters are a good choice if you might want to reuse your formatting logic with other templates.

Template Selectors

Another, more powerful option is to give different items a completely different template. To do this, you need to create a class that derives from DataTemplateSelector. Template selectors work in the same way as the style selectors you considered earlier—they examine the bound object and choose a suitable template by using the logic you supply.

Earlier, you saw how to build a style selector that searches for specific values and highlights them with a style. Here's the analogous template selector, which looks at a property (specified by PropertyToEvaluate) and returns the HighlightTemplate if the property matches a set value (specified by PropertyValueToHighlight) or the DefaultTemplate otherwise:

```
Public Class SingleCriteriaHighlightTemplateSelector
    Inherits DataTemplateSelector

    Private _defaultTemplate As DataTemplate
    Public Property DefaultTemplate() As DataTemplate
        Get
            Return _defaultTemplate
        End Get
        Set(ByVal value As DataTemplate)
            _defaultTemplate = value
        End Set
    End Property

    Private _highlightTemplate As DataTemplate
    Public Property HighlightTemplate() As DataTemplate
        Get
            Return _highlightTemplate
        End Get
        Set(ByVal value As DataTemplate)
            _highlightTemplate = value
        End Set
    End Property
```

```vb
    Private _propertyToEvaluate As String
    Public Property PropertyToEvaluate() As String
        Get
            Return _propertyToEvaluate
        End Get
        Set(ByVal value As String)
            _propertyToEvaluate = value
        End Set
    End Property

    Private _propertyValueToHighlight As String
    Public Property PropertyValueToHighlight() As String
        Get
            Return _propertyValueToHighlight
        End Get
        Set(ByVal value As String)
            _propertyValueToHighlight = value
        End Set
    End Property

    Public Overrides Function SelectTemplate(ByVal item As Object, _
      ByVal container As DependencyObject) As DataTemplate
        Dim product As Product = CType(item, Product)

        ' Use reflection to get the property to check.
        Dim type As Type = product.GetType()
        Dim propertyInfo As PropertyInfo = type.GetProperty(PropertyToEvaluate)

        ' Decide if this product should be highlighted
        ' based on the property value.
        If propertyInfo.GetValue(product, Nothing).ToString() = _
          PropertyValueToHighlight Then
            Return HighlightTemplate
        Else
            Return DefaultTemplate
        End If
    End Function

End Class
```

And here's the markup that creates the two templates and an instance of the SingleCriteriaHighlightTemplateSelector:

```xml
<Window.Resources>
  <DataTemplate x:Key="DefaultTemplate">
    <Border Margin="5" BorderThickness="1" BorderBrush="SteelBlue"
      CornerRadius="4">
      <Grid Margin="3">
        <Grid.RowDefinitions>
          <RowDefinition></RowDefinition>
          <RowDefinition></RowDefinition>
        </Grid.RowDefinitions>
      </Grid.RowDefinitions>
```

```
      <TextBlock
        Text="{Binding Path=ModelNumber}"></TextBlock>
      <TextBlock Grid.Row="1"
        Text="{Binding Path=ModelName}"></TextBlock>
    </Grid>
  </Border>
</DataTemplate>

<DataTemplate x:Key="HighlightTemplate">
  <Border Margin="5" BorderThickness="1" BorderBrush="SteelBlue"
    Background="LightYellow" CornerRadius="4">
    <Grid Margin="3">
      <Grid.RowDefinitions>
        <RowDefinition></RowDefinition>
        <RowDefinition></RowDefinition>
        <RowDefinition></RowDefinition>
      </Grid.RowDefinitions>
      <TextBlock FontWeight="Bold"
        Text="{Binding Path=ModelNumber}"></TextBlock>
      <TextBlock Grid.Row="1" FontWeight="Bold"
        Text="{Binding Path=ModelName}"></TextBlock>
      <TextBlock Grid.Row="2" FontStyle="Italic" HorizontalAlignment="Right">
        *** Great for vacations ***</TextBlock>
    </Grid>
  </Border>
</DataTemplate>
</Window.Resources>
```

And here's the markup that applies the template selector:

```
<ListBox Name="lstProducts" HorizontalContentAlignment="Stretch">
  <ListBox.ItemTemplateSelector>
    <local:SingleCriteriaHighlightTemplateSelector
      DefaultTemplate="{StaticResource DefaultTemplate}"
      HighlightTemplate="{StaticResource HighlightTemplate}"
      PropertyToEvaluate="CategoryName"
      PropertyValueToHighlight="Travel"
    >
    </local:SingleCriteriaHighlightTemplateSelector>
  </ListBox.ItemTemplateSelector>
</ListBox>
```

As you can see, template selectors are far more powerful than style selectors, because each template has the ability to show different elements arranged in a different layout. In this example, the HighlightTemplate adds a TextBlock with an extra line of text at the end (Figure 20-13).

Figure 20-13. *A list with two data templates*

■ **Tip** One disadvantage of this approach is that you'll probably be forced to create multiple templates that are similar. If your templates are complex, this can create a lot of duplication. For best maintainability, you shouldn't create more than a few templates for a single list—instead, use triggers and styles to apply different formatting to your templates.

Templates and Selection

There's a small but irritating quirk in the previous template example. The problem is that the templates you've seen don't take selection into account.

If you select an item in the list, WPF automatically sets the Foreground and Background properties of the item container (in this case, the ListBoxItem object). The foreground is white, and the background is blue. The Foreground property uses property inheritance, so any elements you've added to your template automatically acquire the new white color, unless you've explicitly specified a new color. The Background color doesn't use property inheritance, but the default Background value is Transparent. If you have a transparent border, for example, the new blue background shows through. Otherwise, the color you've set in the template still applies.

This mishmash can alter your formatting in a way you might not intend. Figure 20-14 shows an example.

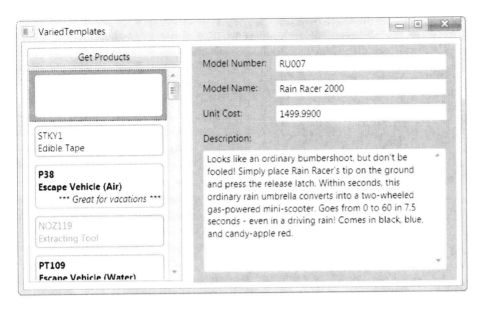

Figure 20-14. *Unreadable text in a highlighted item*

You could hard-code all your colors to avoid this problem, but then you'll face another challenge. The only indication that an item is selected will be the blue background around your curved border.

To solve this problem, you need to use the familiar ItemContainerStyle property to apply different formatting to the selected item:

```
<ListBox Name="lstProducts" HorizontalContentAlignment="Stretch">
  <ListBox.ItemContainerStyle>
    <Style>
      <Setter Property="Control.Padding" Value="0"></Setter>
      <Style.Triggers>
        <Trigger Property="ListBoxItem.IsSelected" Value="True">
          <Setter Property="ListBoxItem.Background" Value="DarkRed" />
        </Trigger>
      </Style.Triggers>
    </Style>
  </ListBox.ItemContainerStyle>
</ListBox>
```

This trigger applies a dark red background to the selected item. Unfortunately, this code doesn't have the desired effect for a list that uses templates. That's because these templates include elements with a different background color that's displayed over the dark red background. Unless you make everything transparent (and allow the red color to wash through your entire template), you're left with a thin red edge around the margin area of your template.

The solution is to explicitly bind the background in part of your template to the value of the ListBoxItem. Background property. This makes sense—after all, you've now gone to the work of choosing the right background color to highlight the selected item. You just need to make sure it appears in the right place.

The markup you need to implement this solution is a bit messy. That's because you can't make do with an ordinary binding expression, which can simply bind to a property in the current data object (in this case, the Product object). Instead, you need to grab the background from the item container (in this case, the ListBoxItem). This involves using the Binding.RelativeSource property to search up the element tree for the first matching ListBoxItem object. Once that element is found, you can grab its background color and use it accordingly.

Here's the finished template, which uses the selected background in the curved border region. The Border element is placed inside a Grid with a white background, which ensures that the selected color does not appear in the margin area outside the curved border. The result is the much slicker selection style shown in Figure 20-15.

```
<DataTemplate>
  <Grid Margin="0" Background="White">
    <Border Margin="5" BorderThickness="1"
      BorderBrush="SteelBlue" CornerRadius="4"
      Background="{Binding Path=Background, RelativeSource={
                          RelativeSource
                          Mode=FindAncestor,
                          AncestorType={x:Type ListBoxItem}
                  }}" >
      <Grid Margin="3">
        <Grid.RowDefinitions>
          <RowDefinition></RowDefinition>
          <RowDefinition></RowDefinition>
        </Grid.RowDefinitions>
        <TextBlock FontWeight="Bold" Text="{Binding Path=ModelNumber}"></TextBlock>
        <TextBlock Grid.Row="1" Text="{Binding Path=ModelName}"></TextBlock>
      </Grid>
    </Border>
  </Grid>
</DataTemplate>
```

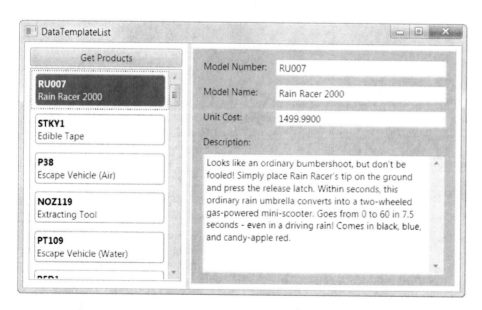

Figure 20-15. *Highlighting a selected item*

SELECTION AND SNAPSTODEVICEPIXELS

You should make one other change to ensure that your template displays perfectly on computers with different system DPI settings (such as 120 dpi rather than the standard 96 dpi). You should set the ListBox. SnapsToDevicePixels property to True. This ensures that the edge of the list doesn't use anti-aliasing if it falls in between pixels.

If you don't set SnapsToDevicePixels to True, you could get a trace of the familiar blue border creeping in between the edge of your template and the edge of the containing ListBox control. (For more information about fractional pixels and why they occur when the system DPI is set to a value other than 96 dpi, see the discussion about WPF's device-independent measuring system in Chapter 1.)

This approach—using a binding expression to alter a template—works well if you can pull the property value you need out of the item container. For example, it's a great technique if you want to get the background and foreground color of a selected item. However, it isn't as useful if you need to alter the template in a more profound way.

For example, consider the list of products shown in Figure 20-16. When you select a product from this list, that item is expanded from a single-line text display to a box with a picture and full description. This example also combines several of the techniques you've already seen, including showing image content in a template and using data binding to set the background color of the Border element when an item is selected.

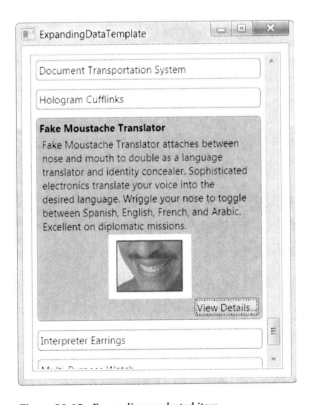

Figure 20-16. *Expanding a selected item*

To create this sort of list, you need to use a variation of the technique used in the previous example. You still need to use the RelativeSource property of a Binding to search for the current ListBoxItem. However, now you don't want to pull out its background color. Instead, you want to examine whether it's selected. If it isn't, you can hide the extra information by setting its Visibility property.

This technique is similar to the previous example but not exactly the same. In the previous example, you were able to bind directly to the value you wanted so that the background of the ListBoxItem became the background of the Border object. But in this case, you need to consider the ListBoxItem.IsSelected property and set the Visibility property of another element. The data types don't match—IsSelected is a Boolean value, while Visibility takes a value from the Visibility enumeration. As a result, you can't bind the Visibility property to the IsSelected property (at least, not without the help of a custom value converter). The solution is to use a data trigger so that when the IsSelected property is changed in the ListBoxItem, you modify the Visibility property of your container.

The place in your markup where you put the trigger is also different. It's no longer convenient to place the trigger in the ItemContainerStyle, because you don't want to change the visibility of the entire item. Instead, you want to hide just a single section, so the trigger needs to be part of a style that applies to just one container.

Here's a slightly simplified version of the template that doesn't have the automatically expanding behavior yet. Instead, it shows all the information (including the picture and description) for every product in the list.

```
<DataTemplate>
  <Border Margin="5" BorderThickness="1" BorderBrush="SteelBlue"
  CornerRadius="4">
    <StackPanel Margin="3">
      <TextBlock Text="{Binding Path=ModelName}"></TextBlock>
      <StackPanel>
        <TextBlock Margin="3" Text="{Binding Path=Description}"
        TextWrapping="Wrap" MaxWidth="250" HorizontalAlignment="Left"></TextBlock>
        <Image Source=
"{Binding Path=ProductImagePath, Converter={StaticResource ImagePathConverter}}">
        </Image>
        <Button FontWeight="Regular" HorizontalAlignment="Right" Padding="1"
        Tag="{Binding}">View Details...</Button>
      </StackPanel>
    </StackPanel>
  </Border>
</DataTemplate>
```

Inside the Border is a StackPanel that holds all the content. Inside that StackPanel is a second StackPanel that holds the content that should be shown only for selected items, which includes the description, image, and button. To hide this information, you need to set the style of the inner StackPanel by using a trigger, as shown here:

```
<StackPanel>
  <StackPanel.Style>
    <Style>
      <Style.Triggers>
        <DataTrigger
          Binding="{Binding Path=IsSelected, RelativeSource={
                            RelativeSource
                            Mode=FindAncestor,
                            AncestorType={x:Type ListBoxItem}
                    }}"
          Value="False">
          <Setter Property="StackPanel.Visibility" Value="Collapsed" />
        </DataTrigger>
```

```
      </Style.Triggers>
    </Style>
  </StackPanel.Style>

  <TextBlock Margin="3" Text="{Binding Path=Description}"
    TextWrapping="Wrap" MaxWidth="250" HorizontalAlignment="Left"></TextBlock>
  <Image Source=
"{Binding Path=ProductImagePath, Converter={StaticResource ImagePathConverter}}">
  </Image>
  <Button FontWeight="Regular" HorizontalAlignment="Right" Padding="1"
    Tag="{Binding}">View Details...</Button>
</StackPanel>
```

In this example, you need to use a DataTrigger instead of an ordinary trigger, because the property you need to evaluate is in an ancestor element (the ListBoxItem), and the only way to access it is by using a data-binding expression.

Now, when the ListBoxItem.IsSelected property changes to False, the StackPanel.Visibility property is changed to Collapsed, hiding the extra details.

▨ **Note**   Technically, the expanded details are always present, just hidden. As a result, you'll experience the extra overhead of generating these elements when the list is first created, not when an item is selected. This doesn't make much difference in the current example, but this design could have a performance effect if used for an extremely long list with a complex template.

Changing Item Layout

Data templates give you remarkable control over every aspect of item presentation. However, they don't allow you to change how the items are organized with respect to each other. No matter what templates and styles you use, the ListBox puts each item into a separate horizontal row and stacks each row to create the list.

You can change this layout by replacing the container that the list uses to lay out its children. To do so, you set the ItemsPanelTemplate property with a block of XAML that defines the panel you want to use. This panel can be any class that derives from System.Windows.Controls.Panel.

The following uses a WrapPanel to wrap items across the available width of the ListBox control (as shown in Figure 20-17):

```
<ListBox Margin="7,3,7,10" Name="lstProducts"
  ItemTemplate="{StaticResource ItemTemplate}"
  ScrollViewer.HorizontalScrollBarVisibility="Disabled">
  <ListBox.ItemsPanel>
    <ItemsPanelTemplate>
      <WrapPanel></WrapPanel>
    </ItemsPanelTemplate>
  </ListBox.ItemsPanel>
</ListBox>
```

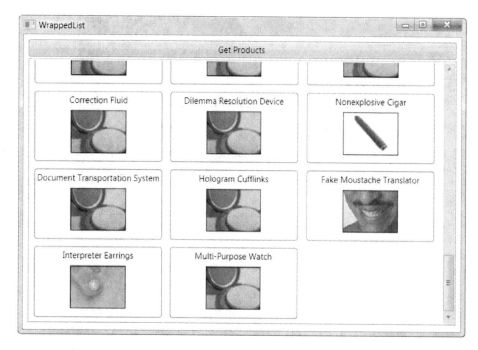

Figure 20-17. *Tiling items in the display area of a list*

For this approach to work, you must also set the attached ScrollViewer.HorizontalScrollBarVisibility property to Disabled. This ensures that the ScrollViewer (which the ListBox uses automatically) never uses a horizontal scrollbar. Without this detail, the WrapPanel will be given infinite width in which to lay out its items, and this example becomes equivalent to a horizontal StackPanel.

There's one caveat with this approach. Ordinarily, most list controls use the VirtualizingStackPanel rather than the standard StackPanel. As discussed in Chapter 19, the VirtualizingStackPanel ensures that large lists of bound data are handled efficiently. When you use the VirtualizingStackPanel, it creates the elements that are required to show the set of currently visible items. When you use the StackPanel, it creates the elements that are required for the entire list. If your data source includes thousands of items (or more), the VirtualizingStackPanel will use far less memory. It will also perform better when you are filling the list and when the user is scrolling through it, because there's far less work for WPF's layout system to do.

Thus, you shouldn't set a new ItemsPanelTemplate unless you're using your list to show a fairly modest amount of data. If you're on the borderline—for example, you're showing only a couple hundred items but you have an extremely complex template—you can profile both approaches, see how performance and memory usage changes, and decide which strategy is best.

The ComboBox

Although styles and data templates are built into the ItemsControl class and supported by all the WPF list controls, so far all the examples you've seen have used the standard ListBox. There's nothing wrong with this fact—after all, the ListBox is thoroughly customizable and can easily handle lists of check boxes, images, formatted text, or a combination of all these types of content. However, other list controls do introduce some new features. In Chapter 22, you'll learn about the frills of the ListView, TreeView, and DataGrid. But even the lowly ComboBox has a few extra considerations, and those are the details you'll explore in this section of this chapter.

Like the ListBox, the ComboBox is a descendant of the Selector class. Unlike the ListBox, the ComboBox is built out of two pieces: a selection box that shows the currently selected item and a drop-down list from which you can choose that item. The drop-down list appears when you click the drop-down arrow at the edge of the combo box. Or, if your combo box is in read-only mode (the default), you can open the drop-down list by clicking anywhere in the selection box. Finally, you can programmatically open or close the drop-down list by setting the IsDropDownOpen property.

Ordinarily, the ComboBox control shows a read-only combo box, which means you can use it to select an item but can type in arbitrary text of your own. However, you can change this behavior by setting the IsReadOnly property to False and the IsEditable property to True. Now the selection box becomes a text box, and you can type in whatever text you want.

The ComboBox control provides a rudimentary form of autocomplete that completes entries as you type. (This shouldn't be confused with the fancier autocomplete that you see in programs such as Internet Explorer, which shows a whole *list* of possibilities under the current text box.) Here's how it works—as you type in the ComboBox control, WPF fills in the remainder of the selection box with the first matching autocomplete suggestion. For example, if you type **Gr** and your list contains *Green*, the combo box will fill in the letters *een*. The autocomplete text is selected, so you'll automatically overwrite it if you keep typing.

If you don't want the autocomplete behavior, simply set the ComboBox.IsTextSearchEnabled property to False. This property is inherited from the base ItemsControl class, and it applies to many other list controls. For example, if IsTextSearchEnabled is set to True in a ListBox, you can type the first level of an item to jump to that position.

■ **Note** WPF doesn't include any features for using the system-tracked autocomplete lists, such as the list of recent URLs and files. It also doesn't provide support for drop-down autocomplete lists.

So far, the behavior of the ComboBox is quite straightforward. However, it changes a bit if your list contains more-complex objects rather than simple strings of text.

You can place more-complex objects in a ComboBox in two ways. The first option is to add them manually. As with the ListBox, you can place any content you want in a ComboBox. For example, if you want a list of images and text, you'd simply place the appropriate elements in a StackPanel and wrap that StackPanel in a ComboBoxItem object. More practically, you can use a data template to insert the content from a data object into a predefined group of elements.

When using nontext content, it's not as obvious what the selection box should contain. If the IsEditable property is False (the default), the selection box will show an exact visual copy of the item. For example, Figure 20-18 shows a ComboBox that uses a data template that incorporates text and image content.

Figure 20-18. A read-only ComboBox that uses templates

■ **Note** The important detail is what the combo box is displaying as its content, not what it has as its data source. For example, imagine you fill a ComboBox control with Product objects and set the DisplayMemberPath property to ModelName so the combo box shows the ModelName property of each item. Even though the combo box retrieves its information from a group of Product objects, your markup creates an ordinary text list. As a result, the selection box will behave the way you expect it to behave. It will show the ModelName of the current product, and if IsEditable is True and IsReadOnly is False, it will allow you to edit that value.

The user won't be able to interact with the content that appears in the selection box. For example, if the content of the currently selected item includes a text box, you won't be able to type in it. If the currently selected item includes a button, you won't be able to click it. Instead, clicking the selection box will simply open the drop-down list. (Of course, there are countless good usability reasons not to put user-interactive controls in a drop-down list in the first place.)

If the IsEditable property is True, the behavior of the ComboBox control changes. Instead of showing a copy of the selected item, the selection box displays a textual representation of it. To create this textual representation, WPF simply calls ToString() on the item. Figure 20-19 shows an example with the same combo box that's shown in Figure 20-19. In this case, the display text DataBinding.Product is simply the fully qualified class name of the currently selected Product object, which is the default ToString() implementation unless you override it in your data class.

Figure 20-19. *An editable ComboBox that uses templates*

The easiest option to correct this problem is to set the attached TextSearch.TextPath property to indicate the property that should be used for the content of the selection box. Here's an example:

```
<ComboBox IsEditable="True" IsReadOnly="True" TextSearch.TextPath="ModelName" ...>
```

Although IsEditable must be True, it's up to you whether you set IsReadOnly to False (to allow editing of that property) or True (to prevent the user from typing in arbitrary text). Figure 20-20 shows the result.

Figure 20-20. *Displaying a property in the selection box*

■ **Tip** What if you want to show richer content than a simple piece of text but you still want the content in the selection box to be different from the content in the drop-down list? The ComboBox includes a SelectionBoxItemTemplate property that defines the template that's used for the selection box. Unfortunately, the SelectionBoxItemTemplate is read-only. It's automatically set to match the current item, and you can't supply a different template. However, you could create an entirely new ComboBox control template that doesn't use the SelectionBoxItemTemplate at all. Instead, this control template could hard-code the selection box template or could retrieve it from the Resources collection in the window.

The Last Word

In this chapter, you delved deeper into data binding, one of the key pillars of WPF.

In the past, many of the scenarios you considered in this chapter would be handled using code. In WPF, the data-binding model (in conjunction with value converters, styles, and data templates) allows you to do much more work declaratively. In fact, data binding is nothing less than an all-purpose way to display any type of information, regardless of where it's stored, how you want it displayed, or whether it's editable. Sometimes this data will be drawn from a back-end database. In other cases, it may come from a web service, a remote object, or the file system, or it may be generated entirely in code. Ultimately, it won't matter—as long as the data model remains constant, your user interface code and binding expressions will remain the same.

CHAPTER 21

Data Views

Now that you've explored the art of converting data, applying styles to the items in a list, and building data templates, you're ready to move on to *data views*, which work behind the scenes to coordinate collections of bound data. Using data views, you can add navigation logic and implement filtering, sorting, and grouping.

■ **What's New**   In this chapter, you'll come across two more data-binding tweaks that are introduced in WPF 4.5. In the "Grouping and Virtualization" section, you'll learn how virtualization now works even with grouped data. In the "Live Shaping" section, you'll learn how WPF can watch your bound data for changes and update the linked view automatically.

The View Object

When you bind a collection (or a DataTable) to an ItemsControl, a data view is quietly created behind the scenes. This view sits between your data source and the bound control. The data view is a window into your data source. It tracks the current item, and it supports features such as sorting, filtering, and grouping. These features are independent of the data object itself, which means you can bind the same data in different ways in different portions of a window (or different parts of your application). For example, you could bind the same collection of products to two different lists but filter them to show different records.

The view object that's used depends on the type of data object. All views derive from CollectionView, but two specialized implementations derive from CollectionView: ListCollectionView and BindingListCollectionView. Here's how it works:

- If your data source implements IBindingList, a BindingListCollectionView is created. This happens when you bind an ADO.NET DataTable.

- If your data source doesn't implement IBindingList but it implements IList, a ListCollectionView is created. This happens when you bind an ObservableCollection, like the list of products.

- If your data source doesn't implement IBindingList or IList but it implements IEnumerable, you get a basic CollectionView.

■ **Tip**   Ideally, you'll avoid the third scenario. The CollectionView offers poor performance for large items and operations that modify the data source (such as insertions and deletions). As you learned in Chapter 19, if you're not binding to an ADO.NET data object, it's almost always easiest to use the ObservableCollection class.

Retrieving a View Object

To get ahold of a view object that's currently in use, you use the shared GetDefaultView() method of the System. Windows.Data.CollectionViewSource class. When you call GetDefaultView(), you pass in the data source—the collection or DataTable that you're using. Here's an example that gets the view for the collection of products that's bound to the list:

```
Dim view As ICollectionView
view = CollectionViewSource.GetDefaultView(lstProducts.ItemsSource)
```

The GetDefaultView() method always returns an ICollectionView reference. It's up to you to cast the view object to the appropriate class, such as a ListCollectionView or BindingListCollectionView, depending on the data source.

```
Dim view As ListCollectionView = _
  CType(CollectionViewSource.GetDefaultView(lstProducts.ItemsSource), _
    ListCollectionView)
```

Navigating with a View

One of the simplest things you can do with a view object is determine the number of items in the list (through the Count property) and get a reference to the current data object (CurrentItem) or current position index (CurrentPosition). You can also use a handful of methods to move from one record to another, such as MoveCurrentToFirst(), MoveCurrentToLast(), MoveCurrentToNext(), MoveCurrentToPrevious(), and MoveCurrentToPosition(). So far, you haven't needed these details because all the examples you've seen have used the list to allow the user to move from one record to the next. But if you want to create a record browser application, you might want to supply your own navigation buttons. Figure 21-1 shows one example.

Figure 21-1. *A record browser*

The bound text boxes that show the data for the bound product stay the same. They need only to indicate the appropriate property, as shown here:

```
<TextBlock Margin="7">Model Number:</TextBlock>
<TextBox Margin="5" Grid.Column="1" Text="{Binding Path=ModelNumber}"></TextBox>
```

However, this example doesn't include any list control, so it's up to you to take control of the navigation. To simplify life, you can store a reference to the view as a member variable in your window class:

```
Private view As ListCollectionView
```

In this case, the code casts the view to the appropriate view type (ListCollectionView) rather than using the ICollectionView interface. The ICollectionView interface provides most of the same functionality, but it lacks the Count property that gives the total number of items in the collection.

When the window first loads, you can get the data, place it in the DataContext of the window, and store a reference to the view:

```
Dim products As ICollection(Of Products) = Application.StoreDB.GetProducts()
Me.DataContext = products

view = CType(CollectionViewSource.GetDefaultView(Me.DataContext), _
  ListCollectionView)
AddHandler view.CurrentChanged, AddressOf view_CurrentChanged
```

The second line does all the magic needed to show your collection of items in the window. It places the whole collection of Product objects in the DataContext. The bound controls on the form will search up the element tree until they find this object. Of course, you want the binding expressions to bind to the current item in the collection, not the collection itself, but WPF is smart enough to figure this out automatically. It automatically supplies them with the current item, so you don't need a stitch of extra code.

The previous example has one additional code statement. It connects an event handler to the CurrentChanged event of the view. When this event fires, you can perform a few useful actions, such as enabling or disabling the previous and next buttons depending on the current position and displaying the current position in a TextBlock at the bottom of the window.

```
Private Sub view_CurrentChanged(ByVal sender As Object, ByVal e As EventArgs)
    lblPosition.Text = "Record " & (view.CurrentPosition + 1).ToString() & _
      " of " & view.Count.ToString()
    cmdPrev.IsEnabled = view.CurrentPosition > 0
    cmdNext.IsEnabled = view.CurrentPosition < view.Count - 1
End Sub
```

This code seems like a candidate for data binding and triggers. However, the logic is just a bit too complex (partly because you need to add 1 to the index to get the record position number that you want to display).

The final step is to write the logic for the previous and next buttons. Because these buttons are automatically disabled when they don't apply, you don't need to worry about moving before the first item or after the last item.

```
Private Sub cmdNext_Click(ByVal sender As Object, ByVal e As RoutedEventArgs)
    view.MoveCurrentToNext()
End Sub
```

```
Private Sub cmdPrev_Click(ByVal sender As Object, ByVal e As RoutedEventArgs)
    view.MoveCurrentToPrevious()
End Sub
```

For an interesting frill, you can add a list control to this form so the user has the option of stepping through the records one at a time with the buttons or using the list to jump directly to a specific item (as shown in Figure 21-2).

Figure 21-2. *A record browser with a drop-down list*

In this case, you need a ComboBox that uses the ItemsSource property (to get the full list of products) and uses a binding on the Text property (to show the right item):

```
<ComboBox Name="lstProducts" DisplayMemberPath="ModelName"
 Text="{Binding Path=ModelName}"
 SelectionChanged="lstProducts_SelectionChanged"></ComboBox>
```

When you first retrieve the collection of products, you'll bind the list:

```
lstProducts.ItemsSource = products
```

This might not have the effect you expect. By default, the selected item in an ItemsControl is not synchronized with the current item in the view. That means that when you make a new selection from the list, you aren't directed to the new record—instead, you end up modifying the ModelName property of the current record. Fortunately, there are two easy approaches to solve the problem.

The brute-force approach is to simply move to the new record whenever an item is selected in the list. Here's the code that does it:

```
Private Sub lstProducts_SelectionChanged(ByVal sender As Object, _
  ByVal e As RoutedEventArgs)
    view.MoveCurrentTo(lstProducts.SelectedItem)
End Sub
```

A simpler solution is to set the ItemsControl.IsSynchronizedWithCurrentItem to True. That way, the currently selected item is automatically synchronized to match the current position of the view with no code required.

USING A LOOKUP LIST FOR EDITING

The ComboBox provides a handy way to edit record values. In the current example, it doesn't make much sense—after all, there's no reason to give one product the same name as another product. However, it's not difficult to think of other scenarios where the ComboBox is a great editing tool.

For example, you might have a field in your database that accepts one of a small set of preset values. In this case, use a ComboBox, and bind it to the appropriate field using a binding expression for the Text property. However, fill the ComboBox with the allowable values by setting its ItemsSource property to point to the list you've defined. And if you want to display the values in the list one way (say, as text) but store them another way (as numeric codes), just add a value converter to your Text property binding.

Another case where a lookup list makes sense is when dealing with related tables. For example, you might want to allow the user to pick the category for a product using a list of all the defined categories. The basic approach is the same: set the Text property to bind to the appropriate field, and fill in the list of options with the ItemsSource property. If you need to convert low-level unique IDs into more meaningful names, use a value converter.

Creating a View Declaratively

The previous example used a simple pattern that you'll see throughout this chapter. The code retrieves the view you want to use and then modifies it programmatically. However, you have another choice—you can construct a CollectionViewSource declaratively in XAML markup and then bind the CollectionViewSource to your controls (such as the list).

■ **Note** Technically, the CollectionViewSource is not a view. It's a helper class that allows you to retrieve a view (using the GetDefaultView() method you've seen in the previous examples) and a factory that can create a view when you need it (as you'll see in this section).

The two most important properties of the CollectionViewSource class are View, which wraps the view object, and Source, which wraps the data source. The CollectionViewSource also adds the SortDescriptions and GroupDescriptions properties, which mirror the identically named view properties you've already learned about. When the CollectionViewSource creates a view, it simply passes the value of these properties to the view.

The CollectionViewSource also includes a Filter event, which you can handle to perform filtering. This filtering works in the same way as the Filter callback that's provided by the view object, except it's defined as an event so you can easily hook up your event handler in XAML.

For example, consider the previous example, which placed products in groups using price ranges. Here's how you would define the converter and CollectionViewSource you need for this example declaratively:

```
<local:PriceRangeProductGrouper x:Key="Price50Grouper" GroupInterval="50"/>
  <CollectionViewSource x:Key="GroupByRangeView">
    <CollectionViewSource.SortDescriptions>
      <component:SortDescription PropertyName="UnitCost" Direction="Ascending"/>
    </CollectionViewSource.SortDescriptions>
```

```
  <CollectionViewSource.GroupDescriptions>
    <PropertyGroupDescription PropertyName="UnitCost"
     Converter="{StaticResource Price50Grouper}"/>
  </CollectionViewSource.GroupDescriptions>
</CollectionViewSource>
```

Notice that the SortDescription class isn't one of the WPF namespaces. To use it, you need to add the following namespace alias:

```
xmlns:component="clr-namespace:System.ComponentModel;assembly=WindowsBase"
```

Once you've set up the CollectionViewSource, you can bind to it in your list:

```
<ListBox ItemsSource="{Binding Source={StaticResource GroupByRangeView}}" ... >
```

At first glance, this looks a bit odd. It seems as though the ListBox control is binding to the CollectionViewSource, not the view exposed by the CollectionViewSource (which is stored in the CollectionViewSource.View property). However, WPF data binding makes a special exception for the CollectionViewSource. When you use it in a binding expression, WPF asks the CollectionViewSource to create its view and then binds that view to the appropriate element.

The declarative approach doesn't really save you any work. You still need code that retrieves the data at runtime. The difference is that now your code must pass the data along to the CollectionViewSource rather than supply it directly to the list:

```
Dim products As ICollection(Of Product) = Application.StoreDB.GetProducts()
Dim viewSource As CollectionViewSource = CType( _
  Me.FindResource("GroupByRangeView"), CollectionViewSource)
viewSource.Source = products
```

Alternatively, you could create the products collection as a resource using XAML markup. You could then bind the CollectionViewSource to your products collection declaratively. However, you still need to use code to populate your products collection.

▦ **Note** People use a few dubious tricks to create code-free data binding. Sometimes, the data collection is defined and filled using XAML markup (with hard-coded values). In other cases, the code for populating the data object is hidden away in the data object's constructor. Both these approaches are severely impractical. I mention them only because they're often used to create quick, off-the-cuff data binding examples.

Now that you've seen the code-based and markup-based approaches for configuring a view, you're probably wondering which one is the better design decision. Both are equally valid. The choice you make depends on where you want to centralize the details for your data view.

However, the choice becomes more significant if you want to use *multiple* views. In this situation, there's a good case to be made for defining all your views in markup and then using code to swap in the appropriate view.

Filtering, Sorting, and Grouping

As you've already seen, views track the current position in a collection of data objects. This is an important task, and finding (or changing) the current item is the most common reason to use a view.

Views also provide a number of optional features that allow you to manage the entire set of items. In the following sections, you'll see how you can use a view to filter your data items (temporarily hiding those you don't want to see), how you can use it to apply sorting (changing the data item order), and how you can use it to apply grouping (creating subcollections that can be navigated separately).

Filtering Collections

Filtering allows you to show a subset of records that meet specific conditions. When working with a collection as a data source, you set the filter using the Filter property of the view object.

The implementation of the Filter property is a little awkward. It accepts a Predicate delegate that points to a custom filtering method (that you create). Here's an example of how you can connect a view to a method named FilterProduct():

```
Dim view As ListCollectionView = _
  CType(CollectionViewSource.GetDefaultView(lstProducts.ItemsSource), _
    ListCollectionView)
view.Filter = New Predicate(Of object)(FilterProduct)
```

The filtering examines a single data item from the collection and returns True if it should be allowed in the list or False if it should be excluded. When you create the Predicate object, you specify the type of object that it's meant to examine. The awkward part is that the view expects you to use a Predicate<object> instance—you can't use something more useful (such as Predicate<Product>) to save yourself the type casting code.

Here's a simple method that shows products only if they exceed $100:

```
Public Function FilterProduct(ByVal item As Object) As Boolean
    Dim product As Product = CType(item, Product)
    Return product.UnitCost > 100
End Function
```

Obviously, it makes little sense to hard-code values in your filter condition. A more realistic application would filter dynamically based on other information, like the user-supplied criteria shown in Figure 21-3.

Figure 21-3. *Filtering the product list*

The best way to implement this approach is to create a dedicated filtering class. The filtering class wraps the filtering criteria and the callback method that performs the filtering. Here's an extremely simple filtering class that filters products that fall below a minimum price:

```
Public Class ProductByPriceFilterer
    Private _minimumPrice As Decimal

    Public Property MinimumPrice() As Decimal
        Get
            Return _minimumPrice
        End Get
        Set(ByVal value As Decimal)
            _minimumPrice = value
        End Set
    End Property

    Public Sub New(ByVal minimumPrice As Decimal)
        Me.MinimumPrice = minimumPrice
    End Sub

    Public Function FilterItem(ByVal item As Object) As Boolean
        Dim product As Product = TryCast(item, Product)
        If product IsNot Nothing Then
            If product.UnitCost > MinimumPrice Then
                Return True
            End If
        End If
```

```
        Return False
    End Function

End Class
```

Here's the code that creates the ProductByPriceFilterer and uses it to apply minimum price filtering:

```
Private Sub cmdFilter_Click(ByVal sender As Object, ByVal e As RoutedEventArgs)
    Dim minimumPrice As Decimal
    If Decimal.TryParse(txtMinPrice.Text, minimumPrice) Then
        Dim view As ListCollectionView
        view = TryCast( _
          CollectionViewSource.GetDefaultView(lstProducts.ItemsSource), _
          ListCollectionView)

        If view IsNot Nothing Then
            filterer = New ProductByPriceFilterer(minimumPrice)
            view.Filter = _
              New Predicate(Of Object)(AddressOf filterer.FilterItem)
        End If
    End If
End Sub
```

It might occur to you to create different filters for filtering different types of data. For example, you might plan to create (and reuse) a MinMaxFilter, a StringFilter, and so on. However, it's usually more helpful to create a single filtering class for each window where you want to apply filtering. That's because you can't chain more than one filter together.

▓ **Note** Of course, you could create a custom implementation that solves this problem—for example, a FilterChain class that wraps a collection of IFilter objects and calls the FilterItem() method of each one to find out whether to exclude an item. However, this extra layer may be more code and complexity than you need.

If you want to modify the filter later without re-creating the ProductByPriceFilter object, you'll need to store a reference to the filter object as a member variable in your window class. You can then modify the filter properties. However, you'll also need to call the Refresh() method of the view object to force the list to be refiltered. Here's some code that adjusts the filter settings whenever the TextChanged event fires in the text box that contains the minimum price:

```
Private Sub txtMinPrice_TextChanged(ByVal sender As Object, _
  ByVal e As TextChangedEventArgs)
    Dim view As ListCollectionView = TryCast( _
      CollectionViewSource.GetDefaultView(lstProducts.ItemsSource), _
      ListCollectionView)

    If Not view Is Nothing Then
        Dim minimumPrice As Decimal
        If Decimal.TryParse(txtMinPrice.Text, minimumPrice) _
          AndAlso (filterer IsNot Nothing) Then
            filterer.MinimumPrice = minimumPrice
            view.Refresh()
        End If
    End If
End Sub
```

■ **Tip** It's a common convention to let the user choose to apply different types of conditions using a series of check boxes. For example, you could create a check box for filtering by price, by name, by model number, and so on. The user can then choose which filter conditions to apply by checking the appropriate check boxes.

Finally, you can completely remove a filter by setting the Filter property to Nothing:

```
view.Filter = Nothing
```

Filtering the DataTable

Filtering works differently with the DataTable. If you've worked with ADO.NET before, you probably already know that every DataTable works in conjunction with a DataView object (which is, like the DataTable, defined in the System. Data namespace along with the other core ADO.NET data objects). The ADO.NET DataView plays much the same role as the WPF view object. Like a WPF view, it allows you to filter records (by field content using the RowFilter property or by row state using the RowStateFilter property). It also supports sorting through the Sort property. Unlike the WPF view object, the DataView doesn't track the position in a set of data. It also provides additional properties that allow you to lock down editing capabilities (AllowDelete, AllowEdit, and AllowNew).

It's quite possible to change the way a list of data is filtered by retrieving the bound DataView and modifying its properties directly. (Remember, you can get the default DataView from the DataTable.DefaultView property.) However, it would be nicer if you had a way to adjust the filtering through the WPF view object so that you can continue to use the same model.

It turns out that this is possible, but there are some limitations. Unlike the ListCollectionView, the BindingListCollectionView that's used with the DataTable doesn't support the Filter property. (BindingListCollectionView.CanFilter returns False, and attempting to set the Filter property causes an exception to be thrown.) Instead, the BindingListCollectionView provides a CustomFilter property. The CustomFilter property doesn't do any work of its own—it simply takes the filter string that you specify and uses it to set the underlying DataView.RowFilter property.

The DataView.RowFilter is easy enough to use but a little messy. It takes a string-based filter expression, which is modeled after the snippet of SQL you'd use to construct the WHERE clause in a SELECT query. As a result, you need to follow all the conventions of SQL, such as bracketing string and date values with single quotes ('). And if you want to use multiple conditions, you need to string them all together using the OR and AND keywords.

Here's an example that duplicates the filtering shown in the earlier, collection-based example so that it works with a DataTable of product records:

```
Dim minimumPrice As Decimal
If Decimal.TryParse(txtMinPrice.Text, minimumPrice) Then
    Dim view As BindingListCollectionView = _
      CType(CollectionViewSource.GetDefaultView(lstProducts.ItemsSource), _
      BindingListCollectionView)

    If view IsNot Nothing Then
        view.CustomFilter = "UnitCost > " & minimumPrice.ToString()
    End If
End If
```

Notice that this example takes the roundabout approach of converting the text in the txtMinPrice text box to a decimal value and then back to a string to use for filtering. This requires a bit more work, but it avoids possible injection attacks and errors with invalid characters. If you simply concatenate the text from the txtMinPrice text box to build your filter string, it could contain filter operations (=, <, >) and keywords (AND, OR) that apply completely different filtering than what you intend. This could happen as part of a deliberate attack or because of user error.

Sorting

You can also use a view to implement sorting. The easiest approach is to sort based on the value of one or more properties in each data item. You identify the fields you want to use using System.ComponentModel.SortDescription objects. Each SortDescription identifies the field you want to use for sorting and the sort direction (ascending or descending). You add the SortDescription objects in the order that you want to apply them. For example, you could sort first by category and then by model name.

Here's an example that applies a simple ascending sort by model name:

```
Dim view As ICollectionView
view = CollectionViewSource.GetDefaultView(lstProducts.ItemsSource)
view.SortDescriptions.Add( _
  New SortDescription("ModelName", ListSortDirection.Ascending))
```

Because this code uses the ICollectionView interface rather than a specific view class, it works equally well no matter what type of data source you're binding. In the case of a BindingListCollectionView (when binding a DataTable), the SortDescription objects are used to build a sorting string that's applied to the underlying DataView. Sort property.

▧ **Note**   In the rare case that you have more than one BindingListCollectionView working with the same DataView, both will share the same filtering and sorting settings, because these details are stored in the DataView, not the BindingListCollectionView. If this isn't the behavior you want, you can create more than one DataView to wrap the same DataTable.

As you'd expect, when sorting strings, values are ordered alphabetically. Numbers are ordered numerically. To apply a different sort order, begin by clearing the existing SortDescriptions collection.

You also can perform a custom sort, but only if you're using the ListCollectionView (not the BindingListCollectionView). The ListCollectionView provides a CustomSort property that accepts an IComparer object that performs the comparison between any two data items and indicates which one should be considered greater than the other. This approach is handy if you need to build a sorting routine that combines properties to get a sorting key. It also makes sense if you have nonstandard sorting rules. For example, you may want to ignore the first few characters of a product code, perform a calculation on a price, convert your field to a different data type or a different representation before sorting, and so on. Here's an example that counts the number of letters in the model name and uses that to determine sort order:

```
Public Class SortByModelNameLength
    Implements System.Collections.IComparer

    Public Function Compare(ByVal x As Object, ByVal y As Object) As Integer _
      Implements System.Collections.IComparer.Compare
        Dim productX As Product = CType(x, Product)
        Dim productY As Product = CType(y, Product)
        Return productX.ModelName.Length.CompareTo(productY.ModelName.Length)
    End Function

End Class
```

Here's the code that connects the IComparer to a view:

```
Dim view As ListCollectionView = CType( _
  CollectionViewSource.GetDefaultView(lstProducts.ItemsSource),
  ListCollectionView)
view.CustomSort = New SortByModelNameLength()
```

In this example, the IComparer is designed to fit a specific scenario. If you have an IComparer that you need to reuse with similar data in different places, you can generalize it. For example, you could change the SortByModelNameLength class to a SortByTextLength class. When creating a SortByTextLength instance, your code would need to supply the name of the property to use (as a string), and your Compare() method could then use reflection to look it up in the data object.

Grouping

In much the same way that they support sorting, views also allow you to apply grouping. As with sorting, you can group the easy way (based on a single property value) or the hard way (using a custom callback).

To perform grouping, you add System.ComponentModel.PropertyGroupDescription objects to the CollectionView.GroupDescriptions collection. Here's an example that groups products by category name:

```
Dim view As ICollectionView
view = CollectionViewSource.GetDefaultView(lstProducts.ItemsSource)
view.GroupDescriptions.Add(New PropertyGroupDescription("CategoryName"))
```

■ **Note**   This example assumes that the Product class has a property named CategoryName. It's more likely that you have a property named Category (which returns a linked Category object) or CategoryID (which identifies the category with a unique ID number). You can still use grouping in these scenarios, but you'll need to add a value converter that examines the grouping information (such as the Category object or CategoryID property) and returns the correct category text to use for the group. You'll see how to use a value converter with grouping in the next example.

This example has one problem. Although your items will now be arranged into separate groups based on their categories, it's difficult to see that any grouping has been applied when you look at the list. In fact, the result is the same as if you simply sorted by category name.

There's actually more taking place—you just can't see it with the default settings. When you use grouping, your list creates a separate GroupItem object for each group, and it adds these GroupItem objects to the list. The GroupItem is a content control, so each GroupItem holds the appropriate container (like ListBoxItem objects) with your actual data. The secret to showing your groups is formatting the GroupItem element so it stands out.

You could use a style that applies formatting to all the GroupItem objects in a list. However, you probably want more than just formatting—for example, you might want to display a group header, which requires the help of a template. Fortunately, the ItemsControl class makes both tasks easy through its ItemsControl.GroupStyle property, which provides a collection of GroupStyle objects. Despite the name, GroupStyle class is not a style. It's simply a convenient package that wraps a few useful settings for configuring your GroupItem objects. Table 21-1 lists the properties of the GroupStyle class.

Table 21-1. *GroupStyle Properties*

Name	Description
ContainerStyle	Sets the style that's applied to the GroupItem that's generated for each group.
ContainerStyleSelector	Instead of using ContainerStyle, you can use ContainerStyleSelector to supply a class that chooses the right style to use, based on the group.
HeaderTemplate	Allows you to create a template for displaying content at the beginning of each group.
HeaderTemplateSelector	Instead of using HeaderTemplate, you can use HeaderTemplateSelector to supply a class that chooses the right header template to use, based on the group.
Panel	Allows you to change the template that's used to hold groups. For example, you could use a WrapPanel instead of the standard StackPanel to create a list that tiles groups from left to right and then down.

In this example, all you need is a header before each group. You can use this to create the effect shown in Figure 21-4.

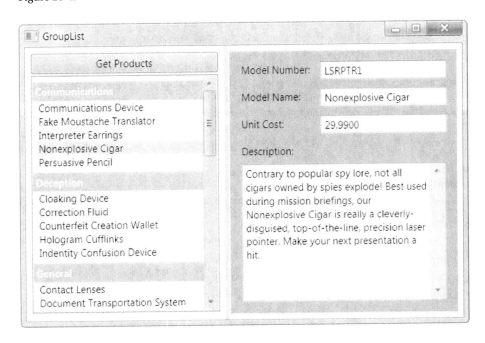

Figure 21-4. *Grouping the product list*

To add a group header, you need to set the GroupStyle.HeaderTemplate. You can fill this property with an ordinary data template, like the ones you saw in Chapter 20. You can use any combination of elements and data binding expressions inside your template.

However, there's one trick. When you write your binding expression, you aren't binding against the data object from your list (in this case, the Product object). Instead, you're binding against the PropertyGroupDescription object for that group. That means if you want to display the field value for that group (as shown in Figure 21-4), you need to bind the PropertyGroupDescription.Name property rather than Product.CategoryName.

Here's the complete template:

```
<ListBox Name="lstProducts" DisplayMemberPath="ModelName">
  <ListBox.GroupStyle>
    <GroupStyle>
      <GroupStyle.HeaderTemplate>
        <DataTemplate>
          <TextBlock Text="{Binding Path=Name}" FontWeight="Bold"
            Foreground="White" Background="LightGreen"
            Margin="0,5,0,0" Padding="3"/>
        </DataTemplate>
      </GroupStyle.HeaderTemplate>
    </GroupStyle>
  </ListBox.GroupStyle>
</ListBox>
```

■ **Tip**   The ListBox.GroupStyle property is actually a collection of GroupStyle objects. This allows you to add multiple levels of grouping. To do so, you need to add more than one PropertyGroupDescription (in the order that you want your grouping and subgrouping applied) and then add a matching GroupStyle object to format each level.

You'll probably want to use grouping in conjunction with sorting. If you want to sort your groups, just make sure that the first SortDescription you use sorts based on the grouping field. The following code sorts the categories alphabetically by category name and then sorts each product within the category alphabetically by model name.

```
view.SortDescriptions.Add(New SortDescription("CategoryName", _
  ListSortDirection.Ascending))
view.SortDescriptions.Add(New SortDescription("ModelName", _
  ListSortDirection.Ascending))
```

Grouping in Ranges

One limitation with the simple grouping approach you see here is that it requires a field with duplicate values to perform its grouping. The previous example works because many products share the same category and have duplicate values for the CategoryName property. However, this approach doesn't work as well if you try to group by another piece of information, such as the UnitCost field. In this situation, you'll end up with a separate group for each product.

This problem has a solution. You can create a class that examines some piece of information and places it into a conceptual group for display purposes. This technique is commonly used to group data objects using numeric or date information that falls into specific ranges. For example, you could create a group for products that are less than $50, another for products that fall between $50 and $100, and so on. Figure 21-5 shows this example.

Figure 21-5. *Grouping in ranges*

To create this solution, you need to supply a value converter that examines a field in your data source (or multiple fields if you implement IMultiValueConverter) and returns the group header. As long as you use the same group header for multiple data objects, these objects are placed into the same logical group.

The following code shows the converter that creates the price ranges shown in Figure 21-5. It's designed to have some flexibility—namely, you can specify the size of the grouping ranges. (In Figure 21-5, the group range is 50 units big.)

```
Public Class PriceRangeProductGrouper
    Implements IValueConverter

    Private _groupInterval As Integer
    Public Property GroupInterval() As Integer
        Get
            Return _groupInterval
        End Get
        Set(ByVal value As Integer)
            _groupInterval = value
        End Set
    End Property
```

```vbnet
Public Function Convert(ByVal value As Object, ByVal targetType As Type, _
  ByVal parameter As Object, ByVal culture As CultureInfo) As Object _
  Implements IValueConverter.Convert
    Dim price As Decimal = CDec(value)
    If price < GroupInterval Then
        Return String.Format(culture, "Less than {0:C}", GroupInterval)
    Else
        Dim interval As Integer = Int(price / GroupInterval)
        Dim lowerLimit As Integer = interval * GroupInterval
        Dim upperLimit As Integer = (interval + 1) * GroupInterval
        Return String.Format(culture, "{0:C} to {1:C}", lowerLimit, upperLimit)
    End If
End Function

Public Function ConvertBack(ByVal value As Object, _
  ByVal targetType As Type, ByVal parameter As Object, _
  ByVal culture As CultureInfo) As Object _
  Implements IValueConverter.ConvertBack
    Throw New NotSupportedException("This converter is for grouping only.")
End Function
```

End Class

To make this class even more flexible so that it can be used with other fields, you could add other properties that allow you to set the fixed part of the header text and a format string to use when converting the numeric values to header text. (The current code assumes the numbers should be treated as currencies, so 50 becomes $50.00 in the header.)

Here's the code that uses the converter to apply the range grouping. Note that the products must first be sorted by price, or you'll end up grouping them based on where they fall in the list.

```vbnet
Dim view As ICollectionView
view = CollectionViewSource.GetDefaultView(lstProducts.ItemsSource)
view.SortDescriptions.Add(New SortDescription("UnitCost", _
  ListSortDirection.Ascending))

Dim grouper As New PriceRangeProductGrouper()
grouper.GroupInterval = 50
view.GroupDescriptions.Add(New PropertyGroupDescription("UnitCost", grouper))
```

Grouping and Virtualization

In Chapter 19, you learned about virtualization, a feature that reduces the memory overhead of a control and increases its speed when you're binding extremely long lists. However, even if your control supports virtualization, it won't use it when you enable virtualization. WPF corrects this oversight with a new VirtualizingStackPanel. IsVirtualizingWhenGrouping property. Set it to True, and your grouped list gets the same performance-boosting virtualization as an ungrouped list:

```xml
<ListBox VirtualizingStackPanel.IsVirtualizingWhenGrouping="True" ...>
```

However, you should still be cautious about using grouping and long lists together, because the work involved to group your data can cause a significant slowdown. For that reason, you'll want to profile your application before you implement this design.

Live Shaping

If you make changes to the filtering, sorting, or grouping of a view that's already in use, you need to call ICollectionViewSource.Refresh() method to refresh the view and make sure the right items appears in the list. You've already seen an example that uses this technique: the price-filtering text box that triggers a refresh whenever the user modifies the minimum price limit.

However, some changes are a little trickier to catch. It's easy enough to remember to refresh a view when you're changing that view, but what if a code routine somewhere in your application changes your *data*? For example, imagine if an edit reduces the price of a product below the minimum that's required by your view's filter condition. Technically, this should cause the record to disappear from the current view, but unless you remember to force a refresh, you won't see any change.

WPF 4.5 introduces a feature called *live shaping* that fills this gap. Essentially, live shaping watches for changes in specific properties. If it detects a change (like a lowered price on a Product object), and it determines that the change affects the current view, it triggers a refresh.

To use live shaping, you need to meet three criteria:

- Your data object must implement INotifyPropertyChanged. It uses this interface to signal when its properties change. The current Product object does that already.

- Your collection must implement ICollectionViewLiveShaping. The standard ListCollectionView and BindingListCollectionView classes both implement ICollectionViewLiveShaping, which means you can use live shaping with any of the examples you've seen in this chapter.

- You must explicitly enable live shaping. You do this by setting several properties on the ListCollectionView or BindingListCollectionView object.

The last point is the most important. Live shaping adds extra overhead, so you need to opt-it to this feature when you need it. You do that with three separate properties: IsLiveFiltering, IsLiveSorting, and IsLiveGrouping. Each one enables live shaping for a different view feature. For example, if you set IsLiveFiltering to True but do not set the other two properties, the collection will check for changes that affect the currently set filtering conditions, but it will ignore changes that could affect the sorting or grouping of the list.

After you've enabled live shaping, you also need to tell the collection what properties to monitor. You do that by adding the property name (as a string) to one of three collection properties: LiveFilteringProperties, LiveSortingProperties, or LiveGroupingProperties. Once again, this design is intended to ensure the best possible performance, by ignoring the properties that aren't important.

For example, consider the price-filtering product example. In this case, it makes sense to turn on IsLiveFiltering and monitor the Product.UnitCost property for changes, because that's the only property that can affect the filtering of the list. (Changes to other properties, like Description or ModelNumber, don't affect whether a product is filtered, and so they aren't important.) To use live shaping in this example, you'd add this code:

```
Dim view As ListCollectionView = CType( _
  CollectionViewSource.GetDefaultView(lstProducts.ItemsSource), ListCollectionView)

view.IsLiveFiltering = True
view.LiveFilteringProperties.Add("UnitCost")
```

Now try editing a record and reducing the price below the filter condition. The Product object reports the change, and the ListCollectionView notices it, reevaluates the condition, and then refreshes the view. The final result is that the low-priced record disappears automatically.

The Last Word

Views are the final piece in the data binding puzzle. They're an invaluable extra layer that sits between your data and the elements that display it, allowing you to manage your position in a collection and giving you the flexibility to implement filtering, sorting, and grouping. In every data binding scenario, there's a view at work. The only difference is whether it's acting behind the scenes or whether you're explicitly taking control of it with code.

You've now considered all the key principles of data binding (and a bit more besides). In the following chapter, you look at three controls that give you still more options for presenting and editing bound data: the ListView, TreeView, and DataGrid.

■ ■ ■

CHAPTER 22

Lists, Trees, and Grids

So far, you've learned a wide range of techniques and tricks for using WPF data binding to display information in the form you need. Along the way, you've seen many examples that revolve around the lowly ListBox control.

Thanks to the extensibility provided by styles, data templates, and control templates, even the ListBox (and its similarly equipped sibling, the ComboBox) can serve as a remarkably powerful tool for displaying data in a variety of ways. However, some types of data presentation would be difficult to implement with the ListBox alone. Fortunately, WPF has a few rich data controls that fill in the blanks, including the following:

> *ListView*: The ListView derives from the plain-vanilla ListBox. It adds support for column-based display and the ability to switch quickly between different "views," or display modes, without requiring you to rebind the data and rebuild the list.

> *TreeView*: The TreeView is a hierarchical container, which means you can create a multilayered data display. For example, you could create a TreeView that shows category groups in its first level and shows the related products under each category node.

> *DataGrid*: The DataGrid is WPF's most full-featured data display tool. It divides your data into a grid of columns and rows, like the ListView, but has additional formatting features (such as the ability to freeze columns and style individual rows), and it supports in-place data editing.

In this chapter, you'll look at these three key controls.

The ListView

The ListView is a specialized list class that's designed for displaying different *views* of the same data. The ListView is particularly useful if you need to build a multicolumn view that displays several pieces of information about each data item.

The ListView derives from the ListBox class and extends it with a single detail: the View property. The View property is yet another extensibility point for creating rich list displays. If you don't set the View property, the ListView behaves just like its lesser-powered ancestor, the ListBox. However, the ListView becomes much more interesting when you supply a view object that indicates how data items should be formatted and styled.

Technically, the View property points to an instance of any class that derives from ViewBase (which is an abstract class). The ViewBase class is surprisingly simple; in fact, it's little more than a package that binds together two styles. One style applies to the ListView control (and is referenced by the DefaultStyleKey property), and the other style applies to the items in the ListView (and is referenced by the ItemContainerDefaultStyleKey property). The DefaultStyleKey and ItemContainerDefaultStyleKey properties don't actually provide the style; instead, they return a ResourceKey object that points to it.

At this point, you might wonder why you need a View property—after all, the ListBox already offers powerful data template and styling features (as do all classes that derive from ItemsControl). Ambitious developers can rework the visual appearance of the ListBox by supplying a different data template, layout panel, and control template.

In truth, you don't need a ListView class with a View property in order to create customizable multicolumned lists. In fact, you could achieve much the same thing on your own by using the template and styling features of the ListBox. However, the View property is a useful abstraction. Here are some of its advantages:

Reusable views: The ListView separates all the view-specific details into one object. That makes it easier to create views that are data-independent and can be used on more than one list.

Multiple views: The separation between the ListView control and the View objects also makes it easier to switch between multiple views with the same list. (For example, you use this technique in Windows Explorer to get a different perspective on your files and folders.) You could build the same feature by dynamically changing templates and styles, but it's easier to have just one object that encapsulates all the view details.

Better organization: The view object wraps two styles: one for the root ListView control and one that applies to the individual items in the list. Because these styles are packaged together, it's clear that these two pieces are related and may share certain details and interdependencies. For example, this makes a lot of sense for a column-based ListView, because it needs to keep its column headers and column data lined up.

Using this model, there's a great potential to create a number of useful prebuilt views that all developers can use. Unfortunately, WPF currently includes just one view object: the GridView. Although the GridView is extremely useful for creating multicolumn lists, you'll need to create your own custom view if you have other needs. The following sections show you how to do both.

■ **Note**   The GridView is a good choice if you want to show a configurable data display, and you want a grid-styled view to be one of the user's options. But if you want a grid that supports advanced styling, selection, or editing, you'll need to step up to the full-fledged DataGrid control described later in this chapter.

Creating Columns with the GridView

The GridView is a class that derives from ViewBase and represents a list view with multiple columns. You define those columns by adding GridViewColumn objects to the GridView.Columns collection.

Both GridView and GridViewColumn provide a small set of useful methods that you can use to customize the appearance of your list. To create the simplest, most straightforward list (which resembles the details view in Windows Explorer), you need to set just two properties for each GridViewColumn: Header and DisplayMemberBinding. The Header property supplies the text that's placed at the top of the column. The DisplayMemberBinding property contains a binding that extracts the piece of information you want to display from each data item.

Figure 22-1 shows a straightforward example with three columns of information about a product.

Figure 22-1. *A grid-based ListView*

Here's the markup that defines the three columns used in this example:

```
<ListView Margin="5" Name="lstProducts">
  <ListView.View>
    <GridView>
      <GridView.Columns>
        <GridViewColumn Header="Name"
         DisplayMemberBinding="{Binding Path=ModelName}" />
        <GridViewColumn Header="Model"
         DisplayMemberBinding="{Binding Path=ModelNumber}" />
        <GridViewColumn Header="Price" DisplayMemberBinding=
"{Binding Path=UnitCost, StringFormat={}{0:C}}" />
      </GridView.Columns>
    </GridView>
  </ListView.View>
</ListView>
```

This example has a few important points worth noticing. First, none of the columns has a hard-coded size. Instead, the GridView sizes its columns just large enough to fit the widest visible item (or the column header, if it's wider), which makes a lot of sense in the flow layout world of WPF. (Of course, this leaves you in a bit of trouble if you have huge column values. In this case, you may choose to wrap your text, as described in the upcoming "Cell Templates" section.)

Also, notice how the DisplayMemberBinding property is set by using a full-fledged binding expression, which supports all the tricks you learned about in Chapter 20, including string formatting and value converters.

Resizing Columns

Initially, the GridView makes each column just wide enough to fit the largest visible value. However, you can easily resize any column by clicking and dragging the edge of the column header. Or you can double-click the edge of the column header to force the GridViewColumn to resize itself based on whatever content is currently visible. For example, if you scroll down the list and find an item that's truncated because it's wider than the column, just double-click the right edge of that column's header. The column will automatically expand itself to fit.

For more micromanaged control over column size, you can set a specific width when you declare the column:

```
<GridViewColumn Width="300" ... />
```

This simply determines the initial size of the column. It doesn't prevent the user from resizing the column by using either of the techniques described previously. Unfortunately, the GridViewColumn class doesn't define properties such as MaxWidth and MinWidth, so there's no way to constrain how a column can be resized. Your only option is to supply a new template for the GridViewColumn's header if you want to disable resizing altogether.

■ **Note**   The user can also reorder columns by dragging a header to a new position.

Using Cell Templates

The GridViewColumn.DisplayMemberBinding property isn't the only option for showing data in a cell. Your other choice is the CellTemplate property, which takes a data template. This is exactly like the data templates you learned about in Chapter 20, except it applies to just one column. If you're ambitious, you can give each column its own data template.

Cell templates are a key piece of the puzzle when customizing the GridView. One feature that they allow is text wrapping. Ordinarily, the text in a column is wrapped in a single-line TextBlock. However, it's easy to change this detail by using a data template of your own devising:

```
<GridViewColumn Header="Description" Width="300">
  <GridViewColumn.CellTemplate>
    <DataTemplate>
      <TextBlock Text="{Binding Path=Description}" TextWrapping="Wrap"></TextBlock>
    </DataTemplate>
  </GridViewColumn.CellTemplate>
</GridViewColumn>
```

Notice that in order for the wrapping to have an effect, you need to constrain the width of the column by using the Width property. If the user resizes the column, the text will be rewrapped to fit. You *don't* want to constrain the width of the TextBlock, because that would ensure that your text is limited to a single specific size, no matter how wide or narrow the column becomes.

The only limitation in this example is that the data template needs to bind explicitly to the property you want to display. For that reason, you can't create a template that enables wrapping and reuse it for every piece of content you want to wrap. Instead, you need to create a separate template for each field. This isn't a problem in this simple example, but it's annoying if you create a more complex template that you would like to apply to other lists (for example, a template that converts data to an image and displays it in an Image element, or a template that uses a TextBox control to allow editing). There's no easy way to reuse any template on multiple columns; instead, you'll be forced to cut and paste the template, and then modify the binding.

■ **Note** It would be nice if you could create a data template that uses the DisplayMemberBinding property. That way, you could use DisplayMemberBinding to extract the specific property you want and use CellTemplate to format that content into the correct visual representation. Unfortunately, this just isn't possible. If you set both DisplayMember and CellTemplate, the GridViewColumn uses the DisplayMember property to set the content for the cell and ignores the template altogether.

Data templates aren't limited to tweaking the properties of a TextBlock. You can also use data templates to s upply completely different elements. For example, the following column uses a data template to show an image. The ProductImagePath converter (shown in Chapter 20) helps by loading the corresponding image file from the file system.

```
<GridViewColumn Header="Picture" >
  <GridViewColumn.CellTemplate>
    <DataTemplate>
      <Image Source=
"{Binding Path=ProductImagePath,Converter={StaticResource ImagePathConverter}}">
      </Image>
    </DataTemplate>
  </GridViewColumn.CellTemplate>
</GridViewColumn>
```

Figure 22-2 shows a ListView that uses both templates to show wrapped text and a product image.

Figure 22-2. *Columns that use templates*

■ **Tip** When creating a data template, you have the choice of defining it inline (as in the previous two examples) or referring to a resource that's defined elsewhere. Because column templates can't be reused for different fields, it's usually clearest to define them inline.

As you learned in Chapter 20, you can vary templates so that different data items get different templates. To do this, you need to create a template selector that chooses the appropriate template based on the properties of the data object at that position. To use this feature, create your selector, and use it to set the GridViewColumn. CellTemplateSelector property. For a full template selector example, see Chapter 20.

CUSTOMIZING COLUMN HEADERS

So far, you've seen how to customize the appearance of the values in every cell. However, you haven't done anything to fine-tune the column headers. If the standard gray boxes don't excite you, you'll be happy to find out that you can change the content and appearance of the column headers just as easily as the column values. In fact, you can use several approaches.

If you want to keep the gray column header boxes but you want to fill them with your own content, you can simply set the GridViewColumn.Header property. The previous examples have the Header property using ordinary text, but you can supply an element instead. Use a StackPanel that wraps a TextBlock and Image to create a fancy header that combines text and image content.

If you want to fill the column headers with your own content, but you don't want to specify this content separately for each column, you can use the GridViewColumn.HeaderTemplate property to define a data template. This data template binds to whatever object you've specified in the GridViewColumn.Header property and presents it accordingly.

If you want to reformat a specific column header, you can use the GridViewColumn.HeaderContainerStyle property to supply a style. If you want to reformat all the column headers in the same way, use the GridView. ColumnHeaderContainerStyle property instead.

If you want to completely change the appearance of the header (for example, replacing the gray box with a rounded blue border), you can supply a completely new control template for the header. Use GridViewColumn. HeaderTemplate to change a specific column, or use GridView.ColumnHeaderTemplate to change them all in the same way. You can even use a template selector to choose the correct template for a given header by setting the GridViewColumn.HeaderTemplateSelector or GridView.ColumnHeaderTemplateSelector property.

Creating a Custom View

If the GridView doesn't meet your needs, you can create your own view to extend the ListView's capabilities. Unfortunately, it's far from straightforward.

To understand the problem, you need to know a little more about the way a view works. Views do their work by overriding two protected properties: DefaultStyleKey and ItemContainerDefaultKeyStyle. Each property returns a specialized object called a ResourceKey, which points to a style that you've defined in XAML. The DefaultStyleKey property points to the style that should be applied to configure the overall ListView. The ItemContainer. DefaultKeyStyle property points to the style that should be used to configure each ListViewItem in the ListView. Although these styles are free to tweak any property, they usually do their work by replacing the ControlTemplate that's used for the ListView and the DataTemplate that's used for each ListViewItem.

Here's where the problems occur. The DataTemplate you use to display items is defined in XAML markup. Imagine you want to create a ListView that shows a tiled image for each item. This is easy enough using a DataTemplate—you simply need to bind the Source property of an Image to the correct property of your data object. But how do you know which data object the user will supply? If you hard-code property names as part of your view, you'll limit its usefulness, making it impossible to reuse your custom view in other scenarios. The alternative—forcing the user to supply the DataTemplate—means you can't pack as much functionality into the view, so reusing it won't be as useful.

■ **Tip**   Before you begin creating a custom view, consider whether you could get the same result by simply using the right DataTemplate with a ListBox or a ListView/GridView combination.

So why go to all the effort of designing a custom view if you can already get all the functionality you need by restyling the ListView (or even the ListBox)? The primary reason is to create a list that can dynamically change views. For example, you might want a product list that can be viewed in different modes, depending on the user's selection. You could implement this by dynamically swapping in different DataTemplate objects (and this is a reasonable approach), but often a view needs to change both the DataTemplate of the ListViewItem and the layout or overall appearance of the ListView itself. A view helps clarify the relationship between these details in your source code.

The following example shows you how to create a grid that can be switched seamlessly from one view to another. The grid begins in the familiar column-separated view but also supports two tiled image views, as shown in Figure 22-3 and Figure 22-4.

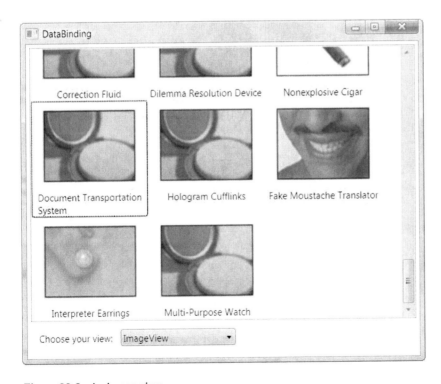

Figure 22-3. *An image view*

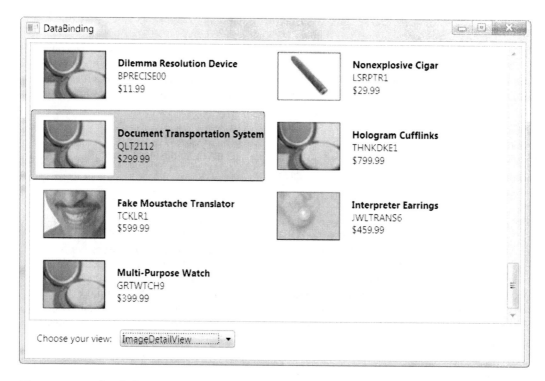

Figure 22-4. *A detailed image view*

The View Class

The first step that's required to build this example is to create the class that represents the custom view. This class must derive from ViewBase. In addition, it usually (although not always) overrides the DefaultStyleKey and ItemContainerDefaultStyleKey properties to supply style references.

In this example, the view is named TileView, because its key characteristic is that it tiles its items in the space provided. It uses a WrapPanel to lay out the contained ListViewItem objects. This view is not named ImageView, because the tile content isn't hard-coded and may not include images at all. Instead, the tile content is defined by using a template that the developer supplies when using the TileView.

The TileView class applies two styles: TileView (which applies to the ListView) and TileViewItem (which applies to the ListViewItem). Additionally, the TileView defines a property named ItemTemplate so the developer using the TileView can supply the correct data template. This template is then inserted inside each ListViewItem and used to create the tile content.

```
Public Class TileView
    Inherits ViewBase

    Private _itemTemplate As DataTemplate
    Public Property ItemTemplate() As DataTemplate
        Get
            Return _itemTemplate
        End Get
        Set(ByVal value As DataTemplate)
            _itemTemplate = value
```

```
                End Set
        End Property

        Protected Overrides ReadOnly Property DefaultStyleKey() As Object
            Get
                Return New ComponentResourceKey(Me.GetType(), "TileView")
            End Get
        End Property

        Protected Overrides ReadOnly Property ItemContainerDefaultStyleKey() _
          As Object
            Get
                Return New ComponentResourceKey(Me.GetType(), "TileViewItem")
            End Get
        End Property
End Class
```

As you can see, the TileView class doesn't do much. It simply provides a ComponentResourceKey reference that points to the correct style. You first learned about the ComponentResourceKey in Chapter 10, when considering how you could retrieve shared resources from a DLL assembly.

The ComponentResourceKey wraps two pieces of information: the type of class that owns the style and a descriptive ResourceId string that identifies the resource. In this example, the type is obviously the TileView class for both resource keys. The descriptive ResourceId names aren't as important, but you'll need to be consistent. In this example, the default style key is named TileView, and the style key for each ListViewItem is named TileViewItem. In the following section, you'll dig into both these styles and see how they're defined.

The View Styles

For the TileView to work as written, WPF needs to be able to find the styles that you want to use. The trick to making sure styles are available automatically is creating a resource dictionary named generic.xaml. This resource dictionary must be placed in a project subfolder named Themes. WPF uses the generic.xaml file to get the default styles that are associated with a class. (You learned about this system when you considered custom control development in Chapter 18.)

In this example, the generic.xaml file defines the styles that are associated with the TileView class. To set up the association between your styles and the TileView, you need to give your style the correct key in the generic.xaml resource dictionary. Rather than using an ordinary string key, WPF expects your key to be a ComponentResourceKey object, and this ComponentResourceKey needs to match the information that's returned by the DefaultStyleKey and ItemContainerDefaultStyleKey properties of the TileView class.

Here's the basic structure of the generic.xaml resource dictionary, with the correct keys:

```
<ResourceDictionary
    xmlns="http://schemas.microsoft.com/winfx/2006/xaml/presentation"
    xmlns:x="http://schemas.microsoft.com/winfx/2006/xaml"
    xmlns:local="clr-namespace:DataBinding">

  <Style x:Key="{ComponentResourceKey TypeInTargetAssembly={x:Type local:TileView},
ResourceId=TileView}"
    TargetType="{x:Type ListView}"
    BasedOn="{StaticResource {x:Type ListBox}}">
    ...
  </Style>
```

```
    <Style x:Key="{ComponentResourceKey TypeInTargetAssembly={x:Type local:TileView},
ResourceId=TileViewItem}"
      TargetType="{x:Type ListViewItem}"
      BasedOn="{StaticResource {x:Type ListBoxItem}}">
      ...
    </Style>

</ResourceDictionary>
```

As you can see, the key of each style is set to match the information provided by the TileView class. Additionally, the styles also set the TargetType property (to indicate which element the style modifies) and the BasedOn property (to inherit basic style settings from more fundamental styles used with the ListBox and ListBoxItem). This saves some work, and it allows you to focus on extending these styles with custom settings.

Because these two styles are associated with the TileView, they'll be used to configure the ListView whenever you've set the View property to a TileView object. If you're using a different view object, these styles will be ignored. This is the magic that makes the ListView work the way you want, so that it seamlessly reconfigures itself every time you change the View property.

The TileView style that applies to the ListView makes three changes:

- It adds a slightly different border around the ListView.

- It sets the attached Grid.IsSharedSizeScope property to True. This allows different list items to use shared column or row settings if they use the Grid layout container (a feature first explained in Chapter 3). In this example, it makes sure each item has the same dimensions in the detailed tile view.

- It changes the ItemsPanel from a StackPanel to a WrapPanel, allowing the tiling behavior. The WrapPanel width is set to match the width of the ListView.

Here's the full markup for this style:

```
<Style x:Key="{ComponentResourceKey TypeInTargetAssembly={x:Type local:TileView},
  ResourceId=TileView}"
  TargetType="{x:Type ListView}" BasedOn="{StaticResource {x:Type ListBox}}">
  <Setter Property="BorderBrush" Value="Black"></Setter>
  <Setter Property="BorderThickness" Value="0.5"></Setter>
  <Setter Property="Grid.IsSharedSizeScope" Value="True"></Setter>

  <Setter Property="ItemsPanel">
    <Setter.Value>
      <ItemsPanelTemplate>
        <WrapPanel Width="{Binding (FrameworkElement.ActualWidth),
                        RelativeSource={RelativeSource
                        AncestorType=ScrollContentPresenter}}">
        </WrapPanel>
      </ItemsPanelTemplate>
    </Setter.Value>
  </Setter>
</Style>
```

These are relatively minor changes. A more ambitious view could link to a style that changes the control template that's used for the ListView, modifying it much more dramatically. This is where you begin to see the benefits of the view model. By changing a single property in the ListView, you can apply a combination of related settings through two styles. The TileView style that applies to the ListViewItem changes a few other details. It sets the padding and content alignment and, most important, sets the DataTemplate that's used to display content.

Here's the full markup for this style:

```
<Style x:Key="{ComponentResourceKey TypeInTargetAssembly={x:Type local:TileView},
 ResourceId=TileViewItem}"
 TargetType="{x:Type ListViewItem}"
 BasedOn="{StaticResource {x:Type ListBoxItem}}">
  <Setter Property="Padding" Value="3"/>
  <Setter Property="HorizontalContentAlignment" Value="Center"></Setter>
  <Setter Property="ContentTemplate" Value="{Binding Path=View.ItemTemplate,
    RelativeSource={RelativeSource Mode=FindAncestor, AncestorType={x:Type ListView}
                    }}"></Setter>
</Style>
```

Remember that to ensure maximum flexibility, the TileView is designed to use a data template that's supplied by the developer. To apply this template, the TileView style needs to retrieve the TileView object (using the ListView.View property) and then pull the data template from the TileView.ItemTemplate property. This step is performed using a binding expression that searches up the element tree (using the FindAncestor RelativeSource mode) until it finds the containing ListView.

■ **Note**   Rather than setting the ListViewItem.ContentTemplate property, you could achieve the same result by setting the ListView.ItemTemplate property. It's really just a matter of preference.

Using the ListView

After you've built your view class and the supporting styles, you're ready to put them to use in a ListView control. To use a custom view, you simply need to set the ListView.View property to an instance of your view object, as shown here:

```
<ListView Name="lstProducts">
  <ListView.View>
    <TileView ... >
  </ListView.View>
</ListView>
```

However, this example demonstrates a ListView that can switch between three views. As a result, you need to instantiate three distinct view objects. The easiest way to manage this is to define each view object separately in the Windows.Resources collection. You can then load the view you want when the user makes a selection from the ComboBox control, by using this code:

```
Private Sub lstView_SelectionChanged(ByVal sender As Object, _
  ByVal e As SelectionChangedEventArgs)
    Dim selectedItem As ComboBoxItem = CType(lstView.SelectedItem, ComboBoxItem)
    lstProducts.View = CType(Me.FindResource(selectedItem.Content), ViewBase)
End Sub
```

The first view is simple enough—it uses the familiar GridView class that you considered earlier to create a multicolumn display. Here's the markup it uses:

```
<GridView x:Key="GridView">
  <GridView.Columns>
    <GridViewColumn Header="Name"
     DisplayMemberBinding="{Binding Path=ModelName}" />
    <GridViewColumn Header="Model"
     DisplayMemberBinding="{Binding Path=ModelNumber}" />
    <GridViewColumn Header="Price"
      DisplayMemberBinding="{Binding Path=UnitCost, StringFormat={}{0:C}}" />
  </GridView.Columns>
</GridView>
```

The two TileView objects are more interesting. Both of them supply a template to determine what the tile looks like. The ImageView (shown in Figure 22-3) uses a StackPanel that stacks the product image above the product title:

```
<local:TileView x:Key="ImageView">
  <local:TileView.ItemTemplate>
    <DataTemplate>
      <StackPanel Width="150" VerticalAlignment="Top">
        <Image Source="{Binding Path=ProductImagePath,
                        Converter={StaticResource ImagePathConverter}}">
        </Image>
        <TextBlock TextWrapping="Wrap" HorizontalAlignment="Center"
         Text="{Binding Path=ModelName}"></TextBlock>
      </StackPanel>
    </DataTemplate>
  </local:TileView.ItemTemplate>
</local:TileView>
```

The ImageDetailView uses a two-column grid. A small version of the image is placed on the left, and more-detailed information is placed on the right. The second column is placed into a shared-size group so that all the items have the same width (as determined by the largest text value).

```
<local:TileView x:Key="ImageDetailView">
  <local:TileView.ItemTemplate>
    <DataTemplate>
      <Grid>
        <Grid.ColumnDefinitions>
          <ColumnDefinition Width="Auto"></ColumnDefinition>
          <ColumnDefinition Width="Auto" SharedSizeGroup="Col2"></ColumnDefinition>
        </Grid.ColumnDefinitions>

        <Image Margin="5" Width="100"
         Source="{Binding Path=ProductImagePath,
                  Converter={StaticResource ImagePathConverter}}">
        </Image>
        <StackPanel Grid.Column="1" VerticalAlignment="Center">
          <TextBlock FontWeight="Bold" Text="{Binding Path=ModelName}"></TextBlock>
          <TextBlock Text="{Binding Path=ModelNumber}"></TextBlock>
          <TextBlock Text="{Binding Path=UnitCost, StringFormat={}{0:C}}">
```

```
          </TextBlock>
        </StackPanel>
      </Grid>
    </DataTemplate>
  </local:TileView.ItemTemplate>
</local:TileView>
```

This is undoubtedly more code than you wanted to generate to create a ListView with multiple viewing options. However, the example is now complete, and you can easily create additional views (based on the TileView class) that supply different item templates and give you even more viewing options.

Passing Information to a View

You can make your view classes more flexible by adding properties that the consumer can set when using the view. Your style can then retrieve these values by using data binding and apply them to configure the Setter objects.

For example, the TileView currently highlights selected items with an unattractive blue color. The effect is all the more jarring because it makes the black text with the product details more difficult to read. As you probably remember from Chapter 17, you can fix these details by using a customized control template with the correct triggers.

But rather than hard-code a set of pleasing colors, it makes sense to let the view consumer specify this detail. To do this with the TileView, you could add a set of properties like these:

```
Private _selectedBackground As Brush = Brushes.Transparent
Public Property SelectedBackground() As Brush
    Get
        Return _selectedBackground
    End Get
    Set(ByVal value As Brush)
        _selectedBackground = value
    End Set
End Property

Private _selectedBorderBrush As Brush = Brushes.Black
Public Property SelectedBorderBrush() As Brush
    Get
        Return _selectedBorderBrush
    End Get
    Set(ByVal value As Brush)
        _selectedBorderBrush = value
    End Set
End Property
```

Now you can set these details when instantiating a view object:

```
<local:TileView x:Key="ImageDetailView" SelectedBackground="LightSteelBlue">
  ...
</local:TileView>
```

The final step is to use these colors in the ListViewItem style. To do so, you need to add a Setter that replaces the ControlTemplate. In this case, a simple rounded border is used with a ContentPresenter. When the item is selected, a trigger fires and applies the new border and background colors:

```
<Style x:Key="{ComponentResourceKey TypeInTargetAssembly={x:Type local:TileView},
 ResourceId=TileViewItem}"
 TargetType="{x:Type ListViewItem}"
 BasedOn="{StaticResource {x:Type ListBoxItem}}">
 ...
 <Setter Property="Template">
   <Setter.Value>
     <ControlTemplate TargetType="{x:Type ListBoxItem}">
       <Border Name="Border" BorderThickness="1" CornerRadius="3">
         <ContentPresenter />
       </Border>
       <ControlTemplate.Triggers>
         <Trigger Property="IsSelected" Value="True">
           <Setter TargetName="Border" Property="BorderBrush"
           Value="{Binding Path=View.SelectedBorderBrush,
                   RelativeSource={RelativeSource Mode=FindAncestor,
                   AncestorType={x:Type ListView}}}"></Setter>
           <Setter TargetName="Border" Property="Background"
           Value="{Binding Path=View.SelectedBackground,
                   RelativeSource={RelativeSource Mode=FindAncestor,
                   AncestorType={x:Type ListView}}}"></Setter>
         </Trigger>
       </ControlTemplate.Triggers>
     </ControlTemplate>
   </Setter.Value>
 </Setter>
</Style>
```

Figure 22-3 and Figure 22-4 show this selection behavior. Figure 22-3 uses a transparent background, and Figure 22-4 uses a light blue highlight color.

■ **Note** Unfortunately, this technique of passing information to a view still doesn't help you make a truly generic view. That's because there's no way to modify the data templates based on this information.

The TreeView

The TreeView is a Windows staple, and it's a common ingredient in everything from the Windows Explorer file browser to the .NET help library. WPF's implementation of the TreeView is impressive, because it has full support for data binding.

The TreeView is, at its heart, a specialized ItemsControl that hosts TreeViewItem objects. But unlike the ListViewItem, the TreeViewItem is not a content control. Instead, each TreeViewItem is a separate ItemsControl, with the ability to hold more TreeViewItem objects. This flexibility allows you to create a deeply layered data display.

■ **Note** Technically, the TreeViewItem derives from HeaderedItemsControl, which derives from ItemsControl. The HeaderedItemsControl class adds a Header property, which holds the content (usually text) that you want to display for that item in the tree. WPF includes two other HeaderedItemsControl classes: the MenuItem and the ToolBar.

Here's the skeleton of a very basic TreeView, which is declared entirely in markup:

```
<TreeView>
  <TreeViewItem Header="Fruit">
    <TreeViewItem Header="Orange"/>
    <TreeViewItem Header="Banana"/>
    <TreeViewItem Header="Grapefruit"/>
  </TreeViewItem>
 <TreeViewItem Header="Vegetables">
    <TreeViewItem Header="Aubergine"/>
    <TreeViewItem Header="Squash"/>
    <TreeViewItem Header="Spinach"/>
  </TreeViewItem>
</TreeView>
```

It's not necessary to construct a TreeView out of TreeViewItem objects. In fact, you have the ability to add virtually any element to a TreeView, including buttons, panels, and images. However, if you want to display nontext content, the best approach is to use a TreeViewItem wrapper and supply your content through the TreeViewItem. Header property. This gives you the same effect as adding non-TreeViewItem elements directly to your TreeView but makes it easier to manage a few TreeView-specific details, such as selection and node expansion. If you want to display a non-UIElement object, you can format it by using data templates with the HeaderTemplate or HeaderTemplateSelector property.

Creating a Data-Bound TreeView

Usually, you won't fill a TreeView with fixed information that's hard-coded in your markup. Instead, you'll construct the TreeViewItem objects you need programmatically, or you'll use data binding to display a collection of objects.

Filling a TreeView with data is easy enough—as with any ItemsControl, you simply set the ItemsSource property. However, this technique fills only the first level of the TreeView. A more interesting use of the TreeView incorporates *hierarchical data* that has some sort of nested structure.

For example, consider the TreeView shown in Figure 22-5. The first level consists of Category objects, and the second level shows the Product objects that fall into each category.

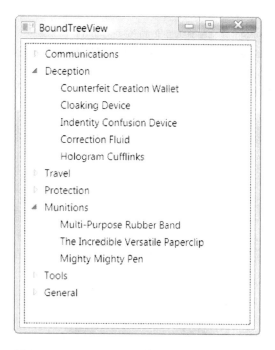

Figure 22-5. *A TreeView of categories and products*

The TreeView makes hierarchical data display easy, whether you're working with handcrafted classes or the ADO.NET DataSet. You simply need to specify the correct data templates. Your templates indicate the relationship between the different levels of the data.

For example, imagine you want to build the example shown in Figure 22-5. You've already seen the Products class that's used to represent a single Product. But to create this example, you also need a Category class. Like the Product class, the Category class implements INotifyPropertyChanged to provide change notifications. The only new detail is that the Category class exposes a collection of Product objects through its Product property.

```
Public Class Category
    Implements INotifyPropertyChanged

    Private _categoryName As String
    Public Property CategoryName() As String
        Get
            Return _categoryName
        End Get
        Set(ByVal value As String)
            _categoryName = value
            OnPropertyChanged(New PropertyChangedEventArgs("CategoryName"))
        End Set
    End Property

    Private _products As ObservableCollection(Of Product)
    Public Property Products() As ObservableCollection(Of Product)
```

```vb
        Get
            Return _products
        End Get
        Set(ByVal value As ObservableCollection(Of Product))
            _products = value
            OnPropertyChanged(New PropertyChangedEventArgs("Products"))
        End Set
    End Property

    Public Event PropertyChanged As PropertyChangedEventHandler _
        Implements INotifyPropertyChanged.PropertyChanged

    Public Sub OnPropertyChanged(ByVal e As PropertyChangedEventArgs)
        If Not PropertyChangedEvent Is Nothing Then
            RaiseEvent PropertyChanged(Me, e)
        End If
    End Sub

    Public Sub New(ByVal categoryName As String, _
        ByVal products As ObservableCollection(Of Product))
        Me.CategoryName = categoryName
        Me.Products = products
    End Sub
End Class
```

■ **Tip** This trick—creating a collection that exposes another collection through a property—is the secret to navigating parent-child relationships with WPF data binding. For example, you can bind a collection of Category objects to one list control, and then bind another list control to the Products property of the currently selected Category object to show the related Product objects.

To use the Category class, you also need to modify the data access code that you first saw in Chapter 19. Now you'll query the information about products and categories from the database. In this example, the window calls the StoreDB.GetCategoriesAndProducts() method to get a collection of Category objects, each of which has a nested collection of Product objects. The Category collection is then bound to the tree so that it will appear in the first level:

```
treeCategories.ItemsSource = Application.StoreDB.GetCategoriesAndProducts()
```

To display the categories, you need to supply a TreeView.ItemTemplate that can process the bound objects. In this example, you need to display the CategoryName property of each Category object. Here's the data template that does it:

```xml
<TreeView Name="treeCategories" Margin="5">
  <TreeView.ItemTemplate>
    <HierarchicalDataTemplate>
      <TextBlock Text="{Binding Path=CategoryName}" />
    </HierarchicalDataTemplate>
  </TreeView.ItemTemplate>
</TreeView>
```

The only unusual detail here is that the TreeView.ItemTemplate is set by using a HierarchicalDataTemplate object instead of a DataTemplate. The HierarchicalDataTemplate has the added advantage that it can wrap a second template. The HierarchicalDataTemplate can then pull a collection of items from the first level and provide that to the second-level template. You simply set the ItemsSource property to identify the property that has the child items, and you set the ItemTemplate property to indicate how each object should be formatted.

Here's the revised data template:

```
<TreeView Name="treeCategories" Margin="5">
  <TreeView.ItemTemplate>
    <HierarchicalDataTemplate ItemsSource="{Binding Path=Products}">
      <TextBlock Text="{Binding Path=CategoryName}" />
      <HierarchicalDataTemplate.ItemTemplate>
        <DataTemplate>
          <TextBlock Text="{Binding Path=ModelName}" />
        </DataTemplate>
      </HierarchicalDataTemplate.ItemTemplate>
    </HierarchicalDataTemplate>
  </TreeView.ItemTemplate>
</TreeView>
```

Essentially, you now have two templates, one for each level of the tree. The second template uses the selected item from the first template as its data source.

Although this markup works perfectly well, it's common to factor out each data template and apply it to your data objects by data type instead of by position. To understand what that means, it helps to consider a revised version of the markup for the data-bound TreeView:

```
<Window x:Class="BoundTreeView" ...
    xmlns:local="clr-namespace:DataBinding">
  <Window.Resources>
    <HierarchicalDataTemplate DataType="{x:Type local:Category}"
     ItemsSource="{Binding Path=Products}">
      <TextBlock Text="{Binding Path=CategoryName}"/>
    </HierarchicalDataTemplate>

    <HierarchicalDataTemplate DataType="{x:Type local:Product}">
      <TextBlock Text="{Binding Path=ModelName}" />
    </HierarchicalDataTemplate>
  </Window.Resources>

  <Grid>
    <TreeView Name="treeCategories" Margin="5">
    </TreeView>
  </Grid>
</Window>
```

In this example, the TreeView doesn't explicitly set its ItemTemplate. Instead, the appropriate ItemTemplate is used based on the data type of the bound object. Similarly, the Category template doesn't specify the ItemTemplate that should be used to process the Products collection. It's also chosen automatically by data type. This tree is now able to show a list of products or a list of categories that contain groups of products.

In the current example, these changes don't add anything new. This approach simplifies the markup and makes it easier to reuse your templates, but it doesn't affect the way your data is displayed. However, if you have deeply nested trees that have looser structures, this design is invaluable. For example, imagine you're creating a tree of Manager objects, and each Manager object has an Employees collection. This collection might contain ordinary

Employee objects or other Manager objects, which would in turn contain more Employees. If you use the type-based template system shown earlier, each object automatically gets the template that's right for its data type.

Binding a DataSet to a TreeView

You can also use a TreeView to show a multilayered DataSet—one that has relationships linking one DataTable to another.

For example, here's a code routine that creates a DataSet, fills it with a table of products and a separate table of categories, and links the two tables together with a DataRelation object:

```
Public Function GetCategoriesAndProducts() As DataSet
    Dim con As New SqlConnection(connectionString)
    Dim cmd As New SqlCommand("GetProducts", con)
    cmd.CommandType = CommandType.StoredProcedure
    Dim adapter As New SqlDataAdapter(cmd)

    Dim ds As New DataSet()
    adapter.Fill(ds, "Products")
    cmd.CommandText = "GetCategories"
    adapter.Fill(ds, "Categories")

    ' Set up a relation between these tables.
    Dim relCategoryProduct As New DataRelation("CategoryProduct", _
      ds.Tables("Categories").Columns("CategoryID"), _
      ds.Tables("Products").Columns("CategoryID"))
    ds.Relations.Add(relCategoryProduct)

    Return ds
End Function
```

To use this in a TreeView, you begin by binding to the DataTable you want to use for the first level:

```
Dim ds As DataSet = Application.StoreDB.GetCategoriesAndProductsDataSet()
treeCategories.ItemsSource = ds.Tables("Categories").DefaultView
```

But how do you get the related rows? After all, you can't call a method such as GetChildRows() from XAML. Fortunately, the WPF data-binding system has built-in support for this scenario. The trick is to use the name of your DataRelation as the ItemsSource for your second level. In this example, the DataRelation was created with the name CategoryProduct, so this markup does the trick:

```
<TreeView Name="treeCategories" Margin="5">
  <TreeView.ItemTemplate>
    <HierarchicalDataTemplate ItemsSource="{Binding CategoryProduct}">
      <TextBlock Text="{Binding CategoryName}" Padding="2" />
        <HierarchicalDataTemplate.ItemTemplate>
          <DataTemplate>
            <TextBlock Text="{Binding ModelName}" Padding="2" />
          </DataTemplate>
        </HierarchicalDataTemplate.ItemTemplate>
    </HierarchicalDataTemplate>
  </TreeView.ItemTemplate>
</TreeView>
```

Now this example works in the same way as the previous example, which used custom Product and Category objects.

Just-in-Time Node Creation

TreeView controls are often used to hold huge amounts of data. That's because the TreeView display is collapsible. Even if the user scrolls from top to bottom, not all the information is necessarily visible. The information that isn't visible can be omitted from the TreeView altogether, reducing its overhead (and the amount of time required to fill the tree). Even better, each TreeViewItem fires an Expanded event when it's opened and a Collapsed event when it's closed. You can use this point in time to fill in missing nodes or discard ones that you don't need. This technique is called *just-in-time node creation*.

Just-in-time node creation can be applied to applications that pull their data from a database, but the classic example is a directory-browsing application. In current times, most people have huge, sprawling hard drives. Although you could fill a TreeView with the directory structure of a hard drive, the process is aggravatingly slow. A better idea is to begin with a partially collapsed view and allow the user to dig down into specific directories (as shown in Figure 22-6). As each node is opened, the corresponding subdirectories are added to the tree—a process that's nearly instantaneous.

Figure 22-6. *Digging into a directory tree*

Using a just-in-time TreeView to display the folders on a hard drive is nothing new. (In fact, the technique is demonstrated in my book *Pro .NET 2.0 Windows Forms and Custom Controls in VB 2005* [Apress, 2005].) However, event routing makes the WPF solution just a bit more elegant.

The first step is to add a list of drives to the TreeView when the window first loads. Initially, the node for each drive is collapsed. The drive letter is displayed in the header, and the DriveInfo object is stored in the TreeViewItem. Tag property to make it easier to find the nested directories later without re-creating the object. (This increases the memory overhead of the application, but it also reduces the number of file-access security checks. The overall effect is small, but it improves performance slightly and simplifies the code.)

Here's the code that fills the TreeView with a list of drives, using the System.IO.DriveInfo class:

```
For Each drive As DriveInfo In DriveInfo.GetDrives()
    Dim item As New TreeViewItem()
    item.Tag = drive
    item.Header = drive.ToString()

    item.Items.Add("*")
    treeFileSystem.Items.Add(item)
Next
```

This code adds a placeholder (a string with an asterisk) under each drive node. The placeholder is not shown, because the node begins in a collapsed state. As soon as the node is expanded, you can remove the placeholder and add the list of subdirectories in its place.

▌ **Note**   The placeholder is a useful tool that can allow you to determine whether the user has expanded this folder to view its contents yet. However, the primary purpose of the placeholder is to make sure the expand icon appears next to this item. Without that, the user won't be able to expand the directory to look for subfolders. If the directory doesn't include any subfolders, the expand icon will simply disappear when the user attempts to expand it, which is similar to the behavior of Windows Explorer when viewing network folders.

To perform the just-in-time node creation, you must handle the TreeViewItem.Expanded event. Because this event uses bubbling, you can attach an event handler directly on the TreeView to handle the Expanded event for any TreeViewItem inside:

```
<TreeView Name="treeFileSystem" TreeViewItem.Expanded="item_Expanded">
</TreeView>
```

Here's the code that handles the event and fills in the missing next level of the tree by using the System.IO.DirectoryInfo class:

```
Private Sub item_Expanded(ByVal sender As Object, ByVal e As RoutedEventArgs)
    Dim item As TreeViewItem = CType(e.OriginalSource, TreeViewItem)
    item.Items.Clear()

    Dim dir As DirectoryInfo
    If TypeOf item.Tag Is DriveInfo Then
        Dim drive As DriveInfo = CType(item.Tag, DriveInfo)
        dir = drive.RootDirectory
    Else
        dir = CType(item.Tag, DirectoryInfo)
    End If
```

```
    Try
        For Each subDir As DirectoryInfo In dir.GetDirectories()
            Dim newItem As New TreeViewItem()
            newItem.Tag = subDir
            newItem.Header = subDir.ToString()
            newItem.Items.Add("*")
            item.Items.Add(newItem)
        Next
    Catch
        ' An exception could be thrown in this code if you don't
        ' have sufficient security permissions for a file or directory.
        ' You can catch and then ignore this exception.
    End Try
End Sub
```

Currently, this code performs a refresh every time the item is expanded. Optionally, you could perform this only the first time it's expanded, when the placeholder is found. This reduces the work your application needs to do, but it increases the chance of out-of-date information. Alternatively, you could perform a refresh every time an item is selected by handling the TreeViewItem.Selected event, or you could use a component such as the System. IO.FileSystemWatcher to wait for operating system notifications when a folder is added, removed, or renamed. The FileSystemWatcher is the only way to ensure that you update the directory tree immediately when a change happens, but it also has the greatest overhead.

CREATING ADVANCED TREEVIEW CONTROLS

There's a lot that you can accomplish when you combine the power of control templates (discussed in Chapter 17) with the TreeView. In fact, you can create a control that looks and behaves in a radically different way simply by replacing the templates for the TreeView and TreeViewItem controls.

Making these adjustments requires some deeper template exploration. You can get started with some eye-opening examples. Visual Studio includes a sample of a multicolumned TreeView that unites a tree with a grid. To browse it, look for the index entry *TreeListView Sample [WPF]* in the Visual Studio help. Another intriguing example is Josh Smith's layout experiment, which transforms the TreeView into something that more closely resembles an organizational chart. You can view the full code at www.codeproject.com/KB/WPF/CustomTreeViewLayout.aspx.

The DataGrid

As its name suggests, the DataGrid is a data-display control that takes the information from a collection of objects and renders it in a grid of rows and cells. Each row corresponds to a separate object, and each column corresponds to a property in that object.

The DataGrid adds much-needed versatility for dealing with data in WPF. Its column-based model gives it remarkable formatting flexibility. Its selection model allows you to choose whether users can select a row, multiple rows, or some combination of cells. Its editing support is powerful enough that you can use the DataGrid as an all-in-one data editor for simple and complex data.

To create a quick-and-dirty DataGrid, you can use automatic column generation. To do so, you need to set the AutoGenerateColumns property to True (which is the default value):

```
<DataGrid x:Name="gridProducts" AutoGenerateColumns="True">
</DataGrid>
```

Now you can fill the DataGrid as you fill a list control, by setting the ItemsSource property:

```
gridProducts.DataSource = products
```

Figure 22-7 shows a DataGrid that uses automatic column generation with the collection of Product objects. For automatic column generation, the DataGrid uses reflection to find every public property in the bound data object. It creates a column for each property.

Figure 22-7. *A DataGrid with automatically generated columns*

To display nonstring properties, the DataGrid calls ToString(), which works well for numbers, dates, and other simple data types, but it won't work as well if your objects include a more complex data object. (In this case, you may want to explicitly define your columns, which gives you the chance to bind to a subproperty, use a value converter, or apply a template to get the correct display content.)

Table 22-1 lists some of the properties you can use to customize a DataGrid's basic appearance. In the following sections, you'll see how to get fine-grained formatting control with styles and templates. You'll also see how the DataGrid deals with sorting and selection, and you'll consider many more properties that underlie these features.

Table 22-1. *Basic Display Properties for the DataGrid*

Name	Description
RowBackground and AlternatingRowBackground	The brush that's used to paint the background behind every row (RowBackground) and whether alternate rows are painted with a different background color (AlternatingRowBackground), making it easier to distinguish rows at a glance. By default, the DataGrid gives odd-numbered rows a white background and even-numbered rows a light-gray background.
ColumnHeaderHeight	The height (in device-independent units) of the row that has the column headers at the top of the DataGrid.

(continued)

Table 22-1. (*continued*)

Name	Description
RowHeaderWidth	The width (in device-independent units) of the column that has the row headers. This is the column at the far left of the grid, which does not show any data. It indicates the currently selected row (with an arrow) and when the row is being edited (with an arrow in a circle).
ColumnWidth	The sizing mode that's used to set the default width of every column, as a DataGridLength object. (The following section explains your column-sizing options.)
RowHeight	The height of every row. This setting is useful if you plan to display multiple lines of text or different content (for example, images) in the DataGrid. Unlike columns, rows cannot be resized by the user.
GridLinesVisibility	A value from the DataGridGridlines enumeration that determines which grid lines are shown (Horizontal, Vertical, None, or All).
VerticalGridLinesBrush	The brush that's used to paint the grid lines between columns.
HorizontalGridLinesBrush	The brush that's used to paint the grid lines between rows.
HeadersVisibility	A value from the DataGridHeaders enumeration that determines which headers are shown (Column, Row, All, None).
HorizontalScrollBarVisibility and VerticalScrollBarVisibility	A value from the ScrollBarVisibility enumeration that determines whether a scrollbar is shown when needed (Auto), always (Visible), or never (Hidden). The default for both properties is Auto.

Resizing and Rearranging Columns

When displaying automatically generated columns, the DataGrid attempts to size the width of each column intelligently, according to the DataGrid.ColumnWidth property.

To set the ColumnWidth property, you supply a DataGridLength object. Your DataGridLength can specify an exact size (in device-independent units) or a special sizing mode, which gets the DataGrid to do some of the work for you. If you choose to use an exact size, simply set ColumnWidth equal to the appropriate number (in XAML) or supply the number as a constructor argument when creating the DataGridLength (in code):

```
grid.ColumnWidth = New DataGridLength(150)
```

The specialized sizing modes are more interesting. You access them through the shared properties of the DataGridLength class. Here's an example that uses the default DataGridLength.SizeToHeader sizing mode, which means the columns are made wide enough to accommodate their header text:

```
grid.ColumnWidth = DataGridLength.SizeToHeader
```

Another popular option is DataGridLength.SizeToCells, which widens each column to fit the widest value that's currently in view. The DataGrid attempts to preserve this intelligent sizing approach when the user starts scrolling through the data. As soon as you come across a row with longer data, the DataGrid widens the appropriate columns to fit it. This automatic sizing is one-way only, so columns don't shrink when you leave large data behind.

Your other special sizing mode choice is DataGridLength.Auto, which works just like DataGridLength.SizeToCells, except that each column is widened to fit the largest displayed value *or* the column header text—whichever is wider.

The DataGrid also allows you to use a proportional sizing system that parallels the star-sizing in the Grid layout panel. Once again, * represents proportional sizing, and you can add a number to split the available space by using the ratios you pick (say, 2* and * to give the first column twice the space of the second). To set up this sort of relationship, or to give your columns different widths or sizing modes, you need to explicitly set the Width property of each column object. You'll see how to explicitly define and configure DataGrid columns in the next section.

The automatic sizing of the DataGrid columns is interesting and often useful, but it's not always what you want. Consider the example shown in Figure 22-7, which contains a Description column that holds a long string of text. Initially, the Description column is made extremely wide to fit this data, crowding the other columns out of the way. (In Figure 22-7, the user has manually resized the Description column to a more sensible size. All the other columns are left at their initial widths.) After a column has been resized, it doesn't exhibit the automatic enlarging behavior when the user scrolls through the data.

■ **Tip** Of course, you don't want to force your users to grapple with ridiculously wide columns. For that reason, you'll also choose to define a different column width or different sizing mode for each column. To do this, you need to define your columns explicitly and set the DataGridColumn.Width property. When set on a column, this property overrides the DataGrid.ColumnWidth default. You'll learn how to define your columns explicitly in the next section.

Ordinarily, users can resize columns by dragging the column edge to either size. You can prevent the user from resizing the columns in your DataGrid by setting the CanUserResizeColumns property to False. If you want to be more specific, you can prevent the user from resizing an individual column by setting the CanUserResize property of that column to False. You can also prevent the user from making the column extremely narrow by setting the column's MinWidth property.

The DataGrid has another surprise frill that lets users customize the column display. Not only can columns be resized, but they can also be dragged from one position to another. If you don't want users to have this reordering ability, set the CanUserReorderColumns property of the DataGrid or the CanUserReorder property of a specific column to False.

Defining Columns

Using automatically generated columns, you can quickly create a DataGrid that shows all your data. However, you give up a fair bit of control. For example, you can't control how columns are ordered, how wide they are, how the values inside are formatted, and what header text is placed at the top.

A far more powerful approach is to turn off automatic column generation by setting AutoGenerateColumns to False. You can then define the columns you want explicitly, with the settings you want and in the order you specify. To do this, you need to fill the DataGrid.Columns collection with the correct column objects.

Currently, the DataGrid supports several types of columns, which are represented by different classes that derive from DataGridColumn:

> *DataGridTextColumn*: This column is the standard choice for most data types. The value is converted to text and displayed in a TextBlock. When you edit the row, the TextBlock is replaced with a standard text box.

> *DataGridCheckBoxColumn*: This column shows a check box. This column type is used automatically for Boolean (or nullable Boolean) values. Ordinarily, the check box is read-only, but when you edit the row, it becomes a normal check box.

> *DataGridHyperlinkColumn*: This column shows a clickable link. If used in conjunction with WPF navigation containers such as the Frame or NavigationWindow, it allows the user to navigate to another URI (typically, an external website).

DataGridComboBox: This column looks like a DataGridTextColumn initially, but changes to a drop-down ComboBox in edit mode. It's a good choice when you want to constrain edits to a small set of allowed values.

DataGridTemplateColumn: This column is by far the most powerful option. It allows you to define a data template for displaying column values, with all the flexibility and power you have when using templates in a list control. For example, you can use a DataGridTemplateColumn to display image data or to use a specialized WPF control (such as a drop-down list with valid values or a DatePicker for date values).

For example, here's a revised DataGrid that creates a two-column display with product names and prices. It also applies clearer column captions and widens the Product column to fit its data:

```
<DataGrid x:Name="gridProducts" Margin="5" AutoGenerateColumns="False">
  <DataGrid.Columns>
    <DataGridTextColumn Header="Product" Width="175"
     Binding="{Binding Path=ModelName}"></DataGridTextColumn>
    <DataGridTextColumn Header="Price"
     Binding="{Binding Path=UnitCost}"></DataGridTextColumn>
  </DataGrid.Columns>
</DataGrid>
```

When you define a column, you almost always set three details: the header text that appears at the top of the column, the width of the column, and the binding that gets the data.

Usually, you'll use a simple string to set the DataGridColumn.Header property, but there's no need to stick to ordinary text. The column header acts as content control, and you can supply any element for the Header property, including an image or a layout panel with a combination of elements.

The DataGridColumn.Width property supports hard-coded values and several automatic sizing modes, just like the DataGrid.ColumnWidth property you considered in the previous section. The only difference is that DataGridColumn.Width applies to a single column, while DataGrid.ColumnWidth sets the default for the whole table. When DataGridColumn.Width is set, it overrides the DataGrid.ColumnWidth.

The most important detail is the binding expression that provides the correct information for the column, as set by the DataGridColumn.Binding property. This approach is different from the simple list controls such as the ListBox and ComboBox. These controls include a DisplayMemberPath property instead of a Binding property. The Binding approach is more flexible—it allows you to use string formatting and value converters without needing to switch to a full-fledged template column.

```
<DataGridTextColumn Header="Price" Binding=
  "{Binding Path=UnitCost, StringFormat={}{0:C}}">
</DataGridTextColumn>
```

■ **Tip** You can dynamically show and hide columns by modifying the Visibility property of the corresponding column object. Additionally, you can move columns at any time by changing their DisplayIndex values.

DataGridCheckBoxColumn

The Product class doesn't include any Boolean properties. If it did, the DataGridCheckBoxColumn would be a useful option.

As with DataGridTextColumn, the Binding property extracts the data—in this case, the True or False value that's used to set the IsChecked property of the CheckBox element inside. The DataGridCheckBoxColumn also adds a property named Content that lets you show optional content alongside the check box. Finally, the DataGridCheckBoxColumn includes an IsThreeState property, which determines whether the check box supports the undetermined state as well as the more obvious checked and unchecked states. If you're using the DataGridCheckBoxColumn to show the information from a nullable Boolean value, you can set IsThreeState property to True. That way, the user can click back to the undetermined state (which shows a lightly shaded check box) to return the bound value to Nothing.

DataGridHyperlinkColumn

The DataGridHyperlinkColumn allows you to display text values that contain a single URL each. For example, if the Product class has a string property named ProductLink, and that property contained values such as http://myproducts.com/info?productID=10432, you could display this information in a DataGridHyperlinkColumn. Every bound value would be displayed using the Hyperlink element, and rendered like this:

```
<Hyperlink NavigateUri="http://myproducts.com/info?productID=10432"
 >http://myproducts.com/info?productID=10432</Hyperlink>
```

Then the user could click a hyperlink to trigger navigation and visit the related page, with no code required. However, there's a major caveat: this automatic navigation trick works only if you've placed your DataGrid in a container that supports navigation events, such as the Frame or NavigationWindow. You'll learn about both controls and the Hyperlink in Chapter 24. If you want a more versatile way to accomplish a similar effect, consider using the DataGridTemplateColumn. You can use it to show underlined, clickable text (in fact, you can even use the Hyperlink control), but you'll have the flexibility of handling click events in your code.

Ordinarily, the DataGridHyperlinkColumn uses the same piece of information for navigation and for display. However, you can specify these details separately if you want. To do so, just set the URI with the Binding property, and use the optional ContentBinding property to get display text from a different property in the bound data object.

DataGridComboBoxColumn

The DataGridComboBoxColumn shows ordinary text initially, but provides a streamlined editing experience that allows the user to pick from a list of available options in a ComboBox control. (In fact, the user will be forced to choose from the list, as the ComboBox does not allow direct text entry.) In the example in Figure 22-8, the user is choosing the product category from a DataGridComboBoxColumn.

Figure 22-8. *Choosing from a list of allowed values*

To use the DataGridComboBoxColumn, you need to decide how to populate the combo box in edit mode. To do that, you simply set the DataGridComboBoxColumn.ItemsSource collection. The absolute simplest approach is to fill it by hand, in markup. The following example adds a list of strings to the combo box:

```
<DataGridComboBoxColumn Header="Category"
 SelectedItemBinding="{Binding Path=CategoryName}">
  <DataGridComboBoxColumn.ItemsSource>
    <col:ArrayList>
      <sys:String>General</sys:String>
      <sys:String>Communications</sys:String>
      <sys:String>Deception</sys:String>
      <sys:String>Munitions</sys:String>
      <sys:String>Protection</sys:String>
      <sys:String>Tools</sys:String>
      <sys:String>Travel</sys:String>
    </col:ArrayList>
  </DataGridComboBoxColumn.ItemsSource>
</DataGridComboBoxColumn>
```

In order for this markup to work as written, you must map the sys and col prefixes to the appropriate .NET namespaces:

```
<Window ...
 xmlns:col="clr-namespace:System.Collections;assembly=mscorlib"
 xmlns:sys="clr-namespace:System;assembly=mscorlib">
```

This works perfectly well, but it's not the best design, as it embeds data details deep into your user interface markup. Fortunately, you have several other options:

- Pull the data collection out of a resource. It's up to you whether you want to define the collection by using markup (as in the previous example) or generate it in code (as in the following example).

- Pull the ItemsSource collection out of a shared method, using the Static markup extension. But for solid code design, limit yourself to calling a method in your window class, not one in a data class.

- Pull the data collection out of an ObjectProvider resource, which can then call a data access class.

- Set the DataGridComboBox.Column property directly in code.

In many situations, the values you display in the list aren't the values you want to store in the data object. One common case occurs when dealing with related data (for example, orders that link to products, billing records that link to customers, and so on).

The StoreDB example includes one such relationship, between products and categories. In the back-end database, each product is linked to a specific category by using the CategoryID field. This fact is hidden in the simplified data model that all the examples have used so far, which gives the Product class a CategoryName property (rather than a CategoryID property). The advantage of this approach is convenience, as it keeps the salient information—the category name for each product—close at hand. The disadvantage is that the CategoryName property isn't really editable, and there's no straightforward way to change a product from one category into another.

The following example considers a more realistic case, where each Product includes a CategoryID property. On its own, the CategoryID number doesn't mean much to the application user. To display the category name instead, you need to rely on one of several possible techniques: you can add an additional CategoryName property to the Product class (which works, but is a bit clumsy), you can use a data converter in your CategoryID bindings (which could look up the matching category name in a cached list), or you can display the CategoryID column with the DataGridComboBoxColumn (which is the approach demonstrated next).

Using this approach, instead of a list of simple strings, you bind an entire list of Category objects to the DataGridComboBoxColumn.ItemsSource property:

```
categoryColumn.ItemsSource = Application.StoreDB.GetCategories()
gridProducts.ItemsSource = Application.StoreDB.GetProducts()
```

You then configure the DataGridComboBoxColumn. You must set three properties:

```
<DataGridComboBoxColumn Header="Category" x:Name="categoryColumn"
  DisplayMemberPath="CategoryName" SelectedValuePath="CategoryID"
  SelectedValueBinding="{Binding Path=CategoryID}"></DataGridComboBoxColumn>
```

DisplayMemberPath tells the column which text to extract from the Category object and display in the list. SelectedValuePath tells the column what *data* to extract from the Category object. SelectedValueBinding specifies the linked field in the Product object.

DataGridTemplateColumn

The DataGridTemplateColumn uses a data template, which works in the same way as the data-template features you explored with list controls earlier. The only difference in the DataGridTemplateColumn is that it allows you to define two templates: one for data display (the CellTemplate) and one for data editing (the CellEditingTemplate), which you'll consider shortly. Here's an example that uses the template data column to place a thumbnail image of each product in the grid (see Figure 22-9):

```
<DataGridTemplateColumn>
  <DataGridTemplateColumn.CellTemplate>
    <DataTemplate>
      <Image Stretch="None" Source=
       "{Binding Path=ProductImagePath, Converter={StaticResource ImagePathConverter}}">
      </Image>
    </DataTemplate>
  </DataGridTemplateColumn.CellTemplate>
</DataGridTemplateColumn>
```

Figure 22-9. *A DataGrid with image content*

This example assumes you've added the ImagePathConverter value converter to the UserControl.Resources collection:

```
<UserControl.Resources>
  <local:ImagePathConverter x:Key="ImagePathConverter"></local:ImagePathConverter>
</UserControl.Resources>
```

Formatting and Styling Columns

You can format a DataGridTextColumn in the same way that you format a TextBlock element, by setting the Foreground, FontFamily, FontSize, FontStyle, and FontWeight properties. However, the DataGridTextColumn doesn't expose all the properties of the TextBlock. For example, there's no way to set the often-used Wrapping property if you want to create a column that shows multiple lines of text. In this case, you need to use the ElementStyle property instead.

Essentially, the ElementStyle property lets you create a style that is applied to the element inside the DataGrid cell. In the case of a simple DataGridTextColumn, that's a TextBlock. In a DataGridCheckBoxColumn, it's a check box. In a DataGridTemplateColumn, it's whatever element you've created in the data template.

Here's a simple style that allows the text in a column to wrap:

```
<DataGridTextColumn Header="Description" Width="400"
 Binding="{Binding Path=Description}">
  <DataGridTextColumn.ElementStyle>
    <Style TargetType="TextBlock">
      <Setter Property="TextWrapping" Value="Wrap"></Setter>
    </Style>
  </DataGridTextColumn.ElementStyle>
</DataGridTextColumn>
```

To see the wrapped text, you must expand the row height. Unfortunately, the DataGrid can't size itself as flexibly as WPF layout containers can. Instead, you're forced to set a fixed row height by using the DataGrid.RowHeight property. This height applies to all rows, regardless of the amount of content they contain. Figure 22-10 shows an example with the row height set to 70 units.

Figure 22-10. *A DataGrid with wrapped text*

▨ **Tip** If you want to apply the same style to multiple columns (for example, to deal with wrappable text in several places), you can define the style in the Resources collection and then refer to it in each column by using a StaticResource.

You can use EditingElementStyle to style the element that's employed when you're editing a column. In the case of DataGridTextColumn, the editing element is the TextBox control.

The ElementStyle, ElementEditingStyle, and column properties give you a way to format all the cells in a specific column. However, in some cases, you might want to apply formatting settings to every cell in every column. The simplest way to do so is to configure a style for the DataGrid.RowStyle property. The DataGrid also exposes a small set of additional properties that allow you to format other parts of the grid, such as the column headers and row headers. Table 22-2 has the full story.

Table 22-2. *Style-Based DataGrid Properties*

Property	Style Applies To...
ColumnHeaderStyle	The TextBlock that's used for the column headers at the top of the grid
RowHeaderStyle	The TextBlock that's used for the row headers
DragIndicatorStyle	The TextBlock that's used for a column header when the user is dragging it to a new position
RowStyle	The TextBlock that's used for ordinary rows (rows in columns that haven't been expressly customized through the ElementStyle property of the column)

Formatting Rows

By setting the properties of the DataGrid column objects, you can control how entire columns are formatted. But in many cases, it's more useful to flag rows that contain specific data. For example, you may want to draw attention to high-priced products or expired shipments. You can apply this sort of formatting programmatically by handling the DataGrid.LoadingRow event.

The LoadingRow event is a powerful tool for row formatting. It gives you access to the data object for the current row, allowing you to perform simple range checks, comparison, and more-complex manipulations. It also provides the DataGridRow object for the row, letting you format the row with different colors or a different font. However, you can't format just a single cell in that row—for that, you need DataGridTemplateColumn and a custom value converter.

The LoadingRow event fires once for each row when it appears onscreen. The advantage of this approach is that your application is never forced to format the whole grid; instead, LoadingRow fires only for the rows that are currently visible. But there's also a downside. As the user scrolls through the grid, the LoadingRow event is triggered continuously. As a result, you can't place time-consuming code in the LoadingRow method unless you want scrolling to grind to a halt.

There's also another consideration: item container recycling. To lower its memory overhead, the DataGrid reuses the same DataGridRow objects to show new data as you scroll through the data. (That's why the event is called LoadingRow rather than CreatingRow.) If you're not careful, the DataGrid can load data into an already-formatted DataGridRow. To prevent this from happening, you must explicitly restore each row to its initial state.

In the following example, high-priced items are given a bright orange background (see Figure 22-11). Regular-price items are given the standard white background:

```
' Reuse brush objects for efficiency in large data displays.
Private highlightBrush As New SolidColorBrush(Colors.Orange)
Private normalBrush As New SolidColorBrush(Colors.White)

Private Sub gridProducts_LoadingRow(ByVal sender As Object, _
  ByVal e As DataGridRowEventArgs)
    ' Check the data object for this row.
    Dim product As Product = CType(e.Row.DataContext, Product)

    ' Apply the conditional formatting.
    If product.UnitCost > 100 Then
```

```
            e.Row.Background = highlightBrush
        Else
            ' Restore the default white background. This ensures that used,
            ' formatted DataGrid objects are reset to their original appearance.
            e.Row.Background = normalBrush
        End If
End Sub
```

Figure 22-11. *Highlighting rows*

Remember, you have another option for performing value-based formatting: you can use a value converter that examines bound data and converts it to something else. This technique is especially powerful when combined with a DataGridTemplateColumn. For example, you can create a template-based column that contains a TextBlock, and bind the TextBlock.Background property to a value converter that sets the color based on the price. Unlike the LoadingRow approach shown previously, this technique allows you to format just the cell that contains the price, rather than the whole row. For more information about this technique, refer to Chapter 20.

▓ **Note** The formatting you apply in the LoadingRow event handler applies only when the row is loaded. If you edit a row, this LoadingRow code doesn't fire (at least, not until you scroll the row out of view and then back into sight).

Displaying Row Details

The DataGrid also supports *row details*—an optional, separate display area that appears just under the column values for a row. The row-details area adds two things that you can't get from columns alone:

- It spans the full width of the DataGrid and isn't carved into separate columns, which gives you more space to work with.

- You can configure the row-details area so that it appears only for the selected row, allowing you to tuck the extra details out of the way when they're not needed.

Figure 22-12 shows a DataGrid that uses both of these behaviors. The row-details area displays the wrapped product description text, and it's shown only for the currently selected product.

Figure 22-12. *Using the row-details area*

To create this example, you need to first define the content that's shown in the row-details area by setting the DataGrid.RowDetailsTemplate property. In this case, the row-details area uses a basic template that includes a TextBlock that shows the full product text and adds a border around it:

```
<DataGrid.RowDetailsTemplate>
  <DataTemplate>
    <Border Margin="10" Padding="10" BorderBrush="SteelBlue" BorderThickness="3"
    CornerRadius="5">
      <TextBlock Text="{Binding Path=Description}" TextWrapping="Wrap"
      FontSize="10">
      </TextBlock>
    </Border>
  </DataTemplate>
</DataGrid.RowDetailsTemplate>
```

Other options include adding controls that allow you to perform various tasks (for example, getting more information about a product, adding it to a shopping list, editing it, and so on).

You can configure the display behavior of the row-details area by setting the DataGrid.RowDetailsVisibilityMode property. By default, this property is set to VisibleWhenSelected, which means the row-details area is shown when the row is selected. Alternatively, you can set it to Visible, which means the details area of every row will be shown at once.

Or you can use Collapsed, which means the details area won't be shown for any row—at least, not until you change the RowDetailsVisibilityMode in code (for example, when the user selects a certain type of row).

Freezing Columns

A *frozen* column stays in place at the left side of the DataGrid, even as you scroll to the right. Figure 22-13 shows how a frozen Product column remains visible during scrolling. Notice how the horizontal scrollbar extends under only the scrollable columns, not the frozen columns.

Figure 22-13. *Freezing the Product column*

Column freezing is a useful feature for very wide grids, especially when you want to make sure certain information (such as the product name or a unique identifier) is always visible. To use it, you set the DataGrid.FrozenColumnCount property to a number greater than 0. For example, a value of 1 freezes just the first column:

```
<DataGrid x:Name="gridProducts" Margin="5" AutoGenerateColumns="False"
  FrozenColumnCount="1">
```

Frozen columns must always be on the left side of the grid. If you freeze one column, it is the leftmost column; if you freeze two columns, they will be the first two on the left; and so on.

Selection

Like an ordinary list control, the DataGrid lets the user select individual items. You can react to the SelectionChanged event when this happens. To find out which data object is currently selected, you can use the SelectedItem property. If you want the user to be able to select multiple rows, set the SelectionMode property to Extended. (Single is the only other option and the default.) To select multiple rows, the user must hold down the Shift or Ctrl key. You can retrieve the collection of selected items from the SelectedItems property.

■ **Tip**   You can set the selection programmatically by using the SelectedItem property. If you're setting the selection to an item that's not currently in view, it's a good idea to follow up with a call to the DataGrid.ScrollIntoView() method, which forces the DataGrid to scroll forward or backward until the item you've indicated is visible.

Sorting

The DataGrid features built-in sorting as long as you're binding a collection that implements IList (such as the List(Of T) and ObservableCollection(Of T) collections). If you meet this requirement, your DataGrid gets basic sorting for free.

To use the sorting, the user needs to click a column header. Clicking once sorts the column in ascending order based on its data type (for example, numbers are sorted from 0 up, and letters are sorted alphabetically). Click the column again, and the sort order is reversed. An arrow appears at the far-right side of the column header, indicating that the DataGrid is sorted based on the values in this column. The arrow points up for an ascending sort and down for a descending sort.

Users can sort based on multiple columns by holding down Shift while they click. For example, if you hold down Shift and click the Category column followed by the Price column, products are sorted into alphabetical category groups, and the items in each category group are ordered by price.

Ordinarily, the DataGrid sorting algorithm uses the bound data that appears in the column, which makes sense. However, you can choose a different property from the bound data object by setting a column's SortMemberPath. And if you have a DataGridTemplateColumn, you need to use SortMemberPath, because there's no Binding property to provide the bound data. If you don't, your column won't support sorting.

You can also disable sorting by setting the CanUserSortColumns property to False (or turn it off for specific columns by setting the column's CanUserSort property).

Editing

One of the DataGrid's greatest conveniences is its support for editing. A DataGrid cell switches into edit mode when the user double-clicks it. But the DataGrid lets you restrict this editing ability in several ways:

DataGrid.IsReadOnly: When this property is True, users can't edit anything.

DataGridColumn.IsReadOnly: When this property is True, users can't edit any of the values in that column.

Read-only properties: If your data object has a property with no property setter, the DataGrid is intelligent enough to notice this detail and disable column editing, just as if you had set DataGridColumn.IsReadOnly to True. Similarly, if your property isn't a simple text, numeric, or date type, the DataGrid makes it read-only (although you can remedy this situation by switching to the DataGridTemplateColumn, as described shortly).

What happens when a cell switches into edit mode depends on the column type. A DataGridTextColumn shows a text box (although it's a seamless-looking text box that fills the entire cell and has no visible border). A DataGridCheckBox column shows a check box that you can check or uncheck. But the DataGridTemplateColumn is by far the most interesting. It allows you to replace the standard editing text box with a more specialized input control.

For example, the following column shows a date. When the user double-clicks to edit that value, it turns into a drop-down DatePicker (see Figure 22-14) with the current value preselected:

```
<DataGridTemplateColumn Header="Date Added">
  <DataGridTemplateColumn.CellTemplate>
    <DataTemplate>
      <TextBlock Margin="4" Text=
 "{Binding Path=DateAdded, Converter={StaticResource DateOnlyConverter}}">
      </TextBlock>
    </DataTemplate>
  </DataGridTemplateColumn.CellTemplate>
  <DataGridTemplateColumn.CellEditingTemplate>
    <DataTemplate>
      <DatePicker SelectedDate="{Binding Path=DateAdded, Mode=TwoWay}">
      </DatePicker>
    </DataTemplate>
  </DataGridTemplateColumn.CellEditingTemplate>
</DataGridTemplateColumn>
```

Figure 22-14. *Editing dates with the DatePicker*

The DataGrid automatically supports the same basic validation system you learned about in the previous chapter, which reacts to problems in the data-binding system (such as the inability to convert supplied text to the appropriate data type) or exceptions thrown by the property setter. Here's an example that uses a custom validation rule to validate the UnitCost field:

```
<DataGridTextColumn Header="Price">
```

```
<DataGridTextColumn.Binding>
  <Binding Path="UnitCost" StringFormat="{}{0:C}">
    <Binding.ValidationRules>
      <local:PositivePriceRule Max="999.99" />
    </Binding.ValidationRules>
  </Binding>
</DataGridTextColumn.Binding>
</DataGridTextColumn>
```

The default ErrorTemplate for the DataGridCell displays a red outline around the invalid value, much the same as other input controls such as the TextBox.

You can implement validation a couple of other ways with a DataGrid. One option is to use the DataGrid's editing events, which are listed in Table 22-3. The order of rows matches the order that the events fire in the DataGrid.

Table 22-3. *DataGrid Editing Events*

Name	Description
BeginningEdit	Occurs when the cell is about to be put in edit mode. You can examine the column and row that are currently being edited, check the cell value, and cancel this operation by using the DataGridBeginningEditEventArgs.Cancel property.
PreparingCellForEdit	Used for template columns. At this point, you can perform any last-minute initialization that's required for the editing controls. Use DataGridPreparingCellForEditEventArgs. EditingElement to access the element in the CellEditingTemplate.
CellEditEnding	Occurs when the cell is about to exit edit mode. DataGridCellEditEndingEventArgs. EditAction tells you whether the user is attempting to accept the edit (for example, by pressing Enter or clicking another cell) or cancel it (by pressing the Esc key). You can examine the new data and set the Cancel property to roll back an attempted change.
RowEditEnding	Occurs when the user navigates to a new row after editing the current row. As with CellEditEnding, you can use this point to perform validation and cancel the change. Typically, you'll perform validation that involves several columns—for example, ensuring that the value in one column isn't greater than the value in another.

If you need a place to perform validation logic that is specific to your page (and so can't be baked into the data objects), you can write custom validation logic that responds to the CellEditEnding and RowEditEnding events. Check column rules in the CellEditEnding event handler, and validate the consistency of the entire row in the RowEditEnding event. And remember that if you cancel an edit, you should provide an explanation of the problem (usually in a TextBlock elsewhere on the page).

The Last Word

In this chapter, you took a closer look at the ItemsControl classes provided by WPF. You learned how to use the ListView to create lists with multiple viewing modes, the TreeView to show hierarchical data, and the DataGrid to view and edit a dense assortment of data in a single place.

The most impressive aspect of all these classes is that they derive from a single base class—the ItemsControl—that defines their essential functionality. The fact that all these controls share the same content model, the same data-binding ability, and the same styling and templating features is one of WPF's small miracles. Remarkably, the ItemsControl defines all the basics for any WPF list control, even those that wrap hierarchical data, such as the TreeView. The only change in the model is that the children of these controls (TreeViewItem objects) are *themselves* ItemsControl objects, with the ability to host their own children.

Windows, Pages, and Rich Controls

Windows

Windows are the basic ingredients in traditional desktop applications—so basic that the operating system itself is named after them.

In the years since the window model was introduced, simplified page-based applications have often challenged the window model. The first and most successful challenger was the Web, with its range of app-like websites that run in the browser. But the page-based model of the Web has also crept into the territory of the desktop. Today, you'll find that Microsoft is busy creating a design framework called Metro, which favors simplified, touch-friendly interfaces that don't use windows at all. And even WPF has its own page-based development model, which you'll consider in Chapter 24. But for complex applications, content creation, and business tools, windows still remain the dominant user interface metaphor.

In this chapter, you'll explore the Window class. You'll learn the various ways to show and position windows, how window classes should interact, and what built-in dialog boxes WPF provides. You'll also look at more exotic window effects, such as nonrectangular windows and windows with transparency. Finally, you'll explore WPF"s support for programming the Windows taskbar.

The Window Class

As you learned in Chapter 6, the Window class derives from ContentControl. That means it can contain a single child (usually a layout container such as the Grid control), and you can paint the background with a brush by setting the Background property. You can also use the BorderBrush and BorderThickness properties to add a border around your window, but this border is added inside the window frame (around the edge of the client area). You can remove the window frame altogether by setting the WindowStyle property to None, which allows you to create a completely customized window, as you'll see later in the "Nonrectangular Windows" section.

Note The *client area* is the surface inside the window boundaries. This is where you place your content. The nonclient area includes the border and the title bar at the top of the window. The operating system manages this area.

In addition, the Window class adds a small set of members that will be familiar to any Windows programmer. The most obvious are the appearance-related properties that let you change the way the nonclient portion of the window appears. Table 23-1 lists these members.

Table 23-1. *Basic Properties of the Window Class*

Name	Description
AllowsTransparency	When set to True, the Window class allows other windows to show through if the background is set to a transparent color. If set to False (the default), the content behind the window never shows through, and a transparent background is rendered as a black background. This property allows you to create irregularly shaped windows when it's used in combination with a WindowStyle of None, as you'll see in the "Nonrectangular Windows" section.
Icon	An ImageSource object that identifies the icon you want to use for your window. Icons appear at the top left of a window (if it has one of the standard border styles), in the taskbar (if ShowInTaskBar is True), and in the selection window that's shown when the user presses Alt + Tab to navigate between running applications. Because these icons are different sizes, your .ico file should include at least a 16 × 16 pixel image and a 32 × 32 pixel image. In fact, the modern Windows icon standard includes both a 48 × 48 pixel image and a 256 × 256 image, which can be sized as needed for other purposes. If Icon is a null reference (Nothing), the window is given the same icon as the application (which you can set in Visual Studio by double-clicking the My Project node in the Solution Explorer and then choosing the Application tab). If this is omitted, WPF will use a standard but unremarkable icon that shows a window.
Top and Left	Set the distance between the top-left corner of the window and the top and left edges of the screen, in device-independent pixels. The LocationChanged event fires when either of these details changes. If the WindowStartupPosition property is set to Manual, you can set these properties before the window appears to set its position. You can always use these properties to move the position of a window *after* it has appeared, no matter what value you use for WindowStartupPosition.
ResizeMode	Takes a value from the ResizeMode enumeration that determines whether the user can resize the window. This setting also affects the visibility of the maximize and minimize boxes. Use NoResize to lock a window's size completely, CanMinimize to allow minimizing only, CanResize to allow everything, or CanResizeWithGrip to add a visual detail at the bottom-right corner of the window to show that the window is resizable.
RestoreBounds	Gets the bounds of the window. However, if the window is currently maximized or minimized, this property provides the bounds that were last used before the window was maximized or minimized. This is extremely useful if you need to store the position and dimensions of a window, as described later in this chapter.
ShowInTaskbar	If set to True, the window appears in the taskbar and the Alt + Tab list. Usually, you will set this to True only for your application's main window.
SizeToContent	Allows you to create a window that enlarges itself automatically. This property takes a value from the SizeToContent enumeration. Use Manual to disable automatic sizing; or use Height, Width, or WidthAndHeight to allow the window to expand in different dimensions to accommodate dynamic content. When using SizeToContent, the window may be sized larger than the bounds of the screen.
Title	The caption that appears in the title bar for the window (and in the taskbar).

(continued)

Table 23-1. (*continued*)

Name	Description
Topmost	When set to True, this window is always displayed on top of every other window in your application (unless these other windows also have TopMost set to True). This is a useful setting for palettes that need to "float" above other windows.
WindowStartupLocation	Takes a value from the WindowStartupLocation enumeration. Use Manual to position a window exactly with the Left and Top properties, CenterScreen to place the window in the center of the screen, or CenterOwner to center the window with respect to the window that launched it. When showing a modeless window with CenterOwner, make sure you set the Owner property of the new window before you show it.
WindowState	Takes a value from the WindowState enumeration. Informs you (and allows you to change) whether the window is currently maximized, minimized, or in its normal state. The StateChanged event fires when this property changes.
WindowStyle	Takes a value from the WindowStyle enumeration, which determines the border for the window. Your options include SingleBorderWindow (the default), None (a very thin raised border with no title bar region), and two other choices that are largely obsolete (ThreeDBorderWindow and ToolWindow), especially if you plan to run your application on Windows 8.

You've already learned about the lifetime events that fire when a window is created, activated, and unloaded (in Chapter 5). In addition, the Window class includes LocationChanged and WindowStateChanged events, which fire when the window's position and WindowState change, respectively.

Showing a Window

To display a window, you need to create an instance of the Window class and use the Show() or ShowDialog() method.

The ShowDialog() method shows a *modal* window. Modal windows stop the user from accessing the parent window by blocking any mouse or keyboard input to it, until the modal window is closed. In addition, the ShowDialog() method doesn't return until the modal window is closed, so any code that you've placed after the ShowDialog() call is put on hold. (However, that doesn't mean other code can't run—for example, if you have a timer running, its event handler will still run.) A common pattern in code is to show a modal window, wait until it's closed, and then act on its data.

Here's an example that uses the ShowDialog() method:

```
Dim winTask As New TaskWindow()
winTask.ShowDialog()
' Execution reaches this point after winTask is closed.
```

The Show() method shows a *modeless* window, which doesn't block the user from accessing any other window. The Show() method also returns immediately after the window is shown, so subsequent code statements are executed immediately. You can create and show several modeless windows, and the user can interact with them all at once. When using modeless windows, synchronization code is sometimes required to make sure that changes in one window update the information in another window to prevent a user from working with invalid information.

Here's an example that uses the Show() method:

```
Dim winMain As New MainWindow()
winMain.Show()
' Execution reaches this point immediately after winMain is shown.
```

Modal windows are ideal for presenting the user with a choice that needs to be made before an operation can continue. For example, consider Microsoft Word, which shows its Options and Print windows modally, forcing you to make a decision before continuing. On the other hand, the windows used to search for text or check the spelling in a document are shown modelessly, allowing the user to edit text in the main document window while performing the task.

Closing a window is equally easy, using the Close() method. Alternatively, you can hide a window from view using Hide() or by setting the Visibility property to Hidden. Either way, the window remains open and available to your code. Generally, it makes sense to hide only modeless windows. That's because if you hide a modal window, your code remains stalled until the window is closed, and the user can't close an invisible window.

Positioning a Window

Usually, you won't need to position a window exactly on the screen. You'll simply use CenterOwner for the WindowState and forget about the whole issue. In other, less common cases, you'll use Manual for the Windows state and set an exact position using the Left and Right properties.

Sometimes you need to take a little more care in choosing an appropriate location and size for your window. For example, you could accidentally create a window that is too large to be accommodated on a low-resolution display. If you are working with a single-window application, the best solution is to create a resizable window. If you are using an application with several floating windows, the answer is not as simple.

You could just restrict your window positions to locations that are supported on even the smallest monitors, but that's likely to frustrate higher-end users (who have purchased better monitors for the express purpose of fitting more information on their screen at a time). In this case, you usually want to make a runtime decision about the best window location. To do this, you need to retrieve some basic information about the available screen real estate using the System.Windows.SystemParameters class.

The SystemParameters class consists of a huge list of shared properties that return information about various system settings. For example, you can use the SystemParameters class to determine whether the user has enabled hot tracking and the "drag full windows" option, among many others. With windows, the SystemParameters class is particularly useful because it provides two properties that give the dimensions of the current screen: FullPrimaryScreenHeight and FullPrimaryScreenWidth. Both are quite straightforward, as this bit of code (which centers the window at runtime) demonstrates:

```
Dim screenHeight As Double = SystemParameters.FullPrimaryScreenHeight
Dim screenWidth As Double = SystemParameters.FullPrimaryScreenWidth
Me.Top= (screenHeight - Me.Height) / 2
Me.Left= (screenWidth - Me.Width) / 2
```

Although this code is equivalent to using CenterScreen for the WindowState property of the window, it gives you the flexibility to implement different positioning logic and to run this logic at the appropriate time.

An even better choice is to use the SystemParameters.WorkArea rectangle to center the window in the *available* screen area. The work area measurement doesn't include the area where the taskbar is docked (and any other "bands" that are docked to the desktop).

```
Dim workHeight As Double = SystemParameters.WorkArea.Height
Dim workWidth As Double = SystemParameters.WorkArea.Width
Me.Top = (workHeight - Me.Height)  / 2
Me.Left = (workWidth - Me.Width) / 2
```

■ **Note** Both window-positioning examples have one minor drawback. When the Top property is set on a window that's already visible, the window is moved and refreshed immediately. The same process happens when the Left property is set in the following line of code. As a result, keen-eyed users may see the window move twice. Unfortunately, the Window class does not provide a method that allows you to set both position properties at once. The only solution is to position the window after you create it but before you make it visible by calling Show() or ShowDialog().

Saving and Restoring Window Location

A common requirement for a window is to remember its last location. This information can be stored in a user-specific configuration file or in the Windows registry.

If you wanted to store the position of an important window in a user-specific configuration file, you would begin by double-clicking the My Project node in the Solution Explorer and choosing the Settings section. Then, add a user-scoped setting with a data type of System.Windows.Rect, as shown in Figure 23-1.

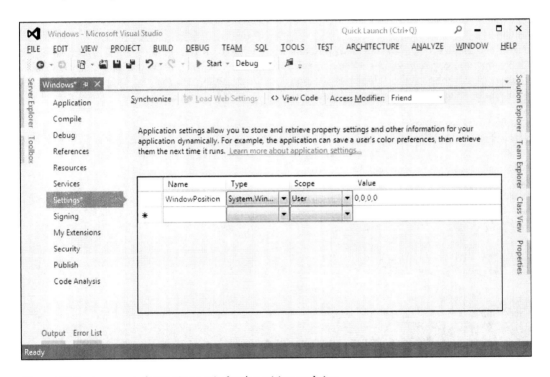

Figure 23-1. *A property for storing a window's position and size*

With this setting in place, it's easy to create code that automatically stores information about a window's size and position, as shown here:

```
My.Settings.WindowPosition = win.RestoreBounds
My.Settings.Save()
```

Notice that this code uses the RestoreBounds property, which gives the correct dimensions (the last nonmaximized, nonminimized size), even if the window is currently maximized or minimized.

It's just as easy to retrieve this information when you need it:

```
Try
    Dim bounds As Rect = My.Settings.Default.WindowPosition
    win.Top = bounds.Top
    win.Left = bounds.Left

    ' Restore the size only for a manually sized
    ' window.
    If win.SizeToContent = SizeToContent.Manual Then
        win.Width = bounds.Width
        win.Height = bounds.Height
    End If

Catch  As System.Exception
    MessageBox.Show("No settings stored.")
End Try
```

The only limitation to this approach is that you need to create a separate property for each window that you want to store. If you need to store the position of many different windows, you might want to design a more flexible system. For example, the following helper class stores a position for any window you pass in, using a registry key that incorporates the name of that window. (You could use additional identifying information if you want to store the settings for several windows that will have the same name.)

```
Public Class WindowPositionHelper
    Public Shared RegPath As String = "Software\MyApp\"

    Public Shared Sub SaveSize(ByVal win As Window)
        ' Create or retrieve a reference to a key where the settings
        ' will be stored.
        Dim key As RegistryKey
        key = Registry.CurrentUser.CreateSubKey(RegPath & win.Name)

        key.SetValue("Bounds", _
          win.RestoreBounds.ToString(CultureInfo.InvariantCulture))
    End Sub

    Public Shared Sub SetSize(ByVal win As Window)
        Dim key As RegistryKey
        key = Registry.CurrentUser.OpenSubKey(RegPath & win.Name)

        If key IsNot Nothing Then
            Dim bounds As Rect = Rect.Parse(key.GetValue("Bounds").ToString())

            win.Top = bounds.Top
            win.Left = bounds.Left

            ' Only restore the size for a manually sized
            ' window.
```

```
            If win.SizeToContent = SizeToContent.Manual Then
                win.Width = bounds.Width
                win.Height = bounds.Height
            End If
        End If
    End Sub
End Class
```

To use this class in a window, you call the SaveSize() method when the window is closing and call the SetSize() method when the window is first opened. In each case, you pass a reference to the window you want the helper class to inspect. Note that in this example, each window must have a different value for its Name property.

Window Interaction

In Chapter 7, you considered the WPF application model, and you took your first look at how windows interact. As you saw there, the Application class provides you with two tools for getting access to other windows: the MainWindow and Windows properties. If you want to track windows in a more customized way—for example, by keeping track of instances of a certain window class, which might represent documents—you can add your own shared properties to the Application class.

Of course, getting a reference to another window is only half the battle. You also need to decide how to communicate. As a general rule, you should minimize the need for window interactions, because they complicate code unnecessarily. If you do need to modify a control in one window based on an action in another window, create a dedicated method in the target window. That makes sure the dependency is well identified, and it adds another layer of indirection, making it easier to accommodate changes to the window's interface.

■ **Tip** If the two windows have a complex interaction, are developed or deployed separately, or are likely to change, you can consider going one step further and formalize their interaction by creating an interface with the public methods and implementing that interface in your window class.

Figures 23-2 and 23-3 show two examples for implementing this pattern. Figure 23-2 shows a window that triggers a second window to refresh its data in response to a button click. This window does not directly attempt to modify the second window's user interface; instead, it relies on a custom intermediate method called DoUpdate().

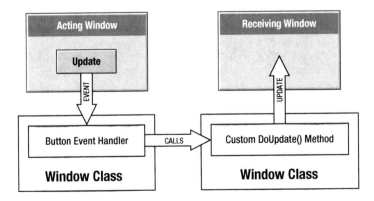

Figure 23-2. A single window interaction

The second example, Figure 23-3, shows a case where more than one window needs to be updated. In this case, the acting window relies on a higher-level application method, which calls the required window update methods (perhaps by iterating through a collection of windows). This approach is better because it works at a higher level. In the approach shown in Figure 23-2, the acting window doesn't need to know anything specific about the controls in the receiving window. The approach in Figure 23-3 goes one step further—the acting window doesn't need to know anything at all about the receiving window class.

Figure 23-3. *A one-to-many window interaction*

■ **Tip** When interacting between windows, the Window.Activate() method often comes in handy. It transfers the activation to the window you want. You can also use the Window.IsActive property to test whether a window is currently the one and only active window.

You can go one step further in decoupling this example. Rather than having the Application class trigger a method in the various windows, it could simply fire an event and allow the windows to choose how to respond to that event.

■ **Note** WPF can help you abstract your application logic through its support for commands, which are application-specific tasks that can be triggered any way you like. Chapter 9 has the full story.

The examples in Figure 23-2 and Figure 23-3 show how separate windows (usually modeless) can trigger actions in one another. But certain other patterns for window interaction are simpler (such as the dialog model) and supplement this model (such as window ownership). You'll consider these features in the following sections.

Window Ownership

.NET allows a window to "own" other windows. Owned windows are useful for floating toolbox and command windows. One example of an owned window is the Find and Replace window in Microsoft Word. When an owner window is minimized, the owned windows are also minimized automatically. When an owned window overlaps its owner, it is always displayed on top.

To support window ownership, the Window class adds two properties. Owner is a reference that points to the window that owns the current window (if there is one). OwnedWindows is a collection of all the windows that the current window owns (if any).

Setting up ownership is simply a matter of setting the Owner property, as shown here:

```
' Create a new window.
Dim winTool As New ToolWindow()

' Designate the current window as the owner.
winTool.Owner = Me

' Show the owned window.
winTool.Show()
```

Owned windows are always shown modelessly. To remove an owned window, set the Owner property to Nothing.

▨ **Note**   WPF does not include a system for building multiple document interface (MDI) applications. If you want more sophisticated window management, it's up to you to build it (or buy a third-party component).

An owned window can own another window, which can own another window, and so forth (although it's questionable whether this design has any practical use). The only limitations are that a window cannot own itself and two windows cannot own each other.

The Dialog Model

Often, when you show a window modally, you are offering the user some sort of choice. The code that displays the window waits for the result of that choice and then acts on it. This design is known as the *dialog model*. The window you show modally is the dialog box.

You can easily accommodate this design pattern by creating some sort of public property in your dialog window. When the user makes a selection in the dialog window, you would set this property and then close the window. The code that shows the dialog box can then check for this property and determine what to do next based on its value. (Remember that even when a window is closed, the window object, and all its control information, still exists until the variable referencing it goes out of scope.)

Fortunately, some of this infrastructure is already hardwired into the Window class. Every window includes a ready-made DialogResult property, which can take a True, False, or Nothing value. Usually, True indicates the user chose to go forward (for example, clicked OK), while False indicates that the user canceled the operation.

Best of all, once you set the dialog result, it's returned to the calling code as the return value of the ShowDialog() method. That means you can create, show, and consider the result of a dialog box window with this lean code:

```
Dim dialog As New DialogWindow()
If dialog.ShowDialog() = True Then
    ' The user accepted the action. Full speed ahead.
Else
    ' The user canceled the action.
End If
```

■ **Note** Using the DialogResult property doesn't prevent you from adding custom properties to your window. For example, it's perfectly reasonable to use the DialogResult property to inform the calling code whether an action was accepted or canceled and to provide other important details through custom properties. If the calling code finds a DialogResult of True, it can then check these other properties to get the information it needs.

You can take advantage of another shortcut. Rather than setting the DialogResult by hand after the user clicks a button, you can designate a button as the accept button (by setting IsDefault to True). Clicking that button automatically sets the DialogResult of the window to True. Similarly, you can designate a button as the cancel button (by setting IsCancel to True), in which case clicking it will set the DialogResult to Cancel. (You learned about IsDefault and IsCancel when you considered buttons in Chapter 6.)

Common Dialog Boxes

The Windows operating system includes many built-in dialog boxes that you can access through the Windows API. WPF provides wrappers for just a few of these.

■ **Note** There are good reasons that WPF doesn't include wrappers for all the Windows APIs. One of the goals of WPF is to decouple it from the Windows API so it's usable in other environments (like a browser) or portable to other platforms. Also, many of the built-in dialog boxes are showing their age and shouldn't be the first choice for modern applications.

The most obvious of these is the System.Windows.MessageBox class, which exposes a shared Show() method. You can use this code to display a standard Windows message box. Here's the most common overload:

```
MessageBox.Show("You must enter a name.", "Name Entry Error", _
    MessageBoxButton.OK, MessageBoxImage.Exclamation)
```

The MessageBoxButton enumeration allows you to choose the buttons that are shown in the message box. Your options include OK, OKCancel, YesNo, and YesNoCancel. (The less user-friendly AbortRetryIgnore isn't supported.) The MessageBoxImage enumeration allows you to choose the message box icon (Information, Exclamation, Error, Hand, Question, Stop, and so on).

Along with the MessageBox class, WPF includes specialized printing support that uses the PrintDialog (which is described in Chapter 29) and, in the Microsoft.Win32 namespace, the OpenFileDialog and SaveFileDialog classes.

The OpenFileDialog and SaveFileDialog classes acquire some additional features (some which are inherited from the FileDialog class). Both support a filter string, which sets the allowed file extensions. The OpenFileDialog class also provides properties that let you validate the user's selection (CheckFileExists) and allow multiple files to be selected (Multiselect). Here's an example that shows an OpenFileDialog and displays the selected files in a list box after the dialog box is closed:

```
Dim myDialog As New OpenFileDialog()

myDialog.Filter = "Image Files(*.BMP;*.JPG;*.GIF)|*.BMP;*.JPG;*.GIF" & _
    "|All files (*.*)|*.*"
myDialog.CheckFileExists = True
myDialog.Multiselect = True
```

```
If myDialog.ShowDialog() = True Then
    lstFiles.Items.Clear()
    For Each file As String In myDialog.FileNames
        lstFiles.Items.Add(file)
    Next
End If
```

You won't find any color pickers, font pickers, or folder browsers (although you can get these ingredients using the System.Windows.Forms classes from .NET 2.0).

Nonrectangular Windows

Irregularly shaped windows are often used in consumer applications such as photo editors, movie makers, and MP3 players. Creating a basic shaped window in WPF is easy. However, creating a slick, professional-looking shaped window takes more work—and, most likely, a talented graphic designer to create the outlines and design the background art.

A Simple Shaped Window

The basic technique for creating a shaped window is to follow these steps:

1. Set the Window.AllowsTransparency property to True.

2. Set the Window.WindowStyle property to None to hide the nonclient region of the window (the blue border). If you don't, you'll get an InvalidOperationException when you attempt to show the window.

3. Set the Background to be transparent (using the color Transparent, which has an alpha value of 0). Or set the Background to use an image that has transparent areas (regions that are painted with an alpha value of 0).

These three steps effectively remove the standard window appearance (known to WPF experts as the window *chrome*). To get the shaped window effect, you now need to supply some nontransparent content that has the shape you want. You have a number of options:

- Supply background art, using a file format that supports transparency. For example, you can use a PNG file to supply the background of a window. This is a simple, straightforward approach, and it's suitable if you're working with designers who have no knowledge of XAML. However, because the window will be rendered with more pixels at higher system DPIs, the background graphic may become blurry. This is also a problem if you choose to allow the user to resize the window.

- Use the shape-drawing features in WPF to create your background with vector content. This approach ensures that you won't lose quality regardless of the window size and system DPI setting. However, you'll probably want to use a XAML-capable design tool like Expression Blend.

- Use a simpler WPF element that has the shape you want. For example, you can create a nicely rounded window edge with the Border element. This gives you a modern Office-style window appearance with no design work.

Here's a bare-bones transparent window that uses the first approach and supplies a PNG file with transparent regions:

```
<Window x:Class="TransparentBackground"...
    WindowStyle="None" AllowsTransparency="True"
    >
  <Window.Background>
    <ImageBrush ImageSource="squares.png"></ImageBrush>
  </Window.Background>
    <Grid>
      <Grid.RowDefinitions>
        <RowDefinition></RowDefinition>
        <RowDefinition></RowDefinition>
        <RowDefinition></RowDefinition>
        <RowDefinition></RowDefinition>
      </Grid.RowDefinitions>
      <Button Margin = "20">A Sample Button</Button>
      <Button Margin = "20" Grid.Row = "2">Another Button</Button>
    </Grid>
</Window>
```

Figure 23-4 shows this window with a Notepad window underneath. Not only does the shaped window (which consists of a circle and square) leave gaps through which you can see the content underneath, but also some buttons drift off the image and into the transparent region, which means they appear to be floating without a window.

Figure 23-4. *A shaped window that uses a background image*

▓ **Note** WPF can perform anti-aliasing between the background of your window and the content underneath, ensuring that your window gets a clean, smoothed edge.

Figure 23-5 shows another, subtler shaped window. This window uses a rounded Border element to give a distinctive look. The layout is also simplified, because there's no way your content could accidentally leak outside the border, and the border can be easily resized with no Viewbox required.

Figure 23-5. *A shaped window that uses a Border*

This window holds a Grid with three rows, which are used for the title bar, the footer bar, and all the content in between. The content row holds a second Grid, which sets a different background and holds any other elements you want (currently, it holds just a single TextBlock).

Here's the markup that creates the window:

```
<Window x:Class="ModernWindow"...
    AllowsTransparency="True" WindowStyle="None"
    Background="Transparent"
    >
  <Border Width="Auto" Height="Auto" Name="windowFrame"
    BorderBrush="#395984" BorderThickness="1"
    CornerRadius="0,20,30,40" >
    <Border.Background>
      <LinearGradientBrush>
        <GradientBrush.GradientStops>
          <GradientStopCollection>
            <GradientStop Color="#E7EBF7" Offset="0.0"/>
            <GradientStop Color="#CEE3FF" Offset="0.5"/>
          </GradientStopCollection>
        </GradientBrush.GradientStops>
      </LinearGradientBrush>
    </Border.Background>
```

715

```
  <Grid>
    <Grid.RowDefinitions>
      <RowDefinition Height="Auto"></RowDefinition>
      <RowDefinition></RowDefinition>
      <RowDefinition Height="Auto"></RowDefinition>
    </Grid.RowDefinitions>

    <TextBlock Text="Title Bar" Margin="1" Padding="5"></TextBlock>

    <Grid Grid.Row="1" Background="#B5CBEF">
      <TextBlock VerticalAlignment="Center" HorizontalAlignment="Center"
        Foreground="White" FontSize="20">Content Goes Here</TextBlock>
    </Grid>

    <TextBlock Grid.Row="2" Text="Footer" Margin="1,10,1,1" Padding="5"
      HorizontalAlignment="Center"></TextBlock>
  </Grid>
  </Border>
</Window>
```

To complete this window, you would want to create buttons that mimic the standard maximize, minimize, and close buttons in the top-right corner.

A Transparent Window with Shaped Content

In most cases, WPF windows won't use fixed graphics to create shaped windows. Instead, they'll use a completely transparent background and then place shaped content on this background. (You can see how this works by looking at the button in Figure 23-4, which is hovering over a completely transparent region.)

The advantage of this approach is that it's more modular. You can assemble a window out of many separate components, all of which are first-class WPF elements. But more important, this allows you to take advantage of other WPF features to build truly dynamic user interfaces. For example, you might assemble shaped content that can be resized, or use animation to produce perpetually running effects right in your window. This isn't as easy if your graphics are provided in a single static file.

Figure 23-6 shows an example. Here, the window contains a Grid with one cell. Two elements share that cell. The first element is a Path that draws the shaped window border and gives it a gradient fill. The other element is a layout container that holds the content for the window, which overlays the Path. In this case, the layout container is a StackPanel, but you could also use something else (such as another Grid or a Canvas for coordinate-based absolute positioning). This StackPanel holds the close button (with the familiar X icon) and the text.

Figure 23-6. *A shaped window that uses a Path*

▓ **Note** Even though Figure 23-4 and Figure 23-6 show different examples, they are interchangeable. In other words, you could create either one using the background-based approach or the shape-drawing approach. However, the shape-drawing approach gives you more abilities if you want to dynamically change the shape later and gives you the best quality if you need to resize the window.

The key piece of this example is the Path element that creates the backgrounds. It's a simple vector-based shape that's composed of a series of lines and arcs. Here's the complete markup for the Path:

```
<Path Stroke="DarkGray" StrokeThickness="2">
  <Path.Fill>
    <LinearGradientBrush StartPoint="0.2,0" EndPoint="0.8,1">
      <LinearGradientBrush.GradientStops>
        <GradientStop Color="White" Offset="0"></GradientStop>
        <GradientStop Color="White" Offset="0.45"></GradientStop>
        <GradientStop Color="LightBlue" Offset="0.9"></GradientStop>
        <GradientStop Color="Gray" Offset="1"></GradientStop>
      </LinearGradientBrush.GradientStops>
    </LinearGradientBrush>
  </Path.Fill>

  <Path.Data>
    <PathGeometry>
      <PathGeometry.Figures>
        <PathFigure StartPoint="20,0" IsClosed="True">
          <LineSegment Point="140,0"/>
          <ArcSegment Point="160,20" Size="20,20" SweepDirection="Clockwise"/>
          <LineSegment Point="160,60"/>
          <ArcSegment Point="140,80" Size="20,20" SweepDirection="Clockwise"/>
          <LineSegment Point="70,80"/>
          <LineSegment Point="70,130"/>
          <LineSegment Point="40,80"/>
          <LineSegment Point="20,80"/>
          <ArcSegment Point="0,60" Size="20,20" SweepDirection="Clockwise"/>
          <LineSegment Point="0,20"/>
          <ArcSegment Point="20,0" Size="20,20" SweepDirection="Clockwise"/>
        </PathFigure>
      </PathGeometry.Figures>
    </PathGeometry>
  </Path.Data>
</Path>
```

Currently, the Path is fixed in size (as is the window), although you could make it resizable by hosting it in the Viewbox container that you learned about in Chapter 12. You could also improve this example by giving the close button a more authentic appearance—probably a vector X icon that's drawn on a red surface. Although you could use a separate Path element to represent a button and handle the button's mouse events, it's better to change the standard Button control using a control template (as described in Chapter 17). You can then make the Path that draws the X icon part of your customized button.

Moving Shaped Windows

One limitation of shaped forms is that they omit the nonclient title bar portion, which allows the user to easily drag the window around the desktop. Fortunately, WPF allows you to initiate window-dragging mode at any time by calling the Window.DragMove() method.

So, to allow the user to drag the shaped form you saw in the previous examples, you simply need to handle the MouseLeftButtonDown event for the window (or an element on the window, which will then play the same role as the title bar):

```
<TextBlock Text="Title Bar" Margin="1" Padding="5"
  MouseLeftButtonDown="titleBar_MouseLeftButtonDown"></TextBlock>
```

In your event handler, you need only a single line of code:

```
Private Sub titleBar_MouseLeftButtonDown(ByVal sender As Object, _
  ByVal e As MouseButtonEventArgs)
    Me.DragMove()
End Sub
```

Now the window follows the mouse around the screen, until the user releases the mouse button.

Resizing Shaped Windows

Resizing a shaped window isn't as easy. If your window is roughly rectangular in shape, the easiest approach is to add a sizing grip to the bottom-right corner by setting the Window.ResizeMode property to CanResizeWithGrip. However, the sizing grip placement assumes that your window is rectangular. For example, if you're creating a rounded window effect using a Border object, as shown earlier in Figure 23-5, this technique may work. The sizing grip will appear in the bottom-right corner, and depending how much you've rounded off that corner, it may appear over the window surface where it belongs. But if you've created a more exotic shape, such as the Path shown earlier in Figure 23-6, this technique definitely won't work; instead, it will create a sizing grip that floats in empty space next to the window.

If the sizing grip placement isn't right for your window, or you want to allow the user to size the window by dragging its edges, you'll need to go to a bit more work. You can use two basic approaches. You can use .NET's platform invoke feature (p/invoke) to send a Win32 message that resizes the window. Or you can simply track the mouse position as the user drags to one side, and resize the window manually, by setting its Width property. The following example uses the latter approach.

Before you can use either approach, you need a way to detect when the user moves the mouse over the edges of the window. At this point, the mouse pointer should change to a resize cursor. The easiest way to do this in WPF is to place an element along the edge of each window. This element doesn't need to have any visual appearance—in fact, it can be completely transparent and let the window show through. Its sole purpose is to intercept mouse events.

A 5-unit wide Rectangle is perfect for the task. Here's how you might place a Rectangle that allows right-side resizing in the rounded-edge window shown in Figure 23-5:

```
<Grid>
    ...
    <Rectangle Grid.RowSpan="3" Width="5"
      VerticalAlignment="Stretch" HorizontalAlignment="Right"
      Cursor="SizeWE" Fill="Transparent"
      MouseLeftButtonDown="window_initiateWiden"
      MouseLeftButtonUp="window_endWiden"
      MouseMove="window_Widen"></Rectangle>
</Grid>
```

The Rectangle is placed in the top row but is given a RowSpan value of 3. That way, it stretches along all three rows and occupies the entire right side of the window. The Cursor property is set to the mouse cursor you want to show when the mouse is over this element. In this case, the "west-east" resize cursor does the trick—it shows the familiar two-way arrow that points left and right.

The Rectangle event handlers toggle the window into resize mode when the user clicks the edge. The only trick is that you need to capture the mouse to ensure you continue receiving mouse events even if the mouse is dragged off the rectangle. The mouse capture is released when the user releases the left mouse button.

```
Private isWiden As Boolean = False

Private Sub window_initiateWiden(ByVal sender As Object, _
  ByVal e As System.Windows.Input.MouseEventArgs)
    isWiden = True
End Sub

Private Sub window_Widen(ByVal sender As Object, _
  ByVal e As System.Windows.Input.MouseEventArgs)
    Dim rect As Rectangle = CType(sender, Rectangle)
    If isWiden Then
        rect.CaptureMouse()
        Dim newWidth As Double = e.GetPosition(Me).X + 5
        If newWidth > 0 Then Me.Width = newWidth
    End If
End Sub

Private Sub window_endWiden(ByVal sender As Object, _
  ByVal e As System.Windows.Input.MouseEventArgs)
    isWiden = False

    ' Make sure capture is released.
    Dim rect As Rectangle = CType(sender, Rectangle)
    rect.ReleaseMouseCapture()
End Sub
```

Figure 23-7 shows the code in action.

Figure 23-7. *Resizing a shaped window*

Putting It All Together: A Custom Control Template for Windows

Using the code you've seen so far, you can build a custom-shaped window quite easily. However, if you want to use a new window standard for your entire application, you'll be forced to manually restyle every window with the same shaped border, header region, close buttons, and so on. In this situation, a better approach is to adapt your markup into a control template that you can use on any window. (If you're a bit sketchy on the inner workings of control templates, you might want to review the information in Chapter 17 before you continue with the rest of this section.)

The first step is to consult the default control template for the Window class. For the most part, this template is pretty straightforward, but it includes one detail you might not expect: an AdornerDecorator element. This element creates a special drawing area called the *adorner layer* over the rest of the window's client content. WPF controls can use the adorner layer to draw content that should appear superimposed over your elements. This includes small graphical indicators that show focus, flag validation errors, and guide drag-and-drop operations. When you build a custom window, you need to ensure that the adorner layer is present, so that controls that use it continue to function.

With that in mind, it's possible to identify the basic structure that the control template for a window should take. Here's a standardized example with markup that creates window like the one shown in Figure 23-7:

```
<ControlTemplate x:Key="CustomWindowTemplate" TargetType="{x:Type Window}">
  <Border Name="windowFrame"...>
    <Grid>
      <Grid.RowDefinitions>
        <RowDefinition Height="Auto"></RowDefinition>
        <RowDefinition></RowDefinition>
        <RowDefinition Height="Auto"></RowDefinition>
      </Grid.RowDefinitions>

      <!-- The title bar. -->
      <TextBlock Text="{TemplateBinding Title}"
       FontWeight="Bold"></TextBlock>
      <Button Style="{StaticResource CloseButton}"
       HorizontalAlignment="Right"></Button>

      <!-- The window content. -->
      <Border Grid.Row="1">
        <AdornerDecorator>
          <ContentPresenter></ContentPresenter>
        </AdornerDecorator>
      </Border>

      <!-- The footer. -->
      <ContentPresenter Grid.Row="2" Margin="10"
       HorizontalAlignment="Center"
       Content="{TemplateBinding Tag}"></ContentPresenter>

      <!-- The resize grip. -->
      <ResizeGrip Name="WindowResizeGrip" Grid.Row="2"
       HorizontalAlignment="Right" VerticalAlignment="Bottom"
       Visibility="Collapsed" IsTabStop="False" />

      <!-- The invisible rectangles that allow dragging to resize. -->
      <Rectangle Grid.Row="1" Grid.RowSpan="3" Cursor="SizeWE"
       VerticalAlignment="Stretch" HorizontalAlignment="Right"
       Fill="Transparent" Width="5"></Rectangle>
```

```
        <Rectangle Grid.Row="2" Cursor="SizeNS"
         HorizontalAlignment="Stretch" VerticalAlignment="Bottom"
         Fill="Transparent" Height="5"></Rectangle>
      </Grid>
    </Border>

    <ControlTemplate.Triggers>
      <Trigger Property="ResizeMode" Value="CanResizeWithGrip">
        <Setter TargetName="WindowResizeGrip"
         Property="Visibility" Value="Visible"></Setter>
      </Trigger>
    </ControlTemplate.Triggers>
  </ControlTemplate>
```

The top-level element in this template is a Border object for the window frame. Inside that is a Grid with three rows. The contents of the Grid break down as follows:

- The top row holds the title bar, which consists of an ordinary TextBlock that displays the window title and a close button. A template binding pulls the window title from the Window. Title property.

- The middle row holds a nested Border with the rest of the window content. The content is inserted using a ContentPresenter. The ContentPresenter is wrapped in the AdornerDecorator, which ensures that the adorner layer is placed over your element content.

- The third row holds another ContentPresenter. However, this content presenter doesn't use the standard binding to get its content from the Window.Content property. Instead, it explicitly pulls its content from the Window.Tag property. Usually, this content is just ordinary text, but it could include any element content you want to use.

▓ **Note** The Tag property is used because the Window class doesn't include any property that's designed to hold footer text. Another option is to create a custom class that derives from Window and adds a Footer property.

- Also in the third row is a resize grip. A trigger shows the resize grip when the Window. ResizeMode property is set to CanResizeWithGrip.

- Finally, two invisible rectangles run along the right and bottom edge of the Grid (and thus the window). They allow the user to click and drag to resize the window.

Two details that aren't shown here are the relatively uninteresting style for the resize grip (which simply creates a small pattern of dots to use as the resize grip) and the close button (which draws a small *X* on a red square). This markup also doesn't include the formatting details, such as the gradient brush that paints the background and the properties that create a nicely rounded border edge. To see the full markup, refer to the sample code provided for this chapter.

The window template is applied using a simple style. This style also sets three key properties of the Window class that make it transparent. This allows you to create the window border and background using WPF elements.

```
<Style x:Key="CustomWindowChrome" TargetType="{x:Type Window}">
  <Setter Property="AllowsTransparency" Value="True"></Setter>
  <Setter Property="WindowStyle" Value="None"></Setter>
  <Setter Property="Background" Value="Transparent"></Setter>
```

```
  <Setter Property="Template"
    Value="{StaticResource CustomWindowTemplate}"></Setter>
</Style>
```

At this point, you're ready to use your custom window. For example, you could create a window like this that sets the style and fills in some basic content:

```
<Window x:Class="CustomWindow"
  xmlns="http://schemas.microsoft.com/winfx/2006/xaml/presentation"
  xmlns:x="http://schemas.microsoft.com/winfx/2006/xaml"
  Title="CustomWindowTest" Height="300" Width="300"
  Tag="This is a custom footer"
  Style="{StaticResource CustomWindowChrome}">

  <StackPanel Margin="10">
    <TextBlock Margin="3">This is a test.</TextBlock>
    <Button Margin="3" Padding="3">OK</Button>
  </StackPanel>
</Window>
```

There's just one problem. Currently, the window lacks most of the basic behavior windows require. For example, you can't drag the window around the desktop, resize it, or use the close button. To perform these actions, you need code.

There are two possible ways to add the code you need: you could expand your example into a custom Window-derived class, or you could create a code-behind class for your resource dictionary. The custom control approach provides better encapsulation and allows you to extend the public interface of your window (for example, adding useful methods and properties that you can use in your application). The code-behind approach is a relatively lightweight alternative that allows you to extend the capabilities of a control template while letting your application continue to use the base control classes. It's the approach that you'll see in this example.

You've already learned how to create a code-behind class for your resource dictionary (see the "User-Selected Skins" section in Chapter 17). Once you've created the code file, it's easy to add the event handling code you need. The only challenge is that your code runs in the resource dictionary object, not inside your window object. That means you can't use the Me keyword to access the current window. Fortunately, there's an easy alternative: the FrameworkElement.TemplatedParent property.

For example, to make the window draggable, you need to intercept a mouse event on the title bar and initiate dragging. Here's the revised TextBlock that wires up an event handler when the user clicks with the mouse:

```
<TextBlock Margin="1" Padding="5" Text="{TemplateBinding Title}"
  FontWeight="Bold" MouseLeftButtonDown="titleBar_MouseLeftButtonDown"></TextBlock>
```

Now you can add the following event handler to the code-behind class for the resource dictionary:

```
Private Sub titleBar_MouseLeftButtonDown(ByVal sender As Object, _
  ByVal e As MouseButtonEventArgs)
    Dim senderElement As FrameworkElement = CType(sender, FrameworkElement)
    Dim win As Window = CType(senderElement.TemplatedParent, Window)
    win.DragMove()
End Sub
```

You can add the event handling code for the close button and resize rectangles in the same way. To see the finished resource dictionary markup and code, along with a template that you apply to any window, refer to the download examples for this chapter.

Of course, there's still a lot of polish needed before this window is attractive enough to suit a modern application. But it demonstrates the sequence of steps you need to follow to build a complex control template, with code, and it achieves a result that would have required custom control development in previous user interface frameworks.

Programming the Windows Taskbar

Both Windows 7 and Windows 8 (in desktop mode) use a revamped taskbar that adds several enhanced features—features that aren't available in Windows Vista. WPF does a good job of supporting these features without forcing developers to add unmanaged API calls or rely on separate assemblies.

First, WPF provides basic support for jump lists (the lists that appear when you right-click a taskbar button). Second, WPF lets you to change the taskbar preview image and the taskbar icon that's used for your application. In the following sections, you'll see how to use these features.

■ **Note** You can safely use the Windows taskbar features even in an application that targets Windows Vista. Any markup or code you use to interact with the enhanced Windows 7 and Windows 8 taskbar is harmlessly ignored on Windows Vista. (The same is true if you're targeting .NET 4, and you build an application that can run on Windows XP computers. WPF simply ignores the taskbar features that don't apply.)

Using Jump Lists

Jump lists are the handy mini-menus that pop up when you right-click a taskbar button. They appear for both currently running applications and applications that aren't currently running but have their buttons pinned to the taskbar. Typically, a jump list provides a quick way to open a document that belongs to the appropriate application—for example, to open a recent document in Word or a frequently played song in Windows Media Player. However, some programs use them more creatively to perform application-specific tasks.

Recent Document Support

The taskbar in Windows 7 and Windows 8 adds a jump list to every document-based application, provided that application is registered to handle a specific file type. For example, in Chapter 7, you learned how to build a single-instance application that was registered to handle .testDoc files (called SingleInstanceApplication). When you run this program and right-click its taskbar button, you'll see a list of recently opened documents, as shown in Figure 23-8.

Figure 23-8. *An automatically generated jump list*

If you click one of the recent documents in the jump list, Windows launches another instance of your application and passes the full document path to it as a command-line argument. Of course, you can code around this behavior if it isn't what want. For example, consider the single-instance application from Chapter 7. If you open a document from its jump list, the new instance quietly passes the file path to the currently running application, and then shuts itself down. The end result is that the same application gets to handle all the documents, whether they're opened from inside the application or from the jump list.

As noted, to get the recent document support, your application must be registered to handle the corresponding file type. There are two easy ways to accomplish this. First, you can add the relevant details to the Windows registry using code, as detailed in Chapter 7. Second, you can do it by hand with Windows Explorer. Here's a quick review of what you need to do:

1. Right-click the appropriate file (for example, one with the extension .testDoc).

2. Choose Open With ➤ Choose Default Program to show the Open With dialog box.

3. Click the Browse button, find your WPF application's .exe file, and select it.

4. Optionally, clear the "Always use selected program to open this kind of file" option. Your application doesn't need to be the default application to get jump list support.

5. Click OK.

When registering a file type, you need to keep a few guidelines in mind:

- When creating a file-type registration, you give Windows the exact path to your executable. So do this *after* you place your application somewhere sensible, or you'll need to reregister it every time you move your application file.

- Don't worry about taking over common file types. As long as you don't make your application into the default handler for that file type, you won't change the way Windows works. For example, it's perfectly acceptable to register your application to handle .txt files. That way, when the user opens a .txt file with your application, it appears in your application's recent document list. Similarly, if the user chooses a document from your application's jump list, Windows launches your application. However, if the user double-clicks a .txt file in Windows Explorer, Windows still launches the default application for .txt files (typically Notepad).

- To test jump lists in Visual Studio, you must switch off running the Visual Studio hosting process. If you're running it, Windows will check the file-type registrations for the hosting process (say, YourApp.vshost.exe) instead of your application (YourApp.exe). To avoid this problem, run your compiled application directly from Windows Explorer, or choose Debug ➤ Start Without Debugging. Either way, you won't get debugging support while you're testing the jump list.

■ **Tip** If you want to stop using the Visual Studio hosting process for a longer period of time, you can change your project configuration. Double-click the My Project node in the Solution Explorer. Then choose the Debug tab and clear the check box next to the "Enable the Visual Studio hosting process" setting.

Not only does Windows give your applications the recent document list for free, but it also supports *pinning*, which allows users to attach their most important documents to the jump list and keep them there permanently. As with the jump list for any other application, the user can pin a document by clicking the tiny thumbnail icon. Windows will then move the chosen file to a separate list category, which is called Pinned. Similarly, the user can remove an item from the recent documents list by right-clicking it and choosing Remove.

Custom Jump Lists

The jump list support you've seen so far is built in to Windows, and doesn't require any WPF logic. However, WPF adds on to this support by allowing you to take control of the jump list and fill it with custom items. To do so, you simply add some markup that defines a < JumpList.List > section in your Application.xaml file, as shown here:

```
<Application x:Class="JumpLists"
 xmlns="http://schemas.microsoft.com/winfx/2006/xaml/presentation"
 xmlns:x="http://schemas.microsoft.com/winfx/2006/xaml"
 StartupUri="MainWindow.xaml">
  <Application.Resources>
  </Application.Resources>

  <JumpList.JumpList>
    <JumpList>
    </JumpList>
  </JumpList.JumpList>
</Application>
```

When you define a custom jump list in this way, Windows stops showing the recent document list. To get it back, you need to explicitly opt in with the JumpList.ShowRecentCategory property:

```
<JumpList ShowRecentCategory="True">
```

You can also add the ShowFrequentCategory property to show a list of the most frequently opened documents that your application is registered to handle.

In addition, you can create your own jump list items and place them in a custom category of your choosing. To do so, you must add JumpPath or JumpTask objects to your JumpList. Here's an example of the JumpPath, which represents a document:

```
<JumpList ShowRecentCategory="True">
  <JumpPath CustomCategory="Sample Documents"
    Path="c:\Samples\samples.testDoc"></JumpPath>
</JumpList>
```

When creating a JumpPath, you can supply two details. The CustomCategory property sets the heading that's shown before the item in the jump list. (If you add several items with the same category name, they will be grouped together.) If you don't supply a category, Windows uses the category name Tasks. The Path property is a file path that points to a document. Your path must use a fully qualified file name, the file must exist, and it must be a file type that your application is registered to handle. If you break any of these rules, the item won't appear in the jump list.

Clicking a JumpPath item is exactly the same as clicking one of the files in the recent documents section. When you do, Windows launches a new instance of the application and passes the document path as a command-line argument.

The JumpTask object serves a slightly different purpose. While each JumpPath maps to a document, each JumpTask maps to an *application*. Here's an example that creates a JumpTask for Windows Notepad:

```
<JumpList>
  <JumpTask CustomCategory="Other Programs" Title="Notepad"
    Description="Open a sample document in Notepad"
    ApplicationPath="c:\windows\notepad.exe"
    IconResourcePath="c:\windows\notepad.exe"
    Arguments=" c:\Samples\samples.testDoc "></JumpTask>
  ...
</JumpList>
```

Although a JumpPath requires just two details, a JumpTask uses several more properties. Table 23-2 lists them all.

Table 23-2. *Properties of the JumpTask Class*

Name	Description
Title	The text that appears in the jump list.
Description	The tooltip text that appears when you hover over the item.
ApplicationPath	The executable file for the application. As with the document path in a JumpList, the ApplicationPath property requires a fully qualified path.
IconResourcePath	Points to the file that has the thumbnail icon that Windows will show next to that item in the jump list. Oddly enough, Windows won't choose a default icon or pull it out of the application executable. If you want to see a valid icon, you must set the IconResourcePath.
IconResourceIndex	If the application or icon resource identified by IconResourcePath has multiple icons, you also need to use IconResourceIndex to pick the one you want.
WorkingDirectory	The working directory where the application will be started. Usually, this will be a folder that contains documents for the application.
ApplicationPath	A command-line parameter that you want to pass to the application, such as a file to open.

Creating Jump List Items in Code

Although it's easy to fill a jump list using markup in the Application.xaml file, there's a serious disadvantage to this approach. As you've seen, both the JumpPath and the JumpTask items require a fully qualified file path. However, this information often depends on the way the application is deployed, and so it shouldn't be hard-coded. For that reason, it's common to create or modify the application jump list programmatically.

To configure the jump list in code, you use the JumpList, JumpPath, and JumpPath classes from the System. Windows.Shell namespace. The following example demonstrates this technique by creating a new JumpPath object. This item allows the user to open Notepad to view a readme.txt file that's stored in the current application folder, no matter where it's installed.

```
Private Sub Application_Startup(ByVal sender As Object, ByVal e As StartupEventArgs)
    ' Retrieve the current jump list.
    Dim jumpList As New JumpList()
    JumpList.SetJumpList(Application.Current, jumpList)

    ' Add a new JumpPath for a file in the application folder.
    Dim path As String = Path.GetDirectoryName(_
      System.Reflection.Assembly.GetExecutingAssembly().Location)
    path = Path.Combine(path, "readme.txt")
    If File.Exists(path) Then
        Dim jumpTask As New JumpTask()
        jumpTask.CustomCategory = "Documentation"
        jumpTask.Title = "Read the readme.txt"
        jumpTask.ApplicationPath = "c:\windows\notepad.exe"
        jumpTask.IconResourcePath = "c:\windows\notepad.exe"
        jumpTask.Arguments = path
        jumpList.JumpItems.Add(jumpTask)
    End If

    ' Update the jump list.
    jumpList.Apply()
End Sub
```

Figure 23-9 shows a customized jump list that includes this newly added JumpTask.

Figure 23-9. A jump list with a custom JumpTask

Launching Application Tasks from the Jump List

So far, all the examples you've seen have used the jump list to open documents or launch applications. You haven't seen an example that uses it to trigger a task inside a running application.

This isn't an oversight in the WPF jump list classes—it's just the way jump lists are designed. To work around it, you need to use a variation of the single-instance technique you used in Chapter 7. Here's the basic strategy:

- When the Application.Startup event fires, create a JumpTask that points to your application. Instead of using a file name, set the Arguments property to a special code that your application recognizes. For example, you could set it to @#StartOrder if you wanted this task to pass a "start order" instruction to your application.

- Use the single-instance code from Chapter 7. When a second instance starts, pass the command-line parameter to the first instance and shut down the new application.

- When the first instance receives the command-line parameter (in the OnStartupNextInstance() method), perform the appropriate task.

- Don't forget to remove the tasks from the jump list when the Application.Exit event fires, unless the tasks' commands will work equally well when your application is launched for the first time.

To see a basic implementation of this technique, refer to the JumpListApplicationTask project with the sample code for this chapter.

Changing the Taskbar Icon and Preview

The taskbar in Windows 7 and Windows 8 adds several more refinements, including an optional progress display and thumbnail preview windows. Happily, WPF makes it easy to work with all these features.

To access any of these features, you use TaskbarItemInfo class, which is found in the same System.Windows.Shell namespace as the jump list classes you considered earlier. Every window can have one associated TaskbarItemInfo object, and you can create it in XAML by adding this markup to your window:

```
<Window x:Class = "JumpLists.MainWindow"
 xmlns = "http://schemas.microsoft.com/winfx/2006/xaml/presentation"
 xmlns:x = "http://schemas.microsoft.com/winfx/2006/xaml"
 Title = "MainWindow" Height = "300" Width = "300">
```

```
<Grid>
  ...
</Grid>

<Window.TaskbarItemInfo>
  <TaskbarItemInfo x:Name="taskBarItem"></TaskbarItemInfo>
</Window.TaskbarItemInfo>
</Window>
```

This step, on its own, doesn't change anything in your window or application. But now you're ready to use the features that are demonstrated in the following sections.

Thumbnail Clipping

Much as Windows gives every application automatic jump list support, it also provides a thumbnail preview window that appears when the user hovers over the taskbar button. Ordinarily, the thumbnail preview window shows a scaled-down version of the client region of the window (everything but the window border). However, in some cases, it might show just a portion of the window. The advantage in this case is that it focuses attention on the relevant part of the window. In a particularly large window, it may make content legible that would otherwise be too small to read.

You can tap into this feature in WPF using the TaskbarItemInfo.ThumbnailClipMargin property. This specifies a Thickness object that sets the margin space between the content you want to show in the thumbnail and the edges of the window. The example shown in Figure 23-10 demonstrates how this works. Every time the user clicks a button in this application, the clipping region is shifted to include just the clicked button. Figure 23-10 shows the preview after clicking the second button.

Figure 23-10. *A window that clips its thumbnail preview*

■ **Note**   You can't change the thumbnail preview to show a graphic of your choosing. Your only option is to direct it to show a portion of the full window.

To create this effect, the code must take several details into account: the coordinates of the button, its size, and the size of the content region of the window (which, helpfully, is the size of the top-level Grid named LayoutRoot, which sits just inside the window and contains all its markup). Once you have these numbers, a few simple calculations are all you need to constrain the preview to the correct region:

```
Private Sub cmdShrinkPreview_Click(ByVal sender As Object, _
  ByVal e As RoutedEventArgs)
    ' Find the position of the clicked button, in window coordinates.
    Dim cmd As Button = CType(sender, Button)
    Dim locationFromWindow As Point = cmd.TranslatePoint(New Point(0, 0), Me)

    ' Determine the width that should be added to every side.
    Dim left As Double = locationFromWindow.X
    Dim top As Double = locationFromWindow.Y
    Dim right As Double = LayoutRoot.ActualWidth - cmd.ActualWidth - left
    Dim bottom As Double = LayoutRoot.ActualHeight - cmd.ActualHeight - top

    ' Apply the clipping.
    taskBarItem.ThumbnailClipMargin = New Thickness(left, top, right, bottom)
End Sub
```

Thumbnail Buttons

Some applications use the preview window for an entirely different purpose. They place buttons into a small toolbar area under the preview. Windows Media Player is one example. If you hover over its taskbar icon, you'll get a preview that includes play, pause, forward, and back buttons, which give you a convenient way to control playback without switching to the application itself.

WPF supports thumbnail buttons—in fact, it makes them easy. You simply need to add one or more ThumbButtonInfo objects to the TaskbarItemInfo.ThumbButtonInfos collection. Each ThumbButtonInfo needs an image, which you supply with the ImageSource property. You can also use a Description that adds tooltip text. You can then hook up the button to a method in your application by handling its Click event.

Here's an example that adds Media Player play and pause buttons:

```
<TaskbarItemInfo x:Name="taskBarItem">
  <TaskbarItemInfo.ThumbButtonInfos>
    <ThumbButtonInfo ImageSource="play.png" Description="Play"
     Click="cmdPlay_Click"></ThumbButtonInfo>
    <ThumbButtonInfo ImageSource="pause.png" Description="Pause"
     Click="cmdPause_Click"></ThumbButtonInfo>
  </TaskbarItemInfo.ThumbButtonInfos>
</TaskbarItemInfo>
```

Figure 23-11 shows these buttons under the preview window.

Figure 23-11. *Adding buttons to the thumbnail preview*

■ **Note**   Remember that the taskbar buttons are not shown in Windows Vista. For that reason, they should duplicate the functionality that's already in your window, rather than provide new features.

As your application performs different tasks and enters different states, some taskbar buttons may not be appropriate. Fortunately, you can manage them using a small set of useful properties, which are listed in Table 23-3.

Table 23-3. *Properties of the ThumbButtonInfo Class*

Name	Description
ImageSource	Sets the image you want to show for the button, which must be embedded in your application as a resource. Ideally, you'll use a .png file that has a transparent background.
Description	Sets the tooltip text that appears when the user hovers over the button.
Command, CommandParameter, and CommandTarget	Designate a command that the button should trigger. You can use these properties instead of the Click event.
Visibility	Allows you to hide or show a button.
IsEnabled	Allows you to disable a button, so it's visible but can't be clicked.
IsInteractive	Allows you to disable a button without dimming its appearance. This is useful if you want the button to act as a sort of status indicator.
IsBackgroundVisible	Allows you to disable the mouseover feedback for the button. If True (the default), Windows highlights the button and displays a border around it when the mouse moves overtop. If False, it doesn't.
DismissWhenClicked	Allows you to create a single-use button. As soon as it is clicked, Windows removes it from the taskbar. (For more control, you can use code to add or remove buttons on the fly, although it's usually just easier to show and hide them with the Visibility property.)

Progress Notification

If you've ever copied a large file in Windows Explorer, you've seen how it uses progress notification to shade the background of the taskbar button in green. As the copy progresses, the green background fills the button area from left to right, like a progress bar, until the operation completes.

What you might not realize is that this feature isn't specific to Windows Explorer. Instead, it's built into the taskbar and available to all your WPF applications. All you need to do is use two properties of the TaskbarItemInfo class: ProgressValue and ProgressState.

ProgressState starts out at None, which means no progress indicator is shown. However, if you set it to TaskbarItemProgressState.Normal, you get the green-colored progress background that Windows Explorer uses. The ProgressValue property determines its size, from 0 (none) to 1 (full, or complete). For example, setting ProgressValue to 0.5 fills half of the taskbar button's background with a green fill.

The TaskbarItemProgressState enumeration provides a few possibilities other than just None and Normal. You can use Pause to show a yellow background instead of green, Error to show a red background, and Indeterminate to show a continuous, pulsing progress background that ignores the ProgressValue property. This latter option is suitable when you don't know how long the current task will take to complete (for example, when calling a web service).

Overlay Icons

The final taskbar feature is the taskbar overlay—the ability to add a small image overtop of the taskbar icon. For example, the Messenger chat application uses different overlays to signal different statuses.

To use an overlay, you simply need a very tiny .png or .ico file with a transparent background. You aren't forced to use a specific pixel size, but you'll obviously want an image that's a fair bit smaller than the taskbar button picture. Assuming you've added this image to your project, you can show it by simply setting the TaskBarItemInfo.Overlay property. Most commonly, you'll set it using an image resource that's already defined in your markup, as shown here:

```
taskBarItem.Overlay = CType(Me.FindResource("WorkingImage"), ImageSource)
```

Alternatively, you can use the familiar pack URI syntax to point to an embedded file, as shown here:

```
taskBarItem.Overlay = New BitmapImage( _
  New Uri("pack://application:,,,/working.png"))
```

Set the Overlay property to a null reference (Nothing) to remove the overlay altogether.

Figure 23-12 shows the pause.png image being used as an overlay over the generic WPF application icon. This indicates that the application's work is currently paused.

Figure 23-12. *Showing an icon overlay*

The Last Word

In this chapter, you explored the WPF window model. You began with the basics: positioning and sizing a window, creating owned windows, and using the common dialog boxes. Then you considered more sophisticated effects, like irregularly shaped windows, and custom window templates.

In the last part of this chapter, you considered the impressive support that WPF includes for the taskbar in Windows 7 and Windows 8 (in desktop mode). You saw how your WPF application can get basic jump list support and add custom items. You also learned how you can focus the thumbnail preview window on a section of your window and give it convenient command buttons. Finally, you learned to use progress notification and overlays with your taskbar icon.

CHAPTER 24

■ ■ ■

Pages and Navigation

Most traditional Windows applications are arranged around a window that contains toolbars and menus. The toolbars and menus *drive* the application—as the user clicks them, actions happen, and other windows appear. In document-based applications, several equally important "main" windows may be open at once, but the overall model is the same. The users spend most of their time in one place, and jump to separate windows when necessary.

Windows applications are so common that it's sometimes hard to imagine different ways to design an application. However, the Web uses a dramatically different page-based navigation model, and desktop developers have realized that it's a surprisingly good choice for designing certain types of applications. In a bid to give desktop developers the ability to build weblike desktop applications, WPF includes its own page-based navigation system. As you'll see in this chapter, it's a remarkably flexible model.

Currently, the page-based model is most commonly used for simple, lightweight applications (or small feature subsets in a more complex window-based application). However, page-based applications are a good choice if you want to streamline application *deployment*. That's because WPF allows you to create a page-based application that runs directly inside Internet Explorer or Firefox. This means that users can run your application without an explicit installation step—they simply point their browsers to the correct location. You'll learn about this model, called XBAP, in this chapter.

Finally, this chapter wraps up with a look at WPF's WebBrowser control, which lets you host HTML web pages in a WPF window. As you'll see, the WebBrowser not only shows web pages, but also allows you to programmatically explore their structure and content (using the HTML DOM). It even allows your application to interact with JavaScript code.

Page-Based Navigation

The average web application looks quite a bit different from traditional rich client software. The users of a website spend their time navigating from one page to another. Unless they're unlucky enough to face pop-up advertising, there's never more than one page visible at a time. When completing a task (such as placing an order or performing a complicated search), the user traverses these pages in a linear sequence from start to finish.

HTML doesn't support the sophisticated windowing capabilities of desktop operating systems, so the best web developers rely on good design and clear, straightforward interfaces. As web design has become increasingly more sophisticated, Windows developers have also begun to see the advantages of this approach. Most important, the web model is simple and streamlined. For that reason, novice users often find websites easier to use than Windows applications, even though Windows applications are obviously much more capable.

In recent years, developers have begun mimicking some of the conventions of the Web in desktop applications. Financial software such as Microsoft Money is a prime example of a weblike interface that leads users through set tasks. However, creating these applications is often more complicated than designing a traditional window-based application, because developers need to re-create basic browser features such as navigation.

■ **Note**   In some cases, developers have built weblike applications by using the Internet Explorer browser engine. This is the approach that Microsoft Money takes, but it's one that would be more difficult for non-Microsoft developers. Although Microsoft provides hooks into Internet Explorer, such as the WebBrowser control, building a complete application around these features is far from easy. It also risks sacrificing the best capabilities of ordinary Windows applications.

In WPF, there's no longer any reason to compromise, because WPF includes a built-in page model that incorporates navigation. Best of all, this model can be used to create a variety of page-based applications, applications that use some page-based features (for example, in a wizard or help system), or applications that are hosted directly in the browser.

Page-Based Interfaces

To create a page-based application in WPF, you need to stop using the Window class as your top-level container for user interfaces. Instead, it's time to switch to the System.Windows.Controls.Page class.

The model for creating pages in WPF is much the same as the model for creating windows. Although you could create page objects with just code, you'll usually create a XAML file and a code-behind file for each page. When you compile that application, the compiler creates a derived page class that combines your code with a bit of automatically generated glue (such as the fields that refer to each named element on your page). This is the same process that you learned about when you considered compilation with a window-based application in Chapter 2.

■ **Note**   You can add a page to any WPF project. Just choose Project ➤ Add Page in Visual Studio.

Although pages are the top-level user interface ingredient when you're designing your application, they aren't the top-level container when you *run* your application. Instead, your pages are hosted in another container. This is the secret to WPF's flexibility with page-based applications, because you can use one of several containers:

- The NavigationWindow, which is a slightly tweaked version of the Window class

- A Frame that's inside another window

- A Frame that's inside another page

- A Frame that's hosted directly in Internet Explorer or Firefox

You'll consider all of these hosts in this chapter.

Creating a Simple Page-Based Application with NavigationWindow

To try an extremely simple page-based application, create a page like this:

```
<Page x:Class="Page1"
    xmlns="http://schemas.microsoft.com/winfx/2006/xaml/presentation"
    xmlns:x="http://schemas.microsoft.com/winfx/2006/xaml"
    WindowTitle="Page1"
    >
```

```
  <StackPanel Margin="3">
    <TextBlock Margin="3">
      This is a simple page.
    </TextBlock>
    <Button Margin="2" Padding="2">OK</Button>
    <Button Margin="2" Padding="2">Close</Button>
  </StackPanel>
</Page>
```

Now modify the Application.xaml file so that the startup page is your page file:

```
<Application x:Class="Application"
    xmlns="http://schemas.microsoft.com/winfx/2006/xaml/presentation"
    xmlns:x="http://schemas.microsoft.com/winfx/2006/xaml"
    StartupUri="Page1.xaml"
    >
</Application>
```

When you run this application, WPF is intelligent enough to realize that you're pointing it to a page rather than a window. It automatically creates a new NavigationWindow object to serve as a container and shows your page inside of it (Figure 24-1). It also reads the page's WindowTitle property and uses that for the window caption.

Figure 24-1. *A page in a NavigationWindow*

■ **Note**   One difference between a page and a window is that you don't typically set the size of a page, because the page size is determined by the host. If you do set the Width and Height properties of the page, the page is made exactly that size, but some content is clipped if the host window is smaller, or it's centered inside the available space if the host window is larger.

The NavigationWindow looks more or less like an ordinary window, aside from the back and forward navigation buttons that appear in the bar at the top. As you might expect, the NavigationWindow class derives from Window, and it adds a small set of navigation-related properties. You can get a reference to the containing NavigationWindow object by using code like this:

```
' Get a reference to the window that contains the current page.
Dim win As NavigationWindow
win = CType(Window.GetWindow(Me), NavigationWindow)
```

This code won't work in the page constructor, because the page hasn't been placed inside its container yet—instead, wait at least until the Page.Loaded event fires.

▓ **Tip** It's best to avoid the NavigationWindow approach if at all possible, and use properties of the Page class (and the navigation service described later in this chapter). Otherwise, your page will be tightly coupled to the NavigationWindow, and you won't be able to reuse it in different hosts.

If you want to create a code-only application, you'd need to create both the navigation window and the page to get the effect shown in Figure 24-1. Here's the code that would do it:

```
Dim win As New NavigationWindow()
win.Content = New Page1()
win.Show()
```

The Page Class

Like the Window class, the Page class allows a single nested element. However, the Page class isn't a content control; it derives directly from FrameworkElement. The Page class is also simpler and more streamlined than the Window class. It adds a small set of properties that allow you to customize its appearance, interact with the container in a limited way, and use navigation. Table 24-1 lists these properties.

Table 24-1. *Properties of the Page Class*

Name	Description
Background	Takes a brush that allows you to set the background fill.
Content	Takes the single element that's shown in the page. Usually, this is a layout container, such as a Grid or a StackPanel.
Foreground, FontFamily, and FontSize	Determine the default appearance of text inside the page. The values of these properties are inherited by the elements inside the page. For example, if you set the foreground fill and font size, by default, the content inside the page gets these details.
WindowWidth, WindowHeight, and WindowTitle	Determine the appearance of the window that wraps your page. These properties allow you to take control of the host by setting its width, height, and caption. However, they have an effect only if your page is being hosted in a window (rather than a frame).
NavigationService	Returns a reference to a NavigationService object, which you can use to programmatically send the user to another page.

(continued)

Table 24-1. *(continued)*

Name	Description
KeepAlive	Determines whether the page object should be kept alive after the user navigates to another page. You'll take a closer look at this property later in this chapter (in the "Navigation History" section), when you consider how WPF restores the pages in your navigation history.
ShowsNavigationUI	Determines whether the host for this page shows its navigation controls (the forward and back buttons). By default, it's True.
Title	Sets the name that's used for the page in the navigation history. The host does not use the title to set the caption in the title bar; instead, the WindowTitle property serves that purpose.

It's also important to notice what's not there—namely, there's no equivalent of the Hide() and Show() methods of the Window class. If you want to show a different page, you'll need to use navigation.

Hyperlinks

The easiest way to allow the user to move from one page to another is by using hyperlinks. In WPF, hyperlinks aren't separate elements. Instead, they're *inline flow elements*, which must be placed inside another element that supports them. (The reason for this design is that hyperlinks and text are often intermixed. You'll learn more about flow content and text layout in Chapter 28.)

For example, here's a combination of text and links in a TextBlock element, which is the most practical container for hyperlinks:

```
<TextBlock Margin="3" TextWrapping="Wrap">
  This is a simple page.
  Click <Hyperlink NavigateUri="Page2.xaml">here</Hyperlink> to go to Page2.
</TextBlock>
```

When rendered, hyperlinks appear as the familiar blue, underlined text (see Figure 24-2).

Figure 24-2. *Linking to another page*

You can handle clicks on a link in two ways. You can respond to the Click event and use code to perform some task, or direct the user to another page. However, there's an easier approach. The Hyperlink class also includes a NavigateUri property, which you set to point to any other page in your application. Then, when users click this hyperlink, they travel to the destination page automatically.

■ **Note** The NavigateUri property works only if you place the hyperlink in a page. If you want to use a hyperlink in a window-based application to let users perform a task, launch a web page, or open a new window, you need to handle the RequestNavigate event and write the code yourself.

Hyperlinks aren't the only way to move from one page to another. The NavigationWindow includes prominent forward and back buttons (unless you set the Page.ShowsNavigationUI property to False to hide them). Clicking these buttons moves you through the navigation sequence one page at a time. And similar to a browser, you can click the drop-down arrow at the edge of the forward button to examine the complete sequence and jump forward or backward several pages at a time (Figure 24-3).

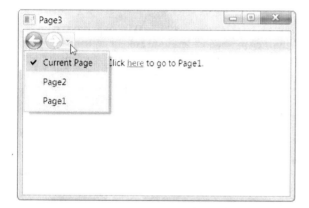

Figure 24-3. *The history of visited pages*

You'll learn more about how the page history works—and its limitations—later in the "Navigation History" section.

■ **Note** If you navigate to a new page, and that page doesn't set the WindowTitle property, the window keeps the title it had on the previous page. If you don't set the WindowTitle on any page, the window caption is left blank.

Navigating to Websites

Interestingly, you can also create a hyperlink that points to web content. When the user clicks the link, the target web page loads in the page area:

```
<TextBlock Margin="3" TextWrapping="Wrap">
  Visit the website
  <Hyperlink NavigateUri="http://www.prosetech.com">www.prosetech.com</Hyperlink>.
</TextBlock>
```

However, if you use this technique, make sure you attach an event handler to the Application. DispatcherUnhandledException or Application.NavigationFailed event. The attempt to navigate to a website could fail if the computer isn't online, the site isn't available, or the web content can't be reached. In this case, the network stack returns an error such as "404: File Not Found," which becomes a WebException. To handle this exception gracefully and prevent your application from shutting down unexpectedly, you need to neutralize it with an event handler such as this:

```
Private Sub Application_NavigationFailed(ByVal sender As Object, _
  ByVal e As System.Windows.Navigation.NavigationFailedEventArgs) _
  Handles Me.NavigationFailed

    If TypeOf e.Exception Is System.Net.WebException Then
        MessageBox.Show("Website " & e.Uri.ToString() & " cannot be reached.")

        ' Neutralize the erorr so the application continues running.
        e.Handled = True
    End If
End Sub
```

NavigationFailed is just one of several navigation events that are defined in the Application class. You'll get the full list later in this chapter, in Table 24-2.

▓ **Note**   After you lead users to a web page, they'll be able to click its links to travel to other web pages, leaving your content far behind. In fact, they'll return to your WPF page only if they use the navigation history to go back or if you're showing the page in a custom window (as discussed in the next section) and that window includes a control that navigates back to your content.

You can't do a number of things when displaying pages from external websites. You can't prevent the user from navigating to specific pages or sites. Also, you can't interact with the web page by using the HTML Document Object Model (DOM). That means you can't scan a page looking for links or dynamically change a page. All of these tasks are possible using the WebBrowser control, which is described at the end of this chapter.

Fragment Navigation

The last trick that you can use with the hyperlink is *fragment navigation*. By adding the number sign (#) at the end of the NavigateUri, followed by an element name, you can jump straight to a specific control on a page. However, this works only if the target page is scrollable. (The target page is scrollable if it uses the ScrollViewer control or if it's hosted in a web browser.) Here's an example:

```
<TextBlock Margin="3">
    Review the <Hyperlink NavigateUri="Page2.xaml#myTextBox">full text</Hyperlink>.
</TextBlock>
```

When the user clicks this link, the application moves to the page named Page2, and scrolls down the page to the element named myTextBox. The page is scrolled down until myTextBox appears at the top of the page (or as close as possible, depending on the size of the page content and the containing window). However, the target element doesn't receive focus.

Hosting Pages in a Frame

The NavigationWindow is a convenient container, but it's not your only option. You can also place pages directly inside other windows or even inside other pages. This makes for an extremely flexible system, because you can reuse the same page in different ways, depending on the type of application you need to create.

To embed a page inside a window, you simply need to use the Frame class. The Frame class is a content control that can hold any element, but it makes particular sense when used as a container for a page. It includes a property named Source, which points to a XAML page that you want to display.

Here's an ordinary window that wraps some content in a StackPanel and places a Frame in a separate column:

```
<Window x:Class="WindowWithFrame"
    xmlns="http://schemas.microsoft.com/winfx/2006/xaml/presentation"
    xmlns:x="http://schemas.microsoft.com/winfx/2006/xaml"
    Title="WindowWithFrame" Height="300" Width="300"
    >
  <Grid Margin="3">
    <Grid.ColumnDefinitions>
      <ColumnDefinition></ColumnDefinition>
      <ColumnDefinition></ColumnDefinition>
    </Grid.ColumnDefinitions>

    <StackPanel>
      <TextBlock Margin="3" TextWrapping="Wrap">
       This is ordinary window content.</TextBlock>
      <Button Margin="3" Padding="3">Close</Button>
    </StackPanel>
    <Frame Grid.Column="1" Source="Page1.xaml"
      BorderBrush="Blue" BorderThickness="1"></Frame>
  </Grid>
</Window>
```

Figure 24-4 shows the result. A border around the frame shows the page content. There's no reason you need to stop at one frame. You can easily create a window that wraps multiple frames, and you can point them to different pages.

Figure 24-4. *A window with a page embedded in a frame*

As you can see in Figure 24-4, this example doesn't include the familiar navigation buttons. This is because the Frame.NavigationUIVisibility property is (by default) set to Automatic. As a result, the navigation controls appear only after there's something in the forward and back list. To try this, navigate to a new page. You'll see the buttons appear inside the frame, as shown in Figure 24-5.

Figure 24-5. *A frame with navigation buttons*

You can change the NavigationUIVisibility property to Hidden if you never want to show the navigation buttons, or change it to Visible if you want them to appear right from the start.

Having the navigation buttons inside the frame is a great design if your frame contains content that's separate from the main flow of the application. (For example, maybe you're using it to display context-sensitive help or the content for a walk-through tutorial.) But in other cases, you may prefer to show the buttons at the top of the window. To do this, you need to change your top-level container from Window to NavigationWindow. That way, your window will include the navigation buttons. The frame inside the window will automatically wire itself up to these buttons, so the user gets a similar experience to what's shown in Figure 24-3, except now the window also holds the extra content.

___

■ **Tip** You can add as many Frame objects as you need to a window. For example, you could easily create a window that allows the user to browse through an application task, help documentation, and an external website, using three separate frames.

___

Hosting Pages in Another Page

Frames give you the ability to create more-complex arrangements of windows. As you learned in the previous section, you can use several frames in a single window. You can also place a frame inside another page to create a *nested* page. In fact, the process is exactly the same—you simply add a Frame object inside your page markup.

Nested pages present a more complex navigation situation. For example, imagine you visit a page and then click a link in an embedded frame. What happens when you click the back button?

Essentially, all the pages in a frame are flattened into one list. So the first time you click the back button, you move to the previous page in the embedded frame. The next time you click the back button, you move to the previously visited parent page. Figure 24-6 shows the sequence you follow. Notice that the back navigation button is enabled in the second step.

Figure 24-6. *Navigation with an embedded page*

Most of the time, this navigation model is fairly intuitive, because you'll have one item in the back list for each page you visit. However, in some cases the embedded frame plays a less important role. For example, maybe it shows different views of the same data or allows you to step through multiple pages of help content. In these cases, stepping through all the pages in the embedded frame may seem awkward or time-consuming. Instead, you may want to use the navigation controls to control the navigation of the parent frame only, so that when you click the back button, you move to the previous parent page right away. To do this, you need to set the JournalOwnership property of the embedded frame to OwnsJournal. This tells the frame to maintain its own distinct page history. By default, the embedded frame will now acquire navigation buttons that allow you to move back and forth through its content (see Figure 24-7). If this isn't what you want, you can use the JournalOwnership property in conjunction with the NavigationUIVisibility property to hide the navigation controls altogether, as shown here:

```
<Frame Source="Page1.xaml"
  JournalOwnership="OwnsJournal" NavigationUIVisibility="Hidden"
  BorderThickness="1" BorderBrush="Blue"></Frame>
```

Figure 24-7. *An embedded page that owns its journal and supports navigation*

Now the embedded frame is treated as though it's just a piece of dynamic content inside your page. From the user's point of view, the embedded frame doesn't support navigation.

Hosting Pages in a Web Browser

The final way that you can use page-based navigation applications is in Internet Explorer or Firefox. However, in order to use this approach, you need to create a *XAML browser application* (which is known as an XBAP). In Visual Studio, the XBAP is a separate project template, and you must select it (rather than the standard WPF Windows application) when creating a project in order to use browser hosting. You'll examine the XBAP model later in this chapter.

GETTING THE RIGHT SIZE WINDOW

There are really two types of page-based applications:

- Stand-alone Windows applications that use pages for part or all of their user interfaces. You'll use this approach if you need to integrate a wizard into your application or you want a simple task-oriented application. This way, you can use WPF's navigation and journal features to simplify your coding.

- Browser applications (XBAPs) that are hosted by Internet Explorer or Firefox, and usually run with limited permissions. You'll use this approach if you want a lightweight, web-based deployment model.

If your application falls into the first category, you probably won't want to set the Application.StartupUri property to point to a page. Instead, you'll create the NavigationWindow manually, and then load your first page inside it (as shown earlier), or you'll embed your pages in a custom window by using the Frame control. Both of these approaches give you the flexibility to set the size of the application window, which is important for making sure your application looks respectable when it first starts up. On the other hand, if you're creating an XBAP, you have no control over the size of the containing web browser window, and you *must* set the StartupUri property to point to a page.

The Page History

Now that you've learned about pages and the different ways to host them, you're ready to delve deeper into the navigation model that WPF uses. In this section, you'll learn how WPF hyperlinks work and how pages are restored when you navigate back to them.

A Closer Look at URIs in WPF

You might wonder how properties such as Application.StartupUri, Frame.Source, and Hyperlink.NavigateUri actually work. In an application that's made up of loose XAML files and run in the browser, it's fairly straightforward: when you click a hyperlink, the browser treats the page reference as a relative URI and looks for the XAML page in the current folder. But in a compiled application, the pages are no longer available as separate resources; instead, they're compiled to Binary Application Markup Language (BAML) and embedded into the assembly. So, how can they be referenced using a URI?

This system works because of the way that WPF addresses application resources. When you click a hyperlink in a compiled XAML application, the URI is still treated as a relative path. However, it's relative to the *base URI* for the application. That's because a hyperlink that points to Page1.xaml is actually expanded to the pack URI shown here:

```
pack://application:,,,/Page1.xaml
```

Chapter 7 describes the pack URI syntax in detail. But the most important detail is the final portion, which includes the resource name.

At this point, you might be wondering why it's important to understand how hyperlink URIs work if the process is so seamless. The chief reason is that you might choose to create an application that navigates to XAML pages stored in another assembly. In fact, there are good reasons for this design. Because pages can be used in different containers, you might want to reuse the same set of pages in an XBAP and an ordinary Windows application. That way, you can deploy two versions of your application: a browser-based version and a desktop version. To avoid duplicating your code, you should place all the pages you plan to reuse in a separate class library assembly (DLL), which can then be referenced by both your application projects.

This necessitates a change in your URIs. If you have a page in one assembly that points to a page in another, you need to use the following syntax:

```
pack://application:,,,/PageLibrary;component/Page1.xaml
```

Here, the component is named PageLibrary and the path ,,,/PageLibrary;component/Page1.xaml points to a page named Page1.xaml that's compiled and embedded inside.

Of course, you probably won't use the absolute path. Instead, it makes more sense to use the following slightly shorter relative path in your URIs:

```
/PageLibrary;component/Page1.xaml
```

Tip   Use the project template called Custom Control Library (WPF) when you create the SharedLibrary assembly to get the correct assembly references, namespace imports, and application settings.

Navigation History

The WPF page history works just like the history in a browser. Every time you navigate to a new page, the previous page is added to the back list. If you click the back button, the page is added to the forward list. If you back out from one page and then navigate to a new page, the forward list is cleared.

The behavior of the back and forward lists is fairly straightforward, but the plumbing that supports them is more complex. For example, imagine you visit a page with two text boxes, type something in, and move ahead. If you head back to this page, you'll find that WPF restores the state of your text boxes—meaning whatever content you placed in them is still there.

▓ **Note**   There's an important difference between returning to a page through the navigation history and clicking a link that takes you to the same page. For example, if you click links that take you from Page1 to Page2 to Page1, WPF creates three separate page objects. The second time you see Page1, WPF creates it as a separate instance, with its own state. However, if you click the back button twice to return to the first Page1 instance, you'll see that your original Page1 state remains.

You might assume that WPF maintains the state of previously visited pages by keeping the page object in memory. The problem with that approach is that the memory overhead may not be trivial in a complex application with many pages. For that reason, WPF can't assume that maintaining the page object is a safe strategy. Instead, when you navigate away from a page, WPF stores the state of all your controls and then destroys the page. When you return to a page, WPF re-creates the page (from the original XAML) and then restores the state of your controls. This strategy has lower overhead because the memory required to save just a few details of control state is far less than the memory required to store the page and its entire visual tree of objects.

This system raises an interesting question: how does WPF decide which details to store? WPF examines the complete element tree of your page, and it looks at the dependency properties of all your elements. Properties that should be stored have a tiny bit of extra metadata—a *journal* flag that indicates they should be kept in the navigation log known as the *journal*. (The journal flag is set by using the FrameworkPropertyMetadata object when registering the dependency property, as described in Chapter 4.)

If you take a closer look at the navigation system, you'll find that many properties don't have the journal flag. For example, if you set the Content property of a content control or the Text property of a TextBlock element by using code, neither of these details will be retained when you return to the page. The same is true if you set the Foreground or Background properties dynamically. However, if you set the Text property of a TextBox, the IsSelected property of a CheckBox, or the SelectedIndex property of a ListBox, all these details will remain.

So what can you do if this isn't the behavior you want? What if you set many properties dynamically, and you want your pages to retain all of their information? You have several options. The most powerful is to use the Page.KeepAlive property, which is False by default. When set to True, WPF doesn't use the serialization mechanism described previously. Instead, it keeps all your page objects alive. Thus, when you navigate back to a page, it's exactly the way you left it. Of course, this option has the drawback of increased memory overhead, so you should enable it only on the few pages that really need it.

▓ **Tip**   When you use the KeepAlive property to keep a page alive, it won't fire the Initialized event the next time you navigate to it. (Pages that aren't kept alive but are "rehydrated" by using WPFs journaling system *will* fire the Initialized event each time the user visits them.) If this behavior isn't what you want, you should instead handle the Unloaded and Loaded events of the Page, which always fire.

Another solution is to choose a different design that passes information around. For example, you can create page functions (described later in this chapter) that return information. Using page functions, along with extra initialization logic, you can design your own system for retrieving the important information from a page and restoring it when needed.

There's one more wrinkle with the WPF navigation history. As you'll discover later in this chapter, you can write code that dynamically creates a page object and then navigates to it. In this situation, the ordinary mechanism of maintaining the page state won't work. WPF doesn't have a reference to the XAML document for the page, so it doesn't know how to reconstruct the page. (And if the page is created dynamically, there may not even *be* a corresponding XAML document.) In this situation, WPF always keeps the page object alive in memory, no matter what the KeepAlive property says.

Maintaining Custom Properties

Ordinarily, any fields in your page class lose their values when the page is destroyed. If you want to add custom properties to your page class and make sure *they* retain their values, you can set the journal flag accordingly. However, you can't take this step with an ordinary property or a field. Instead, you need to create a dependency property in your page class.

You've already taken a look at dependency properties in Chapter 4. To create a dependency property, you need to follow two steps. First, you need to create the dependency property definition. Second, you need an ordinary property procedure that sets or gets the value of the dependency property.

To define the dependency property, you need to create a shared field like this:

```
Private Shared MyPageDataProperty As DependencyProperty
```

By convention, the field that defines your dependency property has the name of your ordinary property, plus the word *Property* at the end.

■ **Note**   This example uses a private dependency property. That's because the only code that needs to access this property is in the page class where it's defined.

To complete your definition, you need a shared constructor that registers your dependency property definition. This is the place where you set the services that you want to use with your dependency property (such as support for data binding, animation, and journaling).

```
Shared Sub New()
    Dim metadata As New FrameworkPropertyMetadata()
    metadata.Journal = True

    MyPageDataProperty = DependencyProperty.Register( _
      "MyPageDataProperty", GetType(String), _
      GetType(PageWithPersistentData), metadata, Nothing)
End Sub
```

Now you can create the ordinary property that wraps this dependency property. However, when you write the getter and setter, you'll use the GetValue() and SetValue() methods that are defined in the base DependencyObject class:

```
Private Property MyPageData() As String
    Set(ByVal value As String)
        SetValue(MyPageDataProperty, value)
    End Set
```

```
Get
        Return CStr(GetValue(MyPageDataProperty))
    End Get
End Property
```

Add all these details to a single page (in this example, one named PageWithPersistentData), and the MyPageData property value will be automatically serialized when users navigate away and restored when they return.

The Navigation Service

So far, the navigation you've seen relies heavily on hyperlinks. When this approach works, it's simple and elegant. However, in some cases, you'll want to take more control of the navigation process. For example, hyperlinks work well if you're using pages to model a fixed, linear series of steps that the user traverses from start to finish (such as a wizard). However, if you want the user to complete small sequences of steps and return to a common page, or if you want to configure the sequence of steps based on other details (such as the user's previous actions), you need something more.

Programmatic Navigation

You can set the Hyperlink.NavigateUri and Frame.Source properties dynamically. However, the most flexible and powerful approach is to use the WPF navigation service. You can access the navigation service through the container that hosts the page (such as Frame or NavigationWindow), but this approach limits your pages so they can be used only in that type of container. The best approach is to access the navigation service through the shared NavigationService.GetNavigationService() method. You pass a reference to your page to the GetNavigationService() method, and it returns a live NavigationService object that lets you perform programmatic navigation:

```
Dim nav As NavigationService
nav = NavigationService.GetNavigationService(Me)
```

This code works no matter which container you're using to host your pages.

■ **Note**   The NavigationService isn't available in a page constructor or when the Page.Initialized event fires. Use the Page.Loaded event instead.

The NavigationService class gives you a number of methods you can use to trigger navigation. The most commonly used is the Navigate() method, which allows you to navigate to a page based on its URI:

```
nav.Navigate(New System.Uri("Page1.xaml", UriKind.RelativeOrAbsolute))
```

or by creating the appropriate page object:

```
Dim nextPage As New Page1()
nav.Navigate(nextPage)
```

If possible, you'll want to navigate by URI, because that allows WPF's journaling system to preserve the page data without needing to keep the tree of page objects alive in memory. When you pass a page object to the Navigate() method, the entire object is always retained in memory.

However, you may decide to create the page object manually if you need to pass information into the page. You can pass in information by using a custom page class constructor (which is the most common approach), or you can call another custom method in the page class after you've created it. If you add a new constructor to the page, make sure your constructor calls InitializeComponent() to process your markup and create the control objects.

■ **Note** If you decide you need to use programmatic navigation, it's up to you whether you use button controls, hyperlinks, or something else. Typically, you'll use conditional code in your event handler to indicate the page to which you navigate.

WPF navigation is asynchronous. As a result, you can cancel the navigation request before it's complete by calling the NavigationService.StopLoading() method. You can also use the Refresh() method to reload a page.

Finally, the NavigationService also provides GoBack() and GoForward() methods, which allow you to move through the back and forward lists. This is useful if you're creating your own navigation controls. Both of these methods raise an InvalidOperationException if you try to navigate to a page that doesn't exist (for example, you attempt to go back when you're on the first page). To avoid these errors, check the Boolean CanGoBack and CanGoForward properties before using the matching methods.

Navigation Events

The NavigationService class also provides a useful set of events that you can use to react to navigation. The most common reason you'll react to navigation is to perform some sort of task when navigation is complete. For example, if your page is hosted inside a frame in a normal window, you might update status bar text in the window when navigation is complete.

Because navigation is asynchronous, the Navigate() method returns before the target page has appeared. In some cases, the time difference could be significant, such as when you're navigating to a loose XAML page on a website (or a XAML page in another assembly that triggers a web download) or when the page includes time-consuming code in its Initialized or Loaded event handler.

The WPF navigation process unfolds like this:

1. The page is located.

2. The page information is retrieved. (If the page is on a remote site, it's downloaded at this point.)

3. Any related resources that the page needs (such as images) are also located and downloaded.

4. The page is parsed, and the tree of objects is generated. At this point, the page fires its Initialized event (unless it's being restored from the journal) and its Loaded event.

5. The page is rendered.

6. If the URI includes a fragment, WPF navigates to that element.

Table 24-2 lists the events that are raised by the NavigationService class during the process. These navigation events are also provided by the Application class and by the navigation containers (NavigationWindow and Frame). If you have more than one navigation container, this gives you the flexibility to handle the navigation in different containers separately. However, there's no built-in way to handle the navigation events for a single *page*. After you attach an event handler to the navigation service in a navigation container, it continues to fire events as you move from page to page (or until you remove the event handler). Generally, this means that the easiest way to handle navigation is at the application level.

Table 24-2. Events of the NavigationService Class

Name	Description
Navigating	Navigation is just about to start. You can cancel this event to prevent the navigation from taking place.
Navigated	Navigation has started, but the target page has not yet been retrieved.
NavigationProgress	Navigation is underway, and a chunk of page data has been downloaded. This event is raised periodically to provide information about the progress of navigation. It provides the amount of information that has been downloaded (NavigationProgressEventArgs.BytesRead) and the total amount of information that's required (NavigationProgressEventArgs.MaxBytes). This event fires every time 1 KB of data is retrieved.
LoadCompleted	The page has been parsed. However, the Initialized and Loaded events have not yet been fired.
FragmentNavigation	The page is about to be scrolled to the target element. This event fires only if you use a URI with fragment information.
NavigationStopped	Navigation was canceled with the StopLoading() method.
NavigationFailed	Navigation has failed because the target page could not be located or downloaded. You can use this event to neutralize the exception before it bubbles up to become an unhandled application exception. Just set NavigationFailedEventArgs.Handled to True.

Navigation events can't be suppressed by using the RoutedEventArgs.Handled property. That's because navigation events are ordinary .NET events, not routed events.

⬛ **Tip**   You can pass data from the Navigate() method to the navigation events. Just look for one of the Navigate() method overloads that take an extra object parameter. This object is made available in the Navigated, NavigationStopped, and LoadCompleted events through the NavigationEventArgs.ExtraData property. For example, you could use this property to keep track of the time a navigation request was made.

Managing the Journal

Using the techniques you've learned so far, you'll be able to build a linear navigation-based application. You can make the navigation process adaptable (for example, using conditional logic so that users are directed to different steps along the way), but you're still limited to the basic start-to-finish approach. Figure 24-8 shows this navigation topology, which is common when building simple task-based wizards. The dashed lines indicate the steps we're interested in—when the user exits a group of pages that represent a logical task.

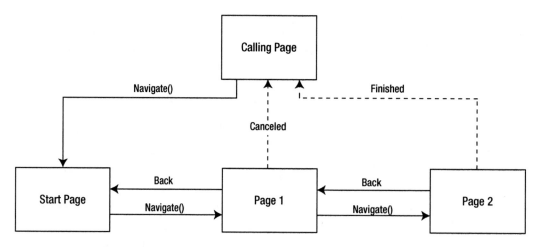

Figure 24-8. *Linear navigation*

If you try to implement this design by using WPF navigation, you'll find that there's a missing detail. Namely, when the user is finished with the navigation process (either because the user canceled the operation during one of the steps or because the user completed the task at hand), you need to wipe out the back history. If your application revolves around a main window that isn't navigation-based, this isn't a problem. When the user launches the page-based task, your application simply creates a new NavigationWindow to take the user through it. When the task ends, you can destroy that window. However, if your entire application is navigation-based, this isn't as easy. You need a way to drop the history list when the task is canceled or complete, so the user can't step back to one of the intermediary steps.

Unfortunately, WPF doesn't allow you to have much control over the navigation stack. It just gives you two methods in the NavigationService class: AddBackEntry() and RemoveBackEntry(). RemoveBackEntry() is the one you need in this example. It takes the most recent item from the back list and deletes it. RemoveBackEntry() also returns a JournalEntry object that describes that item. It tells you the URI (through the Source property) and the name that it uses in the navigation history (through the Name property). Remember that the name is set based on the Page.Title property.

If you want to clear several entries after a task is complete, you'll need to call RemoveBackEntry() multiple times. You can use two approaches. If you've decided to remove the entire back list, you can use the CanGoBack property to determine when you've reached the end:

```
Do While nav.CanGoBack
    nav.RemoveBackEntry()
Loop
```

Alternatively, you can continue removing items until you remove the task starting point. For example, if a page launches a task starting with a page named ConfigureAppWizard.xaml, you could use this code when the task is complete:

```
Dim pageName As String
Do While pageName <> "ConfigureAppWizard.xaml"
    Dim entry As JournalEntry = nav.RemoveBackEntry()
    pageName = System.IO.Path.GetFileName(entry.Source.ToString())
Loop
```

This code takes the full URI that's stored in the JournalEntry.Source property and trims it down to just the page name by using the shared GetFileName() method of the Path class (which works equally well with URIs). Using the Title property would make for more convenient coding, but it isn't as robust. Because the page title is displayed in the navigation history and is visible to the user, it's a piece of information you would need to translate into other languages when localizing your application. This would break code that expects a hard-coded page title. And even if you don't plan to localize your application, it's not difficult to imagine a scenario where the page title is changed to be clearer or more descriptive.

Incidentally, it is possible to examine all the items in the back and forward lists by using the BackStack and ForwardStack properties of the navigation container (such as NavigationWindow or Frame). However, it's not possible to get this information generically through the NavigationService class. In any case, these properties expose simple read-only collections of JournalEntry objects. They don't allow you to modify the lists, and they're rarely needed.

Adding Custom Items to the Journal

Along with the RemoveBackEntry() method, the NavigationService also gives you an AddBackEntry() method. The purpose of this method is to allow you to save "virtual" entries in the back list. For example, imagine you have a single page that allows the user to perform a fairly sophisticated configuration task. If you want the user to be able to step back to a previous state of that window, you can save it by using the AddBackEntry() method. Even though it's only a single page, it may have several corresponding entries in the list.

Contrary to what you might expect, when you call AddBackEntry(), you don't pass in a JournalEntry object. (In fact, the JournalEntry class has a protected constructor and so it can't be instantiated by your code.) Instead, you need to create a custom class that derives from the abstract System.Windows.Navigation.CustomContentState class and stores all the information you need. For example, consider the application shown in Figure 24-9, which allows you to move items from one list to another.

Figure 24-9. *A dynamic list*

Now imagine that you want to save the state of this window every time an item is moved from one list to the other. The first thing you need is a class that derives from CustomContentState and keeps track of this information you need. In this case, you simply need to record the contents of both lists. Because this class will be stored in the journal (so your page can be "rehydrated" when needed), it needs to be serializable:

```
<Serializable()>_
Public Class ListSelectionJournalEntry
    Inherits CustomContentState

    Private _sourceItems As List(Of String)
    Public ReadOnly Property SourceItems() As List(Of String)
        Get
            Return _sourceItems
        End Get
    End Property

    Private _targetItems As List(Of String)
    Public ReadOnly Property TargetItems() As List(Of String)
        Get
            Return _targetItems
        End Get
    End Property
    ...
```

This gets you off to a good start, but there's still a fair bit more to do. For example, you probably don't want the page to appear with the same title in the navigation history multiple times. Instead, you'll probably want to use a more descriptive name. To make this possible, you need to override the JournalEntryName property.

In this example, there's no obvious, concise way to describe the state of both lists. So it makes sense to let the page choose the name when it saves the entry in the journal. This way, the page can add a descriptive name based on the most recent action (such as Added Blue or Removed Yellow). To create this design, you simply need to make the JournalEntryName depend on a variable, which can be set in the constructor:

```
    ...
    Private journalName As String
    Public Overrides ReadOnly Property JournalEntryName() As String
        Get
            Return journalName
        End Get
    End Property
    ...
```

The WPF navigation system calls your JournalEntryName property to get the name it should show in the list.

The next step is to override the Replay() method. WPF calls this method when the user navigates to an entry in the back or forward list so that you can apply the previously saved state.

There are two approaches you can take in the Replay() method. You can retrieve a reference to the current page by using the NavigationService.Content property. You can then cast that into the appropriate page class and call whatever method is required to implement your change. The other approach, which is used here, is to rely on a callback:

```
...
Private replayListChange As ReplayListChange

Public Overrides Sub Replay(ByVal navigationService As NavigationService, _
  ByVal mode As NavigationMode)
    Me.replayListChange(Me)
End Sub
...
```

The ReplayListChange delegate isn't shown here, but it's quite simple. It represents a method with one parameter: the ListSelectionJournalEntry object. The page can then retrieve the list information from the SourceItems and TargetItems properties and restore the page.

With this in place, the last step is to create a constructor that accepts all the information you need: the two lists of items, the title to use in the journal, and the delegate that should be triggered when the state needs to be reapplied to the page:

```
...
Public Sub New(ByVal sourceItems As List(Of String), _
  ByVal targetItems As List(Of String), ByVal journalName As String, _
  ByVal replayListChange As ReplayListChange)
    _sourceItems = sourceItems
    _targetItems = targetItems
    _journalName = journalName
    Me.replayListChange = replayListChange
End Sub
```

End Class

To hook up this functionality into the page, you need to take three steps:

1. Call AddBackReference() at the appropriate time to store an extra entry in the navigation history.

2. Handle the ListSelectionJournalEntry callback to restore your window when the user navigates through the history.

3. Implement the IProvideCustomContentState interface and its single GetContentState() method in your page class. When the user navigates to another page through the history, the GetContentState() method is called by the navigation service. This allows you to return an instance of your custom class that will be stored as the state of the current page.

▦ **Note** The IProvideCustomContentState interface is an easily overlooked but essential detail. When the user navigates using the forward or back list, two things need to happen. Your page needs to add the current view to the journal (using IProvideCustomContentState), and then it needs to restore the selected view (using the ListSelectionJournalEntry callback).

First, whenever the Add button is clicked, you need to create a new ListSelectionJournalEntry object and call AddBackReference() so the previous state is stored in the history. This process is factored out into a separate method so that you can use it in several places in the page (for example, when either the Add button or the Remove button is clicked):

```
Private Sub cmdAdd_Click(ByVal sender As Object, ByVal e As RoutedEventArgs)
    If lstSource.SelectedIndex <> -1 Then
        ' Determine the best name to use in the navigation history.
        Dim nav As NavigationService =_
          NavigationService.GetNavigationService(Me)
        Dim itemText As String = lstSource.SelectedItem.ToString()
        Dim journalName As String = "Added " & itemText

        ' Update the journal (using the method shown below.)
        nav.AddBackEntry(GetJournalEntry(journalName))

        ' Now perform the change.
        lstTarget.Items.Add(itemText)
        lstSource.Items.Remove(itemText)
    End If
End Sub

Private Function GetJournalEntry(ByVal journalName As String) _
  As ListSelectionJournalEntry
    ' Get the state of both lists (using a helper method).
    Dim source As List(Of String)=GetListState(lstSource)
    Dim target As List(Of String)=GetListState(lstTarget)

    ' Create the custom state object with this information.
    ' Point the callback to the Replay method in this class.
    Return New ListSelectionJournalEntry(source, target, journalName, _
      AddressOf Replay)
End Function
```

You can use a similar process when the Remove button is clicked.

The next step is to handle the callback in the Replay() method and update the lists, as shown here:

```
Private Sub Replay(ByVal state As ListSelectionJournalEntry)
    lstSource.Items.Clear()
    For Each item As String In state.SourceItems
        lstSource.Items.Add(item)
    Next

    lstTarget.Items.Clear()
    For Each item As String In state.TargetItems
        lstTarget.Items.Add(item)
    Next

    restoredStateName=state.JournalEntryName
End Sub
```

And the final step is to implement IProvideCustomContentState in the page:

```
Public Class PageWithMultipleJournalEntries
    Implements IProvideCustomContentState
```

IProvideCustomContentState defines a single method named GetContentState(). In GetContentState(), you need to store the state for the page in the same way you do when the Add or Remove button is clicked. The only difference is that you don't add it by using the AddBackReference() method. Instead, you provide it to WPF through a return value:

```
Public Function GetContentState() As CustomContentState _
    Implements IProvideCustomContentState.GetContentState
        ' We haven't stored the most recent action,
        ' so just use the page name for a title.
        Return GetJournalEntry("PageWithMultipleJournalEntries")
End Function
```

Remember that the WPF navigation service calls GetContentState() when the user travels to another page by using the back or forward buttons. WPF takes the CustomContentState object you return and stores that in the journal for the current page. There's a potential quirk here. If the user performs several actions and then travels back through the navigation history reversing them, the "undone" actions in the history will have the hard-coded page name (PageWithMultipleJournalEntries), rather than the more descriptive original name (such as Added Orange). To improve the way this is handled, you can store the journal name for the page by using a member variable in your page class. The downloadable code for this example takes that extra step.

This completes the example. Now when you run the application and begin manipulating the lists, you'll see several entries appear in the history (Figure 24-10).

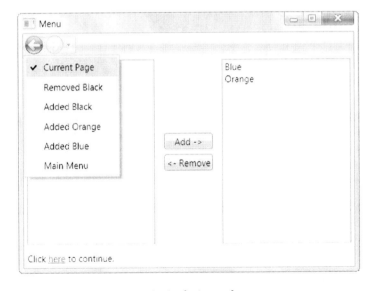

Figure 24-10. *Custom entries in the journal*

Using Page Functions

So far, you've learned how to pass information to a page (by instantiating the page programmatically, configuring it, and then passing it to the NavigationService.Navigate() method), but you haven't seen how to return information *from* a page. The easiest (and least structured) approach is to store information in some sort of shared application variable so that it's accessible to any other class in your program. However, that design isn't the best if you just need a way to transmit simple bits of information from one page to another, and you don't want to keep this information in memory for a long time. If you clutter your application with global variables, you'll have a difficult time figuring out the dependencies (which variables are used by which pages), and it will become much more difficult to reuse your pages and maintain your application.

The other approach that WPF provides is the PageFunction class. A PageFunction is a derived version of the Page class that adds the ability to return a result. In a way, a PageFunction is analogous to a dialog box, while a page is analogous to a window.

To create a PageFunction in Visual Studio, right-click your project in the Solution Explorer, and choose Add ➤ New Item. Next, select the WPF category, choose the Page Function (WPF) template, enter a file name, and click Add. The markup for a PageFunction is nearly identical to the markup you use for a Page. The difference is the root element, which is < PageFunction > instead of < Page >.

Technically, the PageFunction is a generic class. It accepts a single type parameter, which indicates the data type that's used for the PageFunction's return value. By default, every new page function is parameterized by string (which means it returns a single string as its return value). However, you can easily modify that detail by changing the TypeArguments attribute in the < PageFunction > element.

In the following example, the PageFunction returns an instance of a custom class named Product. In order to support this design, the < PageFunction > element maps the appropriate namespace (NavigationAplication) to a suitable XML prefix (local), which is then used when setting the TypeArguments attribute.

```
<PageFunction
    xmlns="http://schemas.microsoft.com/winfx/2006/xaml/presentation"
    xmlns:x="http://schemas.microsoft.com/winfx/2006/xaml"
    xmlns:local="clr-namespace:NavigationApplication"
    x:Class=" SelectProductPageFunction"
    x:TypeArguments="local:Product"
    Title="SelectProductPageFunction"
>
```

The PageFunction needs to handle all its navigation programmatically. When you click a button or a link that finishes the task, your code must call the PageFunction.OnReturn() method. At this point, you supply the object you want to return, which must be an instance of the class you specified in the declaration. Or you can supply a null value (Nothing), which indicates that the task was not completed.

Here's an example with two event handlers:

```
Private Sub lnkOK_Click(ByVal sender As Object, ByVal e As RoutedEventArgs)
    ' Return the selection information.
    Dim item As ListBoxItem = CType(lstProducts.SelectedItem, ListBoxItem)
    Dim product As New Product(item.Content.ToString())
    OnReturn(New ReturnEventArgs(Of Product)(product))
End Sub

Private Sub lnkCancel_Click(ByVal sender As Object, ByVal e As RoutedEventArgs)
    ' Indicate that nothing was selected.
    OnReturn(Nothing)
End Sub
```

Using the PageFunction is just as easy. The calling page needs to instantiate the PageFunction programmatically because it needs to hook up an event handler to the PageFunction.Returned event. (This extra step is required because the NavigationService.Navigate() method is asynchronous and returns immediately.)

```
Dim pageFunction As New SelectProductPageFunction()
AddHandler pageFunction.Return, AddressOf SelectProductPageFunction_Returned
Me.NavigationService.Navigate(pageFunction)
```

When the user finishes using the PageFunction and clicks a link that calls OnReturn(), the PageFunction.Returned event fires. The returned object is available through the ReturnEventArgs.Result property:

```
Private Sub SelectProductPageFunction_Returned(ByVal sender As Object, _
  ByVal e As ReturnEventArgs(Of Product))
    If Not e Is Nothing Then
        lblStatus.Content = "You chose: " & e.Result.Name
    End If
End Sub
```

Usually, the OnReturn() method marks the end of a task, and you don't want the user to be able to navigate back to the PageFunction. You could use the NavigationService.RemoveBackEntry() method to implement this, but there's an easier approach. Every PageFunction also provides a property named RemoveFromJournal. If you set this to True, the page is automatically removed from the history when it calls OnReturn().

By adding the PageFunction to your application, you now have the ability to use a different sort of navigation topology. You can designate one page as a central hub and allow users to perform various tasks through page functions, as shown in Figure 24-11.

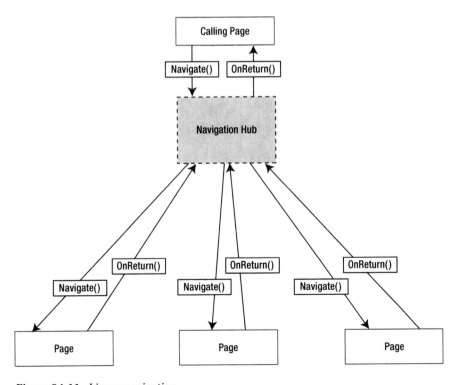

Figure 24-11. *Linear navigation*

Often, a PageFunction will call another page function. In this case, the recommended way to handle the navigation process after it's complete is to use a chained series of OnReturn() calls. In other words, if PageFunction1 calls PageFunction2, which then calls PageFunction3, when PageFunction3 calls OnReturn(), it triggers the Returned event handler in PageFunction2, which then calls OnReturn(), which then fires the Returned event in PageFunction1, which finally calls OnReturn() to end the whole process. Depending on what you're trying to accomplish, it may be necessary to pass your return object up through the whole sequence until it reaches a root page.

XAML Browser Applications

XBAPs are page-based applications that run inside the browser. XBAPs are full-blown WPF applications, with a few key differences:

- *They run inside the browser window.* They can take the entire display area for the web page, or you can place them somewhere inside an ordinary HTML document by using the < iframe > tag (as you'll see shortly).

■ **Note**   The technical reality is that any type of WPF application, including an XBAP, runs as a separate process managed by the Common Language Runtime (CLR). An XBAP appears to run "inside" the browser simply because it displays all its content in the browser window. This is different from the model used by plug-ins and Silverlight applications, which *are* loaded inside the browser process.

- *They usually have limited permissions.* Although it's possible to configure an XBAP so that it requests full trust permissions, the goal is to use XBAP as a lighter-weight deployment model that allows users to run WPF applications without allowing potentially risky code to execute. The permissions given to an XBAP are the same as the permissions given to a .NET application that's run from the Web or local intranet, and the mechanism that enforces these restrictions (code access security) is the same. That means that by default an XBAP cannot write files, interact with other computer resources (such as the Registry), connect to databases, or pop up full-fledged windows.

- *They aren't installed.* When you run an XBAP, the application is downloaded and cached in the browser. However, it doesn't remain installed on the computer. This gives you the instant-update model of the Web. In other words, every time a user returns to use an application, the newest version is downloaded if it doesn't exist in the cache.

The advantage of XBAPs is that they offer a *prompt-free* experience. If .NET is installed, a client can surf to an XBAP in the browser and start using it just like a Java applet, a Flash movie, or a JavaScript-enhanced web page. There's no installation prompt or security warning. The obvious trade-off is that you need to abide by a stringently limited security model. If your application needs greater capabilities (for example, it needs to read or write arbitrary files, interact with a database, use the Windows Registry, and so on), you're far better off creating a stand-alone Windows application. You can then offer a streamlined (but not completely seamless) deployment experience for your application by using ClickOnce deployment, which is described in Chapter 33.

Currently, two browsers are able to launch XBAP applications: Internet Explorer and Firefox. Chrome doesn't support XBAP applications (although you can google your way to some unsupported hacks that some developers have used to make them work on a specific machine). As with any .NET application, the client computer also needs the version of .NET that you targeted (when you compiled your application) in order to run it.

Creating an XBAP

Any page-based application can become an XBAP, although Visual Studio forces you to create a new project with the WPF Browser Application template in order to create one. The difference is four key elements in the .vbproj project file, as shown here:

```
<HostInBrowser>True</HostInBrowser>
<Install>False</Install>
<ApplicationExtension>.xbap</ApplicationExtension>
<TargetZone>Internet</TargetZone>
```

These tags tell WPF to host the application in the browser (HostInBrowser), to cache it along with other temporary Internet files rather than install it permanently (Install), to use the extension .xbap (ApplicationExtension), and to request the permissions for only the Internet zone (TargetZone). The fourth part is optional. As you'll see shortly, it's technically possible to create an XBAP that has greater permissions. However, XBAPs almost always run with the limited permissions available in the Internet zone, which is the key challenge to programming one successfully.

■ **Tip** The .vbproj file also includes other XBAP-related tags that ensure the right debugging experience. The easiest way to change an application from an XBAP into a page-based application with a stand-alone window (or vice versa) is to create a new project of the desired type, and then import all the pages from the old project.

After you've created your XBAP, you can design your pages and code them in exactly the same way as if you were using the NavigationWindow. For example, you set the StartupUri in the Application.xaml file to one of your pages. When you compile your application, an .xbap file is generated. You can then request that .xbap file in Internet Explorer or Firefox, and (provided the .NET Framework is installed) the application runs in limited trust mode automatically. Figure 24-12 shows an XBAP in Internet Explorer.

Figure 24-12. *An XBAP in the browser*

The XBAP application runs just the same as an ordinary WPF application, provided you don't attempt to perform any restricted actions (such as showing a stand-alone window). If you're running your application in Internet Explorer, the browser buttons take the place of the buttons on the NavigationWindow, and they show the back and forward page lists. On previous versions of Internet Explorer and in Firefox, you get a new set of navigation buttons at the top of your page, which isn't quite as nice.

Deploying an XBAP

Although you could create a setup program for an XBAP (and you can run an XBAP from the local hard drive), there's rarely a reason to take this step. Instead, you can simply copy your compiled application to a network share or a virtual directory.

■ **Note**   You can get a similar effect by using loose XAML files. If your application consists entirely of XAML pages with no code-behind files, you don't need to compile it at all. Instead, just place the appropriate .xaml files on your web server and let users browse to them directly. Of course, loose XAML files obviously can't do as much as their compiled counterparts, but they're suitable if you simply need to display a document, a graphic, or an animation, or if you wire up all the functionality you need through declarative binding expressions.

Unfortunately, deploying an XBAP isn't as simple as just copying the .xbap file. You need to copy the following three files to the same folder:

- *ApplicationName.exe*: This file has the compiled IL code, just as it does in any .NET application.

- *ApplicationName.exe.manifest*: This file is an XML document that indicates requirements of your application (for example, the version of the .NET assemblies you used to compile your code). If your application uses other DLLs, you can make these available in the same virtual directory as your application, and they'll be downloaded automatically.

- *ApplicationName.xbap*: The .xbap file is another XML document. It represents the entry point to your application. In other words, this is the file that the user needs to request in the browser to install your XBAP. The markup in the .xbap file points to the application file and includes a digital signature that uses the key you've chosen for your project.

After you've transferred these files to the appropriate location, you can run the application by requesting the .xbap file in Internet Explorer or Firefox. It makes no difference whether the files are on the local hard drive or a remote web server—you can request them in the same way.

■ **Tip**   It's tempting, but don't run the .exe file. If you do, nothing will happen. Instead, double-click the .xbap file in Windows Explorer (or type its path in the address box in your web browser). Either way, all three files must be present, and the browser must be able to recognize the .xbap file extension.

The browser will show a progress page as it begins downloading the .xbap file (Figure 24-13). This downloading process is essentially an installation process that copies the .xbap application to the local Internet cache. When the user returns to the same remote location on subsequent visits, the cached version will be used. (The only exception occurs if there's a newer version of the XBAP on the server, as described in the next section.)

Figure 24-13. *Running an .xbap application for the first time*

When you create a new XBAP application, Visual Studio also includes an automatically generated certificate file with a name such as ApplicationName_TemporaryKey.pfx. This certificate contains a public/private key pair that's used to add a signature to your .xbap file. If you publish an update to your application, you'll need to sign it with the same key to ensure that the digital signature remains consistent.

Rather than using the temporary key, you may want to create a key of your own (which you can then share between projects and protect with a password). To do so, double-click the My Project node under your project in the Solution Explorer and use the options in the Signing tab.

Updating an XBAP

When you debug an XBAP application, Visual Studio always rebuilds your XBAP and loads the latest version in the browser. You don't need to take any extra steps. This isn't the case if you request an XBAP directly in your browser. When running XBAPs in this fashion, there's a potential problem. If you rebuild the application, deploy it to the same location, and then rerequest it in the browser, you won't necessarily get the updated version. Instead, you'll continue running the older cached copy of the application. This is true even if you close and reopen the browser window, click the browser's Refresh button, and increment the assembly version of your XBAP.

You can manually clear the ClickOnce cache, but this obviously isn't a convenient solution. Instead, you need to update the publication information that's stored in your .xbap file so that the browser recognizes that your newly deployed XBAP represents a new version of your application. Updating the assembly version isn't enough to trigger an update; instead, you need to update the *publish version*.

■ **Note** The extra step of updating the publication information is required because the download-and-cache functionality of an .xbap is built by using the plumbing from ClickOnce, the deployment technology that you'll learn about in Chapter 33. ClickOnce uses the publication version to determine when an update should be applied. This allows you to build an application multiple times for testing (each time with a different assembly version number) but increment the publish version only when you want to deploy a new release.

The easiest way to rebuild your application *and* apply a new publication version is to choose Build ➤ Publish [ProjectName] from the Visual Studio menu (and then click Finish). You don't need to use the publication files (which are placed in the Publish folder under your project directory). That's because the newly generated .xbap file in the Debug or Release folder will indicate the new publish version. All you need to do is deploy this .xbap file (along with the .exe and .manifest files) to the appropriate location. The next time you request the .xbap file, the browser will download the new application files and cache them.

You can see the current publish version by double-clicking the My Project item in the Solution Explorer, choosing the Publish tab, and looking at the settings in the Publish Version section at the bottom of the tab. Make sure you keep the Automatically Increment Revision with Each Publish setting switched on so that the publish version is incremented when you publish your application, which clearly marks it as a new release.

XBAP Security

The most challenging aspect to creating an XBAP is staying within the confines of the limited security model. Ordinarily, an XBAP runs with the permissions of the Internet zone. This is true even if you run your XBAP from the local hard drive.

The .NET Framework uses *code access security* (a core feature that it has had since version 1.0) to limit what your XBAP is allowed to do. In general, the limitations are designed to correspond with what comparable Java or JavaScript code could do in an HTML page. For example, you'll be allowed to render graphics, perform animations, use controls, show documents, and play sounds. You can't access computer resources such as files, the Windows Registry, databases, and so on.

One simple way to find out whether an action is allowed is to write some test code and try it. The WPF documentation also has full details. Table 24-3 provides a quick list of significant supported and disallowed features.

Table 24-3. *Key WPF Features and the Internet Zone*

Allowed	Not Allowed
All core controls, including the RichTextBox	Windows Forms controls (through interop)
Pages, the MessageBox, and the OpenFileDialog	Stand-alone windows and other dialog boxes (such as the SaveFileDialog)
Isolated storage	Access to the file system and access to the Registry
2-D and 3-D drawing, audio and video, flow and XPS documents, and animation	Bitmap effects and pixel shaders (presumably because they rely on unmanaged code)
"Simulated" drag-and-drop (code that responds to mouse-move events)	Windows drag-and-drop
ASP.NET (.asmx) web services and Windows Communication Foundation (WCF) services	Most advanced WCF features (non-HTTP transport, server-initiated connections, and WS-* protocols) and communicating with any server other than the one where the XBAP is hosted

So what's the effect if you attempt to use a feature that's not allowed in the Internet zone? Ordinarily, your application fails as soon as it runs the problematic code with a SecurityException. Figure 24-14 shows the result of running an ordinary XBAP that attempts to perform a disallowed action and not handling the resulting SecurityException.

Figure 24-14. *An unhandled exception in an XBAP*

Full-Trust XBAPs

It's possible to create an XBAP that runs with full trust, although this technique isn't recommended. To do so, double-click the My Project node in the Solution Explorer, choose the Security tab, and select This Is a Full Trust Application. However, users won't be able to run your application from a web server or virtual directory anymore. Instead, you'll need to take one of the following steps to ensure that your application is allowed to execute in full trust:

- Run the application from the local hard drive. (You can launch the .xbap file like an executable file by double-clicking it or using a shortcut.) You may want to use a setup program to automate the installation process.

- Add the certificate you're using to sign the assembly (by default, it's a .pfx file) to the Trusted Publishers store on the target computer. You can do this by using the certmgr.exe tool.

- Assign full trust to the website URL or network computer where the .xbap file is deployed. To do this, you need to use the Microsoft .NET 2.0 Framework Configuration tool (which you can find in the Administrative Tools section of the Control Panel, accessed from the Start menu).

The first option is the most straightforward. However, all of these steps require an awkward configuration or deployment step that must be performed on everyone else's computer. As a result, they aren't ideal approaches.

■ **Note**   If your application requires full trust, you should consider building a stand-alone WPF application and deploying it by using ClickOnce (as described in Chapter 33). The real goal of the XBAP model is to create a WPF equivalent to the traditional HTML-and-JavaScript website (or Flash applet).

Combination XBAP/Stand-Alone Applications

So far, you've considered how to deal with XBAPs that may run under different levels of trust. However, there's another possibility. You might take the same application and deploy it as both an XBAP *and* a stand-alone application that uses the NavigationWindow (as described in the beginning of this chapter).

In this situation, you don't necessarily need to test your permissions. It may be enough to write conditional logic that tests the shared BrowserInteropHelper.IsBrowserHosted property and assumes that a browser-hosted application is automatically running with Internet zone permissions. The IsBrowserHosted property is True if your application is running inside the browser.

Unfortunately, changing between a stand-alone application and an XBAP is not an easy feat, because Visual Studio doesn't provide direct support. However, other developers have created tools to simplify the process. One example is the flexible Visual Studio project template found at http://scorbs.com/2006/06/04/vs-template-flexible-application. It allows you to create a single project file and choose between an XBAP and a stand-alone application by using the build configuration list. (Sadly, support is limited to C# only.)

Another option is to place your pages in a reusable class library assembly. Then you can create two top-level projects: one that creates a NavigationWindow and loads the first page inside and another that launches the page directly as an XBAP. This makes it easier to maintain your solution, but will probably still need some conditional code that tests the IsBrowserHosted property and checks specific CodeAccessPermission objects.

Coding for Different Security Levels

In some situations, you might choose to create an application that can function in different security contexts. For example, you may create an XBAP that can run locally (with full trust) or be launched from a website. In this case, it's key to write flexible code that can avoid an unexpected SecurityException.

Every separate permission in the code-access security model is represented by a class that derives from CodeAccessPermission. You can use this class to check whether your code is running with the required permission. The trick is to call the CodeAccessPermission.Demand() method, which requests a permission. This demand fails (throwing a SecurityException) if the permission isn't granted to your application.

Here's a simple function that allows you to check for a given permission:

```
Private Function CheckPermission( _
  ByVal requestedPermission As CodeAccessPermission) As Boolean
    Try
        ' Try to get this permission.
        requestedPermission.Demand()
        Return True
    Catch
        Return False
    End Try
End Function
```

You can use this function to write code like this, which checks to see whether the calling code has permission to write to a file before attempting the operation:

```
' Create a permission that represents writing to a file.
Dim permission As New FileIOPermission(FileIOPermissionAccess.Write, _
  "c:\highscores.txt")
```

```
' Check for this permission.
If CheckPermission(permission) Then
    ' (It's safe to write to the file.)
Else
    ' (It's not allowed. Do nothing or show a message.)
End If
```

The obvious disadvantage with this code is that it relies on exception handling to control normal program flow, which is discouraged (both because it leads to unclear code and because it adds overhead). An alternative would be to simply attempt to perform the operation (such as writing to a file) and then catch any resulting SecurityException. However, this approach makes it more likely that you'll run into a problem halfway through a task, when recovery or cleanup may be more difficult.

Using Isolated Storage

In many cases, you may be able to fall back on less-powerful functionality if a given permission isn't available. For example, although code running in the Internet zone isn't allowed to write to arbitrary locations on the hard drive, it is able to use isolated storage. Isolated storage provides a virtual file system that lets you write data to a small, user-specific and application-specific slot of space. The actual location on the hard drive is obfuscated (so there's no way to know exactly where the data will be written beforehand), and the total space available is typically 1 MB. A typical location is a path in the form c:\Users\[UserName]\AppData\Local\IsolatedStorage\[GuidIdentifier]. Data in one user's isolated store is restricted from all other nonadministrative users.

■ **Note** Isolated storage is the .NET equivalent of persistent cookies in an ordinary web page. It allows small bits of information to be stored in a dedicated location that has specific controls in place to prevent malicious attacks (such as code that attempts to fill the hard drive or replace a system file).

Isolated storage is covered in detail in the .NET reference. However, it's quite easy to use because it exposes the same stream-based model as ordinary file access. You simply use the types in the System.IO.IsolatedStorage namespace. Typically, you'll begin by calling the IsolatedStorageFile.GetUserStoreForApplication() method to get a reference to the isolated store for the current user and application. (Each application gets a separate store.) You can then create a virtual file in that location by using the IsolatedStorageFileStream. Here's an example:

```
' Create a permission that represents writing to a file.
Dim permission As New FileIOPermission(FileIOPermissionAccess.Write, _
    "c:\highscores.txt")

' Check for this permission.
If CheckPermission(permission) Then
    ' Write to local hard drive.
    Try
        Using fs As FileStream = File.Create(filePath)
            WriteHighScores(fs, content)
        End Using
    Catch err As Exception
        MessageBox.Show(err.Message)
    End Try
```

```
Else
    ' Write to isolated storage.
    Try
        Dim store As IsolatedStorageFile
        store = IsolatedStorageFile.GetUserStoreForApplication()
        Using fs As New IsolatedStorageFileStream("highscores.txt", _
          FileMode.Create, store)
            WriteHighScores(fs, content)
        End Using
    Catch err As Exception
        MessageBox.Show(err.Message)
    End Try
End If
```

You can also use methods such as IsolatedStorageFile.GetFileNames() and IsolatedStorageFile.GetDirectoryNames() to enumerate the contents of the isolated store for the current user and application.

Remember that if you've made the decision to create an ordinary XBAP that will be deployed on the Web, you already know that you won't have FileIOPermission for the local hard drive (or anywhere else). If this is the type of application you're designing, there's no reason to use the conditional code shown here. Instead, your code can jump straight to the isolated storage classes.

■ **Tip** To determine the amount of available isolated storage space, check IsolatedStorageFile.AvailableFreeSpace. You should use code that checks this detail and refrains from writing data if the available space is insufficient. To increase the amount of data you can pack into isolated storage, you may want to wrap your file-writing operations with the DeflateStream or GZipStream. Both types are defined in the System.IO.Compression namespace and use compression to reduce the number of bytes required to store data.

Simulating Dialog Boxes with the Pop-up Control

Another limited feature in XBAPs is the ability to open a secondary window. In many cases, you'll use navigation and multiple pages instead of separate windows, and you won't miss this functionality. However, sometimes it's convenient to pop open a window to show some sort of a message or collect input. In a stand-alone Windows application, you'd use a modal dialog box for this task. In an XBAP, there's another possibility—you can use the Popup control that was introduced in Chapter 6.

The basic technique is easy. First, you define the Popup in your markup, making sure to set its StaysOpen property to True so it will remain open until you close it. (There's no point in using the PopupAnimation or AllowsTransparency property, because neither will have any effect in a web page.) Include suitable buttons, such as OK and Cancel, and set the Placement property to Center so the pop-up will appear in the middle of the browser window.

Here's a simple example:

```
<Popup Name="dialogPopUp" StaysOpen="True" Placement="Center" MaxWidth="200">
  <Border>
    <Border.Background>
      <LinearGradientBrush>
        <GradientStop Color="AliceBlue" Offset="1"></GradientStop>
        <GradientStop Color="LightBlue" Offset="0"></GradientStop>
      </LinearGradientBrush>
    </Border.Background>
```

```
    <StackPanel Margin="5" Background="White">
      <TextBlock Margin="10" TextWrapping="Wrap">
       Please enter your name.
      </TextBlock>
      <TextBox Name="txtName" Margin="10"></TextBox>
      <StackPanel Orientation="Horizontal" Margin="10">
        <Button Click="dialog_cmdOK_Click" Padding="3" Margin="0,0,5,0">OK</Button>
        <Button Click="dialog_cmdCancel_Click" Padding="3">Cancel</Button>
      </StackPanel>
    </StackPanel>
  </Border>
</Popup>
```

At the appropriate time (for example, when a button is clicked), disable the rest of your user interface and show the Popup. To disable your user interface, you can set the IsEnabled property of some top-level container, such as a StackPanel or a Grid, to False. (You can also set the Background property of the page to gray, which will draw the user's attention to the Popup.) To show the Popup, simply set its IsVisible property to True.

Here's an event handler that shows the previously defined Popup:

```
Private Sub cmdStart_Click(ByVal sender As Object, ByVal e As RoutedEventArgs)
    DisableMainPage()
End Sub

Private Sub DisableMainPage()
    mainPage.IsEnabled = False
    Me.Background = Brushes.LightGray
    dialogPopUp.IsOpen = True
End Sub
```

When the user clicks the OK or Cancel button, close the Popup by setting its IsVisible property to False, and reenable the rest of the user interface:

```
Private Sub dialog_cmdOK_Click(ByVal sender As Object, _
  ByVal e As RoutedEventArgs)
    ' Copy name from the Popup into the main page.
    lblName.Content = "You entered: " & txtName.Text
    EnableMainPage()
End Sub

Private Sub dialog_cmdCancel_Click(ByVal sender As Object, _
  ByVal e As RoutedEventArgs)
    EnableMainPage()
End Sub

Private Sub EnableMainPage()
    mainPage.IsEnabled = True
    Me.Background = Nothing
    dialogPopUp.IsOpen = False
End Sub
```

Figure 24-15 shows the Popup in action.

Figure 24-15. Simulating a dialog box with the Popup

Using the Popup control to create this work-around has one significant limitation. To ensure that the Popup control can't be used to spoof legitimate system dialog boxes, the Popup window is constrained to the size of the browser window. If you have a large Popup window and a small browser window, this could chop off some of your content. One solution, which is demonstrated with the sample code for this chapter, is to wrap the full content of the Popup control in a ScrollViewer with the VerticalScrollBarVisibility property set to Auto.

There's one other, even stranger option for showing a dialog box in a WPF page. You can use the Windows Forms library from .NET 2.0. You can safely create and show an instance of the System.Windows.Forms.Form class (or any custom form that derives from Form), because it doesn't require unmanaged code permission. In fact, you can even show the form modelessly, so the page remains responsive. The only drawback is that a security balloon automatically appears superimposed over the form and remains until the user clicks the warning message (as shown in Figure 24-16). You're also limited in what you can show *in* the form. Windows Forms controls are acceptable, but WPF content isn't allowed. For an example of this technique, refer to the sample code for this chapter.

Figure 24-16. Using a .NET 2.0 form for a dialog box

Embedding an XBAP in a Web Page

Usually, an XBAP is loaded directly in the browser so it takes up all the available space. However, you can have one other option: you can show an XBAP inside a portion of an HTML page, along with other HTML content. All you need to do is create an HTML page that uses the < iframe > tag to point to your .xbap file, as shown here:

```
<html>
  <head>
    <title>An HTML Page That Contains an XBAP</title>
  </head>
  <body>
    <h1>Regular HTML Content</h1>
    <iframe src="BrowserApplication.xbap"></iframe>
    <h1>More HTML Content</h1>
  </body>
</html>
```

Using an < iframe > is a relatively uncommon technique, but it does allow you to pull off a few new tricks, such as displaying more than one XBAP in the same browser window or making it easy to add your application to a site that's powered by a content-management system such as WordPress.

The WebBrowser Control

As you've seen in this chapter, WPF blurs the boundaries between traditional desktop applications and the Web. Using pages, you can create WPF applications with web-style navigation. Using XBAPs, you can run WPF inside a browser window, like a web page. And using the Frame control, you can perform the reverse trick and put an HTML web page into a WPF window.

However, when you use the Frame to show HTML content, you give up all control over that content. You have no way to inspect it or to follow along as the user navigates to a new page by clicking a link. You certainly have no way to call JavaScript methods in an HTML web page or let them call your WPF code. This is where the WebBrowser control comes into the picture.

▓ **Tip**   The Frame is a good choice if you need a container that can switch seamlessly between WPF and HTML content. The WebBrowser is a better choice if you need to examine the object model of a page, limit or monitor page navigation, or create a path through which JavaScript and WPF code can interact.

Both the WebBrowser and the Frame (when it's displaying HTML content) show a standard Internet Explorer window. This window has all the features and frills of Internet Explorer, including JavaScript, Dynamic HTML, ActiveX controls, and plug-ins. However, the window doesn't include additional details such as a toolbar, address bar, or status bar (although you can add all of these ingredients to your form by using other controls).

The WebBrowser isn't written from scratch in managed code. Like the Frame (when it's displaying HTML content), it wraps the shdocvw.dll COM component, which is a part of Internet Explorer and is included with Windows. As a side effect, the WebBrowser and the Frame have a few graphical limitations that other WPF controls don't share. For example, you can't place other elements on top of the HTML content that's displayed in these controls, and you can't use a transform to skew or rotate it.

■ **Note** As a feature, WPF's ability to show HTML (either through the Frame or the WebBrowser) isn't nearly as useful as the page model or XBAPs. However, you might choose to use it in specialized situations where you have already developed HTML content that you don't want to replace. For example, you might use the WebBrowser to show HTML documentation inside an application, or to allow a user to jump between the functionality in your application and that in a third-party website.

Navigating to a Page

After you've placed the WebBrowser control on a window, you need to point it to a document. The easiest approach is to set the Source property with a URI. Set this to a remote URL (for example, `http://mysite.com/mypage.html`) or a fully qualified file path (such as file:///c:\mydocument.text). The URI can point to any file type that Internet Explorer can open, although you'll almost always use the WebBrowser to show HTML pages.

```
<WebBrowser Source="http://www.prosetech.com"></WebBrowser>
```

■ **Note** You can also direct the WebBrowser to a directory. For example, set the Url property to file:///c:\. In this case, the WebBrowser window becomes the familiar Explorer-style file browser, allowing the user to open, copy, paste, and delete files. However, the WebBrowser doesn't provide events or properties that allow you to restrict this ability (or even monitor it), so tread carefully!

In addition to the Source property, you can navigate to a URL by using any of the navigation methods described in Table 24-4.

Table 24-4. *Navigation Methods for the WebBrowser*

Method	Description
Navigate()	Navigates to the new URL you specify. If you use the overloaded method, you can choose to load this document into a specific frame, post back data, and send additional HTML headers.
NavigateToString()	Loads the content from the string you supply, which should contain the full HTML content of a web page. This provides some interesting options, including the ability to retrieve HTML text from a resource in your application and display it.
NavigateToStream()	Loads the content from a stream that contains an HTML document. This allows you to open a file and feed it straight into the WebBrowser for rendering, without needing to hold the whole HTML content in memory at once.
GoBack() and GoForward()	Move to the previous or next document in the navigation history. To avoid errors, you should check the CanGoBack and CanGoForward properties before using these methods, because attempting to move to a document that does not exist (for example, trying to move back while on the first document in the history) will cause an exception.
Refresh()	Reloads the current document.

All WebBrowser navigation is asynchronous. That means your code continues executing while the page is downloading.

The WebBrowser also adds a small set of events, including the following:

- *Navigating* fires when you set a new URL, or the user clicks a link. You can inspect the URL, and cancel navigation by setting e.Cancel to True.

- *Navigated* fires after Navigating, just before the web browser begins downloading the page.

- *LoadCompleted* fires when the page is completely loaded. This is your chance to process the page.

Building a DOM Tree

Using the WebBrowser, you can create VB code that browses through the tree of HTML elements on a page. You can even modify, remove, or insert elements as you go, using a programming model that's similar to the HTML DOM used in web browser scripting languages such as JavaScript. In the following sections, you'll see both techniques.

Before you can use the DOM with the WebBrowser, you need to add a reference to the Microsoft HTML Object Library (mshtml.tlb). This is a COM library, so Visual Studio needs to generate a managed wrapper. To do so, choose Project ➤ Add Reference, pick the COM tab, select the Microsoft HTML Object Library, and click OK.

The starting point for exploring the content in a web page is the WebBrowser.Document property. This property provides an HTMLDocument object that represents a single web page as a hierarchical collection of IHTMLElement objects. You'll find a distinct IHTMLElement object for each tag in your web page, including paragraphs (<p>), hyperlinks (<a>), images (<img>), and all the other familiar ingredients of HTML markup.

The WebBrowser.Document property is read-only. That means that although you can modify the linked HtmlDocument, you can't create a new HtmlDocument object on the fly. Instead, you need to set the Source property or call the Navigate() method to load a new page. After the WebBrowser.LoadCompleted event fires, you can access the Document property.

■ **Tip** Building the HTMLDocument takes a short but distinctly noticeable amount of time (depending on the size and complexity of the web page). The WebBrowser won't actually build the HTMLDocument for the page until you try to access the Document property for the first time.

Each IHTMLElement object has a few key properties:

- *tagName* is the actual tag, without the angle brackets. For example, an anchor tag takes the form < a href = "..." > ...</a>, and has the tag name A.

- *id* contains the value of the id attribute, if specified. Often, elements are identified with unique id attributes if you need to manipulate them in an automated tool or server-side code.

- *children* provides a collection of IHTMLElement objects, one for each contained tag.

- *innerHTML* shows the full content of the tag, including any nested tags and their content.

- *innerText* shows the full content of the tag and the content of any nested tags. However, it strips out all the HTML tags.

- *outerHTML* and *outerText* play the same role as innerHTML and innerText, except they include the current tag (rather than just its contents).

To get a better understanding of innerText, innerHTML, and outerHTML, consider the following tag:

```
<p>Here is some<i>interesting</i>text.</p>
```

The innerText for this tag is as follows:

```
Here is some interesting text.
```

This is the innerHTML:

```
Here is some<i>interesting</i>text.
```

Finally, the outerHTML is the full tag:

```
<p>Here is some<i>interesting</i>text.</p>
```

In addition, you can retrieve the attribute value for an element by name, by using the IHTMLElement. getAttribute() method.

To navigate the document model for an HTML page, you simply move through the children collections of each IHTMLElement. The following code performs this task in response to a button click, and builds a tree that shows the structure of elements and the content on the page (see Figure 24-17).

```
Private Sub cmdBuildTree_Click(ByVal sender As Object, _
  ByVal e As System.EventArgs)
    ' Analyzing a page takes a nontrivial amount of time.
    ' Use the hourglass cursor to warn the user.
    Me.Cursor = Cursors.Wait

    ' Get the DOM object from the WebBrowser control.
    Dim dom As HTMLDocument = CType(webBrowser.Document, HTMLDocument)

    ' Process all the HTML elements on the page, and display them
    ' in the TreeView named treeDOM.
    ProcessElement(dom.documentElement, treeDOM.Items)

    Me.Cursor = Nothing
End Sub

Private Sub ProcessElement(ByVal parentElement As IHTMLElement, _
  ByVal nodes As ItemCollection)
    ' Scan through the collection of elements.
    For Each element As IHTMLElement In parentElement.children
        ' Create a new node that shows the tag name.
        Dim node As New TreeViewItem()
        node.Header = "<" & element.tagName & ">"
        nodes.Add(node)

        If element.children.length = 0 And element.innerText IsNot Nothing Then
            ' If this element doesn't contain any other elements, add
            ' any leftover text content as a new node.
            node.Items.Add(element.innerText)
```

```
        Else
            ' If this element contains other elements, process them recursively.
            ProcessElement(element, node.Items)
        End If
    Next
End Sub
```

Figure 24-17. *A tree model of a web page*

If you want to find a specific element without digging through all the layers of the web page, you have a couple of simpler options. You can use the HTMLDocument.all collection, which allows you to retrieve any element on the page by using its id attribute. If you need to retrieve an element that doesn't have an id attribute, you can use the HTMLDocument method getElementsByTagName().

Scripting a Web Page with .NET Code

The last trick you'll see with the WebBrowser is something even more intriguing: the ability to react to web-page events in your Windows code.

The WebBrowser makes this technique remarkably simple. The first step is to create a class that will receive the messages from the JavaScript code. To make it scriptable, you must add the ComVisible attribute (from the System. Runtime.InteropServices namespace) to the class declaration:

```
<ComVisible(True)>_
Public Class HtmlBridge
    Public Sub WebClick(ByVal source As String)
        MessageBox.Show("Received: " & source)
    End Sub
End Class
```

Next, you need to register an instance of this class with the WebBrowser. You do this by setting the WebBrowser. ObjectForScripting property:

```
Public Sub New()
    InitializeComponent()
    webBrowser.Navigate("file:///" & System.IO.Path.Combine( _
      Path.GetDirectoryName(Application.ResourceAssembly.Location), "sample.htm"))
    webBrowser.ObjectForScripting = New HtmlBridge()
End Sub
```

Now the sample.html web page will be able to call any public method in the HtmlBridge class, including HtmlBridge.WebClick().

In the web page, you use JavaScript code to trigger the event. Here, the trick is the window.external object, which represents the linked .NET object. Using this object, you specify a method that you want to trigger; for example, use window.external.HelloWorld() if you want to call a public method named HelloWorld in the .NET object.

■ **Caution** If you use JavaScript to trigger an event from your web page, make sure that your class doesn't include any other public methods that aren't related to web access. A nefarious user could theoretically find the HTML source, and modify it to call a different method than the one you intend. Ideally, the scriptable class should contain only web-related methods to ensure security.

To build the JavaScript command into your web page, you first need to decide to which web-page event you want to react. Most HTML elements support a small number of events, and some of the most useful include the following:

- *onFocus* occurs when a control receives focus.

- *onBlur* occurs when focus leaves a control.

- *onClick* occurs when the user clicks a control.

- *onChange* occurs when the user changes the value of certain controls.

- *onMouseOver* occurs when the user moves the mouse pointer over a control.

To write a JavaScript command that responds to one of these events, you simply add an attribute with that name to the element tag. For example, if you have an image tag that looks like this:

```
<img border="0" id="img1" src="buttonC.jpg" height="20" width="100">
```

you can add an onClick attribute that triggers the HelloWorld() method in your linked .NET class whenever the user clicks the image:

```
<img onClick="window.external.HelloWorld()" border="0" id="img1"
src="buttonC.jpg" height="20" width="100">
```

Figure 24-18 shows an application that puts it all together. In this example, a WebBrowser control shows a local HTML file that contains four buttons, each of which is a graphical image. But when the user clicks a button, the image uses the onClick attribute to trigger the HtmlBridge.WebClick() method:

```
<img onClick="window.external.WebClick('Option1')" ... >
```

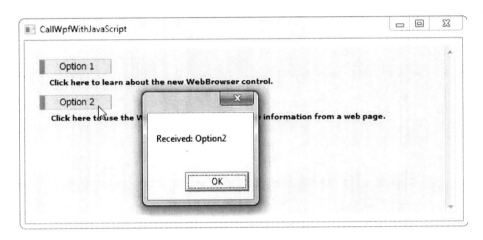

Figure 24-18. *An HTML menu that triggers .NET code*

The WebClick()method then takes over. It could show another web page, open a new window, or modify part of the web page. In this example, it simply displays a message box to confirm that the event has been received. Each image passes a hard-coded string to the WebClick() method, which identifies the button that triggered the method.

■ **Caution**   Keep in mind that unless your HTML document is compiled into your assembly as an embedded resource or retrieved from some secure location (such as a database), it may be subject to client tampering. For example, if you store HTML documents as separate files, users can easily edit them. If this is a concern, use the embedding techniques described in Chapter 7. You can create file resources, retrieve them as strings, and then show them by using the WebBrowser.NavigateToString() method.

The Last Word

In this chapter, you took a close look at the WPF navigation model. You learned how to build pages, host them in different containers, and use WPF navigation to move from one page to the next.

You also delved into the XBAP model that allows you to create a web-style WPF application that runs in a browser. Because XBAPs still require the .NET Framework, they won't replace the existing web applications that we all know and love. However, they just might provide an alternate way to deliver rich content and graphics to Windows users.

Finally, you learned how to embed web content in a WPF application by using the WebBrowser control, and how to allow your web page script code to trigger methods in your WPF application.

CHAPTER 25

Menus, Toolbars, and Ribbons

A few rich controls can appear in virtually any type of application, from document editors to system utilities. Those are the controls that you'll meet in this chapter. They include the following:

- *Menus.* They're one of the oldest user interface controls, and they've changed surprisingly little in the past two decades. WPF includes solid, straightforward support for main menus and pop-up context menus.

- *Toolbars and status bars.* They decorate the top and bottom of countless applications—sometimes when they aren't even needed. WPF supports both controls with its customary flexibility, allowing you to insert virtually any control inside. However, the WPF toolbars and status bars don't have many frills. They support overflow menus, but they don't provide floating and docking capability.

- *Ribbons.* With only a little more effort, you can add an Office-style ribbon to the top of your application window. It requires a separate (free) download, but you'll get some valuable built-in features, such as configurable resizing. You'll also get an Office-style menu feature to match.

What's New   WPF 4.5 adds native Office ribbon functionality. However, it only works for Office applications. In other words, you can use WPF 4.5 to build an Office add-in that extends the ribbon in Word, Excel, PowerPoint, Visio, Outlook, InfoPath, or Project. (For more information, see `http://tinyurl.com/945vpsj`.) However, if you want to add an Office-style ribbon to a custom desktop application, you need to download an extra component, as described in this chapter.

Menus

WPF provides two menu controls: Menu (for main menus) and ContextMenu (for pop-up menus that are attached to other elements). Like all the WPF classes, WPF performs the rendering for the Menu and ContextMenu controls. That means these controls aren't simple wrappers around Windows libraries. This gives them more flexibility, including the ability to be used in browser-hosted applications.

Note   If you use the Menu class in a browser-hosted application, it appears at the top of the page. The browser window wraps your page, and it may or may not include a menu of its own, which will be completely separate.

The Menu Class

WPF doesn't make any assumption about where a stand-alone menu should be placed. Ordinarily, you'll dock it at the top of your window using a DockPanel or the top row of a Grid, and you'll stretch it across the entire width of your window. However, you can place a menu anywhere, even alongside other controls (as shown in Figure 25-1). Furthermore, you can add as many menus in a window as you want. Although it might not make much sense, you have the ability to stack menu bars or scatter them throughout your user interface.

Figure 25-1. *Mixed menus*

This freedom provides some interesting possibilities. For example, if you create a menu with one top-level heading and style it to look like button, you'll end up with a one-click pop-up menu (like the menu that's activated in Figure 25-1). This sort of user interface trickery might help you get the exact effect you want in a highly customized interface. Or, it might just be a more powerful way to confuse users.

The Menu class adds a single new property: IsMainMenu. When True (which is the default value), pressing the Alt key or F10 gives the menu focus, just as in any other Windows application. Along with this small detail, the Menu container has a few of the familiar ItemsControl properties for you to play with. That means you can create data-bound menus using the ItemsSource DisplayMemberPath, ItemTemplate, and ItemTemplateSelector properties. You can also apply grouping, change the layout of menu items inside the menu, and apply styles to your menu items.

For example, Figure 25-2 shows a scrollable sidebar menu. You can create it by supplying a StackPanel for the ItemsPanel property, changing its background, and wrapping the entire Menu in a ScrollViewer. Obviously, you can make more radical changes to the visual appearance of menus and submenus using triggers and control templates. The bulk of the styling logic is in the default control template for the MenuItem.

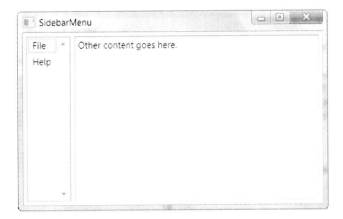

Figure 25-2. *A menu in a StackPanel*

Menu Items

Menus are composed of MenuItem objects and Separator objects. The MenuItem class derives from HeaderedItemsControl, because each menu item has a header (which contains the text for that item) and can hold a collection of MenuItem objects (which represents a submenu). The Separator simply displays a horizontal line separating menu items.

Here's a straightforward combination of MenuItem objects that creates the rudimentary menu structure shown in Figure 25-3:

```
<Menu>
  <MenuItem Header="File">
    <MenuItem Header="New" ></MenuItem>
    <MenuItem Header="Open" ></MenuItem>
    <MenuItem Header="Save" ></MenuItem>
    <Separator ></Separator>
    <MenuItem Header="Exit" ></MenuItem>
  </MenuItem>
  <MenuItem Header="Edit">
    <MenuItem Header="Undo" ></MenuItem>
    <MenuItem Header="Redo" ></MenuItem>
    <Separator ></Separator>
    <MenuItem Header="Cut" ></MenuItem>
    <MenuItem Header="Copy" ></MenuItem>
    <MenuItem Header="Paste" ></MenuItem>
  </MenuItem>
</Menu>
```

Figure 25-3. *A basic menu*

As with buttons, you can use the underscore to indicate an Alt + shortcut key combination. Whereas this is often considered an optional feature in buttons, most menu users expect to have keyboard shortcuts.

WPF allows you to break most of the commonsense rules of structuring a menu. For example, you can have non-MenuItem objects inside a Menu or MenuItem. This allows you to create menus that hold ordinary WPF elements, ranging from the ordinary CheckBox to a DocumentViewer. For a variety of reasons, placing non-MenuItem objects in a menu is almost always a bad way to go. If you place non-MenuItem objects in a menu, they'll exhibit a few oddities that you'll need to track down and correct. For example, a TextBox in a MenuItem will lose focus as soon as you move the mouse out of the bounds of the MenuItem. If you really want a user interface that includes some sort of drop-down menu with controls, consider using another element (such as the Expander) and styling it to suit your needs. Use menus only when you really want the behavior of a menu—in other words, a group of clickable commands.

■ **Note**   Set the MenuItem.StaysOpenOnClick property to True if you want submenus to remain visible when opened until the user clicks somewhere else.

MenuItem objects can also be used *outside* the standard Menu, ContextMenu, and MenuItem containers. These items behave just like ordinary menu items—they glow blue when you hover over them, and they can be clicked to trigger actions. However, any submenus they include won't be accessible. Again, this is an aspect of Menu flexibility you probably won't want to use.

To react when a MenuItem is clicked, you may choose to handle the MenuItem.Click event. You can handle it for individual items, or you can attach an event handler to the root Menu tag. Your other alternative is to use the Command, CommandParameter, and CommandTarget properties to connect a MenuItem to a Command object, as you learned to do with buttons in Chapter 9. This is particularly useful if your user interface includes multiple menus (for example, a main menu and a context menu) that use the same commands or includes a menu and a toolbar that do.

Along with text content (which is supplied through the Header property), MenuItem objects can actually show several more details:

- A thumbnail icon in the margin area just to the left of the menu command.

- A check mark in the margin area. If you set the check mark and an icon, only the check mark appears.

- Shortcut text to the right of the menu text. For example, you might see Ctrl + O to indicate the shortcut key for the Open command.

Setting all these ingredients is easy. To show a thumbnail icon, you set the MenuItem.Icon property. Interestingly, the Icon property accepts any object, which gives you the flexibility to construct a miniature vector drawing. This way, you can take full advantage of WPF's resolution-independent scaling to show more detail at higher system DPI settings. If you want to use an ordinary icon, simply use an Image element with a bitmap source.

To show a check mark next to a menu item, you simply need to set the MenuItem.IsChecked property to True. Additionally, if IsCheckable is True, clicking the menu item will toggle back and forth between its checked and unchecked state. However, there's no way to associate a group of checked menu items. If that's the effect you want, you need to write the code to clear the other check boxes when an item is checked.

You can set the shortcut text for a menu item using the MenuItem.InputGestureText property. However, simply displaying this text doesn't make it active. It's up to you to watch for the key presses you want. This is almost always too much work, so menu items are commonly used with commands, which gives you the shortcut key behavior and the InputGestureText in one step.

For example, the following MenuItem is linked to the ApplicationsCommands.Open command:

```
<MenuItem Command="ApplicationCommands.Open"></MenuItem>
```

This command already has the Ctrl + O keystroke defined in the RoutedUICommand.InputGestures command collection. As a result, Ctrl + O appears for the shortcut text, and the Ctrl + O keystroke triggers the command (assuming you've wired up the appropriate event handler). If a keystroke wasn't defined, you could add it to the InputGestures collection yourself.

■ **Tip** Several useful properties indicate the current state of the MenuItem, including IsChecked, IsHighlighted, IsPressed, and IsSubmenuOpen. You can use these to write triggers that apply different styling in response to certain actions.

The ContextMenu Class

Like the Menu, the ContextMenu class holds a collection of MenuItem objects. The difference is that a ContextMenu can't be placed in a window. Instead, it can be used only to set the ContextMenu property of another element:

```
<TextBox>
  <TextBox.ContextMenu>
    <MenuItem ... >
      ...
    </MenuItem>
  </TextBox.ContextMenu>
</TextBox>
```

The ContextMenu property is defined in the FrameworkElement class, so it's supported by virtually all WPF elements. If you set the ContextMenu property of an element that ordinarily has its own context menu, your menu replaces the standard menu. If you simply want to remove an existing context menu, just set it to a null reference (Nothing).

When you attach a ContextMenu object to an element, it appears automatically when the user right-clicks that control (or presses Shift + F10 while it has focus). The context menu won't appear if the element has IsEnabled set to False, unless you explicitly allow this with the ContextMenuService.ShowOnDisabled attached property:

```
<TextBox ContextMenuService.ShowOnDisabled="True">
  <TextBox.ContextMenu>
    ...
  </TextBox.ContextMenu>
</TextBox>
```

Menu Separators

The Separator is a standard element for dividing menus into groups of related commands. However, the content of the separator is completely fluid, thanks to control templates. By taking a separator and supplying a new template, you can add other, nonclickable elements to your menus, such as subheadings.

You might expect that you could add a subheading simply by adding a non-MenuItem object to a menu, such as a TextBlock with some text. However, if you take this step, the newly added element keeps the menu selection behavior; this means you can step through it with the keyboard, and when you hover over it with the mouse, the edges glow blue. The Separator doesn't exhibit this behavior—it's a fixed piece of content that doesn't react to keyboard or mouse actions.

Here's an example of a Separator that defines a text title:

```
<Separator>
  <Separator.Template>
    <ControlTemplate>
      <Border CornerRadius="2" Padding="5" Background="PaleGoldenrod"
       BorderBrush="Black" BorderThickness="1">
        <TextBlock FontWeight="Bold">
         Editing Commands
        </TextBlock>
      </Border>
    </ControlTemplate>
  </Separator.Template>
</Separator>
```

Figure 25-4 shows the title this creates.

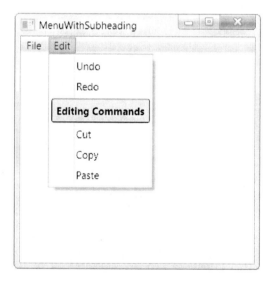

Figure 25-4. *A menu that includes a fixed subheading*

Unfortunately, the Separator isn't a content control, so it's not possible to separate the content you want to show (for example, the string of text) from the formatting you want to use. That means you'll be forced to define the same template each time you use the separator if you want to vary its text. To make this process a bit simpler, you can create a separator style that bundles together all the properties you want to set on the TextBlock inside the Separator, except for the text.

Toolbars and Status Bars

Toolbars and status bars are two well-worn staples of the Windows world. Both are specialized containers that hold a collection of items. Traditionally, a toolbar holds buttons, and a status bar consists primarily of text and other noninteractive indicators (like a progress bar). However, both toolbars and status bars are used with a variety of different controls.

In Windows Forms, toolbars and status bars have their own content model. Although it's still possible to place arbitrary controls inside a toolbar and status bar using a wrapper, the process isn't seamless. The WPF toolbar and status bar don't have this limitation. They support the WPF content model, allowing you to add any element to a toolbar or status bar and giving you unparalleled flexibility. In fact, there are no toolbar-specific or status bar–specific elements. Everything you need is already available in the basic collection of WPF elements.

The ToolBar

A typical WPF ToolBar is filled with Button, ComboBox, CheckBox, RadioButton, and Separator objects. Because these elements are all content controls (except for the Separator), you can place text and image content inside. Although you can use other elements, such as Label and Image to put noninteractive elements into the ToolBar, the effect is often confusing.

At this point, you might be wondering how you can place these common controls in a toolbar without creating an odd visual effect. After all, the content that appears in standard Windows toolbars looks quite a bit different from similar content that appears in a window. For example, the buttons in a toolbar are displayed with a flat, streamlined appearance that removes the border and the shaded background. The toolbar surface shows through underneath, and the button glows blue when you hover over it with the mouse.

In the WPF way of thinking, the button in a toolbar is the same as a button in a window—both are clickable regions you can use to perform an action. The only difference is the visual appearance. Thus, the perfect solution is to use the existing Button class but adjust various properties or change the control template. This is exactly what the ToolBar class does—it overrides the default style of some types of children, including the buttons. You can still have the last word by manually setting the Button.Style property if you want to create your own customized toolbar button, but usually you'll get all the control you need by setting the button content.

Not only does the ToolBar change the appearance of many of the controls its holds, but it also changes the behavior of the ToggleButton and the CheckBox and RadioButton that derive from it. A ToggleButton or CheckBox in a ToolBar is rendered like an ordinary button, but when you click it, the button remains highlighted (until you click it again). The RadioButton has a similar appearance, but you must click another RadioButton in a group to clear the highlighting. (To prevent confusion, it's always best to separate a group of RadioButton objects in a toolbar using the Separator.)

To demonstrate what this looks like, consider the simple markup shown here:

```
<ToolBar>
  <Button Content="{StaticResource DownloadFile}"></Button>
  <CheckBox FontWeight="Bold">Bold</CheckBox>
  <CheckBox FontStyle="Italic">Italic</CheckBox>
  <CheckBox>
    <TextBlock TextDecorations="Underline">Underline</TextBlock>
  </CheckBox>
```

```
<Separator></Separator>
<ComboBox SelectedIndex="0">
  <ComboBoxItem>100%</ComboBoxItem>
  <ComboBoxItem>50%</ComboBoxItem>
  <ComboBoxItem>25%</ComboBoxItem>
</ComboBox>
<Separator></Separator>
</ToolBar>
```

Figure 25-5 shows this toolbar in action, with two CheckBox controls in the checked state and the drop-down list on display.

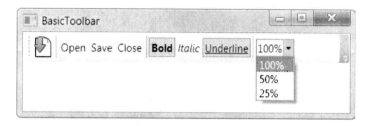

Figure 25-5. *Different controls in a toolbar*

Although the example in Figure 25-5 is limited to buttons that contain text, ToolBar buttons usually hold image content. (You can also combine both by wrapping an Image element and a TextBlock or Label in a horizontal StackPanel.) If you're using image content, you need to decide whether you want to use bitmap images (which may show scaling artifacts at different resolutions), icons (which improve this situation somewhat because you can supply several differently sized images in one file), or vector images (which require the most markup but provide flawless resizing).

The ToolBar control has a few oddities. First, unlike other controls that derive from ItemsControl, it doesn't supply a dedicated wrapper class. (In other words, there is a ToolBarItem class.) The ToolBar simply doesn't require this wrapper to manage items, track selection, and so on, as other list controls. Another quirk in the ToolBar is that it derives from HeaderedItemsControl even though the Header property has no effect. It's up to you to use this property in some interesting way. For example, if you have an interface that uses several ToolBar objects, you could allow users to choose which ones to display from a context menu. In that menu, you could use the toolbar name that's set in the Header property.

The ToolBar has one more interesting property: Orientation. You can create a top-to-bottom toolbar that's docked to one of the sides of your window by setting the ToolBar.Orientation property to Vertical. However, each element in the toolbar will still be oriented horizontally (for example, text won't be turned on its side), unless you use a LayoutTransform to rotate it.

The Overflow Menu

If a toolbar has more content than it can fit in a window, it removes items until the content fits. These extra items are placed into an overflow menu, which you can see by clicking the drop-down arrow at the end of the toolbar. Figure 25-6 shows the same toolbar shown in Figure 25-5 but in a smaller window that necessitates an overflow menu.

Figure 25-6. *The automatic overflow menu*

The ToolBar control adds items to the overflow menu automatically, starting with the last item. However, you can configure the way this behavior works to a limited degree by applying the attached ToolBar.OverflowMode property to the items in the toolbar. Use OverflowMode.Never to ensure that an important item is never placed in the overflow menu, OverflowMode.AsNeeded (the default) to allow it to be placed in the overflow menu when space is scarce, or OverflowMode.Always to force an item to remain permanently in the overflow menu.

■ **Note**   If the toolbar's container (usually, a window) is smaller than the required space to display all the OverflowMode.Always items, the items that don't fit will be clipped off at the bounds of the container and will be inaccessible to the user.

If your toolbar contains more than one OverflowMode.AsNeeded item, the ToolBar removes items that are at the end of the toolbar first. Unfortunately, there's no way to assign relative priorities to toolbar items. For example, there's no way to create an item that's allowed in the overflow menu but won't be placed there until every other relocatable item has already been moved. There's also no way to create buttons that adapt their sizes based on the available space, as you can with the ribbon discussed later in this chapter.

The ToolBarTray

Although you're free to add multiple ToolBar controls to your window and manage them using a layout container, WPF has a class that's designed to take care of some of the work: the ToolBarTray. Essentially, the ToolBarTray holds a collection of ToolBar objects (which are exposed through a property named ToolBars).

The ToolBarTray makes it easier for toolbars to share the same row, or *band*. You can configure the ToolBarTray so that toolbars share a band, while others are placed on other bands. The ToolBarTray provides the shaded background behind the entire ToolBar area. But most important, the ToolBarTray adds support for toolbar drag-and-drop functionality. Unless you set the ToolBarTray.IsLocked property to True, the user can rearrange your toolbars in a ToolBar tray by clicking the grip at the left side. Toolbars can be repositioned in the same band or moved to a different band. However, the user is not able to drag a toolbar from one ToolBarTray to another. If you want to lock down individual toolbars, simply set the ToolBarTray.IsLocked attached property on the appropriate ToolBar objects.

■ **Note**   When moving toolbars, it's possible that some content may be obscured. For example, the user may move a toolbar to a position that leaves very little room for another adjacent toolbar. In this situation, the missing items are added to the overflow menu.

You can place as many ToolBar objects as you want in a ToolBarTray. By default, all your toolbars will be placed in left-to-right order on the topmost band. Initially, each toolbar is given its full desired width. (If a subsequent toolbar doesn't fit, some or all of its buttons are moved to the overflow menu.) To get more control, you can specify which band a toolbar should occupy by setting the Band property using a numeric index (where 0 is the topmost band). You can also set the placement inside the band explicitly by using the BandIndex property. A BandIndex of 0 puts the toolbar at the beginning of the band.

Here's some sample markup that creates several toolbars in a ToolBarTray. Figure 25-7 shows the result.

```
<ToolBarTray>
  <ToolBar>
    <Button>One</Button>
    <Button>Two</Button>
    <Button>Three</Button>
  </ToolBar>
  <ToolBar>
    <Button>A</Button>
    <Button>B</Button>
    <Button>C</Button>
  </ToolBar>
  <ToolBar Band="1">
    <Button>Red</Button>
    <Button>Blue</Button>
    <Button>Green</Button>
    <Button>Black</Button>
  </ToolBar>
</ToolBarTray>
```

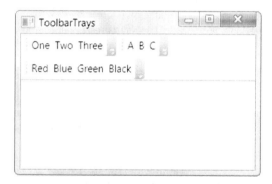

Figure 25-7. *Grouping toolbars in the ToolBarTray*

The StatusBar

Compared to the ToolBar, the StatusBar is a much less glamorous control class. Like the ToolBar, it holds any content (which it wraps implicitly in StatusBarItem objects), and it overrides the default styles of some elements to provide more suitable rendering. However, the StatusBar control doesn't have the support for draggable rearranging or an overflow menu. It's primarily used to display text and image indicators (and the occasional progress bar).

The StatusBar doesn't work very well if you want to use one of the ButtonBase-derived elements or the ComboBox. It doesn't override the styles of any of these controls, so they look out of place in the status bar. If you need to create a status bar that includes these controls, you might consider docking an ordinary ToolBar control to the bottom of your window. It's probably as a result of this general lack of features that the StatusBar is found in the

System.Windows.Controls.Primitives namespace rather than in the more mainstream System.Windows.Controls namespace where the ToolBar control exists.

There's one tip worth noting if you're using a status bar. Ordinarily, the StatusBar control lays its children out from left to right using a horizontal StackPanel. However, applications often use proportionately sized status bar items or keep items locked to the right side of the status bar. You can implement this design by specifying that the status bar should use a different panel using the ItemsPanelTemplate property, which you first considered in Chapter 20.

One way to get proportionally or right-aligned items is to use a Grid for your layout container. The only trick is that you must wrap the child element in a StatusBarItem object in order to set the Grid.Column property appropriately. Here's an example that uses a Grid to place one TextBlock on the left side of a StatusBar and another on the right side:

```
<StatusBar Grid.Row="1">
  <StatusBar.ItemsPanel>
    <ItemsPanelTemplate>
      <Grid>
        <Grid.ColumnDefinitions>
          <ColumnDefinition Width="*"></ColumnDefinition>
          <ColumnDefinition Width="Auto"></ColumnDefinition>
        </Grid.ColumnDefinitions>
      </Grid>
    </ItemsPanelTemplate>
  </StatusBar.ItemsPanel>
  <TextBlock>Left Side</TextBlock>
  <StatusBarItem Grid.Column="1">
    <TextBlock>Right Side</TextBlock>
  </StatusBarItem>
</StatusBar>
```

This highlights one of the key advantages of WPF—other controls can benefit from the core layout model without needing to re-create it. By contrast, Windows Forms included several controls that wrapped some sort of proportionally sized items, including the StatusBar and the DataGridView. Despite the conceptual scenario, these controls were forced to include their own layout model and add their own layout-specific properties to manage child items. In WPF, this isn't the case—every control that derives from ItemsControl can use any panel to arrange its child items.

Ribbons

At this point, you might be feeling that the WPF toolbars are just a bit underwhelming. Other than two built-in features—a basic overflow menu and the ability to be rearranged by the user—they don't provide any modern frills. Even the Windows Forms toolkit has a feature that allows users to drag and dock toolbars to different places in a window.

The reason that toolbars haven't evolved since the first version of WPF is simple: they're a dying trend. Although toolbars are still relatively popular at the moment, the shift is to smarter tab-based controls, such as the ribbon that debuted in Office 2007 and now graces Windows Explorer (in Windows 8) and Office 2013.

With the ribbon, Microsoft found itself faced with a familiar dilemma. To improve the productivity and consistency of all Windows applications, Microsoft wanted to encourage every application to adopt the ribbon. But because Microsoft also wanted to keep its competitive edge, it wasn't in a rush to release the APIs that would make that possible. After all, Microsoft spent thousands of hours of research and development in perfecting its version of the ribbon, so it's no surprise that the company took a few years to enjoy the result.

Fortunately, the wait has ended, and Microsoft has made a version of the ribbon available to WPF developers. The good news is that it's completely free and respectably full-featured, including rich tooltips, drop-down buttons, dialog launchers, a quick access toolbar, and configurable resizing.

However, the ribbon control isn't included with the .NET Framework. Instead, you need to download it from Microsoft's Download Center. Just search for "WPF ribbon" at http://www.microsoft.com/download. At the time of this writing, you can download the latest version at http://tinyurl.com/8aphzsf. Click "Microsoft Ribbon for WPF. msi" to install the compiled class library that houses the ribbon control, which is named RibbonControlsLibrary.dll. You can also click "Microsoft Ribbon for WPF Source and Samples.msi" to install sample projects that use the ribbon, including one that mimics the Home tab in the user interface for Word.

■ **Tip** Before you begin using the ribbon, it's worth reviewing the design guidelines and best practices for the ribbon, which you can read at http://tinyurl.com/4dsbef.

Adding the Ribbon

To start using the ribbon, start by creating a new WPF project and adding a reference to the RibbonControlsLibrary.dll assembly. You'll find it in a folder like Program Files (x86)\Microsoft Ribbon for WPF\V4.0.

As with any control that's not a part of the core WPF libraries, you need to map the control assembly to an XML prefix before you can use it:

```
<Window x:Class="RibbonTest.MainWindow" ... xmlns:r=
    "clr-namespace:Microsoft.Windows.Controls.Ribbon;assembly=RibbonControlsLibrary">
```

You can then add an instance of the Ribbon control anywhere in your window:

```
<r:Ribbon>
</r:Ribbon>
```

By far the best position for the ribbon is at the top of the window, using a Grid or Dock panel. But before you go any further, there's one change worth making. The RibbonControlsLibrary.dll assembly includes a RibbonWindow class—a class that derives from Window but provides additional ribbon integration features. Most significantly, the RibbonWindow class provides a spot for the quick access toolbar (which is a customizable group of commonly used buttons that's displayed above the ribbon), and a spot to put the header for contextual ribbon tabs (these are tabs that only appear for certain tasks). Figure 25-8 compares the difference, with the normal window on the left and the RibbonWindow on the right.

Figure 25-8. *Putting the ribbon in a RibbonWindow*

You'll learn about the quick access toolbar later in this chapter. For now, you can use the outline of a basic ribbon-enabled window shown in the following code. This custom window derives from RibbonWindow and places the ribbon at the top, while reserving the second row of a Grid for the actual window content.

```
<r:RibbonWindow x:Class="RibbonTest.MainWindow"
 xmlns="http://schemas.microsoft.com/winfx/2006/xaml/presentation"
 xmlns:x="http://schemas.microsoft.com/winfx/2006/xaml"
 Title="MainWindow" Height="350" Width="525"
 xmlns:r=
 "clr-namespace:Microsoft.Windows.Controls.Ribbon;assembly=RibbonControlsLibrary">
  <Grid>
    <Grid.RowDefinitions>
      <RowDefinition Height="Auto"></RowDefinition>
      <RowDefinition></RowDefinition>
    </Grid.RowDefinitions>

    <r:Ribbon>
    </r:Ribbon>
  </Grid>
</r:RibbonWindow>
```

This assumes that your window is named MainWindow and your project is named RibbonTest—you'll need to adjust these details in the class declaration to match your names.

The Ribbon control actually consists of three pieces: the quick access toolbar (which sits at the top), an application menu (which is exposed through the button on the far left, before any tabs), and the multitabbed ribbon itself. In the following sections, you'll explore all three parts.

■ **Tip** If you don't like the ribbon's blue color, you can set the Background property with the color of your choice. There's no need to use a fancy gradient brush, either, because the ribbon takes the solid color you supply and automatically adds a subtle gradient effect over the surface of the control.

The Application Menu

The easiest way to get started with the ribbon is to fill the application menu.

The application menu is based on two straightforward classes: RibbonApplicationMenu (which derives from MenuBase) and RibbonApplicationMenuItem (which derives from MenuItem). This establishes a pattern you'll see throughout this section—the ribbon takes the base WPF control class and derives more specialized versions. From a purist point of view, the ToolBar and StatusBar have a cleaner model, because they're able to work with standard WPF controls, which they simply restyle. But the ribbon needs an extra layer of derived classes to support many of its more advanced features. For example, the RibbonApplicationMenu and RibbonApplicationMenuItem are enhanced beyond the ordinary menu classes to support the RibbonCommand.

To create a menu, you create a new RibbonApplicationMenu object and use that to set the Ribbon. ApplicationMenu property. As you probably already expect, the RibbonApplicationMenu includes a collection of RibbonApplicationMenuItem objects, each of which represents a separate clickable menu item.

Here's a basic example outline that creates an application menu with three menu items:

```
<r:Ribbon>
  <r:Ribbon.ApplicationMenu>
    <r:RibbonApplicationMenu>
```

```
      <r:RibbonApplicationMenuItem>...</r:RibbonApplicationMenuItem>
      <r:RibbonApplicationMenuItem>...</r:RibbonApplicationMenuItem>
      <r:RibbonApplicationMenuItem>...</r:RibbonApplicationMenuItem>

    </r:RibbonApplicationMenu>
  </r:Ribbon.ApplicationMenu>
</r:Ribbon>
```

As with an ordinary MenuItem, a RibbonApplicationMenuItem needs a value for the Header property (which provides the menu text). However, instead of using the Icon property inherited from MenuItem, you supply a small picture (typically, one that's 32×32 pixels) through the ImageSource property.

Here's an example that fleshes out the three menu items shown earlier. It also adds an image to the small button that opens the menu. (Unlike the pictures next to each command, this button should be 16×16 pixels.)

```
<r:Ribbon>
  <r:Ribbon.ApplicationMenu>
    <r:RibbonApplicationMenu SmallImageSource="images\window2.png">

      <r:RibbonApplicationMenuItem Header="New"
       ToolTip="Create a new document" ImageSource="images\new.png" />
      <r:RibbonApplicationMenuItem Header="Save"
       ToolTip="Save the current document" ImageSource="images\save.png" />
      <r:RibbonApplicationMenuItem Header="Save As"
       ToolTip="Save the document with a new name"
       ImageSource="images\saveas.png" />

    </r:RibbonApplicationMenu>
  </r:Ribbon.ApplicationMenu>
</r:Ribbon>
```

You handle clicks on the ribbon menu in the same way that you handle clicks in an ordinary menu. You can respond to the Click event, or you can wire up a command using the Command, CommandParameter, and CommandTarget properties. Commands are a particularly good idea with the ribbon menu, because you may want to link the same command to a ribbon menu item and to a ribbon button. They're also required if you want to use the quick access toolbar, as described later.

It's also worth noting that any RibbonApplicationMenuItem can hold more RibbonApplicationMenuItem objects to create a submenu (see Figure 25-9). Each submenu item supports the same text, image, and tooltip options:

```
<r:Ribbon.ApplicationMenu>
  <r:RibbonApplicationMenu SmallImageSource="images\window2.png">
    <r:RibbonApplicationMenuItem Header="New" ImageSource="images\window2.png" />

    <r:RibbonApplicationMenuItem Header="_Save" ImageSource="images\save.png">
      <r:RibbonApplicationMenuItem Header="Save As" ImageSource="images\save.png"/>
      <r:RibbonApplicationMenuItem Header="Save" ImageSource="images\save.png" />
    </r:RibbonApplicationMenuItem>

    <r:RibbonSeparator></r:RibbonSeparator>
    <r:RibbonApplicationMenuItem Header="About" />
    <r:RibbonApplicationMenuItem Header="Exit " />
  </r:RibbonApplicationMenu>
</r:Ribbon.ApplicationMenu>
```

Figure 25-9. *The ribbon application menu with a submenu*

To separate menu items, you can add a thin horizontal dividing line by placing the RibbonSeparator control into your menu. And if you're more ambitious, you can fill the second column of the drop-down menu panel with more information (say, a list of recent documents), and you can add more details to a footer region underneath (for example, a link to a help page). Both regions act like content controls—you simply set the Ribbon.AuxiliaryPaneContent with any element to fill the right-side column, and the Ribbon.FooterPaneContent to fill the footer area. As with any content control, these content properties can hold a layout container with an assortment of interactive elements, or you can supply a data object, which is then interpreted by a template (that you then supply through the AuxiliaryPaneContentTemplate and FooterPaneContent templates).

Tabs, Groups, and Buttons

The ribbon uses the same model to fill its toolbar tabs as it does to fill its application menu, just with a few extra layers.

First, the ribbon holds a collection of tabs. In turn, each tab holds one or more groups, which is an outlined, titled, box-like section of the ribbon. Lastly, each group holds one or more ribbon controls. Figure 25-10 shows this arrangement.

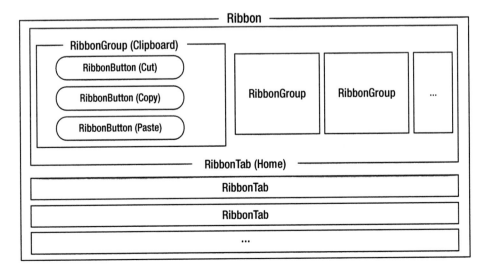

Figure 25-10. *Tabs, groups, and buttons*

Each of these ingredients has a corresponding class. To create a ribbon like the one shown in Figure 25-10, you start by declaring the appropriate RibbonTab objects, fill each one with RibbonGroup objects, and place ribbon controls (like the straightforward RibbonButton) in each group.

When you create a new tab in the ribbon, you use its Header property to supply the text that appears in the tab (above the ribbon). When you create a group in a tab, you use its Header property to supply the text that appears underneath that section of the ribbon. You can also use the SmallImageSource property to set the image that will be used if space is limited and the group is collapsed down to a single button, as shown later, in Figure 25-12.

Here's some markup that gives a ribbon one tab (named "Home"), with one group inside it (named "Clipboard"):

```
<r:Ribbon>
  <r:Ribbon.ApplicationMenu>
    <r:RibbonApplicationMenu>
      ...
    </r:RibbonApplicationMenu>
  </r:Ribbon.ApplicationMenu>

  <r:RibbonTab Header="Home">
    <r:RibbonGroup Header="Clipboard">
      ...
    </r:RibbonGroup>
  </r:RibbonTab>

</r:Ribbon>
```

You can see this part of the ribbon, along with a full set of RibbonCommand buttons, back in Figure 25-9.

As with the application menu, you configure text and image content that appears in each ribbon button. However, the property names are different. Instead of setting Header and ImageSource, you now set Label for the text, and SmallImageSource and LargeImageSource for the image. Two images are needed because the same button can be shown at two different sizes, depending on how you've configured it and how much space is available. You use the familiar Click event or Command property to handle button clicks.

▩ **Note**   The SmallImageSource property sets the image that's used when the item is rendered in small size (16×16 pixels on a standard 96 dpi display). The LargeImageSource property sets the image that's used when the item is rendered in large size (32×32 pixels on a standard 96 dpi display). To avoid scaling artifacts at different pixel densities, you can use a DrawingImage instead of a bitmap for each picture, as explained in Chapter 13.

Here's a portion of ribbon markup that defines the Clipboard group (shown in Figure 25-9) and places three commands inside:

```
<r:Ribbon>
  <r:Ribbon.ApplicationMenu>
    <r:RibbonApplicationMenu>
      ...
    </r:RibbonApplicationMenu>
  </r:Ribbon.ApplicationMenu>

  <r:RibbonTab Header="Home">
    <r:RibbonGroup Header="Clipboard">
```

```
    <r:RibbonButton Label="Cut"
      SmallImageSource="images/cut.png" LargeImageSource="images/cut.png" />
    <r:RibbonButton Label="Copy"
      SmallImageSource="images/copy.png" LargeImageSource="images/copy.png" />
    <r:RibbonButton Label="Paste"
      SmallImageSource="images/paste.png" LargeImageSource="images/paste.png" />
  </r:RibbonGroup>
 </r:RibbonTab>
</r:Ribbon>
```

This markup hasn't yet been connected to any logic (either through the Click event or through a command), so clicking these buttons won't trigger any action.

In this example, the ribbon was entirely made up of RibbonButton objects, which is the most common ribbon control type. However, WPF gives you several more options, which are outlined in Table 25-1. As with the application menu, most of the ribbon classes derive from the standard WPF controls. They simply add extra ribbon functionality on top. For example, all of them include the Label property, which lets you add a text caption next to the control (which appears immediately below a big button, to the right of a small button, to the left of a text box or combo box, and so on).

Table 25-1. *Ribbon Control Classes*

Name	Description
RibbonButton	A clickable text-and-image button, which is the most common ingredient on the ribbon.
RibbonCheckBox	A check box that can be checked or unchecked.
RibbonRadioButton	One clickable option in a group of mutually exclusive options (just like ordinary option buttons).
RibbonToggleButton	A button that has two states: pressed or unpressed. For example, many programs use this sort of button to turn on or off font characteristics such as bold, italic, and underline.
RibbonMenuButton	A button that pops open a menu. You fill the menu with MenuItem objects using the RibbonMenuButton.Items collection.
RibbonSplitButton	Similar to a RibbonMenuButton, but the button is actually divided into two sections. The user can click the top portion (with the picture) to run the command or the bottom portion (with the text and drop-down arrow) to show the linked menu of items. For example, the Paste command in Word is a RibbonSplitButton.
RibbonComboBox	Embeds a combo box in the ribbon, which the user can use to type in text or make a selection, just as with the standard ComboBox control.
RibbonTextBox	Embeds a text box in the ribbon, which the user can use to type in text, just as with the standard TextBox control.
RibbonSeparator	Draws a vertical line between individual controls (or groups of controls) in the ribbon (or a horizontal line between items in a menu).

Rich Tooltips

The ribbon supports an enhanced tooltip model, which displays more detailed tooltip pop-ups that can include a title, description, and image (and a footer with the same). However, all these details are optional, and you need only set the ones you want to use.

If you want to use enhanced tooltips, simply remove the standard ToolTip property, and use any combination of the tooltip properties described in Table 25-2. You can set them on any of the ribbon controls, including RibbonButton, and on RibbonApplicationMenuItem objects. The only limitation is that you can't put actual elements (like links) into a tooltip. You're limited to text and image content.

Table 25-2. *Enhanced Properties for ToolTips*

Property	Description
ToolTipTitle	The title that appears at the top of the tooltip for this item.
ToolTipDescription	The text that appears in the tooltip, under the title.
ToolTipImageSource	The image that appears in the tooltip, under the title and to the left of the text description. The image can be any size.
ToolTipFooterTitle	The text that appears a footer title of a tooltip.
ToolTipFooterDescription	The text that appears in the footer of a tooltip, under the footer title.
ToolTipFooterImageSource	The image that appears to the left of the tooltip footer text. The image can be any size.

Here's an example of an enhanced tooltip:

```
<r:RibbonButton Label="Cut" ToolTipTitle="Cut"
 ToolTipDescription="Copies the selected text to the clipboard and removes it"
 ToolTipImageSource="images/cut.png"
 ToolTipFooterImageSource="images/help.png"
 ToolTipFooterTitle="More Details" ToolTipFooterDescription="Press F1 for Help"
... />
```

Figure 25-11 shows the result.

Figure 25-11. *An enhanced tooltip*

Keyboard Access with KeyTips

Even keyboard users can access the commands in the ribbon. But to do so, you need to assign the appropriate shortcut keys to your tabs, groups, and commands.

Here's how it works if everything's configured properly. First, the user presses the Alt key (and then releases it). The ribbon shows a *keytip*—a single shortcut letter—over the application menu and every tab. The user presses a letter to select a tab (or the application menu), and then the ribbon shows the key tip for each keytip-enabled command in that tab (or menu), as shown in Figure 25-12. Finally, the user presses a letter to trigger the corresponding command. The whole process requires three key presses, and makes it easy for keyboard users to discover the key combination that leads to their command.

Figure 25-12. *The first level of keytips*

To use keytips in the WPF ribbon, you need to set the KeyTip property on the RibbonApplicationMenu, each RibbonTab, and each RibbonMenuItem, RibbonButton, or other ribbon control. Each keytip must be unique in its scope, which means you shouldn't give two tabs the same keytip letter, or assign the same keytip to two buttons in a tab. And unlike Office applications, you need to keep your keytips to a single letter (two-letter combinations aren't supported). If you don't assign a keytip to a control in the ribbon, it won't be accessible via the keyboard. However, as long as you assign a keytip to the RibbonApplicationMenu, all the menu items inside will be keyboard-accessible, even if they don't have keytips, because the user can use the keytip to open the menu and use the arrow keys to move through the menu.

■ **Note** The RibbonMenuItem supports the old-style menu shortcut of using an underscore in the menu text. For example, if you use the menu text "_File" then the F becomes the keytip. However, the same convention doesn't work for commands in the ribbon, so it's probably easiest to always use the KeyTip property and avoid confusion.

Ribbon Sizing

One of the ribbon's most remarkable features is its ability to resize itself to fit the width of the window by reducing and rearranging the buttons in each groups.

When you create a ribbon with WPF, you get basic resizing for free. This resizing, which is built in to the RibbonWrapPanel, uses a different template depending on the number of controls in the group and the size of the group. For example, a group with three RibbonButton objects displays them from left to right, if space permits. If not, the controls on the right are collapsed to small icons, then their text is stripped away to reclaim more space, and finally the whole group is reduced to a single button that, when clicked, shows all the commands in a drop-down list. Figure 25-13 illustrates this process with a ribbon that has three copies of the File group. The first is fully expanded, the second is partially collapsed, and the second is completely collapsed. (It's worth noting that to create this example, the ribbon must be explicitly configured to not collapse the first group. Otherwise, it will always try to partially collapse every group before it fully collapses any group.)

Figure 25-13. *Shrinking the ribbon*

You can use several techniques to change the sizing of a ribbon group. You can use the RibbonTab. GroupSizeReductionOrder property to set which groups should be reduced first. You specify each group using the value of its LabelTitle. Here's an example:

```
<r:RibbonTab Header="Home" GroupSizeReductionOrder="Clipboard,Tasks,File">
```

As you reduce the size of the window, all the groups will be collapsed bit by bit. However, the Clipboard group will switch to a more compact layout first, followed by the Tasks group, and so on. If you continue shrinking the window, there will be another round of group rearrangement, once again led by the Clipboard group. If you don't set the GroupSizeReductionOrder property, the rightmost group leads the way.

A more powerful approach is to create a collection of RibbonGroupSizeDefinition objects that dictates how a group should collapse itself. Each RibbonGroupSizeDefinition is a template that defines a single layout. It specifies which commands should get large icons, which ones should get small icons, and which ones should include display text. Here's an example of a RibbonControlSizeDefinition that sets the layout for a group of four controls, making them all as big as can be:

```
<r:RibbonGroupSizeDefinition>
   <r:RibbonControlSizeDefinition ImageSize="Large" IsLabelVisible="True" />
   <r:RibbonControlSizeDefinition ImageSize="Large" IsLabelVisible="True" />
   <r:RibbonControlSizeDefinition ImageSize="Large" IsLabelVisible="True" />
   <r:RibbonControlSizeDefinition ImageSize="Large" IsLabelVisible="True" />
</r:RibbonGroupSizeDefinition>
```

To understand this, you need to realize that a RibbonGroupSizeDefinition matches controls by order, regardless of their names. So the definition shown provides instructions for the first four controls in the ribbon, regardless of what type of control they are and what text they contain.

To take control of group resizing, you need to define multiple RibbonGroupSizeDefinition objects and order them from largest to smallest in a RibbonGroupSizeDefinitionCollection. As the group is collapsed, the ribbon can then switch from one layout to the next to reclaim more space, while keeping the layout you want (and ensuring that the controls you think are most important remain visible). Usually, you'll place the RibbonGroupSizeDefinitionCollection in the Ribbon.Resources section, so you can reuse the same sequences of templates for more than one four-button group.

```
<r:Ribbon.Resources>
  <r:RibbonGroupSizeDefinitionBaseCollection x:Key="RibbonLayout">

    <!-- All large controls. -->
    <r:RibbonGroupSizeDefinition>
      <r:RibbonControlSizeDefinition ImageSize="Large" IsLabelVisible="True"/>
      <r:RibbonControlSizeDefinition ImageSize="Large" IsLabelVisible="True"/>
      <r:RibbonControlSizeDefinition ImageSize="Large" IsLabelVisible="True"/>
      <r:RibbonControlSizeDefinition ImageSize="Large" IsLabelVisible="True"/>
    </r:RibbonGroupSizeDefinition>

    <!-- A large control at both ends, with two small controls in between. -->
    <r:RibbonGroupSizeDefinition>
      <r:RibbonControlSizeDefinition ImageSize="Large" IsLabelVisible="True"/>
      <r:RibbonControlSizeDefinition ImageSize="Small" IsLabelVisible="True"/>
      <r:RibbonControlSizeDefinition ImageSize="Small" IsLabelVisible="True"/>
      <r:RibbonControlSizeDefinition ImageSize="Large" IsLabelVisible="True"/>
    </r:RibbonGroupSizeDefinition>

    <!-- Same as before, but now with no text for the small buttons. -->
    <r:RibbonGroupSizeDefinition>
      <r:RibbonControlSizeDefinition ImageSize="Large" IsLabelVisible="True"/>
      <r:RibbonControlSizeDefinition ImageSize="Small" IsLabelVisible="False"/>
      <r:RibbonControlSizeDefinition ImageSize="Small" IsLabelVisible="False"/>
      <r:RibbonControlSizeDefinition ImageSize="Large" IsLabelVisible="True"/>
    </r:RibbonGroupSizeDefinition>

    <!-- All small buttons. -->
    <r:RibbonGroupSizeDefinition>
      <r:RibbonControlSizeDefinition ImageSize="Small" IsLabelVisible="True"/>
      <r:RibbonControlSizeDefinition ImageSize="Small" IsLabelVisible="False"/>
      <r:RibbonControlSizeDefinition ImageSize="Small" IsLabelVisible="False"/>
      <r:RibbonControlSizeDefinition ImageSize="Small" IsLabelVisible="True"/>
    </r:RibbonGroupSizeDefinition>

    <!-- All small, no-text buttons. -->
    <r:RibbonGroupSizeDefinition>
      <r:RibbonControlSizeDefinition ImageSize="Small" IsLabelVisible="False"/>
      <r:RibbonControlSizeDefinition ImageSize="Small" IsLabelVisible="False"/>
      <r:RibbonControlSizeDefinition ImageSize="Small" IsLabelVisible="False"/>
      <r:RibbonControlSizeDefinition ImageSize="Small" IsLabelVisible="False"/>
    </r:RibbonGroupSizeDefinition>
```

```
<!-- Collapse the entire group to a single drop-down button. -->
<r:RibbonGroupSizeDefinition IsCollapsed="True" />
  </r:RibbonGroupSizeDefinitionBaseCollection>
</r:Ribbon.Resources>
```

Now you can apply these resizing rules to a group in your ribbon like this:

```
<r:RibbonGroup Header="Files" SmallImageSource="images/save_Small.png"
  GroupSizeDefinitions="{StaticResource RibbonLayout}">
  ...
</r:RibbonGroup>
```

■ **Note**　Not only can the ribbon be resized, it can also be *minimized* (collapsed down so that just the tabs are visible). Users can minimize the ribbon (and expand it back) by double-clicking any tab title, or by right-clicking the ribbon and choosing Minimize the Ribbon.

The Quick Access Toolbar

The final ingredient that you'll consider in the ribbon is the quick access toolbar (or QAT). It's a narrow strip of commonly used buttons that sits either just above or just below the rest of the ribbon, depending on user selection.

Initially, your ribbon won't include a quick access toolbar. If you want to add one, you need to create it by setting the Ribbon.QuickAccessToolBar property. It takes a RibbonQuickAccessToolbar object, which holds a series of RibbonButton objects. When defining the RibbonCommand for these objects, you need only supply the tooltip text and small image, because text labels and large images are never shown.

Here's the definition for the exceedingly simple QAT shown back in Figure 25-8:

```
<r:Ribbon.QuickAccessToolBar>
  <r:RibbonQuickAccessToolBar>
    <r:RibbonButton Label="Undo" SmallImageSource="images\undo.png" />
    <r:RibbonButton Label="Redo" SmallImageSource="images\redo.png" />
    <r:RibbonButton Label="Save" SmallImageSource="images\save_small.png" />
  </r:RibbonQuickAccessToolBar>
</r:Ribbon.QuickAccessToolBar>
```

The real goal of the QAT is to provide a customization avenue for the user. You should put a relatively small number of items into your QAT, but allow users to take their favorite commands from the ribbon and place them into the QAT. This happens pretty much automatically, with two caveats. Most importantly, a button can only be copied into the QAT if it uses a command (in other words, you've set its Command property, and you're using that rather than the Click event to trigger the appropriate action in your application). If you've done that, a user can copy any command into the QAT by right-clicking the ribbon button and choosing Add to Quick Access Toolbar (see Figure 25-14). Similarly, a user can remove a button from the QAT by right-clicking it and choosing Remove from Quick Access Toolbar. You can turn this feature off for specific buttons by setting the CanAddToQuickAccessToolbarDirectly property to False.

Figure 25-14. *Adding a command to the quick access toolbar*

■ **Tip** It's also possible to add items from the application menu, provided they are wired to commands, not Click event handlers. In this case, you'll run into a small issue—the standard menu image, as set by the ImageSource property, is too big for the QAT. The ribbon scales it down automatically, but this can reduce the quality of the image. To avoid this quirk, give each menu command a QAT-compatible picture by adding the QuickAccessToolBarImageSource property.

If the ribbon is stuffed full of items, or the window has been resized to very narrow dimension, some of the items in the QAT will be moved into the overflow menu. To see them, the user must click the drop-down arrow at the right edge of the QAT, which opens a drop-down that shows all the extra commands that don't fit.

The most significant limitation of the QAT is that it cannot save its current state. In other words, there's no way for your application to remember the commands that the user has added and restore them the next time the application is launched (unless you build that functionality yourself).

■ **Tip** There are still several more ribbon features that aren't covered in this chapter, such as ribbon galleries, custom resizing with a custom layout panel, and contextual tabs. For more information, you can refer to Microsoft's ribbon documentation at `http://tinyurl.com/33yx2cl`.

The Last Word

In this chapter you looked at four controls that underpin professional Windows applications. The first three—the Menu, ToolBar, and StatusBar—derive from the ItemsControl class you considered in Chapter 20. But rather than display data, they hold groups of menu commands, toolbar buttons, and status items. This is one more example that shows how the WPF library takes fundamental concepts, such as the ItemsControl, and uses them to standardize entire branches of the control family.

The fourth and final control that you considered is the Ribbon, a toolbar replacement that was introduced as the distinguishing feature of Office 2007 and became a standard ingredient Windows 7. Although the ribbon isn't baked into the .NET runtime, it's a valuable free library for WPF developers.

■ ■ ■

CHAPTER 26

Sound and Video

In this chapter, you'll tackle two more areas of WPF functionality: audio and video. The support WPF provides for audio is a significant step up from the first versions of .NET, but it's far from groundbreaking. WPF gives you the ability to play a wide variety of sound formats, including MP3 files and anything else supported by Windows Media Player. However, WPF's sound capabilities still fall far short of DirectSound (the advanced audio API in DirectX), which allows you to apply dynamic effects and place sounds in a simulated 3-D space. WPF also lacks a way to retrieve spectrum data that tells you the highs and lows of sound, which is useful for creating some types of synchronized effects and sound-driven animations.

WPF's video support is more impressive. Although the ability to play video (such as MPEG and WMV files) isn't earth-shattering, the way it integrates into the rest of the WPF model is dramatic. For example, you can use video to fill thousands of elements at once and combine it with effects, animation, transparency, and even 3-D objects.

In this chapter, you'll see how to integrate video and audio content into your applications. You'll even take a quick look at WPF's support for speech synthesis and speech recognition. But before you get to the more exotic examples, you'll begin by considering the basic code required to play humble WAV audio.

Playing WAV Audio

The simplest way to play audio files in .NET is with the underwhelming SoundPlayer class, which you can find in the underpopulated System.Media namespace. The SoundPlayer is severely limited: it can play only WAV audio files, it doesn't support playing more than one sound at once, and it doesn't provide the ability to control any aspect of the audio playback (for example, details such as volume and balance).

If you can live with the SoundPlayer's significant limitations, it still presents the easiest, most lightweight way to add audio to an application. The SoundPlayer class is also wrapped by the SoundPlayerAction class, which allows you to play sounds through a declarative trigger (rather than writing a few lines of VB code in an event handler). In the following sections, you'll take a quick look at both classes, before you move on to WPF's much more powerful MediaPlayer and MediaElement classes.

The SoundPlayer

To play a sound with the SoundPlayer class, you follow several steps:

1. Create a SoundPlayer instance.

2. Specify the sound content by setting either the SoundLocation property or the Stream property. If you have a file path that points to a WAV file, use the SoundLocation property. If you have a Stream-based object that contains WAV audio content, use the Stream property.

■ **Note**   If your audio content is stored in a binary resource and embedded in your application, you'll need to access it as a stream (see Chapter 7) and use the SoundPlayer.Stream property. That's because the SoundPlayer doesn't support WPF's pack URI syntax.

3. After you've set the Stream or SoundLocation property, you can tell SoundPlayer to actually load the audio data by calling the Load() or LoadAsync() method. The Load() method is the simplest—it stalls your code until all the audio is loaded into memory. LoadAsync() quietly carries its work out on another thread and fires the LoadCompleted event when it's finished.

■ **Note**   Technically, you don't need to use Load() or LoadAsync(). The SoundPlayer will load the audio data if needed when you call Play() or PlaySync(). However, it's a good idea to explicitly load the audio—not only does that save you the overhead if you need to play it multiple times, but it also makes it easy to handle exceptions related to file problems separately from exceptions related to audio playback problems.

4. Now you can call PlaySync() to pause your code while the audio plays, or you can use Play() to play the audio on another thread, ensuring that your application's interface remains responsive. Your only other option is PlayLooping(), which plays the audio asynchronously in an unending loop (perfect for those annoying soundtracks). To halt the current playback at any time, just call Stop().

The following code snippet shows the simplest approach to load and play a sound asynchronously:

```
Dim player As New SoundPlayer()
player.SoundLocation = "test.wav"

Try
    player.Load()
    player.Play()

Catch err As System.IO.FileNotFoundException err
    ' An error will occur here if the file can't be found.

Catch err As FormatException
    ' A FormatException will occur here if the file doesn't
    ' contain valid WAV audio.
End Try
```

So far, the code has assumed that the audio is present in the same directory as the compiled application. However, you don't need to load the SoundPlayer audio from a file. If you've created small sounds that are played at several points in your application, it may make more sense to embed the sound files into your compiled assembly as a binary resource (not to be confused with declarative resources, which are the resources you define in XAML markup).

This technique, which was discussed in Chapter 11, works just as well with sound files as it does with images. For example, if you add the ding.wav audio file with the resource name Ding (just browse to the Properties ➤ Resources node in the Solution Explorer and use the designer support), you could use this code to play it:

```
Dim player As New SoundPlayer()
player.Stream = Properties.Resources.Ding
player.Play()
```

■ **Note** The SoundPlayer class doesn't deal well with large audio files, because it needs to load the entire file into memory at once. You might think that you can resolve this problem by submitting a large audio file in smaller chunks, but the SoundPlayer wasn't designed with this technique in mind. There's no easy way to synchronize the SoundPlayer so that it plays multiple audio snippets one after the other, because it doesn't provide any sort of queuing feature. Each time you call PlaySync() or Play(), the current audio playback stops. Workarounds are possible, but you'll be far better off using the MediaElement class discussed later in this chapter.

The SoundPlayerAction

The SoundPlayerAction makes it more convenient to use the SoundPlayer class. The SoundPlayerAction class derives from TriggerAction (Chapter 11), which allows you to use it in response to any event.

Here's a button that uses a SoundPlayerAction to connect the Click event to a sound. The trigger is wrapped in a style that you could apply to multiple buttons (if you pulled it out of the button and placed it in a Resources collection).

```
<Button>
  <Button.Content>Play Sound</Button.Content>
  <Button.Style>
    <Style>
      <Style.Triggers>
        <EventTrigger RoutedEvent="Button.Click">
          <EventTrigger.Actions>
            <SoundPlayerAction Source="test.wav"></SoundPlayerAction>
          </EventTrigger.Actions>
        </EventTrigger>
      </Style.Triggers>
    </Style>
  </Button.Style>
</Button>
```

When using the SoundPlayerAction, the sound is always played asynchronously.

System Sounds

One of the shameless frills of the Windows operating system is its ability to map audio files to specific system events. Along with SoundPlayer, WPF also includes a System.Media.SystemSounds class that allows you to access the most common of these sounds and use them in your own applications. This technique works best if all you want is a simple chime to indicate the end of a long-running operation or an alert sound to indicate a warning condition.

Unfortunately, the SystemSounds class is based on the MessageBeep Win32 API, and as a result, it provides access only to the following generic system sounds:

- Asterisk

- Beep

- Exclamation

- Hand

- Question

The SystemSounds class provides a property for each of these sounds, which returns a SystemSound object you can use to play the sound through its Play() method. For example, to sound a beep in your code, you simply need to execute this line of code:

```
SystemSounds.Beep.Play()
```

To configure what WAV files are used for each sound, head to the Control Panel and double-click the Sound icon.

The MediaPlayer

The SoundPlayer, SoundPlayerAction, and SystemSounds classes are easy to use but relatively underpowered. In today's world, it's much more common to use compressed MP3 audio for everything except the simplest of sounds, instead of the original WAV format. But if you want to play MP3 audio or MPEG video, you need to turn to two classes: MediaPlayer and MediaElement. Both classes depend on key pieces of technology that are provided through Windows Media Player.

The MediaPlayer class (found in the WPF-specific System.Windows.Media namespace) is the WPF equivalent to the SoundPlayer class. Although it's clearly not as lightweight, it works in a similar way—namely, you create a MediaPlayer object, call the Open() method to load your audio file, and call Play() to begin playing it asynchronously. (There's no option for synchronous playback.) Here's a bare-bones example:

```
Private player As New MediaPlayer()

Private Sub cmdPlayWithMediaPlayer_Click(ByVal sender As Object, _
  ByVal e As RoutedEventArgs)
    player.Open(New Uri("test.mp3", UriKind.Relative))
    player.Play()
End Sub
```

There are a few important details to notice in this example:

- The MediaPlayer is created outside the event handler, so it lives for the lifetime of the window. That's because the MediaPlayer.Close() method is called when the MediaPlayer object is disposed from memory. If you create a MediaPlayer object in the event handler, it will be released from memory almost immediately and probably garbage collected shortly after, at which point the Close() method will be called and playback will be halted.

■ **Tip**   You should create a Window.Unloaded event handler to call Close() to stop any currently playing audio when the window is closed.

- You supply the location of your file as a URI. Unfortunately, this URI doesn't use the application pack syntax that you learned about in Chapter 7, so it's not possible to embed an audio file and play it by using the MediaPlayer class. This limitation exists because the MediaPlayer class is built on functionality that's not native to WPF—instead, it's provided by a distinct, unmanaged component of the Windows Media Player.

- There's no exception-handling code. Irritatingly, the Open() and Play() methods don't throw exceptions (the asynchronous load and playback process is partly to blame). Instead, it's up to you to handle the MediaOpened and MediaFailed events if you want to determine whether your audio is being played.

The MediaPlayer is fairly straightforward but still more capable than SoundPlayer. It provides a small set of useful methods, properties, and events. Table 26-1 has the full list.

Table 26-1. *Key MediaPlayer Members*

Member	Description
Balance	Sets the balance between the left and right speaker as a number from –1 (left speaker only) to 1 (right speaker only).
Volume	Sets the volume as a number from 0 (completely muted) to 1 (full volume). The default value is 0.5.
SpeedRatio	Sets a speed multiplier to play audio (or video) at faster than normal speed. The default value of 1 is normal speed, while 2 is two-times normal speed, 10 is ten-times speed, 0.5 is half-times speed, and so on. You can use any positive Double value.
HasAudio and HasVideo	Indicates whether the currently loaded media file includes audio or video, respectively. To show video, you need to use the MediaElement class described in the next section.
NaturalDuration, NaturalVideoHeight, and NaturalVideoWidth	Indicates the play duration at normal speed and the size of the video window. (As you'll discover later, you can scale or stretch a video to fit different window sizes.)
Position	A TimeSpan indicating the current location in the media file. You can set this property to skip to a specific time position.
DownloadProgress and BufferingProgress	Indicates the percentage of a file that has been downloaded (useful if the Source is a URL pointing to a web or remote computer) or buffered (if the media file you're using is encoded in a streaming format so it can be played before it's entirely downloaded). The percentage is represented as a number from 0 to 1.
Clock	Gets or sets the MediaClock that's associated with this player. The MediaClock is used only when you're synchronizing audio to a timeline (in much the same way that you learned to synchronize an animation to a timeline in Chapter 15). If you're using the methods of the MediaPlayer to perform manual playback, this property is null.
Open()	Loads a new media file.
Play()	Begins playback. Has no effect if the file is already being played.
Pause()	Pauses playback but doesn't change the position. If you call Play() again, playback will begin at the current position. Has no effect if the audio is not playing.
Stop()	Stops playback and resets the position to the beginning of the file. If you call Play() again, playback will begin at the beginning of the file. Has no effect if the audio has already been stopped.

Using these members, you could build a basic but full-featured media player. However, WPF programmers usually use another quite similar element, which is defined in the next section: the MediaElement class.

The MediaElement

The MediaElement is a WPF element that wraps all the functionality of the MediaPlayer class. Like all elements, the MediaElement is placed directly in your user interface. If you're using the MediaElement to play audio, this fact isn't important, but if you're using the MediaElement for video, you place it where the video window should appear.

A simple MediaElement tag is all you need to play a sound. For example, if you add this markup to your user interface:

```
<MediaElement Source="test.mp3"></MediaElement>
```

the test.mp3 audio will be played as soon as it's loaded (which is more or less as soon as the window is loaded).

Playing Audio Programmatically

Usually, you'll want the ability to control playback more precisely. For example, you might want it to be triggered at a specific time, repeated indefinitely, and so on. One way to achieve this result is to use the methods of the MediaElement class at the appropriate time.

The startup behavior of the MediaElement is determined by its LoadedBehavior property, which is one of the few properties that the MediaElement class adds, which isn't found in the MediaPlayer class. The LoadedBehavior takes any value from the MediaState enumeration. The default value is Play, but you can also use Manual, in which case the audio file is loaded, and your code takes responsibility for starting the playback at the right time. Another option is Pause, which also suspends playback but doesn't allow you to use the playback methods. (Instead, you'll need to start playback by using triggers and a storyboard, as described in the next section.)

■ **Note**   The MediaElement class also provides an UnloadedBehavior property, which determines what should happen when the element is unloaded. In this case, Close is really the only sensible choice, because it closes the file and releases all system resources.

So to play audio programmatically, you must begin by changing the LoadedBehavior, as shown here:

```
<MediaElement Source="test.mp3" LoadedBehavior="Manual" Name="media"></MediaElement>
```

You must also choose a name so that you can interact with the media element in code. Generally, interaction consists of the straightforward Play(), Pause(), and Stop() methods. You can also set Position to move through the audio. Here's a simple event handler that seeks to the beginning and starts playback:

```
Private Sub cmdPlay_Click(ByVal sender As Object, ByVal e As RoutedEventArgs)
    media.Position = TimeSpan.Zero
    media.Play()
End Sub
```

If this code runs while playback is already underway, the first line will reset the position to the beginning, and playback will continue from that point. The second line will have no effect, because the media file is already being played. If you try to use this code on a MediaElement that doesn't have the LoadedBehavior property set to Manual, you'll receive an exception.

■ **Note** In a typical media player, you can trigger basic commands such as play, pause, and stop in more than one way. Obviously, this is a great place to use the WPF command model. In fact, there's a command class that already includes some handy infrastructure, the System.Windows.Input.MediaCommands class. However, the MediaElement does not have any default command bindings that support the MediaCommands class. In other words, it's up to you to write the event-handling logic that implements each command and calls the appropriate MediaElement method. The savings to you is that multiple user interface elements can be hooked up to the same command, reducing code duplication. Chapter 9 has more about commands.

Handling Errors

The MediaElement doesn't throw an exception if it can't find or load a file. Instead, it's up to you to handle the MediaFailed event. Fortunately, this task is easy. Just tweak your MediaElement tag:

```
<MediaElement ... MediaFailed="media_MediaFailed"></MediaElement>
```

And, in the event handler, use the ExceptionRoutedEventArgs.ErrorException property to get an exception object that describes the problem:

```
Private Sub media_MediaFailed(ByVal sender As Object, _
  ByVal e As ExceptionRoutedEventArgs)
    lblErrorText.Content = e.ErrorException.Message
End Sub
```

Playing Audio with Triggers

So far, you haven't received any advantage by switching from the MediaPlayer to the MediaElement class (other than support for video, which is discussed later in this chapter). However, by using a MediaElement, you also gain the ability to control audio declaratively, through XAML markup rather than code. You do this by using triggers and storyboards, which you first saw when you considered animation in Chapter 15. The only new ingredient is the MediaTimeline, which controls the timing of your audio or video file and works with MediaElement to coordinate its playback. MediaTimeline derives from Timeline and adds a Source property that identifies the audio file you want to play.

The following markup demonstrates a simple example. It uses the BeginStoryboard action to begin playing a sound when the mouse clicks a button. (Obviously, you could respond equally well to other mouse and keyboard events.)

```
<Grid>
 <Grid.RowDefinitions>
   <RowDefinition Size="Auto"></RowDefinition>
   <RowDefinition Size="Auto"></RowDefinition>
 </Grid.RowDefinitions>
 <MediaElement x:Name="media"></MediaElement>

 <Button>
   <Button.Content>Click me to hear a sound.</Button.Content>
   <Button.Triggers>
     <EventTrigger RoutedEvent="Button.Click">
       <EventTrigger.Actions>
```

```
          <BeginStoryboard>
            <Storyboard>
              <MediaTimeline Source="soundA.wav"
                Storyboard.TargetName="media"></MediaTimeline>
            </Storyboard>
          </BeginStoryboard>
        </EventTrigger.Actions>
      </EventTrigger>
    </Button.Triggers>
  </Button>
</Grid>
```

Because this example plays audio, the positioning of the MediaElement isn't important. In this example, it's placed inside a Grid, behind a Button. (The ordering isn't important, because the MediaElement won't have any visual appearance at runtime.) When the button is clicked, a Storyboard is created with a MediaTimeline. Notice that the source isn't specified in the MediaElement.Source property. Instead, the source is passed along through the MediaTimeline.Source property.

■ **Note** When you use MediaElement as the target of a MediaTimeline, it no longer matters what you set the LoadedBehavior and UnloadedBehavior to. Once you use a MediaTime, your audio or video is driven by a WPF animation clock (technically, an instance of the MediaClock class, which is exposed through the MediaElement.Clock property).

You can use a single Storyboard to control the playback of a single MediaElement—in other words, not only stopping it but also pausing, resuming, and stopping it at will. For example, consider the extremely simple four-button media player shown in Figure 26-1.

Figure 26-1. *A window for controlling playback*

This window uses a single MediaElement, MediaTimeline, and Storyboard. The Storyboard and MediaTimeline are declared in the Window.Resources collection:

```
<Window.Resources>
  <Storyboard x:Key="MediaStoryboardResource">
    <MediaTimeline Storyboard.TargetName="media" Source="test.mp3"></MediaTimeline>
  </Storyboard>
</Window.Resources>
```

The only challenge is that you must remember to define all the triggers for managing the storyboard in one collection. You can then attach them to the appropriate controls by using the EventTrigger.SourceName property.

In this example, the triggers are all declared inside the StackPanel that holds the buttons. Here are the triggers and the buttons that use them to manage the audio:

```
<StackPanel Orientation="Horizontal">
  <StackPanel.Triggers>
    <EventTrigger RoutedEvent="ButtonBase.Click" SourceName="cmdPlay">
      <EventTrigger.Actions>
        <BeginStoryboard Name="MediaStoryboard"
         Storyboard="{StaticResource MediaStoryboardResource}"/>
      </EventTrigger.Actions>
    </EventTrigger>
    <EventTrigger RoutedEvent="ButtonBase.Click" SourceName="cmdStop">
      <EventTrigger.Actions>
        <StopStoryboard BeginStoryboardName="MediaStoryboard"/>
      </EventTrigger.Actions>
    </EventTrigger>
    <EventTrigger RoutedEvent="ButtonBase.Click" SourceName="cmdPause">
      <EventTrigger.Actions>
        <PauseStoryboard BeginStoryboardName="MediaStoryboard"/>
      </EventTrigger.Actions>
    </EventTrigger>
    <EventTrigger RoutedEvent="ButtonBase.Click" SourceName="cmdResume">
      <EventTrigger.Actions>
        <ResumeStoryboard BeginStoryboardName="MediaStoryboard"/>
      </EventTrigger.Actions>
    </EventTrigger>
  </StackPanel.Triggers>

  <MediaElement  Name="media" ></MediaElement>
  <Button Name="cmdPlay" >Play</Button>
  <Button Name="cmdStop" >Stop</Button>
  <Button Name="cmdPause" >Pause</Button>
  <Button Name="cmdResume" >Resume</Button>
</StackPanel>
```

Notice that even though the implementation of MediaElement and MediaPlayer allows you to resume playback after pausing by calling Play(), the Storyboard doesn't work in the same way. Instead, a separate ResumeStoryboard action is required. If this isn't the behavior you want, you can consider adding some code for your play button instead of using the declarative approach.

▪ **Note** The downloadable code samples for this chapter include a declarative media player window and a more flexible code-driven media player window.

Playing Multiple Sounds

Although the previous example showed you how to control the playback of a single media file, there's no reason you can't extend it to play multiple audio files. The following example includes two buttons, each of which plays its own sound. When a button is clicked, a new Storyboard is created, with a new MediaTimeline, which is used to play a different audio file through the same MediaElement.

```
<Grid>
 <Grid.RowDefinitions>
   <RowDefinition Size="Auto"></RowDefinition>
   <RowDefinition Size="Auto"></RowDefinition>
 </Grid.RowDefinitions>
 <MediaElement x:Name="media"></MediaElement>

   <Button>
     <Button.Content>Click me to hear a sound.</Button.Content>
     <Button.Triggers>
       <EventTrigger RoutedEvent="Button.Click">
         <EventTrigger.Actions>
         <BeginStoryboard>
           <Storyboard>
             <MediaTimeline Source="soundA.wav"
              Storyboard.TargetName="media"></MediaTimeline>
           </Storyboard>
         </BeginStoryboard>
         </EventTrigger.Actions>
       </EventTrigger>
     </Button.Triggers>
   </Button>

   <Button Grid.Row="1">
     <Button.Content>Click me to hear a different sound.</Button.Content>
     <Button.Triggers>
       <EventTrigger RoutedEvent="Button.Click">
         <EventTrigger.Actions>
           <BeginStoryboard>
             <Storyboard>
               <MediaTimeline Source="soundB.wav"
                Storyboard.TargetName="media"></MediaTimeline>
             </Storyboard>
           </BeginStoryboard>
         </EventTrigger.Actions>
       </EventTrigger>
     </Button.Triggers>
   </Button>
</Grid>
```

In this example, if you click both buttons in quick succession, you'll see that the second sound interrupts the playback of the first. This is a consequence of using the same MediaElement for both timelines. A slicker (but more resource-heavy) approach is to use a separate MediaElement for each button and point the MediaTimeline to the corresponding MediaElement. (In this case, you can specify the Source directly in the MediaElement tag, because it doesn't change.) Now, if you click both buttons in quick succession, both sounds will play at the same time.

The same applies to the MediaPlayer class—if you want to play multiple audio files, you need multiple MediaPlayer objects. If you decide to use the MediaPlayer or MediaElement with code, you have the opportunity to use more-intelligent optimization that allows exactly two simultaneous sounds, but no more. The basic technique is to define two MediaPlayer objects and flip between them each time you play a new sound. (You can keep track of which object you used last by using a Boolean variable.) To make this technique really effortless, you can store the audio file names in the Tag property of the appropriate element, so all your event-handling code needs to do is find the right MediaPlayer to use, set its Source property, and call its Play() method.

Changing Volume, Balance, Speed, and Position

The MediaElement exposes the same properties as the MediaPlayer (detailed in Table 26-1) for controlling the volume, the balance, the speed, and the current position in the media file. Figure 26-2 shows a simple window that extends the sound player example from Figure 26-1 with additional controls for adjusting these details.

Figure 26-2. *Controlling more playback details*

The Volume and Balance sliders are the easiest to wire up. Because Volume and Balance are dependency properties, you can connect the slider to the MediaElement with a two-way binding expression. Here's what you need:

```
<Slider Grid.Row="1" Minimum="0" Maximum="1"
 Value="{Binding ElementName=media, Path=Volume, Mode=TwoWay}"></Slider>
<Slider Grid.Row="2" Minimum="-1" Maximum="1"
Value="{Binding ElementName=media, Path=Balance, Mode=TwoWay}"></Slider>
```

Although two-way data-binding expressions incur slightly more overhead, they ensure that if the MediaElement properties are changed some other way, the slider controls remain synchronized.

The SpeedRatio property can be connected in the same way:

```
<Slider Grid.Row="3" Minimum="0" Maximum="2"
  Value="{Binding ElementName=media, Path=SpeedRatio}"></Slider>
```

However, this has a few quirks. First, SpeedRatio isn't used in a clock-driven audio (one that uses a MediaTimeline). To use it, you need to set the LoadedBehavior property of SpeedRatio to Manual and take control of its playback manually through the playback methods.

▓ **Tip** If you're using a MediaTimeline, you can get the same effect from the SetStoryboardSpeedRatio action as you get from setting the MediaElement.SpeedRatio property. You learned about these details in Chapter 15.

Second, SpeedRatio isn't a dependency property, and WPF doesn't receive change notifications when it's modified. That means if you include code that modifies the SpeedRatio property, the slider won't be updated accordingly. (One workaround is to modify the slider in your code, rather than modify the MediaElement directly.)

■ **Note** Changing the playback speed of audio can distort the audio and cause sound artifacts, such as echoes.

The last detail is the current position, which is provided by the Position property. Once again, the MediaElement needs to be in Manual mode before you can set the Position property, which means you can't use the MediaTimeline. (If you're using a MediaTimeline, consider using the BeginStoryboard action with an Offset to the position you want, as described in Chapter 15.)

To make this work, you don't use any data binding in the slider:

```
<Slider Minimum="0" Name="sliderPosition"
  ValueChanged="sliderPosition_ValueChanged"></Slider>
```

You use code like this to set up the position slider when you open a media file:

```
Private Sub media_MediaOpened(ByVal sender As Object, _
  ByVal e As RoutedEventArgs)
    sliderPosition.Maximum = media.NaturalDuration.TimeSpan.TotalSeconds
End Sub
```

You can then jump to a specific position when the slider tab is moved:

```
Private Sub sliderPosition_ValueChanged(ByVal sender As Object, _
  ByVal e As RoutedEventArgs)
    ' Pausing the player before moving it reduces audio "glitches"
    ' when the value changes several times in quick succession.
    media.Pause()
    media.Position = TimeSpan.FromSeconds(sliderPosition.Value)
    media.Play()
End Sub
```

The drawback here is that the slider isn't updated as the media advances. If you want this feature, you need to cook up a suitable workaround (for example, a DispatcherTimer that triggers a periodic check while playback is taking place and updates the slider then). The same is true if you're using the MediaTimeline. For various reasons, you can't bind directly to the MediaElement.Clock information. Instead, you'll need to handle the Storyboard. CurrentTimeInvalidated event, as demonstrated in the AnimationPlayer example in Chapter 15.

Synchronizing an Animation with Audio

In some cases, you may want to synchronize another animation to a specific point in a media file (audio or video). For example, if you have a lengthy audio file that features a person describing a series of steps, you might want to fade in different images after each pause.

Depending on your needs, this design may be overly complex, and you may be able to achieve better performance and simpler design by segmenting the audio into separate files. That way, you can load the new audio and perform the correlated action all at once, simply by responding to the MediaEnded event. In other situations, you need to synchronize something with continuous, unbroken playback of a media file.

One technique that allows you to pair playback with other actions is key-frame animation (which was introduced in Chapter 16). You can then wrap this key-frame animation and your MediaTimeline into a single storyboard. That way, you can supply specific time offsets for your animation, which will then correspond to precise times in the audio file. In fact, you can even use a third-party program that allows you to annotate audio and export a list of important times. You can then use this information to set up the time for each key frame.

When using key-frame animation, it's important to set the Storyboard.SlipBehavior property to Slip. This specifies that your key-frame animation should not creep ahead of the MediaTimeline, if the media file is delayed. This is important because the MediaTimeline could be delayed by buffering (if it's being streamed from a server) or, more commonly, by load time.

The following markup demonstrates a basic example of an audio file with two synchronized animations. The first varies the text in a label as specific parts of the audio file are reached. The second shows a small circle halfway through the audio and pulses it in time to the beat by varying the value of the Opacity property.

```
<Window.Resources>
  <Storyboard x:Key="Board" SlipBehavior="Slip">
    <MediaTimeline Source="sq3gm1.mid"
      Storyboard.TargetName="media"/>

      <StringAnimationUsingKeyFrames
        Storyboard.TargetName="lblAnimated"
        Storyboard.TargetProperty="(Label.Content)" FillBehavior="HoldEnd">
        <DiscreteStringKeyFrame Value="First note..." KeyTime="0:0:3.4" />
        <DiscreteStringKeyFrame Value="Introducing the main theme..."
          KeyTime="0:0:5.8" />
        <DiscreteStringKeyFrame Value="Irritating bass begins..."
          KeyTime="0:0:28.7" />
        <DiscreteStringKeyFrame Value="Modulation!" KeyTime="0:0:53.2" />
        <DiscreteStringKeyFrame Value="Back to the original theme."
          KeyTime="0:1:8" />
      </StringAnimationUsingKeyFrames>

      <DoubleAnimationUsingKeyFrames
        Storyboard.TargetName="ellipse"
        Storyboard.TargetProperty="Opacity" BeginTime="0:0:29.36"
        RepeatBehavior="30x">
        <LinearDoubleKeyFrame Value="1" KeyTime="0:0:0" />
        <LinearDoubleKeyFrame Value="0" KeyTime="0:0:0.64" />
      </DoubleAnimationUsingKeyFrames>
  </Storyboard>
</Window.Resources>

<Window.Triggers>
  <EventTrigger RoutedEvent="MediaElement.Loaded">
    <EventTrigger.Actions>
      <BeginStoryboard Name="mediaStoryboard" Storyboard="{StaticResource Board}">
      </BeginStoryboard>
    </EventTrigger.Actions>
  </EventTrigger>
</Window.Triggers>
```

To make this example even more interesting, it also includes a slider that allows you to change your position. You'll see that even if you change the position by using the slider, the three animations are adjusted automatically to the appropriate point by the MediaTimeline. (The slider is kept synchronized by using the Storyboard. CurrentTimeInvalidated event, and the ValueChanged event is handled to seek to a new position after the user drags the slider thumb. You saw both of these techniques in Chapter 15, with the AnimationPlayer example.)

Figure 26-3 shows the program in action.

Figure 26-3. *Synchronized animations*

Playing Video

Everything you've learned about using the MediaElement class applies equally well when you use a video file instead of an audio file. As you'd expect, the MediaElement class supports all the video formats that are supported by Windows Media Player. Although support depends on the codecs you've installed, you can't count on basic support for WMV, MPEG, and AVI files.

The key difference with video files is that the visual and layout-related properties of the MediaElement are suddenly important. Most important, the Stretch and StretchDirection properties determine how the video window is scaled to fit its container (and work in the same way as the Stretch and StretchDirection properties that you learned about on all Shape-derived classes). When setting the Stretch value, you can use None to keep the native size, Uniform to stretch it to fit its container without changing its aspect ratio, Uniform to stretch it to fit its container in both dimensions (even if that means stretching the picture), and UniformToFill to resize the picture to fit the largest dimension of its container while preserving its aspect ratio (which guarantees that part of the video window will be clipped out if the container doesn't have the same aspect ratio as the video).

■ **Tip**   The MediaElement's preferred size is based on the native video dimensions. For example, if you create a MediaElement with a Stretch value of Uniform (the default) and place it inside a Grid row with a Height value of Auto, the row will be sized just large enough to keep the video at its standard size, so no scaling is required.

Video Effects

Because the MediaElement works like any other WPF element, you have the ability to manipulate it in some surprising ways. Here are some examples:

- You can use a MediaElement as the content inside a content control, such as a button.

- You can set the content for thousands of content controls at once with multiple MediaElement objects—although your CPU probably won't bear up very well under the strain.

- You can also combine video with transformations through the LayoutTransform or RenderTransform property. This allows you to move your video window, stretch it, skew it, or rotate it.

■ **Tip**   Generally, RenderTransform is preferred over LayoutTransform for the MediaElement, because it's lighter weight. It also takes the value of the handy RenderTransformOrigin property into account, allowing you to use relative coordinates for certain transforms (such as rotation).

- You can set the Clipping property of the MediaElement to cut down the video window to a specific shape or path and show only a portion of the full window.

- You can set the Opacity property to allow content behind your video window to show through. In fact, you can even stack multiple semitransparent video windows on top of each other (with dire consequences for performance).

- You can use animation to change a property of the MediaElement (or one of its transforms) dynamically.

- You can copy the current content of the video window to another place in your user interface by using a VisualBrush, which allows you to create specific effects such as reflection.

- You can place a video window on a three-dimensional surface and use animation to move the video window as the video is being played (as described in Chapter 27).

For example, the following markup creates the reflection effect shown in Figure 26-4. It does so by creating a Grid with two rows. The top row holds a MediaElement that plays a video file. The bottom row holds a Rectangle that's painted with a VisualBrush. The trick is that the VisualBrush takes its content from the video window above it, using a binding expression. The video content is then flipped over by using the RelativeTransform property and then faded out gradually toward the bottom by using an OpacityMask gradient.

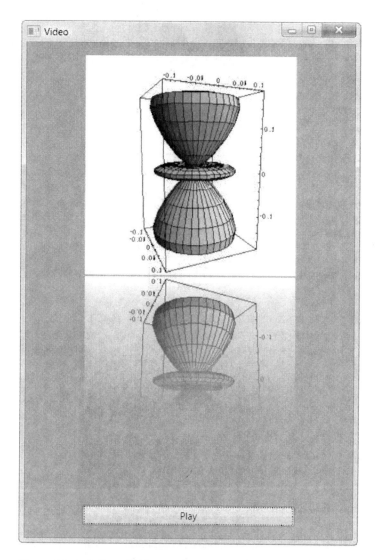

Figure 26-4. *Reflected video*

```
<Grid Margin="15" HorizontalAlignment="Center">
  <Grid.RowDefinitions>
    <RowDefinition Height="Auto"></RowDefinition>
    <RowDefinition></RowDefinition>
  </Grid.RowDefinitions>
  <Grid.ColumnDefinitions>
    <ColumnDefinition Width="Auto"></ColumnDefinition>
  </Grid.ColumnDefinitions>

  <Border BorderBrush="DarkGray" BorderThickness="1" CornerRadius="2">
    <MediaElement x:Name="video" Source="test.mpg" LoadedBehavior="Manual"
     Stretch="Fill"></MediaElement>
  </Border>
```

```
<Border Grid.Row="1" BorderBrush="DarkGray" BorderThickness="1" CornerRadius="2">
  <Rectangle VerticalAlignment="Stretch" Stretch="Uniform">
  <Rectangle.Fill>
    <VisualBrush Visual="{Binding ElementName=video}">
      <VisualBrush.RelativeTransform>
        <ScaleTransform ScaleY="-1" CenterY="0.5"></ScaleTransform>
      </VisualBrush.RelativeTransform>
    </VisualBrush>
  </Rectangle.Fill>

  <Rectangle.OpacityMask>
    <LinearGradientBrush StartPoint="0,0" EndPoint="0,1">
      <GradientStop Color="Black" Offset="0"></GradientStop>
      <GradientStop Color="Transparent" Offset="0.6"></GradientStop>
    </LinearGradientBrush>
  </Rectangle.OpacityMask>
  </Rectangle>
  </Border>
</Grid>
```

This example performs fairly well. The reflection effect has a similar rendering overhead to two video windows, because each frame must be copied to the lower rectangle. In addition, each frame needs to be flipped and faded to create the reflection effect. (WPF uses an intermediary rendering surface to perform these transformations.) But on a modern computer, the extra overhead is barely noticeable.

This isn't the case with other video effects. In fact, video is one of the few areas in WPF where it's extremely easy to overtask the CPU and create interfaces that perform poorly. Average computers can't handle more than a few simultaneous video windows (depending, obviously, on the size of your video file—higher resolutions and higher frame rates obviously mean more data, which is more time-consuming to process).

THE VIDEODRAWING CLASS

WPF includes a VideoDrawing class that derives from the Drawing class you learned about in Chapter 13. The VideoDrawing can be used to create a DrawingBrush, which can then be used to fill the surface of an element, creating much the same effect as demonstrated in the previous example with the VisualBrush.

However, there's a difference that may make the VideoDrawing approach more efficient. That's because VideoDrawing uses the MediaPlayer class, while the VisualBrush approach requires the use of the MediaElement class. The MediaPlayer class doesn't need to manage layout, focus, or any other element details, so it's more lightweight than the MediaElement class. In some situations, using the VideoDrawing and DrawingBrush instead of the MediaElement and VisualBrush can avoid the need for an intermediary rendering surface and thus improve performance (although in my testing, I didn't notice much of a difference between the two approaches).

Using the VideoDrawing takes a fair bit more work, because the MediaPlayer needs to be started in code (by calling its Play() method). Usually, you'll create all three objects—the MediaPlayer, VideoDrawing, and DrawingBrush—in code. Here's a basic example that paints the video on the background of the current window:

```
' Create the MediaPlayer.
Dim player As New MediaPlayer()
player.Open(New Uri("test.mpg", UriKind.Relative))
```

817

```
' Create the VideoDrawing.
Dim videoDrawing As New VideoDrawing()
videoDrawing.Rect = New Rect(150, 0, 100, 100)
videoDrawing.Player = player

' Assign the DrawingBrush.
Dim brush As New DrawingBrush(videoDrawing)
Me.Background = brush

' Start playback.
player.Play()
```

The downloadable examples for this chapter include a demonstration of video effects: an animation that rotates a video window as it plays. The need to wipe out each video frame and redraw a new one at a slightly different angle runs relatively well on modern video cards but causes a noticeable flicker on lower-tier cards. If in doubt, you should profile your user interface plans on a lesser-powered computer to see whether they stand up and should provide a way to opt out of the more complex effects your application provides or gracefully disable them on lower-tier cards.

Speech

Audio and video support is a core pillar of the WPF platform. However, WPF also includes libraries that wrap two less commonly used multimedia features: speech synthesis and speech recognition.

Both of these features are supported through classes in the System.Speech.dll assembly. By default, Visual Studio doesn't add a reference to this assembly in a new WPF project, so it's up to you to add one to your project.

■ **Note** Speech is a peripheral part of WPF. Although the speech support is technically considered to be part of WPF and was released with WPF in the .NET Framework 3.0, the speech namespaces start with System.Speech, not System.Windows.

Speech Synthesis

Speech synthesis is a feature that generates spoken audio based on text you supply. Speech synthesis isn't built into WPF—instead, it's a Windows accessibility feature. System utilities such as Narrator, a lightweight screen reader included with Windows, use speech synthesis to help blind users navigate basic dialog boxes. More generally, speech synthesis can be used to create audio tutorials and spoken instructions, although prerecorded audio provides better quality.

■ **Note** Speech synthesis makes sense when you need to create audio for *dynamic* text—in other words, when you don't know at compile time what words need to be spoken at runtime. But if the audio is fixed, prerecorded audio is easier to use, is more efficient, and sounds better. The only other reason you might consider speech synthesis is if you need to narrate a huge amount of text and prerecording it all would be impractical.

Modern versions of Windows have speech synthesis built in. They use a relatively natural female voice named Anna, although you can download and install additional voices.

Playing speech is deceptively simple. All you need to do is create an instance of the SpeechSynthesizer class from the System.Speech.Synthesis namespace and call its Speak() method with a string of text. Here's an example:

```
Dim synthesizer As New SpeechSynthesizer()
synthesizer.Speak("Hello, world")
```

When using this approach—passing plain text to the SpeechSynthesizer—you give up a fair bit of control. You may run into words that aren't pronounced properly, emphasized appropriately, or spoken at the correct speed. To get more control over spoken text, you need to use the PromptBuilder class to construct a definition of the speech. Here's how you could replace the earlier example with completely equivalent code that uses the PromptBuilder:

```
Dim prompt As New PromptBuilder()
prompt.AppendText("Hello, world")

Dim synthesizer As New SpeechSynthesizer()
synthesizer.Speak(prompt)
```

This code doesn't provide any advantage. However, the PromptBuilder class has a number of other methods that you can use to customize the way text is spoken. For example, you can emphasize a specific word (or several words) by using an overloaded version of the AppendText() method that takes a value from the PromptEmphasis enumeration. Although the precise effect of emphasizing a word depends on the voice you're using, the following code stresses the *are* in the sentence "How are you?"

```
Dim prompt As New PromptBuilder()
prompt.AppendText("How ")
prompt.AppendText("are ", PromptEmphasis.Strong)
prompt.AppendText("you")
```

The AppendText() method has two other overloads—one that takes a PromptRate value that lets you increase or decrease speed and one that takes a PromptVolume value that lets you increase or decrease the volume.

If you want to change more than one of these details at the same time, you need to use a PromptStyle object. The PromptStyle wraps PromptEmphasis, PromptRate, and PromptVolume values. You can supply values for all three details or just the one or two you want to use.

To use a PromptStyle object, you call PromptBuilder.BeginStyle(). The PromptStyle you've created is then applied to all the spoken text until you can EndStyle(). Here's a revised example that uses emphasis and a change in speed to put the stress on the word *are*:

```
Dim prompt As New PromptBuilder()
prompt.AppendText("How ")
Dim style As New PromptStyle()
style.Rate = PromptRate.ExtraSlow
style.Emphasis = PromptEmphasis.Strong
prompt.StartStyle(style)
prompt.AppendText("are ")
prompt.EndStyle()
prompt.AppendText("you")
```

> **Note** If you call BeginStyle(), you must call EndStyle() later in your code. If you fail to do so, you'll receive a runtime error.

The PromptEmphasis, PromptRate, and PromptVolume enumerations provide relatively crude ways to influence a voice. There's no way to get finer-grained control or introduce nuances or subtler specific speech patterns into spoken text. However, the PromptBuilder includes an AppendTextWithHint() method that allows you to deal with telephone numbers, dates, times, and words that need to be spelled out. You supply your choice by using the SayAs enumeration. Here's an example:

```
prompt.AppendText("The word laser is spelled ")
prompt.AppendTextWithHint("laser", SayAs.SpellOut)
```

This produces the narration "The word laser is spelled l-a-s-e-r."

Along with the AppendText() and AppendTextWithHint() methods, the PromptBuilder also includes a small collection of additional methods for adding ordinary audio to the stream (AppendAudio()), creating pauses of a specified duration (AppendBreak()), switching voices (StartVoice() and EndVoice()), and speaking text according to a specified phonetic pronunciation (AppendTextWithPronounciation()).

The PromptBuilder is really a wrapper for the Speech Synthesis Markup Language (SSML) standard, which is described at www.w3.org/TR/speech-synthesis. As such, it shares the limitations of that standard. As you call the PromptBuilder methods, the corresponding SSML markup is generated behind the scenes. You can see the final SSML representation of your code by calling PromptBuilder.ToXml() at the end of your work, and you can call PromptBuilder.AppendSsml() to take existing SSML markup and read it into your prompt.

Speech Recognition

Speech recognition is a feature that translates user-spoken audio into text. As with speech synthesis, speech recognition is a built-in feature of the Windows operating system.

> **Note** If speech recognition isn't currently running, the speech recognition toolbar will appear when you instantiate the SpeechRecognizer class. If you attempt to instantiate the SpeechRecognizer class and you haven't configured speech recognition for your voice, Windows will automatically start a wizard that leads you through the process.

Speech recognition is also a Windows accessibility feature. For example, it allows users with disabilities to interact with common controls by voice. Speech recognition also allows hands-free computer use, which is useful in certain environments.

The most straightforward way to use speech recognition is to create an instance of the SpeechRecognizer class from the System.Speech.Recognition namespace. You can then attach an event handler to the SpeechRecognized event, which is fired whenever spoken words are successfully converted to text:

```
Dim recognizer As New SpeechRecognizer()
AddHandler recognizer.SpeechRecognized, AddressOf recognizer_SpeechRecognized
```

You can then retrieve the text in the event handler from the SpeechRecognizedEventArgs.Result property:

```
Private Sub recognizer_SpeechRecognized(ByVal sender As Object, _
  ByVal e As SpeechRecognizedEventArgs)
    MessageBox.Show("You said: " & e.Result.Text)
End Sub
```

The SpeechRecognizer wraps a COM object. To avoid unseemly glitches, you should declare it as a member variable in your window class (so the object remains alive as long as the window exists) and you should call its Dispose() method when the window is closed (to remove your speech-recognition hooks).

■ **Note** The SpeechRecognizer class raises a sequence of events when audio is detected. First, SpeechDetected is raised if the audio appears to be speech. SpeechHypothesized then fires one or more times, as the words are tentatively recognized. Finally, the SpeechRecognizer raises a SpeechRecognized if it can successfully process the text or a SpeechRecognitionRejected event if it cannot. The SpeechRecognitionRejected event includes information about what the SpeechRecognizer believes the spoken input might have been, but its confidence level is not high enough to accept the input.

It's generally not recommended that you use speech recognition in this fashion. That's because WPF has its own UI Automation feature that works seamlessly with the speech-recognition engine. When configured, it allows users to enter text in text controls and trigger button controls by speaking their automation names. However, you could use the SpeechRecognition class to add support for more-specialized commands to support specific scenarios. You do this by specifying a *grammar* based on the Speech Recognition Grammar Specification (SRGS).

The SRGS grammar identifies what commands are valid for your application. For example, it may specify that commands can use only one of a small set of words (*in* or *off*) and that these words can be used only in specific combinations (*blue on, red on, blue off*, and so on).

You can construct an SRGS grammar in two ways. You can load it from an SRGS document, which specifies the grammar rules by using an XML-based syntax. To do this, you need to use the SrgsDocument from the System.Speech. Recognition.SrgsGrammar namespace:

```
Dim doc As New SrgsDocument("app_grammar.xml")
Dim grammar As New Grammar(doc)
recognizer.LoadGrammar(grammar)
```

Alternatively, you can construct your grammar declaratively by using the GrammarBuilder. The GrammarBuilder plays an analogous role to that of the PromptBuilder you considered in the previous section—it allows you to append grammar rules bit by bit to create a complete grammar. For example, here's a declaratively constructed grammar that accepts two-word input, where the first words has five possibilities and the second word has just two:

```
Dim grammar As New GrammarBuilder()
grammar.Append(New Choices("red", "blue", "green", "black", "white"))
grammar.Append(New Choices("on", "off"))

recognizer.LoadGrammar(New Grammar(grammar))
```

This markup allows commands such as *red on* and *green off*. Alternate input such as *yellow on* or *on red* won't be recognized.

The Choices object represents the SRGS *one-of* rule, which allows the user to speak one word out of a range of choices. It's the most versatile ingredient when building a grammar. Several more overloads to the GrammarBuilder. Append() method accept different input. You can pass an ordinary string, in which case the grammar will require the user to speak exactly that word. You can pass a string followed by a value from the SubsetMatchingMode enumeration to require the user to speak some part of a word or phrase. Finally, you can pass a string followed by a number of minimum and maximum repetitions. This allows the grammar to ignore the same word if it's repeated multiple times, and it also allows you to make a word optional (by giving it a minimum repetition of 0).

Grammars that use all these features can become quite complex. For more information about the SRGS standard and its grammar rules, refer to `www.w3.org/TR/speech-grammar`.

The Last Word

In this example, you explored how to integrate sound and video into a WPF application. You learned about two ways to control the playback of media files—either programmatically by using the methods of the MediaPlayer or MediaTimeline classes or declaratively by using a storyboard.

As always, the best approach depends on your requirements. The code-based approach gives you more control and flexibility, but it also forces you to manage more details and introduces additional complexity. As a general rule, the code-based approach is best if you need fine-grained control over audio playback. However, if you need to combine media playback with animations, the declarative approach is far easier.

CHAPTER 27

■ ■ ■

3-D Drawing

WPF includes an expansive 3-D model that allows you to build complex 3-D scenes out of straightforward markup. Helper classes provide hit-testing, mouse-based rotation, and other fundamental building blocks. And virtually any computer can display the 3-D content, thanks to WPF's ability to fall back on software rendering when video card support is lacking.

The most remarkable part of WPF's libraries for 3-D programming is that they are designed to be a clear, consistent extension of the WPF model you've already learned about. For example, you use the same set of brush classes to paint 3-D surfaces as you use to paint 2-D shapes. You use a similar transform model to rotate, skew, and move 3-D objects, and a similar geometry model to define their contours. More dramatically, you can use the same styling, data binding, and animation features on 3-D objects as you use with 2-D content. It's this support of high-level WPF features that makes WPF's 3-D graphics suitable for everything from eye-catching effects in simple games to charting and data visualization in a business application. (The one situation where WPF's 3-D model *isn't* sufficient is high-powered real-time games. If you're planning to build the next Halo, you're much better off with the raw power of DirectX.)

Even though WPF's model for 3-D drawing is surprisingly clear and consistent, creating rich 3-D interfaces is still difficult. In order to code 3-D animations by hand (or just understand the underlying concepts), you need to master more than a little math. And modeling anything but a trivial 3-D scene with handwritten XAML is a huge, error-prone chore—it's far more involved than the 2-D equivalent of creating a XAML vector image by hand. For that reason, you're much more likely to rely on a third-party tool to create 3-D objects, export them to XAML, and then add them to your WPF applications.

Entire books have been written about all these issues—3-D programming math, 3-D design tools, and the 3-D libraries in WPF. In this chapter, you'll learn enough to understand the WPF model for 3-D drawing, create basic 3-D shapes, design more-advanced 3-D scenes with a 3-D modeling tool, and use some of the useful code released by the WPF team and other third-party developers.

3-D Drawing Basics

A 3-D drawing in WPF involves four ingredients:

- A viewport, which hosts your 3-D content

- A 3-D object

- A light source that illuminates part or all of your 3-D scene

- A camera, which provides the vantage point from which you view the 3-D scene

Of course, more-complex 3-D scenes will feature multiple objects and may include multiple light sources. (It's also possible to create a 3-D object that doesn't require a light source, if the 3-D object itself gives off light.) However, these basic ingredients provide a good starting point.

Compared to 2-D graphics, it's the second and third points that really make a difference. Programmers who are new to 3-D programming sometimes assume that 3-D libraries are just a simpler way to create an object that has a 3-D appearance, such as a glowing cube or a spinning sphere. But if that's all you need, you're probably better off creating a 3-D drawing by using the 2-D drawing classes you've already learned about. After all, there's no reason that you can't use the shapes, transforms, and geometries you learned about in Chapter 12 and Chapter 13 to construct a shape that appears to be 3-D—in fact, it's usually easier than working with the 3-D libraries.

So what's the advantage of using the 3-D support in WPF? The first advantage is that you can create effects that would be extremely complex to calculate using a simulated 3-D model. One good example is light effects such as reflection, which become very involved when working with multiple light sources and different materials with different reflective properties. The other advantage to using a 3-D drawing model is that it allows you to interact with your drawing as a set of 3-D objects. This greatly extends what you can do programmatically. For example, after you build the 3-D scene you want, it becomes almost trivially easy to rotate your object or rotate the camera around your object. Doing the same work with 2-D programming would require an avalanche of code (and math).

Now that you know what you need, it's time to build an example that has all these pieces. This is the task you'll tackle in the following sections.

The Viewport

If you want to work with 3-D content, you need a container that can host it. This container is the Viewport3D class, which is found in the System.Windows.Controls namespace. Viewport3D derives from FrameworkElement, and so it can be placed anywhere you'd place a normal element. For example, you can use it as the content of a window or a page, or you can place it inside a more complex layout.

The Viewport3D class only hints at the complexity of 3-D programming. It adds just two properties—Camera, which defines your lookout onto the 3-D scene, and Children, which holds all the 3-D objects you want to place in the scene. Interestingly enough, the light source that illuminates your 3-D scene is itself an object in the viewport.

■ **Note**   Among the inherited properties in the Viewport3D class, one is particularly significant: ClipToBounds. If set to True (the default), content that stretches beyond the bounds of the viewport is trimmed out. If set to False, this content appears on top of any adjacent elements. This is the same behavior you get from the ClipToBounds property of the Canvas. However, there's an important difference when using the Viewport3D: performance. Setting Videport3D.ClipToBounds to False can dramatically improve performance when rendering a complex, frequently refreshed 3-D scene.

3-D Objects

The viewport can host any 3-D object that derives from Visual3D (from the System.Windows.Media.Media3D namespace, where the vast majority of the 3-D classes live). However, you'll need to perform a bit more work than you might expect to create a 3-D visual. In version 1.0, the WPF library lacks a collection of 3-D shape primitives. If you want a cube, a cylinder, a torus, and so on, you'll need to build it yourself.

One of the nicest design decisions that the WPF team made when building the 3-D drawing classes was to structure them in a similar way as the 2-D drawing classes. That means you'll immediately be able to understand the purpose of a number of core 3-D classes (even if you don't yet know how to use them). Table 27-1 spells out the relationships.

Table 27-1. *2-D Classes and 3-D Classes Compared*

2-D Class	3-D Class	Notes
Visual	Visual3D	Visual3D is the base class for all 3-D objects (objects that are rendered in a Viewport3D container). As with the Visual class, you could use the Visual3D class to derive lightweight 3-D shapes or to create more-complex 3-D controls that provide a richer set of events and framework services. However, you won't get much help. You're more likely to use one of the classes that derive from Visual3D, such as ModelVisual3D or ModelUIElement3D.
Geometry	Geometry3D	The Geometry class is an abstract way to define a 2-D figure. Often geometries are used to define complex figures that are composed of arcs, lines, and polygons. The Geometry3D class is the 3-D analogue—it represents a 3-D surface. However, while there are several 2-D geometries, WPF includes just a single concrete class that derives from Geometry3D: MeshGeometry3D. The MeshGeometry3D class has a central importance in 3-D drawing because you'll use it to define all your 3-D objects.
GeometryDrawing	GeometryModel3D	There are several ways to use a 2-D Geometry object. You can wrap it in a GeometryDrawing and use that to paint the surface of an element or the content of a Visual. The GeometryModel3D class serves the same purpose—it takes a Geometry3D, which can then be used to fill your Visual3D.
Transform	Transform3D	You already know that 2-D transforms are incredibly useful tools for manipulating elements and shapes in all kinds of ways, including moving, skewing, and rotating them. Transforms are also indispensable when performing animations. Classes that derive from Transform3D perform the same magic with 3-D objects. In fact, you'll find surprisingly similar transform classes such as RotateTransform3D, ScaleTransform3D, TranslateTransform3D, Transform3DGroup, and MatrixTransform3D. Of course, the options provided by an extra dimension are considerable, and 3-D transforms are able to warp and distort visuals in ways that look quite different.

At first, you may find it a bit difficult to untangle the relationships between these classes. Essentially, the Viewport3D holds Visual3D objects. To actually give a Visual3D some content, you'll need to define a Geometry3D that describes the shape and wrap it in a GeometryModel3D. You can then use that as the content for your Visual3D. Figure 27-1 shows this relationship.

Figure 27-1. *How a 3-D object is defined*

This two-step process—defining the shapes you want to use in abstract and then fusing them with a visual—is an optional approach for 2-D drawing. However, it's mandatory for 3-D drawing because there are no prebuilt 3-D classes in the library. (The members of the WPF team and others have released some sample code online that starts to fill this gap, but it's still evolving.)

The two-step process is also important because 3-D models are a bit more complex than 2-D models. For example, when you create a Geometry3D object, you specify not only the vertexes of your shape, but also the *material* out of which it's composed. Different materials have different properties for reflecting and absorbing light.

Geometry

To build a 3-D object, you need to start by building the geometry. As you've already learned, there's just one class that fills this purpose: MeshGeometry3D.

Unsurprisingly, a MeshGeometry3D object represents a *mesh*. If you've ever dealt with 3-D drawing before (or if you've read a bit about the technology that underlies modern video cards), you may already know that computers prefer to build 3-D drawings out of triangles. That's because a triangle is the simplest, most granular way to define a surface. Triangles are simple because every triangle is defined by just three points (the vertexes at the corner). Arcs and curved surfaces are obviously more complex. Triangles are granular because other straight-edged shapes (squares, rectangles, and more-complex polygons) can be broken down into a collection of triangles. For better or worse, modern day graphics hardware and graphics programming is built on this core abstraction.

Obviously, most of the 3-D objects you want won't look like simple, flat triangles. Instead you'll need to combine triangles—sometimes just a few, but often hundreds or thousands that line up with one another at varying angles. A mesh is this combination of triangles. With enough triangles, you can ultimately create the illusion of anything, including a complex surface. (Of course, there are performance considerations involved, and 3-D scenes often map some sort of bitmap or 2-D content onto a triangle in a mesh to create the illusion of a complex surface with less overhead. WPF supports this technique.)

Understanding how a mesh is defined is one of the first keys to 3-D programming. If you look at the MeshGeometry3D class, you'll find that it adds the four properties listed in Table 27-2.

Table 27-2. *Properties of the MeshGeometry3D Class*

Name	Description
Positions	Contains a collection of all the points that define the mesh. Each point is a vertex in a triangle. For example, if your mesh has 10 completely separate triangles, you'll have 30 points in this collection. More commonly, some of your triangles will join at their edges, which means one point will become the vertex of several triangles. For example, a cube requires 12 triangles (two for each side), but only 8 distinct points. Making matters even more complicated, you may choose to define the same shared vertex multiple times, so that you can better control how separate triangles are shaded with the Normals property.
TriangleIndices	Defines the triangles. Each entry in this collection represents a single triangle by referring to three points from the Positions collection.
Normals	Provides a vector for each vertex (each point in the Positions collection). This vector indicates how the point is angled for lighting calculations. When WPF shades the face of a triangle, it measures the light at each of the three vertexes using the normal vector. Then, it interpolates between these three points to fill the surface of the triangle. Getting the right normal vectors makes a substantial difference to how a 3-D object is shaded—for example, it can make the divisions between triangles blend together or appear as sharp lines.
TextureCoordinates	Defines how a 2-D texture is mapped onto your 3-D object when you use a VisualBrush to paint it. The TextureCoordinates collection provides a 2-D point for each 3-D point in the Positions collection.

You'll consider shading with normals and texture mapping later in this chapter. But first, you'll learn how to build a basic mesh.

The following example shows the simplest possible mesh, which consists of a single triangle. The units you use aren't important because you can move the camera closer or farther away, and you can change the size or placement of individual 3-D objects by using transforms. What *is* important is the coordinate system, which is shown in Figure 27-2. As you can see, the X and Y axes have the same orientation as in 2-D drawing. What's new is the Z axis. As the Z axis value decreases, the point moves farther away. As it increases, the point moves closer.

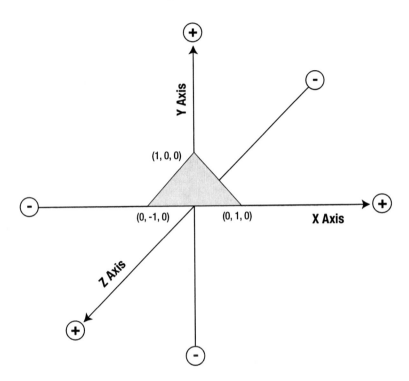

Figure 27-2. *A triangle in 3-D space*

Here's the MeshGeometry element that you can use to define this shape inside a 3-D visual. The MeshGeometry3D object in this example doesn't use the Normals property or the TextureCoordinates property because the shape is so simple and will be painted with a SolidColorBrush:

```
<MeshGeometry3D Positions="-1,0,0  0,1,0  1,0,0" TriangleIndices="0,2,1" />
```

Here, there are obviously just three points, which are listed one after the other in the Positions property. The order you use in the Positions property isn't important because the TriangleIndices property clearly defines the triangle. Essentially, the TriangleIndices property states that there is a single triangle made of point #0, #2, and #1. In other words, the TriangleIndices property tells WPF to draw the triangle by drawing a line from (−1, 0 ,0) to (1, 0, 0) and then to (0, 1, 0).

3-D programming has several subtle, easily violated rules. When defining a shape, you'll face the first one—namely, you must list the points in a counterclockwise order around the Z axis. This example follows that rule. However, you could easily violate it if you changed the TriangleIndices to 0, 1, 2. In this case, you'd still define the same triangle, but that triangle would be backward—in other words, if you look at it down the Z axis (as in Figure 27-2), you'll actually be looking at the *back* of the triangle.

■ **Note** The difference between the back of a 3-D shape and the front is not a trivial one. In some cases, you may paint both with a different brush. Or you may choose not to paint the back at all in order to avoid using any resources for a part of the scene that you'll never see. If you inadvertently define the points in a clockwise order, and you haven't defined the material for the back of your shape, it will disappear from your 3-D scene.

Geometry Model and Surfaces

After you have the properly configured MeshGeometry3D that you want, you need to wrap it in a GeometryModel3D.

The GeometryModel3D class has just three properties: Geometry, Material, and BackMaterial. The Geometry property takes the MeshGeometry3D that defines the shape of your 3-D object. In addition, you can use the Material and BackMaterial properties to define the surface out of which your shape is composed.

The surface is important for two reasons. First, it defines the color of the object (although you can use more-complex brushes that paint textures rather than solid colors). Second, it defines how that material responds to light.

WPF includes four material classes, all of which derive from the abstract Material class in the System.Windows.Media.Media3D namespace). They're listed in Table 27-3. In this example, we'll stick with DiffuseMaterial, which is the most common choice because its behavior is closest to a real-world surface.

Table 27-3. *Material Classes*

Name	Description
DiffuseMaterial	Creates a flat, matte surface. It diffuses light evenly in all directions.
SpecularMaterial	Creates a glossy, highlighted look (think metal or glass). It reflects light back directly, like a mirror.
EmissiveMaterial	Creates a glowing look. It generates its own light (although this light does not reflect off other objects in the scene).
MaterialGroup	Lets you combine more than one material. The materials are then layered on top of one another in the order they're added to the MaterialGroup.

DiffuseMaterial offers a single Brush property that takes the Brush object you want to use to paint the surface of your 3-D object. (If you use anything other than a SolidColorBrush, you'll need to set the MeshGeometry3D.TextureCoordinates property to define the way it's mapped onto the object, as you'll see later in this chapter.)

Here's how you can configure the triangle to be painted with a yellow matte surface:

```
<GeometryModel3D>
  <GeometryModel3D.Geometry>
    <MeshGeometry3D Positions="-1,0,0  0,1,0  1,0,0" TriangleIndices="0,2,1" />
  </GeometryModel3D.Geometry>

  <GeometryModel3D.Material>
    <DiffuseMaterial Brush="Yellow" />
  </GeometryModel3D.Material>
</GeometryModel3D>
```

In this example, the BackMaterial property is not set, so the triangle will disappear if viewed from behind.

All that remains is to use this GeometryModel3D to set the Content property of a ModelVisual3D and then place that ModelVisual3D in a viewport. But in order to see your object, you'll also need two more details: a light source and a camera.

Light Sources

In order to create realistically shaded 3-D objects, WPF uses a lighting model. The basic idea is that you add one (or several) light sources to your 3-D scene. Your objects are then illuminated based on the type of light you've chosen, its position, direction, and intensity.

Before you delve into WPF lighting, it's important that you realize that the WPF lighting model doesn't behave like light in the real world. Although the WPF lighting system is constructed to emulate the real world, calculating true light reflections is a processor-intensive task. WPF uses a number of simplifications that ensure the lighting model is practical, even in animated 3-D scenes with multiple light sources. These simplifications include the following:

- Light effects are calculated for objects *individually*. Light reflected from one object will not reflect off another object. Similarly, an object will not cast a shadow on another object, no matter where it's placed.

- Lighting is calculated at the vertexes of each triangle and then interpolated over the surface of the triangle. (In other words, WPF determines the light strength at each corner and blends that to fill in the triangle.) As a result of this design, objects that have relatively few triangles may not be illuminated correctly. To achieve better lighting, you'll need to divide your shapes into hundreds or thousands of triangles.

Depending on the effect you're trying to achieve, you may need to work around these issues by combining multiple light sources, using different materials, and even adding extra shapes. In fact, getting the precise result you want is part of the art of 3-D scene design.

▨ **Note** Even if you don't provide a light source, your object will still be visible. However, without a light source, all you'll see is a solid black silhouette.

WPF provides four light classes, all of which derive from the abstract Light class. Table 27-4 lists them all. In this example, we'll stick with a single DirectionalLight, which is the most common type of lighting.

Table 27-4. *Light Classes*

Name	Description
DirectionalLight	Fills the scene with parallel rays of light traveling in the direction you specify.
AmbientLight	Fills the scene with scattered light.
PointLight	Radiates light in all directions, beginning at a single point in space.
SpotLight	Radiates light outward in a cone, starting from a single point.

Here's how you can define a white DirectionalLight:

```
<DirectionalLight Color="White" Direction="-1,-1,-1" />
```

In this example, the vector that determines the path of the light starts at the origin (0, 0, 0) and goes to (–1, –1, –1). That means that each ray of light is a straight line that travels from top-right front toward the bottom-left back. This makes sense in this example because the triangle (shown in Figure 27-2) is angled to face this light.

When calculating the light direction, it's the angle that's important, not the length of your vector. That means a light direction of (–2, –2, –2) is equivalent to the normalized vector (–1, –1, –1) because the angle it describes is the same.

In this example, the direction of the light doesn't line up exactly with the triangle's surface. If that's the effect you want, you'll need a light source that sends its beams straight down the Z axis, using a direction of (0, 0, –1). This distinction is deliberate. Because the beams strike the triangle at an angle, the triangle's surface will be shaded, which creates a more pleasing effect.

Figure 27-3 shows an approximation of the (–1, –1, –1) directional light as it strikes the triangle. Remember, a directional light fills the entire 3-D space.

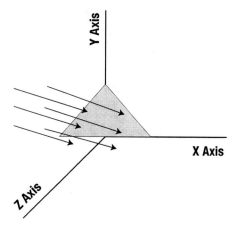

Figure 27-3. *The path of a (–1, –1, –1) directional light*

■ **Note** Directional lights are sometimes compared to sunlight. That's because the light rays received from a faraway light source (such as the sun) become almost parallel.

All light objects derive indirectly from GeometryModel3D. That means that you treat them exactly like 3-D objects by placing them inside a ModelVisual3D and adding them to a viewport. Here's a viewport that includes both the triangle you saw earlier and the light source:

```
<Viewport3D>
  <Viewport3D.Camera>...</Viewport3D.Camera>

  <ModelVisual3D>
    <ModelVisual3D.Content>
      <DirectionalLight Color="White" Direction="-1,-1,-1" />
    </ModelVisual3D.Content>
  </ModelVisual3D>
```

```
<ModelVisual3D>
  <ModelVisual3D.Content>
    <GeometryModel3D>
      <GeometryModel3D.Geometry>
        <MeshGeometry3D Positions="-1,0,0 0,1,0 1,0,0" TriangleIndices="0,2,1" />
      </GeometryModel3D.Geometry>
      <GeometryModel3D.Material>
        <DiffuseMaterial Brush="Yellow" />
      </GeometryModel3D.Material>
    </GeometryModel3D>
  </ModelVisual3D.Content>
</ModelVisual3D>

</Viewport3D>
```

There's one detail that's left out of this example—the viewport doesn't include a camera that defines your vantage point on the scene. That's the task you'll tackle in the next section.

A CLOSER LOOK AT 3-D LIGHTING

Along with DirectionalLight, AmbientLight is another all-purpose lighting class. Using AmbientLight on its own gives 3-D shapes a flat look, but you can combine it with another light source to add some illumination that brightens up otherwise darkened areas. The trick is to use an AmbientLight that's less than full strength. Instead of using a white AmbientLight, use one-third white (set the Color property to #555555) or less. You can also set the DiffuseMaterial. AmbientColor property to control how strongly an AmbientLight affects the material in a given mesh. Using white (the default) gives the strongest effect, while using black creates a material that doesn't reflect any ambient light.

The DirectionalLight and AmbientLight are the most useful lights for simple 3-D scenes. The PointLight and SpotLight give the effect you want only if your mesh includes a large number of triangles—typically hundreds. This is due to the way that WPF shades surfaces.

As you've already learned, WPF saves time by calculating the lighting intensity only at the vertexes of a triangle. If your shape uses a small number of triangles, this approximation breaks down. Some points will fall inside the range of the SpotLight or PointLight, while others won't. The result is that some triangles will be illuminated while others will remain in complete darkness. Rather than getting a soft, rounded circle of light on your object, you'll end up with a group of illuminated triangles, giving the illuminated area a jagged edge.

The problem here is that PointLight and SpotLight are used to create soft, circular lighting effects, but you need a very large number of triangles to create a circular shape. (To create a perfect circle, you need one triangle for each pixel that lies on the perimeter of the circle.) If you have a 3-D mesh with hundreds or thousands of triangles, the pattern of partially illuminated triangles can more easily approximate a circle, and you'll get the lighting effect you want.

The Camera

Before a 3-D scene can be rendered, you need to place a camera at the correct position and orient it in the correct direction. You do this by setting the Viewport3D.Camera property with a Camera object.

In essence, the camera determines how a 3-D scene is projected onto the 2-D surface of a Viewport. WPF includes three camera classes: the commonly used PerspectiveCamera and the more exotic OrthographicCamera and MatrixCamera. The PerspectiveCamera renders the scene so that objects that are farther away appear smaller. This is the behavior that most people expect in a 3-D scene. The OrthographicCamera flattens 3-D objects so that the exact scale is preserved, no matter where a shape is positioned. This looks a bit odd, but it's useful for some types of visualization tools. For example, technical drawing applications often rely on this type of view. (Figure 27-4 shows the difference between the PerspectiveCamera and the OrthographicCamera.) Finally, the MatrixCamera allows you to specify a matrix that's used to transform the 3-D scene to 2-D view. It's an advanced tool that's intended for highly specialized effects and for porting code from other frameworks (such as Direct3D) that use this type of camera.

Orthographic Projection   **Perspective Projection**

Figure 27-4. Perspective in different types of cameras

Choosing the right camera is relatively easy, but placing and configuring it is a bit trickier. The first detail is to specify a point in 3-D space where the camera will be positioned by setting its Position property. The second step is to set a 3-D vector in the LookDirection property that indicates how the camera is oriented. In a typical 3-D scene, you'll place the camera slightly off to one corner by using the Position property, and then tilt it to survey the view by using the LookDirection property.

■ **Note** The position of the camera determines how large your scene appears in the viewport. The closer the camera, the larger the scale. In addition, the viewport is stretched to fit its container and the content inside is scaled accordingly. For example, if you create a viewport that fills a window, you can expand or shrink your scene by resizing the window.

You need to set the Position and LookDirection properties in concert. If you use Position to offset the camera but fail to compensate by turning the camera back in the right direction by using LookDirection, you won't see the content you've created in your 3-D scene. To make sure you're correctly oriented, pick a point that you want to see square on from your camera. You can then calculate the look direction by using this formula:

```
CameraLookDirection = CenterPointOfInterest - CameraPosition
```

In the triangle example, the camera is placed in the top-left corner by using a position of (–2, 2, 2). Assuming you want to focus on the origin point (0, 0, 0), which falls in the middle of the triangle's bottom edge, you would use this look direction:

```
CameraLookDirection = (0, 0, 0) - (-2, 2, 2)
                    = (2, -2, -2)
```

This is equivalent to the normalized vector (1, –1, –1) because the direction it describes is the same. As with the Direction property of a DirectionalLight, it's the direction of the vector that's important, not its magnitude.

After you've set the Position and LookDirection properties, you may also want to set the UpDirection properties. UpDirection determines how the camera is tilted. Ordinarily, UpDirection is set to (0, 1, 0), which means the up direction is straight up, as shown in Figure 27-5.

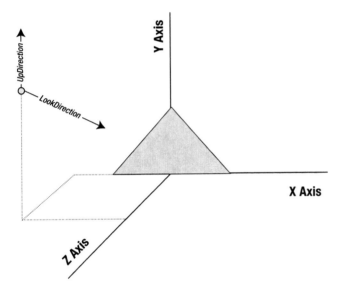

Figure 27-5. *Positioning and angling the camera*

If you offset this slightly—say to (0.25, 1, 0)—the camera is tilted around the X axis, as shown in Figure 27-6. As a result, the 3-D objects will appear to be tilted a bit in the other direction. It's just as if you'd cocked your head to one side while surveying the scene.

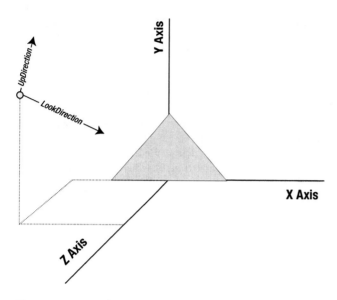

Figure 27-6. *Another way to angle the camera*

With these details in mind, you can define the PerspectiveCamera for the simple one-triangle scene that's been described over the previous sections:

```
<Viewport3D>
  <Viewport3D.Camera>
    <PerspectiveCamera Position="-2,2,2" LookDirection="2,-2,-2"
    UpDirection="0,1,0" />
  </Viewport3D.Camera>
  ...
</Viewport3D>
```

Figure 27-7 shows the final scene.

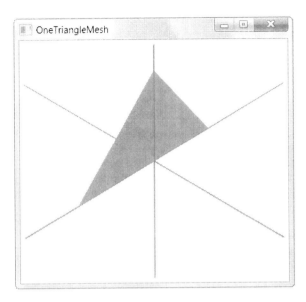

Figure 27-7. *A complete 3-D scene with one triangle*

AXIS LINES

There's one added detail in Figure 27-7: the axis lines. These lines are a great testing tool, as they make it easy to see where your axes are placed. If you render a 3-D scene and nothing appears, the axis lines can help you isolate the potential problem, which could include a camera pointing in the wrong direction or positioned off to one side, or a shape that's flipped backward (and thus invisible). Unfortunately, WPF doesn't include any class for drawing straight lines. Instead, you need to render long, vanishingly narrow triangles.

Fortunately, there's a tool that can help. The WPF 3-D team has created a handy ScreenSpaceLines3D that solves the problem in a freely downloadable class library that's available (with C# source code) at http://3dtools.codeplex.com. This project includes several other useful code ingredients, including the Trackball described later in this chapter in the "Interactivity and Animations" section.

The ScreenSpaceLines3D class allows you to draw straight lines with an invariant width. In other words, these lines have the fixed thickness that you choose no matter where you place the camera. (They do not become thicker as the camera gets closer, and thinner as it recedes.) This makes these lines useful to create wireframes, boxes that indicate content regions, vector lines that indicate the normal for lighting calculations, and so on. These applications are most useful when building a 3-D design tool or when debugging an application. The example in Figure 27-5 uses the ScreenSpaceLines3D class to draw the axis lines.

There are a few other camera properties that are often important. One of these is FieldOfView, which controls how much of your scene you can see at once. FieldOfView is comparable to a zoom lens on a camera—as you decrease the FieldOfView, you see a smaller portion of the scene (which is then enlarged to fit the Viewport3D). As you increase the FieldOfView, you see a larger part of the scene. However, it's important to remember that changing the field of view is *not* the same as moving the camera closer or farther away from the objects in your scene. Smaller fields of view tend to compress the distance between near and far objects, while wider fields of view exaggerate the perspective difference between near and far objects. (If you've played with camera lenses before, you may have noticed this effect.)

> ▓ **Note** The FieldOfView property applies to only the PerspectiveCamera. The OrthographicCamera includes a Width property that's analogous. The Width property determines the viewable area but it doesn't change the perspective because no perspective effect is used for the OrthographicCamera.

The camera classes also include NearPlaneDistance and FarPlaneDistance properties that set the blind spots of the camera. Objects closer than the NearPlaneDistance won't appear at all, and objects farther than the FarPlaneDistance are similarly invisible. Ordinarily, NearPlaneDistance defaults to 0.125, and FarPlaneDistance defaults to Double.PositiveInfinity, which renders both effects negligible. However, in some cases you'll need to change these values to prevent rendering artifacts. The most common example occurs when a complex mesh is extremely close to the camera, which can cause z-fighting (also known as *stitching*). In this situation, the video card is unable to correctly determine which triangles are closest to the camera and should be rendered. The result is a pattern of artifacts of the surface of your mesh.

Z-fighting usually occurs because of floating-point round-off errors in the video card. To avoid this problem, you can increase the NearPlaneDistance to clip objects that are extremely close to the camera. Later in this chapter, you'll see an example that animates the camera so it flies through the center of a torus. To create this effect without causing z-fighting, it's necessary to increase the NearPlaneDistance.

> ▓ **Note** Rendering artifacts are almost always the result of objects close to the camera and a NearPlaneDistance that's too large. Similar problems with very distant objects and the FarPlaneDistance are much less common.

Deeper into 3-D

Going to the trouble of cameras, lights, materials, and mesh geometries is a lot of work for an unimpressive triangle. However, you've now seen the bare bones of WPF's 3-D support. In this section, you'll learn how to use it to introduce more-complex shapes.

After you've mastered the lowly triangle, the next step up is to create a solid, faceted shape by assembling a small group of triangles. In the following example, you'll create the markup for the cube shown in Figure 27-8.

Figure 27-8. *A 3-D cube*

The first challenge to building your cube is determining how to break it down into the triangles that the MeshGeometry object recognizes. Each triangle acts like a flat, 2-D shape.

A cube consists of six square sides. Each square side needs two triangles. Each square side can then be joined to the adjacent side at an angle. Figure 27-9 shows how a cube breaks down into triangles.

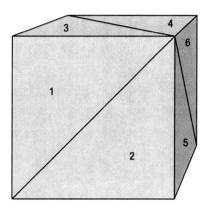

Figure 27-9. *Breaking the cube into triangles*

To reduce overhead and improve performance in a 3-D program, it's common to avoid rendering shapes that you won't see. For example, if you know you'll never look at the underside of the cube shown in Figure 27-8, there's no reason to define the two triangles for that side. However, in this example you'll define every side so you can rotate the cube freely.

Here's a MeshGeometry3D that creates a cube:

```
<MeshGeometry3D Positions="0,0,0    10,0,0    0,10,0    10,10,0
                           0,0,10  10,0,10  0,10,10  10,10,10"
              TriangleIndices="0,2,1  1,2,3  0,4,2  2,4,6
                               0,1,4  1,5,4  1,7,5  1,3,7
                               4,5,6  7,6,5  2,6,3  3,6,7" />
```

First, the Positions collection defines the corners of the cube. It begins with the four points in the back (where z = 0) and then adds the four in the front (where z = 10). The TriangleIndices property maps these points to triangles. For example, the first entry in the collection is 0, 2, 1. It creates a triangle from the first point (0, 0, 0) to the second point (0, 0, 10) to the third point (0, 10, 0). This is one of the triangles required for the back side of the square. (The index 1, 2, 3 fills in the other backside triangle.)

Remember, when defining triangles, you must define them in counterclockwise order to make their front side face forward. However, the cube appears to violate that rule. The squares on the front side are defined in counterclockwise order (see the index 4, 5, 6 and 7, 6, 5, for instance), but those on the back side are defined in clockwise order, including the index 0, 2, 1 and 1, 2, 3. This is because the back side of the cube must have its triangle facing backward. To better visualize this, imagine rotating the cube around the Y axis so that the back side is facing forward. Now, the backward-facing triangles will be facing forward, making them completely visible, which is the behavior you want.

Shading and Normals

There's one issue with the cube mesh demonstrated in the previous section. It doesn't create the faceted cube shown in Figure 27-8. Instead, it gives you the cube shown in Figure 27-10, with clearly visible seams where the triangles meet.

Figure 27-10. A cube with lighting artifacts

This problem results from the way that WPF calculates lighting. In order to simplify the calculation process, WPF computes the amount of light that reaches each vertex in a shape—in other words, it pays attention to only the corners of your triangles. It then blends the lighting over the surface of the triangle. While this ensures that every triangle is nicely shaded, it may cause other artifacts. For example, in this situation it prevents the adjacent triangles that share a cube side from being shaded evenly.

To understand why this problem occurs, you need to know a little more about normals. Each normal defines how a vertex is oriented toward the light source. In most cases, you'll want your normal to be perpendicular to the surface of your triangle.

Figure 27-11 illustrates the front face of a cube. The front face has two triangles and a total of four vertexes. Each of these four vertexes should have a normal that points outward at a right angle to the square's surface. In other words, each normal should have a direction of (0, 0, 1).

Figure 27-11. *Normals on the front side of a cube*

■ **Tip** Here's another way to think about normals. When the normal vector lines up with the light direction vector, but in opposite directions, the surface will be fully illuminated. In this example, that means a directional light with a direction of (0, 0, –1) will completely light up the front surface of the cube, which is what you expect.

The triangles on the other sides of the square need their own normals as well. In each case, the normals should be perpendicular to the surface. Figure 27-12 fills in the normals on the front, top, and right sides of the cube.

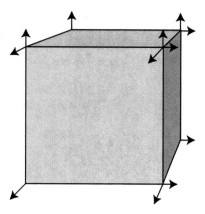

Figure 27-12. *Normals on the visible faces of a cube*

The cube diagrammed in Figure 27-12 is the same cube shown in Figure 27-8. When WPF shades this cube, it examines it one triangle at a time. For example, consider the front surface. Each point faces the directional light in exactly the same way. For that reason, each point will have exactly the same illumination. As a result, when WPF blends the illumination at the four corners, it creates a flat, consistently colored surface with no shading.

So why doesn't the cube you've just created exhibit this lighting behavior? The culprit is the shared points in the Positions collection. Although normals apply to the way triangles are shaded, they're defined on only the vertexes of the triangle. Each point in the Positions collection has just a single normal defined for it. That means if you share points between two triangles, you also end up sharing normals.

That's what's happened in Figure 27-10. The different points on the same side are illuminated differently because they don't all have the same normal. WPF then blends the illumination from these points to fill in the surface of each triangle. This is a reasonable default behavior, but because the blending is performed on each triangle, different triangles won't line up exactly, and you'll see the seams of color where the separate triangles meet.

One easy (but tedious) way to solve this problem is to make sure no points are shared between triangles by declaring each point several times (once for each time it's used). Here's the lengthier markup that does this:

```
<MeshGeometry3D Positions="0,0,0    10,0,0    0,10,0    10,10,0
                           0,0,0    0,0,10    0,10,0    0,10,10
                           0,0,0    10,0,0    0,0,10    10,0,10
                           10,0,0   10,10,10  10,0,10   10,10,0
                           0,0,10   10,0,10   0,10,10   10,10,10
                           0,10,0   0,10,10   10,10,0   10,10,10"
                TriangleIndices="0,2,1      1,2,3
                                 4,5,6      6,5,7
                                 8,9,10     9,11,10
                                 12,13,14   12,15,13
                                 16,17,18   19,18,17
                                 20,21,22   22,21,23" />
```

In this example, this step saves you from needing to code the normals by hand. WPF correctly generates them for you, making each normal perpendicular to the triangle surface, as shown in Figure 27-11. The result is the faceted cube shown in Figure 27-8.

▦ **Note** Although this markup is much longer, the overhead is essentially unchanged. That's because WPF always renders your 3-D scene as a collection of distinct triangles, whether or not you share points in the Positions collection.

It's important to realize that you don't always want your normals to match. In the cube example, it's a requirement to get the faceted appearance. However, you might want a different lighting effect. For example, you might want a blended cube that avoids the seam problem shown earlier. In this case, you'll need to define your normal vectors explicitly.

Choosing the right normals can be a bit tricky. However, to get the result you want, keep these two principles in mind:

- To calculate a normal that's perpendicular to a surface, calculate the cross product of the vectors that make up any two sides of your triangle. However, make sure to keep the points in counterclockwise order so that the normal points out from the surface (instead of into it).

- If you want the blending to be consistent over a surface that includes more than one triangle, make sure all the points in all the triangles share the same normal.

To calculate the normal you need for a surface, you can use a bit of VB code. Here's a simple code routine that can help you calculate a normal that's perpendicular to the surface of a triangle based on its three points:

```
Private Function CalculateNormal(ByVal p0 As Point3D, _
  ByVal p1 As Point3D, ByVal p2 As Point3D) As Vector3D
    Dim v0 As New Vector3D(p1.X - p0.X, p1.Y - p0.Y, p1.Z - p0.Z)
    Dim v1 As New Vector3D(p2.X - p1.X, p2.Y - p1.Y, p2.Z - p1.Z)
    Return Vector3D.CrossProduct(v0, v1)
End Function
```

Next, you need to set the Normals property by hand by filling it with vectors. Remember, you must add one normal for each position.

The following example smooths the blending between adjacent triangles on the same side of a rectangle by sharing normals. The adjacent triangles on a cube face share two of the same points. Therefore, it's only the two nonshared points that need to be adjusted. As long as they match, the shading will be consistent over the entire surface:

```
<MeshGeometry3D Positions="0,0,0 10,0,0 0,10,0 10,10,0
                           0,0,10 10,0,10 0,10,10 10,10,10"
                TriangleIndices="0,2,1 1,2,3 0,4,2 2,4,6
                                 0,1,4 1,5,4 1,7,5 1,3,7
                                 4,5,6 7,6,5 2,6,3 3,6,7"
                Normals="0,1,0 0,1,0 1,0,0 1,0,0
                         0,1,0 0,1,0 1,0,0 1,0,0" />
```

This creates the smoother cube shown in Figure 27-13. Now large portions of the cube end up sharing the same normal. This causes an extremely smooth effect that blends the edges of the cube, making it more difficult to distinguish the sides.

Figure 27-13. *An extremely smooth cube*

This effect isn't correct or incorrect—it simply depends on the effect you're trying to achieve. For example, faceted sides create a more geometric look, while blended sides look more organic. One common trick is to use blending with a large multifaceted polygon to make it look like a sphere, a cylinder, or another sort of curved shape. Because the blending hides the edges of the shape, this effect works remarkably well.

More Complex Shapes

Realistic 3-D scenes usually involve hundreds or thousands of triangles. For example, one approach to building a simple sphere is to split the sphere into bands and then split each band into a faceted series of squares, as shown in the leftmost example in Figure 27-14. Each square then requires two triangles.

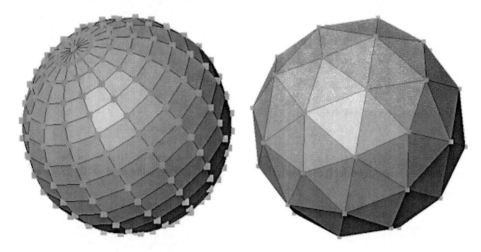

Figure 27-14. *Two ways to model a basic sphere*

To build this sort of nontrivial mesh, you need to construct it in code or use a dedicated 3-D modeling program. The code-only approach requires significant math. The design approach requires a sophisticated 3-D design application.

Fortunately, there are several tools for building 3-D scenes that you can use in WPF applications. Here are a few:

- Blender is an open source toolkit for 3-D modeling. It's available at `www.blender.org`, and there's an experimental XAML export script at `http://xamlexporter.codeplex.com`. Taken together, these provide a sophisticated and completely free platform for building 3-D content for WPF applications.

- Export plug-ins are available for a range of professional 3-D modeling programs such as Autodesk Maya and Newtek's LightWave. For a list of some, check out `http://tinyurl.com/bumqt2y`.

All 3-D modeling programs include basic primitives, such as the sphere, that are built out of smaller triangles. You can then use these primitives to construct a scene. 3-D modeling programs also let you add and position your light sources and apply textures. Some, such as Electric Rain ZAM 3D, also allow you to define animations you want to perform on the objects in your 3-D scene.

Model3DGroup Collections

When working with complex 3-D scenes, you'll usually need to arrange multiple objects. As you already know, a Viewport3D can hold multiple Visual3D objects, each of which uses a different mesh. However, this isn't the best way to build a 3-D scene. You'll get far better performance by creating as few meshes as possible and combining as much content as possible into each mesh.

Obviously, there's another consideration: flexibility. If your scene is broken down into separate objects, you have the ability to hit test, transform, and animate these pieces individually. However, you don't need to create distinct Visual3D objects to get this flexibility. Instead, you can use the Model3DGroup class to place several meshes in a single Visual3D.

Model3DGroup derives from Model3D (as do the GeometryModel3D and Light classes). However, it's designed to group together a combination of meshes. Each mess remains a distinct piece of your scene that you can manipulate individually.

For example, consider the 3-D character shown in Figure 27-15. This character was created in ZAM 3D and exported to XAML. His individual body parts—head, torso, belt, arm, and so on—are separate meshes grouped into a single Model3DGroup object.

Figure 27-15. *A 3-D character*

The following is a portion of the markup, which draws the appropriate meshes from a resource dictionary:

```
<ModelVisual3D>
  <ModelVisual3D.Content>
    <Model3DGroup x:Name="Scene" Transform="{DynamicResource SceneTR20}">
      <AmbientLight ... />
      <DirectionalLight ... />
      <DirectionalLight ... />
      <Model3DGroup x:Name="CharacterOR22">
        <Model3DGroup x:Name="PelvisOR24">
          <Model3DGroup x:Name="BeltOR26">
            <GeometryModel3D x:Name="BeltOR26GR27"
             Geometry="{DynamicResource BeltOR26GR27}"
             Material="{DynamicResource ER_Vector___Flat_Orange___DarkMR10}"
             BackMaterial="{DynamicResource ER_Vector___Flat_Orange___DarkMR10}" />
          </Model3DGroup>
          <Model3DGroup x:Name="TorsoOR29">
            <Model3DGroup x:Name="TubesOR31">
              <GeometryModel3D x:Name="TubesOR31GR32"
               Geometry="{DynamicResource TubesOR31GR32}"
               Material="{DynamicResource ER___Default_MaterialMR1}"
```

```
            BackMaterial="{DynamicResource ER___Default_MaterialMR1}"/>
        </Model3DGroup>

        ...

   </ModelVisual3D.Content>
</ModelVisual3D>
```

The entire scene is defined in a single ModelVisual3D, which contains a Model3DGroup. That Model3DGroup contains other nested Model3DGroup objects. For example, the top-level Model3DGroup contains the lights and the character, while the Model3DGroup for the character contains another Model3DGroup that contains the torso, and that Model3DGroup contains details such as the arms, which contain the palms, which contain the thumbs, and so on, leading eventually to the GeometryModel3D objects that actually define the objects and their material. As a result of this carefully segmented, nested design (which is implicit in the way you create these objects in a design tool such as ZAM 3D), you can animate these body parts individually, making the character walk, gesture, and so on. (You'll take a look at animating 3-D content a bit later in this chapter in the "Interactivity and Animations" section.)

▓ **Note**   Remember, the lowest overhead is achieved by using the fewest number of meshes and the fewest number of ModelVisual3D objects. The Model3DGroup allows you to reduce the number of ModelVisual3D objects you use (there's no reason to have more than one) while retaining the flexibility to manipulate parts of your scene separately.

Materials Revisited

So far, you've used just one of the types of material that WPF supports for constructing 3-D objects. The DiffuseMaterial is by far the most useful material type—it scatters light in all directions, like a real-world object.

When you create a DiffuseMaterial, you supply a Brush. So far, the examples you've seen have used solid-color brushes. However, the color you see is determined by the brush color and the lighting. If you have direct, full-strength lighting, you'll see the exact brush color. But if your lighting hits a surface at an angle (as in the previous triangle and cube examples), you'll see a darker, shaded color.

▓ **Note**   Interestingly, WPF does allow you to make partially transparent 3-D objects. The easiest approach is to set the Opacity property of the brush that you use with the material to a value less than 1.

The SpecularMaterial and EmissiveMaterial types work a bit differently. Both are additively blended into any content that appears underneath. For that reason, the most common way to use both types of material is in conjunction with a DiffuseMaterial.

Consider the SpecularMaterial. It reflects light much more sharply than DiffuseMaterial. You can control how sharply the light is reflected by using the SpecularPower property. Use a low number, and light is reflected more readily, no matter at what angle it strikes the surface. Use a higher number, and direct light is favored more strongly. Thus, a low SpecularPower produces a washed out, shiny effect, while a high SpecularPower produces sharply defined highlights.

On its own, placing a SpecularMaterial over a dark surface creates a glasslike effect. However, SpecularMaterial is more commonly used to add highlights to a DiffuseMaterial. For example, using a white SpecularMaterial on top of a DiffuseMaterial creates a plastic-like surface, while a darker SpecularMaterial and DiffuseMaterial produce a more metallic effect. Figure 27-16 shows two versions of a torus (a 3-D ring). The version on the left uses an ordinary DiffuseMaterial. The version on the right adds a SpecularMaterial on top. The highlights appear in several places because the scene includes two directional lights that are pointed in different directions.

To combine two surfaces, you need to wrap them in a MaterialGroup. Here's the markup that creates the highlights shown in Figure 27-16:

```
<GeometryModel3D>
  <GeometryModel3D.Material>
    <MaterialGroup>
      <DiffuseMaterial>
        <DiffuseMaterial.Brush>
          <SolidColorBrush Color="DarkBlue" />
        </DiffuseMaterial.Brush>
      </DiffuseMaterial>
      <SpecularMaterial SpecularPower="24">
        <SpecularMaterial.Brush>
          <SolidColorBrush Color="LightBlue" />
        </SpecularMaterial.Brush>
      </SpecularMaterial>
    </MaterialGroup>
  </GeometryModel3D.Material>

  <GeometryModel3D.Geometry>...</GeometryModel3D.Geometry>
<GeometryModel3D>
```

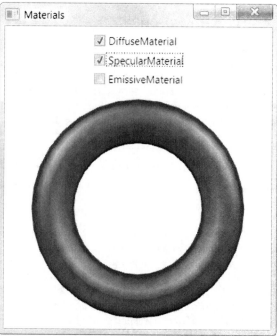

Figure 27-16. *Adding a SpecularMaterial*

■ **Note**   If you place a SpecularMaterial or an EmissiveMaterial on a white surface, you won't see anything at all. That's because the SpecularMaterial and EmissiveMaterial contribute their color additively, and the color white is already maxed out with the maximum possible red, green, and blue contributions. To see the full effect of SpecularMaterial or EmissiveMaterial, place them on a black surface (or use them over a black DiffuseMaterial).

The EmissiveMaterial is stranger still. It emits light, which means that a green EmissiveMaterial that's displayed over a dark surface shows up as a flat green silhouette, regardless of whether your scene includes any light sources.

Once again, you can get a more interesting effect by layering an EmissiveMaterial over a DiffuseMaterial. Because of the additive nature of EmissiveMaterial, the colors are blended. For example, if you place a red EmissiveMaterial over a blue DiffuseMaterial, your shape will acquire a purple tinge. The EmissiveMaterial will contribute the same amount of red over the entire surface of the shape, while the DiffuseMaterial will be shaded according to the light sources in your scene.

■ **Tip**   The light "radiated" from an EmissiveMaterial doesn't reach other objects. To create the effect of a glowing object that illuminates other nearby objects, you may want to place a light source (such as PointLight) near your EmissiveMaterial.

Texture Mapping

So far, you've used the SolidColorBrush to paint your objects. However, WPF allows you to paint a DiffuseMaterial object by using any brush. That means you can paint it with gradients (LinearGradientBrush and RadialGradientBrush), vector or bitmap images (ImageBrush), or the content from a 2-D element (VisualBrush).

There's one catch. When you use anything other than a SolidColorBrush, you need to supply additional information that tells WPF how to map the 2-D content of the brush onto the 3-D surface you're painting. You supply this information by using the MeshGeometry.TextureCoordinates collection. Depending on your choice, you can tile the brush content, extract just a part of it, and stretch, warp, and otherwise mangle it to fit curved and angular surfaces.

So how does the TextureCoordinates collection work? The basic idea is that each coordinate in your mesh needs a corresponding point in TextureCoordinates. The coordinate in the mesh is a point in 3-D space, while the point in the TextureCoordinates collection is a 2-D point because the content of a brush is always 2-D. The following sections show you how to use texture mapping to display image and video content on a 3-D shape.

Mapping the ImageBrush

The easiest way to understand how TextureCoordinates work is to use an ImageBrush that allows you to paint a bitmap. Here's an example that uses a misty scene of a tree at dawn:

```
<GeometryModel3D.Material>
  <DiffuseMaterial>
    <DiffuseMaterial.Brush>
      <ImageBrush ImageSource="Tree.jpg"></ImageBrush>
    </DiffuseMaterial.Brush>
  </DiffuseMaterial>
</GeometryModel3D.Material>
```

In this example, the ImageBrush is used to paint the content of the cube you created earlier. Depending on the TextureCoordinates you choose, you could stretch the image, wrapping it over the entire cube, or you could put a separate copy of it on each face (as we do in this example). Figure 27-17 shows the end result.

Figure 27-17. *A textured cube*

■ **Note** This example adds one extra detail. It uses a Slider at the bottom of the window that allows the user to rotate the cube, viewing it from all angles. This is made possible by a transform, as you'll learn in the next section.

Initially, the TextureCoordinates collection is empty and your image won't appear on the 3-D surface. To get started with the cube example, you may want to concentrate on mapping just a single face. In the current example, the cube is oriented so that its left side is facing the camera. Here is the mesh for the cube. The two triangles that make up the left (front-facing) side are in bold:

```
<MeshGeometry3D
    Positions="0,0,0    10,0,0    0,10,0    10,10,0
               0,0,0    0,0,10    0,10,0    0,10,10
               0,0,0    10,0,0    0,0,10    10,0,10
               10,0,0   10,10,10  10,0,10   10,10,0
               0,0,10   10,0,10   0,10,10   10,10,10
               0,10,0   0,10,10   10,10,0   10,10,10"
    TriangleIndices="
               0,2,1      1,2,3
               4,5,6      6,5,7
               8,9,10     9,11,10
               12,13,14   12,15,13
               16,17,18   19,18,17
               20,21,22   22,21,23"  />
```

Most of the mesh points aren't mapped at all. In fact, the only points that are mapped are these four, which define the face of the cube that's oriented toward the camera:

(0,0,0) (0,0,10) (0,10,0) (0,10,10)

Because this is actually a flat surface, mapping is relatively easy. You can choose a set of TextureCoordinates for this face by removing the dimension that has a value of 0 in all four points. (In this example, that's the X coordinate because the visible face is on the left side of the cube.)
Here's the TextureCoordinates that fill this requirement:

(0,0) (0,10) (10,0) (10,10)

The TextureCoordinates collection uses relative coordinates. To keep things simple, you may want to use 1 to indicate the maximum value. In this example, that transformation is easy:

(0,0) (0,1) (1,0) (1,1)

This set of TextureCoordinates essentially tells WPF to take the point (0, 0) at the bottom left of the rectangle that represents the brush content, and map that to the corresponding point (0, 0, 0) in 3-D space. Similarly, take the bottom-right corner (0, 1) and map that to (0, 0, 10), make the top-left corner (1, 0) map to (0, 10, 0), and make the top-right corner (1, 1) map to (0, 10, 10).
Here's the cube mesh that uses this texture mapping. All the other coordinates in the Positions collection are mapped to (0, 0), so that the texture is not applied to these areas:

```
<MeshGeometry3D
  Positions="0,0,0   10,0,0    0,10,0    10,10,0
             0,0,0    0,0,10    0,10,0    0,10,10
             0,0,0   10,0,0     0,0,10   10,0,10
            10,0,0   10,10,10  10,0,10   10,10,0
             0,0,10  10,0,10    0,10,10  10,10,10
             0,10,0   0,10,10  10,10,0   10,10,10"
  TriangleIndices="..."
  TextureCoordinates="
             0,0   0,0  0,0  0,0
             0,0   0,1  1,0  1,1
             0,0   0,0  0,0  0,0
             0,0   0,0  0,0  0,0
             0,0   0,0  0,0  0,0
             0,0   0,0  0,0  0,0"  />
```

This markup maps the texture to a single face on the cube. Although it is mapped successfully, the image is turned on its side. To get a top-up image, you need to rearrange your coordinates to use this order:

1,1 0,1 1,0 0,0

You can extend this process to map each face of the cube. Here's a set of TextureCoordinates that does exactly that and creates the multifaceted cube shown in Figure 27-17:

```
TextureCoordinates="0,0 0,1 1,0 1,1
                    1,1 0,1 1,0 0,0
                    0,0 1,0 0,1 1,1
                    0,0 1,0 0,1 1,1
                    1,1 0,1 1,0 0,0
                    1,1 0,1 1,0 0,0"
```

There are obviously many more effects you can create by tweaking these points. For example, you could stretch your texture around a more complex object such as a sphere. Because the meshes required for this sort of object typically include hundreds of points, you won't fill the TextureCoordinates collection by hand. Instead, you'll rely on a 3-D modeling program (or a math-crunching code routine that does it at runtime). If you want to apply different brushes to different portions of your mesh, you'll need to split your 3-D object into multiple meshes, each of which will have a different material that uses a different brush. You can then combine those meshes into one Model3DGroup for the lowest overhead.

Video and the VisualBrush

Ordinary images aren't the only kind of content you can map to a 3-D surface. You can also map content that changes, such as gradient brushes that have animated values. One common technique in WPF is to map a video to a 3-D surface. As the video plays, its content is displayed in real time on the 3-D surface.

Achieving this somewhat overused effect is surprisingly easy. In fact, you can map a video brush to the faces of a cube, with different orientations, using the exact same set of TextureCoordinates you used in the previous example to map the image. All you need to do is replace the ImageBrush with a more capable VisualBrush and use a MediaElement for your visual. With the help of an event trigger, you can even start a looping playback of your video without requiring any code.

The following markup creates a VisualBrush that performs playback and rotates the cube at the same time, displaying its different axes. (You'll learn more about how you can use animation and rotation to achieve this effect in the next section.)

```
<GeometryModel3D.Material>
  <DiffuseMaterial>
    <DiffuseMaterial.Brush>
      <VisualBrush>
        <VisualBrush.Visual>
          <MediaElement>
            <MediaElement.Triggers>
              <EventTrigger RoutedEvent="MediaElement.Loaded">
                <EventTrigger.Actions>
                  <BeginStoryboard>
                    <Storyboard >
                      <MediaTimeline Source="test.mpg" />
                      <DoubleAnimation Storyboard.TargetName="rotate"
                        Storyboard.TargetProperty="Angle"
                        To="360" Duration="0:0:5" RepeatBehavior="Forever" />
                    </Storyboard>
                  </BeginStoryboard>
                </EventTrigger.Actions>
              </EventTrigger>
```

```
                </MediaElement.Triggers>
              </MediaElement>
            </VisualBrush.Visual>
          </VisualBrush>
        </DiffuseMaterial.Brush>
      </DiffuseMaterial>
    </GeometryModel3D.Material>
```

Figure 27-18 shows a snapshot of this example in action.

Figure 27-18. *Displaying video on several 3-D surfaces*

Interactivity and Animations

To get the full value out of your 3-D scene, you need to make it *dynamic*. In other words, you need to have some way to modify part of the scene, either automatically or in response to user actions. After all, if you don't need a dynamic 3-D scene, you'd be better off creating a 3-D image in your favorite illustration program and then exporting it as an ordinary XAML vector drawing. (Some 3-D modeling tools, such as ZAM 3D, provide exactly this option.)

In the following sections, you'll learn how to manipulate 3-D objects by using transforms and how to add animation and move the camera. You'll also consider a separately released tool: a Trackball class that allows you to rotate a 3-D scene interactively. Finally, you'll learn how to perform hit testing in a 3-D scene and how to place interactive 2-D elements, such as buttons and text boxes, on a 3-D surface.

Transforms

As with 2-D content, the most powerful and flexible way to change an aspect of your 3-D scene is to use transforms. This is particularly the case with 3-D, as the classes you work with are relatively low-level. For example, if you want to scale a sphere, you need to construct the appropriate geometry and use the ScaleTransform3D to animate it. If you had a 3-D sphere primitive to work with, this might not be necessary because you might be able to animate a higher-level property such as Radius.

Transforms are obviously the answer to creating dynamic effects. However, before you can use transforms, you need to decide how you want to apply them. There are several possible approaches:

- Modify a transform that's applied to your Model3D. This allows you to change a single aspect of a single 3-D object. You can also use this technique on a Model3DGroup, as it derives from Model3D.

- Modify a transform that's applied to your ModelVisual3D. This allows you to change an entire scene.

- Modify a transform that's applied to your light. This allows you to change the lighting of your scene (for example, to create a "sunrise" effect).

- Modify a transform that's applied to your camera. This allows you to move the camera through your scene.

Transforms are so useful in 3-D drawing that it's a good idea to get into the habit of using a Transform3DGroup whenever you need a transform. That way, you can add additional transforms afterward without being forced to change your animation code. The ZAM 3D modeling program always adds a set of four placeholder transforms to every Model3DGroup, so that the object represented by that group can be manipulated in various ways:

```
<Model3DGroup.Transform>
  <Transform3DGroup>
    <TranslateTransform3D OffsetX="0" OffsetY="0" OffsetZ="0"/>
    <ScaleTransform3D ScaleX="1" ScaleY="1" ScaleZ="1"/>
    <RotateTransform3D>
      <RotateTransform3D.Rotation>
        <AxisAngleRotation3D Angle="0" Axis="0 1 0"/>
      </RotateTransform3D.Rotation>
    </RotateTransform3D>
    <TranslateTransform3D OffsetX="0" OffsetY="0" OffsetZ="0"/>
  </Transform3DGroup>
</Model3DGroup.Transform>
```

Notice that this set of transforms includes two TranslateTransform3D objects. That's because translating an object before it's been rotated produces a different result than translating it after it's been rotated, and you may want to use both effects.

Another handy technique is to name your transform objects in XAML by using the x:Name attribute. Even though the transform objects don't have a name property, this creates a private member variable you can use to access them more easily without being forced to dig through a deep hierarchy of objects. This is particularly important because complex 3-D scenes often have multiple layers of Model3DGroup objects, as described earlier. Walking down this element tree from the top-level ModelVisual3D is awkward and error-prone.

Rotations

To get a taste of the ways you might use transforms, consider the following markup. It applies a RotateTransform3D, which allows you to rotate a 3-D object around an axis you specify. In this case, the axis of rotation is set to line up exactly with the Y axis in your coordinate system:

```
<ModelVisual3D.Transform>
  <RotateTransform3D>
    <RotateTransform3D.Rotation>
      <AxisAngleRotation3D x:Name="rotate" Axis="0 1 0" />
    </RotateTransform3D.Rotation>
  </RotateTransform3D>
</ModelVisual3D.Transform>
```

Using this named rotation, you can create a data-bound Slider that allows the user to spin the cube around its axis:

```
<Slider Grid.Row="1"  Minimum="0" Maximum="360" Orientation="Horizontal"
  Value="{Binding ElementName=rotate, Path=Angle}" ></Slider>
```

Just as easily, you can use this rotation in an animation. Here's an animation that spins a torus (a 3-D ring) simultaneously along two axes. It all starts when a button is clicked:

```
<Button>
  <Button.Content>Rotate Torus</Button.Content>
    <Button.Triggers>
      <EventTrigger RoutedEvent="Button.Click">
        <BeginStoryboard>
          <Storyboard RepeatBehavior="Forever">
            <DoubleAnimation Storyboard.TargetName="ring"
              Storyboard.TargetProperty="rotate1" To="360" Duration="0:0:2.5"/>
            <DoubleAnimation Storyboard.TargetName="ring"
              Storyboard.TargetProperty="rotate2" To="360" Duration="0:0:2.5"/>
          </Storyboard>
        </BeginStoryboard>
      </EventTrigger>
    </Button.Triggers>
</Button>
```

Figure 27-19 shows four snapshots of the torus in various stages of rotation.

Figure 27-19. *A rotating 3-D shape*

A Flyover

A common effect in 3-D scenes is to move the camera around the object. This task is conceptually quite easy in WPF. You simply need a TranslateTransform to move the camera. However, two considerations apply:

- Usually, you'll want to move the camera along a route rather than in a straight line from a start point to an end point. There are two ways to solve this challenge—you can use a path-based animation to follow a geometrically defined route, or you can use a key-frame animation that defines several smaller segments.

- As the camera moves, it also needs to adjust the direction in which it's looking. You'll also need to animate the LookDirection property to keep focused on the object.

The following markup shows an animation that flies through the center of a torus, spins around its outer edge, and eventually drifts back to the starting point. To see this animation in action, check out the samples for this chapter:

```
<StackPanel Orientation="Horizontal">
  <Button>
    <Button.Content>Begin Fly-Through</Button.Content>
    <Button.Triggers>
      <EventTrigger RoutedEvent="Button.Click">
        <BeginStoryboard>
          <Storyboard>
            <Point3DAnimationUsingKeyFrames
              Storyboard.TargetName="camera"
              Storyboard.TargetProperty="Position">
              <LinearPoint3DKeyFrame Value="0,0.2,-1" KeyTime="0:0:10"/>
              <LinearPoint3DKeyFrame Value="-0.5,0.2,-1" KeyTime="0:0:15"/>
              <LinearPoint3DKeyFrame Value="-0.5,0.5,0" KeyTime="0:0:20"/>
              <LinearPoint3DKeyFrame Value="0,0,2" KeyTime="0:0:23"/>
            </Point3DAnimationUsingKeyFrames>
```

```
          <Vector3DAnimationUsingKeyFrames
            Storyboard.TargetName="camera"
            Storyboard.TargetProperty="LookDirection">
            <LinearVector3DKeyFrame Value="-1,-1,-3" KeyTime="0:0:4"/>
            <LinearVector3DKeyFrame Value="-1,-1,3" KeyTime="0:0:10"/>
            <LinearVector3DKeyFrame Value="1,0,3" KeyTime="0:0:14"/>
            <LinearVector3DKeyFrame Value="0,0,-1" KeyTime="0:0:22"/>
          </Vector3DAnimationUsingKeyFrames>
        </Storyboard>
      </BeginStoryboard>
    </EventTrigger>
  </Button.Triggers>
 </Button>
</StackPanel>
```

For a bit more fun, you can start both animations (the rotation shown earlier and the flyover effect shown here), which will cause the camera to pass through the edge of the ring as it rotates. You can also animate the UpDirection property of the camera to wiggle it as it moves:

```
<Vector3DAnimation
   Storyboard.TargetName="camera" Storyboard.TargetProperty="UpDirection"
   From="0,0,-1" To="0,0.1,-1" Duration="0:0:0.5" AutoReverse="True"
   RepeatBehavior="Forever" />
```

3-D PERFORMANCE

Rendering a 3-D scene requires much more work than rendering a 2-D scene. When you animate a 3-D scene, WPF attempts to refresh the parts that have changed 60 times per second. Depending on the complexity of your scene, this can easily use up the memory resources on your video card, which will cause the frame rate to fall and the animation to become choppy.

There are a few basic techniques you can use to get better 3-D performance. Here are some strategies for tweaking the viewport to reduce the 3-D rendering overhead:

- If you don't need to crop content that extends beyond the bounds of your viewport, set Viewport3D.ClipToBounds to False.

- If you don't need to provide hit testing in your 3-D scene, set Viewport3D.IsHitTestVisible to False.

- If you don't mind lower quality—jagged edges on 3-D shapes—set the attached property RenderOptions.EdgeMode to Aliased on the Viewport3D.

- If your Viewport3D is larger than it needs to be, resize it to be smaller.

It's also important to ensure that your 3-D scene is as lightweight as possible. Here are a few critical tips for creating the most efficient meshes and models:

- Whenever possible, create a single complex mesh rather than several smaller meshes.

- If you need to use different materials for the same mesh, define the MeshGeometry object once (as a resource) and then reuse it to create multiple GeometryModel3D objects.

- Whenever possible, wrap a group of GeometryModel3D objects in a Model3DGroup, and place that group in a single ModelVisual3D object. Don't create a separate ModelVisual3D object for each GeometryModel3D.

- Don't define a back material (using GeometryModel3D.BackMaterial) unless the user will actually see the back of the object. Similarly, when defining meshes, consider leaving out triangles that won't be visible (for example, the bottom surface of a cube).

- Prefer solid brushes, gradient brushes, and the ImageBrush over the DrawingBrush and VisualBrush, both of which have more overhead. When using the DrawingBrush and VisualBrush to paint static content, you can cache the brush content to improve performance. To do so, use the attached property RenderOptions.CachingHint on the brush and set it to Cache.

If you keep these guidelines in mind, you'll be well on the way to ensuring the best possible 3-D drawing performance, and the highest possible frame rate for 3-D animation.

The Trackball

One of the most commonly requested behaviors in a 3-D scene is the ability to rotate an object by using the mouse. One of the most common implementations is called a *virtual trackball*, and it's found in many 3-D graphics and 3-D design programs. Although WPF doesn't include a native implementation of a virtual trackball, the WPF 3-D team has released a free sample class that performs this function. This virtual trackball is a robust, extremely popular piece of code that finds its way into most of the 3-D demo applications that are provided by the WPF team.

The basic principle of the virtual trackball is that the user clicks somewhere on the 3-D object and drags it around an imaginary center axis. The amount of rotation depends on the distance the mouse is dragged. For example, if you click in the middle of the right side of a Viewport3D and drag the mouse to the left, the 3-D scene will appear to rotate around an imaginary vertical line. If you move the mouse all the way to the left side, the 3-D scene will be flipped 180 degrees to expose its back, as shown in Figure 27-20.

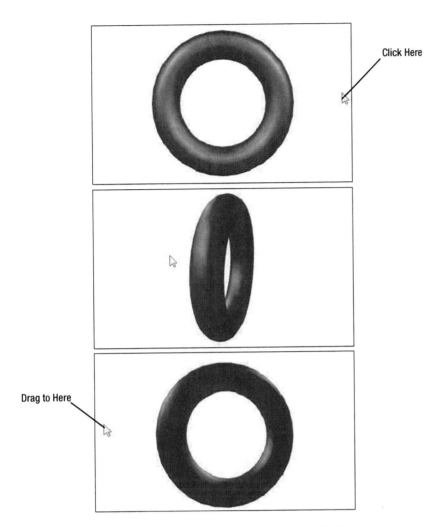

Figure 27-20. Changing your viewpoint with the virtual trackball

Although the virtual trackball appears to rotate the 3-D scene, it actually works by moving the camera. The camera always remains equally distant from the center point of the 3-D scene—essentially, the camera is moved along the contour of a big sphere that contains the entire scene. You can download the virtual trackball code with the 3-D tools projects described earlier at http://3dtools.codeplex.com.

▨ **Note** Because the virtual trackball moves the camera, you shouldn't use it in conjunction with your own camera-moving animation. However, you can use it in conjunction with an animated 3-D scene (for example, a 3-D scene that contains a rotating torus like the one described earlier).

Using the virtual trackball is absurdly easy. All you need to do is wrap your Viewport3D in the TrackballDecorator class. The TrackballDecorator class is included with the 3-D tools project, so you'll need to begin by adding an XML alias for the namespace:

```
<Window xmlns:tools="clr-namespace:_3DTools;assembly=3DTools" ...>
```

Then you can easily add the TrackballDecorator to your markup:

```
<tools:TrackballDecorator>
  <Viewport3D>
    ...
  </Viewport3D>
</tools:TrackballDecorator>
```

After you take this step, the virtual trackball functionality is automatically available—just click with the mouse and drag.

Hit Testing

Sooner or later, you'll want to create an interactive 3-D scene—one where the user can click 3-D shapes to perform different actions. The first step to implementing this design is *hit testing*, the process by which you intercept a mouse click and determine what region was clicked. Hit testing is easy in the 2-D world, but it's not quite as straightforward in a Viewport3D.

Fortunately, WPF provides sophisticated 3-D hit-testing support. You have three options for performing hit-testing in a 3-D scene:

- You can handle the mouse events of the viewport (such as MouseUp or MouseDown). Then you can call the VisualTreeHelper.HitTest() method to determine what object was hit. In the first version of WPF (released with .NET 3.0), this was the only possible approach.

- You can create your own 3-D control by deriving a custom class from the abstract UIElement3D class. This approach works, but it requires a lot of work. You need to implement all the UIElement-type plumbing on your own.

- You can replace one of your ModelVisual3D objects with a ModelUIElement3D object. The ModelUIElement3D class is derived from UIElement3D. It fuses the all-purpose 3-D model you've used so far with the interactive capabilities of a WPF element, including mouse handling.

To understand how 3-D hit testing works, it helps to consider a simple example. In the following section, you'll add hit testing to the familiar torus.

Hit Testing in the Viewport

To use the first approach to hit testing, you need to attach an event handler to one of the mouse events of the Viewport3D, such as MouseDown:

```
<Viewport3D MouseDown="viewport_MouseDown">
```

The MouseDown event handler uses hit-testing code at its simplest. It takes the current position of the mouse and returns a reference for the topmost ModelVisual3D that the point intercepts (if any):

```
Private Sub viewport_MouseDown(ByVal sender As Object, _
  ByVal e As MouseButtonEventArgs)
    Dim viewport As Viewport3D = CType(sender, Viewport3D)
    Dim location As Point = e.GetPosition(viewport)
    Dim hitResult As HitTestResult = VisualTreeHelper.HitTest( _
      viewport, location)

    If (hitResult IsNot Nothing) AndAlso _
      (hitResult.VisualHit Is ringVisual) Then
        ' The click hit the ring.
    End If
End Sub
```

Although this code works in simple examples, it's usually not sufficient. As you learned earlier, it's almost always better to combine multiple objects in the same ModelVisual3D. In many cases, all the objects in your entire scene will be placed in the same ModelVisual3D, so the hit doesn't provide enough information.

Fortunately, if the click intercepts a mesh, you can cast the HitTestResult to the more capable RayMeshGeometry3DHitTestResult object. You can find out which ModelVisual3D was hit by using the RayMeshGeometry3DHitTestResult:

```
Dim meshHitResult As RayMeshGeometry3DHitTestResult
meshHitResult = TryCast(hitResult, RayMeshGeometry3DHitTestResult)

If (meshHitResult IsNot Nothing) AndAlso _
  (meshHitResult.ModelHit Is ringModel) Then
    ' Hit the ring.
End If
```

Or for even more fine-grained hit testing, you can use the MeshHit property to determine which specific mesh was hit. In the following example, the code determines whether the mesh representing the torus was hit. If it has been hit, the code creates and starts a new animation that rotates the torus. Here's the trick—the rotation axis is set so that it runs through the center of the torus, perpendicular to an imaginary line that connects the center of the torus to the location where the mouse was clicked. The effect makes it appear that the torus has been "hit" and is rebounding away from the click by twisting slightly away from the foreground and in the opposite direction.

Here's the code that implements that effect:

```
Private Sub viewport_MouseDown(ByVal sender As Object, _
  ByVal e As MouseButtonEventArgs)
    Dim viewport As Viewport3D = CType(sender, Viewport3D)
    Dim location As Point = e.GetPosition(viewport)
    Dim hitResult As HitTestResult = VisualTreeHelper.HitTest( _
      viewport, location)
    Dim meshHitResult As RayMeshGeometry3DHitTestResult
    meshHitResult = TryCast(hitResult, RayMeshGeometry3DHitTestResult)

    If (meshHitResult IsNot Nothing) _
      AndAlso (meshHitResult.MeshHit Is ringMesh) Then
        ' Set the axis of rotation.
        axisRotation.Axis = New Vector3D( _
          (meshHitResult.PointHit.Y * -1), meshHitResult.PointHit.X, 0)
```

```
' Start the animation.
Dim animation As New DoubleAnimation()
animation.To = 40
animation.DecelerationRatio = 1
animation.Duration = TimeSpan.FromSeconds(0.15)
animation.AutoReverse = true
axisRotation.BeginAnimation(AxisAngleRotation3D.AngleProperty, _
    animation)
        End If
    End Sub
End Sub
```

This approach to hit testing works perfectly well. However, if you have a scene with a large number of 3-D objects and the interaction you require with these objects is straightforward (for example, you have a dozen buttons), this approach to hit testing makes for more work than necessary. In this situation, you're better off using the ModelUIElement3D class, which is introduced in the next section.

The ModelUIElement3D

The ModelUIElement3D is a type of Visual3D. Like all the Visual3D objects, it can be placed in a Viewport3D container.

Figure 27-21 shows the inheritance hierarchy for all the classes that derive from Visual3D. The three key classes that derive from Visual3D are ModelVisual3D (which you've used up to this point), UIElement3D (which defines the 3-D equivalent of the WPF element), and Viewport2DVisual3D (which allows you to place 2-D content in a 3-D scene, as described in the section "2-D Elements on 3-D Surfaces" later in this chapter).

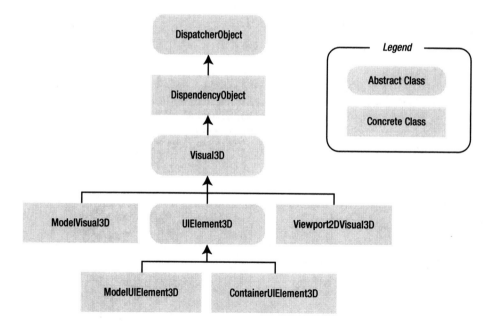

Figure 27-21. *The 3-D visual classes*

The UIElement3D class plays an analogous role to the UIElement class in the 2-D world, by adding support for mouse, keyboard, and stylus events, along with focus tracking. However, UIElement3D doesn't support any sort of layout system.

Although you can create a custom 3-D element by deriving from UIElement3D, it's far easier to use the ready-made classes that derive from UIElement3D: ModelUIElement3D and ContainerUIElement3D.

Using a ModelUIElement3D is not much different from using the ModelVisual3D class with which you're already familiar. The ModelUIElement3D class supports transforms (through the Transform property) and allows you to define its shape with a GeometryModel3D object (by setting the Model property, not the Content property as you do with ModelVisual3D).

Hit Testing with the ModelUIElement3D

Right now, the torus consists of a single ModelVisual3D, which contains a Model3DGroup. This group includes the torus geometry and the light sources that illuminate it. To change the torus example so that it uses the ModelUIElement3D, you simply need to replace the ModelVisual3D that represents the torus with a ModelUIElement3D:

```
<Viewport3D x:Name="viewport">
  <Viewport3D.Camera>...</Viewport3D.Camera>

  <ModelUIElement3D>
    <ModelUIElement3D.Model>
      <Model3DGroup>...<Model3DGroup>
    </ModelUIElement3D.Model>
  </ModelUIElement3D>

</Viewport3D>
```

Now you can perform hit testing directly with the ModelUIElement3D:

```
<ModelUIElement3D MouseDown="ringVisual_MouseDown">
```

The difference between this example and the previous one is that now the MouseDown event will fire only when the ring is clicked (rather than every time a point inside the viewport is clicked). However, the event-handling code still needs a bit of tweaking to get the result you want in this example.

The MouseDown event provides a standard MouseButtonEventArgs object to the event handler. This object provides the standard mouse event details, such as the exact time the event occurred, the state of the mouse buttons, and a GetPosition() method that allows you to determine the clicked coordinates relative to any element that implements IInputElement (such as the Viewport3D or the MouseUIElement3D). In many cases, these 2-D coordinates are exactly what you need. (For example, they are a requirement if you're using 2-D content on a 3-D surface, as described in the next section. In this case, anytime you move, resize, or create elements, you're positioning them in 2-D space, which is then mapped to a 3-D surface based on a preexisting set of texture coordinates.)

However, in the current example it's important to get the 3-D coordinates on the torus mesh so that the appropriate animation can be created. That means you still need to use the VisualTreeHelper.HitTest() method, as shown here:

```
Private Sub ringVisual_MouseDown(ByVal sender As Object, _
  ByVal e As MouseButtonEventArgs)
    ' Get the 2-D coordinates relative to the viewport.
    Dim location As Point = e.GetPosition(viewport)
```

```
' Get the 3-D coordinates relative to the mesh.
Dim meshHitResult As RayMeshGeometry3DHitTestResult
meshHitResult = CType(VisualTreeHelper.HitTest(viewport, location), _
    RayMeshGeometry3DHitTestResult)

' Create the animation.
axisRotation.Axis = New Vector3D( _
    -meshHitResult.PointHit.Y, meshHitResult.PointHit.X, 0)
Dim animation As New DoubleAnimation()
animation.To = 40
animation.DecelerationRatio = 1
animation.Duration = TimeSpan.FromSeconds(0.15)
animation.AutoReverse = True
axisRotation.BeginAnimation(AxisAngleRotation3D.AngleProperty, animation)
End Sub
```

Using this sort of realistic 3-D behavior, you could create a true 3-D "control," such as a button that deforms when you click it.

If you simply want to react to clicks on a 3-D object and you don't need to perform calculations that involve the mesh, you won't need to use the VisualTreeHelper at all. The fact that the MouseDown event fired tells you that the torus was clicked.

▓ **Tip** In most cases, the ModelUIElement3D provides a simpler approach to hit testing than using the mouse events of the viewport. If you simply want to detect when a given shape is clicked (for example, you have a 3-D shape that represents a button and triggers an action), the ModelUIElement3D class is perfect. On the other hand, if you want to perform more-complex calculations with the clicked coordinates or examine *all* the shapes that exist at a clicked location (not just the topmost one), you'll need more-sophisticated hit-testing code, and you'll probably want to respond to the mouse events of the viewport.

The ContainerUIElement3D

The ModelUIElement3D class is intended to represent a single control-like object. If you want to place more than one ModelUIElement3D in a 3-D scene and allow the user to interact with them independently, you need to create ModelUIElement3D objects and wrap them in a single ContainerUIElement3D. You can then add that ContainerUIElement3D to the viewport.

The ContainerUIElement3D has one other advantage. It supports any combination of objects that derive from Visual3D. That means it can hold ordinary ModelVisual3D objects, interactive ModelUIElement3D objects, and Viewport2DVisual3D objects, which represent 2-D elements that have been placed in 3-D space. You'll learn more about this trick in the next section.

2-D Elements on 3-D Surfaces

As you learned earlier in this chapter, you can use texture mapping to place 2-D brush content on a 3-D surface. You can use this to place images or videos in a 3-D scene. Using a VisualBrush, you can even take the visual appearance of an ordinary WPF element (such as a button), and place it in your 3-D scene.

However, the VisualBrush is inherently limited. As you already know, the VisualBrush can copy the visual appearance of an element, but it doesn't actually duplicate the element. If you use the VisualBrush to place the visual for a button in a 3-D scene, you'll end up with a 3-D picture of a button. In other words, you won't be able to click it.

The solution to this problem is the Viewport2DVisual3D class. The Viewport2DVisual3D class wraps another element and maps it to a 3-D surface by using texture mapping. You can place the Viewport2DVisual3D directly in a Viewport3D, alongside other Visual3D objects (such as ModelVisual3D objects and ModelUIElement3D objects). However, the element inside the Viewport2DVisual3D retains its interactivity and has all the WPF features you're accustomed to, including layout, styling, templates, mouse events, drag-and-drop, and so on.

Figure 27-22 shows an example. A StackPanel containing a TextBlock, Button, and TextBox is placed on one of the faces of a 3-D cube. The user is in the process of typing text into the TextBox, and you can see the I-beam cursor that shows the insertion point.

Figure 27-22. *Interactive WPF elements in 3-D*

In your Viewport3D, you can place all the usual ModelVisual3D objects. In the example shown in Figure 27-22, there's a ModelVisual3D for the cube. To place your 2-D element content in the scene, you use a Viewport2DVisual3D object instead. The Viewport2DVisual3D class provides the properties listed in Table 27-5.

Table 27-5. *Properties of the InteractiveVisual3D*

Name	Description
Geometry	The mesh that defines the 3-D surface.
Visual	The 2-D element that will be placed on the 3-D surface. You can use only a single element, but it's perfectly legitimate to use a container panel to wrap multiple elements together. The example in Figure 27-22 uses a Border that contains a StackPanel with three child elements.
Material	The material that will be used to render the 2-D content. Usually, you'll use a DiffuseMaterial. You must set the attached Viewport2DVisual3D.IsVisualHostMaterial on the DiffuseMaterial to True so that the material is able to show element content.
Transform	A Transform3D or Transform3DGroup that determines how your mesh should be altered (rotated, scaled, skewed, and so on).

Using the 2-D on 3-D technique is relatively straightforward, provided you're already familiar with texture mapping (as described in the "Texture Mapping" section earlier in this chapter). Here's the markup that creates the WPF elements shown in Figure 27-22:

```
<Viewport2DVisual3D>
  <Viewport2DVisual3D.Geometry>
    <MeshGeometry3D
      Positions="0,0,0 0,0,10 0,10,0 0,10,10"
      TriangleIndices="0,1,2 2,1,3"
      TextureCoordinates="0,1 1,1 0,0 1,0"
    />
  </Viewport2DVisual3D.Geometry>

  <Viewport2DVisual3D.Material>
    <DiffuseMaterial Viewport2DVisual3D.IsVisualHostMaterial="True" />
  </Viewport2DVisual3D.Material>

  <Viewport2DVisual3D.Visual>
    <Border BorderBrush="Yellow" BorderThickness="1">
      <StackPanel Margin="10">
        <TextBlock Margin="3">This is 2D content on a 3D surface.</TextBlock>
        <Button Margin="3">Click Me</Button>
        <TextBox Margin="3">[Enter Text Here]</TextBox>
      </StackPanel>
    </Border>
  </Viewport2DVisual3D.Visual>

  <Viewport2DVisual3D.Transform>
    <RotateTransform3D>
      <RotateTransform3D.Rotation>
        <AxisAngleRotation3D
          Angle="{Binding ElementName=sliderRotate, Path=Value}"
          Axis="0 1 0" />
      </RotateTransform3D.Rotation>
    </RotateTransform3D>
  </Viewport2DVisual3D.Transform>
</Viewport2DVisual3D>
```

In this example, the Viewport2DVisual3D.Geometry property supplies a mesh that mirrors a single face of the cube. The TextureCoordinates of the mesh define how the 2-D content (the Border that wraps the StackPanel) should be mapped to the 3-D surface (the cube face). The texture mapping that you use with the Viewport2DVisual3D works in the same way as the texture mapping you used earlier with the ImageBrush and VisualBrush.

■ **Note** When defining the TextureCoordinates, it's important to make sure you have the element facing the camera. WPF does not render anything for the back surface of Viewport2DVisual3D, so if you flip it around and stare at its back, the element will disappear. (If this isn't the result you want, you can use another Viewport2DVisual3D to create content for the back side.)

This example also uses a RotateTransform3D to allow the user to turn the cube around by using a slider underneath the Viewport3D. The ModelVisual3D that represents the cube includes the same RotateTransform3D, so the cube and 2-D element content move together.

Currently, this example doesn't use any event handling in the Viewport2DVisual3D content. However, it's easy enough to add an event handler:

```
<Button Margin="3" Click="cmd_Click">Click Me</Button>
```

WPF handles mouse events in a clever way. It uses texture mapping to translate the virtual 3-D coordinates (where the mouse is) to ordinary, non-texture-mapped 2-D coordinates. From the element's point of view, the mouse events are exactly the same in the 3-D world as they are in the 2-D world. This is part of the magic that holds the solution together.

The Last Word

The most impressive part of WPF's 3-D features is their ease of use. Although it's possible to create complex code that creates and modifies 3-D meshes by using intense math, it's just as possible to export 3-D models from a design tool and manipulate them by using straightforward transformations. And key features such as a virtual trackball implementation and 2-D element interactivity are provided by high-level classes that take no expertise at all.

This chapter provided a tour of the core pillars of WPF's 3-D support and introduced some of the indispensable tools that have emerged since WPF 1.0 was released. However, 3-D programming is a detailed topic, and it's certainly possible to delve much more deeply into 3-D theory. If you want to brush up on the math that underlies 3-D development, you may want to consider the old but classic book *3D Math Primer for Graphics and Game Development* by Fletcher Dunn (Wordware Publishing, 2002).

The easiest way to continue your exploration into the world of 3-D is to head to the Web and check out the resources and sample code provided by the WPF team and other independent developers. Here's a short list of useful links, including some that have already been referenced in this chapter:

- http://3dtools.codeplex.com provides an essential library of tools for developers doing 3-D work in WPF, including the virtual trackball and the ScreenSpaceLines3D class discussed in this chapter.

- http://tinyurl.com/bumqt2y provides a list of WPF tools, including 3-D design programs that use XAML natively and export scripts that can transform other 3-D formats (including Maya, LightWave, Blender, and Autodesk 3ds Max) to XAML.

- http://tinyurl.com/np295l includes classes that wrap the meshes required for three common 3-D primitives: a cone, a sphere, and a cylinder.

- http://tinyurl.com/97kwul2 provides a SandBox3D project that allows you to load simple 3-D meshes and manipulate them with transforms.

Documents and Printing

Documents

Using the WPF skills you've picked up so far, you can craft windows and pages that include a wide variety of elements. Displaying fixed text is easy—you simply need to add the TextBlock and Label elements to the mix.

However, using the Label and TextBlock elements isn't a good solution if you need to display large volumes of text (such as a newspaper article or detailed instructions for online help). Large amounts of text are particularly problematic if you want your text to fit in a resizable window in the best possible way. For example, if you pile a large swath of text into a TextBlock and stretch it to fit a wide window, you'll end up with long lines that are difficult to read. Similarly, if you combine text and pictures by using the ordinary TextBlock and Image elements, you'll find that they no longer line up correctly when the window changes size.

To deal with these issues, WPF includes a set of higher-level features that work with *documents*. These features allow you to display large amounts of content in a way that makes them easy to read regardless of the size of the containing window. For example, WPF can hyphenate words (if you have only a narrow space available) or place your text into multiple columns (if you have a wide space to work with).

In this chapter, you'll learn how to use *flow documents* to display content. You'll also learn how to let users edit flow document content with the RichTextBox control. After you've mastered flow documents, you'll take a quick look at XPS, Microsoft's technology for creating print-ready documents. Finally, you'll consider WPF's annotation feature, which allows users to add comments and other markers to documents and store them permanently.

Understanding Documents

WPF separates documents into two broad categories:

> *Fixed documents*: These are typeset, print-ready documents. The positioning of all content is fixed (for example, the way text is wrapped over multiple lines and hyphenated can't change). Although you might choose to read a fixed document on a computer monitor, fixed documents are intended for print output. Conceptually, they're equivalent to Adobe PDF files. WPF includes a single type of fixed document, which uses Microsoft's XPS (XML Paper Specification) standard.

> *Flow documents*: These documents are designed for viewing on a computer. Like fixed documents, flow documents support rich layout. However, WPF can optimize a flow document based on the way you want to view it. WPF can lay out the content dynamically based on details such as the size of the view window, the display resolution, and so on. Conceptually, flow documents are used for many of the same reasons as HTML documents, but they have more-advanced text-layout features.

Although flow documents are obviously more important from an application-building point of view, fixed documents are important for documents that need to be printed without alteration (such as forms and publications).

WPF provides support for both types of documents by using different containers. The DocumentViewer allows you to show fixed documents in a WPF window. The FlowDocumentReader, FlowDocumentPageViewer, and FlowDocumentScrollViewer give you different ways to look at flow documents. All of these containers are read-only. However, WPF includes APIs for creating fixed documents programmatically, and you can use the RichTextBox to allow the user to edit flow content.

In this chapter, you'll spend most of your time exploring flow documents and the ways they can be used in a WPF application. Toward the end of this chapter, you'll take a look at fixed documents, which are more straightforward.

Flow Documents

In a flow document, the content adapts itself to fit the container. Flow content is ideal for onscreen viewing. In fact, it avoids many of the pitfalls of HTML.

Ordinary HTML content uses flow layout to fill the browser window. (This is the same way WPF organizes elements if you use a WrapPanel.) Although this approach is very flexible, it gives a good result for only a small range of window sizes. If you maximize a window on a high-resolution monitor (or, even worse, a wide-screen display), you'll end up with long lines that are extremely difficult to read. Figure 28-1 shows this problem with a portion of a web page from Wikipedia.

Figure 28-1. *Long lines in flow content*

Many websites avoid this problem by using some sort of fixed layout that forces content to fit a narrow column. (In WPF, you can create this sort of design by placing your content in a column inside a Grid container and setting the ColumnDefinition.MaxWidth property.) This prevents the readability problem, but it results in a fair bit of wasted screen space in large windows. Figure 28-2 shows this problem on a portion of a page from the New York Times website.

Figure 28-2. *Wasted space in flow content*

Flow document content in WPF improves upon these current-day approaches by incorporating better pagination, multicolumn display, sophisticated hyphenation and text flow algorithms, and user-adjustable viewing preferences. The end result is that WPF gives the user a much better experience when reading large amounts of content.

Understanding Flow Elements

You build a WPF flow document by using a combination of flow elements. Flow elements have an important difference from the elements you've seen so far. They don't inherit from the familiar UIElement and FrameworkElement classes. Instead, they form an entirely separate branch of classes that derive from ContentElement and FrameworkContentElement.

The content element classes are simpler than the noncontent element classes that you've seen throughout this book. However, content elements support a similar set of basic events, including events for keyboard and mouse handling, drag-and-drop operations, tooltip display, and initialization. The key difference between content and noncontent elements is that content elements do not handle their own rendering. Instead, they require a container that can render all its content elements. This deferred rendering allows the container to introduce various optimizations. For example, it allows the container to determine the best way to wrap lines of text in a paragraph, even though a paragraph is a single element.

Note   Content elements can accept focus, but ordinarily they don't (because the Focusable property is set to False by default). You can make a content element focusable by setting Focusable to True on individual elements, by using an element type style that changes a whole group of elements, or by deriving your own custom element that sets Focusable to True. The Hyperlink is an example of a content element that sets its Focusable property to True.

Figure 28-3 shows the inheritance hierarchy of content elements.

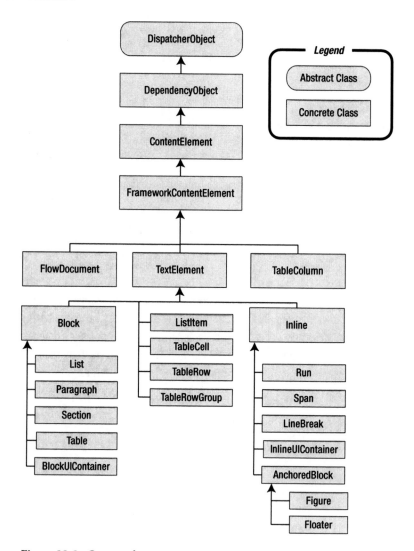

Figure 28-3. *Content elements*

There are two key branches of content elements:Block elements: These elements can be used to group other content elements. For example, a Paragraph is a block element. It can hold text that's formatted in various ways. Each section of separately formatted text is a distinct element in the paragraph.*Inline elements*: These elements are nested inside a block element (or another inline element). For example, the Run element wraps a bit of text, which can then be nested in a Paragraph element.

The content model allows multiple layers of nesting. For example, you can place a Bold element inside an Underline element to create text that's both bold and underlined. Similarly, you might create a Section element that wraps together multiple Paragraph elements, each of which contains a variety of inline elements with the actual text content. All of these elements are defined in the System.Windows.Documents namespace.

Tip If you're familiar with HTML, this model will seem more than a little familiar. WPF adopts many of the same conventions (such as the distinction between block and inline elements). If you're an HTML pro, you might consider using the surprisingly capable HTML-to-XAML translator at `http://tinyurl.com/mg9f6y`. With the help of this translator, which is implemented in C# code, you can use an HTML page as the starting point for a flow document.

Formatting Content Elements

Although the content elements don't share the same class hierarchy as noncontent elements, they feature many of the same formatting properties as ordinary elements. Table 28-1 lists some properties that you'll recognize from your work with noncontent elements.

Table 28-1. *Basic Formatting Properties for Content Elements*

Name	Description
Foreground and Background	Accept brushes that will be used to paint the foreground text and the background surface. You can also set the Background property on the FlowDocument object that contains all your markup.
FontFamily, FontSize, FontStretch, FontStyle, and FontWeight	Allow you to configure the font that's used to display text. You can also set these properties on the FlowDocument object that contains all your markup.
ToolTip	Allows you to set a tooltip that will appear when the user hovers over this element. You can use a string of text, or a full ToolTip object, as described in Chapter 6.
Style	Identifies the style that should be used to set the properties of an element automatically.

Block elements also add the properties shown in Table 28-2.

Table 28-2. *Additional Formatting Properties for Block Elements*

Name	Description
BorderBrush and BorderThickness	Allow you to create a border that will be shown around the edge of an element.
Margin	Sets the spacing between the current element and its container (or any adjacent elements). When the margin is not set, flow containers add a default space of about 18 units between block elements and the edges of the container. If you don't want this spacing, you can explicitly set smaller margins. However, to reduce the space between two paragraphs, you'll need to shrink both the bottom margin of the first paragraph and the top margin of the second paragraph. If you want all paragraphs to start out with reduced margins, consider using an element-type style rule that acts on all paragraphs.
Padding	Sets the spacing between its edges and any nested elements inside. The default padding is 0.

(continued)

Table 28-2. (*continued*)

Name	Description
TextAlignment	Sets the horizontal alignment of nested text content (which can be Left, Right, Center, or Justify). Ordinarily, content is justified.
LineHeight	Sets the spacing between lines in the nested text content. Line height is specified as a number of device-independent pixels. If you don't supply this value, the text is single-spaced based on the characteristics of the font you're using.
LineStackingStrategy	Determines how lines are spaced if they contain mixed font sizes. The default option, MaxHeight, makes the line as tall as the largest text inside. The alternative, BlockLineHeight, uses the height configured in the LineHeight property for all lines, which means the text is spaced based on the font of the paragraph. If this font is smaller than the largest text in the paragraph, the text in some lines may overlap. If it's equal or larger, you'll get a consistent spacing that leaves extra whitespace between some lines.

Along with the properties described in these two tables, there are some additional details that you can tweak in specific elements. Some of these pertain to pagination and multicolumn displays and are discussed in the "Creating Pages and Columns" section later in this chapter. A few other properties of interest include the following:

- TextDecorations, which is provided by the Paragraph and all Inline-derived elements. It takes a value of strikethrough, overline, or (most commonly) underline. You can combine these values to draw multiple lines on a block of text, although it's not common.

- Typography, which is provided by the top-level FlowDocument element, as well as TextBlock and all TextElement-derived types. It provides a Typography object that you can use to alter a variety of details about the way text is rendered (most of which apply to only OpenType fonts).

Constructing a Simple Flow Document

Now that you've taken a look at the content element model, you're ready to assemble some content elements into a simple flow document.

You create a flow document by using the FlowDocument class. Visual Studio allows you to create a new flow document as a separate file, or you can define it inside an existing window by using one of the supported containers. For now, start building a simple flow document by using the FlowDocumentScrollViewer as a container. Here's how your markup should start:

```
<Window x:Class="FlowContent"
    xmlns="http://schemas.microsoft.com/winfx/2006/xaml/presentation"
    xmlns:x="http://schemas.microsoft.com/winfx/2006/xaml"
    Title="FlowContent" Height="381" Width="525" >

  <FlowDocumentScrollViewer>
    <FlowDocument>
      . . .
    </FlowDocument>
  </FlowDocumentScrollViewer>

</Window>
```

You might assume that you could begin typing your text inside the FlowDocument element, but you can't. Instead, the top level of a flow document must use a block-level element. Here's an example with a Paragraph:

```
<FlowDocumentScrollViewer>
  <FlowDocument>
    <Paragraph>Hello, world of documents.</Paragraph>
  </FlowDocument>
</FlowDocumentScrollViewer>
```

There's no limit on the number of top-level elements you can use. So this example with two paragraphs is also acceptable:

```
<FlowDocumentScrollViewer>
  <FlowDocument>
    <Paragraph>Hello, world of documents.</Paragraph>
    <Paragraph>This is a second paragraph.</Paragraph>
  </FlowDocument>
</FlowDocumentScrollViewer>
```

Figure 28-4 shows the modest result.

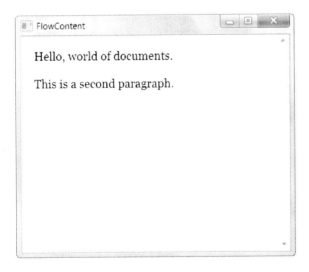

Figure 28-4. *A bare-bones flow document*

The scrollbar is added automatically. The font (Segoe UI) is picked up from the Windows system settings, not the containing window.

■ **Note** Ordinarily, the FlowDocumentScrollViewer allows text to be selected (as in a web browser). This way, a user can copy portions of a document to the Windows clipboard and paste them in other applications. If you don't want this behavior, set the FlowDocumentScrollViewer.IsSelectionEnabled property to False.

Using Block Elements

Creating a basic document is easy, but to get the result you really want, you need to master a range of elements. Among them are the five block elements described in the following sections.

Paragraph and Run

You've already seen the Paragraph element, which represents a paragraph of text. Technically, paragraph doesn't contain text—instead, it contains a collection of inline elements, which are stored in the Paragraph.Inlines collection.

This fact has two consequences. First, it means that a paragraph can contain a whole lot more than text. Second, it means that in order for a paragraph to contain text, the paragraph needs to contain an inline Run element. The Run element contains the actual text, as shown here:

```
<Paragraph>
  <Run>Hello, world of documents.</Run>
</Paragraph>
```

This long-winded syntax wasn't required in the previous example. That's because the Paragraph class is intelligent enough to create a Run implicitly when you place text directly inside.

However, in some cases it's important to understand the behind-the-scenes reality of how a paragraph works. For example, imagine you want to retrieve the text from a paragraph programmatically and you have the following markup:

```
<Paragraph Name="paragraph">Hello, world of documents.</Paragraph>
```

You'll quickly discover that the Paragraph class doesn't contain a Text property. In fact, there's no way to get the text from the paragraph. Instead, to retrieve the text (or change it), you need to grab the nested Run object, as shown here:

```
CType(paragraph.Inlines.FirstInline, Run).Text = "Hello again."
```

You can improve the readability of this code by using a Span element to wrap the text you want to modify. You can then give the Span element a name and access it directly. The Span element is described in the "Using Inline Elements" section.

The Paragraph class includes a TextIndent property that allows you to set the amount that the first line should be indented. (By default, it's 0.) You supply a value in device-independent units.

The Paragraph class also includes a few properties that determine how it splits lines over column and page breaks. You'll consider these details in the "Creating Pages and Columns" section later in this chapter.

List

The List element represents a bulleted or numeric list. You choose by setting the MarkerStyle property. Table 28-3 lists your options. You can also set the distance between each list item and its marker by using the MarkerOffset property.

Table 28-3. *Values from the TextMarkerStyle Enumeration*

Name	Appears As . . .
Disc	A solid bullet. This is the default.
Box	A solid square box.
Circle	A bullet with no fill.
Square	A square box with no fill.
Decimal	An incrementing number (1, 2, 3). Ordinarily, it starts at 1, but you can adjust the StartingIndex to begin counting at a higher number. Despite the name, a MarkerStyle of Decimal will not show fractional values, just integral numbers.
LowerLatin	A lowercase letter that's incremented automatically (a, b, c).
UpperLatin	An uppercase letter that's incremented automatically (A, B, C).
LowerRoman	A lowercase Roman numeral that's incremented automatically (i, ii, iii, iv).
UpperRoman	An uppercase Roman numeral that's incremented automatically (I, II, III, IV).
None	Nothing.

You nest ListItem elements inside the List element to represent individual items in the list. However, each ListItem must itself include a suitable block element (such as a Paragraph). Here's an example that creates two lists, one with bullets and one with numbers:

```
<Paragraph>Top programming languages:</Paragraph>
<List>
  <ListItem>
    <Paragraph>C#</Paragraph>
  </ListItem>
  <ListItem>
    <Paragraph>C++</Paragraph>
  </ListItem>
  <ListItem>
    <Paragraph>Perl</Paragraph>
  </ListItem>
  <ListItem>
    <Paragraph>Logo</Paragraph>
  </ListItem>
</List>
```

```
<Paragraph Margin="0,30,0,0">To-do list:</Paragraph>
<List MarkerStyle="Decimal">
  <ListItem>
    <Paragraph>Program a WPF application</Paragraph>
  </ListItem>
  <ListItem>
    <Paragraph>Bake bread</Paragraph>
  </ListItem>
</List>
```

Figure 28-5 shows the result.

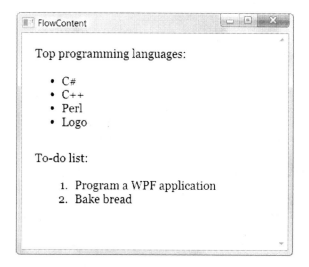

Figure 28-5. *Two lists*

Table

The Table element is designed to display tabular information. It's modeled after the HTML <table> element. To create a table, you must follow these steps:

- Place a TableRowGroup element inside the Table. The TableRowGroup holds a group of rows, and every table consists of one or more TableRowGroup elements. On its own, the TableRowGroup doesn't do anything. However, if you use multiple groups and give them each different formatting, you get an easy way to change the overall look of your table without setting repetitive formatting properties on each row.

- Place a TableRow element inside your TableRowGroup for each row.

- Place a TableCell element inside each TableRow to represent each column in the row.

- Place a block element (typically a Paragraph) in each TableCell. This is where you'll add your content for that cell.

Here are the first two rows of the simple table shown in Figure 28-6:

```
<Paragraph FontSize="20pt">Largest Cities in the Year 100</Paragraph>
<Table>
  <TableRowGroup Paragraph.TextAlignment="Center">
    <TableRow FontWeight="Bold" >
      <TableCell>
        <Paragraph>Rank</Paragraph>
      </TableCell>
      <TableCell>
        <Paragraph>Name</Paragraph>
      </TableCell>
      <TableCell>
        <Paragraph>Population</Paragraph>
      </TableCell>
    </TableRow>
    <TableRow>
      <TableCell>
        <Paragraph>1</Paragraph>
      </TableCell>
      <TableCell>
        <Paragraph>Rome</Paragraph>
      </TableCell>
      <TableCell>
        <Paragraph>450,000</Paragraph>
      </TableCell>
    </TableRow>
    ...
  </TableRowGroup>
</Table>
```

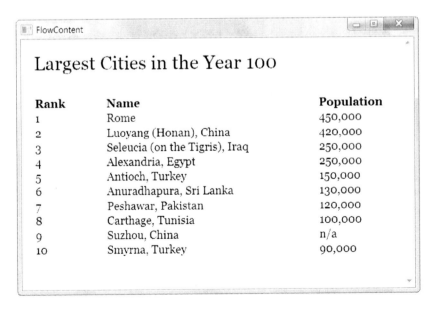

Figure 28-6. *A basic table*

■ **Note**   Unlike a Grid, cells in a Table are filled by position. You must include a TableCell element for each cell in the table, and you must place each row and value in the correct display order.

If you don't supply explicit column widths, WPF splits the space evenly between all its columns. You can override this behavior by supplying a set of TableColumn objects for the Table.Rows property and setting the Width of each one. Here's the markup that the previous example uses to make the middle column three times as big as the first and last columns:

```
<Table.Columns>
  <TableColumn Width="*"></TableColumn>
  <TableColumn Width="3*"></TableColumn>
  <TableColumn Width="*"></TableColumn>
</Table.Columns>
```

There are a few more tricks you can perform with a table. You can set the ColumnSpan and RowSpan properties of a cell to make it stretch over multiple rows. You can also use the CellSpacing property of the table to set the number of units of space that are used to pad between cells. You can also apply individual formatting (such as text and background colors) to different cells. However, don't expect to find good support for table borders. You can use the BorderThickness and BorderBrush properties of the TableCell, but this forces you to draw a separate border around the edge of each cell with separate borders. These borders don't look quite right when you use them on a group of contiguous cells. Although the Table element provides the BorderThickness and BorderBrush properties, these allow you to draw a border around only the entire table. If you're hoping for a more sophisticated effect (for example, adding lines between columns), you're out of luck.

Another limitation is that columns must be sized explicitly or proportionately (using the asterisk syntax shown previously). However, you can't combine the two approaches. For example, there's no way to create two fixed-width columns and one proportional column to receive the leftover space, as you can with the Grid.

■ **Note**   Some content elements are similar to other noncontent elements. However, the content elements are designed solely for use inside a flow document. For example, there's no reason to try to swap a Grid with a Table. The Grid is designed to be the most efficient option when laying out the controls in a window, while a Table is optimized to present text in the most readable way possible in a document.

Section

The Section element doesn't have any built-in formatting of its own. Instead, it's used to wrap other block elements in a convenient package. By grouping elements in a Section element, you can apply common formatting to an entire portion of a document. For example, if you want the same background color and font in several contiguous paragraphs, you can place these paragraphs in a section and then set the Section.Background property, as shown here:

```
<Section FontFamily="Palatino" Background="LightYellow">
  <Paragraph>Lorem ipsum dolor sit amet... </Paragraph>
  <Paragraph>Ut enim ad minim veniam...</Paragraph>
  <Paragraph>Duis aute irure dolor in reprehenderit...</Paragraph>
</Section>
```

This works because the font settings are inherited by the contained paragraphs. The background value is not inherited, but because the background of every paragraph is transparent by default, the section background shows through.

Even better, you can set the Section.Style property to format your section by using a style:

```
<Section Style="IntroText">
```

The Section element is analogous to the <div> element in HTML.

Tip　Many flow documents use style extensively to categorize content formatting based on its type. For example, a book reviewing site might create separate styles for review titles, review text, emphasized pull quotes, and bylines. These styles could then define whatever formatting is appropriate.

BlockUIContainer

The BlockUIContainer allows you to place noncontent elements (classes that derive from UIElement) inside a document, where a block element would otherwise go. For example, you can use the BlockUIContainer to add buttons, check boxes, and even entire layout containers such as the StackPanel and Grid to a document. The only rule is that the BlockUIContainer is limited to a single child.

You might wonder why you would ever want to place controls inside a document. After all, isn't the best rule of thumb to use layout containers for user-interactive portions of your interface, and flow layout for length, read-only blocks of content? However, in real-world applications many types of documents need to provide some sort of user interaction (beyond what the Hyperlink content element provides). For example, if you're using the flow layout system to create online help pages, you might want to include a button that triggers an action.

Here's an example that places a button under a paragraph:

```
<Paragraph>
  You can configure the foof feature using the Foof Options dialog box.
</Paragraph>
<BlockUIContainer>
  <Button HorizontalAlignment="Left" Padding="5">Open Foof Options</Button>
</BlockUIContainer>
```

You can connect an event handler to the Button.Click event in the usual way.

Tip　Mingling content elements and ordinary noncontent elements makes sense if you have a user-interactive document. For example, if you're creating a survey application that lets users fill out different surveys, it may make sense to take advantage of the advanced text layout provided by the flow document model, without sacrificing the user's ability to enter values and make choices via common controls.

Using Inline Elements

WPF provides a larger set of inline elements, which can be placed inside block elements or other inline elements. Most of the inline elements are quite straightforward. Table 28-4 lists your options.

Table 28-4. Inline Content Elements

Name	Description
Run	Contains ordinary text. Although you can apply formatting to a Run element, it's generally preferred to use a Span element instead. Run elements are often created implicitly (such as when you add text to a paragraph).
Span	Wraps any amount of other inline elements. Usually, you'll use a span to specifically format a piece of text. To do so, you wrap the Span element around a Run element and set the properties of the Span element. (For a shortcut, just place text inside the Span element, and the nested Run element will be created automatically.) Another reason to use a Span is to make it easy for your code to find and manipulate a specific piece of text. The Span element is analogous to the \<span\> element in HTML.
Bold, Italic, and Underline	Apply bold, italic, and underline formatting. These elements derive from Span. Although you can use these tags, it usually makes more sense to wrap the text you want to format inside a Span element and then set the Span.Style property to point to a style that applies the formatting you want. That way, you have the flexibility to easily adjust the formatting characteristics later on, without altering the markup of your document.
Hyperlink	Represents a clickable link inside a flow document. In a window-based application, you can respond to the Click event to perform an action (for example, showing a different document). In a page-based application, you can use the NavigateUri property to let the user browse directly to another page (as explained in Chapter 24).
LineBreak	Adds a line break inside a block element. Before using a line break, consider whether it would be clearer to use increased Margin or Padding values to add whitespace between elements.
InlineUIContainer	Allows you to place noncontent elements (classes that derive from UIElement) where an inline element would otherwise go (for example, in a Paragraph element). The InlineUIContainer is similar to the BlockUIElement, but it's an inline element rather than a block element.
Floater and Figure	Allow you to embed a floating box of content that you can use to highlight important information, display a figure, or show related content (such as advertisements, links, code listings, and so on).

Preserving Whitespace

Ordinarily, whitespace in XML is collapsed. Because XAML is an XML-based language, it follows the same rules.

As a result, if you include a string of spaces in your content, that string is converted to single space. That means this markup

```
<Paragraph>hello      there</Paragraph>
```

is equivalent to this:

```
<Paragraph>hello there</Paragraph>
```

Spaces between content and tags are also collapsed. So this line of markup

```
<Paragraph>         Hello there</Paragraph>
```

becomes

```
<Paragraph>Hello there</Paragraph>
```

For the most part, this behavior makes sense. It allows you to indent your document markup by using line breaks and tabs where convenient, without altering the way that content is interpreted.

Tabs and line breaks are treated in the same way as spaces. They're collapsed to a single space when they appear inside your content, and ignored when they appear on the edges of your content. However, there's one exception to this rule. If you have a space before an inline element, WPF preserves that space. (And if you have several spaces, WPF collapses these spaces to a single space.) That means you can write markup like this:

```
<Paragraph>A common greeting is <Bold>hello</Bold>.</Paragraph>
```

Here, the space between the content "A common greeting is" and the nested Bold element is retained, which is what you want. However, if you rewrote the markup like this, you'd lose the space:

```
<Paragraph>A common greeting is<Bold> hello</Bold>.</Paragraph>
```

In this case, you'll see the text "A common greeting ishello" in your user interface.

In some situations, you might want to add space where it would ordinarily be ignored or include a series of spaces. You can do this by using the xml:space attribute with the value *preserve*, which is an XML convention that tells an XML parser to keep all the whitespace characters in nested content:

```
<Paragraph xml:space="preserve">This     text     is     spaced     out</Paragraph>
```

This seems like the perfect solution, but there are still a few headaches. Now that the XML parser is paying attention to whitespace, you can no longer use line breaks and tabs to indent your content for easier reading. In a long paragraph, this is a significant trade-off that makes the markup more difficult to understand. (Of course, this won't be an issue if you're using another tool to generate the markup for your flow document, in which case you really don't care what the serialized XAML looks like.)

Because you can use the xml:space attribute on any element, you can pay attention to whitespace more selectively. For example, the following markup preserves whitespace in the nested Run element only:

```
<Paragraph>
  <Run xml:space="preserve">This     text     </Run> is spaced out.
</Paragraph>
```

Floater

The Floater element gives you a way to set some content off from the main document. Essentially, this content is placed in a "box" that floats somewhere in your document. (Often, it's displayed off to one side.) Figure 28-7 shows an example with a single line of text.

Figure 28-7. *A floating pull quote*

To create this floater, you simply insert a Floater element somewhere inside another block element (such as a paragraph). The Floater itself can contain one or more block elements. Here's the markup used to create the example in Figure 28-7. (The ellipsis indicates omitted text.)

```
<Paragraph>
  It was a bright cold day in April, and the clocks were striking thirteen ...
</Paragraph>
<Paragraph>The hallway smelt of boiled cabbage and old rag mats.
  <Run xml:space="preserve"> </Run>
  <Floater Style="{StaticResource PullQuote}">
    <Paragraph>"The hallway smelt of boiled cabbage"</Paragraph>
  </Floater>
  At one end of it a coloured poster, too large for indoor display ...
</Paragraph>
```

Here's the style that this Floater uses:

```
<Style x:Key="PullQuote">
  <Setter Property="Paragraph.FontSize" Value="30"></Setter>
  <Setter Property="Paragraph.FontStyle" Value="Italic"></Setter>
  <Setter Property="Paragraph.Foreground" Value="Green"></Setter>
  <Setter Property="Paragraph.Padding" Value="5"></Setter>
  <Setter Property="Paragraph.Margin" Value="5,10,15,10"></Setter>
</Style>
```

Ordinarily, the flow document widens the floater so that all its content fits on one line or, if that's not possible, so that it takes the full width of one column in the document window. (In the current example, there's only one column, so the Floater takes the full width of the document window.)

If this isn't what you want, you can specify the width in device-independent units by using the Width property. You can also use the HorizontalAlignment property to indicate whether the floater is centered, placed on the left edge, or placed on the right edge of the line where the Floater element is placed. Here's how you can create the left-aligned floater shown in Figure 28-8:

```
<Floater Style="{StaticResource PullQuote}" Width="205" HorizontalAlignment="Left">
  <Paragraph>"The hallway smelt of boiled cabbage"</Paragraph>
</Floater>
```

Figure 28-8. *A left-aligned floater*

The Floater will use the specified width, unless it stretches beyond the bounds of the document window (in which case the floater gets the full width of the window).

By default, the floating box that's used for the Floater is invisible. However, you can set a shaded background (through the Background property) or a border (through the BorderBrush and BorderThickness properties) to clearly separate this content from the rest of your document. You can also use the Margin property to add space between the floating box and the document, and the Padding property to add space between the edges of the box and its contents.

■ **Note** Ordinarily, the Background, BorderBrush, BorderThickness, Margin, and Padding properties are available only to block elements. However, they're also defined in the Floater and Figure classes, which are inline elements.

You can also use a floater to show a picture. But oddly enough, there is no flow content element that's up to the task. Instead, you'll need to use the Image element in conjunction with the BlockUIContainer or the InlineUIContainer.

However, there's a catch. When inserting a floater that wraps an image, the flow document assumes the figure should be as wide as a full column of text. The Image inside will then stretch to fit, which could result in problems if you're displaying a bitmap and it has to be scaled up or down a large amount. You could change the Image.Stretch property to disable this image-resizing feature, but in that case the floater will still take the full width of the column—it simply leaves extra blank space at the sides of the figure.

The only reasonable solution when embedding a bitmap in a flow document is to set a fixed size for the floater box. You can then choose how the image sizes itself in that box by using the Image.Stretch property. Here's an example:

```
<Paragraph>
  It was a bright cold day in April,
  <Floater Width="100" Padding="5,0,5,0" HorizontalAlignment="Right">
    <BlockUIContainer>
      <Image Source="BigBrother.jpg"></Image>
    </BlockUIContainer>
  </Floater>
  and the clocks ...
</Paragraph>
```

Figure 28-9 shows the result. Notice that the image actually stretches out over two paragraphs, but this doesn't pose a problem. The flow document wraps the text around all the floaters.

Figure 28-9. *A floater with an image*

■ **Note**   Using a fixed-size floater also gives the most sensible result when you use zooming. As the zoom percentage changes, so does the size of your floater. The image inside the floater can then stretch itself as needed (based on the Image.Stretch property) to fill or center itself in the floater box.

Figure

The Figure element is similar to the Floater element, but it gives a bit more control over positioning. Usually, you'll use floaters and give WPF a little more control to arrange your content. But if you have a complex, rich document, you might prefer to use figures to make sure your floating boxes aren't bumped too far away as the window is resized, or to put boxes in specific positions.

So what does the Figure class offer that the Floater doesn't? Table 28-5 describes the properties you have to play with. However, there's one caveat: many of these properties (including HorizontalAnchor, VerticalOffset, and HorizontalOffset) aren't supported by the FlowDocumentScrollViewer that you've been using to display your flow document. Instead, they need one of the more sophisticated containers you'll learn about later in the "Using Read-Only Flow Document Containers" section. For now, replace the FlowDocumentScrollViewer tags with tags for the FlowDocumentReader if you want to use the figure placement properties.

Table 28-5. *Figure Properties*

Name	Description
Width	Sets the width of the figure. You can size a figure just as you size a floater, using device-independent pixels. However, you have the additional ability of sizing the figure proportionately, respective to the overall window or the current column. For example, in your XAML, you can supply the text *0.25 content* to create a box that takes 25 percent of the width of the window, or *2 Column* to create a box that's two columns wide.
Height	Sets the height of the figure. You can also set the exact height of a figure in device-independent units. (By comparison, a floater makes itself as tall as required to fit all its content in the specified width.) If your use of the Width and Height properties creates a floating box that's too small for all of its content, some content will be truncated.
HorizontalAnchor	Replaces the HorizontalAlignment property in the Floater class. However, along with three equivalent options (ContentLeft, ContentRight, and ContentCenter), it also includes options that allow you to orient the figure relative to the current page (such as PageCenter) or column (such as ColumnCenter).
VerticalAnchor	Allows you to align the image vertically with respect to the current line of text, the current column, or the current page.
HorizontalOffset and VerticalOffset	Set the figure alignment. These properties allow you to move the figure from its anchored position. For example, a negative VerticalOffset will shift the figure box up the number of units you specify. If you use this technique to move a figure away from the edge of the containing window, text will flow into the space you free up. (If you want to increase spacing on one side of a figure but you don't want text to enter that area, adjust the Figure.Padding property instead.)
WrapDirection	Determines whether text is allowed to wrap on one side or both sides (space permitting) of a figure.

Interacting with Elements Programmatically

So far, you've seen examples of how to create the markup required for flow documents. It should come as no surprise that flow documents can also be constructed programmatically. (After all, that's what the XAML parser does when it reads your flow document markup.)

Creating a flow document programmatically is fairly tedious because of a number of disparate elements that need to be created. As with all XAML elements, you must create each element and then set all its properties, as there are no constructors to help you out. You also need to create a Run element to wrap every piece of text, as it won't be generated automatically.

Here's a snippet of code that creates a document with a single paragraph and some bolded text. It then displays the document in an existing FlowDocumentScrollViewer named docViewer:

```
' Create the first part of the sentence.
Dim runFirst As New Run()
runFirst.Text = "Hello world of "

' Create bolded text.
Dim bold As New Bold()
Dim runBold As New Run()
runBold.Text = "dynamically generated"
bold.Inlines.Add(runBold)

' Create last part of sentence.
Dim runLast As New Run()
runLast.Text = " documents"

' Add three parts of sentence to a paragraph, in order.
Dim paragraph As New Paragraph()
paragraph.Inlines.Add(runFirst)
paragraph.Inlines.Add(bold)
paragraph.Inlines.Add(runLast)

' Create a document and add this paragraph.
Dim document As New FlowDocument()
document.Blocks.Add(paragraph)

' Show the document.
docViewer.Document = document
```

The result is the sentence "Hello world of **dynamically generated** documents."

Most of the time, you won't create flow documents programmatically. However, you might want to create an application that browses through portions of a flow document and modifies them dynamically. You can do this in the same way that you interact with any other WPF elements: by responding to element events, and by attaching a name to the elements that you want to change. However, because flow documents use deeply nested content with a free-flowing structure, you may need to dig through several layers to find the actual content you want to modify. (Remember, this content is always stored in a Run element, even if the run isn't declared explicitly.)

There are some properties that can help you navigate the structure of a flow document:

- To get the block elements in a flow document, use the FlowDocument.Blocks collection. Use FlowDocument.Blocks.FirstBlock or FlowDocument.Blocks.LastBlock to jump to the first or last block element.

- To move from one block element to the next (or previous) block, use the Block.NextBlock property (or Block.PreviousBlock). You can also use the Block.SiblingBlocks collection to browse all the block elements that are at the same level.

- Many block elements can contain other elements. For example, the List element provides a ListItem collection, the Section provides a Blocks collection, and the Paragraph provides an Inlines collection.

If you need to modify the text inside a flow document, the easiest way is to isolate exactly what you want to change (and no more) by using a Span element. For example, the following flow document highlights selected nouns, verbs, and adverbs in a block of text so they can be modified programmatically. The type of selection is indicated with an extra bit of information—a string that's stored in the Span.Tag property.

■ **Tip**   Remember, the Tag property in any element is reserved for your use. It can store any value or object that you want to use later on.

```
<FlowDocument Name="document">
  <Paragraph FontSize="20" FontWeight="Bold">
    Release Notes
  </Paragraph>
  <Paragraph>
    These are the release <Span Tag="Plural Noun">notes</Span>
    for <Span Tag="Proper Noun">Linux</Span> version 1.2.13.
  </Paragraph>
  <Paragraph>
    Read them <Span Tag="Adverb">carefully</Span>, as they
    tell you what this is all about, how to <Span Tag="Verb">boot</Span>
    the <Span Tag="Noun">kernel</Span>, and what to do if
    something goes wrong.
  </Paragraph>
</FlowDocument>
```

This design allows you to create the straightforward Mad Libs game shown in Figure 28-10. In this game, the user gets the chance to supply values for all the span tags before seeing the source document. These user-supplied values are then substituted for the original values to humorous effect.

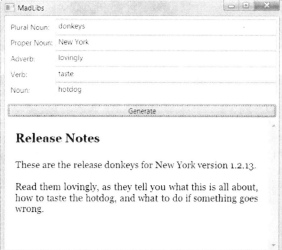

Figure 28-10. *Dynamically modifying a flow document*

To make this example as generic as possible, the code doesn't have any specific knowledge about the document that you're using. Instead, it's written generically so that it can pull the named Span elements out of all the top-level paragraphs in any document. It simply walks through the Blocks collection looking for paragraphs and then walks through the Inlines collection of each paragraph looking for spans. Each time it finds a Span object, it creates the text box that the user can use to supply a new value and adds it to a grid above the document (along with a descriptive label). And to make the substitution process easier, each text box stores a reference (through the TextBox.Tag property) to the Run element with the text inside the corresponding Span element:

```
Private Sub WindowLoaded(ByVal sender As Object, ByVal e As RoutedEventArgs)
    ' Clear grid of text entry controls.
    gridWords.Children.Clear()

    ' Look at paragraphs.
    For Each block As Block In document.Blocks
        Dim paragraph As Paragraph = TryCast(block, Paragraph)

        ' Look for spans.
        For Each inline As Inline In paragraph.Inlines
            Dim span As Span = TryCast(inline, Span)
            If Not span Is Nothing Then
                Dim row As New RowDefinition()
                gridWords.RowDefinitions.Add(row)

                Dim lbl As New Label()
                lbl.Content = inline.Tag.ToString() & ":"
                Grid.SetColumn(lbl, 0)
                Grid.SetRow(lbl, gridWords.RowDefinitions.Count - 1)
                gridWords.Children.Add(lbl)

                Dim txt As New TextBox()
                Grid.SetColumn(txt, 1)
                Grid.SetRow(txt, gridWords.RowDefinitions.Count - 1)
                gridWords.Children.Add(txt)

                txt.Tag = span.Inlines.FirstInline
            End If
        Next
    Next
End Sub
```

When the user clicks the Generate button, the code walks through all the text boxes that were added dynamically in the previous step. It then copies the text from the text box to the related Run in the flow document:

```
Private Sub cmdGenerate_Click(ByVal sender As Object, _
  ByVal e As RoutedEventArgs)
    For Each child As UIElement In gridWords.Children
        If Grid.GetColumn(child) = 1 Then
            Dim txt As TextBox = CType(child, TextBox)

            If txt.Text <> "" Then
                CType(txt.Tag, Run).Text = txt.Text
            End If
```

```
        End If
    Next
    docViewer.Visibility = Visibility.Visible
End Sub
```

It might occur to you to do the reverse—in other words, walk through the document again, inserting the matching text each time you find a Span. However, this approach is more problematic because you can't enumerate through the collections of inline elements in a paragraph at the same time that you're modifying its content.

Text Justification

You may have already noticed that text content in a flow document is, by default, justified so that every line stretches from the left to the right margin. You can change this behavior by using the TextAlignment property, but most flow documents in WPF are justified.

To improve the readability of justified text, you can use a WPF feature called *optimal paragraph layout* that ensures that whitespace is distributed as evenly as possible. This avoids the distracting rivers of whitespace and oddly spaced-out words that can occur with more-primitive line-justification algorithms (such as those provided by web browsers).

Note   Basic line-justification algorithms work on one line at a time. WPF's optimal paragraph justification uses a total-fit algorithm that looks ahead at the lines to come. It then chooses line breaks that balance the word spacing throughout the entire paragraph and result in the minimal cost over all lines.

Ordinarily, WPF's optimal paragraph feature isn't enabled. Presumably, this is because of the additional overhead in the total-fit algorithm. However, in most cases you'll find that the responsiveness of your application (how it "feels" as you resize the window) is the same with optimal paragraphs enabled.

To enable optimal paragraphs, set the FlowDocument.IsOptimalParagraphEnabled property to True. Figure 28-11 compares the difference by placing a flow document that uses normal paragraphs on top, and one that uses the total-fit algorithm below.

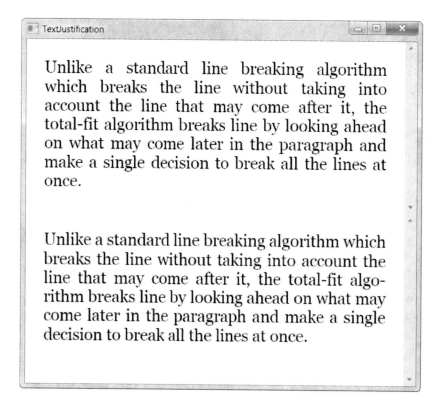

Figure 28-11. *Comparing ordinary justification (top) with optimal paragraphs (bottom)*

To further improve text justification, particularly in narrow windows, set the FlowDocument.IsHyphenationEnabled property to True. This way, WPF will break long words where necessary to keep the space between words small. Hyphenation works well with the optimal paragraph feature, and it's particularly important when using multicolumn displays. WPF uses a hyphenating dictionary to make sure that hyphens fall in the appropriate places (between syllables, as in *algo-rithm* rather than *algori-thm*).

Read-Only Flow Document Containers

WPF provides three read-only containers that you can use to display flow documents:

- FlowDocumentScrollViewer shows the entire document with a scrollbar to let you move through it if the document exceeds the size of the FlowDocumentScrollViewer. The FlowDocumentScrollViewer doesn't support pagination or multicolumn displays (although it does support printing and zooming, as all containers do). All of the examples you've seen up to this point have used the FlowDocumentScrollViewer.

- FlowDocumentPageViewer splits a flow document into multiple pages. Each page is as large as the available space, and the user can step from one page to the next. The FlowDocumentPageViewer has more overhead than the FlowDocumentScrollViewer (because of the additional calculations required for breaking content into pages).

- FlowDocumentReader combines the features of the FlowDocumentScrollViewer and FlowDocumentPageViewer. It lets the user choose whether to read content in a scrollable or paginated display. It also includes searching functionality. The FlowDocumentReader has the most overhead of any flow document container.

Switching from one container to another is simply a matter of modifying the containing tag. For example, here's a flow document in a FlowDocumentPageViewer:

```
<FlowDocumentPageViewer>
  <FlowDocument>
    <Paragraph>Hello, world of documents.</Paragraph>
  </FlowDocument>
</FlowDocumentPageViewer>
```

Each of these containers provides additional features, such as zooming, pagination, and printing. You'll learn about them in the following sections.

THE TEXTBLOCK

You can display small amounts of flow content by using the familiar TextBlock, a text display element that you've seen extensively over the past chapters. Although the TextBlock is often used to hold ordinary text (in which case the TextBlock creates a Run object to wrap that text), you can place any combination of inline elements inside. They'll all be added to the TextBlock.Inlines collection.

The TextBlock provides text wrapping (through the TextWrapping property), and a TextTrimming property that allows you to control how text is treated when it can't fit in the bounds of the TextBlock. When this occurs, the extra text is trimmed off, but you can choose whether an ellipsis is used to indicate that trimming has taken place. Your options are the following:

- *None*: The text is trimmed with no ellipsis. "This text is too big" might become "This text is to".

- *WordEllipse*: The ellipsis is inserted after the last word that fits (as in "This text is . . .").

- *CharacterEllipse*: The ellipsis is inserted after the last character that fits (as in "This text is t . . .").

The TextBlock can't match the scrolling and paging features of the more sophisticated FlowDocument containers. For that reason, the TextBlock is best for displaying small amounts of flow content, such as control labels and hyperlinks. The TextBlock can't accommodate block elements at all.

Zooming

All three document containers support *zooming*: the ability for you to shrink or magnify the displayed content. The Zoom property of the container (for example, FlowDocumentScrollViewer.Zoom) sets the size of the content as a percentage value. Ordinarily, the Zoom value begins at 100, and the FontSize values correspond to any other elements in your window. If you increase the Zoom value to 200, the text size is doubled. Similarly, if you reduce it to 50, the text size is halved (although you can use any value in between).

Obviously, you can set the zoom percentage by hand. You can also change the zoom programmatically by using the IncreaseZoom() and DecreaseZoom() methods, which change the Zoom value by the amount specified by the ZoomIncrement property. You can also wire up other controls to these features by using commands (Chapter 9). But there's no need to go to any of this trouble. The simplest approach is to let users set the zoom percentage to match their preferences. The FlowDocumentScrollViewer includes a toolbar with a zoom slider bar for just this purpose. To make it visible, set IsToolbarVisible to True, as shown here:

```
<FlowDocumentScrollViewer MinZoom="50" MaxZoom="1000"
  Zoom="100" ZoomIncrement="5" IsToolbarVisible="True">
```

Figure 28-12 shows a flow document with a zoom slider bar at the bottom.

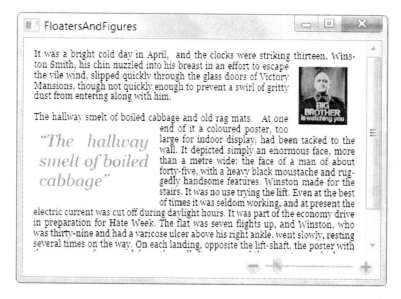

Figure 28-12. *Scaling down a document*

If you're using the FlowDocumentPageViewer or FlowDocumentReader, the zoom slider is always visible (although you can still configure the zoom increment and the minimum and maximum allowed zoom values).

■ **Tip** Zooming affects the size of anything that's set in device-independent units (not just font sizes). For example, if your flow document uses floater or figure boxes with explicit widths, these widths are also sized proportionately.

Creating Pages and Columns

The FlowDocumentPageViewer can split a long document into separate pages. This makes it easier to read long content. (When scrolling, readers are constantly forced to stop reading, scroll down, and then find the point where they left off. But when readers browse through a series of pages, they know exactly where to start reading—at the top of each page.)

The number of pages depends on the size of the window. For example, if you allow a FlowDocumentPageViewer to take the full size of a window, you'll notice that the number of pages changes as you resize the window, as shown in Figure 28-13.

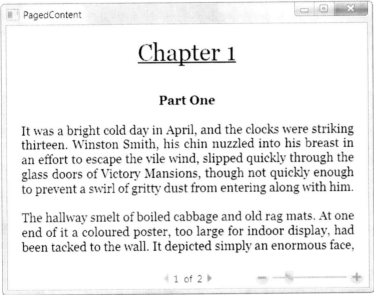

Figure 28-13. *Dynamically repaginated content*

If you make the window wide enough, the FlowDocumentPageViewer splits the text into multiple columns to make it easier to read (Figure 28-14). Figure 28-13 and Figure 28-14 show the same window. This window simply adjusts itself to make the best use of the available space.

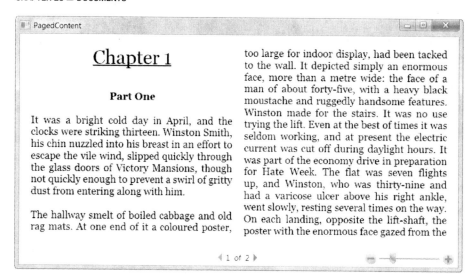

Figure 28-14. Automatic columns

■ **Note**   Remember, Floater elements like to make themselves as wide as a single column. You can make them smaller by setting an explicit width, but not wider. On the other hand, Figure elements can easily span multiple columns.

Although the standard settings give good page breaking and column breaking, you can tweak them in a number of ways to get exactly the result you want. There are two key extensibility points that you can use: the FlowDocument class that contains the content (which provides the properties listed in Table 28-6) and individual Paragraph elements in the document (which provide the properties listed in Table 28-7).

Table 28-6. *FlowDocument Properties for Controlling Columns*

Name	Description
ColumnWidth	Specifies the preferred size of text columns. This acts as a minimum size, and the FlowDocumentPageViewer adjusts the width to make sure all the space is used on the page.
IsColumnWidthFlexible	Determines whether the document container can adjust the column size. If False, the exact column width specified by the ColumnWidth property is used. The FlowDocumentPageViewer will not create partial columns, so this may leave some blank space at the right edge of the page (or on either side if FlowDocumentMaxPageWidth is less than the width of the document window). If True (the default), the FlowDocumentPageViewer splits the space evenly to create columns, respecting the ColumnWidth property as a minimum.
ColumnGap	Sets the blank space between columns.
ColumnRuleWidth and ColumnRuleBrush	Allow you to draw a vertical line between columns. You can choose the width and fill of that line.

Table 28-7. Paragraph Properties for Controlling Columns

Name	Description
KeepTogether	Determines whether a paragraph can be split over a page break. If True, this paragraph will not be split over a page break. Usually, it will all be bumped to the next page. (This setting makes sense for small amounts of text that need to be read in one piece.)
KeepWithNext	Determines whether a pair of paragraphs can be separated by a page break. If True, this paragraph will not be divided from the following paragraph over a page break. (This setting makes sense for headings.)
MinOrphanLines	Controls how a paragraph can be split over a page break. When this paragraph is split over a page break, this is the minimum number of lines that needs to appear on the first page. If there isn't enough space for this number of lines, the entire paragraph will be bumped to the next page.
MinWindowLines	Controls how a paragraph can be split over a page break. When this paragraph is split over a page break, this is the minimum number of lines that needs to appear on the second page. The FlowDocumentPageViewer will move lines from the first page to the second to meet this criteria.

■ **Note** Obviously, in some situations the column-break properties of the Paragraph element can't be met. For example, if a paragraph is too large to fit on a single page, it doesn't matter whether you set KeepTogether to True, as the paragraph must be broken.

The FlowDocumentPageViewer isn't the only container that supports pagination. The FlowDocumentReader allows the user to choose between a scroll mode (which works exactly like the FlowDocumentScrollViewer) and two page modes. You can choose to see one page at a time (which works exactly like the FlowDocumentPageViewer), or two pages side by side. To switch between viewing modes, you simply click one of the icons in the bottom-right corner of the FlowDocumentReader toolbar.

Loading Documents from a File

So far, the examples you've seen declare the FlowDocument inside its container. However, it's no stretch to imagine that after you've created the perfect document viewer, you might want to reuse it to show different document content. (For example, you might show different topics in a help window.) To make this possible, you need to dynamically load content into the container by using the XamlReader class in the System.Windows.Markup namespace.

Fortunately, it's a fairly easy task. Here's the code you need (without the obligatory error-handling you'd use to catch file-access problems):

```
Using fs As FileStream = File.Open(documentFile, FileMode.Open)
    Dim document As FlowDocument = TryCast(XamlReader.Load(fs), FlowDocument)

    If document Is Nothing Then
        MessageBox.Show("Problem loading document.")
    Else
        flowContainer.Document = document
    End If
End Using
```

It's just as easy to take the current content of a FlowDocument and save it to a XAML file by using the XamlWriter class. This functionality is less useful (after all, the containers you've seen so far don't allow the user to make changes). However, it's a worthwhile technique if you need to make programmatic changes to a document based on user actions (for example, you want to save the text from the completed Mad Libs game shown earlier), or you want to construct a FlowDocument programmatically and save it directly to disk.

Here's the code that serializes a FlowDocument object to XAML:

```
Using fs As FileStream = File.Open(documentFile, FileMode.Create)
    XamlWriter.Save(flowContainer.Document, fs)
End Using
```

Printing

If you want to print a flow document, it's easy. Just use the Print() method of the container. (All flow document containers support printing.) The Print() method shows the Windows Print dialog box, where the user can choose the printer and other printing preferences, such as the number of copies, before choosing to cancel the operation or to go ahead and send the job to the printer.

Printing, like many of the features in the flow document containers, works through commands. As a result, if you want to wire a control up to this functionality, you don't need to write code that calls the Print() method. Instead, you can simply use the appropriate command, as shown here:

```
<Button Command="ApplicationCommands.Print" CommandTarget="docViewer">Print</Button>
```

Along with printing, the flow document containers also support commands for searching, zooming, and page navigation.

Commands may also have key bindings. For example, the Print command has a default key binding that maps the Ctrl+P keystroke. As a result, even if you don't include a button or code to call the Print() method, the user can still hit Ctrl+P to trigger it and show the Print window. If you don't want this behavior, you need to remove the key binding from the command.

■ **Note**   It's possible to customize the printout of a flow document. You'll learn how to do this, and how to print other types of content, in Chapter 29.

Editing a Flow Document

All the flow document containers you've seen so far are read-only. They're ideal for displaying document content, but they don't allow the user to make changes. Fortunately, there's another WPF element that fills the gap: the RichTextBox control.

Programming toolkits have included rich text controls, in some form or another, for more than a decade. However, the RichTextBox control that WPF includes is significantly different from its predecessors. It's no longer bound to the dated RTF standard that's found in word processing programs. Instead, it now stores its content as a FlowDocument object.

The consequences of this change are significant. Although you can still load RTF content into a RichTextBox control, internally the RichTextBox uses the much more straightforward flow content model that you've studied in this chapter. That makes it far easier to manipulate document content programmatically.

The RichTextBox control also exposes a rich programming model that provides plenty of extensibility points so you can plug in your own logic, which allows you to use the RichTextBox as a building block for your own customized text editor. The one drawback is speed. The WPF RichTextBox, like most of the rich text controls that have preceded it, can be a bit sluggish. If you need to hold huge amounts of data, use intricate logic to handle key presses, or add effects such as automatic formatting (for example, Visual Studio's syntax highlighting or Word's spelling-checker underlining), the WPF RichTextBox probably won't provide the performance you need.

■ **Note** The RichTextBox doesn't support all the features that read-only flow document containers do. Zooming, pagination, multicolumn displays, and search are all features that the RichTextBox doesn't provide.

Loading a File

To try out the RichTextBox, you can declare one of the flow documents you've already seen inside a RichTextBox element, as shown here:

```
<RichTextBox>
  <FlowDocument>
    <Paragraph>Hello, world of editable documents.</Paragraph>
  </FlowDocument>
</RichTextBox>
```

More practically, you may choose to retrieve a document from a file and then insert it in the RichTextBox. To do this, you can use the same approach that you used to load and save the content of a FlowDocument before displaying it in a read-only container—namely, the shared XamlReader.Load() method. However, you might want the additional ability to load and save files in other formats (namely, .rtf files). To do this, you need to use the System.Windows. Documents.TextRange class, which wraps a chunk of text. The TextRange is a miraculously useful container that allows you to convert text from one format to another and apply formatting (as described in the next section).

Here's a simple code snippet that translates an .rtf document into a selection of text in a TextRange and then inserts it into a RichTextBox:

```
Dim openFile As New OpenFileDialog()
openFile.Filter = "RichText Files (*.rtf)|*.rtf|All Files (*.*)|*.*"

If openFile.ShowDialog() = True Then
    ' Create a TextRange around the entire document.
    Dim documentTextRange As New TextRange( _
      richTextBox.Document.ContentStart, richTextBox.Document.ContentEnd)

    Using fs As FileStream = File.Open(openFile.FileName, FileMode.Open)
        documentTextRange.Load(fs, DataFormats.Rtf)
    End Using
End If
```

Notice that before you can do anything, you need to create a TextRange that wraps the portion of the document you want to change. Even though there's currently no document content, you still need to specify the starting point and ending point of the selection. To select the whole document, you can use the FlowDocument.ContentStart and FlowDocument.ContentEnd properties, which provide the TextPointer objects the TextRange requires.

After the TextRange has been created, you can fill it with data by using the Load() method. However, you need to supply a string that identifies the type of data format you're attempting to convert. You can use one of the following:

- DataFormat.Xaml for XAML flow content

- DataFormats.Rtf for rich text (as in the previous example)

- DataFormats.XamlPackage for XAML flow content with embedded images
- DataFormats.Text for plain text

■ **Note** The DataFormats.XamlPackage format is essentially the same as DataFormats.Xaml. The only difference is that DataFormats.XamlPackage stores the binary data for any embedded images (which is left out if you use the ordinary DataFormats.Xaml serialization). The XAML package format is not a true standard—it's just a feature that WPF provides to make it easier to serialize document content and support other features you might want to implement, such as cut-and-paste or drag-and-drop.

Although the DataFormats class provides many additional fields, the rest aren't supported. For example, you won't have any luck attempting to convert an HTML document to flow content by using DataFormats.Html. Both the XAML package format and RTF require unmanaged code permission, which means you can't use them in a limited-trust scenario (such as a browser-based application).

The TextRange.Load() method works only if you specify the correct file format. However, it's quite possible that you might want to create a text editor that supports both XAML (for best fidelity) and RTF (for compatibility with other programs, such as word processors). In this situation, the standard approach is to let the user specify the file format or make an assumption about the format based on the file extension, as shown here:

```
Using fs As FileStream = File.Open(openFile.FileName, FileMode.Open)
    If Path.GetExtension(openFile.FileName).ToLower() = ".rtf" Then
        documentTextRange.Load(fs, DataFormats.Rtf)
    Else
        documentTextRange.Load(fs, DataFormats.Xaml)
    End If
End Using
```

This code will encounter an exception if the file isn't found, can't be accessed, or can't be loaded using the format you specify. For all these reasons, you should wrap this code in an exception handler.

Remember, no matter how you load your document content, it's converted to a FlowDocument in order to be displayed by the RichTextBox. To study exactly what's taking place, you can write a simple routine that grabs the content from the FlowDocument and converts it to a string text by using the XamlWriter or a TextRange. Here's an example that displays the markup for the current flow document in another text box:

```
' Copy the document content to a MemoryStream.
Using stream As New MemoryStream()
    Dim range As New TextRange(richTextBox.Document.ContentStart, _
      richTextBox.Document.ContentEnd)
    range.Save(stream, DataFormats.Xaml)
    stream.Position = 0

    ' Read the content from the stream and display it in a text box.
    Using r As New StreamReader(stream)
        txtFlowDocumentMarkup.Text = r.ReadToEnd()
    End Using
End Using
```

This trick is extremely useful as a debugging tool for investigating how the markup for a document changes after it's been edited.

Saving a File

You can also save your document by using a TextRange object. You need to supply two TextPointer objects—one that identifies the start of the content, and one that demarcates the end. You can then call the TextRange.Save() method and specify the desired export format (text, XAML, XAML package, or RTF) by using a field from the DataFormats class. Once again, the XAML package and RTF formats require unmanaged code permission.

The following block of code saves the document in the XAML format unless the file name has an .rtf extension. (Another, more explicit approach is to give the user the choice of using a save feature that uses XAML and an export feature that uses RTF.)

```
Dim saveFile As New SaveFileDialog()
saveFile.Filter = _
  "XAML Files (*.xaml)|*.xaml|RichText Files (*.rtf)|*.rtf|All Files (*.*)|*.*"

If saveFile.ShowDialog() = True Then
    ' Create a TextRange around the entire document.
    Dim documentTextRange As New TextRange( _
      richTextBox.Document.ContentStart, richTextBox.Document.ContentEnd)

    ' If this file exists, it's overwritten.
    Using fs As FileStream = File.Create(saveFile.FileName)
        If Path.GetExtension(saveFile.FileName).ToLower() = ".rtf" Then
            documentTextRange.Save(fs, DataFormats.Rtf)
        Else
            documentTextRange.Save(fs, DataFormats.Xaml)
        End If
    End Using
End If
```

When you use the XAML format to save a document, you probably assume that the document is stored as an ordinary XAML file with a top-level FlowDocument element. This is close, but not quite right. Instead, the top-level element must be a Section element.

As you learned earlier in this chapter, the Section is an all-purpose container that wraps other block elements. This makes sense—after all, the TextRange object represents a section of selected content. However, make sure that you don't try to use the TextRange.Load() method with other XAML files, including those that have a top-level FlowDocument, Page, or Window element, as none of these files will be parsed successfully. (Similarly, the document file can't link to a code-behind file or attach any event handlers.) If you have a XAML file that has a top-level FlowDocument element, you can create a corresponding FlowDocument object by using the XamlReader.Load() method, as you did with the other FlowDocument containers.

Formatting Selected Text

You can learn a fair bit about the RichTextBox control by building a simple rich text editor, like the one shown in Figure 28-15. Here, toolbar buttons allow the user to quickly apply bold formatting, italic formatting, and underlining. But the most interesting part of this example is the ordinary TextBox control underneath, which shows the XAML markup for the FlowDocument object that's currently displayed in the RichTextBox. This allows you to study how the RichTextBox modifies the FlowDocument object as you make edits.

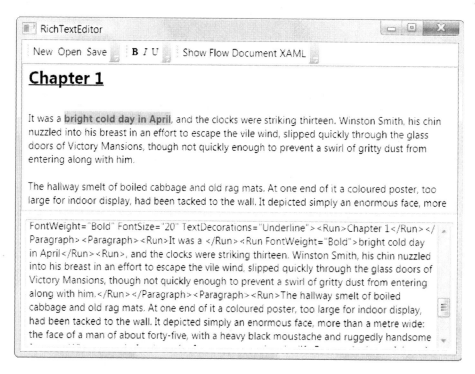

Figure 28-15. *Editing text*

■ **Note** Technically, you don't need to code the logic for bolding, italicizing, and underlining selected text. That's because the RichTextBox supports the ToggleBold, ToggleItalic, and ToggleUnderline commands from the EditingCommands class. You can wire your buttons up to these commands directly. However, it's still worth considering this example to learn more about how the RichTextBox works. The knowledge you gain is indispensable if you need to process text in another way. (The downloadable code for this chapter demonstrates both the code-based approach and the command-based approach.)

All of the buttons work in a similar way. They use the RichTextBox.Selection property, which provides a TextSelection object that wraps the currently selected text. (TextSelection is a slightly more advanced class that derives from the TextRange class you saw in the previous section.)

Making changes with the TextSelection object is easy enough, but not obvious. The simplest approach is to use ApplyPropertyValue() to change a dependency property in the selection. For example, you could apply bold formatting to any text elements in the selection by using this code:

```
richTextBox.Selection.ApplyPropertyValue( _
    TextElement.FontWeightProperty, FontWeights.Bold)
```

There's more happening here than meets the eye. For example, if you try this out on a small piece of text inside a larger paragraph, you'll find that this code automatically creates an inline Run element to wrap the selection and then applies the bold formatting to just that run. This way, you can use the same line of code to format individual words, entire paragraphs, and irregular selections that involve more than one paragraph (in which case you'll end up with a separate run being created in each affected paragraph).

Of course, this code as written isn't a complete solution. If you want to toggle the bold formatting, you'll also need to use the TextSelection.GetPropertyValue() to check whether bold formatting is already applied:

```
Dim obj As Object = richTextBox.Selection.GetPropertyValue( _
  TextElement.FontWeightProperty)
```

This method is a little trickier. If your selection encloses text that is all unambiguously bold or unambiguously normal, you'll receive the FontWeights.Bold or FontWeights.Normal property. However, if your selection contains some bold text and some normal text, you'll get a DependencyProperty.UnsetValue instead.

It's up to you how you want to handle a mixed selection. You might want to do nothing, always apply the formatting, or decide based on the first character (which is what the EditingCommands.ToggleBold command does). To do this, you'd need to create a new TextRange that wraps just the starting point of the selection. Here's the code that implements the latter approach and checks the first letter in ambiguous cases:

```
Dim obj As Object = richTextBox.Selection.GetPropertyValue( _
  TextElement.FontWeightProperty)

If obj Is DependencyProperty.UnsetValue Then
    Dim range As New TextRange(richTextBox.Selection.Start, _
      richTextBox.Selection.Start)

    obj = range.GetPropertyValue(TextElement.FontWeightProperty)
End If

Dim fontWeight As FontWeight = CType(obj, FontWeight)
If fontWeight = FontWeights.Bold Then
    fontWeight = FontWeights.Normal
Else
    fontWeight = FontWeights.Bold
End If

richTextBox.Selection.ApplyPropertyValue( _
  TextElement.FontWeightProperty, fontWeight)
```

In some cases, a user might trigger the bold command without any selected text at all. Just for fun, here's a code routine that checks for this condition and then checks the formatting that's applied to the entire paragraph that contains this text. The font weight of that paragraph is then flipped from bold to normal or from normal to bold:

```
If richTextBox.Selection.Text = "" Then
    Dim fontWeight As FontWeight = _
      richTextBox.Selection.Start.Paragraph.FontWeight

    If fontWeight = FontWeights.Bold Then
        fontWeight = FontWeights.Normal
    Else
        fontWeight = FontWeights.Bold
    End If

    richTextBox.Selection.Start.Paragraph.FontWeight = fontWeight
End If
```

■ **Tip**   To get the plain, unformatted text in a selection, use the TextRange.Text property.

There are many more methods for manipulating text in a RichTextBox. For example, the TextRange class and RichTextBox class both include a range of properties that let you get character offsets, count lines, and navigate through the flow elements in a portion of a document. To get more information, consult the MSDN help.

Getting Individual Words

One frill that the RichTextBox lacks is the ability to isolate specific words in a document. Although it's easy enough to find the flow document element that exists in a given position (as you saw in the previous section), the only way to grab the nearest word is to move character by character, checking for whitespace. This type of code is tedious and extremely difficult to write without error.

Prajakta Joshi of the WPF editing team has posted a reasonably complete solution at http://tinyurl.com/ylbla4v that detects word breaks. Using this code, you can quickly create a host of interesting effects, such as the following routine that grabs a word when the user right-clicks, and then displays that word in a separate text box. Another option might be to show a pop-up with a dictionary definition, launch an e-mail program or a web browser to follow a link, and so on:

```
Private Sub richTextBox_MouseDown(ByVal sender As Object, _
  ByVal e As MouseEventArgs)

    If e.RightButton = MouseButtonState.Pressed Then
        ' Get the nearest TextPointer to the mouse position.
        Dim location As TextPointer
        location = richTextBox.GetPositionFromPoint( _
          Mouse.GetPosition(richTextBox), True)

        ' Get the nearest word using this TextPointer.
        Dim word As TextRange = WordBreaker.GetWordRange(location)

        ' Display the word.
        txtSelectedWord.Text = word.Text
    End If
End Sub
```

■ **Note**   This code doesn't actually connect to the MouseDown event, because the RichTextBox intercepts and suppresses MouseUp and MouseDown. Instead, this event handler is attached to the PreviewMouseDown event, which occurs just before MouseDown.

PLACING UIELEMENT OBJECTS IN A RICHTEXTBOX

As you learned earlier in this chapter, you can use the BlockUIContainer and InlineUIContainer classes to place noncontent elements (classes that derive from UIElement) inside a flow document. However, if you use this technique to add interactive controls (such as text boxes, buttons, check boxes, hyperlinks, and so on) to a RichTextBox, they'll be disabled automatically and will appear grayed out.

You can opt out of this behavior and force the RichTextBox to enable embedded controls, much like the read-only FlowDocument containers do. To do so, simply set the RichTextBox.IsDocumentEnabled property to True.

Although it's easy, you may want to think twice before you set IsDocumentEnabled to True. Including element content inside a RichTextBox introduces all sorts of odd usability quirks. For example, controls can be deleted and undeleted (using Ctrl+Z or the Undo command), but undeleting them loses their event handlers. Furthermore, text can be inserted between adjacent containers, but if you attempt to cut and paste a block of content that includes UIElement objects, they'll be discarded. For reasons like these, it's probably not worth the trouble to use embedded controls inside a RichTextBox.

Fixed Documents

Flow documents allow you to dynamically lay out complex, text-heavy content in a way that's naturally suited to onscreen reading. Fixed documents—those that use XPS (the XML Paper Specification)—are much less flexible. They serve as print-ready documents that can be distributed and printed on any output device with full fidelity to the original source. Toward that end, they use a precise, fixed layout, have support for font embedding, and can't be casually rearranged.

XPS isn't just a part of WPF. It's a standard that's tightly integrated into the Windows operating system. Windows includes a print driver that can create XPS documents (in any application) and a viewer that allows you to display them. These two pieces work similarly to Adobe Acrobat, allowing users to create, review, and annotate print-ready electronic documents. Additionally, Microsoft Office allows you to save your documents as XPS or PDF files.

■ **Note** Under the hood, XPS files are actually ZIP files that contain a library of compressed files, including fonts, images, and text content for individual pages (using a XAML-like XML markup). To browse the inner contents of an XPS file, just rename the extension to .zip and open it. You can also refer to `http://tinyurl.com/yg7jqjb` for an overview of the XPS file format.

You can display an XPS document just as easily as you display a flow document. The only difference is the viewer. Instead of using one of the FlowDocument containers (FlowDocumentReader, FlowDocumentScrollViewer, or FlowDocumentPageViewer), you use the simply named DocumentViewer. It includes controls for searching and zooming (Figure 28-16). It also provides a similar set of properties, methods, and commands as the FlowDocument containers.

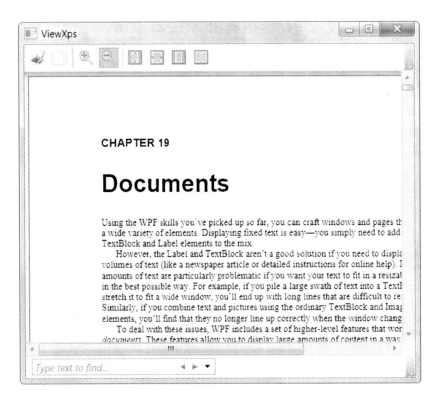

Figure 28-16. *A fixed document*

Here's the code you might use to load an XPS file into memory and show it in a DocumentViewer:

```
Dim doc As New XpsDocument("filename.xps", FileAccess.Read)
docViewer.Document = doc.GetFixedDocumentSequence()
doc.Close()
```

The XpsDocument class isn't terribly exciting. It provides the GetFixedDocument-Sequence() method used previously, which returns a reference to the document root with all its content. It also includes an AddFixedDocument() method for creating the document sequence in a new document, and two methods for managing digital signatures (SignDigitally() and RemoveSignature()).

XPS documents are closely associated with the concept of printing. A single XPS document is fixed at a particular page size and lays out its text to fit the available space. As with flow documents, you can get straightforward support for printing a fixed document by using the ApplicationCommands.Print command. In Chapter 29, you'll learn how to get fine-grained control of printing, and you'll see how the XPS model allows you to create a straightforward print preview feature.

Annotations

WPF provides an annotation feature that allows you to add comments and highlights to flow documents and fixed documents. These annotations can be used to suggest revisions, highlight errors, or flag important pieces of information.

Many products provide a wide range of annotation types. For example, Adobe Acrobat allows you to draw revision marks and shapes on a document. WPF isn't quite as flexible. It allows you to use two types of annotations:Highlighting: You can select some text and give it a colored background of your choice. (Technically, WPF highlighting applies a partially transparent color *over* your text, but the effect makes it seem as if you were changing the background.)*Sticky notes*: You can select some text and attach a floating box that contains additional text information or ink content.

Figure 28-17 shows the sample you'll learn how to build in this section. It shows a flow document with a highlighted text region and two sticky notes, one with ink content and one with text content.

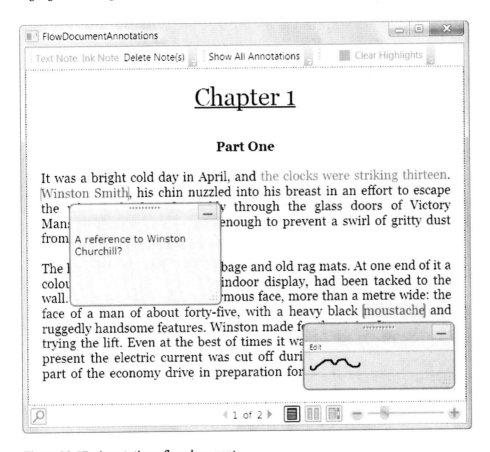

Figure 28-17. *Annotating a flow document*

All four of the WPF document containers—FlowDocumentReader, FlowDocumentScrollViewer, FlowDocumentPageViewer, and DocumentViewer—support annotations. But in order to use annotations, you need to take two steps. First, you need to manually enable the annotation service by using a bit of initialization code. Second, you need to add controls (such as toolbar buttons) that allow users to add the types of annotations you want to support.

Understanding the Annotation Classes

WPF's annotation system relies on several classes from the System.Windows.Annotations and System.Windows. Annotations.Storage namespaces. Here are the key players:

> *AnnotationService*: This class manages the annotations feature. In order to use annotations, it's up to you to create this object.
>
> *AnnotationStore*: This class manages the storage of your annotations. It defines several methods that you can use to create and delete individual annotations. It also includes events that you can use to react to annotations being created or changed. AnnotationStore is an abstract class, and there's currently just one class that derives from it: XmlStreamStore. XmlStreamStore serializes annotations to an XML-based format and allows you to store your annotation XML in any stream.
>
> *AnnotationHelper*: This class provides a small set of shared methods for dealing with annotations. These methods bridge the gap between the stored annotations and the document container. Most of the AnnotationHelper methods work with the currently selected text in the document container (allowing you to highlight it, annotate it, or remove its existing annotations). The AnnotationHelper also allows you to find where a specific annotation is placed in a document.

In the following sections, you'll use all three of these key ingredients.

■ **Tip** Both the AnnotationStore and the AnnotationHelper provide methods for creating and deleting annotations. However, the methods in the AnnotationStore class work with the currently selected text in a document container. For that reason, the AnnotationStore methods are best for programmatically manipulating annotations without user interaction, while the AnnotationHelper methods are best for implementing user-initiated annotation changes (for example, adding an annotation when the user selects some text and clicks a button).

Enabling the Annotation Service

Before you can do anything with annotations, you need to enable the annotation service with the help of an AnnotationService and AnnotationStream object.

In the example shown in Figure 28-17, it makes sense to create the AnnotationService when the window first loads. Creating the service is simple enough—you just need to create an AnnotationService object for the document reader and call AnnotationService.Enable(). However, when you call Enable(), you need to pass in an AnnotationStore object. The AnnotationService manages the information for your annotations, while the AnnotationStore manages the storage of these annotations.

Here's the code that creates and enables annotations:

```
' A stream for storing annotation.
Private annotationStream As MemoryStream

' The service that manages annotations.
Private service As AnnotationService

Protected Sub window_Loaded(ByVal sender As Object, _
   ByVal e As RoutedEventArgs)
     ' Create the AnnotationService for your document container.
     service = New AnnotationService(docReader)
```

```
    ' Create annotation storage.
    annotationStream = New MemoryStream()
    Dim store As New XmlStreamStore(annotationStream)

    ' Enable annotations.
    service.Enable(store)
End Sub
```

Notice that in this example, annotations are stored in a MemoryStream. As a result, they'll be discarded as soon as the MemoryStream is garbage collected. If you want to store annotations so they can be reapplied to the original document, you have two choices. You can create a FileStream instead of a MemoryStream, which ensures that the annotation data is written as the user applies it. Or you can copy the data in the MemoryStream to another location (such as a file or a database record) after the document is closed.

■ Tip   If you aren't sure whether annotations have been enabled for your document container, you can use the shared AnnotationService.GetService() method and pass in a reference to the document container. This method returns a null reference (Nothing) if annotations haven't been enabled yet.

At some point, you'll also need to close your annotation stream and switch off the AnnotationService. In this example, these tasks are performed when the user closes the window:

```
Protected Sub window_Unloaded(ByVal sender As Object, _
  ByVal e As RoutedEventArgs)
    If Not service Is Nothing AndAlso service.IsEnabled Then
        ' Flush annotations to stream.
        service.Store.Flush()

        ' Disable annotations.
        service.Disable()
        annotationStream.Close()
    End If
End Sub
```

This is all you need to enable annotations in a document. If there are any annotations defined in the stream object when you call AnnotationService.Enable(), these annotations will appear immediately. However, you still need to add the controls that will allow the user to add or remove annotations. That's the topic of the next section.

■ Tip   Every document container can have one instance of the AnnotationService. Every document should have its own instance of the AnnotationStore. When you open a new document, you should disable the AnnotationService, save and close the current annotation stream, create a new AnnotationStore, and then reenable the AnnotationService.

Creating Annotations

There are two ways to manipulate annotations. You can use one of the methods of the AnnotationHelper class that allows you to create annotations (CreateTextStickyNoteForSelection() and CreateInkStickyNoteForSelection()), delete them (DeleteTextStickyNotesForSelection() and DeleteInkStickyNotesForSelection()), and apply highlighting (CreateHighlightsForSelection() and ClearHighlightsForSelection()). The *ForSelection* part of the method name indicates that these methods apply the annotation to whatever text is currently selected.

Although the AnnotationHelper methods work perfectly well, it's far easier to use the corresponding commands that are exposed by the AnnotationService class. You can wire these commands directly to the buttons in your user interface. That's the approach we'll take in this example.

Before you can use the AnnotationService class in XAML, you need to map the System.Windows.Annotations namespace to an XML namespace, as it isn't one of the core WPF namespaces. You can add a mapping like this:

```
<Window x:Class="FlowDocumentAnnotations"
  xmlns:annot=
  "clr-namespace:System.Windows.Annotations;assembly=PresentationFramework" ... >
```

Now you can create a button like this, which creates a text note for the currently selected portion of the document:

```
<Button Command="annot:AnnotationService.CreateTextStickyNoteCommand">
  Text Note
</Button>
```

Now when the user clicks this button, a green note window will appear. The user can type text inside this note. (If you create an ink sticky note with the CreateInkStickyNoteCommand, the user can draw inside the note window instead.)

■ **Note** This Button element doesn't set the CommandTarget property. That's because the button is placed in a toolbar. As you learned in Chapter 9, the Toolbar class is intelligent enough to automatically set the CommandTarget to the element that has focus. Of course, if you use the same command in a button outside a toolbar, you'll need to set the CommandTarget to point to your document viewer.

Sticky notes don't need to remain visible at all times. If you click the minimize button in the top-right corner of the note window, it will disappear. All you'll see is the highlighted portion of the document where the note is set. If you hover over this highlighted region with the mouse, a note icon appears (see Figure 28-18)—click this to restore the sticky note window. The AnnotationService stores the position of each note window. Therefore, if you drag one somewhere specific in your document, close it and then reopen it, the note window will reappear in its previous place.

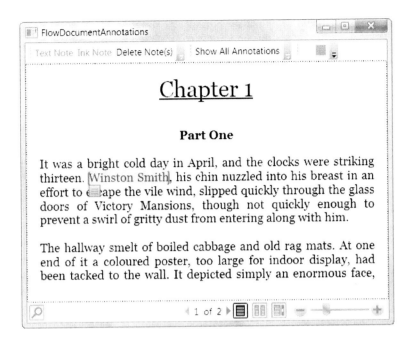

Figure 28-18. *A "hidden" annotation*

In the previous example, the annotation is created without any author information. If you plan to have multiple users annotating the same document, you'll almost certainly want to store some identifying information. Just pass a string that identifies the author as a parameter to the command, as shown here:

```
<Button Command="annot:AnnotationService.CreateTextStickyNoteCommand"
 CommandParameter="{StaticResource AuthorName}">
  Text Note
</Button>
```

This markup assumes that the author name is set as a resource:

```
<sys:String x:Key="AuthorName">[Anonymous]</sys:String>
```

This allows you to set the author name when the window first loads, at the same time as you initialize the annotation service. You can use a name that the user supplies, which you'll probably want to store in a user-specific .config file as an application setting. Alternatively, you can use the following code to grab the current user's Windows user account name with the help of the System.Security.Principal.WindowsIdentity class:

```
Dim identity As WindowsIdentity = WindowsIdentity.GetCurrent()
Me.Resources("AuthorName") = identity.Name
```

To create the window shown in Figure 28-17, you'll also want to create buttons that use the CreateInkStickyNoteCommand (to create a note window that accepts hand-drawn ink content) and DeleteStickyNotesCommand (to remove previously created sticky notes):

```
<Button Command="annot:AnnotationService.CreateInkStickyNoteCommand"
 CommandParameter="{StaticResource AuthorName}">
  Ink Note
</Button>
<Button Command="annot:AnnotationService.DeleteStickyNotesCommand">
  Delete Note(s)
</Button>
```

The DeleteStickyNotesCommand removes all the sticky notes in the currently selected text. Even if you don't provide this command, the user can still remove annotations by using the Edit menu in the note window (unless you've given the note window a different control template that doesn't include this feature).

The final detail is to create the buttons that allow you to apply highlighting. To add a highlight, you use the CreateHighlightCommand and you pass the Brush object that you want to use as the CommandParameter. However, it's important to make sure you use a brush that has a partially transparent color. Otherwise, your highlighted content will be completely obscured, as shown in Figure 28-19.

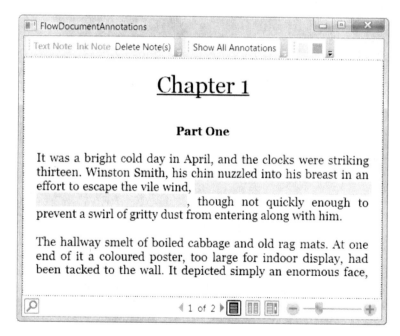

Figure 28-19. *Highlighting content with a nontransparent color*

For example, if you want to use the solid color #FF32CD32 (for lime green) to highlight your text, you should reduce the alpha value, which is stored as a hexadecimal number in the first two characters. (The alpha value ranges from 0 to 255, where 0 is fully transparent and 255 is fully opaque.) For example, the color #54FF32CD32 gives you a semitransparent version of the lime green color, with an alpha value of 84 (or 54 in hexadecimal notation).

The following markup defines two highlighting buttons, one for applying yellow highlights and one for green highlights. The button itself doesn't include any text. It simply shows a 15-by-15 square of the appropriate color. The CommandParameter defines a SolidColorBrush that uses the same color but with reduced opacity so the text is still visible:

```
<Button Background="Yellow" Width="15" Height="15" Margin="2,0"
 Command="annot:AnnotationService.CreateHighlightCommand">
  <Button.CommandParameter>
    <SolidColorBrush Color="#54FFFF00"></SolidColorBrush>
  </Button.CommandParameter>
</Button>

<Button Background="LimeGreen" Width="15" Height="15" Margin="2,0"
 Command="annot:AnnotationService.CreateHighlightCommand">
  <Button.CommandParameter>
    <SolidColorBrush Color="#5432CD32"></SolidColorBrush>
  </Button.CommandParameter>
</Button>
```

You can add a final button to remove highlighting in the selected region:

```
<Button Command="annot:AnnotationService.ClearHighlightsCommand">
  Clear Highlights
</Button>
```

■ **Note**   When you print a document that includes annotations by using the ApplicationCommands.Print command, the annotations are printed just as they appear. In other words, minimized annotations will appear minimized, visible annotations will appear on top of content (and may obscure other parts of the document), and so on. If you want to create a printout that doesn't include annotations, simply disable the annotation service before you begin your printout.

Examining Annotations

At some point, you may want to examine all the annotations that are attached to a document. There are many possible reasons—you may want to display a summary report about your annotations, print an annotation list, export annotation text to a file, and so on.

The AnnotationStore makes it relatively easy to get a list of all the annotations it contains by using the GetAnnotations() method. You can then examine each annotation as an Annotation object:

```
Dim annotations As IList(Of Annotation) annotations
annotations = service.Store.GetAnnotations()

For Each annotation As Annotation In annotations
   ...
Next
```

In theory, you can find annotations in a specific portion of a document by using the overloaded version of the GetAnnotations() method that takes a ContentLocator object. In practice, however, this is tricky, because the ContentLocator object is difficult to use correctly and you need to match the starting position of the annotation precisely.

After you've retrieved an Annotation object, you'll find that it provides the properties listed in Table 28-8.

Table 28-8. Annotation Properties

Name	Description
Id	A global identifier (GUID) that uniquely identifies this annotation. If you know the GUID for an annotation, you can retrieve the corresponding Annotation object by using the AnnotationStore.GetAnnotation() method. (Of course, there's no reason you'd know the GUID of an existing annotation unless you had previously retrieved it by calling GetAnnotations(), or you had reacted to an AnnotationStore event when the annotation was created or changed.)
AnnotationType	The XML element name that identifies this type of annotation, in the format *namespace:localname*.
Anchors	A collection of zero, one, or more AnnotationResource objects that identify what text is being annotated.
Cargos	A collection of zero, one, or more AnnotationResource objects that contain the user data for the annotation. This includes the text of a text note, or the ink strokes for an ink note.
Authors	A collection of zero, one, or more strings that identify who created the annotation.
CreationTime	The date and time when the annotation was created.
LastModificationTime	The date and time the annotation was last updated.

The Annotation object is really just a thin wrapper over the XML data that's stored for the annotation. One consequence of this design is that it's difficult to pull information out of the Anchors and Cargos properties. For example, if you want to get the actual text of an annotation, you need to look at the second item in the Cargos selection. This contains the text, but it's stored as a Base64-encoded string (which avoids problems if the note contains characters that wouldn't otherwise be allowed in XML element content). If you want to actually view this text, it's up to you to write tedious code like this to crack it open:

```
' Check for text information.
If annotation.Cargos.Count > 1 Then
    ' Decode the note text.
    Dim base64Text As String = annotation.Cargos(1).Contents(0).InnerText
    Dim decoded As Byte() = Convert.FromBase64String(base64Text)

    ' Write the decoded text to a stream.
    Dim m As New MemoryStream(decoded)

    ' Using the StreamReader, convert the text bytes into a more
    ' useful string.
    Dim r As New StreamReader(m)
    Dim annotationXaml As String = r.ReadToEnd()
    r.Close()

    ' Show the annotation content.
    MessageBox.Show(annotationXaml)
End If
```

This code gets the text of the annotation, wrapped in a XAML <Section> element. The opening <Section> tag includes attributes that specify a wide range of typography details. Inside the <Section> element are more <Paragraph> and <Run> elements.

■ **Note** Like a text annotation, an ink annotation will also have a Cargos collection with more than one item. However, in this case the Cargos collection will contain the ink data but no decodable text. If you use the previous code on an ink annotation, you'll get an empty message box. Thus, if your document contains both text and ink annotations, you should check the Annotation.AnnotationType property to make sure you're dealing with a text annotation before you use this code.

If you just want to get the text without the surrounding XML, you can use the XamlReader to deserialize it (and avoid using the StreamReader). The XML can be deserialized into a Section object, using code like this:

```
' Check for text information.
If annotation.Cargos.Count > 1 Then
    ' Decode the note text.
    Dim base64Text As String = annotation.Cargos(1).Contents(0).InnerText
    Dim decoded As Byte() = Convert.FromBase64String(base64Text)

    ' Write the decoded text to a stream.
    Dim m As New MemoryStream(decoded)

    ' Deserialize the XML into a Section object.
    Dim section As Section = CType(XamlReader.Load(m), Section)
    m.Close()

    ' Get the text inside the Section.
    Dim range As New TextRange(section.ContentStart, section.ContentEnd)

    ' Show the annotation content.
    MessageBox.Show(range.Text)
End If
```

As Table 28-8 shows, text isn't the only detail you can recover from an annotation. It's easy to get the annotation author, the time it was created, and the time it was last modified.

You can also retrieve information about where an annotation is anchored in your document. The Anchors collection isn't much help for this task, because it provides a low-level collection of AnnotationResource objects that wrap additional XML data. Instead, you need to use the GetAnchorInfo() method of the AnnotationHelper class. This method takes an annotation and returns an object that implements IAnchorInfo.

```
Dim anchorInfo As IAnchorInfo
anchorInfo = AnnotationHelper.GetAnchorInfo(service, annotation)
```

IAnchorInfo combines the AnnotationResource (the Anchor property), the annotation (Annotation), and an object that represents the location of the annotation in the document tree (ResolvedAnchor), which is the most useful detail. Although the ResolvedAnchor property is typed as an object, text annotations and highlights always return a TextAnchor object. The TextAnchor describes the starting point of the anchored text (BoundingStart) and the ending point (BoundingEnd).

Here's how you could determine the highlighted text for an annotation by using the IAnchorInfo:

```
Dim anchor As IAnchorInfo = AnnotationHelper.GetAnchorInfo(service, annotation)
Dim resolvedAnchor As TextAnchor = TryCast(anchor.ResolvedAnchor, TextAnchor)

If resolvedAnchor IsNot Nothing Then
    Dim startPointer As TextPointer = CType(resolvedAnchor.BoundingStart, _
        TextPointer)
    Dim endPointer As TextPointer = CType(resolvedAnchor.BoundingEnd, _
        TextPointer)

    Dim range As New TextRange(startPointer, endPointer)
    MessageBox.Show(range.Text)
End If
```

You can also use the TextAnchor objects as a jumping-off point to get to the rest of the document tree, as shown here:

```
' Scroll the document so the paragraph with the annotated text is displayed.
Dim tp As TextPointer = CType(resolvedAnchor.BoundingStart, TextPointer)
tx.Paragraph.BringIntoView()
```

The samples for this chapter include an example that uses this technique to create an annotation list. When an annotation is selected in the list, the annotated portion of the document is shown automatically.

In both cases, the AnnotationHelper.GetAnchorInfo() method allows you to travel from the annotation to the annotated text, much as the AnnotationStore.GetAnnotations() method allows you to travel from the document content to the annotations.

Although it's relatively easy to examine existing annotations, the WPF annotation feature isn't as strong when it comes to manipulating these annotations. It's easy enough for the user to open a sticky note, drag it to a new position, change the text, and so on, but it's not easy for you to perform these tasks programmatically. In fact, all the properties of the Annotation object are read-only. There are no readily available methods to modify an annotation, so annotation editing involves deleting and re-creating the annotation. You can do this by using the methods of the AnnotationStore or the AnnotationHelper (if the annotation is attached to the currently selected text). However, both approaches require a fair bit of grunt work. If you use the AnnotationStore, you need to construct an Annotation object by hand. If you use the AnnotationHelper, you need to explicitly set the text selection to include the right text before you create the annotation. Both approaches are tedious and unnecessarily error-prone.

Reacting to Annotation Changes

You've already learned how the AnnotationStore allows you to retrieve the annotations in a document (with GetAnnotations()) and manipulate them (with DeleteAnnotation() and AddAnnotation()). The AnnotationStore provides one additional feature—it raises events that inform you when annotations are changed.

The AnnotationStore provides four events: AnchorChanged (which fires when an annotation is moved), AuthorChanged (which fires when the author information of an annotation changes), CargoChanged (which fires when annotation data, including text, is modified), and StoreContentChanged (which fires when an annotation is created, deleted, or modified in any way).

The online samples for this chapter include an annotation-tracking example. An event handler for the StoreContentChanged event reacts when annotation changes are made. It retrieves all the annotation information (using the GetAnnotations() method) and then displays the annotation text in a list.

> ■ **Note** The annotation events occur after the change has been made. That means there's no way to plug in custom logic that extends an annotation action. For example, you can't add just-in-time information to an annotation or selectively cancel a user's attempt to edit or delete an annotation.

Storing Annotations in a Fixed Document

The previous examples used annotations on a flow document. In this scenario, annotations can be stored for future use, but they must be stored separately—for example, in a distinct XML file.

When using a fixed document, you can use the same approach, but you have an additional option—you can store annotations directly in the XPS document file. In fact, you could even store multiple sets of distinct annotations, all in the same document. You simply need to use the package support in the System.IO.Packaging namespace.

As you learned earlier, every XPS document is actually a ZIP archive that includes several files. When you store annotations in an XPS document, you are actually creating another file inside the ZIP archive.

The first step is to choose a URI to identify your annotations. Here's an example that uses the name AnnotationStream:

```
Dim annotationUri As Uri = PackUriHelper.CreatePartUri( _
    New Uri("AnnotationStream", UriKind.Relative))
```

Now you need to get the Package for your XPS document by using the shared PackageStore.GetPackage() method:

```
Dim package As Package = PackageStore.GetPackage(doc.Uri)
```

You can then create the package part that will store your annotations inside the XPS document. However, you need to check whether the annotation package part already exists (in case you've loaded the document before and already added annotations). If it doesn't exist, you can create it now:

```
Dim annotationPart As PackagePart
If package.PartExists(annotationUri) Then
    annotationPart = package.GetPart(annotationUri)
Else
    annotationPart = package.CreatePart(annotationUri, "Annotations/Stream")
End If
```

The last step is to create an AnnotationStore that wraps the annotation package part, and then enable the AnnotationService in the usual way:

```
Dim store As New XmlStreamStore(annotationPart.GetStream())
service = New AnnotationService(docViewer)
service.Enable(store)
```

In order for this technique to work, you must open the XPS file by using FileMode.ReadWrite mode rather than FileMode.Read, so the annotations can be written to the XPS file. For the same reason, you need to keep the XPS document open while the annotation service is at work. You can close the XPS document when the window is closed (or you choose to open a new document).

Customizing the Appearance of Sticky Notes

The note windows that appear when you create a text note or ink note are instances of the StickyNoteControl class, which is found in the System.Windows.Controls namespace. Like all WPF controls, you can customize the visual appearance of the StickyNoteControl by using style setters or applying a new control template.

For example, you can easily create a style that applies to all StickyNoteControl instances by using the Style. TargetType property. Here's an example that gives every StickyNoteControl a new background color:

```
<Style TargetType="{x:Type StickyNoteControl}">
  <Setter Property="Background" Value="LightGoldenrodYellow"/>
</Style>
```

To make a more dynamic version of the StickyNoteControl, you can write a style trigger that responds to the StickyNoteControl.IsActive property, which is True when the sticky note has focus.

For more control, you can use a completely different control template for your StickyNoteControl. The only trick is that the StickyNoteControl template varies depending on whether it's used to hold an ink note or a text note. If you allow the user to create both types of notes, you need a trigger that can choose between two templates. Ink notes must include an InkCanvas, and text notes must contain a RichTextBox. In both cases, this element should be named PART_ContentControl.

Here's a style that applies the bare minimum control template for both ink and text sticky notes. It sets the dimensions of the note window and chooses the appropriate template based on the type of note content:

```
<Style x:Key="MinimumStyle" TargetType="{x:Type StickyNoteControl}">
  <Setter Property="OverridesDefaultStyle" Value="true" />
  <Setter Property="Width" Value="100" />
  <Setter Property="Height" Value ="100" />
  <Style.Triggers>
    <Trigger Property="StickyNoteControl.StickyNoteType"
     Value="{x:Static StickyNoteType.Ink}">
      <Setter Property="Template">
        <Setter.Value>
          <ControlTemplate>
            <InkCanvas Name="PART_ContentControl" Background="LightYellow" />
          </ControlTemplate>
        </Setter.Value>
      </Setter>
    </Trigger>
    <Trigger Property="StickyNoteControl.StickyNoteType"
     Value="{x:Static StickyNoteType.Text}">
      <Setter Property="Template">
        <Setter.Value>
          <ControlTemplate>
              <RichTextBox Name="PART_ContentControl" Background="LightYellow"/>
          </ControlTemplate>
        </Setter.Value>
      </Setter>
    </Trigger>
  </Style.Triggers>
</Style>
```

The Last Word

Most developers already know that WPF offers its own, specialized model for drawing, layout, and animation. However, WPF's rich document features are often overlooked.

In this chapter, you've seen how to create flow documents, lay out text inside them in a variety of ways, and control how that text is displayed in different containers. You also learned how to use the FlowDocument object model to change portions of the document dynamically, and you considered the RichTextBox, which provides a solid base for advanced text-editing features.

Finally, you took a quick look at fixed documents and the XpsDocument class. The XPS model provides the plumbing for WPF's printing feature, which is the subject of the next chapter.

Printing

WPF includes a revamped printing model that organizes all your coding around a single ingredient: the PrintDialog class in the System.Windows.Controls namespace. Using the PrintDialog class, you can show a Print dialog box where the user can pick a printer and change its setting, and you can send elements, documents, and low-level visuals directly to the printer. In this chapter, you'll learn how to use the PrintDialog class to create properly scaled and paginated printouts.

Basic Printing

Although WPF includes dozens of print-related classes (most of which are found in the System.Printing namespace), there's a single starting point that makes life easy: the PrintDialog class.

The PrintDialog wraps the familiar Print dialog box that lets the user choose the printer and a few other standard print options, such as the number of copies (see Figure 29-1). However, the PrintDialog class is more than just a pretty window—it also has the built-in ability to trigger a printout.

Figure 29-1. *Showing the PrintDialog*

To submit a print job with the PrintDialog class, you need to use one of two methods:

- *PrintVisual()* works with any class that derives from System.Windows.Media.Visual. This includes any graphic you draw by hand and any element you place in a window.

- *PrintDocument()* works with any DocumentPaginator object. This includes the ones that are used to split a FlowDocument (or XpsDocument) into pages and any custom DocumentPaginator you create to deal with your own data.

In the following sections, you'll consider a variety of strategies that you can use to create a printout.

Printing an Element

The simplest approach to printing is to take advantage of the model you're already using for onscreen rendering. Using the PrintDialog.PrintVisual() method, you can send any element in a window (and all its children) straight to the printer.

To see an example in action, consider the window shown in Figure 29-2. It contains a Grid that lays out all the elements. In the topmost row is a Canvas, and in that Canvas is a drawing that consists of a TextBlock and a Path (which renders itself as a rectangle with an elliptic hole in the middle).

Figure 29-2. *A simple drawing*

To send the Canvas to the printer, complete with all the elements it contains, you can use this snippet of code when the Print button is clicked:

```
Dim printDialog As New PrintDialog()
If printDialog.ShowDialog() = True Then
    printDialog.PrintVisual(canvas, "A Simple Drawing")
End Of
```

The first step is to create a PrintDialog object. The next step is to call ShowDialog() to show the Print dialog box. ShowDialog returns a nullable Boolean value. A return value of True indicates that the user clicked OK, a return value of False indicates that the user clicked Cancel, and a null reference (Nothing) indicates that the dialog box was closed without either button being clicked.

When calling the PrintVisual() method, you pass two arguments. The first is the element that you want to print, and the second is a string that's used to identify the print job. You'll see it appear in the Windows print queue (under the Document Name column).

When printing this way, you don't have much control over the output. The element is always lined up with the top-left corner of the page. If your element doesn't include nonzero Margin values, the edge of your content might land in the nonprintable area of the page, which means it won't appear in the printed output.

The lack of margin control is only the beginning of the limitations that you'll face using this approach. You also can't paginate your content if it's extremely long, so if you have more content than can fit on a single page, some will be left out at the bottom. Finally, you have no control over the scaling that's used to render your job to the printing. Instead, WPF uses the same device-independent rendering system based on 1/96th-inch units. For example, if you have a rectangle that's 96 units wide, that rectangle will appear to be an inch wide on your monitor (assuming you're using the standard 96 dpi Windows system setting) and an inch wide on the printed page. Often, this results in a printout that's quite a bit smaller than what you want.

▨ **Note** Obviously, WPF fills in much more detail in the printed page, because virtually no printer has a resolution as low as 96 dpi (600 dpi and 1200 dpi are much more common printer resolutions). However, WPF keeps your content the same size in the printout as it is on your monitor.

Figure 29-3 shows the full-page printout of the Canvas from the window shown in Figure 29-2.

Figure 29-3. *A printed element*

```
┌──────────────────────────────────────────────────────────────────────┐
│                        PRINTDIALOG QUIRKS                              │
└──────────────────────────────────────────────────────────────────────┘
```

The PrintDialog class wraps a lower-level internal .NET class named Win32PrintDialog, which in turns wraps the Print dialog box that's exposed by the Win32 API. Unfortunately, these extra layers remove a little bit of your flexibility.

One potential problem is the way that the PrintDialog class works with modal windows. Buried in the inaccessible Win32PrintDialog code is a bit of logic that always makes the Print dialog box modal with respect to your application's *main* window. This leads to an odd problem if you show a modal window from your main window and then call the PrintDialog.ShowDialog() method from that window. Although you'd expect the Print dialog box to be modal to your second window, it will actually be modal with respect to your main window, which means the user can return to your second window and interact with it (even clicking the Print button to show multiple instances of the Print dialog box)! The somewhat clumsy solution is to manually change your application's main window to the current window before you call PrintDialog.ShowDialog() and then switch it back immediately afterward.

There's another limitation to the way the PrintDialog class works. Because your main application thread owns the content you're printing, it's not possible to perform your printing on a background thread. This becomes a concern if you have time-consuming printing logic. Two possible solutions exist. If you construct the visuals you want to print on the background thread (rather than pulling them out of an existing window), you'll be able to perform your printing on the background thread. However, a simpler solution is to use the PrintDialog box to let the user specify the print settings and then use the XpsDocumentWriter class to actually print the content instead of the printing methods of the PrintDialog class. The XpsDocumentWriter can send content to the printer asynchronously, and it's described in the "Printing Through XPS" section later in this chapter.

Transforming Printed Output

You may remember (from Chapter 12) that you can attach the Transform object to the RenderTransform or LayoutTransform property of any element to change the way it's rendered. Transform objects could solve the problem of inflexible printouts, because you could use them to resize an element (ScaleTransform), move it around the page (TranslateTransform), or both (TransformGroup). Unfortunately, visuals can lay themselves out only one way at a time. That means there's no way to scale an element one way in a window and another way in a printout—instead, any Transform objects you apply will change both the printed output and the onscreen appearance of your element.

If you aren't intimidated by a bit of messy compromise, you can work around this issue in several ways. The basic idea is to apply your transform objects just before you create the printout and then remove them. To prevent the resized element from appearing in the window, you can temporarily hide it.

You might expect to hide your element by changing its Visibility property, but this hides your element from both the window and the printout, which obviously isn't what you want. One possible solution is to change the Visibility of the parent (in this example, the layout Grid). This works because the PrintVisual() method considers only the element you specify and its children, not the details of the parent.

Here's the code that puts it all together and prints the Canvas shown in Figure 29-2, but five times bigger in both dimensions:

```
Dim printDialog As New PrintDialog()
If printDialog.ShowDialog() = True Then
    ' Hide the Grid.
    grid.Visibility = Visibility.Hidden

    ' Magnify the output by a factor of 5.
    canvas.LayoutTransform = New ScaleTransform(5, 5)
```

```
    ' Print the element.
    printDialog.PrintVisual(canvas, "A Scaled Drawing")

    ' Remove the transform and make the element visible again.
    canvas.LayoutTransform = Nothing
    grid.Visibility = Visibility.Visible
End If
```

This example has one missing detail. Although the Canvas (and its contents) is stretched, the Canvas is still using the layout information from the containing Grid. In other words, the Canvas still believes it has an amount of space to work with that's equal to the dimensions of the Grid cell in which it's placed. In this example, this oversight doesn't cause a problem, because the Canvas doesn't limit itself to the available space (unlike some other containers). However, you will run into trouble if you have text and you want it to wrap to fit the bounds of the printed page or if your Canvas has a background (which, in this example, will occupy the smaller size of the Grid cell rather than the whole area behind the Canvas).

The solution is easy. After you set the LayoutTransform (but before you print the Canvas), you need to trigger the layout process manually using the Measure() and Arrange() methods that every element inherits from the UIElement class. The trick is that when you call these methods, you'll pass in the size of the page, so the Canvas stretches itself to fit. (Incidentally, this is also why you set the LayoutTransform instead of the RenderTransform property, because you want the layout to take the newly expanded size into account.) You can get the page size from the PrintableAreaWidth and PrintableAreaHeight properties.

■ **Note**   Based on the property names, it's reasonable to assume that PrintableAreaWidth and PrintableAreaHeight reflect the *printable* area of the page—in other words, the part of the page on which the printer can actually print. (Most printers can't reach the very edges, usually because that's where the rollers grip onto the page.) But in truth, PrintableAreaWidth and PrintableAreaHeight simply return the *full* width and height of the page in device-independent units. For a sheet of 8.5×11 paper, that's 816 and 1056. (Try dividing these numbers by 96 dpi, and you'll get the full paper size.)

The following example demonstrates how to use the PrintableAreaWidth and PrintableAreaHeight properties. To be a bit nicer, it leaves off 10 units (about 0.1 of an inch) as a border around all edges of the page.

```
Dim printDialog As New PrintDialog()
If printDialog.ShowDialog() = True Then
    ' Hide the Grid.
    grid.Visibility = Visibility.Hidden

    ' Magnify the output by a factor of 5.
    canvas.LayoutTransform = New ScaleTransform(5, 5)

    ' Define a margin.
    Dim pageMargin As Integer = 5

    ' Get the size of the page.
    Dim pageSize As New Size(printDialog.PrintableAreaWidth - pageMargin * 2, _
      printDialog.PrintableAreaHeight - 20)
```

```
' Trigger the sizing of the element.
canvas.Measure(pageSize)
canvas.Arrange(New Rect(pageMargin, pageMargin, _
  pageSize.Width, pageSize.Height))

' Print the element.
printDialog.PrintVisual(canvas, "A Scaled Drawing")

' Remove the transform and make the element visible again.
canvas.LayoutTransform = Nothing
grid.Visibility = Visibility.Visible
End If
```

The end result is a way to print any element and scale it to suit your needs (see the full-page printout in Figure 29-4). This approach works perfectly well, but you can see the (somewhat messy) glue that's holding it all together.

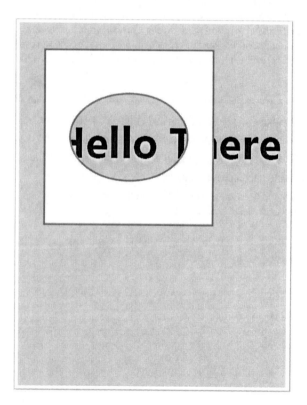

Figure 29-4. *A scaled printed element*

Printing Elements Without Showing Them

Because the way you want to show data in your application and the way you want it to appear in a printout are often different, it sometimes makes sense to create your visual programmatically (rather than using one that appears in an existing window). For example, the following code creates an in-memory TextBlock object, fills it with text, sets it to wrap, sizes it to fit the printed page, and then prints it:

```
Dim printDialog As New PrintDialog()
If printDialog.ShowDialog() = True Then
    ' Create the text.
    Dim textRun As New Run("This is a test of the printing functionality" & _
        "in the Windows Presentation Foundation.")

    ' Wrap it in a TextBlock.
    Dim visual As New TextBlock()
    TextBlock.Inlines.Add(textRun)

    ' Use margin to get a page border.
    visual.Margin = New Thickness(15)

    ' Allow wrapping to fit the page width.
    visual.TextWrapping = TextWrapping.Wrap

    ' Scale the TextBlock up in both dimensions by a factor of 5.
    ' (In this case, increasing the font would have the same effect,
    ' because the TextBlock is the only element.)
    visual.LayoutTransform = New ScaleTransform(5, 5)

    ' Size the element.
    Dim pageSize As New Size(printDialog.PrintableAreaWidth, _
        printDialog.PrintableAreaHeight)
    visual.Measure(pageSize)
    visual.Arrange(New Rect(0, 0, pageSize.Width, pageSize.Height))

    ' Print the element.
    printDialog.PrintVisual(visual, "A Scaled Drawing")
End If
```

Figure 29-5 shows the printed page that this code creates.

This is a test of the printing functionality in the Windows Presentation Foundation.

Figure 29-5. *Wrapped text using a TextBlock*

This approach allows you to grab the content you need out of a window but customize its printed appearance separately. However, it's of no help if you have content that needs to span more than one page (in which case you'll need the printing techniques described in the following sections).

Printing a Document

The PrintVisual() method may be the most versatile printing method, but the PrintDialog class also includes another option. You can use PrintDocument() to print the content from a flow document. The advantage of this approach is that a flow document can handle a huge amount of complex content and can split that content over multiple pages (just as it does onscreen).

You might expect that the PrintDialog.PrintDocument() method would require a FlowDocument object, but it actually takes a DocumentPaginator object. The DocumentPaginator is a specialized class whose sole role in life is to take content, split it into multiple pages, and supply each page when requested. Each page is represented by a DocumentPage object, which is really just a wrapper for a single Visual object with a little bit of sugar on top. You'll find just three more properties in the DocumentPage class. Size returns the size of the page, ContentBox is the size of the box where content is placed on the page after margins are added, and BleedBox is the area where print production-related bleeds, registration marks, and crop marks appear on the sheet, outside the page boundaries.

What this means is that PrintDocument() works in much the same way as PrintVisual(). The difference is that it prints several visuals—one for each page.

▓ **Note**   Although you could split your content into separate pages without using a DocumentPaginator and make repeated calls to PrintVisual(), this isn't a good approach. If you do, each page will become a separate print job.

So how do you get a DocumentPaginator object for a FlowDocument? The trick is to cast the FlowDocument to an IDocumentPaginatorSource and then use the DocumentPaginator property. Here's an example:

```
Dim printDialog As New PrintDialog()
If printDialog.ShowDialog() = True Then
    Dim paginatorSource As IDocumentPaginatorSource
    paginatorSource = CType(docReader.Document, IDocumentPaginatorSource)

    printDialog.PrintDocument(paginatorSource.DocumentPaginator, _
      "A Flow Document")
End If
```

This code may or may not produce the desired result, depending on the container that's currently housing your document. If your document is in-memory (but not in a window) or if it's stored in RichTextBox or FlowDocumentScrollViewer, this codes works fine. You'll end up with a multipaged printout with two columns (on a standard sheet of 8.5×11 paper in portrait orientation). This is the same result you'll get if you use the ApplicationCommands.Print command.

▓ **Note**   As you learned in Chapter 9, some controls include built-in command wiring. The FlowDocument containers (like the FlowDocumentScrollViewer used here) is one example. It handles the ApplicationCommands.Print command to perform a basic printout. This hardwired printing code is similar to the code shown previously, although it uses the XpsDocumentWriter, which is described in the "Printing Through XPS" section of this chapter.

However, if your document is stored in a FlowDocumentPageViewer or a FlowDocumentReader, the result isn't as good. In this case, your document is paginated the same way as the current view in the container. So if there are 24 pages required to fit the content into the current window, you'll get 24 pages in the printed output, each with a tiny window worth of data. Again, the solution is a bit messy, but it works. (It's also essentially the same solution that the ApplicationCommands.Print command takes.) The trick is to force the FlowDocument to paginate itself for the printer. You can do this by setting the FlowDocument.PageHeight and FlowDocument.PageWidth properties to the boundaries of the page, not the boundaries of the container. (In containers such as the FlowDocumentScrollViewer, these properties aren't set because pagination isn't used. That's why the printing feature works without a hitch—it paginates itself automatically when you create the printout.)

```
Dim doc As FlowDocument = docReader.Document

doc.PageHeight = printDialog.PrintableAreaHeight
doc.PageWidth = printDialog.PrintableAreaWidth
printDialog.PrintDocument( _
  CType(doc, IDocumentPaginatorSource).DocumentPaginator, _
  "A Flow Document")
```

You'll probably also want to set properties such as ColumnWidth and ColumnGap so you can get the number of columns you want. Otherwise, you'll get whatever is used in the current window.

The only problem with this approach is that once you've changed these properties, they apply to the container that displays your document. As a result, you'll end up with a compressed version of your document that's probably too small to read in the current window. A proper solution takes this into account by storing all these values, changing them, and then reapplying the original values.

Here's the complete code printing a two-column printout with a generous margin (added through the FlowDocument.PagePadding property):

```
Dim printDialog As New PrintDialog()
If printDialog.ShowDialog() = True Then
    Dim doc As FlowDocument = docReader.Document

    ' Save all the existing settings.
    Dim pageHeight As Double = doc.PageHeight
    Dim pageWidth As Double = doc.PageWidth
    Dim pagePadding As Thickness = doc.PagePadding
    Dim columnGap As Double = doc.ColumnGap
    Dim columnWidth As Double = doc.ColumnWidth

    ' Make the FlowDocument page match the printed page.
    doc.PageHeight = printDialog.PrintableAreaHeight
    doc.PageWidth = printDialog.PrintableAreaWidth
    doc.PagePadding = New Thickness(50)

    ' Use two columns.
    doc.ColumnGap = 25
    doc.ColumnWidth = (doc.PageWidth - doc.ColumnGap _
      - doc.PagePadding.Left - doc.PagePadding.Right) / 2

    printDialog.PrintDocument( _
      CType(doc, IDocumentPaginatorSource).DocumentPaginator, _
      "A Flow Document")

    ' Reapply the old settings.
    doc.PageHeight = pageHeight
    doc.PageWidth = pageWidth
    doc.PagePadding = pagePadding
    doc.ColumnGap = columnGap
    doc.ColumnWidth = columnWidth
End If
```

This approach has a few limitations. Although you're able to tweak properties that adjust the margins and number of columns, you don't have much control. Of course, you can modify the FlowDocument programmatically (for example, temporarily increasing its FontSize), but you can't tailor the printout with details such as page numbers. You'll learn one way to get around this restriction in the next section.

PRINTING ANNOTATIONS

WPF includes two classes that derive from DocumentPaginator. FlowDocumentPaginator paginates flow documents—it's what you get when you examine the FlowDocument.DocumentPaginator property. Similarly, FixedDocumentPaginator paginates XPS documents, and it's used automatically by the XpsDocument class. However, both of these classes are marked internal and aren't accessible to your code. Instead, you can interact with these paginators by using the members of the base DocumentPaginator class.

WPF includes just one public, concrete paginator class, AnnotationDocumentPaginator, which is used to print a document with its associated annotations. (Chapter 28 discussed annotations.) AnnotationDocumentPaginator is public so that you can create it, if necessary, to trigger a printout of an annotated document.

To use the AnnotationDocumentPaginator, you must wrap an existing DocumentPaginator in a new AnnotationDocumentPaginator object. To do so, simply create an AnnotationDocumentPaginator, and pass in two references. The first reference is the original paginator for your document, and the second reference is the annotation store that contains all the annotations. Here's an example:

```
' Get the ordinary paginator.
Dim oldPaginator As DocumentPaginator
oldPaginator = CType(doc, IDocumentPaginatorSource).DocumentPaginator

' Get the (currently running) annotation service for a
' specific document container.
Dim service As AnnotationService = AnnotationService.GetService(docViewer)

' Create the new paginator.
Dim newPaginator As New AnnotationDocumentPaginator( _
  oldPaginator, service.Store)
```

Now, you can print the document with the superimposed annotations (in their current minimized or maximized state) by calling PrintDialog.PrintDocument() and passing in the AnnotationDocumentPaginator object.

Manipulating the Pages in a Document Printout

You can gain a bit more control over how a FlowDocument is printed by creating your own DocumentPaginator. As you might guess from its name, a DocumentPaginator divides the content of a document into distinct pages for printing (or displaying in a page-based FlowDocument viewer). The DocumentPaginator is responsible for returning the total number of pages based on a given page size and providing the laid-out content for each page as a DocumentPage object.

Your DocumentPaginator doesn't need to be complex—in fact, it can simply wrap the DocumentPaginator that's provided by the FlowDocument and allow it to do all the hard work of breaking up the text into individual pages. However, you can use your DocumentPaginator to make minor alterations, such as adding a header and a footer. The basic trick is to intercept every request the PrintDialog makes for a page and then alter that page before passing it along.

The first ingredient of this solution is building a HeaderedFlowDocumentPaginator class that derives from DocumentPaginator. Because DocumentPaginator is an abstract class, HeaderedFlowDocument needs to implement several methods. However, HeaderedFlowDocument can pass most of the work on to the standard DocumentPaginator that's provided by the FlowDocument.

Here's the basic skeleton of the HeaderedFlowDocumentPaginator class:

```vb
Public Class HeaderedFlowDocumentPaginator
    Inherits DocumentPaginator

    ' The real paginator (which does all the pagination work).
    Private flowDocumentPaginator As DocumentPaginator

    ' Store the FlowDocument paginator from the given document.
    Public Sub New(ByVal document As FlowDocument)
        flowDocumentPaginator = CType(document, _
      IDocumentPaginatorSource).DocumentPaginator
    End Sub

    Public Overrides ReadOnly Property IsPageCountValid() As Boolean
        Get
            Return flowDocumentPaginator.IsPageCountValid
        End Get
    End Property

    Public Overrides ReadOnly Property PageCount() As Integer
        Get
            Return flowDocumentPaginator.PageCount
        End Get
    End Property

    Public Overrides Property PageSize() As System.Windows.Size
        Get
            Return flowDocumentPaginator.PageSize
        End Get
        Set(ByVal value As System.Windows.Size)
            flowDocumentPaginator.PageSize = value
        End Set
    End Property

    Public Overrides ReadOnly Property Source() As IDocumentPaginatorSource
        Get
            Return flowDocumentPaginator.Source
        End Get
    End Property

    Public Overrides Function GetPage(ByVal pageNumber As Integer) _
      As DocumentPage
        ...
    End Function

End Class
```

Because the HeaderedFlowDocumentPaginator hands off its work to its private DocumentPaginator, this code doesn't indicate how the PageSize, PageCount, and IsPageCountValid properties work. The PageSize is set by the DocumentPaginator consumer (the code that's using the DocumentPaginator). This property tells the DocumentPaginator how much space is available in each printed page (or onscreen). The PageCount and IsPageCountValid properties are provided *to* the DocumentPaginator consumer to indicate the pagination result. Whenever PageSize is changed, the DocumentPaginator will recalculate the size of each page. (Later in this chapter, you'll see a more complete DocumentPaginator that was created from scratch and includes the implementation details for these properties.)

The GetPage() method is where the action happens. This code calls the GetPage() method of the real DocumentPaginator and then gets to work on the page. The basic strategy is to pull the Visual object out of the page and place it in a new ContainerVisual object. You can then add the text you want to that ContainerVisual. Finally, you can create a new DocumentPage that wraps the ContainerVisual, with its newly inserted header.

> **Note** This code uses visual-layer programming (Chapter 14). That's because you need a way to create visuals that represent your printed output. You don't need the full overhead of elements, which include event handling, dependency properties, and other plumbing. Custom print routines (as described in the next section) almost always use visual-layer programming and the ContainerVisual, DrawingVisual, and DrawingContext classes.

Here's the complete code:

```
Public Overrides Function GetPage(ByVal pageNumber As Integer) As DocumentPage
    ' Get the requested page.
    Dim page As DocumentPage = flowDocumentPaginator.GetPage(pageNumber)

    ' Wrap the page in a Visual. You can then add a transformation and extras.
    Dim newVisual As New ContainerVisual()
    newVisual.Children.Add(page.Visual)

    ' Create a header.
    Dim header As New DrawingVisual()
    Using context As DrawingContext = header.RenderOpen()
        Dim typeface As New Typeface("Times New Roman")
        Dim text As New FormattedText("Page" & (pageNumber + 1).ToString(), _
          CultureInfo.CurrentCulture, FlowDirection.LeftToRight, _
          typeface, 14, Brushes.Black)

        ' Leave a quarter-inch of space between the page edge and this text.
        context.DrawText(text, New Point(96*0.25, 96*0.25))
    End Using

    ' Add the title to the visual.
    newVisual.Children.Add(header)

    ' Wrap the visual in a new page.
    Dim newPage As New DocumentPage(newVisual)
    Return newPage
End Function
```

This implementation assumes the page size doesn't change because of the addition of your header. Instead, the assumption is that there's enough empty space in the margin to accommodate the header. If you use this code with a small margin, the header will be printed overtop of your document content. This is the same way headers work in programs such as Microsoft Word. Headers aren't considered part of the main document, and they're positioned separately from the main document content.

There's one minor messy bit. You won't be able to add the Visual object for the page to the ContainerVisual while it's displayed in a window. The workaround is to temporarily remove it from the container, perform the printing, and then add it back.

```
Dim document As FlowDocument = docReader.Document
docReader.Document = Nothing

Dim paginator As New HeaderedFlowDocumentPaginator(document)
printDialog.PrintDocument(paginator, "A Headered Flow Document")

docReader.Document = document
```

The HeaderedFlowDocumentPaginator is used for the printing, but it's not attached to the FlowDocument, so it won't change the way the document appears onscreen.

Custom Printing

By this point, you've probably realized the fundamental truth of WPF printing. You can use the quick-and-dirty techniques described in the previous section to send content from a window to your printer and even tweak it a bit. But if you want to build a first-rate printing feature for your application, you'll need to design it yourself.

Printing with the Visual Layer Classes

The best way to construct a custom printout is to use the visual-layer classes. Two classes are particularly useful:

- *ContainerVisual* is a stripped-down visual that can hold a collection of one or more other Visual objects (in its Children collection).

- *DrawingVisual* derives from ContainerVisual and adds a RenderOpen() method and a Drawing property. The RenderOpen() method creates a DrawingContext object that you can use to draw content in the visual (such as text, shapes, and so on), and the Drawing property lets you retrieve the final product as a DrawingGroup object.

Once you understand how to use these classes, the process for creating a custom printout is fairly straightforward.

1. Create your DrawingVisual. (You can also create a ContainerVisual in the less common case that you want to combine more than one separate drawn DrawingVisual object on the same page.)

2. Call DrawingVisual.RenderOpen() to get the DrawingContext object.

3. Use the methods of the DrawingContext to create your output.

4. Close the DrawingContext. (If you've wrapped the DrawingContext in a using block, this step is automatic.)

5. Using PrintDialog.PrintVisual() to send your visual to the printer.

Not only does this approach give you more flexibility than the print-an-element techniques you've used so far, it also has less overhead.

Obviously, the key to making this work is knowing what methods the DrawingContext class has for you to create your output. Table 29-1 describes the methods you can use. The Push*Xxx*() methods are particularly interesting, because they apply settings that will apply to future drawing operations. You can use Pop() to reverse the most recent Push*Xxx*() method. If you call more than one Push*Xxx*() method, you can switch them off one at a time with subsequent Pop() calls.

Table 29-1. DrawingContext Methods

Name	Description
DrawLine(), DrawRectangle(), DrawRoundedRectangle(), and DrawEllipse()	Draws the specified shape at the point you specify, with the fill and outline you specify. These methods mirror the shapes you saw in Chapter 12.
DrawGeometry () and DrawDrawing()	Draws more complex Geometry and Drawing objects. You saw these in Chapter 13.
DrawText()	Draws text at the specified location. You specify the text, font, fill, and other details by passing a FormattedText object to this method. You can use DrawText() to draw wrapped text if you set the FormattedText.MaxTextWidth property.
DrawImage()	Draws a bitmap image in a specific region (as defined by a Rect).
Pop()	Reverses the last Push*Xxx*() method that was called. You use the Push*Xxx*() method to temporarily apply one or more effects and the Pop() method to reverse them.
PushClip()	Limits drawing to a specific clip region. Content that falls outside of this region isn't drawn.
PushEffect ()	Applies a BitmapEffect to subsequent drawing operations.
PushOpacity()	Applies a new opacity setting to make subsequent drawing operations partially transparent.
PushTransform()	Sets a Transform object that will be applied to subsequent drawing operations. You can use a transformation to scale, displace, rotate, or skew content.

These are all the ingredients that are required to create a respectable printout (along with a healthy dash of math to work out the optimum placement of all your content). The following code uses this approach to center a block of formatted text on a page and add a border around the page:

```
Dim printDialog As New PrintDialog()
If printDialog.ShowDialog() = True Then
    ' Create a visual for the page.
    Dim visual As New DrawingVisual()
```

```vb
    ' Get the drawing context
    Using dc As DrawingContext = visual.RenderOpen()
        ' Define the text you want to print.
        Dim text As New FormattedText(txtContent.Text, _
            CultureInfo.CurrentCulture, FlowDirection.LeftToRight, _
            New Typeface("Calibri"), 20, Brushes.Black)

        ' You must pick a maximum width to use wrapping with a
        ' FormattedText object.
        text.MaxTextWidth = printDialog.PrintableAreaWidth / 2

        ' Get the size required for the text.
        Dim textSize As New Size(text.Width, text.Height)

        ' Find the top-left corner where you want to place the text.
        Dim margin As Double = 96 * 0.25
        Dim point As New Point( _
            (printDialog.PrintableAreaWidth - textSize.Width) / 2 - margin, _
            (printDialog.PrintableAreaHeight - textSize.Height) / 2 - margin)

        ' Draw the content.
        dc.DrawText(text, point)

        ' Add a border (a rectangle with no background).
        dc.DrawRectangle(Nothing, New Pen(Brushes.Black, 1), _
            New Rect(margin, margin, _
                printDialog.PrintableAreaWidth - margin * 2, _
                printDialog.PrintableAreaHeight - margin * 2))
    End Using

    ' Print the visual.
    printDialog.PrintVisual(visual, "A Custom-Printed Page")
End If
```

■ **Tip** To improve this code, you'll probably want to move your drawing logic to a separate class (possibly the document class that wraps the content you're printing). You can then call a method in that class to get your visual and pass the visual to the PrintVisual() method in the event handling in your window code.

Figure 29-6 shows the output.

Marley was dead: to begin with There is no doubt whatever about that. The register of his burial was signed by the clergyman, the clerk, the undertaker, and the chief mourner. Scrooge signed it: and Scrooge's name was good upon 'Change, for anything he chose to put his hand to. Old Marley was as dead as a door-nail.

Figure 29-6. *A custom printout*

Custom Printing with Multiple Pages

A visual can't span pages. If you want a multipage printout, you need to use the same class you used when printing a FlowDocument: the DocumentPaginator. The difference is that you need to create the DocumentPaginator yourself from scratch. And this time you won't have a private DocumentPaginator on the inside to take care of all the heavy lifting.

Implementing the basic design of a DocumentPaginator is easy enough. You need to add a method that splits your content into pages, and you need to store the information about those pages internally. Then, you simply respond to the GetPage() method to provide the page that the PrintDialog needs. Each page is generated as a DrawingVisual, but the DrawingVisual is wrapped by the DocumentPage class.

The tricky part is separating your content into pages. There's no WPF magic here—it's up to you to decide how to divide your content. Some content is relatively easy to separate (like the long table you'll see in the next example), while some types of content are much more problematic. For example, if you want to print a long, text-based document, you'll need to move word by word through all your text, adding words to lines and lines to pages. You'll need to measure each separate piece of text to see whether it fits in the line. And that's just to split text content using ordinary left justification—if you want something comparable to the best-fit justification used for the FlowDocument, you're better off using the PrintDialog.PrintDocument() method, as described earlier, because there's a huge amount of code to write and some very specialized algorithms to use.

The following example demonstrates a typical not-too-difficult pagination job. The contents of a DataTable are printed in a tabular structure, putting each record on a separate row. The rows are split into pages based on how many lines fit on a page using the chosen font. Figure 29-7 shows the final result.

Model Number	Model Name
RU007	Rain Racer 2000
STKY1	Edible Tape
P38	Escape Vehicle (Air)
NOZ119	Extracting Tool
PT109	Escape Vehicle (Water)
RED1	Communications Device
LK4TLNT	Persuasive Pencil
NTMBS1	Multi-Purpose Rubber Band
NE1RPR	Universal Repair System
BRTLGT1	Effective Flashlight
INCPPRCLP	The Incredible Versatile Paperclip
DNTRPR	Toaster Boat
TGFDA	Multi-Purpose Towelette
WOWPEN	Mighty Mighty Pen
ICNCU	Perfect-Vision Glasses
LKARCKT	Pocket Protector Rocket Pack
DNTGCGHT	Counterfeit Creation Wallet
WRLD00	Global Navigational System
CITSME9	Cloaking Device
BME007	Indentity Confusion Device
SHADE01	Ultra Violet Attack Defender
SQUKY1	Guard Dog Pacifier
CHEW99	Survival Bar
COOLCMB1	Telescoping Comb
FF007	Eavesdrop Detector
LNGWADN	Escape Cord
1MOR4ME	Cocktail Party Pal
SQRTME1	Remote Foliage Feeder
ICUCLRLY00	Contact Lenses
OPNURMIND	Telekinesis Spoon

Model Number	Model Name
ULOST007	Rubber Stamp Beacon
BSUR2DUC	Bullet Proof Facial Tissue
NOBOOBOO4U	Speed Bandages
BHONST93	Correction Fluid
BPRECISE00	Dilemma Resolution Device
LSRPTR1	Nonexplosive Cigar
QLT2112	Document Transportation System
THNKDKE1	Hologram Cufflinks
TCKLR1	Fake Moustache Translator
JWLTRANS6	Interpreter Earrings
GRTWTCH9	Multi-Purpose Watch

Figure 29-7. *A table of data split over two pages*

In this example, the custom DocumentPaginator contains the code for splitting the data into pages and the code for printing each page to a Visual object. Although you could factor this into two classes (for example, if you want to allow the same data to be printed in the same way but paginated differently), usually you won't because the code required to calculate the page size is tightly bound to the code that actually prints the page.

The custom DocumentPaginator implementation is fairly long, so I'll break it down piece by piece. First, the StoreDataSetPaginator stores a few important details in private variables, including the DataTable that you plan to print and the chosen typeface, font size, page size, and margin:

```
Public Class StoreDataSetPaginator
    Inherits DocumentPaginator

    Private dt As DataTable

    Private typeface As Typeface
    Private fontSize As Double
    Private margin As Double

    Private _pageSize As Size
    Public Overrides Property PageSize() As Size
        Get
            Return _pageSize
        End Get
```

```
        Set(ByVal value As Size)
            _pageSize = value
            PaginateData()
        End Set
    End Property

    Public Sub New(ByVal dt As DataTable, ByVal typeface As Typeface, _
        ByVal fontSize As Double, ByVal margin As Double, ByVal pageSize As Size)
        Me.dt = dt
        Me.typeface = typeface
        Me.fontSize = fontSize
        Me.margin = margin
        Me._pageSize = pageSize
        PaginateData()
    End Sub
```

...

Notice that these details are supplied in the constructor and then can't be changed. The only exception is the PageSize property, which is a required abstract property from the DocumentPaginator class. You could create properties to wrap the other details if you wanted to allow your code to alter these details after creating the paginator. You'd simply need to make sure you call PaginateData() when any of these details are changed.

The PaginateData() isn't a required member. It's just a handy place to calculate how many pages are needed. The StoreDataSetPaginator paginates its data as soon as the DataTable is supplied in the constructor.

When the PaginateData() method runs, it measures the amount of space required for a line of text and compares that against the size of the page to find out how many lines will fit on each page. The result is stored in a field named rowsPerPage.

...

```
Private rowsPerPage As Integer
Private _pageCount As Integer

' This helper method splits the data into pages.
' In some cases you'll need to store objects representing the per-page data.
' Here, a rowsPerPage value is enough because every page is the same.
Private Sub PaginateData()
    ' Create a test string for the purposes of measurement.
    Dim text As FormattedText = GetFormattedText("A")

    ' Count the lines that fit on a page.
    rowsPerPage = CInt((_pageSize.Height - margin * 2) / text.Height)

    ' Leave a row for the headings
    rowsPerPage -= 1

    _pageCount = CInt(Math.Ceiling(CDbl(dt.Rows.Count) / rowsPerPage))
End Sub
```
...

This code assumes that a capital letter *A* is sufficient for calculating the line height. However, this might not be true for all fonts, in which case you'd need to pass a string that includes a complete list of all characters, numbers, and punctuation to GetFormattedText().

▓ **Note**   To calculate the number of lines that fit on a page, you use the FormattedText.Height property. You *don't* use FormattedText.LineHeight, which is 0 by default. The LineHeight property is provided for you to override the default line spacing when drawing a block with multiple lines of text. However, if you don't set it, the FormattedText class uses its own calculation, which uses the Height property.

In some cases, you'll need to do a bit more work and store a custom object for each page (for example, an array of strings with the text for each line). However, this isn't required in the StoreDataSetPaginator example because all the lines are the same, and there isn't any text wrapping to worry about.

The PaginateData() uses a private helper method named GetFormattedText(). When printing text, you'll find that you need to construct a great number of FormattedText objects. These FormattedText objects will always share the same culture and left-to-right text flow options. In many cases, they'll also use the same typeface. The GetFormattedText() encapsulates these details and so simplifies the rest of your code. The StoreDataSetPaginator uses two overloaded versions of GetFormattedText(), one of which accepts a different typeface to use:

```
...
Private Function GetFormattedText(ByVal text As String) As FormattedText
    Return GetFormattedText(text, typeface)
End Function

Private Function GetFormattedText(ByVal text As String, _
  ByVal typeface As Typeface) As FormattedText
    Return New FormattedText(text, CultureInfo.CurrentCulture, _
      FlowDirection.LeftToRight, typeface, fontSize, Brushes.Black)
End Function
...
```

Now that you have the number of pages, you can implement the remainder of the required DocumentPaginator properties:

```
...
' Always returns true, because the page count is updated immediately,
' and synchronously, when the page size changes.
' It's never left in an indeterminate state.
Public Overrides ReadOnly Property IsPageCountValid() As Boolean
    Get
        Return True
    End Get
End Property

Public Overrides ReadOnly Property PageCount() As Integer
    Get
        Return _pageCount
    End Get
End Property
```

```
Public Overrides ReadOnly Property Source() As IDocumentPaginatorSource
    Get
        Return Nothing
    End Get
End Property
...
```

There's no factory class that can create this custom DocumentPaginator, so the Source property returns a null reference (Nothing).

The last implementation detail is also the longest. The GetPage() method returns a DocumentPage object for the requested page, with all the data.

The first step is to find the position where the two columns will begin. This example sizes the columns relative to the width of one capital letter A, which is a handy shortcut when you don't want to perform more detailed calculations.

```
...
Public Overrides Function GetPage(ByVal pageNumber As Integer) _
    As DocumentPage
    ' Create a test string for the purposes of measurement.
    Dim text As FormattedText = GetFormattedText("A")

    Dim col1_X As Double = margin
    Dim col2_X As Double = col1_X + text.Width * 15
    ...
```

The next step is to find the offsets that identify the range of records that belong on this page:

```
...
' Calculate the range of rows that fits on this page.
Dim minRow As Integer = pageNumber * rowsPerPage
Dim maxRow As Integer = minRow + rowsPerPage
...
```

Now the print operation can begin. There are three elements to print: column headers, a separating line, and the rows. The underlined header is drawn using DrawText() and DrawLine() methods from the DrawingContext class. For the rows, the code loops from the first row to the last row, drawing the text from the corresponding DataRow in the two columns and then increasing the Y-coordinate position by an amount equal to the line height of the text.

```
...
' Create the visual for the page.
Dim visual As New DrawingVisual()

' Set the position to the top-left corner of the printable area.
Dim point As New Point(margin, margin)

' Print the column values.
Using dc As DrawingContext = visual.RenderOpen()
    ' Draw the column headers.
    Dim columnHeaderTypeface As New Typeface(typeface.FontFamily, _
        FontStyles.Normal, FontWeights.Bold, FontStretches.Normal)
    point.X = col1_X
    text = GetFormattedText("Model Number", columnHeaderTypeface)
    dc.DrawText(text, point)
```

```
            text = GetFormattedText("Model Name", columnHeaderTypeface)
            point.X = col2_X
            dc.DrawText(text, point)

            ' Draw the line underneath.
            dc.DrawLine(New Pen(Brushes.Black, 2), _
              New Point(margin, margin + text.Height), _
              New Point(_pageSize.Width - margin, margin + text.Height))

            point.Y += text.Height

            ' Draw the column values.
            For i As Integer = minRow To maxRow - 1
                ' Check for the end of the last (half-filled) page.
                If i > (dt.Rows.Count - 1) Then
                    Exit For
                End If

                point.X = col1_X
                text = GetFormattedText(dt.Rows(i)("ModelNumber").ToString())
                dc.DrawText(text, point)

                ' Add second column.
                text = GetFormattedText(dt.Rows(i)("ModelName").ToString())
                point.X = col2_X
                dc.DrawText(text, point)
                point.Y += text.Height
            Next
        End Using
        Return New DocumentPage(visual, pageSize, New Rect(pageSize), _
          New Rect(pageSize))
    End Function

End Class
```

Now that the StoreDateSetDocumentPaginator is complete, you can use it whenever you want to print the contents of the DataTable with the product list, as shown here:

```
Dim printDialog As New PrintDialog()
If printDialog.ShowDialog() = True Then
    Dim paginator As New StoreDataSetPaginator(ds.Tables(0), _
      New Typeface("Calibri"), 24, 96 * 0.75, _
      New Size(printDialog.PrintableAreaWidth, printDialog.PrintableAreaHeight))

    printDialog.PrintDocument(paginator, "Custom-Printed Pages")
End If
```

The StoreDataSetPaginator has a certain amount of flexibility built in—for example, it can work with different fonts, margins, and paper sizes—but it can't deal with data that has a different schema. Clearly, there's still room in the WPF library for a handy class that could accept data, column and row definitions, headers and footers, and so on, and then print a properly paginated table. WPF doesn't have anything like this currently, but you can expect third-party vendors to provide components that fill the gaps.

Print Settings and Management

So far, you've focused all your attention on two methods of the PrintDialog class: PrintVisual() and PrintDocument(). This is all you need to use to get a decent printout, but you have more to do if you want to manage printer settings and jobs. Once again, the PrintDialog class is your starting point.

Maintaining Print Settings

In the previous examples, you saw how the PrintDialog class allows you to choose a printer and its settings. However, if you've used these examples to make more than one printout, you may have noticed a slight anomaly. Each time you return to the Print dialog box, it reverts to the default print settings. You need to pick the printer you want and adjust it all over again.

Life doesn't need to be this difficult. You have the ability to store this information and reuse it. One good approach is to store the PrintDialog as a member variable in your window. That way, you don't need to create the PrintDialog before each new print operation—you just keep using the existing object. This works because the PrintDialog encapsulates the printer selection and printer settings through two properties: PrintQueue and PrintTicket.

The PrintQueue property refers to a System.Printing.PrintQueue object, which represents the print queue for the selected printer. And as you'll discover in the next section, the PrintQueue also encapsulates a good deal of features for managing your printer and its jobs.

The PrintTicket property refers to a System.Printing.PrintTicket object, which defines the settings for a print job. It includes details such as print resolution and duplexing. If you want, you're free to tweak the settings of a PrintTicket programmatically. The PrintTicket class even has a GetXmlStream() method and a SaveTo() method, both of which let you serialize the ticket to a stream, and a constructor that lets you re-create a PrintTicket object based on the stream. This is an interesting option if you want to persist specific print settings between application sessions. (For example, you could use this ability to create a "print profile" feature.)

As long as these PrintQueue and PrintTicket properties remain consistent, the selected printer and its properties will remain the same each time you show the Print dialog box. So even if you need to create the PrintDialog box multiple times, you can simply set these properties to keep the user's selections.

Printing Page Ranges

You haven't yet considered one of the features in the PrintDialog class. You can allow the user to choose to print only a subset of a larger printout using the Pages text box in the Page Range box. The Pages text box lets the user specify a group of pages by entering the starting and ending page (for example, *4–6*) or pick a specific page (for example, *4*). It doesn't allow multiple page ranges (such as *1–3,5*).

The Pages text box is disabled by default. To switch it on, you simply need to set the PrintDialog.UserPageRangeEnabled property to True before you call ShowDialog(). The Selection and Current Page options remain disabled, because they aren't supported by the PrintDialog class. You can also set the MaxPage and MinPage properties to constrain the pages that the user can pick.

After you've shown the Print dialog box, you can determine whether the user entered a page range by checking the PageRangeSelection property. If it provides a value of UserPages, there's a page range present. The PageRange property provides a PageRange property that indicates the starting page (PageRange.PageFrom) and ending page (PageRange.PageTo). It's up to your printing code to take these values into account and print only the requested pages.

Managing a Print Queue

Typically, a client application has a limited amount of interaction with the print queue. After a job is dispatched, you may want to display its status or (rarely) provide the option to pause, resume, or cancel the job. The WPF print classes go far beyond this level and allow you to build tools that can manage local or remote print queues.

The classes in the System.Printing namespace provide the support for managing print queues. You can use a few key classes to do most of the work, and they're outlined in Table 29-2.

Table 29-2. *Key Classes for Print Management*

Name	Description
PrintServer and LocalPrintServer	Represents a computer that provides printers or another device that does. (This "other device" might include a printer with built-in networking or a dedicated piece of network hardware that acts as a print server.) Using the PrintServer class, you can get a collection of PrintQueue objects for that computer. You can also use the LocalPrintServer class, which derives from PrintServer and always represents the current computer. It adds a DefaultPrintQueue property that you can use to get (or set) the default printer and a shared GetDefaultPrintQueue() method that you can use without creating a LocalPrintServer instance.
PrintQueue	Represents a configured printer on a print server. The PrintQueue class allows you to get information about that printer's status and manage the print queue. You can also get a collection of PrintQueueJobInfo objects for that printer.
PrintSystemJobInfo	Represents a job that's been submitted to a print queue. You can get information about its status and modify its state or delete it.

Using these basic ingredients, you can create a program that launches a printout without any user intervention.

```
Dim dialog As New PrintDialog()

' Pick the default printer.
dialog.PrintQueue = LocalPrintServer.GetDefaultPrintQueue()

' Print something.
dialog.PrintDocument(someContent, "Automatic Printout")
```

You can also create and apply a PrintTicket object to the PrintDialog to configure other print-related settings. More interestingly, you can delve deeper in the PrintServer, PrintQueue, and PrintSystemJobInfo classes to study what's taking place.

Figure 29-8 shows a simple program that allows you to browse the print queues on the current computer and see the outstanding jobs for each one. This program also allows you to perform some basic printer management tasks, such as suspending a printer (or a print job), resuming the printer (or print job), and canceling one job or all the jobs in a queue. By considering how this application works, you can learn the basics of the WPF print management model.

Figure 29-8. *Browsing printer queues and jobs*

This example uses a single PrintServer object, which is created as a member field in the window class:

```
private printServer As New PrintServer()
```

When you create a PrintServer object without passing any arguments to the constructor, the PrintServer represents the current computer. Alternatively, you could pass the UNC path that points to a print server on the network, like this:

```
private printServer As New PrintServer("\\Warehouse\PrintServer")
```

Using the PrintServer object, the code grabs a list of print queues that represent the printers that are configured on the current computer. This step is easy—all you need to do is call the PrintServer.GetPrintQueues() method when the window is first loaded:

```
Private Sub Window_Loaded(ByVal sender As Object, ByVal e As EventArgs)
    lstQueues.DisplayMemberPath = "FullName"
    lstQueues.SelectedValuePath = "FullName"
    lstQueues.ItemsSource = printServer.GetPrintQueues()
End Sub
```

The only piece of information this code snippet uses is the PrintQueue.FullName property. However, the PrintQueue class is stuffed with properties you can examine. You can get the default print settings (using properties such as DefaultPriority, DefaultPrintTicket, and so on), you can get the status and general information (using properties such as QueueStatus and NumberOfJobs), and you can isolate specific problems using Boolean Is*Xxx* and Has*Xxx* properties (such as IsManualFeedRequired, IsWarmingUp, IsPaperJammed, IsOutOfPaper, HasPaperProblem, and NeedUserIntervention).

The current example reacts when a printer is selected in the list by displaying the status for that printer and then fetching all the jobs in the queue. The PrintQueue.GetPrintJobInfoCollection() performs this task.

```
Private Sub lstQueues_SelectionChanged(ByVal sender As Object, _
  ByVal e As SelectionChangedEventArgs)
    Try
        Dim queue As PrintQueue
        queue = printServer.GetPrintQueue(lstQueues.SelectedValue.ToString())

        lblQueueStatus.Text = "Queue Status:" & queue.QueueStatus.ToString()
        lblJobStatus.Text = ""
        lstJobs.DisplayMemberPath = "JobName"
        lstJobs.SelectedValuePath = "JobIdentifier"

        lstJobs.ItemsSource = queue.GetPrintJobInfoCollection()
    Catch Err As Exception
        MessageBox.Show(err.Message, _
          "Error on " & lstQueues.SelectedValue.ToString())
    End Try
End Sub
```

Each job is represented as a PrintSystemJobInfo object. When a job is selected in the list, this code shows its status:

```
Private Sub lstJobs_SelectionChanged(ByVal sender As Object, _
  ByVal e As SelectionChangedEventArgs)
    If lstJobs.SelectedValue Is Nothing Then
        lblJobStatus.Text = ""
    Else
        Dim queue As PrintQueue
        queue = printServer.GetPrintQueue(lstQueues.SelectedValue.ToString())

        Dim job As PrintSystemJobInfo
        job = queue.GetJob(CInt(Fix(lstJobs.SelectedValue)))

        lblJobStatus.Text = "Job Status: " & job.JobStatus.ToString()
    End If
End Sub
```

The only remaining detail is the event handlers that manipulate the queue or job when you click one of the buttons in the window. This code is extremely straightforward. All you need to do is get a reference to the appropriate queue or job and then call the corresponding method. For example, here's how to pause a PrintQueue:

```
Dim queue As PrintQueue
queue = printServer.GetPrintQueue(lstQueues.SelectedValue.ToString())
queue.Pause()
```

And here's how to pause a print job:

```
Dim queue As PrintQueuequeue = printServer.GetPrintQueue(lstQueues.SelectedValue.ToString())

Dim job As PrintSystemJobInfo = queue.GetJob(CInt(lstJobs.SelectedValue))
job.Pause()
```

▓ **Note** It's possible to pause (and resume) an entire printer or a single job. You can do both tasks using the Printers icon in the Control Panel. Right-click a printer to pause or resume a queue, or double-click a printer to see its jobs, which you can manipulate individually.

Obviously, you'll need to add error handling when you perform this sort of task, because it won't necessarily succeed. For example, Windows security might stop you from attempting to cancel someone else's print job or an error might occur if you try to print to a networked printer after you've lost your connection to the network.

WPF includes quite a bit of print-related functionality. If you're interested in using this specialized functionality (perhaps because you're building some sort of tool or creating a long-running background task), check out the classes in the System.Printing namespace in the MSDN help.

Printing Through XPS

As you learned in Chapter 28, WPF supports two complementary types of documents. Flow documents handle flexible content that flows to fit any page size you specify. XPS documents store print-ready content that's based on a fixed-page size. The content is frozen in place and preserved in its precise, original form.

As you'd expect, printing an XpsDocument is easy. The XpsDocument class exposes a DocumentPaginator, just like the FlowDocument. However, the DocumentPaginator of an XpsDocument has little to do, because the content is already laid out in fixed, unchanging pages.

Here's the code you might use to load an XPS file into memory, show it in a DocumentViewer, and then send it to the printer:

```
' Display the document.
Dim doc As New XpsDocument("filename.xps", FileAccess.ReadWrite)
docViewer.Document = doc.GetFixedDocumentSequence()
doc.Close()

' Print the document.
If printDialog.ShowDialog() = True Then
    printDialog.PrintDocument(docViewer.Document.DocumentPaginator, _
       "A Fixed Document")
End If
```

Obviously, you don't need to show a fixed document in a DocumentViewer before you print it. This code includes that step because it's the most common option. In many scenarios, you'll load up the XpsDocument for review and print it after the user clicks a button.

As with the viewers for FlowDocument objects, the DocumentViewer also handles the ApplicationCommands. Print command, which means you can send an XPS document from the DocumentViewer to the printer with no code required.

Creating an XPS Document for a Print Preview

WPF also includes all the support you need to programmatically create XPS documents. Creating an XPS document is conceptually similar to printing some content—once you've built your XPS document, you've chosen a fixed page size and frozen your layout. So why bother taking this extra step? There are two good reasons:

- *Print preview.* You can use your generated XPS document as a print preview by displaying it in a DocumentViewer. The user can then choose whether to go ahead with the printout.

- *Asynchronous printing.* The XpsDocumentWriter class includes both a Write() method for synchronous printing and a WriteAsync() method that lets you send content to the printer asynchronously. For a long, complex print operation, the asynchronous option is preferred. It allows you to create a more responsive application.

The basic technique for creating an XPS document is create an XpsDocumentWriter object using the shared XpsDocument.CreateXpsDocumentWriter() method. Here's an example:

```
Dim xpsDocument As New XpsDocument("filename.xps", FileAccess.ReadWrite)
Dim writer As XpsDocumentWriter
writer = XpsDocument.CreateXpsDocumentWriter(xpsDocument)
```

The XpsDocumentWriter is a stripped-down class—its functionality revolves around the Write() and WriteAsync() methods that write content to your XPS document. Both of these methods are overloaded multiple times, allowing you to write different types of content, including another XPS document, a page that you've extracted from an XPS document, a visual (which allows you to write any element), and a DocumentPaginator. The last two options are the most interesting, because they duplicate the options you have with printing. For example, if you've created a DocumentPaginator to enable custom printing (as described earlier in this chapter), you can also use it to write an XPS document.

Here's an example that opens an existing flow document and then writes it to a temporary XPS document using the XpsDocumentWriter.Write() method. The newly created XPS document is then displayed in a DocumentViewer, which acts as a print preview.

```
Using FileStream fs = File.Open("FlowDocument1.xaml", FileMode.Open)

    Dim doc As flowDocument = CType(XamlReader.Load(fs), FlowDocument)
    writer.Write(CType(doc, IDocumentPaginatorSource).DocumentPaginator)

    ' Display the new XPS document in a viewer.
    docViewer.Document = xpsDocument.GetFixedDocumentSequence()
    xpsDocument.Close()
End Using
```

You can get a visual or paginator in a WPF application in an endless variety of ways. Because the XpsDocumentWriter supports these classes, it allows you to write any WPF content to an XPS document.

Writing to an In-Memory XPS Document

The XpsDocument class assumes that you want to write your XPS content to a file. This is a bit awkward for situations like the one shown previously, where the XPS document is a temporary stepping stone that's used to create a preview. Similar problems occur if you want to serialize XPS content to some other storage location, like a field in a database record.

It's possible to get around this limitation, and write XPS content directly to a MemoryStream. However, it takes a bit more work, as you first need to create a package for your XPS content. Here's the code that does the trick:

```
' Get ready to store the content in memory.
Dim ms As New MemoryStream()

' Create a package usign the static Package.Open() method.
Dim package As Package = Package.Open(ms, FileMode.Create, FileAccess.ReadWrite)

' Every package needs a URI. Use the pack:// syntax.
' The actual file name is unimportant.
Dim documentUri As New Uri("pack://InMemoryDocument.xps")

' Add the package.
PackageStore.AddPackage(documentUri, package)

' Create the XPS document based on this package. At the same time, choose
' the level of compression you want for the in-memory content.
Dim xpsDocument As New XpsDocument(package, CompressionOption.Fast, _
    DocumentUri.AbsoluteUri)
```

When you're finished using the XPS document, you can close the stream to recover the memory.

▦ **Note**   Don't use the in-memory approach if you might have a larger XPS document (for example, if you're generating an XPS document based on content in a database, and you don't know how many records there will be). Instead, use a method like Path.GetTempFileName() to get a suitable temporary path for a file-based XPS document.

Printing Directly to the Printer via XPS

As you've learned in this chapter, the printing support in WPF is built on the XPS print path. If you use the PrintDialog class, you might not see any sign of this low-level reality. If you use the XpsDocumentWriter, it's impossible to miss.

So far, you've been funneling all your printing through the PrintDialog class. This isn't necessary—in fact, the PrintDialog delegates the real work to the XpsDocumentWriter. The trick is to create an XpsDocumentWriter that wraps a PrintQueue rather than a FileStream. The actual code for writing the printed output is identical—you simply rely on the Write() and WriteAsync() methods.

Here's a snippet of code that shows the Print dialog box, gets the selected printer, and uses it to create an XpsDocumentWriter that submits the print job:

```
Dim filePath As String = Path.Combine(appPath, "FlowDocument1.xaml")

If printDialog.ShowDialog() = True Then
    Dim queue As PrintQueue = printDialog.PrintQueue
    Dim writer As XpsDocumentWriter = PrintQueue.CreateXpsDocumentWriter(queue)

    Using FileStream fs = File.Open(filePath, FileMode.Open)
        Dim doc As FlowDocument = CType(XamlReader.Load(fs), FlowDocument)
        writer.Write(CType(doc, IDocumentPaginatorSource).DocumentPaginator)
    End Using
End If
```

Interestingly, this example still uses the PrintDialog class. However, it simply uses it to display the standard Print dialog box and allow the user to choose a printer. The actual printing is performed through the XpsDocumentWriter.

Asynchronous Printing

The XpsDocumentWriter makes asynchronous printing easy. In fact, you can convert the previous example to use asynchronous printing by simply replacing the call to the Write() method with a call to WriteAsync().

▪ **Note** In Windows, all print jobs are printed asynchronously. However, the process of *submitting* the print job takes place synchronously if you use Write() and asynchronously if you use WriteAsync(). In many cases, the time taken to submit a print job won't be significant, and you won't need this feature. Another consideration is that if you want to build (and paginate) the content you want to print asynchronously, this is often the most time-consuming stage of printing, and if you want this ability, you'll need to write the code that runs your printing logic on a background thread. You can use the techniques described in Chapter 31 (such as the BackgroundWorker) to make this process relatively easy.

The signature of the WriteAsync() method matches the signature of the Write() method—in other words, WriteAsync() accepts a paginator, visual, or one of a few other types of objects. Additionally, the WriteAsync() method includes overloads that accept an optional second parameter with state information. This state information can be any object you want to use to identify the print job. This object is provided through the WritingCompletedEventArgs object when the WritingCompleted event fires. This allows you to fire off multiple print jobs at once, handle the WritingCompleted event for each one with the same event handler, and determine which one has been submitted each time the event fires.

When an asynchronous print job is underway, you can cancel it by calling the CancelAsync() method. The XpsDocumentWriter also includes a small set of events that allow you to react as a print job is submitted, including WritingProgressChanged, WritingCompleted, and WritingCancelled. Keep in mind that the WritingCompleted event fires when the print job has been written to the print queue, but this doesn't mean the printer has printed it yet.

The Last Word

In this chapter, you learned about WPF's printing model. First you considered the easiest entry point: the all-in-one PrintDialog class that allows users to configure print settings and allows your application to send a document or visual to the printer. After considering a variety of ways to extend the PrintDialog and use it with onscreen and dynamically generated content, you looked at the lower-level XPS printing model. You then learned about the XpsDocumentWriter, which supports the PrintDialog and can be used independently. The XpsDocumentWriter gives you an easy way to create a print preview (because WPF doesn't include any print preview control), and it allows you to submit your print job asynchronously.

Additional Topics

Interacting with Windows Forms

In an ideal world, once developers master a new technology such as WPF, they'd leave the previous framework behind. Everything would be written using the latest, most capable toolkit, and no one would ever worry about legacy code. Of course, this ideal world is nothing like the real world, and most WPF developers will need to interact with the Windows Forms platform at some point for two reasons: to leverage existing code investments and to compensate for missing features in WPF.

In this chapter, you'll look at strategies for integrating Windows Forms and WPF content. You'll consider how to use both types of windows in a single application, and you'll explore the more impressive trick of mixing content from both platforms in a single window. But before you delve into WPF and Windows Forms interoperability, it's worth taking a step back and assessing the reasons you should (and shouldn't) use WPF interoperability.

■ **What's New**   Early betas of WPF 4.5 included a mechanism that solved the airspace issue (the inability to overlap content that's created by WPF with content that's created by Windows Forms). However, this feature was dropped from the final release, leaving WPF's interoperability support unchanged.

Assessing Interoperability

There's no tool to transform Windows Forms interfaces into similar WPF interfaces (and even if there were, such a tool would be only a starting point of a long and involved migration process). Of course, there's no *need* to transplant a Windows Forms application into the WPF environment—most of the time, you're better off keeping old applications as is and using WPF for new projects. However, life isn't always that simple. You might decide that you want to add a WPF feature (such as an eye-catching 3-D animation) to an existing Windows Forms application. Or you might decide that you want to migrate an existing Windows Forms application to WPF piece by piece, as you release updated versions. Either way, the interoperability support in WPF can help you make the transition gradually and without sacrificing the work that's invested in your legacy code.

Before you toss WPF elements and Windows Forms controls together, it's important to assess your overall goals. In many situations, developers are faced with deciding between incrementally enhancing a Windows Forms application (and gradually moving it into the WPF world) or replacing it with a newly rewritten WPF masterpiece. Obviously, the first approach is faster and easier to test, debug, and release. However, in a suitably complex application that needs a major WPF injection, there may come a point where it's simpler to start over in WPF and import the legacy bits that you need.

■ **Note**   As always, when moving from one user interface platform to another, you should be forced to migrate only the user interface. Other details, such as data access code, validation rules, file access, and so on, should be abstracted away in separate classes (and possibly even separate assemblies), which you can plug into a WPF front-end just as easily as a Windows Forms application. Of course, this level of componentization isn't always possible, and sometimes other details (such as data-binding considerations and validation strategies) can lead you to shape your classes a certain way and inadvertently limit their reusability.

Mixing Windows and Forms

The cleanest way to integrate WPF and Windows Forms content is to place each in a separate window. That way, your application consists of well-encapsulated window classes, each of which deals with just a single technology. Any interoperability details are handled in the *glue* code—the logic that creates and shows your windows.

Adding Forms to a WPF Application

The easiest approach to mixing windows and forms is to add one or more forms (from the Windows Forms toolkit) to an otherwise ordinary WPF application. Visual Studio makes this easy—just right-click the project name in the Solution Explorer and choose Add ➤ New Item. Then select the Windows Forms category on the left side and choose the Windows Form template. Finally, give your form a file name and click Add. The first time you add a form, Visual Studio adds references to all the required Windows Forms assemblies, including System.Windows.Forms.dll and System.Drawing.dll.

You can design a form in a WPF project in the same way that you design it in a Windows Forms project. When you open a form, Visual Studio loads the normal Windows Forms designer and fills the Toolbox with Windows Forms controls. When you open the XAML file for a WPF window, you get the familiar WPF design surface instead.

■ **Tip**   For better separation between WPF and Windows Forms content, you might choose to place the "foreign" content in a separate class library assembly. For example, a Windows Forms application might use the WPF windows defined in a separate assembly. This approach makes especially good sense if you plan to reuse some of these windows in both Windows Forms and WPF applications.

Adding WPF Windows to a Windows Forms Application

The reverse trick is a bit more awkward. Visual Studio doesn't directly allow you to create a new WPF window in a Windows Forms application. (In other words, you won't see it as one of the available templates when you right-click your project and choose Add ➤ New Item.) However, you can add the existing .vb and .xaml files that define a WPF window from another WPF project. To do so, right-click your project in the Solution Explorer, choose Add ➤ Existing Item, and find both these files. You'll also need to add references to the core WPF assemblies (PresentationCore.dll, PresentationFramework.dll, and WindowsBase.dll).

■ **Tip** There's a shortcut to adding the WPF references you need. You can add a WPF user control (which Visual Studio *does* support), which causes Visual Studio to add these references automatically. You can then delete the user control from your project. To add a WPF user control, right-click the project, choose Add ➤ New Item, pick the WPF category, and select the User Control (WPF) template.

After you add a WPF window to a Windows Forms application, that window is treated correctly. When you open it, you'll be able to use the WPF designer to modify it. When you build the project, the XAML will be compiled, and the automatically generated code will be merged with your code-behind class, just as it is in a full-fledged WPF application.

Creating a project that uses forms and windows isn't too difficult. However, there are a few extra considerations when you show these forms and windows at runtime. If you need to show a window or form modally (as you would with a dialog box), the task is straightforward, and your code is essentially unchanged. But if you want to show a window modelessly, you need a bit of extra code to ensure proper keyboard support, as you'll see in the following sections.

Showing Modal Windows and Forms

Showing a modal form from a WPF application is effortless. You use exactly the same code you'd use in a Windows Forms project. For example, if you have a form class named Form1, you'd use code like this to show it modally:

```
Dim frm As New Form1()
If frm.ShowDialog() = System.Windows.Forms.DialogResult.OK Then
    MessageBox.Show("You clicked OK in a Windows Forms form.")
End If
```

You'll notice that the Form.ShowDialog() method works in a slightly different way than WPF's Window. ShowDialog() method. While Window.ShowDialog() returns True, False, or Nothing, Form.ShowDialog() returns a value from the DialogResult enumeration.

The reverse trick—showing a WPF window from a form—is just as easy. Once again, you simply interact with the public interface of your Window class, and WPF takes care of the rest:

```
Dim win As New Window1()
If win.ShowDialog() = True Then
    MessageBox.Show("You clicked OK in a WPF window.")
End If
```

Showing Modeless Windows and Forms

It's not quite as straightforward if you want to show windows or forms modelessly. The challenge is that keyboard input is received by the root application and needs to be delivered to the appropriate window. In order for this to work between WPF and Windows Forms content, you need a way to forward these messages along to the right window or form.

If you want to show a WPF window modelessly from inside a Windows Forms application, you must use the shared ElementHost.EnableModelessKeyboardInterop() method. You'll also need a reference to the WindowsFormsIntegration.dll assembly, which defines the ElementHost class in the System.Windows.Forms. Integration namespace. (You'll learn more about the ElementHost class later in this chapter.)

You call the EnableModelessKeyboardInterop() method after you create the window but before you show it. When you call it, you pass in a reference to the new WPF window, as shown here:

```
Dim win As New Window1()
ElementHost.EnableModelessKeyboardInterop(win)
win.Show()
```

When you call EnableModelessKeyboardInterop(), the ElementHost adds a message filter to the Windows Forms application. This message filter intercepts keyboard messages when your WPF window is active and forwards them to your window. Without this detail, your WPF controls won't receive any keyboard input.

If you need to show a modeless Windows Forms application inside a WPF application, you use the similar WindowsFormsHost.EnableWindowsFormsInterop() method. However, you don't need to pass in a reference to the form you plan to show. Instead, you simply need to call this method once before you show any form. (One good choice is to call this method at application startup.)

```
WindowsFormsHost.EnableWindowsFormsInterop()
```

Now you can show your form modelessly without a hitch:

```
Dim frm As New Form1()
frm.Show()
```

Without the call to EnableWindowsFormsInterop(), your form will still appear, but it won't recognize all keyboard input. For example, you won't be able to use the Tab key to move from one control to the next.

You can extend this process to multiple levels. For example, you could create a WPF window that shows a form (modally or modelessly), and that form could then show a WPF window. Although you won't need to do this very often, it's more powerful than the element-based interoperability support you'll learn about later. This support allows you to integrate different types of content in the same window but doesn't allow you to nest more than one layer deep (for example, creating a WPF window that contains a Windows Forms control that, in turn, hosts a WPF control).

Enabling Visual Styles for Windows Forms Controls

When you show a form in a WPF application, that form uses the shockingly old-fashioned (pre–Windows XP) styles for buttons and other common controls. That's because support for the newer styles must be explicitly enabled by calling the Application.EnableVisualStyles() method. Ordinarily, Visual Studio adds this line of code to the Main() method of every new Windows Forms application. However, when you create a WPF application, this detail isn't included.

To resolve this issue, just call the EnableVisualStyles() method once before showing any Windows Forms content. A good place to do this is at the start of the application, as shown here:

```
Public Class Application

    Private Sub App_Startup(ByVal sender As Object, _
      ByVal e As System.Windows.StartupEventArgs) Handles Me.Startup
        System.Windows.Forms.Application.EnableVisualStyles()
    End Sub

End Class
```

Notice that the EnableVisualStyles() method is defined in the System.Windows.Forms.Application class, *not* the System.Windows.Application class that forms the core of your WPF application.

Creating Windows with Mixed Content

In some cases, the clean window-by-window separation isn't suitable. For example, you might want to place WPF content in an existing form alongside Windows Forms content. Although this model is conceptually messier, WPF handles it quite gracefully.

In fact, including Windows Forms content in a WPF application (or vice versa) is more straightforward than adding ActiveX content to a Windows Forms application. In the latter scenario, Visual Studio must generate a wrapper class that sits between the ActiveX control and your code, which manages the transition from managed to unmanaged code. This wrapper is *component-specific*, which means each ActiveX control you use requires a separate customized wrapper. And because of the quirks of COM, the interface exposed by the wrapper might not match the interface of the underlying component exactly.

When integrating Windows Forms and WPF content, you don't need a wrapper class. Instead, you use one of a small set of containers, depending on the scenario. These containers work with any class, so there's no code-generation step. This simpler model is possible because even though Windows Forms and WPF are dramatically different technologies, they are both firmly grounded in the world of managed code.

The most significant advantage of this design is that you can interact with Windows Forms controls and WPF elements in your code directly. The interoperability layer comes into effect only when this content is rendered in the window. This part takes place automatically without requiring any developer intervention. You also don't need to worry about keyboard handling in modeless windows because the interoperability classes you'll use (ElementHost and WindowsFormsHost) handle that automatically.

Understanding WPF and Windows Forms "Airspace"

To integrate WPF and Windows Forms content in the same window, you need to be able to segregate a portion of your window for "foreign" content. For example, it's completely reasonable to throw a 3-D graphic into a Windows Forms application because you can place that 3-D graphic in a distinct region of a window (or even make it take up the entire window). However, it's not easy or worthwhile to reskin all the buttons in your Windows Forms application by making them WPF elements, because you'll need to create a separate WPF region for each button.

Along with the considerations of complexity, some things just aren't possible with WPF interoperability. For example, you can't *combine* WPF and Windows Forms content by overlapping it. That means you can't have a WPF animation send an element flying over a region that's rendered with Windows Forms. Similarly, you can't overlap partially transparent Windows Forms content over a WPF region to blend them together. Both of these violate what's known as the *airspace rule*, which dictates that WPF and Windows Forms must always have their own distinct window regions, which they manage exclusively. Figure 30-1 shows what's allowed and what isn't.

Allowed

Not Allowed

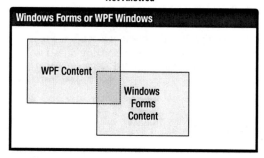

Figure 30-1. *The airspace rule*

Technically, the airspace rule results from the fact that in a window containing WPF content and Windows Forms content, both regions have a separate window handle, or *hwnd*. Each hwnd is managed, rendered, and refreshed separately.

Window handles are managed by the Windows operating system. In classic Windows applications, every control is a separate window, which means each control has ownership of a distinct piece of screen real estate. Obviously, this type of "window" isn't the same as the top-level windows that float around your screen—it's simply a self-contained region (rectangular or otherwise). In WPF, the model is dramatically different—there's a single, top-level hwnd, and the WPF engine does the compositing for the entire window, which allows more-pleasing rendering (for example, effects such as dynamic anti-aliasing) and far greater flexibility (for example, visuals that render content outside their bounds).

■ **Note** A few WPF elements use separate window handles. These include menus, tooltips, and the drop-down portion of a combo box, all of which need the ability to extend beyond the bounds of the window.

The implementation of the airspace rule is fairly straightforward. If you place Windows Forms content on top of WPF content, you'll find that the Windows Forms content is always on top, no matter where it's declared in the markup or what layout container you use. That's because the WPF content is a single window, and the container with Windows Forms content is implemented as a separate window that's displayed on top of a portion of the WPF window.

If you place WPF content in a Windows Forms form, the result is a bit different. Every control in Windows Forms is a distinct window and therefore has its own hwnd. So, WPF content can be layered anywhere with relation to other Windows Forms controls in the same window, depending on its z-index. (The z-index is determined by the order in which you add controls to the parent's Controls collection, so that controls added later appear on top of those added before.) However, the WPF content still has its own completely distinct region. That means you can't use transparency or any other technique to partially overwrite (or combine your element with) Windows Forms content. Instead, the WPF content exists in its own self-contained region.

Hosting Windows Forms Controls in WPF

To show a Windows Forms control in a WPF window, you use the WindowsFormsHost class in the System.Windows. Forms.Integration namespace. The WindowsFormsHost is a WPF element (it derives from FrameworkElement) that has the ability to hold exactly one Windows Forms control, which is provided in the Child property.

It's easy enough to create and use WindowsFormsHost programmatically. However, in most cases, it's easiest to create it declaratively in your XAML markup. The only disadvantage is that Visual Studio doesn't include much designer support for the WindowsFormsHost control. Although you can drag and drop it onto a window, you need to fill in its content (and map the required namespace) by hand.

The first step is to map the System.Windows.Forms namespace so you can refer to the Windows Forms control you want to use:

```
<Window x:Class="HostWinFormControl"
    xmlns="http://schemas.microsoft.com/winfx/2006/xaml/presentation"
    xmlns:x="http://schemas.microsoft.com/winfx/2006/xaml"
    xmlns:wf="clr-namespace:System.Windows.Forms;assembly=System.Windows.Forms"
    Title="HostWinFormControl" Height="300" Width="300" >
```

Now you can create the WindowsFormsHost and the control inside just as you would any other WPF element. Here's an example that uses the MaskedTextBox from Windows Forms:

```
<Grid>
  <WindowsFormsHost>
    <wf:MaskedTextBox x:Name="maskedTextBox"></wf:MaskedTextBox>
  </WindowsFormsHost>
</Grid>
```

▓ **Note** The WindowsFormsHost can hold any Windows Forms control (that is, any class that derives from System.Windows. Forms.Control). It can't hold Windows Forms components that aren't controls, such as the HelpProvider or the NotifyIcon.

Figure 30-2 shows a MaskedTextBox in a WPF window.

Figure 30-2. *A masked text box for a phone number*

You can set most of the properties of your MaskedTextBox directly in your markup. That's because Windows Forms uses the same TypeConverter infrastructure (discussed in Chapter 2) to change strings into property values of a specific type. This isn't always convenient—for example, the string representation of a type may be awkward to enter by hand—but it usually allows you to configure your Windows Forms controls without resorting to code. For example, here's a MaskedTextBox equipped with a mask that shapes user input into a seven-digit phone number with an optional area code:

```
<wf:MaskedTextBox x:Name="maskedTextBox" Mask="(999)-000-0000"></wf:MaskedTextBox>
```

You can also use ordinary XAML markup extensions to fill in null values, use shared properties, create type objects, or use objects that you've defined in the Resources collection of the window. Here's an example that uses the type extension to set the MaskedTextBox.ValidatingType property. This specifies that the MaskedTextBox should change the supplied input (a phone number string) into an Int32 when the Text property is read or the focus changes:

```
<wf:MaskedTextBox x:Name="maskedTextBox" Mask="(999)-000-0000"
  ValidatingType="{x:Type sys:Int32}"></wf:MaskedTextBox>
```

One markup extension that won't work is a data-binding expression because it requires a dependency property. (Windows Forms controls are constructed out of normal .NET properties.) If you want to bind a property of a Windows Forms control to the property of a WPF element, there's an easy workaround—just set the dependency property on the WPF element and adjust the BindingDirection as required. (Chapter 8 has the full details.)

Finally, it's important to note that you can hook events up to your Windows Forms control by using the familiar XAML syntax. Here's an example that attaches an event handler for the MaskInputRejected event, which occurs when a keystroke is discarded because it doesn't suit the mask:

```
<wf:MaskedTextBox x:Name="maskedTextBox" Mask="(999)-000-0000"
  MaskInputRejected="maskedTextBox_MaskInputRejected"></wf:MaskedTextBox>
```

Obviously, these aren't routed events, so you can't define them at higher levels in the element hierarchy.

When the event fires, your event handler responds by showing an error message in another element. In this case, it's a WPF label that's located elsewhere on the window:

```
Private Sub maskedTextBox_MaskInputRejected(ByVal sender As Object, _
  ByVal e As System.Windows.Forms.MaskInputRejectedEventArgs)
    lblErrorText.Content = ("Error: " & e.RejectionHint.ToString())
End Sub
```

■ **Tip** Don't import the Windows Forms namespaces (such as System.Windows.Forms) in a code file that already uses WPF namespaces (such as System.Windows.Controls). The Windows Forms classes and the WPF classes share many names. Basic ingredients (such as Brush, Pen, Font, Color, Size, and Point) and common controls (such as Button, TextBox, and so on) are found in both libraries. To prevent naming clashes, it's best to import just one set of namespaces in your window (WPF namespaces for a WPF window, Windows Forms namespaces for a form) and use fully qualified names or a namespace alias to access the others.

This example illustrates the nicest feature about WPF and Windows Forms interoperability: it doesn't affect your code. Whether you're manipulating a Windows Forms control or a WPF element, you use the familiar class interface for that object. The interoperability layer is simply the magic that lets both ingredients coexist in the window. It doesn't require any extra code.

■ **Note** To have Windows Forms controls use more up-to-date control styles introduced with Windows XP, you must call EnableVisualStyles() when your application starts, as described in the "Visual Styles for Windows Forms Controls" section earlier in this chapter.

Windows Forms content is rendered by Windows Forms, not WPF. Therefore, display-related properties of the WindowsFormsHost container (properties such as Transform, Clip, and Opacity) have no effect on the content inside. This means that even if you set a rotational transform, set a narrow clipping region, and make your content 50 percent transparent, you'll see no change. Similarly, Windows Forms uses a different coordinate system that sizes controls by using physical pixels. As a result, if you increase the system DPI setting of your computer, you'll find that the WPF content resizes cleanly to be more detailed, but the Windows Forms content does not.

Using WPF and Windows Forms User Controls

One of the most significant limitations of the WindowsFormsHost element is that it can hold only a single Windows Forms control. To compensate, you could use a Windows Forms container control. Unfortunately, Windows Forms container controls don't support XAML content models, so you'll need to fill in the contents of the container control programmatically.

A much better approach is to create a Windows Forms user control. This user control can be defined in a separate assembly that you reference, or you can add it directly to your WPF project (using the familiar Add ➤ New Item command). This gives you the best of both worlds—you have full design support to build your user control and an easy way to integrate it into your WPF window.

In fact, using a user control gives you an extra layer of abstraction similar to using separate windows. That's because the containing WPF window won't be able to access the individual controls in your user control. Instead, it will interact with the higher-level properties you've added to your user control, which can then modify the controls inside. This makes your code better encapsulated and simpler because it limits the points of interaction between the WPF window and your Windows Forms content. It also makes it easier to migrate to a WPF-only solution in the future, simply by creating a WPF user control that has the same properties and swapping that in place of the WindowsFormsHost. (And once again, you can further improve the design and flexibility of your application by moving the user control into a separate class library assembly.)

▦ **Note** Technically, your WPF window can access the controls in a user control by accessing the Controls collection of the user control. However, to use this back door, you need to write error-prone lookup code that searches for specific controls by using a string name. That's always a bad idea.

As long as you're creating a user control, it's a good idea to make it behave as much like WPF content as possible so it's easier to integrate into your WPF window layout. For example, you may want to consider using the FlowLayoutPanel and TableLayoutPanel container controls so that the content inside your user controls flows to fit its dimensions. Simply add the appropriate control and set its Dock property to DockStyle.Fill. Then place the controls you want to use inside. For more information about using the Windows Forms layout controls (which are subtly different from the WPF layout panels), refer to my book *Pro .NET 2.0 Windows Forms and Custom Controls in VB 2005* (Apress, 2005).

ACTIVEX INTEROPERABILITY

WPF has no direct support for ActiveX interoperability. However, Windows Forms has extensive support in the form of *runtime callable wrappers* (RCWs), dynamically generated interop classes that allow a managed Windows Forms application to host an Active component. Although there are .NET-to-COM quirks that can derail some controls, this approach works reasonably well for most scenarios, and it works seamlessly if the person who creates the component also provides a *primary interop assembly*, which is a handcrafted, fine-tuned RCW that's guaranteed to dodge interop issues.

So, how does this help if you need to design a WPF application that uses an ActiveX control? In this case, you need to layer two levels of interoperability. First you place the ActiveX control in a Windows Forms user control or form. You then place that user control in your WPF window or show the form from your WPF application.

Hosting WPF Controls in Windows Forms

The reverse approach—hosting WPF content in a form built with Windows Forms—is just as easy. In this situation, you don't need the WindowsFormsHost class. Instead, you use the System.Windows.Forms.Integration.ElementHost class, which is part of the WindowsFormsIntegration.dll assembly.

The ElementHost has the ability to wrap any WPF element. However, the ElementHost is a genuine Windows Forms control, which means you can place it in a form alongside other Windows Forms content. In some respects, the ElementHost is more straightforward than the WindowsFormsHost, because every control in Windows Forms is displayed as a separate hwnd. Thus, it's not terribly difficult for one of these windows to be rendered with WPF instead of User32/GDI+.

Visual Studio provides some design-time support for the ElementHost control, but only if you place your WPF content in a WPF user control. Here's what to do:

1. Right-click the project name in the Solution Explorer, and choose Add ➤ New Item. Pick the User Control (WPF) template, supply a name for your custom component class, and click Add.

■ **Note** This example assumes you're placing the WPF user control directly in your Windows Forms project. If you have a complex user control, you must choose to use a more structured approach and place it in a separate class library assembly.

---

2. Add the WPF controls you need to your new WPF user control. Visual Studio gives you the usual level of design-time support for this step, so you can drag WPF controls from the Toolbox, configure them with the Properties window, and so on.

3. When you're finished, rebuild your project (choose Build ➤ Build Solution). You can't use your WPF user control in a form until you've compiled it.

4. Open to the Windows Forms form where you want to add your WPF user control (or create a new form by right-clicking the project in the Solution Explorer and choosing Add ➤ Windows Form).

5. To place the WPF user control in a form, you need the help of the ElementHost control. The ElementHost control appears on the WPF Interoperability tab of the Toolbox. Drag it onto your form, and size it accordingly.

■ **Tip** For better separation, it's a good idea to add the ElementHost to a specific container rather than directly to the form. This makes it easier to separate your WPF content from the rest of the window. Typically, you'll use the Panel, FlowLayoutPanel, or TableLayoutPanel.

---

6. To choose the content for the ElementHost, you use the smart tag. If the smart tag isn't visible, you can show it by selecting the ElementHost and clicking the arrow in the top-right corner. In the smart tag you'll find a drop-down list named Select Hosted Content. Using this list, you can pick the WPF user control you want to use, as shown in Figure 30-3.

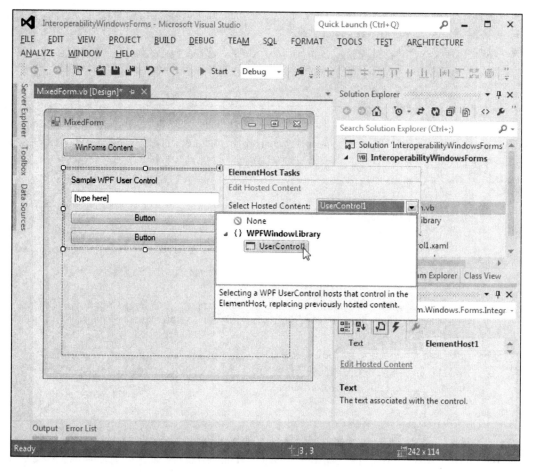

Figure 30-3. *Selecting WPF content for an ElementHost*

7. Although the WPF user control will appear in your form, you can't edit its content there. To jump to the corresponding XAML file in a hurry, click the Edit Hosted Content link in the ElementHost smart tag.

Technically, the ElementHost can hold any type of WPF element. However, the ElementHost smart tag expects you to choose a user control that's in your project (or a referenced assembly). If you want to use a different type of control, you'll need to write code that adds it to the ElementHost programmatically.

Access Keys, Mnemonics, and Focus

The WPF and Windows Forms interoperability works because the two types of content can be rigorously separated. Each region handles its own rendering and refreshing and interacts with the mouse independently. However, this segregation isn't always appropriate. For example, it runs into potential problems with keyboard handling, which sometimes needs to be global across an entire form. Here are some examples:

- When you tab from the last control in one region, you expect focus to move to the first control in the next region.

- When you use a shortcut key to trigger a control (such as a button), you expect that button to respond no matter what region of the window it's located in.

- When you use a label mnemonic, you expect the focus to move to the linked control.

- Similarly, if you suppress a keystroke by using a preview event, you don't expect the corresponding key event to occur in either region, no matter what control currently has focus.

The good news is that all these expected behaviors work without any customization needed. For example, consider the WPF window shown in Figure 30-4. It includes two WPF buttons (top and bottom) and a Windows Forms button (in the middle).

Figure 30-4. *Three buttons with shortcut keys*

Here's the markup:

```
<Grid>
  <Grid.RowDefinitions>
    <RowDefinition></RowDefinition>
    <RowDefinition></RowDefinition>
    <RowDefinition></RowDefinition>
  </Grid.RowDefinitions>
```

```
<Button Click="cmdClicked">Use Alt+_A</Button>
<WindowsFormsHost Grid.Row="1">
  <wf:Button Text="Use Alt+&amp;B" Click="cmdClicked"></wf:Button>
</WindowsFormsHost>
<Button Grid.Row="2" Click="cmdClicked">Use Alt+_C</Button>
</Grid>
```

■ **Note** The syntax for identifying accelerator keys is slightly different in WPF (which uses an underscore) than in Windows Forms. Windows Forms uses the & character, which must be escaped as & in XML because it's a special character.

When this window first appears, the text in all buttons is normal. When the user presses and holds the Alt key, all three shortcuts are underlined. The user can then trigger any one of the three buttons by pressing the A, B, or C key (while holding down Alt).

The same magic works with mnemonics, which allows labels to forward the focus to a nearby control (typically a text box). You can also tab through the three buttons in this window as though they were all WPF-defined controls, moving from top to bottom. Finally, the same example continues to work if you host a combination of Windows Forms and WPF content in a Windows Forms form.

Keyboard support isn't always this pretty, and there are a few focus-related quirks that you may run into. Here's a list of issues to watch out for:

- Although WPF supports a keystroke forwarding system to make sure every element and control gets a chance to handle keyboard input, the keyboard-handling models of WPF and Windows Forms still differ. For that reason, you won't receive keyboard events from the WindowsFormsHost when the focus is in the Windows Forms content inside. Similarly, if the user moves from one control to another inside a WindowsFormsHost, you won't receive the GotFocus and LostFocus events from the WindowsFormsHost.

■ **Note** Incidentally, the same is true for WPF mouse events. For example, the MouseMove event won't fire for the WindowsFormsHost while you move the mouse inside its bounds.

- Windows Forms validation won't fire when you move the focus from a control inside the WindowsFormsHost to an element outside the WindowsFormsHost. Instead, it will fire only when you move from one control to another inside the WindowsFormsHost. (When you remember that the WPF content and the Windows Forms content are essentially separated windows, this makes perfect sense, because it's the same behavior you experience if you switch between different applications.)

- If the window is minimized while the focus is somewhere inside a WindowsFormsHost, the focus may not be restored when the window is restored.

Property Mapping

One of the most awkward details in interoperability between WPF and Windows Forms is the way they use similar but different properties. For example, WPF controls have a Background property that allows you to supply a brush that paints the background. Windows Forms controls use a simpler BackColor property that fills the background with a color based on an ARGB value. Obviously, there's a disconnect between these two properties, even though they're often used to set the same aspect of a control's appearance.

Most of the time, this isn't a problem. As a developer, you'll simply be forced to switch between both APIs, depending on the object you're working with. However, WPF adds a little bit of extra support through a feature called *property translators*.

Property translators won't allow you to write WPF-style markup and have it work with Windows Forms controls. In fact, property translators are quite modest. They simply convert a few basic properties of the WindowsFormsHost (or ElementHost) from one system to another so that they can be applied on the child control.

For example, if you set the WindowsFormsHost.IsEnabled property, the Enabled property of the control inside is modified accordingly. This isn't a necessary feature (you could do much the same thing by modifying the Enabled property of the child directly, instead of the IsEnabled property of the container), but it can often make your code a bit clearer.

To make this work, the WindowsFormsHost and ElementHost classes both have a PropertyMap collection, which is responsible for associating a property name with a delegate that identifies a method that performs the conversion. By using a method, the property map system is able to handle sticky conversions such as BackColor to Background, and vice versa. By default, each is filled with a default set of associations. (You're free to create your own or replace the existing ones, but this degree of low-level fiddling seldom makes sense.)

Table 30-1 lists the standard property map conversions that are provided by the WindowsFormHost and ElementHost classes.

Table 30-1. *Property Maps*

WPF Property	Windows Forms Property	Comments
Foreground	ForeColor	Converts any ColorBrush into the corresponding Color object. In the case of a GradientBrush, the color of the GradientStop with the lowest offset value is used instead. For any other type of brush, the ForeColor is not changed, and the default is used.
Background	BackColor or BackgroundImage	Converts any SolidColorBrush to the corresponding Color object. Transparency is not supported. If a more exotic brush is used, the WindowsFormsHost creates a bitmap and assigns it to the BackgroundImage property instead.
Cursor	Cursor	
FlowDirection	RightToLeft	
FontFamily, FontSize, FontStretch, FontStyle, FontWeight	Font	
IsEnabled	Enabled	
Padding	Padding	
Visibility	Visible	Converts a value from the Visibility enumeration into a Boolean value. If Visibility is Hidden, the Visible property is set to True so that the content size can be used for layout calculations but the WindowsFormsHost does not draw the content. If Visibility is Collapsed, the Visible property is not changed (so it remains with its currently set or default value), and the WindowsFormsHost does not draw the content.

▉ **Note** Property maps work dynamically. For example, if the WindowsFormsHost.FontFamily property is changed, a new Font object is constructed and applied to the Font property of the child control.

WIN32 INTEROPERABILITY

WPF certainly doesn't limit its interoperability to Windows Forms applications—if you want to work with the Win32 API or place WPF content in a C++ MFC application, you can do that too.

You can host Win32 in WPF by using the System.Windows.Interop.HwndHost class, which works analogously to the WindowsFormsHost class. The same limitations that apply to WindowsFormsHost apply to HwndSource (for example, the airspace rule, focus quirks, and so on). In fact, WindowsFormsHost derives from HwndHost.

The HwndHost is your gateway to the traditional world of C++ and MFC applications. However, it also allows you to integrate managed DirectX content. Currently, WPF does not include any DirectX interoperability features, and you can't use the DirectX libraries to render content in a WPF window. However, you can use DirectX to build a separate window and then host that inside a WPF window by using the HwndHost. Although DirectX is far beyond the scope of this book (and an order of magnitude more complex than WPF programming), you can learn more at http://msdn.microsoft.com/directx.

The complement of HwndHost is the HwndSource class. While HwndHost allows you to place any hwnd in a WPF window, HwndSource wraps any WPF visual or element in an hwnd so it can be inserted in a Win32-based application, such as an MFC application. The only limitation is that your application needs a way to access the WPF libraries, which are managed .NET code. This isn't a trivial task. If you're using a C++ application, the simplest approach is to use the Managed Extensions for C++. You can then create your WPF content, create an HwndSource to wrap it, set the HwndHost.RootVisual property to the top-level element, and then place the HwndSource into your window.

The Last Word

In this chapter you considered the interoperability support that allows WPF applications to show Windows Forms content (and vice versa). Then you examined the WindowsFormsHost element, which lets you embed a Windows Forms control in a WPF window, and the ElementHost, which lets you embed a WPF element in a form. Both of these classes provide a simple, effective way to manage the transition from Windows Forms to WPF.

CHAPTER 31

Multithreading

As you've discovered over the previous 30 chapters, WPF revolutionizes almost all the conventions of Windows programming. It introduces a new approach to everything from defining the content in a window to rendering 3-D graphics. WPF even introduces a few new concepts that aren't obviously UI-focused, such as dependency properties and routed events.

Of course, a great number of coding tasks fall outside the scope of user interface programming and haven't changed in the WPF world. For example, WPF applications use the same classes as other .NET applications when contacting databases, manipulating files, and performing diagnostics. There are also a few features that fall somewhere between traditional .NET programming and WPF. These features aren't strictly limited to WPF applications, but they do have specific WPF considerations. One example is the *add-in model*, which allows your WPF application to dynamically load and use separately compiled components with useful bits of functionality. (It's described in the next chapter.) And in this chapter, you'll look at *multithreading*, which allows your WPF application to perform background work while keeping a responsive user interface.

■ **Note**　Both multithreading and the add-in model are advanced topics that could provide an entire book worth of material; therefore, you won't get an exhaustive examination of either feature in this book. However, you will get the basic outline you need to use them with WPF, and you'll establish a solid foundation for future exploration.

Understanding the Multithreading Model

Multithreading is the art of executing more than one piece of code at once. The goal of multithreading is usually to create a more responsive interface—one that doesn't freeze up while it's in the midst of other work—although you can also use multithreading to take better advantage of dual-core CPUs when executing a processor-intensive algorithm or to perform other work during a high-latency operation (for example, to perform some calculations while waiting for a response from a web service).

Early in the design of WPF, the creators considered a new threading model. This model—called *thread rental*—allowed user interface objects to be accessed on any thread. To reduce the cost of locking, groups of related objects could be grouped under a single lock (called a *context*). Unfortunately, this design introduced additional complexity for single-threaded applications (which needed to be context-aware) and made it more difficult to interoperate with legacy code (such as the Win32 API). Ultimately, the plan was abandoned.

The result is that WPF supports a *single-threaded apartment* model that's very much like the one used in Windows Forms applications. It has a few core rules:

- WPF elements have *thread affinity*. The thread that creates them owns them, and other threads can't interact with them directly. (An *element* is a WPF object that's displayed in a window.)

- WPF objects that have thread affinity derive from DispatcherObject at some point in their class hierarchy. DispatcherObject includes a small set of members that allow you to verify whether code is executing on the right thread to use a specific object— and if not, to switch it over.

- In practice, one thread runs your entire application and owns all WPF objects. Although you could use separate threads to show separate windows, this design is rare.

In the following sections, you'll explore the DispatcherObject class and learn the simplest way to perform an asynchronous operation in a WPF application.

The Dispatcher

A *dispatcher* manages the work that takes place in a WPF application. The dispatcher owns the application thread and manages a queue of work items. As your application runs, the dispatcher accepts new work requests and executes one at a time.

Technically, a dispatcher is created the first time you instantiate a class that derives from DispatcherObject on a new thread. If you create separate threads and use them to show separate windows, you'll wind up with more than one dispatcher. However, most applications keep things simple and stick to one user interface thread and one dispatcher. They then use multithreading to manage data operations and other background tasks.

■ **Note**   The dispatcher is an instance of the System.Windows.Threading.Dispatcher class. All the dispatcher-related objects are also found in the small System.Windows.Threading namespace, which is new to WPF. (The core threading classes that have existed since .NET 1.0 are found in System.Threading.)

You can retrieve the dispatcher for the current thread by using the shared Dispatcher.CurrentDispatcher property. Using this Dispatcher object, you can attach event handlers that respond to unhandled exceptions or respond when the dispatcher shuts down. You can also get a reference to the System.Threading.Thread that the dispatcher controls, shut down the dispatcher, or marshal code to the correct thread (a technique you'll see in the next section).

The DispatcherObject

Most of the time, you won't interact with a dispatcher directly. However, you'll spend plenty of time using instances of DispatcherObject, because every visual WPF object derives from this class. A DispatcherObject is simply an object that's linked to a dispatcher—in other words, an object that's bound to the dispatcher's thread.

The DispatcherObject introduces just three members, listed in Table 31-1.

Table 31-1. Members of the DispatcherObject Class

Name	Description
Dispatcher	Returns the dispatcher that's managing this object
CheckAccess()	Returns True if the code is on the right thread to use the object; returns False otherwise
VerifyAccess()	Does nothing if the code is on the right thread to use the object; throws an InvalidOperationException otherwise

WPF objects call VerifyAccess() frequently to protect themselves. They don't call VerifyAccess() in response to every operation (because that would impose too great a performance overhead), but they do call it often enough that you're unlikely to use an object from the wrong thread for very long.

For example, the following code responds to a button click by creating a new System.Threading.Thread object. It then uses that thread to launch a small bit of code that changes a text box in the current window.

```
Private Sub cmdBreakRules_Click(ByVal sender As Object, _
  ByVal e As RoutedEventArgs)
    Dim thread As New Thread(AddressOf UpdateTextWrong)
    thread.Start()
End Sub

Private Sub UpdateTextWrong()
    ' Simulate some work taking place with a five-second delay.
    Thread.Sleep(TimeSpan.FromSeconds(5))

    txt.Text = "Here is some new text."
End Sub
```

This code is destined to fail. The UpdateTextWrong() method will be executed on a new thread, and that thread isn't allowed to access WPF objects. In this case, the TextBox object catches the violation by calling VerifyAccess(), and an InvalidOperationException is thrown.

To correct this code, you need to get a reference to the dispatcher that owns the TextBox object (which is the same dispatcher that owns the window and all the other WPF objects in the application). Once you have access to that dispatcher, you can call Dispatcher.BeginInvoke() to marshal some code to the dispatcher thread. Essentially, BeginInvoke() schedules your code as a task for the dispatcher. The dispatcher then executes that code.

Here's the corrected code:

```
Private Sub cmdFollowRules_Click(ByVal sender As Object, _
  ByVal e As RoutedEventArgs)
    Dim thread As New Thread(AddressOf UpdateTextRight)
    thread.Start()
End Sub

Private Sub UpdateTextRight()
    ' Simulate some work taking place with a five-second delay.
    Thread.Sleep(TimeSpan.FromSeconds(5))

    ' Get the dispatcher from the current window, and use it to invoke
    ' the update code.
```

```
    Me.Dispatcher.BeginInvoke(DispatcherPriority.Normal, _
      New ThreadStart(AddressOf UpdateProcess))
End Sub

Private Sub UpdateProcess()
    txt.Text = "Here is some new text."
End Sub
```

The Dispatcher.BeginInvoke() method takes two parameters. The first indicates the priority of the task. In most cases, you'll use DispatcherPriority.Normal, but you can also use a lower priority if you have a task that doesn't need to be completed immediately and that should be kept on hold until the dispatcher has nothing else to do. For example, this might make sense if you need to display a status message about a long-running operation somewhere in your user interface. You can use DispatcherPriority.ApplicationIdle to wait until the application has finished all other work or the even more laid-back DispatcherPriority.SystemIdle to wait until the entire system is at rest and the CPU is idle.

You can also use an above-normal priority to get the dispatcher's attention right away. However, it's recommended that you leave higher priorities to input messages (such as key presses). These need to be handled nearly instantaneously, or the application will feel sluggish. On the other hand, adding a few milliseconds of extra time to a background operation won't be noticeable, so a priority of DispatcherPriority.Normal makes more sense in this situation.

The second BeginInvoke() parameter is a delegate that points to the method with the code you want to execute. This could be a method somewhere else in your code, or you can use an anonymous method to define your code inline (as in this example). The inline approach works well for simple operations, like this single-line update. However, if you need to use a more complex process to update the user interface, it's a good idea to factor this code into a separate method.

■ **Note** The BeginInvoke() method also has a return value, which isn't used in the earlier example. BeginInvoke() returns a DispatcherOperation object, which allows you to follow the status of your marshaling operation and determine when your code has actually been executed. However, the DispatcherOperation is rarely useful, because the code you pass to BeginInvoke() should take very little time.

Remember, if you're performing a time-consuming background operation, you need to perform this operation on a separate thread and *then* marshal its result to the dispatcher thread (at which point you'll update the user interface or change a shared object). It makes no sense to perform your time-consuming code in the method that you pass to BeginInvoke(). For example, this slightly rearranged code still works but is impractical:

```
Private Sub UpdateTextRight()
    ' Get the dispatcher from the current window, and use it to invoke
    ' the update code.
    Me.Dispatcher.BeginInvoke(DispatcherPriority.Normal, _
      New ThreadStart(AddressOf UpdateProcess))
End Sub

Private Sub UpdateProcess()
    ' Now the delay happens on the UI thread.
    ' Simulate some work taking place with a five-second delay.
    Thread.Sleep(TimeSpan.FromSeconds(5))

    txt.Text = "Here is some new text."
End Sub
```

The problem here is that all the work takes place on the dispatcher thread. That means this code ties up the dispatcher in the same way a non-multithreaded application would.

■ **Note** The dispatcher also provides an Invoke() method. Like BeginInvoke(), Invoke() marshals the code you specify to the dispatcher thread. But unlike BeginInvoke(), Invoke() stalls your thread until the dispatcher executes your code. You might use Invoke() if you need to pause an asynchronous operation until the user has supplied some sort of feedback. For example, you could call Invoke() to run a snippet of code that shows an OK/Cancel dialog box. After the user clicks a button and your marshaled code completes, the Invoke() method will return, and you can act upon the user's response.

The BackgroundWorker

You can perform asynchronous operations in many ways. You've already seen one no-frills approach—creating a new System.Threading.Thread object by hand, supplying your asynchronous code, and launching it with the Thread.Start() method. This approach is powerful, because the Thread object doesn't hold anything back. You can create dozens of threads at will, set their priorities, control their status (for example, pausing, resuming, and aborting them), and so on. However, this approach is also a bit dangerous. If you access shared data, you need to use locking to prevent subtle errors. If you create threads frequently or in large numbers, you'll generate additional, unnecessary overhead.

The techniques to write good multithreading code—and the .NET classes you'll use—aren't WPF-specific. If you've written multithreaded code in a Windows Forms application, you can use the same techniques in the WPF world. In the remainder of this chapter, you'll consider one of the simplest and safest approaches: the System.ComponentModel.BackgroundWorker component.

The BackgroundWorker was introduced in .NET 2.0 to simplify threading considerations in Windows Forms applications. However, the BackgroundWorker is equally at home in WPF. The BackgroundWorker component gives you a nearly foolproof way to run a time-consuming task on a separate thread. It uses the dispatcher behind the scenes and abstracts away the marshaling issues with an event-based model.

As you'll see, the BackgroundWorker also supports two frills: progress events and cancel messages. In both cases, the threading details are hidden, making for easy coding.

■ **Note** The BackgroundWorker is perfect if you have a single asynchronous task that runs in the background from start to finish (with optional support for progress reporting and cancellation). If you have something else in mind—for example, an asynchronous task that runs throughout the entire life of your application or an asynchronous task that communicates with your application while it does its work, you'll need to design a customized solution using .NET's threading support.

A Simple Asynchronous Operation

To try the BackgroundWorker, it helps to consider a sample application. The basic ingredient for any test is a time-consuming process. The following example uses a common algorithm for finding prime numbers in a given range, called the *sieve of Eratosthenes*, which was invented by Eratosthenes himself in about 240 BC. With this algorithm, you begin by making a list of all the integers in a range of numbers. You then strike out the multiples of all primes less than or equal to the square root of the maximum number. The numbers that are left are the primes.

In this example, I won't go into the theory that proves the sieve of Eratosthenes works or show the fairly trivial code that performs it. (Similarly, don't worry about optimizing it or comparing it against other techniques.) However, you will see how to perform the sieve of Eratosthenes algorithm asynchronously.

The full code is available with the online examples for this chapter. It takes this form:

```
Public Class Worker

    Public Shared Function FindPrimes(ByVal fromNumber As Integer, _
        ByVal toNumber As Integer) As Integer()
            ' Find the primes between fromNumber and toNumber,
            ' and return them as an array of integers.
    End Function

End Class
```

The FindPrimes() method takes two parameters that delimit a range of numbers. The code then returns an integer array with all the prime numbers that occur in that range.

Figure 31-1 shows the example we're building. This window allows the user to choose the range of numbers to search. When the user clicks Find Primes, the search begins, but it takes place in the background. When the search is finished, the list of prime numbers appears in the list box.

Figure 31-1. *A completed prime number search*

Creating the BackgroundWorker

To use the BackgroundWorker, you begin by creating an instance. Here, you have two options:

- You can create the BackgroundWorker in your code and attach all the event handlers programmatically.

- You can declare the BackgroundWorker in your XAML. The advantage of this approach is that you can hook up your event handlers by using attributes. Because the BackgroundWorker isn't a visible WPF element, you can't place it just anywhere. Instead, you need to declare it as a resource for your window.

Both approaches are equivalent. The downloadable sample uses the second approach. The first step is to make the System.ComponentModel namespace accessible in your XAML document through a namespace import. To do this, you need to map the namespace to an XML prefix:

```
<Window x:Class="BackgroundWorkerTest"
    xmlns="http://schemas.microsoft.com/winfx/2006/xaml/presentation"
    xmlns:x="http://schemas.microsoft.com/winfx/2006/xaml"
    xmlns:cm="clr-namespace:System.ComponentModel;assembly=System"
    ... >
```

Now you can create an instance of the BackgroundWorker in the Window.Resources collection. When doing this, you need to supply a key name so the object can be retrieved later. In this example, the key name is backgroundWorker:

```
<Window.Resources>
  <cm:BackgroundWorker x:Key="backgroundWorker"></cm:BackgroundWorker>
</Window.Resources>
```

The advantage of declaring the BackgroundWorker in the Window.Resources section is that you can set its properties and attach its event handlers by using attributes. For example, here's the BackgroundWorker tag you'll end up with at the end of this example, which enables support for progress notification and cancellation and attaches event handlers to the DoWork, ProgressChanged, and RunWorkerCompleted events:

```
<cm:BackgroundWorker x:Key="backgroundWorker"
  WorkerReportsProgress="True" WorkerSupportsCancellation="True"
  DoWork="backgroundWorker_DoWork"
  ProgressChanged="backgroundWorker_ProgressChanged"
  RunWorkerCompleted="backgroundWorker_RunWorkerCompleted">
</cm:BackgroundWorker>
```

To get access to this resource in your code, you need to pull it out of the Resources collection. In this example, the window performs this step in its constructor so that all your event-handling code can access it more easily:

```
Public Class BackgroundWorkerTest
    Private backgroundWorker As BackgroundWorker
```

```
    Public Sub New()
        InitializeComponent()
        backgroundWorker = CType(Me.FindResource("backgroundWorker"), _
            BackgroundWorker)
    End Sub

    ...
End Class
```

Running the BackgroundWorker

The first step to using the BackgroundWorker with the prime-number search example is to create a custom class that allows you to transmit the input parameters to the BackgroundWorker. When you call BackgroundWorker.RunWorkerAsync(), you can supply any object, which will be delivered to the DoWork event. However, you can supply only a single object, so you need to wrap the *to* and *from* numbers into one class, as shown here:

```
Public Class FindPrimesInput

    Private _to As Integer
    Public Property [To]() As Integer
        Get
            Return _to
        End Get
        Set(ByVal value As Integer)
            _to = value
        End Set
    End Property

    Private _from As Integer
    Public Property From() As Integer
        Get
            Return _from
        End Get
        Set(ByVal value As Integer)
            _from = value
        End Set
    End Property

    Public Sub New(ByVal fromValue As Integer, ByVal toValue As Integer)
        Me.To = toValue
        Me.From = fromValue
    End Sub

End Class
```

To start the BackgroundWorker on its way, you need to call the BackgroundWorker.RunWorkerAsync() method and pass in the FindPrimesInput object. Here's the code that does this when the user clicks the Find Primes button:

```
Private Sub cmdFind_Click(ByVal sender As Object, ByVal e As RoutedEventArgs)
    ' Disable the button and clear previous results.
    cmdFind.IsEnabled = False
```

```vb
        cmdCancel.IsEnabled = True
        lstPrimes.Items.Clear()

        ' Get the search range.
        Dim fromValue, toValue As Integer
        If (Not Int32.TryParse(txtFrom.Text, fromValue)) Then
            MessageBox.Show("Invalid From value.")
            Return
        End If
        If (Not Int32.TryParse(txtTo.Text, toValue)) Then
            MessageBox.Show("Invalid To value.")
            Return
        End If

        ' Start the search for primes on another thread.
        Dim input As New FindPrimesInput(fromValue, toValue)
        backgroundWorker.RunWorkerAsync(input)
End Sub
```

When the BackgroundWorker begins executing, it grabs a free thread from the CLR thread pool and then fires the DoWork event from this thread. You handle the DoWork event and begin your time-consuming task. However, you need to be careful not to access shared data (such as fields in your window class) or user interface objects. Once the work is complete, the BackgroundWorker fires the RunWorkerCompleted event to notify your application. This event fires on the dispatcher thread, which allows you to access shared data and your user interface, without incurring any problems.

After the BackgroundWorker acquires the thread, it fires the DoWork event. You can handle this event to call the Worker.FindPrimes() method. The DoWork event provides a DoWorkEventArgs object, which is the key ingredient for retrieving and returning information. You retrieve the input object through the DoWorkEventArgs.Argument property and return the result by setting the DoWorkEventArgs.Result property.

```vb
Private Sub backgroundWorker_DoWork(ByVal sender As Object, _
  ByVal e As DoWorkEventArgs)
    ' Get the input values.
    Dim input As FindPrimesInput = CType(e.Argument, FindPrimesInput)

    ' Start the search for primes and wait.
    Dim primes As Integer() = Worker.FindPrimes(input.From, _
      input.To, backgroundWorker)

    ' Return the result.
    e.Result = primes
End Sub
```

After the method completes, the BackgroundWorker fires the RunWorkerCompletedEventArgs on the dispatcher thread. At this point, you can retrieve the result from the RunWorkerCompletedEventArgs.Result property. You can then update the interface and access window-level variables without worry.

```vb
Private Sub backgroundWorker_RunWorkerCompleted(ByVal sender As Object, _
  ByVal e As RunWorkerCompletedEventArgs)
    If Not e.Error Is Nothing Then
        ' An error was thrown by the DoWork event handler.
        MessageBox.Show(e.Error.Message, "An Error Occurred")
```

```
    Else
        Dim primes As Integer() = CType(e.Result, Integer())
        For Each prime As Integer In primes
            lstPrimes.Items.Add(prime)
        Next
    End If

    cmdFind.IsEnabled = True
    cmdCancel.IsEnabled = False
    progressBar.Value = 0
End Sub
```

Notice that you don't need any locking code, and you don't need to use the Dispatcher.BeginInvoke() method. The BackgroundWorker takes care of these issues for you.

Behind the scenes, the BackgroundWorker uses a few multithreading classes that were introduced in .NET 2.0, including AsyncOperationManager, AsyncOperation, and SynchronizationContext. Essentially, the BackgroundWorker uses AsyncOperationManager to manage the background task. The AsyncOperationManager has some built-in intelligence—namely, it's able to get the synchronization context for the current thread. In a Windows Forms application, the AsyncOperationManager gets a WindowsFormsSynchronizationContext object, whereas a WPF application gets a DispatcherSynchronizationContext object. Conceptually, these classes do the same job, but their internal plumbing is different.

Tracking Progress

The BackgroundWorker also provides built-in support for tracking progress, which is useful for keeping the client informed about how much work has been completed in a long-running task.

To add support for progress, you need to first set the BackgroundWorker.WorkerReportsProgress property to True. Actually, providing and displaying the progress information is a two-step affair. First, the DoWork event-handling code needs to call the BackgroundWorker.ReportProgress() method and provide an estimated percent complete (from 0 percent to 100 percent). You can do this as little or as often as you like. Every time you call ReportProgress(), the BackgroundWorker fires the ProgressChanged event. You can react to this event to read the new progress percentage and update the user interface. Because the ProgressChanged event fires from the user interface thread, there's no need to use Dispatcher.BeginInvoke().

The FindPrimes() method reports progress in 1 percent increments, using code like this:

```
Dim iteration As Integer = CInt(list.Length / 100)
For i As Integer = 0 To list.Length - 1
    ...

    ' Report progress only if there is a change of 1%.
    ' Also, don't bother performing the calculation if there
    ' isn't a BackgroundWorker or if it doesn't support
    ' progress notifications.
    If (i Mod iteration = 0) And _
      (backgroundWorker IsNot Nothing) AndAlso _
      backgroundWorker.WorkerReportsProgress Then
        backgroundWorker.ReportProgress(i \ iteration)
    End If
Next
```

After you've set the BackgroundWorker.WorkerReportsProgress property, you can respond to these progress notifications by handling the ProgressChanged event. In this example, a progress bar is updated accordingly:

```
Private Sub backgroundWorker_ProgressChanged(ByVal sender As Object, _
  ByVal e As ProgressChangedEventArgs)
    progressBar.Value = e.ProgressPercentage
End Sub
```

Figure 31-2 shows the progress meter while the task is in progress.

Figure 31-2. *Tracking progress for an asynchronous task*

Supporting Cancellation

It's just as easy to add support for canceling a long-running task with the BackgroundWorker. The first step is to set the BackgroundWorker.WorkerSupportsCancellation property to True.

To request a cancellation, your code needs to call the BackgroundWorker.CancelAsync() method. In this example, the cancellation is requested when a Cancel button is clicked:

```
Private Sub cmdCancel_Click(ByVal sender As Object, _
  ByVal e As RoutedEventArgs)
    backgroundWorker.CancelAsync()
End Sub
```

Nothing happens automatically when you call CancelAsync(). Instead, the code that's performing the task needs to explicitly check for the cancel request, perform any required cleanup, and return. Here's the code in the FindPrimes() method that checks for cancellation requests just before it reports progress:

```
For i As Integer = 0 To list.Length - 1
    ...

    If (i Mod iteration = 0) And (backgroundWorker IsNot Nothing) Then
        If backgroundWorker.CancellationPending Then
            ' Return without doing any more work.
            Return
        End If

        If backgroundWorker.WorkerReportsProgress Then
            backgroundWorker.ReportProgress(i / iteration)
        End If
    End If
Next
```

The code in your DoWork event handler also needs to explicitly set the DoWorkEventArgs.Cancel property to True to complete the cancellation. You can then return from that method without attempting to build up the string of primes.

```
Private Sub backgroundWorker_DoWork(ByVal sender As Object, _
  ByVal e As DoWorkEventArgs)
    ' Get the input values.
    Dim input As FindPrimesInput = CType(e.Argument, FindPrimesInput)

    ' Start the search for primes and wait.
    Dim primes() As Integer = Worker.FindPrimes( _
      input.From, input.To, backgroundWorker)

    If backgroundWorker.CancellationPending Then
        e.Cancel = True
        Return
    End If

    ' Return the result.
    e.Result = primes
End Sub
```

Even when you cancel an operation, the RunWorkerCompleted event still fires. At this point, you can check whether the task was canceled and handle it accordingly.

```
Private Sub backgroundWorker_RunWorkerCompleted(ByVal sender As Object, _
  ByVal e As RunWorkerCompletedEventArgs)
    If e.Cancelled Then
        MessageBox.Show("Search cancelled.")
    ElseIf Not e.Error Is Nothing Then
        ' An error was thrown by the DoWork event handler.
        MessageBox.Show(e.Error.Message, "An Error Occurred")
```

```
        Else
            Dim primes As Integer() = CType(e.Result, Integer())
            For Each prime As Integer In primes
                lstPrimes.Items.Add(prime)
            Next
        End If

        cmdFind.IsEnabled = True
        cmdCancel.IsEnabled = False
        progressBar.Value = 0
End Sub
```

Now the BackgroundWorker component allows you to start a search and end it prematurely.

The Last Word

To design a safe and stable multithreading application, you need to understand WPF's threading rules. In this chapter, you explored these rules and learned how to safely update controls from other threads. You also saw how to build in progress notification, provide cancellation support, and make multithreading easy with BackgroundWorker.

■ ■ ■

The Add-in Model

Add-ins (also known as *plug-ins*) are separately compiled components that your application can find, load, and use dynamically. Often an application is designed to use add-ins so that it can be enhanced in the future without needing to be modified, recompiled, and retested. Add-ins also give you the flexibility to customize separate instances of an application for a particular market or client. But the most common reason to use the add-in model is to allow third-party developers to extend the functionality of your application. For example, add-ins in Adobe Photoshop provide a wide range of picture-processing effects. Add-ins in Firefox provide enhanced web-surfing features and entirely new functionality. In both cases, the add-ins are created by third-party developers.

Since .NET 1.0, developers have had all the technology they need to create their own add-in system. The two basic ingredients are *interfaces* (which allow you to define the contracts through which the application interacts with the add-in and the add-in interacts with the application) and *reflection* (which allows your application to dynamically discover and load add-in types from a separate assembly). However, building an add-in system from scratch requires a fair bit of work. You need to devise a way to locate add-ins, and you need to ensure that they're managed correctly (in other words, that they execute in a restricted security context and can be unloaded when necessary).

Fortunately, .NET has a prebuilt add-in model that saves you the trouble. It uses interfaces and reflection, like the add-in model that you'd probably write yourself. However, it handles the low-level plumbing for tedious tasks such as discovery and hosting. In this chapter, you'll learn how to use the add-in model in a WPF application.

Choosing Between MAF and MEF

Before you can get started building an extensible application with add-ins, you need to deal with an unexpected headache. Namely, .NET doesn't have just one add-in framework; it has two.

.NET 3.5 introduced an add-in model called the Managed Add-in Framework (MAF). But to make matters even more interesting (and a whole lot more confusing), .NET 4 added a new model called the Managed Extensibility Framework (MEF). Developers, who had to create their own add-in system not long ago, suddenly have two completely separate technologies that share the same ground. So, what's the difference?

MAF is the more elaborate framework of the two. It allows you to decouple your add-ins from your application so they depend on nothing more than the interface you define. This gives you welcome flexibility if you want to handle versioning scenarios—for example, if you need to change the interface but continue to support old add-ins for backward compatibility. MAF also allows your application to load add-ins into a separate application domain so that they can crash harmlessly, without affecting the main application. All of these features mean that MAF works well if you have one development team working on an application and another one (or several) working on its add-ins. MAF is also particularly well suited for supporting third-party add-ins.

But MAF's features come at a cost. MAF is a complex framework, and setting up the add-in pipeline is tedious, even for a simple application. This is where MEF comes in. It's a lighter-weight option that aims to make extensibility as easy as copying related assemblies into the same folder. But MEF also has a different underlying philosophy than MAF. Whereas MAF is a strict, interface-driven add-in model, MEF is a free-wheelin' system that allows an application to be built out of a collection of parts. Each part can export functionality, and any part can import the functionality of any other part. This system gives developers far more flexibility, and it works particularly well for designing *composable applications* (modular programs that are developed by a single development team but need to be assembled in different ways, with differently implemented features, for separate releases). The obvious danger is that MEF is too loose, and a poorly designed application can quickly become a tangle of interrelated parts.

If you think MAF is the add-in system for you, keep reading—it's the technology that's discussed in this chapter. If you want to check out MEF, you can learn more at Microsoft's MEF community site at http://tinyurl.com/37s2jdx. And if your real interest is not in add-ins but in composable applications, you'll want to check out Microsoft's Composite Application Library (CAL), which is also known by its old code name, Prism. Although MEF is a general-purpose solution for building any sort of modular .NET application, CAL is tailored for WPF. It includes UI-oriented features, such as the ability to let different modules communicate with events and show content in separate display regions. CAL also has support for creating "hybrid" applications that can be compiled for the WPF platform or the browser-based Silverlight platform. You can find the documentations and downloads for CAL at http://tinyurl.com/5ljve8.

■ **Note** From this point on, when the text refers to *the add-in model*, it means the MAF add-in model.

Understanding the Add-in Pipeline

The key advantage of the add-in model is that you don't need to write the underlying plumbing for tasks such as discovery. The key disadvantage is the add-in model's sheer complexity. The designers of .NET have taken great care to make the add-in model flexible enough to handle a wide range of versioning and hosting scenarios. The end result is that you must create at least seven (!) separate components to implement the add-in model in an application, even if you don't need to use its most sophisticated features.

The heart of the add-in model is the add-in *pipeline,* which is a chain of components that allow the hosting application to interact with an add-in (see Figure 32-1). At one end of the pipeline is the hosting application. At the other end is the add-in. In between are the five components that govern the interaction.

Figure 32-1. *Communicating through the add-in pipeline*

At first glance, this model seems a bit excessive. A simpler scenario would put a single layer (the contract) between the application and the add-in. However, the additional layers (the views and adapters) allow the add-in model to be much more flexible in certain situations (as described in the sidebar "More Advanced Adapters").

How the Pipeline Works

The *contract* is the cornerstone of the add-in pipeline. It includes one or more interfaces that define how the host application can interact with its add-ins and how the add-ins can interact with the host application. The contract assembly can also include custom serializable types that you plan to use to transmit data between the host application and the add-in.

The add-in pipeline is designed with extensibility and flexibility in mind. It's for this reason that the host application and the add-in don't directly use the contract. Instead, they use their own respective versions of the contract, called *views*. The host application uses the host view, while the add-in uses the add-in view. Typically, the view includes MustInherit classes that closely match the interfaces in the contract.

Although they're usually quite similar, the contracts and views are completely independent. It's up to the *adapters* to link these two pieces together. The adapters perform this linkage by providing classes that simultaneously inherit from the view classes and implement the contract interfaces. Figure 32-2 shows this design.

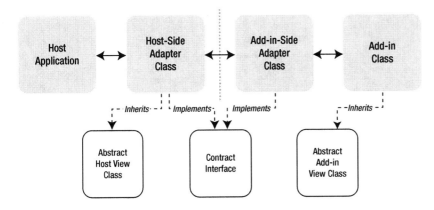

Figure 32-2. *Class relationships in the pipeline*

Essentially, the adapters bridge the gap between the views and the contract interface. They map calls on a view to calls on the contract interface. They also map calls on the contract interface to the corresponding method on the view. This complicates the design somewhat but adds an all-important extra layer of flexibility.

To understand how the adapters work, consider what happens when an application uses an add-in. First, the host application calls one of the methods in the host view. But remember, the host view is a MustInherit class. Behind the scenes, the application is actually calling a method on the host adapter *through* the host view. (This is possible because the host adapter class derives from the host view class.) The host adapter then calls the corresponding method in the contract interface, which is implemented by the add-in adapter. Finally, the add-in adapter calls a method in the add-in view. This method is implemented by the add-in, which performs the actual work.

MORE ADVANCED ADAPTERS

If you don't have any specialized versioning or hosting needs, the adapters are fairly straightforward. They simply pass the work along through the pipeline. However, the adapters are also an important extensibility point for more-sophisticated scenarios. One example is versioning. Obviously, you can independently update an application or its add-ins without changing the way they interact, as long as you continue to use the same interfaces in the contract. However, in some cases you might need to change the interfaces to expose new features. This causes a bit of a problem, because the old interfaces must still be supported for backward compatibility with old add-ins. After a few revisions, you'll end up with a complex mess of similar yet different interfaces, and the application will need to recognize and support them all.

With the add-in model, you can take a different approach to backward compatibility. Instead of providing multiple interfaces, you can provide a single interface in your contract and use adapters to create different views. For example, a version 1 add-in can work with a version 2 application (which exposes a version 2 contract) as long as you have an add-in adapter that spans the gap. Similarly, if you develop an add-in that uses the version 2 contract, you can use it with the original version 1 application (and version 1 contract) by using a different add-in adapter.

It's possible to work similar magic if you have specialized hosting needs. For example, you can use adapters to load add-ins with different isolation levels or even share them between applications. The hosting application and the add-in don't need to be aware of these details, because the adapters handle all the details.

Even if you don't need to create custom adapters to implement specialized versioning and hosting strategies, you still need to include these components. However, all your add-ins can use the same view and adapter components. In other words, after you've gone to the trouble of setting up the complete pipeline for one add-in, you can add more add-ins without much work, as illustrated in Figure 32-3.

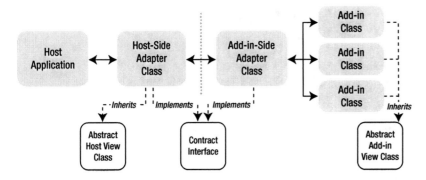

Figure 32-3. *Multiple add-ins that use the same pipeline*

In the following sections, you'll learn how to implement the add-in pipeline for a WPF application.

The Add-in Folder Structure

To use the add-in pipeline, you must follow a strict directory structure. This directory structure is separate from the application. In other words, it's perfectly acceptable to have your application residing at one location and all the add-ins and pipeline components residing at another location. However, the add-in components must be arranged in specifically named subdirectories with respect to one another. For example, if your add-in system uses the root directory c:\MyApp, you need the following subdirectories:

        c:\MyApp\AddInSideAdapters

        c:\MyApp\AddInViews

        c:\MyApp\Contracts

        c:\MyApp\HostSideAdapters

        c:\MyApp\AddIns

Finally, the AddIns directory (shown last in this list) must have a separate subdirectory for each add-in your application is using, such as c:\MyApp\AddIns\MyFirstAddIn, c:\MyApp\AddIns\MySecondAddIn, and so on.

In this example, it's assumed that the application executable is deployed in the c:\MyApp subdirectory. In other words, the same directory does double duty as the application folder and as the add-in root. This is a common deployment choice, but it's certainly not a requirement.

■ **Note** If you've been paying close attention to the pipeline diagrams, you may have noticed that there's a subdirectory for each component except the host-side views. That's because the host views are used directly by the host application, so they're deployed alongside the application executable. (In this example, that means they are in c:\MyApp.) The add-in views aren't deployed in the same way, because it's likely that several add-ins will use the same add-in view. Thanks to the dedicated AddInViews folder, you need to deploy (and update) just one copy of each add-in view assembly.

Preparing a Solution That Uses the Add-in Model

The add-in folder structure is mandatory. If you leave out one of the subdirectories listed in the previous section, you'll encounter a runtime exception when you search for add-ins.

Currently, Visual Studio doesn't have a template for creating applications that use add-ins. Thus, it's up to you to create these folders and set up your Visual Studio project to use them.

Here's the easiest approach to follow:

1. Create a top-level directory that will hold all the projects you're about to create. For example, you might name this directory c:\AddInTest.

2. Create a new WPF project for the host application in this directory. It doesn't matter what you name the project, but you must place it in the top-level directory you created in step 1 (for example, c:\AddInTest\HostApplication).

3. Add a new class library project for each pipeline component, and place them all in the same solution. At a bare minimum, you'll need to create a project for one add-in (for example, c:\AddInTest\MyAddIn), one add-in view (c:\AddInTest\MyAddInView), one add-in-side adapter (c:\AddInTest\MyAddInAdapter), one host view (c:\AddInTest\HostView), and one host-side adapter (c:\AddInTest\HostAdapter). Figure 32-4 shows an example from the downloadable code for this chapter, which you'll consider in the following sections. It includes an application (named HostApplication) and two add-ins (named FadeImageAddIn and NegativeImageAddIn).

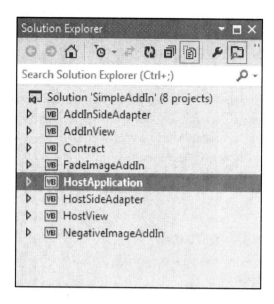

Figure 32-4. *A solution that uses the add-in pipeline*

■ **Note** Technically, it doesn't matter what project names and directory names you use when you create the pipeline components. The required folder structure, which you learned about in the previous section, will be created when you build the application (provided you configure your project settings properly, as described in the following two steps). However, to simplify the configuration process, it's strongly recommended that you create all the project directories in the top-level directory you established in step 1.

---

4. Now you need to create a build directory inside the top-level directory. This is where your application and all the pipeline components will be placed after they're compiled. It's common to name this directory Output (as in c:\AddInTest\Output).

5. As you design the various pipeline components, you'll modify the build path of each one so that the component is placed in the right subdirectory. For example, your add-in adapter should be compiled to a directory such as c:\AddInTest\Output\ AddInSideAdapters. To modify the build path, double-click the My Project node in the Solution Explorer. Then click the Compile tab and look for the Build Output Path text box. You need to use a relative output path that travels one level up the directory tree and then uses the Output directory. For example, the output path for an add-in adapter would be ..\ Output\AddInSideAdapters. As you build each component in the following sections, you'll learn which build path to use. Figure 32-5 shows a preview of the final result, based on the solution shown in Figure 32-4.

- SimpleAddIn
  - ▷ AddInSideAdapter
  - ▷ AddInView
  - ▷ Contracts
  - ▷ FadeImageAddIn
  - ▷ HostApplication
  - ▷ HostSideAdapter
  - ▷ HostView
  - ▷ NegativeImageAddIn
  - Output
    - ▷ AddIns
    - AddInSideAdapters
    - AddInViews
    - Contracts
    - HostSideAdapters

Figure 32-5. *The folder structure for a solution that uses the add-in pipeline*

There's one more consideration when developing with the add-in model in Visual Studio: references. Some pipeline components need to reference other pipeline components. However, you don't want the referenced assembly to be copied with the assembly that contains the reference. Instead, you rely on the add-in model's directory system.

To prevent a referenced assembly from being copied, you need to first configure Visual Studio to show references in the Solution Explorer by selecting the project in the Solution Explorer and choosing Project ➤ Show All Files (or clicking the Show All Files icon at the top of the Solution Explorer window). You'll then see the References node in the Solution Explorer, which you can expand to see all the referenced assemblies. To prevent a specific assembly from being copied, you need to select the assembly in the Solution Explorer. Then set Copy Local to False in the Properties window. As you build each component in the following sections, you'll learn which references to add.

■ **Tip** Correctly configuring an add-in project can take a bit of work. To start off on the right foot, you can use the add-in example that's discussed in this chapter, which is available with the downloadable code for this book.

Creating an Application That Uses Add-Ins

In the following sections, you'll create an application that uses the add-in model to support different ways of processing a picture (Figure 32-6). When the application starts, it lists all the add-ins that are currently present. The user can then select one of the add-ins from the list and use it to modify the currently displayed picture.

Figure 32-6. *An application that uses add-ins to manipulate a picture*

The Contract

The starting point for defining the add-in pipeline for your application is to create a contract assembly. The contract assembly defines two things:

- The interfaces that determine how the host will interact with the add-in and how the add-in will interact with the host.

- Custom types that you use to exchange information between the host and add-in. These types must be serializable.

The example shown in Figure 32-6 uses an exceedingly simple contract. Plug-ins provide a method named ProcessImageBytes() that accepts a byte array with image data, modifies it, and returns the modified byte array. Here's the contract that defines this method:

```
<AddInContract> _
Public Interface IImageProcessorContract
    Inherits IContract

    Function ProcessImageBytes(ByVal pixels As Byte()) As Byte()
End Interface
```

When creating a contract, you must derive from the IContract interface, and you must decorate the class with the AddInContract attribute. Both the interface and the attribute are found in the System.AddIn.Contract namespace. To have access to them in your contract assembly, you must add a reference to the System.AddIn.Contract.dll assembly.

Because the image-processing example doesn't use custom types to transmit data (just ordinary byte arrays), no types are defined in the contract assembly. Byte arrays can be transmitted between the host application and add-in because arrays and bytes are serializable.

The only additional step you need is to configure the build directory. The contract assembly must be placed in the Contracts subdirectory of the add-in root, which means you can use an output path of ..\Output\Contracts in the current example.

Note In this example, the interfaces are kept as simple as possible to avoid clouding the code with extra details. In a more realistic image-processing scenario, you might include a method that returns a list of configurable parameters that affect how the add-in processes the image. Each add-in would have its own parameters. For example, a filter that darkens a picture might include an Intensity setting, a filter that skews a picture might have an Angle setting, and so on. The host application could then supply these parameters when calling the ProcessImageBytes() method.

The Add-in View

The add-in view provides a MustInherit class that mirrors the contract assembly and is used on the add-in side. Creating this class is easy:

```
<AddInBase> _
Public MustInherit Class ImageProcessorAddInView
    Public MustOverride Function ProcessImageBytes(ByVal pixels As Byte()) _
      As Byte()
End Class
```

Notice that the add-in view class must be decorated with the AddInBase attribute. This attribute is found in the System.AddIn.Pipeline namespace. The add-in view assembly requires a reference to the System.AddIn.dll assembly in order to access it.

The add-in view assembly must be placed in the AddInViews subdirectory of the add-in root, which means you can use an output path of ..\Output\AddInViews in the current example.

The Add-In

The add-in view is a MustInherit class that doesn't provide any functionality. To create a usable add-in, you need a concrete class that derives from the MustInherit view class. This class can then add the code that actually does the work (in this case, processing the image).

The following add-in inverts the color values to create an effect that's similar to a photo negative. Here's the complete code:

```
<AddIn("Negative Image Processor", Version:="1.0.0.0", _
  Publisher:="Imaginomics", _
  Description:="Inverts colors to look like a photo negative")> _
Public Class NegativeImageProcessor
    Inherits AddInView.ImageProcessorAddInView
```

```vbnet
    Public Overrides Function ProcessImageBytes(ByVal pixels As Byte()) _
      As Byte()
        For i As Integer = 0 To pixels.Length - 2 - 1
            ' Assuming 24-bit, color, each pixel has three bytes of data.
            pixels(i) = CByte(255 - pixels(i))
            pixels(i + 1) = CByte(255 - pixels(i + 1))
            pixels(i + 2) = CByte(255 - pixels(i + 2))
        Next
        Return pixels
    End Function
End Class
```

■ **Note** In this example, the byte array is passed into the ProcessImageBytes() method through a parameter, modified directly, and then passed back to the calling code as the return value. However, when you call ProcessImageBytes() from a different application domain, this behavior isn't as simple as it seems. The add-in infrastructure actually makes a *copy* of the original byte array and passes that copy to the add-in's application domain. After the byte array is modified and has been returned from the method, the add-in infrastructure copies it back into the host's application domain. If ProcessImageBytes() didn't return the modified byte array in this way, the host would never see the changed picture data.

To create an add-in, you simply need to derive a class from the MustInherit view class and decorate it with the AddIn attribute. Additionally, you can use the properties of the AddIn attribute to supply an add-in name, version, publisher, and description, as done here. This information is made available to the host during add-in discovery.

The add-in assembly requires two references: one to the System.AddIn.dll assembly and one to the add-in view project. However, you must set the Copy Local property of the add-in view reference to False (as described earlier in the section "Preparing a Solution That Uses the Add-in Model"). That's because the add-in view isn't deployed with the add-in—instead, it's placed in the designated AddInViews subdirectory.

The add-in must be placed in its own subdirectory in the AddIns subdirectory of the add-in root. In the current example, you would use an output path such as ..\Output\AddIns\NegativeImageAddIn.

The Add-in Adapter

The current example has all the add-in functionality that you need, but there's still a gap between the add-in and the contract. Although the add-in view is modeled after the contract, it doesn't implement the contract interface that's used for communication between the application and the add-in.

The missing ingredient is the add-in adapter. It implements the contract interface. When a method is called in the contract interface, it calls the corresponding method in the add-in view. Here's the code for the most straightforward add-in adapter that you can create:

```vbnet
<AddInAdapter> _
Public Class ImageProcessorViewToContractAdapter
    Inherits ContractBase
    Implements Contract.IImageProcessorContract

    Private view As AddInView.ImageProcessorAddInView
```

```
    Public Sub New(ByVal view As AddInView.ImageProcessorAddInView)
        Me.view = view
    End Sub

    Public Function ProcessImageBytes(ByVal pixels As Byte()) As Byte() _
      Implements Contract.IImageProcessorContract.ProcessImageBytes
        Return view.ProcessImageBytes(pixels)
    End Function
End Class
```

All add-in adapters must derive from ContractBase (from the System.AddIn.Pipeline namespace). ContractBase derives from MarshalByRefObject, which allows the adapter to be called over an application domain boundary. All add-in adapters must also be decorated with the AddInAdapter attribute (from the System.AddIn.Pipeline namespace). Furthermore, the add-in adapter must include a constructor that receives an instance of the appropriate view as an argument. When the add-in infrastructure creates the add-in adapter, it automatically uses this constructor and passes in the add-in itself. (Remember, the add-in derives from the MustInherit add-in view class expected by the constructor.) Your code simply needs to store this view for later use.

The add-in adapter requires three references: one to System.AddIn.dll, one to System.AddIn.Contract.dll, and one to the contract project. You must set the Copy Local property of the contract reference to False (as described earlier in the section "Preparing a Solution That Uses the Add-in Model").

The add-in adapter assembly must be placed in the AddInSideAdapters subdirectory of the add-in root, which means you can use an output path of ..\Output\AddInSideAdapters in the current example.

The Host View

The next step is to build the host side of the add-in pipeline. The host interacts with the host view. Like the add-in view, the host view is a MustInherit class that closely mirrors the contract interface. The only difference is that it doesn't require any attributes.

```
Public MustInherit Class ImageProcessorHostView
    Public MustOverride Function ProcessImageBytes(ByVal pixels As Byte()) _
      As Byte()
End Class
```

The host view assembly must be deployed along with the host application. You can adjust the output path manually (for example, so the host view assembly is placed in the ..\Output folder in the current example). Or, when you add the host view reference to the host application, you can leave the Copy Local property set to True. This way, the host view will be copied automatically to the same output directory as the host application.

The Host Adapter

The host-side adapter derives from the host view. It receives an object that implements the contract, which it can then use when its methods are called. This is the same forwarding process that the add-in adapter uses, but in reverse. In this example, when the host application calls the ProcessImageBytes() method of the host view, it's actually calling ProcessImageBytes() in the host adapter. The host adapter calls ProcessImageBytes() on the contract interface (which is then forwarded across the application boundary and transformed into a method call on the add-in adapter).

Here's the complete code for the host adapter:

```
<HostAdapter> _
Public Class ImageProcessorContractToViewHostAdapter
    Inherits HostView.ImageProcessorHostView

    Private contract As Contract.IImageProcessorContract
    Private contractHandle As ContractHandle

    Public Sub New(ByVal contract As Contract.IImageProcessorContract)
        Me.contract = contract
        contractHandle = New ContractHandle(contract)
    End Sub

    Public Overrides Function ProcessImageBytes(ByVal pixels As Byte()) _
      As Byte()
        Return contract.ProcessImageBytes(pixels)
    End Function
End Class
```

You'll notice that the host adapter uses two member fields. It stores a reference to the current contract object, and it stores a reference to a System.AddIns.Pipeline.ContractHandle object. The ContractHandle object manages the lifetime of the add-in. If the host adapter doesn't create a ContractHandle object (and keep a reference to it), the add-in will be released immediately after the constructor code ends. When the host application attempts to use the add-in, it will receive an AppDomainUnloadedException.

The host adapter project needs references to System.Add.dll and System.AddIn.Contract.dll. It also needs references to the contract assembly and the host view assembly (both of which must have Copy Local set to False). The output path is the HostSideAdapters subdirectory in the add-in root (in this example, it's ..\Output\HostSideAdapters).

The Host

Now that the infrastructure is in place, the final step is to create the application that uses the add-in model. Although any type of executable .NET application could be a host, this example uses a WPF application.

The host needs just one reference that points to the host view project. The host view is the entry point to the add-in pipeline. In fact, now that you've done the heavy lifting in implementing the pipeline, the host doesn't need to worry about how it's managed. It simply needs to find the available add-ins, activate the ones it wants to use, and then call the methods that are exposed by the host view.

The first step—finding the available add-ins—is called *discovery*. It works through the shared methods of the System.AddIn.Hosting.AddInStore class. To load add-ins, you simply supply the add-in root path and call AddInStore.Update(), as shown here:

```
' In this example, the path where the application is running
' is also the add-in root.
Dim path As String = Environment.CurrentDirectory
AddInStore.Update(path)
```

After calling Update(), the add-in system will create two files with cached information. A file named PipelineSegments.store will be placed in the add-in root. This file includes information about the different views and adapters. A file named AddIns.store will be placed in the AddIns subdirectory, with information about all the available add-ins. If new views, adapters, or add-ins are added, you can update these files by calling AddInStore.Update() again.

(This method returns quite quickly if there are no new add-ins or pipeline components.) If there is reason to expect that there is a problem with existing add-in files, you can call AddInStore.Rebuild() instead, which always rebuilds the add-in files from scratch.

After you've created the cache files, you can search for the specific add-ins. You can use the FindAddIn() method to find a single specific add-in, or you can use the FindAddIns() method to find all the add-ins that match a specified host view. The FindAddIns() method returns a collection of tokens, each of which is an instance of the System.AddIn.Hosting.AddInToken class.

```
Dim tokens As IList(Of AddInToken)
tokens = AddInStore.FindAddIns(GetType(HostView.ImageProcessorHostView), path)
lstAddIns.ItemsSource = tokens
```

You can get information about the add-in through a few key properties (Name, Description, Publisher, and Version). In the image-processing application (shown in Figure 32-6), the token list is bound to a ListBox control, and some basic information is shown about each add-in by using the following data template:

```
<ListBox Name="lstAddIns" Margin="3">
  <ListBox.ItemTemplate>
    <DataTemplate>
      <StackPanel Margin="3,3,0,8" HorizontalAlignment="Stretch">
        <TextBlock Text="{Binding Path=Name}" FontWeight="Bold" />
        <TextBlock Text="{Binding Path=Publisher}" />
        <TextBlock Text="{Binding Path=Description}"
          FontSize="10" FontStyle="Italic" />
      </StackPanel>
    </DataTemplate>
  </ListBox.ItemTemplate>
</ListBox>
```

You can create an instance of the add-in by calling the AddInToken.Activate<T> method. In the current application, the user clicks the Go button to activate an add-in. The information is then pulled out of the current image (which is shown in the window) and passed to the ProcessImageBytes() method of the host view. Here's how it works:

```
Private Sub cmdProcessImage_Click(ByVal sender As Object, _
  ByVal e As RoutedEventArgs)
    ' Copy the image information from the image to a byte array.
    Dim source As BitmapSource = CType(img.Source, BitmapSource)
    Dim stride As Integer
    stride = CInt(source.PixelWidth * source.Format.BitsPerPixel / 8)
    stride = stride + (stride Mod 4) * 4
    Dim pixelLength as Integer = CInt( _
      stride * source.PixelHeight * source.Format.BitsPerPixel / 8 - 1)
    Dim originalPixels As Byte() = New Byte(pixelLength) {}
    source.CopyPixels(originalPixels, stride, 0)

    ' Get the selected add-in token.
    Dim token As AddInToken = CType(lstAddIns.SelectedItem, AddInToken)
```

```
' Get the host view.
Dim addin As HostView.ImageProcessorHostView
addin = token.Activate(Of HostView.ImageProcessorHostView) _
  (AddInSecurityLevel.Internet)

' Use the add-in.
Dim changedPixels As Byte() = addin.ProcessImageBytes(originalPixels)

' Create a new BitmapSource with the changed image data, and display it.
Dim newSource As BitmapSource = BitmapSource.Create(source.PixelWidth, _
  source.PixelHeight, source.DpiX, source.DpiY, source.Format, _
  source.Palette, changedPixels, stride)
img.Source = newSource
End Sub
```

When you call the AddInToken.Activate<T> method, quite a few steps unfold behind the scenes:

1. A new application domain is created for the add-in. Alternatively, you can load the add-in into the application domain of the host application or into a completely separate process. However, the default is to place it in a distinct application domain in the current process, which usually gives the best compromise between stability and performance. You can also choose the level of permissions that are given to the new application domain. (In this example, they're limited to the Internet set of permissions, which is a heavily restricted permission set that's applied to code that's executed from the Web.)

2. The add-in assembly is loaded into the new application domain. The add-in is then instantiated through reflection, using its no-argument constructor. As you've already seen, the add-in derives from a MustInherit class in the add-in view assembly. As a result, loading the add-in also loads the add-in view assembly into the new application domain.

3. The add-in adapter is instantiated in the new application domain. The add-in is passed to the add-in adapter as a constructor argument. (The add-in is typed as the add-in view.)

4. The add-in adapter is made available to the host's application domain (through a remoting proxy). However, it's typed as the contract that it implements.

5. In the host application domain, the host adapter is instantiated. The add-in adapter is passed to the host adapter through its constructor.

6. The host adapter is returned to the host application (typed as the host view). The application can now call the methods of the host view to interact with the add-in through the add-in pipeline.

There are other overloads for the Activate<T> method that allow you to supply a custom permission set (to fine-tune security), a specific application domain (which is useful if you want to run several add-ins in the same application domain), and an outside process (which allows you to host the add-in in a completely separate EXE application for even greater isolation). All of these examples are illustrated in the Visual Studio help.

This code completes the example. The host application can now discover its add-ins, activate them, and interact with them through the host view.

ADD-IN LIFETIME

You don't need to manage the lifetime of your add-ins by hand. Instead, the add-in system will automatically release an add-in and shut down its application domain. In the previous example, the add-in is released when the variable that points to the host view goes out of scope. If you want to keep the same add-in active for a longer time, you could assign it to a member variable in the window class.

In some situations, you might want more control over the add-in lifetime. The add-in model gives the host application the ability to shut down an add-in automatically by using the AddInController class (from the System. AddIn.Hosting namespace), which tracks all the currently active add-ins. The AddInControls provides a shared method named GetAddInController(), which accepts a host view and returns an AddInController for that add-in. You can then use the AddInController.Shutdown() method to end it, as shown here:

```
Dim controller As AddInController = AddInController.GetAddInController(addin)
controller.Shutdown()
```

At this point, the adapters will be disposed, the add-in will be released, and the add-in's application domain will be shut down if it doesn't contain any other add-ins.

More Add-Ins

Using the same add-in view, it's possible to create an unlimited number of distinct add-ins. In this example there are two, which process images in different ways. The second add-in uses a crude algorithm to darken the picture by removing part of the color from random pixels:

```
<AddIn("Fade Image Processor", Version:="1.0.0.0", Publisher:="SupraImage", _
  Description := "Darkens the picture")> _
Public Class FadeImageProcessor
    Inherits AddInView.ImageProcessorAddInView

    Public Overrides Function ProcessImageBytes(ByVal pixels As Byte()) _
      As Byte()
        Dim rand As New Random()
        Dim offset As Integer = rand.Next(0, 10)
        For i As Integer = 0 To pixels.Length - 1 - offset - 1
            If (i + offset) Mod 5 = 0 Then
                pixels(i) = 0
            End If
        Next
        Return pixels
    End Function
End Class
```

In the current example, this add-in builds to the output path ..\Output\AddIns\FadeImageAddIn. There's no need to create additional views or adapters. After you deploy this add-in (and then call the Rebuild() or Update() method of the AddInStore class), your host application will find both add-ins.

Interacting with the Host

In the current example, the host is in complete control of the add-in. However, the relationship is often reversed. A common example is an add-in that drives an area of application functionality. This is particularly common with visual add-ins (the subject of the next section), such as custom toolbars. Often this process of allowing the add-in to call the host is called *automation*.

From a conceptual standpoint, automation is quite straightforward. The add-in simply needs a reference to an object in the host's application domain, which it can manipulate through a separate interface. However, the add-in system's emphasis on versioning flexibility makes the implementation of this technique a bit more complicated. A single host interface is not enough, because it tightly binds the host and the add-in together. Instead, you'll need to implement a pipeline with views and adapters.

To see this challenge, consider the slightly updated version of the image-processing application, which is shown in Figure 32-7. It features a progress bar at the bottom of the window that's updated as the add-in processes the image data.

Figure 32-7. *An add-in that reports progress*

■ **Tip**   The rest of this section explores the changes you need to make to the image processor to support host automation. To see how these pieces fit together and examine the full code, download the code samples for this chapter.

For this application to work, the add-in needs a way to pass progress information to the host while it works. The first step in implementing this solution is to create the interface that defines how the add-in can interact with the host. This interface should be placed in the contract assembly (or in a separate assembly in the Contracts folder).

Here's the interface that describes how the add-in should be allowed to report progress, by calling a method named ReportProgress() in the host application:

```
Public Interface IHostObjectContract
    Inherits IContract

    Sub ReportProgress(ByVal progressPercent As Integer)
End Interface
```

As with the add-in interface, the host interface must inherit from IContract. Unlike the add-in interface, the host interface does not use the AddInContract attribute, because it isn't implemented by an add-in.

The next step is to create the add-in view and host view. As when designing an add-in, you simply need a MustInherit class that closely corresponds to the interface you're using. To use the IHostObjectContract interface shown earlier, you simply need to add the following class definition to both the add-in view and host view projects.

```
Public MustInherit Class HostObject
    Public MustOverride Sub ReportProgress(ByVal progressPercent As Integer)
End Class
```

Notice that the class definition does not use the AddInBase attribute in either project.

The actual implementation of the ReportProgress() method is in the host application. It needs a class that derives from the HostObject class (in the host view assembly). Here's a slightly simplified example that uses the percentage to update a ProgressBar control:

```
Public Class AutomationHost
    Inherits HostView.HostObject

    Private progressBar As ProgressBar

    Public Sub New(ByVal progressBar As ProgressBar)
        Me.progressBar = progressBar
    End Sub

    Public Overrides Sub ReportProgress(ByVal progressPercent As Integer)
        progressBar.Value = progressPercent
    End Sub
End Class
```

You now have a mechanism that the add-in can use to send progress information to the host application. However, there's one problem—the add-in doesn't have any way to get a reference to the HostObject. This problem doesn't occur when the host application is using an add-in, because it has a discovery feature that it can use to search for add-ins. There's no comparable service for add-ins to locate their host.

The solution is for the host application to pass the HostObject reference to the add-in. Typically, this step will be performed when the add-in is first activated. By convention, the method that the host application uses to pass this reference is often called Initialize().

Here's the updated contract for image processor add-ins:

```
<AddInContract> _
Public Interface IImageProcessorContract
    Inherits IContract
```

```
Function ProcessImageBytes(ByVal pixels As Byte()) As Byte()
    Sub Initialize(ByVal hostObj As IHostObjectContract)
End Interface
```

When Initialize() is called, the add-in will simply store the reference for later use. The add-in can then call the ReportProgress() method whenever that is appropriate, as shown here:

```
<AddIn> _
Public Class NegativeImageProcessor
    Inherits AddInView.ImageProcessorAddInView

    Private host As AddInView.HostObject
    Public Overrides Sub Initialize(ByVal hostObj As AddInView.HostObject)
        host = hostObj
    End Sub

    Public Overrides Function ProcessImageBytes(ByVal pixels As Byte()) _
        As Byte()
        Dim iteration As Integer = CInt(pixels.Length / 100)

        For i As Integer = 0 To pixels.Length - 2 - 1
            pixels(i) = CByte(255 - pixels(i))
            pixels(i + 1) = CByte(255 - pixels(i + 1))
            pixels(i + 2) = CByte(255 - pixels(i + 2))

            If i Mod iteration = 0 Then
                host.ReportProgress(i \ iteration)
            End If
        Next
        Return pixels
    End Function

End Class
```

So far, the code hasn't posed any real challenges. However, the last piece—the adapters—is a bit more complicated. Now that you've added the Initialize() method to the add-in contract, you need to also add it to the host view and add-in view. However, the signature of the method can't match the contract interface. That's because the Initialize() method in the interface expects an IHostObjectContract as an argument. The views, which are not linked to the contract in any way, have no knowledge of the IHostObjectContract. Instead, they use the MustInherit HostObject class that was described earlier:

```
Public MustInherit Class ImageProcessorHostView
    Public MustOverride Function ProcessImageBytes(ByVal pixels As Byte()) _
        As Byte()

    Public MustOverride Sub Initialize(ByVal host As HostObject)
End Class
```

The adapters are the tricky part. They need to bridge the gap between the HostObject view classes and the IHostObjectContract interface. For example, consider the ImageProcessorContractToViewHostAdapter on the host side. It derives from the MustInherit ImageProcessorHostView class, and as a result it implements the version of Initialize() that receives a HostObject instance. This Initialize() method needs to convert this view to the contract and then call the IHostObjectContract.Initialize() method.

The trick is to create an adapter that performs this transformation (much like the adapter that performs the same transformation with the add-in view and add-in interface). The following code shows the new HostObjectViewToContractHostAdapter that does the work and the Initialize() method that uses it to make the jump from the view class to the contract interface:

```
Public Class HostObjectViewToContractHostAdapter
    Inherits ContractBase
    Implements Contract.IHostObjectContract

    Private view As HostView.HostObject
    Public Sub New(ByVal view As HostView.HostObject)
        Me.view = view
    End Sub

    Public Sub ReportProgress(ByVal progressPercent As Integer) _
        Implements Contract.IHostObjectContract.ReportProgress
            view.ReportProgress(progressPercent)
    End Sub
End Class

<HostAdapter> _
Public Class ImageProcessorContractToViewHostAdapter
    Inherits HostView.ImageProcessorHostView

    Private contract As Contract.IImageProcessorContract
    Private contractHandle As ContractHandle

    ...

    Public Overrides Sub Initialize(ByVal host As HostView.HostObject)
        Dim hostAdapter As New HostObjectViewToContractHostAdapter(host)
        contract.Initialize(hostAdapter)
    End Sub
End Class
```

A similar transformation takes place in the add-in adapter, but in reverse. Here, the ImageProcessorViewToContractAdapter implements the IImageProcessorContract interface. It needs to take the IHostObjectContract object that it receives in its version of the Initialize() method and then convert the contract to a view. Next, it can pass the call along by calling the Initialize() method in the view. Here's the code:

```
<AddInAdapter> _
Public Class ImageProcessorViewToContractAdapter
    Inherits ContractBase
    Implements Contract.IImageProcessorContract
```

```vb
    Private view As AddInView.ImageProcessorAddInView

    ...

    Public Sub Initialize(ByVal hostObj As Contract.IHostObjectContract) _
      Implements Contract.IImageProcessorContract.Initialize
        view.Initialize(New HostObjectContractToViewAddInAdapter(hostObj))
    End Sub
End Class

Public Class HostObjectContractToViewAddInAdapter
    Inherits AddInView.HostObject

    Private contract As Contract.IHostObjectContract
    Private handle As ContractHandle

    Public Sub New(ByVal contract As Contract.IHostObjectContract)
        Me.contract = contract
        Me.handle = New ContractHandle(contract)
    End Sub

    Public Overrides Sub ReportProgress(ByVal progressPercent As Integer)
        contract.ReportProgress(progressPercent)
    End Sub
End Class
```

Now, when the host calls Initialize() on an add-in, it can flow through the host adapter (ImageProcessorContractToViewHostAdapter) and the add-in adapter (ImageProcessorViewToContractAdapter), before being called on the add-in. When the add-in calls the ReportProgress() method, it flows through similar steps, but in reverse. First it flows through the add-in adapter (HostObjectContractToViewAddInAdapter), and then it passes to the host adapter (HostObjectViewToContractHostAdapter).

This walk-through completes the example—sort of. The problem is that the host application calls the ProcessImageBytes() method on the main user interface thread. As a result, the user interface is effectively locked up. Although the calls to ReportProgress() are handled and the progress bar is updated, the window isn't refreshed until the operation is complete.

A far better approach is to perform the time-consuming call to ProcessImageBytes() on a background thread, either by creating a Thread object by hand or by using the BackgroundWorker. Then, when the user interface needs to be updated (when ReportProgress() is called and when the final image is returned), you must use the Dispatcher.BeginInvoke() method to marshal the call back to the user interface thread. All of these techniques were demonstrated earlier in this chapter. To see the threading code in action in this example, refer to the downloadable code for this chapter.

Visual Add-Ins

Considering that the WPF is a display technology, you've probably started to wonder whether there's a way to have an add-in generate a user interface. This isn't a small challenge. The problem is that the user interface elements in WPF aren't serializable. Thus, they can't be passed between the host application and the add-in.

Fortunately, the designers of the add-in system created a sophisticated workaround. The solution is to allow WPF applications to display user interface content that's hosted in separate application domains. In other words, your host application can display controls that are actually running in the application domain of an add-in. If you interact with these controls (clicking them, typing in them, and so on), the events are fired in the add-in's application domain. If you need to pass information from the add-in to the application, or vice versa, you use the contract interfaces, as you've explored in the previous sections.

Figure 32-8 shows this technique in action in a modified version of the image-processing application. When an add-in is selected, the host application asks the add-in to provide a control with suitable content. That control is then displayed at the bottom of the window.

Figure 32-8. *A visual add-in*

In this example, the negative image add-in has been selected. It provides a user control that wraps an Image control (with a preview of the effect) and a Slider control. As the slider is adjusted, the intensity of the effect is changed, and the preview is updated. (The update process is sluggish, because of the poorly optimized image-processing code. Much better algorithms could be used, possibly incorporating unsafe code blocks for maximum performance.)

Although the plumbing that makes this work is fairly sophisticated, it's surprisingly easy to use. The key ingredient is the INativeHandleContract interface from the System.AddIn.Contract namespace. It allows a window handle to be passed between an add-in and the host application.

Here's the revised IImageProcessorContract from the contract assembly. It replaces the ProcessImageBytes() method with a GetVisual() method that accepts similar image data but returns a chunk of user interface:

```
<AddInContract> _
Public Interface IImageProcessorContract
    Inherits IContract

    Function GetVisual(ByVal imageStream As Stream) As INativeHandleContract
End Interface
```

You don't use the INativeHandlerContract in the view classes, because it isn't directly usable in your WPF applications. Instead, you use the type you expect to see—a FrameworkElement. Here's the host view:

```
Public MustInherit Class ImageProcessorHostView

    Public MustOverride Function GetVisual(ByVal imageStream As Stream) _
      As FrameworkElement
End Class
```

And here's the nearly identical add-in view:

```
<AddInBase> _
Public MustInherit Class ImageProcessorAddInView

    Public MustOverride Function GetVisual(ByVal imageStream As Stream) _
      As FrameworkElement
End Class
```

This example is surprisingly similar to the automation challenge in the previous section. Once again, you have a different type being passed in the contract from the one that's used in the views. And once again, you need to use the adapters to perform the contract-to-view and view-to-contract conversion. However, this time the work is done for you by a specialized class called FrameworkElementAdapters.

FrameworkElementAdapters is found in the System.AddIn.Pipeline namespace, but it's actually part of WPF, and it's part of the System.Windows.Presentation.dll assembly. The FrameworkElementAdapters class provides two shared methods that perform the conversion work: ContractToViewAdapter() and ViewToContractAdapter().

Here's how the FrameworkElementAdapters.ContractToViewAdapter() method bridges the gap in the host adapter:

```
<HostAdapter> _
Public Class ImageProcessorContractToViewHostAdapter
    Inherits HostView.ImageProcessorHostView

    Private contract As Contract.IImageProcessorContract
    Private contractHandle As ContractHandle
    ...

    Public Overrides Function GetVisual(ByVal imageStream As Stream) _
      As FrameworkElement
```

```
        Return FrameworkElementAdapters.ContractToViewAdapter( _
            contract.GetVisual(imageStream))
    End Function

End Class
```

And here's how the FrameworkElementAdapters.ViewToContractAdapter() method bridges the gap in the add-in adapter:

```
<AddInAdapter> _
Public Class ImageProcessorViewToContractAdapter
    Inherits ContractBase
    Implements Contract.IImageProcessorContract

    Private view As AddInView.ImageProcessorAddInView
    ...

    Public Function GetVisual(ByVal imageStream As Stream) _
      As INativeHandleContract _
      Implements Contract.IImageProcessorContract.GetVisual

        Return FrameworkElementAdapters.ViewToContractAdapter( _
            view.GetVisual(imageStream))
    End Function

End Class
```

Now the final detail is to implement the GetVisual() method in the add-in. In the negative image processor, a new user control named ImagePreview is created. The image data is passed to the ImagePreview control, which sets up the preview image and handles slider clicks. (The user control code is beside the point for this example, but you can see the full details by downloading the samples for this chapter.)

```
<AddIn> _
Public Class NegativeImageProcessor
    Inherits AddInView.ImageProcessorAddInView

    Public Overrides Function GetVisual(ByVal imageStream As Stream) _
      As FrameworkElement
        Return New ImagePreview(imageStream)
    End Function
End Class
```

Now that you've seen how to return a user interface object from an add-in, there's no limit to what type of content you can generate. The basic infrastructure—the INativeHandleContract interface and the FrameworkElementAdapters class—remains the same.

The Last Word

In this chapter, you dove into the deeply layered add-in model. You learned how its pipeline works, why it works the way it does, and how to create basic add-ins that support host automation and provide visual content.

There's quite a bit more you can learn about the add-in model. If you plan to make add-ins a key part of a professional application, you may want to take a closer look at specialized versioning and hosting scenarios and deployment, best practices for dealing with unhandled add-in exceptions, and how to allow more-complex interactions between the host and add-in and between separate add-ins. To get the details, you can visit two old (and now discontinued) Microsoft blogs that still provide technical information about the add-in model. They are `http://blogs.msdn.com/clraddins` (with posts by the Microsoft developers who created the add-in system) and `http://blogs.msdn.com/zifengh` (with posts by Jason He, who writes about his experience adapting Paint.NET to use the add-in model).

CHAPTER 33

■ ■ ■

ClickOnce Deployment

Sooner or later, you'll want to unleash your WPF applications on the world. Although you can use dozens of ways to transfer an application from your development computer to an end user's desktop, most WPF applications use one of the following deployment strategies:

Run in the browser: If you create a page-based WPF application, you can run it right in the browser. You don't need to install anything. However, your application needs to be able to function with a very limited set of privileges. (For example, you won't be allowed to access arbitrary files, use the Windows Registry, pop up new windows, and so on.) You learned about this approach in Chapter 24.

Deploy via the browser: WPF applications integrate closely with the ClickOnce setup feature, which allows users to launch a setup program from a browser page. Best of all, applications that are installed through ClickOnce can be configured to check for updates automatically. On the negative side, you have little ability to customize your setup and no way to perform system configuration tasks (such as modifying the Windows Registry, creating a database, and so on).

Deploy via a traditional setup program: This approach still lives on in the WPF world. If you choose this option, it's up to you whether you want to create a full-fledged Windows Installer setup or a more streamlined (but more limited) ClickOnce setup. After you've built your setup, you can choose to distribute it by placing it on a CD, in an e-mail attachment, on a network share, and so on.

In this chapter, you'll focus on the second approach: deploying your application with the ClickOnce deployment model.

Understanding Application Deployment

Although it's technically possible to move a .NET application from one computer to another just by copying the folder that contains it, professional applications often require a few more frills. For example, you might need to add multiple shortcuts to the Start menu, add registry settings, and set up additional resources (such as a custom event log or a database). To get these features, you need to create a custom setup program.

You have many options for creating a setup program. You can use a retail product such as Flexera Software's InstallShield, or you can create a Windows Installer setup by using the Setup Project template in Visual Studio. Traditional setup programs give you a familiar setup wizard, with plenty of features for transferring files and performing a variety of configuration actions.

Your other choice is to use the ClickOnce deployment system that's closely integrated in WPF. ClickOnce has plenty of limitations (most of them by design), but it offers two important advantages:

- Support for installing from a browser page (which can be hosted on an internal network or placed on the Web)

- Support for automatically downloading and installing updates

These two features might not be enough to entice developers to give up the features of a full-fledged setup program. But if you need a simple, lightweight deployment that works over the Web and supports automatic updates, ClickOnce is perfect.

CLICKONCE AND PARTIAL TRUST

Ordinary WPF applications require full trust because your application needs unmanaged code permission to create a WPF window. This means that installing a stand-alone WPF application using ClickOnce presents the same security roadblock as installing any type of application from the Web—namely, the web browser will present a security warning. If the user goes ahead, the installed application will have the ability to do anything that the current user can do.

WPF does have a way to combine partial-trust programming and a ClickOnce-based installation experience. The trick is to use the XBAP model described in Chapter 24. In this situation, your application runs in the browser; therefore, it doesn't need to create any windows and doesn't need unmanaged code permission. Even better, because the application is accessed through a URL (and then cached locally), the user always runs the latest, most up-to-date version. Behind the scenes, the automatic XBAP download uses the same ClickOnce technology that you'll use in this chapter.

XBAPs aren't covered in this chapter. For more information about XBAPs and partial-trust programming, refer to Chapter 24.

ClickOnce is designed with simple, straightforward applications in mind. It's particularly suitable for line-of-business applications and internal company software. Typically, these applications perform their work with the data and services on middle-tier server computers. As a result, they don't need privileged access to the local computer. These applications are also deployed in enterprise environments that may include thousands of workstations. In these environments, the cost of application deployment and updating isn't trivial, especially if it needs to be handled by an administrator. As a result, it's more important to provide a simple, streamlined setup process than to pack in features.

ClickOnce may also make sense for consumer applications that are deployed over the Web, particularly if these applications are updated frequently and don't have extensive installation requirements. However, the limitations of ClickOnce (such as the lack of flexibility for customizing the setup wizard) don't make it practical for sophisticated consumer applications that have detailed setup requirements or need to guide the user through a set of proprietary configuration steps. In these cases, you'll need to create a custom setup application.

■ **Note** For ClickOnce to install a WPF application, the computer must already have the .NET Framework runtime. When you first launch a ClickOnce setup, a bootstrapper runs that verifies this requirement. If the .NET Framework runtime isn't installed, the bootstrapper shows a message box that explains the issue and prompts the user to install .NET from Microsoft's website.

The ClickOnce Installation Model

Although ClickOnce supports several types of deployment, the overall model is designed to make web deployment practical and easy. Here's how it works: You use Visual Studio to publish your ClickOnce application to a web server. Then the user surfs to an automatically generated web page (named publish.htm) that provides a link to install the application. When the user clicks that link, the application is downloaded, installed, and added to the Start menu. Figure 33-1 shows this process.

Figure 33-1. *Installing a ClickOnce application*

Although ClickOnce is ideal for web deployment, the same basic model lends itself to other scenarios, including the following:

- Deploying your application from a network file share

- Deploying your application from a CD or DVD

- Deploying your application to a web server or network file share and then sending a link to the setup program via e-mail

The installation web page isn't created when deploying to a network share, a CD, or a DVD. Instead, in these cases users must install the application by running the setup.exe program directly.

The most interesting part of a ClickOnce deployment is the way it supports updating. Essentially, you (the developer) have control over several update settings. For example, you can configure the application to check for updates automatically or periodically at certain intervals. When users launch your application, they actually run a shim that checks for newer versions and offers to download them.

You can even configure your application to use a weblike online-only mode. In this situation, the application must be launched from the ClickOnce web page. The application is still cached locally for optimum performance, but users won't be able to run the application unless they're able to connect to the site where the application was published. This ensures that users always run the latest, most up-to-date version of your application.

ClickOnce Limitations

ClickOnce deployment doesn't allow for much configuration. Many aspects of its behavior are completely fixed, either to guarantee a consistent user experience or to encourage enterprise-friendly security policies.

The limitations of ClickOnce include the following:

- ClickOnce applications are installed for a single user. You cannot install an application for all users on a workstation.

- ClickOnce applications are always installed in a system-managed user-specific folder. You cannot change or influence the folder where the application is installed.

- If ClickOnce applications are installed in the Start menu, you get just two shortcuts: one that launches the application and one that launches a help web page in the browser. You can't change this, and you can't add a ClickOnce application to the Startup group, the Favorites menu, and so on.

- You can't change the user interface of the setup wizard. That means you can't add new dialog boxes, change the wording of existing ones, and so on.

- You can't change the installation page that ClickOnce applications generate. However, you can edit the HTML by hand after it's generated.

- A ClickOnce setup can't install shared components in the global assembly cache (GAC).

- A ClickOnce setup can't perform custom actions (such as creating a database or configuring Registry settings).

You can work around some of these issues. For example, you could configure your application to add Registry settings the first time it's launched on a new computer. However, if you have complex setup requirements, you're much better off creating a full-fledged custom setup program. You can use a third-party tool such as InstallShield, or you can create a setup project in Visual Studio.

Finally, it's worth noting that .NET makes it possible to build a custom installer that uses ClickOnce deployment technology. This gives you the option of designing an advanced setup application without sacrificing the automatic updating feature that ClickOnce provides. However, there are also some drawbacks. This approach not only forces you to write (and debug) a fair bit of code, it also requires that you use the legacy classes from the Windows Forms toolkit to build your setup user interface. Mixing custom setup applications with ClickOnce is beyond the scope of this book, but if you're interested, you can get started with the example at http://tinyurl.com/9qx9ckp.

Setting Up a Simple ClickOnce Publication

Before you get started with ClickOnce publishing, you need to set some basic information about your project. First, double-click the My Project node in the Solution Explorer, and then click the Publish tab. You'll see the settings shown in Figure 33-2.

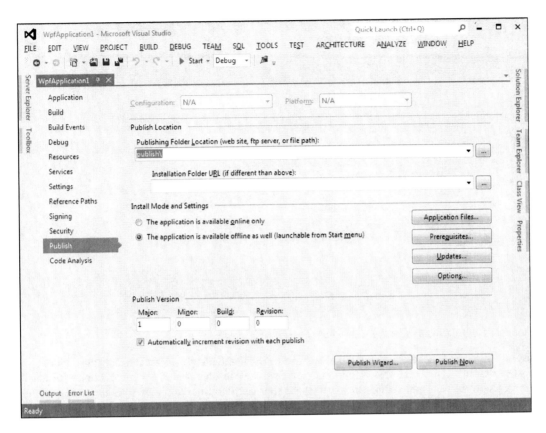

Figure 33-2. *ClickOnce project settings*

You'll learn your way around the settings in this window later in this chapter. But first you need to supply some basic publication details.

Setting the Publisher and Production

Before you can install your application, it needs a basic identity, including a publisher name and a product name that can be used in the setup prompts and the Start menu shortcuts. To supply this information, click the Options button to show the Publish Options dialog box. It displays a slew of additional settings, separated into several groups. Although Description is selected (in the list on the left), you'll see text boxes that allow you to supply three key details: the publisher name, suite name, and product name (see Figure 33-3).

Figure 33-3. *Supplying some basic information about your project*

These details are important because they're used to create the Start menu hierarchy. If you supply the optional suite name, ClickOnce creates a shortcut for your application in the form [Publisher Name] ➤ [Suite Name] ➤ [Product Name]. If you don't supply the suite name, ClickOnce creates the shortcut [Publisher Name] ➤ [Product Name]. From the example shown in Figure 33-3, the shortcut will be generated as Acme Software ➤ ClickOnceTest (see Figure 33-4).

Figure 33-4. *The ClickOnce shortcuts (based on the information in Figure 33-3)*

If you specify a support URL, ClickOnce will create an additional shortcut named [Product Name] Online Support. When the user clicks this shortcut, it launches the default web browser and sends it to the page you've specified.

The error URL specifies a website link that will be shown (in a dialog box) if an error occurs while attempting to install the application.

You'll learn about the other groups of settings at the end of this chapter. For now, click OK after you've filled in the publisher name, product name, and any other details you choose to supply.

Starting the Publish Wizard

The easiest way to configure your ClickOnce settings is to click the Publish Wizard button at the bottom of the property page shown in Figure 33-2. This launches a wizard that walks you through a few short steps to gather the essential information. The wizard doesn't give you access to all the ClickOnce features you'll learn about in this chapter, but it's a quick way to get started.

The first choice you're faced with in the Publish Wizard is choosing the location where you want to publish the application (see Figure 33-5).

Figure 33-5. Choosing a publish location

There's nothing particularly important about the location where you first publish your application, because this isn't necessarily the same location you'll use to host the setup files later. In other words, you could publish to a local directory and then transfer the files to a web server. The only caveat is that you need to know the ultimate destination of your files when you run the Publish Wizard, because you need to supply this information. Without it, the automatic update feature won't work.

Of course, you could choose to publish the application directly to its final destination, but it's not necessary. In fact, building the installation locally is often the easiest option. To get a better sense of how this works, start by choosing a local file path location (such as c:\Temp\ClickOnceApp). Then click Next. You're now faced with the real question—where users will go to install this application (see Figure 33-6).

Figure 33-6. *Choosing the installation type*

This bit is important, because it influences your update strategy. The choices you make are stored in a manifest file that's deployed with your application.

■ **Note**   There is one case in which you won't see the dialog box in Figure 33-6. If you enter a virtual directory to a web server for the publish location (in other words, a URL starting with http://), the wizard assumes this is the final installation location.

In Figure 33-6, you have essentially three choices. You can create an installation for a network file share, a web server, or CD or DVD media. The following sections explain each approach.

Publishing for a Network File Share

In this case, all the users in your network will access the installation by browsing to a specific UNC path and running a file named setup.exe at that location. A UNC path is a network path in the form *ComputerName**ShareName*. You can't use a networked drive, because networked drives depend on system settings (so different users might have their drives mapped differently). To provide automatic updates, the ClickOnce infrastructure needs to know exactly where it can find the installation files, because this is also the location where you'll deploy updates.

Publishing for a Web Server

You can create an installation for a web server on a local intranet or the Internet. Visual Studio will generate an HTML file named publish.htm that simplifies the process. Users request this page in a browser and click a link to download and install the application.

You have several options for transferring your files to a web server. If you want to take a two-step approach (publish the files locally and then transfer them to the right location), you simply need to copy the files from the local directory to your web server by using the appropriate mechanism (such as FTP). Make sure you preserve the directory structure.

If you want to publish your files straight to the web server without any advance testing, you have two choices. If you are using IIS and the current account you're running has the necessary permissions to create a new virtual directory on the web server (or upload files to an existing one), you can publish files straight to your web server. Just supply the virtual directory path in the first step of the wizard. For example, you could use the publish location `http://ComputerName/VirtualDirectoryName` (in the case of an intranet) or `http://DomainName/VirtualDirectoryName` (for a server on the Internet).

You can also publish straight to a web server by using FTP. This is often required in Internet (rather than intranet) scenarios. In this case, Visual Studio will contact your web server and transfer the ClickOnce files over FTP. You'll be prompted for user and password information when you connect.

■ **Note** FTP is used to transfer files—it's not used for the actual installation process. Instead, the idea is that the files you upload become visible on a web server, and users install the application from the publish.htm file on that web server. As a result, when you use an FTP path in the first step of the wizard (Figure 33-5), you'll still need to supply the corresponding web URL in the second step (Figure 33-6). This is important, because the ClickOnce publication needs to return to this location to perform its automatic update checks.

PUBLISHING TO THE LOCAL WEB SERVER

If you're publishing your application to a virtual directory on the local computer, you'll need to ensure that Internet Information Services (IIS) is installed by using the Programs and Features entry in the Control Panel, which allows you to turn Windows features on or off. When you choose to install IIS, make sure you include the .NET Extensibility option and the IIS 6 Management Compatibility option (which allows Visual Studio to interact with IIS).

Additionally, you need to run Visual Studio as an administrator before you can publish to a virtual directory. The easiest way to do this is to right-click the Microsoft Visual Studio shortcut in the Start menu and choose Run as Administrator. You can also configure your computer to always run Visual Studio as an administrator, which is a trade-off between convenience and security that needs to be weighed carefully. To put this in place, right-click the Visual Studio shortcut, choose Properties, and then head to the Compatibility tab, where you'll find an option named Run This Program as an Administrator.

Publishing for a CD or DVD

If you choose to publish to setup media such as a CD or DVD, you still need to decide whether you plan to support the automatic update feature. Some organizations will use CD-based deployment exclusively, while others will use it to supplement their existing web-based or networked-based deployment. You choose which option applies for use in the third step of the wizard (see Figure 33-7).

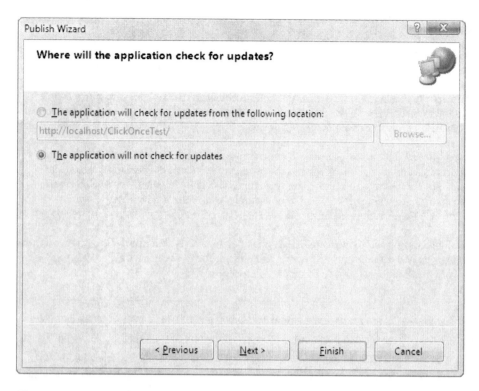

Figure 33-7. *Support for automatic updates*

Here, you have three options:

- You can supply a URL or UNC path that the application will check for updates. This assumes that you plan to publish the application to that location.

- You can omit this information and bypass the automatic update feature altogether.

- You can omit this information but tell the ClickOnce application to use the installation location as the update location. For example, if you use this strategy and someone installs the application from \\CompanyServer-B\MyClickOnceApp, the application will automatically check this location (and only this location) for updates each time it runs. This looser approach gives you more flexibility, but it also risks causing problems (most commonly, not being able to find updated versions if users install it from the wrong path). You can't choose this behavior through the Publish Wizard. If you want it, you need to set the Exclude Deployment Provider URL setting, as described in the "Publish Options" section later in this chapter.

■ **Note** The Publish Wizard doesn't give you an option for how often to check for updates. By default, ClickOnce applications check for an update whenever they're launched. If a new version is found, .NET prompts the user to install it before launching the application. You'll learn how to change these settings in the "Updates" section later in this chapter.

Choosing Online or Offline

If you're creating a deployment for a web server or network share, you'll get one additional option, as shown in Figure 33-8.

Figure 33-8. *Support for offline use*

The default choice is to create an online/offline application that runs whether or not the user can connect to the published location. In this case, a shortcut for the application is added to the Start menu.

If you choose to create an online-only application, the user needs to return to the published location to run the application. (To help make this clear, the publish.htm web page will show a button labeled Run instead of Install.) This ensures that an old version of the application can't be used after you roll out an update. This part of the deployment model is analogous to a web application.

When you create an online-only application, the application will still be downloaded (into a locally cached location) the first time it's launched. Thus, while startup times may be longer (because of the initial download), the application will still run as quickly as any other installed Windows application. However, the application can't be launched when the user isn't connected to the network or Internet, which makes it unsuitable for mobile users (such as laptop users who don't always have an Internet connection available).

If you choose to create an application that supports offline use, the setup program will add a Start menu shortcut. The user can launch the application from this shortcut, regardless of whether the computer is online or offline. If the computer is online, the application will check for new versions in the location where the application was published. If an update exists, the application will prompt the user to install it. You'll learn how to configure this policy later.

▪ **Note** If you choose to publish for a CD installation, you don't have the option of creating an online-only application.

This is the final choice in the Publish Wizard. Click Next to see the final summary, and click Finish to generate the deployment files and copy them to the location you chose in step 1.

▪ **Tip** From this point on, you can quickly republish your application by clicking the Publish Now button or by choosing Build ▶ Publish [ApplicationName] from the menu.

Understanding the Deployed File Structure

ClickOnce uses a fairly straightforward directory structure. It creates a setup.exe file in the location you chose and a subdirectory for the application.

For example, if you deployed an application named ClickOnceTest to the location c:\ClickOnceTest, you'll end up with files like these:

C:\ClickOnceTest\setup.exe

C:\ClickOnceTest\publish.htm

C:\ClickOnceTest\ClickOnceTest.application

C:\ClickOnceTest\ClickOnceTest_1_0_0_0.application

C:\ClickOnceTest\ClickOnceTest_1_0_0_0\ClickOnceTest.exe.deploy

C:\ClickOnceTest\ClickOnceTest_1_0_0_0\ClickOnceTest.exe.manifest

The publish.htm file is present only if you're deploying to a web server. The .manifest and .application files store information about required files, update settings, and other details. (You can get a low-level look at these files and their XML file in the MSDN Help.) The .manifest and .application files are digitally signed at the time of publication, so these files can't be modified by hand. If you do make a change, ClickOnce will notice the discrepancy and refuse to install the application.

As you publish newer versions of your application, ClickOnce adds new subdirectories for each new version. For example, if you change the publish version of your application to 1.0.0.1, you'll get a new directory like this:

C:\ClickOnceTest\ClickOnceTest_1_0_0_1\ClickOnceTest.exe.deploy

C:\ClickOnceTest\ClickOnceTest_1_0_0_1\ClickOnceTest.exe.manifest

When you run the setup.exe program, it handles the process of installing any prerequisites (such as the .NET Framework) and then installs the most recent version of your application.

Installing a ClickOnce Application

To see ClickOnce in action with a web deployment, follow these steps:

1. Make sure you have the optional IIS web server component installed (as described in the "Publishing to the Local Web Server" sidebar earlier in this chapter).

2. Using Visual Studio, create a basic Windows application, and compile it.

3. Launch the Publish Wizard (by clicking the Publish Wizard button or choosing Build ➤ Publish), and select http://localhost/ClickOnceTest for the publish location. The localhost portion of the URL points to the current computer. As long as IIS is installed and you are running with sufficient privileges, Visual Studio will be able to create this virtual directory.

4. Choose to create an online and offline application, and then click Finish to end the wizard. The files will be deployed to a folder named ClickOnceTest in the IIS web server root (by default, the directory c:\Inetpub\wwwroot).

5. Run the setup.exe program directly, or load up the publish.htm page in Internet Explorer (shown in Figure 33-9) and click Install. You'll receive a security message asking whether you want to trust the application (similar to when you download an ActiveX control in a web browser).

Figure 33-9. The publish.htm installation page

LAUNCHING A CLICKONCE SETUP FROM A DIFFERENT BROWSER

Installing a ClickOnce application from Internet Explorer is easy. You simply visit the publish.htm page and click the Install button. This starts the setup process immediately.

You can also install ClickOnce applications from other browsers, but you need at least one extra step. For example, if you click the Install button in Google Chrome or Mozilla Firefox, you'll actually start downloading the setup program. After the download is complete, you can choose to launch the file to start the setup process (although the browser will give you an extra warning to explain that executable files can harm your computer).

If you want to make other browsers as adept as Internet Explorer at handling ClickOnce applications, you can install a plug-in that does the job. Chrome offers one at `http://tinyurl.com/492nyw9`, and there's one for Firefox at `http://tinyurl.com/7cxq4vw`. These plug-ins allow you to launch ClickOnce installations with a single-click, just as the name promises.

6. If you choose to continue, the application will be downloaded, and you'll be asked to verify that you want to install it.

7. After the application is installed, you can run it from the Start menu shortcut or uninstall it by using the Add/Remove Programs dialog box.

The shortcut for ClickOnce applications isn't the standard shortcut to which you're probably accustomed. Instead, it's an application reference—a text file with information about the application name and the location of the deployment files. The actual program files for your application are stored in a location that's difficult to find and impossible to control. The location follows this pattern:

```
c:\Documents and Settings\[UserName]\Local Settings\Apps\2.0\[...]\[...]\[...]
```

The final three portions of this path are opaque, automatically generated strings such as C6VLXKCE.828. Clearly, you aren't expected to access this directory directly.

Updating a ClickOnce Application

To see how a ClickOnce application can update itself automatically, follow these steps with the installation from the previous example:

1. Make a minor but noticeable change in the application (for example, adding a button).

2. Recompile the application, and republish it to the same location.

3. Run the application from the Start menu. The application will detect the new version and ask you whether you'd like to install it (see Figure 33-10).

Figure 33-10. *Detecting a newer version of a ClickOnce application*

4. After you accept the update, the new version of the application will install and start.

In the following sections, you'll learn how to customize some additional ClickOnce options.

▪ **Note** The ClickOnce engine, dfsvc.exe, handles updates and downloads.

Additional ClickOnce Options

The Publish Wizard is a quick way to create a ClickOnce deployment, but it doesn't allow you to adjust all the possible options. For that, you need to take a closer look at the Publish tab in the application properties window shown earlier.

Many of the settings here duplicate details you've already seen in the wizard. For example, the first two text boxes allow you to set the publishing location (the place where the ClickOnce files will be placed, as set in step 1 of the wizard) and the installation location (the place from which the user will run the setup, as set in step 2 of the wizard). The Install Mode setting allows you to choose whether the application should be installed on the local computer or run in an online-only mode, as described earlier. However, there are also some settings you haven't already seen, which are discussed in the following sections.

Publish Version

The Publish Version section sets the version of your application that's stored in the ClickOnce manifest file. This isn't the same as the assembly version, which you can set on the Application tab, although you might set both to match.

The key difference is that the publish version is the criteria used to determine whether a new update is available. If a user launches version 1.5.0.0 of an application, and version 1.5.0.1 is available, the ClickOnce infrastructure will show the update dialog box shown in Figure 33-10.

By default, the Automatically Increment Revision with Each Publish check box is set, in which case the final part of the publish version (the revision number) is incremented by 1 after each publication, so 1.0.0.0 becomes 1.0.0.1, then 1.0.0.2, and so on. If you want to publish the same version of your application to multiple locations by using Visual Studio, you should switch off this option. However, keep in mind that the automatic update feature springs into action only if it finds a higher version number. The date stamp on the deployed files has no effect (and isn't reliable).

It may seem horribly inelegant to track separate assembly and publication version numbers. However, sometimes it makes sense. For example, while testing an application, you may want to keep the assembly version number fixed without preventing testers from getting the latest version. In this case, you can use the same assembly version number but keep the autoincrementing publish version number. When you're ready to release an official update, you can set the assembly version and the publish version to match. Also, a published application might contain multiple assemblies with different version numbers. In this case, it wouldn't be realistic to use the assembly version number—instead, the ClickOnce infrastructure needs to consider a single version number to determine whether an update is warranted.

Updates

Click the Updates button to show the Application Updates dialog box (Figure 33-11), where you can choose your update strategy.

Figure 33-11. Setting update options

■ **Note** The Updates button isn't available if you're creating an online-only application. An online-only application always runs from its published location on a website or network share.

You first choose whether the application performs update checking. If it does, you can choose when updates are performed. You have two options:

> *Before the application starts*: If you use this model, the ClickOnce infrastructure checks for an application update (on the website or network share) every time the user runs the application. If an update is detected, it's installed, and *then* the application is launched. This option is a good choice if you want to make sure the user gets an update as soon as it's available.

After the application starts: If you use this model, the ClickOnce infrastructure checks for a new update after the application is launched. If an updated version is detected, this version is installed the *next* time the user starts the application. This is the recommended option for most applications, because it improves load times.

If you choose to perform checks after the application starts, the check is performed in the background. You can choose to perform it every time the application is run (the default option) or in less-frequent intervals. For example, you can limit checks to once per number of hours, days, or weeks.

You can also specify a minimum required version. You can use this to make updates mandatory. For example, if you set the publish version to 1.5.0.1 and the minimum version to 1.5.0.0 and then publish your application, any user who has a version older than 1.5.0.0 will be forced to update before being allowed to run the application. (By default there is no minimum version, and all updates are optional.)

■ **Note**   Even if you specify a minimum version and require the application to check for updates before starting, a user could end up running an old version of your application. This happens if the user is offline, in which case the update check will fail without an error. The only way around this limitation is to create an online-only application.

File Associations

ClickOnce allows you to set up to eight file associations. These are file types that will be linked to your application so that double-clicking a file of this type in Windows Explorer automatically launches your application.

To create a file association, begin by clicking the Options button in the Publish tab. This shows the Publish Options dialog box. Then click File Associations in the list on the left. This shows a grid where you can enter the information for a file association, as shown in Figure 33-12.

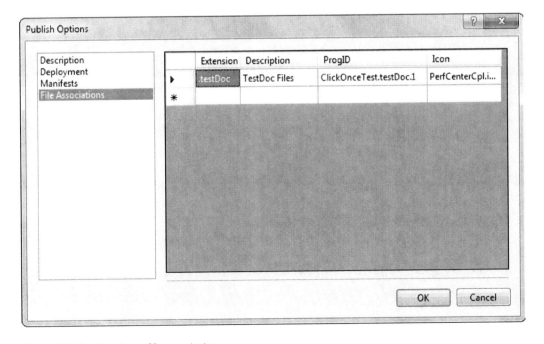

Figure 33-12. *Creating a file association*

CHAPTER 33 ■ CLICKONCE DEPLOYMENT

Every file association requires four pieces of information: the file extension, text description, ProgID, and icon file. The ProgID is a text code that uniquely identifies your file type. By convention, it should be based on the application name and version, as in MyApplication.testDoc.1.0, although the format doesn't really matter as long as it's unique. The icon points to a file in your project. In order for this file to be included in your ClickOnce setup, you must select it in the Solution Explorer and set the Build Action to Content.

■ **Note** One detail you don't need to specify for your file association is the name or path of your program. That's because ClickOnce already has this information.

There's one potential stumbling block when using file associations with ClickOnce. Contrary to what you might expect, when a user double-clicks a registered file, it isn't passed to your application as a command-line argument. Instead, you must retrieve it from the current AppDomain, as shown here:

```
string commandLineFile =
    AppDomain.CurrentDomain.SetupInformation.ActivationArguments.ActivationData[0];
```

Another tricky point is that the file location is passed in URI format, as in file:///c:\MyApp\MyFile.testDoc. That means you need code like this to get the true file path and clean up escaped spaces (which are translated in the %20 character in a URI):

```
Uri fileUri = new Uri(commandLineFile);
string filePath = Uri.UnescapeDataString(fileUri.AbsolutePath);
```

You can now check for the existence of the file and attempt to open it, as you normally would.

Publish Options

As you've already seen, you can click the Options button to see the Publish Options dialog box with even more options. You use the list on the left to pick the group of settings you want to tweak.

You've already looked through the settings in the Description and File Association groups. Table 33-1 describes the settings in the Deployment group, and Table 33-2 describes the settings in the Manifest group.

Table 33-1. ClickOnce Deployment Settings

Setting	Description
Deployment web page	Sets the name of the installation page in web deployments (which is publish.htm by default).
Automatically generate deployment web page after every publish	If set (the default), the web page is re-created during every publish operation.
Open deployment web page after publish	If set (the default), Visual Studio launches the installation page in your web browser after a successful publication so you can test it.
Use ".deploy" file extension	If set (the default), the installation web page always has the file extension .deploy. You shouldn't change this detail, because the .deploy file extension is registered on the IIS web server and locked down to prevent malicious users from snooping through it.
For CD installations, automatically start Setup when CD is inserted	If set, Visual Studio generates an autorun.inf file to tell CD or DVD players to launch the setup program immediately when the CD is inserted into the drive.
Verify files uploaded to a web server	If set, the publish process downloads each file after publishing it to verify that it can be downloaded. If a file cannot be downloaded, you'll receive a notification that explains the problem.

Table 33-2. ClickOnce Manifest Settings

Setting	Description
Block application from being activated via a URL	If set, the user will be able to launch the application from the Start menu only after it's installed, not from the web browser.
Allow URL parameters to be passed to application	If set, this allows the application to receive URL information from the browser that launches it, such as query string arguments. You can retrieve the URI through the ApplicationDeployment class in the System. Deployment.Application namespace. Just use the ApplicationDeployment. CurrentDeployment.ActivationUri property.
Use application manifest for trust information	If set, you can re-sign the application manifest after you publish the application. Usually, you'll do this so you can use a certificate with your company name. This information will then appear in the trust message the user sees when installing the application.
Exclude deployment provider URL	If set, the application will automatically check its installation location for updates. You can use this option if you don't know the exact deployment location but you still want to use ClickOnce automatic updating.
Create desktop shortcut	If set, the setup will create a desktop icon in addition to the Start menu icon.

The Last Word

This chapter gave a quick tour of the ClickOnce deployment model, which was introduced in .NET 2.0 and remains a good choice for deploying stand-alone WPF applications. As with XBAPs, ClickOnce entails certain compromises—for example, you need to accept that there are certain client configuration details you can't control. But now that most computers have web browsers that support ClickOnce, it's become a truly practical way to deploy applications that have modest setup requirements.

Index

■ E

█ **F**

▨ M

N

▒ O

U

V

■ W

▒ X, Y

CPSIA information can be obtained at www.ICGtesting.com
Printed in the USA
LVOW09s1033281214

420633LV00005B/15/P